Using
CorelDRAW!™ 5, Special Edition

Ed Paulson

with
Paul Bodensiek
Thomas Budlong
Cyndie Klopfenstein
Linda Miles
Stephen R. Poland
Rick Wallace

Using CorelDRAW! 5, Special Edition

Copyright© 1994 by Que® Corporation

All rights reserved. Printed in the United States of America. No part of this book may be used or reproduced in any form or by any means, or stored in a database or retrieval system, without prior written permission of the publisher except in the case of brief quotations embodied in critical articles and reviews. Making copies of any part of this book for any purpose other than your own personal use is a violation of United States copyright laws. For information, address Que Corporation, 201 W. 103rd St., Indianapolis, IN 46290.

Library of Congress Catalog No.: 94-66722

ISBN: 1-56529-764-4

This book is sold *as is*, without warranty of any kind, either express or implied, respecting the contents of this book, including but not limited to implied warranties for the book's quality, performance, merchantability, or fitness for any particular purpose. Neither Que Corporation nor its dealers or distributors shall be liable to the purchaser or any other person or entity with respect to any liability, loss, or damage caused or alleged to have been caused directly or indirectly by this book.

97 96 95 94   6 5 4 3 2 1

Interpretation of the printing code: the rightmost double-digit number is the year of the book's printing; the rightmost single-digit number, the number of the book's printing. For example, a printing code of 94-1 shows that the first printing of the book occurred in 1994.

Screen reproductions in this book were created using Collage Plus from Inner Media, Inc., Hollis, NH.

Using CorelDRAW! 5, Special Edition, is based on CorelDRAW! version 5.

Photos in color plates 39–41 and on pages 632, 635, and 641–644 ©1994 Aris Multimedia Entertainment, Inc.

Publisher: David P. Ewing

Associate Publisher: Corinne Walls

Publishing Director: Lisa A. Bucki

Managing Editor: Anne Owen

Product Marketing Manager: Greg Wiegand

Credits

Publishing Manager
Tom Bennett

Acquisitions Editor
Nancy Stevenson

Product Director
Jim Minatel

Production Editors
Chris Nelson
Elsa Bell

Editors
Jo Anna Arnott
Danielle Bird
Geneil Breeze
Patrick Kanouse
Heather Kaufman
Maureen Schneeberger
Kathy Simpson

Technical Editors
Toby A. Asplin
Discovery Computer, Inc.
Pat Gibson
Chris Morton
Ed Quillen
Jolie Renee
Ray Werner

Composed in *Stone Serif* and *MCPdigital* by Que Corporation

Figure Specialist
Cari Ohm

Book Designer
Amy Peppler-Adams

Editorial Assistants
Theresa Mathias
Ruth Slates

Production Team
Stephen Adams
Angela D. Bannan
Stephen Carlin
Kim Cofer
Karen Dodson
Aren Howell
Greg Kemp
Bob LaRoche
Beth Lewis
G. Alan Palmore
Nanci Sears Perry
Caroline Roop
S.A. Springer
Michael Thomas
Marcella Thompson
Tina Trettin
Donna Winter
Robert Wolf
Lillian Yates

Indexer
Rebecca Mayfield

About the Authors

Ed Paulson has been a CorelDRAW! user since 1989. He is a member of the Austin chapter of Corel Artists and thoroughly enjoys working with CorelDRAW! and its associated applications. He is the author of numerous published articles and several technology-related books, including a telecommunications textbook, and has taught at the university level. His educational credits include bachelor's and master's degrees in engineering from the University of Illinois and an MBA from the University of Texas at Austin. He is also the author of *Using CorelDRAW! 4*.

He is the executive director of Applied Concepts, an Austin, Texas based technology training and consulting company. Applied Concepts, an authorized CorelDRAW! training center, develops and markets its training curricula to organizations around the country and is a provider of authorized CorelDRAW! training materials.

Mr. Paulson has over 20 years of high-technology industry experience and has worked extensively with such notable companies as Seagate Technology, Plantronics, IBM, WANG Laboratories, and AT&T. He believes that effective training is the most expedient route to improving worker productivity and appreciates the opportunity to share his experience in print, in the classroom, and as a speaker.

He can be reached at:

Applied Concepts
A Technology and Communications, Inc. Company
7701 North Lamar Blvd., Suite 501
Austin, TX 78752
(512) 458-9700
(512) 458-9794 [fax]
CompuServe: 74201,2664

Paul Bodensiek is a mechanical engineer specializing in innovative heating element design and technical writing. He also runs ParaGrafix, an advertising and desktop publishing company. In his spare time, he writes short fiction, sails tall ships, and is working toward his private pilot's license. Mr. Bodensiek is blessed to share his life with wife, Mary, and daughter, Melissa.

Thomas Budlong, a writer and mechanical engineer, resides with his wife and daughter in Los Angeles. He has written technical manuals and published several articles, some in outdoor periodicals. Tom has used CorelDRAW! to map trails for trail guides. He enjoys walking in the woods and mountain climbing.

Cyndie Klopfenstein has a 20-year background in the printing and prepress industries. She has worked for the past eight years as a corporate trainer for companies that are converting to electronic prepress. She also produces a series of videos and other books geared toward the electronic graphics community.

Linda Miles, a writer and electronic publishing trainer, lives in San Diego with her husband and her cats. She has written other materials concerning illustration and has used this talent to write and co-illustrate works on cats.

Stephen R. Poland is an entrepreneur in the toy and novelty industry and computer consultant specializing in writing about application software topics for IBM PCs, PC compatibles, and the Apple Macintosh. He uses CorelDRAW! extensively to promote his business, producing engineering drawings and marketing materials such as mechanical drawings, electronic schematics, package designs, and sales brochures. Steve is the author of *Easy CorelDRAW!* and the *10 Minute Guide to the Mac*. He is a contributing author to several computer books including *Microsoft Office 6 in 1*, *The Idiot's Guide to Buying and Upgrading Computers*, and *The First Book of Personal Computing*.

Rick Wallace spent 20 years as an award-winning reporter, investigator, and news director in the radio and television news business before discovering computers. In the 10 years since then, a voyage of computer curiosity has taken him on several ventures, including serving as president of a company that produced videotape tutorials on computers and software, producing seminar programs to help real estate agents get computerized, writing a series of books on computer-aided law practice management, and publishing newsletters full of computer tips and company news. He also has written previously for Que: *Using PageMaker 5 for the Mac*, Special Edition.

Acknowledgments

The preparation of a book of this scope involves the people at Corel who developed a wonderful software package, the people at Que who turned the text and figures into a beautiful final product, and the people who assisted with the writing of the various chapters. A heartfelt thank you to the many people who were integral to this project's completion.

I also want to thank those people around me who realized that writing a book requires extraordinary effort and time, and who gave me the support to complete it without interference. Thank you to Elizabeth Purzer, Wanda Fletcher, Robert Turk, and Jan Gillespie along with my other associates and neighbors who did not write me off their list while I was out of pocket.

I also want to thank these people from Que: Nancy Stevenson for pushing me and the project, Lisa Bucki for assembling an outline that truly meets the Corel user's needs, and the developmental, editorial, technical editing, and production staffs. Thanks also to the local Austin Hill Country Association of Corel Artists and Designers (ACAD) for their input on topics and emphasis that would make this book more valuable to them.

Thank you, Patsy Hogan and Kelly Greig at Corel Systems, for your support during the Beta phase and beyond.

These people wrote various sections of the book and deserve a thank you for taking their work seriously and applying a professional touch under tight deadlines: Paul Bodensiek, Thomas Budlong, Cyndie Klopfenstein, Linda Miles, Stephen R. Poland, and Rick Wallace.

Thank you for purchasing *Using CorelDRAW! 5*, Special Edition. Your feedback is welcome so that we can make this book an ever-improving resource for its readers.

Trademarks

All terms mentioned in this book that are known to be trademarks or service marks have been appropriately capitalized. Que cannot attest to the accuracy of this information. Use of a term in this book should not be regarded as affecting the validity of any trademark or service mark.

Contents at a Glance

Introduction		1
Getting Started		**9**
1	An Overview of CorelDRAW! 5	11
2	A Quick Start	35

Learning CorelDRAW! Basics		**59**
3	A Detailed Look at Object Drawing	61
4	Mastering Object Manipulations	93
5	Modifying Object Outlines and Interior Fills	137
6	Scaling, Rotating, and Distorting Objects	183
7	Adding Text to a Drawing	207
8	Advanced Text Techniques	249

Working with Files		**259**
9	File-Related Operations and CorelMOSAIC	261
10	Printing and Merging Files	297

Working with Scanners		**317**
11	Scanning Images into CorelDRAW!	319

Becoming an Expert		**339**
12	Using Color for Commercial Success	341
13	Advanced Line and Curve Techniques	377
14	Creating Special Effects with Perspective	413
15	Creating Special Effects with Envelope	423
16	Creating Special Effects with Blending	441
17	Creating Special Effects with Extruding	461
18	Creating Special Effects with Contouring	477
19	Creating Special Effects with PowerLine	485
20	Creating Special Effects with Lens	499
21	Creating Special Effects with PowerClip	507
22	Combining and Reusing Effects	515
23	Multipage Documents and the Object Data Manager	541
24	Customizing CorelDRAW! to Fit Your Needs	559

Using the Other Corel Applications — 589

- 25 Photograph Touch-Up with CorelPHOTO-PAINT — 591
- 26 Advanced CorelPHOTO-PAINT — 629
- 27 Tracing Bitmap Images with CorelTRACE — 657
- 28 Creating Presentation Charts with CorelCHART — 695
- 29 Making Presentations with CorelSHOW — 751
- 30 Adding Animation with CorelMOVE — 777

Learning from the Pros — 817

- 31 Fast and Sure: Getting the Job Done — 819
- 32 One-Page DTP Design with CorelDRAW! — 829
- 33 Artful Type: Depth and Dimension — 839
- 34 Pattern Making with a Master Mask Artist — 851
- 35 Painless and Powerful Slide Production — 861

Appendixes — 869

- A Installation Considerations — 871
- B Special Characters — 877
- Index of Common Problems — 881
- Glossary — 893
- Index — 925

Contents

Introduction   1

Who Should Use This Book? 1
    A Special Note to CorelDRAW! 3 Users 2
    A Reference Guide for CorelDRAW! 4 Users 3
How This Book Is Organized 3
How to Use This Book..5
Conventions Used in This Book 6
Where to Find More Help 7
Closing Comments 7

I Getting Started   9

1 An Overview of CorelDRAW! 5   11

What to Expect from CorelDRAW! 5 12
    CorelDRAW! 12
    CorelMOSAIC 13
    CorelCHART 13
    CorelMOVE 13
    CorelPHOTO-PAINT 14
    CorelTRACE 14
    CorelSHOW 14
    CorelQUERY 15
PostScript versus Non-PostScript Issues 15
New Release 5 Features 15
Starting CorelDRAW! 16
Learning the Parts of the CorelDRAW! Screen 18
Viewing Your Work 20
Reviewing the Toolbox Tools 23
How CorelDRAW! Creates Objects 24
Understanding Object Outlines, Fills, and Defaults 25
Using Roll-Up Windows 25
Using Roll-Up Windows and Styles 27
Getting On-Line Help 29
Exiting CorelDRAW! 31
Planning Ahead 31
    Printing Considerations (Monochrome versus Color) 32
    Object Linking and Embedding 32
From Here... 33

2 A Quick Start — 35

Creating a Simple Drawing 35
    Setting the Page Size and Orientation 36
    Drawing Rectangles for the Business Card Logo 37
    Shading the Square 39
    Enhancing the Logo with Circles 40
    Adding Initials to the Logo Background 41
    Adding a Border and Company Name and Address 42
    Saving the Drawing 46
Creating a Drawing with Symbols and Clipart 47
    Retrieving Clipart into a Drawing 48
    Modifying the Clipart 50
    Adding Text 53
    Creating a Border and a Drop Shadow 54
    Adding Symbols 55
    Previewing and Printing 56
Considering Copyright When Using Clipart 57
From Here… 57

II Learning CorelDRAW! Basics — 59

3 A Detailed Look at Object Drawing — 61

Understanding Object Components 62
Drawing Straight Lines 63
    Drawing a Straight Line in Freehand Mode 63
    Drawing a Straight Line in Bézier Mode 64
    Drawing a Single Object Using Several Straight Lines 65
Drawing Curved Lines 68
    Drawing a Curved Line in Freehand Mode 68
    Drawing a Curved Line in Bézier Mode 69
    Drawing a Curve-Sided Object 71
Reshaping a Curve or Object by Changing Its Nodes
    and Control Points 72
Creating Rectangular and Square Objects 78
    Drawing a Rectangle or a Square from a Corner Point 78
    Drawing a Rectangle from a Center Point 79
    Rounding the Corners of a Rectangle or Square 80
Drawing Circular Shapes 81
    Drawing an Ellipse or a Circle from a Corner Point 82
    Drawing an Ellipse or a Circle from the Center Point 83
    Drawing a Pie Wedge or an Arc 84
Drawing Callouts on Objects 86
Understanding Open and Closed Path Objects 89
    Drawing Open and Closed Path Objects 90
    Converting an Open Path Object to a Closed
        Path Object 90
From Here… 91

4 Mastering Object Manipulations · 93

Selecting Objects 94
    Selecting Individual Objects with the Pick Tool 94
    Selecting Individual Objects with the Tab Key 95
    Selecting Multiple Objects with the Pick Tool 96
    Selecting Nonadjacent Objects with the Shift Key 98
    Selecting All Objects on the Page 99
Undoing Mistakes 99
Deleting Objects 100
Moving Objects 100
    Moving an Object with the Mouse 100
    Moving Using the Transform Roll-Up 101
    Moving Objects with Nudge 101
Laying Objects on Top of or beneath Each Other 102
Copying Objects 105
    Duplicating Objects 105
    Setting the Automatic Duplication Defaults 106
    Duplicating Objects Using the Clipboard 107
    Cloning Objects 107
Aligning Objects 109
    Using the Grid to Facilitate Alignment 109
    Aligning to Other Objects 113
    Simultaneously Aligning Several Objects 116
    Using the Guidelines to Ease Alignment 117
Combining and Grouping Objects 119
    Distinguishing between Grouping and Combining
        Objects 120
    Grouping Objects 120
    Ungrouping Objects 122
    Accessing Objects within a Group (Child Objects) 122
    Combining Objects 124
Using Tricks and Techniques 127
    Combining Object Outlines 128
    Aligning with No-Width Lines 130
Understanding CorelDRAW! Layers 131
    Understanding How CorelDRAW! Layers Objects
        in a Drawing 132
    Grouping and Combining Objects from Different
        Layers 133
    Using the Desktop Layer 133
    Creating and Using a Master Layer 134
From Here… 134

5 Modifying Object Outlines and Interior Fills · 137

Modifying Object Outline Characteristics 137
    Introducing the Outline Menus and Dialog Boxes 138
    Changing the Outline Color 141
    Changing the Outline Style 142

　　　　Adding Arrowheads 142
　　　　Creating a Nonprinting Outline 144
　　　　Copying Outline Styles Between Objects 144
　　　　Establishing a Default Outline Style 145
　　Working with Interior Fills 146
　　　　Introducing the Fill Menus and Dialog Boxes 147
　　　　Copying Fills between Objects 148
　　　　Establishing a Default Fill 148
　　Working with Solid Fills 150
　　　　Adding a Solid-Color Fill 151
　　　　Making an Object Transparent 151
　　Using Patterned Fills 152
　　　　Using Two-Color Patterns 152
　　　　Using Full-Color Patterns 160
　　　　Using PostScript Textures 165
　　　　Using PostScript Halftones 167
　　Working with Gradated (Fountain) Fills 170
　　　　Introducing the Fountain Fill Menus and
　　　　　Dialog Boxes 170
　　　　Choosing the Fountain Type 171
　　　　Choosing Colors 172
　　　　Controlling the Edge Padding 173
　　　　Controlling the Number of Steps 174
　　　　Setting the Angle for Linear, Conical, and
　　　　　Square Fountains 176
　　　　Specifying the Center Offset for Radial, Conical,
　　　　　and Square Fountain Fills 177
　　　　Creating Custom Fountain Gradations 178
　　Using Texture Fills 180
　　From Here... 181

6 Scaling, Rotating, and Distorting Objects　　183

　　Learning the Basic Tools and Techniques 183
　　　　Scaling and Sizing an Object 184
　　　　Mirroring an Object 188
　　Rotating an Object 189
　　Skewing an Object 192
　　Using Transformation Tricks and Techniques 194
　　　　Increasing Precision with the Mouse 195
　　　　Leaving Copies of the Original Object 196
　　　　Repeating and Undoing Transformations 196
　　Practicing Using the Effects with the Mouse 197
　　　　Scaling Objects 197
　　　　Stretching Objects 198
　　　　Creating Mirror Images 199
　　　　Rotating Objects 200
　　　　Rotating an Object Off Center 202
　　　　Skewing Objects 203
　　　　Creating an Object with Multiple Transformations 204
　　From Here... 204

7 Adding Text to a Drawing　　　　　　　　　　　207

Understanding the Fundamentals of Text Design 208
    Typefaces 208
    Point Size 210
    Character and Line Spacing 210
    Serif versus Sans Serif Typefaces 210
    Outline 211
    Fill 211
Differentiating between Paragraph and Artistic Text 211
Working with Artistic Text 212
    Adding Artistic Text 212
    Editing Artistic Text 212
    Changing Artistic Text Attributes 214
Working with Paragraph Text 218
    Adding Paragraph Text 218
    Editing Paragraph Text 219
    Modifying Paragraph Text Attributes 219
    Changing the Fill and Outline Type 221
    Changing Typeface, Style, and Size 221
    Setting Paragraph Text Tabs, Margins, and Indents 221
    Setting Tabs 221
    Creating Bulleted Lists 224
Working with Artistic and Paragraph Text 226
    Importing Text 226
    Finding and Replacing Text 227
    Using the Spelling Checker and Thesaurus 228
Using Type Assist 231
Working with Text Frame 233
    Setting Column Numbers and Gutter Width 233
    Creating Text Frame Envelopes 234
    Flowing Paragraph Text between Frames 235
    Using Styles and Templates 236
Using Text Artistically 239
    Scaling, Rotating, and Skewing Text 239
    Fitting Text to a Path 240
    Modifying an Individual Character's Attributes 243
    Straightening Text and Aligning to a Baseline 244
    Copying Attributes from One Text String to Another 244
Understanding Advanced Text Design 245
    Extracting Text 246
    Editing Extracted Text 246
    Restoring (Merging Back) Text 246
From Here… 248

8 Advanced Text Techniques　　　　　　　　　　　249

Converting Text Characters to Curved Objects for Shaping 249
Adding a Graphic Symbol 250
Adding a Special Character 252

Working with Typefaces 253
    About TrueType Fonts 253
    Creating Custom Typefaces (Exporting Text) 253
From Here… 257

III Working with Files   259

9 File-Related Operations and CorelMOSAIC   261

Saving and Retrieving Files 261
    Saving Drawings 262
    Saving a Copy of an Open File 263
    Adding Keywords and Notes to Files 264
    Changing Keywords, Notes, and the Preview
        Image Header 264
    Finding and Opening Files 265
    Sorting Files 266
    Saving and Retrieving Earlier Version Files 267
Sharing Drawings—Export, Import, and the Clipboard 268
    Exporting versus Saving 269
    Exporting in Encapsulated PostScript (EPS) Format 270
    Exporting Bitmaps 271
    Opening and Importing a Drawing 273
    Import Format Compatibilities 274
    Importing a CorelTRACE File 276
    Importing a Photo CD File 277
    Getting More Information on Importing and
        Exporting 278
    Using the Clipboard instead of File Transfers 280
Using CorelMOSAIC 282
    Running CorelMOSAIC 283
    Making and Editing Libraries and Catalogs 283
    Using Libraries and Catalogs 289
Converting Files to Another Format with MOSAIC 293
From Here… 295

10 Printing and Merging Files   297

General Printing Procedures 298
Previewing before Printing 299
Printing—the Details 299
Printing Specific Layers of a Drawing 304
Printing without Starting CorelDRAW! 305
Printing Color Files 307
Halftone Patterns, Screen Frequency, and Angle
    Considerations 307
PostScript and Non-PostScript Printing 307
Merging Text into a CorelDRAW! Drawing 310
    An Overview of the Merge Process 311

Creating the Word Processing Text File 311
Preparing the Drawing for a Merge 312
Performing the Merge 313
From Here… 315

IV Working with Scanners — 317

11 Scanning Images into CorelDRAW! — 319

Choosing from Flatbed, Hand-Held, and Drum Scanners 320
Installing CorelDRAW! for Scanning 320
    Using TWAIN Technology 321
    SCSI Devices and Boards 321
    Accessing Your Scanner with CorelPHOTO-PAINT
      or CorelTRACE 322
Planning for the Best Scan Possible 323
    Input (Scan) Resolution and Output Resolution 325
    The Effects of Enlarging and Reducing on Input
      Resolution 325
    DPI and LPI 326
    Defining and Compensating for Dot Gain 329
    The Importance of Calibration 331
    Choosing the Best Output 332
Recognizing Vector- and Pixel-Based Artwork 333
Scanning Photos with CorelPHOTO-PAINT 333
Scanning Line Art for Tracing with CorelTRACE 335
    Figuring the Input Resolution for Line Art 335
    Tips for Tracing 335
Ending the Scanning Session (Saving) 335
OCR Text Scanning 336
From Here… 337

V Becoming an Expert — 339

12 Using Color for Commercial Success — 341

Commercial Printing Process Primer 342
Selecting Fill and Outline Colors 343
    Selecting Fill Colors 344
Using CorelDRAW!'s Color Capabilities 347
    Defining the Color Palettes 348
    Spot versus Process Colors 348
    Creating Custom Colors 351
    Converting from One Color Scheme to Another 355
    Displaying the Color Palette 357
Printing Process Color Drawings 357
    Getting the Color You Want 358

Understanding CorelDRAW! 5's Color Management
    System 359
  Using the Color Correction Command 361
Creating Color Separations in CorelDRAW! 362
  Exploring the Print Options Dialog Box 363
  Additional Color Printing Considerations 367
  The Cost of Printing in Color 368
Using CorelDRAW! for Maximum Color-Related Benefit 369
Drawing Some Simple Color Illustrations 370
From Here… 375

13 Advanced Line and Curve Techniques   377

Changing Object Shapes 378
  Using the Shape Tool with the Node Edit Roll-Up 379
  Understanding Line Segments and Nodes 379
  Using the Shape Tool To Move Nodes 386
Adding and Deleting Nodes 390
  Adding Nodes 391
  Deleting Nodes 391
  Using the AutoReduce Feature 392
Joining and Breaking Nodes 392
Aligning Nodes between Objects 393
Adding and Creating Arrowheads 396
Modifying Line Thickness, Color, and Style 400
  Using the Outline Fly-Out Menu 401
  Using the Pen Roll-Up 401
  Using the Outline Pen Dialog Box 402
Using Dimension Lines 403
Applying Advanced Curve Techniques 408
From Here… 410

14 Creating Special Effects with Perspective   413

Watching the Status Line 414
Working from the Menu 415
  Using One-Point Perspective 416
  Using Two-Point Perspective 416
Understanding the Vanishing Point 417
  Finding the Vanishing Point 417
  Moving the Vanishing Point 418
  Aligning Vanishing Points 418
Copying Perspective 419
Clearing Perspective 420
From Here… 420

15 Creating Special Effects with Envelope   423

Watching the Status Line 424
Working from the Menu 424

Using the Envelope Roll-Up Window 424
    Add New 424
    Add Preset 425
    How an Envelope Fits Objects 425
    Envelope Edit 427
    Mapping 430
    Keep Lines 433
    Reset Envelope 433
    Apply 433
Enveloping Objects 434
    Creating an Envelope for an Object 434
    Creating an Envelope from an Object 435
Enveloping Text 435
    Creating an Envelope for Artistic Text 436
    Using Create From to Make an Envelope for a
        Paragraph of Text 437
    Using the Preset List to Make an Envelope for
        Paragraph Text 437
    Editing Text in an Envelope 438
Clearing Applied Envelopes 439
From Here… 440

16 Creating Special Effects with Blending   441

Watching the Status Line 442
Working from the Menus 442
Using the Blend Roll-Up Window 443
    Steps, Spacing, and Rotation 443
    Loop 444
    Color 444
    Start Nodes 446
    Split Blend 447
    Fuse Blend 448
    Start Objects 448
    End Objects 449
    Blends on a Path 449
Working with Blends 451
    Identifying the Parts of a Blend 451
    Making Just a Blend 452
    Making a Blend Follow a Path 454
    Making a Chain of Blends 456
    Making a Compound Blend 456
    Reversing the Direction of a Blend 457
    Using Blends To Highlight 457
    Clearing a Blend 458
    Copying a Blend 458
    Cloning a Blend 458
From Here… 459

17 Creating Special Effects with Extruding — 461

Watching the Status Line 462
Working from the Menu 463
Using the Extrude Roll-Up Window 463
    Extrude Preset Button 464
    Depth Control Button 464
    Rotating Perspective and Parallel Extrusions 467
    Light Source Button 467
    Color Button 469
    Save As Button 471
    Apply Button 472
Working with Extrusions 472
    Extruding Objects 472
    Editing an Extrude Node 473
    Changing the Center of Rotation 473
    Working with the Vanishing Point 474
    Clearing an Extrude 475
    Copying an Extrude 475
    Cloning an Extrude 476
From Here... 476

18 Creating Special Effects with Contouring — 477

Watching the Status Line 478
Working from the Menu 479
Using the Contour Roll-Up Window 479
    To Center 479
    Inside 480
    Outside 480
    Offset 480
    Steps 480
    Outline 481
    Fill 481
    Apply 481
Creating Contours for Objects 482
Editing Contours 482
Copying Contours 483
Cloning a Contour 483
Clearing a Contour 483
From Here... 484

19 Creating Special Effects with PowerLine — 485

Watching the Status Line 486
Working from the Menu 486
Using the PowerLine Roll-Up Window 486
    PowerLine Button 487
    Apply When Drawing Lines 487
    Preset List Box 487
    Maximum Width 488

Nib Shape 489
Speed, Spread, Ink Flow, and Scale With Image 490
Save As 493
Apply 493
Drawing with PowerLines 493
Node Editing PowerLines 494
Copying a PowerLine 495
Cloning a PowerLine 496
Removing a PowerLine 496
From Here… 497

20 Creating Special Effects with Lens 499

Watching the Status Line 500
Working from the Menu 500
Using the Lens Roll-Up Window 500
Type of Lens 501
Color 503
Apply 504
Creating a Lens for Objects 504
Copying Lens Effect 505
From Here… 506

21 Creating Special Effects with PowerClip 507

Watching the Status Line 508
Working from the Menu 509
Making a PowerClip 509
Making a PowerClip from a Group 510
Locking and Unlocking PowerClip 510
Editing the Contents of a PowerClip 511
Combining a PowerClip with Other Special Effects 511
Copying a PowerClip Effect 512
Cloning a PowerClip Effect 513
Removing a PowerClip 513
From Here… 514

22 Combining and Reusing Effects 515

Diminishing with Perspective 516
Simple Perspective with a Blend 516
Perspective for Artistic Text 518
Fitting to Envelopes 520
Subtle Envelopes 521
Defined Envelope Styles 522
Using Blend Between Objects 523
Extruding for Depth 525
Adding Contours to an Object 527
Making Powerful Lines 529
Looking at Art Through Lenses 530

Using the Power of Clipping 530
Creating Preset Templates, Styles, and Macros 533
    Styles 534
    Applying Styles to Graphics Objects 535
    Templates 536
    Macros 537
From Here... 539

23 Multipage Documents and the Object Data Manager   541

Multipage Document Fundamentals 542
    Choosing a Page Layout and Display Style 542
    Changing, Adding, and Deleting Pages 545
    Designing a Master Layer 547
    Printing and the Page Layout Styles 548
Object Data Manager Basic Concepts 549
    Designing the Object Database 550
    Adding, Editing, and Printing Object Data 554
    Grouping and Data Hierarchy 556
From Here... 558

24 Customizing CorelDRAW! to Fit Your Needs   559

Customizing CorelDRAW! at Windows Startup 560
    Minimizing the CorelDRAW! Program Group 560
    Starting CorelDRAW! When You Start Windows 560
Program Startup Defaults 561
Setting General Preferences 561
    Setting Positioning, Constraint, and Undo Defaults 562
    Customizing the Mouse 564
Customizing Screen Display Characteristics 567
    Positioning the Roll-Up Windows 568
    Positioning Rulers on the Display 570
    Defining Display Preferences 570
    Establishing Preview Color Defaults 572
Customizing Backup Defaults 574
Establishing Grid-Related and Display Dimension Defaults 575
Customizing the Toolbox 577
    Relocating the Toolbox 577
    Making All Tools and Icons Appear on the Toolbox 577
    Hiding the Toolbox 578
Defining Defaults for Object Attributes 578
Setting Default Dimension Line Attributes 580
Using CorelDRAW! Templates 581
Customizing Text Attributes 582
Setting Curve Preferences 584
    Setting the Auto-Reduce Feature Default 585
    Setting Tracking and Threshold Defaults 586
Customizing INI Files 587
From Here... 588

VI Using the Other Corel Applications   589

25 Photograph Touch-Up with CorelPHOTO-PAINT   591

Understanding Memory Limitations 592
Basic CorelPHOTO-PAINT Operation 593
    Starting CorelPHOTO-PAINT 593
    Saving an Image 596
    Printing an Image 597
Getting To Know the CorelPHOTO-PAINT Screen 598
    Sizing and Rearranging Windows 600
    Magnifying and Reducing the Image View 601
    Working with Duplicate Windows 602
CorelPHOTO-PAINT Tools 603
Editing Images in CorelPHOTO-PAINT 606
    Selecting Image Areas 606
    Manipulating Image Cutouts 609
    Cutting, Copying, and Pasting Parts of an Image 610
    Replacing Colors 611
Acquiring Images 613
    Scanning a Picture with CorelPHOTO-PAINT 613
    Capturing a Screen 615
Working with Color 616
    Working with Color Images 616
    Working with Grayscale Images 617
    Automatically Changing Color Modes 618
Painting the Photo 618
    Painting with the Brushes and Spray Tools 619
    Drawing Lines with the Line, Curve, and Pen Tools 620
    Adding Shapes to the Photo 621
    Filling Objects 622
    Cloning 623
    Smudge, Smear, and Sharpen Tools 624
    Changing the Effects of Brushes and Tools 624
    Defining the Drawing Canvas 625
    Changing Color Palettes 626
Adding Text to the Picture 627
From Here… 628

26 Advanced CorelPHOTO-PAINT   629

Editing Image Color 629
Working with Detail and Sharpness 630
Changing Overall Photo Contrast Characteristics 633
Image Transformations 634
Working with Special Effects 637
Using CorelPHOTO-PAINT Masks 644
    Using CorelPHOTO-PAINT Mask Tools 644
    Editing Mask Sizes and Shapes 646
    Combining Mask Designs 647

Creating Color Masks 649
Using the Transparency Masks 652
Loading and Saving Masks 653
Designing Your Own Brushes 654
From Here... 656

27 Tracing Bitmap Images with CorelTRACE   657

Some Considerations before Tracing 658
What Are the Advantages of Tracing? 658
Scanning Hints for Improving CorelTRACE Results 659
Working with Large Bitmap Files 660
Using Manual Tracing and AutoTrace 661
Manually Tracing an Object with the Pencil Tool 661
Tracing a Simple Drawing with AutoTrace 662
Customizing the AutoTrace Operation 665
Tracing an Image with CorelTRACE 667
Placing Images into CorelTRACE 668
Understanding the CorelTRACE Window 670
The File-Related Icons 671
Choosing a Tracing Method 675
Defining the Accuracy of the Traced Image 680
Modifying Additional Image Settings 681
Saving the Traced Image 687
Tracing Only Part of a Bitmap 687
Tracing and Saving Multiple Files Simultaneously 688
Using the Bitmap Header Information 689
Using CorelTRACE Images with Other Applications 690
Using Traced Images in CorelDRAW! 691
Using Traced Images in Other Applications 691
Conceptual Overview: Tracing a Logo 692
From Here... 693

28 Creating Presentation Charts with CorelCHART   695

Understanding How CorelCHART Works 697
Learning Basic CorelCHART Concepts and Terminology 698
Starting CorelCHART 699
Creating a New Chart 700
Opening an Existing Chart 704
Entering Data Using the Data Manager 704
Entering Data 705
Selecting Data Cel Ranges 707
Speeding Up Data Entry 707
Automatically Filling Ranges of Cels 707
Performing Calculations in the Data Manager 710
Entering Formulas 711
Using the Functions in Formulas 712
Using the Separators 714
Moving, Copying, and Pasting Data 714
Manipulating Columns and Rows 716

Contents   **xxiii**

Importing Data from Other Applications 717
    Obtaining Database Information with CorelQUERY 718
    Formatting Text, Numbers, and Cells 723
    Centering Text across Several Cells 724
    Tagging the Data Cells 725
    Printing Data from the Data Manager Window 727
    Reversing the Orientation of Data 727
    Sorting Data Items 729
Modifying Chart Elements Using Chart View 729
    Using the Toolbox 730
    Selecting Chart Elements 732
    Using the Context-Sensitive Pop-Up Menu 732
    Formatting Numbers 733
    Adding Color with the Color Palette 734
    Modifying a Chart Using a Template 734
    Importing Graphics into a Chart 734
    Exporting Charts into Other Applications 735
    Editing Chart Objects 735
    Changing the Chart Style 735
    Controlling the Display of the Underlying Chart Data ... 736
    Controlling the Alignment of Graphics and Text 741
    Refreshing a Window 741
    Formatting Text with the Text Ribbon 742
Customizing Your Charts 743
    Creating Text Annotations 743
    Creating Graphic Annotations 744
    Creating Customized Fills 744
    Adding Pictographs 745
    Creating 3D Charts 746
From Here… 749

29 Making Presentations with CorelSHOW   751

Starting CorelSHOW and the CorelSHOW Screen 752
    Opening an Existing Presentation 752
    Starting a New Presentation 752
    Setting Up the Printer 754
    The CorelCHART Screen 754
Creating CorelSHOW Presentations 755
    Understanding Design Principles 755
    Adding Text 756
    Including Graphic Objects 757
    Creating Chart Slides 760
    Organizing the Presentation 761
    Display and Timing of Slide Object Transition Effects 762
    Working with Backgrounds 764
    Using OLE with CorelSHOW 767
    Saving and Retrieving a Presentation or Background 768

Contents

Presenting Your Work 769
    Adding Sound 770
    Adding Animation 771
    Adding Cues and Using the Timelines 772
Running a Stand-Alone Screen Show 773
Printing Speaker Notes and Audience Handouts 775
From Here... 776

30 Adding Animation with CorelMOVE   777

Understanding CorelMOVE's Basic Concepts 778
    What Is CorelMOVE? 778
    An Overview of the Animation Process 779
Starting, Saving, and Retrieving a Movie 780
    Retrieving a Movie 780
    Starting a New Movie 782
    Saving a Movie 782
Setting the Animation Window Size and
    Playback Attributes 782
Creating Props and Single-Cel Actors 784
    Creating a New Prop or Actor 785
    Using the CorelMOVE Paint Facility 788
    Creating Special Effects with Paint 791
Adding Multicel Actors, Movement, and Sound 793
    Creating Multicel Actors Using Paint 794
    Setting the Path Registration Point 796
    Arranging Object Orientation 796
    Adding Actor Movement 797
    Adding Sound to the Animation 799
    Adding and Editing Cues 802
Viewing and Editing Animation Timing 803
Morphing: Blending from One Bitmap into Another 805
Animation Design Considerations 807
Creating and Using Libraries 807
Applying the Cel Sequencer 809
Using CorelDRAW! Images in CorelMOVE 810
Exporting Animation Objects 814
From Here... 815

VII Learning from the Pros   817

31 Fast and Sure: Getting the Job Done   819

Randy Tobin, President, Association of Corel Designers
    and Artists, Burbank, California 819

32 One-Page DTP Design with CorelDRAW!   829

Robert Davis, Owner, Davis Advertising, Inc.,
    Roswell, Georgia 829

33 Artful Type: Depth And Dimension — 839

Janie Owen-Bugh, Janie Owen-Bugh Electronic Publishing,
Dallas, Texas 839

34 Pattern Making with a Master Mask Artist — 851

Nick Pregent, Creative Imagery, North Hills, California 851

35 Painless and Powerful Slide Production — 861

David Wood, Director, Graphic Computer Services,
Woodland Hills, California 861

Appendixes — 869

A Installation Considerations — 871

Understanding the Basic Installation Options 872
    Full Installation 872
    Custom Installation 872
    Installing Fonts 874
Installing CorelDRAW! to Run from the CD-ROM 875
Installing CorelDRAW! on a Network 875

B Special Characters — 877

Index of Common Problems — 881

Glossary — 893

Index — 925

Introduction

The ability to draw and print images used to be reserved for an elite few, but with the advent of products like CorelDRAW!, this drawing ability is more and more commonplace. Once you learn CorelDRAW!'s basic operation and thinking mode, you can use a wide array of functions and features that allows you to take your imagination and translate it into computer-generated pictures.

I have used CorelDRAW! since 1989 and have watched it evolve from its early stages into one of the most flexible graphics packages in the world. The concept of vector graphics, which saw its first major public introduction with CorelDRAW!, was a novelty in the late 1980s and is now the industry standard drawing mode. What makes CorelDRAW! different from the other packages that followed is that Corel Systems never stands still. It continually improves the package so that what you see in release 5 is a solid step in the CorelDRAW! product evolution. In addition, most of the operational aspects covered in *Using CorelDRAW! 5, Special Edition*, also apply to versions 3 and 4 also.

Who Should Use This Book?

This book is designed as a complete reference to CorelDRAW! and its associated other applications, which include CorelPHOTO-PAINT, CorelMOVE, CorelSHOW, CorelTRACE, CorelMOSAIC, CorelCHART, CorelCAPTURE, and CorelQUERY. The emphasis of the book is not to treat each package as a stand-alone application but to reinforce the synergy that exists between the packages. The Corel suite of products takes full advantage of the Windows DDE/OLE environment and allows you to use work created in one Corel application while creating a new image in another application. The special "Learning from the Pros" chapters have been added to this edition to address the design aspects of the applications. *Using CorelDRAW! 5*, Special Edition, is not only a technical reference, but also an idea source for you to use on your own projects.

If you are a beginner, start with Chapter 1, which introduces you to various CorelDRAW! 5 applications. Chapter 2 leads you through the basics of CorelDRAW!. If you are an experienced CorelDRAW! user, you will find the book a complete reference to all of the various features, options, and applications encountered with the Corel suite of applications. The organization of this book makes the information pertinent to your needs easy to find. Personal experience-based recommendations are included as they apply to the particular sections.

The emphasis in the early part of the book is not on drawing various types of pictures, although that is ultimately important. The emphasis is on informing you, in a structured way, on the uses and benefits associated with the various CorelDRAW! product features. When you become familiar with the various features, use your imagination to discover new ways of using them. The original special effects chapter has been expanded from one to nine chapters. Use these chapters to investigate the CorelDRAW! special effects in great detail so that you can present their wide array of uses in an informative yet imaginative format.

If you work at a service bureau, keep this book around as an authoritative reference on how to make the applications perform as your clients require. Much of what you need is already included with CorelDRAW!, and it would be a shame to reinvent the wheel if an image or feature that matched your needs was included with CorelDRAW! 5.

A Special Note to CorelDRAW! 3 Users

Basic object creation and manipulation in CorelDRAW! 3 is virtually identical to version 5, and CorelDRAW! 3 users will find the early chapters useful for the operation of their version. Most of the operational concepts presented in *Using CorelDRAW! 5*, Special Edition, such as combining and grouping, also apply to CorelDRAW! versions 3 and 4, although the number of drawing features is more limited in the earlier versions and the same commands may appear under different menu headings. Working with Artistic text is similar; however, in version 3, text is entered in a text box, whereas versions 4 and 5 allow direct editing in the drawing area. Paragraph text did not exist in version 3, but appears in versions 4 and 5. Several of the special effects are not part of version 3, nor is CorelMOVE animation.

You will find that the chapters on CHART, TRACE, PHOTO-PAINT, SHOW, and MOSAIC provide effective introductions to those programs, both for version 3 and for many of the user interface changes and additional features covered in version 5. Although CorelDRAW! 5 contains numerous new applications and features compared to CorelDRAW! 3, version 3 is an excellent entry point for learning computer-based graphics, and you can always upgrade to versions 4 or 5 at a later date.

A Reference Guide for CorelDRAW! 4 Users

CorelDRAW! 4 users will find much of the basic information provided in *Using CorelDRAW! 5*, Special Edition, applicable to their version. The jump between versions 4 and 5 is much smaller than from version 3 to version 5. If you use CorelDRAW! 4 on a regular basis, you will appreciate the new CorelDRAW! 5 ribbon bar, the improved user interface, and the new special effects included with the various applications. But many of the images and operations pertaining to version 5 that are discussed in this book, will closely, and often exactly, track with CorelDRAW! 4 operation. In particular, Part VII, "Learning from the Pros," and the color inserts will fire your imagination and push you to new levels of CorelDRAW! 4 use.

How This Book Is Organized

This book is organized to follow the natural order of learning and using CorelDRAW! 5, progressing from the basic and essential topics to more complex and often optional issues. To help you see this organization, the book is divided into seven parts:

Part I	Getting Started	Chapters 1–2
Part II	Learning CorelDRAW! Basics	Chapters 3–8
Part III	Working with Files	Chapters 9–10
Part IV	Working with Scanners	Chapter 11
Part V	Becoming an Expert	Chapters 12–24
Part VI	Using the Other Corel Applications	Chapters 25–30
Part VII	Learning from the Pros	Chapters 31–35

Part I is designed to provide the reader with information relevant to the use of this book and the overall capabilities of the Corel suite of products. Because CorelDRAW! is the germinating application upon which the operation of the other applications is defined, CorelDRAW! and its capabilities are covered first.

Part II introduces all of the basic drawing and image-editing techniques.

Part III deals with the various file format issues, file organization and management, and output mechanisms.

Part IV is a new part that covers the increasingly important scanning process. In conjunction with the enhanced CorelPHOTO-PAINT capabilities, this chapter is important reading.

Part V covers the more advanced CorelDRAW! features with emphasis on the special effects, and includes a chapter dedicated to the useful multipage document feature and the innovative Object Database Manager. Make sure to check out the color insert to see how the topics covered in the early chapters can be combined to create beautiful artwork. Working effectively with commercial printers and service bureaus is also covered.

Part VI introduces several of the other applications included with CorelDRAW! 5. The CorelPHOTO-PAINT chapters show you how to capture, enhance, and combine bitmap images for use with other applications. A special new chapter covers the advanced PHOTO-PAINT features and use. The CorelTRACE chapter illustrates the procedures used for changing those bitmaps into vector graphic objects that are easily scaled and modified for use in the other applications. CorelCHART coverage was expanded substantially since the product is now a full spreadsheet. Spreadsheet creation is covered along with the graphic aspects of graphs and charts used in formal presentations. CorelQUERY coverage is included in the CorelCHART chapter to illustrate its use in acquiring data from a database product and its use for charting purposes. The CorelMOVE chapter covers the animation features of CorelDRAW! 5. The CorelSHOW chapter covers the combination of objects created in the various applications into a unified presentation.

Part VII is new to this edition and looks at CorelDRAW! 5 from the professional artist's perspective. These chapters provide you with a look at how a professional artist addresses a graphic design project using CorelDRAW! 5. These chapters force your imagination and your designs to a new level of excellence and fun. Don't miss the exciting color insert included in Part VII to see what can really be done with the tools already in your hands.

The book also includes two appendixes. Appendix A covers CorelDRAW! 5 installation. Appendix B provides tables showing the codes for inserting special characters in CorelDRAW! 5 and Windows 3.1. Also included is a short glossary of useful terms related to this product, and the Index of Common Problems, which you can turn to for help with CorelDRAW! 5 applications.

Using CorelDRAW! 5, Special Edition, gives you a tremendous graphics background that prepares you well for working with any of the Corel applications, while also laying the groundwork for understanding the technology associated with any graphically related software package.

How to Use This Book

Each chapter is designed as a complete unit, with references to those other sections of the book where specific topics are covered in more detail. New users are encouraged to work their way through Chapters 1 and 2 to acquire a quick introduction to the Corel application thinking process. If you are familiar with CorelDRAW! but unfamiliar with commercial printing procedures, review Chapters 10 and 12 on printing and using color. The information in these chapters becomes important as you become more proficient with the product.

If you are an experienced CorelDRAW! 3 or 4 user, you can update yourself by reviewing the basic new features such as live dimensioning with dimension lines, numerous new special effects such as the lens, and useful features like trimming.

Experienced users also greatly benefit from Part VII, "Learning from the Pros." This is the next best thing to an active user's group in that the tips and tricks that mark a proficient user are included for your use.

Do yourself a favor and read Part VI, "Using the Other Corel Applications." Many people think of CorelDRAW! as a drawing package, whereas it's really an image processing and design suite of applications. CorelPHOTO-PAINT includes numerous new special effects and a much friendlier user interface. Give your presentations life by using the other CorelDRAW! 5 applications in concert with each other to make your work stand out from the crowd.

You are encouraged to bounce around in the book using the table of contents or index as a guide. You are also encouraged to read the opening comments in each chapter because they outline the information that follows. In addition, the overall procedures associated with a specific operation are often outlined at the beginning and then explained in detail throughout the rest of the chapter.

▶ See "Starting CorelDRAW!," p. 16

Frequently, you will encounter topics in this book that relate closely to other topics, or to different aspects the same topic. In many such cases, cross-references occur in the margin to direct you to the relevant section of the book (such as the sample cross-reference alongside this paragraph). Referenced sections from earlier parts of the book are indicated by a left-pointing icon (◀), and later sections by a right-pointing icon (▶).

Conventions Used in This Book

The conventions used in this book have been established to help you learn to use CorelDRAW! 5 quickly and easily. The directions are not keyboard or mouse specific. Choose the method that you are most comfortable with. Many procedures may be easier with the mouse while others may be better accomplished with the keyboard. This is largely a matter of personal preference.

In many instances, there are three ways that you can access a command: you can click it with the mouse, you can press a letter key (indicated by boldface), or press a function key. Commands that require multiple letters to be chosen consecutively have more than one letter in boldface. These letters are usually underlined on the screen in Corel. Where appropriate, the function key alternatives follow the command. The keys are separated by a + sign if more than one key must be pressed at once. For instance, Ctrl+F1 means to press the Ctrl key and the F1 function key at the same time.

In some cases, there is now a fourth way to access a command. Many common commands are now buttons on the new CorelDRAW! ribbon bars. In fact, there are many tools represented by icons in CorelDRAW!, such as those shown on the ribbon bars, toolboxes, and associated fly-out menus. Where appropriate, these icons are displayed in the margin when discussing the commands.

Directions for mouse operations, such as clicking and dragging, refer to the primary mouse button, which is generally the left mouse button. If you have changed your primary mouse button to the right button, all the referrals to the right (secondary) mouse button actually refer to the left button.

This book uses several typeface enhancements to indicate special text or terms. Text that you are supposed to type while performing a task is set off in **bold type**. On-screen messages are set in a special `computer type`. New terms are set in *italic type*.

Where to Find More Help

If you find yourself stuck at a particular point in CorelDRAW!, the built-in help feature may answer your questions. Help is explained in Chapter 1. In addition, you can use this book or the Corel documentation to answer most questions.

This book contains many Troubleshooting sections that anticipate problems that might arise during various situations. In these sections, the problems are stated, followed by explanations of how to solve the problems. The Troubleshooting sections are referenced in the Index of Common Problems mentioned earlier.

If all else fails, you can try the Corel technical support number or look for help from the local chapter of the Association of Corel Artists and Designers (ACAD). The national number is (818) 563-ACAD. There is also a network of Corel Authorized Training Centers located in North America and around the world. These people are checked out by Corel, which ensures that they will provide training and information to aid the installed user base.

Get help directly from Corel by calling (613) 728-1990 for the Corel interactive, automated help line. If this system cannot answer your questions, for a fee you can call the provided 800 number to get access to a technical support representative. Other technical support options are detailed in the front of the Corel manual.

If you have a CompuServe membership, help is available through the Corel forum. Type **GO CORELAPPS** (all caps) to access this forum.

Closing Comments

CorelDRAW! 5 is more than just a drawing package. It is a suite of products that provides a wide array of image processing, desktop publishing, and database access functions. As you learn the operation of the various applications, think about how you can use each in conjunction with the other applications to create images that are far beyond those you currently use. We intend for *Using CorelDRAW! 5*, Special Edition, to become a reference guide and design aid while also providing an overall framework for using the Corel applications as a unified offering.

Thank you for making *Using CorelDRAW! 5*, Special Edition, a part of your computer library. This is where the fun starts, again!

Ed Paulson

Austin, Texas

Part I

Getting Started

1 An Overview of CorelDRAW! 5

2 A Quick Start

Chapter 1

An Overview of CorelDRAW! 5

by Stephen R. Poland

You can use the components of CorelDRAW! 5 most effectively if you have a realistic set of expectations about the capabilities of the program. This chapter outlines the different applications of CorelDRAW! 5 and explains how they can be used in conjunction with one another. CorelDRAW! 5 is a graphics and publishing package that combines powerful technical drawing and illustration, animation, presentation graphics and charting, file conversion, tracing, editing of color bitmaps (usually photographs), desktop publishing and layout, object-oriented image database management, and screen-capture applications.

CorelDRAW! does some of these things exceptionally well and others only adequately. But taken as a whole, it is one of the most comprehensive software packages on the market today. If you learn CorelDRAW! and its associated features, you are well on your way to understanding how to navigate through any Windows-based software application.

In this chapter, you learn the following:

- The basics of each of the Corel applications
- The new features available in CorelDRAW! 5
- How to start and exit CorelDRAW!
- About the CorelDRAW! application window
- The ins and outs of the toolbox
- The ways to use menus, dialog boxes, and roll-up windows
- How to get help using CorelDRAW!'s Help system

What to Expect from CorelDRAW! 5

The CorelDRAW! 5 name is a bit misleading, because the product really is a combination of several software application packages. CorelDRAW! is only one of the applications provided with the package. Other applications that enhance the use of CorelDRAW! or capitalize on work created in CorelDRAW! have been added as the product has evolved.

Think of the Corel suite of products as a set of image-processing and publishing tools. CorelDRAW! is the illustration and drawing tool. The other tools enhance the overall product by providing capabilities that users need to work with quality images in today's computing environment. The following sections list the tools that come with CorelDRAW! 5, explain their functions, and discuss how they complement one another.

You can start any of these Corel applications by choosing the appropriate icon in the Windows Corel application group.

CorelDRAW!

As the umbrella application in the suite, CorelDRAW! is a sophisticated drawing tool that you can use to create everything from simple line art to technical drawings to complex full-color artwork. CorelDRAW! determines the menu structure and icon arrangement used in the other applications.

Basic features include the capability to draw shapes and lines and to define outline and fill attributes. CorelDRAW! provides a helpful Shape tool that allows for easy modification of those shapes into any design you want. CorelDRAW! uses a special vector-graphic format for all objects, so the quality of the image does not degrade as the objects are scaled or rotated.

CorelDRAW! also comes with a set of special effects that handle shading, highlighting, transitions from one object to another, and envelope shaping of entire objects. With the tools provided by CorelDRAW!, you can take on the most complex drawing tasks; the possibilities are limited only by your imagination. The only restraint is that CorelDRAW! works according to well-defined rules that you must follow. Learning to use the program properly will keep you from getting frustrated and discouraged.

You can transfer objects created in CorelDRAW! to other Corel applications by exporting the appropriate files or by using the Windows Clipboard. Exporting file information is covered in Chapter 9, "File-Related Operations and CorelMOSAIC."

CorelMOSAIC

Because these products ultimately deal with images, Corel provides MOSAIC to enable you to view images when you call up a file directory. Files are displayed as *thumbnail* images, which enable you to select files based on their image contents rather than on their name or date of creation. MOSAIC is a separate application that can be started on its own or from CorelDRAW!. This application sometimes slows the file-opening process, but it can be a lifesaver when you are working with several different files and cannot remember when a file was created or what it was named.

You also can use MOSAIC to print multiple files at the same time. Simply select the desired files in the MOSAIC screen and then choose the desired action (Print, in this case). MOSAIC loads the required applications and then performs the print functions, relieving the user of the routine tasks associated with this type of printing operation.

CorelCHART

CorelCHART is a presentation graphics application that enables you to create sophisticated charts and graphs of numeric data. With CHART, you can import or enter data that you want to present in graphical form and then select the chart style you want to use for the display. The finished charts are not actually presented by CHART; they are imported into SHOW for the final presentation. But you can use CHART to print or export your graph in file formats that other applications can use.

CHART provides a wide variety of chart styles—including 3D, area, pie, and scatter graph—so you should be able to find a style appropriate for your charting needs. Because CHART cannot easily create some conventional presentation products, such as single slides containing charts with bulleted text, it cannot be considered an equivalent to other programs such as Lotus Freelance Graphics or Microsoft PowerPoint. But you can use CHART's image-handling capabilities to customize virtually every facet of a chart.

CorelMOVE

CorelMOVE enables you to create simple computer animation. Now you can create an object with MOVE's set of drawing tools and design the object to move around on-screen. You also can use CorelDRAW! to create objects for a MOVE animation. You can add sound and user-driven cues, which make the animation interact with the viewer.

One feature new to MOVE in Version 5 is morphing, which enables you to blend from one object to another and view all the objects in between. The procedures required to create animation are relatively complicated; Chapter 30, "Adding Animation Using CorelMOVE," takes you through the process step by step. MOVE is an exciting feature that you are sure to have fun with.

CorelPHOTO-PAINT

CorelPHOTO-PAINT is an editing application that enables you to scan an image, edit images with bitmap graphic tools, and apply filters (such as pointillism or fractal texture overlay) that add artistic touches to an underlying image. You also can create your own painting with PHOTO-PAINT. Several styles of brushes and special-effect options enable you to create paintings in unique styles. PHOTO-PAINT makes many types of image modifications possible; you will have fun exploring their use. Images created in PHOTO-PAINT can be used as backgrounds in SHOW or as images in the other applications.

CorelTRACE

CorelTRACE transforms a PHOTO-PAINT image (or other bitmap image) into a vector format that CorelDRAW! can use, enabling you to use the full power of CorelDRAW! to edit and apply special effects to the image. This lets you acquire shapes that would be difficult to draw manually. An artist might scan an image of an iguana for inclusion in a zoo newsletter, for example, and then need to scale or modify it slightly before final printing. Using TRACE to convert the image, the artist can export it to CorelDRAW! and edit it as needed.

TRACE images are stored as Encapsulated PostScript (EPS) files so that they can be used in other applications.

CorelSHOW

A formal presentation requires a flow of information that you can organize in CorelSHOW. Graphs created in CHART, logos created in CorelDRAW!, pictures scanned and edited in PHOTO-PAINT, and animations developed in MOVE can be combined with other things (such as sound) in SHOW to create a coherent presentation with dramatic effects.

SHOW does not provide much intrinsic editing capability, because most of the editing is done in the source applications. Consequently, SHOW makes extensive use of the Windows 3.1 object-linking and data-exchange capability. With SHOW, you also can create stand-alone presentations that do not require CorelDRAW! or SHOW to run on standard PCs.

CorelQUERY

CorelQUERY is a powerful database extraction tool that you can use to incorporate database information into CHART. Rather than retype long rows and columns of numbers, you can use QUERY to extract selected information from your ODBC-compliant database and place that information in CHART's Data Manager.

PostScript versus Non-PostScript Issues

Some printing capabilities of CorelDRAW! are not available on non-PostScript printers. You should verify your printer type and be aware of the limits that a non-PostScript printer places on your final output. Not all the textures and fill patterns in CorelDRAW! are available without PostScript; however, you can create color separations on non-PostScript printers.

New Release 5 Features

Noteworthy changes and additions to all the applications in the CorelDRAW! suite include the following:

- A new ribbon bar for easy access to commonly used commands
- OLE2 support, including the capability to drag and drop images from the MOSAIC image manager
- MOSAIC's availability as a roll-up window in most Corel applications

New features of CorelDRAW! include the following:

- Two new special effects: Lenses and PowerClip
- The capability to create and save macro effects
- Precise sizing and positioning of objects
- The capability to delete all guidelines at one time

New features of PHOTO-PAINT include the following:

- The capability to use industry-standard plug-in filters
- New artistic filters: Pinch, Swirl, Spherize, 3D Perspective, and Mesh Warp
- The capability to create floating objects and place them in layers in a painting

New CHART features include the following:

- Ten new chart types, bringing the total number of chart types to 90
- More than 300 new spreadsheet functions that can be used in Data Manager view
- Direct access to CorelDRAW! fills and outlines for application to charts and the Data Manager

New MOVE features include the following:

- A new morphing special effect
- More than 300 new actors, props, and sounds, bringing the total to more than 1,000

New SHOW features include the following:

- On-screen text entry for easy creation of bullet points
- The capability to create speaker's notes to accompany a presentation

Users of previous versions of CorelDRAW! will find that things are located differently in the new release and that some keyboard shortcuts have changed, so some adjustment is necessary at first. After you get used to the new layout, however, you will find that it enhances your efficiency and creative possibilities.

Note

Look for the Release 5 feature icon throughout the book to locate features that are new to CorelDRAW! 5 or that are substantial improvements on previous versions.

Starting CorelDRAW!

After installation, the Windows Corel application group contains all the Corel-related applications. Each one is represented by a different Windows icon (see fig. 1.1). You can start each program by double-clicking its associated icon.

To start Corel, follow these steps:

1. Locate the Corel applications group icon and double-click it. The Corel group window opens.

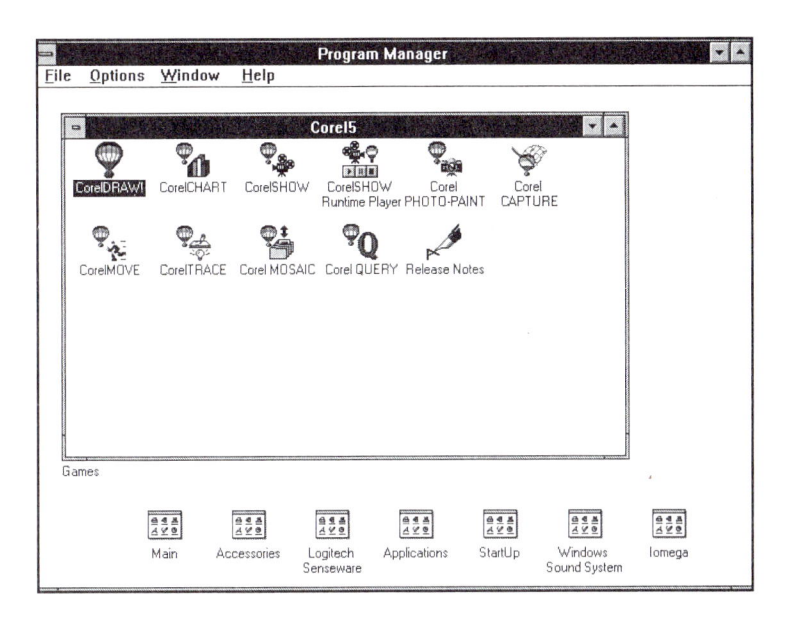

Starting CorelDRAW! 17

Fig. 1.1
By default, the CorelDRAW! 5 program icons are installed in a program group called Corel 5, along with an icon for release notes.

2. Double-click the CorelDRAW! icon. The CorelDRAW! 5 application window opens, as shown in figure 1.2.

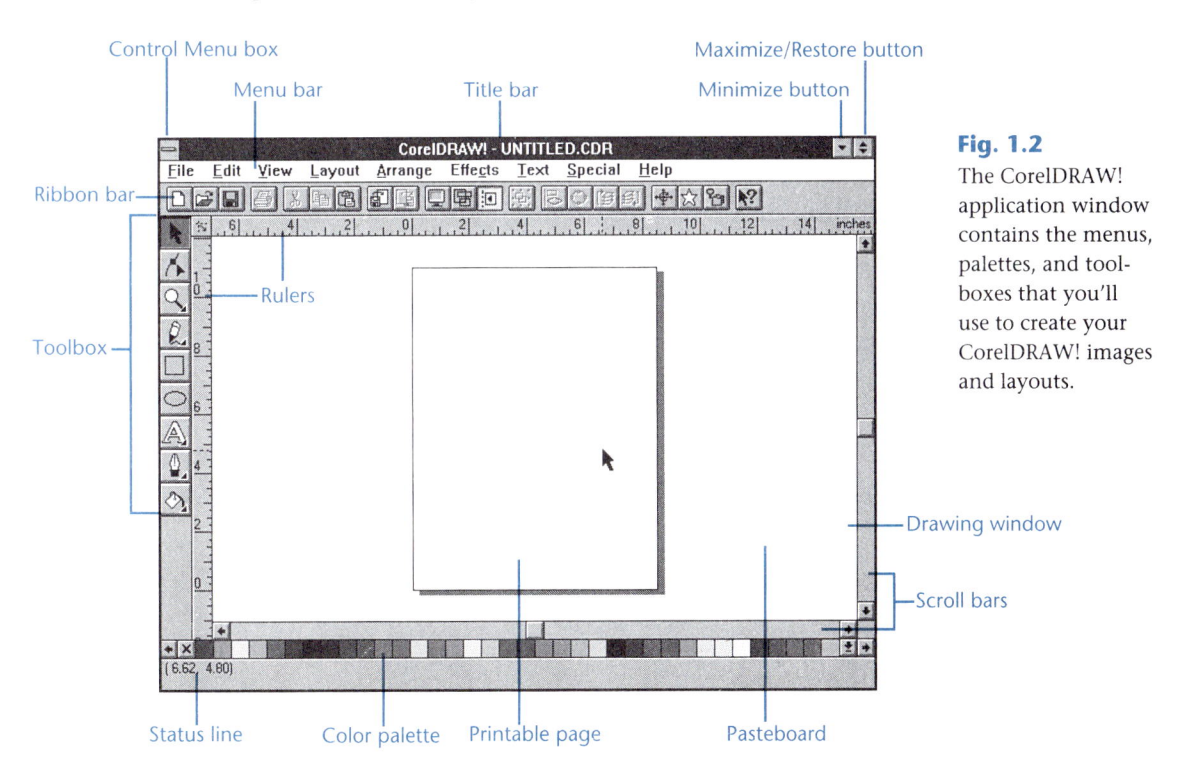

Fig. 1.2
The CorelDRAW! application window contains the menus, palettes, and toolboxes that you'll use to create your CorelDRAW! images and layouts.

The basic layout of the CorelDRAW! toolbox and menus is similar to that of the other Corel applications. The time you spend familiarizing yourself with this setup makes the other Corel applications easier to learn.

> **Troubleshooting**
>
> *I can't find the Corel application group or any of the Corel icons.*
>
> Check to see whether you accidentally deleted the program group or application icon. If the group is missing, go to Program Manager, open the **F**ile menu, and choose the **N**ew command. Select New Program Group (file is for an individual application) and click OK. Give the group a description (such as Corel 5) and click OK. To add missing application icons to the Corel group, go to Program Manager, open the **F**ile menu, and choose the **N**ew command. Select New Program Item and click OK. Click the Browse button, look for the COREL50 directory (or whatever directory you installed Corel in), and select the application from the Programs subdirectory. If you cannot find a directory with the CorelDRAW! 5 applications, you may have deleted them from your hard drive. In that case, you need to reinstall CorelDRAW!.
>
> *An older version of CorelDRAW! starts when I double-click the icon.*
>
> Version 3 of CorelDRAW! created a program group called Corel Graphics. Version 4 created a program group called Corel 4. Look at the title bar of the program-group window or at the name under the group icon. If the name is Corel Graphics or Corel 4, you have an older version. Look for a group with the name Corel 5; this is the new version. If you cannot find the group in Program Manager, open the **W**indow menu and choose **M**ore Windows. If the Corel group is not in this list of groups, see the preceding suggestion.

Learning the Parts of the CorelDRAW! Screen

Corel applications have a similar appearance, and the overall operation of the windows is the same. This section provides an overview of the basic Corel screen tools and sections.

At the top of the active Corel application window is the title bar, which shows the application name. CorelDRAW! also shows the name of the file currently being edited. Because the file in figure 1.2 does not yet have a name, CorelDRAW! calls it UNTITLED.CDR.

Learning the Parts of the CorelDRAW! Screen

> **Note**
>
> All CorelDRAW! file names have a CDR extension. All CorelDRAW! backup files have a BAK extension. This extension is useful when you are trying to locate CorelDRAW! files in the Windows File Manager.

At the far left end of the title bar is the control menu box, a small box with a horizontal line. Double-clicking this box terminates CorelDRAW! and returns you to Windows.

As in all Windows applications, clicking the Minimize button shrinks the application to an icon. Keep in mind that the application is still running even though it's shrunk to an icon.

Click the Maximize button to enlarge the CorelDRAW! window so that it takes up the maximum amount of allowable screen space. To restore the window to its original size, click the Restore button (a double-headed arrow), which replaces the Maximize button.

The menu bar, which is located below the title bar, contains the various pull-down menus used to operate the Corel applications.

New to CorelDRAW! 5, the ribbon bar, located directly below the menu bar, holds buttons used to access commands that perform common operations, such as saving, printing, cutting, and pasting.

The status line is located at the bottom of the screen. The status line provides important information about the current state of CorelDRAW! objects, such as their screen location, size, line, number of objects selected, and interior fill characteristics. The status line is displayed by default, but you can hide it or change its location by selecting options in the Preferences dialog box (available through the Special menu).

The toolbox, which runs along the left side of the window, contains the tools you use to create and modify the basic shapes that comprise a finished drawing. You take a detailed look at the toolbox later in this chapter in "Reviewing the Toolbox Tools."

The rulers are located below the ribbon bar and along the side of the toolbox. Rulers help you place and size objects in the drawing window. Ruler increments are user-defined. The page-origin location defaults to the lower-left corner of the page so that all measurements are positive.

Tip
Leave the page grid origin at its default location unless you have a specific reason for moving it. This location makes all the page-location numbers positive instead of a combination of positive and negative numbers.

The drawing window is located in the middle of the screen. This window is where the actual editing and layout of the drawing takes place. Contained within the drawing window is the printable page, which is a display representation of the currently active drawing. You can drag objects between the printable page and the drawing window. The area outside the boundaries of the printable page is known as the *pasteboard area*. The pasteboard area provides a place to keep objects you draw that you do not want to print on the printable page. It's a handy area to draw objects in without disturbing the objects you placed on the printable page. Remember, you can draw anywhere in the drawing window, but only the objects in the printable page will print.

As in other Windows applications, you use the horizontal and vertical scroll bars to scroll the drawing window. Click the arrow located at either end of the scroll bar to move in that direction. You also can use the horizontal and vertical scroll bars to move the image in larger increments; with the mouse, drag the scroll box across or up and down the scroll bar.

CorelDRAW! enables you to create and edit multiple-page documents. If you've added pages to the current CorelDRAW! file, a small section at the left end of the horizontal scroll bar displays the number of the current page and the number of pages in the file.

> **Note**
>
> The page-number area is displayed only in multiple-page files.

The color palette is located at the bottom of the window. You use the color palette to add fill and outline colors to the images in the drawing window. You can also choose among various color palettes by pulling down the View menu and choosing Color Palette. In the Color Palette submenu, you can set different options, such as the Palette Type (for example, Custom, Process, and Spot).

Viewing Your Work

You have three ways to view your work on-screen in CorelDRAW!: Editable Preview, Wireframe view, and Full-Screen Preview. The default drawing view is called Editable Preview. This view shows objects in full color with all their attributes, such as line thickness, pattern fills, and special effects (see fig. 1.3). Fills that use PostScript Textures and halftone screens, however, are not displayed in Editable Preview mode.

Fig. 1.3
Viewing work in Editable Preview.

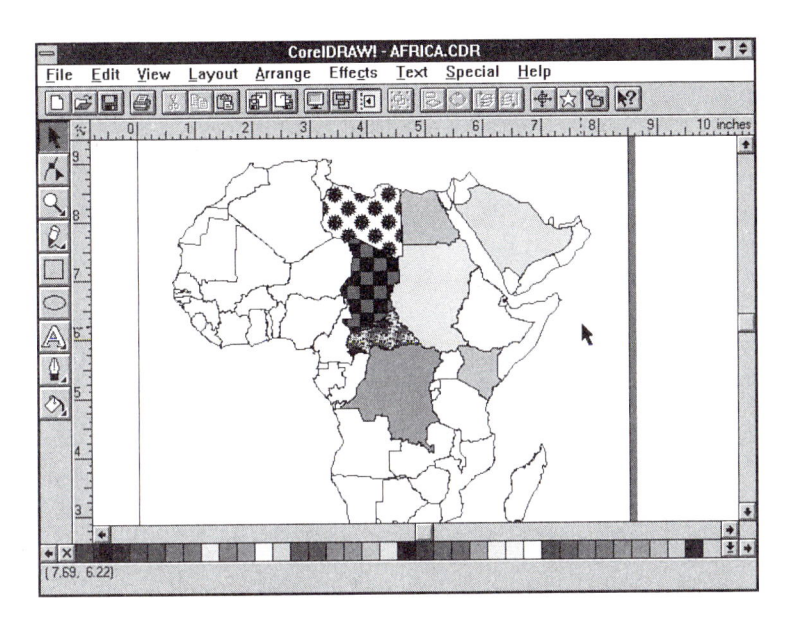

Wireframe view features quicker screen redraws because it shows only the skeleton form of the various objects, not their outlines or fill characteristics (see fig. 1.4). To change to Wireframe view, open the **V**iew menu and choose the Wir**e**frame option, or choose the Wireframe button on the ribbon bar.

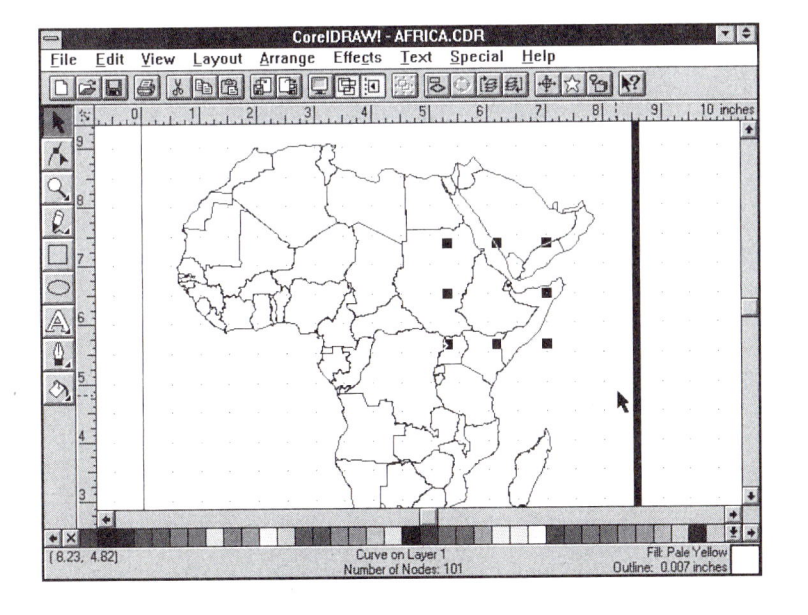

Fig. 1.4
Viewing work in Wireframe view speeds up the display of drawings by showing only the outline of the objects in the drawing window.

Tip

To switch between Editable Preview and Wireframe view, press Shift+F9.

When you edit in Wireframe view, all object characteristics are displayed at the right end of the status line. When you become familiar with CorelDRAW! operation, you may find that Wireframe view used in conjunction with the status-line information provides optimal drawing performance.

All CorelDRAW! tools and commands work in both Wireframe view and Editable Preview. In either view, you can use the Zoom tool to enlarge or reduce the drawing or to zoom in on a specific detail. Both views also have scroll bars at the edges of the window so that you can scroll your viewing window to see other portions of your drawing. You also can display facing pages on-screen (useful for multipage documents) in both views.

The third way to view your drawing on-screen is in Full-Screen Preview mode. Full-Screen Preview displays the drawing at its actual size and in full color, and removes all CorelDRAW! features from the screen (see fig. 1.5).

Fig. 1.5

Viewing work in Full-Screen Preview removes CorelDRAW! menus and shows the images in the drawing window as they will actually print.

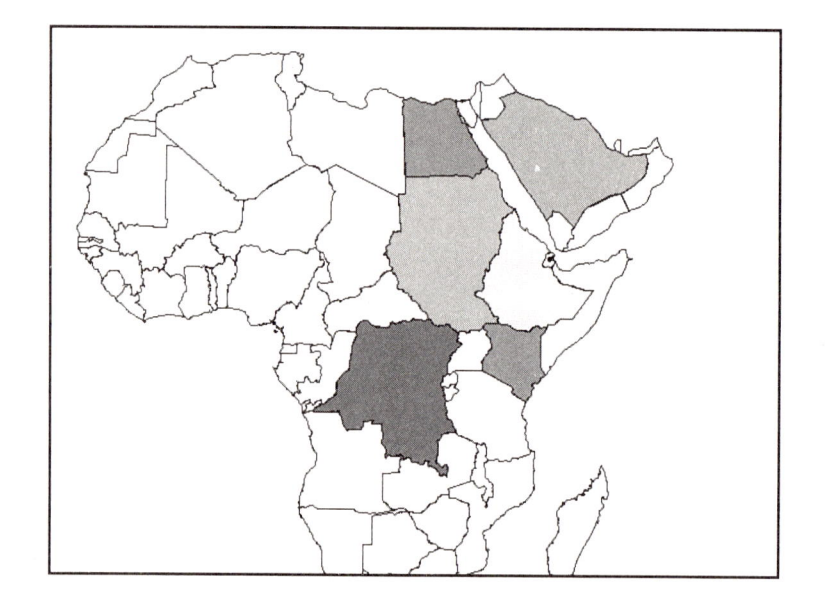

Full-Screen Preview is the most accurate representation of how your image will actually print. You cannot edit a drawing in this mode, however.

To preview your drawing, open the **V**iew menu and choose Full-Screen **P**review, or press the F9 key. Click the right mouse button to return to the drawing window.

Reviewing the Toolbox Tools

Just as a carpenter uses a box of tools to build a house, you use the CorelDRAW! tools to build your drawings. The following descriptions start with the top tool and move top to bottom through the toolbox.

The Pick tool is the arrow icon at the top of the toolbox. Use this tool to select and move the objects on which you want to work. You can select an object in numerous ways; the most fundamental method is clicking the object.

CorelDRAW! objects are constructed by a set of nodes. The Shape tool, shaped like an arrowhead, enables you to change the location, alignment, and performance characteristics of the nodes.

The Zoom tool has a fly-out menu that provides different levels of drawing magnification. The Zoom In tool (+) enlarges your drawing; the Zoom Out tool (-) reduces the drawing.

You use the Pencil, Rectangle, and Ellipse tools to draw lines, boxes, and circles.

The Text tool fly-out menu enables you to enter text in the drawing. Users of earlier versions of CorelDRAW! can access the Symbol roll-up window by clicking the star button in the ribbon bar or by opening the **S**pecial menu and choosing Symbols **R**oll-Up.

The Outline Pen tool provides a fly-out menu that enables you to change the outline characteristics of the selected objects. Use the Outline Pen fly-out menu to control the thickness, color, pattern, and endpoints of lines.

The Fill tool provides a fly-out menu of tools that control the fill attributes of the selected object. Use the Fill fly-out menu to control object colors, patterns, and other fill effects.

> **Tip**
> Press the space bar to activate the Pick tool. Press again to return to the drawing tool you used before Pick.

> **Tip**
> To set the right mouse button to automatically magnify 2X when you click it, select **S**pecial **P**references and click the General tab. Choose 2X Zoom from the pop-up list in the Right Mouse Button section of the dialog box.

Troubleshooting

I click the tools, but no fly-out menus appear.

Not all tools have fly-out menus associated with them. In Corel 5, the tools with a small black triangle in the lower right corner of their icons have fly-out menus. Some fly-out menus open immediately when you click the tool, such as the Fill tool, and other fly-outs open only after you click on the tool icon and hold the mouse button for a second. Tool icons in CorelDRAW! 4 do not indicate fly-outs with the small triangle, so you'll have to experiment to locate the fly-out.

(continues)

> (continued)
>
> I select the Zoom In tool from the Zoom tools fly-out menu, but after I use it once, I have to reopen the Zoom tools fly-out menu and reselect the Zoom In tool.
>
> Although somewhat inconvenient, this is the way many tools on the fly-out menus work. Tools such as Zoom In and other Zoom tools are available only for the next operation you perform. However, the F2, F3, and F4 keys provide quick ways to activate the Zoom In, Zoom Out, and Zoom-to-Fit-in-Window modes, respectively.

How CorelDRAW! Creates Objects

Early computer-based drawings were composed of a series of dots that combined to form a screen-based image. Each dot was an isolated black or white spot. You could perform certain manipulations with the screen images by turning on and off individual dots of the image, but substantial changes or precise control over the shape of objects in the image were extremely difficult to perform.

CorelDRAW! uses a method of image creation called *vector graphics*. This technique is relatively common today, but was revolutionary when it was introduced. In vector images, the dots are part of an overall object. Corel retains information about the object (such as size, line thickness, and fill) and combines the dots to form the desired image. This idea is the essence of vector-graphic imaging.

To retain this object information, CorelDRAW! recognizes the size and shape of the underlying object and then creates a mathematical model based on nodal points and the angle of the lines connected to the node. The number of node points used depends on the complexity of the object. When the user changes the size of the object, CorelDRAW! calculates the new information and connects the nodes with the appropriate dots. The change does not affect the quality of the object, because all object information is contained in the nodes, which are kept current.

In essence, a Corel drawing is nothing more than a mathematical combination of nodes that represent objects. As the objects are placed on top of one another and given various attributes, such as line thickness or fill type, the user creates a final illustration. Objects are simplified or made more complex based on the number and type of nodes used.

Thinking of your drawings as combinations of objects with specific attributes instead of as dots connected on-screen, is important. When you make this transformation in your thinking, CorelDRAW! becomes relatively simple to understand, and you begin to appreciate the true power of this package.

Understanding Object Outlines, Fills, and Defaults

CorelDRAW! does not really know that a drawing exists. It only knows that there are a certain number of objects, each of which has specific defining characteristics, and that it is supposed to draw these objects in a certain order and orientation.

Most objects consist of two basic components: an outline and an interior fill. The outline is a line that defines the appearance of the perimeter of the object; the interior fill determines the color and texture of the space within that perimeter.

Tip
If no object is selected when you choose Apply in a roll-up window, a dialog box appears, enabling you to set the defaults for the selected object types in this session and future sessions.

> **Note**
> You can make your drawing life a lot simpler by setting the default Outline and Interior Fill characteristics early in the life of your drawing. *Defaults*, or settings that the program uses automatically for a feature, provide more consistency across the various drawing objects and greatly speed the drawing process. Every time you change the default, CorelDRAW! applies the new default to all objects you subsequently create.

Even text characters have an outline and interior fill, which means that each character is individually controlled, making for some very interesting color and texture combinations. Both the outline and fill can have various designs, colors, and styles. CorelDRAW! enables you to define default characteristics for outlines and fills, which saves you time when you are creating graphic objects, Artistic text, and Paragraph text.

▶ See "Defining Defaults for Object Attributes," p. 578

Using Roll-Up Windows

CorelDRAW! provides roll-up windows that streamline the application of numerous attributes to selected objects. For example, the Pen roll-up window shown in figure 1.6 provides ready access to the fly-out menu options, such as line thickness, arrows, patterns, and color. Many of the more widely used CorelDRAW! features (blend, fill, extrude, lens, and so on) have their own

26 Chapter 1—An Overview of CorelDRAW! 5

roll-up windows. Unlike dialog boxes, which must be closed before you can continue to work on a drawing, roll-up windows can remain open as you work. You can open and close the roll-up windows as you need them.

Fig. 1.6
The Pen roll-up window enables you to change the line thickness, color, and other attributes of the currently selected object.

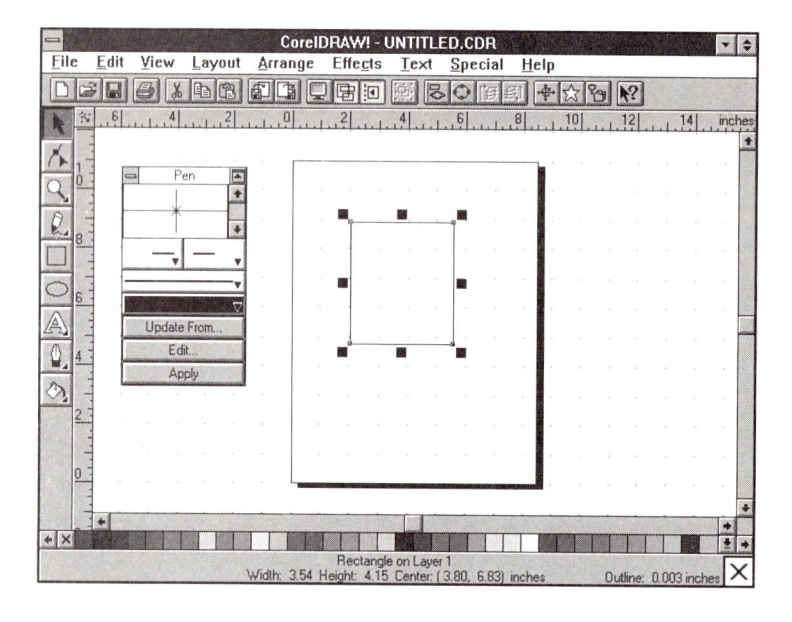

To access a roll-up window, click the roll-up window icon in a tool's fly-out menu, choose the desired roll-up from a menu, or click one of the three roll-up buttons in the ribbon bar at the top of the screen. The appropriate roll-up window appears.

Click the up arrow in the upper-right corner to roll up the window. The window rolls up, leaving only the title bar of the roll-up window. Click the down arrow to reopen the window. You also can move the roll-up window to any desired screen location by dragging it by the title bar. To compress the roll-up window and move it to the upper-left or upper-right corner of the editing screen, click the control menu box in the upper-left corner of the roll-up window and choose A**r**range All.

Tip
After applying text, fill, and/or outline attributes to an object, if you want to apply identical such attributes to another object all at once, use Copy Attributes From on the Edit menu.

To use a roll-up window, select the object to which you want to apply the attribute or attributes, click the attribute or attributes (such as line thickness, dashing, and color) in the roll-up window, and then click Apply in the roll-up window. CorelDRAW! applies the attributes to the selected object. After you choose the attributes you want from a roll-up window, you can apply these attributes to any number of objects simply by selecting each object and clicking Apply in the roll-up window. This procedure is much easier than individually choosing each attribute for each object from a menu.

> **Note**
>
> To arrange all open roll-up windows as title bars in the upper-left or upper-right corner of the screen, open the Control menu in any open roll-up window and choose the Arrange All command. Similarly, you can close all open roll-up windows from the same control menu. You may encounter Insufficient Memory messages if you attempt to arrange all available roll-ups.

Troubleshooting

I click a button in a roll-up window, but nothing happens.

Most buttons in roll-up windows only work when an object is selected. Be sure you select the object; then click the button. Also, be sure the button is appropriate to the type of object you have selected. For instance, none of the buttons in the Node Edit roll-up have any effect unless you select a node or nodes instead of an object.

I made several changes to the settings in a roll-up window, but none of the changes seem to affect the object I selected.

To change an object using a roll-up window, you must select an object, make the changes to the roll-up settings, and click the Apply button to apply the roll-up settings to the selected object. The settings in the roll-up remain as you changed them until you close the roll-up. The roll-up returns to its default settings once it is closed.

Using Roll-Up Windows and Styles

The roll-up windows provide ready access to multiple attributes that are related to the same function so that you can apply these attributes at one time instead of separately. You can use roll-up windows effectively to apply a *style*—a consistent combination of attributes—to a set of objects by defining the roll-up selections, selecting the object, and clicking Apply. You also can apply styles to artistic and paragraph text. Artistic text, created with the Artistic text tool, is used in your drawings when you need small amounts of text, such as figure labels or other short text strings. You can apply CorelDRAW!'s special effects to artistic text. Paragraph text, created using the Paragraph Text tool, should be used for longer passages of text that do not require special effects.

Styles include all the attributes needed to accurately define the appearance of the selected object. When you create a style, you give it a name. You access styles by selecting the object, clicking the right mouse button (if you haven't reassigned the right mouse button to an action other than Object Menu), and choosing Apply Styles to display all applicable style names. Styles are a combination of different object attributes, but the other defaults deal only with one particular aspect of an object (for example, fill or outline). CorelDRAW! stores these styles in templates that you can access from within any drawing.

The major benefit associated with using styles is consistency of appearance. Drawings become "busy" when the various text or graphic objects have many different appearances. Defining and applying styles speed your operation of CorelDRAW! and also give your drawings a professional appearance.

Follow these steps to define a style:

1. Create the graphic object or text.

2. Apply the desired formatting characteristics, such as line thickness, color, and fill.

3. Select the object, and click the right mouse button to display the object menu (see fig. 1.7).

Fig. 1.7
The Object menu lists options that enable you to create and modify object styles.

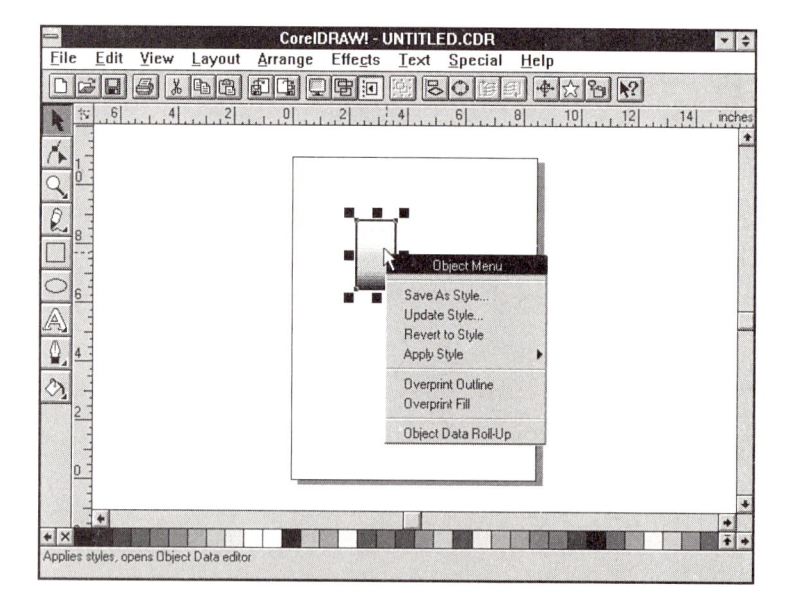

4. Choose the Save As Style option to display the Save Style As dialog box (see fig. 1.8). Notice the various options that a particular object's style definition includes.

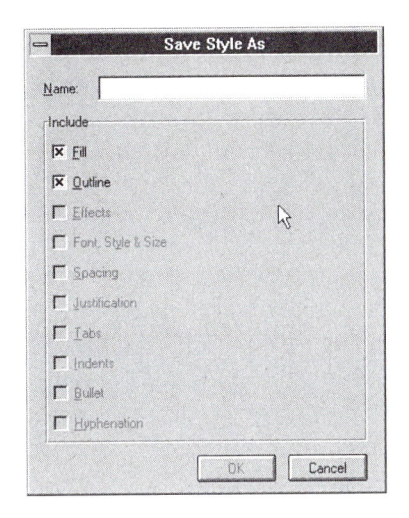

Fig. 1.8
The Save Style As dialog box lists the attributes of the selected object, such as Fill and Outline.

5. Choose the various options you want to include in the style, type a style name, and click OK.

The style now appears in the Style roll-up window. You can create styles for text and graphic objects.

Getting On-Line Help

CorelDRAW! comes with an on-line help facility that truly puts a reference at your fingertips. The Help lookup procedures follow the standard Windows conventions, so if you know how to use Help in other Windows applications, you should be able to run the CorelDRAW! Help menus. This section covers the features available in CorelDRAW! 5.

> **Note**
>
> Corel 5 gives you additional help by way of its Bubble Help feature. This feature automatically gives the name of any button in the toolbox or ribbon bars. Simply position the pointer over the button, and after a moment, the name of the button appears in a yellow bubble next to the pointer. Remove the pointer from over the button to close the bubble.

Clicking Help in the menu bar reveals a drop-down menu that contains several options: Contents, Screen/Menu Help, Search For Help On, Tutorial, and About CorelDRAW!. Each option has a useful and unique function.

Choosing Contents (F1) reveals the help window's table of contents, shown in icon form. To see specific help information, simply click the appropriate item and follow the layers of dialog boxes to your desired topic. When you finish, click the Back button as many times as necessary to return to the Contents screen, or close the dialog box to exit Help altogether.

Choosing Screen/Menu Help (Shift+F1) changes the cursor to an arrow and a question mark. Moving this cursor to any currently accessible screen location or active menu command (boldfaced, not dimmed) opens the Help information for that particular feature. This Help function is particularly handy when you are becoming familiar with various tools and menu commands. Right-clicking on any button on the ribbon bar will activate Help specific to the function of that button.

The Search For Help On (Ctrl+F1) menu selection opens the Search dialog box, shown in figure 1.9. You can scroll through the topics in the display list and then double-click your desired topic. Alternatively, type the name of the topic in the text box at the top of the dialog box and then click Show Topics to reveal various topics related to your selection. Double-click the topic (or select the topic and then click Go To) to display the help section pertaining to your selection.

Fig. 1.9
The Search dialog box lists the CorelDRAW! help topics. Type a partial topic name to jump to that name in the topics list.

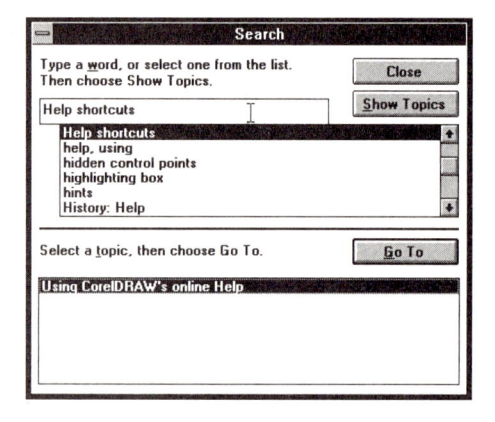

Choosing Tutorial opens the CorelDRAW! tutorial window. The tutorial provides several lessons on using the basic tools of CorelDRAW!. As you move through the tutorial, you can get hands-on practice by performing the lesson steps in CorelDRAW!. If you are new to CorelDRAW!, the tutorial will get you off to a flying start.

Choosing About CorelDRAW! displays a dialog box that contains information about the licensed owner, the serial and version number of your Corel application, and image information (such as the number of groups, number of objects, and free disk space). This information is handy as a benchmark for determining the complexity of your drawing.

> **Troubleshooting**
>
> *When I try to open the Help menu while a dialog box is open, nothing happens.*
>
> The menu commands are not available while a dialog box is open. Press F1 to get help while a dialog box is open. Help opens a window related to the topics in the open dialog box.
>
> *When I select Contents or Search for Help On from the Help menu, I get a message saying* `Can Not Open Help`.
>
> It is likely that the CorelDRAW! help files were not installed. You must run SETUP.EXE on the first CorelDRAW! application disk and install the help files for the application. See Appendix A for more information on installing the Corel applications.

Exiting CorelDRAW!

Once you're done exploring the CorelDRAW! screens, menus, tools, and other features, you can exit the application by selecting Exit from the File menu. If you created a drawing or made changes to an existing drawing that you opened, you'll be prompted to save the changes made to the file. Select Yes if you want to save the changes, or select No to abandon the changes and exit the program. If you decide you are not ready to quit, you can choose Cancel to return to the CorelDRAW! application window.

And, as with most menu commands in Corel, you can use a keyboard shortcut to issue the exit command, Alt+F4.

Planning Ahead

The only way that CorelDRAW!'s WYSIWYG (What-You-See-Is-What-You-Get) capability can work properly is if the computer display is formatted to comply with the capabilities of the output device, such as a printer. If you don't consider the desired output form before you start drawing, you may have to redo a great deal of work.

It is helpful to remember that CorelDRAW! actually is several different software packages (CorelDRAW!, CHART, MOSAIC, and so on) sold in one box, as opposed to many different capabilities provided in a single application. The Windows 3.1 feature called *Object Linking and Embedding* (OLE) enables you to use the Corel packages in a complementary way. Keeping this feature in mind early in the design process strengthens your work.

Printing Considerations (Monochrome versus Color)

Just as audio speakers determine the perceived sound quality of a stereo system, the quality of your final drawing is only as good as the output device. You must design your drawing around the limitations of that device.

If the final device is a color PostScript printer, you have a wide variety of high-quality print options, and your imagination can soar. If the final device is a monochrome (black-and-white) laser printer, such as a Hewlett-Packard LaserJet 4, the quality still is excellent, but the screen colors may assume unpredictable shades of gray as they are converted from the screen colors to a printer-compatible format.

If you do not take your output device into consideration early in the design process, you may have to correct some of your design work to accommodate the requirements of the final output device. Simple things (for example, choosing portrait or landscape printing) can dramatically affect the amount of work involved in creating drawings.

▶ See "Printing—the Details," p. 299

▶ See "Choosing a Page Layout and Display Style," p. 542

The good news in CorelDRAW! is that most Corel objects are created in a vector-graphic format as opposed to a bitmap format. A vector-graphic format enables you to make major changes in the size and shape of objects without negatively affecting the quality of the final output. If you need to change the output device, you should be able to modify the drawings to accommodate the change. A little advance planning, however, helps prevent this situation. For tips, procedures, and suggestions on creating high-quality output for commercial printers, see Chapter 12, "Using Color for Commercial Success."

Object Linking and Embedding

A major benefit of working in the Windows environment is the standard Object Linking and Embedding (OLE) feature. These features become particularly handy when you work with the various Corel applications.

Object linking provides automatic updating of information between one application file (called the *source*) and another application (called the *destination*). When changes are made to the source file's contents, affected sections of the destination file are updated—either automatically or at a time that you determine—to reflect those changes. Effective use of these features can greatly increase your efficiency when you are working with the various Corel applications and Windows applications (such as Microsoft Word for Windows).

You make substantial use of Windows features later in this book, where the various Corel applications are used in concert to make effective business-related presentations, documents, and illustrations. Whenever possible, look for ways that linking data can make your work more efficient and productive.

From Here...

This chapter covers much of the basic information needed to understand CorelDRAW!. For other information related to the topics in this chapter, consider these chapters:

- Chapter 2, "A Quick Start," walks you through the basic drawing tools by creating a simple drawing. Printing and saving a drawing is also covered.

- Chapter 3, "A Detailed Look at Object Drawing," gives detailed instructions for using and understanding CorelDRAW!'s drawing tools.

Chapter 2
A Quick Start

by Stephen R. Poland

The best way to learn a package is to perform simple tasks that enable you to work with many of the application features. This chapter takes you step by step through some of the basic features of CorelDRAW! 5 so that you can begin creating drawings immediately. As you become more comfortable with the program, you will want to experiment with the advanced concepts covered in later chapters.

In this chapter, you learn how to do the following:

- Draw circles, rectangles, and lines
- Fill objects with color
- Add text to drawings
- Move, select, and rotate objects
- Save a CorelDRAW! drawing
- Create a drawing using clipart and symbols
- Preview and print your drawings

Creating a Simple Drawing

The first part of this chapter introduces the basic drawing tools. In this section, you create the simple logotype and business card drawing shown in figure 2.1.

Fig. 2.1
Using CorelDRAW!'s drawing tools, you can combine simple shapes to create interesting designs.

```
         S R Postalthwait
               &
           Associates
       Certified Tax Preparation

           378 Audit Drive
          Revenue, NJ 40302
          Tel 415.555.1122
          Fax 415.555.2233
```

Setting the Page Size and Orientation

▶ See "Choosing a Page Layout and Display Style," p. 542

Before you begin drawing, it's a good idea to set up the size of the page and its orientation. The page size setting determines how large the printable page border in the drawing window is. If you choose a page size of 11 by 17 inches, the page border in the drawing window is scaled to 11 by 17 inches. Page orientation setting tells CorelDRAW! how you want the page positioned in the drawing window—either in portrait or landscape position. Portrait orientation positions the page so that it's taller than it is wide. Landscape orientation positions the page with the long side horizontal, essentially on its side.

To set the page size and orientation, follow these steps:

1. From the Layout menu, choose Page Setup. The Page Setup dialog box appears (see fig. 2.2).

Fig. 2.2
The Page Setup dialog box enables you to choose the size, layout, and display of the printable page in the drawing window.

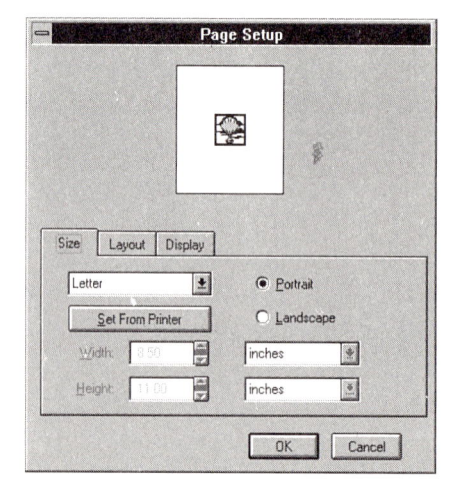

Creating a Simple Drawing   37

2. Click the down arrow to open the Page Size drop-down list. Select a page size from the list. Note that the custom page size allows you to manually define your page dimensions—that is, 3½-by-2 inches for a business card.

3. Click either Portrait or Landscape to choose a page orientation. Notice the page preview area at the top of the dialog box displays a preview image of a page depicting the size and orientation options you've selected.

4. Click OK to complete the page setup operation. When the Page Setup dialog box closes, the printable page border in the drawing window reflects the page setup changes you made.

Drawing Rectangles for the Business Card Logo

For this drawing, you are going to make the company logo first and then add the text to complete the business card. The logo is made from two squares, two circles, and three initials created by using the Artistic Text tool. You'll start the logo with the Rectangle tool to draw the two squares.

▶ See "Drawing a Rectangle or a Square from a Corner Point," p. 78

Follow these steps to draw the squares that make up the background of the business card:

1. Click the Zoom tool to open the Zoom Tools fly-out menu. Click the Actual Size icon (1:1) to enlarge the drawing window.

2. Click the Rectangle tool (F6). The pointer changes to cross hairs.

3. Position the cross hairs near the center of the drawing window.

4. Press and hold down the Ctrl key, and then click and drag the mouse down and to the right. The outline of the square appears as you drag.

> **Note**
>
> Holding down the Ctrl key makes the rectangle as long as it is wide, thus creating a square. If you do not hold down the Ctrl key, you create an rectangle as you drag.

5. Stop dragging when the square is the size you want—about 1.2 inches, in this case. Release the mouse button and then release the Ctrl key. You should have a square like the one shown in figure 2.3.

6. Draw the center square of the logo by repeating steps 2 through 4, but make the square about 1 inch on a side. At this point, don't worry about where the square is on the page.

Tip
The size of the square appears in the status line below the drawing as you draw the circle.

38 Chapter 2—A Quick Start

Fig. 2.3
Pressing the Ctrl key while drawing with the Rectangle tool creates a perfect square.

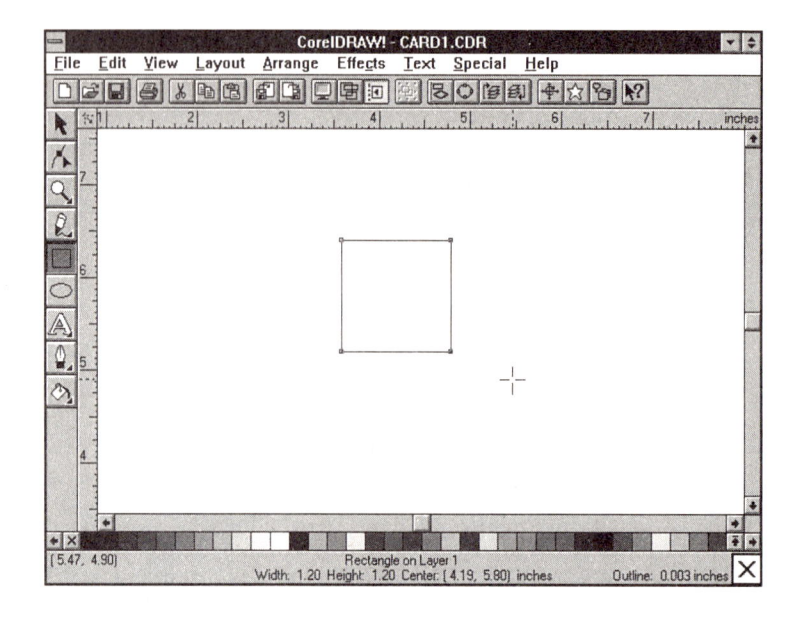

▶ See "Selecting Individual Objects with the Pick Tool," p. 94

7. Click the Pick tool or press the space bar. The square you just drew should be selected, as indicated by the small black squares (*handles*) that appear around it.

   If the square is not selected, position the Pick tool so that it touches the square and click the left mouse button. The handles that appear indicate that the square is selected (see fig. 2.4). After an object is selected, you can move, shape, or perform other operations on it.

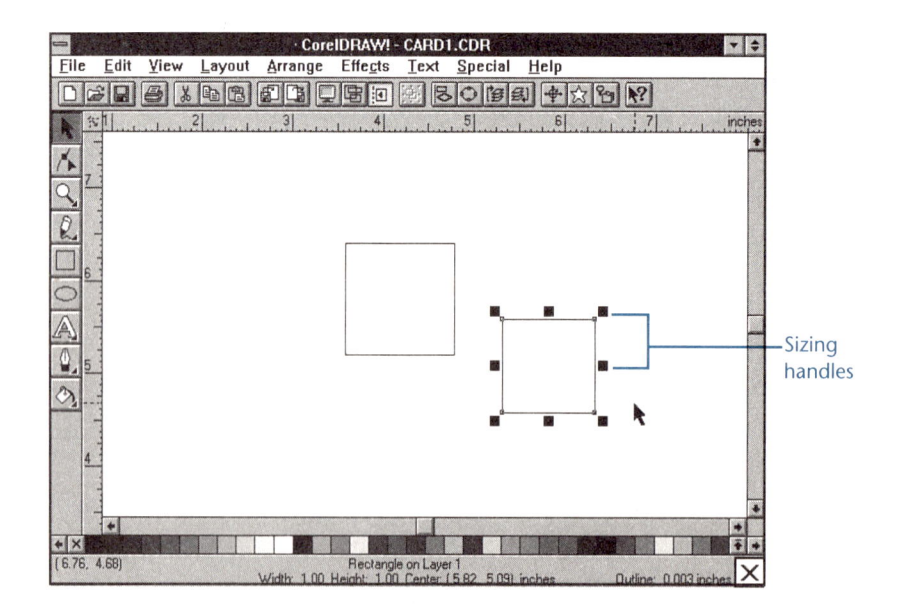

Fig. 2.4
Sizing handles appear around objects selected with the Pick tool.

8. With the mouse pointer touching the square, drag the mouse. The pointer changes to four arrows, and a dashed outline shows the location of the square (see fig. 2.5).

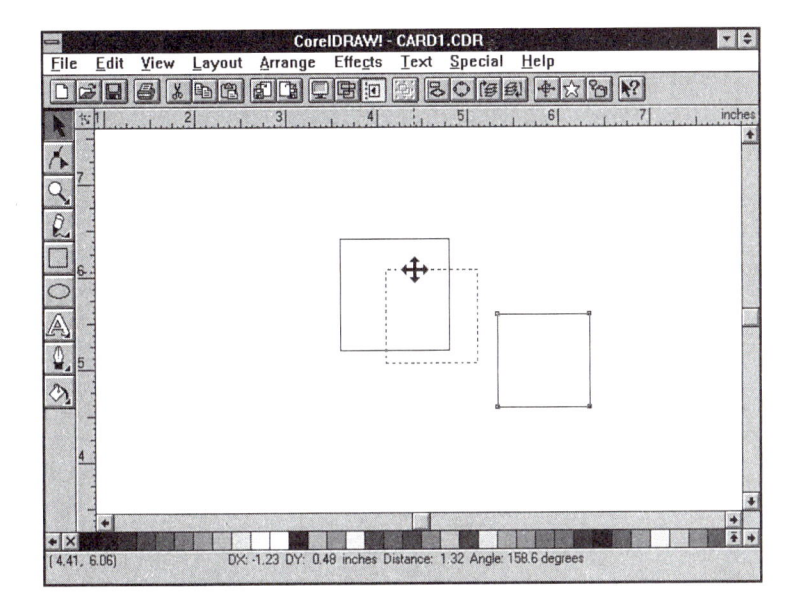

Fig. 2.5
As you drag an object, a dashed outline shows the location of the object.

9. When the dashed outline is centered in the first square, release the mouse button.

Tip
If the smaller square appears to keep aligning to the grid, choose Layout and turn off Snap to Grid so that the check mark disappears.

> **Note**
>
> If the second square isn't exactly where you want it, use the Pick tool to select the square, and then move it again.

Shading the Square

The interior square of the logo needs to be filled with color. You can choose any color you like for this design.

▶ See "Working with Solid Fills," p. 150

To shade the center of the logo, follow these steps:

1. Click the Pick tool.
2. Click the inner square to select it. Sizing handles appear around the square.

Fig. 2.6
Filling objects is as simple as selecting the object and clicking a color in the color palette.

Tip
The Ellipse tool works like the Rectangle tool. Hold down the Ctrl key while dragging to create a circle. The status line shows the size of the circle as you draw it.

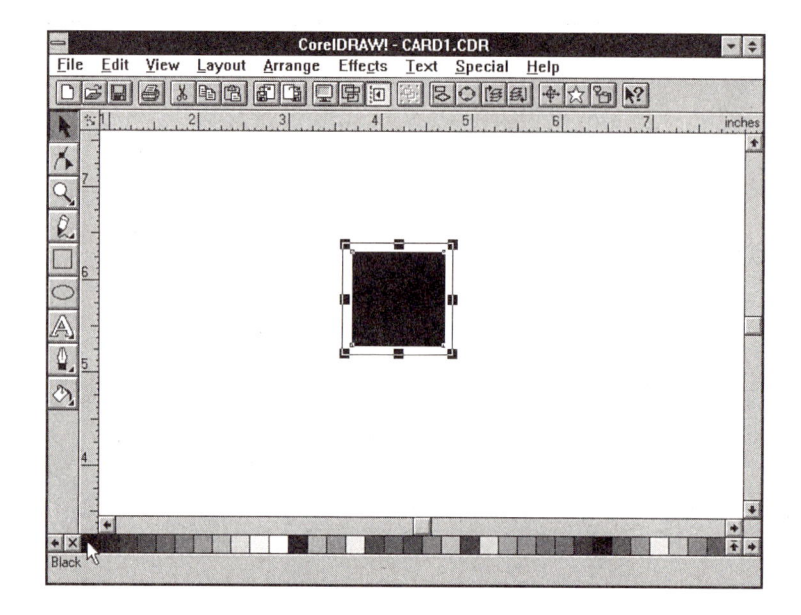

▶ See "Drawing an Ellipse or a Circle from a Corner Point," p. 82

3. Fill the square with one of the black shades located in the color palette by left-clicking the dark tones you want to use (see fig. 2.6). If you don't see the black shades on the color palette, open the View menu and choose Color Palette, Uniform Colors.

Enhancing the Logo with Circles

To add variety to our squares, we'll take a bite out of two corners by placing white circles over the two opposite corners. For this part of the drawing, use the Ellipse tool to draw the circles.

To draw the circles for the logo, follow these steps:

1. Click the Ellipse tool or press F7.

2. In a blank part of the drawing area, click and drag the mouse to make a small circle about 0.2 inches across. Watch the status line at the bottom of the screen to size the circle properly.

3. Release the mouse button.

4. Click the Pick tool. The small circle is selected automatically.

5. Open the **E**dit menu and choose **D**uplicate to create a duplicate of the circle, or use the shortcut Ctrl+D. The second circle appears slightly above and to the right of the first circle. The position of the duplicate is determined by your settings in General Preferences for placing duplicates.

Creating a Simple Drawing   41

6. Fill the circles with a white color by selecting each circle with the Pick tool and clicking a white color in the color palette at the bottom of the screen.

7. Drag one circle to the upper-right corner of the two squares, and drag the other circle to the lower-left corner. Make sure the circle outline does not touch the outside square.

8. Change the outline of one circle to white by selecting a circle and clicking the white color in the color palette with the right mouse button. The outline of the circle changes to white. Repeat the operation for the other circle. Figure 2.7 shows the logo to this point.

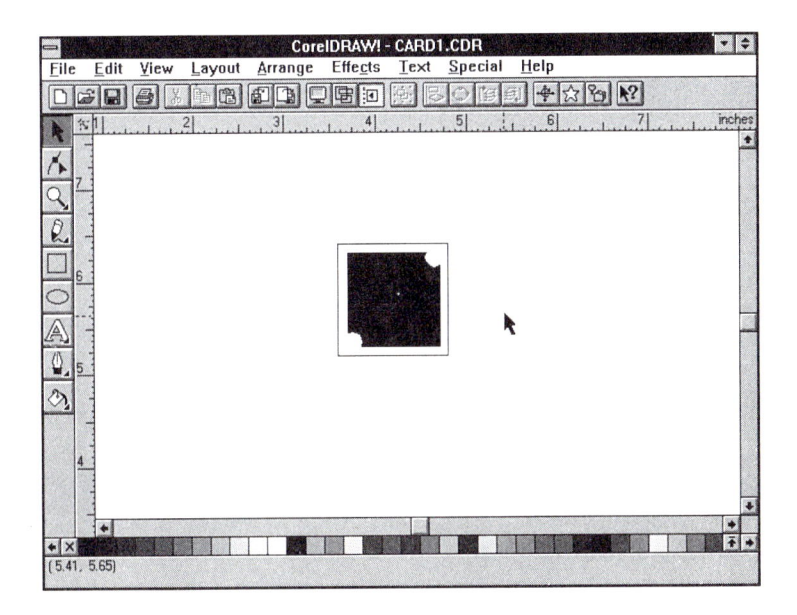

Fig. 2.7
The company logo with two white circles covering opposite corners.

Adding Initials to the Logo Background

You have now completed the background of a corporate logo. To finish the logo, you use the Artistic Text tool to add the initials to the background (for more information, see Chapter 7, "Adding Text to a Drawing").

To add the initials to the logo, follow these steps:

1. Click the Text tool or press F8. The pointer changes to cross hairs when you move it into the drawing window. Position the pointer in a blank area of the drawing window and click once. Now the pointer changes to an I-beam.

2. Type a capital letter **S**. The letter appears where you clicked the mouse.

3. Move the pointer to another blank area of the drawing window and click once. Type a capital letter **R**. Move the pointer again and type a capital letter **P**.

4. Click the Pick tool. Select the letter S. Sizing handles appear around the letter.

5. From the **T**ext menu, choose Text **R**oll-Up. The Text roll-up window appears (see fig. 2.8).

Fig. 2.8
The Text roll-up window enables you select fonts, type sizes, and text alignment.

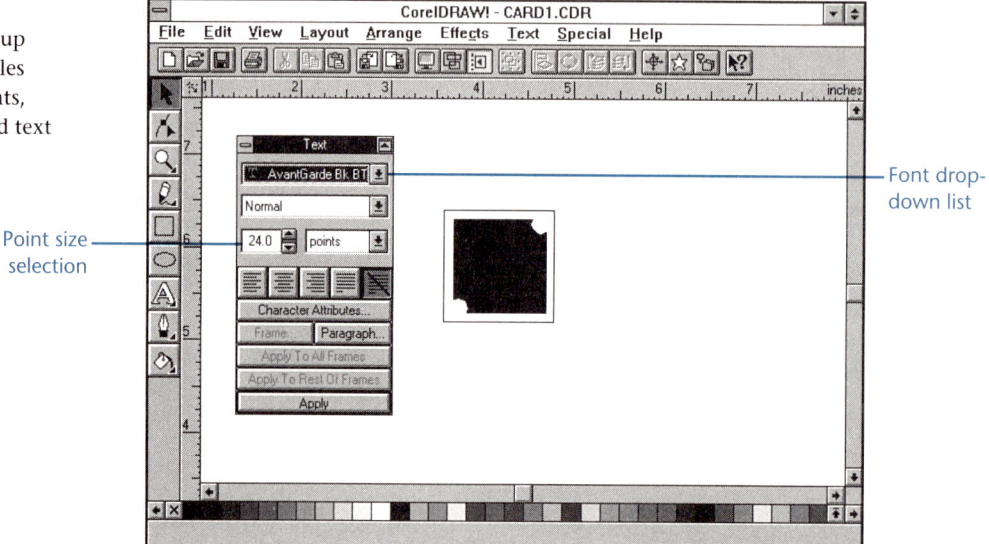

6. Click the down arrow to open the font drop-down list.

7. Scroll down the list and click Times New Roman. Click the font-size down arrow until the point size reaches 42.

8. Click Apply. The letter S changes to 42 point Times New Roman. Repeat steps 4–7 for the letters R and P.

9. Finally, complete the logo by filling each letter with white and dragging it to the center of the logo background. Arrange the letters in a stair-step pattern. Figure 2.9 shows the completed logo.

Adding a Border and Company Name and Address

You are now ready to draw a frame for the business card and add the company name and address.

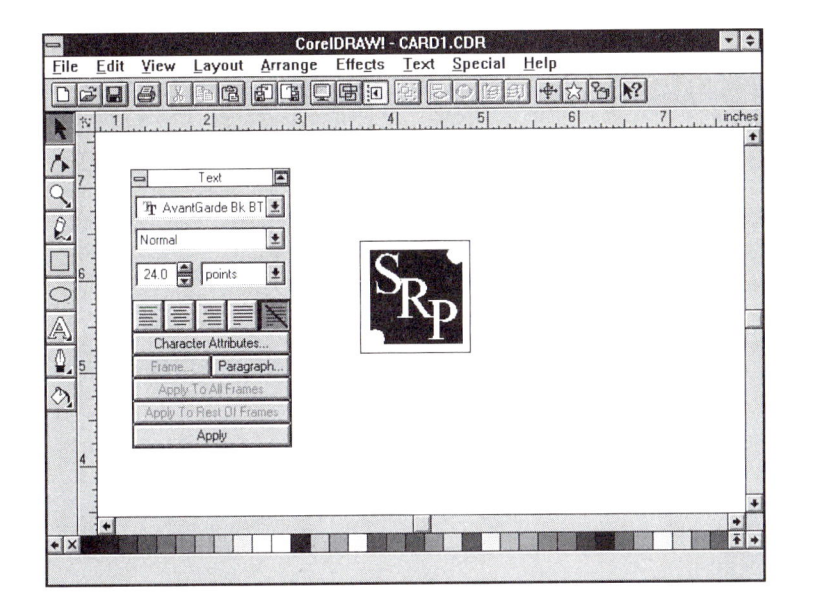

Fig. 2.9
The completed company logo.

To draw a frame for the business card, follow these steps:

1. Click the Rectangle tool or press F6.

2. Move the pointer to the drawing window and draw a rectangle 2 inches wide by 3.5 inches tall.

3. Click the Pick tool. Drag the rectangle so the company logo is positioned at the top center of the rectangle.

To add the company name and address text, follow these steps:

1. Click the Text tool. Type the following text in a blank area of the drawing window. Be sure to press the Enter key at the end of each line.

> **S R Postalthwait**
> **&**
> **Associates**
> **Certified Tax Preparation**
>
> 378 Audit Drive
> Revenue, NJ 40302
> Tel 415.555.1122
> Fax 415.555.2233

44 Chapter 2—A Quick Start

2. Click the Pick tool. The text you typed in step 1 is selected.

3. Click the down arrow in the Text roll-up to open the font-selection drop-down list. Scroll down the font list and click on Times New Roman.

4. Click the font-size-selection down arrow until the font size reads 42 point.

5. Click the Center Alignment button in the Text roll-up. Click Apply. The text is changed to center aligned Times New Roman 42 point (see fig. 2.10).

Fig. 2.10
Text is center aligned by clicking the Center Alignment button in the Text roll-up.

Center alignment button

6. Click the Pick tool. Drag the text to the lower center of the business card.

To round out the appearance of the business card, let's draw a rule between the company name and the business description. A *rule* is a horizontal or vertical line that separates various elements of text or graphics. You use the Freehand tool to draw a horizontal rule. Follow these steps:

1. Click the Freehand tool or press F5. The pointer changes to a cross-hair pointer as you move it to the drawing window or press F5.

2. Position the pointer below and to the left of the word Associates.

Creating a Simple Drawing   45

3. Press and hold the Ctrl key. Click the left mouse button once. This action plants the first end point of the line segment. Note that the status line (at the bottom of the screen) now displays start and end points.

4. Drag the pointer to the right. As you drag, a line is drawn from the first point to the pointer (see fig. 2.11). Click again when the line is evenly positioned under the word Associates.

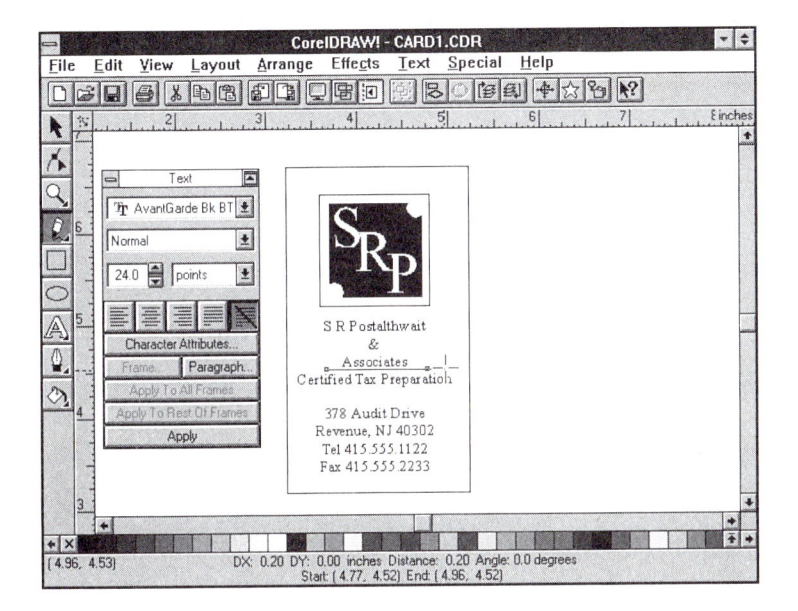

Fig. 2.11
Holding the Ctrl key while drawing with the Freehand tool constrains the line created to 15 degree angles as it's stretched and moved to the next end point.

Tip
If the line is slightly out of center from the rest of the text, click the Pick tool and drag the line to center it with the text.

Finally, let's group all the objects in the business card so that you can move the card as one unit in the drawing window. To group the objects in the business card, follow these steps:

1. Click the Pick tool or press the space bar.

2. Position the mouse pointer above and to the left of the business card.

3. Press and hold the mouse button. Drag the pointer down and to the left until the entire business card is enclosed in the dashed box that appears (see fig. 2.12).

4. Release the mouse button. Now all card objects are selected and you can work with all of them at the same time. The status line should indicate that ten objects are selected. This method of dragging a box around several objects is called *marquee selecting*.

5. Choose the **G**roup option from the **A**rrange menu to form the entire arrangement into a single group. You can now move the entire business card as one object.

46 Chapter 2—A Quick Start

Fig. 2.12
You can select several objects by dragging a marquee box around the objects to be selected.

Congratulations! You have created your first drawing in CorelDRAW!.

Saving the Drawing

At this point, you have put a lot of work into this business card. Not saving it would be a real shame. Maybe you will want to come back and change the address or phone numbers.

To save your business card drawing, follow these steps:

1. Open the **F**ile menu and choose Save **A**s to display the Save Drawing dialog box (see fig. 2.13).

Fig. 2.13
The Save Drawing dialog box.

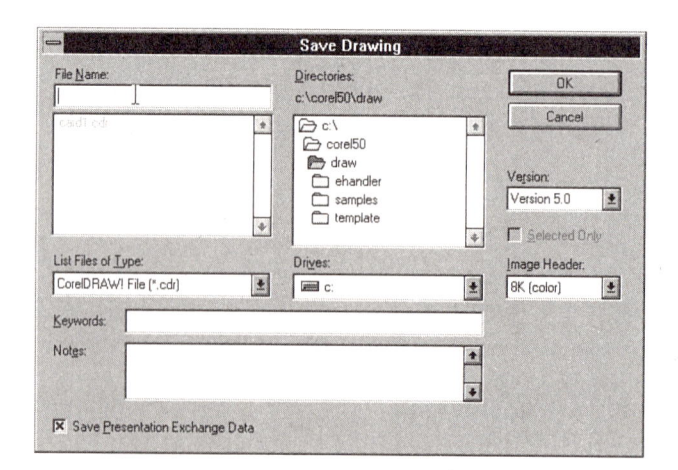

2. In the File **N**ame text box, type the name **card1**. CorelDRAW! automatically adds the extension CDR. This will overwrite the highlighted *.CDR.

3. Select the appropriate directory and drive.

4. Click OK to save the drawing in CorelDRAW!-compatible format.

You can save the file again later under the same name by pressing Ctrl+S, or by opening the **F**ile menu and choosing **S**ave.

Tip
CorelDRAW! provides numerous file formats. Saving and converting these formats is covered in Chapter 10, "Printing and Merging Files."

Troubleshooting

I try to draw circles using the Ellipse tool and I press the Ctrl key before I draw, but I keep getting ellipses, not circles.

To draw perfect circles using the Ellipse tool, you must press and hold the Ctrl key while you draw. Release the Ctrl key only after you release the mouse button to complete the circle. If you release the Ctrl key before releasing the mouse button, the circle in progress becomes an ellipse.

I attempt to fill an object with color, but no color appears when I click a color in the color palette.

Either you did not select the object to be filled, or you are probably working in Wireframe view. To see object fills and other object attributes, change to Editable Preview mode by choosing View, Wireframe to deselect the Wireframe option or use the Shift+F9 keys.

I try to move an unfilled object but it just changes shape.

You are clicking and dragging the object's sizing handles instead of clicking the object's outline and dragging. To drag a filled object, you can position the pointer anywhere on the object before dragging.

Creating a Drawing with Symbols and Clipart

Two kinds of art are available in CorelDRAW!—clipart and symbols. The distinction between them is not absolute, but symbols generally are simple and clipart usually is detailed. This section explains how to access symbols and clipart, add a symbol or clipart to your drawing, modify the added element, and combine it with other symbols and clipart to create a new picture.

Chapter 2—A Quick Start

The best way to consider the differences between clipart and symbols is to consider their place in your drawing. Clipart usually should be seen as a starting point of a drawing, one that you probably will not want to modify extensively. The complexity of clipart can make it hard to work with, and the drawing typically will be complete as it stands. Using a great deal of clipart can create a large file and, depending on your printer, may be difficult or time-consuming to print. Symbols use much less memory and do not significantly increase the size of your file. If you want to get fancier with your artwork, you can combine clipart and symbols to create complex, professional-looking drawings.

Retrieving Clipart into a Drawing

To get some practice in combining clipart and symbols in your drawing, in this section, you create a flyer announcing a company picnic. You begin this flyer by importing a clipart image of the sun.

To import the sun image, follow these steps:

1. Start a new page by choosing **F**ile, **N**ew. If you made additional changes to the logo file in the previous example, be sure to save the file again before proceeding.

2. Open the **F**ile menu and choose Mosaic Roll-Up**.** The Mosaic roll-up, shown in figure 2.14, appears.

Fig. 2.14
You can drag images from the Mosaic roll-up and drop them directly into your drawing.

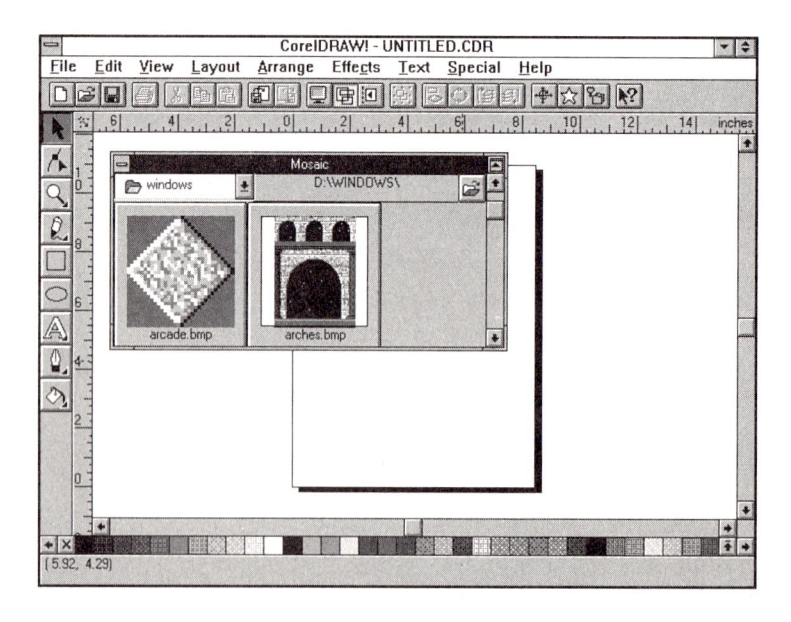

Creating a Drawing with Symbols and Clipart 49

3. Click the directory tree drop-down arrow and navigate to the Clipart subdirectory.

> **Note**
>
> The majority of clipart in CorelDRAW! 5 is located on CD-ROM. If you have a CD-ROM, insert the Clipart CD in the CD-ROM drive and change to your CD-ROM drive in the MOSAIC roll-up. The clipart images are displayed in the roll-up. If you only have floppy disks, some clipart will be installed in the clipart subdirectory.

4. Select the Sun file (SUN062.CDR) and drag it to the drawing window.

5. Close the Mosaic roll-up by double-clicking its Control Menu box in the upper-left corner of the window.

6. Before making any changes, choose **F**ile, **S**ave.

7. In the File **N**ame box, type the name **picnic**, and then click OK. Figure 2.15 shows the sun saved as a new drawing.

Fig. 2.15
Saving the sun clipart as a new drawing.

8. Click the Zoom tool to open the Zoom Tools fly-out menu. Click the Zoom In tool and move it to the center of the drawing window. Click once. The drawing window enlarges to show more of the sun image.

Modifying the Clipart

You may find that the clipart doesn't exactly fit your needs. Maybe your company makes sunglasses and the glasses in the drawing look too much like those made by the competition. You can modify the clipart to meet your needs.

To separate the parts of the sun so that you can make changes, follow these steps:

1. Click the Pick tool.

2. Click the sun object to select it.

3. Open the **A**rrange menu and choose the **U**ngroup option (Ctrl+U).

4. Deselect the sun drawing by clicking a blank portion of the page. The various objects that comprise the sun now are individually accessible.

Enlarging your view of the drawing makes it easy to select objects when several are close together. Follow these steps to zoom in on and remove the sunglasses:

1. Click the Zoom tool in the toolbox.

2. In the fly-out menu, click the Zoom In tool.

3. Move the mouse pointer (which looks like a magnifying glass) to the sunglasses and drag a marquee box around them (see fig. 2.16). The image enlarges to fill the screen.

Fig. 2.16
The Zoom In tool enables you to easily select an area of your drawing to magnify.

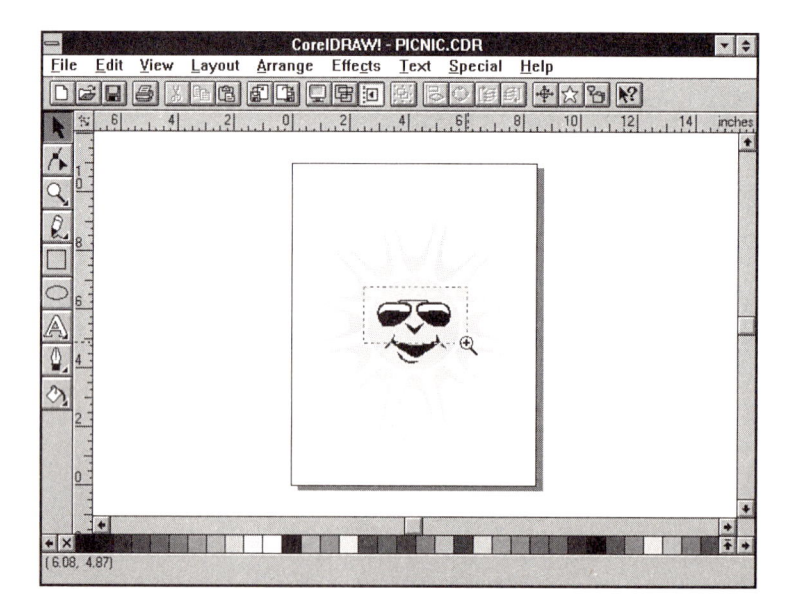

Creating a Drawing with Symbols and Clipart 51

4. Select the sunglasses by using the Pick tool (see fig. 2.17).

Fig. 2.17
The enlarged sun with glasses selected.

5. Open the menu and choose **E**dit, De**l**ete to remove the sunglasses from the drawing, or simply press Delete.

6. Point to the Zoom tool and hold down the mouse button until the fly-out menu opens. Then click the Zoom Out tool—the magnifying glass with the – sign (F3). The view is restored to the way it was before, and the new sun looks like the one shown in figure 2.18.

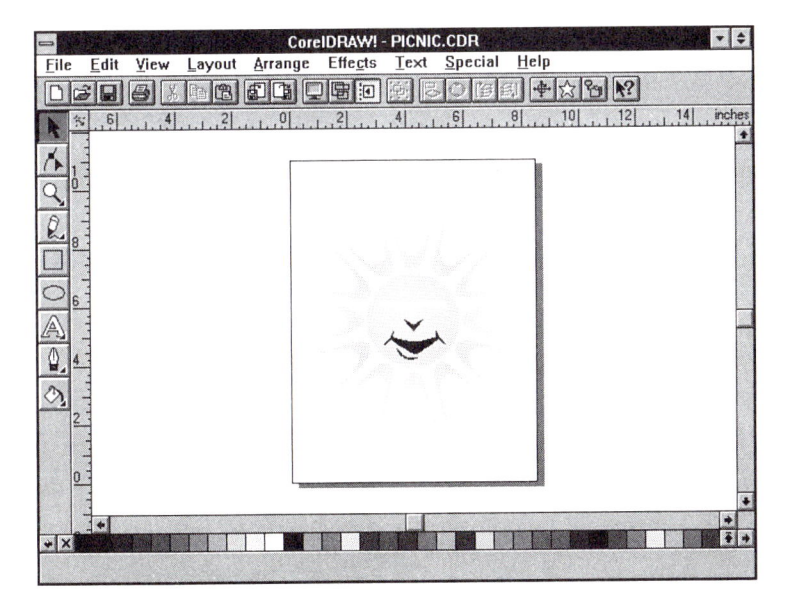

Fig. 2.18
The modified sun clipart (with sunglasses deleted).

52 Chapter 2—A Quick Start

Not only does Mr. Sun not have sunglasses, he doesn't have eyes. Follow these steps to give him eyes:

1. Select the remaining white eye slits, and choose **Edit, Delete** to remove them.

2. Click the Ellipse tool (F7) and draw an ellipse. Give it a black fill by clicking the black palette color.

3. Draw a second, smaller ellipse with a solid white fill. Place this second ellipse on the first, near the bottom (see fig. 2.19).

Fig. 2.19
Using the Ellipse tool, you can create circles and ellipses of any size.

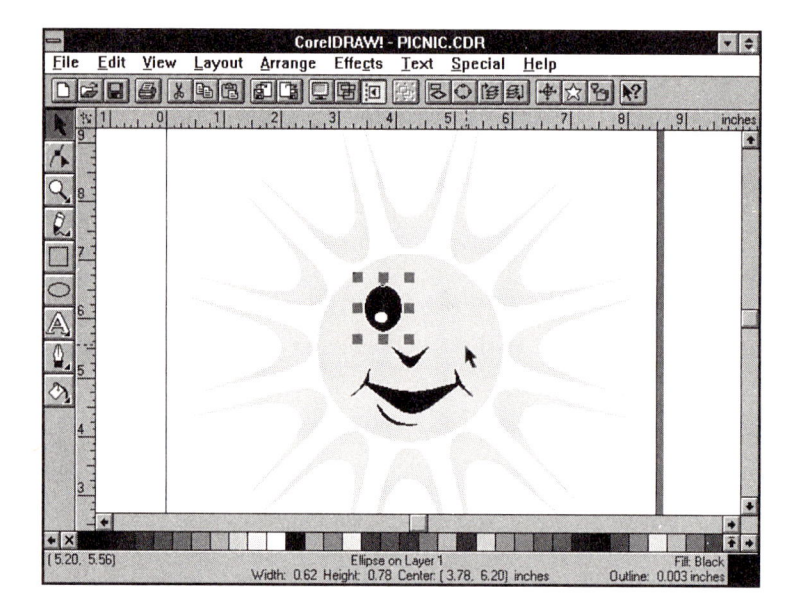

4. Select the black-and-white ellipses by dragging a marquee box around them with the Pick tool. (Begin your marquee on a blank area of the page near the two ellipses.)

5. Open the **A**rrange menu and choose the **G**roup option (Ctrl+G) to combine these two objects in a group that represents Mr. Sun's first eye.

6. Next, you need to copy the eye group and move the copy into place as the second eye. Select the first eye group. Change the size of the eye, if necessary.

7. Open the **E**dit menu and choose **D**uplicate, or press Ctrl+D to create a duplicate of the object.

8. Move the eyes into the desired positions inside Mr. Sun's face.

Creating a Drawing with Symbols and Clipart   **53**

9. Select all the components of the sun drawing by opening the **E**dit menu and choosing Select **A**ll. Then open the **A**rrange menu and choose the **G**roup option from the **A**rrange menu to form the entire arrangement into a single group. Figure 2.20 shows the result.

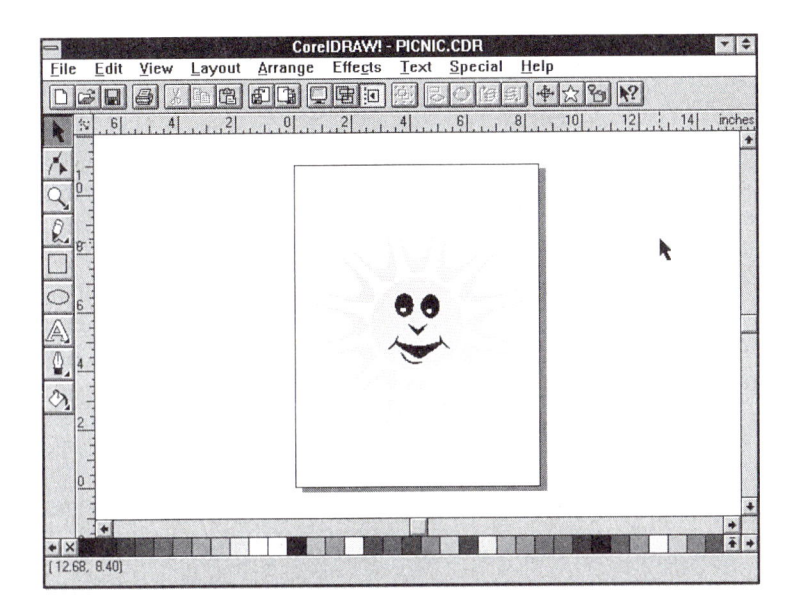

Fig. 2.20
The modified sun clipart (with new eyes added).

10. Because you just made a major change to the drawing, you should save the drawing again. Press Ctrl+S or open the **F**ile menu and choose **S**ave.

Adding Text

The picnic flyer is off to a good start, but it isn't very useful without some text explaining what the flyer is all about. To add text to your flyer, follow these steps:

1. Choose the Text tool or press F8. The pointer changes to a crossbar pointer when you move it to the drawing window.

2. Place the crossbar pointer above the sun you just created, click once, and type the words **PICNIC TIME!**

> **Note**
>
> For more information on working with text, see Chapter 9, "File-Related Operations and CorelMOSAIC."

54 Chapter 2—A Quick Start

Tip
You may need to move the text to correctly align with respect to the rest of the document. With the Pick tool, click and drag the text as you would any other object.

3. Move the crossbar pointer below the sun, click once, and type the following text. Press Enter at the end of each line:

   COME ONE, COME ALL

   The Acme Company Picnic

   Saturday, June 10th at

   The Old Camp Grounds

4. Click the Pick tool to add the text to the drawing.

5. Select the lower text with the Pick tool, and then open the **T**ext menu and choose Text Roll-Up. The Text roll-up appears.

6. Click the **C**enter button in the Text roll-up and then click Apply. If your text looks different from that shown in the figure, check the point size and change it accordingly.

Figure 2.21 shows the text added to the sun drawing.

Fig. 2.21
The modified sun clipart with text added.

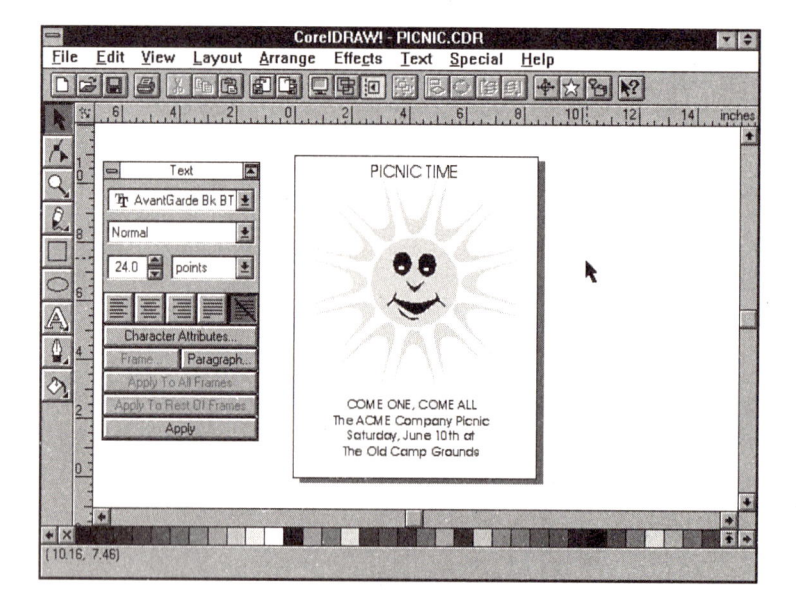

Creating a Border and a Drop Shadow

A border and a drop shadow will give your flyer a more complete look. To add these elements, follow these steps:

Creating a Drawing with Symbols and Clipart   55

1. Click the Rectangle tool (F6) and draw a rectangle around the picture.

2. Using the Pick tool, select the rectangle you just drew and make a duplicate by opening the **E**dit menu and choosing **D**uplicate, or by pressing Ctrl+D.

3. Move the second rectangle up and slightly to the right.

4. Change the fill of the second rectangle to black and then place it at the back of the other objects by choosing **A**rrange, **O**rder To **B**ack.

5. Change the fill of the original rectangle to white and then move it to the back of the other objects by opening the **A**rrange menu and choosing **O**rder To **B**ack.

6. Open the **A**rrange menu and choose **O**rder Forward **O**ne to place the white rectangle in front of the black rectangle and under the other objects. The result should look like figure 2.22.

Fig. 2.22
Adding the drop shadow to the flyer.

7. Save your drawing by opening the **F**ile menu and choosing **S**ave (Ctrl+S).

Adding Symbols

Now you can add a few related symbols to finish your flyer. Follow these steps:

1. Click the Star Symbol button in the ribbon bar to display the Symbols roll-up window (see fig. 2.23).

56 Chapter 2—A Quick Start

Fig. 2.23
The Symbols roll-up enables you to choose a symbol from one of several categories and drag it to your drawing.

2. Click the down arrow in the upper-right corner of the roll-up window to display the drop-down list box. Scroll through the symbol groups and select the desired symbols group. In the lower left of the Symbols roll-up, choose a size of one inch.

3. Select an appropriate symbol and drag it from its location in the symbols group to the upper-left corner of your drawing.

4. Select another symbol, and drag it to the upper-right corner of the drawing.

Previewing and Printing

You can preview your drawing at any time by choosing **V**iew, Full-Screen **P**review, or by pressing the F9 key. CorelDRAW! shows you exactly how your picture will optimally print. (The only exception occurs if you do not have a color printer. Even though your drawing may have color, the resulting printout will not.) If you have a properly installed printer online, you can print the drawing by following these steps:

1. Open the **F**ile menu and choose the **P**rint option. The Print dialog box appears (see fig. 2.24). Click on the Options button if the Preview Image check box is checked; the picture displays with margin cutoffs, which appear as dashed lines near the edge of the page. (These typically are 0.25 inch wide around the picture. Any portion of the picture beyond these lines will not print.)

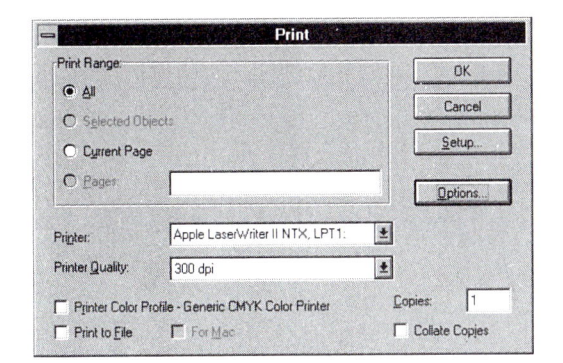

Fig. 2.24
The default options in the Print dialog box enable you to print one copy of each page of your drawing.

2. Click OK.

You may want to save your drawing now by opening the **F**ile menu and choosing **S**ave, or by pressing Ctrl+S to update the version of the file you already saved to disk.

Considering Copyright When Using Clipart

One final note about clipart is in order. The clipart provided by CorelDRAW! is yours to use as you like, within the copyright restrictions imposed by United States federal law. You should be cognizant of the copyright laws that apply to artwork and of the limitations on its use. Corel requests that all clipart be designated as Corel copyright material, but this designation is not always required if the clipart has been substantially modified. If you have any doubts about the legality of your use of a piece of clipart, consult a copyright attorney before you use the art.

Corel provides a statement pertaining to licensing in the copyright pages of the user's manual. If you plan to use the clipart for professional applications, you should review this information before proceeding.

From Here...

This chapter merely scratches the surface of the total capabilities of CorelDRAW! and its companion applications. For other information related to the topics in this chapter, consider these chapters:

- Chapter 3, "A Detailed Look at Object Drawing," gives detailed instructions for using and understanding CorelDRAW!'s drawing tools.

- Chapter 4, "Mastering Object Manipulations," explains in detail how to select, delete, move, copy, and align objects.
- Chapter 5, "Modifying Object Outlines and Interior Fills," shows you how to modify object outlines and interior fills, including full-color pattern fills and fountain fills.

Part II

Learning CorelDRAW! Basics

3 A Detailed Look at Object Drawing

4 Mastering Object Manipulations

5 Modifying Object Outlines and Interior Fills

6 Scaling, Rotating, and Distorting Objects

7 Adding Text to a Drawing

8 Advanced Text Techniques

Chapter 3
A Detailed Look at Object Drawing

by Paul Bodensiek

The preceding chapter introduced you to the three tools CorelDRAW! provides for drawing objects: the Pencil tool, the Rectangle tool, and the Ellipse tool. With only these three tools, you can create complex graphics and virtually unlimited illustrations. All three tools use the same technique to draw an object: click the tool; click on the start point; then drag to the end point. You have many options available to you while drawing an object and many ways to change it after you finish.

This chapter leads you through the basics of creating and reshaping an object; later chapters cover the many advanced commands and options you have when creating an illustration in CorelDRAW!, such as PowerLines and Dimension Lines. This chapter gives you an understanding of lines, shapes, and objects and prepares you for creating your own complex illustrations.

In this chapter, you learn to

- Draw straight lines
- Draw curves
- Create fillable objects
- Edit node points
- Draw rectangles and squares
- Create round cornered rectangles and squares
- Draw circles and ellipses
- Work with closed and open path objects

Understanding Object Components

▶ See "Modifying Object Outline Characterics," p. 137

The squares, circles, lines, and curves you create in this chapter are all CorelDRAW! objects, as are any symbols, text blocks, bitmapped art, or other graphics you import. All objects have dimensions, starting points, and ending points, and are on a specific layer within the CorelDRAW! document. All objects also have an outline (the border around the edges) of a certain thickness in a certain color, and have a fill in a certain color or pattern. Objects you create are assigned default values for these outlines and fills, but you can change these values later.

One way to determine the characteristics of an object is to click the Pick tool and then select the object by clicking its outline (see fig. 3.1). When you select an object, a set of eight black squares, or *scaling handles*, appears to mark the boundary of the object's highlighting box. Read the status line at the bottom of the CorelDRAW! window for information, such as the object type, on which layer it resides, its measurements, its center point location, the thickness of the line on its outside edge, and the color of the fill, if any. You can also find out how many *nodes*, or anchoring points, an object has.

Fig. 3.1
The status line gives instant information about a variety of object characteristics from the object type to the outline and fill styles.

Tip
An X in the fill area on the status line indicates that the object selected has no fill, which makes the object transparent in relation to the objects beneath it.

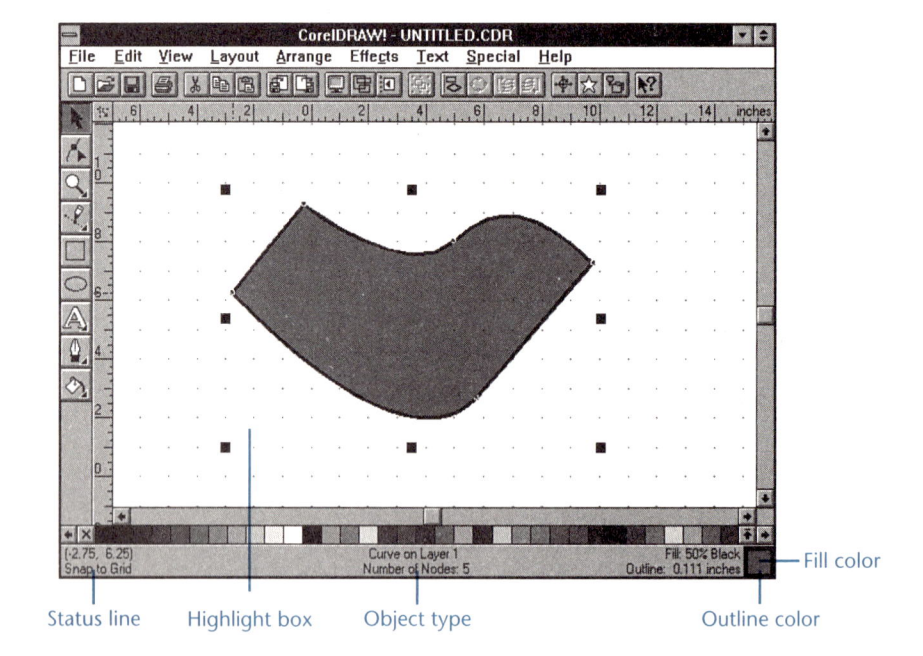

Drawing Straight Lines

You create straight lines with the Pencil tool, which you can set to draw in one of two modes: Freehand and Bézier. Freehand mode is much like drawing on the screen with a pencil, but Bézier mode requires you to establish anchor points, or nodes, which CorelDRAW! then connects with lines. The two modes work similarly when drawing straight lines, except that Freehand mode draws one line at a time whereas Bézier automatically links each line segment.

To change from one mode to the other, click the Pencil tool and hold down the mouse button for a moment until you see the fly-out menu (see fig. 3.2). The first button in the fly-out menu is for the Freehand mode, and the second is for Bézier. (The three other buttons are for creating Dimension Lines for technical drawings, which are covered later.) Click either the Freehand or Bézier button to choose that drawing mode. The toolbar pencil icon changes to indicate which drawing mode you are in.

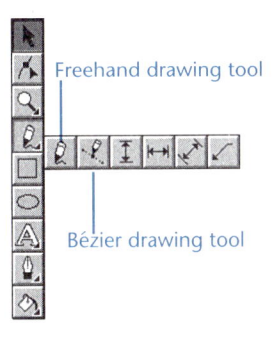

Fig. 3.2
The Pencil tool fly-out menu provides access to the Freehand and Bézier drawing tools.

Drawing a Straight Line in Freehand Mode

Freehand is the most commonly used drawing mode because you actually see your line as you draw it. This section introduces Freehand drawing techniques.

To draw a straight line in Freehand mode, follow these steps:

1. Click the Pencil tool and hold down the mouse button to display the fly-out menu.

   > **Note**
   >
   > Double-clicking the left mouse button on the Pencil tool in version 5 no longer reveals the fly-out menu.

2. Click the Freehand mode button. As you move the cursor into the drawing area, it changes from an arrow to cross hairs.

64 Chapter 3—A Detailed Look at Object Drawing

Tip
Open the **S**pecial menu and choose P**r**eferences (Ctrl+J); then choose **C**onstrain Angle to change the degree of this angle. The default is 15 degrees.

3. Position the cross hairs where you want the line to begin; then click and release the mouse button.

4. Release the mouse button and move the cross hairs. You see a line stretching from the original point to the cross hairs. Position the cursor at the point where you want the line to end and click again.

CorelDRAW! connects these two points for you with a straight line (see fig. 3.3). If you hold down Ctrl while you draw a straight line in Freehand mode, you constrain the line to horizontal, vertical, or to an angle that is a multiple of 15 degrees.

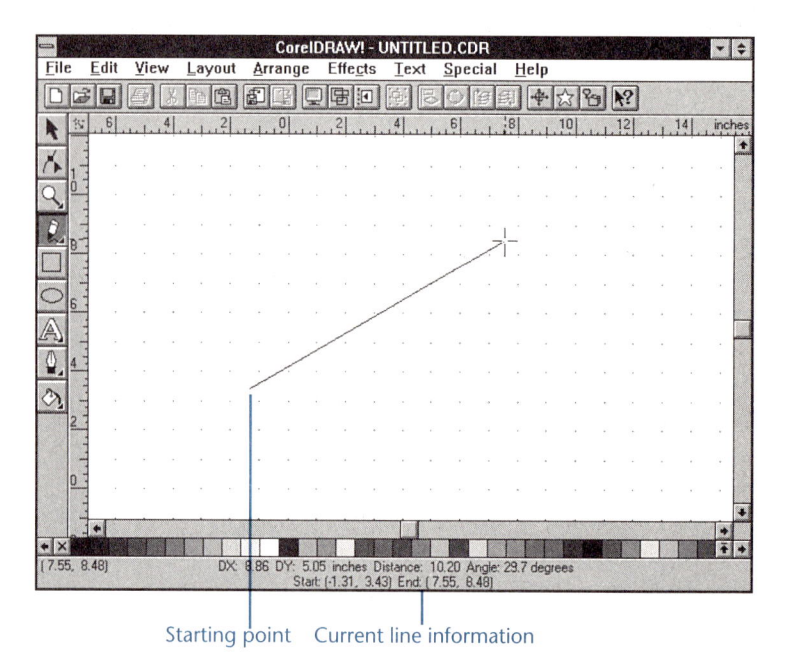

Fig. 3.3
As you draw a straight line in Freehand mode, watch the status line for information about the line length, starting point locations, and ending point locations.

Starting point   Current line information

Drawing a Straight Line in Bézier Mode

Follow these steps to draw a straight line in Bézier mode:

1. Click the Pencil tool and hold down the mouse button for a few moments to display the fly-out menu.

2. Click the Bézier mode button. The cursor changes to cross hairs, which appear after you move the cursor to the drawing area.

3. Position the cross hairs where you want the line to begin; then click and release the mouse button. Make sure to release the mouse button before you move the cross hairs or CorelDRAW! will think you want to draw a curve.

4. Position the cursor at the point where you want the line to end and click again (see fig. 3.4). CorelDRAW! connects these two points for you with a straight line.

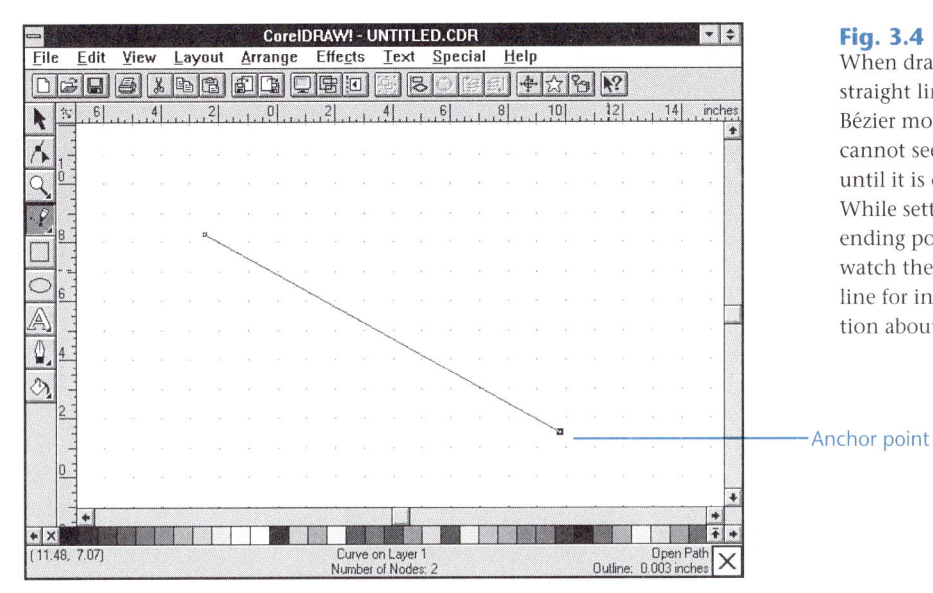

Fig. 3.4
When drawing a straight line in Bézier mode, you cannot see the line until it is done. While setting the ending point, watch the status line for information about the line.

Anchor point

Drawing a Single Object Using Several Straight Lines

To create multiple straight lines connected as one object, continue using the Pencil tool and click again where your last line ends. As long as you are within five pixels of where your last line ends, CorelDRAW! assumes that you want to join the lines. If you make a mistake, open the **E**dit menu and choose **U**ndo to delete the last line segment, or press Ctrl+Z.

> **Note**
>
> To change the distance CorelDRAW! gives you when connecting lines and curves, open the **S**pecial menu and choose Pr**e**ferences; then choose C**u**rves and adjust the figure in the Auto**J**oin option. Make the number higher than five pixels to increase the maximum distance at which CorelDRAW! automatically connects lines. Don't make the value too high, however, or you'll run into the problem of connecting lines and curves that you don't want to connect.

To draw an object using straight lines, follow these steps:

1. Click the Pencil tool and hold down the mouse button a moment to display the fly-out menu.

66 Chapter 3—A Detailed Look at Object Drawing

2. Choose either Freehand or Bézier mode by clicking on the appropriate button. The cursor changes to cross hairs.

3. Position the cross hairs where you want the beginning of one line segment of the object. Click once to anchor the line.

4. Move the cross hairs to where you want the beginning of the next line segment of the object. Click twice in Freehand mode, once in Bézier mode. This completes one side of your object and anchors the line for the next line segment (see fig. 3.5).

Fig. 3.5
When ending one straight line segment, double-click in Freehand mode and single-click in Bézier mode to set this point as the beginning of the next segment.

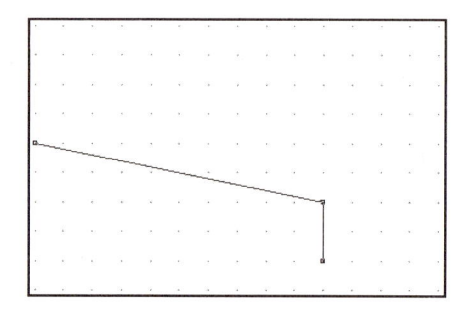

▶ See "Understanding Open and Closed Path Objects," p. 89

5. Continue moving your cross hairs and double-clicking in Freehand mode or single-clicking in Bézier mode to end one line segment and begin another.

6. When you come back to the original point of your object, or wherever you want to end the object, click one last time (see fig. 3.6).

Fig. 3.6
Complete the object by again clicking on the original point, which makes the object a closed path that can be filled.

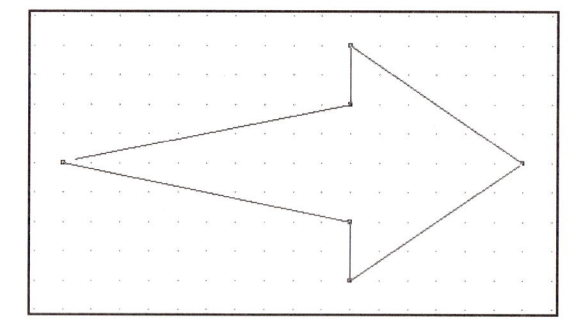

Troubleshooting

When I try to draw a straight line with the Freehand tool, I get a curved line that traces every wiggle I make with the mouse.

To draw a straight line, don't hold the mouse button while moving from the beginning of the line to the end. Click once at the beginning, move the mouse, and then click again.

When I try to draw a straight line with the Bézier tool, I get a slightly curved line that has most of its curve at the beginning and/or end of the line.

To draw a straight line, make sure that you only click the mouse button momentarily at both ends. As with the Freehand tool, click once at the beginning of the line, move the mouse, then click again at the end. (See the "Drawing a Curved Line in Bézier Mode" section later in this chapter.)

I need to draw a line exactly 1 inch long, but I can't get it exactly that length with the mouse.

The Snap to Grid feature can help by making the line start and end at specific points on the page. To set the grid, open the **L**ayout menu and choose **G**rid Setup. Enter the Horizontal and Vertical unit preferences in the Grid Frequency area and press OK.

▶ See "Using the Grid to Facilitate Alignment," p. 109

When I try to draw two individual lines with the Bézier tool, I end up getting a single object with several straight lines.

Between drawing the first and second lines, press the space bar twice. This selects the pick tool, and then it selects the Bézier tool again.

▶ See "Establishing Grid Frequencies," p. 111

When I try to draw a single object with many straight lines using the Freehand tool, I end up with two or more sections that aren't linked together.

Remember to double-click at the end of each line segment. This tells CorelDRAW! that you want to start a new line segment connected to the first, at this point. If you move the cross hairs too much between the first and second click, CorelDRAW! assumes you want to start a new object. You can set the distance within which CorelDRAW! will link line segments by using the AutoJoin feature in the Preferences dialog box (press Ctrl+J to open the dialog box).

I want to draw a line straight up.

Using the Freehand tool, click to start the line at the desired point then press Ctrl to constrain the line to 15 degree increments. Keeping the cross hairs within plus or minus 15 degrees on either side of vertical will make sure the line goes straight up.

Drawing Curved Lines

You also use the Pencil tool to create curved lines. With curved lines, the mode you choose has a great effect on your control of the line.

Drawing in Freehand mode is much like drawing with a pencil. Although CorelDRAW! 5 now optimizes a freehand curve as you draw it, you may find the effect too rough and comprising unexpected sharp angles. Drawing in Bézier mode gives you elegant curves with smooth transitions.

▶ See "Adding and Deleting Nodes," p. 390

For more control when creating a line with many segments, pause before drawing each new segment to allow the CorelDRAW! screen to redraw so you can view the curve. Relax, and remember that you can reshape lines created in both Freehand and Bézier modes by moving, adding, deleting, or altering nodes using the Shape tool, which is covered in "Reshaping a Curve or Object by Changing Its Nodes and Control Points," later in this chapter.

> **Note**
>
> To simplify your drawings, draw curved lines using as few nodes as possible; fewer nodes make drawings easier to work with and speed up screen refresh times. You can always use the Shape tool later to add more nodes if needed.

Drawing a Curved Line in Freehand Mode

To draw a curved line in Freehand mode, follow these steps:

1. Click the Pencil tool to display the fly-out menu.
2. Click the Freehand mode button. The cursor becomes cross hairs.
3. Position the cross hairs where you want the line to begin.
4. Click and drag, drawing the curve as if you were drawing with a pencil on-screen (see fig. 3.7).

▶ See "Using the Grid to Facilitate Alignment," p. 109

> **Note**
>
> The snap feature does not constrain your curve when drawing in Freehand mode.

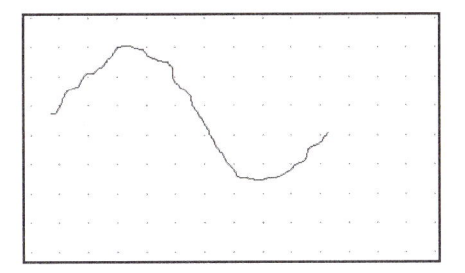

Fig. 3.7
When drawing a curved line in Freehand mode, drag the cross hairs along the path you want the curve to take.

> **Note**
>
> If you make a mistake before you end the line, hold down Shift while continuing to drag and go back over the line segment you just drew. Release Shift to return to regular Drawing mode. This technique does not work if you have ended the line by releasing the mouse button.

5. When you reach the end of the curve, release the mouse button. If your curve has ten or fewer nodes, notice that CorelDRAW! shows them at each point on the curve where the direction of the curve changes.

> **Note**
>
> You can add a curve to an existing line or curve by using the Pick tool to select the existing curve and then using the Freehand drawing tool to click at either end node and continue drawing. AutoJoin joins the curve or line segment with the one that you select.

Drawing a Curved Line in Bézier Mode

A Bézier curve is a line that you form by setting anchor points and then shaping the curve using control points. Using Bézier mode to create curves minimizes the number of nodes (see fig. 3.8).

Drawing curved lines in Bézier mode may appear complex in written instructions, but a little practice can familiarize you with the process. Use this mode when accuracy is critical.

Fig. 3.8
The Bézier tool can be used to create curves which flow evenly from one endpoint to the other.

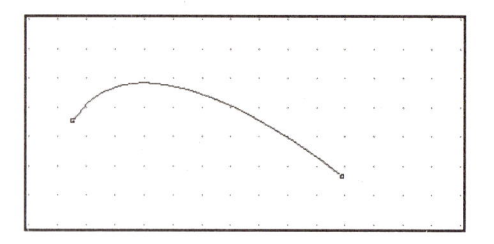

To draw a curved line in Bézier mode, follow these steps:

1. Click the Pencil tool and hold down the mouse button to display the fly-out menu.

2. Click the Bézier mode button. The cursor changes to cross hairs.

3. Position the cross hairs where you want the line to begin.

4. Press and hold down the mouse button to set the first anchor point. A node appears to indicate that this is the start of the curve.

5. Still holding down the mouse button, start to drag the cursor. Two control points appear on opposite sides of the node (see fig. 3.9). One of these control points follows your cursor. The dashed line connecting the control points is tangent to the curve you are creating.

Fig. 3.9
The control points of a curve node are tangent to the curve you draw.

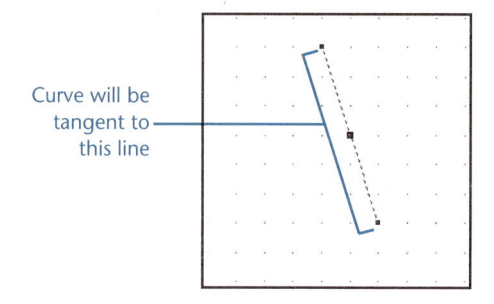

Curve will be tangent to this line

Tip
Hold down Ctrl to constrain the control points to move in 15-degree increments.

To set the height or depth of the curve, make the distance between the control points larger or smaller. The larger the distance is between the node and the control points, the larger the curve. The smaller the distance is between the node and control points, the tighter the curve. The angle of the line connecting the control points determines the slope of the curve.

6. When the control points are where you want them, release the mouse button.

Drawing Curved Lines

> **Note**
>
> When drawing in Bézier mode, the snap feature constrains both the node and control points. For more freedom while laying out your curves, turn Snap off.

▶ See "Using the Grid to Facilitate Alignment," p. 109

7. Move the cross hairs to the point where you want the curve to end, and click the mouse button. CorelDRAW! places the second node at that point and then connects the node to the first node with a curved line showing the characteristics you chose during your placement of the control points (see fig. 3.10).

To specify the characteristics of the second curve point, hold down the mouse button and drag the control points instead of releasing the mouse button.

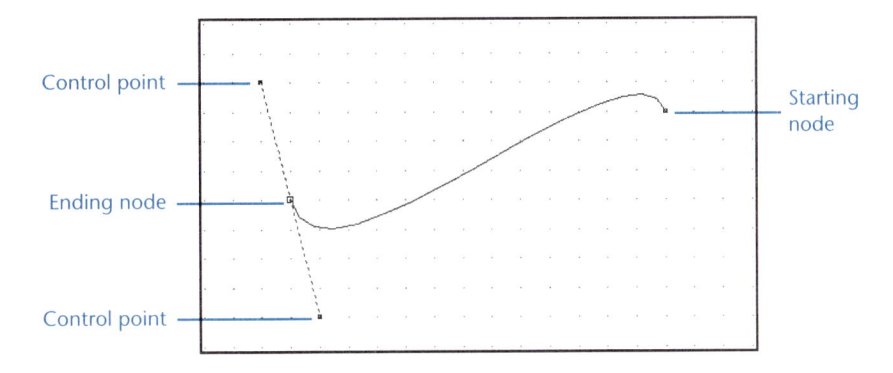

Fig. 3.10
After placing the second end point, CorelDRAW! places a curve tangent to the control points at both ends.

> **Note**
>
> To add a curve to an existing line or curve using the Bézier tool, use the Pick tool to select the existing curve; then use the Bézier drawing tool to click at either end node and continue drawing. AutoJoin joins the curve or line segment with the one that you select.

Drawing a Curve-Sided Object

Drawing a curve-sided object in Freehand mode emulates drawing with a pencil: you click where you want the object to begin; hold down the mouse button; and draw. If you want to draw a closed object so that you can fill it later, make sure you end by clicking your original point again so that CorelDRAW! knows to connect all the line segments.

In Bézier mode, however, you repeat a series of steps to set the nodes and the curve characteristics. To draw a curve-sided object in Bézier mode, follow these steps:

1. Follow the steps for drawing a curved line in Bézier mode.

2. While still holding down the mouse button, drag to set the control points for the second curved line segment. If you want a smooth curve with one bump for this line segment, continue to drag in the direction the curve is moving in the first line segment. If you want a smooth curve with two bumps (for example, an S shape, indicating that the curve has changed direction), drag in the opposite direction that the curve is moving in the first line segment.

3. Release the mouse button, and CorelDRAW! redraws the line segment to include the new node (see fig. 3.11).

Fig. 3.11
This curve sided object, drawn in Bézier mode, shows examples of both single bump and double bump curve segments.

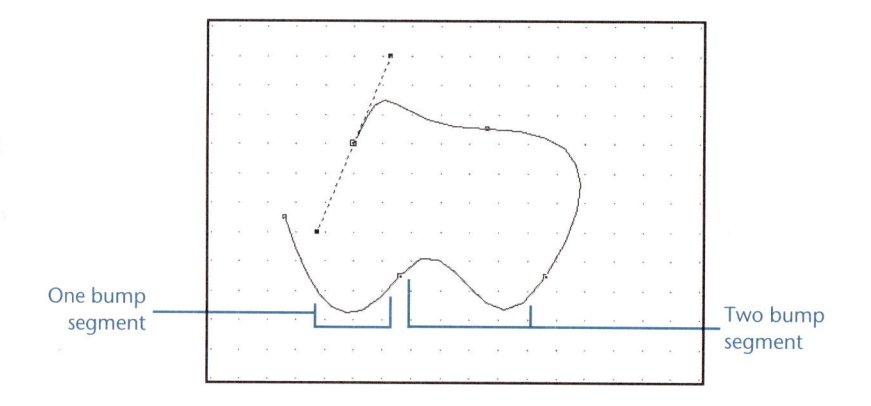

▶ See "Understanding Open and Closed Path Objects," p. 89

4. Repeat these steps to finish the curved object. If you want a closed shape, place the final node on top of the first node. Just click within five pixels of the first node.

Reshaping a Curve or Object by Changing Its Nodes and Control Points

You can make adjustments to a straight line or curved segment you created in either Freehand or Bézier mode. Every line segment in CorelDRAW! has two nodes, which you can move with the Shape tool. On a curved line segment, each node has one or two control points associated with it. You move the control points to reshape the curve. You can delete or add nodes, or create a break in a line segment, all of which also change the curve. The control points show the nodal slope characteristics of the approaching or departing line segment.

You also can change the curve node to a different type, depending on what characteristics you want the curve to have. The three types of curve nodes are cusp, smooth, and symmetrical.

▶ See "Changing Object Shapes," p. 378

Changing a Curve by Moving Its Nodes

To reshape a curve by moving its nodes, follow these steps:

1. Click the Shape tool.
2. Click the curve you want to reshape. The nodes of the curve become visible.
3. Click the single node you want to move. Nodes become filled black squares when selected.

▶ See "Using the Shape Tool to Move Nodes," p. 386

> **Note**
>
> You may select multiple nodes for editing in the same way as multiple objects. Select multiple nodes by holding down Shift and clicking the cursor on each node in turn ("Shift-clicking"), or by dragging the cursor to create a box around the nodes (a "marquee box").

▶ See "Selecting Individual Objects With the Pick Tool," p. 94

4. Click and drag the node(s) until the curve is the shape you want.

▶ See "Selecting Multiple Objects With the Pick Tool," p. 96

Changing a Curve by Moving Its Control Points

To reshape a curve by moving its control points, follow these steps:

1. Click the Shape tool.
2. Click the curve you want to reshape. The nodes of the curve become visible.
3. Click the single node you want to change. The control points for the node become visible.
4. Click and drag the control points until the curve is the shape you want.

Tip

To select the first node on a certain curve, press the Home key. To select the last node, press the End key.

▶ See "Changing the Curvature," p. 388

> **Note**
>
> CorelDRAW! also enables you to drag directly on the line with the Shape tool to shape the curve. Control points don't actually need to be selected at all, but they do give greater control over the curve.

74 Chapter 3—A Detailed Look at Object Drawing

Changing a Curve by Editing Its Nodes

▶ See "Examining Characteristics of Nodes," p. 383

The three different types of nodes are defined by how their control points move.

- A *cusp* node has one or two control points; the control points move independently of each other so line segments can change direction sharply on either side of the node (see fig. 3.12).

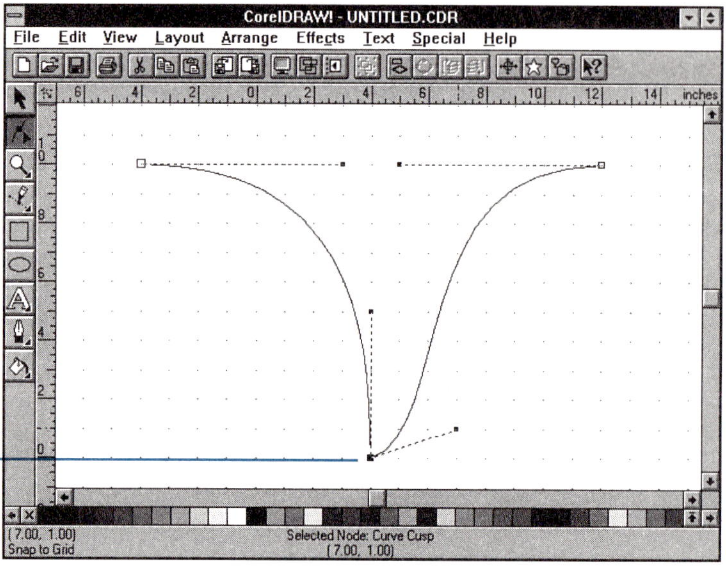

Fig. 3.12
The middle solid black node of this curve is a cusp: the control points extend from the node in different directions. Notice that the status line states the type of node.

Selected cusp node

- A *smooth* node with a curved segment on both sides of it always has two control points that lie on a straight line that passes through the node. This way the curve stays smooth between the two line segments it connects; the control points can be different distances from the node (see fig. 3.13).

  A *smooth node* with a straight line segment on one side of it has only one control point that is always in a direct line with the straight line segment.

- A *symmetrical* node always has two control points connected by a straight line, and the control points are always an equal distance from the node for a smooth and balanced curve. Symmetrical is the default setting for nodes on a curve created with the Bézier tool (see fig. 3.14).

Drawing Curved Lines

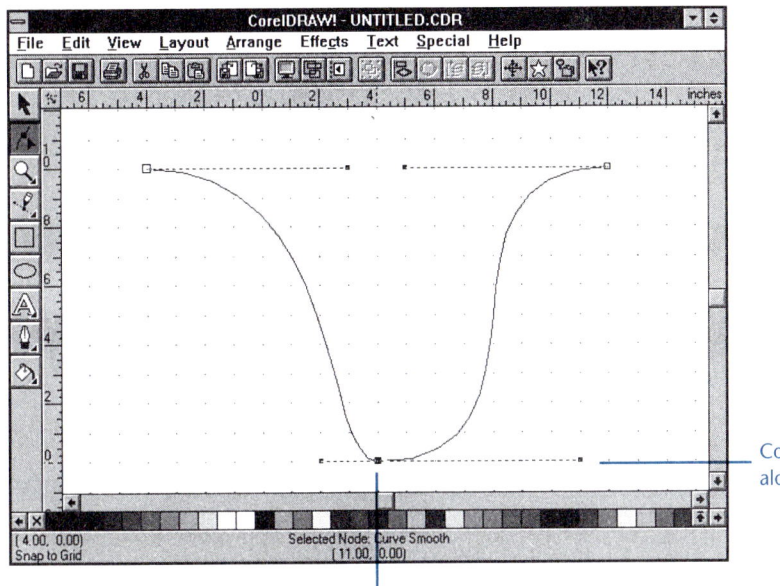

Fig. 3.13
The selected (middle) node in this curve is smooth, as the status line indicates. Each control point lies along the same line, but may be different distances from the node.

Control points along straight line

Selected smooth node

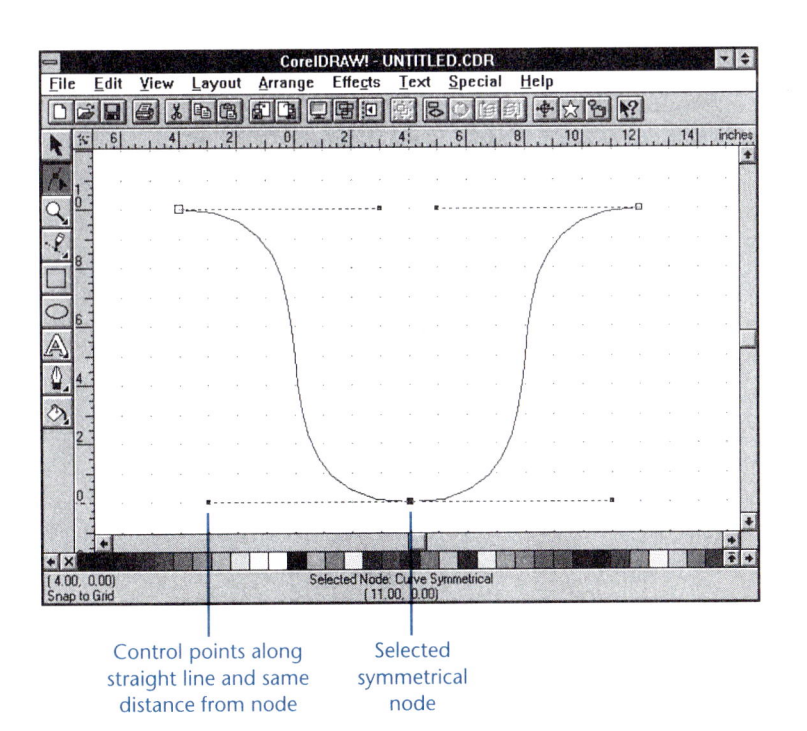

Fig. 3.14
A symmetrical node, shown in the middle of this curve, has two control points located equal distances from the node along the same line.

Control points along straight line and same distance from node

Selected symmetrical node

Chapter 3—A Detailed Look at Object Drawing

To reshape a curve by editing its nodes, follow these steps:

1. Click the Shape tool.

2. Click the curve you want to reshape. The nodes of the curve become visible.

▶ See "Using the Shape Tool with the Node Edit Roll-up," p. 379

3. Click the single node you want to edit, or Shift-click to select more than one node. Nodes become filled black squares when selected.

4. Double-click the last (or only) node you want to edit to activate the Node Edit roll-up window (see fig. 3.15). Grayed options are not available. The options for editing a node or line segment are the following:

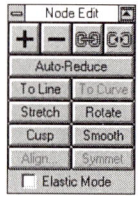

Fig. 3.15
This roll-up window provides access to commands for adding, deleting, and changing the characteristics of nodes and curve segments between them.

Option	Purpose
➕	Adds nodes
➖	Deletes nodes and segments
(join icon)	Joins two end nodes
(break icon)	Breaks the curve at a node
Auto-Reduce	Deletes extraneous nodes
To Line	Changes curve segments to lines
To Curve	Converts line segments to curves
Stretch	Stretches and changes a segment
Rotate	Rotates and skews a segment
Cusp	Turns a smooth or symmetrical node into a cusp node
Smooth	Turns a cusp or symmetrical node into a smooth node

Option	Purpose
Align	Aligns nodes
Symmet	Turns a smooth or cusp node into a symmetrical node
Elastic mode	Makes movement of nodes a factor of how close they are to the base node (the one you drag)

> **Troubleshooting**
>
> *The status line says that I have a picked a smooth node, but there is only one control point. How do I edit the curve segment on the other side of the node?*
>
> There are two possibilities for what is happening: 1) the other curve is actually a straight line or 2) the control point is so close to the node that the node covers it up.
>
> If the segment is a straight line, you can convert it to a curve by double-clicking in the middle of the segment, then clicking To Curve in the Node Edit dialog box and editing the curve as normal.
>
> If the control point is too close to the node, either drag on the curve, changing the shape of the curve directly (the control point should then become visible); or hold down Shift and drag the control point out from under node.
>
> *I changed the curve segment on one side of a node and now there is a sharp corner where there was a smooth curve before.*
>
> The node is a cusp. To change it to a smooth node, select the node and click Smooth in the Node Edit dialog box.
>
> *I changed the curve segment on one side of a node, but both segments bordering the node changed.*
>
> The node is either smooth or symmetrical. To change it to a cusp (so that changes on one side of the node don't affect the segment on the other), select the node and click Cusp in the Node Edit dialog box.
>
> *When I try to move a node, suddenly I am dragging control points out from it and the curve changes.*
>
> The node is probably symmetrical. Change it to a smooth node, and you can move it easily without affecting the control points.

78   Chapter 3—A Detailed Look at Object Drawing

Creating Rectangular and Square Objects

Tip
The status line gives you the exact dimensions of the rectangle or square as you draw.

You draw both rectangles and squares using the Rectangle tool. You can build your rectangle or square either from one corner to its diagonal or from a center point outward. After you draw the rectangle or square, you have the option of adding rounded corners. If you later decide you want square corners instead, you can easily change them back.

Drawing a Rectangle or a Square from a Corner Point

To draw a rectangle or square from a corner point, follow these steps:

1. Click the Rectangle tool (or press F6). The cursor changes to cross hairs.

2. Position the cross hairs at the point where you want one corner of the rectangle.

3. Click and drag in any direction until the rectangle is the desired size; then release the mouse button to complete the rectangle. CorelDRAW! creates a rectangle shape with one corner fixed at the original point (see fig. 3.16).

Fig. 3.16
Draw a rectangle from a corner point by dragging the cross hairs from the beginning corner and then releasing it when the object is the desired size (the status line shows the size of the rectangle).

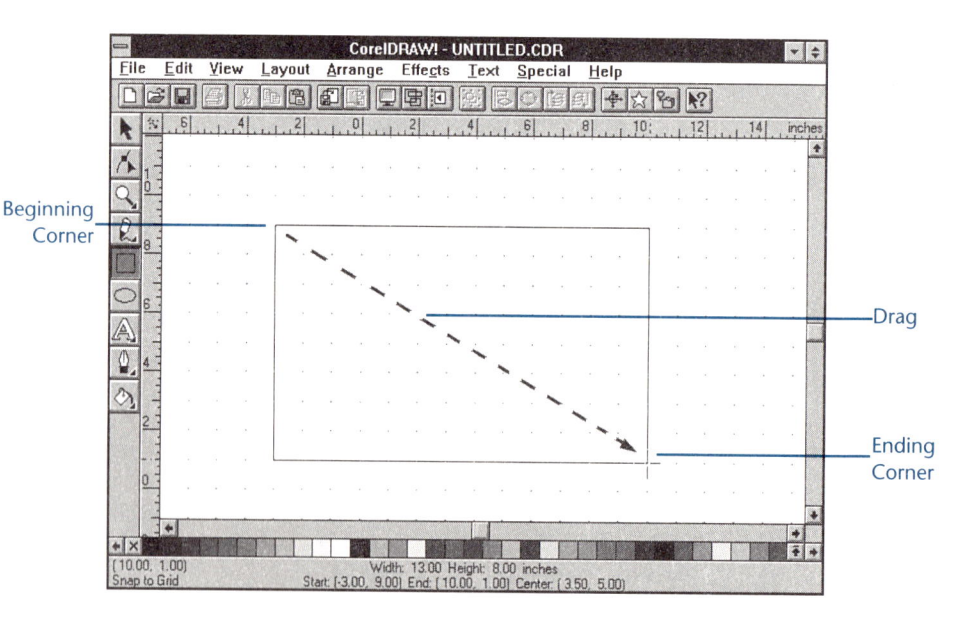

Creating Rectangular and Square Objects 79

To create a square, press Ctrl while dragging the cross hairs. Both sides of the rectangle are sized equally to create a square when you release the mouse button.

▶ See "Scaling and Sizing an Object," p. 184

Drawing a Rectangle from a Center Point

To draw a rectangle or a square from a center point, follow these steps:

1. Click the Rectangle tool; the cursor changes to cross hairs.

2. Position the cross hairs at the point where you want the center of the rectangle.

3. Hold down Shift and then click and drag from that center point to get the correct width and depth of the rectangle. When the rectangle is the desired size, release the mouse button (see fig. 3.17). Make sure that you do not release Shift until after you release the mouse button, or you automatically draw a rectangle from a corner point.

   To draw a square from its center point, press and hold down both Ctrl and Shift while dragging the Rectangle tool.

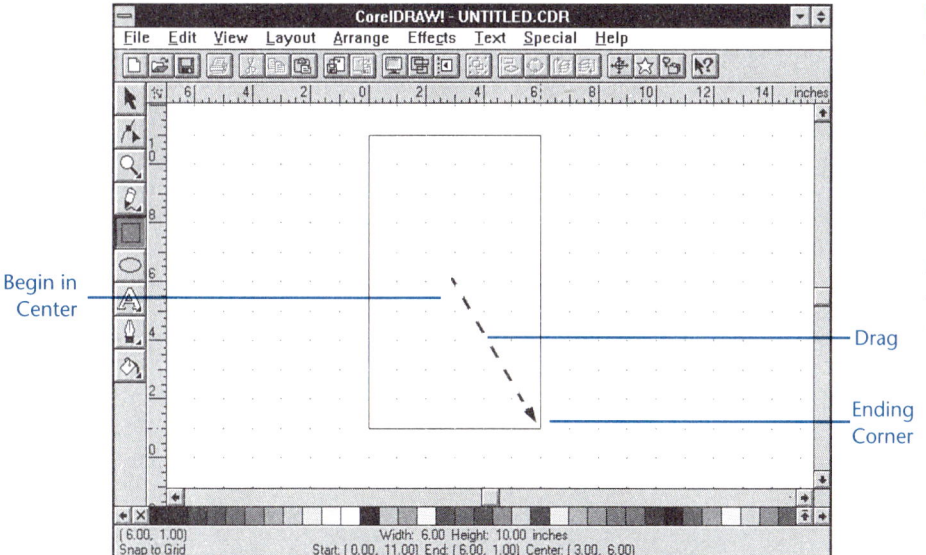

Fig. 3.17
To draw a rectangle from the center point, press Ctrl while dragging the cross hairs out until the object is the right size. The status line shows the exact size of the square.

80 Chapter 3—A Detailed Look at Object Drawing

Rounding the Corners of a Rectangle or Square

To round the corners of a rectangle or square, follow these steps:

1. Click the Shape tool.

2. Click any one of the lines of the rectangle or square you want to change so that the corner nodes appear.

3. Click any one of the corner nodes and, while holding down the mouse button, slide the node down either side of the rectangle and away from the corner. As you move one corner node, all the other nodes move at the same time.

4. When the corners of the rectangle are rounded to the desired radius, release the mouse button (see fig. 3.18).

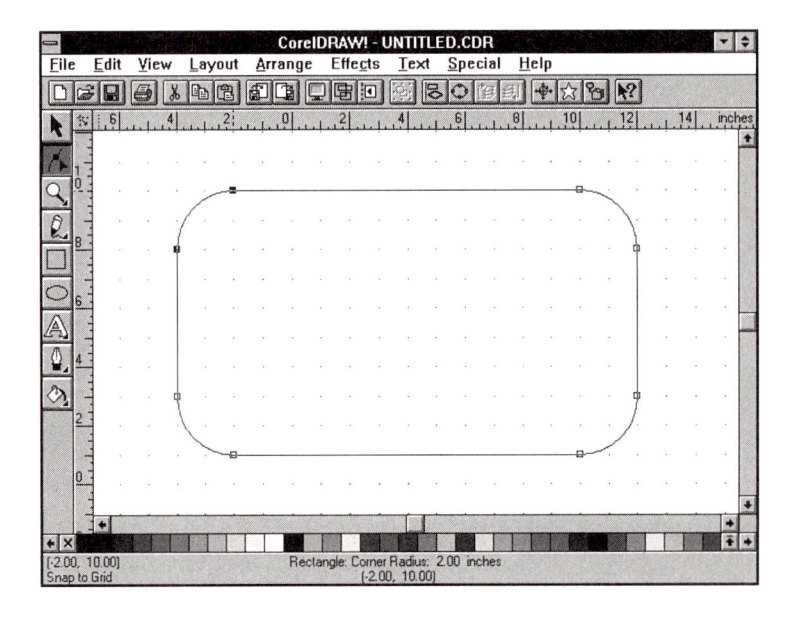

Tip
Change from corner- to center-draw mode by pressing or releasing Shift while drawing a rectangle, as long as the cursor is moving as the key is pressed or released.

Fig. 3.18
Using the Shape tool, drag a rectangle's corner nodes to add a radius to the corners.

5. To return to square corners, drag a corner node back to the corner position.

Tip
The status line indicates the corner radius. Use this readout while rounding the corners to get the right radius.

Note

To create a rectangle or square with a specific corner radius, activate Snap To Grid so that the corner nodes align automatically from one grid increment to the next. Open the **L**ayout menu and choose **S**nap To Grid.

> **Troubleshooting**
>
> *When I scale a rectangle with rounded corners (changed more in the horizontal or vertical direction than it is in the other) the corners get distorted and become elliptical, rather than circular arcs.*
>
> *This also happens if the rectangle is scaled before the rounded corners are added.*
>
> The corner radius is scaled with the rectangle and becomes elliptical if scaled more in one direction than the other.
>
> To solve this problem, draw another rectangle, using the first one as a template. Then delete the original rectangle and put the right size radius on the corners of the new rectangle.
>
> *I try to draw a rectangle from the center by holding down Shift, but the rectangle draws from the corner.*
>
> Press Shift before beginning to draw the rectangle and don't release the key until you have released the mouse button.
>
> *I try to draw a square by holding down Ctrl, but it comes out rectangular.*
>
> Make sure that Ctrl is held down the entire time you are drawing and don't release it until you release the mouse button.

▶ See "Scaling and Sizing an Object," p. 184

Drawing Circular Shapes

You draw both a circle and an ellipse (an oblong circle) in CorelDRAW! with the same Ctrl and Shift operations you use to draw a rectangle and a square. You also use the same two methods of sizing an ellipse or circle, either from one corner to the other, or from a center point out. To figure out where exactly to put your cursor when creating a circular shape, imagine that an ellipse fits inside an imaginary rectangle and that a circle fits inside an imaginary square. Think of this imaginary square or rectangle as the *defining rectangle* (see fig. 3.19).

Fig. 3.19
When drawing a circle or an ellipse, imagine that the object is surrounded by a "defining rectangle" whose corners are placed by the cross hairs.

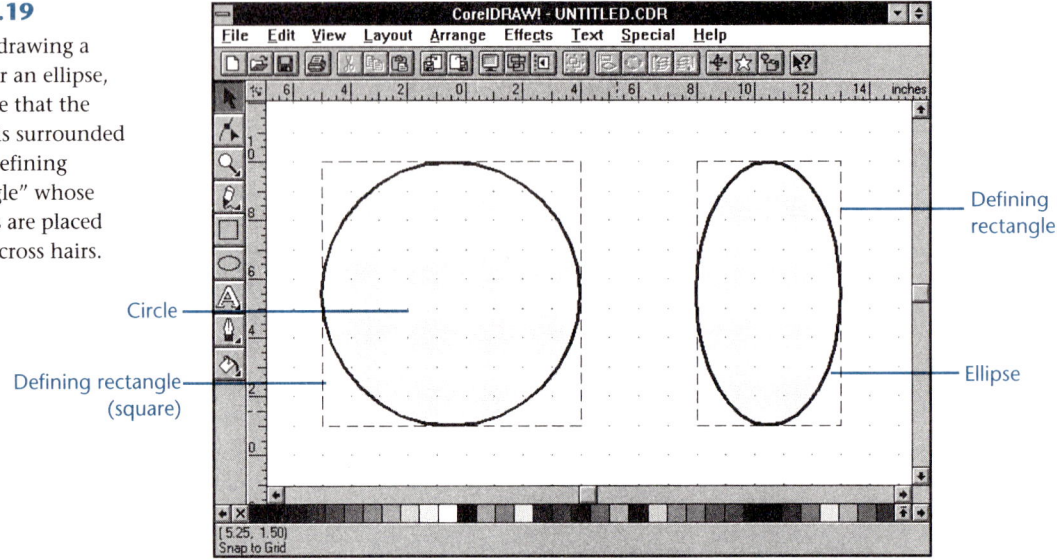

Circle

Defining rectangle (square)

Defining rectangle

Ellipse

Drawing an Ellipse or a Circle from a Corner Point

To draw an ellipse or a circle from a corner point, follow these steps:

1. Click the Ellipse tool (or press F7); the cursor changes to cross hairs.

2. Position the cross hairs where you want one corner of the defining rectangle of the ellipse.

3. Click and drag in any direction until the ellipse is the desired size, then release the mouse button. As you click and drag, CorelDRAW! creates an ellipse shape with one corner fixed at the original point (see fig. 3.20). The release of the mouse button creates the opposite corner of the defining rectangle.

To create a circle, press and hold down Ctrl, then click and drag the cross hairs. Release Ctrl after you have released the mouse button.

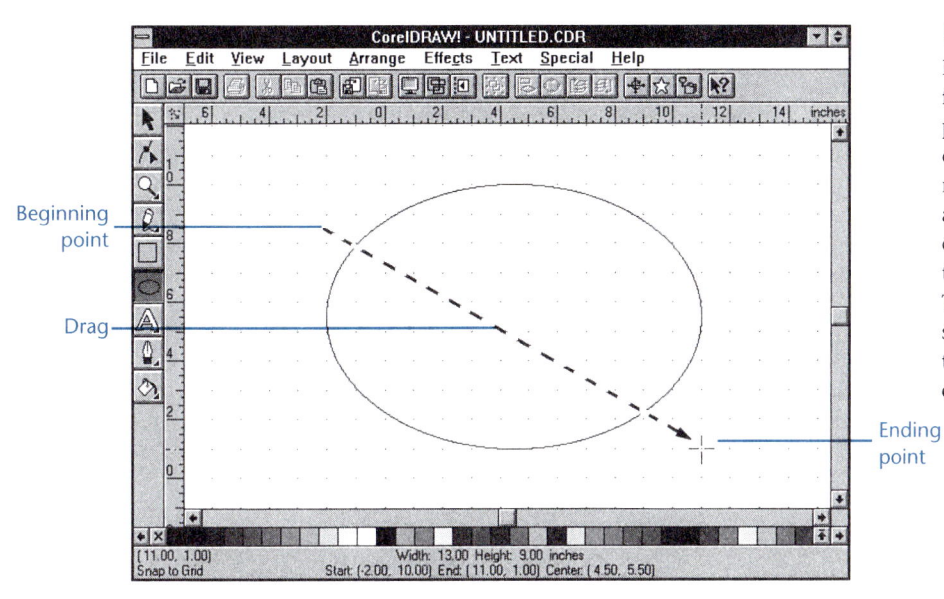

Fig. 3.20
Draw an ellipse from the corner point by starting at one of the defining rectangle corners and dragging the cross hairs toward the other corner. The status line shows the size of the ellipse as you draw it.

Drawing an Ellipse or a Circle from the Center Point

To draw an ellipse or a circle from the center point, follow these steps:

1. Click the Ellipse tool so that the cursor changes to cross hairs.

2. Position the cross hairs where you want the center of the ellipse.

3. Hold down Shift, and then click and drag from that center point to get the correct width and depth of the ellipse. When the ellipse is the desired size, release the mouse button (see fig. 3.21). Make sure that you do not release Shift until after you release the mouse button, or you automatically draw the ellipse from a corner point.

   To create a circle, press and hold down both Ctrl and Shift. Then click and drag the Ellipse tool.

Tip
Change from corner- to center-draw mode by pressing or releasing Shift while drawing an ellipse as long as the cursor is moving as you press or release the key.

Fig. 3.21
Draw an ellipse from the center point by pressing Shift while dragging the cross hairs toward a corner of the imaginary defining rectangle. The status line shows the size of the ellipse.

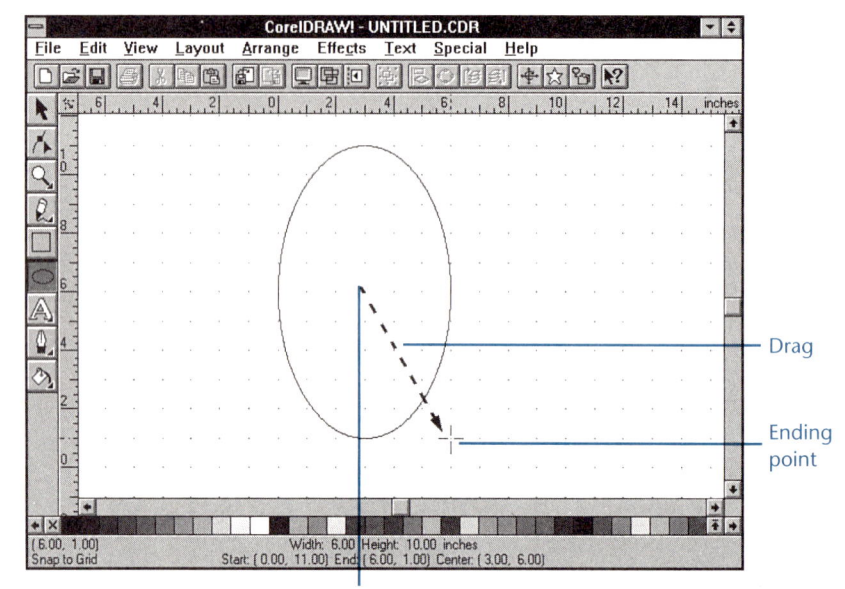

Drawing a Pie Wedge or an Arc

You can modify an ellipse to create a pie wedge or an arc. Even after you modify an ellipse into a pie wedge or arc, however, CorelDRAW! shows you the full ellipse shape in the highlight box.

Drawing a Pie Wedge

To draw a pie wedge, follow these steps:

1. Follow the steps for drawing an ellipse or circle.

Tip
Hold down Ctrl while you make modifications to constrain the angle of the nodes to 15-degree increments.

2. Click the Shape tool and then click the outline of the ellipse. A single node appears on the ellipse.

3. Click the node and drag it in either direction, with the pointer inside the ellipse perimeter, to create a pie wedge. Release the mouse button when the wedge is the size you want (see fig. 3.22). The status line shows the beginning, ending, and included angles of the pie shape.

Drawing an Arc

To draw an arc, follow these steps:

1. Follow the steps for drawing an ellipse or a circle.

2. Click the Shape tool and then click the outline of the ellipse. A single node appears on the ellipse.

3. Click this node and drag it in either direction, with the pointer outside the ellipse, until the arc is the size you want and then release the mouse button (see fig. 3.23). The status line shows the beginning, ending, and included angles of the arc.

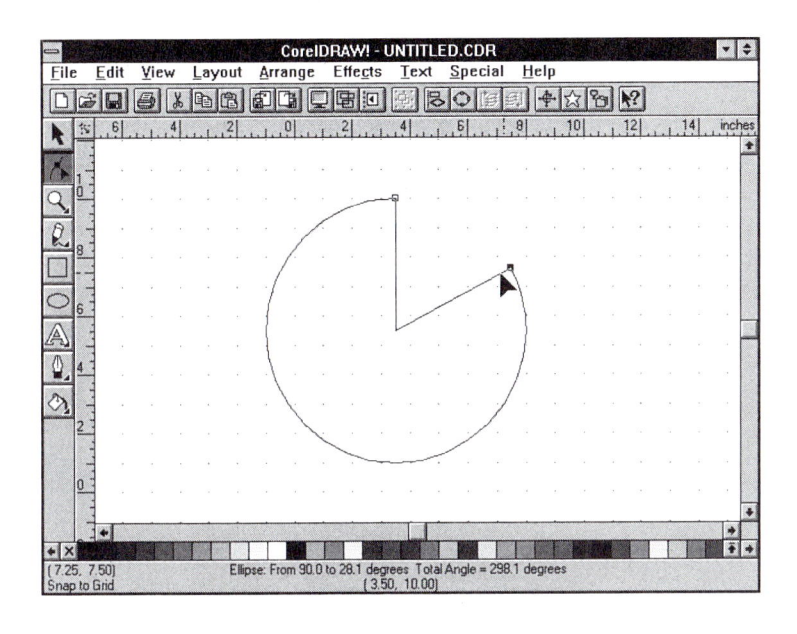

Fig. 3.22
Starting with a circle or ellipse, create a pie wedge by dragging the object's node point while keeping the cursor within its radius.

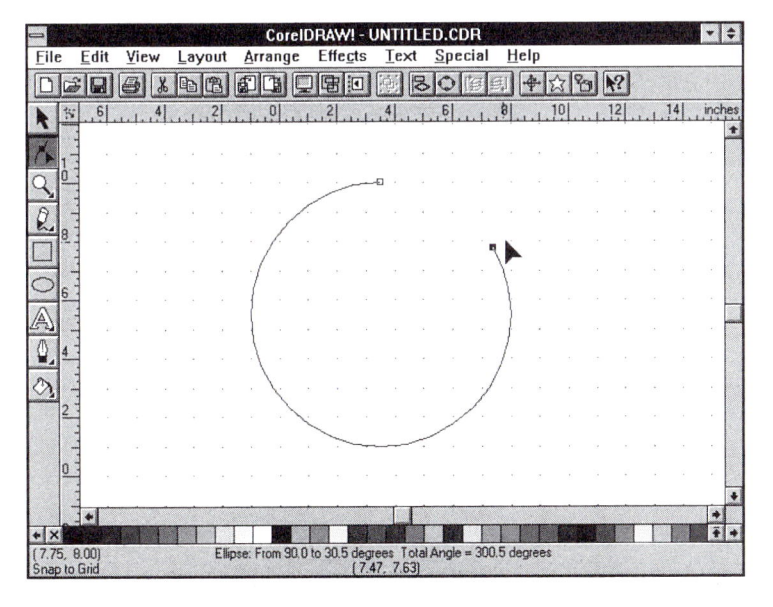

Fig. 3.23
Draw a circular arc by dragging the circle or ellipse's node point while keeping the cursor outside the object's radius.

> **Troubleshooting**
>
> *When I try to draw an ellipse from the center, it looks fine while I am drawing it. But when I release the mouse, it looks as though I drew it from the corner.*
>
> Make sure that you release Shift after you have released the mouse button.
>
> *I want to draw a circle, but I can't get both dimensions the same.*
>
> Hold Ctrl while using the ellipse tool, and release Ctrl after you let up on the mouse button.
>
> *When drawing pie wedges, all that remains is a small curved line.*
>
> Keep the cursor within the radius of the circle or ellipse. Imagine you are dragging a line from the outside of the circle toward the center. When you draw an arc, keep the cursor outside the circle as though you are keeping the line from moving toward the center.
>
> *I want to line up the edge of a circle along two lines on my drawing, but the circle pulls away from the lines as I draw it.*
>
> This can happen when you are drawing a circle or ellipse from the corner. Chapter 4 "Mastering Object Manipulations," tells you how to align objects after you draw them.

▶ See "Aligning Objects," p. 109

Drawing Callouts on Objects

▶ See "Adding Text to a Drawing," p. 207

Callouts are used to draw attention to things. In the illustrations for this book, callouts show you which object the caption is talking about or what part is most important. Callouts can be used in illustrations, advertising, and engineering drawings.

In CorelDRAW!, a Callout is composed of two parts, the callout line and its text. The callout line connects the text to the object it describes. The callout text and line are attached to each other so that if you move either one, the other is dragged along with it (see fig. 3.24).

To create a two-segment callout, follow these steps:

1. Press and hold the Pen tool to access the Pen fly-out menu and select the Callout tool. The cursor changes to cross hairs.

2. Click where you want the callout line to begin and move the cursor away from that point. A line with a rectangular box on its end extends from the starting point to the cursor (see fig. 3.25).

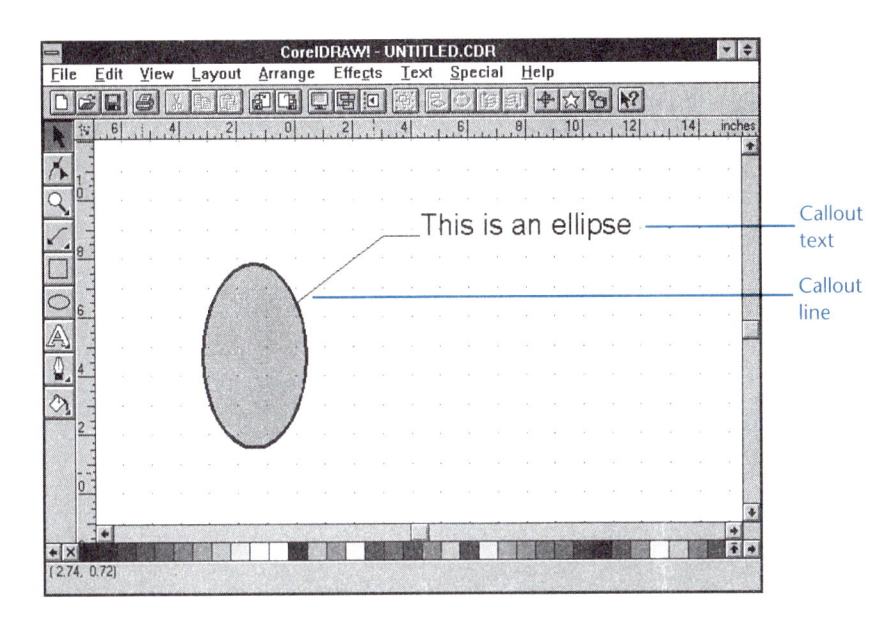

Fig. 3.24
The Callout tool makes it simple to draw a line from an object and to type in text to describe it.

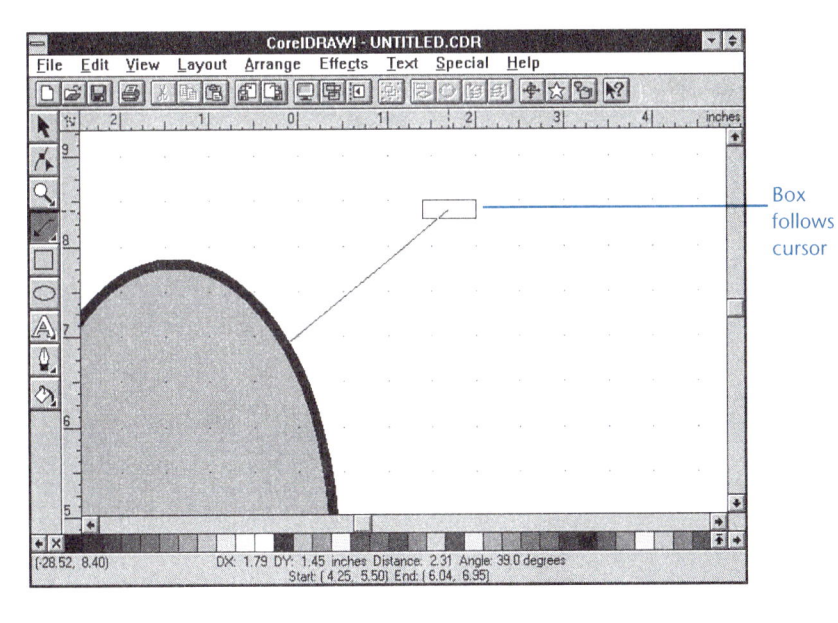

Fig. 3.25
As you draw the callout line, a box follows the cursor. When you are done, this box will disappear, to be replaced by the text you type in the box.

3. Click where you want the first segment of the callout line to end and where you want the second to begin. A second, horizontal, line segment extends from the end of the first segment.

4. Click at a point to end the second segment. A thick vertical line begins just to one side of the second segment. This is a text insertion point.

5. Type in the text you want to appear on the callout.

6. When you finish entering text, select the Pick tool.

Sometimes callouts have only one line connecting the object and the text. To create a single-segment callout, follow these steps:

1. Press and hold the Pen tool to access the Pen fly-out menu and select the Callout tool. The cursor changes to cross hairs.

2. Click where you want the callout line to begin and move the cursor away from that point. A line with a rectangular box on its end extends from the starting point to the cursor.

3. Double-click where you want the callout line to end. A thick vertical line begins just to one side of the second segment. This is a text insertion point.

4. Type in the text you want to appear on the callout.

5. When you finish entering text, select the Pick tool.

▶ See "Modifying Object Outline Characteristics," p. 137

Troubleshooting

I want to have an arrowhead at the end of my callout.

Select the callout line, then open the Pen roll-up window. Select the arrowhead type you want and press Apply.

After I finish drawing a callout line, it disappears before I type in the callout text.

Make sure that you only click the mouse button once when you finish drawing the second segment of a two-segment callout, and click the mouse button twice for a one-segment callout. Otherwise, CorelDRAW! will remove the callout line.

Every time I move callout text, the callout line follows it without my wanting the line to move.

Open the **A**rrange menu and choose **S**eparate. This breaks the callout into two individual objects which can be moved at will.

The callout line and callout text are too close together.

To put a little more distance between the callout line and text, press the space bar one or more times before entering the callout text.

Understanding Open and Closed Path Objects

The main difference between an *open* and *closed path object* is that the closed path object can accept an interior fill (a color or texture), but the open path object cannot (see fig. 3.26). Curved lines, straight lines, and some curved and polygon shapes are usually open path objects. Rectangles, circles, squares, and text are closed path objects. Sometimes an object appears to be an enclosed shape, or to have closed paths, when really the line segments are open paths that merely intersect. You can check whether an object is unfillable by choosing the Pick tool, clicking on the object, and checking whether the status line says Open Path on the Fill Indicator. For example, an ellipse modified to be an arc using the preceding method is an open path and cannot be filled. The pie shape, on the other hand, is a closed path that is fillable.

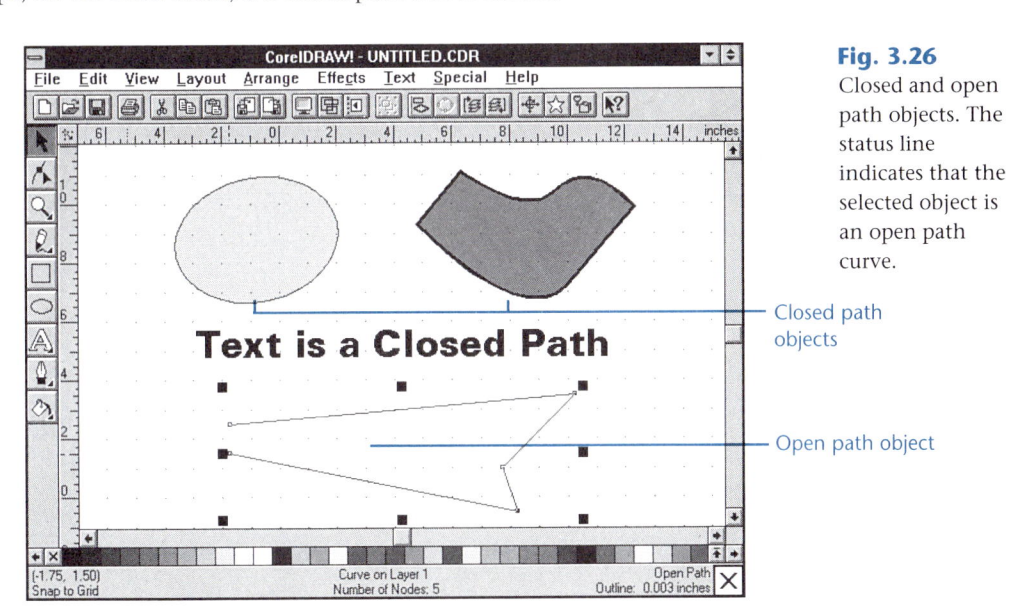

Fig. 3.26
Closed and open path objects. The status line indicates that the selected object is an open path curve.

The color or pattern inside a closed object is its *fill*. CorelDRAW! gives you a wide assortment of fills in various patterns and colors. Most fills have their own controls and special menus. You also can make or import your own colors, fills, or graphics done in CorelDRAW! or other programs. To fill an open path, you must close it first by joining the two end-line segments. See "Modifying Object Outlines and Interior Fills" in Chapter 5.

Drawing Open and Closed Path Objects

▶ See "Understanding Open and Closed Curve Objects," p. 385

To draw an open path object, use the Pencil tool in either Freehand or Bézier mode and draw a straight line object or a curved line object. Do not connect the final line segment to the original node.

When you draw a straight line object or a curved line object and complete the shape by clicking back on the beginning node, CorelDRAW! often completes the closed path for you. If you attempt to fill the object and the status line tells you it is an Open Path, you can easily convert it.

Converting an Open Path Object to a Closed Path Object

▶ See "Joining and Breaking Nodes," p. 392

Use the Join command in the Node Edit roll-up window if you want to join the end nodes of an open path to create a closed path. The Join command joins two end nodes (you also can accomplish a Join command on several pairs of nodes simultaneously). Before you can join nodes on two separate objects, you must first combine the objects. Select the objects; then open the **A**rrange menu and choose **C**ombine (Ctrl+L).

To convert an open path object to a closed path object, follow these steps:

1. Find the end nodes on the open path object that you want to close.
2. Click the Shape tool and then select the two nodes to join by Shift-clicking them.
3. Double-click one of the selected nodes (or press Ctrl+F10), and the Node Edit roll-up window appears on-screen (see fig. 3.27).

Fig. 3.27
You can join the beginning and end nodes of a curve to make a closed path object.

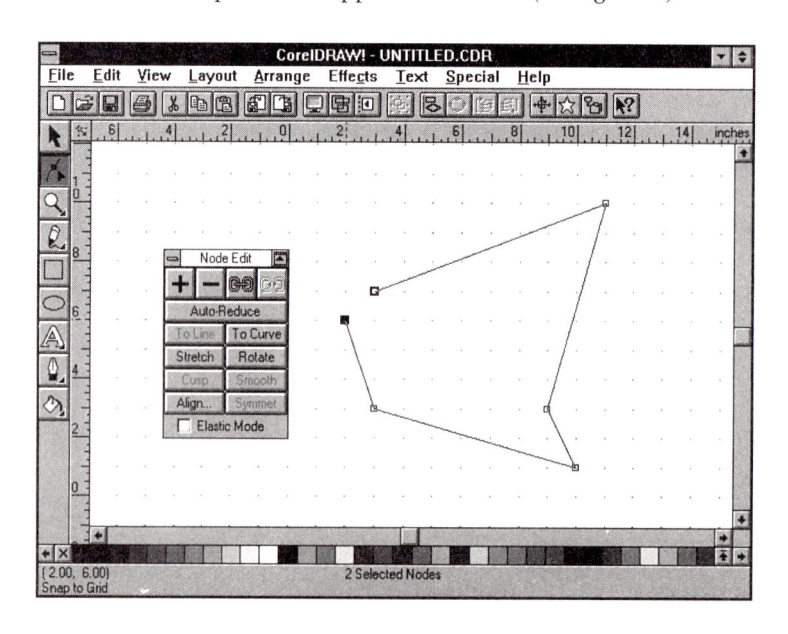

4. Click the Join icon in the roll-up window. CorelDRAW! redraws the object as a closed path that can then be filled.

> **Note**
>
> To automatically select the first and last node in a curve, first select the curve with the Shape tool. Press Home, and then press Shift+End. Then use Join to make a closed shape.

You can convert a closed path into an open path by first selecting a node and then choosing the Break icon located in the Node Edit roll-up window.

From Here...

In this chapter, you learned how to create lines and curves in both Freehand and Bézier modes using the Pencil tool. You learned how to create rectangles and squares and how to give these objects rounded corners. You also learned how to create ellipses, circles, pie wedges, and arcs. In addition, you learned how to draw callouts. Open and closed path objects, as well as converting one to the other, were also covered.

- Chapter 4, "Mastering Object Manipulations," shows you how to change additional object characteristics and work with many objects at once.

- Chapter 5, "Modifying Object Outlines and Interior Fills," covers how to change the color, shape, and texture of outlines and interiors of objects.

- Chapter 6, "Scaling, Rotating, and Distorting Objects," teaches you how to size objects and change their overall shape.

- Chapter 13, "Using Advanced Line and Curve Techniques," deals with a more advanced description of editing nodes, working with different line styles, and dimensioning a drawing.

Chapter 4
Mastering Object Manipulations

by Paul Bodensiek

CorelDRAW! gives you the ability to manipulate graphic objects to achieve artistic effect. Achieving many of the desired results requires aligning, layering, and duplicating objects. CorelDRAW! provides numerous techniques that make working with objects easy and more productive. This chapter introduces you to these basic object-related operations.

Knowing how to use these techniques efficiently is a key to creating drawings in CorelDRAW!. Several sections in this chapter include some detailed examples that you can duplicate. These examples are shown in addition to the general procedures you can follow as a reference while creating your own drawings.

In this chapter you learn how to

- Select single and multiple objects
- Lay objects on top of or below each other
- Copy, duplicate, and clone objects
- Use the grid
- Align objects
- Create scales for drawings
- Create guidelines and guide objects
- Work with groups of objects

Chapter 4—Mastering Object Manipulations

- Undo mistakes
- Combine and weld objects together
- Move objects
- Access different layers

Selecting Objects

◀ See "A Detailed Look at Object Drawing," p. 61

You must first select an object before CorelDRAW! can assign attributes to it. CorelDRAW! drawings may involve hundreds of objects, so the ability to select a particular object, or group of objects, out of many is critical. This section explains the various ways of selecting objects in CorelDRAW!.

The concepts are easiest to understand if you are in Wireframe view. To change to Wireframe view, open the **V**iew menu and then choose Wir**e**frame (Shift+F9). This section uses the rectangle, square, ellipse, and circle as shown in figure 4.1 to illustrate the procedures with a concrete example. You can practice the selection and grouping techniques on these simple objects or on any objects of your own.

◀ See "Viewing Your Work," p. 20

Fig. 4.1
When creating the objects for this example, make sure that they are sized and laid out according to this figure.

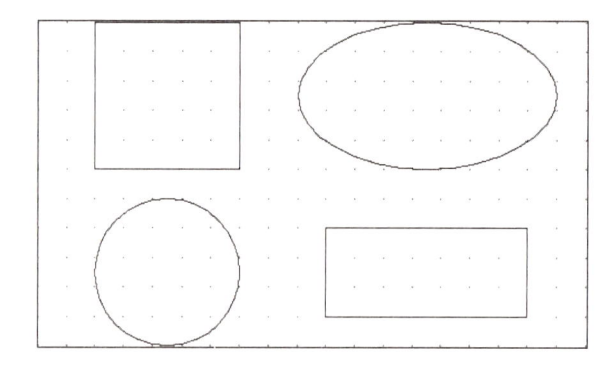

Selecting Individual Objects with the Pick Tool

To select an individual object, first click the Pick tool and then click the desired object's outline. When selected, the object is surrounded by handles, as shown in figure 4.2.

Fig. 4.2
The black boxes (handles) show that this object is selected. The status line indicates that the selected object is a rectangle.

Tip
The cursor must be precisely on the object's outline when selecting in Wireframe view. When in Editable Preview, you can click anywhere on the object's outline or fill to select the object.

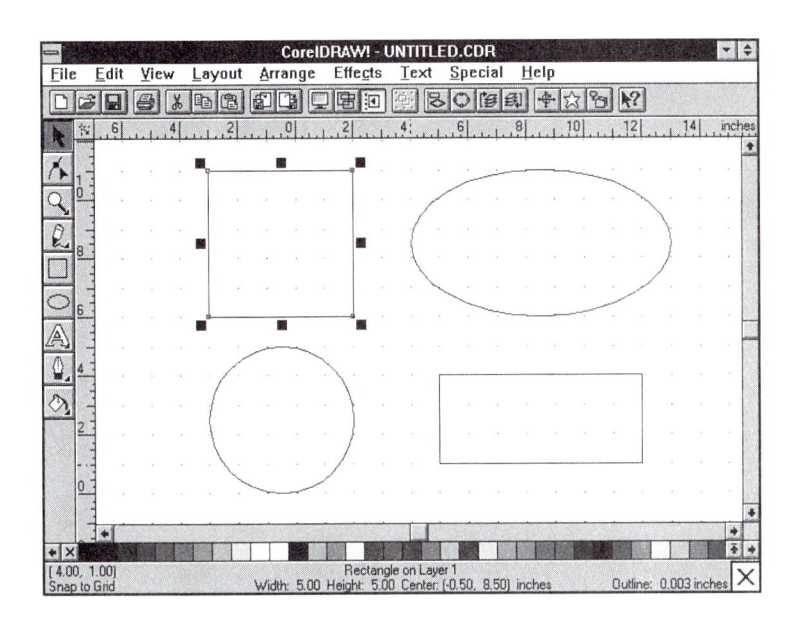

Selected objects are always surrounded by this series of handles. In addition, CorelDRAW! also shows the corner nodes of the selected object. All CorelDRAW! objects have nodes associated with them, and these nodes appear each time you select the object.

Selecting Individual Objects with the Tab Key

You also can select an object using the Pick tool in combination with the Tab key. Select an object with the Pick tool and then press Tab to individually select each of the existing objects in the order of the objects' top to bottom order. (For more information, see the "Laying Objects on Top of or beneath Each Other" section later in this chapter.) Pressing Shift+Tab reverses the selection order. Keeping Tab depressed cycles the selection quickly through each object in sequence.

Tip
Remember that you cannot edit the nodes with the Pick tool; you must use the Shape tool to modify nodal characteristics.

This selection technique is particularly valuable when the drawing contains hundreds of closely aligned objects. Selecting an object with only the Pick tool is often impossible simply due to the proximity of the objects. Adjacent objects are often drawn in sequence, and this technique enables you to get in the neighborhood of the desired object and press Tab until the object is selected.

◀ See "Reshaping a Curve or Object by Changing Its Nodes and Control Points," p. 72

> **Note**
>
> You don't have to use the Pick tool to select a first object—pressing Tab with nothing selected automatically picks the most recently created object. In a drawing with relatively few objects, it is sometimes more convenient just to press Tab a few times.

You can deselect an object, or group of objects, by either pressing Esc or clicking an empty portion of the editing window.

Selecting Multiple Objects with the Pick Tool

The Pick tool provides a convenient way for selecting multiple objects at once by enabling you to drag a marquee box around the desired group of objects.

To select multiple objects using a marquee box, follow these steps:

1. Click the Pick tool.

2. Click the Pick tool in the top-left corner of the area that includes all the objects you want to select. Drag the tool to the bottom-right corner of the area. A marquee box appears around the area as you drag the tool, as shown in figure 4.3.

3. Release the mouse button. All objects contained within the marquee are selected.

> **Note**
>
> You may find it easier to set up your marquee properly if you change the cursor to cross hairs rather than the pointer. To use the cross-hair cursor, open the Special Preferences dialog box (press Ctrl+J). Pick the View pane and click the box next to Cross Hair Cursor so that an × appears in the box.

You must include the entire object within the marquee for CorelDRAW! to include it in part of the selection. On the other hand, if the entire object is included in the marquee, it is selected whether you want it or not (refer to fig. 4.3). If you want to select nonadjacent objects or objects in a drawing that contains many objects, you may need to use a different selection method or combination of methods.

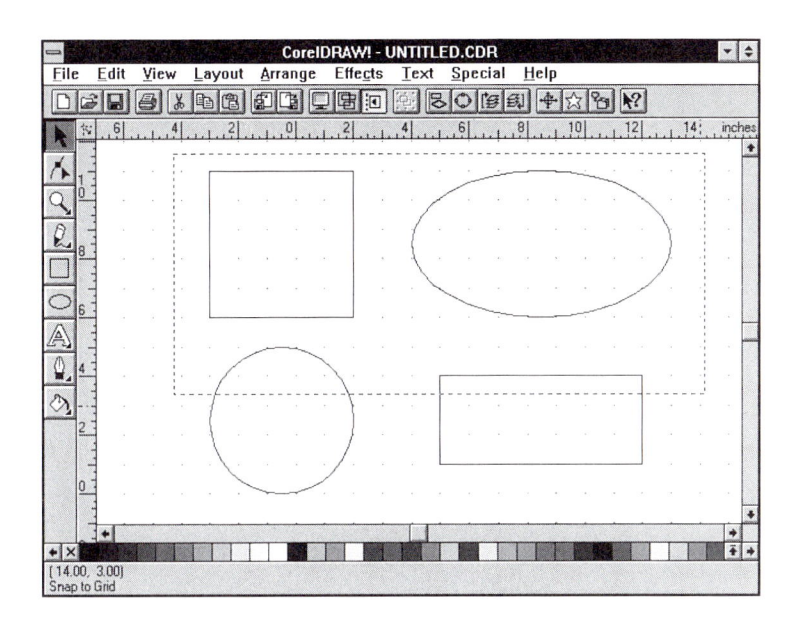

Fig. 4.3
Marquee selecting multiple objects. Because only the top two objects are surrounded by the marquee box, only they will be selected.

If you need some practice with marquee selection, follow these steps:

1. Draw the four objects shown in figure 4.3 if they are not already on-screen. Make sure that their size and location are as shown in the drawing so that the marquee will be able to select the appropriate objects. (For more information on drawing objects, see Chapter 3, "A Detailed Look at Object Drawing.")
2. Select only the top two objects.
3. Select only the bottom two objects.
4. Select the upper-right and bottom-left objects without including the other two.

Troubleshooting

A curve has been completely surrounded with the marquee, but it won't select.

CorelDRAW! includes the control points as part of an object. On some curves, the control points extend far outside the visible edge of the object. It's pretty difficult to come up with a rule of thumb for accessing these types of objects.

If most of the objects you want to select *are* being selected when you use the marquee, it's probably easiest to leave those objects selected and then pick the remaining objects you want using the Shift+click combination explained in the next section.

(continues)

> (continued)
>
> *I marquee selected some objects on-screen, but the status line indicates more objects are selected than I see.*
>
> You probably have objects hidden behind filled objects that also are selected. Open the **V**iew menu and choose Wir**e**frame. Now all the objects are shown as outlines only, and you should be able to see selected objects that were previously hidden. If you don't want these additional objects selected, Shift+click to deselect them.

Selecting Nonadjacent Objects with the Shift Key

You can select combinations of several individual objects by using the Pick tool in conjunction with the Shift key. Use this selection technique when you cannot use the marquee method because unwanted objects would be selected within the marquee.

To select multiple objects that are not adjacent, follow these steps:

1. Select the first object with the Pick tool by clicking the object or using a marquee box.

2. Press and hold down Shift (Shift+click) while you click the next object you want to select. You can also Shift+marquee to select objects (pressing Shift while making a marquee box).

3. Repeat step 2 for any additional objects you want to select. The status line shows the number of objects selected.

Tip
Shift+clicking or Shift+marqueeing an already selected object deselects it.

To practice this technique using the objects in figure 4.1, follow these steps:

1. Select the upper-right object on-screen.

2. Press Shift while clicking the lower-left object.

   The six handle boxes appear around the two objects and their nodes are displayed. Even though the handles appear to surround all four objects, only two are actually selected by CorelDRAW!. You can tell that the other two objects are not selected because their nodes are not displayed, and the status line shows that only two objects are selected, not four.

3. Press Shift and click either of the two remaining objects.

   The status line now shows that three objects are selected, and the handle boxes move to include the third object. The nodes of the rectangular object you selected also become visible. You can repeat this process for any number of objects.

> **Note**
>
> For large groups where Shift+clicking is too cumbersome, it may be easier to marquee select more objects than you really want and Shift+click to remove the unwanted objects.

Selecting All Objects on the Page

Many times, all the objects in a drawing must be manipulated at the same time. Although you can marquee select or Shift+click all the individual objects in the drawing, it is generally easier to use the Select All option. To select all objects, open the **E**dit menu and choose Select **A**ll.

Undoing Mistakes

Everyone makes mistakes. Being able to fix mistakes easily can keep them from becoming catastrophes. CorelDRAW! provides the Undo command to enable you to reverse the effect of your last edit or edits (i.e. adding or deleting an object, changing object colors, and so on).

In addition, CorelDRAW! 5 gives you the opportunity to undo up to your last 99 actions in sequence. The number of undos executed by CorelDRAW! is dependent upon the Undo levels set in the Preferences dialog box, which is accessed by opening the **S**pecial menu and choosing **P**references (Ctrl+J). The maximum number of Undo levels is 99.

To use the Undo command, open the **E**dit menu and choose **U**ndo (action), or press Ctrl+Z. CorelDRAW! fills in what it will undo in place of the word "action." For example, if you have just deleted an object accidentally and want to recover it, the Edit menu choice will read Undo Delete. Delete is covered in the next section.

Related to the Undo command is Redo. This command works exactly the same as Undo and basically undoes an Undo. To Redo an Undo, open the **E**dit menu and choose R**e**do (action). Like Undo, Redo can have up to 99 levels, which are set along with the Undo levels.

CorelDRAW! also gives you the Repeat command. With Repeat, you can select a new object and perform the same editing procedures on it that were just done. Say you have just stretched an object and want to stretch another object by the same amount. To use the Repeat command, simply select the new object, and then open the **E**dit menu and choose **R**epeat (action). CorelDRAW! does not allow you to repeat drawing an object, but it does allow just about any other editing procedure.

Tip

If you are trying to conserve memory in CorelDRAW!, set the number of Undo levels to a lower number, because each Undo level uses system memory.

▶ See "Stretching Objects," p. 198

> **Troubleshooting**
>
> *I accidentally opened a new drawing without saving my old one, and Undo will not bring back the old drawing.*
>
> Once a new drawing has been loaded, CorelDRAW! clears its memory of all its Undos. You cannot undo loading or saving a file.
>
> *I selected Redo by accident and CorelDRAW! repeated the last thing I did.*
>
> Simply use the Undo command. CorelDRAW! allows you to Undo Redos just as you would any other command you have made.
>
> *I just reset my Undo Levels to 10, but I can only undo my last 4 actions.*
>
> CorelDRAW! only saves as many actions as are currently set. CorelDRAW! will now add steps to be undone up to the limit you set, but it has not memorized any steps further back.

Deleting Objects

The procedures for deleting objects are simple. Select the objects that you want to delete and then delete them either by pressing the Delete key or by opening the **E**dit menu and choosing De**l**ete.

Selecting and then cutting an object(s) to the Windows Clipboard (open the **E**dit menu and select Cu**t**) removes the object from the drawing and makes it available for pasting into other applications or CorelDRAW! drawings.

If you delete an object by accident, open the **E**dit menu and select **U**ndo to restore the object.

Moving Objects

During the course of creating a drawing, objects and groups often have to be moved from one part of a drawing to another. There are three main ways of doing this in CorelDRAW!: dragging the object with the mouse, using the Transform roll-up window, and nudging the object with the arrow keys.

Moving an Object with the Mouse

The most common way to move an object is to drag it with the mouse. To do this, simply select the object and then drag it to its new location.

Moving Using the Transform Roll-Up

You also can move an object by using the Move option in the Transform roll-up window. This gives you numerical precision in assigning the location of the object.

To position an object using the Move option, follow these steps:

1. Select an object.

2. Open the Effects menu and select Transform Roll-Up.

3. Press the Move button (see fig. 4.4).

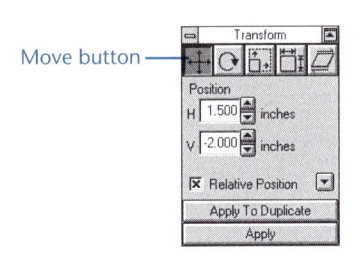

Fig. 4.4
The Transform roll-up window, showing the Position options.

4. To position the object at a *specific place on the page*, enter the numbers corresponding to numbers in the H and V boxes.

   To position the object *relative to its current position*, check the Relative Position box so that it is filled with an × and input the appropriate numbers.

5. Press Apply to place the object at the indicated position.

> **Note**
>
> When moving the object to a specific page location, CorelDRAW! defaults to moving it to the location you have input, based on the center of the object. To change the basis for this move, press the down arrow next to Relative Position and select the handle position for the object.

Moving Objects with Nudge

Use the arrow keys to move, or *nudge*, a selected object a precisely defined distance. To nudge an object, select the object and then press the arrow key that points in the direction of desired movement.

102 Chapter 4—Mastering Object Manipulations

To set the amount of offset caused by each nudge, open the **S**pecial menu and choose Pr**e**ferences to display the dialog box shown in figure 4.5. Type the new nudge displacement value (0.25 inch, for example) in the Nudge box.

Fig. 4.5
Set the nudge distance by using the Preferences dialog box. This value must be between 0.0 and 2.0 inches.

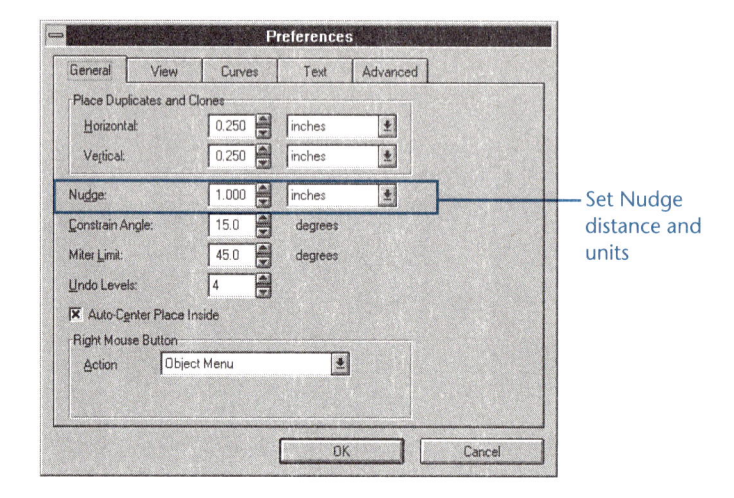

Set Nudge distance and units

> **Note**
>
> With CorelDRAW! 5, you also can nudge a node by first selecting it with the Shape tool and then nudging it with the arrow keys. The same nudge displacement preferences apply to node nudges. Although version 4 also enabled you to do this, often the moved node printed in the same place it was before the nudge, or returned to its original position when saved. For more information on object nodes, see "Reshaping a Curve or Object by Changing Its Nodes and Control Points" in Chapter 3.

Laying Objects on Top of or beneath Each Other

CorelDRAW! always places the most recently drawn object on top of the ones drawn previously. You change the position of objects with respect to each other by moving them on top of or beneath other objects. This is useful for achieving many different overlapping effects, such as a fanned out set of playing cards arranged in a particular order.

If you want to move an object forward (closer to the front or top layer) in the back-to-front order of objects, follow these steps:

Laying Objects on Top of or beneath Each Other   **103**

1. Click the Pick tool and click the object you want to reposition close to the top layer.

2. Open the **A**rrange menu and choose **O**rder; then choose Forward **O**ne (Ctrl+PgUp). This option moves the object forward one place in the order.

If you want to move an object to the top layer (the front object) in the back-to-front order of objects, follow these steps:

1. Click the Pick tool and click the object you want to bring to the top.

2. Open the **A**rrange menu and choose **O**rder; then choose To **F**ront (Shift+PgUp). This option makes the object the top object.

The steps are similar for moving an object backward in the order. You use Back O**n**e (Ctrl+PgDn) to move an object back one place in the order, or To **B**ack (Shift+PgDn) to make it the bottom object.

The following steps illustrate the use of the Front and Back commands when orienting objects, follow these steps:

1. Draw the objects shown in figure 4.6 and pay special attention to their relative size and orientation. Draw the square-cornered rectangle first; the round-cornered rectangle second; the ellipse third; and the triangle last to ensure the proper front-to-back orientation for the beginning of this exercise. (See Chapter 3, "A Detailed Look at Object Drawing," for information on drawing objects.)

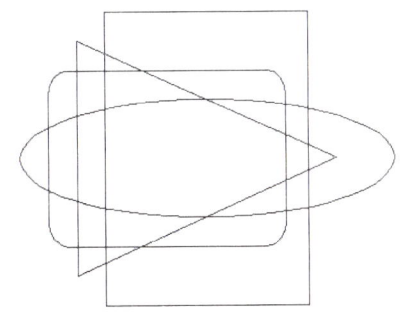

Fig. 4.6
The objects to be used for the object ordering exercise shown in Wireframe view.

Tip
Although figure 4.6 is in Wireframe view, this exercise is best run in Editable Preview, which is used for the subsequent figures.

2. Give each of these objects a solid fill at random. Make sure, however, that each color stands out well against the others so that you can see them easily. (See Chapter 5, "Modifying Object Outlines and Interior Fills," for information on fills.)

104 Chapter 4—Mastering Object Manipulations

3. Select the triangle and then open the **A**rrange menu and choose **O**rder; then select the Back O**n**e option. The triangle is now between the ellipse and the round-cornered rectangle as shown in figure 4.7.

Fig. 4.7
The objects in the example, viewed in Editable Preview, as they appear at the end of step 3.

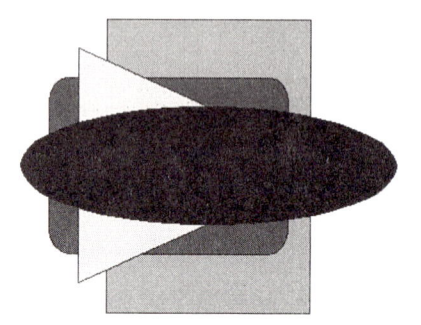

4. Open the **A**rrange menu and choose **O**rder; then choose Back O**n**e again to move the triangle between the two rectangles as shown by the small amount of triangle showing at the top and bottom of the round-cornered rectangle.

5. Select the ellipse and move it behind the other objects by opening the **A**rrange menu and choosing **O**rder, and then choosing To **B**ack. Your drawing should look like figure 4.8.

Fig. 4.8
The objects in the example as they appear after step 5.

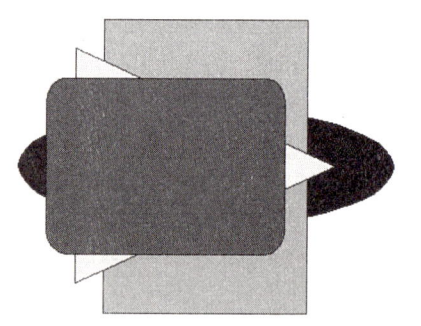

6. Select the square-cornered rectangle. Open the **A**rrange menu and choose **O**rder, and then choose Forward **O**ne. This action moves the object forward one level.

7. Open the **A**rrange menu and choose **O**rder; then choose Forward **O**ne to move the square-cornered rectangle in front of the other objects.

To reverse the entire order of the objects, select the group of objects to be reordered. Open the **A**rrange menu and choose **O**rder; then choose **R**everse Order.

Copying Objects

The two basic types of copies are *duplicates* and *clones*. A duplicate is a new object exactly like the original. A clone also is an exact copy of the original object, but it remains connected to the original object so that modifications to the original object are made to the clones. The following sections explain how to duplicate and clone objects.

Duplicating Objects

Effective use of the CorelDRAW! duplicating techniques can save you time when you work on drawings.

All duplicating techniques follow the same two-step procedure:

1. Select the object(s) or group of objects for duplication.

2. Duplicate the object(s) or group using any of the following three methods:

   Open the **E**dit menu and choose **D**uplicate (Ctrl+D). This creates a copy a specific distance from the original.

   Press the + key on the numeric keypad, which places a duplicate on top of the original object(s).

   Copy (Ctrl+C) and Paste (Ctrl+V) the object via the Clipboard.

CorelDRAW! automatically selects the duplicated object(s) so that you can then work with the new object(s), moving or sizing them at will.

The following steps illustrate the duplication process:

1. Clear the drawing by opening the **F**ile menu and choosing **N**ew (select **N**o when asked if you want to save changes), or by deleting all objects by opening the **E**dit menu and choosing Select **A**ll, and then pressing the Delete key.

2. Draw an object (rectangle, ellipse, line, and so on).

3. Click the Pick tool. The object is automatically selected.

4. Open the **E**dit menu and choose **D**uplicate. The object is duplicated to the side and on top of the original.

5. Open the **E**dit menu and choose **D**uplicate again, and a new copy is placed in the same relative orientation to the second object as the second object was to the first. (The position used for the duplicated object

> **Tip**
> Using Copy and Paste can be lengthy if you are copying many objects, due to a very slow Copy procedure.

106 Chapter 4—Mastering Object Manipulations

is a user-defined default setting. Setting this position is covered in the next section.)

Setting the Automatic Duplication Defaults

Precisely locating a duplicated object automatically when it is created can greatly increase your drawing efficiency. This is particularly true when creating forms, which are essentially lines or boxes of the same shape and size copied to various screen locations.

To specify where CorelDRAW! positions duplicates, follow these steps:

1. Open the **S**pecial menu and choose **P**references. The Preferences dialog box opens, as shown in figure 4.9.

Fig. 4.9
Use the Preferences dialog box to set the location for placing a duplicate or clone object.

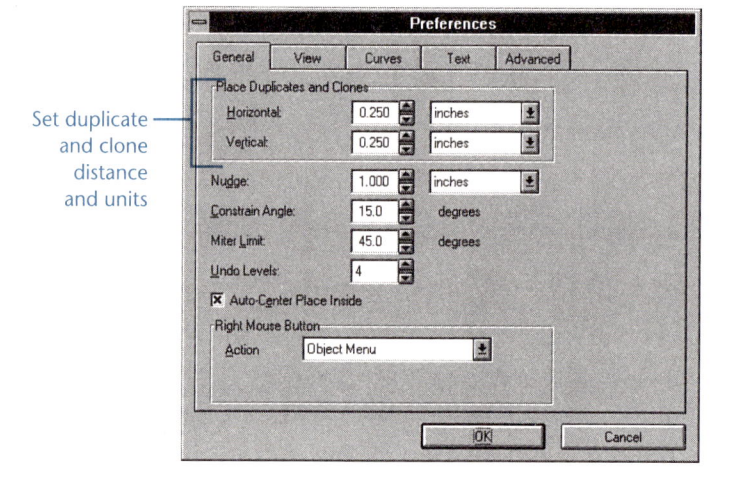

Set duplicate and clone distance and units

2. Click the General tab.

3. Change the vertical and horizontal values shown in the Place Duplicates and Clones section as desired. Keep in mind that these distances are relative to the original position of the object that you're copying.

    Positive numbers place the duplicate object to the right (horizontal) and above (vertical). Negative numbers move the object in the opposite direction, respectively. Mixing positive horizontal and negative vertical settings (and vice versa) also is allowed.

4. Click OK. The next time you duplicate an object, CorelDRAW! places the duplicate according to the settings you entered.

> **Note**
>
> You also can set the values by clicking the small up and down arrows, or by dragging up or down on the separator bar located between the up and down arrows. The cursor turns into a double arrow when placed on the separator bar.
>
> These options only enable you to change the numbers by 0.01 inch, so greater control is best done by entering the exact number you want through the keyboard.

Duplicating Objects Using the Clipboard

In addition to using the direct duplication command, CorelDRAW! also allows you to use the Windows Clipboard to store a copy of an object for later use. This can be especially helpful when creating multiple duplicates or when you want to add objects to other documents.

To place an object in the Clipboard, follow these steps:

1. Select an object using the Pick tool.

2. Open the **E**dit menu and choose **C**opy (Ctrl+C) to leave the original object in your drawing.

   To delete the original object, open the **E**dit menu and choose Cu**t**.

To paste an object from the Clipboard, open the **E**dit menu and choose **P**aste.

Cloning Objects

Cloning makes many CorelDRAW! operations faster, easier, and less tedious. Cloning is a unique method of duplicating objects. Cloned objects remain related to the original, or master, object so that changes to the master affect all cloned objects.

> **Tip**
> To create a duplicate or clone positioned directly on top of the master, make the horizontal and vertical Place Duplicates and Clones settings zero.

The following steps outline the cloning procedure:

1. Select the object to be cloned.

2. Open the **E**dit menu and choose Cl**o**ne. CorelDRAW! creates the clone at the screen location defined in the Preferences dialog box. You can drag the cloned object to another screen location.

3. Repeat steps 1 and 2 to create as many clones as needed.

Chapter 4—Mastering Object Manipulations

> **Note**
>
> You cannot clone a clone. You can only clone the master. To determine whether an object is a master or clone, select the object and read the status line. If the object is a master object, the status line will read `Control`.
>
> Clicking the object with the right mouse button displays a fly-out menu. The bottom of the menu shows *Select Master* if the object is a clone, or *Select Clones* if the object is the master (see fig. 4.10). Pressing the Select Master button automatically picks the master object.

Fig. 4.10
The fly-out menu tells you an object is a clone when it reads `Select Master` at the bottom.

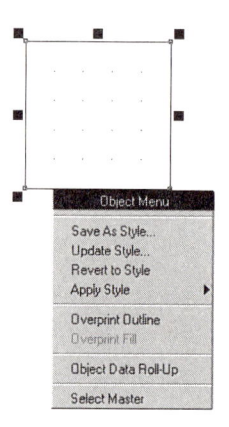

To simultaneously make changes to all object clones, select the master object and then make any changes you need. All the clones automatically change too.

You make changes to individual clones just like any other CorelDRAW! object: select it and make the changes. However, if you change a clone's attributes, those attributes are no longer linked to the master. For example, if you change the line thickness on a clone, any changes to the line thickness of the master do not affect that clone.

To familiarize yourself with the cloning process, try the following exercise:

1. Either select a current object or draw and select a new one. (For more information about drawing objects, refer to Chapter 3, "A Detailed Look at Object Drawing.")

▶ See "Creating Special Effects with Perspective," p. 413

2. Open the **E**dit menu and choose Cl**o**ne. CorelDRAW! creates the clone at the Duplicate Preferences location.

> **Note**
>
> You can clone master objects that include special effects (such as blending, extruding, contouring, PowerLines, and so on) and have those effects carry to the clones. Changing these characteristics on the master affects the clones as long as you originally apply the characteristics to the master *before* cloning. Adding these effects to the master after cloning does not affect the clones. (See Part V, "Becoming an Expert," for chapters covering CorelDRAW! 5 special effects.)

3. Drag the clone to your desired screen location. (See the "Moving Objects" section earlier in this chapter.)

4. Modify all clone attributes by selecting the master object and changing its attributes. The clone will be changed to adopt the new master object attributes, such as color, size, rotation, and outline.

Aligning Objects

CorelDRAW! is equipped with a series of tools to make it easy to provide exact alignment for objects and collections of objects.

Using the Grid to Facilitate Alignment

A grid defines specific intervals upon which object outlines can fall. Although they are described as lines, the grid is displayed as a series of points at the intersections of the grid lines. A grid is particularly useful when working with rectangular objects because all of its sides are constrained to fall on a grid line, which greatly simplifies object alignment. When drawing objects that do not require rigorous alignment, such as illustrations, you should disable Snap To Grid so that you have complete freedom in creating and moving the objects.

▶ See "Modifying Object Outlines and Interior Fills," p. 137

▶ See "Scaling, Rotating, and Distorting Objects," p. 183

Establishing the Grid

To establish the grid, follow these steps:

1. Open the **L**ayout menu and choose G**r**id Setup to display the Grid Setup dialog box shown in figure 4.11.

2. Enter the horizontal and vertical grid frequencies you want to use for the grid. (These options are discussed in detail in the next section, so you may just want to accept the defaults for now.)

Fig. 4.11
The Grid & Scale Setup dialog box enables you to manipulate the on-screen grid.

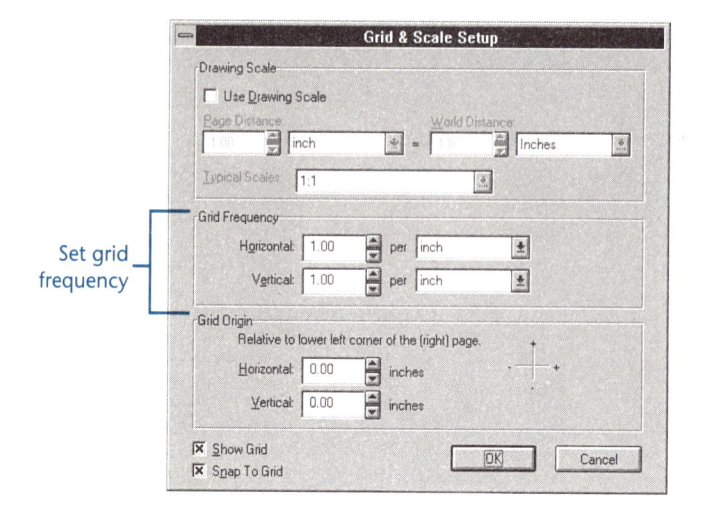

Set grid frequency

3. Choose the Snap To Grid option located at the bottom left of the dialog box to align newly created objects along grid lines.

4. If you want to see the grid while you are drawing or editing, choose the Show Grid option located at the bottom left of the dialog box. You can show the grid whether you are snapping to it or not.

5. Click OK to return to the editing screen.

Tip
You also can activate or deactivate Snap To Grid by opening the **L**ayout menu and choosing **S**nap To Grid.

◄ See "Reviewing the Toolbox Tools," p. 23

> **Note**
>
> When you are zoomed out, the grid changes its *visible* frequency so that the screen does not get too confusing with grid intersection points. You can still snap to the actual grid points that may lie between the visible grid dots.

To draw objects aligned to the grid, draw them as you normally would. The edges of the objects now only align along gridlines.

Establishing Scale Settings

Many times you will want to create a drawing much larger than your CorelDRAW! page. Establishing a scale enables you to "fool" CorelDRAW! into thinking that you've increased the size of your drawing space. This is especially helpful if you are making technical illustrations. The drawing still prints out on your normal sized paper.

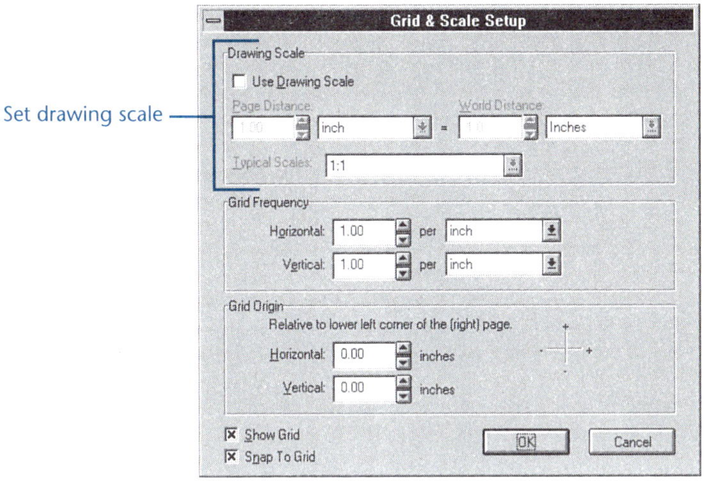

Fig. 4.12
You can set the scale for a drawing by using the Grid & Scale Setup dialog box.

To set the drawing scale, open the **L**ayout menu and choose **G**rid & Scale Setup. In the Drawing Scale section (see fig. 4.12), you can have CorelDRAW! display the units pertinent to a particular drawing (such as meters) and determine how big that particular unit appears on your drawing (say, one inch equals one meter). You can choose from various unit types by clicking the down arrow next to the unit listed to display the drop-down list and then choosing the one you want. Many preset scales also can be accessed through the Typical Scales pull-down menu.

After you establish these settings, CorelDRAW! calculates all display dimension units accordingly. All objects are described on the status line in the display unit you set (kilometers in fig. 4.12), which makes scale drawing creation much simpler.

Tip
When drawing rough house plans, the industry standard scales are 1/8' = 1" and 1/4' = 1".

Establishing Grid Frequencies

The Horizontal and Vertical grid frequencies sections of the Grid Setup dialog box establish the location of the various grid alignment lines. For example, a setting of 8 grid lines per inch (unit) creates a 1/8-inch grid network. The maximum number of grid lines per unit follows:

Unit	Grid Lines
Inch	72 lines
Pica	12 lines
Point	1 line
Millimeter	About 2.8 lines

The grid frequency you choose depends upon the type of drawing you are doing. Very accurate drawings need a tighter grid (higher number of lines), whereas less accurate drawings can generally get away with a looser grid (smaller number of lines).

Often you find that a portion of a drawing needs a grid setting different from the rest of the drawing. To make it easier to line up that portion of the drawing with the rest, it is generally best to make the new grid frequency a multiple of the original. For example, say the original setting is 4 lines per inch and you need a tighter grid; 8 lines per inch would enable you to have more detail, while still lining up on the original grid at every other grid point.

Establish a grid frequency for each new image and then stick with it, or a multiple of the original frequency. Keep in mind that working with a drawing containing a very tight grid network can be difficult when you are zoomed out, and each new drawing may require a different grid frequency.

To set the grid frequency, follow these steps:

1. Open the **L**ayout menu and choose **G**rid & Scale Setup. The Grid & Scale Setup dialog box appears.

2. In the Grid Frequency area, set the Horizontal and Vertical unit preferences.

3. Click OK.

Establishing the Grid Origin

The grid origin is the assumed 0,0 location for the drawing, and all page locations are referenced from that origin point. In general, the origin is located at the lower-left corner of the drawing so that all page locations are shown as positive numbers. Moving the origin to another page location so that all dimensions are referenced from that new location is occasionally useful.

You can either specify the precise page location using the Grid Setup dialog box, or you can drag the icon located at the intersection of the horizontal and vertical rulers to the desired new origin location. All screen locations shown on the status line from that time forward show dimensions based on the new origin location.

To specify the precise location of the origin using the Grid Setup dialog box, follow these steps:

1. Open the **L**ayout menu and choose **G**rid & Scale Setup. The Grid & Scale Setup dialog box appears.

2. Choose Horizontal (or Vertical) in the Grid Origin section of the Grid Setup dialog box.

3. Type the desired new horizontal (and/or vertical) location for the origin.

> **Note**
>
> You can also use the up and down buttons or the separator bar located next to the numbers. Because these only allow you to set the origin in 0.1" increments, you should set the numbers using the keyboard if you need tighter control.

4. Click OK.

Aligning to Other Objects

In addition to snapping to the grid, you also can snap to other objects in a drawing. Effective use of this feature can greatly increase your drawing speed.

Objects are snapped to each other by their nodes. When you enable the Snap To Objects feature, object nodes are "magnetically" aligned with each other. Keep in mind that Snap To Grid should be off for Snap To Objects to work properly because the grid overrides other snap options.

◀ See "Reshaping a Curve or Object by Changing Its Nodes and Control Points," p. 72

To use the Snap To Objects feature, follow these steps:

1. Open the **L**ayout menu and choose Snap To **O**bjects.

2. Select an object.

3. Drag the selected object toward another object. Whenever any of the nodes of your selected object get close to those of the other, the selected object jumps into alignment with that node.

◀ See "Moving Objects," p. 100

4. Drag the mouse pointer toward the desired location on the second object and release the object when it "snaps to" the correct location.

Most CorelDRAW! objects have node points used as "magnets" during the Snap To Object process. These node points are located differently for different object shapes and types (see table 4.1). When node points from various objects are brought near each other, they attract each other along those node points.

114 Chapter 4—Mastering Object Manipulations

Table 4.1 Node Points for CorelDRAW! Objects

Object Type	Node Points
Rectangular and square objects	Along the edge of the object in the same relative location as the scaling handles, and one in the center
Rectangular and square objects with rounded corners	In the center of the rectangle and objects with rounded corners at the ends of each arc segment in each corner
Closed ellipses and circles	In the center and at the end of each major and minor axis along the object's perimeter
Modified ellipses and circles	At the same points as for the closed ellipse, and also at the endpoints associated with removed wedge
Open line paths	At the ends and at as many other locations along the path as are required to complete the curve
Bitmaps	In the corners and center of the bitmap image (See Chapter 25, "Photograph Touch-Up with CorelPHOTO-PAINT.")
Artistic text	At the standard scaling handle locations and in the center (See Chapter 7, "Adding Text to a Drawing".)
Paragraph text	At the standard scaling handle locations and in the center
Dimension lines	Will snap to other objects using the place you grabbed the dimension line. Objects cannot be snapped to dimension lines or their text.
Callouts	Will snap to other objects using the place you grabbed the callout or its text. Object will only snap to callout text (using the text locations noted above) but not to the callout line.

◀ See "Creating Rectangular and Square Objects," p. 78

◀ See "Drawing Circular Shapes," p. 81

◀ See "Understanding Open and Closed Path Objects," p. 89

▶ See "Using Dimension Lines," p. 403

◀ See "Drawing Callouts on Objects," p. 86

Figure 4.13 shows the node locations for each type of object.

Note

You can use the Snap To Objects feature to automatically resize objects to each other by first dragging the two objects on top of each other and then allowing the snap to magnetism to do the rest as you drag the nodes towards each other.

For example, follow along with the following procedure:

1. Activate Snap To Objects by opening the **L**ayout menu and choosing Snap To **O**bjects.

2. Draw a large rectangle and a small circle on top of each other on the drawing page.

Aligning Objects 115

3. Select the circle with the Pick tool and drag the right scaling handle to the rectangle's right side. The sides should snap to each other. You may have to move the cursor toward the center or corner of the desired side for CorelDRAW! to know you wat to snap to the rectangle.

4. With the circle still selected, drag the left scaling handle toward the left side of the rectangle. It should snap to the rectangle's mid-span.

5. Now drag the circle's top and bottom scaling handles toward the top and bottom of the rectangle, respectively, and notice that they also snap to the rectangle's side nodes. The circle is now exactly sized to fit within the rectangle and is now elliptical in shape.

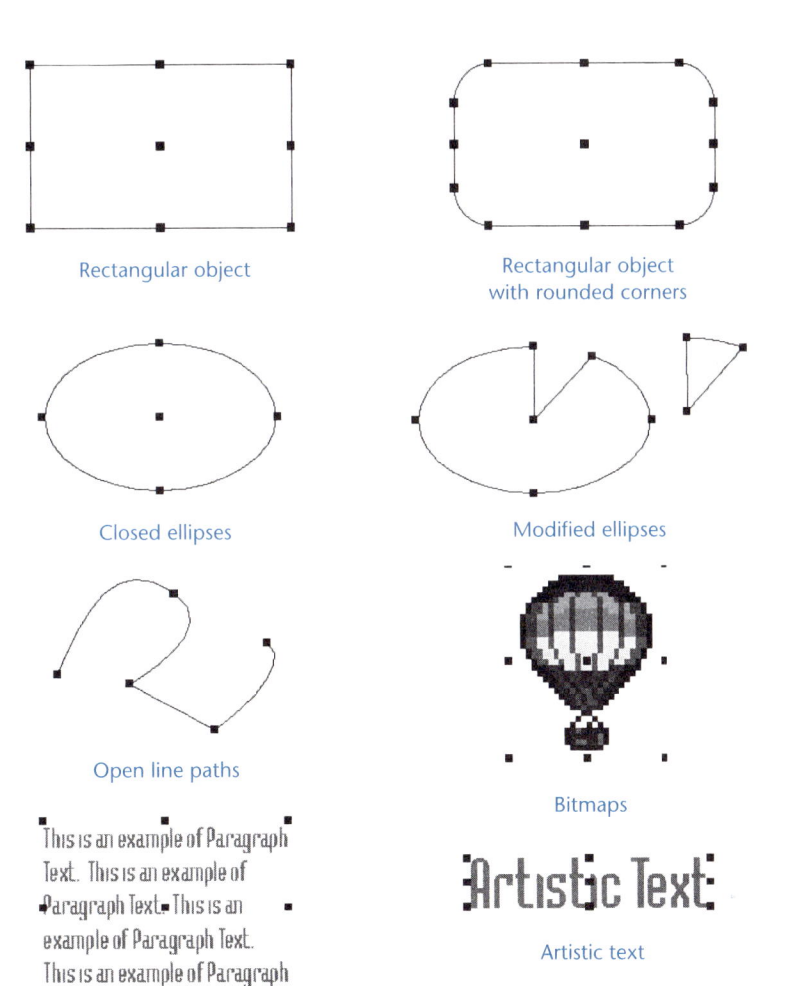

Rectangular object

Rectangular object with rounded corners

Closed ellipses

Modified ellipses

Open line paths

Bitmaps

Paragraph text

Artistic text

Fig. 4.13
When using Snap To Object mode, other objects will snap to the locations shown in this figure.

Simultaneously Aligning Several Objects

The Align command enables you to simultaneously align several objects along their edges or center in a horizontal or vertical direction. This feature is particularly useful when the objects are of different shapes and were created with Snap To Grid deactivated.

To align objects using the Align command, follow these steps:

1. Select all the objects you want to align.

2. Open the **A**rrange menu and choose **A**lign (Ctrl+A) to display the Align dialog box (see fig. 4.14).

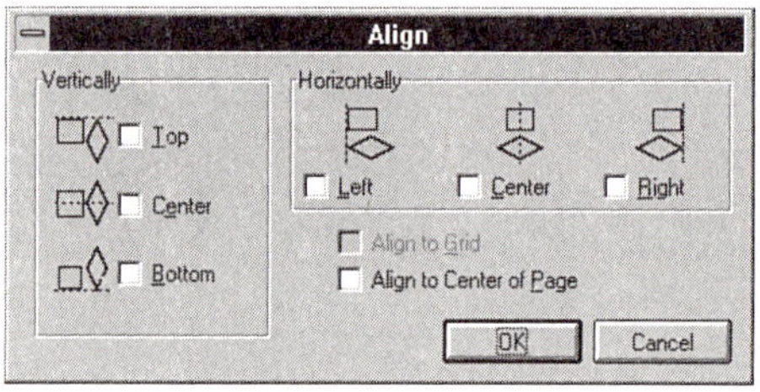

Fig. 4.14
The Align dialog box allows you to set various combinations of vertical and horizontal alignment for multiple objects.

3. Select the arrangement option you want and click OK.

The diagrams shown in the dialog box indicate the relative alignment of objects performed by each alignment type. You can choose vertical options and horizontal options individually or jointly. If you only choose an option for one direction, CorelDRAW! ignores the other direction's alignment. For example, vertical center alignment causes the objects to move up or down so that the centers align, but no horizontal movement is performed. Horizontal center alignment works the same way but in the horizontal, rather than vertical, direction. Choosing both horizontal and vertical center aligns the centers of all selected objects with each other and in both directions.

All the objects will align either around the last object selected or the bottom-most object, depending on your selection method. When objects are picked individually by Shift+clicking, they align on the last selected object. When objects are marquee-selected, they align on the bottom-most object.

CorelDRAW! also enables you to align objects to the center of the page by using the Align command with the Align To Center Of Page option activated. The object alignment selections tell CorelDRAW! which part of the objects to align with the center of the page. For example, selecting Align to center of page and then setting Vertical-Bottom aligns the bottom center of all selected objects with the center of the page as shown in figure 4.15.

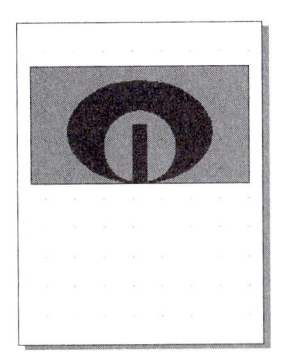

Fig. 4.15

These objects are all aligned with their bottoms and horizontal centers on the center of the page.

The Align To Grid option instructs CorelDRAW! to align the selected objects in the chosen orientation, but to lay the aligned objects along the closest grid line. This option does not align multiple objects to each other.

Using the Guidelines to Ease Alignment

CorelDRAW! provides guidelines to allow for easy alignment of objects along straight vertical and horizontal paths.

The general procedure for setting up guidelines with the mouse is as follows:

1. Click the vertical ruler and drag the cursor to the right. A dashed, vertical guide line follows the cursor. Release the mouse button when the guideline is at the desired point.

2. Click the horizontal ruler and drag the cursor downward. A dashed, horizontal guide line follows the cursor. Release the mouse button when the guideline is at the desired point.

3. Open the **L**ayout menu and choose Snap To Guidelin**e**s.

4. To align objects along guidelines you have created, drag the objects to the guideline, and their nodes align along the guidelines (see fig. 4.16).

The Guidelines Setup dialog box allows for creation, deletion, and precise page locating of guidelines. These features become particularly helpful when the overall page formatting must conform to precise standards. CorelDRAW! stores the guidelines on their own layer, which may be visible or invisible. When the layer is invisible, you cannot snap to the guidelines.

Fig. 4.16
The objects in this figure have all been aligned to the dashed guidelines using the Snap To Guidelines feature.

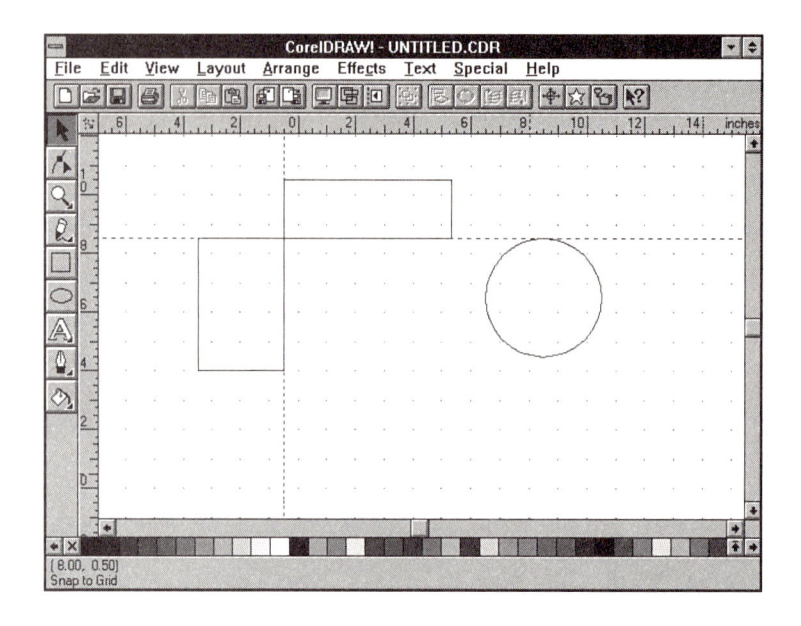

The Guidelines Setup dialog box enables you to numerically designate the guideline locations relative to the current ruler origin. The following is the general procedure for setting up guidelines with the dialog box:

1. Open the **L**ayout menu and choose G**u**idelines Setup. This opens the Guidelines Setup dialog box shown in figure 4.17.

Fig. 4.17
The Guidelines Setup dialog box allows you to precisely set the locations of both horizontal and vertical guidelines.

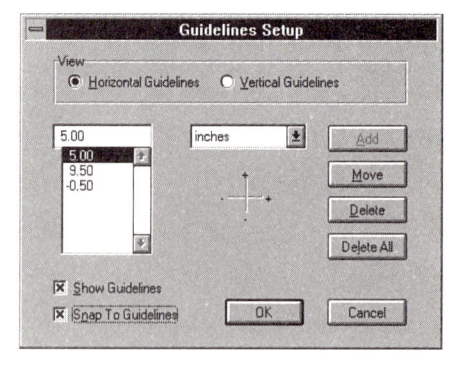

2. Choose Horizontal or Vertical; the list shows all previously set up guidelines of the selected type.

3. Input the position for the desired guideline in the input box. The position is measured from the current ruler origin, and these numbers change if you move the origin, while retaining the same position

relative to the page. (See the "Establishing the Grid Origin" section earlier in this chapter.)

4. Choose Show Guidelines and Snap to Guidelines.

5. Click OK when done.

6. To align objects along the guidelines you have created, drag the objects to the guideline; and their nodes align along the guidelines (refer to fig. 4.16).

> **Troubleshooting**
>
> *I have the grid set, but the cursor seems to snap between the grid points on the screen.*
>
> Double-check your grid setting. When you are zoomed out, not every grid point is visible (to keep the screen from becoming too confusing). If you want to have the screen show every grid point, either zoom in closer on the drawing or reset the grid frequency so that it corresponds with what is displayed on the screen.
>
> *I try to align to guidelines, but my objects snap to points slightly away from the guides.*
>
> Turn off Snap To Grid, if it is active. Snap To Grid overrides all other snap options, so that even when Snap To Guidelines is set, if there is a grid line close to the guideline, the object will snap to the grid.
>
> *When I try to align several objects to the center of the page, they all end up on top of each other instead of keeping their original layout relative to each other.*
>
> When you align several objects at once, each is treated individually so that they align to the page center. Group the objects together, and then align the group to the page. You can then ungroup the object if you want. (See the "Grouping Objects" section later in this chapter.)

Combining and Grouping Objects

Often when you are drawing, you will want to work on groups of objects together as one object. Or you will have labored to precisely align all the objects in a drawing, and you want to keep them aligned even if you move or resize them. Combining objects is useful for speeding the redraw process during screen refresh because combining reduces the number of objects to be drawn.

The following sections explain how to group and combine objects and how to work with these object types. These sections also explain how to separate grouped objects.

Distinguishing between Grouping and Combining Objects

Grouping objects is used often with CorelDRAW! because alignment of separate objects to each other is often critical, hard to establish, and necessary to keep after established. Each object in a group retains its own identity, but it becomes part of a group of objects. Selecting any member of the group selects the entire group of objects.

Combining, on the other hand, creates a single object out of many different objects and is used primarily to decrease the size of CorelDRAW! files and increase screen redraw speed.

Grouping Objects

Group objects any time the relationship between objects is critical and you want to maintain it. Grouping objects enables you to select a number of objects at once for actions such as rotating, sizing, or moving. You also can form groups of individual groups, called subgroups.

Tip
CorelDRAW! allows up to ten levels of subgrouping. Look to the status line to determine whether the selected objects are part of a subgroup, also called a *child group*.

You will probably use grouping extensively because much of the work done with CorelDRAW! involves the relationships between groups. For example, you may create a drawing of an automobile. The windows, doors, tires, and so on are all distinct objects that create the final automobile image. After you complete the automobile image, you work with the total automobile not just the image of the tires. The automobile group is the single image of the automobile, which is composed of many separate objects. Selecting any object within the automobile group selects the entire group.

To group a number of objects, follow these steps:

1. Select the objects to be grouped.
2. Open the **A**rrange menu and select **G**roup (Ctrl+G).

For practice in grouping objects, follow this example:

1. Draw a big circle and two smaller ellipses to create a drawing similar to that in figure 4.18.

▶ See "Working with Interior Fills," p. 146

Combining and Grouping Objects   **121**

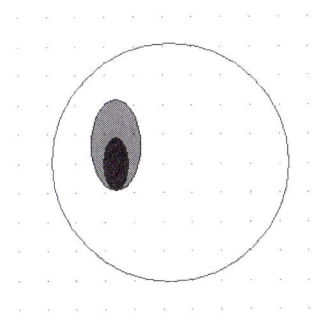

Fig. 4.18
Use this figure as a guide to lay out the circle and ellipses used for this example.

> **Note**
>
> Drawing and aligning the two smaller ellipses is a good opportunity to practice the snap to objects and/or align objects procedures outlined earlier in this chapter.

2. Select the objects to be grouped (the two ellipses in this example) using any of the previously mentioned object selection procedures.

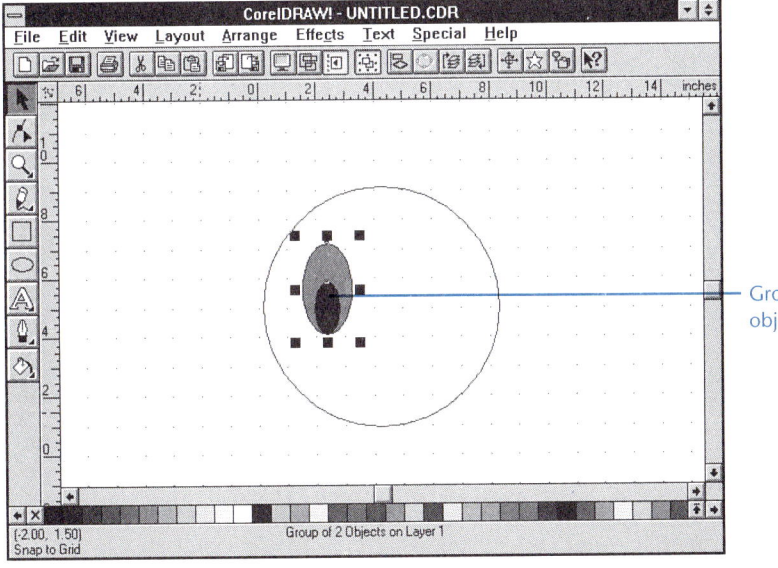

Fig. 4.19
The status line shows that the "eye" is a group composed of two objects.

Group of two objects

3. Open the **A**rrange menu and choose **G**roup (Ctrl+G). The status line now indicates that this is a group of objects (see fig. 4.19).

122 Chapter 4—Mastering Object Manipulations

You now can perform any standard object operations on the new object group. For example, figure 4.20 shows the result of duplicating and moving a group.

Fig. 4.20
Duplicating a single eye means that you have to draw it only once, but you still can to use its design for both eyes in the figure.

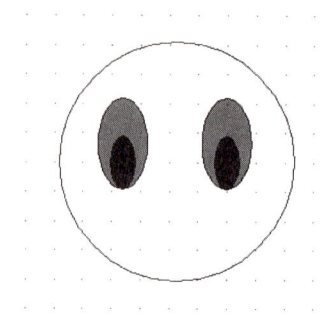

> **Note**
>
> Changing the fill or outline of a group of objects applies the change to all objects within the group, sometimes with unwanted results. For instructions on changing the attributes on a single object in a group, see "Accessing Objects within a Group" later in this chapter.

Ungrouping Objects

Ungrouping objects is simply a matter of selecting the group, opening the **A**rrange menu, and choosing **U**ngroup (Ctrl+U). If the group is comprised of several subgroups, you may need to ungroup each of them also.

Tip
The group button on the ribbon bar acts as an "ungroup" button when a group is selected.

The primary reason for ungrouping is to make changes to or remove an individual object rather than the entire group. Make sure that you regroup the objects after making the modifications to the single object, or you can lose the alignment of the whole group.

Accessing Objects within a Group (Child Objects)

A simpler way to change the characteristics of an individual object within a group is to select it as a *child object*. While an object is selected as a child object, you can treat it as though it were a stand-alone object. When you deselect the object, it reverts to being a member of the group.

To work with a child object within a group, follow these steps:

1. Select the object group.

2. Press and hold down Ctrl and click the object within the group that you want to work with. The status line indicates that a child object is

Combining and Grouping Objects

selected, and the black handle squares around the group become black circles around the child object.

3. Make any changes you want to the child object.

4. Click anywhere on-screen, and the child object is no longer selected and is again treated as part of the group.

Tip
You may need to Ctrl+click several times to work through the levels of the group until you can access the desired child object.

To give you a clearer understanding of this concept, the following steps illustrate how to select and modify a child object using the drawing from the preceding section:

1. Click the pupil of the left eye of the character drawn in the preceding exercise. The standard scaling handles appear around the left group of objects.

2. Ctrl+click the left pupil. The black squares around the left eye group turn into small circles around the left pupil, indicating that the pupil is a child object (see fig. 4.21).

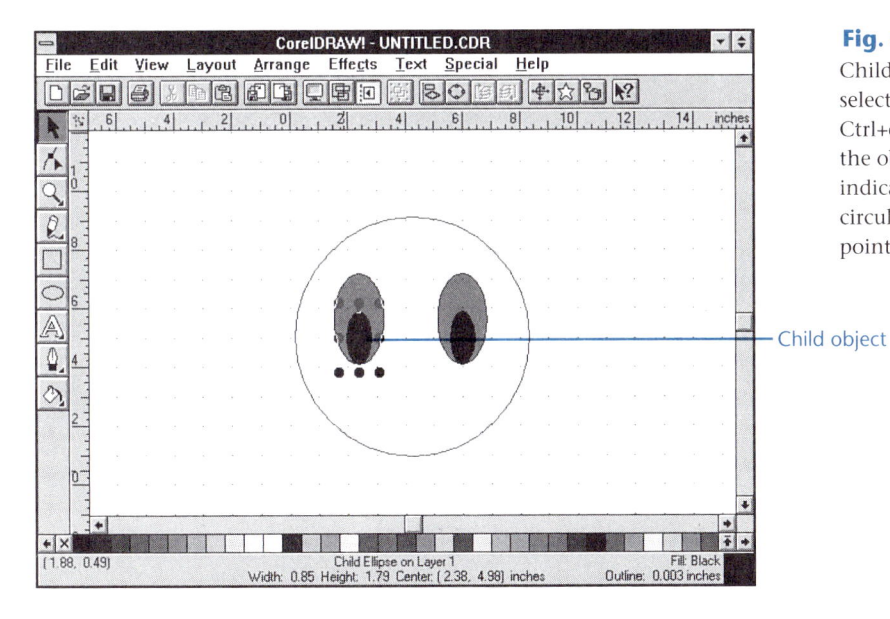

Fig. 4.21
Child objects, selected by Ctrl+clicking the object, are indicated by the circular handle points.

— Child object

3. Change the interior fill to a shaded design and then click elsewhere on-screen.

▶ See "Working with Interior Fills," p. 146

4. Click the left pupil again and notice that the entire original group is once again selected. However, the left pupil now has a shaded fill instead of black. Repeat this procedure to return the pupil to a black fill, or open the **E**dit menu and choose **U**ndo Fill.

> **Note**
>
> You cannot delete a child object. To delete part of a group, follow these steps:
>
> 1. Select the group.
>
> 2. Ungroup it, as described earlier.
>
> 3. Shift+click the object you want to delete to deselect it.
>
> 4. Regroup the remaining objects.
>
> 5. Pick the object you want to delete.
>
> 6. Open the **E**dit menu and choose **D**elete.

Combining Objects

You combine objects when they have the same attributes so that they do not need to be treated as separate objects. Cross-hatching is a good example of the benefits of combining. Each line in the cross-hatch is a separate object and must be drawn individually. This process adds time and complexity to the drawing. Because cross-hatching lines have the same attributes, you can combine them into one single object even though some of the lines are not actually touching. Combining greatly speeds up the drawing time and decreases the amount of storage space required for a drawing.

To combine multiple objects into one, select all the objects to be combined; then open the **A**rrange menu and choose **C**ombine (Ctrl+L). CorelDRAW! now treats the objects as a single curve with many nodes. You can separate combined objects by opening the **A**rrange menu and choosing Brea**k** Apart (Ctrl+K).

The following example gives a general idea of the benefits associated with combining objects and the basic procedures to follow. You are going to give your character creation from the preceding examples some hair.

1. Click the Pencil tool and draw a series of lines on the top of the head of the grouped object character (see fig. 4.22).

2. Draw a marquee around the hair strands. The status line displays the number of objects selected.

3. Open the **A**rrange menu and choose **C**ombine. The status line indicates that the large number of objects is now treated as a single curve with many nodes.

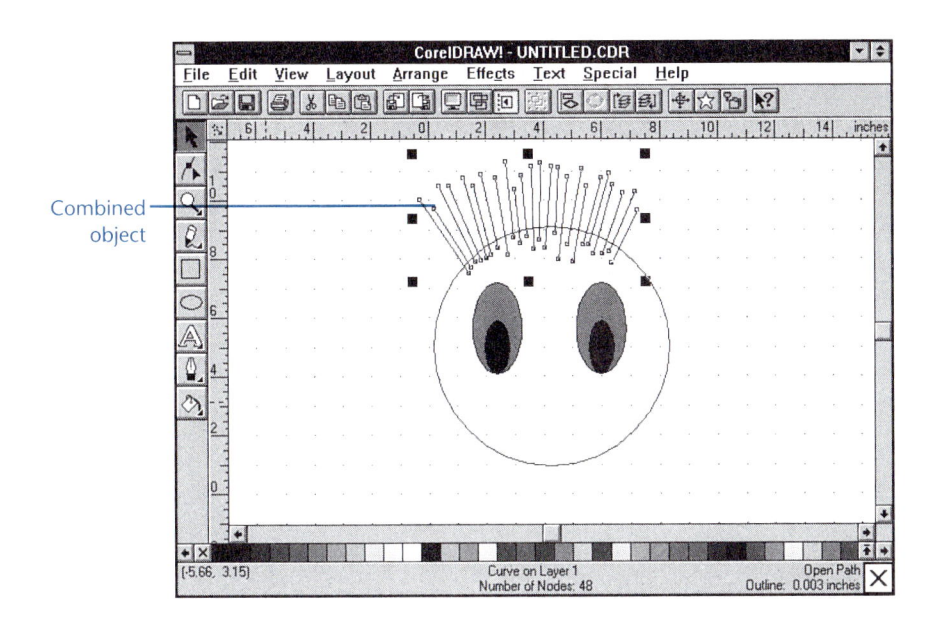

Fig. 4.22

The combined hair on the figure's head can be manipulated as one object and take less time for CorelDRAW! to redraw.

Combined object

4. Select a hair strand. This action now selects the entire hair object because the strands are all combined into one object.

5. Shift+click the head to add the rest of the character to the selection.

6. Open the **A**rrange menu and choose **G**roup to group this new hair combination with the rest of the character.

The Combine command has a few major characteristics you should consider whenever you use it:

- Before CorelDRAW! combines an object, it first turns the object into curves. This characteristic applies to text, rectangles, ellipses, and other objects that may not have started out as curves. After text is converted to curves, you can change it back only by using Undo.

- Combining objects decreases screen redraw time and greatly enhances drawing efficiency.

- All combined objects adopt the attributes of the bottom object, or the one selected last. Select the object with the desired attributes as the last object, or move it to the back, and then, using the marquee method, select the objects to be combined.

- Objects do not need to touch to be combined.

▶ See "Converting Text Characters to Curved Objects for Shaping," p. 249

▶ See "Converting Objects to Curves," p. 380

Fig. 4.23

The mask, made by combining the text and the rectangle, allows the animals to be viewed through the cutout hole.

▶ See "Adding Artistic Text," p. 212

◀ See "Creating Rectangular and Square Objects," p. 78

▶ See "Adding a Graphic Symbol," p. 184

▶ See "Scaling and Sizing an Object," p. 184

> **Note**
>
> You can use clipping holes, or masks, for impressive effects. Combine enables you to easily accomplish this otherwise complicated procedure. In this example, you create the mask shown in figure 4.23:
>
> 1. Enter the text Animals by using the typeface Stamp. Set the type size to about 200 points and give the text a black fill.
> 2. Draw a rectangle around the text.
> 3. Click the Pick tool and Shift+click the Animals text.
> 4. Open the Arrange menu and choose Combine to make the two objects one. The combined object contains a "knockout" where the Animals text previously existed. The combined object adopted the attributes of the text because it was the last item selected. (See the section "Selecting Objects," earlier in this chapter.)
> 5. Add symbols or backgrounds as needed for effect. In this case, the gorilla and kangaroo symbols were taken from the Animals symbol group.
> 6. Move the symbols to the back and size them so that they are partially masked by the combined object.
>
> This masking technique is nicely used when overlaying a city skyline with the city's name. For example, you can place the Chicago skyline behind a combined object containing a white fill and a center knockout of the word "Chicago."

> **Troubleshooting**
>
> *When I combine a number of objects, they all end up with the same fills and outlines, but I want them to still look the same as they did before I combined them.*
>
> You want to *group* the objects rather than *combine* them. This way each object will retain its own, original attributes.
>
> *When I ungroup a group with a large number of objects, the status line says that there are only two objects selected, instead of a much larger number.*
>
> When a group and an object are selected, the status line says that there are two objects selected. This means that the group you just ungrouped contained a child group, which you can ungroup to access individual objects.
>
> *Objects with many nodes look fine on-screen, but create a printer error or fail to print.*
>
> An object has a maximum node limit between 1,000 and 2,000 nodes, depending on the printer capabilities. This is sometimes a problem with a combined object because each object put together as one may exceed this limit. Although the object displays, it may not print. To fix this, follow these steps:
>
> 1. Select the object.
> 2. Break it apart as described earlier.
> 3. Choose about one-half of the individual objects.
> 4. Combine these into one object.
> 5. Choose the remaining individual objects.
> 6. Combine these into another object.
> 7. For convenience, you may want to group these two new objects.
>
> For particularly complex objects, you may find that this still doesn't work, and you will have to break these new objects into still smaller objects. To do this, just repeat the preceding procedure for each of the new objects.

Using Tricks and Techniques

You can combine each of the techniques discussed in this chapter to create interesting final effects. In addition, *welding* provides an easy way to create complicated outlines from several objects, and *nudging* provides a convenient and precise way for moving objects into exactly the desired orientation using the keyboard rather than the mouse. You also can use lines for alignment even when they do not print. The following sections introduce all these techniques.

Combining Object Outlines

The Weld, Intersection, and Trim features are similar to combine except that, in addition to making multiple objects into a single object, they create a composite of the outline of the objects involved. These features eliminate the need to perform relatively complicated node-related actions to achieve the same effect. When objects are combined using any of these techniques, CorelDRAW! applies the outline and fill of the bottom-most object if selected with the marquee, or the last selected object if selected by Shift+clicking.

- *Weld* creates an outline based on the outermost outline of all the objects selected. The original objects are deleted, leaving only the welded object (see fig. 4.25).

- *Intersection* makes its outline based on the area(s) common to all the objects selected. The original objects remain, and a new object is created (see fig. 4.26).

- *Trim* removes the area common to the selected objects. The last object selected or the lowermost object in the stack is modified, and the other object(s) remain as they were (see fig. 4.27).

To weld, trim, or intersect objects, follow these steps:

1. Select the desired objects. The status line indicates the number of objects selected.

2. Open the **A**rrange menu and choose **W**eld, **I**ntersect, or **T**rim, as appropriate.

You now can perform any operation on the new object, such as filling it.

▶ See "Converting Objects to Curves," p. 380

Caution

Trying to weld, intersect, or trim text can sometimes cause the computer to crash. To avoid this problem, convert the text to curves before trying to weld it.

The following procedure demonstrates the uses of and benefits associated with the Weld, Intersect, and Trim features:

1. Draw the rectangle, circle, and ellipse shown in figure 4.24, making sure that the relative size and orientation of the objects matches that shown in the figure.

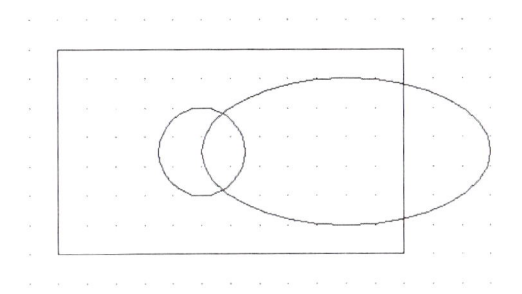

Fig. 4.24
Draw these objects for use in the Weld/Intersect/Trim example. Make sure that their relative size and orientation are as shown.

2. Select all three objects. The status line indicates that three objects are selected.

3. Open the **A**rrange menu and choose **W**eld. The status line now indicates a single object with the aggregate outline of the previously separate objects (see fig. 4.25). Notice that the circle has not contributed to the final object.

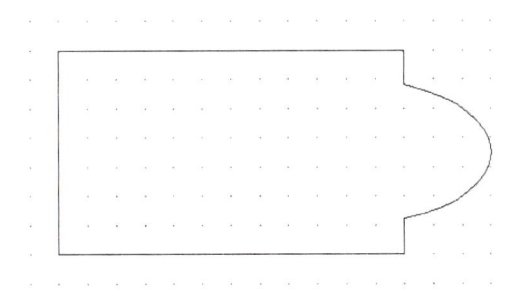

Fig 4.25
The objects as they appear after they have been welded together in step 3.

4. Open the **E**dit menu and choose **U**ndo (Ctrl+Z) to return the objects to their original, separate state.

5. Open the **A**rrange menu and choose **I**ntersection. A new object that includes only the area common to all three objects is created and selected.

6. Open the Fill fly-out menu and give the object a 50% fill (see fig. 4.26).

▶ See "Adding a Solid Color Fill," p. 151

Fig. 4.26
The new object created by using the Intersection command as it appears after it has been filled.

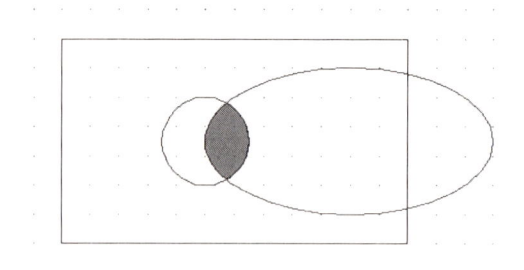

7. Open the Edit menu and choose De**l**ete to remove the new object.

8. Select all three remaining objects.

9. Open the **A**rrange menu and choose **T**rim. The rectangle is trimmed so that its outline now traces around the circle and the ellipse.

10. Open the Fill fly-out menu and give the object a 50% fill to view it more easily (see fig. 4.27).

Fig. 4.27
The result of the rectangle being trimmed to the circle and ellipse and then filled.

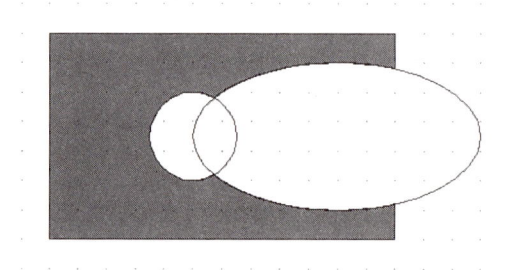

Aligning with No-Width Lines

▶ See "Modifying Object Outline Characteristics," p. 137

You may occasionally want to align objects along a common border, but not necessarily show the line along which they are aligned. Although guidelines can create this effect, they include some disadvantages such as the inability to align to an existing object. You can achieve this effect by drawing an alignment line and giving it no thickness. This is not the same as giving a line the same color as the background because a colored line may still show up against other objects in the drawing.

The alignment line shows up in Wireframe view but does not display in the Editable Preview because it has no display attributes.

To align objects by using no-width lines, follow these steps:

1. Enter Wireframe view (if not already active) by opening the **V**iew menu and choosing Wir**e**frame (Shift+F9).

2. Create the objects you want to align.

3. Create a horizontal line.

4. Click the × at the left end of the on-screen color palette using the right mouse button. The status line indicates that the object has no outline.

5. Shift+click one of the objects you want to align. Both this object and the line are now selected.

6. Open the **A**rrange menu and choose **A**lign. The Align dialog box opens.

7. Select **B**ottom and **C**enter, and then press OK. The objects are aligned as indicated.

8. Select the other object and then Shift+click the line to select it as well.

9. Open the Align dialog box as noted above.

10. Select **T**op and **C**enter, and then press OK. The second object is aligned so that its top is flush with the bottom of the first object.

◀ See "Viewing Your Work," p. 20

The no-width line may now be deleted if you will not be using it again.

The above steps can be used with any combination of the Align options or number of objects.

Understanding CorelDRAW! Layers

Complicated drawings may involve hundreds of objects. Drawing is less confusing, and the redraw time is faster if you work with fewer objects at a given time. The CorelDRAW! Layers feature enables you to select certain objects that appear on a specific layer, or plane, of the drawing. You then can display only those layers that directly pertain to your current editing needs and display all the objects only as needed.

Think of the layers as clear pieces of plastic upon which the objects are drawn. Selecting a layer places that piece of plastic into the viewing area. You can specify overlays so that you can view specific layers in combination.

Understanding How CorelDRAW! Layers Objects in a Drawing

Layer 1 is the default layer for object drawing. The guides exist on their own layer (which you can edit), and the grid exists on its own layer (which you cannot edit). In addition, there are the desktop and master layers, used for multipage documents.

Layers are selected, created, and deleted and objects are moved between layers using the Layers roll-up window, shown in figure 4.28. You can edit objects on any visible layer that is not locked, although, as described below, some actions change the layer of an object.

Fig. 4.28
Use the Layers roll-up window and command menu to set attributes for individual drawing layers.

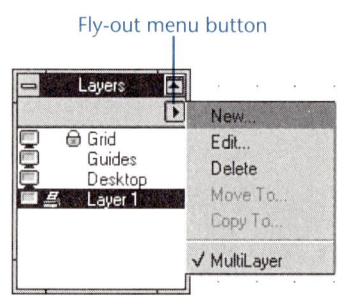

You can change the order of layers by dragging the layer name higher or lower in the layer name list shown in the Layers roll-up window. The first layer is at the top of the list, and the last layer is at the bottom.

Activate objects added to the Guides layer by opening the **L**ayout menu and choosing Snap To Guidelin**e**s. The ability to create custom guides is handy when creating drawings with specific layout issues, such as plotting information along angular lines.

You add and delete layers using the fly-out menu displayed after clicking the small arrow pointing to the right in the upper-right corner of the Layers roll-up window. Figure 4.28 shows the fly-out menu.

The MultiLayer option contained in the fly-out menu instructs CorelDRAW! to allow access to objects contained on all layers of the drawing. Deselecting MultiLayer restricts object access to those on the currently active layer.

Clicking New or Edit displays the Edit Layers dialog box shown in figure 4.29.

Enter custom layer names using the Edit Layers dialog box. You can use up to 32 characters in the name. Clicking OK adds the new layer name in the roll-up window.

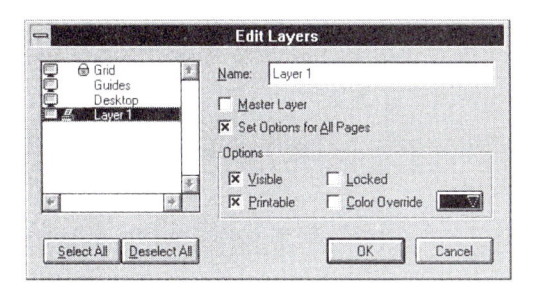

Fig. 4.29
The Edit Layers dialog box enables you to set attributes for the various drawing layers.

Use the Edit Layers dialog box items to determine whether the layer displays, prints, or is locked so that accidental changes do not occur. Turn off the display for layers you do not currently need, and the screen refreshes faster. Turn them on again when you want to see the entire object with all its layers.

Use the Color Override option to specify a color for a particular layer so that objects belonging to this layer are clearly displayed. Using Color Override displays the objects in Wireframe view, so only object outlines are displayed. The actual object fill and outline attributes remain untouched. The Override Color is for your benefit only. Deselecting Color Override returns the object display to its normal state.

Tip
Double-clicking any of the layer names opens the Edit Layers dialog box for that particular layer.

Grouping and Combining Objects from Different Layers

You can group objects contained on different layers. The process is similar to the standard grouping procedure except that you must consider the different layers. First, select the layer on which you want the final group of objects to reside. Select all desired objects; then open the **A**rrange menu and choose **G**roup (Ctrl+G). The group is now formed on the active layer.

Follow the same procedure to combine objects except open **A**rrange-**C**ombine after you select the objects. Selecting multilayer objects with the marquee method causes the combined object to reside on the layer of the most recently created object, not necessarily the currently active layer.

Tip
To use an object that's on the Desktop layer on many different pages of a document, duplicate it by pressing + before dragging it into the printable page. It's then available for other pages.

Using the Desktop Layer

When working with multipage documents, any object that is moved off the printable page is automatically placed on the Desktop layer. Objects on the Desktop layer are visible on all pages of the document. Once an object is on the Desktop layer, it can be added to an individual page by simply dragging it into the printable page area. The status line does not indicate that an object is on the Desktop layer.

Creating and Using a Master Layer

Master Layers are used in multipage documents to allow you to include information on every page, such as headers and footers or a company logo. Any object on a layer tagged with the Master Layer option will appear on all pages of the document.

To make a layer a Master Layer, follow these steps:

1. Open the **L**ayout menu and choose **L**ayers Roll-Up.

2. Double-click the layer containing the information you want to appear on each page. The Edit Layers dialog box opens.

3. Select the Master Layer option so that an × appears in the box.

4. Press OK. All objects on that layer will appear on all pages.

Troubleshooting

When I create new objects, they appear on-screen as dashed outlines and won't print.

Check the active layer. It is most likely the Guides layer or another layer with similar attributes. Set the active layer to Layer 1 (or another appropriate drawing layer). The objects you have already drawn may be moved to this layer by selecting them and then selecting Move To on the Layers roll-up window's fly-out menu and clicking the appropriate layer.

When I create new objects in a multipage document, they appear on every page, not just the one on which I created them.

These objects have been created on a Master Layer. Select the objects and move them to another layer that does not have the Master Layer attribute set.

When I try to create new objects, a dialog box opens saying `Operation Cannot Be Completed. The active layer "layername" is locked or invisible.`

Set the active layer to either Layer 1 or another layer which is not locked and has an × in the Visible box of the Edit Layers dialog box. Objects can now be created.

From Here...

The techniques introduced in this chapter are used repeatedly in CorelDRAW!. As your drawings get more complicated, you will benefit from the information provided in the layering section. Review and practice these techniques until they become second nature, and you can concentrate on the task of creating your drawing.

You can move, align, rotate, and size entire groups of objects at once using the techniques outlined in this chapter and those listed below.

- Chapter 5, "Modifying Object Outlines and Interior Fills," expands on the capability to make objects and their outlines different colors and textures.

- Chapter 6, "Scaling, Rotating, and Distorting Objects," teaches you how to size objects and change their overall shape.

- Chapter 18, "Combining and Reusing Effects," helps you to refine your use of cloning and copying in this chapter.

Chapter 5

Modifying Object Outlines and Interior Fills

by Paul Bodensiek

All CorelDRAW! objects have interiors and outlines that can be colored, shaded, and/or textured. The wide variety of options that CorelDRAW! provides gives the creative individual numerous artistic opportunities. This chapter discusses various techniques for changing object fill and outline attributes.

In this chapter, you learn to

- Modify an object outline's width, color, and style
- Fill objects with solid colors
- Create and use two-color and full-color patterns
- Create PostScript textures and halftones
- Work with gradated (fountain) fills

Modifying Object Outline Characteristics

You can enhance an object's outline in many ways. You can change the color, width, corner shapes, end shape, and style of the outline, and even vary the width as the outline changes direction so that the result resembles calligraphy.

◄ See "Viewing Your Work," p. 20

> **Note**
> CorelDRAW! has two modes for editing a drawing: Editable Preview and Wireframe. In Editable Preview, you see your drawing with its colors, line styles, and shades as they will print (with some exceptions, which are noted later in this chapter). In Wireframe, as its name implies, you view only the outlines of the shapes in your drawing.

Introducing the Outline Menus and Dialog Boxes

CorelDRAW! provides five basic menus and dialog boxes for changing the outline characteristics. In general, all these elements work the same way: you select the object, change the appropriate dialog-box settings, and click OK or Apply.

All objects are drawn with defaults (a certain line width, color, and so on). These defaults can be changed by accident if you follow the procedures outlined in this chapter without first selecting an object. However, you gain a great measure of control over the defaults if you use the techniques outlined later in this chapter in "Establishing a Default Outline Style."

Following are the elements you use to change outline attributes:

► See "Using the Outline Fly-Out Menu," p. 401

- *The Outline fly-out menu.* This menu provides direct access to a limited number of outline style presets, as well as the other outline menus and dialog boxes.

  To access this menu, click the Outline Pen tool in the toolbar (see fig. 5.1). Changes are made automatically when you choose an option.

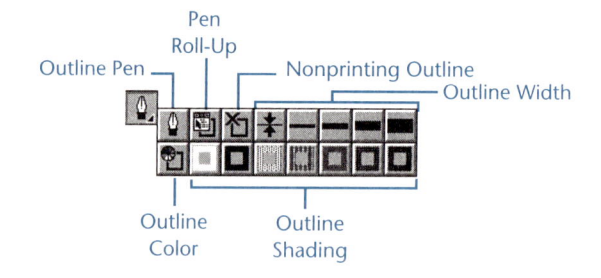

Fig. 5.1
The Outline Pen fly-out menu allows you to set many basic pen attributes directly and access other menus and dialog boxes for more settings.

- *The on-screen Color Palette.* The palette along the bottom of the screen displays colors that you can assign to an outline simply by selecting an object and clicking the desired color with the right mouse button (see fig. 5.2). Changes are made automatically when you click a color.
To view additional colors, click the scroll arrows or the roll-up arrow.

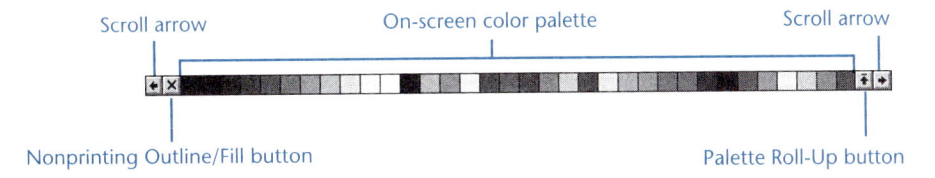

Scroll arrow — On-screen color palette — Scroll arrow
Nonprinting Outline/Fill button — Palette Roll-Up button

Fig. 5.2
The on-screen color palette allows you to directly add colors and shades to an outline by clicking on the color using the right mouse button.

- *The Pen roll-up window.* This window provides direct access to a larger number of styles than the Outline Pen fly-out menu does (see fig. 5.3). It also gives you more freedom in the way you use those styles.

To open this menu, click the Pen Roll-Up button in the Outline fly-out menu. After you make the appropriate settings, click Apply.

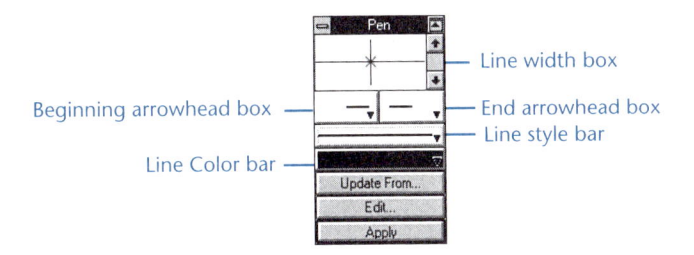

Beginning arrowhead box — Line width box — End arrowhead box — Line style bar
Line Color bar

Fig. 5.3
Using the Pen roll-up window, you can set most pen attributes directly by clicking the appropriate button.

- *The Outline Color dialog box.* With this dialog box, you have complete control of the almost limitless assortment of colors and PostScript shading options available through CorelDRAW! (see fig. 5.4).

To access this dialog box, click the Outline Color tool in the Outline fly-out menu. Alternatively, click More when choosing colors in the Pen roll-up window or the Edit Outline dialog box. When selected from the Pen roll-up window, this dialog box is titled "Select Color."

▶ See "Using the Pen Roll-Up," p. 401

▶ See "Creating Custom Colors," p. 351

Fig. 5.4
The Outline Color dialog box provides complete control over the outline colors, shades, and PostScript textures.

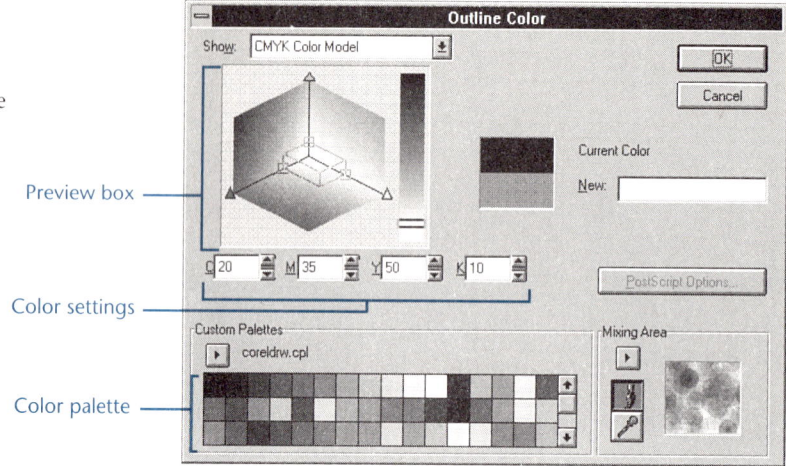

Preview box
Color settings
Color palette

- *The Outline Pen dialog box.* This dialog box provides much finer control of a wider range of line-style settings than either the Outline Pen fly-out menu or the Pen roll-up window (see fig. 5.5).

  To open this dialog box, click the Outline Pen dialog box tool in the Outline fly-out menu or the Edit button in the Pen roll-up window.

Fig. 5.5
The Outline Pen dialog box allows you to set pen widths, line styles and line end types.

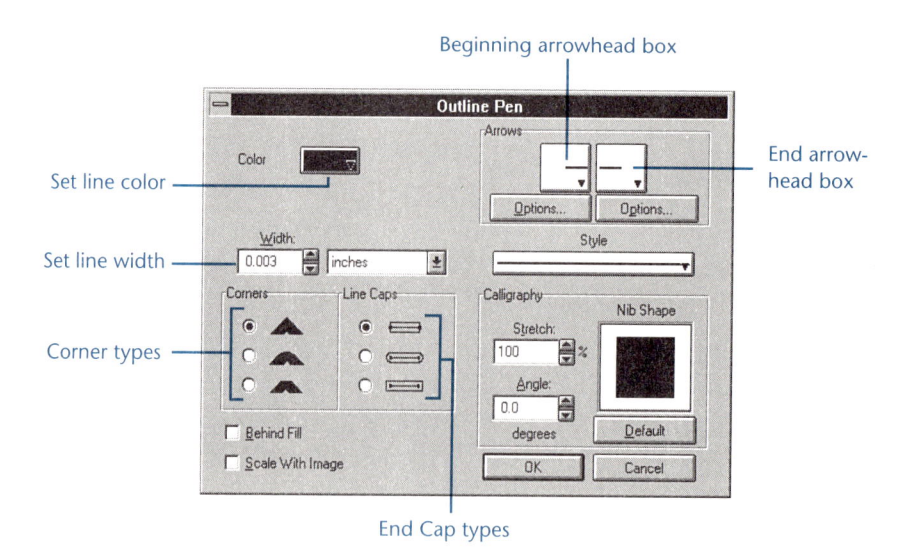

Set line color
Set line width
Corner types
Beginning arrowhead box
End arrowhead box
End Cap types

In addition, CorelDRAW! has PowerLines, which can give your outlines an artist's-brush effect. For more information, see Chapter 19, "Creating Special Effects with PowerLine."

The next few sections cover the Pen roll-up window. You can access all the options for changing a line from this dialog box; you don't have to repeatedly open the fly-out menu, which closes after you select each new option. You also can set multiple options before applying them all at the same time.

Changing the Outline Color

To change the outline color from the Pen roll-up window, follow these steps:

1. Select the object.

2. Click the color selector to drop down a palette of outline colors (see fig. 5.6).

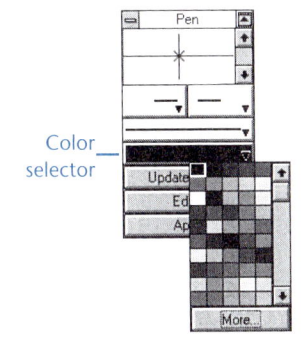

Color selector

Fig. 5.6
Many preset colors and shades are included in the Pen roll-up's palette, and others can be selected by clicking "More."

3. Click the color you want to use. You return to the Pen roll-up window.

   If you don't want to choose a new color, press the Esc key to return to the roll-up window.

4. Click Apply to apply the color to your object.

Tip
You can also close the palette by clicking away from the palette and the roll-up.

> **Note**
>
> You also can change the outline color through the Outline Pen dialog box, the on-screen Color Palette, or the Outline Color dialog box.

Changing the Outline Style

CorelDRAW! provides many outline styles, ranging from solid lines to dashed and dotted lines.

To change the outline style from the Pen roll-up window, follow these steps:

1. Select the object.

2. Click the line style selector to drop down the line-selection box (see fig. 5.7).

Fig. 5.7
The line selection box contains a number of line styles which may be added to any object's outline.

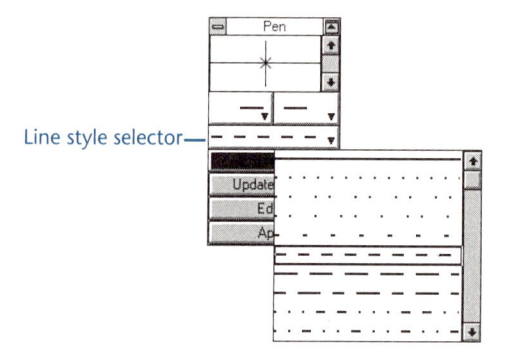

3. Click the outline style you want to use. You return to the Pen roll-up window.

   If you don't want to choose a new outline style, press the Esc key to return to the roll-up window.

4. Click Apply to apply the outline style to your object.

> **Note**
> You also can change the outline style through the Outline Pen dialog box using similar techniques.

◄ See "Understanding Open and Closed Path Objects," p. 89

Adding Arrowheads

Arrowheads come in more varieties than arrows: CorelDRAW! gives you many different options, including circles, dots, and even airplanes. Arrowheads may be added to any open path object.

Modifying Object Outline Characteristics

To add arrowheads to an open path object, follow these steps:

1. Select the object.

2. Open the beginning or end arrowhead box, as shown in figure 5.8.

Beginning arrowhead box — End arrowhead box

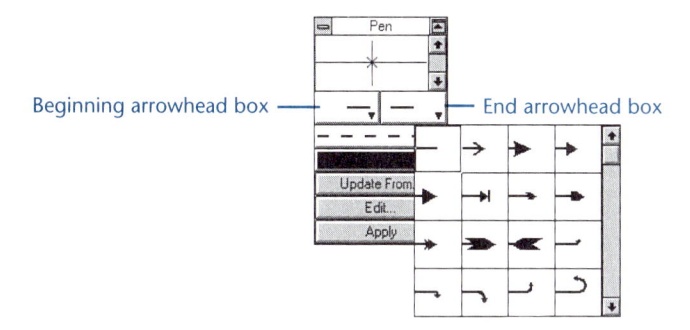

Fig. 5.8
CorelDRAW! provides a large assortment of arrowhead styles which may be added to any open path object.

3. Click the arrowhead style you want to use. You return to the Pen roll-up window.

If you don't want to choose an arrowhead, press the Esc key to return to the roll-up window.

4. Click Apply to apply the arrowhead to your object.

Tip
Remember that the far right end of a line may be the beginning of an arrowhead, and vice versa, even though the beginning and ending arrowhead boxes are on the left and right.

◀ See "Reshaping a Curve or Object by Changing its Nodes and Control Points," p. 72

Troubleshooting

I added an arrowhead to an open path object, but instead of only being at the end, there are arrowheads at every node of the curve.

Even though it looks like the curve is continuous, this object is made up of a number of disconnected segments. Join the nodes where the arrowheads appear (except the beginning and end nodes) to remove the extra arrowheads.

I added an arrowhead to a line, but it is too small to see in the final drawing.

The size of an arrowhead is related to the width of its line. Increase the width of the line until the arrowhead is the size you want it.

Creating a Nonprinting Outline

◄ See "Aligning with No-Width Lines," p. 130

You can create an object that has no visible outline. To create a nonprinting outline from the Pen roll-up window, follow these steps:

1. Select the object.

2. Open the Outline Pen fly-out menu and click the Pen Roll-Up button.

3. Click the scroll arrow button in the line-width box until an X appears in the box.

4. Click Apply to make the outline nonprinting.

To create a nonprinting outline from the on-screen color palette, follow these steps:

1. Select the object.

2. Click the X button at the left edge of the color palette with the right mouse button.

Troubleshooting

Small text looks muddy or mottled.

The most likely cause is an outline associated with the text. A line that is 0.003 inch wide isn't even noticeable in 36-point type, but it can significantly change the appearance of the letters in 6-point type.

Remove the outline (create a nonprinting outline). The text should look much clearer.

When new objects are created, I can't see them.

To make sure the objects have been created, change to Wireframe mode (Shift+F9). If they show up in Wireframe mode but not Editable Preview mode, you have set the default line type to no outline. Follow the instructions in the section "Establishing a Default Outline Style" later in this chapter, to make sure that new objects can be seen in Editable Preview mode.

Copying Outline Styles Between Objects

Many times, you work very hard to develop just the right outline for an object. You may have taken 10 minutes to adjust the color, width, style, and arrowhead, and the thought of going through it again for another object is about to drive you up a tree. CorelDRAW! provides three ways you can give one object exactly the same outline characteristics as another without having to search for your climbing pitons.

If you have just created your outline from the Pen roll-up window, simply follow these steps:

1. Select the new object.

2. Click the Apply button in the Pen roll-up window to give the new object the same outline characteristics as the last one.

To use the Pen roll-up window to copy outline characteristics from one object to another, follow these steps:

1. Select the object whose outline you want to update.

2. Click the Update From button in the Pen roll-up window. The mouse pointer changes to a big black arrow.

3. Click the tip of the arrow on the object whose outline you want to copy. The Pen roll-up window automatically changes all its settings to those of the selected object.

4. Click Apply to give all these characteristics to the selected object.

To copy the outline characteristics from the Edit menu, follow these steps:

1. Select the object whose outline you want to update.

2. Open the **E**dit menu and choose Copy Attributes **F**rom. The Copy Attributes dialog box opens.

3. Choose Outline **P**en, Outline **C**olor, or both.

4. Click OK and the cursor changes to a big black arrow.

5. Click the tip of the arrow on the object whose outline you want to copy.

Establishing a Default Outline Style

If you will be doing a lot of work with one outline style, you may want to reset the default outline style rather than go back and edit it later. CorelDRAW! allows you to set separate default line style types for graphic objects (ellipses, rectangles, and so on), artistic text, and paragraph text.

To reset the default outline style, follow these steps:

1. Deselect any objects in your drawing by clicking an empty space or pressing the Esc key.

2. Set the outline characteristics you want to use, following the procedures outlined in the previous section "Modifying Object Outline Characteristics."

3. Apply the characteristics using the method appropriate to the window or dialog box you are using. The Outline Pen dialog box opens (see fig. 5.9).

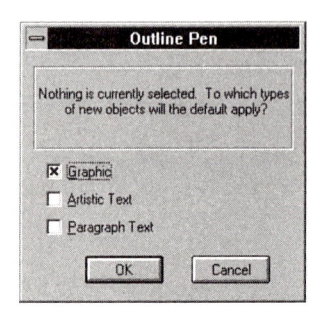

Fig. 5.9
Set the type(s) of objects for which you want to define a default outline using the Outline Pen dialog box.

4. Select the object type(s) to which you want these outline characteristics to apply (graphic object, artistic text, and/or paragraph text).

5. Click OK. All objects of this type that you create hereafter will have these outline characteristics.

Tip
CorelDRAW! remembers these settings from one session to the next. If you don't want to use these options for your next session, reset them by reversing steps 1 through 5 before quitting CorelDRAW!.

Working with Interior Fills

CorelDRAW! provides beautiful colors and patterns that you can use as interior fills for closed objects. The fills include uniform colors and shades (including grays), fountains (linear, radial, and conical), two-color and full-color patterns, halftones, and PostScript and bitmap textures. These interior fills are independent of the outline style.

> **Note**
>
> In Editable Preview, you see your drawing with its colors and shades as they will print, with the exception of PostScript textures and halftones. These fills are specific to PostScript devices and will not print on non-PostScript printers.

Introducing the Fill Menus and Dialog Boxes

Following are the two main ways to access all the fill options:

- *The Fill fly-out menu.* This menu provides easy access to solid fills in black, white, and four intermediate shades of gray, as well as the no-fill option in the seven buttons along the bottom of the menu. The menu also enables you to open all the dialog boxes, windows, and menus for specifying the other fill options.

   To open this menu, click the Fill tool in the toolbar (see fig. 5.10). Changes are made automatically when you choose an option.

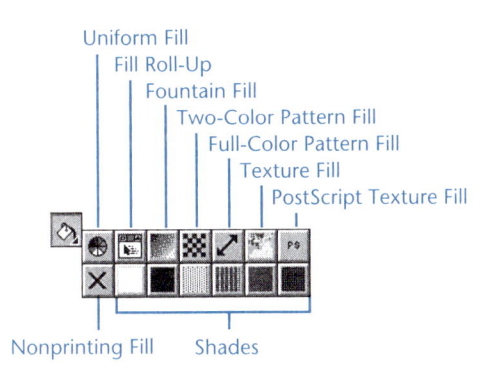

Fig. 5.10
The Fill fly-out menu allows you to set many basic fill attributes directly and access other menus and dialog boxes for more settings.

- *The Fill roll-up window.* Like the Fill fly-out menu, the Fill roll-up window gives you access to the various dialog boxes, windows, and menus for specifying CorelDRAW!'s great variety of fill options (see fig. 5.11). For solid fills, this menu also has a color palette for choosing colors. The Edit button brings up the Uniform Fill dialog box.

   Open the Fill roll-up window by clicking the Roll-Up button in the Fill fly-out menu. After you make the appropriate settings, click Apply.

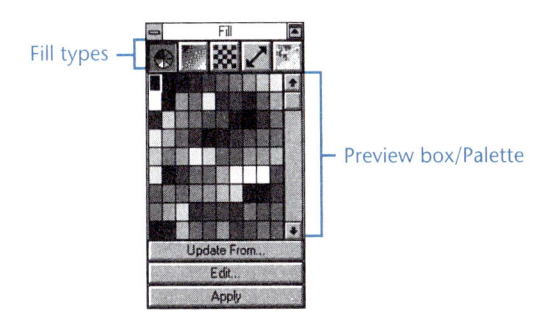

Fig. 5.11
The Fill roll-up window provides access to all of CorelDRAW!'s fill styles and options.

Copying Fills between Objects

Fills can be very difficult to set for an object. CorelDRAW! provides a number of easy ways to copy a fill from one object to another. See the previous section, "Introducing the Fill Menus and Dialog Boxes," for more information.

If you just created your fill from the Fill roll-up window, simply follow these steps:

1. Select the new object.
2. Click the Apply button in the Fill roll-up window to give the new object the same fill characteristics as the last one.

To use the Fill roll-up window to copy fill characteristics from one object to another, follow these steps:

1. Select the object whose fill you want to update.
2. Click the Update From button in the Fill roll-up window. The mouse pointer changes to a big black arrow.
3. Click the tip of the arrow on the object whose fill you want to copy. The Fill roll-up window automatically changes all its settings to those of the selected object.
4. Click Apply to give all these characteristics to the selected object.

To copy the fill characteristics from the Edit menu, follow these steps:

1. Select the object whose fill you want to update.
2. Open the **E**dit menu and choose Copy Attributes **F**rom. The Copy Attributes dialog box opens.
3. Choose **F**ill.
4. Click OK and the cursor changes to a big black arrow.
5. Click the tip of the arrow on the object whose fill you want to copy.

Establishing a Default Fill

If you will be doing lots of work with one fill style, you may want to reset the default fill rather than go back and edit it later. CorelDRAW! allows you to set separate default fills for graphic objects (ellipses, rectangles, and so on), artistic text, and paragraph text.

To reset the default fill, follow these steps:

1. Deselect any objects in your drawing by clicking an empty space or pressing the Esc key.

2. Set the fill characteristics you want to use, following the procedures outlined in the sections "Working with Solid Fills," "Using Patterned Fills," "Working with Gradated (Fountain) Fills" and "Using Fractal Fills."

3. When you apply the characteristics using the method appropriate to the window or dialog box you are using, the Fill dialog box opens.

    Figure 5.12 shows the Fill dialog box for setting a Uniform default fill, though this dialog box can also be used for patterned, fountain, and texture fills. The only difference in the dialog box is the name of the fill type being used.

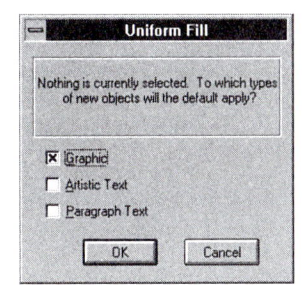

Fig. 5.12

Set the type(s) of objects for which you want to define a default fill type using the Fill dialog box.

4. Select the object type(s) to which you want these outline characteristics to apply (graphic object, artistic text, and/or paragraph text).

5. Click OK. All objects of this type that you create from now on will have these outline characteristics.

Troubleshooting

When I zoom in and try to copy the fill style from an object that is outside of the visible page, CorelDRAW! will not let me move the view using the scroll bars to pick the object to copy from.

Select the object you want to copy the fill to, and then scroll the view to show the object you want to copy from before opening the **E**dit menu and choosing the Copy Attributes **F**rom option.

(continues)

150 Chapter 5—Modifying Object Outlines and Interior Fills

> (continued)
>
> *Whenever I create new objects, they're filled with a pattern, and I want them to be created without a fill.*
>
> Using the techniques listed in the previous section, set the default fill type to no fill.

Working with Solid Fills

As the name implies, solid fills make an object one solid color (not counting the outline, of course). CorelDRAW! gives you four ways to specify a solid fill, with varying levels of precision to match the level of work you are doing. In addition to the two methods that you use to choose fill options, you can use the following two methods only for solid fills:

- *Color palette.* Located along the bottom edge of the screen, the color palette has a wide range of solid fill colors, including the no-fill option. To see more colors, click the scroll buttons, or click the Roll-Up button next to the right scroll button to see a larger palette.

▶ See "Creating Custom Colors," p. 351

- *Uniform Fill dialog box.* This dialog box provides the most extensive options for specifying solid fills, from choosing the color model you will use to setting the numerical amounts of colors to be mixed to make just the color you want (see fig. 5.13).

Open the Uniform Fill dialog box by clicking the Uniform Fill button in the Fill fly-out menu.

Fig. 5.13
You can set fills of solid colors and shades using the Uniform Fill dialog box.

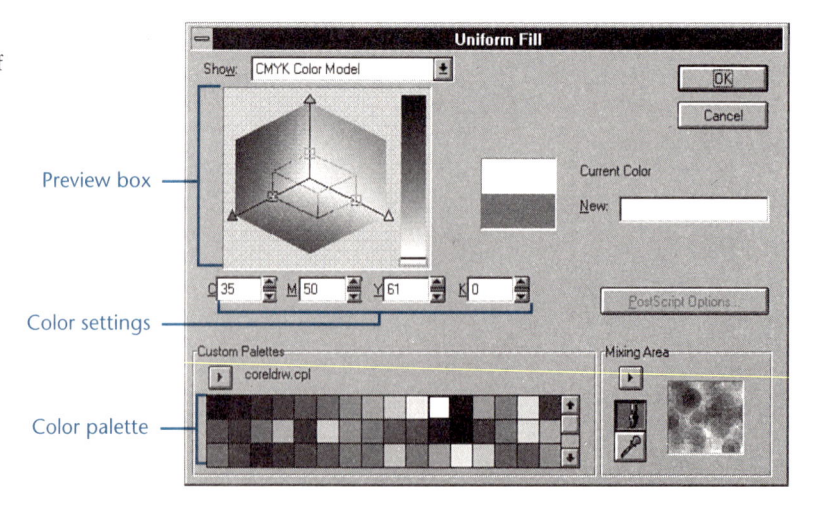

Working with Solid Fills   **151**

CorelDRAW! 5 enables you to mix colors in a way similar to the way you mix paint. The new mixing area enables you to take two colors from the palette and mix them in varying amounts. Chapter 12, "Using Color for Commercial Success," explains how to create and mix new colors.

Adding a Solid-Color Fill

To change the fill color of an object from the Fill roll-up window, follow these steps:

▶ See "Selecting Fill and Outline Colors," p. 343

1. Select the object whose fill color you want to change.

2. Open the Fill roll-up window by clicking the Fill tool and then clicking the Fill Roll-Up button. If solid fill is not active, click the color wheel button along the top of the roll-up window.

3. Choose the color you want from the roll-up's color palette. If you don't see the color you want, scroll through the palette or click the Edit button to reveal the Uniform Fill dialog box.

4. Click Apply to apply the color to your object.

Making an Object Transparent

An object may have a transparent fill (also called no-fill) that enables you to see objects located below it in the stack. To specify a transparent fill, follow these steps:

1. Select the object you want to fill.

2. Click the × button on the left side of the color palette (see fig. 5.14).

   or

   Open the Fill fly-out menu and click the × button.

Scroll arrow · On-screen color palette · Scroll arrow

No Fill button · Palette Roll-Up button

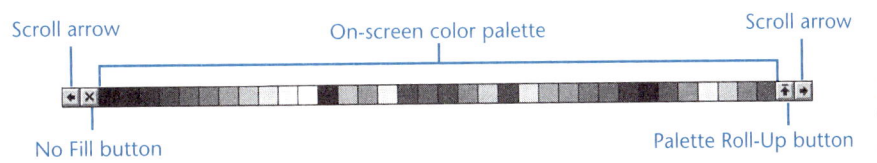

Fig. 5.14
The on-screen color palette provides direct access to a large number of colors for object fills.

> **Troubleshooting**
>
> *Objects filled with a solid color block out the objects underneath them. Can I make an object translucent instead of opaque?*
>
> CorelDRAW!'s new Lens tool, explained in Chapter 20, "Creating Special Effects with Lens," teaches you how to do this.
>
> *After I fill a large object, I can't see or pick any of the objects that it covers up.*
>
> Select the large object and place it beneath the other objects by opening the **A**rrange menu and choosing **O**rder. Depending on how many levels the object must be moved, select Back O**n**e (Ctrl+PgDn) a number of times or select To **B**ack (Shift+PgDn).
>
> *An object with no fill is transparent to the objects below it. I want to have the object look as though it has no fill, but I don't want to see the other objects.*
>
> Set the object's fill to the color of the page (usually white).

Using Patterned Fills

Patterned fills give you an additional level of creativity in defining objects. Using a patterned fill is like tiling an object with ceramic tiles (without the fuss of cutting the tiles and using adhesive), because the patterns are repeated in the horizontal and vertical directions. You can work with CorelDRAW!'s existing patterns, import a pattern from another program, or create a pattern of your own.

In CorelDRAW!, you can work with two-color and full-color patterns. Although the process of using the two types is basically similar, you deal with them in different dialog boxes, which accommodate the options that are different. The following section, "Using Two-Color Patterns," describes the basic procedures that apply to both types of patterns. Information that is specific to full-color patterns is covered in "Using Full-Color Patterns."

Using Two-Color Patterns

Two-color patterns generally are black and white, but you can use any other colors you like.

Choosing a Pattern

To choose a pattern in the Fill roll-up window, follow these steps:

1. Select the object to which you want to apply the pattern.

2. Open the Fill fly-out menu and click the Roll-Up button.

3. Click the Two-Color Pattern button. The Two-Color preview box appears in the roll-up window.

4. Click the preview box. The pattern palette appears.

5. To choose a pattern, double-click it, or single-click it and then click OK.

6. To apply the pattern to the selected object, click the Apply button.

A Two-Color pattern can also be added to an object using the Two-Color Pattern dialog box, in essentially the same manner you use with the Fill roll-up window.

Specifying the Tile Size

As noted earlier, a pattern is made of *tiles* that repeat to fill an object. You can adjust the tile size to specify how many times the pattern repeats in your object.

Remember that patterns are bitmaps that are made up of a specific number of dots, called *pixels*. If the tiles are too big, they will look jagged when displayed or printed. If the tiles are too small, they may look muddy or just print as blobs.

To specify the tile size, follow these steps:

1. If the object with which you want to work does not have a patterned fill, give it one by using the instructions in the previous section.

2. Select the object.

3. Open the Fill fly-out menu and click the Two-Color Pattern button. The Two-Color Pattern dialog box appears.

4. Click the Tiling button. The dialog box enlarges, adding more options.

Tip
You can alter the appearance of a pattern for dramatic effect by making the width and height measurements different. Of course, this can make some patterns look strange, too.

5. Adjust the tile size by clicking the small, medium, or large radio buttons. (The Width and Height settings change to 0.25, 0.5, and 1.0 inch, respectively.)

or

Enter the exact tile size you want by entering numbers in the Width and Height settings.

The preview box shows the relative changes as you make them.

6. Apply the tile-size changes by clicking the OK button.

You also can use the Fill roll-up window to set the tile size. Follow these steps:

1. Select an object that contains a pattern.

2. Open the Fill fly-out menu and click the Roll-Up button.

3. Click the Two-Color Pattern button at the top of the roll-up window. The preview box appears.

4. If the pattern in the preview box is not the one that is in your object, click the Update From button. The mouse pointer changes to a large black arrow. Click the current object. Its pattern appears in the preview box.

5. Click the Tile button in the Fill roll-up window. Two squares appear in the upper-left corner of the selected object. These squares show the relative positions of two repeats of the pattern fill.

6. Click and drag the small box below and between the two squares to change the tile size.

7. When the tile is the size you want, release the mouse button and then click the Apply button.

Choosing Colors

You are not stuck with having Two-Color patterns appear only in black and white. You can change either color to any color you can create in CorelDRAW!.

The two colors in a Two-Color pattern are named the Front and Back colors. In a black-and-white pattern, the front color is typically black and the back color, white. This conforms to the standard used in many paint programs that use a white background.

Using Patterned Fills   **155**

To change the pattern colors in the Fill roll-up window, follow these steps:

1. Select an object with a Two-Color pattern.

2. Open the Fill fly-out menu and click the Roll-Up button.

3. Click the Two-Color Pattern button at the top of the roll-up window. The preview box appears.

4. If the pattern in the preview box is not the one that is in your object, click the Update From button. The mouse pointer changes to a large black arrow. Click the current object. Its pattern appears in the preview box.

5. Click the Color bar for the color (front or back) you want to change. A color palette appears.

6. Choose the color you want. You can see more colors by using the scroll bar.

    If you do not see the color you want, click the More button to open the Color dialog box. Make the setting you want, and click OK.

    ▶ See "Creating Custom Colors," p. 351

7. If you want to change the other color (front or back), do it now as instructed in steps 5 and 6.

8. Apply the new color settings to your object by clicking the Apply button.

Controlling the Tile Offset

Sometimes, the pattern tiles do not line up exactly as you want. For example, the pattern may start too high or too far to the right, making the outline of the object look odd.

To change where the tiling starts in an object, follow these steps:

1. Select an object with a two-color pattern.

2. Open the Two-Color Pattern dialog box from the Fill fly-out menu or the Fill roll-up window.

3. If you open the dialog box from the fly-out menu, click the Tiling button to display the additional options. These options appear automatically if you open the dialog box from the roll-up window.

Chapter 5—Modifying Object Outlines and Interior Fills

4. Specify the amount of offset in the First Tile Offset section as a percentage of the tile height and width. Specifying a shift in the X direction shifts the tiles to the right by that percentage; specifying a shift in the Y direction shifts the tiles down.

5. Transfer the offset settings to your object by clicking the OK button (see fig. 5.15).

If you opened the Two-Color dialog box from the roll-up window, you also have to click the Apply button after you click OK.

Fig. 5.15

As shown, offsetting the starting tile lines up a two-color pattern differently within the object it fills.

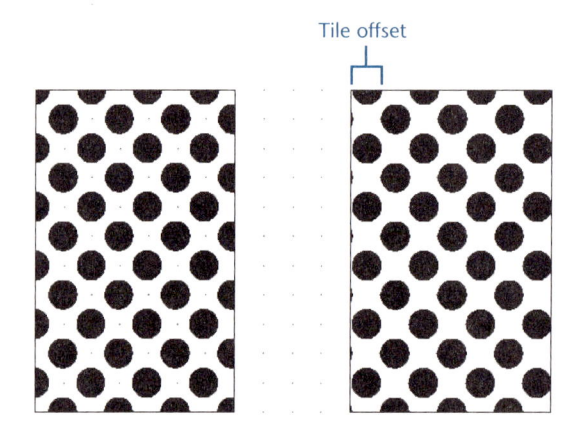

To set the offset directly from the roll-up window, follow these steps:

1. Select an object with a two-color pattern.

2. Open the Fill roll-up window and click the Two-Color Pattern button. The preview box appears.

3. Click the Tile button. Two boxes appear in the upper-left corner of the object.

4. Click and drag the left box down and to the right to set where you want the first tile to begin.

5. When the tile is where you want it, release the mouse button, and then click the Apply button. Another partial tile fills the space above and to the left of this tile.

Specifying the Row and Column Offsets

The repeat of rows or columns can be offset from each other. This technique may not be appropriate for some patterns, however, because the adjacent parts of the tiles will not line up properly (see fig. 5.16).

Fig. 5.16
For some patterns, changing the row offset may not be appropriate because of the way the pattern lines up.

To specify the row or column offset, follow these steps:

1. Select an object with a two-color fill.

2. Open the Two-Color Pattern dialog box from the Fill fly-out menu or the Fill roll-up window.

3. If you open the dialog box from the fly-out menu, click the Tiling button to expand the window. These options appear automatically if you open the dialog box from the roll-up window.

4. Specify whether you want to offset rows or columns by clicking the Row or Column radio button in the Row/Column Offset section.

5. Specify the amount of offset as a percentage of the tile height or width (depending on which way you are performing your offset).

    Specifying a row shift offsets each row of tiles to the right by that percentage; specifying a column shift offsets each column of tiles down.

6. Transfer the offset setting to your object by clicking the OK button.

    If you opened the Two-Color dialog box from the roll-up window, you also have to click the Apply button after pressing OK.

To set the offset from the roll-up window, follow these steps:

1. Select an object with a two-color pattern.

2. Open the Fill roll-up window and click the Two-Color Pattern button. The preview box appears.

3. Click the Offset icon. Two boxes appear in the upper-left corner of the object.

4. To set column offset, click and drag the right box down to where you want the second column to begin.

   To set row offset, click and drag the right box down. When this box reaches the bottom of the left box, it automatically begins to move along the bottom edge.

5. When the tile is where you want, release the mouse button, and then click the Apply button.

Importing a Pattern

You can import bitmaps for use as patterns from scanned images, bitmap editing programs such as CorelPHOTO-PAINT, and any of the growing number of clip-art galleries available. CorelDRAW! also can import vector art and convert it to bitmaps. The Import dialog box, detailed later in this section, contains a list of all acceptable file formats.

Two-color graphics work best for two-color patterns, because images with more colors are rendered as black-and-white objects with dot patterns to simulate the various shades of color. Although you still can specify the foreground and background colors, the quality will not be as good.

Tip

Any white space around a pattern is considered to be part of the pattern and will influence the size when tiled. Before importing the pattern, you should crop any unwanted white space with your paint program.

A two-color pattern is created at the same resolution as the bitmap from which it was imported, unless the pattern is made up of more than 256 dots in either direction. Any pattern that exceeds this limit is squished in the offending direction(s) to a maximum size of 256 by 256 dots. This can make the pattern look weird and may alter straight lines.

To import a two-color pattern, follow these steps:

1. Select an object.

2. Open the Two-Color Pattern dialog box from the Fill fly-out menu or the Fill roll-up window.

3. Click the Import button to open the Import dialog box (see fig. 5.17).

Using Patterned Fills 159

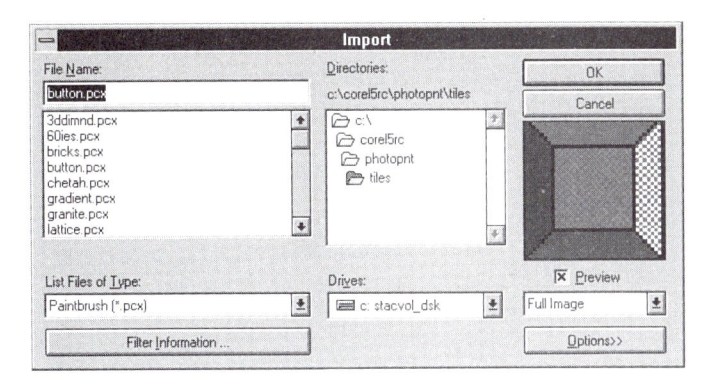

Fig. 5.17
Using the Import dialog box, you can load a bitmap file for use as a two-color pattern.

4. Select the image you want to import, setting drive, directory, and file-type information if necessary.

5. Click the OK button. The selected pattern appears in the preview box.

6. Add the new pattern to your object by clicking the OK button.

    If you opened the Two-Color Pattern dialog box from the roll-up window, you also have to click the Apply button after clicking OK.

Creating a Pattern

You can create a pattern of your own design or edit an existing one in the Two-Color Pattern Editor dialog box (see fig. 5.18). To open the Editor, click the Create button in the Two-Color Pattern dialog box.

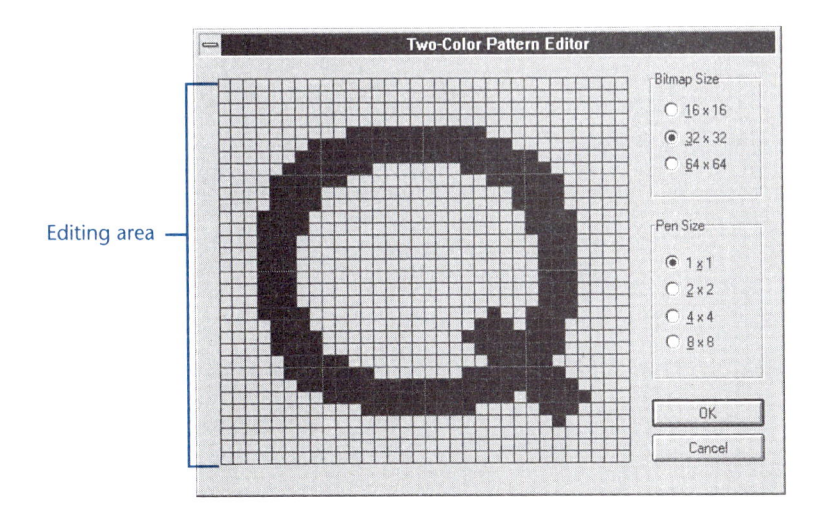

Fig. 5.18
The Two-Color Pattern Editor dialog box looks and works like a simplified paint program.

Tip

If you want to design a fairly complicated pattern or one that includes any kind of shape, you are better off to create it in CorelPHOTO-PAINT and import it as outlined in "Importing a Pattern."

The Two-Color Pattern Editor essentially is a miniature, extremely limited bitmap editing program. Clicking on the drawing area with the left mouse button adds dots (pixels), while using the right mouse button erases them.

Troubleshooting

When printed out, the pattern fill of an object looks jagged, but it looks fine on-screen.

This happens because printers have higher resolution than computer screens. Make the tile size smaller, or create a new pattern with a higher resolution to the tile (more pixels).

At the edges of an object, the pattern gets cut off and makes the object look jagged.

Add an outline to the object so that it has a definite edge.

Can I have the pattern rotate with an object?

No. Patterns always remain lined up with the page.

Using Full-Color Patterns

Full-color patterns are designs that can be composed of any color your computer system can display and tiled to fill your object. You use and manipulate full-color patterns in much the same way as you do two-color patterns.

Choosing a Pattern

To choose a full-color pattern, follow these steps:

1. Select the object to which you want to apply the pattern.

2. Open the Fill fly-out menu and click the Full-Color Pattern button. The Full-Color Pattern dialog box opens (see fig. 5.19).

   The large preview box in the dialog box shows the current pattern (if any).

3. To view the palette of patterns, click anywhere in the preview box (see fig. 5.20). You can use the scroll bar to view additional patterns.

4. Choose a pattern by double-clicking it or by single-clicking it and then clicking the OK button. This pattern now appears in the preview box.

5. Apply the pattern to the selected object by clicking OK.

Using Patterned Fills

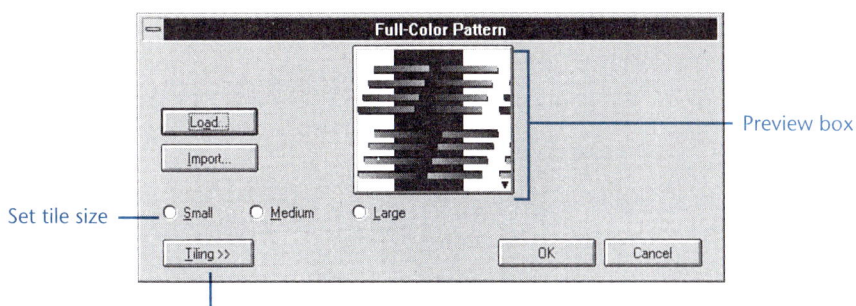

Fig. 5.19
The Full-Color Pattern dialog box provides full control over selecting and using full-color patterns.

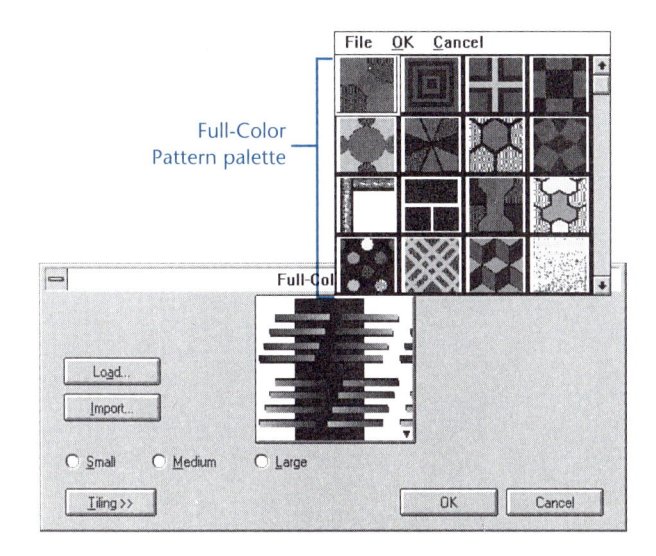

Fig. 5.20
Clicking the preview box opens a palette of patterns. Additional patterns may be viewed by using the scroll bars.

To choose a pattern in the Fill roll-up window, follow these steps:

1. Select the object to which you want to apply the pattern.
2. Open the Fill fly-out menu and click the Roll-Up button.
3. Click the Full-Color Pattern button. The preview box appears in the roll-up window.
4. Click the preview box. The pattern palette appears.
5. To choose a pattern, double-click it, or single-click it and then click OK.
6. To apply the pattern to the selected object, click the Apply button.

162 Chapter 5—Modifying Object Outlines and Interior Fills

Loading a Pattern

Loading a full-color pattern is similar to importing a two-color pattern, except that you are limited to PAT files (CorelDRAW!'s pattern files).

To load a full-color pattern, follow these steps:

1. Select the object to which you want to apply the pattern.

2. Open the Full-Color Pattern dialog box from the Fill fly-out menu or the Fill roll-up window.

3. Click the Load button to open the Load dialog box (see fig. 5.21).

Fig. 5.21
In addition to those patterns shown in the pattern palette, you can load CorelDRAW! PAT files using the Load dialog box.

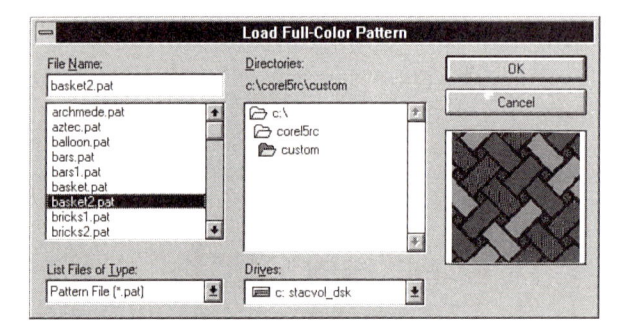

4. Select the image you want to load, setting the drive and directory information as needed.

5. Click the OK button. The selected pattern appears in the preview box.

6. Add the new pattern to your object by clicking the OK button.

    If you opened the Full-Color Pattern dialog box from the roll-up window, you also have to click the Apply button after you click OK.

Importing a Pattern

Importing a full-color pattern gives you more flexibility in the choice of files you can use as a pattern. Any graphic file that the CorelDRAW! filter can import, you can use as a full-color pattern. A list of acceptable file formats is in the dialog box.

To import a full-color pattern, follow these steps:

1. Select the object to which you want to apply the pattern.

2. Open the Full-Color Pattern dialog box from the Fill fly-out menu or the Fill roll-up window.

3. Click the Import button to open the Import dialog box (see fig. 5.22).

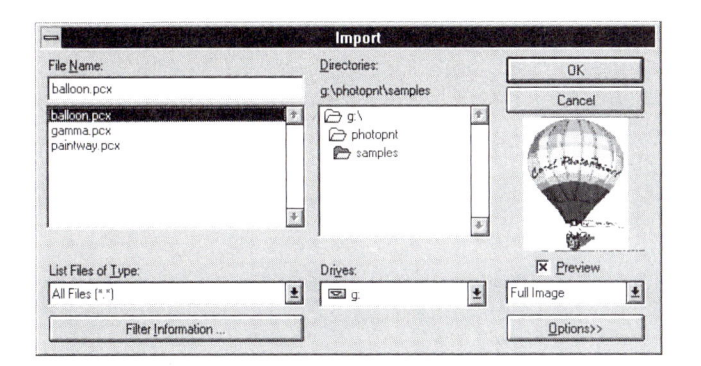

Fig. 5.22
The Import dialog box allows you to import graphic files for use as full-color patterns.

4. Select the image you want to load, setting drive, directory, and file-type information as needed.

5. Click the OK button. The selected pattern appears in the preview box. Objects that don't appear cannot be used as fills.

6. Add the new pattern to your object by clicking the OK button.

   If you opened the Full-Color Pattern dialog box from the roll-up window, you also have to click the Apply button after clicking OK.

Editing a Pattern

CorelDRAW! full-color patterns, as opposed to patterns that you import, are stored as PAT files. These files are, for all intents and purposes, standard CorelDRAW! files that contain additional information that enables them to be tiled.

To edit a full-color pattern, follow these steps:

1. Open the **F**ile menu and choose **O**pen.

2. Select Pattern File (*.PAT) in the List Files of **T**ype box.

3. Select the PAT file you want to edit, and click OK.

4. Ungroup the pattern object, and edit it as you would any other CorelDRAW! drawing.

    ◀ See "Ungrouping Objects," p. 122

5. Save the file under a new name by opening the **F**ile menu and choosing Save **A**s. Enter the new name in the File **N**ame box. Make sure that Pattern File (*.PAT) appears in the List Files of **T**ype box.

6. Click OK.

Chapter 5—Modifying Object Outlines and Interior Fills

If you have made major changes in the PAT file, you may have moved the pattern from its invisible bounding box. You also may want to change the way that CorelDRAW! tiles this file.

To save the file with a new bounding box, follow the preceding steps 1–4, and then perform the following additional steps:

1. Open the **S**pecial menu and choose **C**reate Pattern. The Create Pattern dialog box opens (see fig. 5.23).

Fig. 5.23
After you design your pattern, use the Create Pattern dialog box to specify its properties.

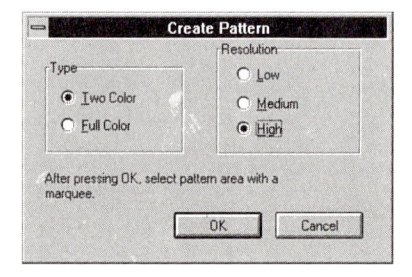

2. Click the **F**ull Color radio button; then click OK. A pair of cross hairs replaces the cursor.

3. Drag the cross-hair cursor to indicate the rectangular area to be saved as the boundary of the pattern.

4. When the rectangle is the right size, release the mouse button, and then click OK in the Create Pattern dialog box. The Save Full-Color Pattern dialog box opens.

5. Enter a name for the pattern in the File **N**ame portion of the dialog box, and then click OK.

Creating a Pattern

You can create a full-color pattern in CorelDRAW!. Follow these steps:

1. Open the **F**ile menu and choose **N**ew to open an empty drawing file.

2. Draw the pattern you want, using the standard CorelDRAW! drawing tools.

3. When the pattern is right, open the **S**pecial menu and choose **C**reate Pattern.

4. Click the **F**ull Color radio button, and then click OK. A pair of cross hairs replaces the cursor.

5. Drag the cross-hair cursor to indicate the rectangular area to be saved as the boundary of the pattern.

6. When the rectangle is the right size, release the mouse button, and then click OK in the Create Pattern dialog box. The Save Full-Color Pattern dialog box opens.

7. Enter a name for the pattern in the File **N**ame portion of the dialog box, and then click OK.

> **Troubleshooting**
>
> *When I rotate an object with a pattern, the pattern does not rotate with it.*
>
> Patterns cannot be rotated.
>
> *The pattern lines up oddly in the object, with half a tile cut off. How can I get the pattern to line up in the object?*
>
> There are two ways to make a pattern line up better in an object: change the tile offset or change the tile size, using the same techniques as those specified earlier in this chapter for a two-color pattern.

Using PostScript Textures

You can fill objects with PostScript textures only if you will be printing to a PostScript printer or sending your files to a service bureau that supports PostScript. PostScript textures are very complex, and as a result, they may print extremely slowly.

To add a PostScript texture, follow these steps:

1. Select the object you want to fill.

2. Open the Fill fly-out menu and click the PostScript button. The PostScript Texture dialog box appears (see fig. 5.24).

Tip
Unless you have a specific reason for using PostScript textures, you probably will enjoy better results with other fills, such as Texture Fills.

166 Chapter 5—Modifying Object Outlines and Interior Fills

Fig. 5.24
All of the parameters for PostScript Textures are set from within the PostScript Texture dialog box.

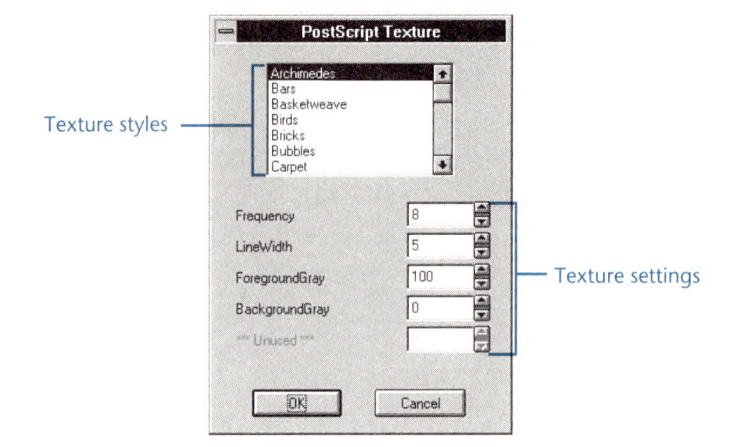

3. Select the name of the texture you want to use (use the scroll bar if necessary).

4. Set the options for the texture. These options change for each texture.

   When setting texture options, frequency is given in number of patterns per inch, and thickness is set in thousandths of an inch. When colors are to be set, 100% gray is black, while 0% is white.

   Setting a large frequency number (smaller pattern) with a high line thickness can result in a solid black texture.

5. Click OK.

On-screen, the object fill is composed of tiled PSs, which indicate a PostScript texture. The only way to see the outcome of different option settings is to print the file to a PostScript device.

▶ See "PostScript and Non-PostScript Printing," p. 307

> **Troubleshooting**
>
> *I have specified a PostScript Texture, but it won't print.*
>
> Make sure that you're printing to a PostScript printer. If you are, and the Texture still won't print, try printing just the object with the texture, using the Print Only Selected option in the Print dialog box. If the object still won't print, make sure that all the options for the texture are set to their defaults. Sometimes PostScript Textures can be so complex that they won't print on some printers.

Using Patterned Fills   **167**

> *I have added a PostScript Texture to an object, but it doesn't display on the screen.*
>
> Because PostScript Textures require a PostScript interpreter, they can only be displayed and printed on PostScript devices, such as a Linotronics printer.
>
> *I want to check the effect of changing PostScript Texture parameters, but it takes so long to print them.*
>
> To speed up the printing time for test prints, select the object with the Texture and print using the Print Only Selected option in the Print dialog box.

Using PostScript Halftones

PostScript halftone screens produce some wonderful effects, but you must print to a PostScript device to see them. A *screen* is a pattern of shapes that becomes heavier or lighter depending on the percent tint you use. You can use PostScript halftones only with certain color palettes, such as PANTONE Spot Colors.

In addition to solid fills, which the following examples demonstrate, PostScript halftones can be used with gradient fills.

Setting the Screen Type

Screen types include dots, lines, grids, and diamonds. To set the screen type, follow these steps:

1. Select the object you want to fill.

2. Open the Fill fly-out menu and click the Fill Color Tool button. The Uniform Fill dialog box appears.

3. In the Sho**w** box, choose Pantone Spot Colors. The text in the PostScript Options button turns from gray to black to show that these options are available.

4. Select the color you want to use with the object.

5. Set the **T**int percentage. For most screen types, a setting between 40 and 60 percent yields the best results.

6. Click the **P**ostScript Options button. The PostScript Options dialog box opens (see fig. 5.25).

Fig. 5.25
When printing to a PostScript printer, you can specify the pattern used to produce different shades of a color.

   7. In the **T**ype box, select the screen type, which determines what pattern the screen will be made from.

   8. Click OK. You return to the Uniform Fill dialog box.

   9. Click OK again. Your object is filled with a solid color, but will print with the settings you selected.

Setting the Screen Frequency

The screen-frequency setting changes the number of lines (or dots or diamonds, depending on what screen type you're using) per inch of output (lpi). The higher the lpi, the fewer individual shades can be printed in, say, a fountain fill. The lower the lpi, the greater the number of shades that can be printed, but the object may be too small to effectively show all the shades.

The number of shades available is equal to $(resolution/lpi)^2$. CorelDRAW! automatically sets the screen frequency based on your printer's resolution. For custom work, the frequency setting you use will depend on the effect you are trying to achieve.

In general, you should follow these guidelines:

- Use a value of 100 or more if the output is going to a high-resolution device (such as a Linotronic film printer) and you want the screen pattern to blend into your drawing without standing out.

- Use a value between 60 and 80 if you are printing to a 300-dpi laser or inkjet printer.

- Use a maximum value of 60 if your output is going to be photocopied.

To set the screen frequency, follow these steps:

1. Select the object you want to fill.
2. Open the Fill fly-out menu and click the Fill Color Tool button. The Uniform Fill dialog box appears.
3. From the Show menu, select the PANTONE Spot Color palette.
4. Click the **P**ostScript Options button. The PostScript Options dialog box opens.
5. Select a screen type.
6. Enter the appropriate number in the **F**requency box.
7. Click OK. You return to the Uniform Fill dialog box.
8. Click OK again. Your object is filled with a solid color but will print with the settings you selected.

Setting the Screen Angle

The screen-angle setting enables you to select an angle for the PostScript Halftone pattern. You can create many interesting effects with this setting.

To set the screen angle, follow these steps:

1. Select the object you want to fill.
2. Open the Fill fly-out menu and click the Color Wheel button. The Uniform Fill dialog box appears.
3. Click the **P**ostScript Options button. The PostScript Options dialog box opens.
4. Enter the appropriate number in the **A**ngle box.
5. Click OK. You return to the Uniform Fill dialog box.
6. Click OK again. Your object is filled with a solid color but will print with the settings you selected.

Tip
Be careful when you set the screen angle because the screen angle remains the same relative to the page, not to the object.

> **Troubleshooting**
>
> *When I print a PostScript Halftone that is a light shade, some of the lines or dots that I am using fade out.*
>
> Either decrease the lines per inch (lpi) setting in the halftone, or use a darker shade to increase the size of the screen shapes.
>
> *When I rotate an object, the halftone pattern doesn't rotate.*
>
> PostScript Halftone patterns do not automatically rotate with objects. After you rotate an object, manually change the screen angle for the halftone to match that of the object.
>
> *I have a non-PostScript printer. How do I produce a draft output of a PostScript halftone before I send my artwork to be printed at a service bureau?*
>
> PostScript Halftones print only on PostScript printers. To get a draft output, you have to print on a PostScript printer, though service bureaus charge much less for a standard 300 or 600 dpi proof.

Working with Gradated (Fountain) Fills

Tip
When you use spot colors to make color separations, create fountain fills between two shades of the same spot color. If you're printing directly to a color printer, ignore this rule.

Fountain fills blend an object between two colors or tints of the same color. The effect is similar to shading a rounded object. This feature gives the designer easy three-dimensional shading to achieve realistic effects. Fountain fills are frequently used with lettering to achieve chrome-like effects.

Introducing the Fountain Fill Menus and Dialog Boxes

CorelDRAW! gives you two ways to specify a fountain fill:

- *The Fountain Fill dialog box.* This dialog box enables you to make all the settings for fountain fills with numerical precision (see fig. 5.26).

- *The Fill roll-up window.* This roll-up window enables you to use your mouse to set up a fountain fill interactively, without having to set specific numbers (see fig. 5.27).

Working with Gradated (Fountain) Fills   **171**

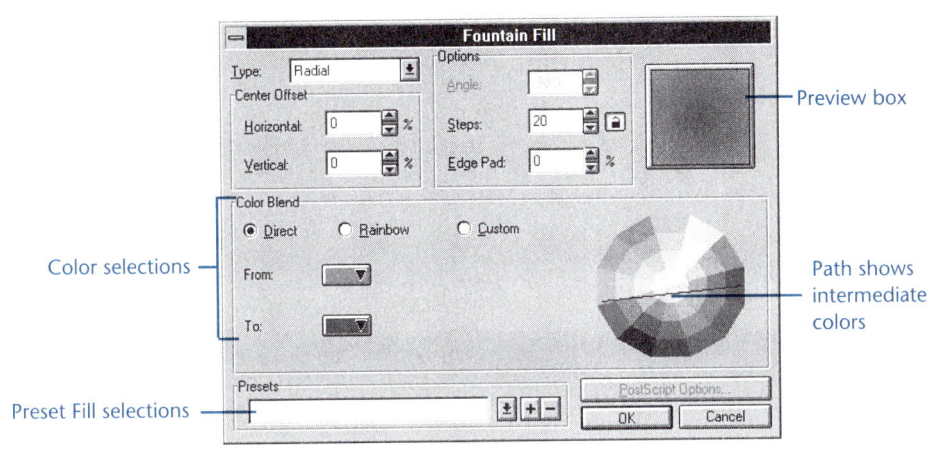

Fig. 5.26
All parameters for fountain fills can be set with mathematical precision using the Fountain Fill dialog box.

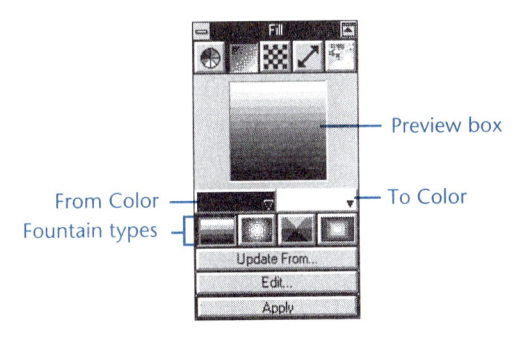

Fig. 5.27
When using the Fountain Fill roll-up window, fill parameters are set interactively with the results shown immediately in the preview box.

Choosing the Fountain Type

CorelDRAW! provides four fountain-fill types: linear, radial, conical, and (new in CorelDRAW! 5) square. Figure 5.28 shows these fountain types.

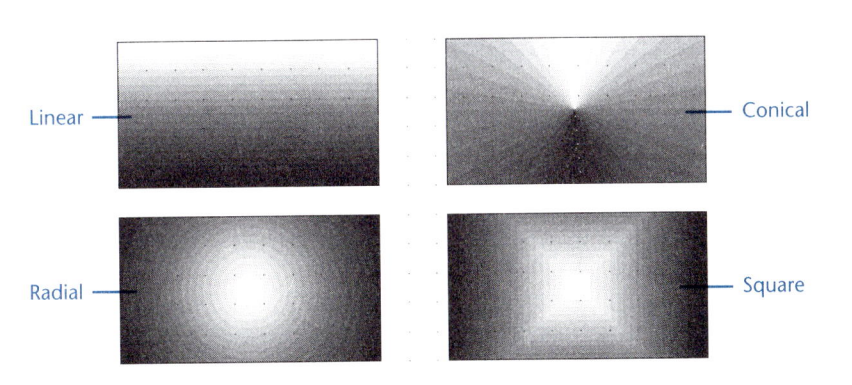

Fig. 5.28
The four types of fountain fill: linear, radial, conical, and square.

To choose a fountain type in the Fountain Fill dialog box, follow these steps:

1. Select the object you want to fill.

2. Open the Fill fly-out menu and click the Fountain Fill button. The Fountain Fill dialog box appears (refer to fig. 5.26).

3. In the **T**ype box, select the fountain-fill type you want to use.

4. Click OK to apply the fountain fill to your object.

To choose a fountain type in the Fill roll-up window:

1. Select the object you want to fill.

2. Open the Fill fly-out menu and click the Fill Roll-Up button. The Fill roll-up window appears.

3. Click the Fountain Fill button. The preview box and fountain-fill options appear.

4. From the type box, select the type of fountain fill you want to use. Select from linear, radial, conical, and square.

5. Click Apply to fill your object.

Choosing Colors

To choose the beginning and ending colors in the Fountain Fill dialog box, follow these steps:

1. Select the object you want to fill.

2. Open the Fill fly-out menu and click the Fountain Fill button. The Fountain Fill dialog box appears.

3. Click the From button in the Color Blend section to change the beginning color of the fountain. When you do, a color palette appears.

4. Choose the color you want by clicking on the palette.

5. Click on the To button in the Color Blend section to change the ending color of the fountain. When you do, another color palette appears.

6. Select the color you want to use.

7. Click OK to apply the fountain fill you just defined to your object.

Working with Gradated (Fountain) Fills   **173**

To choose the beginning and ending colors in the Fill roll-up window, follow these steps:

1. Select the object you want to fill.

2. Open the Fill fly-out menu and click the Roll-Up button.

3. Click the Fountain Fill button.

4. Click one of the color bars. A color palette appears.

5. Select the color you want.

6. If you want to set the other color, click the other color bar. Another color palette appears.

7. Select the other color.

8. Click the Apply button to apply the fountain fill you just defined to your object.

Controlling the Edge Padding

Fountain fills are defined in a box that is just big enough to hold the object that is being filled. In a way, the object merely acts as a mask for the fountain-fill box. Depending on the shape of the object, the start and end colors of the fountain fill may not be visible. You can use edge padding to ensure that you see the to and from colors by increasing their width in relation to the object (see fig. 5.29).

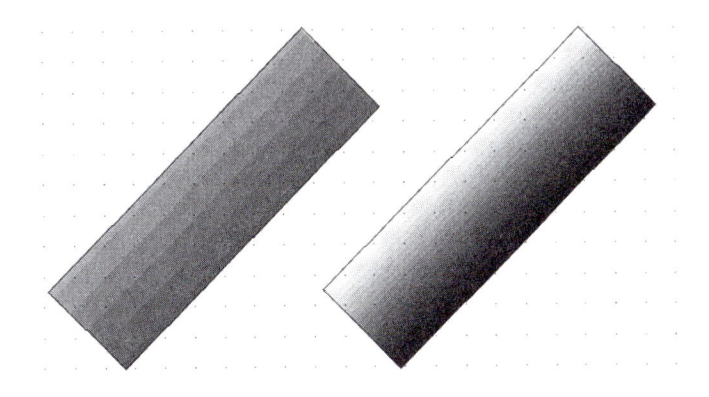

Fig. 5.29
These two objects are identical except for their edge pad settings. The to and from colors are visible only in the object on the right.

174   Chapter 5—Modifying Object Outlines and Interior Fills

To set the edge-padding amount, follow these steps:

1. Select a fountain-filled object.

2. Open the Fill fly-out menu and click the Fountain Fill button. The Fountain Fill dialog box appears.

3. In the Options section, set the amount of **E**dge Pad you want to use. The default value is 10 percent; the maximum setting is 45 percent.

4. Click OK. The fountain fill changes to reflect the new setting.

You also can set the edge padding in the Fill roll-up window by clicking the Edit button to open the Fountain Fill dialog box.

Troubleshooting

Text that includes a linear fountain fill turns to a solid color when rotated.

The object that is filled with a fountain (text in this case) acts only as a mask for the fountain fill, which is bounded by a rectangle. When the text is rotated, the bounding rectangle is not; it merely changes to a different shape that still encloses the text. The fountain may start and end at opposing corners, leaving only part of the fill in the text itself.

To fix this problem, increase the edge padding slightly. As the screen redraws, watch the bounding rectangle, and estimate how far the fountain fill has to travel before it reaches the text. Set the edge padding to this amount. You may have to do some tweaking to get the edge padding just right.

Controlling the Number of Steps

Although you may not be able to tell in many fountain fills, the shift of color from the beginning to the ending color is not continuous. The shift actually takes place in a number of discrete steps. CorelDRAW! automatically sets the number of steps based on the resolution of the selected printer. You can override this number to produce interesting effects, as shown in figure 5.30.

To specify the number of steps in a fountain fill, follow these steps:

1. Select an object that already contains a fountain fill.

2. Open the Fill fly-out menu and click the Fountain Fill button. The Fountain Fill dialog box appears.

Working with Gradated (Fountain) Fills   175

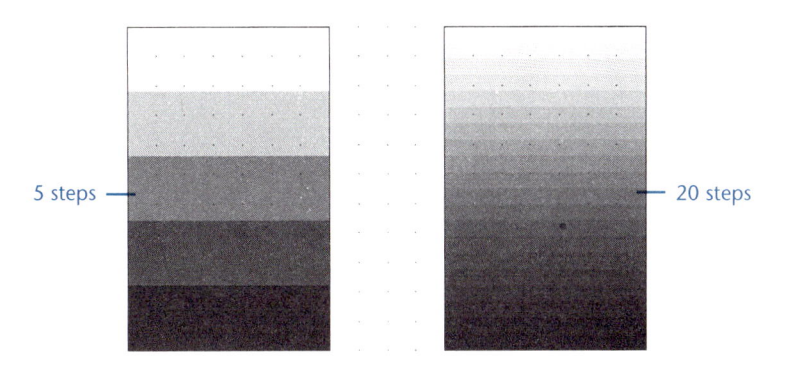

5 steps — 20 steps —

Fig. 5.30
These two fountain fills have the same two and from colors, but have different numbers of steps.

3. In the Options area, click the lock button next to the **S**teps box to allow override of CorelDRAW!'s default settings. The word Steps and the scroll arrows turn from gray to black.

4. Specify the number of steps you want the fountain to make.

5. Click OK. Your object changes to reflect the changes you made.

Troubleshooting

When printed, a fountain fill contains many more steps than it did when displayed on-screen.

PostScript creates up to 256 shades of each of the four process colors. The true number of shades you can use, however, depends on the resolution of your output device (in dots per inch, or dpi) and the frequency of the halftone screen being used (in lines per inch, or lpi). The equation $(dpi/lpi)^2$ provides the number of shades available. For example, using a 300 dpi laser printer to print a halftone with 30 lines per inch provides 100 printable shades.

The range of colors you cover in a blend can make it difficult to determine the percent change in a shade. These rules of thumb can help you print better halftones:

- In general, take the color that changes the most and use it as the color that determines your percentage change for the equation.

- Never use two Pantone spot colors in a blend. All you can do with Pantone is blend from a color to an absence of color. Using two different spot colors is bound to produce strange and unpredictable results if you have a high-resolution output device, because the screen angles are not adjusted to reduce moiré patterns or muddiness.

(continues)

> (continued)
>
> - If the fountain covers less than the full range (1 to 100 percent), the number of available shades is proportionately smaller. A gradation ranging from 30 to 80 percent, for example, creates a range of 50 percent of the 256 shades, or a total 128 shades.
>
> *All fountain fills only print with 5 steps instead of the number I specify.*
>
> Check the Options tab of the Print dialog box. The Fountain Steps option may have been set to five. This option has a default setting of 128, and it overrides other settings.

Setting the Angle for Linear, Conical, and Square Fountains

You can specify the characteristic angle between the two colors in linear, conical, and square fountains. If you rotate an object that contains one of these fills, the fountain angle changes to maintain its original angle relative to the object (see fig. 5.31). Note that a radial fountain fill has no characteristic angle.

Fig. 5.31
When an object is rotated, the fountain fill will rotate along with it.

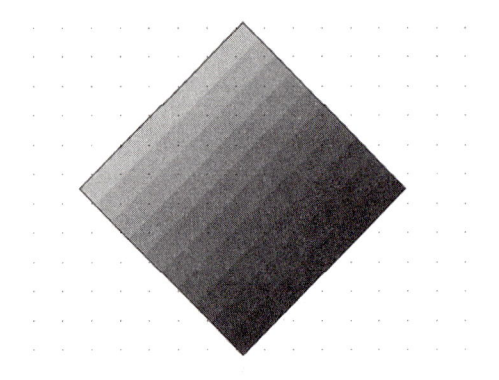

To set the angle with numerical precision, follow these steps:

1. Select an object that has a linear, conical, or square fountain fill.

2. Open the Fill fly-out menu and click the Fountain Fill button. The Fountain Fill dialog box opens.

3. In the Options section, enter the angle you want to use in the **A**ngle box. (This number can be between positive and negative 360.) The result appears in the preview box.

4. Click the OK button. Your object's fill is rotated to the angle you specify.

To set the angle interactively, using the mouse, follow these steps:

1. Select an object that has a linear, conical, or square fountain fill.

2. Open the Fill fly-out menu and click the Fountain Fill button or the Roll-Up button. The appropriate window opens.

3. If you opened the Fill roll-up window, click the Fountain Fill button. The preview box appears.

   If you opened the Fountain Fill dialog box, the preview box opens with the dialog box.

4. Position the mouse pointer in the preview box in either window, and drag the angle to its desired position. Hold down the Ctrl key while you drag to constrain the angle to increments of 15 degrees.

5. Release the mouse button, and then click OK or Apply. Your object's fill is rotated to the angle you specified.

Specifying the Center Offset for Radial, Conical, and Square Fountain Fills

The centers of radial, conical, and square fountain fills do not necessarily have to occur at the centers of your objects. Note that linear fountain fills do not have a center to be offset.

To specify the center offset of fountain fills numerically, follow these steps:

1. Select an object that has a radial, conical, or square fountain fill.

2. Open the Fill fly-out menu and click the Fountain Fill button. The Fountain Fill dialog box appears.

3. In the Center Offset section, enter the desired numbers in the **H**orizontal and **V**ertical boxes. The preview box shows the effect of the changes.

4. Click OK. The object changes to reflect the options you selected.

To specify the center offset using the mouse, follow these steps:

1. Select an object that has a radial, conical, or square fountain fill.

2. Open the Fill fly-out menu and click the Fountain Fill button or the Roll-Up button. The Fountain Fill dialog box or the Fill roll-up window opens.

3. If you opened the roll-up window, click the Fountain Fill button to display the preview box. If you opened the Fountain fill dialog box, the preview box opens automatically.

4. Click the spot in the preview box where you want the fill to be centered.

5. Click OK or Apply. The object's fill moves according to the location you specified.

Creating Custom Fountain Gradations

Customizing fountain fill colors gives you the opportunity to create the specific fills you need to complement your designs. There are three color-gradation systems:

- *Direct*. This is the default gradation system. The intermediate fountain colors are taken as though a straight line were drawn across the color sheet from the beginning to the ending color.

- *Rainbow*. As its name implies, this option provides a wide spectrum of colors to the fountain, because the intermediate colors are taken from a path around the color wheel. To choose the Rainbow option, simply click the Rainbow radio button in the Fountain Fill dialog box, and then click OK. You also can specify the direction that the path takes by clicking the clockwise or counterclockwise button next to the color wheel.

- *Custom Blend*. This option enables you to choose up to 99 intermediate colors from the palette.

Working with Gradated (Fountain) Fills

To create a custom blend, follow these steps:

1. Select the object you want to fill.

2. Open the Fill fly-out menu and click the Fountain Fill button. The Fountain Fill dialog box opens.

3. In the Color Blend section, click the **C**ustom radio button. A color palette and a preview stripe appear.

4. Double-click just above the preview stripe to create a color marker. This marker specifies where the intermediate color will be located (see figure 5.32).

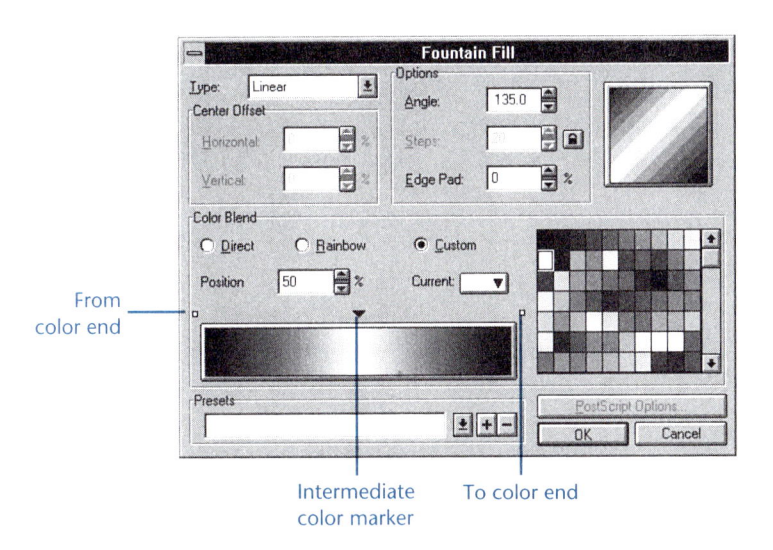

Fig. 5.32
When customizing a fountain fill, intermediate color locations can be specified in the preview stripe.

5. If you placed the marker in the wrong place, click and drag it to a new location.

6. Choose a new color for the marker's location from the color palette.

7. You can specify up to 99 different intermediate colors by repeating steps 4–6.

8. When you finish changing the fill, click OK. Your object is updated.

180 Chapter 5—Modifying Object Outlines and Interior Fills

Using Texture Fills

Using texture fills is a fairly straightforward way to produce some beautiful effects (see fig. 5.33). You can use the texture-fills settings to customize each style; these settings are based on the individual patterns.

Fig. 5.33
Texture fills can produce vibrant, natural looking patterns, like the one shown, for your artwork.

To set up a texture fill, follow these steps:

1. Select the object you want to fill.

2. Open the Fill fly-out menu and click the Texture Fill button. The Texture Fill dialog box opens (see fig. 5.34).

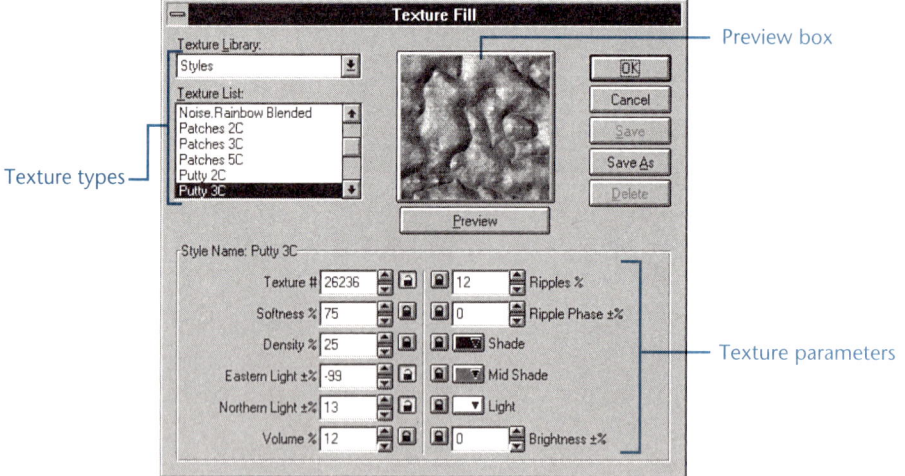

Fig. 5.34
With the Texture Fill dialog box, you can select a texture and set its parameters.

3. Select a texture fill from the Texture list. For more choices, open different libraries of textures from the Texture Library list.

4. Change the settings at the bottom of the dialog box, and click the Preview button to see the results.

5. When you finish making changes, click OK to update your object.

Tip
The best advice on using texture fills is to experiment. Every setting you make can change the fill in new and unexpected ways.

From Here...

Without the techniques described in this chapter, the objects in your drawings look like stick figures. With CorelDRAW!'s outline and fill features, your objects gain aesthetic enhancement and substance. These objects also gain practical value because the enhancements help to distinguish one object from another; one color, for example, can represent a certain unique value in your drawing.

- Chapter 12, "Using Color for Commercial Success." This chapter builds on the color techniques you just learned and shows you how to use them for obtaining printed results that work for you.

- Chapter 14, "Creating Special Effects with Perspective." Now that you know how to shade objects effectively, this chapter will show you exciting ways to use these techniques.

Chapter 6

Scaling, Rotating, and Distorting Objects

by Paul Bodensiek

The major advantage of using vector graphics is that you can substantially modify an object without sacrificing image quality. Whereas a bitmap graphic created in a paint program can become hopelessly distorted as you make changes in its size and shape, a vector graphic of the type created by CorelDRAW! retains the nice sharp edges it had before you "distorted" it.

This chapter covers the following object transformations:

- *Scaling*—making an object larger or smaller
- *Sizing*—scaling an object to an exact size
- *Stretching*—scaling in only one direction
- *Mirroring*—making an object backward or upside down
- *Rotating*—adding a clockwise or counterclockwise spin to an object
- *Skewing*—slanting an object vertically or horizontally

Learning the Basic Tools and Techniques

This section introduces the basic tools and techniques you use to transform objects. In figure 6.1, each transformation has been applied to the character string that represents its name (except Moving).

Fig. 6.1

Each of the transformations is shown in this figure. The black text shows the object before transformation, while the gray version is the object afterward.

◀ See "Accessing Objects within a Group (Child Objects)," p. 122

◀ See "Ungrouping Objects" p. 122

◀ See "Selecting Objects," p. 94

You can apply object transformations to all objects, including text strings, closed objects, curve segments, and even bitmaps. You can apply them to a single object or to a group of objects. Transformations apply to an entire object or group of objects. To transform an individual object within a group, select it as a child object, or break the group apart to access each object by itself.

Before you can transform an object, you must select it. The simplest way to select a single object is to click its outline or fill with the Pick tool. Handles then appear around the object. There are two types of handles: stretch/mirror handles, and rotate/skew handles. *Stretch/mirror handles* are the black squares you see when you click an object to select it; *rotate/skew handles* are the small double-headed arrows that appear when you click a selected object again.

New to CorelDRAW! 5 is the Transform roll-up window, which replaces the individual Stretch & Mirror and Rotate & Skew dialog boxes in CorelDRAW! version 4.

Scaling and Sizing an Object

Making an object larger or smaller, or changing its scale, is one of the most common and useful of all object transformations. Scaling an object changes its size without affecting its shape.

Stretching, on the other hand, increases or decreases one dimension of an object (its width or height). With the Stretch transformation, you can quickly lengthen or shorten a line segment, transform a circle into an ellipse, or change the appearance of text.

To scale an object with the mouse, follow these steps:

1. Select the object you want to transform. The handles appear (see fig. 6.2).

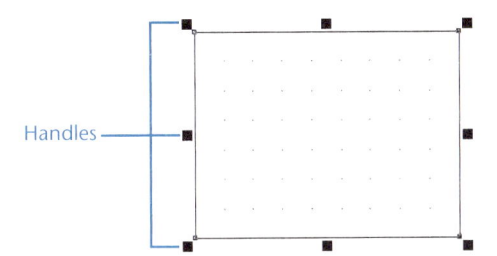

Fig. 6.2
Dragging the corner handles sizes the object proportionally, while the side, top, and bottom handles size the object in only the direction dragged.

2. Position the mouse pointer on one of the four corner handles. The pointer changes to small cross hairs.

3. Drag the handle away from the object to make it bigger, or drag toward the center of the object to make it smaller. The marquee box that follows the mouse shows the object's changing size.

4. Release the mouse button. The object remains the same shape, no matter what size it is now.

To stretch an object with the mouse, follow these steps:

1. Select the object you want to transform. The handles appear.

2. Position the mouse pointer on one of the four side handles. The pointer changes to small cross hairs.

3. Drag the handle away from the object to make it bigger, or drag toward the center of the object to make it smaller. The object changes shape only in the direction in which you are dragging, as shown by the marquee box that follows the mouse (see fig. 6.3).

4. Release the mouse button when the object is the size and shape you want.

Chapter 6—Scaling, Rotating, and Distorting Objects

Fig. 6.3

While scaling an object, watch the marquee box for a visual cue on the object's size. The status line displays the change numerically.

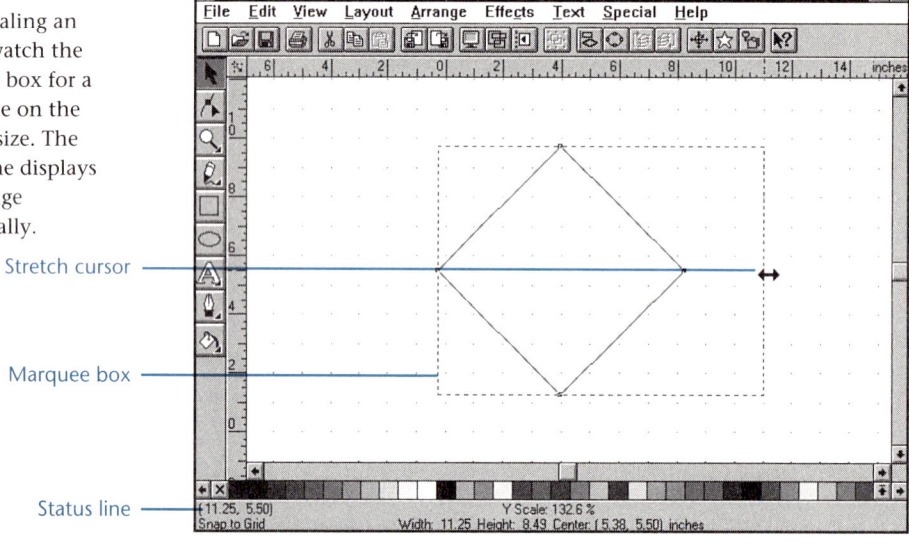

Stretch cursor

Marquee box

Status line

To scale or stretch an object by using the Transform roll-up window, follow these steps:

1. Select the object. The handles appear.

2. Open the Effects menu and choose Transform Roll-Up. The Transform roll-up window appears.

3. Click the Scale button. The scale options appear (see fig. 6.4).

Fig. 6.4

To stretch or mirror an object precisely, use the Transform roll-up with the scale options.

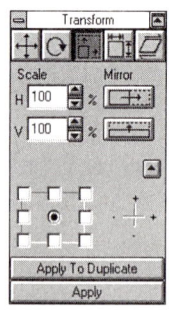

4. Input the percentage difference you want the object to be. For example, 100 percent is full size, 50 percent is half size, and 200 percent is double size. The largest number you can enter with the keyboard is 3276.0 percent (almost 33 times the size). Use the arrow buttons or the separator bar to allow numbers of up to 3,000 percent (30 times size).

Learning the Basic Tools and Techniques   **187**

If you want to scale the object, make sure that the numbers in the H (horizontal) and V (vertical) boxes indicate the same percentage.

If you want to stretch the object, you can use any required numbers in the H and V boxes.

5. Click the Apply button. Your object changes in size by the indicated percentage.

Typically, when an object is scaled, the center of the object remains anchored. If two objects are aligned along their left sides, however, this transformation leaves them unaligned. CorelDRAW! provides a method for setting the anchor point for a transformation.

To change the anchor point for a scale transformation:

1. Follow steps 1 through 4 in the preceding procedure for scaling or stretching an object using the Transform roll-up window.

2. Click the fly-out button to reveal the anchor point options shown in figure 6.5.

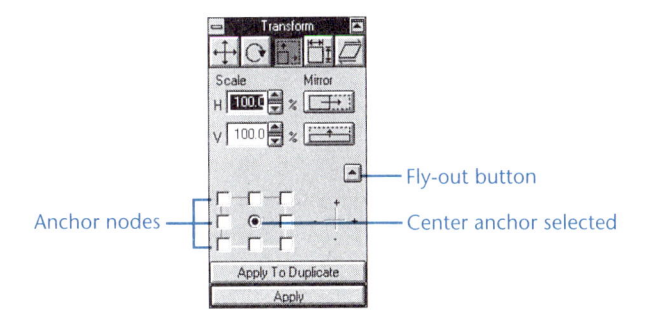

Fig. 6.5
Set a fixed point about which to stretch or mirror an object using the anchor point boxes, each of which corresponds to a location on the object.

3. Click the appropriate anchor point.

Each check box is located at the point in the object that will remain fixed. The default setting is the center position.

4. Click Apply. The object is transformed, with the selected location fixed.

Sizing essentially is identical to Scaling and Stretching, except that instead of entering a percentage change in object size, you enter the desired new object size itself. This is a mixed blessing. If you know the overall size that you want an object to be, you do not have to figure out what the percentage change is, but it may be difficult to determine what the horizontal and vertical changes must be to keep the object looking the same (scaling).

Fig. 6.6
Sizing an object allows you to scale it by setting a precise size instead of having to input a percentage.

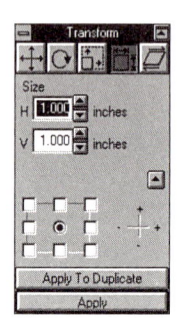

Tip
The object's (or group's) current overall size is entered in the H and V boxes. This display can help when you're working with a group because the status line doesn't provide it.

To Size an object, follow these steps:

1. Select the object. The handles appear.

2. Open the Effects menu and choose **T**ransform Roll-Up. The Transform roll-up window appears.

3. Click the Size button. The size options appear (see fig. 6.6).

4. Enter the horizontal and vertical size that you want the object to be.

   If you want to Scale the object, you must increase the horizontal and vertical settings by the same percentage.

   If you want to Stretch the object, you can use any number for the horizontal and vertical settings.

5. Click the Apply button. Your object changes to the indicated size.

Mirroring an Object

Creating a mirror image of an object often is useful. You can easily create a precisely symmetrical object, for example, by making half of the object and then creating a mirror image of it. Creating a mirror image of an object really is just a special application of the Stretch transformation.

To mirror an object with the mouse, follow these steps:

1. Select an object. The handles appear.

2. Drag one of the four side handles toward the center of the object and back past its opposite side. As the marquee box passes the other side of the object, the number in the status line becomes negative.

3. Release the mouse button when the marquee box is the size that you want the mirror image to be.

To mirror an object by using the Transform roll-up window, follow these steps:

1. Select the object.
2. Open the Effects menu and choose Transform Roll-Up.
3. Click the Scale button. The scale options appear.
4. Click the Horizontal and/or Vertical mirror button, as needed.
5. Click the Apply button to make a mirror image.

> **Troubleshooting**
>
> *I want to scale an object, but when I drag a handle on the side, it only gets bigger in that direction, not overall.*
>
> To scale an object (make it bigger in both directions), drag the corner handles. The side handles are used for stretching.
>
> *When I try to stretch an object by dragging a corner handle, the handle moves away from the cursor. I want the object to be stretched more in one direction at the same time.*
>
> You want to stretch the object. The corner handles only scale an object. Making it larger or smaller in different amounts for both directions is a two-step process: first stretch the object in one direction, then stretch it in the other.
>
> *When I mirror an object with the mouse, I can't get it to come out the same size as the original.*
>
> As you are dragging the handles, press Ctrl to constrain the object to 100 percent changes in size (–100 percent for a mirror). See "Increasing Precision with the Mouse" later in this chapter for more information.

Rotating an Object

Rotating an object turns it clockwise or counterclockwise around its center point, which is designated by a bull's-eye marker.

To rotate an object with the mouse, follow these steps:

1. Select an object. The handles appear.
2. Click the object again. The handles change from squares to double-headed arrows, indicating that the object now is in Rotate/Skew mode (see fig. 6.7).

Fig. 6.7
The double-headed arrows show that the object is in Rotate/Skew mode.

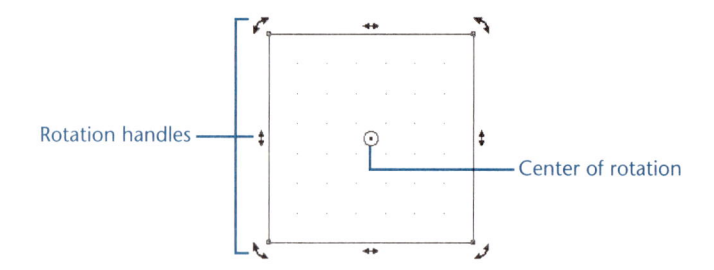

Rotation handles

Center of rotation

3. Position the mouse pointer on one of the four corner arrow handles. The pointer changes to cross hairs.

4. Drag the arrow handle around the center of the object. A marquee box the approximate size of the object rotates with the cursor, showing how the object will be placed (see fig. 6.8). Also, the status line shows the angle at which that the object is rotated.

Fig. 6.8
While rotating an object, watch the marquee box and the status line to indicate the angle of rotation.

Rotation cursor

Marquee box

Rotation Angle

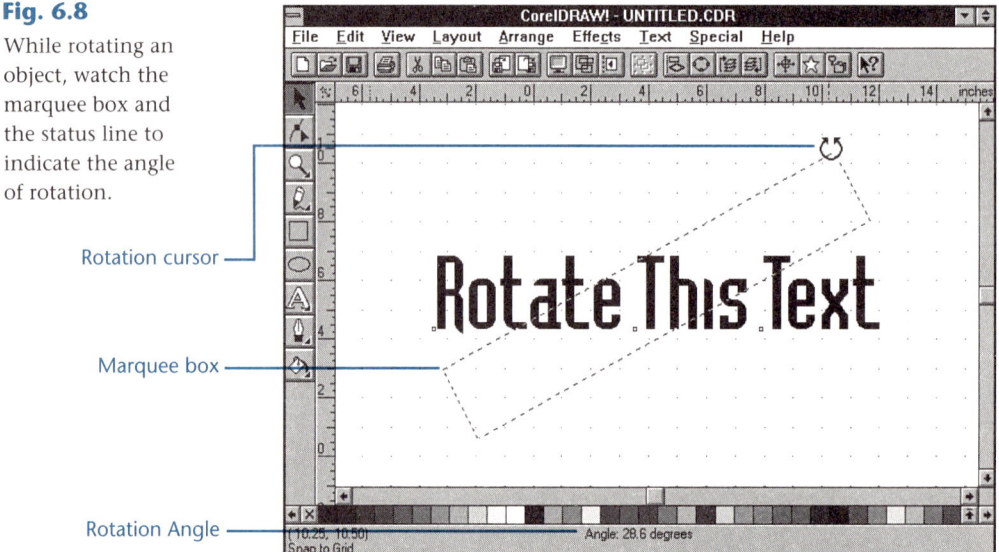

5. Release the mouse button when the marquee box is at the right angle. CorelDRAW! redraws the object in this position.

To rotate an object by using the Transform roll-up window, follow these steps:

1. Select the object.

Rotating an Object   191

2. Open the Effects menu and choose **T**ransform Roll-Up.

3. Click the Rotate button. The rotate options appear (see fig. 6.9).

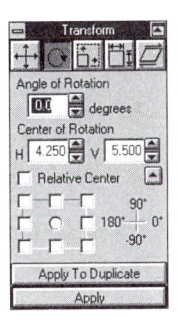

Fig. 6.9
Rotate an object to a precise angle using the Transform roll-up window.

4. Enter the desired angle of rotation. Positive numbers rotate an object counterclockwise; negative numbers rotate it clockwise.

5. Click the Apply button.

By default, both of the preceding methods of rotating an object use the object's center as its axis of rotation. Many times, however, you will want to rotate an object around some other point.

To change the center of rotation with the mouse, follow these steps:

1. Select an object.

2. Click the object again to enter Rotate/Skew mode. The bull's-eye marker indicates the center of rotation.

3. Drag the bull's-eye to the desired center of rotation.

4. You now can rotate the object as described in the preceding steps.

To change the center of rotation numerically, using the Transform roll-up window, follow these steps:

1. Select an object.

2. Open the Effects menu and choose **T**ransform Roll-Up.

3. Click the Rotate button. The rotate options appear.

4. To place the center of rotation relative to the page, enter the appropriate numbers in the H and V boxes in the Center of Rotation area. Leave the Relative Center box unchecked.

To place the center of rotation relative to the object, click the Relative Center box to fill it with an X, and then enter the appropriate numbers.

The Transform roll-up window also provides a simplified method for setting the center of rotation. The eight check boxes and single radio box, shown in figure 6.9, can be used to set the center of rotation to any one of either locations along the outside edge of an object or at the object's center.

5. Click the Apply button now to change only the center of rotation, or enter the desired angle of rotation, as outlined above in the instructions for rotating an object using the Transform roll-up window.

Troubleshooting

When I try to rotate an object using the mouse, I deselect the object when trying to drag the handles.

Because the rotate handles are smaller than the scale handles, they're more difficult to click on. It can take some practice to precisely locate the cursor for grabbing these handles, and you must wait until the cursor turns into cross hairs before dragging a rotation handle.

How do I get the center of rotation back to the center of an object?

There are two methods to do this:

When using the mouse, turn on Snap to Object mode (open the Layout menu and choose Snap to Object). Drag the center of rotation (bull's eye) toward the center of the object. The bull's eye snaps to the center of the object.

When using the Transform roll-up, set the Angle of Rotation to zero. Click the fly-out button and choose the center radio button. Then click Apply. The center of rotation moves to the center of the object.

Skewing an Object

You can make interesting changes to the appearance of objects by slanting them at an angle. This transformation is called skewing. With the skew transformation, you can slant text, transform a rectangle into a parallelogram, or change the shape of a curve.

Skewing an Object

To skew an object with the mouse, follow these steps:

1. Select an object. The handles appear.

2. Click the object again. The handles change from squares to double-headed arrows, indicating that the object is in Rotate/Skew mode.

3. Position the mouse pointer on one of the four side arrow handles. The pointer changes to cross hairs.

4. Drag the arrow handle along the edge of the object. A marquee box the approximate size of the object moves with the cursor, showing how the object will be placed (see figure 6.10). Also, the status line shows the angle at which the object is skewed.

Fig. 6.10
When skewing an object, watch the marquee box and the status line to show the angle of skew.

5. Release the mouse button when the marquee box is at the right angle. CorelDRAW! redraws the object in this position.

To skew an object by using the Transform roll-up window, follow these steps:

1. Select the object.

2. Open the Effects menu and choose Transform Roll-Up.

3. Click the Skew button. The skew options appear (see fig. 6.11).

Fig. 6.11
To skew an object to a precise angle, use the Transform roll-up window.

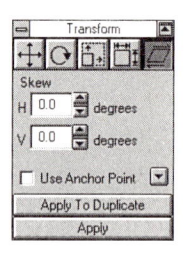

4. Enter the desired angle of skew. Positive horizontal numbers skew an object left; negative numbers skew it right. Positive vertical numbers skew an object up; negative numbers skew it down.

5. Click the Apply button.

> **Troubleshooting**
>
> *I want to skew an object by 18 degrees using the mouse, but the status line says it will only skew to 17.8 or 18.1 degrees.*
>
> The easiest way to make a precision skew is to use the Transform roll-up. If you need to use the mouse, open the **S**pecial menu and choose **P**references; then set the Constraint Angle to 18 degrees and press OK. When you rotate the object, hold down the Ctrl key while dragging the handle and release the key when you have finished. For more information, see "Increasing Precision with the Mouse," later in this chapter.
>
> *When I skew an object horizontally, a positive number in the Transform dialog box moves the top of the object to the left (the negative direction).*
>
> Skewing an object is related to rotating it, so the numbers you input are rotations, not movements. Remember that positive rotations in CorelDRAW! are counterclockwise, so skewing an object in effect rotates the top of the object counterclockwise, or left.

Using Transformation Tricks and Techniques

The effects introduced in the preceding sections are very useful, and you will find that many of your drawings rely on them. If you find yourself using these effects often, however, you will want to find a faster way to make precise changes. Also, in many drawings you may want to make changes to a copy of an object but leave the original unchanged. Another useful feature is repeating the same effects on several objects. And it is likely that you occasionally will make a mistake or change your mind, and want to return the object to its original form. The following sections discuss all these operations, which CorelDRAW! makes easy.

Increasing Precision with the Mouse

Although the menu commands give you the most precise control of object transformations, you also can achieve a considerable amount of precision by using the Pick tool and the mouse.

While you are transforming an object with the mouse, the center of the status line displays the percent change in the object's dimensions or the degree change in the angle of the object. By using the following methods to constrain these changes to specified increments, you can work with effects more precisely.

- Hold down the Ctrl key as you drag the mouse in Stretch and Mirror transformations to constrain the percent change to increments of 100 percent.

- Hold down the Ctrl key in Rotate and Skew transformations to constrain the angle to increments of 15 degrees.

> **Note**
>
> To change the constraint angle, open the **S**pecial menu and choose Pr**e**ferences (Ctrl+J). In the Preferences dialog box, enter the desired angle in the **C**onstraint Angle box.
>
> Also, be aware that the percent or degree increment represents the change from the last transformation, not from when the object was created.

- Hold down the Shift key before you begin dragging the mouse in Stretch and Mirror transformations to keep the transformed object centered on the center point of the original object. The object is transformed around the center of the object instead of the center of rotation, which may have been moved.

> **Note**
>
> When you use the Ctrl and/or Shift key to constrain changes, be sure to release the mouse button before you release Ctrl and/or Shift.

Notice that a dashed *marquee* outline, rather than the object itself, moves with the cursor until the mouse button is released. This feature enables you to keep the original object as a reference point while you are transforming it, and also speeds the process by giving CorelDRAW! a simple object to redraw during the transformation process.

Leaving Copies of the Original Object

One of the most useful features of object transformations in CorelDRAW! is your ability to transform a copy of the object, rather than the object itself.

When you perform transformations with the mouse, click the secondary mouse button (usually the right one) just before releasing the primary button. An alternative method of transforming a copy of the original object is to press the plus key (+) in the numeric keypad while you drag the mouse.

When you transform objects from the Transform roll-up window, click the Apply to Duplicate button instead of the Apply button.

Repeating and Undoing Transformations

You can repeat the last transformation by opening the **E**dit menu and choosing **R**epeat (Ctrl+R). Repeating a transformation several times on copies of the original object can result in interesting patterns and images. This is a great way to make a flower-like shape that consists of a petal making a series of rotations around a bottom-relative center. You also can select another object and apply the same transformation to it by issuing the Repeat command.

◀ See "Undoing Mistakes," p. 99

You can undo individual object transformations by opening the **E**dit menu and choosing **U**ndo (Ctrl+Z). The Undo feature, however, is limited to the number of levels specified in the Preferences dialog box. Regardless of the number of Undo layers, however, you can clear all transformations and return an object to its original shape by opening the Effects menu and choosing **C**lear Transformations. This command resets all object dimensions to 100 percent and all angle changes to 0 degrees, and resets the center point to the middle of the object. It also clears the effects of any changes made in the Effects menu's Envelope and Perspective options.

> **Note**
>
> Clear Transformations, when applied to a group of objects, clears only those transformations applied to the group. It does not clear transformations applied to the individual objects before they were grouped. You can, however, ungroup the objects and continue to clear transformations on individual objects in the group.

> **Troubleshooting**
>
> *I pressed the plus key (+) to leave the original of the object I was transforming, but both the original and the duplicate were transformed.*
>
> This sometimes happens when you're working in Snap to Grid and other modes. To overcome this, press the plus key before you perform the transformation. This action duplicates the object directly over the original, and you then can work with the duplicate.
>
> Alternatively, click the secondary mouse button just before releasing the primary button at the end of the transformation.
>
> *When I use the Shift key while scaling an object, the object gets redrawn scaled from the corner, not from the center.*
>
> Make sure that you hold down the Shift key the entire time that you drag the mouse. Also, release the mouse button before releasing the Shift key.

◀ See "Duplicating Objects," p. 105

Practicing Using the Effects with the Mouse

Many of the effects are difficult to visualize without some practice. If you want to try your hand at a few examples, the rest of the chapter takes you through each of the five types of object transformations, using some concrete examples.

Scaling Objects

Use the following procedure to practice changing the scale of an object:

1. Create a large circle in the middle of the drawing area.
2. Click the Pick tool. The circle is selected.
3. Move the mouse pointer to one of the corner handles. The pointer changes to cross hairs.
4. Press and hold down the Shift key to keep the transformation centered, and then drag the handle toward the object until the object is about 80 percent of its original size (as shown in the status line). The object's dashed marquee box follows the handle to show you what the object's size will be.

5. Click the secondary mouse button.

6. Release the primary mouse button, and then release the Shift key. Your drawing now should be two concentric circles.

7. Repeat steps 4 through 6 three more times, using 60 percent, 40 percent, and 20 percent reductions of the *original* circle. You have created a bull's-eye (see fig. 6.12).

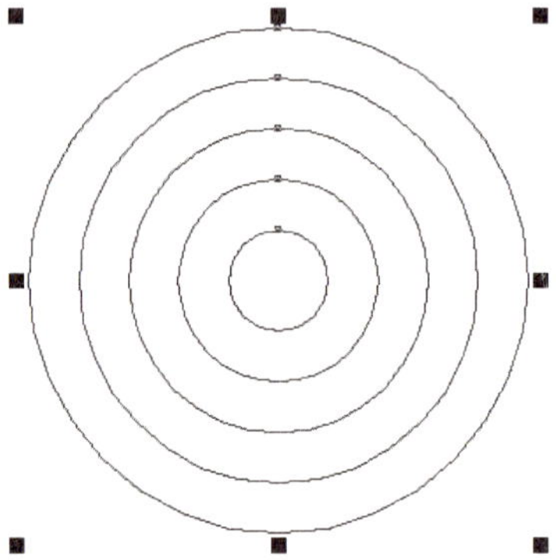

Fig. 6.12
The object you created by repeatedly scaling and duplicating a circle while keeping the transformation centered.

Tip
If your circles aren't centered, or if you have one circle only, you released the Shift key or clicked the secondary mouse button at the wrong time. Choose **E**dit and then **U**ndo (Ctrl+Z), and try again from step 4.

Stretching Objects

The basic procedure for Stretching objects with the Pick tool and the mouse is the same as that used in scaling, except that you use the side handles. When you Stretch an object with the mouse, you are constrained to dragging the side handle along a horizontal or vertical path toward or away from the center of the object.

Practice using the Stretch transformation by turning a circle into an ellipse, making its vertical dimension 50 percent longer than its horizontal dimension. Follow these steps:

1. Create a small circle in the center of the drawing area.

2. Click the Pick tool. The circle is selected.

3. Place the mouse pointer on the top side handle. The pointer changes from an arrow to cross hairs.

4. Press and hold down the Shift key to Stretch from the center of the object.

5. Drag the handle upward until the status line shows approximately 150 percent. Your screen should look like figure 6.13.

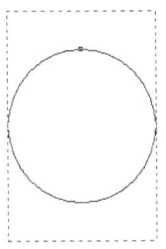

Fig. 6.13
The marquee box shows the relative size of the circle while it is being transformed.

6. Release the mouse button before you release the Shift key, and CorelDRAW! redraws the circle as an ellipse (see fig. 6.14).

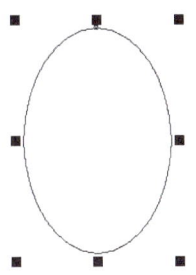

Fig. 6.14
By dragging on the top handle while holding down shift key, the circle has been transformed into an ellipse.

Creating Mirror Images

You create a mirror image with the Pick tool and the mouse by dragging one of the side handles all the way through the object to the other side. Try the following exercise to create a kite shape by Mirroring a triangle with the Pick tool and the mouse. Follow these steps:

1. Using the Pencil tool in Freehand mode, draw a vertical line and two connected line segments to make a triangle.

2. Click the triangle to select it.

3. Place the mouse pointer on the left handle; then hold down the Ctrl key and drag the handle across the object. This action creates an accurate mirror image by making the new object 100 percent of the original size, as shown in the middle of the status line. A dashed box similar to the one shown in figure 6.15 indicates the object's destination.

◀ See "Drawing a Single Object Using Several Straight Lines," p. 65

Fig. 6.15
The status line indicates that this triangle has been mirrored by exactly 100 percent.

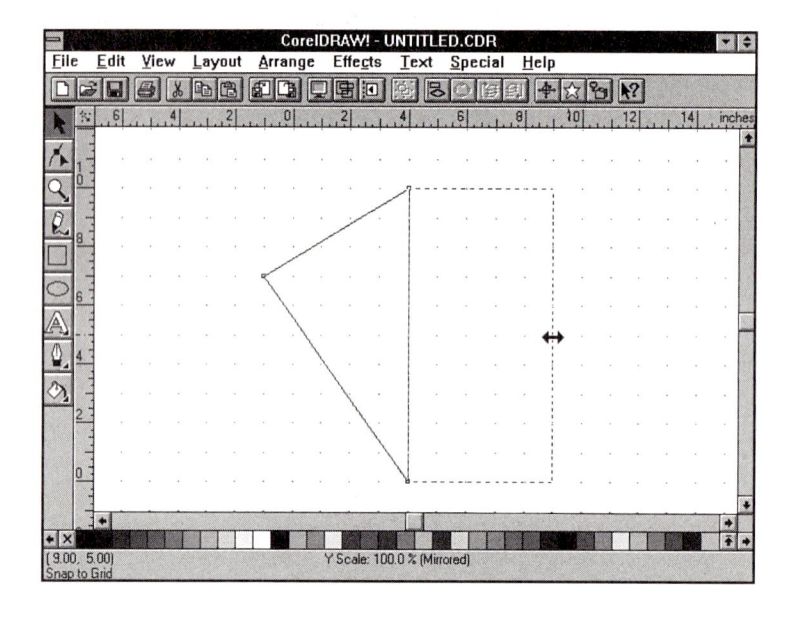

4. Click the secondary mouse button or (if you are very dexterous) press the plus key (+) in the numeric keypad as you drag to retain a copy of the original triangle.

5. Release the primary mouse button, and observe the symmetry of the kite shape you created (see fig. 6.16).

Fig. 6.16
Mirroring the left hand triangle resulted in the kite shape shown in this figure.

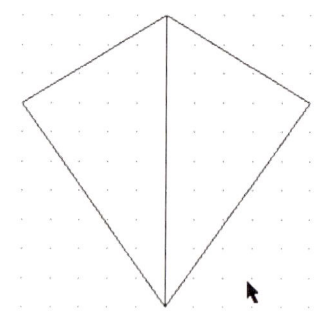

Rotating Objects

You may want to change an object's orientation on the page without changing the object's size or shape. For example, you might want to take a horizontal string of text and position it diagonally across the page.

You can change the angle of orientation of any object easily, and very precisely, by using the mouse and the Pick tool in Rotate/Skew mode. Practice this technique on the triangle you created in the last exercise. Follow these steps:

1. Delete the mirror image of the triangle, or draw a new triangle.

2. Activate Rotate/Skew mode by double-clicking the triangle's outline. The handles change to double-headed arrows, and the center-of-rotation symbol (a bull's-eye) appears in the middle of the object.

3. Move the mouse pointer to one of the corner handles. When the pointer is on the handle, it changes to cross hairs.

4. Drag the handle clockwise or counterclockwise. Notice that the object's dashed marquee box moves with the mouse and rotates around the center point.

5. Hold down the Ctrl key as you drag the mouse to constrain the angle of rotation to increments of 15 degrees, depending of what is set in Preferences for the Constrain Angle. Drag the mouse until the status line shows an angle of 45 degrees (see fig. 6.17).

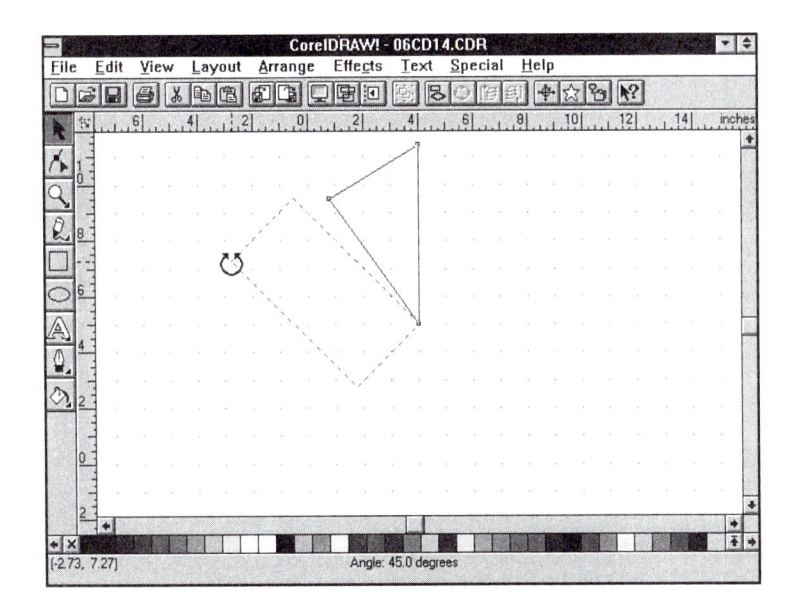

Fig. 6.17
The status line indicates the current angle while you rotate an object.

6. Release the mouse button. CorelDRAW! redraws the triangle at a 45-degree angle.

Rotating an Object Off Center

In the preceding example, an object was rotated around its center. You can create unusual objects or special effects by rotating copies of an original object around some other point.

Tip
Hold down the Ctrl key while dragging the center point to constrain it to the center of the object or one of the eight handles.

When you enter Rotate/Skew mode, a center-point symbol (a bull's-eye) appears in the middle of the selected object. CorelDRAW! rotates the object around this point. You can move the center point to a new location by dragging it with the mouse.

In the following exercise, you create a pinwheel by rotating a triangle about its tip. Follow these steps:

1. Select the triangle you used in the last exercise, or create a new one that is similar to it.

2. Activate Rotate/Skew mode by clicking the triangle's outline.

3. Place the mouse pointer on the bull's-eye. The pointer becomes a cross hair.

4. Drag the bull's-eye toward the narrowest tip of the triangle, holding down the Ctrl key to constrain the bull's-eye to the corner.

5. When the bull's-eye is on the tip of the triangle, release the mouse button and Ctrl key.

6. Rotate the triangle 45 degrees, using either the mouse or the Transform roll-up window. Leave the original triangle by clicking the secondary mouse button while dragging or by clicking Apply to Duplicate in the roll-up window.

7. Repeat the rotation (Ctrl+R) six times. You have created the pinwheel shown in figure 6.18.

Fig. 6.18
This pinwheel was created by rotating and duplicating a triangle around one of its corners.

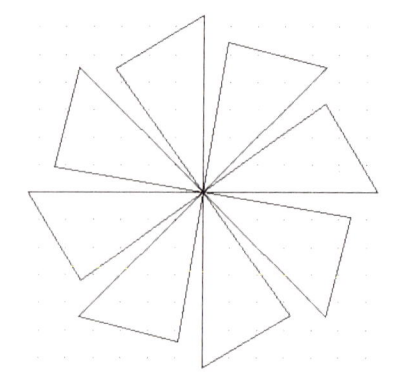

Skewing Objects

As with the rotate transformation, you can skew objects very precisely with the mouse by holding down the Ctrl key, which constrains the angle to 15-degree increments or to whatever you specify as the constrain angle in the Preferences dialog box.

To skew an object using the mouse, follow these steps:

1. Create a rectangle.

2. Activate Rotate/Skew mode by clicking the outline of the square until the rotate/skew handles appear.

3. Move the mouse pointer to the top center handle. The pointer changes from an arrow to cross hairs.

4. Drag the handle to the left and then to the right. Notice that only the top and sides of the dashed marquee box move; the bottom remains in a fixed position.

5. Hold down the Ctrl key while dragging the handle to constrain the change in angle to 15-degree increments. Drag until the status line shows a 30-degree angle (see fig. 6.19).

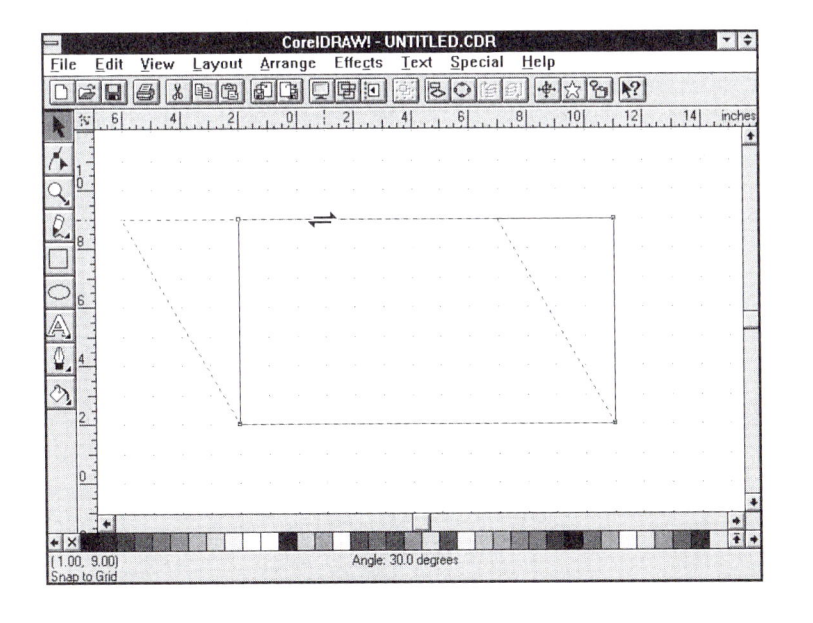

Fig. 6.19
While you are skewing an object, the status line indicates the angle of skew.

6. Release the mouse button. CorelDRAW! transforms the square into a parallelogram.

Creating an Object with Multiple Transformations

Now that you know how to perform individual transformations on objects, you can perform successive transformations on a simple object to produce an interesting pattern. In the following example, you start with a square and transform it into an entirely different object. Follow these steps:

1. Create a square.

2. Rotate it 45 degrees in any direction.

3. Stretch it 100 percent in either dimension.

4. Rotate it 45 degrees, this time leaving the original.

5. Repeat step 4 two times.

6. Open the **E**dit menu and choose Select **A**ll.

7. Open the **A**rrange menu and choose **W**eld. You have created an eight-pointed star (see fig. 6.20). Fill with a yellow-orange gradient, conical fill for a 3-D look.

Fig. 6.20
This eight-pointed star shape was created with multiple transformations and then welded together.

From Here...

This chapter covers techniques for transforming the overall appearance of objects without altering their basic shape. You can transform objects with the mouse by using the Pick tool, or by entering precise values in the Transform roll-up menu.

■ Chapter 7, "Adding Text to a Drawing." Using text is the last basic skill you need to master. This chapter teaches you the basics of typography and shows you how to enter artistic and paragraph text and work with the proofing techniques.

- Chapter 14, "Creating Special Effects with Perspective." Perspective and Extrude are more advanced transformations that help create a 3-D effect in a drawing.

- Chapter 15, "Creating Special Effects with Envelope." The envelope builds on the capabilities of the transformations you learned.

Chapter 7

Adding Text to a Drawing

by Paul Bodensiek

CorelDRAW! is unique because it enables you to manipulate text to achieve almost any design or layout. Not only can you edit text, but you also can color it, add a border, change the slant, and even arrange text on a curve or in a circle.

You can add text to your drawings in one of three ways: typing text directly into a drawing; importing text data files from other applications such as word processing or desktop publishing programs; or pasting it through the Windows Clipboard. After you place text within your drawing, you can edit and format it much as you do using traditional word processing applications. You also can export text to a file, open it in a word processor, and later return it to the drawing.

This chapter teaches you how to

- Understand basic text-related terminology
- Work with Artistic and Paragraph text
- Create multiple text columns
- Check the spelling and add synonyms in your text
- Add an artistic flair to your text characters

Understanding the Fundamentals of Text Design

Most text-design terms derive from those used by printers before the advent of computers. These terms remain with us today. Understanding these terms can help you make more informed decisions about the designs you create. The following sections explain typeface, point size, kerning, spacing, outline, and fill.

The text spacing, size, and font characteristics discussed in this chapter are generic to any text-processing application and are not necessarily unique to CorelDRAW!. However, the capability to modify the text display attributes, such as outlines and fills, in combination with the artistic capabilities discussed later in this chapter distinguish CorelDRAW! from the other drawing packages on the market.

◄ See "How CorelDRAW! Creates Objects," p. 24

Part of the reason for this distinction is CorelDRAW!'s effective use of vector graphics as opposed to bitmapped images. Early graphics packages used a series of dots to represent their objects; CorelDRAW! actually calculates an object's characteristics based on a mathematical representation and then displays the results. This method means that when you modify the CorelDRAW! objects, CorelDRAW! simply recalculates the new orientation numbers and refreshes the display. Bitmapped objects must re-create a facsimile of the original dot-patterned design, but without an understanding of the underlying objects, the computer changes can distort the object. This difference in technology provides CorelDRAW! with a superior capability to manipulate text and objects.

Typefaces

A collection of letters and symbols displaying common characteristics is called a *typeface* or *font*. Creating a particular type of text is an artistic endeavor with each letter and symbol regarded as a separate drawing. When an artist creates a typeface, he or she usually copyrights it; thus, you may see very similar typefaces with different names. Some of the more common typefaces are Times Roman, Helvetica, and Courier.

Although the terms *font* and *typeface* are often used interchangeably, a distinction exists. A typeface literally refers to the face, or design, of a type, whereas font refers to a particular combination of the typeface design—the style (for example, bold or italic) and the size of the type (you learn more about this in the next section). In other words, a font is a subset of a typeface.

CorelDRAW!—Compatible Typefaces

CorelDRAW! supports the industry type standards TrueType (TTF) and Adobe Type 1 (PFB), in addition to the WFN font used by earlier versions of CorelDRAW!.

Third-Party Typefaces

The huge success of desktop publishing has made a seemingly limitless range of typefaces available to the computer artist. Adobe, Bitstream, and many other large type foundries (a term left over from the days of forged type) have huge libraries of professionally designed typefaces available for reasonable prices.

Less costly alternatives are available from computer bulletin boards and the burgeoning number of shareware outlets. These shareware (and freeware) typefaces are often similar in design to their counterparts from the larger companies and are an excellent way to work with type on a limited budget. Any number of CD-ROMs with hundreds or thousands of shareware typefaces are available for less money than one typeface from the large foundries.

CorelDRAW! provides a large number of typefaces (around 75 in the disk version and 750 in the CD version), some in TrueType and some Adobe Type 1 format. It is very likely that many readers can fulfill most of their type needs from the Corel CD. If Corel doesn't contain just the right typeface, Image Club Graphics (800-661-9410) has a catalog of thousands of commercial typefaces in every style and format. Quantum Axcess' Font Axcess CD contains over 1300 shareware fonts and is available from MEI Microcenter (800-634-3478) for about $10 (plus a small registration fee for each font used). Also, electronic bulletin boards, such as CompuServe and Prodigy, have forums for downloading shareware typefaces.

> **Note**
>
> When saving money by using a shareware or freeware typeface, investigate the typeface very carefully before using it in a project. Some low-cost typefaces are worth what you pay for them. On the other hand, some are created by extremely talented type designers working on their own, and using their products can be very rewarding. As with everything else in graphics, the key word is *experiment*.

Point Size

Tip

A general rule of thumb is to use 9, 10, 11, or 12 point for body text; 12 or 14 for subheadings; 18, 24, 36, or 48 for headings; and 60 or 72 for headlines or displays.

The height of a character is generally measured in *points*. Points, in turn, are measured in *picas*. There are approximately six picas in an inch, and one pica equals 12 points (or about 72 points to an inch). The higher the point size, the larger the type. Thus, 12-point type is half the size of 24 point.

Character and Line Spacing

When you deal with text, you must deal with the interline (*leading*) and intercharacter (*kerning*) spacing.

The character height, or point size, determines interline spacing. The interline spacing must be greater than the actual character height, or the lines will overlap each other. For example, an interline spacing of 8 points used with a 10-point type character makes the first line overlap the second.

Intercharacter spacing, or kerning, is used to differentiate between two types of typefaces. *Proportional* typefaces have different spacing requirements for different characters. The letter M, for example, takes up more room on the line than the letter I. Proportional typefaces take this relative size difference into account when placing the characters on the line; *monospaced* (nonproportional) typefaces keep the intercharacter spacing constant. Most contemporary typefaces are proportional, but some old standards like Courier are monospaced.

CorelDRAW! enables you to change the leading, kerning, and interword spacing using some simple mouse techniques. You also can do this with more precision using CorelDRAW!'s dialog boxes. For more information, see the section "Changing Word, Character, and Line Spacing" later in this chapter.

Serif versus Sans Serif Typefaces

In addition to spacing, typefaces have another basic characteristic used to distinguish two separate types—the serif. A *serif* is a small extension at the end of a character that gives it a flowing appearance and makes it easier to read. Some typefaces have, and some do not have, serifs. A typeface without serifs is called *sans serif* (literally, "without serif").

This book was set in the serif typeface Stone Serif, which was picked because of its easy flow and good reading characteristics. The chapter heads and notes use the sans serif typeface Stone Sans.

Outline

The line that marks the edge of a letter (or any other CorelDRAW! object) is called the *outline*. You can display a letter with or without an outline and give the outline a custom thickness, style, and color, which creates a text character border. For more information, see the section "Changing the Fill and Outline Type" later in this chapter.

◀ See "Modifying Object Outline Characteristics," p. 137

Fill

The interior portion of a letter—whether the letter is outlined or not—is the *fill*. In CorelDRAW!, you specify the fill design and color independent of the outline specifications.

◀ See "Working with Interior Fills," p. 146

Differentiating between Paragraph and Artistic Text

CorelDRAW! divides text into two types: *Paragraph* and *Artistic*. In general, you use Artistic text for accent and Paragraph text for longer written information. They have much in common, but keep their differences in mind—especially when initially deciding which one to use.

Paragraph text is like traditional text you use in a word processing program, but you can manipulate it in many more ways. In addition to standard text formatting and editing, you can rotate Paragraph text and even arrange it on a curve. Paragraph text's best use is for creating longer passages that flow over multiple columns or pages. It also enables you to add bullets, indents, tabs, and hyphenation automatically. For more information, see the section "Working with Paragraph Text" later in this chapter.

Artistic text acts less like traditional word processor text and more like a graphic object that you also can edit. You can apply many of the artistic capabilities described elsewhere in this book to Artistic text (see fig. 7.1). For more information, see the next section, "Working with Artistic Text."

This is an example of Artistic Text

Fig. 7.1
Although limited in the length of a passage, Artistic text can be manipulated using many of CorelDRAW!'s special effects.

The type of text you choose depends on what you want to do with it. If you want to perform special artistic effects, choose Artistic text. If you don't expect to manipulate the text, except for formatting (using tabs, indenting, and setting columns), Paragraph text is better suited to your needs.

Artistic text has a 8000-character limit per Artistic text *string*, but you can have an unlimited number of strings in your drawing. (Text string refers to the collection of characters in an object.) Paragraph text has an 850-paragraph limit per drawing, and each paragraph can contain up to 4,000 characters. A single paragraph is a block of text that ends with a paragraph (return) mark. (Artistic text can have these types of characters.)

You can edit Artistic or Paragraph text either directly on the CorelDRAW! screen or within the Edit Text dialog box.

Working with Artistic Text

Artistic text is the basis for many of CorelDRAW!'s most striking artistic features. This section introduces the basic operations pertaining to Artistic text, such as entering, deleting, and editing Artistic text.

Adding Artistic Text

To add Artistic text to your drawing, follow these steps:

1. Click the Artistic Text tool in the toolbox. If it is not showing, click and hold down the Text tool to display the fly-out menu and then click the Artistic Text tool.

2. Place the cursor where you want text to appear in the document.

3. Type the text. When you finish typing, click elsewhere on the page.

Tip
You must click the cursor on-screen to end the previous block's editing procedure and move to the next text block. To end working with the Artistic Text tool, click the Pick tool.

CorelDRAW! always inserts text to the left of the current cursor position. While using the Artistic Text tool, if you click the text at a specific point in any text string, the existing text to the right moves over as CorelDRAW! adds the typed text to the drawing. If you select a section of text by using any of the standard selection techniques such as dragging the mouse over the text or double-clicking a word, text you type after that point replaces the highlighted text.

Editing Artistic Text

After adding text to your drawing, you can edit text either on-screen or from within the Edit Text dialog box. Editing on-screen is similar to using any standard word processor.

To edit the text using the Edit Text dialog box, follow these steps:

1. Select the text object that you want to edit.

2. Open the Text menu and choose Edit Text (Ctrl+Shift+T). The Edit Text dialog box appears (see fig. 7.2).

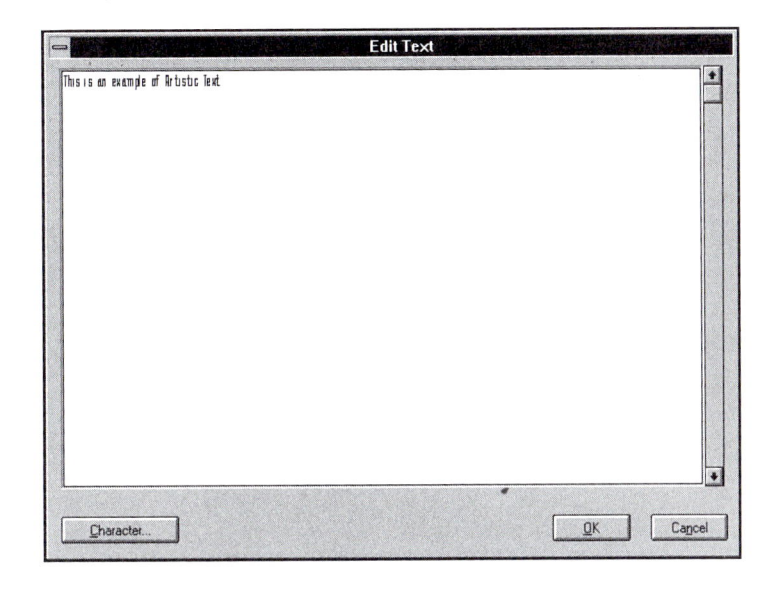

Fig. 7.2
The Edit Text dialog box allows any type of text to be edited in its preview window.

Tip
Pressing the space bar does not automatically switch you to the Pick tool when working with text.

3. Click the cursor in the editing window where you want to edit.

4. Use the keyboard to make deletions or changes.

5. Click OK when finished.

Follow these steps to edit text on-screen:

1. Select the text object you want to edit.

2. Click the Artistic Text tool from the toolbox. The cursor becomes the text I-beam, like that used in a standard word processor.

3. Click the I-beam in the text string where you want to edit the text.

4. Use standard word processor techniques to alter the text.

5. Click the cursor off the text string or click the Pick tool when you are finished.

Changing Artistic Text Attributes

You can change fonts, alignment, spacing, point size, and style by using the Character Attributes dialog box (see fig. 7.3) or the Text roll-up window (see fig. 7.4). The examples in the following sections describe the use of the Character Attributes dialog box, but using the Text roll-up window is essentially the same.

Tip
When you want to change only specific letters, remember to highlight the letters first.

Either the entire text string or individual letters can be altered. When working with the Pick tool, if the string is bounded by the scaling handles, any changes made using the Character Attributes dialog box are made to the entire string. When you are using the Text tool, changes are made only to specifically highlighted letters.

Fig. 7.3
Change a character's font, alignment, point size, and style using the Character Attributes dialog box.

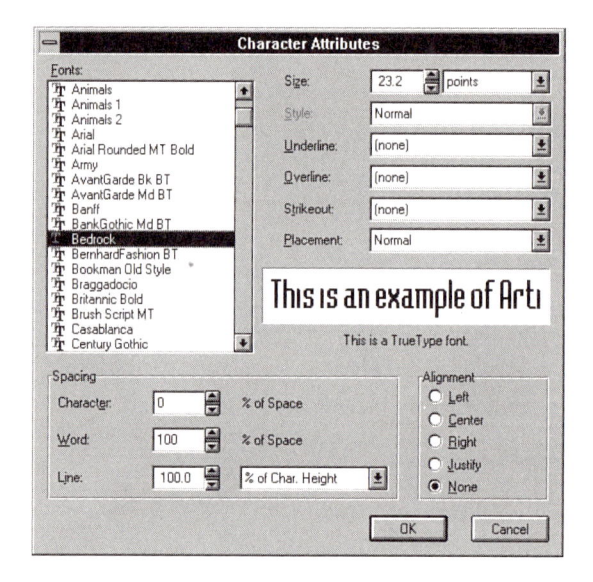

Fig. 7.4
You can also change a character's font, alignment, point size, and style by using the Text roll-up window.

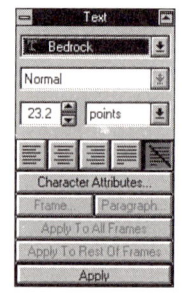

Changing the Typeface and Character Attributes

CorelDRAW! gives you the ability to change the typeface and the full range of associated fonts—bold, italic, and normal.

To change the character attributes, perform the following steps:

1. Select the character string you want to modify.

   If you want to alter only certain letters, click the Text tool and highlight those letters by dragging the cursor over them.

2. Open the **T**ext menu and choose **C**haracter. The Character Attributes dialog box opens.

3. Change the font, style, and size boxes as required.

4. Press OK to transfer these changes to your text.

Changing the Alignment Style

The five alignment types are left, right, center, justified, and none.

The *Left* alignment option aligns text so that the left side lines up where you click the cursor to begin entering text. *Center* aligns the text evenly, left and right, around where you click the cursor. *Right* aligns the text so that the right side of the text string lines up where you originally click the cursor. *Justify* is used only with Paragraph text and forces the text to line up evenly along the left and right sides. *None* sets the default alignment, but does not automatically modify character spacing if the Shape tool is later used to modify individual character attributes.

To change the alignment style, follow these steps:

1. Select the text string you want to modify.

2. Open the Character Attributes dialog box (or press Ctrl+T).

3. Select the alignment type.

   > **Note**
   >
   > Alignment cannot be selectively applied to Artistic text, even if separate "paragraphs" are in it.

4. Click OK.

Tip
Not all typefaces support all character styles. Only those options appropriate to a certain typeface are displayed in the style box when that typeface is selected.

Tip
If you need to have different parts of an Artistic text string align differently, use multiple strings or Paragraph text.

Changing Word, Character, and Line Spacing

You also can change spacing between characters, words, and lines for Artistic text. Follow these steps to change the spacing of a text string:

1. Select the text string.

2. Open the **T**ext menu and choose **C**haracter.

3. Set the spacing options as appropriate. The options are described in the following paragraphs.

4. Click OK.

The three main spacing options are as follows:

- *Character* determines the amount of space between characters. Zero represents standard spacing. A positive percentage indicates more than standard spacing or expanded, whereas a negative percent indicates less than standard spacing or compressed.

- *Word* enables you to set the percentage of a standard character space used between words; for example, 100 percent means that 100 percent of the size of the space character in the selected font appears between words.

- *Line* defines the amount of space used for the height of each line of text. When set at 100 percent, the spacing is set at the height necessary to accommodate the current character height. Settings of more than 100 percent increase the line height, and those less than 100 percent decrease the line spacing. You also can set the line height in points, or percentage of point size rather than percent of character height, by selecting points from the drop-down list to the far right of the option.

You also can set the line, character, and word spacing by using the mouse in conjunction with the Shape tool. To change spacing with the mouse, click the Shape tool and then click the text string. This displays small boxes near each letter and arrows on the ends of the text string that point to the right and down (see fig. 7.5). Then do any of the following procedures to change the spacing:

- Drag on the down arrow to set the line spacing.

- Drag on the right arrow to set the character spacing.

- Drag on the right arrow while pressing Ctrl to set the word spacing.

Working with Artistic Text 217

This is an example of Artistic Text

Drag up or down for interline spacing

Drag left or right for intercharacter spacing; Ctrl+drag for interword spacing

Fig. 7.5
By dragging the arrows as shown in this figure, text spacing can be changed without accessing the Character or Paragraph dialog boxes.

Changing Fill and Outline Options

You can select the type and color of your text's fill and outline just as you can with any other CorelDRAW! object. You can achieve many interesting effects by using these two attributes in conjunction with each other.

◄ See "Working with Interior Fills," p. 146

The procedure for changing the fill type is simple and requires the following steps:

1. Select the text using the Pick tool. Handles appear to show the text you selected.

2. Choose a solid fill from the current color pallet by left-clicking on a color, or click the Fill tool in the toolbox.

3. Choose the fill type from the fly-out menu, just as you choose fill for graphic elements (see fig. 7.6).

The procedure for setting the outline type and color is the same as with any other object. Select the text; click the Outline tool; and select the design and color (see fig. 7.6).

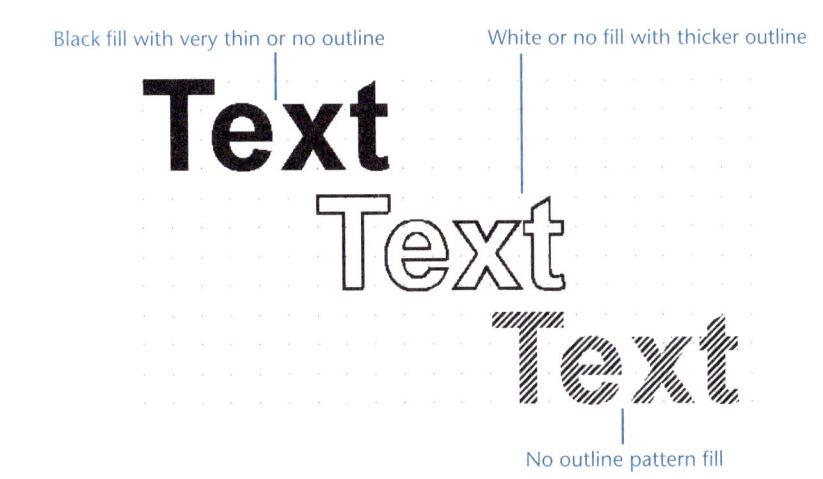

Black fill with very thin or no outline

White or no fill with thicker outline

Text

Text

Text

No outline pattern fill

Fig. 7.6
The typeface and size for all three pieces of text in this figure are the same. Only the outline and interior fill are different.

> **Troubleshooting**
>
> *I typed in a large amount of text. It looked fine on-screen, but when I clicked the Pick tool, a dialog box opened and said I had an "application error."*
>
> This is only one of the problems that can result when you try to type too much Artistic text. Remember that Artistic text has a limit of 8000 characters per text string. You can sometimes input more than 250 characters, but the results can be unpredictable.
>
> *When I use small text, it looks indistinct or muddy.*
>
> It probably has an outline, which at a small size changes the appearance of the typeface. Remove any outline that the text may have. It also may have reached the small print threshold where it becomes greeked text.
>
> *When I try to change the spacing on individual letters using the Shape tool, I can't keep them in line with the other letters.*
>
> While you are dragging the letters, press the Ctrl key to constrain the letters to the baseline of the other letters.
>
> *When I try to find a certain word in a block of text, nothing happens when I press Find Next.*
>
> Make sure that you have selected the Text tool before opening the Find dialog box.

Tip
If your text is small, use the Zoom tool to zoom in and enlarge the text.

Working with Paragraph Text

Much of the information covered in the preceding section on Artistic text also applies to Paragraph text. Whereas Artistic text is added using the Artistic Text tool, Paragraph text is added using the Paragraph Text tool located on the text fly-out menu (see fig. 7.7).

Fig. 7.7
Clicking and holding down the Text tool in the toolbox opens the Text fly-out menu, which provides access to the Artistic and Paragraph Text tools.

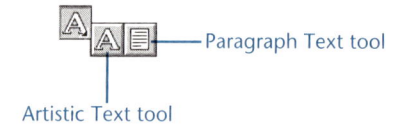

Adding Paragraph Text

To add Paragraph text to your drawing, follow these steps:

1. Click and hold down the cursor on the Text tool until a fly-out menu appears.

2. Click the Paragraph Text icon.

3. Place the cursor where you want to place the upper left-hand corner of the text.

4. Click and drag the cursor to the place where you want the lower right-hand corner of the text to be and release the mouse button. A frame appears outlining the boundaries of the text box. The insertion point in the upper left-hand side of the frame blinks to indicate where your Paragraph text begins.

5. Type the text.

6. Click the Pick tool. You have completed the Paragraph text entry process, and the frame is no longer selected.

Note

Your text frame may not be large enough to display all the characters you enter. The characters are still entered, but are not displayed. You can enlarge the frame by selecting the text frame with the Pick tool and then dragging the handles horizontally or vertically until the text frame is sized as needed.

Tip

Scaling the text frame using the scaling handles only changes the frame size, not the size of the text characters within it.

Editing Paragraph Text

You edit Paragraph text as you would Artistic text, either on-screen or using the Edit Text dialog box (Ctrl+Shift+T).

Modifying Paragraph Text Attributes

You can change many of the attributes of Paragraph text, such as spacing, fill, and outline, in much the same way you make changes to Artistic text.

Changing Text Spacing

Line spacing works the same way with Paragraph text as it does with Artistic text (see the earlier section "Changing Word, Character, and Line Spacing" for more information).

220 Chapter 7—Adding Text to a Drawing

You also can set the height of the line preceding and following a paragraph of text by using the Paragraph dialog box, shown in figure 7.8. Access the Paragraph dialog box by opening the **T**ext menu and choosing **P**aragraph.

This spacing option works the same way as the normal line spacing options described for Artistic text.

Fig. 7.8
The Paragraph dialog box gives you additional options over the Character dialog box for setting up the spacing before and after paragraphs.

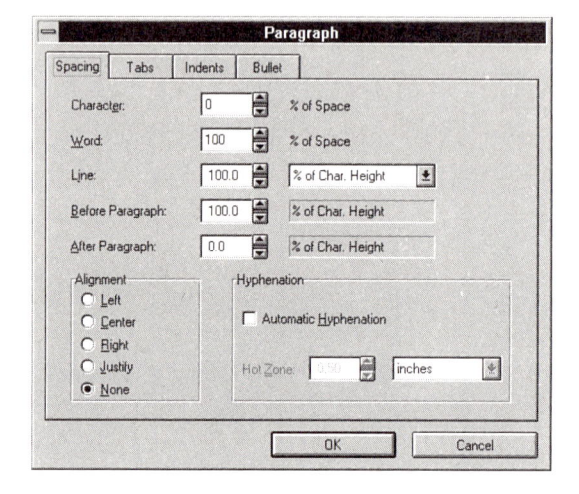

Aligning Text

You can set the alignment by clicking the desired option in the Alignment box. The alignment options are the same as those for Artistic text, with the addition that you can align different paragraphs of a block in different ways. Also, the text now aligns to the text box, not to the initial cursor location. For more information, refer to the earlier section "Changing the Alignment Style."

Use the following steps to align a specific paragraph:

1. Select the Paragraph text block using the Pick tool.
2. Click the Text tool (either one) in the toolbox.
3. Move the cursor over the paragraph you want to change. The cursor changes from cross hairs to the I-beam when it is over the Paragraph text.
4. Click the cursor anywhere in the appropriate paragraph. If you selected the Artistic Text tool, the toolbox now displays the Paragraph Text tool.
5. Open the **T**ext menu and choose **P**aragraph.

6. Set the required alignment.

7. Click OK.

Hyphenating Paragraph Text

You also can select hyphenation options in the Paragraph dialog box. You can set hyphenation to automatic by choosing the Automatic Hyphenation option, and you can define the *hot zone* by clicking the Hot Zone option.

The hot zone is the distance the last letter on a line can be from the right margin before CorelDRAW! tries to hyphenate the first word of the next line. With unjustified text, a larger value for the hot zone results in few hyphenations, but a more ragged right margin, while a small value creates a lot of hyphenations and a less ragged margin.

Changing the Fill and Outline Type

Paragraph text objects have interior fills and outline types just as all other CorelDRAW! objects. You set these attributes exactly as you do for Artistic text and other CorelDRAW! objects.

◀ See "Modifying Object Outline Characteristics," p. 137

Changing Typeface, Style, and Size

CorelDRAW! applies the default font to any text you enter as Paragraph text. After entering the text, you can change the typeface, style, and size from within the Character Attributes dialog box (Ctrl+T), which operates exactly as outlined in the earlier section "Changing the Typeface and Character Attributes."

◀ See "Working with Interior Fills," p. 146

As noted for Artistic text, if you highlight specific characters within the text block, only those characters are modified.

Setting Paragraph Text Tabs, Margins, and Indents

You can set formatting options such as margins, tabs, and indents by using the Paragraph dialog box (accessed by opening the **T**ext menu and choosing **P**aragraph). Click the desired "tab" in the list at the top of the box to provide access to the appropriate window.

Setting Tabs

You can set tabs incrementally, spacing them as close together or as far apart as you like. You can set them to align text at the left, right, or center; or you can use the decimal point to align a list of numbers.

222   Chapter 7—Adding Text to a Drawing

To set tabs, follow these steps:

1. Select the Paragraph text for which you want to set tabs.

2. Open the **T**ext menu and choose **P**aragraph. The Paragraph dialog box appears.

3. Click the Tabs tab to display the Paragraph/Tabs dialog box, shown in figure 7.9.

    The ruler at the top displays the tab settings indicated by the vertical arrows.

Fig. 7.9
The Paragraph/Tabs dialog box enables you to set tabs either interactively by dragging the icons on the ruler, or by entering data via the keyboard.

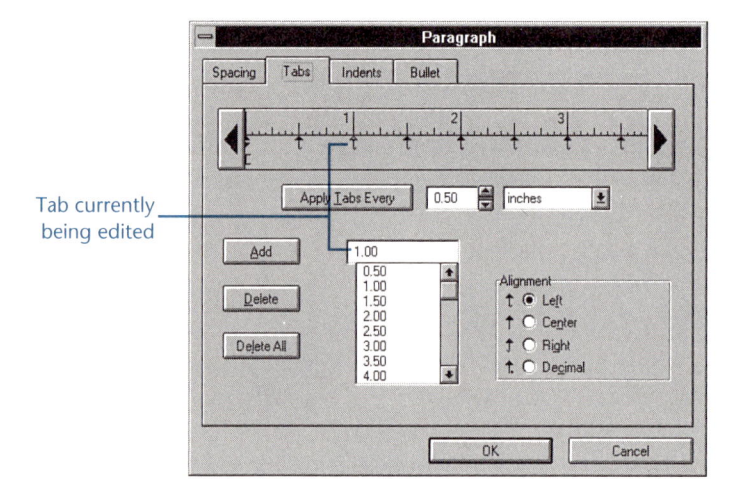

4. Make the tab settings you want as described in the following steps:

    ■ To set tabs at a given interval, such as every one-half inch, choose Apply **T**abs Every and enter the interval in the box to the right.

    ■ To add a tab at a specific location, type the location in the box to the right of **A**dd and then press **A**dd. You also can choose a number from the drop-down list, edit it, and then choose **A**dd.

    ■ To clear a tab, select it from the location shown in the list; then choose Clear. To clear all tabs from the list, choose Clear **A**ll.

    ■ To interactively set the tab locations with the mouse, drag the tab indicators directly on the ruler. Set the tab type by clicking the tab marker and then clicking the desired tab alignment type. The tab marker changes shape to reflect the alignment selected.

To change the alignment for any tab, select it in the list or on the ruler and then select the alignment type from the box. If you look carefully at the ruler, you see that the tab position indicator is different for each type of tab.

5. When you finish editing the tab settings, click OK to return to the drawing screen or choose one of the other categories at the left to change other paragraph settings.

Setting the Margin and Indents

You can set the margin and indents by clicking the Indents "tab" in the Paragraph dialog box to get the Paragraph/Indents dialog box shown in figure 7.10.

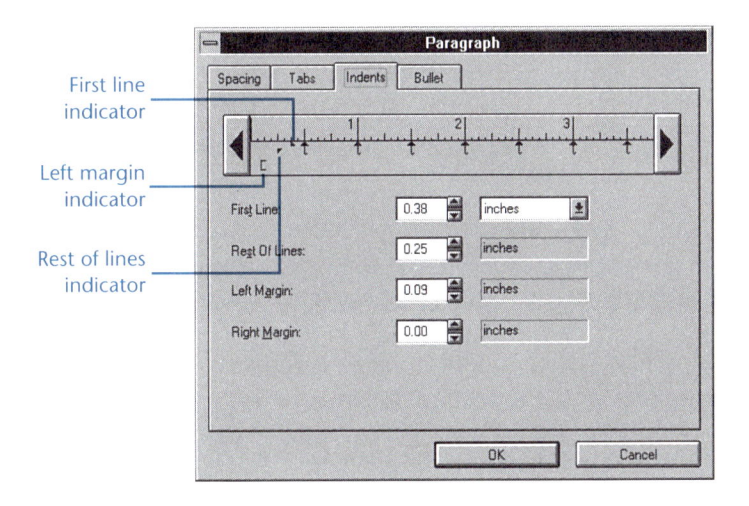

Fig. 7.10
The Paragraph/Indents dialog box enables you to set the indents and margins for Paragraph Text frames using the mouse or the keyboard.

The margin setting is established from the left edge of the Paragraph text frame, not the edge of the page, unless the two just happen to be the same. A zero margin setting places the text precisely on the frame edge.

CorelDRAW! measures indents from the margin location. So, first set the margins and then set the indents to provide consistency in Paragraph text formatting.

Think of a paragraph as two separate parts: the first line and the rest of the paragraph. You set the two parts separately by using their respective setting boxes. The right margin setting determines how closely the text tracks the right side of the text frame. In general, you set the left and right margins to the same number to achieve symmetry in the paragraph box.

> **Note**
>
> You can change the units of measure used for margins and indent by selecting a unit of measure from the drop-down list to the right of the First Line box.

You can set the indents and margins by dragging the indicators on the ruler. Dragging the margin indicator moves all the indents along with it. Moving the rest-of-lines indicator also moves the first-line indicator; moving the first-line indicator only affects its settings. You cannot move the rest-of-lines or first-line indicators to the left of the margin setting, although you can move the first-line indicator to the left of the rest-of-lines indicator to create a hanging indent.

Creating Bulleted Lists

▶ See "Adding a Graphic Symbol," p. 250

A *bulleted list* is a list of items (each usually no longer than one line) preceded by a single symbol known as a bullet. A bullet can take a variety of shapes. Most commonly, it's a black dot; sometimes it is square. You can use almost any CorelDRAW! symbol as a bullet.

If you do not specify a size for the bullet, CorelDRAW! automatically sizes it to match the text point size. In addition, you can specify the amount of indent desired for the bullet and the associated text. Some manipulation of these two values is required if the bullet extends beyond the ruler setting for the first line indent. Insert a paragraph mark (Enter) at the beginning of paragraphs that contain bullets. The Bullet Indent setting replaces the left margin setting when the bullets are activated by choosing **B**ullet On from the Paragraph/Bullet dialog box.

Follow these steps to create a bulleted list:

1. Enter the Paragraph text. Use a flush alignment and a paragraph return between each item in the list.

2. Open the **T**ext menu and choose **P**aragraph to display the Paragraph dialog box.

3. Click the Bullet tab at the top to display the dialog box shown in figure 7.11.

Working with Paragraph Text **225**

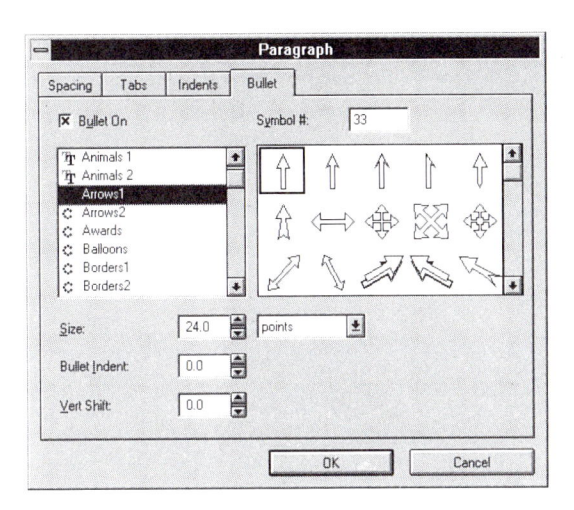

Fig. 7.11
Bulleted lists can be created using the Paragraph/Bullets dialog box and selecting the desired bullet and indents.

4. Click the box labeled **Bu**llet On.

5. Choose the symbol name that contains the specific bullet you want.

6. Select a bullet style from the symbol group displayed.

7. If necessary, make changes to the default values for point size, indentation, and vertical shift.

    Size is determined in points and defaults to the text size currently active. Bullet Indent is set in whatever units are displayed in the drop-down list (for example, points or inches). This dimensional setting affects all the settings made in the Paragraph/Bullets dialog box.

    The Bullet Indent setting replaces the Left Margin setting in the Indents dialog box, so you should set the drop-down list to points when you are setting the Size and set the list to page-relative units, such as inches, when setting the Bullet Indent. Either way, the setting always displays in page-related units on the Indents screen.

8. When finished, click OK.

Troubleshooting

When I type a large amount of Paragraph text, the last things I type in disappear from the frame.

Text frames do not expand to include all the text you type. To see all the text you typed, either make the type size smaller or make the frame larger.

(continues)

> (continued)
>
> *When I try to scale Paragraph text, the frame gets larger but the text remains the same size.*
>
> The handles on Paragraph text only affect the frame, not the characters. To change the size of Paragraph text characters, use the Text roll-up window or Character Attributes dialog box.
>
> *When I create a bulleted list, the text crowds the bullets.*
>
> In the Paragraph dialog box, set a left tab at about a distance appropriate to the bullet and text size you are using and the Rest of Lines setting to the same amount. Then, when editing text, insert a tab between each bullet and the first character of each bulleted line.

Working with Artistic and Paragraph Text

CorelDRAW! provides you with several text tools that can be used on both Paragraph and Artistic text. These tools enable you to import text from other applications, find and replace text, spell check text, and use a thesaurus. These tools help create professional, polished CorelDRAW! documents.

Importing Text

Tip

You also can paste text from the Clipboard. CorelDRAW! normally pastes text characters as Paragraph text.

You can bring text you created elsewhere into any CorelDRAW! drawing. CorelDRAW! recognizes a number of text formats, including ASCII, WordPerfect, Microsoft Word, and Ami Pro. Text you import with these file formats retains its tabs, indents, and other formatting information. Note that if a paragraph frame is not already defined, the imported text assumes that the entire page is the frame size and adjusts accordingly.

To import text using the File menu, follow these steps:

1. Open the **F**ile menu and choose **I**mport. The Import dialog box appears, enabling you to select the text file name and import format.

2. Choose the file format from the List Files of **T**ype box and choose the file name from the list.

3. Click OK. CorelDRAW! imports the text and displays it in a frame. The size of the frame is determined by the size of the current CorelDRAW! page. If the text takes up more than one page, additional pages are automatically added to the drawing.

Finding and Replacing Text

You can locate and/or change words or phrases in a block of Paragraph or Artistic text using the Find and Replace commands on the Text menu. You must first activate the appropriate text tool before you have access to these commands.

To find a word or phrase, follow these steps:

1. Select the Artistic or Paragraph text using the Text tool.

2. Open the **T**ext menu and choose **F**ind. The Find dialog box appears (see fig. 7.12).

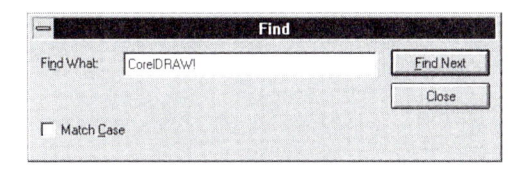

Fig. 7.12
Locating words in long passages of Paragraph text is made easy by entering the word into the Find What box and clicking **F**ind Next.

3. Type the text you want to find in the Fi**n**d What text box. (The maximum number of characters you can type is 100.)

4. If the case of the word or phrase is important, click the box labeled Match **C**ase.

5. Click **F**ind Next, and the search begins. When CorelDRAW! finds an occurrence of the word or phrase, it stops searching and highlights it.

6. To continue searching, click **F**ind Next again. To stop searching, click Cancel.

Tip
To find a word or phrase in upper- or lowercase letters, leave the Match Case box blank. Otherwise, CorelDRAW! finds only exact matches.

It is often useful to have CorelDRAW! find a word and automatically replace it with a new one. To find and replace a word or phrase, follow these steps:

1. Select the Artistic or Paragraph text.

2. Open the **T**ext menu and choose Repl**a**ce. The Replace dialog box appears (see fig. 7.13).

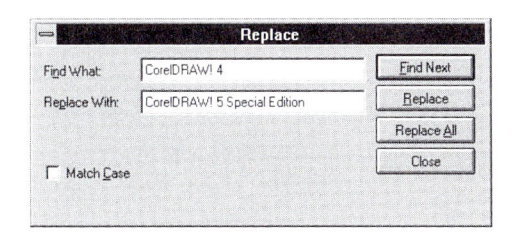

Fig. 7.13
The Replace dialog box enables you to replace single or multiple occurrences of a word automatically.

3. Type the text you want to replace in the Fi**n**d What text box.

4. Type the replacement text in the Re**p**lace With text box. A maximum of 100 characters can be typed in the Find What or Replace With boxes.

5. If the case of the word or phrase is important, click the box labeled Match **C**ase.

6. Choose **F**ind Next to go to the first occurrence of the word or phrase, which is highlighted on-screen.

Tip
Use the Esc key to cancel the replacement operation at any time. Use the Undo command to reverse the replacement immediately after you complete it.

7. Choose either **R**eplace to change this one occurrence or Replace **A**ll to have CorelDRAW! automatically find each additional match and make the replacement. If you choose Replace, CorelDRAW! stops at each occurrence and waits for you to confirm the replacement.

Using the Spelling Checker and Thesaurus

You can use the Spelling Checker to check a single word or a group of words, in either Paragraph or Artistic text, for spelling errors. The Thesaurus provides synonyms for individual words you select. Remember that a Spelling Checker checks only spelling and not grammar. If a word is spelled correctly, CorelDRAW!'s Spelling Checker lets it pass, even if it doesn't make sense (for example, *Merry had a little lamb*).

The Spelling Checker finds spelling errors, suggests corrections, and enables you to manually correct the error, automatically correct the error, or add the word to a supplemental dictionary. You can use the supplemental dictionary to add words to the Spelling Checker not normally found in a standard dictionary. It is particularly useful when you frequently use technical or unusual terms, such as those used in science or law or names of people.

Using the Spelling Checker

To check the spelling of a single word or a group of words, follow these steps:

1. Select the paragraph text, word, or group of words you want to check with the text cursor or Pick tool, respectively.

2. Open the **T**ext menu and choose Spell C**h**ecker. The Spell Check dialog box appears (see fig. 7.14).

3. Click **B**egin Check to begin the spell checking procedures. The Spelling Checker selects and displays in the Unknown Word box any incorrectly spelled words or words not in its dictionary.

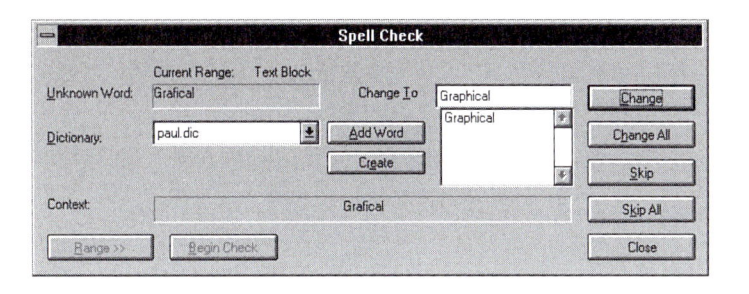

Fig. 7.14
With the Spell Check dialog box, you can check the spelling of any CorelDRAW! text, whether it's a single word or an entire newsletter.

4. CorelDRAW! suggests words that might be the correct spelling in the Change To box and the list below it.

5. If you want the Spelling Checker to replace the word in question with one of the suggested words, click the appropriate word and choose **C**hange, or double-click the properly spelled word from the list.

6. If you want the Spelling Checker to replace every occurrence of the misspelled word, select the desired replacement word from the list or type in the proper spelling and then choose C**h**ange All.

7. If you don't want to replace a word (it may be spelled correctly and CorelDRAW! doesn't have it in its dictionary, or it may be incorrect and neither you nor CorelDRAW! has the correct spelling), choose **S**kip. To ignore every occurrence of the same unknown or misspelled word, choose S**k**ip All.

8. If you often use special words that CorelDRAW! does not find (such as technical or medical terms or names of people or places), you probably do not want CorelDRAW! to flag them as misspelled at every occurrence. To create a personal dictionary to hold the spelling of people's names and other unusually spelled words, click Cr**e**ate and then type the desired name of the dictionary. In figure 7.14, the dictionary name is PAUL. CorelDRAW! creates the paul.dic file to hold the personal spelling dictionary. You can only create a new personal dictionary after you've begun the spell check.

9. To add a word to your personal dictionary, choose **A**dd Word when the Spelling Checker lists it in the Unknown Word box.

10. When CorelDRAW! completes the spelling check, click OK in the message box that appears. To stop the spelling check before CorelDRAW! finishes, choose Close from the Spell Check dialog box at any time. Remember to load your personal dictionary before you run the spell checker next time.

Finding a Synonym

The Thesaurus provides words with similar meanings to the word in question. To find a synonym for a word, follow these steps:

1. Select the word that you want to check with the appropriate text tool.

2. Open the **T**ext menu and choose Thes**au**rus to display the Thesaurus dialog box (see fig. 7.15).

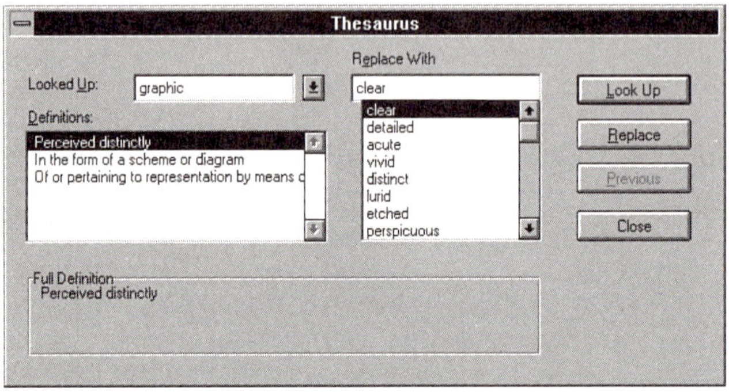

Fig. 7.15
The Thesaurus dialog box provides a quick and easy way to find synonyms and even look up definitions of words in your CorelDRAW! drawings.

3. If CorelDRAW! does not display any information in the Definitions box, click the **L**ook Up button. One or more definitions usually appear in the Definitions list box. Synonyms for the highlighted definition of the word appear in the Replace With list box.

4. If you want to see synonyms for any of the other definitions, select the definition and check out its associated synonyms.

5. When you select one of the synonyms, it appears in the Replace With box.

6. To replace the word you searched for with the selected synonym, choose **R**eplace. If you don't find a word you want to use as a replacement, click Close.

Tip
The Thesaurus also provides a brief dictionary. If you are trying to determine the meaning of a word, simply type it in and use the thesaurus to find the definition.

Troubleshooting

When I try to find a particular word in a block of text by using the Find dialog box, nothing happens when I press Find Next.

Make sure that you have selected the text using the Text tool or Pick tool before opening the Find dialog box.

> *When I paste text from another application using the Clipboard, it is placed on the drawing as a "Document Object" and I am unable to edit the text.*
>
> When you import text via the Clipboard, make sure that you have selected the Text tool (either Artistic or Paragraph) and click a location on-screen or create a text frame, just as you would to type in text. Then paste from the Clipboard as you normally would.

Using Type Assist

In addition to the standard Spell Checker and Thesaurus, CorelDRAW! 5 now includes Type Assist. Type Assist can automatically capitalize certain words, insert words for shorthand abbreviations, and change straight quotes to typographical quotes as you type the text.

To activate Type Assist, follow these steps:

1. Select your empty or non-empty paragraph text box with the pick tool, or choose the Paragraph or Artistic Text tools and set your insertion point. Open the **T**ext menu and choose Typ**e** Assist. The Type Assist dialog box opens (see fig. 7.16).

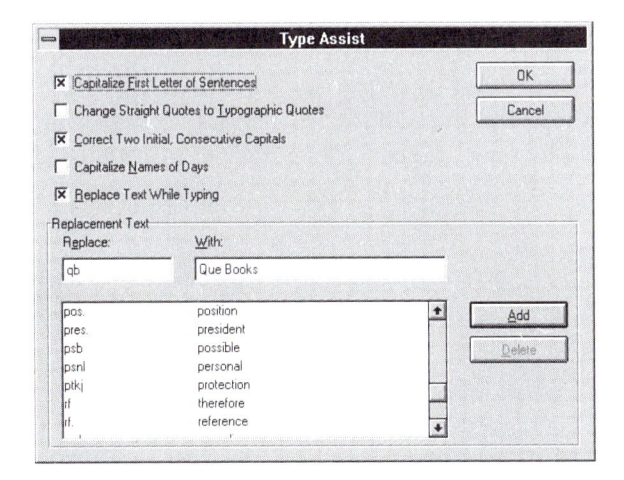

Fig. 7.16
The Type Assist dialog box allows you to set options to have CorelDRAW! automatically edit your text as you type it.

2. Set the options that you want by clicking the appropriate check boxes.

   - *Capitalize **F**irst Letter of Sentences* makes CorelDRAW! automatically capitalize the first letter following a period, exclamation mark, or question mark.

- *Change Straight Quotes to **T**ypographic Quotes* makes quotations turn in at both ends of a quotation instead of turning both in the same direction.

- ***C**orrect Two Initial, Consecutive Capitals* automatically fixes the capitalization any time you type a word such as "David or USA." If you type U.S.A., it will not be corrected.

- *Capitalize **N**ames of Days* makes sure that all the days of the week are capitalized.

- ***R**eplace Text While Typing* converts abbreviations to full words. CorelDRAW! has a number of built-in replacements and you can add your own.

3. Press OK. CorelDRAW! now performs the options you set.

To add your own replacement text pairs, follow these steps:

1. Open the **T**ext menu and choose Typ**e** Assist. The Type Assist dialog box opens.

2. Type the abbreviation text in R**e**place box (for example, **qb**).

3. Type the text you want to replace it with in the **W**ith box (for example, **Que Books**.)

4. Press **A**dd. The pair of words is added to the Replacement Text list.

5. Press OK to accept the addition and return to your drawing. Now every time you type "**qb**," CorelDRAW! replaces it with Que Books.

Troubleshooting

When I type the word "oh" (as in, "oh, my!") in a sentence, it is replaced with the word Ohio. How do I get just the word "oh"?

You have Replace Text While Typing activated and the word "Ohio" has been set up to replace "oh." Change the abbreviation used for Ohio to a combination of letters that does not form a word that might be typed. You could use OH instead to be replaced by Ohio if you didn't turn on the option for Correct Two Initial, Consecutive Capitals.

I type a lot of text that includes measurements in it. When I type two sets of numbers in inches (such as 15" and 20"), the first quotation mark gets turned backwards.

Turn off Change Straight Quotes to Typographic Quotes in the Type Assist dialog box.

Working with Text Frame

You often want more than one column for your Paragraph text, especially when laying out newsletters and promotional literature. You also might want to define different styles for the frame outlining the text and for the way text aligns itself around objects that lie within the frame. These important desktop publishing capabilities are the topic of this section.

Setting Column Numbers and Gutter Width

CorelDRAW! enables you to define up to eight columns within a Paragraph text box. You also can define the distance between columns, called the *gutter*. Although you can define the width of individual columns in the units most appropriate to your situation, the gutter width is always defined in inches. You set these items within the Frame Attributes dialog box, which you can access by opening the **T**ext menu and choosing **F**rame, or by choosing Frame from the Text roll-up window.

To set the number of columns and the gutter width, follow these steps:

1. Use the Pick tool to select the frame containing the text you want in columns.

2. Open the Frame Attributes dialog box as described earlier (see fig. 7.17).

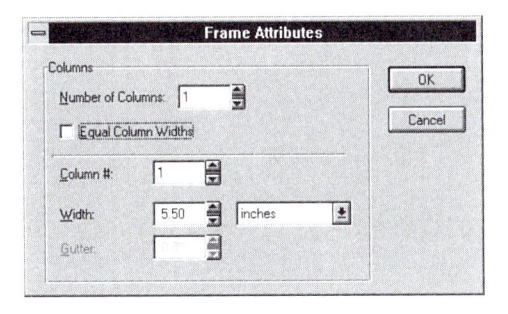

Fig. 7.17

The Frame Attributes dialog box allows you to create multiple columns of text within one text frame.

3. Set the attributes you want:

   In the **N**umber of Columns box, enter the number of columns.

   If you want all columns to be the same width, make sure that an x is in the **E**qual Column Widths box.

   Set the column width in the **W**idth box. If the columns aren't all the same width, select the column you want to work with in the **C**olumn # box and set its width.

Set the distance between columns in the **G**utter box.

Click a unit of measurement from the drop-down list by clicking the down arrow if the current measurement isn't the one you want to work in.

4. Click OK. CorelDRAW! reformats the image text with the number of columns and the gutter width you selected.

> **Note**
>
> Beware that the indents, margins, and tabs you set in the Text Paragraph dialog box apply to each column as though it is a separate document page. You probably need to set the margins, indents, and tabs to meet your layout needs after you define the desired column widths and gutters. If the display does not match what you expect, check these settings before becoming discouraged.

Once text is set in columns, you can edit it as you would any other Paragraph text. As you add or delete new text, the characters wrap from one column to the next.

Creating Text Frame Envelopes

▶ See "Enveloping Text," p. 435

You can use the Envelope feature to wrap Paragraph text around an object. To create a text frame envelope, follow these steps:

1. Select the text frame.

2. Open the Effe**c**ts menu and choose **E**nvelope Roll-Up (see fig. 7.18).

Fig. 7.18
The Envelope roll-up window is used for the creation of text wrapping around images and oddly shaped text frames.

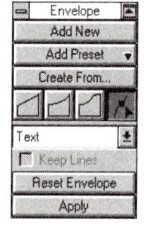

3. Click Add New from within the roll-up window.

4. Shape the envelope as needed. Notice that the envelope type selected is Text, which happens automatically when an envelope is applied to Paragraph text.

5. Click Apply. The text conforms to the new envelope shape (see fig. 7.19). However, results may not always be what you hoped for.

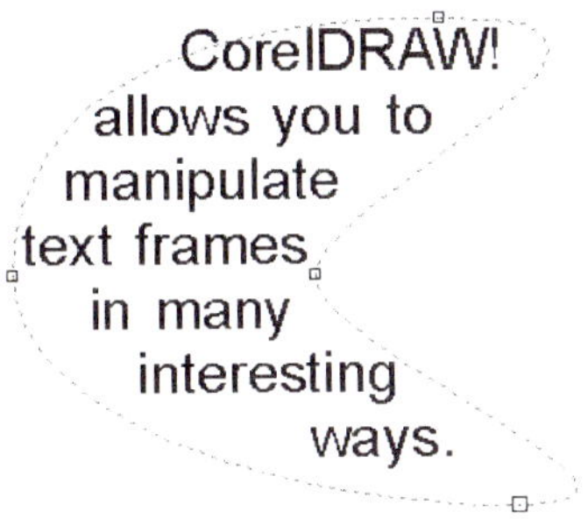

> CorelDRAW!
> allows you to
> manipulate
> text frames
> in many
> interesting
> ways.

Fig. 7.19
Text can be put into almost any shaped envelope as long as the letters themselves can fit into the shape.

Remember that you can make the envelope as complicated as needed to shape around objects or create interesting shapes by adding nodes and Bézier control points.

◀ See "Reshaping a Curve or Object by Changing Its Nodes and Control Points," p. 72

Flowing Paragraph Text between Frames

When you use desktop publishing, having a passage begin in one frame and end in another is common. To make using multiple frames easier, CorelDRAW! provides a way of linking the frames to make the text flow naturally from one frame to another. If the dimensions or characteristics of one frame change, the text in the other(s) automatically adjusts to accommodate the change.

Documents are linked via the hollow box that appears at the top or bottom of the text frame. The hollow box often appears at the top of the frame, meaning that the frame is linked from the top to previous text in the document. You can link from top to bottom or bottom to top between text frames, as long as the box is hollow before linking. In general, you start the text in an initial frame and link from that frame's bottom hollow box to the top of the next frame to contain text. The subsequent frames, because they are linked together, can be on different pages of the document.

Tip
The + in the box indicates that the frame is linked from that point to another frame within the active document.

To create linked frames on the same or different pages, follow these steps:

1. Create the first frame of Paragraph text and select the text frame with the Pick tool.

2. Click the hollow box at the bottom (top) of the frame. The cursor changes to a Paragraph Text icon with an arrow.

3. Move the new cursor to the desired location of the second frame and drag another Paragraph text frame.

When you finish, CorelDRAW! creates a link between the two text frames and continues to flow (display) the text to the top of the new frame. You can repeat this procedure as many times as needed until the entire story flows between text frames (or pages) the way you want.

If you change the size of the text, frame, or other components related to the text involved, the passage automatically adjusts itself within the frames to accommodate the changes.

If you click anywhere on the page after selecting the hollow box on the first frame, CorelDRAW! creates a text box that takes up the whole page and inserts the Paragraph text into that frame. You can now shape and size this frame as needed. If you click an existing text frame after selecting the hollow box, CorelDRAW! flows the text into that frame. It is best to link to new frames not linked to other frames; but you can link to a frame with existing linked text as long as you link-in from a direction containing a hollow box, and a + isn't present.

The text may display in strange ways, or not at all, when linked to a prior frame. This situation is generally a result of the margin setting for the text frame being too large for the frame size itself so there is no room for the text. Use the Text Paragraph Indent dialog box to set the margins to reasonable sizes for the text frame in use. Right/Left Margins and Other Lines at 0.25" and First Line at 0.33" are good starting points.

In addition, you can change the text attributes for the entire story that flows between the frames by first selecting the text in a frame and then applying the changes. The text roll-up has options for applying attribute changes to all frames, this frame, or rest of frames.

You can remove text from a frame, which causes the removed text not to flow into the remaining frames. To remove the text, select the frame with the Pick tool; open the **A**rrange menu and then click **S**eparate. The text within the frame is removed, and the balance of the text flows into the remaining linked frames.

▶ See "Multipage Document Fundamentals," p. 542

The procedure for flowing text between pages is the same except that you move to the destination page before dragging the second frame. To move between pages in a document, open the **L**ayout menu and choose **G**o To Page and then enter the desired page number and press OK.

Using Styles and Templates

CorelDRAW!'s Style option enables you to save many of the formatting characteristics of text you created as a style and apply them to other pieces of text. A *style* is a subdivision of a template; CorelDRAW! differentiates between them by regarding a *template* as a collection of styles. You can create a text style from Paragraph or Artistic text. Styles make working with objects and text much more efficient while providing a consistency between objects that makes your drawings look more professional. This section explains how to create and apply styles and templates.

Saving a New Style

After you create text with a set of attributes that you want to use again, follow these steps to save those attributes as a style:

1. Select the text with the characteristics you want to use.
2. Click the object with the secondary mouse button to call up the Object menu. You must have the Mouse Second button in the Preferences dialog box set to Object Menu for this to work.
3. Select Save As Style from the menu. The Save Style As dialog box appears.
4. Select the characteristics you want to save from the selected text.
5. Type a name for the style.
6. Click OK.

▶ See "Customizing the Mouse," p. 564

Tip
Make the style's name descriptive so that later you will know what it does.

Saving Multiple Styles as a Template

You may find that you have a number of styles that are appropriate for one type of drawing, but not for another. You can organize styles into *templates*, which contain a number of related styles.

To create a style template, follow these steps:

1. Open the **L**ayout menu and choose S**t**yle Roll-Up. The Styles roll-up window appears.
2. Click the black arrow to display the Styles pull-down menu (see fig. 7.20).
3. Click Save Template to display the Save Template dialog box.
4. Accept the default file name or type a different name.
5. Click OK. The dialog box closes, but the roll-up window remains.

Tip
Organize your styles within templates so that you only have to use one template per document; save a style in all the different templates you want to use it with.

Fig. 7.20
Sets of attributes such as outline width and color, fill type, and typeface can be saved using the Styles pull-down menu and applied to almost any CorelDRAW! object.

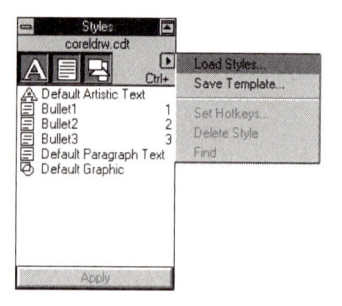

> **Note**
>
> The default extension for a template file is CDT, and the default CorelDRAW! template is CORELDRW.CDT. It is a good idea to create a new template instead of modifying the default template in case something goes wrong with your template modification process.

Applying a Style to a Piece of Text

Now that you have saved a particular style, you need to know how to apply it to unformatted text. Follow these steps to apply a style from the library of available templates:

1. Select the text whose characteristics you want to change to those of a saved style.

2. Open the **L**ayout menu and choose S**t**yle Roll-Up. The Styles roll-up window appears.

3. Click the right-arrow button and choose Load Styles. Pick the desired template and click OK.

4. Select the desired style name from the list.

5. Click Apply to apply the style to the selected text item. Pressing the Enter key has the same result as clicking Apply.

> **Troubleshooting**
>
> *When I create a frame with multiple columns, it ends up being twice as wide as when it started.*
>
> CorelDRAW! automatically sets each column to be the width of the original text frame. To keep this from happening, reset the column width before you press OK.
>
> *When I create a Text Frame Envelope, sometimes the text goes outside the envelope.*
>
> Enveloping text is based on the location of the character handles on the baseline, not the overall characters. You may have to adjust the envelope slightly to have it move characters in just the way you want.

Using Text Artistically

Text doesn't have to remain simply text. After being created or imported, text can be manipulated in much the same way as any CorelDRAW! object. Options include rotating or skewing both Artistic and Paragraph text and fitting Artistic text to a path or baseline. You also can copy the attributes of one text string to another text string.

Scaling, Rotating, and Skewing Text

Paragraph and Artistic text can be scaled, rotated, or skewed horizontally or vertically. You can perform these transformations by using the menu commands or the mouse. This section presents commands that use the mouse. The procedure for rotating and skewing text is identical to that used to rotate and skew objects. This topic is covered in great detail in Chapter 6, "Scaling, Rotating, and Distorting Objects."

To *scale* text objects, simply click an already selected text object to reveal the small solid black scaling handles. Place the cursor on the scaling handle and wait until the cursor changes to cross hairs. Dragging the corner handles scales the object evenly in both the horizontal and vertical directions.

Dragging the handles along the sides of the object scales the text in the horizontal direction (*stretch*). Dragging the handles in the middle of the top and bottom scales the object vertically. Notice that the point size displayed on the status line changes with the scaling operation.

Double-clicking a text object reveals the rotation and skewing arrows. Dragging on the rounded arrows in the corners of the object rotates the object either clockwise or counter-clockwise (see fig. 7.21). You also can move the

Tip

The application of various artistic effects may require some trial and error. You can use the Undo command to remove any unwanted effects up to the number of undo levels you define in Preferences. Remember, the key word is *experiment*.

240 Chapter 7—Adding Text to a Drawing

bull's-eye to the desired rotation center point just as you can with any other CorelDRAW! object.

Fig. 7.21
Text can be rotated clockwise or counter-clockwise using the mouse or the Transform roll-up window.

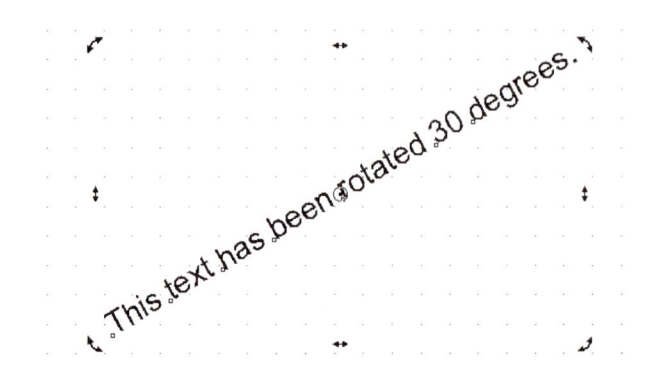

This text has been rotated 30 degrees.

Dragging on the double arrows skews the object either horizontally or vertically (see fig. 7.22). Hold down Ctrl while dragging to constrain the rotation or skewing to a predefined angle increment.

Fig. 7.22
Text can be skewed to the right or left and up or down using the mouse or the Transform roll-up menu.

This text has been skewed 30 degrees.

Fitting Text to a Path

A *path* is any line you select, define, or create in your drawing. The path even can be another object or letter converted into curves. Only Artistic text can be fit to a path.

To fit Artistic text to a path, follow these steps:

1. Select the piece of text and the line you want it to follow. (Hold down Shift to select more than one item in the drawing.)

2. Open the **T**ext menu and click Fit **T**ext to Path. A roll-up window opens, showing you two fit alignment options (see fig. 7.23). The alignment options are listed in figures 7.24 through 7.27.

3. If you want more precise modifications of the horizontal offset of the text and its distance from the path, click Edit to display the Fit Text to Path Offsets dialog box (see fig. 7.28). Click OK to return to the Fit Text to Path roll-up window after you make the modifications.

4. Click Apply to fit the text to the path (see fig. 7.29).

Using Text Artistically   241

[Figure with labels: Vertical alignment options, Text arrangement options, Horizontal alignment options — Fit Text To Path roll-up, with sample "This text will be fit to a path"]

Fig. 7.23
The Fit Text to Path roll-up window provides all the options required to fit any piece of Artistic text to a curve or object.

[Figure with labels: Text perpendicular to path, Text vertical and skewed horizontally, Text vertical and skewed vertically, Text always vertical]

Fig. 7.24
The four different ways in which individual letters can be aligned to a curve when text is fit to a path.

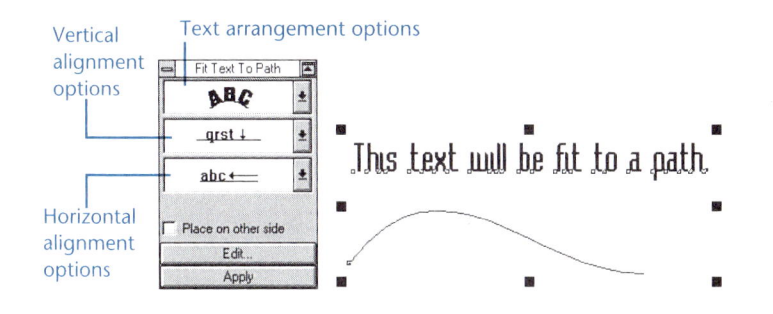

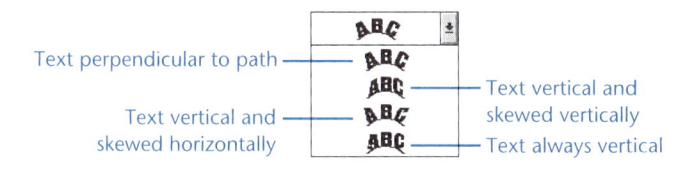

The options in the Fit Text to Path dialog box are as follows:

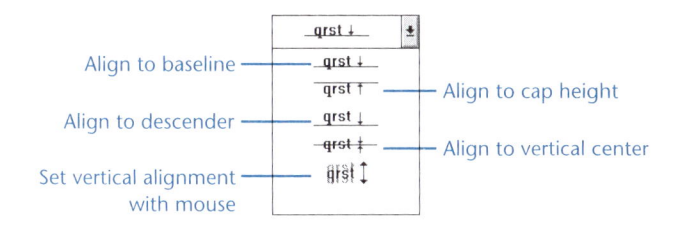

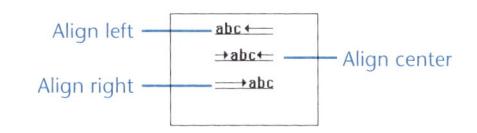

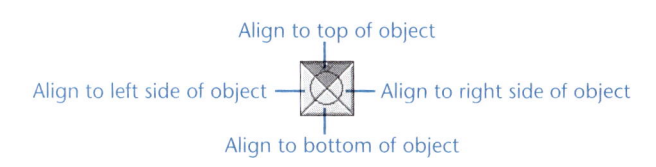

[Figure with labels: Align to baseline, Align to descender, Set vertical alignment with mouse, Align to cap height, Align to vertical center]

Fig. 7.25
The Vertical alignment options allow you to specify what part of the letters will be lined up to the path.

[Figure with labels: Align left, Align right, Align center]

Fig. 7.26
As with any text string, text that has been fit to a path can be aligned to the left, center, or right.

[Figure with labels: Align to top of object, Align to left side of object, Align to right side of object, Align to bottom of object]

Fig. 7.27
When fitting text to an ellipse or rectangle, use the four quadrants to determine how the text will align.

Fig. 7.28
The Fit Text to Path Offsets dialog box sets text a precise distance from the curve or object to which it is being aligned.

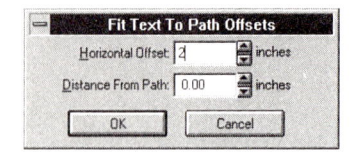

Press Ctrl while clicking the text to separate it from the path-text group and then press Ctrl+T; or open the **T**ext menu and click Edit Te**x**t to edit the contents of the text string. If you want to fit the text to a path that was previously a letter, you must first convert the letter to curves and then fit the text to the path of the letter's outline. You may want to remove the text character path's thickness or color to make it invisible.

◀ See "Creating a Non-Printing Outline," p. 144

Note

If you edit the control curve to which you aligned the text, the text is automatically updated to follow the new curve. To keep the curve in your drawing without having it print, set its outline to none. You can then edit it in Wireframe mode.

Fig. 7.29
Once all the options have been set, press Enter to fit text to a path.

Putting Text on the Opposite Side of the Line

If you want the text to appear on the opposite side of the line to which it is attached, follow these steps:

1. Select the text and the path to which it will be aligned.

2. Open the **T**ext menu and click Fit **T**ext to Path. The Fit Text to Path roll-up window appears.

3. Click the Place On Other Side box.

4. Click Apply.

Separating Text from a Path

Editing the nodes of the path automatically alters the path of the text. It is often advantageous to break this link so that you can use the curve for other purposes in the drawing. To separate text from a path, follow these steps:

1. Select the text.
2. Open the **A**rrange menu and click **S**eparate.

The text is now separated from the curve, which can be altered without affecting the text.

To restore text to straight line, open the **T**ext menu and click **S**traighten Text.

Modifying an Individual Character's Attributes

You can modify almost every aspect of an individual character in a longer text string by using the Shape tool rather than the Pick or Text tools. After the text is selected with the Shape tool, small squares appear at the bottom left of each character (see fig. 7.30). You use these squares to select an individual character or a group of characters using either the marquee select or Shift-click selection procedures with the Shape tool.

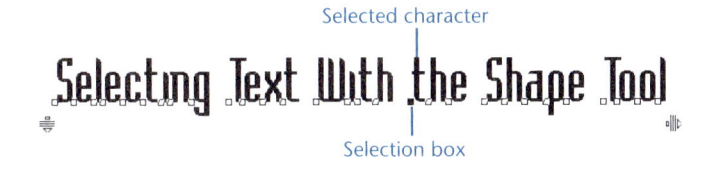

Selected character

Selecting Text With the Shape Tool

Selection box

Fig. 7.30
Individual and multiple letters can be selected using the Shape tool. The attributes of these letters can then be altered using any of the standard text editing techniques.

Double-clicking any of the character boxes opens the Character Attributes dialog box, which is used to set the attributes associated with this particular character (see fig. 7.31). The character retains its text status, but is modified in accordance with this screen's settings.

- *Font Size* and *Style* of this particular character are set just as with prior screens.

- *Placement* options include normal, superscript, and subscript.

- *Horizontal Shift* and *Vertical Shift* settings define a percentage of an *em shift* you want for this particular character with respect to the others. An em shift is the width and height of a capital letter M for the text's typeface.

- *Angle* enables you to define a rotation for the character that does not affect the other characters in the text string.

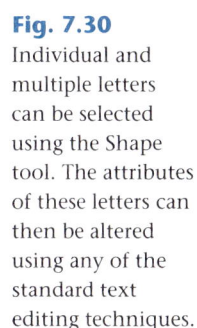

Fig. 7.31
The attributes of single or multiple letters can be set using the Character Attributes dialog box without affecting the other characters in a text string.

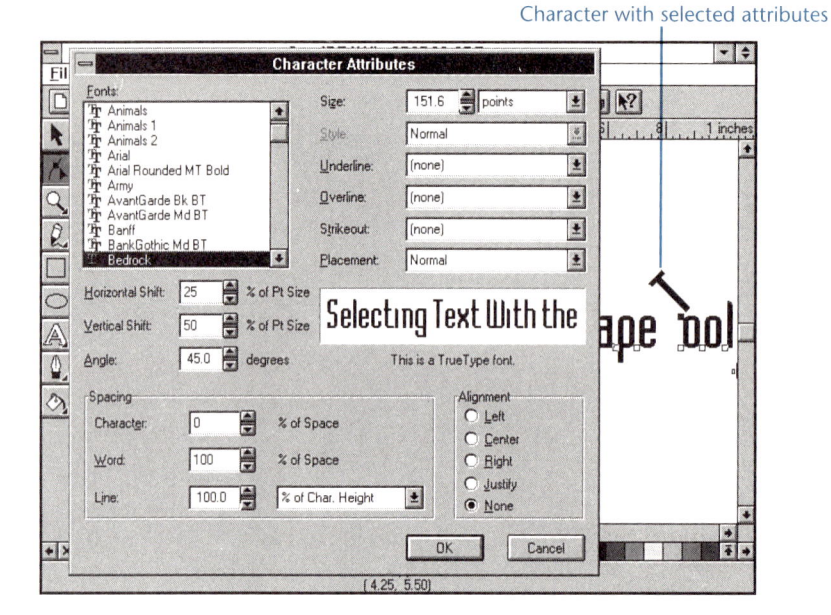

Straightening Text and Aligning to a Baseline

After you modify text by using the Shape tool, you may need to straighten it back to how it was before you applied the modifications. To straighten text, use one of the following two methods:

- Select text on a path. Open the Arrange menu and choose Separate. Select the text with the Shape tool; then open the **T**ext menu and click **S**traighten Text to straighten the selected text and remove any horizontal, vertical, and angular changes.

- Select text on a path. Open the Arrange menu and choose Separate. Select the text; then open the **T**ext menu and click Align to Base**l**ine to remove all vertical shifts applied to the characters. Leave all other transformations in place. This option is useful for lining characters along a common line from which they can be rotated or moved horizontally.

Copying Attributes from One Text String to Another

You can copy the attributes you assigned to a selected string of text to another string. To copy the attributes, follow these steps:

1. Select the text you want to update.

2. Open the **E**dit menu and click Copy Attributes **F**rom. The Copy Style dialog box appears. Several options are available for copying: Outline Pen and Outline Color, Fill, and Text Attributes.

3. Select the attributes you want to copy.

4. Click OK. The From? cursor appears on-screen.

5. Select the text from which you want to copy the attributes. CorelDRAW! applies the attributes you selected earlier to the target text.

Troubleshooting

When I try to select individual characters to change their typeface, none of the letters get selected.

Make sure that the text is not part of a group. If it is, select it as a child object. If it is not, you may find it easier to select the text with the Shape tool and drag a marquee box around the node points to the left of the characters you want to change. The nodes will fill in black to show that they have been selected.

When I change the spacing on individual letters using the Shape tool, I can't keep them in line with the other letters.

While you are dragging the letters, press the Ctrl key to constrain the letters to the baseline of the other letters.

The top of text that has been fit to a path gets all bunched up at some points.

The default method for having individual letters fit a curve is for them to always be perpendicular to the path. This can cause this problem when the path has a tight curve. Either pick one of the other methods of alignment or change the path so that it does not have quite so tight a curve.

Understanding Advanced Text Design

You may find yourself creating original copy in CorelDRAW! that you want to transfer to another word processor for more extensive editing. After you edit the text in the word processor, you can bring the file back into CorelDRAW!. The procedure is simple, but it requires that you adhere to certain rules. This section introduces you to these rules and the basic text transfer procedures.

Text created in CorelDRAW! can be extracted, or removed from CorelDRAW!, into a separate ASCII text file that you can access and edit using a standard word processing application, such as Word for Windows or the Windows Notepad. You can return the edited ASCII text file to your drawing using the Merge Back option in the Special menu.

> **Note**
>
> Do not erase any codes inserted as part of the extraction process because CorelDRAW! does not know what to do with the file when it attempts to use Merge Back unless those codes are present.

Extracting Text

To extract a piece of text, follow these steps:

1. Select the text.

2. Open the **S**pecial menu and click E**x**tract. If you made modifications to the drawing since the last time you saved, CorelDRAW! prompts you to save your drawing before displaying the Extract dialog box.

   After you save the drawing, CorelDRAW! displays the Extract dialog box.

3. Enter save options as appropriate (file name and/or file path).

4. Click OK.

Tip
Using the file name that CorelDRAW! suggests is a good idea because it is the same name as the drawing, with a TXT extension rather than a CDR extension. This naming process makes it easier for you to determine which extracted text file goes with your drawings.

Editing Extracted Text

You can edit the extracted text with many ASCII-capable word processing programs. You must be very careful not to alter any of the contents except for the text. Altering other characters in the file can have dire consequences that affect the Merge Back procedure.

For example, the first line encodes the CorelDRAW! file from which the text was extracted, and the <CDR> at the end represents the end of the file (see fig. 7.32). Removing either of these precludes the Merge Back operation.

After you finish editing the file, you can close it and merge the contents back into your drawing. You must close the edited text file before merging it back into CorelDRAW! because a datafile cannot be used by two programs at the same time.

Restoring (Merging Back) Text

After the text is edited, open the **S**pecial menu and click Merge Bac**k** to insert the text back into its original file location. Select or enter the name and path of the text file you want to bring back. The file is restored and any changes made to the file while in the word processor are made to the text in the drawing. Note that text may only be merged back into the drawing from which it was extracted.

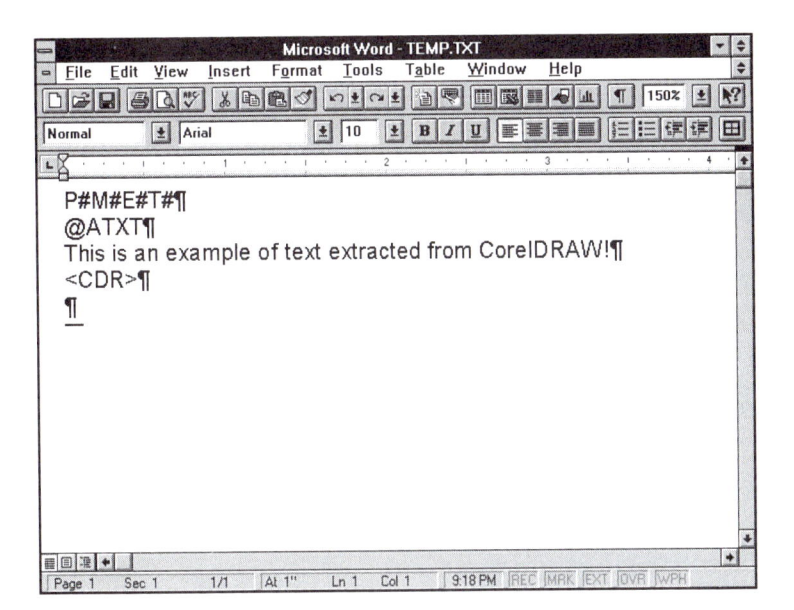

Fig. 7.32
CorelDRAW! text can be edited using any word processing program, including Word for Windows, the Windows Notepad, and many others.

Troubleshooting

I have grouped some objects, including text, in my drawing and now CorelDRAW! won't let me merge back my text file.

Grouping and changing the relative levels of text objects can adversely affect the way CorelDRAW! lets you merge back text. Whenever possible, do not change a CorelDRAW! file between when you extract text and when you merge it back.

When I edit an extracted text file, all the text from the drawing is included. How do I find the correct section of text to edit?

The extracted text file has text in order of its relative level: text at the top level is at the beginning of the text file, while text at lower levels are further on in the file. In simple drawings, this order corresponds to the order in which you created it with the most recently created text at the beginning of the file and the oldest text at the end.

I merged edited text back into a drawing and some of the character attributes have changed.

If you have modified the attributes of individual characters in a text string, only those characters that precede any changed text in the text string will be merged back with their formatting intact.

From Here...

If you are familiar with the features found in most word processors, you shouldn't have much trouble with Corel's text functions. With CorelDRAW!, you can choose the text spacing, alignment, fill, outine characteristics, typeface, point size, and style. You can create a bulleted list, control the spacing between words, characters, lines and paragraphs, as well as impose standard word processing features like tabs, indentation, and automatic hyphenation. CorelDRAW! also provides a spell checker and thesaurus.

- Chapter 8, "Advanced Text Techniques," deals further with using text as artistic objects, including creating your own typefaces and altering existing ones.

- Chapter 15, "Creating Special Effects with Envelope," teaches you techniques that can help you use Paragraph text envelopes and add further artistic flair to your drawings.

- Chapter 23, "Multipage Documents and the Object Data Manager," discusses how to deal with longer documents and works with the information you just learned about flowing text between different frames that may span these pages.

Chapter 8
Advanced Text Techniques

by Paul Bodensiek

CorelDRAW!'s text handling features don't stop at simply working with text as text. Text can be manipulated by CorelDRAW!'s full battery of artistic tools. In addition, you can use CorelDRAW! to create custom TrueType and Adobe Type 1 typefaces for use with any Windows program. The Adobe Type 1 fonts can also be used by any DOS program that supports them.

In this chapter, you learn how to do the following:

- Convert text to curves
- Work with graphic symbols
- Enter special text characters
- Create a custom typeface

Converting Text Characters to Curved Objects for Shaping

To control the shape of the characters in a string of artistic text, you must convert artistic text to curves so that the object nodes can be modified. You cannot convert paragraph text to curves. Many dramatic effects achieved with CorelDRAW! are accomplished by entering the artistic text, selecting a font that closely matches the final design, and then converting the text to curves for final design.

◀ See "Reshaping a Curve or Object by Changing Its Nodes and Control Points," p. 72

After CorelDRAW! converts text to curves, it loses its text attributes and becomes a series of combined objects.

To convert the text, follow these steps:

1. Select the text using the Pick tool.

2. Open the **A**rrange menu and choose the Con**v**ert To Curves option (Ctrl+Q). The text is no longer treated as text but as a combination of graphic objects.

3. To work on individual letters in the string, open the **A**rrange menu and choose Brea**k** Apart.

You can now work on each letter with the Shape or Pick tool as if each letter were a separate object. Remember, the objects are no longer text characters, even though they look the same as before. They're artistic objects that happen to look like text. You can have fun with this feature.

Tip
The spelling and content of your text must be accurate before you convert that text to curve, because you can't go back except by using Undo.

> **Troubleshooting**
>
> *After text has been converted to curves and broken apart, letters like "b" get all filled in.*
>
> Letters with holes in them will break apart into two or more objects because the letters are made up of more than one closed path. After you've broken a text string apart, combine the various parts of individual letters together to retain the "holes" in them.

Adding a Graphic Symbol

CorelDRAW! comes with thousands of symbols that can be used as simple drawing accents or as starting points for more complicated drawings. To add a symbol to an image, follow these steps:

1. Open the **S**pecial menu and choose Sym**b**ols Roll-Up (Ctrl+F11) (see fig. 8.1).

2. Select the symbol group you want to work with from the drop-down list at the top of the roll-up menu.

3. Select the individual symbol you want from the preview box. You can see more symbols using the scroll bar.

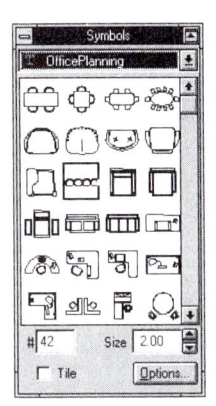

Fig. 8.1
The Symbols Roll-Up Menu allows you to choose from literally hundreds of different symbols to be used in your drawings.

4. Click a symbol and drag it onto the drawing page to include it in your drawing. You can treat the symbol just as you treat any other object.

You can set the initial size of the symbol by entering a number (in inches) in the Size box in the Symbols roll-up window or by using the arrows at its right.

The symbol number is shown at the bottom left of the dialog box. If you know the symbol number, enter it into this box, and CorelDRAW! finds it for you.

The Tile option is used to duplicate the symbol in both a horizontal and vertical direction across the screen (see fig. 8.2).

Clicking the Options button reveals the Tile dialog box, in which you can set the size of the grid the tiled symbols are aligned along. Set these values to the number of inches between each symbol grid line. Make sure that these numbers are larger than the symbol size, or you may get overlap between the symbols when they tile on the page. Selecting Proportional makes the horizontal and vertical number of tiles equal, meaning that you only need to define one number and the other automatically changes with it.

> **Note**
>
> You can make interesting wallpaper (desktop pattern) for Windows with this function. Export your drawing in a BMP file format to the Windows directory. You can also create a small pattern and allow Windows to do the tiling itself by setting the Tile radio button in the Desktop control panel.

Fig. 8.2
Tiling a symbol automatically repeats it in both the horizontal and vertical directions across the screen.

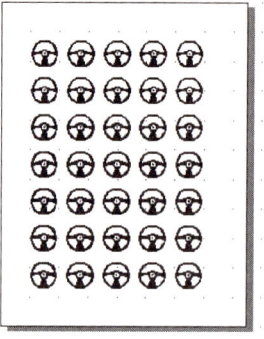

Adding a Special Character

You can add special ASCII characters, such as the copyright and registered trademark symbols, to your text by following these steps:

◀ See "Adding Artistic Text," p. 212

◀ See "Adding Paragraph Text," p. 218

1. Click the text string with the cursor in the place where you want the special character to appear.

2. Press Alt and the ASCII code number for the special character using the keypad, remembering to precede the number with a zero. (For example, Alt+0169 is the copyright symbol.)

3. Release Alt to insert the special character. (A full list of the extended character set is included in Appendix B.)

Troubleshooting

The chart in the DOS manual shows a set of ASCII characters that have only three numbers to fill in instead of four.

When working with CorelDRAW!, all character codes begin with 0. Numbers over 99 have four digits instead of three in DOS (i.e. 0101 instead of 101). Appendix B contains a listing of the character codes for a typical typeface.

I entered text with special characters. They looked fine, but when I changed the typeface, the special characters changed.

Different typefaces use different numbering for special characters and not all typefaces contain the same characters. If in doubt, check with the manufacturer of the font for information on the available special characters.

Working with Typefaces

Adobe Type Manager, Bitstream's FaceLift (a popular set of fonts available separately for Windows applications), TrueType, and the CorelDRAW! WFN fonts are all different from each other. For this reason, the CorelDRAW! font names do not match those of any other typeface. (A simpler reason for this is that typefaces are copyrighted and royalties must be paid for their use. Corel, as well as other software vendors, is able to avoid this requirement by creating their own slightly different version of a popular typeface.)

◀ See "Understanding the Fundamentals of Text Design," p. 208

The CD version of CorelDRAW! provides over 750 different fonts in both TrueType and Adobe Type I (PFB) designs. You are encouraged to work with the TrueType or WFN font designs until you are well-acquainted with the font-related intricacies, at which time you may want to design your own. Until you become very advanced, you may find that everything you want to do can be accomplished with the standard fonts provided.

About TrueType Fonts

Microsoft Windows provides a built-in set of fonts known as TrueType. These fonts are available to any Windows application. Use these TrueType fonts to best ensure that when printed, the text will appear as it does on-screen, also known as WYSIWYG ("what you see is what you get"). In addition, TrueType fonts are scaleable, meaning they can change size without any loss of text quality. This feature is particularly important when you're dealing with high-quality graphics and large text sizes, as you may often do with CorelDRAW!.

A small selection of TrueType fonts is available with Windows, and CorelDRAW! installs a large additional set that is available to all other Windows applications running on your machine. CorelDRAW! also can create a custom typeface or font and then export it for later use.

The major benefit of creating a custom font is that you can then access the font characters just as you would any letter in the alphabet. But this character may be a graphic image, such as your signature or a custom-designed text character. You can have lots of fun with this feature and save yourself a lot of time if you set it up properly.

Creating Custom Typefaces (Exporting Text)

Although it's not likely that you'll create a totally new font, you can convert a portion of a drawn (or customized) text to a font. Keep in mind, however, that you shouldn't attempt to change the existing typefaces or create new ones unless you feel comfortable with typesetting terminology and restrictions.

Chapter 7, "Adding Text to a Drawing," introduced you to some of the basic terms; some others are listed in figure 8.3, but to truly understand typography, study one of many excellent textbooks available on the subject.

> **Note**
>
> A typeface doesn't have to include an entire alphabet full of characters. You can export a single WFN symbol for use in other Windows applications.
>
> In addition, a scanned and traced signature can be exported as a text character for use in mass mailings or to add a personal touch to documents sent via fax/modem. See Chapter 11, "Scanning Images into CorelDraw!," and Chapter 27, "Tracing Bitmap Images," for more information.

Fig. 8.3
Like most disciplines, typography has developed its own vocabulary. This figure shows some of the basic terms used to describe letters.

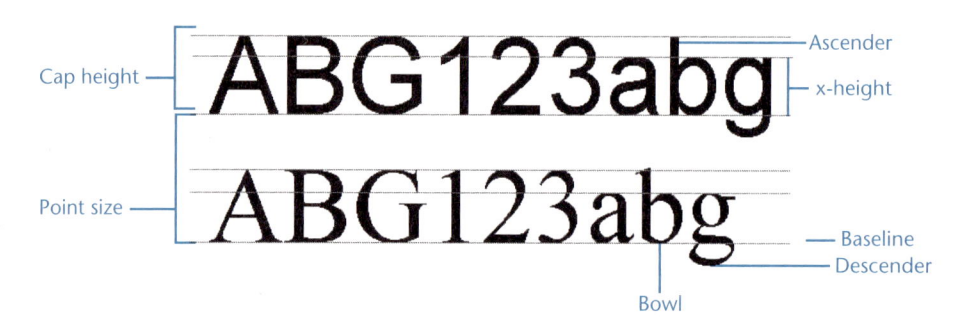

Here are a few restrictions CorelDRAW! places on you when you make a custom font:

◀ See "Combining and Grouping Objects," p. 119

- The character must be a single object, so make it all at one time or use the combine feature.

◀ See "Creating a Nonprinting Outline," p.144

- The object should contain no outline color or thickness attributes.

- The overlapping objects that comprise the character should align to make a continuous outline as opposed to a jagged interior edge.

◀ See "Aligning Objects," p. 109

Creating a typeface that can be effectively used by CorelDRAW! and other programs is much easier if you do the following:

- Work with a *large* object. The export filter is sensitive to size, and a large object is easier to work with. Set the paper size to 750 points (about 10.4 inches) in both the horizontal and vertical directions. Fill the new page with your letter, making it about 720 points (10 inches) high.

- Set the character's baseline at the origin (lower left-hand) corner of the page. This affects how it will line up with other letters in the typeface.

- Guidelines will not be exported into the typeface. You will find it easier to design your typeface if you use these guidelines to set the baseline, x-height, descender depth, and cap height for the letter.

Tip
Give your object a solid fill so that it will be visible in the Export preview window.

You can create and save the typeface one character at a time using the following procedure:

1. Create or modify a single character using the guidelines listed above.

2. Open the **F**ile menu and choose **E**xport.

3. Select either Adobe Type 1 Font or TrueType Font (depending upon your need) from the List Files of **T**ype box.

   If you've created a new typeface, type a name for the file in the File **N**ame box.

   To add a character to an existing typeface, select the typeface name from the listed files. (Be sure to select the proper path; for example, the TrueType fonts are usually in the Windows/System subdirectory.)

4. Choose OK. The TrueType/Adobe Type 1 Export dialog box opens. See the following information for details of the options in this dialog box (see fig. 8.4).

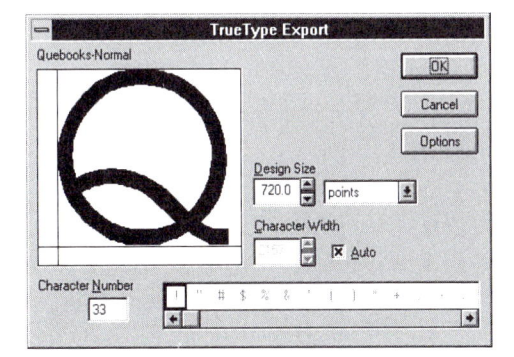

◀ See "Using the Guidelines to Ease Alignment," p. 117

Fig. 8.4
Use the TrueType/Adobe Type 1 Export dialog box to enter information concerning the typeface being created or modified.

> **Note**
>
> The Options dialog box appears when you initially save a font. It allows for detailed definition of the style, grid size, and space width associated with the font in question. See the following information for details of this dialog box.

5. Type the family name for the typeface in the **F**amily Name box.

6. Set the **S**tyle, **G**rid Size, and Spa**c**e Width for the typeface and select OK. A font family export dialog box appears for either TrueType or Adobe, depending upon the font type you choose.

7. Make the desired changes to the **D**esign Size and Character Width.

8. Choose the appropriate character number either numerically, from the Character **N**umber box, or by scrolling through the selection list next to the box.

9. Click OK.

Both the TrueType and the Adobe Type 1 dialog boxes contain the following options:

- *Design Size*. This is the size of the character that you are exporting. If you followed the suggestions above, this size is 720 points.

- *Character Width*. This number sets the width of the character relative to the grid size (see Width in the Options dialog box description below). Typically, you will not want to set this number, and instead allow CorelDRAW! to calculate it if you have the **A**uto box checked.

- *Character Number*. This is the location of the character in the typeface listing (its ASCII number). Next to the number box is a list of the standard ASCII characters indicating where this number is located.

The following options are available in the Options dialog box (see fig. 8.5). You will probably want to leave most of these settings alone when you're first learning to design a typeface. When you get more confident, experiment.

- *Family name*. This is the name that programs display in the typeface selection list. It does not have to be the same as the typeface file name.

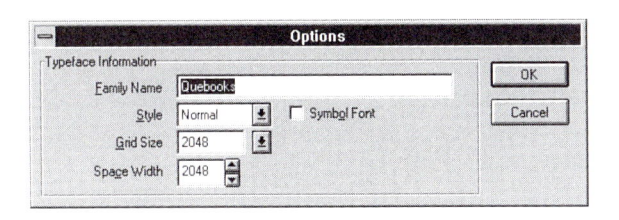

Fig. 8.5
The Options dialog box allows you to enter more detailed information concerning the typeface you are creating.

- *Style*. The standard styles—normal, bold, italic, bold-italic—are available for new typefaces. This does not change the typeface you are creating, but gives you the option of creating multiple variations of the same typeface.

- *Symbol font*. If you check this box, Windows treats the font as a symbol font and will not typically make it available for standard word processing. When you load the font into Windows (using the Control Panel), it will be listed in CorelDRAW!'s symbol menu.

- *Grid Size*. This number sets the number of points used to describe a typeface. The default setting for TrueType fonts is 2048 (which can be changed), and the setting for Adobe Type 1 is 1000 (which cannot be changed). If you plan to use your typeface at very large sizes, you may want to set it higher to give more detailed results. Once set, this number cannot be changed.

- *Space Width*. This sets the width of a space (character number 32). You can reset this number; however, if you will be using the typeface only with CorelDRAW!, you can also set this number in the spacings section of the Character dialog box.

- *Width*. This number overrides the drawn width of the character you designed.

From Here...

CorelDRAW!'s text handling options extend far beyond simply typing in text. You can convert text into a curved object for manipulation by other options in the program, add graphic symbols, and even create brand new typefaces for use in other programs.

- With Chapter 12, "Using Color for Commercial Success," you now have all of the basic skills needed to use CorelDRAW!. Your next step is to take this knowledge and make it work for you.

- Chapter 13, "Using Advanced Line and Curve Techniques," teaches you how to work effectively with lines and curves. The information in this chapter can be invaluable in helping you to create new and exciting typefaces.

- The techniques you learn in Chapter 15, "Creating Special Effects with Envelope," will help you deal with paragraph text envelopes and add further artistic flair to your drawings.

Part III

Working with Files

9	File-Related Operations and CorelMOSAIC
10	Printing and Merging Files

Chapter 9
File-Related Operations and CorelMOSAIC

by Thomas Budlong

Much of CorelDRAW!'s value stems from its capability to import and export files in various formats. Some people buy the package simply for its graphic file conversion capability. This chapter introduces basic saving and retrieving processes and then deals with file conversion and the use of CorelMOSAIC, Corel's file manager.

In this chapter, you learn to

- Save drawings on disk
- Find drawing files on disk
- Use foreign graphics in drawings (Import)
- Send drawings to other applications (Export)
- Work with drawings from earlier versions
- Use CorelMOSAIC to organize drawing files and help work with them
- Use CorelMOSAIC to convert drawing files to a new format

Saving and Retrieving Files

CorelDRAW! file functions follow Windows conventions, so if you are familiar with other Windows applications you will have little problem here. Be aware that CorelDRAW! cannot have more than one drawing open at a time. If you open a new drawing while doing edits, CorelDRAW! asks if you want to save the edits.

Chapter 9—File-Related Operations and CorelMOSAIC

DOS's eight character file names are notoriously poor for identification. CorelDRAW! recognizes this and provides additional ways of identifying files. Keywords, descriptive notes, and thumbnail pictures can be attached to files to aid in identification when you want to retrieve them. The CorelMOSAIC application that comes with CorelDRAW! enables you to organize files in groups, so that you do not have to look everywhere if you know a file's category. These identification aids are described in detail in this chapter.

Saving Drawings

▶ See "Customizing Backup Defaults," p. 574

As you work on a drawing, save it regularly by opening the **F**ile menu and choosing **S**ave. If you don't and the power to your computer is interrupted or the computer malfunctions, you likely will lose your work. Nothing is more frustrating than losing several hours of work because you didn't take a few moments to save your file.

Similar to most applications, the CorelDRAW! File menu contains Save and Save As.

To save your drawing in the currently active directory under its existing file name, click the Save icon in the toolbar, open the **F**ile menu and choose **S**ave, or press Ctrl+S. This updates the file with changes made since the last File Save. Depending on your backup settings, the earlier version is either saved in a backup file (with a BAK extension) or over-written.

If you open the **F**ile menu and choose **S**ave before your drawing is named, the Save Drawing dialog box shown in figure 9.1 appears so that you can enter a name and specify the directory for the file.

Fig. 9.1
Use the Save Drawing dialog box to name a drawing, determine where to save it, and add information that helps you identify it later.

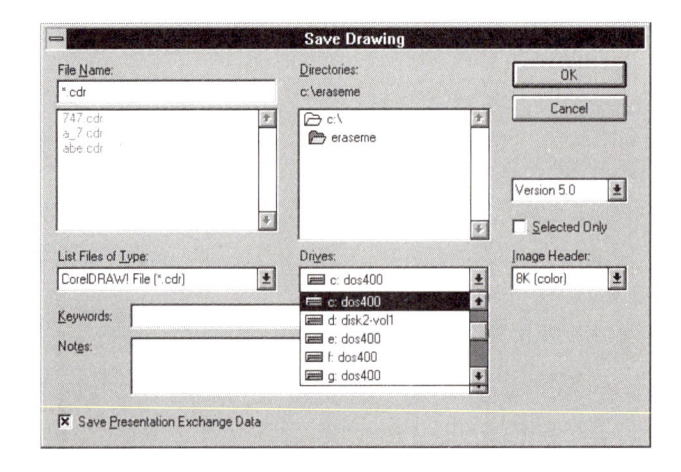

The List Files of Type box at the lower left of the Save Drawing dialog box has several choices. Select CorelDRAW! File (*.cdr) to save your work as a drawing. Type the desired file name in the File Name text box. Don't enter an extension—CorelDRAW! automatically adds CDR.

You can include an *image header* with each file—a small image to help identify the file later. It shows up in the Open dialog box and is used by the CorelMOSAIC application. You don't have to include one, but you might find these little pictures really are worth a thousand words. To access the various Image Header options, click the arrow to the right of the Image Header drop-down list box. The larger headers look better, but take more room and time to display. Unless you have a slow computer or are very tight on disk space, use the larger size—the penalty is relatively small for the benefit.

The Selected Only option is so that you can save part of a drawing. With the drawing on-screen, select the objects you want to save. Open the **F**ile menu and choose Save **A**s; then check Selected Only. If Selected Only is not available, then no objects are selected and you can only save the entire drawing.

To save the current drawing in a format compatible with earlier versions of CorelDRAW!, select the version from the list at the right of the dialog box. With this option, you can provide files to service bureaus or persons still using older versions of CorelDRAW!. CorelDRAW! 5 can read files made by earlier versions, but earlier versions of CorelDRAW! cannot read CorelDRAW! 5 files. The format differs from version to version—if you don't know what version a file was created in, the only way to find out is to open the file and see how CorelDRAW! reacts.

If you open the **F**ile menu and choose Save **A**s using the Version option without changing the file name, the active file is replaced with the earlier version format. You can avoid this situation by saving the earlier version file under a different name or to a different drive/directory. In fact, if you are planning to transfer the file to another party you might want to save the earlier version file to a floppy disk to avoid later confusion.

Saving a Copy of an Open File

Use the File menu's Save As command to save the current drawing in a new file. The original drawing, as it was when last saved, is preserved in the original file. This procedure enables you to save changes without affecting the initial drawing. Note that after using the Save As command, the current drawing—the one you are now editing—is the one with the changes, not the unedited-edited original.

To use the Save As command, follow these steps:

1. Open the **F**ile menu and choose Save **A**s. This brings up the same Save Drawing dialog box as choosing **F**ile **S**ave (see fig. 9.1).

2. Choose the desired drive (A, B, C…).

3. Choose the desired directory.

◀ See "Using Styles and Templates," p. 236

4. Choose CorelDRAW! File (*.cdr) in the List Files of Type box.

5. Type the file name. Don't enter an extension—CorelDRAW! automatically adds CDR.

▶ See "Using CorelDRAW! Templates," p. 581

6. Click OK.

Adding Keywords and Notes to Files

When you save a drawing, the Save Drawing dialog box has space for entering keywords and notes. The Open Drawing dialog box enables you to use these keywords to find files and shows you the notes to help remind you of the file's content. (And of course the image header—called a Preview in the Open Drawing dialog—is a further aid to file identification.)

Place keywords in the Keywords box during the Save operation. They should be single words. You can add as many keywords as you want—separate them with commas. Of course, use words that describe the important aspects of the drawing. Enter note text in the Notes box, also during the Save operation. Keywords and notes are saved in the drawing file.

> **Note**
>
> Get in the habit of giving all your drawing files keywords and notes. Later, when you want to pick a specific file from all files on the disk, you will either appreciate keywords and notes or pay for not using them. CorelDRAW! provides a nice function, missing in so many applications. Use it!

Changing Keywords, Notes, and the Preview Image Header

You can change keywords (but not the notes) with CorelMOSAIC. Refer to the "Editing Keywords" section at the end of this chapter.

To change keywords and notes from CorelDRAW!, you must use Save As, because no direct function is available to edit these. Follow these steps:

1. With the drawing on-screen, open the **F**ile menu and choose Save **A**s. The Save Drawing dialog box appears (see fig. 9.1).

2. The keywords and notes show in the dialog box. Edit them.

3. The drawing's file name is already in the File Name box. Leave it there.

4. Click OK.

5. The system knows the file already exists on disk and asks if you want to replace it. Answer Yes. You are replacing it with itself, including the edited keywords, notes, and image header.

Finding and Opening Files

File names given to drawings are difficult to remember (sometimes impossible!), especially if you have a lot of files or you saved them a while ago. If you don't know a file's name, the keywords described in the preceding section are the answer to finding them. The notes and image header (sometimes called a *preview*) help identify the file after you think you've found it.

The following instructions describe finding drawing files from within CorelDRAW!. You also can use CorelMOSAIC to call a drawing into CorelDRAW! for editing. Refer to the CorelMOSAIC description later in this chapter.

1. Open the **F**ile menu and choose **O**pen to bring up the Open Drawing dialog box (see fig. 9.2).

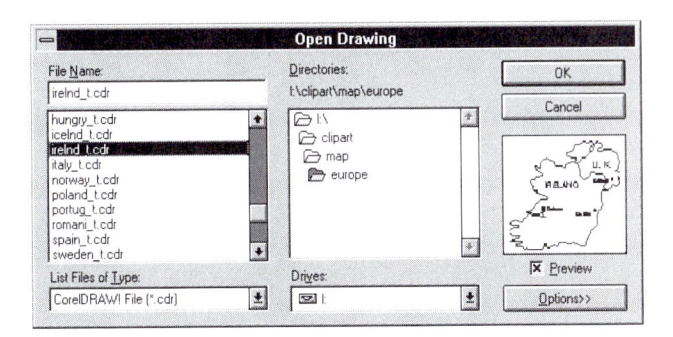

Fig. 9.2
Use the Open Drawing dialog box to bring a saved drawing to the screen for editing or other work.

2. If you know the file name and its directory, select them in the dialog box and click OK. Skip the rest of these instructions. To use keywords to locate a file, continue with step 3.

3. Click **O**ptions, to expand the dialog box. The new area shows the keywords and notes for the file selected in the File Name box.

4. Click **F**ind to get the Keyword Search dialog box (see fig. 9.3).

Fig. 9.3
Use the Keyword Search dialog box to restrict the File Name list to drawings with the keywords you enter.

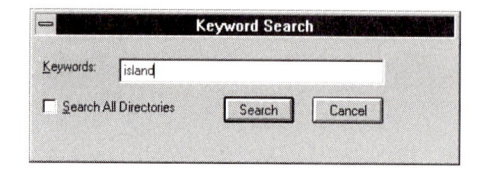

5. Enter the keyword(s) to search for. Separate them with commas.

6. To search all directories on the disk, check Search all Directories. If unchecked, only the current directory is searched.

7. Click Search.

Tip
If you suspect the File Name box doesn't show all the files in a directory, check the Find button. You may have some keywords there.

All drawing files (extension CDR) with the specified keywords are shown in the file name box. Now you can select one and click OK to bring it on-screen, or do more keyword searching if you haven't found it.

Note

Choosing Options when the full dialog box with options is displayed returns you to the shorter dialog box.

After a file is selected, notes and keywords attached to it are shown (Options must be on). To see the preview (also called the *image header*) make sure that the Preview box is checked. A diagonal line in the Preview window means no file is selected or no preview information is available for the selected file.

Sorting Files

Files in the File Name box of the Open Drawing dialog box can be listed by name or by date. Sorting by name is handy, of course, when you know the name of the file you want. Sorting by date puts the most recently saved files at the top of the list—these are usually the files you are most interested in.

To sort by name or date, follow these steps:

1. Open the **F**ile menu and choose **O**pen. The Open Drawing dialog box appears.

2. Click Options to expand it.

3. In the Sort By list, select Name or Date.

Saving and Retrieving Earlier Version Files

Version 5 is the latest in a progressive string of improvements to CorelDRAW!. Each new version brings new capabilities and necessarily changes the format of drawing files. Corel Systems recognize that users of previous versions can't be expected to redraw all of their old work. So they provide capability to read old format files and even save drawings in the old formats. Just the same, you should follow some general guidelines:

- Work with version 5 files as much as you can and encourage anyone you share files with to move to version 5.

- Convert files from previous versions to version 5 and work with them in the version 5 format. When saving edits to drawing files in the format of old versions, save in version 5 format. Although CorelDRAW! enables you to save in the old format, doing so increases the probability of getting into formatting trouble somewhere.

- Save in the format of a previous version only if you must transfer a drawing to a system that has not been upgraded to version 5.

- CorelDRAW! does not provide compatibility with very old versions, such as version 2.

- Version 5 should save and load version 3 and version 4 files correctly. Because some of the typefaces used in earlier versions may be different, problems can occur when drawings are converted to the older formats. Version 3, for example, has no way of interpreting characters in the newer typeface, and strange things, such as weird text spacing, can happen. You can avoid this situation by selecting typefaces common to both versions, or by converting all text to curves before saving in version 3 format. If you convert the text to curves, letters are treated as objects rather than text and the problem is resolved, but at the expense of a more complicated drawing. You may want to try to save and verify the results before trying any fancy work-around procedures.

Under any circumstances, do not expect earlier versions of the CorelDRAW! program to read drawings saved in version 5.

Troubleshooting

File Open doesn't list enough files.

You may have some words in the Keyword filter. To see if you do, click Options in the File Open dialog box, and then click Find to see the Keyword Search dialog box. If any words are shown, only files that have them are listed—others do not show.

Preview in the File Open dialog box shows a diagonal line, not a preview picture.

This problem can have several causes: the Preview check box must be checked. The file may not have a preview picture with it. The name in the File Name box is not a real file name.

In the Open Drawing dialog box, it's difficult to find a file name when the list of file names is long.

If Sort By is set to Date, the files are listed by date not alphabetically. The most recently saved/updated files are listed first.

Sharing Drawings—Export, Import, and the Clipboard

Of course, you can put CorelDRAW! drawings in documents made with other applications. This is one of the major reasons to use CorelDRAW!. You might want to use a CorelDRAW!-created logo in a page-layout document, for example. And you might want to do the opposite—incorporate something created in another application in a CorelDRAW! drawing. Just as common is taking objects from one CorelDRAW! drawing into another CorelDRAW! drawing.

You can accomplish these tasks using the Windows Clipboard, or you can use the Export and Import options in the File menu. The Clipboard is the quick-and-dirty way to do it. Sometimes you may find the Clipboard isn't big enough to do the job (Windows tells you it's having trouble), and you have to go to Export and Import. Export and Import allow more precise control over the transfer process. Because Export makes files, it's a more permanent way of doing the transfer—the Clipboard is ephemeral.

Export and import use export and import filters. Install puts them on the hard disk, but only if you ask for them. If you are running from the hard disk and don't see the filter you want during export or import, it may not be installed. To install an export or import filter, follow these steps:

1. Run install again.

2. Select only CorelDRAW!. Click Continue.

3. Select only Filters, and click Customize. This displays the filter selection window.

4. Select the export or import filter you want from the dialog box that appears.

If you are running from the CD-ROM, all the filters are always available; if you don't see what you want, it doesn't exist.

▶ See "Installing CorelDRAW! to Run from the CD-ROM," p. 875

Exporting versus Saving

The Save command in the File menu saves the drawing in CorelDRAW! format. Other applications may not recognize CorelDRAW!'s format. The File menu's Export command enables you to save in a wide range of other formats; you almost always can find a format that the destination application understands. Export sends the drawing through a *filter* to convert it.

To export a file, follow these steps:

1. Open the **F**ile menu and choose **E**xport to display the Export dialog box (see fig. 9.4).

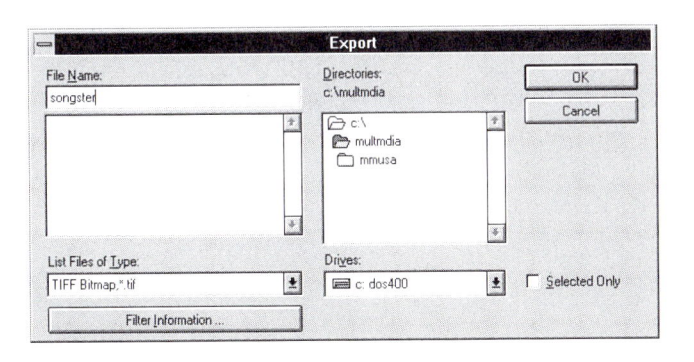

Fig. 9.4
The Export dialog box is for saving drawings in non-CorelDRAW! formats. You select the format from the Files of Type list.

Tip

Before Exporting, save the drawing in CorelDRAW! format. It's easier to make modifications later in this file—importing an exported image sometimes loses information.

2. Select the export file format type from the List Files of **T**ype drop-down list.

3. Check Selected Only if you want to export only selected objects. (Refer to the "Saving Drawings" section earlier in this chapter for Selected Only details.)

4. Select the destination drive and directory in the Drives and Directories boxes.

5. Type the file name in the File Name box. Don't include the extension—the appropriate extension (based on the file type selected in step 2) is added automatically.

6. Click OK.

Depending upon the file type selected, CorelDRAW! presents another dialog box (described later) to gather additional information. CorelDRAW! then translates the drawing and stores the results.

Exporting in Encapsulated PostScript (EPS) Format

Encapsulated PostScript (EPS) is an industry standard file format that can support the complexity of CorelDRAW! images. EPS files created by CorelDRAW! can be used in Ventura Publisher and Page-Maker, but these files keep the bitmap images at low resolution. Remember, save your images as CDR files before exporting to EPS format so that you can edit the images later if necessary.

When you choose the File menu's Export command and select the EPS file type, choose OK to open the Export EPS dialog box shown in figure 9.5.

Fig. 9.5
The Export EPS dialog box controls how EPS files written from CorelDRAW! are formatted.

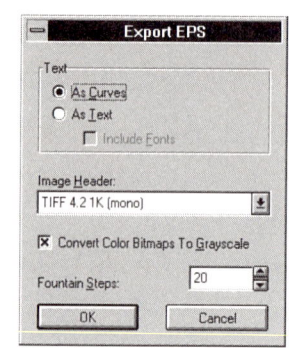

The Text section of this dialog box determines whether the text embedded in the image is exported as text or converted to curves before being exported. Choosing the As Curves option makes the object more complex and might cause your printer to hang up due to unacceptable complexity. If you choose the As Text option and choose Include Fonts, the CorelDRAW! fonts are included in the EPS file and are used for printing. If you don't check Include Fonts, CorelDRAW! assumes that all text fonts are already resident in the printer and that the Adobe versions of typefaces should be used rather than the CorelDRAW! fonts. If a font is not resident when printing the file, the text either prints in Courier or doesn't print at all.

If you are wondering which fonts are resident, refer to the CORELFNT.INI file, which shows a listing of the CorelDRAW! fonts on the left and the equivalent PostScript font on the right followed by either 0, 1, or 3. These fonts are listed in the [PSResidentFonts] section. A trailing 0 means that the typeface is not resident in the printer; a 1 means that the typeface is resident in all PostScript printers; and a 3 means that the typeface is resident in printers that support the 3J standard PostScript typefaces.

EPS files containing color bitmaps do not print on black-and-white PostScript level 1 printers. To resolve this issue, check the Convert Color Bitmaps To Grayscale option.

The Fountain Steps setting determines the quality of fountain fill printing. Keep this number low when printing proofs to speed up the printing process, but set it to the desired level when printing your final output. Settings below 20 are considered low; settings over 40 are considered high. As you increase the number of steps, you reach a point of diminishing returns at which you can no longer tell much of a difference. Play with the settings to determine which levels suit your equipment and drawings.

The Image Header drop-down list enables you to specify inclusion of a small bitmap representation of the drawing. You can choose None, TIFF 5.0 format, or TIFF 4.2 format. Each entry tells how much space it takes.

▶ See "Customizing INI Files," p. 587

Some older applications do not read TIFF 5.0 file formats, which means that the image is not adopted by the importing applications. If you know your files will be going to such an application, save the headers in TIFF 4.2 format.

Exporting Bitmaps

If you choose a bitmap format from the Export dialog box, the Bitmap Export dialog box appears (see fig. 9.6). The controls in the dialog box may be different, depending on the bitmap format chosen, because different bitmap formats have different requirements.

Fig. 9.6
The Bitmap Export dialog box is for setting parameters specific to the bitmap format.

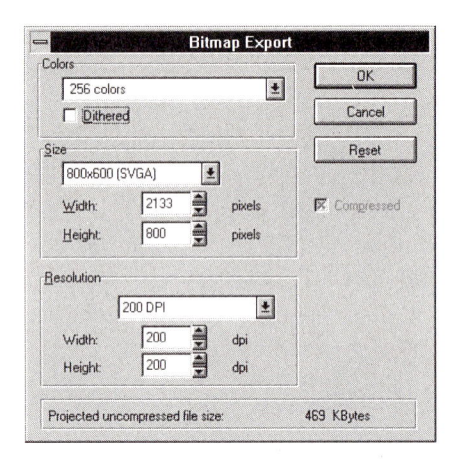

Tip
If you are unsure if a format is bitmap or vector, try it. If you get the Bitmap Export dialog, it's a bitmap format.

Tip
To minimize bitmap storage size, use a 1:1 size ratio, lower bitmap resolutions, and set the image to the desired size within CorelDRAW! before exporting.

Use the Bitmap Export dialog box to set horizontal and vertical resolution, the type of coloring, and the aspect ratio—the width-to-height ratio. It also estimates the size of the exported file. The options are as follows:

- *Colors.* Make your choice depending on where the bitmap is going—high or low resolution, black-and-white or color printers or display devices.

- *Dither.* You should generally use dithering with 16-level grayscale, with 16 to 256-color images, or with images that you will not rescale or touch up in the final application. If you are using 16 million colors or plan to rescale the image in the final application, do not use dithering.

- *Size.* This controls the size and aspect ratio of the bitmap. 1:1 keeps the same size and aspect ratio as the drawing. The screen sizes (640 × 480, 800 × 600, and 1024 × 768) are for use when the drawing is intended for display on a screen. To set any other size, change the Width and Height—the Size box changes to Custom to indicate the size is nonstandard.

- *Resolution.* Select from several resolutions (300 to 75), or one of the two fax resolutions.

Note

To maintain maximum image clarity, set your image to the desired size using the CorelDRAW! vector graphics format *before* exporting. Avoid sizing bitmapped images because it usually degrades image quality.

Table 9.1 shows a list of the Export file filters provided by CorelDRAW!

Table 9.1 CorelDRAW! Export Filters

Format	File Names
Adobe Illustrator	*.AI, *.EPS
Adobe Type 1 Font	*.PFB
AutoCAD DXF	*.DXF
CompuServe Bitmap	*.GIF
Computer Graphics Metafile	*.CGM
GEM Files	*.GEM
HPGL Plotter File	*.PLT
IBM PIF	*.PIF
JPEG Bitmaps	*.JPG, *.JFF, *.JTF, *.CMP
Macintosh PICT	*.PCT
Matrix/Imapro SCODL	*.SCD
OS/2 Bitmap	*.BMP
Paintbrush	*.PCX
EPS (Placeable)	*.EPS
Scitex CT Bitmap	*.CT
Targa Bitmap	*.TGA, *.VDA, *.ICB, *.VST
TIFF Bitmap	*.TIF
TrueType Font	*.TTF
Windows Bitmap	*.BMP, *.DIB, *.RLE
Windows Metafile	*.WMF
WordPerfect Graphic	*.WPG

Opening and Importing a Drawing

The File Open command retrieves a drawing saved by CorelDRAW! in a CorelDRAW! format. The retrieved drawing replaces the drawing that was on-screen.

◀ See "Importing Text," p. 226

The File menu's Import command, on the other hand, adds images and information to the current drawing without otherwise changing it. You can use import to do just that—add components. But if you import to an empty drawing (the result of File New), it's almost like using File Open, except that you are bringing in a drawing from non-CorelDRAW! format.

To import a file, follow these steps:

1. With the drawing to receive the imported file on-screen, open the File menu and choose Import. This displays the Import dialog box, which looks very much like the Open File dialog box.

2. Select the drive and directory where the drawing to be imported resides, using the Drives and Directories window.

3. Select the format of the drawing to be imported from the List Files of Type list. Note the All Files selection in case you know the file name but are unsure of the format. The files in the selected directory that meet the specifications in the List Files of Type list are listed in the File Name window.

4. In the File Name window, select the file to be imported.

5. To check the file contents before importing, check Preview to show a preview of the drawing in the window on the right of the dialog box.

6. Click OK to import the drawing. You can just double-click the file name in the File Name list, but you will not be able to see the preview.

> **Note**
>
> CorelMOSAIC can import drawings from the CorelMOSAIC application and with the CorelMOSAIC roll-up window. (To get the roll-up, click the CorelMOSAIC icon in the ribbon bar, or open the File menu and choose MOSAIC Roll-Up.) Refer to the CorelMOSAIC description later in this chapter.

Import Format Compatibilities

Importing uses filters to translate from an external format, such as PCX, TIF, or WPG. Table 9.2 shows a list of these import filters.

Table 9.2 CorelDRAW! Import Filters

Format	File Names
Adobe Illustrator 1.1, 88, 3.0	*.AI, *.EPS
Ami Professional 2.0, 3	*.SAM
AutoCAD DXF	*.DXF
CompuServe Bitmap	*.GIF
Computer Graphics Metafile	*.CGM
CorelDRAW!	*.CDR
CorelTRACE	*.EPS
Encapsulated PostScript	*.EPS, *,PS
EPS (Placeable)	*.EPS, *.PS, *.AI
Excel for Windows 3, 4.0	*.XLS
GEM file	*.GEM
HPGL Plotter File	*.PLT
IBM PIF	*.PIF
JPEG Bitmap	*.JPG
Kodak Photo CD Image	*.PCD
Lotus 1-2-3 1A, 2.0	*.WK?
Lotus 1-2-3 3.0	*.WK?
Lotus PIC	*.PIC
Macintosh PICT	*.PCT
MacWrite II 1.0, 1.1	*.*
Micrographx 2.x, 3.x	*.DRW
Microsoft Word 5.0, 5.5	*.*
Microsoft Word for Mac 4.0	*.*
Microsoft Word for Mac 5.0	*.*

(continues)

Chapter 9—File-Related Operations and CorelMOSAIC

Table 9.2 Continued

Format	File Names
Microsoft Word for Windows 1.x	*.*
Microsoft Word for Windows 2.x	*.*
Paintbrush	*.PCX
Rich Text Format	*.RTF
Scitex CT Bitmap	*.CT
TARGA Bitmaps	*.TGA, *.VDA, *.ICB, *.VST
Text	*.TXT
TIFF Bitmaps	*.TIF, *.JTF, *.SEP
Windows Bitmaps	*.BMP
Windows Metafile	*.WMF
WordPerfect 6.0	*.WP
WordPerfect 5.0	*.*
WordPerfect 5.1	*.WP
WordPerfect Graphic	*.WPG

▶ See "Using Traced Images in CorelDRAW!," p. 691

As you can see, CorelDRAW! supports many foreign graphics formats. In the rare event you have an unsupported format, bring the foreign document on-screen in the other application and try transferring it to the drawing with the Windows Clipboard. Or if the other application exports the file to a format supported by CorelDRAW!, try that. For example, if the native file format for your favorite paint program is not supported by CorelDRAW! but does export to PCX files, export your drawings to PCX from the paint program and then import the PCX files into CorelDRAW!.

Importing a CorelTRACE File

CorelDRAW! can import CorelTRACE-generated EPS files. You can select image portions or objects from the currently active CorelTRACE EPS file and export them in the desired format, including CDR. In this way, a scanned image can be converted into a vector graphic using CorelTRACE, which can then be exported and scaled within CorelDRAW! for use in other applications.

Importing a Photo CD File

Images in the new Photo CD format can be imported into CorelDRAW! drawings. You must have the Photo CD filter installed. If it is not installed, rerun the CorelDRAW! installation procedure, specifying the Photo CD filter. And of course, because almost all Photo CDs are on CD-ROMs, you must have a CD-ROM drive that can read Photo CDs installed in your computer.

Follow these steps to import a Photo CD image:

1. Open the **F**ile menu and choose **I**mport.
2. Select the drive and directory that contains the file to be imported.
3. In the List Files of Type box, select Kodak Photo CD (*.PCD).
4. Select the file to be imported; it appears in the File Name box.
5. Click OK. The Photo CD Options dialog box appears (see fig. 9.7).

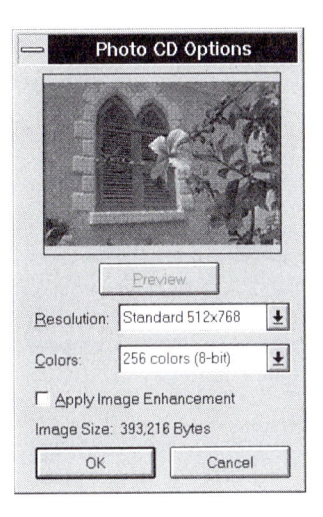

Fig. 9.7
With the Photo CD Options dialog box, you choose the import resolution and number of colors.

6. Choose a resolution. Photos on Photo CDs are stored in several resolutions; larger resolutions take up more room in the drawing. For the best quality, import the resolution you want in the drawing—don't adjust the resolution after it's in the drawing. Photo CDs are bitmap images, and bitmap images always lose quality when they are resized.

7. Select the number of colors. For viewing on-screen, 256 colors is usually sufficient. For high-quality color printing, use more colors. Use 256 grayscale for monochrome and laser printers. Of course, more colors make a larger drawing file.

278 Chapter 9—File-Related Operations and CorelMOSAIC

8. Click OK. The image is brought into the CorelDRAW! drawing. You can then drag it into the correct position.

Getting More Information on Importing and Exporting

CorelDRAW! provides extensive help files for the file formats that it can import and export. Each file format topic is listed in the help system, with details about various aspects of the file format, including supported formats, unsupported features, special import or export considerations, and so forth.

To get help on import file formats, follow these steps:

1. Open the **H**elp menu and choose **S**earch for Help On, or press Ctrl+F1. The Search dialog box appears.

2. Type **Importing Files** in the search text box. The topics list displays the importing topics with Importing File: File Formats highlighted.

3. Click the **S**how Topics button. The Go To section of the dialog box displays the available topics for Importing Files (see fig. 9.8).

4. Click the **G**o To button. The help screen for Import File Formats appears (see fig. 9.9).

Fig. 9.8
The Help systems Search dialog box displays the search topics for Importing Files.

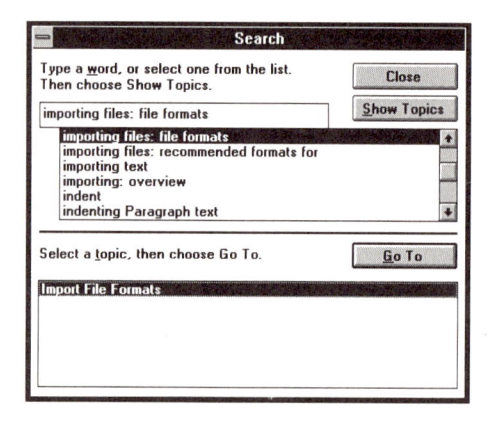

5. To get brief information about a listed file format, click the file format name. The description displays in a pop-up window (see fig. 9.10). Click the mouse button to close the description window.

6. To get extensive information about a listed file format, click the + button next to the file name. The CorelDRAW! Technical Notes for that file format display (see fig. 9.11).

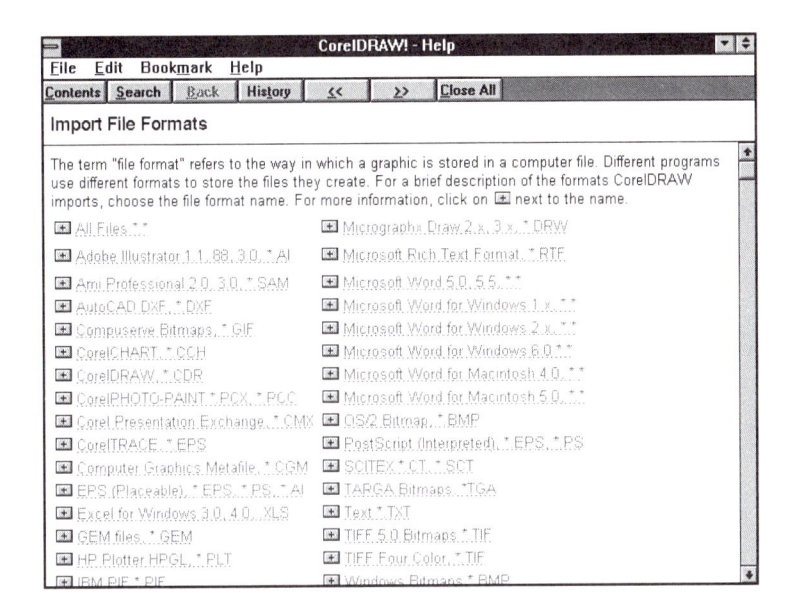

Sharing Drawings—Export, Import, and the Clipboard   279

Fig. 9.9
The Import File Formats Help screen lists all the file formats that CorelDRAW! 5 is capable of importing.

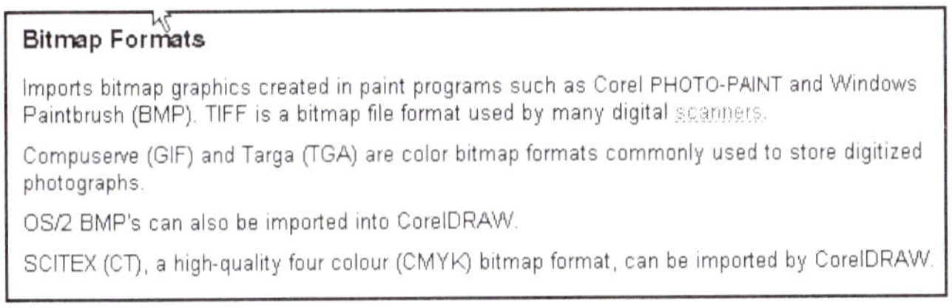

Fig. 9.10
A file format description window gives brief information and occasional notes pertaining to the file format at hand.

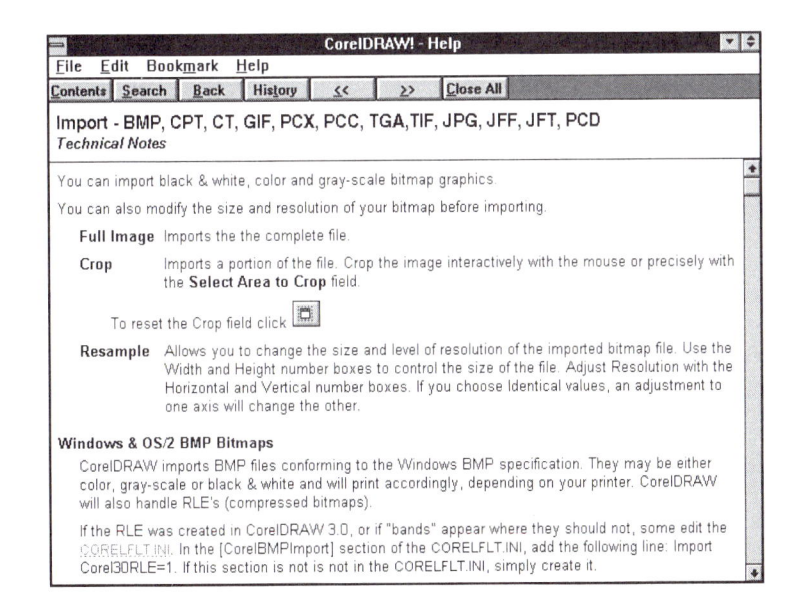

Fig. 9.11
CorelDRAW! Technical Notes Help files give detailed information regarding importing files into CorelDRAW!.

7. When you finish reading the file format information, click **B**ack to return to the complete file list. Click **C**lose All to exit the Help system.

To obtain detailed information on exporting files from CorelDRAW!, follow these steps:

1. Open the **H**elp menu and choose **S**earch for Help On, or press Ctrl+F1. The Search dialog box appears.

2. Type **Exporting: File Formats** in the search text box. The Topics list displays the exporting topics with Exporting: File Formats highlighted.

3. Click the **S**how Topics button. The Go To section of the dialog box displays the available topics for Exporting Files.

4. Click the **G**o To button. The Help screen for Export File Formats appears.

5. To get brief information about a listed file format, click the file format name. The file format description displays in a pop-up window. Click the mouse button to close the description window.

6. To get extensive information about a listed file format, click the + button next to the file name. The CorelDRAW! Technical Notes for that file format are displayed.

7. When you are finished reading the file format information, click **B**ack to return to the complete file list. Click **C**lose All to exit the Help system.

◀ See "Copying Objects," p. 105

Using the Clipboard instead of File Transfers

Refer to the earlier section, "Opening and Importing a Drawing," for hints about using Export/Import or the Clipboard. If you decide to use the Clipboard, you will find that CorelDRAW!'s Clipboard functions follow the Windows standard exactly: Edit Copy copies selected objects to the Windows Clipboard; Edit Cut copies them to the Clipboard and removes them from the drawing; and Edit Paste adds the Clipboard contents to the drawing. You can use the standard keyboard shortcuts—Ctrl+X, Ctrl+C, and Ctrl+V for Cut, Copy, and Paste respectively.

Following are some things you should know about CorelDRAW! with respect to Cut, Copy, and Paste:

- Information pasted into a drawing from the Clipboard comes in at the same size and location as the original. You usually have to resize it and move it to the right location after pasting.

- If the pasted object is in a vector format, such as Metafile, then resizing causes no loss in object image quality. Resizing a bitmap coming from the Clipboard does reduce its quality. The quality reduction can be negligible to severe, depending on the amount of resizing.

- CorelDRAW! does not support these Windows Metafile features: background commands, pattern fills, clipping regions, flood fills, individual pixel manipulations, WINDING polygon fill mode (ALTERNATE mode is supported), and ROP2 modes other than R2_COPYPEN.

- When text is pasted from the Clipboard, CorelDRAW! applies several rules to determine its spacing and text type:

    - Pasted text is imported from the Clipboard as Paragraph text (when not pasted as an OLE object) unless you mark the destination position with the Artistic Text tool.

    - The fill, outline, typeface, and point size of the text are set to the currently active CorelDRAW! default values.

    - Artistic text spacing defaults to 0 percent of intercharacter space width; 100 percent of interword space width; and 100 percent of character point size interline width.

    - Paragraph text defaults to the same values as Artistic text.

- Copying fountain fills via the Clipboard often is a slow process. You can speed things up and achieve a similar result by blending two objects together with the same relative size, location, and color as the radial fills. Remove the object outlines and then blend the two objects together. The final result looks much like a fountain fill with a radial offset, and it does not create the Clipboard copying problems associated with fountain fills.

- CorelDRAW! supports Windows Metafile and CorelMetafile (CMF) formats when cutting or copying information to the Clipboard. Objects containing pattern fills, PostScript textures, and bitmap fills cannot be copied or cut to the Clipboard. Windows Metafile, ASCII text, Rich Text Format (RTF) text, and Windows Bitmaps can be pasted from the Clipboard into a CorelDRAW! image.

► See "Customizing INI Files," p. 587

As you become an advanced CorelDRAW! user, you may need to customize the way the Clipboard handles PostScript calligraphic outlines and text (whether it is converted to curves or retains its text attributes).

These settings are established by opening the Special menu and choosing Preferences. Click the Text tab. To keep calligraphic outlines, select Calligraphic Text (which is the default). To paste text as text, rather than as curves, select Text in Metafile (unselected by default). When finished, choose OK. Stay with the defaults until you are at an advanced level with CorelDRAW!.

Any changes you make take effect immediately.

> **Troubleshooting**
>
> *The print quality of an imported image is poor.*
>
> The image may be a bitmap, and you have changed its size. Bitmaps can lose quality when resized. Vector images don't lose quality.

Using CorelMOSAIC

Managing many drawing files is difficult without some help. CorelMOSAIC is a small application, included with CorelDRAW!, that provides that help. The conveniences of CorelMOSAIC enable you to

- Select files by thumbnail picture and by keyword, as well as by file name.
- Automatically call up the parent program (for example, CorelDRAW! for CDR files) for editing.
- Edit keywords belonging to a CorelDRAW! drawing file.
- Organize files into catalogs and libraries.
- Print multiple drawings with one command. Without CorelMOSAIC, you must open them in CorelDRAW! one at a time and print them individually.
- Extract a drawing's text to an editable text file, and merge it back into the drawing after editing.

Using CorelMOSAIC as a management tool initially requires some discipline, but soon becomes habit after the functions become familiar. As soon as you get so many drawing files on disk that you are having trouble finding them, or they are taking up too much room, you will want to start using CorelMOSAIC. When your files are in catalogs or libraries, you can use CorelMOSAIC to locate them and get them directly into CorelDRAW! or another associated application to work on them. Also from CorelMOSAIC, you can import a drawing to be a component in a CorelDRAW! drawing.

Running CorelMOSAIC

You can run CorelMOSAIC in the following two ways:

- *Standalone.* This treats CorelMOSAIC as a separate application. All functions are available. Double-click the CorelMOSAIC icon in the Windows Program Manager.

- *Roll-up window.* From CorelDRAW! open the **F**ile menu and choose Mosaic Ro**l**l-up to open the CorelMOSAIC roll-up window. This method is only for importing drawings into CorelDRAW!—none of CorelMOSAIC's other functions are available.

◀ See "Using Roll-Up Windows," p. 25

Note

The CorelMOSAIC roll-up window also is available in all other Corel applications, except for CorelQUERY.

Making and Editing Libraries and Catalogs

To help keep track of files, CorelMOSAIC has two organizational structures: *catalogs* and *libraries*. Although they are operationally similar, they serve completely different functions, as follows:

- *Catalog files.* Use these files to make convenient groupings of drawings, regardless of their location on the system or their format. A catalog holds, for each drawing file you choose, the drawing thumbnail and the file path and name. Then, by looking at that single catalog file, you can see the thumbnails of the files it contains; select the one you want; and work with it.

- *Library files.* These files are for compressing drawings to save disk space. A library file holds the full drawings (catalogs only hold the thumbnail) in compressed format. After a drawing is put in a library, the original file can be deleted.

Together, CorelMOSAIC refers to libraries and catalogs as *collections*.

You must choose to either catalog a file or place it in a library, but not both. If you put a drawing in a library and delete the original to save disk space, it is not available as a separate file for inclusion in a catalog. If you put it in a catalog before you place it in a library and delete the original, the catalog cannot find the original.

Creating Libraries and Catalogs

You can create and edit libraries and catalogs only in Standalone mode, not in Roll-up mode. Follow these steps:

1. Open the **F**ile menu and choose **N**ew Collection; the Create New Collection dialog box appears (see fig. 9.12).

Fig. 9.12
The Create New Collection dialog box is for making new libraries and new catalogs.

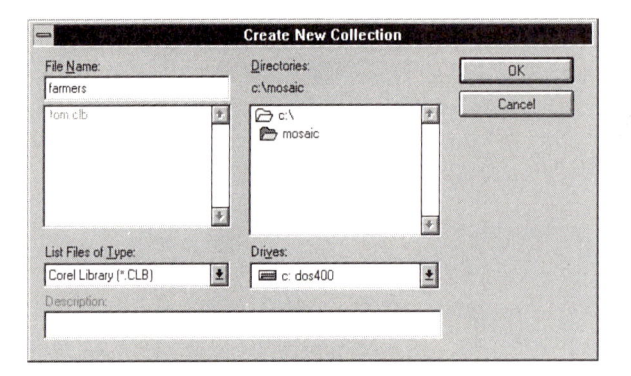

2. In the List Files of Type list box, select Corel Catalog (*.CLC) to make a catalog file to hold drawing thumbnails and locations, or select Corel Library (*.CLB) to make a library file to hold drawing files.

3. Select the drive and directory for the file.

4. Enter a file name. Do not enter an extension—CorelMOSAIC automatically adds .CLC or .CLB.

5. Optional: Enter a file description in the box at the bottom of the dialog. This is free-form text and could be something like "Invertebrates at the Bronx Zoo."

6. Click OK. An empty window appears in the CorelMOSAIC window. You are now ready to put drawing files in this new window.

Adding Drawing Files to Libraries and Catalogs

You add a drawing by dragging its thumbnail from a directory window to the library or catalog window. Both windows must be open.

Open the Library or Catalog File. Follow these steps if the library or catalog file is not open:

1. Open the **F**ile menu and choose **O**pen Collection to get the Open Collection dialog box (see fig. 9.13).

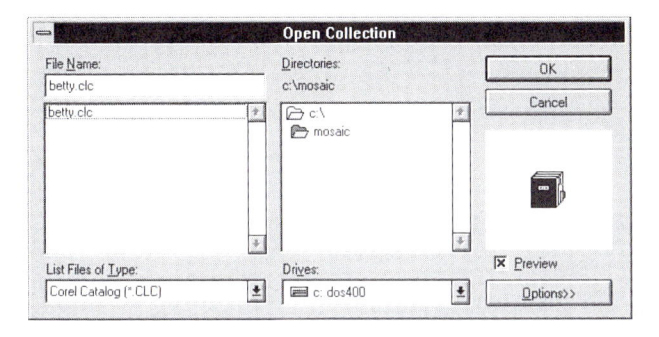

Fig. 9.13
The Open Collection dialog box is used to open libraries and catalogs. You also use it to open directories.

2. In the List Files of Type list box, select Corel Catalog (*.CLC) to open a catalog file or Corel Library (*.CLB) to open a library file. Only files of the selected type appear in the File Name list.

3. Select the drive and directory for the file and the name of the file in the File Name box.

4. Click OK, or double-click the file name.

A window for the library or catalog file opens, and thumbnails of drawings in it are shown in the window (see fig. 9.14).

Open the Directory. To open a directory, no file name is needed. Follow these steps:

1. Open the **F**ile menu and choose **O**pen Collection to get the Open Collection dialog box (refer to fig. 9.13).

2. Select the drive and the directory.

Fig. 9.14
A CorelMOSAIC window with a single open library window.

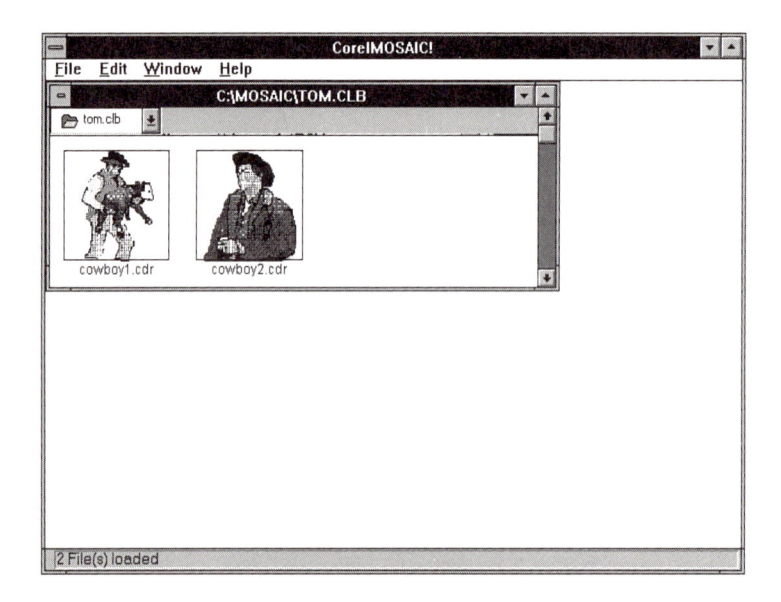

3. In the List Files of Type list box, select the class of files you want to see when the directory opens. CorelMOSAIC won't show any other kind of files in the File Name list. The top item in the list is All Files, in case you want to show everything in the directory. Don't choose Corel Library (*.CLB) or Corel Catalog (*.CLC). If you do, CorelMOSAIC will think you want to open a library or a catalog rather than the directory.

4. Optional: To further restrict the thumbnails that show, click the Options button to expand the dialog box and then click the Find button. This gets the dialog box to select by keyword, as shown in figure 9.15.

   Enter the appropriate keywords, with the appropriate AND and OR conditions.

5. Click OK, or Start Search if you are doing a keyword search (step 4).

A new window opens showing thumbnails and names of all files in the directory that satisfy the List Files of Type and keyword specifications (see fig. 9.16).

Using CorelMOSAIC 287

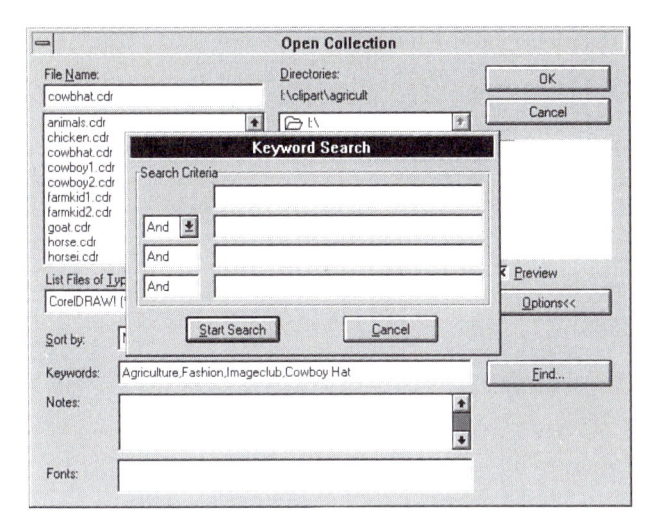

Fig. 9.15
Expanded Open Collection dialog box, with Keyword Search dialog box.

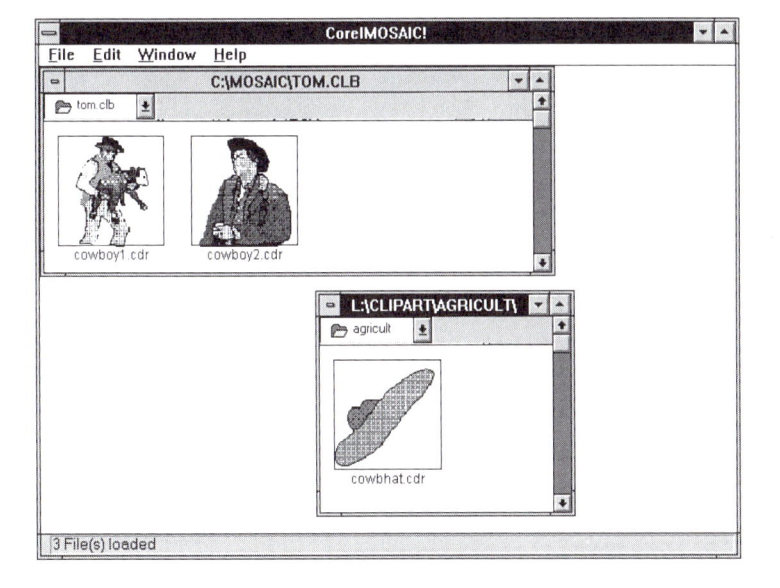

Fig. 9.16
The CorelMOSAIC window with open library and directory windows. Put a drawing in the library by dragging it from the directory window to the library window.

Drag To Add Drawings to the Library or Catalog. Place files in the library or catalog by dragging the thumbnails from the directory window, as outlined in the following steps:

1. Make sure that the directory window is selected (not the library or catalog window), and then select the thumbnails to be added.

2. Drag the selected thumbnails to the library or catalog window. The cursor changes shape when you are dragging.

You can select thumbnails by using the following methods:

- Click a single thumbnail to select it.
- Ctrl+click a thumbnail to select it without deselecting any others.
- Shift+click a thumbnail to select it and all thumbnails between it and the next closest selected thumbnail.
- Open the **E**dit menu and choose Select **A**ll to select all thumbnails in the window.
- Open the **E**dit menu and choose **C**lear All to deselect all thumbnails in the window.
- Open the **E**dit menu and choose Select by **K**eyword to select based on keywords. Enter the keywords with the appropriate AND and OR conditions in the Keyword Search dialog that appears (refer to fig. 9.15).

> **Note**
>
> You can use CorelMOSAIC to copy files from one directory to another instead of using the Windows File Manager. Follow the preceding instructions, but open the destination directory window and drag the thumbnail into it, rather than to a library or catalog window.

Tip
Dragging to a library may take a few seconds while the drawing file is compressed.

Tip
Files already in compressed format (for example, compressed TIFF) are not further compressed.

When you close the library or catalog window, the updated library or catalog file is saved automatically.

Deleting from Libraries and Catalogs

Follow these steps to delete files, but be careful—a relatively simple error can remove a drawing from the disk:

1. In the CorelMOSAIC window, open the library or catalog file with the drawing file to be deleted. (See the earlier section, "Open the Library or Catalog File.")

2. Select the thumbnail to be deleted. The various ways to select, including selecting multiple thumbnails, are described in the preceding section, "Drag To Add Drawings to the Library or Catalog."

3. Open the **E**dit menu and choose **D**elete. A dialog box asks for confirmation. Here is where you must be careful because delete is different if you are deleting from a library, a catalog, or if by mistake, a directory. It's easy to make a mistake because the windows for all three look similar.

Using CorelMOSAIC   289

The following table shows the results of deleting from various files.

Delete From...	What delete does
A catalog (CLC suffix, shown in the window title bar.)	**SAFE** Removes the drawing thumbnail and path from the catalog. This is safe because it does not remove the drawing file from the disk.
A library (CLB suffix, shown in the window title bar.)	**DANGER!** Removes the compressed drawing file from the library file. If there is no copy of the file elsewhere on the disk, the file is gone. There is no undo to restore the drawing if you delete by mistake.
A directory (The title bar shows no file name, just directory.)	**DANGER!** Removes the file from the disk. Although CorelMOSAIC has no undo command to restore files, you may be able to use a DOS or Windows utility to unerase, and therefore recover, the file.

Using Libraries and Catalogs

Now that you know how to make and modify libraries and catalogs, you can begin to put them to use.

Editing from a Library or Catalog

To edit a drawing in a library or catalog, open the library or catalog in a window to show the thumbnails. Double-click on the thumbnail of the drawing you want to edit. Or highlight the thumbnail, open the **E**dit menu, and choose Edi**t**.

CorelMOSAIC automatically opens the application associated with the file name suffix and brings the drawing or graphic into the application so that you can edit it.

Tip
You can edit from a directory window also. Open the directory window (refer to the preceding section, "Open the Directory"), and double-click the thumbnail shown.

> **Note**
>
> *Association* is a Windows function. Windows keeps a list of file extensions and the application to which each belongs. That's how Windows knows, for example, to call up CorelDRAW! when you tell it to edit a file with a CDR extension. (Of course, CDR must be in the association list, associated to CorelDRAW!.) You tell Windows about associations in the Windows File Manager. Open the File Manager's **F**ile menu and choose **A**ssociate to get the dialog box to set up associations.

To edit a drawing contained in a library, you must expand the drawing from the library file to a separate file. When you double-click to edit, a dialog box appears in which you can name a directory to hold the expanded file.

CorelMOSAIC then opens the application and the drawing. Make your edits and close the file to preserve them on disk. Because this does not update the drawing in the library file, you must add the modified drawing back to the library, as described in the preceding section, "Adding Drawing Files to Libraries and Catalogs." If you want, you can then delete the edited file from the disk, to preserve disk space.

Because a catalog only references a drawing file (the path and file name are in the catalog, not the drawing itself), editing from a catalog is simpler than editing from a library. No expansion is needed, and the edited version is available from the catalog immediately after it is saved from the application.

Importing from a Library or Catalog

You can import graphics from catalogs and libraries into a CorelDRAW! drawing, as shown in the following steps:

1. In CorelDRAW!, open the drawing that will receive the graphic.

2. Switch to CorelMOSAIC. Open it if it is not already open.

3. In CorelMOSAIC, open the library or catalog in a window to show the thumbnails.

4. Highlight the thumbnail to be imported.

5. Open the **E**dit menu and choose **I**mport Into CorelDRAW!.

Squeezing Many Thumbnails into a Window

If you have many drawings in a catalog, library, or directory, you probably want to see as many thumbnails as you can at one time in its window. You can reduce the wasted space between thumbnails, and make sure that the thumbnails are as small as possible by following these steps:

1. Open the **F**ile menu and choose Pre**f**erences. The Preferences dialog box appears as shown in figure 9.17.

2. In the Thumbnail list box, select Regular Thumbnail.

Tip
You can save even more space by just showing the file names. Select Text Only in the Thumbnail list-box.

3. In the Spacing box, enter values for Horizontal and Vertical. These are the gaps between adjacent thumbnails. For maximum squeeze, take them all the way down to zero.

4. Adjust the font with the Font button. This is the font used for the file name under the thumbnail—if it is too large you won't see all the name. You probably have to experiment to find the best size. Of course, choose a font you like.

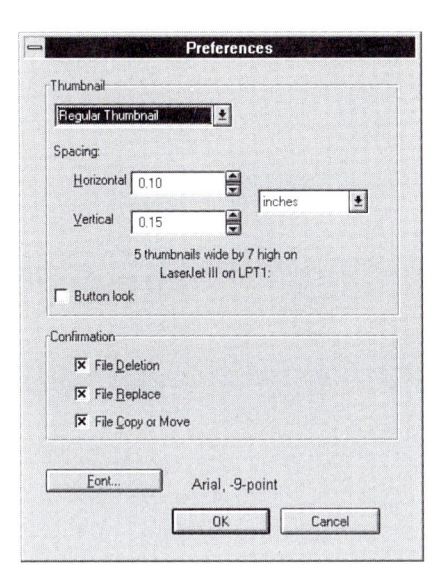

Fig. 9.17
The Preferences dialog box. Use these parameters to control thumbnail density in the library, catalog, and directory windows.

5. Click OK; examine the resultant thumbnail spacing and font; and readjust them if needed.

Editing Keywords

You can change the keywords assigned to a CorelDRAW! drawing file, as follows:

- *Directory*. You can make keyword changes only from a directory.

- *Library*. If a drawing is placed in a library, you must expand it to a separate file; change the keyword in the expanded file; and add the expanded file back to the library. You then can delete the separate file to conserve disk space.

- *Catalog*. You can't change the keywords from a catalog window. Instead, find the file in its directory and change the keywords from there.

Follow these steps to change keywords in a directory:

1. Open a directory to show the thumbnails of CorelDRAW! drawings in it. Refer to the preceding section, "Open the Directory," for instruction on how to open a directory.

2. Select the thumbnail by clicking on it.

3. Open the **E**dit menu and choose Key**w**ords. A dialog box appears that shows the existing keywords and lets you enter new ones and delete unwanted ones (see fig. 9.18).

Fig. 9.18
The dialog box for editing keywords from a directory window.

4. To add a keyword, enter it in the New Keyword box and click Add. To delete a keyword, highlight the keyword in the Current Keywords box and click Delete. To change Thumbnails, Click Next or Previous to switch to the next or previous thumbnail in the directory window.

5. Click Done to remove the dialog box. Close the directory window to record the changes.

Printing Multiple Drawings

With CorelMOSAIC, you can easily print many drawings with one command. In a library, catalog, or directory window, select the drawings to be printed. Open the **F**ile menu and choose **P**rint Files to get the standard Print dialog box. Click OK to print the drawings.

Extracting and Merging Text

You can use CorelMOSAIC to edit text in a drawing. You usually want to do this when you have so much text that a text editor or word processor is useful. In CorelMOSAIC, the text is extracted to a text file in which you edit it. Then from CorelMOSAIC again, you merge the edited text back into the drawing. The procedure is as follows:

1. In a library, catalog, or directory window select the drawing to be edited.

2. Open the **E**dit menu and choose E**x**tract Text.

3. The Extract dialog box opens, in which you define the text file name and location. Select the drive and directory from the Drives and Directories windows. CorelMOSAIC suggests the same file name as the

drawing file (it's usually simplest to use that name). The suffix is TXT, indicating a text file. Click OK to tell CorelMOSAIC to do the extraction and save the text file.

4. Use an editor, such as the Notepad or Write applications that come with Windows, to edit the text. Edit just your text. Be careful not to change any of the other characters that appear in the file. CorelMOSAIC needs these to merge the edited text back to the drawing.

5. Close the file in the editor.

6. From CorelMOSAIC, make sure that the drawing is selected. Open the **E**dit menu and choose **M**erge-Back Text.

7. The Merge Back dialog box opens, in which you select the text file. Usually, the edited file is suggested, and you only have to click OK. The edited text is merged into the drawing, replacing the original text.

8. You can immediately print the file to check how the modified drawing looks. Open the **F**ile menu and choose **P**rint Files.

Converting Files to Another Format with MOSAIC

You can select one or more images in a MOSAIC collection and convert those images to another file format. The advantage to using MOSAIC for this operation is that you can handle files in batches rather than endure the tedium of using another application to convert the images one by one.

MOSAIC lets you convert the images in a collection to any of the following formats:

Windows Bitmap (.BMP, .DIB, .RLE)

CompuServe Bitmap (.GIF)

Computer Graphics Metafile (.CGM)

JPEG Bitmap (.JPG, .JFF, .JTL, .CMP)

OS/2 Bitmap (.BMP)

Paintbrush (.PCX)

Scitex CT Bitmap (.SCT, .CT)

Targa Bitmap (.TGA, .VDA, .JCB)

TIFF Bitmap (.TIF)

Adobe Illustrator (.AI, .EPS)

AutoCAD DXF (.DXF)

GEM File (.GEM)

HPGL Plotter File (.PLT)

IBM PIF (.PIF)

Macintosh PICT (.PIC)

Matrix IMapro SCODL (.SCD)

WordPerfect Graphic (.WPG)

Follow these steps to convert one or more images to a new file format:

1. Open a catalog of images in MOSAIC.

2. Select the thumbnail(s) for the image(s) you want to convert to a new format.

3. Open the **F**ile menu and choose Con**v**ert. The Convert Image(s) dialog box appears.

4. Choose an option from the Convert to Files of **T**ype drop-down list.

5. Type a new file name in the File **N**ame text box. You don't need to type in a file extension—MOSAIC adds it automatically based on your choice in the preceding step.

6. Change the Dri**v**es and **D**irectories settings if necessary to specify where the converted file(s) is stored.

7. Click OK. MOSAIC converts the selected file(s).

From Here...

The first portion of this chapter covered the various file-related activities used in CorelDRAW!, such as the standard Open, Close, Save, and Save As processes. You also learned about using keywords and descriptions to assist in locating and identifying drawing files.

Importing and exporting as they relate to using various file formats in CorelDRAW! or with other applications were then discussed, including importing directly from another file or importing using the Windows Clipboard.

Finally, this chapter covered CorelMOSAIC, the utility application for compressing, cataloging, and printing drawings.

The next chapter deals with creating the actual output of your images and merging images and text. For other information related to drawings saved in files on disk, consider these chapters:

- Chapter 10, "Printing and Merging Files," describes printing drawing files from within CorelDRAW! and without opening CorelDRAW! yourself. It also tells how to merge a text file with a drawing to make multiple copies of the drawing with only the text changed.

- Chapter 28, "Creating Presentation Charts with CorelCHART," teaches you how to spruce up data charts with saved drawings. You can even use saved drawings to make bars in bar charts.

- Chapter 29, "Making Presentations with CorelSHOW," discusses how to include your drawing files in an on-screen slide show.

- Chapter 30, "Adding Animation with CorelMOVE," covers how to make drawings move around on-screen.

Chapter 10

Printing and Merging Files

by Thomas Budlong

Eventually, all drawings are sent to a laser printer, 35mm slide developer, color printer, Linotype, or other output device. In some cases, as with CorelSHOW, the output device may be the computer screen itself. This final category is discussed in Chapter 29, "Making Presentations with CorelSHOW." The others are discussed here.

This chapter investigates printing methods provided by CorelDRAW! and suggests ways to use CorelDRAW!'s automated features to speed up the final steps of drawing creation. CorelDRAW! lets you scale the output from 1/10th of its original size up to 10 times that size. You can even print large drawings in *tiles* (multiple sheets that form the full picture when assembled). This chapter covers printing procedures in general. Chapter 12, "Using Color for Commercial Success," covers many of the details, including color printing.

This chapter also describes *merging*, a technique to combine text from a text file with a CorelDRAW! drawing. A classic merge application is the creation of certificates or awards. The CorelDRAW! document serves as the certificate shell, and the merged text can include information such as student names and class dates. The basic concept is the same as with any word-processing merge procedure (for example, creating mailing labels), except that a CorelDRAW! image is merged with text to create a combined document.

In this chapter, you learn the following:

- Previewing a drawing on-screen before printing
- Details of printing controls

- "Automated" printing without CorelDRAW! open
- Color and Postscript printing
- Merging text files and drawings

General Printing Procedures

Consider the output device before you make a drawing.

◄ See "Changing the Outline Color," p. 141

◄ See "Working with Interior Fills," p. 146

◄ See "Setting the Page Size and Orientation," p. 36

► See "Choosing a Page Layout and Display Style," p. 542

- *Color versus Monochrome.* Draw in color when the target output device is color. Draw in black and white or gray shades when the target output device is monochrome. To draw in color when the output device is monochrome, for example, is to set yourself up for disappointment. The conversion from color to monochrome is often difficult to predict—you're better off working with shades of gray to ensure that what you see is what you (*really*) get.

- *Page Size.* Set the page size (open the **L**ayout menu and choose **P**age Setup, and then the Size tab) to match the output device before you begin drawing. For example, when making a slide, set the Paper Size to Slide so that the dimensions and the horizontal-to-vertical ratios seen on-screen are those of the slide format. If you make the drawing using Letter Size and later convert to Slide, the drawing probably will need modification because it won't have its original appearance in the new format.

The general printing procedure is as follows:

1. Open the **F**ile menu and choose **P**rint (or press Ctrl+P) to display the Print dialog box.

2. Set up the output device:

   Use the Printer box in the middle of the Print dialog box to select the output device. It may already show the one you want to use.

   Click the Setup button to access printer options. These settings are specific to the output device chosen and are not described in this book—you have to go to the documentation for the output device to learn about them. Sometimes on-line help is available.

3. Set the number of copies.

4. Click the Options key to get the Print Options dialog box. This describes the printed page layout. The Separations and Options tabs appear here, as well, for further refinements relative to the output device.

5. Adjust the size of the drawing and its position on the printed sheet with the Left, Top, Width, and Height controls. Set the drawing's position on the page with the Fit to Page, Center, Maintain Aspect Ratio, and Print Tiled Pages check boxes. The best way to see what these controls do is to check the Preview Image box to turn on the preview.

▶ See "Exploring the Print Options Dialog Box," p. 363

The following sections cover these basic steps in more detail. The other choices you see in the Print dialog box, Options and Color, are described in Chapter 12, "Using Color for Commercial Success."

Tip
To print just some objects, select them, open the File menu, and choose Print; then check Selected Objects Only in the Print dialog box.

Previewing before Printing

As you saw in the preceding section, the Print Options dialog box gives you an idea of what the output looks like. (You must check Preview Image below the preview window.)

You can get a better preview of the output by displaying the standard Editable View. Open the View menu and uncheck Wireframe.

Or you can get an even more detailed preview by opening the View menu and choosing Full-Screen Preview (or press F9). This uses the entire screen for the display. Press F9 or Esc, or click the right mouse button to return to normal view.

You can full-screen preview just selected objects. Open the View menu and choose Preview Selected. Select the objects and perform the full-screen preview described earlier.

Printing—the Details

To print, follow these steps:

1. Open the File menu and choose Print (or press Ctrl+P) to display the Print dialog box (see fig. 10.1). This dialog box provides access to the CorelDRAW! printing features and settings.

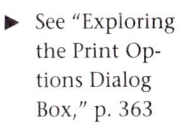

Fig. 10.1
Use the Print dialog box to send the drawing to the printer. Sizing, positioning, and other controls are under the Options button.

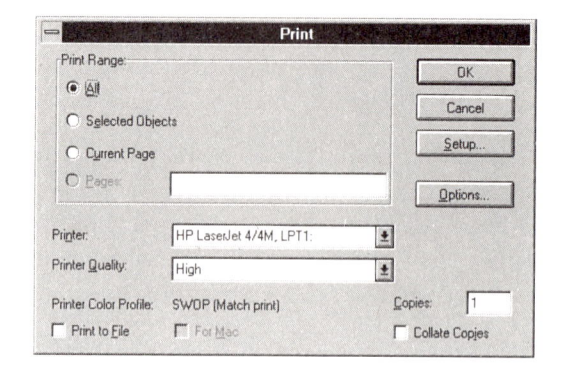

2. Select a print range. The following options are available:

   - *All*. The whole drawing is printed, whether it consists of one page or ten.
   - *Selected Objects*. Only the objects selected in the drawing print. You must select them before entering the Print dialog box. Often you use this to check a particular section of the drawing you have been working on.
   - *Current Page*. For multipage drawings, this option prints only the page on-screen when you entered the Print dialog box.
   - *Pages*. For multipage drawings, you can select which pages to print. Separate the page numbers with commas and indicate page ranges with a dash, for example: 2,5,7-10,12.

3. Choose a Printer. A Printer drop-down menu lists available output devices. To choose a different output device, click the down arrow and select a device from the list. The list shows the output device drivers installed on your computer. You can, for example, fax an image from within CorelDRAW! by selecting the desired fax output device (such as WinFax Pro) from the drop-down list and following the printing procedures provided with the fax software.

> **Note**
>
> Setting the printer here does not change the Windows system default printer or the current printer for any other applications you have running. The setting is for CorelDRAW! only.

4. Choose printer quality. A drop-down menu enables you to choose High, Medium, or Low quality, or specifies a list of dpi settings. Of course, higher quality prints more slowly, but you must use it for final output. For checking and proofing, you can use a lower quality. You have to experiment to see which quality suits your particular requirements.

5. In the Print dialog box, click the Setup button to display the Windows Printer Setup dialog box like the one shown in figure 10.2. (This is the same dialog box you get by selecting the Printers icon in the Windows Control Panel and then choosing Setup from the dialog box that opens, or by opening the **F**ile menu and choosing P**r**int Setup.) The dialog box varies based on the output device chosen and its associated options. In general, you can select the quality of output, the number of copies, and the output orientation (portrait or landscape) from this dialog box. Choosing Options, if available, from the Setup dialog box gives you access to other features associated with the output device. The printing screen frequency (the number of printed dots per inch) used is the frequency set in the Options tab of the CorelDRAW! Print Options dialog box.

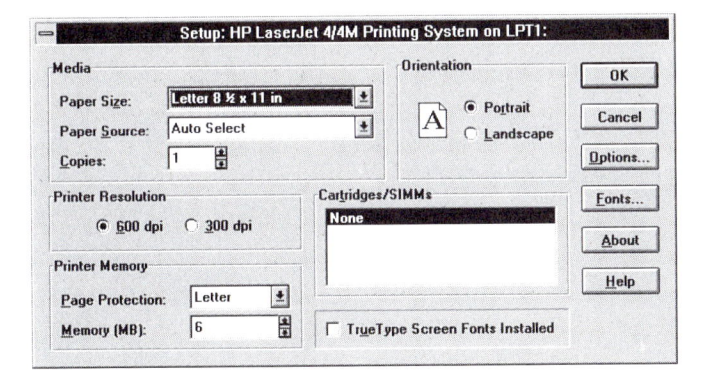

Fig. 10.2
A typical Printer Setup dialog box. Different printers have different Setup dialog boxes.

6. Print to File tells CorelDRAW! to send the output to a disk file instead of directly to an output device. When you print with Print to File checked, you see a dialog box in which you can specify a directory and enter a file name. If you don't include an extension with the file name, CorelDRAW! adds .PRN; if you do include an extension, it is preserved.

   You later can send this file to a printer directly from DOS without CorelDRAW! running. This option can be particularly valuable when you must print from a system without CorelDRAW!. Or you can give the file to a service bureau for printing.

7. The For Mac option sends output in a format compatible with the Apple Macintosh computer, commonly used by service bureaus. During the save process it removes codes such as ^D that stop the Mac from properly printing a PostScript file.

Chapter 10—Printing and Merging Files

> **Note**
>
> Make sure that you match your PostScript output device dpi setting to that intended for the final output. In essence, print-to-file creates a final image of the document just as if it were going to the intended printer; the document is just saved to disk instead of being sent to the printer. If these settings don't match those of the final print devices, the output results may be unacceptable. If adjustable for the selected printer, the dpi value is set by using the File menu's Print Setup or Print options.

Most Macs these days can read DOS disks. But if you run across an older Mac that can't, you must convert the disk to Mac format. The service bureau should be able to help you handle this task.

8. In the Copies box, indicate how many copies you want.

9. Click the Options button to display the Print Options dialog box (see fig. 10.3).

Fig. 10.3
Use the Print Options dialog box to set the size of the printed image and its position on the paper.

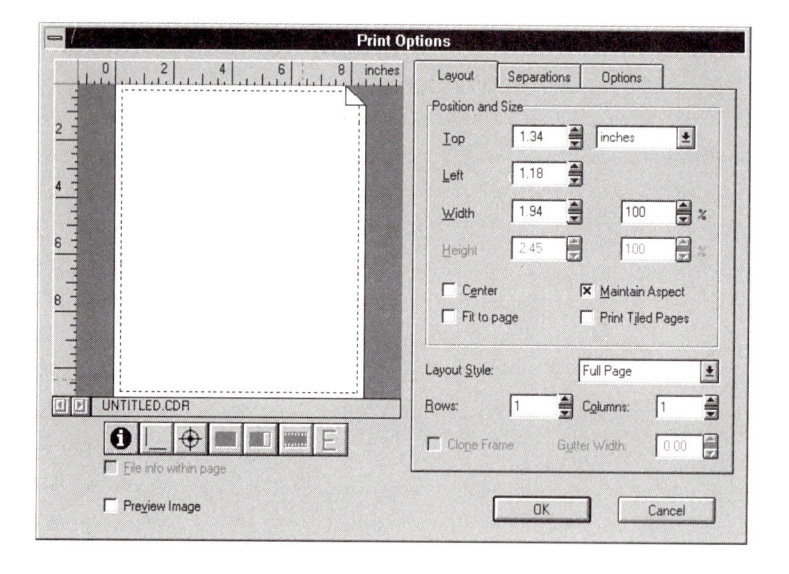

10. Click the Layout tab. Adjust the controls as follows:

   - *Preview Window.* The large box at the left shows a preview of the drawing as it will print on the page with the current settings. Enable this preview box by checking Preview Image below the preview window. The lines near the edge of the preview page represent the printer cutoffs—the selected output device can't print outside these lines. For many laser printers, this cutoff point is 0.25 inches from each edge of the page.

- *Position—Left and Top.* In the Position and Size section, the settings in the Top and Left boxes control the location of the printed image on the page. Left determines the distance from the left edge of the page to the left side of the image. Top determines the distance from the top of the page to the top of the image. These may not be available if the image location is already set with the check boxes at the bottom of this section.

- *Size—Height and Width.* You can define a specific printed image size using the Width and Height boxes in the Position and Size section of the dialog box. If Maintain Aspect is checked, setting one value automatically adjusts the other to keep the height-to-width ratio the same. The scale values, shown to the right of the Height and Width boxes, change automatically.

- *Units.* You can work in inches, centimeters, millimeters, points, or picas. Click the down arrow on the units pull-down list in the lower-right corner of the dialog box and make your selection.

- *Scale.* You can set the scale of the image directly. Scale settings are made in the boxes to the right of the Height and Width boxes. If you know the size for your final image, you can use the Scale box to determine what scaling is required. Scaling and positioning the image changes only the printed output size, not the object itself. If the Maintain Aspect Ratio box is checked, the options for Height are disabled.

> **Note**
>
> If you're sending drawings to a commercial print house, you can use the value that appears in the Scale box to determine scaling requirements. This information is often necessary when dealing with printers who are making final plates for printing. They might need to reduce the image to a certain size; your ability to provide them with a percentage scaling factor makes the process easier.

- *Center.* This check box option aligns the center of the drawing with the center of the page. Width and Height dimensions and scaling are then done around the center point.

- *Fit to Page.* This check box option reduces or enlarges the drawing to fill the printed sheet. This option commonly is used for proofreading.

- *Maintain Aspect.* Check this box to keep the ratio of height-to-width the same as the drawing. This makes sure that the printed drawing doesn't look stretched in the horizontal or vertical direction.

- *Print Tiled Pages.* Use this to print larger than the currently selected page size. The drawing is printed on multiple sheets. You manually assemble the sheets to make the larger finished image. Notice that Fit to Page and Print Tiled Pages cannot be active at the same time because they perform mutually exclusive operations.

Printing Specific Layers of a Drawing

◄ See "Understanding CorelDRAW! Layers," p. 131

You might want to print the layers of a drawing on separate pages. Open the **L**ayout menu and choose **L**ayers Roll-Up (or press Ctrl+F3) to show the Layers roll-up window. Then double-click any of the layer names to display the Edit Layers dialog box (see fig. 10.4).

Fig. 10.4
The Edit Layers dialog box lets you select which layers to print.

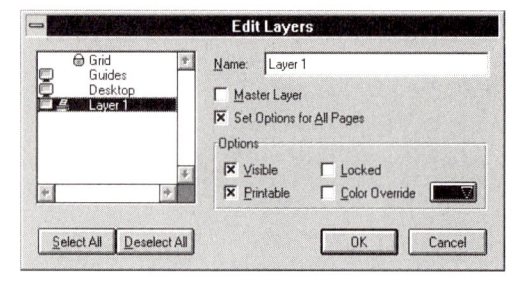

► See "Creating Color Separations in CorelDRAW!," p. 362

To enable/disable printing a layer, select the layer in the box on the left. Then check or uncheck Printable. Only those layers with Printable checked will print. You can make color separations in this way if you restrict certain colors to specific layers, but it's easier and more accurate to use the Color Separations feature included with the Print functions.

> **Troubleshooting**
>
> *The printout is "garbage." Characters and lots of paper comes out of the printer.*
>
> The wrong printer driver is selected. Select the right printer from the list in the middle of the File Print dialog box.
>
> *Only part of the drawing is printed. It's as if someone snipped off an edge with scissors.*
>
> The printer does not have enough memory, or some of its memory is being used for something else. Check the memory in the printer and if you think it has enough, reset the printer with either a software command from the printer's control panel, or by turning the printer off, and then on again. Also, check your Print Preview image and the Top and Left Position settings.
>
> *Print asks for a file name.*
>
> You have told it to print to a file—that is, to save the printing instructions in a disk file instead of sending them out of the computer directly to a printer. Uncheck Print to File (in the lower left corner of the Print dialog box).

Printing without Starting CorelDRAW!

You have four ways to print drawings without starting CorelDRAW!: choosing File Print from the Windows File Manager; using the drag-and-drop feature of Windows 3.1; using MOSAIC as the print manager (see Chapter 9, "File-Related Operations and CorelMOSAIC," for details); and printing a PRN file from the DOS prompt.

- *Choosing File Print from the File Manager.* In the Windows File Manager, select the drawing file with the CDR extension to be printed. Then, from the File Manager's menu, choose **F**ile **P**rint. This automatically opens CorelDRAW!, opens the drawing file you had selected, and displays CorelDRAW!'s Print dialog box—you don't have to do the work. Make the desired entries in the Print dialog box (number of copies and so forth) and click OK. The drawing prints, and the system even closes CorelDRAW! after printing.

- *Windows Drag and Drop.* Windows 3.1 has a wonderful feature called Drag and Drop, similar to printing from the file manager.

    The Print Manager must be running (double-click its icon in the Main group) and iconized. Open the Windows File Manager, find the drawing file with the CDR extension, and drag it to the Print Manager icon. From here on the operation is just like a File Print operation—CorelDRAW! opens, gets the Print dialog, and closes after printing.

Actually, these two methods work with any Windows application that is associated with a file extension. (For example, CDR files are associated with CorelDRAW!, XLS files are associated with Excel, DOC files are associated with Word for Windows.)

> **Note**
>
> *Association* is a Windows function. Windows keeps a list of file extensions and the application each belongs to. That's how it knows, for instance, to call up CorelDRAW! when you tell it to print a file with a CDR extension. (Of course, CDR must be in the association list, associated to CorelDRAW!.) You tell Windows about associations in the Windows File Manager. Open the File Manager's File menu and choose Associate to display the dialog box in which you set up associations. Chances are that these associations were made when you first installed the application.

These two methods can't print multiple files at once. Use CorelMOSAIC for this operation.

- *CorelMOSAIC*. This application, included with CorelDRAW!, is a multi-purpose image management application that, among other things, enables you to print multiple files at once. See Chapter 9, "File-Related Operations and CorelMOSAIC!," for details of MOSAIC and its file management operations. You are encouraged to review this chapter because the procedures outlined there streamline many of CorelDRAW!'s routine and time-consuming operations.

- *Print from DOS*. Use this procedure to print files on systems without CorelDRAW!. Using your system, which has CorelDRAW! installed, you perform normal printing in CorelDRAW! except that you choose Print to File (described earlier in this chapter). Make sure that the printer selected in the Print dialog box is the printer on the destination system. This procedure creates a file with extension PRN containing all the necessary printer instructions. Take the file to the other system and type the following command string at the DOS prompt:

    Copy *filename.PRN* [/b] LPT*x*:

The string *filename.PRN* should be replaced, of course, with the name of the print file. The /b parameter (which indicates a binary file) must be included when printing to non-PostScript printers, and LPT*x*: represents the system port designation for the printer device (*x* usually equals a number from 1 to 4 for networked systems).

Printing Color Files

Creating color output used to be expensive. The per-page cost was high if done by a service bureau, and only the most dedicated companies bought expensive color printers. But now things are different. Color inkjet printers are becoming common, and 35mm slide-makers are inexpensive enough for companies to justify creating slide presentations using presentation software, including the Corel family of products.

To best ensure that colors received from your commercial printer match those that you expect, use industry standard color-matching systems, such as PANTONE and TRUMATCH. You easily can acquire color-matching charts for these systems.

Halftone Patterns, Screen Frequency, and Angle Considerations

Halftone screens are applied to drawings to meet specific commercial printing requirements or for special artistic effect. If you are using a PostScript printer, you can define the halftone screen applied when the image is printed. The screens are defined by the user at the time of object creation in the form of an outline, fill, or patterned fill type. You cannot view the effect of a halftone screen on the display—you must print it to see the effect.

PostScript and Non-PostScript Printing

Many PostScript printers have an internal processor to do the rather extensive calculations needed. Consequently, they tend to print rapidly because the computer's processor does not have to perform those functions. PostScript emulators, which are generally software-based, allow for PostScript printing to non-Postscript printers. However, they increase the processing load of the computer because the computer, not the printer, must do the calculations. Therefore they slow the printing process. If you are using a non-PostScript printer such as a non-PostScript LaserJet, your processing time increases because your computer must perform printing-related calculations.

When using PostScript printers, be sure to use an up-to-date Windows PostScript driver. If you don't, CorelDRAW! may not print properly. To see which printer driver version you have installed, in the Windows Print Manager open the **O**ptions menu and choose **P**rinter Setup. Select the PostScript printer, click **S**etup, and click **A**bout. The driver version number is displayed. Microsoft product support can tell you whether this is the latest driver. Microsoft also maintains a BBS with the latest drivers—you can download a new PostScript driver if needed.

Most printers have built-in fonts, called *resident fonts*. Using these fonts requires less interaction with the computer, speeding printing. You have control over using these built-in fonts as follows:

1. In the Print Options dialog box, select the Options tab (see fig. 10.3).

2. To use the printer's built-in fonts, uncheck Download Type 1 fonts. If the drawing contains non-Type 1 postscript fonts, the printer substitutes the closest equivalent font, or uses the printer's default font.

3. If the drawing uses Type 1 fonts not resident in the printer, check Download Type 1 fonts. This slows printing a bit, but the printed drawing is closer to what you designed on-screen.

4. If the drawing uses TrueType fonts and you want these converted to (built-in) Type 1 fonts, check Convert TrueType to Type 1. Your print file will be smaller than if the TrueType font information in your file were converted to curves or bitmaps when sent to the printer.

A non-PostScript laser printer stores the information it receives until it has a full page, and then prints the page. Laser printers with limited memory (500KB, for example) can't hold a full page, and pages print prematurely. In this case, drawings are printed in bands on separate pages.

More complex drawings need more printer memory. If you are using a PostScript printer, increasing curve *flatness* reduces the drawing complexity and, therefore, the printer memory required. To access the Flatness controls, open the **F**ile menu and choose **P**rint to display the Print dialog box. Click the Options button. From the next dialog box, click the Options tab (see fig. 10.5).

The Set Flatness To option defaults to 1.00, where 1 equals the number of segments that PostScript printers use to draw a curve; you can manually set it to a maximum of 100. If you have trouble printing because of memory-related issues, try incrementing the Flatness value by 4 or 5 and printing again. To minimize your involvement with this process, DRAW provides the Auto Increase Flatness option, which automatically increases the flatness in increments of 1 until the value exceeds the original Set Flatness To value by 10 points. The printer then skips the object creating the problems and moves on to print the next object.

◀ See "Adding Text to a Drawing," p. 207

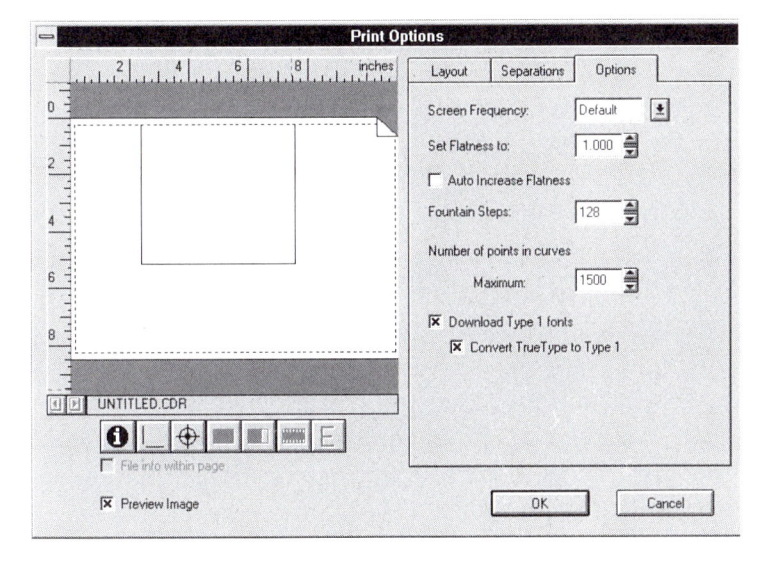

Fig. 10.5

The Options dialog box for setting flatness.

If the flatness setting becomes too high to accommodate the printing function, the curves may lose much of their character. You can take several steps to print your drawing as you created it without crashing the printer. Try to break the complex object causing the problems into several smaller objects by using the Shape tool and the Node Edit features. Remove all unnecessary nodes and objects because they take up memory space and add complexity. The AutoReduce feature may help you to reduce the number of required nodes without compromising drawing quality. Try not to convert large text strings to curves unless absolutely necessary, or at least break curved text objects into smaller objects that are treated individually when printing. These steps slow printing but they can help avoid going beyond the complexity limit of your printer.

> **Note**
>
> Printers that print a line at a time, such as most inkjet and dot-matrix printers, don't have these problems because they need only enough memory to print a single line. However, these printers are often slower and of lower quality.

▶ See "Understanding Memory Limitations," p. 592

To speed up printing draft images, try setting the output resolution to 150 or 75 dpi. Reducing resolution saves toner and also helps if you have trouble printing the entire image on a single page because less printer memory is required. Of course, this reduces print quality. If you want your drawings to look their best, you should seriously consider increasing the printer memory.

Bitmapped images tend to use a great deal of memory, especially at higher resolutions. Keeping them as small as possible and using lower resolution helps minimize printer memory problems. If you know that a scanned image will shrink between the time you scan it and the time it is used, you should scan it at a lower resolution, crop it, and modify its attributes using CorelPHOTO-PAINT!.

To test images being prepared for high-resolution output devices, Corel recommends printing them on a PostScript printer at 300 dpi with a flatness of 0.20. This combination simulates printing at 1270 dpi. If your image prints, you should not run into any problems printing to a higher resolution device. If problems occur, try to decrease the image complexity using some of the previously mentioned techniques.

The Screen Frequency option (in the same dialog box as the Flatness controls) pertains to the halftone screen frequency used while printing. Non-PostScript printers generally use the printer's default screen because individual control is not provided. PostScript printers allow access to this setting. Check with your printer or service bureau about their preferred screen frequencies to ensure that the drawing is printed without annoying blotches or Moiré patterns.

Merging Text into a CorelDRAW! Drawing

You can merge text from a word processing file into a CorelDRAW! drawing. You wouldn't do this for a single drawing, but if you want to make a set of individualized drawings that are all the same except for the text, Merge makes it practical. A typical application might be making Certificates of Completion for a computer software training center. An ASCII text file holds each student's name, class type, date, and instructor, and the certificate is a standard CorelDRAW! drawing. Using Print Merge, the information from the text file is inserted into the drawing to make a customized certificate for each student.

An Overview of the Merge Process

Two files are required to perform a merge in CorelDRAW!: a DRAW image file and an ASCII text file. To work correctly, the ASCII file name must have a TXT extension. In this explanation, the text contained in the image file (text that will be replaced during the merge) is referred to as *primary text,* and the text contained in the ASCII file (text to be inserted during the merge) is called *secondary text.* You can't use the merge process to replace paragraph text in an image file; only artistic text can be replaced.

The ASCII secondary text file contains information that guides the replacement of artistic text strings in the image file with the text contained in the secondary file. The secondary file contains *records*, each of which corresponds to a complete set of information for a single certificate in the example case. And each record contains *fields*, each of which corresponds to a particular text entry to be inserted in the certificate (student name, course name, date of completion, and so on). The structure of the secondary file is critical to performing a Print Merge successfully, so be sure to follow the instructions carefully.

Creating the Word Processing Text File

The text file contains the information to be merged into the drawing. It must be in ASCII or Text format. Almost any word processor can save in ASCII format. The Windows Notepad application and the DOS EDIT command (not in early DOS versions) are simple and adequate ASCII editors. It also must have the extension TXT.

The data, like most files that carry data, are organized into records and fields. A *record* is all the information for one copy of the drawing. In the example of Certificates of Completion, a record has all the data for one student. Each record is on a separate line. A *field* is one piece of a record's data. In the example, the student name is one field and the class type is another. Each field goes to a different place in the drawing.

The format of the ASCII file must be as outlined in the following list:

- The first line is a number, which is the number of fields in each record. Note that each record must have the same number of fields.

- The second line contains the field names. The line must begin with a single backslash and it must end with a single backslash. Each field must have a name, and the names must be separated with double-backslashes. When you see the structure of the merge drawing, you will see how the field names from this line are used to direct where the field text goes in the drawings.

- All lines below the field name line are the actual field data, with one record per line. The arrangement of backslashes is the same as in the second line. You can have as many lines (records) as you want. Empty fields are allowed, just don't put anything between the surrounding backslashes.

Figure 10.6 shows the data for a few Certificates of Completion. Note where double and single backslashes are used.

Fig. 10.6
The text file for the merge example.

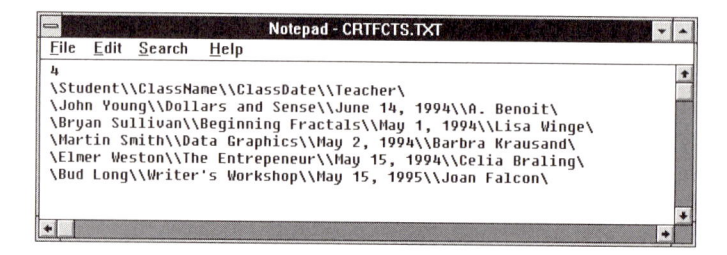

```
4
\Student\\ClassName\\ClassDate\\Teacher\
\John Young\\Dollars and Sense\\June 14, 1994\\A. Benoit\
\Bryan Sullivan\\Beginning Fractals\\May 1, 1994\\Lisa Winge\
\Martin Smith\\Data Graphics\\May 2, 1994\\Barbra Krausand\
\Elmer Weston\\The Entrepeneur\\May 15, 1994\\Celia Braling\
\Bud Long\\Writer's Workshop\\May 15, 1995\\Joan Falcon\
```

Save the file on disk. Don't leave it open in the word processor or text editor because CorelDRAW! will have problems if the text file is open somewhere else.

Preparing the Drawing for a Merge

Follow these steps to make a drawing for merging:

1. Create or open a drawing.

2. Put the field names on the drawing as artistic text—paragraph text won't work.

◄ See "Adding Artistic Text," p. 212

You enter artistic text by using the Artistic Text tool (the capital A). Put the field names where you want them to be in the merged drawing. The merge process will replace the field names with the field text from the ASCII text file. You have to think ahead a bit to avoid collisions—the merged texts can be longer than the field names and can bump into each other or other parts of the drawing if they come in too big.

The field names in the drawing must exactly match the field names in the ASCII text file. This rule includes spaces, punctuation, and capitalization. If they don't match exactly, the merge will not work.

3. Assign text attributes (type style, typeface, and point size) to the field names in the drawing. These attributes will be applied to the text from the ASCII text file when it is merged in.

If, for example, you want the merged text of a field to be centered and bold, give the artistic text field name those attributes. If you are tempted to get fancy by twisting the characters of the field names with the Shape tool, experiment before you do the final merge. The results can be interesting, but also can be unpredictable.

Performing the Merge

After creating the ASCII text file and the CorelDRAW! file, you can merge them. Follow these steps:

1. Put the drawing with the artistic text on the screen. In the example, this is the Certificate of Completion shown in figure 10.7.

Fig. 10.7
The sample certificate of completion, with the field names shown.

2. Open the **F**ile menu and choose Print **M**erge. The Print Merge dialog box appears (it looks like a standard Open dialog box).

3. Select the TXT file with the merge information, and then click OK.

4. From the Print dialog box, select the desired options and click OK. CorelDRAW! performs the merge and sends the results to the printer.

Figure 10.8 shows a sample printed Certificate of Completion.

The drawing with the fields file is not permanently changed during this process. Its information is modified for printing purposes only.

Fig. 10.8
A printed Certificate of Completion.

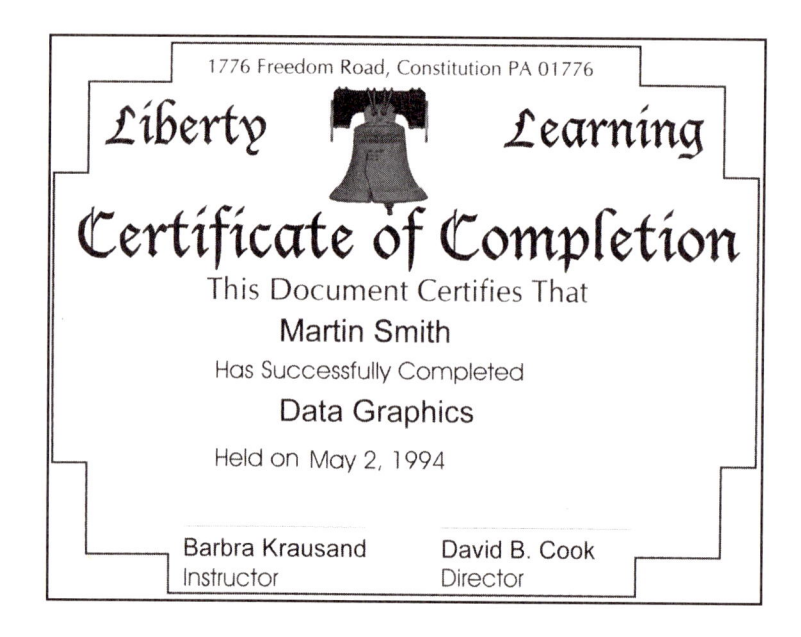

> 1776 Freedom Road, Constitution PA 01776
>
> *Liberty* *Learning*
>
> # Certificate of Completion
>
> This Document Certifies That
>
> **Martin Smith**
>
> Has Successfully Completed
>
> **Data Graphics**
>
> Held on May 2, 1994
>
> Barbra Krausand   David B. Cook
> Instructor   Director

Troubleshooting

Print Merge displays the message `Wrong file format or could not open.`

The text file doesn't agree with the drawing. Look for the following:

- The number on the first line of the ASCII text file must be exactly the number of fields on the second line.

- The field names on the second line must be the same as the artistic text they will replace in the drawing. Punctuation and capitalization must match exactly.

Data from the text file lands in the wrong fields in the drawing.

Two causes are as follows:

- The backslashes between the fields are incorrect. Look at figure 10.6 again. Each line must start and end with a \, and there are two \s between each field.

- The number of fields in one or more records is incorrect. Check to make sure that all lines have the same number of fields. If you have a field without any data, don't omit it. The two backslashes before and the two backslashes after the field will all be adjacent because there is no data to go between them.

From Here...

In this chapter, you learned about general CorelDRAW! printing and merging procedures. Specifically, you learned to preview drawings, print entire or parts of drawings, print without starting CorelDRAW!, and perform color and PostScript printing. You also learned to merge text from a text file with a drawing.

For other information related to printing, see the following chapters:

- Chapter 9, "File-Related Operations and MOSAIC," tells you how to print from MOSAIC, including printing multiple files with one command.

- Chapter 12, "Using Color for Commercial Success," gives more detail about color printing.

Part IV

Working with Scanners

11   Scanning Images into CorelDRAW!

Chapter 11

Scanning Images into CorelDRAW!

by Cyndie Klopfenstein

Other than drawing artwork with the CorelDRAW! tools, creating a painting in CorelPHOTO-PAINT, or importing presaved art, the only way to get text, words, or pictures into an electronic format is to scan them. You must consider several things before and during the scan. This chapter teaches you how to capture the best scan. You learn about setting up before the scan, saving and editing the scan, outputting the completed file, and then finally printing press nuances.

Setting up for a scan requires some preparation. Unless your computer is already suited, you may have to add additional hardware or software. You might also need to reinstall portions of the CorelDRAW! disks; and you need to consider the effects of output calibration and the type of printing press or monitor that creates the end product. The next section gives you some specifics.

To capture a high-quality scan that prints that way, too, read on to learn about the following:

- Determining input and output resolutions
- Deciding when to trace logos for optimum quality
- Recognizing the difference between halftones and line art
- Compensating for printing press dot gain
- Scanning text to an electronic file that can be edited, spell checked, and formatted

Choosing from Flatbed, Hand-Held, and Drum Scanners

The first step in the planning session is choosing a scanner. Deciding the quality requirements of the final product is the most important consideration in choosing a scanner. The three basic categories for scanners are *hand-held*, *flatbed*, and *drum*.

As a general rule, hand-held scanners yield the poorest results, but also are the least expensive of the scanning hardware options. They have a very narrow field of vision, which may require that you scan the artwork or text in several passes and then manipulate the parts together; or you may have to reduce the image before scanning, which contributes to further image degradation.

Flatbed scanners yield fair to fairly high-quality results, depending on the scanner. They are also about midway on the pricing scale. You can get a reasonably good flatbed scanner for about a thousand dollars. The Hewlett-Packard line of flatbed scanners is especially adept at good, but not quite the highest quality halftone scanning, and the scanners are TWAIN-compliant devices. (TWAIN is discussed later in this chapter.)

A drum scanner is usually considered the highest quality of the three options—and the highest priced. Of course, the garbage-in/garbage-out rule applies even with an expensive scanner, so capturing a good scan requires more than just a good scanner (or, just the best scanner for the job).

Installing CorelDRAW! for Scanning

▶ See "Custom Installation," p. 872

If this is the first time you're using your scanner, you may need to install the scanning drivers resident on both the CorelDRAW! 5 disks and CD-ROM. Under the Scanner button, make sure that you select the scanner type that matches your scanner from the drop-down list. Click OK to proceed with the installation. This part of the installation places the ID and name of your scanner in the Acquire drop-down list of the File menu of CorelTRACE or CorelPHOTO-PAINT.

Using TWAIN Technology

TWAIN is a fairly recent development on the scanning front. It's both Macintosh and Windows based and also works across different applications. In other words, you can use TWAIN on either a Macintosh or DOS machine, and it can be used with any application that supports TWAIN. It's not exclusive to CorelDRAW! It enables you to select a scanner (using the TWAIN interface even when CorelDRAW! installation disks have no driver for your scanner type) from the drop-down list and access that device through the TWAIN driver. The scanner must be a TWAIN-compliant device, and the software that you are using to acquire a TWAIN-compliant device must also be TWAIN compliant—CorelDRAW! and its subcomponents are, particularly PHOTO-PAINT and TRACE. CorelDRAW! installs TWAIN drivers at the time of installation if so directed.

SCSI Devices and Boards

Many scanners are connected to the host computer through a *Small Computer System Interface* (SCSI) board. This board might already be resident in your computer, or it might already be connected to another device. You can add another board for your scanner or connect the two SCSI devices together and let them read into the same SCSI slot. This is called *daisy chaining* the devices. The SCSI board was probably shipped with software for accessing the scanner or other devices after they are successfully connected to the board with a SCSI cable. Use this software to ensure that your connection is made properly and that the scanner is identified as such.

Install the SCSI board following the directions that come with it. Also add the software to your hard disk. If the scanner doesn't use a SCSI board, attach the scanner to your computer following the manufacturer's directions.

If you have already installed CorelDRAW!, you may have to return to the installation disks to add the software scanner drivers. You can do this by clicking the Customize button during the installation procedure and then clicking the Scanner button. This will take you to a new dialog box specifically for adding scanner drivers. Refer back to the beginning of the chapter if you need help from this point.

Once you've finished adding the drivers, launch either CorelPHOTO-PAINT or CorelTRACE to access the scanning interface.

Accessing Your Scanner with CorelPHOTO-PAINT or CorelTRACE

▶ See "Basic CorelPHOTO-PAINT Operation," p. 593

▶ See "Tracing an Image with CorelTRACE," p. 667

If you are scanning a photo, you can attain the best results and have the most editing features available in CorelPHOTO-PAINT. This subcomponent of CorelDRAW! is wonderful for editing, resizing, combining, and coloring photos. If you're planning to scan a company logo, CorelTRACE might be your best option. Most scanners are shipped right along with software for accessing and capturing the scan, but working inside CorelPHOTO-PAINT or CorelTRACE keeps all the editing tools right where you need them. After you have launched CorelPHOTO-PAINT or CorelTRACE, use these steps to capture a scan:

1. Select the scanner by opening the **F**ile menu; then choose Acquire Image and Select Source.

2. From the drop-down list, choose the name of the scanner you wish to select, or choose TWAIN.

3. Return to the **F**ile menu and choose Acquire. This prompts the dialog box for the scanner interface.

4. When the Scanning dialog window opens, you're ready to begin the scanning procedure (see fig. 11.1).

Fig. 11.1
From the File menu of CorelPHOTO-PAINT or CorelTRACE, you can access a properly connected scanner. This default scan window may look different if you have chosen a different device driver.

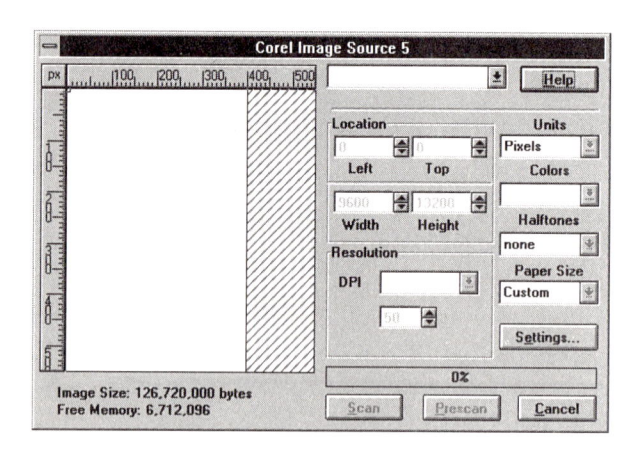

From this point, your processes may differ slightly or immensely. It all depends on the scanner driver that you have installed. There are some rudimentary similarities as explained in the steps that follow. These steps are for a typical desktop flatbed scanner:

1. Make sure the top drop-down list displays the name of your scanner. Then click the Prescan button to preview the image in the scanner.

2. Use the bounding box handles to select the area that you wish to capture. Only the image within the bounding box is captured into an electronic file.

3. When you have moved the bounding box to encompass only the area you want to capture, click the Scan button.

After the scanner has completed its pass, the image becomes like any other image created in CorelTRACE or CorelPHOTO-PAINT, in that it can be manipulated, edited, and saved just as though it was native to that application.

> **Troubleshooting**
>
> *When I try to access Select Source from inside of CorelTRACE or CorelPHOTO-PAINT, there are no scanners listed in the drop-down menu.*
>
> You need to install the scanner drivers. If you didn't do this at the time you installed CorelDRAW!, do it now by using the Custom installation options.
>
> *When I choose a scanner using Select Source and then click the Prescan button, nothing happens.*
>
> Your scanner is not properly connected to the computer. Check the cable connections and ensure that the scanner is plugged in and turned on.
>
> *I can't find CorelTRACE or CorelPHOTO-PAINT.*
>
> When installing CorelDRAW! you are given the opportunity to select the additional applications you wish to install. Make sure that you have chosen CorelTRACE and CorelPHOTO-PAINT. If you didn't, install them using the custom installation procedures.

Planning for the Best Scan Possible

Many outside factors affect how good your scan is. Of course, you can just click the buttons in the Scanner dialog box, and CorelPHOTO-PAINT or CorelTRACE goes to work capturing the scan. But remember the old adage: *garbage in, garbage out.* This phrase is never quite so apparent as with a bad scan. It is nearly impossible to make a bad scan look good after it is captured.

324 Chapter 11—Scanning Images into CorelDRAW!

On the other hand, you usually can make a pretty good scan out of a bad photo or logo, just by planning ahead (see fig. 11.2).

Fig. 11.2
This photo starts out bad, and without proper planning the scan doesn't improve. The file size also turns out to be extremely large—over 5M. At the bottom: a well-prepared scan.

Input (Scan) Resolution and Output Resolution

After you choose a scanner, you can move on to the next step, which is learning about the outside forces that should be considered. The first part of that lesson is terminology. *Input resolution* is the number of dots per inch used to create the image when you scan. If you enlarge a scan thousands of percentages, you find that any scan is made up of dots. These dots, when placed very close together, give the impression of a solid shaded area. If the dots are farther apart, the area is very light in color, and lines can appear dotted or dashed. When you scan an image, you must decide on an input resolution—how many dots per inch to draw the image on-screen. More is not necessarily better, as you learn in a moment.

Output resolution is the number of dots used to draw the image when printing. All images are printed with dots. Even lines drawn with the Pen tool of CorelDRAW!, which appear to be contiguous, are printed with dots. That's the limitation of laser printers, not the software. Choosing a higher number of dots is not necessarily better. The image that you are printing might look better with fewer dots spaced farther apart. Both input resolution and output resolution are measured in *dots per inch* (dpi). Look at the samples in figure 11.3 (on the following page). Notice how well or poorly thin lines hold up at different input and output resolutions. Conversely, with a high output resolution on the desktop laser printer, the dots of the halftone meld together and make detail hard to discern.

The Effects of Enlarging and Reducing on Input Resolution

When you scan, input resolution is not changed as you enlarge or reduce the image size. In fact, as you scan you might find that the image appears on your monitor many times larger than the image you scanned. This is because most monitors—not all—have a screen resolution of about 72 pixels per inch. If you scan the image at 300 dpi, the image previews so that one dot is equal to one pixel. You can reduce the view, but the input resolution remains the same. The reduced view may be represented with two or more dots equal to one pixel.

Fig. 11.3
Examples of different input and output resolutions.

100-dpi input, 300-dpi output

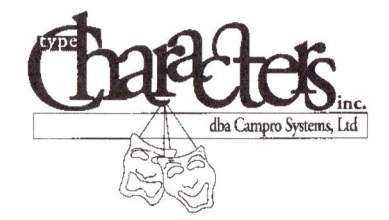

200-dpi input, 1,200-dpi output

300-dpi input, 1,200-dpi output

DPI and LPI

As stated earlier, if you scan a halftone with an input resolution of 300 dpi, it has 300 dots per inch; but that might not be how many lines per inch (lpi) it has. Lines per inch is generally chosen at print time. This is the number of lines (actually lpi might be elliptical, round, or square dots, lines, circles, textures, and so on) used to render *halftones* (from black-and-white, color, or grayscale images) and *screened* (or tinted) areas on your page. You specify this frequency by placing an "lpi" after the number. The most common frequencies are 65, 85, 100, 120, 133, 150, 200, and 300 lpi. This is not the same as output resolution, which is a measure of the number of dots used per inch to draw the image during printing (output). A halftone of 85 lines per inch (lpi) can be output at a resolution of 2,400 dots per inch (dpi), and this only means that more smaller and finer dots are used to draw each dot of the halftone and tinted areas. It's a concept similar to your monitor using 72 pixels per inch to draw each dot in a scan.

Have you ever noticed that no matter how good a picture looks on your monitor, it rarely looks as good on the 300-dpi paper laser printouts? This is due to the size of the dot used to draw the image (both on-screen and on paper) and the components that make up the dot. In the monitor's case, a very small electron beam of light (72 of them per inch, usually) is shot with varying intensity onto the inside surface of your monitor, causing phosphor pixels to glow in combinations of red, green, and blue. That specific beam of electrons may be on or off. With a desktop laser printer (I specify desktop because a high-resolution imagesetter is also a type of laser printer), the dots are much larger. Although the datasheet on the desktop laser printer indicates that it is 300 dpi, if you specify a 100-lpi halftone, all you get is mud as in the second example in figure 11.4. The dots that this type of laser printer uses are very large compared to a high-resolution imagesetter. Choosing a halftone screen (lpi) of a number more like 55 or 60 yields the best results.

Fig. 11.4
This halftone is printed at 55 lpi/300 dpi, 100 lpi/300 dpi, 100 lpi/1,200 dpi, and 150 lpi/1,200 dpi.

55 lpi/300 dpi

100 lpi/300 dpi

100 lpi/1200 dpi

150 lpi/1200 dpi

With a high-end imagesetter, the number of dots and the size make a drastic change. The dots are so small that 1,200, 2,400, or even 3,600 of them fit in a linear inch (dpi). These dots seem minute compared to a monitor that displays the image with only 72 dpi, and compared to the desktop laser printer that prints at 300 dpi. You should now understand why a picture looks so much better from an imagesetter. These same rules apply to printing out line art or even just text on the page. With the imagesetter, many more dots per inch are used to draw the image.

Defining and Compensating for Dot Gain

When you output your file to an imagesetter, you are probably preparing your file for a traditional printer. During the printing process, the printer might need to make a film negative of your artwork (if you printed a positive piece); or if you provide a negative, make duplicates for a job that prints more that one of the same image per page. The process used here can be equated to making a photocopy of your artwork. When you choose a line frequency, you are also choosing a dot size. On a high-resolution printer (an imagesetter), a line frequency of 300 has smaller dots than a line frequency of 85. In tinted areas or halftones, the dots change size again. How much of its area a dot uses is its percentage size. For instance, if you have a 20-percent tinted area, you are using dots that take up 20 percent of their allotted area. Look at figure 11.5 to see this illustrated. White area around smaller dots tricks the eye into believing that it sees lighter colors. So a 50-percent black area looks like a medium gray. A 10-percent black is a very light gray.

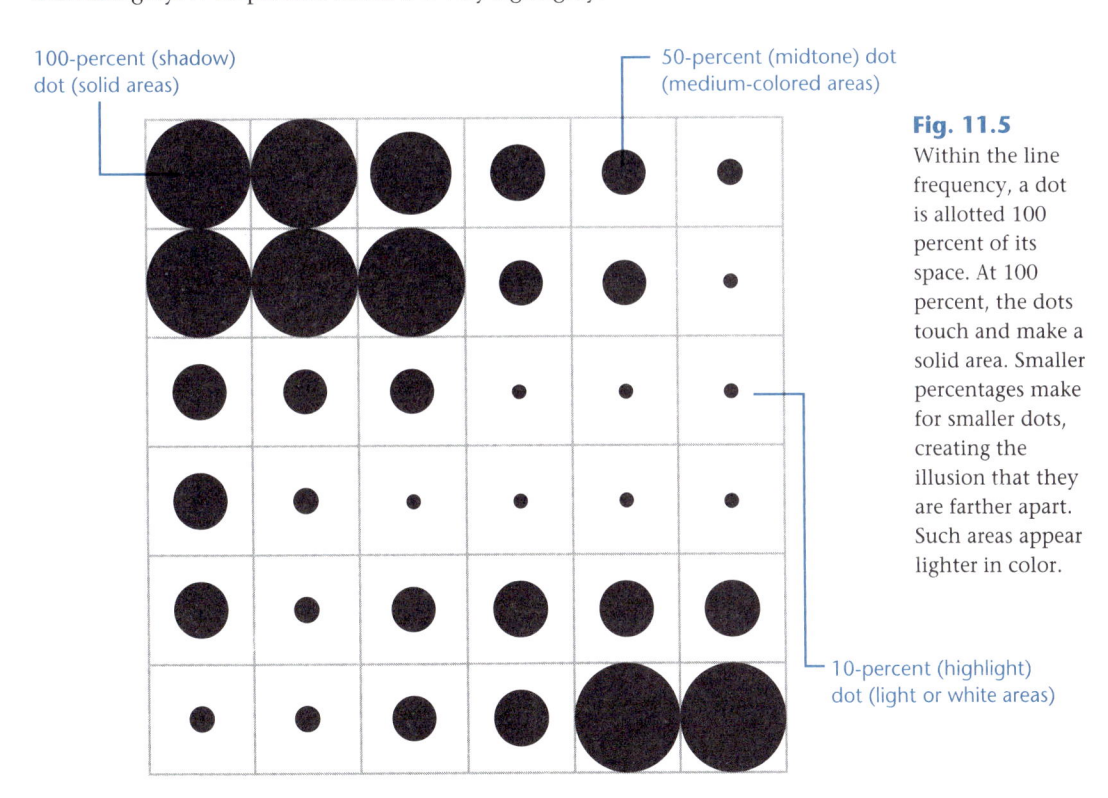

100-percent (shadow) dot (solid areas)

50-percent (midtone) dot (medium-colored areas)

Fig. 11.5
Within the line frequency, a dot is allotted 100 percent of its space. At 100 percent, the dots touch and make a solid area. Smaller percentages make for smaller dots, creating the illusion that they are farther apart. Such areas appear lighter in color.

10-percent (highlight) dot (light or white areas)

The dot size that you so carefully choose and the output are made slightly larger when the page is copied, and, if the copy is photocopied again, the dots become larger still. Each time you make another generation of the artwork, the dot gets bigger—this is called *dot gain*. It happens when the printer makes a negative of your artwork; when the plate for the printing press is made; and again when the image is offset printed to the paper.

You can't stop dot gain from happening; it's a natural process of printing. What you can do, however, is compensate for it. For example, say that the screened or tinted areas of your image need to be very light and you choose a 20-percent tinted area, which looks wonderful on your monitor. After output, the image still looks acceptable, but at printing you discover you've picked up a 30-percent dot. In a bright color, this might be totally unacceptable. Talking with the printer, you learn that you can expect a 5-percent dot gain at 20 percent, and past experience tells you that your service bureau picks up between 5 and 7 percent at 20 percent. What can you do? Define a lighter shade, and then with all the dot gain factored in the end result is a much closer match.

Now suppose that you're working with halftones—many of them are very dark, and most of the dots that make up the halftone are over 80 percent (take up 80 percent of their allotted area)—and you get a great deal of dot gain. Think about what this might do to the shadow areas of the halftones. They are probably all going to turn black. Again, you need to compensate.

This is all part of making the best scan possible. Watch the dark and light areas of intended scans; take into consideration who is going to work with it and what their contribution to the quality will be; and then compensate. In figure 11.6, contrast and brightness were adjusted downward making the dots smaller to allow for the dot gain. If this isn't done, the big dots get bigger, until they overlap and turn to mud. Hence, the phrase "muddy halftone."

Fig. 11.6
By adjusting the brightness and contrast levels of a halftone, you can make room for the impending dot gain.

The Importance of Calibration

Other help in the way of dot gain is available—although admittedly it's not a widely practiced system. When choosing the service bureau for outputting your files to an imagesetter, make sure that the service bureau calibrates its equipment. *Calibrating* is the operation of altering the size of dot that the imagesetter creates in halftones and screened areas to provide leeway for dot gain. Each dot size (3, 12, 70, and all other percentages between 1 and 100) can be altered to accommodate some gain. Typically, dot gain is about 3–5 percent in a 5-percent tinted area (or the 5-percent highlight areas of a halftone); around 12 percent at a 50-percent midtone range; and back down again to around 3 or 4 percent at a 95-percent tint. Because dot gain is a reality, all imagesetters should be calibrated, but every printer and every printing press have different amounts of dot gain. Therefore, it's not very feasible that a service bureau recalibrate for every output job, but it is reasonable to expect them to maintain a tolerance of plus or minus 5 percent. Nearly all offset printers operate within this range, so an imagesetter should actually create a 3-percent dot in the 5-percent highlight areas; around a 40-percent dot in the midtone range; and perhaps a 91-percent dot in the 95-percent shadows. Now when the output is duplicated or printed, you have some room for the dots to gain in size, without them touching one another and producing a muddy looking tint or halftone.

It is useless to calibrate a desktop laser printer, even the 1200-dpi models, because such printers use the dry toner method of creating the image on the page. Toner is placed on the paper as it passes through the paper path and then is heated up. As the toner gets hot, it melts. This is dot gain at its worst.

Choosing the Best Output

Now that you know you're going to have dot gain, how do you decide onthe best output medium (laser paper, high-resolution paper, or high-resolution negative) to minimize the amount of duplication of the artwork and, therefore, the dot gain? Communication with the offset printer is vital. The printer can tell you exactly what his or her presses perform best with.

Negative or Positive

If the quality of the job does not require negatives, you probably want to output the job to paper positive—sometimes called *RC paper* (resin coated). If no halftones or tints are used, a simple desktop laser printer page may suffice. If the image has many halftones, you probably don't want to output to paper, but go straight to negatives to eliminate a generation of dot gain.

Emulsion Up or Down

If the job is being output to negative, but the printer is running the job *4 up*, or *8 up*, and so on (*up* means more than one image exactly the same on a sheet of paper—the way business cards are printed), the negative either needs to be duplicated, or you need to print a negative for each of the images printed on the page. With business cards, this is simple because you can fit as many as 12 business cards on a single 8½-by-11-inch sheet. But what if you're printing 400,000 sheets of company letterhead? The printer most likely prints the letterhead 8 up. If you provide only one negative, you must contend with dot gain, so output eight negatives. If that's not cost effective (although it should be—you'll pay someone for the eight sheets of film whether it's the printer or the service bureau), let the printer duplicate the negative; but you can save the printer one generation by asking for the emulsion side of the film to be printed up.

The *emulsion side* of film is the side with the chemicals on it. When a printer duplicates a sheet of film, he or she contacts it with another sheet of film (the receiver). The emulsion side of the sheets of film (the original and the sheet being duplicated) must be facing one another. If you print the negative emulsion down and the duplicate negative is made, the printer has a negative with the emulsion going the wrong way. This negative is emulsion up (remember, the chemically coated sides were touching). It is called the *inner negative* because it's the inner step to creating the next duplicate, which ends up being emulsion down. The inner negative is then used to make seven more duplicates. You can save one generation of duplicates, and hence, dot gain, by creating the inner negative for the printer. Output the job to be duplicated emulsion up. (Stripped-up negatives must be emulsion down so that the chemical side contacts with the chemical side of the metal plate that they are exposed to.)

Recognizing Vector- and Pixel-Based Artwork

Now that you've chosen the best scanner for the job, connected it properly, and placed the image in the scanner, you are ready to scan. Take a good look at the artwork and decide whether it should be rendered as a color or grayscale bitmap (lools like a continuous-tone image) or line art. Will it take additional editing beyond your scanning preparation to make it look its best? If so, consider these factors. The two basic styles of electronic art are *pixel based* and *vector based*. When you scan, all artwork material becomes pixel based—that is, rendered with dots. Corporate logos, however, look very low quality when they are rendered with dots. Usually, the original logo is made up of lines; this is where the term *line art* comes from. If you're scanning line art, consider that the best quality is generally attained by tracing the image and thereby creating a vector-based image of the logo that has extremely high quality even at huge enlargements and very small reductions. The best place for a scan of line art is CorelTRACE if you intend to illustrate the logo for quality, and CorelPHOTO-PAINT for just a pixel-based scan. If the artwork is a photo, naturally the best place is CorelPHOTO-PAINT. Make sure that you scan continuous-tone images in at the best input resolution for the output you are planning. The following section discusses a formula for determining that resolution.

Scanning Photos with CorelPHOTO-PAINT

Working with photos is a little simpler than line art. You usually don't have to make decisions about whether to trace the image. You just need to capture it in the best quality possible. The best input resolution for your image can be figured with this simple formula:

> lpi × 1.5 (pixels) = input resolution

This formula instructs the scan interface to scan the image using one and a half pixels to represent each dot of the line per inch (screen frequency)—not the dot per inch. The line per inch is the halftone screening discussed at the beginning of the chapter. Nearly all scanning software companies agree that this factor should be between 1.5 and 2.5. If you use more pixels to represent your lpi, you get a bigger file size, not usually a better looking halftone. The best advice however, is to try scanning the same photo at 1.5, 2, and 2.5 pixels per lpi and place them all on the same page. Output them to the imagesetter where your final job is being output and compare the end results. All imagesetters are different (and calibrated differently), so you want to make sure that you know what to expect.

Earlier, you learned that when you scan, enlarging or reducing an image does not increase or decrease the lpi or dpi. It just makes the scanned image appear larger on-screen by using more pixels of the monitor to display each dot of the input resolution. If you do not increase the input resolution, and you enlarge or reduce the image when you output the file, the resulting halftone looks grainy with an enlargement and muddy with a reduction. For this reason, you need to factor the reduction or enlargement into the preceding scanning formula. The formula now is as follows:

$1.5 \times lpi \times$ width of finished size (in inches) $\div$ width of original size

For instance, if you are scanning a 2-inch wide photo, enlarging it 200 percent (the final width is 4 inches) with a screen frequency of 133 lpi, the sample formula is as follows:

$133 \times 1.5 = 199.5 \times 4$ (inches) $\div 2$ (inches) $= 399$-dpi input resolution

This formula affords you the best possible scan with the smallest possible file size.

The steps for scanning in CorelPHOTO-PAINT are the same for CorelTRACE, and they differ depending on which scanner you are using. The most general of rules apply here. Choose Prescan to view the image in the Scan window. Use the cross-hair cursor to crop to the image area you need. Select a scan resolution and click Scan. After you capture the image, it can be edited in either CorelTRACE or CorelPHOTO-PAINT.

Scanning Line Art for Tracing with CorelTRACE

If your plans for the scan are to trace the image—for example, a company logo—or to use a photo as a template for a drawing, use CorelTRACE. The interface is the same as CorelPHOTO-PAINT if you select the same scanner from the Select Source option of the File menu.

Figuring the Input Resolution for Line Art

With line art, generally, more is better. Whether you are tracing the object or you intend to use the pixel-based scan, the more dots drawing the lines, the smoother the art appears. The drawback is the more dpi, the larger the file. A scan of two inches wide at 1,200 dpi might easily produce a 2M file. That's a lot, and it is very slow to render on-screen. It is better to stay with safe numbers. For most instances, between 300 and 500 provide enough detail for tracing, or enough dots for smooth lines.

Tips for Tracing

Before scanning line art to be illustrated, enlarge the original placed on the scanner bed to eight inches wide. This is because with a flatbed scanner, you have a maximum scan width of 8.5 inches. Then when scanning, use an input resolution of 300 or slightly more. This way, you have a nice large image that is easy to trace and a high enough resolution to efficiently render all the nuances of the logo. Even if when enlarging the image you lose some quality, it is drawn in manually as the illustration takes shape. Also, always work in Wireframe view until the illustration is nearly complete. This allows the screen to redraw very quickly without being burdened with color, texture, and so on.

Ending the Scanning Session (Saving)

A finished scan must be saved to be of much use. You must save before you can move it to other areas of CorelDRAW!, or for that matter to other programs. Using the File menu, you choose a file name, destination, and file type for the scan. After the scan is saved, it can be reopened for editing at any future date.

OCR Text Scanning

Using CorelTRACE, you can even scan text and save it as a fully editable, and much smaller, text file as opposed to a graphic file. Follow these steps for capturing an OCR (Optical Character Recognition) scan:

1. Operate the scanner as normal using a high-input resolution (300 dpi or more). Set the scanner for black and white, or convert the image to black and white after scanning it.

2. Open the **T**race menu and choose OC**R** B&W to trace the image.

> **Note**
>
> If you enable **C**heck Spelling first in the Trace Options dialog box (choose **T**race, **E**dit Options, OCR), none of the misspelled words are traced, but this is acceptable because you can type in the corrected word after you have finished capturing the scan.

3. When CorelTRACE finishes tracing the text, open the **F**ile menu and choose Save Text **A**s; then choose ASCII as the format.

You now have a text file that can be read by nearly any word processor. This file can be edited, spell checked, and formatted. It has no limitations that normally apply to text scanned as a graphic.

One more time, the garbage-in/garbage-out rule applies. Make sure that the text you're scanning is the best it can be. If it's too light, try photocopying it at a darker setting. If the words are all run together, try for a better original. Unrecognized words are considered misspellings and not scanned.

> **Troubleshooting**
>
> *I can't get my scanner to work.*
>
> There are hundreds of possible problems here, but try a logical troubleshooting progression. Is the scanner turned on? Is the cable connected properly? Is the SCSI board seated properly? Are the scanner drivers installed? (You should notice this during boot-up if the driver is loaded at that time.) Did you choose Select Source from the File menu? If all else fails, read the manual that comes with your scanner and SCSI interface kit. If you have scanner "test" software (normally included with scanners), try running that.
>
> *When I adjust the brightness to compensate for dot gain, my halftones look posterized.*

> With a halftone, only a small range of editing in this manner is possible before the edits stick out like sore thumbs. Black-and-white images, for example, usually are scanned as grayscales for subsequent ease of manipulation.
>
> *When I scan, the image is too big for a floppy disk, and I can't get it to my service bureau.*
>
> Scans are large files. The higher the input resolution, the larger the file. If you can sacrifice quality, scan at a lower resolution. You're probably better off finding a larger transportable media, such as a SyQuest or Bernouilli drive, if you intend to scan a great deal.

From Here...

Scanning is an easy way to get help with other CorelDRAW! documents. You might find that scanning and tracing an image is easier than trying to draw something from scratch. Scanning text, if the original is good, is always easier than typing it. Use these other chapters for help with ideas about using and editing the scans.

- Chapter 25, "Photograph Touch-Up with CorelPHOTO-PAINT," gives specific tips on lightening, darkening, and editing scanned photos.

- Chapter 26, "Advanced CorelPHOTO-PAINT," offers tips on high-end photo editing.

- Chapter 27, "Tracing Bitmap Images with CorelTRACE," answers all the questions about rendering your line art scan into a vector-based image.

Part V

Becoming an Expert

12	Using Color for Commercial Success
13	Advanced Line and Curve Techniques
14	Creating Special Effects with Perspective
15	Creating Special Effects with Envelope
16	Creating Special Effects with Blending
17	Creating Special Effects with Extruding
18	Creating Special Effects with Contouring
19	Creating Special Effects with PowerLine
20	Creating Special Effects with Lens
21	Creating Special Effects with PowerClip
22	Combining and Reusing Effects
23	Multipage Documents and the Object Data Manager
24	Customizing CorelDRAW! to Fit Your Needs

Chapter 12

Using Color for Commercial Success

by Stephen R. Poland

The difference between black-and-white and color illustrations goes beyond an appealing appearance. Using color well can be part of your signature, the way you communicate. Color can direct the viewer's attention, add emphasis, simplify a complex illustration, or create an emotional reaction. The design aspects of color were covered in earlier chapters; this chapter discusses color in the context of the commercial graphics industry, especially commercial printing.

This chapter is particularly important because your drawings ultimately must be printed. If you do not pay attention to the standards of good reproducible design, your drawings may be prohibitively expensive to reproduce.

Every object in CorelDRAW! has an outline and a fill—even letters and words of text. You set the width, color, and pattern of object outlines, as well as the color and pattern of an object's fill. You can stay with the user-defined default values for these characteristics, or you can exercise sophisticated control over color choice through the color palettes and the myriad of additional colors and texture patterns you create.

In earlier chapters, you learned about object creation and attribute definition. In this chapter, you learn how to use color professionally to communicate to your advantage and why every choice should be based on the final use of the illustration and its method of reproduction. Also, keep in mind that the color displayed on your computer monitor is only a rough approximation of final, or printed, color. After you create a few drawings of the type you need, you will discover a format that works for you and is cost-effective.

In this chapter, you learn to do the following:

- Understand the commercial printing process
- The difference between spot and process color
- How to use CorelDRAW's numerous color palettes
- How to create color separations
- How to use color swatching systems
- How to use Corel 5's Color Management System

Commercial Printing Process Primer

The many powerful features of CorelDRAW! enable you to produce full-color artwork of professional quality. Understanding the basics of the commercial printing process can help you use these features to your best advantage. This section gives you some direction, but you might want to discuss the plans and intentions of your project with your printer even before you present him or her with the final art. An understanding of the steps it takes to transform your original illustration into several thousand or more color reproductions can help you make cost-effective design decisions.

The commercial printing process has come a long way since the Gutenberg press, and the capabilities of commercial printers continue to grow. In the past few years, commercial printing has become an electromechanical process of great sophistication. Commercial printing, which includes letterpress, mimeograph, silk screen, and offset lithography, uses a master from which many copies are produced. (Photocopying and photography, in comparison, take one shot or exposure of the original art to make each copy.) The printing method used by most quick print services is *offset lithography,* also called *photo offset*. Lithography uses a flat plate with an image chemically etched or burned onto it. Ink sticks to the etched portions of the plate and is repelled by water from the nonetched portions. Paper, or other stock, becomes imprinted with the ink when it contacts the plate.

It is important to remember that, unlike photography, printing does not duplicate the original art exactly, but creates an illusion of the original with tiny dots of overlapping ink. The human eye blends these dots of the four process colors (abbreviated CMYK)—the three primary colors plus black—into the full spectrum of color. Because these process inks are transparent, blue overlaid on red, possibly with some black, for example, creates purple. When offset printing in spot (often called PMS colors), blends and screens of the specific PMS inks—usually black and one or two other colors—also are printed in these tiny dots. See the spot and process colors section in this chapter for more details.

In the usual commercial printing method, the original artwork must be transferred into several printer's plates. Offset lithography uses a special camera and light-sensitive plates to transfer the original image. You need a plate for each of the colors (four if the project is a process-color job). This procedure is called *prepress,* and includes such procedures as making negatives, assembling and aligning the negatives, positioning the image, creating special effects, and making the plates.

After you've done the prepress work, the physical printing begins. If a multiple color job runs on a one-color press, each color requires a separate trip through the press, increasing the cost of printing. A basic one-color printing job, like black, only has to go through the press once. Many larger printers have presses that run two, four, or even more colors on the same press. In any case, the more plates required, the higher the cost, the harder it is to align all the different colors, and the harder it is to produce consistent color.

The most advanced printing technology uses no printer's plates at all. An image digitizer turns the original art into data that can be read by a computer that then controls a bank of ink jets to print the image. Sometimes the graphic artist completes the prepress process electronically and delivers to the printer the data needed to create the image on the printing presses already on a computer disk or tape. CorelDRAW! supports this type of electronic prepress as well as color separations from disk (so you don't need any original artwork from which to shoot transparencies). This method is very expensive and has limited availability.

Selecting Fill and Outline Colors

CorelDRAW! gives you so many sophisticated options for color, fill, texture, and outline that some procedures might require opening a series of dialog boxes to set many different parameters. Keep in mind that simple ways are available to accomplish the basic commands, as outlined in the following list:

◀ See "Changing the Outline Color," p. 141

◀ See "Working with Interior Fills," p. 146

■ Click a color in the palette with the left mouse button to fill the selected object with that color.

Chapter 12—Using Color for Commercial Success

- Click a color in the palette with the right mouse button to change the outline of the selected object to that color.

- Click the X button at the left of the color palette with the left mouse button to remove an object's fill.

- Click the X with the right mouse button to remove an object's outline.

Selecting Fill Colors

◀ See "Working with Solid Fills," p. 150

An object's *fill* is the area inside its outline. CorelDRAW! gives you many ways to fill an object; previous chapters covered these in detail. In general, the status line tells you the fill of the currently selected object. An X in the fill box means the object has no fill.

Tip
To open the Uniform Fill dialog box, select the object to fill and press Shift+F11.

At the most basic level, you can fill an object with one color. This is called a *uniform fill* and can consist of any solid color, including black, white, and shades of gray. You also can select a screen of the Uniform fill color, if it is from the PANTONE Spot color palette, in whatever percentage you choose by setting a value in the %Tint box available in the Uniform Fill dialog box or Outline Fill dialog box.

◀ See "Working with Gradated (Fountain) Fills," p. 170

You also can use two colors to fill one object in a fountain fill (see fig. 12.1). You choose how the colors blend and change: a *linear fountain* changes color in a straight line, and a *radial fountain* changes color in concentric circles. Use a linear fountain when shading a background from dark to light, for example. Carefully choosing the colors and placement of a radial fountain can give your object the illusion of three dimensions.

Fig. 12.1
The Fountain Fill dialog box enables you to blend from one color to another.

Tip
To open the Fountain Fill dialog box, select the object to fill and press F11.

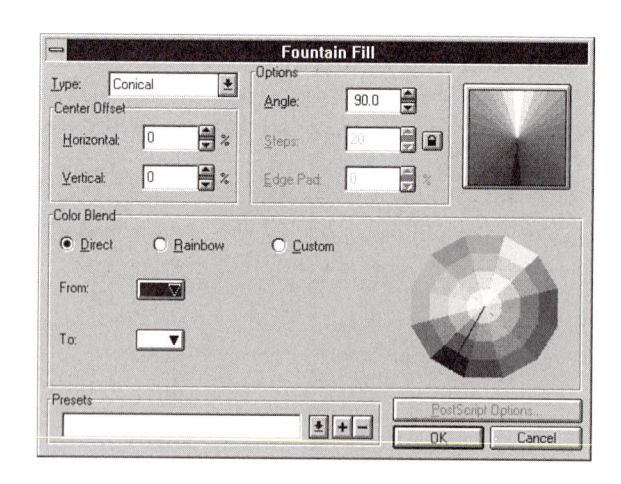

With CorelDRAW! 4 and 5, you also can choose a *conical fountain*. A conical fountain changes colors in rays from the center of the object (like a sun).

You also can fill one object with many colors—even create a rainbow effect—by creating custom fountain fills using one of three options: Direct, Rainbow, and Custom. The Direct option enables you to choose a start color and an end color on the displayed color wheel; then CorelDRAW! fills in the intermediate colors between these two in a straight line. The Rainbow option enables you to draw an arc through the color wheel to specify the color choices in either a clockwise or counterclockwise direction, and then CorelDRAW! fills in the start, end, and intermediate colors. The Custom option enables you to specify up to 99 intermediate colors by clicking them in any order from the Custom Palette at the bottom of the dialog box. To access these custom fills, choose Color Blend, Custom in the Fountain Fill dialog box.

> **Tip**
> If you plan to print color separations with your drawing and are using spot color, you should use two tints of the same spot color when you create fountain fills.

Bitmap fills are patterns made from bitmap tiles, either from CorelDRAW! or from TIFF and PCX files imported into CorelDRAW!. Because a bitmap is just an arrangement of dots forming a pattern and has a fixed resolution, even when you rotate the object, the bitmap fill inside it stays oriented the same way. You can select the height and width of the pattern and how the bitmap tiles line up. You also can select the foreground and background colors in a bitmap pattern. Vector patterns, however, are fill patterns that you can resize without losing any of the pattern's sharpness. These also stay in a fixed orientation and size inside the object they fill, but you can edit the vector pattern file to make changes. You can create vector and bitmap fills as patterns in CorelDRAW! that you can then save and use.

> ◄ See "Using Patterned Fills," p. 152

> **Tip**
> You cannot fill color and grayscale bitmaps because they are not closed-path objects.

Selecting Outline Colors

All objects in CorelDRAW! have outlines, although they may be hard to see—or even invisible. When you click an object, the status line tells you the width of the outline. Adding color to an outline is like using Uniform Fill under the Fill tool. Although you can't create fountain fills or textures for the outline of an object, you can add colors in several different ways. One way to add outline color is by accessing the colors on the predefined color palettes. The quick and simple way covered earlier is as follows:

1. Select the object.
2. Select a color on the color palette at the bottom of the screen by clicking it with the right mouse button.

After the object is selected, you also can click the Outline tool and open the Pen roll-up window, in which you can access the current color palette either by clicking the colored fill bar (see fig. 12.2), or by choosing Edit and clicking the Color button.

> **Tip**
> To view the actual effect of a fill, choose Full-Screen Preview or print the drawing. Wireframe view shows no fill information at all. Information is provided on the status line.

Fig. 12.2
Using the Pen roll-up window, you can easily select colors for the objects you create.

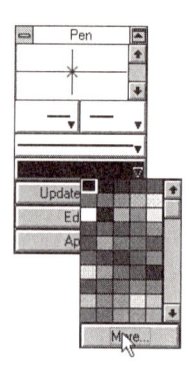

Tip
If you know right away that you want to create a new color, a quicker way to get to the Outline Color dialog box is to simply click the Outline tool and then click the color wheel button.

Tip
F12 is the shortcut to selecting the Outline Pen dialog box. Shift+F12 is the shortcut to the Outline Color dialog box.

The color palette that displays from both of these last two options includes a More button. Click this button to display the Outline Color dialog box, which enables you to create your own process colors or to specify tints of PMS colors. If you plan to commercially print your drawing, it is less confusing for the printer if the same model for creating new colors is used throughout the drawing, but you can change from one to the other at any time. If you do not plan to commercially print your drawing, use whatever colors and color combinations you want on the outline colors.

Troubleshooting

I want to apply an outline color of an existing object to the other objects in my drawing, but I can't find the color in the color palette.

A quick way to apply the color of an existing object to other objects is to open the Outline Pen roll-up and click Update From. The pointer changes to a black arrow. Simply point to the object that contains the outline color you want, and click. The Outline Pen roll-up is updated with the color and outline attributes of the object you clicked on. Now, select the object you want to apply the roll-up's color to and click Apply.

I attempt to add a square fountain fill to a circle, but it does not seem to create the square fountain inside the circle.

A quirk in CorelDRAW! is that an object's fill technically covers its entire highlight box, even though only the fill inside the object is visible. Because the highlight box is always a rectangle or square, an irregularly shaped or rotated object, like a circle or ellipse, can have some "lost" fountain fill. To adjust for this lost fill, open the Fountain Fill dialog box and adjust the Edge Pad amount from 0 to 45 percent.

Using CorelDRAW!'s Color Capabilities

Open a CorelDRAW! drawing, and you see a wealth of color options laid out for you at the bottom of your screen. In Chapter 5, "Modifying Object Outlines and Interior Fills," you learned that these groups of colors are called *color palettes*, but these colors represent only a fraction of the colors you can specify. Over one hundred colors are preprogrammed into these color palettes, and you can create millions of new ones. CorelDRAW! enables you to organize this abundance of color choices into arrangements that work for you.

After you create a document, you can reproduce it in color by using the following three basic methods:

- Print it on a color PostScript or non-PostScript printer (on either paper stock or film stock for transparencies) and then make color photocopies
- Display it on a color computer monitor
- Print it commercially, using spot or process color

The method you use plays an important role in color choice.

The first method, printing the drawing to a color PostScript or non-PostScript printer, such as a Hewlett-Packard inkjet or a color thermography printer, takes time for each copy and causes wear on the printer. It works best when you need only limited copies.

The second method displays the document on a computer monitor, as in presentation packages. The CMYK model for creating new colors in CorelDRAW! uses a color-specifying system that emulates computer monitor color production and gives more consistent colors when the document is transferred to new systems.

The last method, commercial printing, is an industry with a long history and a vocabulary all its own. Commercial printing is the best choice for hundreds, even thousands, of copies of a drawing even though it is often an expensive process. This is true especially if the drawing has many colors or if you want to use the full spectrum of colors found in nature.

Defining the Color Palettes

CorelDRAW! provides you with one Spot color palette and four Process color palettes. The CorelDRAW! window displays only one of these palettes at a time (although the others can be accessed from other dialog windows). You can revise these palettes or create custom palettes of your own. The process color palettes differ in the range of colors they display, and whether the on-screen colors display as dithered or pure. The default process color palette contains about 100 colors, but you can create many more process colors using the three process color models provided with CorelDRAW!. After you create a color, you can add it to the active palette or create a new palette containing several new colors. It is usually easier to revise an existing palette. The next few sections deal with creating and editing color palettes.

You can create up to 16 million colors with CorelDRAW!, but only if your computer has enough memory. Systems that support 16/256 colors use dithering to emulate the wide array of color possible with color output devices. *Dithering* is a process that intersperses on-screen pixels of different colors in a gradual pattern to form the best rendition possible of the desired output color. Dithering can look choppy and only approximates the color on the monitor. Remember, even though a dithered color looks choppy on the monitor, it looks much better on a high-resolution color output devices such as a color PostScript printer.

Spot versus Process Colors

Commercially printing in spot color is usually substantially cheaper than printing in process color. Still, when a drawing contains more than three different colors (a tint or screen of a color is not considered a different color), it's usually best to go to four-color process printing. That way, you have access to the full range of colors found in nature for the price of only four colors of ink. CorelDRAW! contains color palettes in both spot and process color to make it easier later when you take the project to a printer. The simple procedure for converting a spot color to a process color is covered in the next section. However, you cannot convert a process color to a spot color. If you are going to display your final work on a computer screen, use process colors because they provide the widest variety of colors. If, however, you eventually plan to print your file, make the process or spot color decision up-front, or you may be surprised by unexpected expenses and radically changed output.

Spot Color

Spot color is generally used when a drawing contains black and one or two other colors for decoration or emphasis. Because fewer inks and fewer press runs are required, spot color can be commercially printed comparatively inexpensively. Almost all commercial printers are familiar with the system used to specify spot colors, or you can reproduce the work on a color PostScript printer using the PostScript halftone screen patterns. If a drawing has four or more colors and is to be commercially printed, it is usually more cost-effective to create it in process color.

Spot colors typically use the PANTONE Matching System and are called PMS colors. Other color matching systems, such as TRUMATCH, are available for spot colors and process colors, but they are less widely used. The Spot color palette provided in CorelDRAW! contains over 700 PMS colors, each with its own unique number (for example, PMS 131 is a brownish yellow). The colors you see on your computer screen are only approximations of the actual PMS colors, however. You can view the true PMS colors by looking at a PMS book—available at most art supply stores—which has swatches of each PMS color. A PMS book is a basic tool for anyone doing graphics and illustrations for reproduction. Some printers even suggest that you buy a new PMS book yearly because the inks tend to fade with age and new formulas are added regularly.

Process Color
Process colors, on the other hand, are best used when your drawing has four or more colors, or when you want to reproduce color photographs in your drawing. Reproduction of process colors, as in full-color magazines, usually requires a commercial printer with sophisticated equipment, but you also can output your illustration to a color PostScript or non-PostScript printer. Process color is based on the theory that over 16 million colors can be specified as some mixture of the inks used in four-color printing: CMYK, for cyan (or bluish), magenta (or reddish), yellow, and K (for black). In effect, these are the three primary colors and black. These four inks, in various percentages, combine to make up literally millions of colors.

You can save time and money when commercially printing your full-color drawing because CorelDRAW! separates process colors into their CMYK components, provided you use a PostScript printer and choose Process Color Separations when printing. You can match your on-screen process colors to the process colors achieved in commercial printing by selecting colors according to one of the three color palette choices in CorelDRAW! 5—Pantone Process, TRUMATCH, and Focoltone. To use one of these swatching systems, choose a color from the color swatch book, note its color number, and select that number from the corresponding CorelDRAW! color palette. CorelDRAW! displays each color's unique number in the status line when a color is selected.

Converting Spot Colors to Process Colors

Although you can send an illustration that combines both spot and process colors to a commercial printer, you can save money on the final printed piece by converting any spot colors to their process color equivalents. You do lose a little control over the color of the final piece, because the printed results can show a slight variation between the process and spot color. To do this conversion, follow these steps:

1. Select the object with the spot color.

2. Click the Fill or Outline tool, depending on the attribute to be changed, and then click the Color Wheel icon on the fly-out menu to open the appropriate dialog box.

3. The spot color of the selected object will be selected in the dialog box's color palette.

4. Click the Sho**w** drop-down list to choose one of the process color models, and click it (see fig. 12.3).

Fig. 12.3
Selecting a spot color.

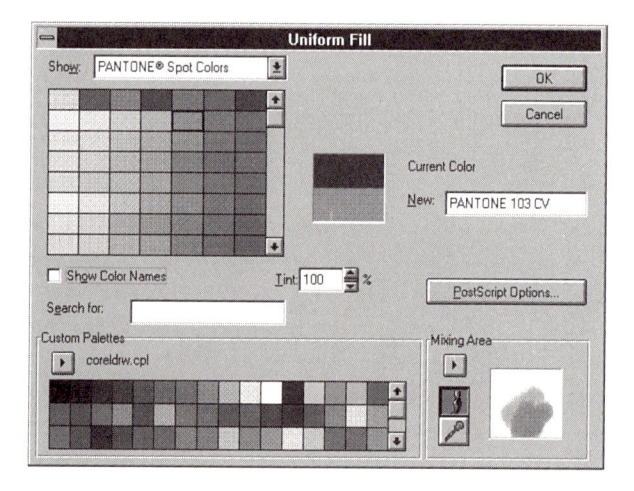

The dialog box now shows you what percentages of the four CMYK inks simulate the spot color (see fig. 12.4).

Using CorelDRAW!'s Color Capabilities   **351**

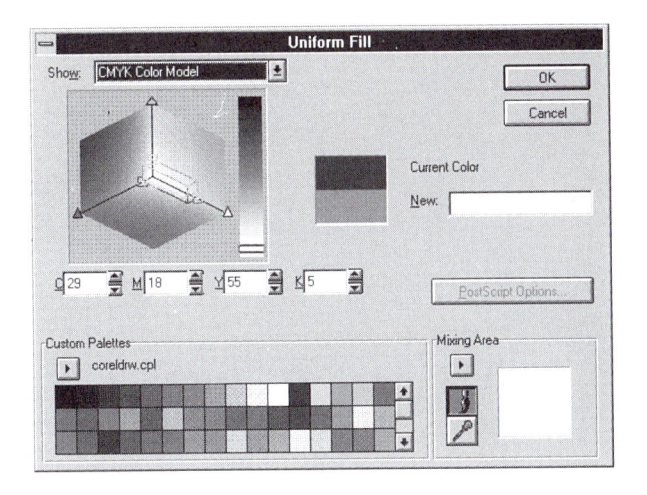

Fig. 12.4
You can convert from one color scheme to another by changing the Show selection in the Uniform Fill and Outline Color dialog boxes.

5. Give the newly created process color a name and click OK.

6. To store the converted color in a palette so you can use it later, click the small black triangle in the Custom Palettes section of the dialog and then choose Add Color. CorelDRAW! adds the new color to the end of the active palette. Click the small black triangle and choose **S**ave or Save **A**s to save the changes to the palette.

Creating Custom Colors

Even though CorelDRAW! gives you hundreds of color choices in both spot colors and process colors, you might have a project that requires a color not available on one of CorelDRAW!'s color palettes. If you find yourself in this situation, you can create a new custom process color or custom tint of a spot color.

Creating a Tinted Spot Color

Using the PANTONE Spot Color palette, you can select among the 700 or so industry-standard PMS or spot colors, or you can select a screened-back version of any PMS color by specifying a percentage tint in the Tint box (see fig. 12.5). The effect of screening or tinting a PMS color is the same as screening black to make gray—you get a paler version of the color. You can then include this new tint in the PANTONE Spot Color palette for later use.

Fig. 12.5
Specifying a screened (tinted) version of a spot color.

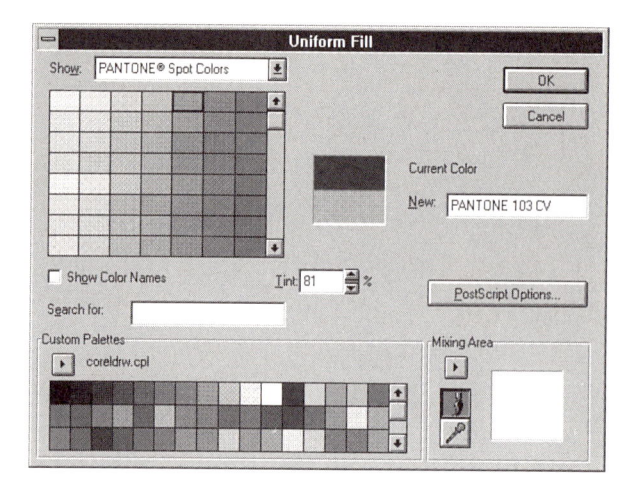

To add a tint of spot color to the palette, follow these steps:

1. Select the object with the spot color.

2. Click the Fill or Outline tool, depending on the location of the spot color to be changed.

3. Click the Color Wheel icon. In the window that appears, the spot color is already selected (or select a new spot color if you want to change it at this time).

4. Reset the Tint figure. (The changes might be too subtle to change your on-screen display.)

5. Click the Custom Palettes button and then choose Add Color. The new tint is added to the end of the active palette displayed in the Custom Palettes section of the dialog box. Click OK.

Creating a Custom Process Color

You also can create your own new colors from process colors using one of the three process color models. Of these three process color creation models, only the CMYK model enables you to specify the TRUMATCH colors that your commercial printer can more easily match. The new process color's name is added to the list of named colors; if you switch models after creating a color, CorelDRAW! converts the new color into the new format for you. After you are in the dialog box that enables you to create new process colors, you have a choice of methods: typing in the percentages of CMYK, or using the visual selector (see fig. 12.6). The visual selector enables you to drag three markers to indicate the amount of cyan, magenta, and yellow (using the markers in the large box) and the amount of black (using the marker in the narrow vertical box).

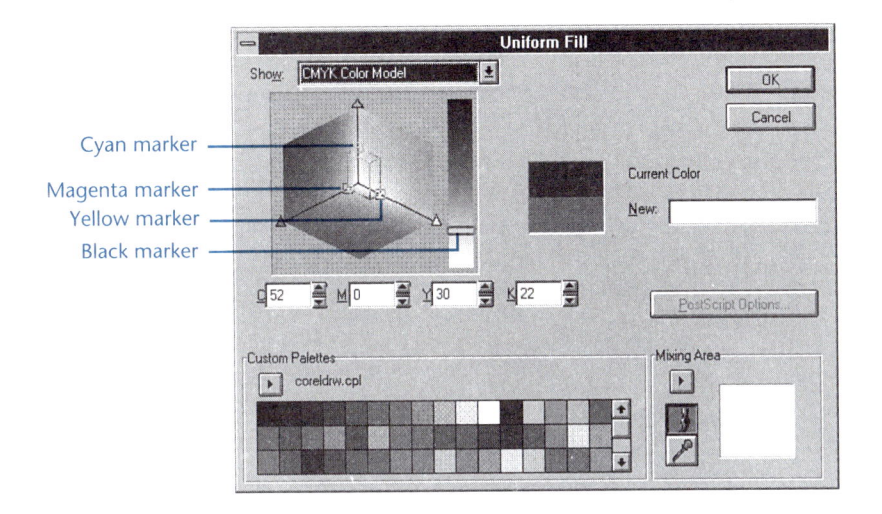

Fig. 12.6
Using the visual selector, you can create new process colors.

> **Note**
>
> TRUMATCH colors are industry-standard process colors. Many printers have TRUMATCH color swatch books that you also can buy at your local art supply store. CorelDRAW! also gives you a TRUMATCH process color palette with the unique number of each color included to make it easier to achieve the printed colors you want. Small print shops still use PMS.

If you want to add to the 100 premixed colors in your Process color palette, CorelDRAW! gives you the following three color models for creating process colors:

- *CMYK.* This uses the four colors from commercial printing (cyan, magenta, yellow, and black).

- *RGB.* This uses various intensities (from 0 to 100) of the colors red, green, and blue.

- *HSB.* This varies three parameters to create colors—hue, saturation, and brightness.

With CMYK, you specify the percentages of the inks, or use the visual selector color wheel to specify the color, and CorelDRAW! creates a screen approximation of it.

The RGB model emulates color reproduction by the RGB pixels on your computer screen, so it is often the best choice when creating color illustrations that are to be transferred to another computer system, as in presentation software (see fig. 12.7). You produce white by setting all three intensities to 255; you produce black by setting them all to 0.

Fig. 12.7
The RGB model of process colors is often used for drawings that are to be displayed on computer screens, not printed on color imagesetters.

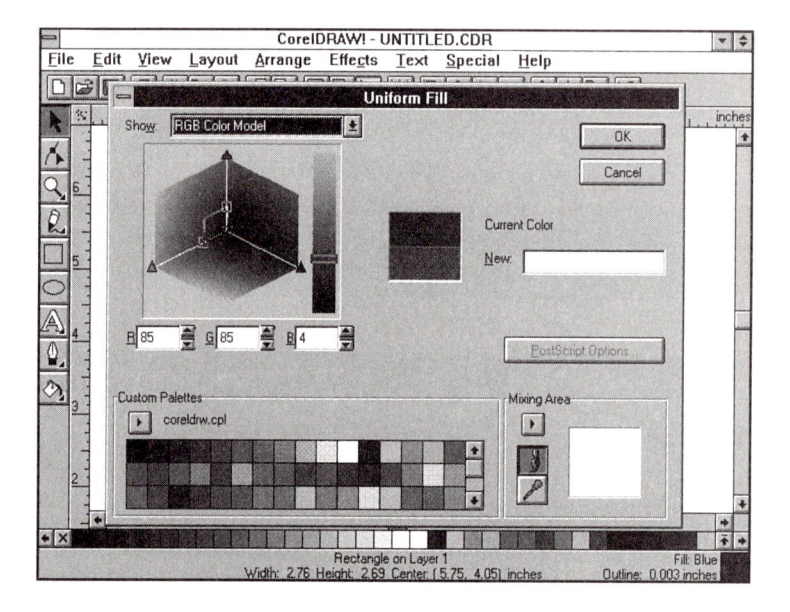

The HSB model varies three parameters to create colors—hue (the color itself such as red or green), saturation (the purity or intensity of the hue), and brightness (the percentage of black in the color where 0 percent is black and 100 percent is white). Hue is set by defining a number that corresponds to rotational degrees on a circle. For example, 0 equals red, and 180 equals cyan. Create the HSB color you want and then save it as a color for later use (see fig. 12.8).

Using CorelDRAW!'s Color Capabilities   355

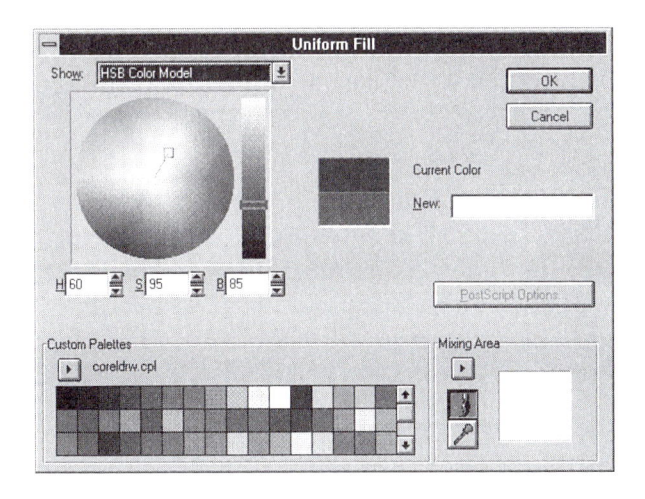

Fig. 12.8
The HSB model of creating process colors.

To create a custom process color, follow these steps:

1. Select the object you want to fill or outline with the new color.

2. Click the Fill or Outline tool, depending on the location of the color, and then click the Color Wheel icon.

3. Choose one of the three models for creating process colors from the Show box. Your choices are CMYK, RGB, or HSB. Note that other color systems are listed in the Show drop-down list, but only the CMYK, RGB, and HSB choices enable you to create a custom process color.

4. Define the new color by moving the color-adjustment markers in the visual selector box, or by entering exact percentages in the text boxes.

5. To save the color in the palette to use later, give it a name in the New Color box.

6. Click the Custom Palettes button, choose Add Color, and then click OK.

7. Click the Custom Palette button again and choose **S**ave or Save **A**s to save the changes to the palette.

Converting from One Color Scheme to Another

As you have seen, CorelDRAW!'s default palettes relate to how your document will ultimately be reproduced. You may decide to change from spot to process color later, and CorelDRAW! supports that. It is also a good idea to use different palettes, or color schemes, for certain projects for consistency and to prevent confusion. You also can create a specific color scheme and use

Tip
For quick recall, name new colors according to their percentage mix, using up to 21 letters or numbers. For example, 66B22R0Y10K is 66 percent cyan/blue, 22 percent magenta/red, 0 percent yellow, and 10 percent black.

it for all drawings related to specific projects by revising an existing palette and renaming it or creating a whole new palette for the project. Keep in mind that the PANTONE Spot color palette is for a different commercial printing process than any of the Process color palettes.

CorelDRAW! shows only one of the many color palettes at the bottom of your screen. More color options in the displayed palette can be accessed by using the palette's scroll arrow or by clicking the up arrow on the right end of the palette. Clicking the up arrow displays five rows of color choices and enables you to find a color more quickly than scrolling left or right using the scroll arrows.

You can reset the color palette in two ways. A quick way to reset to one of the basic palettes is to access the View pull-down menu and choose the Color Palette option; a window appears with several choices, including None. Make your choice by clicking it, and the palette at the bottom of the screen changes.

To choose one of the other preprogrammed palettes or a palette you have created yourself, follow these steps:

1. Select an object and click the Outline or Fill tool; then click the Color Wheel icon to bring up a color dialog box called Uniform Fill (for the Fill tool) or Outline Color (for the Outline tool).

2. At the bottom of this dialog box is a Custom Palettes section. Click the small arrow button, and then click Open from the menu that appears. The Open Palette dialog box appears (see fig. 12.9).

Fig. 12.9
The Open Palette dialog box displays a list of the custom color palettes available in the CUSTOM subdirectory.

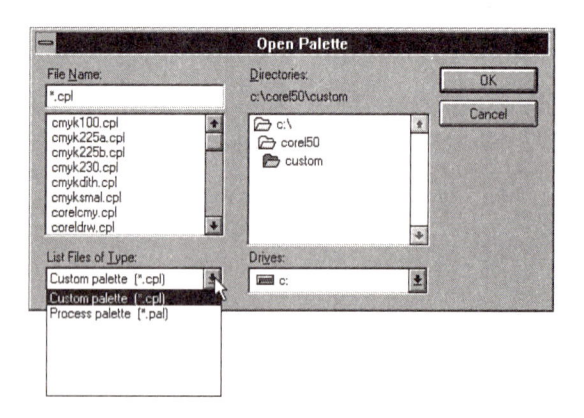

3. Select either Custom Palette or Process Palette from the List Files of Type option box. A list of Process color palette files appears, indicated by the extension PAL, or a single custom color palette file, indicated by the extension CPL.

4. Make a selection from either list to replace the current palette, and then click OK.

5. Click OK again to return to the drawing.

6. To display and use the new palette, select **V**iew, Co**l**or Palette, **C**ustom Colors. The new palette is displayed at the bottom of the screen.

The default CorelDRAW! palette is a Process color palette called CORELDRW.CPL. If you modify this palette and then want to return to the default colors, choose the backup palette PURE100.PAL, also provided. These two palettes were identical when you first installed CorelDRAW!.

Displaying the Color Palette

The color palette displayed along the bottom of your CorelDRAW! window can be toggled on or off by opening the **V**iew menu, choosing the Co**l**or Palette command, and then choosing **N**one. The submenu that appears also enables you to change the color palette to one of the other defaults.

CorelDRAW! also enables you to rearrange the colors on a given palette by moving to either the Uniform Fill or Outline Color dialog boxes and clicking and dragging the color to a new location in the Custom Palettes area. You might want to put the four most-used colors in a drawing grouped at the beginning of the palette, for example. You also can create totally new arrangements of colors specifically for a certain job or project. Save this special arrangement by opening the Custom Palettes menu and choosing the Save **A**s option. CorelDRAW! loads the new palette automatically on startup.

Tip
Never save changes to the PURE100.PAL palette. This way, you always have a true copy of the original CorelDRAW! default palette.

Printing Process Color Drawings

CorelDRAW! gives you a wealth of options for having your drawing commercially printed; using these in an educated way can save you time and printing costs. Of course, if you plan to print just one or a few copies of your color drawing on your office printer, CorelDRAW! enables you to print your process color drawings on a variety of PostScript and even non-PostScript color printers. Hopefully, you knew that you meant to print using commercial process color or spot color while you were creating your drawing so that you could choose the best palettes and color specification models to cause the least amount of confusion for your printer. It is a good rule to discuss your print job with your commercial printer before beginning your design. The printer can offer you production tips that help you avoid problems. Find out what your printer's requirements are.

Commercial spot/PMS color and four-color process printing both require many steps between the original art and the full-color final result. Because spot color usually involves fewer inks and requires fewer press runs, commercially printing PMS color often is substantially cheaper than four-color process printing. The process of getting the original art to the printing press is called *prepress* and can involve shooting the image with a special camera, digitizing the colors into the four process color basics, creating a negative for each of the four colors, and assembling these negatives to expose the printer's plates. Many of these manual prepress steps can be replaced by computer technology that CorelDRAW! supports.

Getting the Color You Want

The first rule of creating color output using CorelDRAW! (or any other application for that matter) can be stated simply: the colors you see on-screen are not the colors you get on paper.

Accurate color reproduction has plagued the computer graphics industry since its beginning. The basic problem is that your computer monitor creates a color image very differently from how a printing press or color printer creates a color image. A color monitor shows images by shooting electrons at a phosphorus coating on the inside of the monitor. It makes colors by lighting up various amounts of red, green, and blue phosphorus to transmit the color you see on-screen. A printing press or color printer creates colors by laying down color inks on paper. The processes are very different and very difficult to coordinate. Many advances have been made to solve the problem, but no one solution is completely effective.

CorelDRAW! 5 offers a Color Manager to help you calibrate your monitor, printer, scanner, and other devices so that they each represent color accurately. You learn more about the Color Manager later in this chapter.

Even if you are not concerned with reproducing color exactly, such as having photographs showing perfect flesh tones, keep in mind that even a simple drawing with relatively few colors can print differently from screen colors. For example, suppose that you create a packaging design for a Halloween product. You want a background blending from a deep midnight purple to a rich jack-o-lantern orange. If you create the background based on the colors on-screen, the deep midnight purple probably will print as a bright pink, and the rich orange will print as a sharp yellow—not even close to the simple Halloween colors you wanted. The lesson is that the colors you see on-screen are not what prints on a color printer, or at a commercial printer.

As mentioned earlier, the solution to this problem is to use one of the color swatching systems such as the Pantone Matching System (PMS), TRUMATCH, or Focoltone. These systems are available in book form or rectangular color panels that fan open. You can get PMS books for both spot colors and process colors. TRUMATCH and Focoltone books also are available for process colors. Make sure that you get the matching system on the type of paper you intend to print on—either coated stock or matte finish. The colors appear differently on different types of paper.

To use a color swatch book to get the color you want, find the color swatch that you want to add to your drawing and locate that color's number on CorelDRAW!'s color palettes. Then apply the color to your drawing. Ignore the fact that the color on-screen looks nothing like the color in the PMS book. When the image is printed, the printer will print the right PMS colors if it is calibrated to match to the proper PMS color.

Understanding CorelDRAW! 5's Color Management System

CorelDRAW! 5 includes a Color Manager system that enables you to calibrate color reproduction across your monitor, printer, and scanner. The Color Manager attempts to adjust the colors captured (scanner), displayed (monitor), and output (printer) from CorelDRAW!. Ideally, using Color Manager, the color you see on a photograph to be scanned is the color you see on the monitor and the color that prints on a printer.

Color Manager creates a System Color Profile based on the type of monitor, printer, and scanner your system has. The Color Profile reconciles the differences in color display and capture among the devices of your system so that each device reproduces a specific color the same way.

To use the Color Manager to create a System Profile for your system, follow these steps:

1. Open the **F**ile menu and choose **C**olor Manager. The System Color Profile dialog box appears (see fig. 12.10).

Fig. 12.10
The System Color Profile dialog box enables you to select your monitor, printer, and scanner types.

2. Choose your monitor type from the Monitor field. If your monitor is not listed, choose Other from the drop-down list. A Monitor Calibration dialog box appears, enabling you to enter the characteristics of your monitor (see fig. 12.11). You should find the dialog box values for your monitor in its user manual.

Fig. 12.11
The Monitor Calibration dialog box enables you to enter specific parameters of your monitor that help CorelDRAW! display colors more accurately.

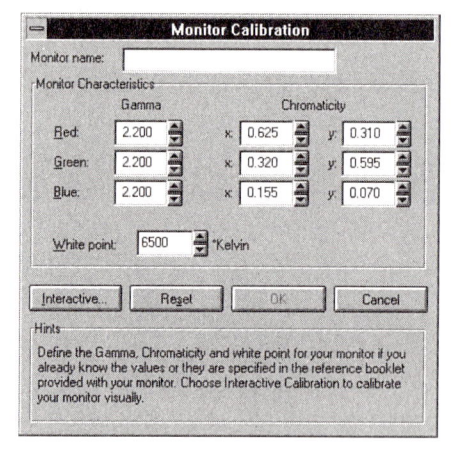

3. Choose your printer from the Printer field. If your printer is not listed, choose Other and enter the characteristics of your printer. Consult your printer's documentation for details.

4. If you have a scanner attached to your system, choose your scanner from the Scanner list. If your scanner type is not listed, select Other from the list and enter your scanner's characteristics.

5. Click Generate. A dialog box appears requesting a System Profile file name.

6. Type a unique file name for your system's System Color Profile. Click OK.

7. A progress dialog box appears showing the progress of the building of the System Color Profile.

8. Click OK in the System Color Profile dialog box to complete the operation.

Tip
CorelDRAW! documentation provides a cross-reference list of monitor, printer, and scanner types that can be selected in place of your equipment when selecting equipment types in the Color Manager dialog box. Make sure that you check this list before choosing Other to create a new device definition.

With the new System Color Profile in use, the colors you see on your monitor should better match the colors produced on your color printer and the colors scanned by your scanner. Keep in mind, however, that if your output requirements demand precise color control, use one of the color matching systems, such as PANTONE, to ensure color accuracy in your printouts.

Using the Color Correction Command

CorelDRAW! 5 introduces another command to assist in accurate color display and, consequently, color output. The Color Correction command found on the View menu enables you to adjust the degree of accuracy that color is displayed on your monitor. The four color correction options are as follows:

- *None.* Selecting this option turns off color correction, allowing the fastest screen redraw.

- *Fast.* This option performs some color correction when displaying colors on-screen. The color correction is based on the System Color Profile generated using the Color Manager command.

- *Accurate.* This option uses the most information available in the System Color Profile to accurately display color on-screen. It does, however, slow the redraw of bitmapped images in drawings.

- *Simulate Printer.* This option corrects color based on your printer's color capabilities.

Creating Color Separations in CorelDRAW!

If you want to print several hundred or even thousands of copies of your color drawings, you need to create color separations of your image for the commercial printer. The basic process is as follows:

1. Print color separations of your drawing to a file.

2. Send the file to a service bureau.

3. The service bureau makes a separate piece of film for each of the four process colors (if you are using process color), or one piece of film for each of the spot colors in your image. They send the film to a commercial printer, and the printer makes plates (flexible metal sheets) for each of the four process colors or each spot color in your image.

4. The printer then sets up the press with the plates and runs the print job.

> **Note**
>
> If you need only a handful of copies of your drawing, consider taking the file to a color quick printer or service bureau. They can print a single copy on plain paper (or the stock of your choice) using a color PostScript printer. For additional copies, they can create color photocopies of the printed image. This is much more economical than paying high prices for a commercial print job. Consider this method if your quantities are under a few hundred, and the print quality does not have to be exact.

◀ See "Printing—the Details," p. 299

As noted earlier, printing a file as color separations creates a page for each of the process colors (cyan/blue, magenta/red, yellow, black) and/or a page for each of the spot (PMS) colors. Your black-and-white printer can produce the separations, but it is likely that you'll need a high-resolution printer to get decent quality. That's why you need to create a separations disk file and send it to a service bureau that can output the separations to a high-resolution printer. Your commercial printer combines the separations to produce full-color output. If you combine process and spot colors, a page is printed for each one. In the Print Options dialog box (accessed by choosing File, Print, Options), you have other choices that can be of benefit when you go to a commercial printer (see fig. 12.12).

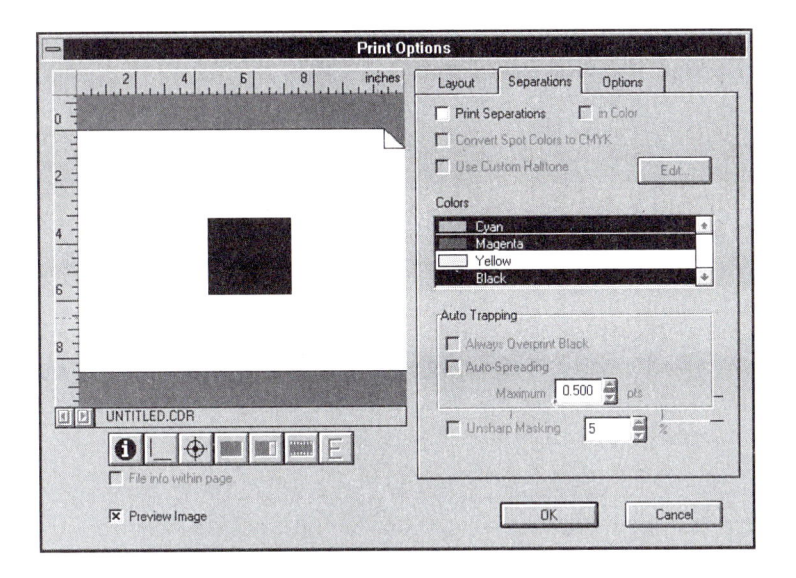

Fig. 12.12
The Print Options dialog box with Separations option selected.

You need to check with your printer to confirm whether the company will accept your printed separations or would prefer electronic files. Look for Corel-authorized service bureaus in your area. These Corel experts can help you successfully separate color images.

Exploring the Print Options Dialog Box

To send your color separation file to a printer or service bureau, you need to print the separations to a file on your hard disk.

Choose **F**ile **P**rint to open the Print dialog box. In the Print dialog box, select the Print to **F**ile check box and the For **M**ac check box if your service bureau uses Apple Macintoshes. Next, select the **O**ptions button to display the Print Options dialog box. Click the Separations tab to display the Separations options in the Print Options dialog box. Printing as color separations means that each process color and each spot color in your drawing is printed on a separate page. Your printer can use these images to create the plates needed for color printing.

Tip
If spot colors appear in the Colors list and you want to print using only process colors, click the Convert Spot Colors to CMYK check box to convert the spot colors to CMYK colors. Alternatively, you can revisit your drawing and apply new process colors in place of spot colors you've used.

364 Chapter 12—Using Color for Commercial Success

> **Note**
>
> If your service bureau uses Macintoshes, call in advance to make sure they can successfully work with your CorelDRAW! files.

Click the Print **S**eparations check box to indicate that you want to print color separations.

Notice that the Colors section of the dialog box shows the names of the colors used in your drawing. If you used only process colors, each of the four process color names appears in the list. If your drawing uses spot colors, the names and numbers of the spot colors are listed.

◀ See "PostScript and Non-PostScript Printing," p. 307

If you are printing to a PostScript printer, the Use Custom Halftone option is available. This option enables you to reset from the default halftone screen frequency. The *halftone screen frequency* refers to the number of dots, lines, or circles printed per inch. The screen angle and frequency settings affect the number of grays, the sharpness, and the intensity of the printed image.

Printing Reference Information

You can print several informational items on your pages to help you identify the document, check registration or colors, mark the edges of the printable page, and other useful things.

Sometimes the CorelDRAW! illustration uses only a portion of the page, or a drawing may have a *bleed,* which means that the color extends to the edge of the page. To get the bleed effect, the printer must print a little past the edges of the drawing and then trim the paper back. The Crop Marks button option prints crop marks to indicate four corners of the image. For this to print out, your CorelDRAW! document must be smaller than the paper on which you are printing.

The File Information button is used to put file and related information on the same page as the output.

> **Note**
>
> If you plan to print color separations with your drawing and are using spot color, you should use two tints of the same spot color when you create fountain fills and not fills of two different colors.

The Registration Marks button prints registration marks on the four corners of a color separation. The printer uses these marks to align the negatives while creating the photos required for each page and to precisely place the four ink colors to achieve the desired color mix.

> **Note**
>
> If you want printed output for an 8½-by-11-inch document that includes registration and crop marks, check with a service bureau. Many can output larger sizes of paper, such as 11 by 14 inch, and provide full-size output without cutting off the crop and registration marks.

The Densitometer Scale button option creates a grid showing the levels of intensity of each of the four CMYK, from 0 to 100, on color separations. This enables you and your printer to check the consistency and accuracy of ink coverage for the printed output.

> **Note**
>
> Choosing screens of process colors for type can give your text a ragged look. Use 100 percent cyan, magenta, or black (not yellow) in the mix to fix this.

The Print Negative button reduces prepress degradation by one generation and specifies a type of printing onto film that a printer can then use to make printer's plates.

The Emulsion Up button specifies an image facing up and is the default setting. Clicking this button changes the setting to Emulsion Down (the backwards facing E) and specifies that the image is to be printed facing down.

The Calibration bar button specifies a color calibration bar to be printed. The calibration bar is used as reference to match printed colors with the colors specified in Corel.

> **Note**
>
> If you are printing the separations yourself, check with your service bureau or printer for the appropriate color separation settings.

Trapping

Most drawings have at least two areas of different colors touching one another. Adjusting these areas in your drawing to overlap slightly is a process called *trapping*. Trapping is done to prevent the color of the paper from showing through when the alignment on two adjacent colors is off a fraction. CorelDRAW! offers two options that aid the program in autotrapping. In the Print Options dialog box with the Separations tab selected, select the first option, Always Overprint Black, if you want all objects containing 95 percent or more black to be trapped. The second option, Auto-Spreading, automatically adds trap to objects meeting the following three conditions:

- They are filled with a uniform fill.
- They have no outline.
- They have not been selected to overprint from the Object menu.

Auto-Spreading has a related value, Maximum Points, that is used to set the maximum outline width for the object. The outline color added for trap matches the fill color of the object.

Many commercial printers request no trap on digital separations and charge fees to do trapping prepress by hand. Understanding trap and applying it judiciously can save you unnecessary expense.

Trapping should be done as a final step if the drawing is to be commercially printed. You can do this manually if you understand the process, or the autotrapping feature does this preventative step for you.

Selecting the Auto Trapping option causes Corel to perform automatic trapping of colors when the separations are printed.

The final step in creating a color separation file is selecting the type of printer the file will be output on. Even though you print the separation information to a disk file, CorelDRAW! must know which type of printer your service bureau uses to print separation film.

Select the printer type that will be used to print the color separation film from the Printer list in the Print dialog box. If the service bureau's printer type is not listed, you must install the printer using Windows' Control Panels.

> **Note**
>
> If possible, find a service bureau that accepts CorelDRAW! files (.CDR extension) and will print the separations from CorelDRAW! on their system. This eliminates the need for you to print separations to a disk file. You just send them your CorelDRAW! file, and they make all the choices needed to print the proper color separations. Using a service bureau that works with CorelDRAW! .CDR files saves you headaches and money.

After you select all the printing options in the Separations portion of the Print Options dialog box, you're ready to print the separations file to disk. Click OK in the Print Options dialog box to return to the Print dialog box, and then click OK to begin printing the separations file. You are prompted for a file name for the separations file. Choose an appropriate name and click OK. The .PRN extension is automatically added to the file name.

After the separations file is created, you can send it to a service bureau to output it on a high-resolution image processor, such as a Linotronic 300 or similar device.

Additional Color Printing Considerations

Some other suggestions when printing in full color are as follows:

- Printers need a registration mark on each different sheet of your final illustration if it has process or spot colors. If you do not use the Color Separation option when printing, which automatically prints registration marks, use the circle with cross hairs found in the Geographic font and make sure that each symbol prints at 100 percent of all the colors (CMYK or PMS) in the drawing so that the marks appear on each sheet.

- In the Fountain Fill dialog box, the PostScript Options dialog box enables you to specify halftone screens, frequency, and angles.

- If you are sending your final illustration to a printer, add a percentage of the three other process colors for a richer black. (Ask your printer for the best ratios.)

- Stick with the same method (CMYK, RGB, or HSB) of creating new process colors throughout your drawing to make it easier to later match printed colors.

Avoiding Fountain Fill Banding

Fountain fills can sometimes have a problem with *banding*, or visible stair-stepping of the colors, if offset printed in process color. The illustration may look fine when the illustration is professionally printed, but the banding appears only when the image is printed on a laser printer or color printer. This is because office PostScript printers have a relatively low resolution (a few hundred dots per inch) and can only produce a maximum of 256 shades of each of the four process colors. Professional printing equipment has a much higher resolution (a few thousand dots per inch). The number of shades available in fountain fills is a factor of this resolution and the halftone screen frequency used, which is measured in lines per inch.

To create smooth fountains, you can calculate the number of shades as follows:

1. Divide the number of dots per inch in the equipment by the number of lines per inch of the halftone resolution, as in dpi/lpi.

2. Multiply the resulting number by itself to get its square, which gives you the number of shades, as in: $(dpi/lpi)^2$.

3. If the fountain used does not contain the full range of shades from 1 percent to 100 percent, figure what fraction it does use. For example: a gradation going from 20 percent to 80 percent uses 60 percent (or a factor of .6) of the shades available.

4. Multiply the number in step 2 by the factor, if any, in step 3, as in $(dpi/lpi)^2 \times 6$.

5. Measure the distance between the end points of the blend in points.

6. Divide this distance by the number of shades from step 4 (or step 2 if the full range of shades is used). This gives you the size of each step in the fountain fill.

If the result is greater than 1, banding is likely. You can prevent banding by changing one or more factors: increase the percentage of the gradation, decrease the distance, raise the output resolution, or lower the frequency of the screen.

The Cost of Printing in Color

You can commercially print just about anything you create in CorelDRAW!, if you are willing to pay the price. Printing in color, especially four color, may be more than your budget can allow. The cost of commercial printing is related to the materials and services used. Effective use of CorelDRAW! can eliminate or reduce some of the printer's work, saving you money on your print job. A printer might charge extra for film and plates, doing a press proof, shooting and assembling the negatives, and more. Special effects, like dropouts, reverses, special screen, retouching, all can add extra costs. Bleeds (in which the ink goes to the edge of the paper) and trapping are also additional.

Color printing costs more than black-and-white (or single color) printing because it requires more negatives, extra printer's plates, and more impressions. It takes more time for the strippers (who shoot and assemble the negatives) and the press operators to get the job right. It also usually requires more expensive paper stock. Setup costs related to commercial printing are fixed, no matter how many units you choose to print.

Using CorelDRAW! for Maximum Color-Related Benefit

The reality of printing in more than one color is that *registration*, aligning the paper stock correctly for each press run, often can be a problem. Usually only large commercial printers with sophisticated offset printing equipment can handle many colors and tight registration. Ask your printer what type of equipment she or he uses, what she or he needs from you to do the job more efficiently, and what design elements can create added printing costs.

Remember, CorelDRAW! makes matching commercially printed colors easy if you use the provided PANTONE, Focoltone, or TRUMATCH color palettes with their respective color reference books.

If you have a color printer attached to your system, you can test its color fidelity using the file COLORBAR.CDR included with your CorelDRAW! samples. To do this, follow these steps:

1. Load and print the file by opening the File menu, choosing Open, and then choosing COLORBAR.CDR. A disk file of the CMYK Color Chart card appears on-screen.

2. Open the File menu again and choose Print.

3. Compare this printed illustration with the CMYK in a clipart manual, for example, to see how the process colors on-screen appear when commercially printed.

Drawing Some Simple Color Illustrations

Some illustrations are created for no purpose other than the artist's enjoyment. CorelDRAW! gives you more than enough tools if this is your goal. If, however, you plan to create a drawing to be used later in a proposal, or copied and disseminated in a PC "slide show," or even commercially printed in mass quantities in a 16 × 20 poster, CorelDRAW! has many features that make it easy to get the effect you want. As an example, the following steps demonstrate some of the vivid colors available in CorelDRAW! in an eye-catching illustration that can be printed on a color PostScript printer:

1. Use the various CorelDRAW! tools to draw an artist's palette in a rectangle background with six blobs of "paint" (see fig. 12.13). Before you select the color fills for the various paint blobs, reflect on how the illustration will be reproduced. Because you will be printing on your color office printer, the PANTONE Spot Colors palette or any of the process color palettes are all suitable.

Fig. 12.13
Sample illustration—drawing a palette.

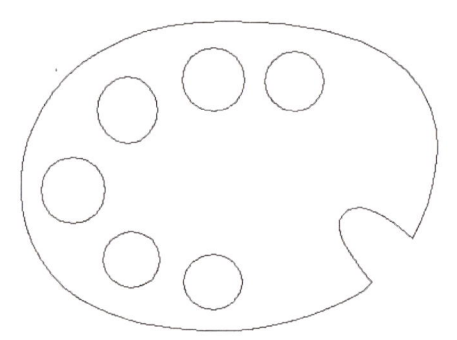

2. Open the **V**iew menu, choose the Co**l**or Palette, and then choose PANTONE **S**pot Colors.

3. Click a paint blob shape to make it active and then click one of the color choices in the palette at the bottom of the screen with the left mouse button. The color fills the interior of the paint blob shape (see fig. 12.14).

4. Continue to fill the other paint blob shapes with other colors from the PANTONE Spot Color palette. Fill the palette shape itself with one of the PMS brown shades.

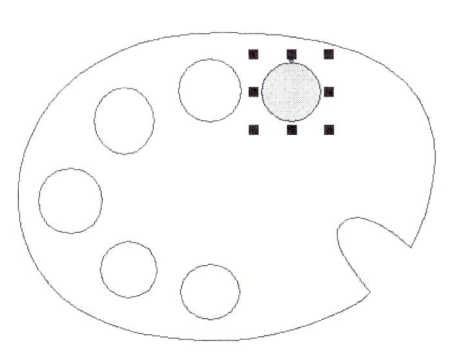

Fig. 12.14
Choosing color fills.

5. Choose a two-color pattern to fill the rectangle forming the backdrop (see fig. 12.15) by clicking the Fill tool and using the two-color Pattern icon. Click in the Colors boxes to set the background and foreground colors from the PANTONE Spot Colors palette.

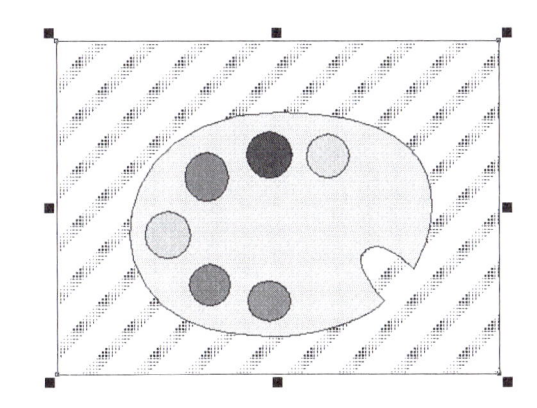

Fig. 12.15
Choosing color pattern fills.

6. Click the Text tool in Paragraph format and type the words:

    CorelDRAW! features a rainbow of ways to communicate using color!

7. Use Center Alignment on this sentence.

8. Set the typeface at 24-point Times New Roman.

9. Click the Pick tool and click the text to select it.

10. Click the Fill tool and choose the Color Wheel icon, or press Shift+F11. This opens the Uniform Fill dialog box. (You used the mouse button to fill objects before; this is just another way to set the fill of an object, even text.)

11. Select a red color of your choice or type **PANTONE 498 CV** in the Search for: box (see fig. 12.16).

Fig. 12.16
Adding color fill to text.

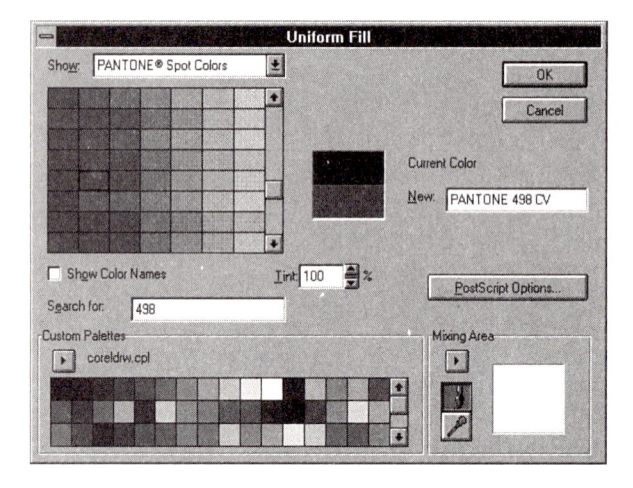

12. Click OK, and the text is given a red-colored fill.

13. At this point, the illustration is ready to print. Open the **F**ile menu and choose **P**rint, or press Ctrl+P. If you want more than one copy so that you can show it off to your colleagues, change the number in the copies box. Because you are not preparing your illustration for commercial printing, you do not have to select any other options.

14. Click OK to print the document (or Cancel if you are not attached to a color printer and are just practicing).

What if you wanted 1,000 copies of this illustration, on a 16-by-20-inch poster, to be printed by a commercial offset printer? Remember that you used six PMS colors for the six paint blobs, another PMS color for the brown palette, two PMS colors in the backdrop rectangle, and another PMS color for the text. Printing these ten different PMS colors requires ten different inks and up to ten press runs. Going to four-color process is cheaper and probably looks better. Using CorelDRAW!'s prepress features, you can save the cost of intermediate steps with your printer and/or service bureau.

To convert your illustration and get it ready for four-color process printing, follow these steps:

1. Click the Pick tool to activate it and then select the text.

Drawing Some Simple Color Illustrations   **373**

2. Click the Fill tool to get the fly-out menu and then choose the Color Wheel icon. You see the PANTONE Warm Red in the visual calibrator and the color name or number in the Search for: box.

3. Choose the CMYK Color Model from the Show drop-down list, and the PANTONE color is assigned a process color—you may or may not get a name in the New box; you can create your own name if not (see fig. 12.17).

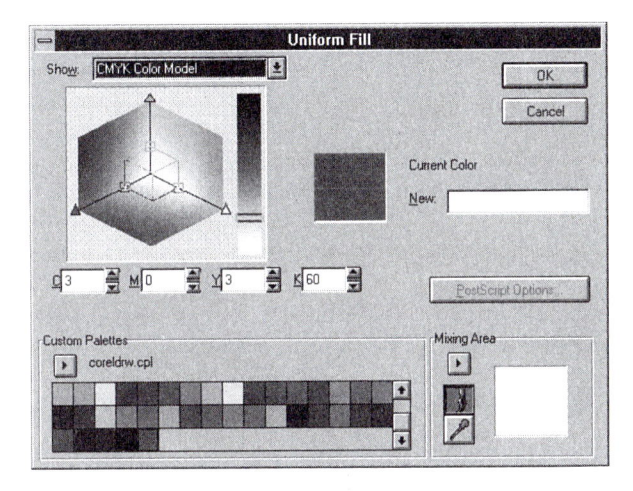

Fig. 12.17
Converting PANTONE spot color fills to process colors.

4. Click OK to convert the PANTONE color to a process color.

5. Continue to select and convert fills for each element in the illustration.

   You want to provide the illustration already separated into its four CMYK color components so that the printer does not have to create color separations manually (usually by shooting a slide photo to get a transparency and then running the transparency through an electronic color scanner). Steps 6 through 8 describe how to do this.

6. Open the **F**ile menu and choose **P**rint, or press Ctrl+P. Then click the **O**ptions button. Now you see the Print Options dialog box.

7. Click the Separations tab, and you see the Separations options for the dialog box (see fig. 12.18).

8. Click Print **S**eparations and both the Auto Trapping options because your illustration has several places in which colors touch other colors, and you want to be sure registration is not a problem. This creates enough spread and overprinting to prevent the color of the paper stock from showing through along these critical color edges.

Fig. 12.18

The Separations options in the Print Options dialog box.

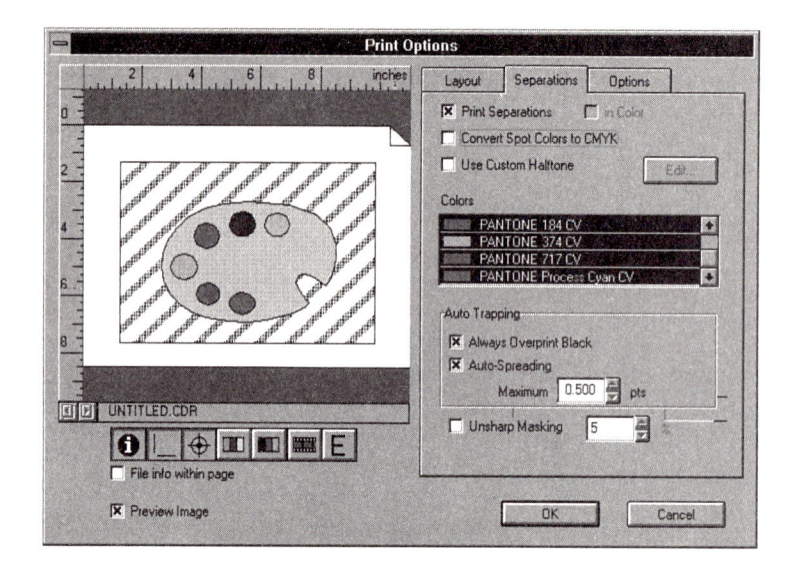

9. If you have PMS colors showing in the list of colors, click the Convert Spot Colors to CMYK option to remove them.

10. Click OK to return to the main Print window.

11. If you have chosen to print multiple copies previously, change this in the Print dialog box to avoid multiple separation print copies.

12. If you want to print to your office printer now, choose OK. You will get four different versions of this same illustration, one for each of the CMYK process ink colors. The cyan separation, for example, shows everywhere that blue ink prints, and in what percent screens.

or

Choose the Print to **F**ile option and then choose OK. This way you can give your printer the information electronically, on a disk or tape. CorelDRAW! asks you to name the printer file and specify a path for it.

Again, talk to your service bureau and your commercial printer before you finalize your project to learn the best formats and ways to transfer the information. You also may want to specify TRUMATCH process color numbers so that the final printed piece more accurately reflects your vision. You can write this information on one of the printouts you make on your color laser printer and give it to your printer along with the tape or disk.

From Here...

In this chapter, you took the knowledge and skills from previous chapters—specifying colors and fills for an object's interior and outline—and learned how to make effective color choices that reflected how your drawing would be used and reproduced (if indeed it would).

For information related to the topics in this chapter, consider these chapters:

- Chapter 13, "Advanced Line and Curve Techniques," explains advanced line and curve techniques that can improve your drawing efficiency.

- Chapter 16, "Creating Special Effects with Blending," explains Corel's Blend roll-up that enables you to transform one object into another.

- Chapter 20, "Creating Special Effects with Lens," discusses the Lens feature that can add photographic effects to your drawings.

Chapter 13

Advanced Line and Curve Techniques

by Linda Miles

In Chapter 3, "A Detailed Look at Object Drawing," you learned how to draw line segments, curve segments, rectangles, and ellipses. Most of your drawings will start out with these kinds of simple objects. To develop your drawings fully, however, you need to be able to change objects from basic shapes having a few nodes into complicated shapes having multiple layers and hundreds of nodes. The first part of this chapter covers changing the shapes of objects, using the Shape tool and the Node Edit roll-up.

Chapter 5, "Modifying Object Outlines and Interior Fills," dealt with the basics of modifying the thickness and color of object outlines. In the second part of this chapter, you learn about more advanced outline features, including line style (dashed lines, dotted lines), calligraphy, arrowheads, and alignment of the outlines of several objects.

With these advanced line and curve techniques, you can put to use all of CorelDRAW.'s curve editing features and increase your efficiency when creating drawings.

In this chapter, you learn the following:

- Changing object shapes using the Shape tool and Node Edit roll-up
- Converting objects and lines to curves
- Using cusp, smooth, and symmetrical nodes
- Understanding open- and closed-path objects
- Selecting and moving nodes with the Shape tool

- Changing object shape by moving nodes
- Changing curvature by moving control points or by dragging the curved line
- Adding and deleting nodes
- Using the Auto-Reduce feature to reduce the number of nodes
- Joining, breaking, and aligning nodes
- Adding and creating arrowheads
- Using dimension lines
- Drawing a sine wave

Changing Object Shapes

Drawing objects with CorelDRAW! involves creating objects such as rectangles, circles, lines, and multisided objects, and then changing their shapes to meet your particular needs. This section covers techniques for using the object nodes, the Shape tool, and the Node Edit roll-up to change the shapes of objects.

CorelDRAW! is set up to think of most objects as being composed of line and curve segments. At each end of a line or curve segment is a node, which looks like a small box. The node of a curve segment has one or two control points attached to the node by dotted lines. A control point is a tiny box about one-quarter the size of a node. Figure 12.1 shows several nodes and their control points on segments of a curve. Nodes and control points are important items—nodes can be moved to change the length of segments; control points can be moved around the nodes to which they are attached to change the shape of a curve.

A line has two nodes at each end. A line has a fixed slope, which means that you have no way to change the angle of the line, entering or leaving an ending node.

A curve, on the other hand, also has nodes at the ends of its segments, but each segment enters and leaves the nodes at different angles, depending on the amount of curvature present. Understanding how curves work is extremely important in using CorelDRAW! effectively.

Using the Shape Tool with the Node Edit Roll-Up

As its name suggests, the Shape tool enables you to change the shape of an object. You use the Shape tool to move and alter the nodes of an object, which in turn affects the object's shape. To select the Shape tool, click the Shape tool icon in the toolbox, or press F10.

The power of the Shape tool is expanded when you use it in conjunction with the Node Edit roll-up shown in figure 13.1. To open this roll-up, select an object with the Shape tool and double-click an object node.

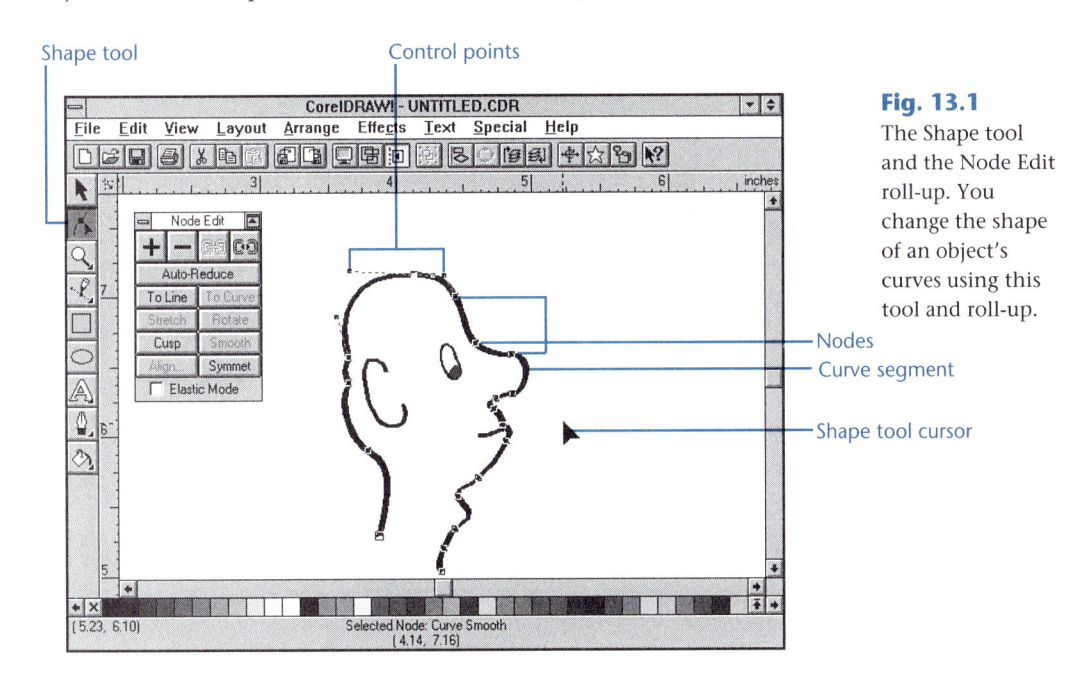

Fig. 13.1
The Shape tool and the Node Edit roll-up. You change the shape of an object's curves using this tool and roll-up.

With the Node Edit roll-up, you can add and delete nodes, fuse nodes together, break nodes apart, or change the line segment type (straight line or curve) or node type characteristics (cusp, smooth, or symmetrical). These tasks are discussed in the following sections.

Understanding Line Segments and Nodes

Before you start to reshape objects, you need a basic understanding of how CorelDRAW! draws objects. CorelDRAW! considers an object as nodes connected by a path. The path can be a straight line with two nodes on each end, or a curve made up of two or more nodes with the segments connecting the nodes. The path can also be a combination of straight line and curved segments The node type and control point angle control the shape of the curve on either side of the node. You change the shape of a curved object by dragging segments, moving nodes, adding and deleting nodes, and modifying the types and line angle characteristics of nodes.

Many of your drawings start out with lines, rectangles, and ellipses. As your drawing proceeds, you often want to change the shapes of these objects, but soon discover that CorelDRAW! does not let you do so. The program assumes that a geometric object is of a certain size and cannot be modified from that basic characteristic (for example, a circle cannot easily become a square). You can, however, convert these objects to curves so that you can edit the nodes and modify the object's shape, literally turning a square into a circle.

Converting Objects to Curves

In CorelDRAW!, basically two kinds of objects exist: curve objects and non-curve objects. Even a straight line is regarded as a curve. You can change the shape of curve objects freely by moving or modifying the nodes with the Shape tool. With non-curve objects, you are much more limited in what you can do with the nodes.

◀ See "Creating Rectangular and Square Objects," p. 78

◀ See "Drawing Circular Shapes," p. 81

Two of the basic types of objects you create with CorelDRAW!—rectangles and ellipses—are non-curve objects and cannot be reshaped with the Shape tool, except for the special corner-rounding and arc/pie techniques described in Chapter 3, "A Detailed Look at Object Drawing." But you can convert one of these objects to a curve object by selecting it, opening the Arrange menu (or pressing Ctrl+Q), and choosing the Convert to Curves command. The status line now refers to the object as a curve instead of a rectangle, for example. Although the object looks the same after being converted, CorelDRAW! no longer constrains its shape, and you can move the nodes with the Shape tool.

> **Caution**
>
> Sometimes you may want to convert a curve object back to a rectangle or ellipse to round out corners or make a pie-cut. Be aware that the only way to convert a curve object back to a rectangle or an ellipse is with the Undo command from the Edit menu. If you have specified three levels of Undo in the Preferences-General property sheet, and you performed three operations after converting a rectangle to curves (four operations in all), you cannot recover the rectangle. You will have to redraw it with the rectangle tool.

You also can convert artistic text to curves, which enables you to reshape individual characters with the Shape tool. You might use this technique to create a company logo, for example. You cannot, however, convert nonartistic or paragraph text to curves.

Objects have specific node point locations. A circle or ellipse, for example, has a node point at each 90 degree point. When a circle is still a circle (rather than a curve), it has only one point that you drag to create the arc and pie shapes you saw previously in Chapter 3. After being converted to a curve, an ellipse has four nodes, and text letters have many nodes (see fig. 13.2).

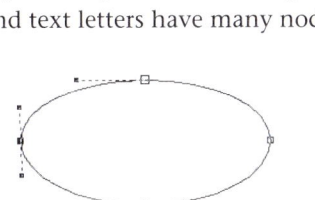

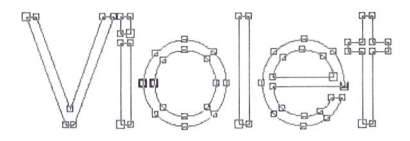

◀ See "Reshaping a Curve or Object by Changing Its Nodes and Control Points," p. 72

Fig. 13.2
An ellipse and artistic text, converted to curves. The converted ellipse is the same shape, but now has four nodes. The text also looks the same but has many nodes. The nodes allow you to change the shape of the objects.

After you convert an object to a curve, you can modify the nodes just as you can with any object to achieve many of the dramatic effects that CorelDRAW! is renowned for creating.

Troubleshooting

I created a square with the rectangle tool but I can't delete a corner node. I want to make a triangle.

Convert the square to curves so the nodes can be selected with the Shape tool. To convert the square, select Convert to Curves in the Arrange menu. Then select the Shape tool and click on a corner node and press the Delete key. The node will disappear and the square will become a triangle.

Why can't I round the corners of my rectangle by moving one of the corner nodes?

You have converted the rectangle to curves. After it has been converted to curves, the rectangle's corner nodes can no longer be manipulated in this way. Try using the Undo command. If this doesn't work, you will have to create another rectangle, round its edges, and then convert it to curves.

Converting Lines to Curves

Curve objects can be composed of any number of connected line and curve segments. Every segment has a beginning node and an end node. The end node determines whether the segment is a line or a curve. If it is a line node, the path connecting it to the previous node is constrained to be linear; you cannot alter its shape and can change only the line's angle. You can convert the segment from a line to a curve, however, and then modify its shape, as you can any other curve. The basic procedure is as follows:

1. Create a line of four or five nodes with the Pencil tool in Bézier mode. When you create the last two nodes, do not pull on a control point. Instead, just click and move to another location and click.

2. Select the line by clicking on it with the Shape tool. Notice that the line has a node on each end (represented by an unfilled box), and that one of the boxes is larger than the others. The larger box is the origin or *first node* of the line (see fig. 13.3). The smaller box at the other end of the path is an end node.

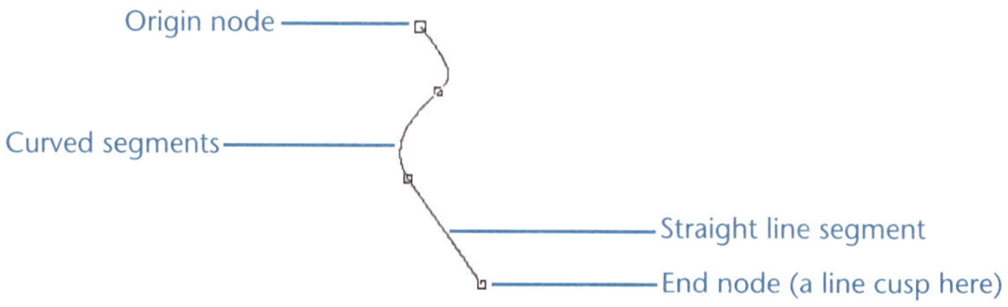

Fig. 13.3

A path consisting of a straight line segment and curved segments. The node (end node) at the lower end of this path is a line cusp node. The segment above it cannot be shaped until you select the end node with the Shape tool and convert the node from a line cusp to a curve cusp.

Origin node

Curved segments

Straight line segment

End node (a line cusp here)

3. Select the end node of the line (represented by the smaller box) by clicking on it with the Shape tool. Notice that the status line identifies the selected node as a *line cusp*.

4. Double-click the node to open the Node Edit roll-up, and click the To Curve button. The status line identifies the selected node as a *curve cusp*.

5. Click the segment between the nodes with the Shape tool. Notice that you now can change the shape of the segment by dragging on it with the mouse cursor (if Elastic mode is selected) or by moving its control points.

To change a curve into a line, follow the same procedure, but start with a curve and choose To Line rather than To Curve.

In general, CorelDRAW! chooses the proper line segment type for a drawing. Illustrations tend to use more complicated curved segments, and technical drawings tend to use more lines and simple curved objects. Making a curved segment look like a straight line is time-consuming and often frustrating, and making a line act like a curve is impossible. If you have difficulty in drawing the kind of line you need, reread the sections in Chapter 3 entitled "Drawing

Straight Lines" and "Drawing Curved Lines." These sections give detailed instructions on how to draw lines and curves. On your part, careful choice concerning when to single click and double-click, and how far and in what direction to pull control points early in the drawing process can cut down on the amount of time you spend adjusting nodes and control points after you create curves and lines.

> **Note**
>
> Many professional artists prefer the Bézier mode to the Freehand mode because it creates fewer nodes. If you can slightly pull the control point of each node as you create it roughly toward the direction the path is headed, you can create drawings quickly. (Click-short-pull, click-short pull, etc.) This technique produces a sketch of the object which can then be refined. With practice you will learn to pull at just the right angle while drawing to get the curve you want.

Examining Characteristics of Nodes

As mentioned previously, the characteristics of nodes control the shape of the curve, and you can change the shape by altering these characteristics. A node can be cusp, smooth, or symmetrical.

A *cusp node* represents a sharp change in the shape of the curve when passing through the node. The segment on one side of the node can be a different shape and size from the segment on the other side. The angles of the line entering and leaving the node are independently controlled by the Bézier control points on either side. Changes to one side do not affect the other. Figure 13.4 shows examples of cusp nodes.

Fig. 13.4
Cusp nodes. The lines entering and leaving the node can be independently controlled by the control points so that the segment on one side of the node can be a different shape and size, and emerge at a different angle from the segment on the other side.

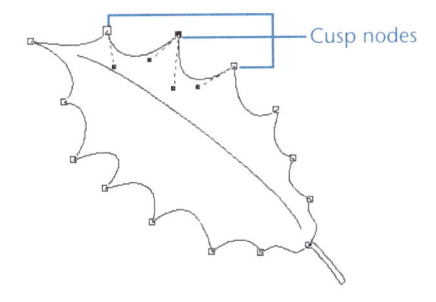

A *smooth node* constrains the curve to a gradual change in shape and requires that the line passing through the node enter and leave at the same angle. Moving the control point on one side of a smooth node changes the angle of the line on the other. Changing the length of the control arm on one side of the node does not affect the size of the control arm on the other. The curve angle is the same on both sides, but the amount of curve deflection varies based on the size of the control arms. If one side of a smooth node is a line segment and the other is a curve segment, the angle of the curve segment is constrained by the line because the line's curve is fixed by the other end's node. No angle changes are possible with this situation, and you should convert the line to a curve so that you can alter the line's curvature. Figure 13.5 shows an example of a smooth node.

Fig. 13.5
A smooth node. The curve angle is the same on both sides of the node. The length of the control arms on each side can be different, making the curve on one side a different shape than the curve on the other.

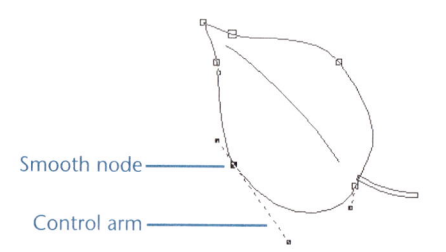

A *symmetrical node* further constrains the shape of the curve so that the curve on one side is symmetrical (or equal) to the other. The control points are always equally distant from the node and are always connected by their control arms in a straight line. Changing one side of a symmetrical node makes the exact same change occur to the other side. Figure 13.6 shows an example of a symmetrical node.

Fig. 13.6
A symmetrical node. The curve on one side of the node is symmetrical to the curve on the other side. The control points are equidistant from the node.

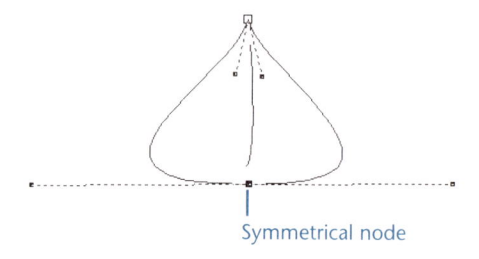

Curve nodes have control points that control the shape of the curve segments on either side of the node. Line nodes also have a control point if the next segment is a curve segment, but the angle of the curve is constrained to the angle of the line segment.

You can change the shape of curve segments by dragging the nodes and their respective control points with the Shape tool. How much flexibility you have in moving the control points depends on whether the node is cusp, smooth, or symmetrical. You can change the overall look of a line dramatically by simply changing a series of nodes from one type to another.

> **Troubleshooting**
>
> *I can't change the shape of a line when I drag it with my mouse, even though the nearest node is a smooth node. What am I doing wrong?*
>
> One side of the smooth node is probably a line segment. The line's curve is fixed by the end node. No angle changes are possible. You will need to convert the end node to a curve so that you can alter the line's curvature. Select the end node with the Shape tool and click on To Curve in the Node Edit roll-up.

Understanding Open and Closed Curve Objects

Objects also can be either open path or closed path (see fig. 13.7). An *open-path object* has two unconnected end points and does not completely enclose a space. A freestanding line or curve segment is an example of an open-path object. *Closed-path objects* do not have end points, and the path or curve between the nodes returns to the point of origin.

◀ See "Understanding Open- and Closed-Path Objects," p. 89

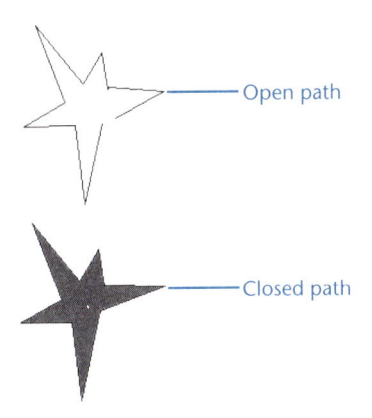

Fig. 13.7
Open- and closed-path objects. A closed-path object can contain a fill.

Because open-path objects do not enclose space, they cannot contain a fill. In some cases, you may want to put a tiny break in a closed-path object to keep it from adopting a fill.

One special characteristic of open-path objects is that you can apply special treatments, called *arrowheads*, to the end points. (For more information, see this chapter's section on "Adding and Creating Arrowheads.") You also can join the end points of an open-path object, or multiple open-path objects, to create a closed-path object that can then be filled. (For more information, see this chapter's section on "Joining and Breaking Nodes.")

Using the Shape Tool To Move Nodes

This section covers the basic techniques for using the Shape tool to modify object shapes by moving individual nodes and their control points. The following section covers using the Node Edit roll-up with the Shape tool.

> **Note**
>
> Object modifications made with the Shape tool differ from those made with the Pick tool because the Pick tool changes the overall object characteristics, such as size and rotation, and the Shape tool deals only with the nodes that comprise the object.

Selecting Objects and Nodes

You must select an object before you can view, move, or modify its nodes with the Shape tool. To select an object while in Wireframe mode, click its outline with the Shape tool. To select an object while in Editable Preview mode, click anywhere in the object interior if it has a fill. If an object has been selected by the Pick tool already when you select the Shape tool, the object remains selected, as shown by the display of nodes. When you are manipulating node points, the Wireframe mode allows you to work faster. It also allows you to view and select the lines, curves, and nodes of lower layers.

You can work on only one object at a time with the Shape tool. If several objects are selected with the Pick tool, and you change to the Shape tool, all objects will be deselected. If you select an object with the Shape tool and then try to select another object while pressing the Shift key, the first object will be deselected, leaving only the second object selected. You generally modify one node at a time, but you can use the Shape tool to drag a dotted selection marquee around several nodes to select them. Then you can simultaneously modify all the selected nodes.

Unselected nodes appear as open squares on the object and become solid black squares when selected. When you select a single node, information about the segment and node type (such as `Curve Cusp` or `Line Smooth`) displays in the center of the status line. In addition, the control points affecting the two adjacent segments are displayed (see fig. 13.8).

If you've already selected a node and you click a second node, the first node is deselected. Pressing the Tab key deselects the current node and selects the next node on the object's path. Pressing Shift+Tab cycles the node selection in the opposite direction.

Changing Object Shapes 387

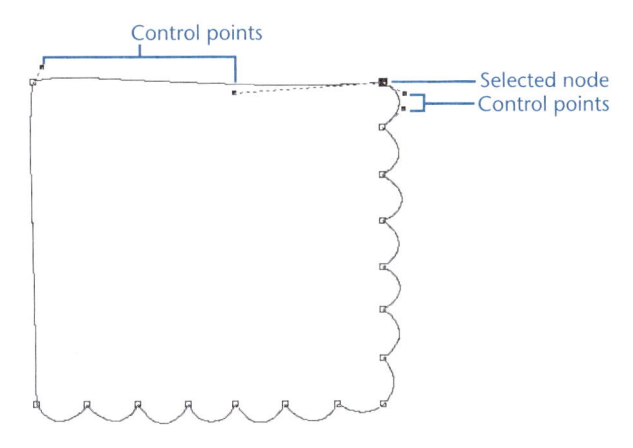

Fig. 13.8
Selecting a single node on an object.

You may want to select more than one node so that you can move them or change their characteristics simultaneously, or join two nodes together. To select multiple nodes, press the Shift key while clicking each node. You also can drag a selection marquee around a group of nodes using the Shape tool. A dashed marquee box appears around the nodes as you drag, and the nodes are selected when you release the mouse button. Click white space with the Shape tool or press the Esc key to deselect all nodes.

Changing Object Shape by Moving Nodes

You can change the shape of an object in creative ways by moving its nodes with the Shape tool. To move a selected node, click and drag it to its new position and release the mouse button. The other nodes remain where they were, and the line or curve segments connected to the node stretch as you move the node. The object remains a closed or an open path but adopts the new shape.

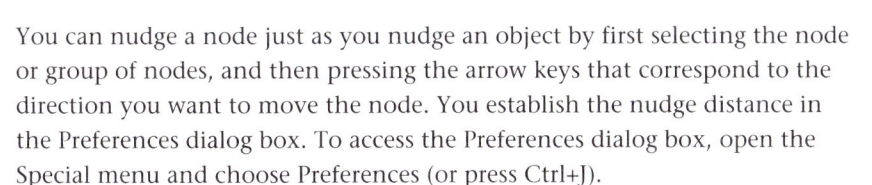

You can nudge a node just as you nudge an object by first selecting the node or group of nodes, and then pressing the arrow keys that correspond to the direction you want to move the node. You establish the nudge distance in the Preferences dialog box. To access the Preferences dialog box, open the Special menu and choose Preferences (or press Ctrl+J).

You can scale a segment of a curve by first selecting the nodes that correspond to the segment and then selecting Stretch from the Node Edit roll-up. The Stretch function provides the same sizing boxes used in conjunction with the Pick tool and overall object sizing, except these sizing boxes now apply only to the selected line segments. When the small black boxes (handles) appear, you can drag them to new locations, which scales the

Tip
When multiple nodes are selected, they all move together. To move all the selected nodes, drag one of the nodes with the Shape tool.

selected line segments while leaving the other nodes and their related segments in their original positions. As you scale, you'll see the percentage scaled in the status line only when you stop stretching the selected nodes.

> **Note**
>
> Dragging a handle while pressing the Ctrl key changes the selected segments in 100-percent increments. Dragging while pressing the Shift key scales the selected segments from the center of the line, and pressing Ctrl+Shift while dragging scales from the center in 100-percent increments when the Ctrl key is pressed. You can increase in only 100-percent increments. CorelDRAW! doesn't decrease in 50-percent increments, but provides 100-percent scaling that corresponds to a mirror.

This simple exercise with an object composed of line segments illustrates the range of possibilities for modifying object shapes by moving nodes with the Shape tool. Follow these steps:

1. Create a rectangle with the Rectangle tool. Convert the rectangle to a curve object by selecting it. Then open the **A**rrange menu and choose the Con**v**ert to Curves command (or press Ctrl+Q).

2. Click one of the nodes with the Shape tool, and drag the node around. Notice that you can move the node in any direction and for any distance, and that the two line segments attached to the node stretch and change their angle of orientation in response to the movements of the node.

3. Select an additional node by holding down the Shift key and clicking, or by using marquee select. Then click one of the nodes with the Shape tool, and drag the node around. Notice that this time, both the nodes move together.

Tip

To move a node or group of selected nodes in a precise horizontal or vertical movement, hold down the Ctrl key as you drag them. Release the mouse button first and then the Ctrl key.

Changing the Curvature

Although you cannot change the shape of a line segment (it does not have control points), you can change the shape of a curve segment by using the Bézier control points attached to the nodes, or by dragging the curved line itself. Typically, you make the curve the basic shape you want by dragging the curve segment itself, and then fine-tune the shape by moving the control points associated with the nodes. The Elastic mode of operation is valuable when working with multiple nodes because the nodes move proportionally rather than independently at exactly the same time.

The control points have different effects on each curved segment, depending on the type of node attached to the segment's end point. A cusp node affects only one side or the other of the node; a smooth node affects both sides from an angle in/out of the node but leaves the amount of line curvature on the opposite side alone; a symmetrical node changes both sides of the node equally. Refer to the control points shown in figures 13.3 through 13.5. The amount of line curvature is related to the length of the control arm. Tremendous flexibility is provided with the CorelDRAW! Bézier-curve editing. Realize that it takes lots of practice and experimentation with control points before you can draw a series of curved segments exactly right the first time around.

All nodes on a curve have two control points. You may occasionally click a node and find only one control point. The second control point is probably hiding under the node. Press the Shift key as you drag the node. The control point should appear, but the node stays in the same place.

The easiest way to change a curved line's curvature is to drag the line itself with the Shape tool. If the control points are visible as you drag the line, you see them update themselves based on the new line design. If the control points aren't present, you can still drag the line and change its shape.

You can move selected nodes and stretch multiple segments proportionally with respect to the node dragged. This means that the curves move like a rubber band as opposed to separate segments which retain their lengths. Follow these steps:

1. Open the Node Edit roll-up.

2. Select **E**lastic Mode. A check mark should appear in the box to the left of the option label.

3. Select two or more nodes you want to move together. You must select multiple nodes.

4. Drag any of the selected nodes. Notice that some of the other nodes move a distance that's proportional to the selected node's movement.

> **Note**
>
> At least one node will remain stationary as an anchor point, depending on whether the selected nodes include an end node, and whether the node being dragged is not an end node.

Tip

You can always polish the curves you draw *after* you create an object. Don't worry too much about getting the right node type or curve shape as you are drawing the object.

In summary, you can drag the node itself, the control points associated with the node, or the line itself to change the shape of a curved line. You can change a line's appearance dramatically by changing the segments from lines to curves (or vice versa) and choosing different node types such as cusp, smooth, and symmetrical. The Elastic mode of operation makes selected nodes move in proportion to the movement of the dragged node, which gives the line's rate of deformation a more realistic appearance and shapes the object segments as a total entity instead of as separate segments.

> **Troubleshooting**
>
> *Sometimes I can't find the control points on a corner node. How do I get them to show up?*
>
> First make sure the object is a curved object. Click on its outline with the Shape tool. If the status line says Rectangle, you must convert the object to a curved object by selecting Convert to Curves in the Arrange menu. Then click on each corner node you want to change and convert it to a curve cusp by selecting To Curve in the Node Edit roll-up. After you convert the corner nodes, control points will appear when you click on one of those nodes.
>
> If your object is already a curved object, click on a node with the Shape tool, if the status line says Line Cusp, select To Curve in the Node Edit roll-up to convert the node to a curve cusp. Depending on what type of node is next on the path, one or two control points will appear.
>
> *When I select several nodes to move, they don't move together the same distance as the node I drag.*
>
> Check to see whether Elastic mode is selected in the Node Edit roll-up. With the Elastic mode unselected, the selected nodes will move together the same distance as the node you drag. With the Elastic mode selected, the nodes move more like rubber bands than solid segments. The segments between the nodes stretch, and the selected nodes move proportionately but not necessarily the same distance on the line.

Adding and Deleting Nodes

After you draw an object, you need to refine the curves so that they exhibit the desired shape. This usually requires you to add or delete nodes. If you want an extra bend in a path, you may need to add a node. If you want to make a path smoother, you may need to delete a few nodes. If you have trouble fitting a curve the way you want, you may have too few or too many nodes.

The more complicated the curve you want, the larger the number of nodes you need. When you draw in Freehand mode. CorelDRAW! inserts nodes when it senses the movements of your mouse, even though some of the movements are unintentional. Unless you have a very steady hand, you may end up with too many nodes on a path.

In general, the number of nodes inserted corresponds to the number of times the line changes directions (called an *inflection point*). Also, the more pauses you make while drawing a curve, the more nodes you're likely to have. When a line moving in one direction changes direction in an angle that surpasses 120 degrees, a node is placed at that point. Actually, you don't have to know this as you draw because it is difficult, if not impossible, to sense when small movements of the hand are exceeding the inflection point and thus producing unwanted nodes. Because hand movements with a mouse are unsteady, you will need to delete excess nodes produced while drawing in the Freehand mode.

In this section, you learn how to add nodes, delete nodes, and use the Auto-Reduce option to eliminate unnecessary nodes.

Adding Nodes

To add a node, first double-click the curve with the Shape tool where you want the new node. Then click the + symbol in the Node Edit roll-up or press the + key. You then can change the node to the type you need.

If you decide you really didn't want to add a node, you can select Undo Curve Edit in the Edit menu. If you have performed too many operations since you added the node for the Undo to work, simply delete the node according to the instructions in the next section.

Deleting Nodes

Deleting a node is just as easy as adding one. Click the node with the Shape tool, and click the – symbol in the Node Edit roll-up or press the – key or Delete key. The curve shape may change dramatically when a node is deleted, depending on the type of the deleted node, its position, and the position and length of its control points. Deleting a node also deletes a line segment.

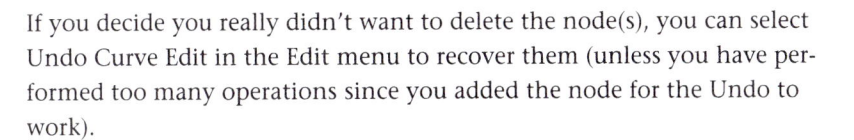

If you decide you really didn't want to delete the node(s), you can select Undo Curve Edit in the Edit menu to recover them (unless you have performed too many operations since you added the node for the Undo to work).

Tip
Select several nodes and delete them all at once by choosing the – button in the Node Edit roll-up, or the – key or Delete key.

Using the AutoReduce Feature

▶ See "Setting the Auto-Reduce Feature Default," p. 585

When you draw a line freehand, CorelDRAW! does the best it can to approximate your drawing. Many little variations added by your hand movement may be unnecessary to the drawing, but sensed by CorelDRAW!. These variations may require nodes to match accurately, which means that simple-looking lines sometimes end up with an exceptional number of nodes. You can delete each node using the – button in the Node Edit roll-up, or the – key or Delete key on the keyboard, but first try the AutoReduce option provided in the Node Edit roll-up. This method is much faster when numerous nodes must be deleted. AutoReduce deletes unneeded nodes in a curve segment and reduces the number of nodes used to fit the curve.

Tip
Traced images or scanned objects can have large numbers of nodes. AutoReduce helps simplify these images.

The AutoReduce procedure is straightforward. Select the nodes included in the segments you want affected, and choose AutoReduce from the Node Edit roll-up. CorelDRAW! uses the AutoReduce setting in the Curves property sheet of the Preferences dialog box to determine which nodes are needed to maintain the general direction of the curve and the frequency at which it deletes the unneeded nodes for those segments you selected (see fig. 13.9).

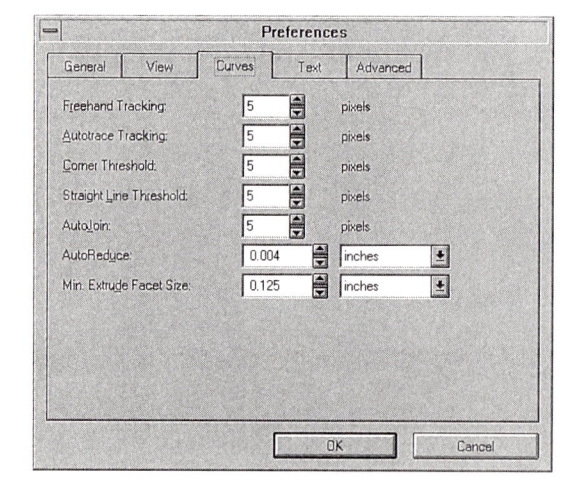

Fig 13.9
The Preferences dialog box with the Curves tab selected.

Joining and Breaking Nodes

You can always join or break nodes by using the Join and Break icons located in the Node Edit roll-up. Use Join to connect nodes and to create a closed path that can be filled. Break divides one node into two, which either opens a closed path or enables you to create multiple objects after separation.

To join two nodes, select them, and then select the join icon from the Node Edit roll-up.

> **Note**
>
> When you join two nodes of an object, the object's shape will change depending on the distance of the nodes from each other. The further apart the nodes, the more the shape will change. If you want to retain the shape of the object, don't join the nodes. Instead, select the object with the Shape tool and then select the Bézier tool. Click on one end node of the object and then on the other end node. This procedure adds a segment between the nodes and makes the object a closed path without changing the shape of the original curves.

To break two joined nodes, simply click the nodes, and then select the Break icon from the Node Edit roll-up. You can drag either of the newly unjoined nodes to a new location.

Tip
Joining nodes changes an open-path object into a closed-path object that can accept a fill. Join the beginning and ending nodes to complete the path so that you can assign a fill.

Aligning Nodes between Objects

Often two objects that you created separately need to share the same boundary. Trying to perform this operation by hand is difficult and usually time-consuming. You can, however, use the Align option in the Node Edit roll-up to align the nodes and control points associated with the nodes. Each object then shares the same shape along the interface (boundary) between the objects.

To align nodes between two closed-path objects, follow these steps:

1. Use the Pick tool to select both objects.

2. Combine them by choosing the **C**ombine option from the **A**rrange menu.

3. Choose the Shape tool. Double-click any node to open the Node Edit roll-up.

4. Make sure that the interface lines along both objects have the same number of nodes. If they do not, use the Node Edit roll-up's + and – options to adjust the number of nodes, preferably keeping them in the same relative positions on their respective lines. Figure 13.10 shows two objects before alignment.

Fig. 13.10
The objects and nodes before alignment.

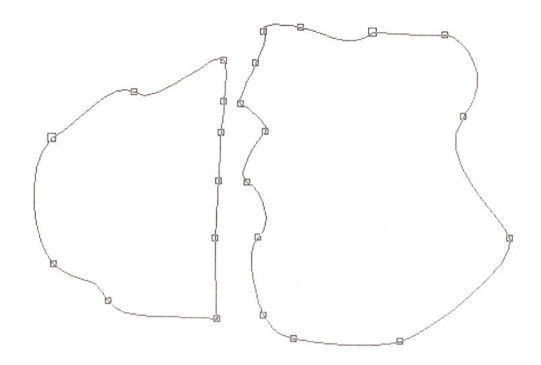

5. Using the Shape tool, select the node that you want to move during the alignment process.

6. While holding down the Shift key, select the node that is to remain stationary. The first node you selected will be moved in the next steps to align to the second node you selected.

7. Choose **A**lign from the Node Edit roll-up. The Node Align dialog box appears, as shown in figure 13.11.

Fig. 13.11
The Node Align dialog box. The default setting is for all three objects to be selected.

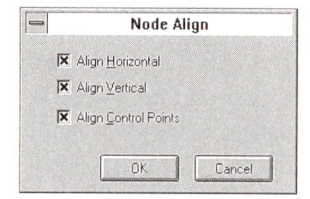

8. Select the appropriate alignment options. The default setting is for all three options to be selected.

   Align Horizontal moves the first selected node so that it rests on the same horizontal line as the reference (second) node.

   Align Vertical moves the first selected node so that it rests on the same vertical line as the reference (second) node.

   Selecting only one of these two dims the Align Control Points option because you must have both vertical and horizontal alignment before the control points can align.

   Selecting Align Control Points in combination with the other two options aligns the node location and the slope of the line entering and leaving that node, because the control points exactly overlay each other.

9. Click OK, and watch the two nodes align in accordance with your settings, as shown in figure 13.12.

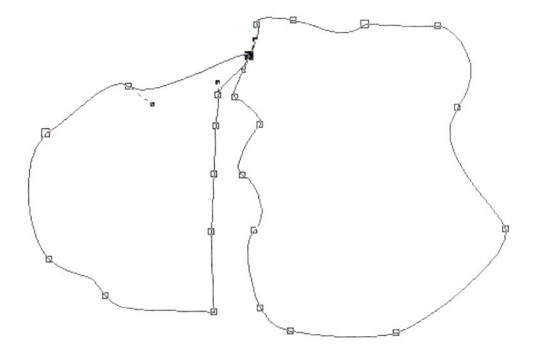

Fig. 13.12
The first two nodes aligned. The left node moved to align with the stationary right node.

10. One node remains stationary and the other moves. Align the remaining pairs of nodes (see fig. 13.13). You may need to adjust the control points to align segments.

You will probably get more consistent results if you start aligning nodes from one end of the overall line segments and then sequentially align each of the nodes to the other end. After you align the object nodes, you can divide the combination into two objects, as shown in figure 13.13, by first selecting the combined objects and then choosing Break Apart from the Arrange menu.

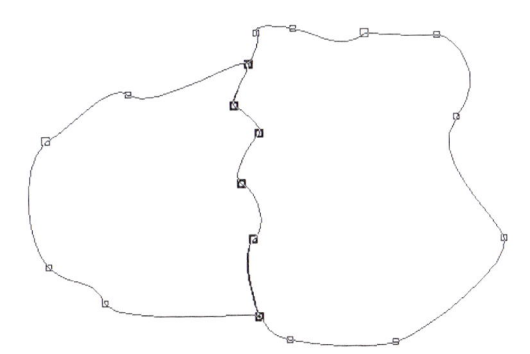

Fig 13.13
Object nodes after all six pairs have been aligned. These nodes were aligned in sequence from top to bottom.

Fig. 13.14
Breaking apart two aligned objects.

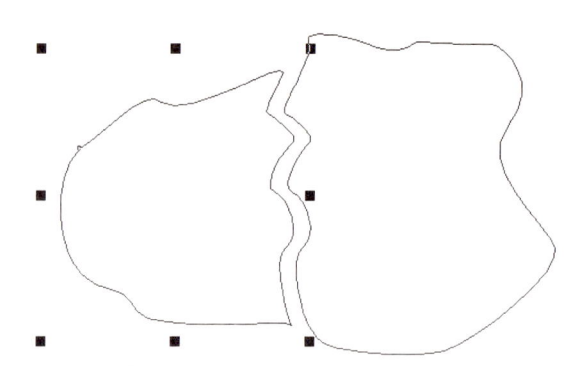

> **Troubleshooting**
>
> *When I select Align in the Arrange menu, the nodes do not align.*
>
> CorelDRAW! has two Align commands, and you selected the wrong one. Select Align in the Node Edit roll-up to align nodes. Align in the Arrange menu is for aligning selected objects on a plane with respect to their handles.
>
> *I have tried to select two nodes so that I can align them, but I can't select them both at one time.*
>
> You will need to first combine the two objects before you can select nodes on each object. To do this, select both objects with the Pick tool, and then choose Combine in the Arrange menu. When the objects are combined, you can select a node on one object, press the Shift key, and select a node on the other object.
>
> *When I aligned the nodes the segments between didn't align. They showed gaps between the lines.*
>
> This is normal. You may still have to adjust control points to align the segments.

Adding and Creating Arrowheads

CorelDRAW! comes with a wide variety of standard arrow designs. You can place these designs at a line's beginning, end, or both. The design for each end does not have to be the same type. To add an arrowhead, you use the Pen roll-up. To add arrowheads to a line, follow these steps:

1. Choose the Outline tool. The Outline fly-out menu appears.

2. Choose the Pen roll-up tool (second icon from the left in the top row). The Pen roll-up shown in figure 13.15 appears.

Adding and Creating Arrowheads   **397**

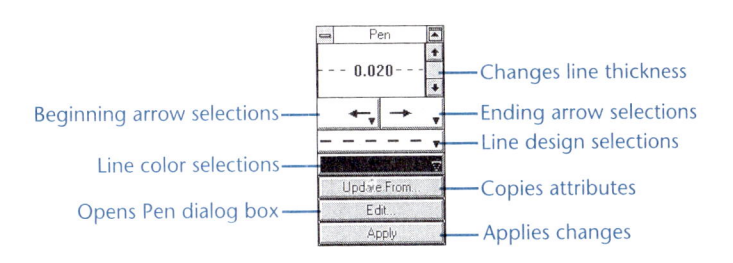

Fig. 13.15
The Pen roll-up.

- Changes line thickness
- Beginning arrow selections
- Ending arrow selections
- Line design selections
- Line color selections
- Copies attributes
- Opens Pen dialog box
- Applies changes

3. To display the available standard arrow selections, click the small triangle in the bottom-right corner of the Ending Arrow Select box. Figure 13.16 shows a few of the arrowhead types available.

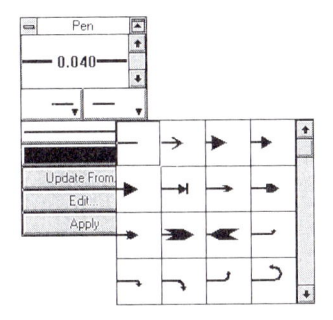

Fig. 13.16
A few of the arrowhead selections. Use the scroll bar to view additional designs.

4. Scroll through the various designs, using the scroll bar located at the right.

5. Click the design of your choice to add it to the dialog box display, selecting it for the beginning arrow.

6. To add an arrowhead to the beginning of the line, repeat steps 3 through 5 but use the Beginning Arrow Select box. Remember, your two arrowheads do not have to be the same.

7. Click Apply to add the arrowheads to the selected line.

You also can add an arrowhead to the line by using the Outline Pen dialog box shown in figure 13.17. To access this dialog box, select the Outline Dialog tool (the pen icon) in the upper-left corner of the Outline fly-out menu.

The Arrows box in the upper-right corner of this dialog box includes two arrow selection buttons that give you access to the beginning and ending arrow designs. You select designs in the same way as in the Pen roll-up, using the left button to select the beginning arrowhead and the right button to select the ending arrowhead. Click OK to apply the arrow designs to the selected line.

Tip
To determine which arrowheads appear at the ends of a selected line, select the line with the Shape tool, and then press the Home key to highlight the beginning node. Press the End key to highlight the ending node.

Fig. 13.17
The Outline Pen dialog box. Use this dialog box to specify line thickness, design, color, and arrowhead endings.

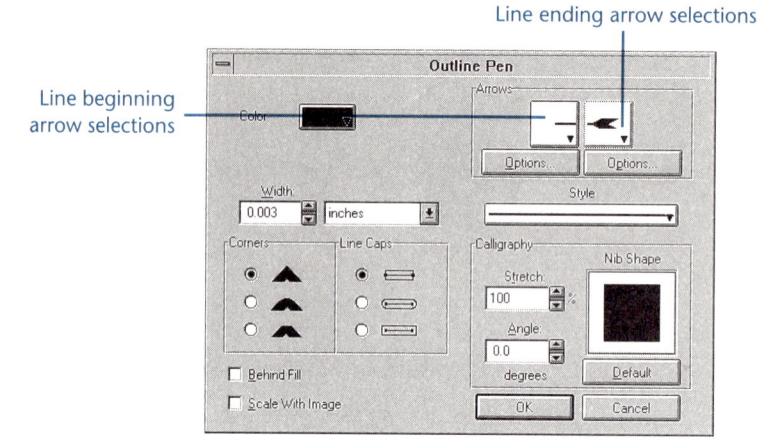

Although CorelDRAW! gives you many designs from which to choose, you may have something else in mind for your arrowhead. You can customize the standard arrowheads to meet your specific needs. The procedure for accessing the Arrowhead Editor is straightforward, and editing the arrowheads follows many of the standard CorelDRAW! object-editing conventions.

To edit an arrowhead, follow these steps:

1. Select the arrow you want to edit from the Outline Pen dialog box's arrow selection boxes.

2. Click the **O**ptions button under the arrow selection box.

3. Choose Edit from the menu. The Arrowhead Editor dialog box appears, as shown in figure 13.8.

Fig. 13.18
The Arrowhead Editor dialog box.

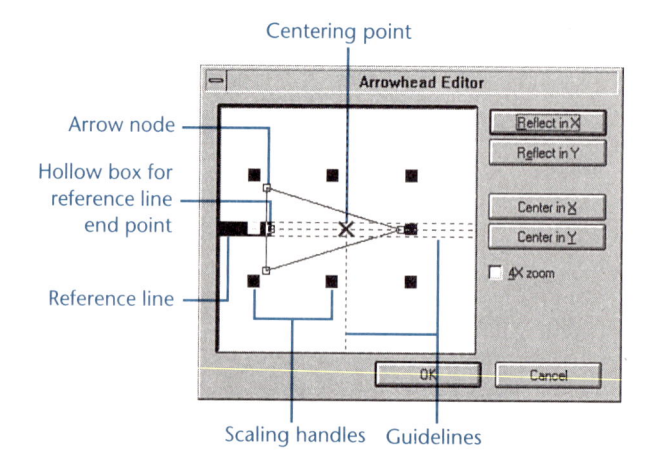

This dialog box shows a detail of the selected arrowhead design. Many of the components, such as the scaling handles, guidelines, and nodes, should now look familiar to you.

4. Use the scaling handles to change the size of the arrowhead, following the same conventions you use to scale objects. The corner handles scale simultaneously in both X and Y directions, and the other handles scale in X or Y only, based on their location.

5. Use the guidelines to align the arrowhead object within the editing screen. The arrowhead object nodes "stick" to the guidelines, just as when you align any other object. The three horizontal guidelines enable you to align with the top, center, and bottom of the reference line. The vertical guideline enables you to align in the horizontal direction with respect to the reference line. If you want the arrowhead applied to the end of the reference line, drag the hollow box that represents the end of the reference line to the vertical guideline, and then drag the back nodes of the arrowhead to the vertical guideline. They line up perfectly because of the guideline's magnetic effect.

6. Use the **R**eflect in X and **R**eflect in Y options if you want to make a mirror image of the arrowhead around the X and Y axes, respectively. The initial arrowhead is erased, and the new, reflected arrowhead takes its place. The reflections occur around the X-marker centering point in the middle of the editing screen.

7. Use the Center in **X** and Center in **Y** options if you want to position the arrowhead center with the X-marker centering point in the middle of the editing screen.

8. Use the **4**X Zoom option to view a close-up of the arrowhead, centered on the X-marker centering point.

9. Click OK when you finish in the Arrowhead Editor dialog box.

You also can apply the complete power of CorelDRAW! to creating your own custom arrowheads, which you then can access from the standard arrowhead lists. Up to 100 arrows are allowed in the arrowhead file.

To create your own arrow, follow these steps:

1. Create the arrowhead design, just as you would any CorelDRAW! object. If you use a rectangle, ellipsis, or text character, convert it to curves. If you have drawn more than one object for the arrowhead

design, select and combine the objects using the Combine command in the Arrange menu.

2. Make sure that the object is selected, and choose Create **A**rrow from the **S**pecial menu.

3. Answer Yes to the dialog box question about creating the arrowhead.

Look at the arrowhead selections in the Pen roll-up and notice that the new design is there at the end of the list. If you see a straight horizontal line at the end of your list, your arrowhead design didn't work. Remember that an arrowhead adopts the attributes of the reference line, so fill and outline colors are irrelevant in arrowhead creation. Also, remember that you can edit the new arrowhead by using the Arrowhead Editor, so don't be too concerned about getting the arrowhead design perfect the first time.

> **Troubleshooting**
>
> *I tried to make an arrowhead using a design with a circle and curved line. When I selected both with the Pick tool and opened the Special menu, the Create Arrow command was light gray and I could not select it. Why can't I create an arrowhead?*
>
> Did you convert the circle to curves? Geometric objects must be curved objects before they can become arrowheads. Did you combine the two objects before you tried to create the arrowhead? You must combine all objects before you attempt to create an arrowhead.

Modifying Line Thickness, Color, and Style

CorelDRAW! provides three ways to modify line thicknesses and colors after the line is drawn. One is through the Outline fly-out menu; another is through the Pen roll-up; the third is through the Outline Pen dialog box. The Pen roll-up is by far the fastest way to modify lines while working on a drawing.

◀ See "Copying Outline Styles Between Objects," p. 144

In addition, after you create a line style in a roll-up or as a template style, you can apply it to multiple lines by following the styles application procedure in Chapter 5, "Modifying Object Outlines and Interior Fills."

Using the Outline Fly-Out Menu

Object outlines can be modified using the Outline tool fly-out menu shown in figure 13.19. Continually having to select the Outline tool is cumbersome and unnecessary if you use the Pen roll-up. The options in the Outline Fly-out Menu are discussed in detail in Chapter 5, "Modifying Object Outlines and Interior Fills."

◀ See "Modifying Object Outline Characteristics," p. 137

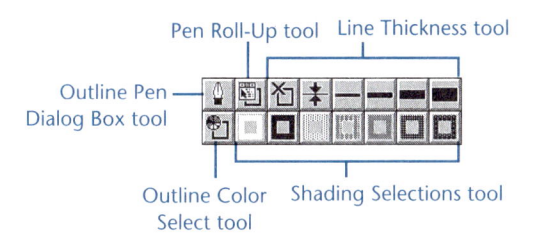

Fig. 13.19
The Outline fly-out menu.

Using the Pen Roll-Up

Choose the Pen Roll-Up tool from the Outline fly-out menu to activate the Pen roll-up, which contains many options you can use to modify the appearance of your lines. The Pen roll-up is shown in figure 13.15 in this chapter.

Use the top portion of the window to select a line thickness. First, select the line you want to modify. Then scroll through the line thickness options until you reach the thickness you want to use, and click Apply to apply it to the selected line. The no thickness option is represented by a large X that extends completely across the display window. The hairline thickness is represented by a small x intersecting in the center of the window. The other thicknesses are shown numerically in inches.

As you learned in this chapter's section on "Adding and Creating Arrowheads," you use the two buttons below the line thickness box to select arrowhead designs.

To set the line design, select your line and click the small triangle in the thin horizontal space below the arrowhead selection buttons. A list of various line designs, including dashed, dotted, and mixed, appears (see fig. 13.20). The top of the list shows the current design. Change this design to another by scrolling to a design and selecting it. Click Apply to apply the design to the currently selected line.

Click the horizontal bar above the Update From button to display an array of colors that you can apply to the selected line (see fig. 13.21). Click More to display the Color dialog box, which is discussed in more detail in Chapter 11, "Scanning Images into CorelDRAW!."

Fig. 13.20
Viewing various line designs.

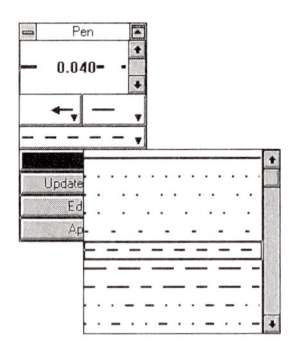

Fig. 13.21
The color palette. The gray line was given a 30% black outline. The selected dashed line is waiting for a color specification. It has a default 100% black outline.

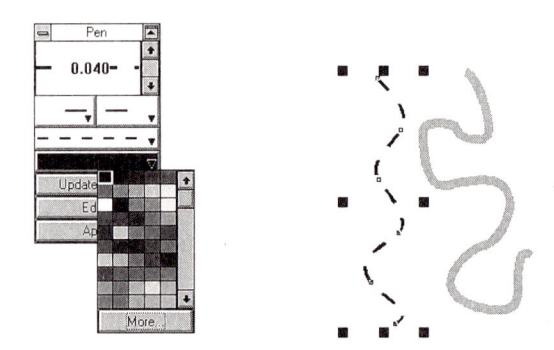

Using the Outline Pen Dialog Box

Tip
Select an object and press F12 to open the Outline Pen dialog box.

Click the Pen tool in the upper-left corner of the Outline fly-out menu to reveal the Outline Pen dialog box.

To change the color of the line, click the Color box in the upper-left corner to display your color choices and choose one.

Adjust the thickness of your line by entering a number in the **W**idth box.

The Corners options determine the shape of a corner. Corners can be mitered, rounded, or beveled as shown in figure 13.22.

The Line Caps options determine the design added to the end points of each line. End points can be butt flat, round, or square. The three styles of line caps are shown in figure 13.22. A butt flat or square design gives the drawing a technical, sharp feel. The rounded line caps soften the drawing.

Select **B**ehind Fill from the Outline Pen dialog box to move the outline behind the fill when displaying the object. Otherwise, the outline displays in front of the fill. Use the **S**cale With Image option to ensure that the outline of the object increases and decreases in thickness proportionally to any scaling done on the base object. Otherwise, the line thickness remains constant as the image is scaled, which gradually looks unacceptable.

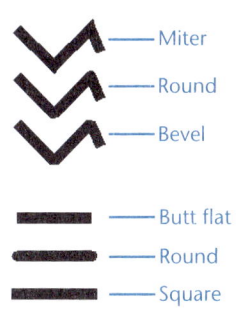

Fig. 13.22
Corners and Line Caps.

After you select a line, you can set the line style by clicking the Style box. A listing of various line designs, including dashed, dotted, and mixed, appears. The top of the list shows the currently active design, and you change this design to another by scrolling to a design and selecting it.

In the lower-right corner of the Outline Pen dialog box is a set of Calligraphy options, which you use to control the nib shape. The *nib* is the imaginary brush tip used to draw the lines. The nib shape is determined by a combination of the corner style, the angle of the imaginary paintbrush, and the stretch (the thickness of the nib). The second corner design shown in the Outline Pen dialog box provides a round nib, and the other two produce rectangular nibs. You can change the stretch and angle of the nib by dragging the nib shape with the mouse. If you get lost and want to return to the original design, click the **D**efault button.

The effect of the pen tip is to provide a less harsh look to the lines and give them a more pen-and-ink quality. By changing features such as the line thickness, nib design, and attributes, you can take an ordinary-looking design and make it into something unique.

Using Dimension Lines

CorelDRAW! provides a convenient way for you to label object dimensions: dimension lines. This feature is particularly useful for technical drawings in which the measurements of objects are a critical part of the drawing. A dimension line can be linked to an object so that when effects or transformations are applied to the object, the dimension line and text reflect the changes.

There are three dimension line tools located on the Pencil fly-out menu: Vertical, Horizontal, and Angular. As shown in figure 13.23, the illustrations on the tool buttons consist of lines with arrows at each end. To access these tools, click the Pencil tool and click the desired tool on the fly-out menu.

Fig. 13.23
The Pencil fly out menu contains drawing tools, three dimension line tools, and the Callout tool.

The procedure for using dimension lines is relatively simple after you understand the overall concept. CorelDRAW! senses where you click to begin the dimension line and where you click to end the line. The program then calculates the distance based on the currently active measurement (as set in the Preferences dialog box) and waits for you to define where to print the dimension value. You specify the spot where you want the dimensions to print when you click the next time. CorelDRAW! not only draws the dimension line, but calculates the dimensional values based on the dimension line drawn.

You use the vertical dimension line tool for defining dimensions along a vertical axis (even if the object itself is not vertical).

You use the horizontal dimension line tool to draw lines and measurements along the horizontal axis.

The diagonal dimension line creates a dimension line that extends along the side of the object at the angle you prescribe.

The Callout tool creates lines for pointing out parts of drawings. Identifying text is linked to the line. If you move the line, the text moves with it.

Note

◄ See "Drawing Callouts on Objects," p. 86

Activate the **S**nap To **O**bjects feature by choosing that option from the **L**ayout menu before drawing dimension lines. This links the object to the dimension line. The lines snap to the nodes of the underlying object and give you an easy, accurate measurement of the object dimensions. Changes made to a linked object automatically update in the dimension line.

Floor plans use dimension lines extensively. Before you draw floor plans, you need to first tell the computer which units of measure on your drawing are equivalent to the units of your building floor. To do this, follow these steps.

1. Open the Layout menu and choose Grid & Scale Setup. The Grid & Scale Setup dialog box appears (see fig. 13.24).

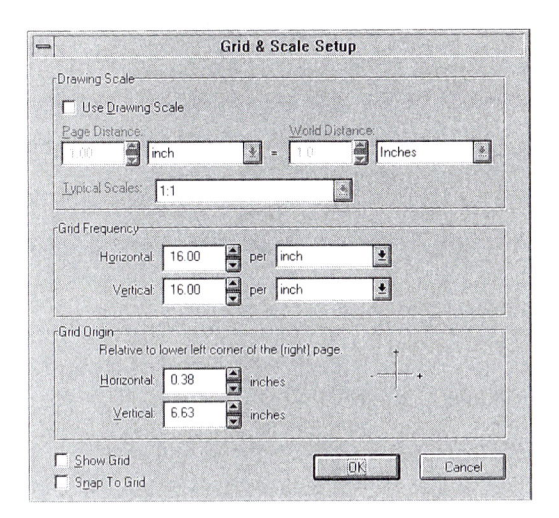

Fig. 13.24
The Grid and Scale Setup dialog box.

2. Click the Use **D**rawing Scale box to activate it. Enter the units first for Page Distance in the second box from the left ("inches" is the default) and then enter the value in the first box.

3. For World Distance, enter the units first in the fourth box from the left ("inches" is the default) and then the value in the third box from the left.

As an example, if you're drawing house floor plans, one inch on your drawing page (Page Distance) could equal twelve inches on the floor space (World Distance).

Figure 13.25 shows an example of a wedged object. To get some practice drawing dimension lines, follow these steps to add linked dimension lines to this object:

1. Make sure that the **S**nap To **O**bjects option, accessed from the **L**ayout menu, is selected, and draw the simple wedge-shaped object shown in figure 13.25.

Tip
Dimension lines are useful for determining the size of grouped objects. The status line provides information on only the number of objects in the group. It shows no dimensional information.

Fig. 13.25

Dimensioning a wedged object. You can change the text characteristics of the dimension value just as you change any other text.

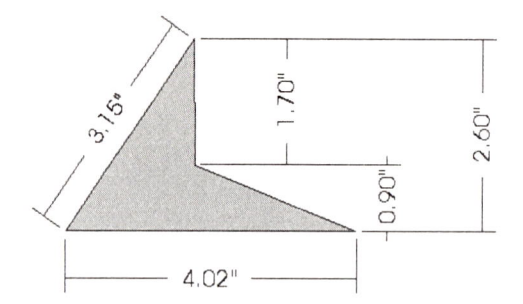

2. Click the Pencil tool, and hold the mouse button until the Pencil fly-out menu appears.

3. Choose the Horizontal Dimension Line tool. You use this tool to create the bottom (4.02") dimension line.

4. Click at the left node of the object bottom; then move the cursor to the right side of the object bottom and click again. This step defines the overall dimensions. You must next tell CorelDRAW! where you want it to print the dimensions.

5. Move the cursor to the center of the bottom and just below the object. Notice that the extension lines follow the cursor. When you are in the appropriate position, click. The dimension line and its numeric measurement are added to the object.

6. To draw the angular dimension line, click the Horizontal Dimension Line tool and hold the mouse button until the fly-out menu appears. Select the Angular Dimension tool. Click at the top and then at the bottom-left corner of the object. Click at the distance from the object where you want the text printed. The dimension value will appear (3.15" in the example).

7. To draw the vertical dimension lines on the right side of the object, click the Diagonal Dimension Line tool and hold the mouse button until the fly-out menu appears; then select the Vertical Dimension tool.

8. Move the cursor to the top of the object and click; then move to the center right node and click again. This step adds the dimension of the segment above the inner "elbow" of the shape.

9. To insert the dimension number, move the cursor to the same relative position as the number shown in figure 13.25, and click again. CorelDRAW! inserts the dimension (1.70" in the example) where you designated.

Using Dimension Lines 407

10. Repeat the procedure for the segment below the inner "elbow" by clicking the center node, then the bottom node, and finally where you want the dimension value (0.90" in the example) printed.

11. Create the longest overall vertical dimension line by clicking at the top node of the object, then at the bottom right node, and finally at the location where you want the dimension value (2.60" in the example) printed.

Selecting and deleting a dimension line deletes not only the line, but the associated dimensioning text. You also can choose Undo from the Edit menu to correct recently inserted dimension lines.

You set the color of dimension lines just as you do with any other line. Click the right mouse button on the color palette at the bottom of the screen, or use the Pen roll-up.

Dimension line text is automatically given the default font and point size. You can change these attributes just as you can normal text by using the Text roll-up or by dragging with the mouse after selecting the Text tool (see Chapter 7, "Adding Text to a Drawing").

◀ See "Working with Artistic Text," p. 212

You can apply most of CorelDRAW!'s effects and transformations to dimension lines. But you can't add perspective, extrude, or apply an envelope to an object with a dimension line. If a line has been linked to an object that has been changed by effects or transformations, the dimension line also moves, and the text indicates the new dimensions. For example, when you select and scale both the object and its dimension lines, the dimension lines and values increase or decrease accordingly, as shown in figure 13.25. In figure 13.26, an object and its dimension lines have been scaled down 50%. The text size remains the same.

Original object and dimension lines

Object and dimension lines scaled down 50%

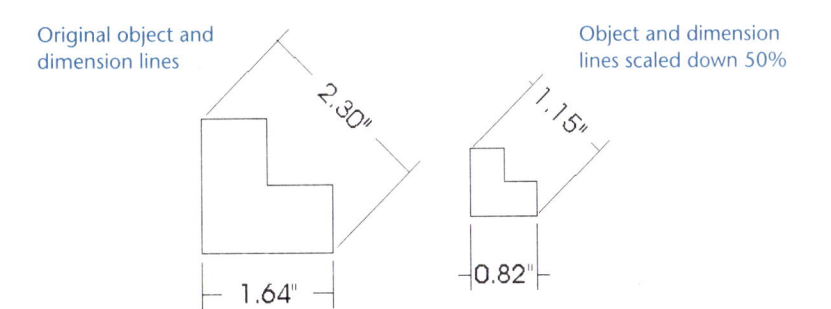

Fig. 13.26
Scaling an object and its dimension lines.

Tip
Use unlinked dimension lines of varying lengths as portable rulers for measuring elements of your drawing.

When you rotate a linked object, the dimension line won't move unless it's an angular dimension line. Angular dimension lines move with the rotated object. When you select an unlinked object and not the dimension line, and rotate, skew, or stretch the object, the dimension line and text will not change.

You can set default attributes for dimension lines that tell CorelDRAW! the units of measurement you prefer to use, and how you always want text to be positioned. Detailed instructions for setting the attributes are in Chapter 23, "Customizing CorelDRAW! to Fit Your Needs."

▶ See "Setting Default Dimension Line Attributes," p. 580

> **Troubleshooting**
>
> *I can't seem to get the crosshair cursor on the exact edges of objects when I click to make the dimension lines. I get a different value every time I try it. How do I get accurate readings?*
>
> Make sure the Snap to Object option in the Layout menu is turned on before you make the dimension lines. You should have no problem obtaining accurate readings if this option is active.

Applying Advanced Curve Techniques

A sine wave like the one shown in figure 13.27 is a common object used in technical drawings. Sine waves are difficult to draw freehand, but easy to draw if you use the automated features of CorelDRAW!. The following procedure leads you through the design of a sine wave. The procedure applies many of the topics discussed in this chapter and provides a good summary of curve modification techniques.

Fig. 13.27
A sine wave drawing. A grid, ruler guidelines, and smooth and symmetrical nodes make this common shape in technical illlustrations easy to draw.

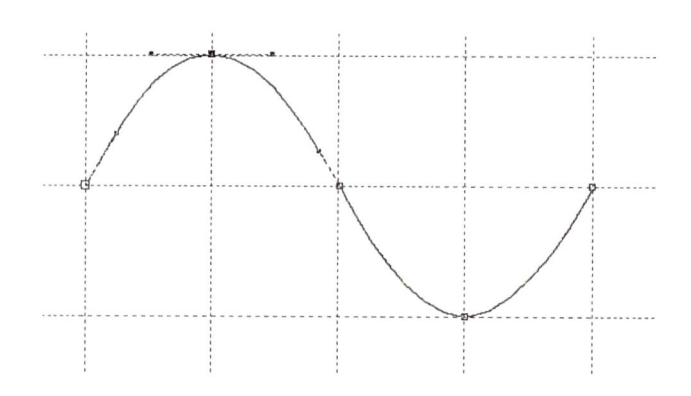

Follow these steps to draw the sine wave:

1. Set up a working grid that corresponds to the beginning, middle, end, top, and bottom of the sine wave, as shown in figure 13.27.

2. Drag a horizontal guideline (from the top ruler) to a whole number ruler marker location (such as the 2-inch mark). This ruler represents the neutral axis of the sine wave.

3. Drag another horizontal guideline to a location 1 inch above and another to 1 inch below the neutral axis.

4. Drag a vertical guideline from the left ruler to a whole number ruler marker. This ruler corresponds to the 0-degree point.

5. Drag guidelines to each 1-inch marker to the right of the initial guideline until you have four more guidelines.

6. Select the Pencil tool.

7. Click at the 0-degree point; double-click at the guideline intersection points that correspond to the top, center, bottom, and end of the wave.

8. The lines connecting the nodes are straight lines and not curves, so you need to change them to curves. Select the first line segment and click To **C**urve in the Node Edit roll-up. Repeat this procedure for each of the other line segments.

9. You need to change the maximum (top) and minimum (bottom) nodes to the symmetrical type to make the alignment of the curve on each side of the node match the symmetrical nature of the sine wave. Click the maximum node, and select the S**y**mmet option from the Node Edit roll-up. Do the same for the minimum node. Finally, repeat the same procedure for the center node (neutral axis), but select S**m**ooth rather than Symmet. The nodes and segments are now ready for the final step of adjusting the curvature.

10. Click the maximum (top) node, and move one of the control points to around the 1/2-inch point on the guidlines. Notice that the other side moves, too. Repeat this procedure for the minimum (bottom) node location. Click the center node, and move the control point until it lies on the curve. Repeat this procedure for the other nodes, and the sine wave is complete.

You can now size, rotate, expand, contract, and combine this basic shape into many forms that you may need for technical drawings. You can create a series of sine waves, for example, and then apply an envelope to the series and replicate an amplitude modulation signal, or you can scale the signals and attach them to each other to create a frequency modulation signal as shown in figure 13.28.

Fig. 13.28
A frequency modulation signal using the sine wave.

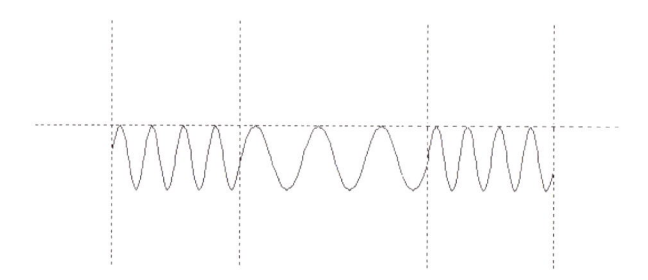

From Here...

For information relating to the topics in this chapter, you may want to review the following major sections of this book:

- Chapter 1, "An Overview of CorelDRAW! 5," provides basic information about CorelDRAW!, including the basics of creating objects and using roll-ups. It also describes the drawing and dimension tools.

- Chapter 3, "A Detailed Look at Object Drawing," provides detailed instructions on drawing lines and shapes and manipulating their nodes, including sections on open and closed paths and joining and breaking nodes.

- Chapter 4, "Mastering Object Manipulations," describes object selection, alignment, transformation, duplication, and arrangement. It includes a detailed section on how to use the grid.

- Chapter 5, "Modifying Object Outlines and Interior Fills," describes adding fills and outlines. It provides detailed instructions on using the Outline and Fill roll-ups, including how to copy styles between objects. Chapter 5 also describes the tools in the Outline fly-out.

- Chapter 7, "Adding Text to a Drawing," describes how to add text to drawings. It includes instructions on how to add attributes to text.

- Chapter 8, "Advanced Text Techniques," describes advanced techniques for manipulating text. It includes a section on how to convert text characters to curved objects.

- Chapter 24, "Customizing CorelDRAW! to Fit Your Needs," describes how to set defaults so that you can be more efficient working with the program. It includes sections on Roll-up preferences, curve preferences, and default Dimension Line attributes.

Chapter 14

Creating Special Effects with Perspective

by Cyndie Klopfenstein

Perspective as an applied effect makes an object smaller at one end. The object has a diminishing point—an end that diminishes in size as it nears the vanishing point. More distant objects are closer to the vanishing point. The closer an object is to the vanishing point, the smaller it is.

In figure 14.1, for example, the left edge of the bridge is larger than the right edge of the bridge. The back diminishes in size because it's farther away. When drawing objects in CorelDRAW!, it's not just how it appears—it actually is smaller. You can draw the back of the object smaller if you choose, but that's a great deal of work for an effect that's fully automated in CorelDRAW!.

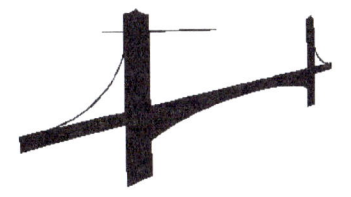

Fig. 14.1
With the automated perspective effect, drawing objects like this bridge is a snap.

In this chapter, you learn about perspective and the vanishing point. You also learn how to do the following:

- Adjust the depth of the perspective by moving the vanishing points
- Identify your progress by checking the status line

- Align the vanishing point of multiple items to give a more realistic look
- Add one- and two-point perspective to both objects and text
- Copy the perspective from one object to another

Watching the Status Line

The status line is an area of your CorelDRAW! window that shows information about an object or the action to perform with the tool or menu item you selected. It is at the bottom of the screen by default. Keep an eye on the status line as you run through the process of adding perspective.

As you work through this chapter, you learn the skills to add perspective to a single item (such as the box on the left in figure 14.2), to text, or to grouped items. Use the Pick tool to select an object for adding perspective. After you apply the special effect, your status line looks something like the one in figure 14.3.

The two types of perspective are one and two point. Each point refers to a vanishing point marked with an X. With two point perspective, you have two Xs; with one point, one X. These vanishing points are moveable.

Fig. 14.2
Here are three basic examples of perspective. One-point perspective was added to the box, and two point to the text and the road.

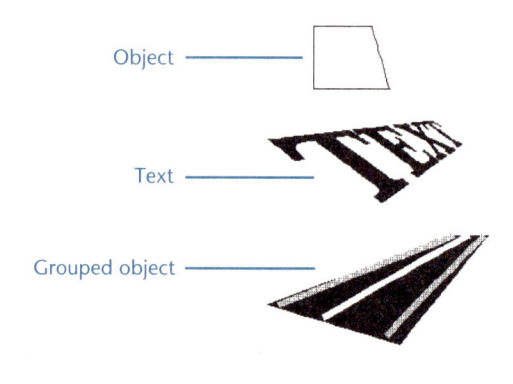

Fig. 14.3
The status line can prompt you about the next move.

Working from the Menu

Unlike other special effects, **A**dd Perspective doesn't have a roll-up window; its options are always chosen from the Effects menu. You use the same procedure to add one- or two-point perspective, and with either way, you first must select the Pick tool.

To add perspective to a selected object or group, follow these steps:

1. With the Pick tool, select an object, grouped objects, or artistic text.

2. Open the Effe**c**ts menu and choose **A**dd Perspective. A dashed-line bounding box now surrounds the object with a handle at each of the four corners.

3. Move to any of the four handles, and the cursor changes to cross hairs.

4. If you're trying to create a one-point perspective, hold down the mouse button and drag the handle, as was done in the left part of figure 14.4. For a two-point perspective (the example on the right), drag diagonally (don't hold down Ctrl) away from the object to pull the object from the vanishing point, and toward the object to push in the direction of the vanishing point.

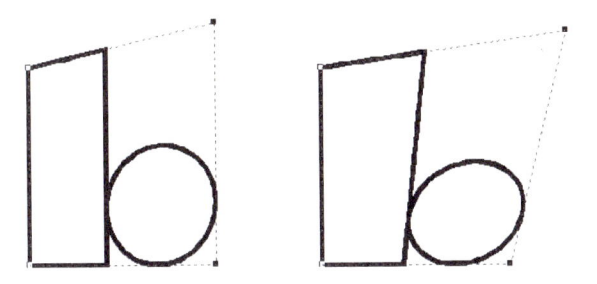

Fig. 14.4
Click and drag any of the four handles horizontally, vertically (one-point), or diagonally (two-point) to change the perspective.

Note

If you hold down Ctrl as you drag, you can drag only horizontally or vertically. Ctrl constrains your movements to only the X or Y axis. If you hold down Ctrl and Shift when you drag a handle, the opposite handle moves the same distance but in an opposing direction.

Using One-Point Perspective

As you create one-point perspective, you're actually shortening or lengthening a single side of the object. Because only one side is involved, it's called one-point perspective. It is also only two-dimensional. Figure 14.5 shows several examples of how you can use one-point perspective.

Fig. 14.5
Here are examples of symbols from the Symbols roll-up window with perspective applied. In each of the four examples, the original shape is the left object, and the right object is after one-point perspective has been applied.

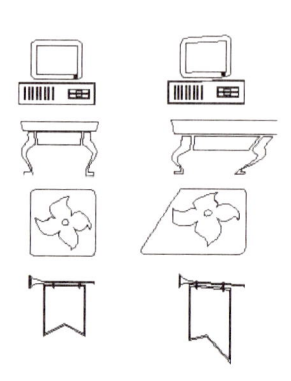

Using Two-Point Perspective

Two-point perspective is sort of the advanced version of perspective. Using this option, you shorten or lengthen the object on two sides—therefore, two-point. Figure 14.6 shows you the different looks you can achieve with two-point perspective on a collection of objects.

Fig. 14.6
Here are several simple and complex examples of two-point perspective.

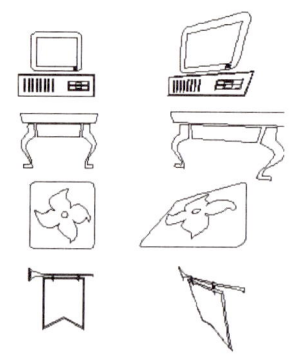

> **Troubleshooting**
>
> *I want two-point perspective, but I only get one-point perspective. What am I doing wrong?*
>
> To get a two-point perspective, you must drag a handle diagonally. If you hold down Ctrl while you drag, the mouse doesn't move diagonally.
>
> *I can't find the Perspective roll-up window.*
>
> Unlike other special effects, perspective does not have a roll-up window; all its functions are performed using the menu options.

Understanding the Vanishing Point

Any time you add perspective to an object, you create a vanishing point, which is the place where the object is diminishing to. The vanishing point is marked on your document page by an ×, and is the point on the horizon to which the perspective stretches. A document can have several objects that you added perspective to, and each object can have its own vanishing point or two vanishing points. If your drawing is to be more life-like, however, all objects should share a common vanishing point. In the next sections, you learn how to find, move, and share vanishing points.

Finding the Vanishing Point

If you add one-point perspective to your object, you have a single vanishing point designated by an ×, like the one in figure 14.7. Two-point perspective has two vanishing points. Where they are and whether you have one or two depends on the way you originally dragged the handles to create the perspective. Did you drag only horizontally or vertically (a single vanishing point); or did you drag diagonally (two vanishing points)?

Fig. 14.7
One-point perspective has one vanishing point, like on the left. To the right, the handle was dragged diagonally, and the result is two vanishing points.

Moving the Vanishing Point

Click and drag to move the vanishing point. Move the vanishing point in a straight line closer to the object, and the edge of the object nearest the vanishing point becomes shorter. If you move the vanishing point away from the object, the farthest edge remains stationary, but the nearer edge is drawn out along with the vanishing point. Both examples are shown in figure 14.8, with the original positions shown first.

Fig. 14.8
Move the vanishing points at any time to change perspective.

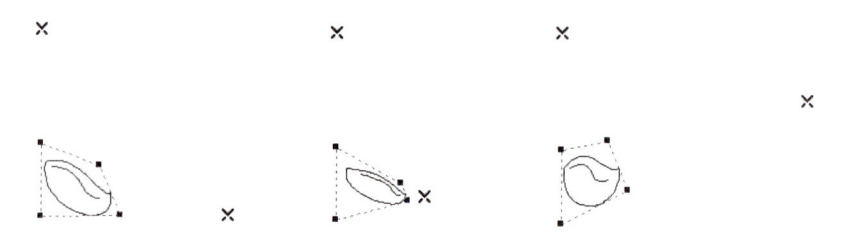

Aligning Vanishing Points

Often, you want more than one object (or group of objects) to diminish toward the same vanishing point. This is more like real life. Escher is a famous artist known for using many vanishing points and conflicting perspectives in his artwork. Unless you're creating an Escher-like drawing, you probably want to have more than one object diminish to the same point on the horizon.

◀ See "Using the Guidelines to Ease Alignment," p. 117

When you select an object with the Shape tool, its vanishing point appears and is indicated by an ×. It's simple to pull guidelines from the rulers out (by clicking on the ruler and dragging the guideline) to align on this symbol (see fig. 14.9). After you do that, click another object with the Shape tool to select it so that its vanishing point becomes visible, and drag the × to align on the guidelines marking the first object's point. If you have a two-point perspective and you've now aligned one of the points, repeat the process for the remaining vanishing point as well.

Troubleshooting

I can't find the vanishing point for my object.

An object must be selected with the Shape tool for its vanishing point to be visible.

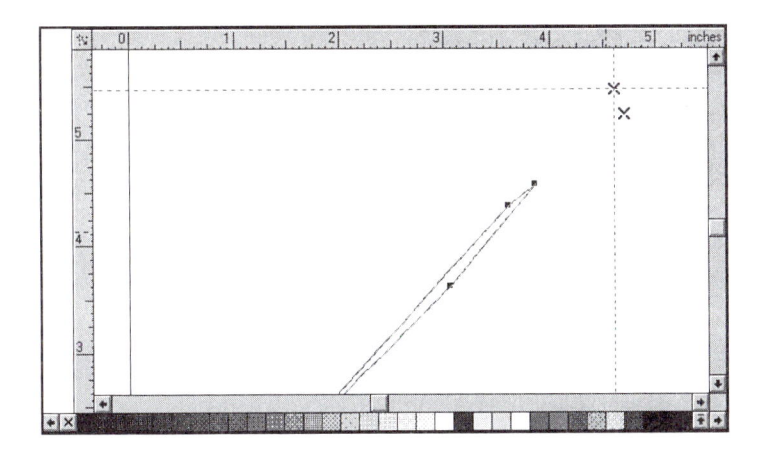

Fig. 14.9
Place guidelines on the vanishing point icon to easily align multiple vanishing points.

Copying Perspective

Returning to the Effects menu, you find the option for copying perspective. This can be much the same as aligning the respective objects' vanishing points. With copying and cloning, you have two objects: the source (where you get your information), and the destination (where you take the information). To copy, you must identify both these objects, although the destination object does not need a perspective bounding box (the box or handles that appear when you click an object). Choosing Copy Perspective From adds a bounding box for you. Follow these steps to copy perspective:

1. Select the destination object or group of objects with the Pick tool.
2. Open the Effects menu and choose Copy. A drop-down menu appears.
3. From the drop-down menu, choose Perspective From. Your cursor becomes an arrow.
4. Click the source object. This applies the perspective to the destination object.

> **Note**
>
> Copy Perspective From has no effect if an object has an envelope (another special effect) applied on top of its perspective bounding box. To copy, you must first remove the envelope. See the section, "Clearing Perspective," later in this chapter.

Clearing Perspective

▶ See "Clearing Applied Envelopes," p. 439

To clear any perspective changes, open the Effects menu and choose Clear Perspective. The selected object reverts to its original form by removing the bounding box. If you applied more than one bounding box, Clear Perspective reverts to the point of the addition of the last bounding box. If the object also has an envelope, Clear Perspective has no effect. You first must remove the envelope, but when you do this, the object loses the shape that the envelope applied.

If you like that envelope shape and don't want to rebuild it from scratch, duplicate the object with the envelope still intact. Then clear perspective on the original and either apply a new perspective or just copy your envelope back to the original from the copy you made. Use the Copy *Effect* (see note) command to do this. In this case, the command is Copy Envelope. Envelope and copying envelope shapes are discussed in Chapter 15, "Creating Special Effects with Envelope."

> **Note**
>
> The Copy command takes on the name of whatever special effect you are performing. For example, while using the Envelope feature, it reads Copy Envelope; during Blend, it reads Copy Blend; and so on.

From Here...

Adding perspective to objects can be as simple as making choices from the menu, or as difficult as minute fine-tuning of each vanishing point of each object. Combining perspective with other special effects can make the process even more difficult, but the results are much more detailed and realistic. Use the information from other chapters to add pizzazz or reality, or even to contradict reality in your drawings.

- Chapter 15, "Creating Special Effects with Envelope," covers in detail the creation and use of Envelopes.

- Chapter 17, "Creating Special Effects with Extruding," explains how to use another powerful special effect—Extrude.

- Chapter 21, "Creating Special Effects with PowerClip," helps you to draw lines as though you were using a pen or paintbrush—another way to add the feel of realism.

- Chapter 22, "Combining and Reusing Effects," provides additional explanation and ideas for beautifying your work.

Chapter 15

Creating Special Effects with Envelope

by Cyndie Klopfenstein

Imagine taking your drawing and warming it up enough so that it's liquefied, but not so much that it loses any of its distinction. Then imagine pouring that artwork into a mold. The mold might be heart-shaped, or box-shaped, or more complex—maybe octagonal-shaped—and yet your artwork fits to the mold quite snugly.

That's what Envelope does: it takes a piece of artwork—something you've drawn or one of CorelDRAW!'s clipart collection—and makes it fit into or around a shape. With Envelope, you can create your own shapes or use a predefined one. You can choose to print the shape and the drawing, or just the drawing. With this flexibility, you soon may find that Envelope is one of your favorite special effects.

Any special effect adds versatility to your drawing, but Envelope especially has great capabilities. In this chapter, you learn to do the following:

- Create envelopes for Artistic text
- Use envelopes to shape predrawn symbols
- Copy envelopes from objects
- Use straight, single arc, and two curves for easy-to-edit envelopes
- Clone applied envelope styles

Watching the Status Line

After you select an object with the Pick tool and click the Add New Envelope button from the Envelope roll-up window (found in the Effects menu), the status line at the bottom of the screen looks like the one in figure 15.1. The status line is a very good place to watch for prompts when you're trying out new special effects. It displays information about either what you've done or what the next move is expected to be.

Fig. 15.1
Even advanced users can watch the status line for prompts.

Working from the Menu

◀ See "Reshaping a Curve or Object by Changing Its Nodes and Control Points," p. 72

Most features of Envelope are found in the Envelope roll-up window. To bring this window on-screen, open the Effects menu and choose Envelope Roll-Up, or press Ctrl+F7. The Node Edit roll-up window is found in the View menu; you learn more about that in the "Node Edit Roll-Up Window" section later in this chapter.

Using the Envelope Roll-Up Window

The Envelope roll-up window is placed in the active window area when you choose Envelope roll-up from the Effects menu (see fig. 15.2). Each button of this roll-up window has a different function dedicated solely to the creation and editing of envelopes. Some buttons prompt other windows or change the content of the primary Envelope roll-up window. The following sections discuss each of the options before you create an envelope.

Fig. 15.2
All the options you need for creating and editing envelopes are contained in the Envelope roll-up window.

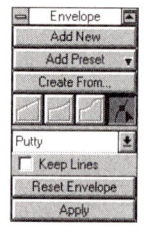

Add New

You begin with the Add New button. Click this button to add an envelope to a selected object. When you click here, you add an envelope bounding box to your artwork. The bounding box has eight handles—one at each corner and one in the middle of each line—as you see in figure 15.3. You can change the editing mode of the envelope by clicking one of the editing mode buttons, as discussed later. Don't forget to click Apply after Add New; otherwise, nothing will happen. The Apply button also is discussed shortly.

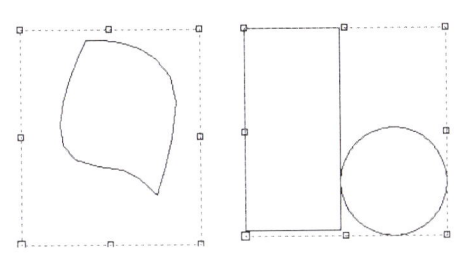

Fig. 15.3
Click the Add New button and then Apply to add an Envelope to an object (left), grouped set of objects (center), or text (right).

You aren't limited to just one envelope per object. Click the Add New button and Apply again to add another envelope over the top of the existing one for further shape editing. Use the Clear Envelope command from the Effects menu to remove each envelope added. See the section, "Clearing Applied Envelopes," later in this chapter.

Add Preset

To try one of the custom shapes CorelDRAW! already includes, click Add Preset, and the scrollable window you see in figure 15.4 appears. The small icons representing envelope shapes make it easy to pick an envelope shape. If you don't like the effect your chosen shape has on the object, clear the first one; return to the Envelope roll-up window; and click the Add Preset button to choose a different one.

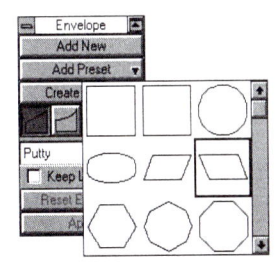

Fig. 15.4
Use the Add Preset button to choose from a scrollable list of predefined envelope shapes.

How an Envelope Fits Objects

Because all predefined envelopes are styled after a basic shape, they're editable, just as any other object is. You can apply these shapes to objects or text, or even paragraphs of text. If you apply an envelope to an object, the *object* stretches itself to fit the envelope. That's when you might decide that

◀ See "Combining and Grouping Objects," p. 119

426 Chapter 15—Creating Special Effects with Envelope

it's not the right shape for your object. If you apply the envelope to a paragraph of text, the *envelope* stretches to fit the paragraph's bounding box. Look at the examples in figure 15.5. The same preset envelope is applied to a single object, a group of objects, text, and a paragraph of text. Notice how the object is distorted in the first three examples, and the envelope is distorted in the last example.

Fig. 15.5
The first three examples are considered objects; even though the third is text, it's not Paragraph Text. The Paragraph Text, the fourth example, distorts the envelope to fit the paragraph bounding box.

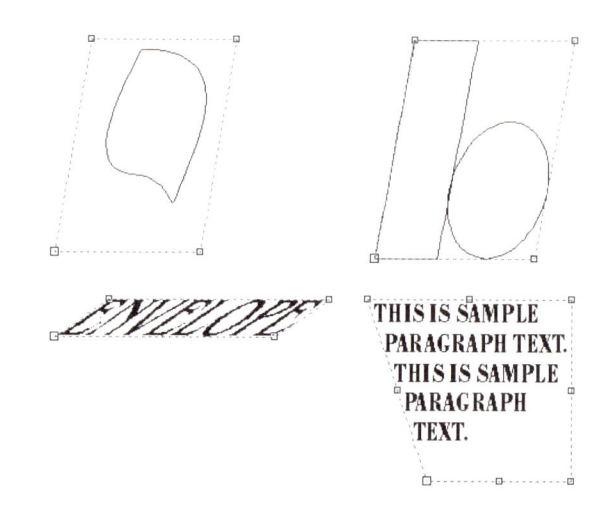

Sometimes the perfect envelope shape is actually an object drawn for something else. Perhaps, as in figure 15.6, the text needs to fit in the shape of the balloon that you've already drawn. Use the Create From button to apply the balloon's shape to the text. Click an object that you want to envelope with your custom shape and then click the Create From button. The cursor changes into a black arrow, and you click the source object. (This is where the envelope information comes from.)

Fig. 15.6
The text on the left was molded to the shape of the balloon and then moved on top of the balloon.

Envelope Edit

All envelopes are editable. You can change the way the lines bend and curve when you click and drag them, and also add new handles for even finer tuning. Each of the four buttons described in the following sections is for editing an envelope's shape. If you don't like the way your envelope shape is bending when you edit the shape, click the Reset Envelope button and then click one of the other editing mode buttons. Reset Envelope is discussed more thoroughly later in this chapter in the section, "Reset Envelope."

The four types of envelopes can be divided into two groups: constrained and unconstrained. Using one of the first three—Straight Line, Single Arc, and Two Curves—limits the shape and editing possibilities of an envelope. That is, the movements are constrained. For instance, a Straight Line envelope is constrained to only allow edits that create straight lines. In the Not Constrained mode, your edits are not limited. Therefore, they are unconstrained. You can add as many straight and curved lines as you like.

> **Note**
>
> When you select an editing mode button, that information isn't stored with the envelope bounding box. In other words, you can't click an envelope and see which of these buttons was used to edit the shape.

> **Note**
>
> With the Straight Line, Single Arc, and Two Curves editing modes, you can further edit nodes by using Ctrl and Shift. Press and hold down the Shift key when you click a node, and the node you select, along with the node opposite it, move in opposing directions. Press and hold down Ctrl when clicking and dragging a node, and that node and the one opposite it move in the same direction. Press and hold down both Ctrl and Shift, and all the corner nodes move in opposing directions.

Straight Line

With Straight Line mode, you have the least amount of movement available for editing. First, you can only move one handle at a time, and if you look at figure 15.7, you can see exactly what the limitations are—straight lines. In fact, you might find that this mode looks much like Add Perspective, which you can read about in Chapter 14, "Creating Special Effects with Perspective."

428   Chapter 15—Creating Special Effects with Envelope

Fig. 15.7
An example of an object, grouped objects, text, and a paragraph of text using a Straight Line envelope.

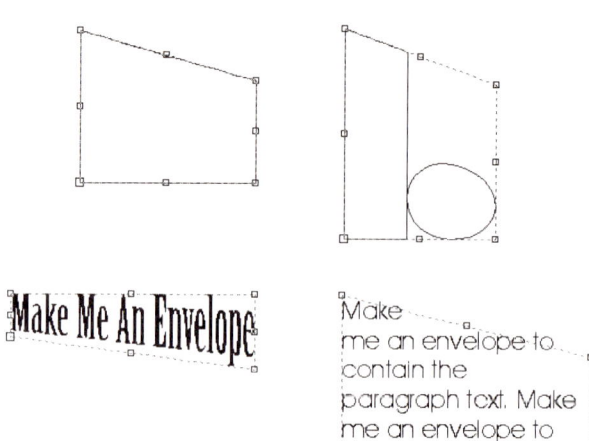

Single Arc

With Single Arc mode, you get just that, a single arc. Figure 15.8 shows some examples of how you can use this shape. Here again, you're limited to moving only one handle at a time, and of course, limited to one arc.

Fig. 15.8
Here are the same examples of figure 15.7. An object, grouped objects, text, and a paragraph of text using the Single Arc editing mode.

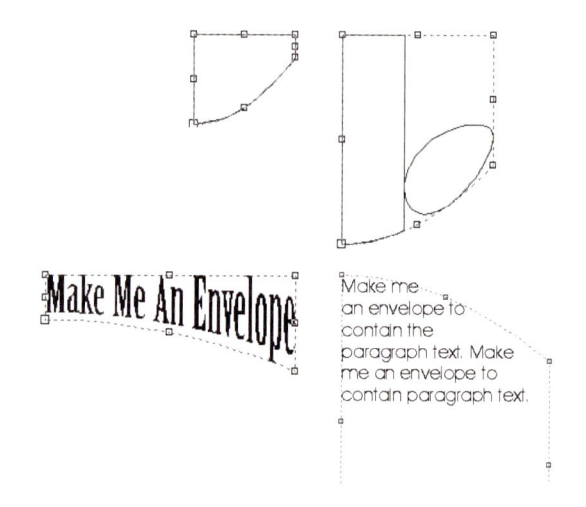

Two Curves

Two Curves mode is the last constrained mode. With this mode, you can have two arcs, but you still are limited to moving only one handle at a time. Figure 15.9 shows the same four examples, but this time using the Two Curves editing mode. Use these examples for ideas on how you can apply a Two Curves envelope to your objects.

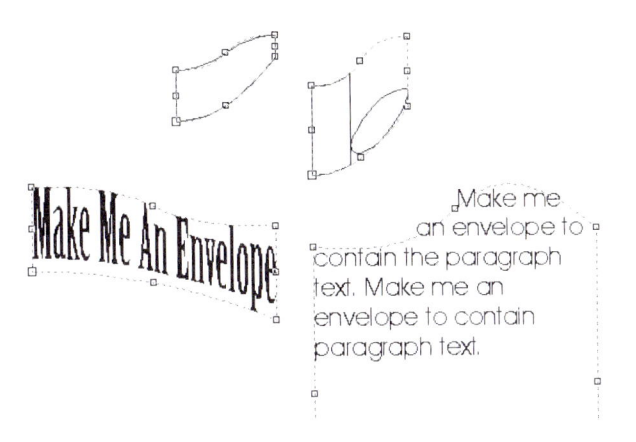

Fig. 15.9
The last of the three constrained editing modes: the same object, group of objects, text, and paragraph text using a Two Curves envelope shape.

Not Constrained

The power lies within Not Constrained mode. Figure 15.10 shows an example of editing a Not Constrained envelope. This mode provides all sorts of capabilities not available with the other three editing modes. You can edit multiple handles at the same time. You can use the Node Edit roll-up window to add and delete nodes, convert curved parts of the bounding box to straight lines and straight lines to curved, and make an individual node smooth, symmetrical, or cusped. The specifics of these operations are discussed later in this chapter in the sections, "Enveloping Objects" and "Enveloping Text."

◀ See "Reshaping a Curve or Object by Changing Its Nodes or Control Points," p. 72

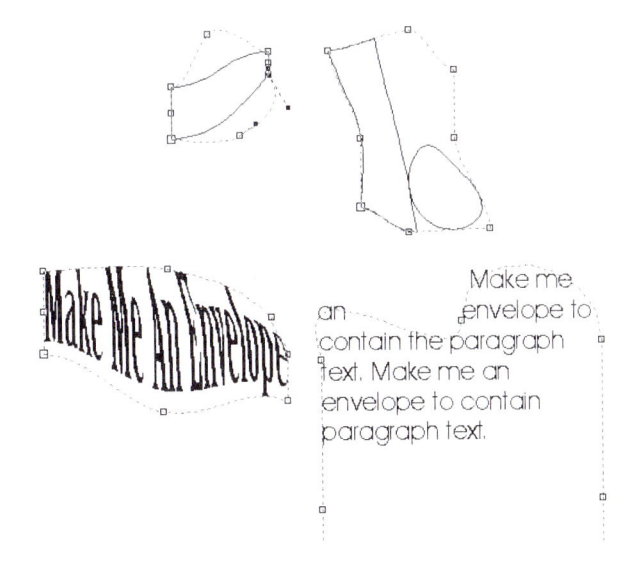

Fig. 15.10
With the Not Constrained editing mode, you get the most versatility. Here is an example of the same four objects after dragging different handles and groups of handles on their envelopes.

Node Edit Roll-Up Window. To edit a node while using a Not Constrained envelope, double-click a handle. Figure 15.11 shows the different buttons of this roll-up window, but a more complete discussion about the Node Edit roll-up window appears in Chapter 1, "An Overview of CorelDRAW! 5."

Fig. 15.11
With the Not Constrained editing mode, you can double-click a node to prompt the Node Edit roll-up window.

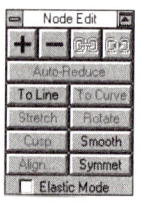

◄ See "Reshaping a Curve or Object by Changing its Nodes and Control Points," p. 72

Editing Nodes with the Keyboard. To add and delete nodes in the Not Constrained mode, click the bounding box of the envelope and press the + (plus sign) to add a node, or click a node and press the – (minus sign) to delete a node. This works regardless of whether the Node Edit roll-up window is open.

Mapping

Mapping is creating a relationship between two points. The first set of points is on the object's highlighting box; the second is on the envelope that you add to the object. When you add an envelope, CorelDRAW! uses the position of these handles to calculate the shape of the object after you add an envelope. You can make choices that affect the mapping between two handles by using the Mapping option of the Envelope roll-up window, and thereby change the effect that an envelope has on an object. You can find these options in the scrollable window just below the envelope styles buttons. Each of the four mapping options (Putty, Original, Horizontal, and Vertical) can be used with any of the four editing modes. Sometimes combining a particular mapping with a different editing mode instead of trying different envelope shapes helps you to achieve the effect you're looking for.

With the Envelope editing mode, the object information is not stored as a part of the envelope, but the mapping information is. With this feature, you can click a previously applied envelope, and the scrollable list places the mapping mode used with that envelope in the window.

Original

Original is so named because it was the only option of CorelDRAW! 3.0—the original. (If you're updating 3.0 documents into this version of CorelDRAW!, make sure that you select this option so that envelopes don't lose their shape.) Using the Original mapping option, the corner handles of the selected item's bounding box are mapped directly to the corner handles of the envelope's bounding box. The intermediate handles are made with Bezier control arcs between the mapped corner nodes. Figure 15.12 shows how this affects an object. This is probably the most predictable of the four options.

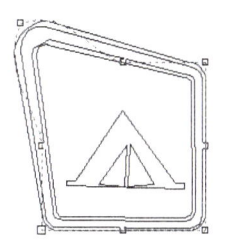

Fig. 15.12
With the Original mapping option, corner handles of the two bounding boxes are mapped to one another.

Putty

The Putty mapping option is the default mode (so make sure that you change it to Original before opening 3.0 documents). This option generally changes the shapes of objects less drastically than Original does because only the corner handles are mapped, and interior nodes are stretched to fill the envelope shape. All other arcs and nodes are disregarded. Figure 15.13 shows the same object from figure 15.12 mapped using the Putty mode.

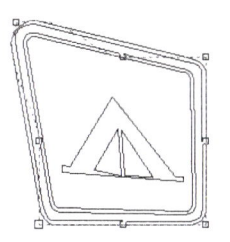

Fig. 15.13
Putty mapping mode is the default and tends to produce milder results than the Original mode.

Vertical

In figure 15.14, the Vertical mapping mode is clearly apparent. Its benefits to objects with vertical lines are easily identified. Here, the object is stretched vertically to fit the envelope and then pulled to the width. This way the vertical lines are not pulled out horizontally like they are in the example of an Original mapping mode.

Fig. 15.14
With objects containing vertical lines, such as text, the Vertical mapping mode generally yields the best results.

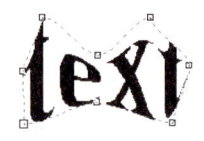

Horizontal

As compared to Vertical, the Horizontal mapping mode constrains the horizontal lines of the object. Figure 15.15 shows the same object with the Original mapping mode on the left and the Horizontal mapping mode on the right. The horizontal lines are pulled to the width of the envelope, and then the object is stretched to fit the shape.

Fig. 15.15
Objects with distinctive horizontal lines fare best with the Horizontal mapping.

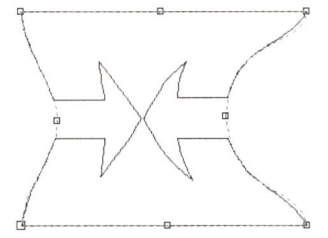

Text

If you select paragraph text with the Pick tool, a fifth option for mapping becomes available. While the paragraph is selected this is the only mode available to you. Paragraphs are different because the envelope is stretched to fit the object (the paragraph), rather than the other way around.

Troubleshooting

There must be a simple method for pulling handles out equally in the edit modes.

Use Ctrl and Shift for constraining and aligning nodes. Ctrl and Shift together pull all four corners out in opposing directions by the same amount.

What if I change my mind after I've chosen an envelope style? Do I need to delete my object and redraw?

The Reset Envelope button is designed for those who change their minds. Click this button to remove the last envelope and its edits. Continue to click to remove each envelope added. You can also use Clear Envelope from the Effects menu.

I'd like to add additional nodes to my envelope bounding box. Can I?

Only if you are using the Not Constrained mode. If you are, then use the keyboard plus sign to add a node to a bounding box and the minus sign to remove a selected node.

Do I have to draw every envelope shape?

Use the Preset styles or Copy From (in the Effects menu) to copy the envelope style and or shape from an existing object that you've drawn.

Keep Lines

The Keep Lines option is simple. Click it to keep the straight lines of an object from curving when you apply an envelope shape (see fig. 15.16).

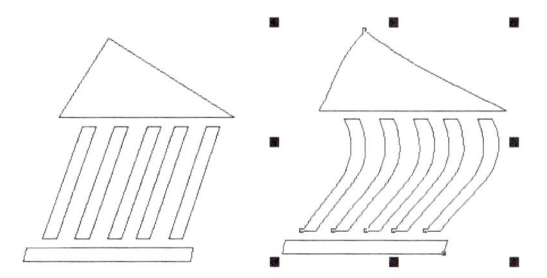

Fig. 15.16
Here's the same object with (left) and without the Keep Lines button checked.

Reset Envelope

This is the backup system. If you don't like the reshaping you've just applied to the envelope, choose Reset Envelope. This option removes editing (even added or deleted nodes) that you've applied to an envelope.

Apply

Anyone can build a great envelope—the steps are simple—but you have to *apply it!* If the envelope is not doing what you think it should be, make sure that you click the Apply button. CorelDRAW! doesn't know you're finished with your creation until you tell it, and this is where you do that. Remember, click Apply after you edit the envelope.

> **Troubleshooting**
>
> *I've made changes to my envelope shape, but nothing happens.*
>
> Click the Apply button.
>
> *When I add an envelope to my object, the lines of the object bend. Can I stop this from happening?*
>
> Choose the Keep Lines command from the Envelope roll-up window. Your object will not follow the envelope shape as closely, but the lines will not bend.

Enveloping Objects

Now that you've learned the operation of all the buttons, you are ready to try making some envelopes. First you get the steps for enveloping an object and creating an envelope *from* an object; the next section works with text.

Using these steps, you can customize an envelope for any object. Don't be timid about choosing editing or mapping mode options. For the most part, after you get the hang of adding an envelope and editing the nodes, all the options work so similarly that you'll be right at home in any mode.

When you copy an envelope shape from an object, CorelDRAW! makes a new envelope around the destination object using the four nodes of the source shape closest to the four nodes of its bounding box. These four become the corners of the envelope, but only if these corner nodes can be reached when following the object's path. If it can't reach them this way, the envelope that CorelDRAW! creates may not match the object's shape very well. To help CorelDRAW! match the shape, try adding additional nodes along the outline edge of the source object so that there are more nodes to choose from, and hence, more nodes that might be closer to a corner.

Creating an Envelope for an Object

To create an envelope for an object, follow these steps:

1. Select an object.

2. Open the Effects menu and choose the Envelope roll-up, or press Ctrl+F7. The Envelope roll-up window appears.

3. Click the Add New button (or choose from the Preset list). An envelope bounding box is added around the selected object.

4. Choose an editing mode.

5. Choose a mapping mode.

6. Choose whether you want to Keep Lines (straight).

7. Click Apply.

8. Edit handles by clicking and dragging. Press and hold down Ctrl, Shift, or Ctrl+Shift when you click on a node to edit opposite handles at the same time. Remember to click Apply each time you edit the envelope.

9. Use the Node Edit roll-up window to redefine or edit nodes.

Creating an Envelope from an Object

To create an envelope from an object, follow these steps:

1. Select the object to which you want to apply the envelope (destination object).

2. Click the Create From button in the Envelope roll-up window. The cursor changes to a black arrow.

3. Click the object you want to copy (the source object). A dotted line of the object now appears over the destination object.

4. Click Apply (sample results are shown in figure 15.17). The destination object now takes on the shape of the applied envelope.

5. Edit the shape of the envelope using the Shape tool.

6. Use the Node Edit roll-up window to redefine or edit nodes. Remember to click Apply each time you edit the envelope.

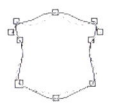

Fig. 15.17
The shape of the object on the right was used to create an envelope.

Enveloping Text

Creating an envelope around a single word or even a couple of words is similar to creating an envelope around an object. It differs a great deal from putting an envelope around an entire paragraph (turn forward to figure 15.20). The steps for both are given here. Aside from this method of creating envelopes for text, you might also choose to use the Copy From feature, although its first attempt might not look as you'd like. Add additional nodes for a closer fit as discussed in the section "Using Create From To Make an Envelope for a Paragraph of Text," later in this chapter.

Some typefaces do not fit the Straight Lines, Single Arc, or Two Curves editing modes well. In the example in figure 15.18, the fonts with rounded letters often display unexpected results when the envelope is applied. Try using the Not Constrained mode, or just choose a different typeface.

Fig. 15.18
Some typefaces return unexpected results with the constrained editing modes. Notice how the envelope doesn't match the text very closely.

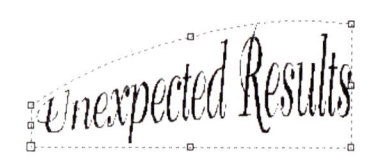

Creating an Envelope for Artistic Text

Adding an envelope to Artistic text is one of the easiest ways to form text into shapes—much easier than trying to adjust the characters after converting them to curves. Use these steps if you need help applying envelopes:

1. Open the Effects menu and choose Envelope, or press Ctrl+F7. The Envelope roll-up window appears.

2. Select the text.

3. Move the text over the shape that will become the guide for the envelope.

4. Scale the text so that it closely matches the size of the shape. At least two corners of the text bounding box need to lie on the shape's outline.

5. While the text is selected, click Add New in the Envelope roll-up window.

6. Choose the Not Constrained editing mode.

7. Make sure that you are using the Putty mapping mode.

8. Move the handles of the envelope's bounding box to roughly match the shape.

9. Edit the control points of the handles for finer adjustments (see fig. 15.19).

10. Click Apply.

11. Leave text over the shape; delete the shape; or move the text away from the shape.

Fig. 15.19
This illustration shows the results of creating an envelope of the same shape.

The bounding box, or frame, of a paragraph is actually replaced by the envelope after it is applied. You can have the paragraph flow around an object or fill the object by applying an envelope of that shape. Envelope shapes can be drawn, chosen from the preset list, or chosen from the Symbols roll-up window, but must be a closed shape. In any event, the Text mapping option is automatically selected in the Envelope roll-up window as soon as you click the paragraph text object. The other mapping options can't be used with paragraph text.

Using Create From to Make an Envelope for a Paragraph of Text

Adding an envelope to paragraph text is somewhat different. Here the envelope size changes to house all the text. These steps walk you through the process of adding the envelope.

1. Select the Pick tool from the tool box and click the bounding box of a paragraph of text.

2. Open the Effects menu and choose Envelope, or press Ctrl+F7. The Envelope roll-up window appears.

3. Click the Create From button. The cursor changes into an arrow.

4. Click the source object (where you get the information).

5. Click Apply.

6. If necessary, use the Shape tool to edit the shape of the envelope and click Apply again.

Using the Preset List to Make an Envelope for Paragraph Text

With the options available in the Preset List box, you may not have to create very many custom envelope styles. To apply a preset style to a selected Paragraph Text, follow these steps:

1. Select the Pick tool from the toolbox and click the bounding box of a paragraph of text.

2. Open the Effects menu and choose Envelope, or press Ctrl+F7. The Envelope roll-up window appears.

3. Choose a shape from the Preset list.

4. Click Apply.

5. If necessary, use the Shape tool to edit the shape of the envelope and click Apply again.

Editing Text in an Envelope

Text remains editable even after an envelope is applied. You just need to use the correct tool—the Text tool. Click the text with the Text tool, or use the cursor to drag through the text. Then open the Text menu and choose Edit Text, or press Ctrl+Shift+T; the Text Editing dialog box appears (see fig. 15.20). Begin editing the text. Click OK when finished, and the new text is placed into the envelope.

Fig. 15.20
Use the Text Editing dialog box for editing text with an envelope applied.

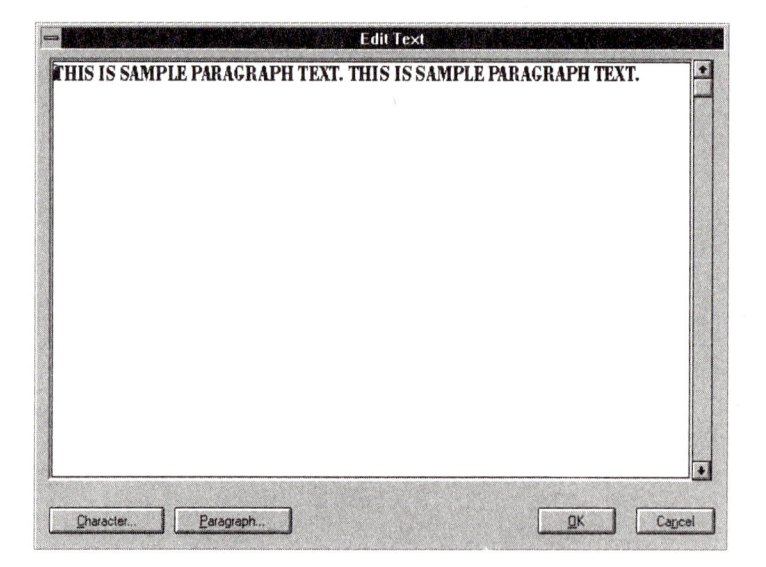

Troubleshooting

The text fit to an envelope does not closely match the bounding box of the envelope. What am I doing wrong?

Some fonts, just by the nature of their design, do not want to follow the shape of an envelope. Try creating a Not Constrained envelope or choosing a different font.

Clearing Applied Envelopes

Earlier, the Reset Envelope option was discussed. With this option, you can reverse edits made to a particular envelope. There are two additional layers of removing applied envelope styles. The first is Clear Envelope. Click the object; open the Effects menu and choose Clear Envelope. The envelope and all its edits are deleted. If you applied more than one envelope, continue clicking until you remove all the layers you want. CorelDRAW! removes them in reverse order. The last one created is the first to be deleted and so on. To remove all envelopes simultaneously, click the object; open the Effects menu and choose Clear Transformations. The object reverts back to its original shape—the way it looked when it was created.

If you combined the Envelope command with perspective, you cannot choose Clear Transformations. First you must remove the perspective. If you want to retain the perspective and remove all the envelopes, follow these steps:

◀ See "Copying Perspective," p. 419

1. Duplicate the object.

2. Remove the perspective from the original object by opening the Effects menu and choosing Clear Transformations.

3. Click on the stripped original and choose Copy from the Effects menu. A drop-down menu appears.

4. From the drop-down menu, choose Perspective From. The cursor changes to an arrow.

5. Click the arrow on the duplicate object. The perspective from the object is copied to the original.

6. Delete the duplicate.

Troubleshooting

I want to remove all the envelopes I've added, but the Clear Transformations options is dimmed in the Effects menu.

You have probably also added perspective to the object, which must be removed before you can choose Clear Transformations.

From Here...

Working with envelopes is just one of the many special effects that can transform your art in ways that might be very difficult without the automation of CorelDRAW!. In the following chapters, you can further your skills with special effects, or learn more about the underlying framework of CorelDRAW!:

- Chapter 1, "An Overview of CorelDRAW! 5" provides the foundation for working with special effects. You learn the layout of CorelDRAW! and how the roll-up windows work.

- Chapter 5, "Modifying Object Outlines and Interior Fills," teaches you how adding color and textures to envelopes can really spice them up.

- Chapter 14, "Creating Special Effects with Perspective," discusses using perspective features, some of which are similar to the envelope features.

- Chapter 22, "Combining and Reusing Effects," provides a host of examples to give you ideas and show you how things work with the special effects. Read through this chapter for a step-by-step tour.

Chapter 16
Creating Special Effects with Blending

by Cyndie Klopfenstein

You can use the Blend special effect to create realistic highlighting, a beautiful airbrush look, or to smoothly meld one object into another. Figure 16.1 shows examples of these different effects, all achieved with the Blend effect. Other color examples are included in Chapter 22, "Combining and Reusing Effects."

Fig. 16.1
Examples of how you can use the Blend effect.

Blend can be a very versatile tool. In this chapter, you learn about its versatility as you:

- Tour the Blend roll-up window
- Transform one object into another
- Flow a transformation along a path
- Create highlighting effects
- Add depth and dimension to otherwise plain drawings

- Change the fill of objects with Blend
- Create distinctive blends by mapping nodes

Watching the Status Line

As with all functions of CorelDRAW!, the status line keeps you up to date on the functions you're working with, or the move expected with the tool you've chosen on the active roll-up window. Many of CorelDRAW!'s effects are rather specialized and beginners don't have occasion to use them frequently. An easy way to forget what you're supposed to be doing with a tool is to only use it once in a blue moon. So don't be too proud to sneak a peek here—CorelDRAW! always remembers how to use a tool. When a blend is selected, the status line looks something like the one shown in figure 16.2.

Fig. 16.2
Use the status line to prompt you for the next expected move.

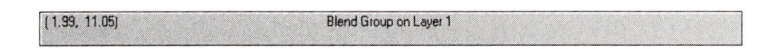

`[ 1.99, 11.05]                                 Blend Group on Layer 1`

The status line for a blend is a little different. First, it displays that it is a blend group. It also displays the number of objects of the blend if you separate the Blend group. If you select a control object, it displays that information as well as the shape of the control object. As you go through this chapter, you'll learn that sometimes control objects belong to more than one blend, in which case the status line is likely to report a total number of objects that is not at first apparent. As you make it through this chapter, you'll begin to understand more of what the status line tells you about the selected blends.

Working from the Menus

◀ See "Combining and Grouping Objects," p. 119

The Blend Roll-Up command is in the Effects menu, as are all other special effects. After you select it from the menu, you see the roll-up window (see fig. 16.3). You return to the menu for options such as Clear Transformations and Clear Blend, but primarily you use the roll-up window. Commands in the Arrange menu are also used a great deal with blends. When a blend is created, the Start and End objects (also known as *Control objects* because they control the intermediate objects) and all intermediate objects are automatically grouped together. Some changes to the group require you to break the group apart first. You can do this by choosing Separate. You'll also find the commands Reverse Order and Group here; both commands are used in this chapter.

Using the Blend Roll-Up Window   **443**

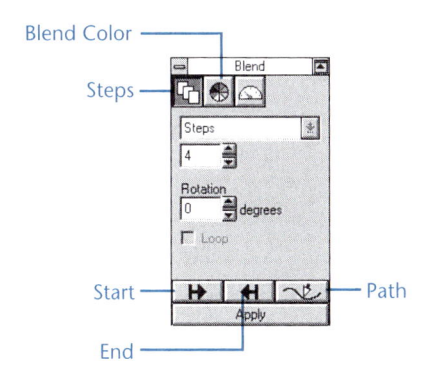

Blend Color
Steps
Start
End
Path

Fig. 16.3
Each button of the Blend roll-up window helps to define the type of blend you want.

Using the Blend Roll-Up Window

Each button of the roll-up window has a different function; some buttons combine functions to make other, more sophisticated blends. In this section, you tour the buttons and move on to step-by-step usage. Refer to figure 16.3 if you can't locate the button on your roll-up window.

Steps, Spacing, and Rotation

The first control you encounter is the Steps, Spacing, and Rotation controls. Here you dictate how many duplicate objects are created between the Start and End Object, how far apart the objects are when blending on a path, and if they rotate, by what degree. Click this button to choose Steps, Spacing, and Rotation from the fields that appear when this option is selected. In the first field now visible, click to choose Steps (the default) or Spacing.

Specifying the Number of Steps

The more intermediate objects you create, the closer the objects are to one another, and the smoother the blend looks. Similarly, the fewer objects you create, the more space is between objects and the more defined is each object (see fig. 16.4).

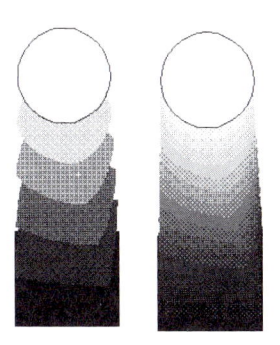

Fig. 16.4
The example on the left shows how a blend looks rougher when there are fewer intermediate objects.

Becoming an Expert

V

Specifying the Spacing

When applying a blend to a path, CorelDRAW! draws the number of objects necessary to traverse the distance if you specify a distance between objects. CorelDRAW! figures the number of steps for you. (If you specify the number of objects, CorelDRAW! determines equal spacing between objects.)

Specifying the Rotation Value

You can specify rotation with either Steps or Spacing chosen. You can type a value in the field or use the scroll arrows. Positive values rotate clockwise, and negative values rotate counterclockwise. Rotation begins with the Start object. If you rotate the blend 180 degrees, the intermediate objects make a complete flip between the Start object and the End object. Figure 16.5 shows this flip; the blend shown was made by mapping nodes. Notice that the top of the Start object has been turned upside down to become the bottom of the End object. (See the sections "Start Objects," "End Objects," and "Start Nodes" later in this chapter.)

Fig. 16.5
On the left is a blend with no rotation. On the right is a blend with 180-degree rotation.

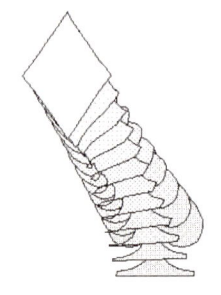

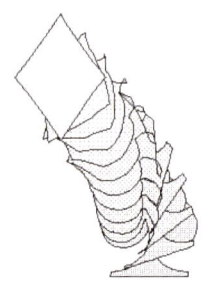

Loop

In figure 16.5, the last example is that of a blend that doesn't make a loop. To create this effect, don't click the Loop check box. When the Loop box is checked, the blend flies out more in an arc.

Color

◀ See "Working with Interior Fills," p. 146

Click the Color button if you want to change the colors of the objects. In the table below, you can find rules about how the intermediate objects of a blend change color and fill depending on what the color and fill of the Start and End Objects are. Figure 16.6 shows the Color window. In Chapter 22, "Combining and Reusing Effects," you find several examples of blends and the fills of intermediate blends. Table 16.1 discusses the fill of the intermediates.

Using the Blend Roll-Up Window

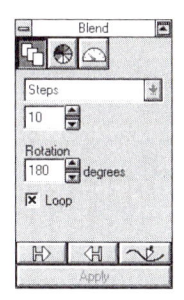

Fig. 16.6
With this color wheel, you can choose the color of the fill of Start and End objects.

Table 16.1 The Color of Intermediate Objects

Start or End Object's Fill	Intermediate Objects' Fill
No fill in Start or End object	No fill in objects
Uniform fill and a fountain fill	Blend from a uniform fill to a fountain
Uniform fill and a pattern fill	Uniform fill
Radial fill and a linear fill	Radial fountain
Radial fill and a uniform fill	Radial fountain
Same type of fountain in Start and End object	Fountain
Pattern in either Start or End object	The fill of the object not containing a pattern
Pattern in both Start and End object	The pattern of the object on top
Spot color in Start or End	Process color with process color in other object
Different spot colors in Start and End	Process color
Same style of texture fill	Blended with texture fills in both objects
Texture fill in Start or End object	The fill of the object not containing a texture
Different texture fills in Start and End object	The texture fill of the start object

The Rainbow Option

The Rainbow check box works in conjunction with the Color button. If you don't mark the Rainbow check box, the intermediate objects of a blend are colored in a direct line across the color wheel. The color wheel shows this path on the color wheel with the endpoints of the path marking the color of the Start object and that of the End object. If you check Rainbow, the intermediate colors are filled with colors from around the color wheel. Here, the Start and End objects are marked by the endpoints of the arc (as opposed to a straight line). The name *Rainbow* implies that the colors of the rainbow are used to fill intermediate colors, and this in the general sense is true.

You can choose the direction of the Rainbow blend by clicking one of the Rotation buttons. Of course, your options are limited to clockwise and counterclockwise. Click the Left button and then click the Right button to watch the difference the direction can make to the fills of intermediate objects. Turn to Chapter 22, "Combining and Reusing Effects," to see examples that demonstrate these differences.

◀ See "Modifying Object Outline Characteristics," p. 137

Each option, such as Rainbow, can apply to the outline colors if you so choose. To see the effect, however, your objects need to have no fill, only an outline.

Blending Unequal Subpaths

When you blend Start and End objects with an unequal number of subpaths, CorelDRAW! has a difficult time filling them. Sometimes one or more of the intermediate objects is drawn as an open path, and then the subpaths might not print. Or the subpaths may print as an outline only. You can circumvent this problem by ensuring that your Start and End object have an equal number of subpaths.

◀ See "Mapping," p. 430

Start Nodes

When CorelDRAW! sets out to create a blend, it finds the first node of the Start object and maps that to the first node of the End object. You can see the first node on a selected item right before you blend the two. It is marked with a small open box icon. (We covered some mapping when we worked with Envelope.) But the first node may not be where you want the blend to start. To select a different start node, click the Map Node button in the Blend rollup window. After you've clicked the button, the pointer changes into a special bent arrow character so that you can choose a start node on the Start object. After you've done that, the pointer changes again. Now the arrow is bent downward, ready for you to select a start node on the End object, which is already displayed for you.

The left blend in figure 16.7 shows how it appears if the lower-left node is the first node of the Start object and the top, middle node is the first node of the End object. The center illustration shows the arrow for choosing the first node (mapping the two together), and the illustration on the right shows the end result of changing the mapping of the top-left node of the Start and top-center node of the End object together.

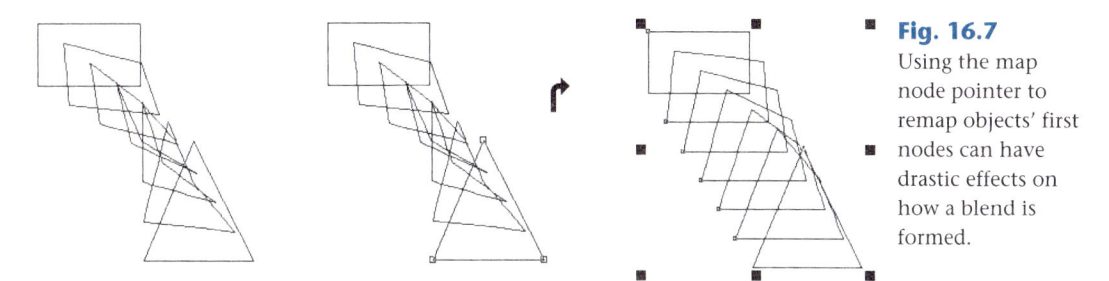

Fig. 16.7
Using the map node pointer to remap objects' first nodes can have drastic effects on how a blend is formed.

Split Blend

CorelDRAW! calls a blend *a dynamically linked object*. In layman's terms, this means that it is a group, controlled and edited by making changes to the Start or End object. Because these changes occur immediately (after you click Apply), it is considered a dynamic change. Because the Start and End object control the intermediate objects, they are the control objects. You cannot change the intermediate objects except by changing the Start and End. You can, however, change an intermediate object into a control object by using the Map Nodes button of the Blend roll-up window. The look of the Blend roll-up window changes (see fig. 16.8). When this icon is selected, the Split button is available, and a special pointer is assigned to the cursor (see fig. 16.9).

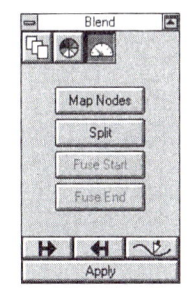

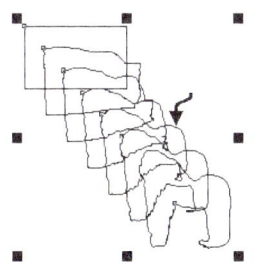

Fig. 16.8
Clicking the Map Nodes button prompts a different window in the Blend roll-up.

Fig. 16.9
Use the special cursor icon to select an intermediate object as a control object. First you need to split the blend.

Now that you've selected a new control object, a bounding box appears around that object to identify it as a new control object. This control object is both the End of the first blend and the Start of the next blend. Making changes to this control object affects both blends dynamically. Some changes require you to click the Apply button at the bottom of the Blend roll-up window before the change takes effect.

Fuse Blend

Now that you have this totally separate intermediate object that is both a Start and an End object, you have the option of fusing it back as an intermediate object to either the first blend or to the following blend. In the first blend, the new control object is the End object; in the next blend, it is the Start object.

What happens when you fuse a split blend is best shown in an illustration. Look at figure 16.10 and see how a blend that followed a bent path is straightened once it is fused. Press the Ctrl key and click one of the split blend groups, and then click the Fuse End or Fuse Start button. Because these blends overlap, it's easy to see how the selected intermediate object becomes both the Start and the End and why it is both the first and last object.

Fig. 16.10
Fusing split blends can change the path that they follow.

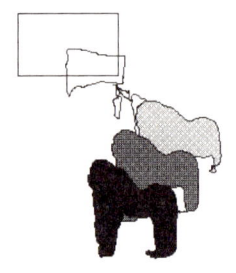

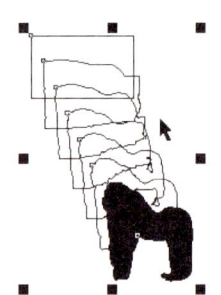

Start Objects

If you have difficulty finding the Start object of a blend, click the blend, the Start button, and Show Start. The Start object is now surrounded with a bounding box and handles (see fig. 16.11). To define a Start object, click the Start button and choose New Start. The cursor changes to the Start icon and you can click an object to make it a Start. You must always click the Apply button to see your changes take effect. If you don't like the results, open the Edit menu and choose Undo.

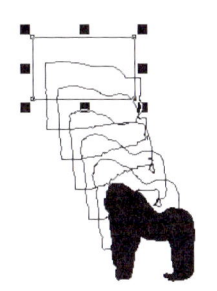

Fig. 16.11
Click Show Start, and the starting object is surrounded with a bounding box.

End Objects

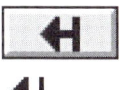

Finding and creating End objects requires the same steps as finding and creating Start objects (see the preceding section). Use the Pick tool to click the Blend, and then click the Show End button. The bounding box moves to surround only the object that is the end of that blend.

Blends on a Path

After you create a blend, you can instruct it to follow a path. Rather, you can instruct its center of rotation to follow a path. This distinction is important because the center of rotation follows the path (the blend pushes away) by the distance that the center is moved (see fig. 16.12). In this illustration, the object on the right has the center of rotation moved to the left. Notice that the center of rotation is exactly aligned to the path, whereas the end object is to the right of the path. This center of rotation was moved to the left and when the Apply button was clicked, the object moved to the right so that the center of rotation once again aligns to the path.

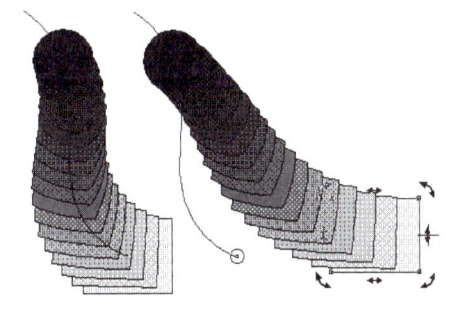

◄ See "Rotating Objects," p. 200

Fig. 16.12
These blends follow a path. On the right, the center of rotation was moved so that the center follows the path, and the blend strays away.

The step-by-step process is presented later in this chapter, but to briefly explain how to make a blend follow a path, draw a path and click the Path icon. In the new window of the roll-up window, choose New Path, and then click the path you want to meld the blend to. At this point, you can choose

450 Chapter 16—Creating Special Effects with Blending

from a few different options from the list box at the top of the Blend roll-up window: Full Path, Rotate All, or Spacing. If you click Full Path, the blend extends the full length of the path and the objects are spaced evenly the full distance. Click Rotate All to rotate the objects at the same degree at the arc of a path. If you click Spacing, you can set the amount of space you want between each object. See figure 16.13 for examples of how these options affect how the blend follows the path.

Fig. 16.13
Use the options of the Path portion of the Blend roll-up window for directing the type of blend you want.

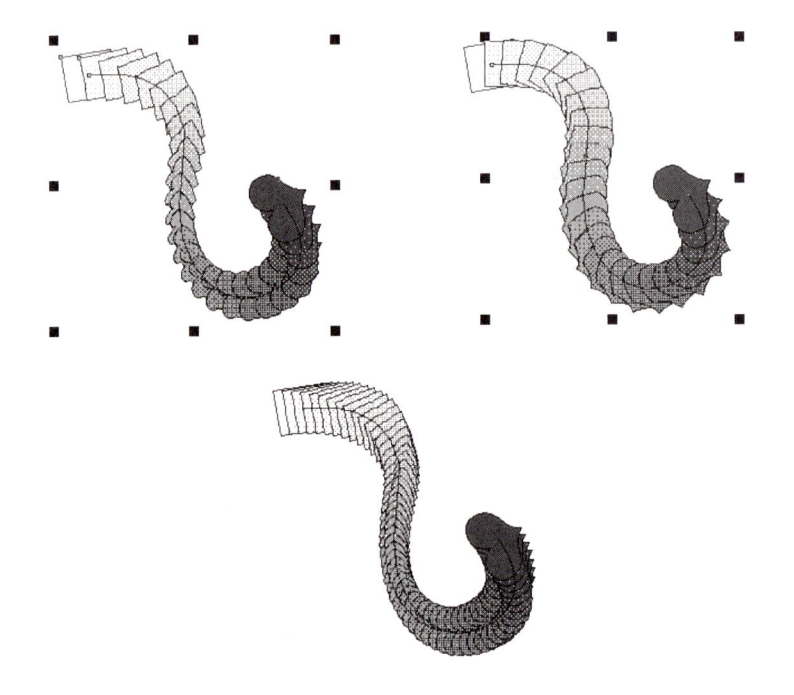

Because of the color or fill of the path, it's sometimes difficult to find the path for editing. Select the Blend group that is using a path. Choose Show Path to select the path and Detach path to pull the path from the blend. It's also possible to add another path by choosing the New Path option again (see fig. 16.14).

Fig. 16.14
Use the Path drop-down menu to edit and create paths.

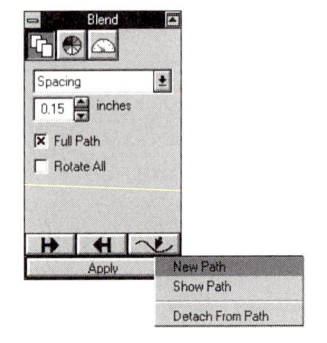

Working with Blends

Now that you know about the elements of the Blend roll-up window, you can use them together to build blends with your artwork. The next section describes all steps necessary to create a Simple blend, a Compound blend, and even a blend along a path. Other topics, such as deleting, copying, and cloning blends, are also discussed.

Identifying the Parts of a Blend

The components of a blend include the Start object, the End object, a Split blend, and the blend following a path with the center of rotation moved from the End object. The Start and End objects are the control objects. A Split blend creates a new control object. See figure 16.15 for examples of each of the components of a blend.

Start object

End object

New start/end path

Center of rotation

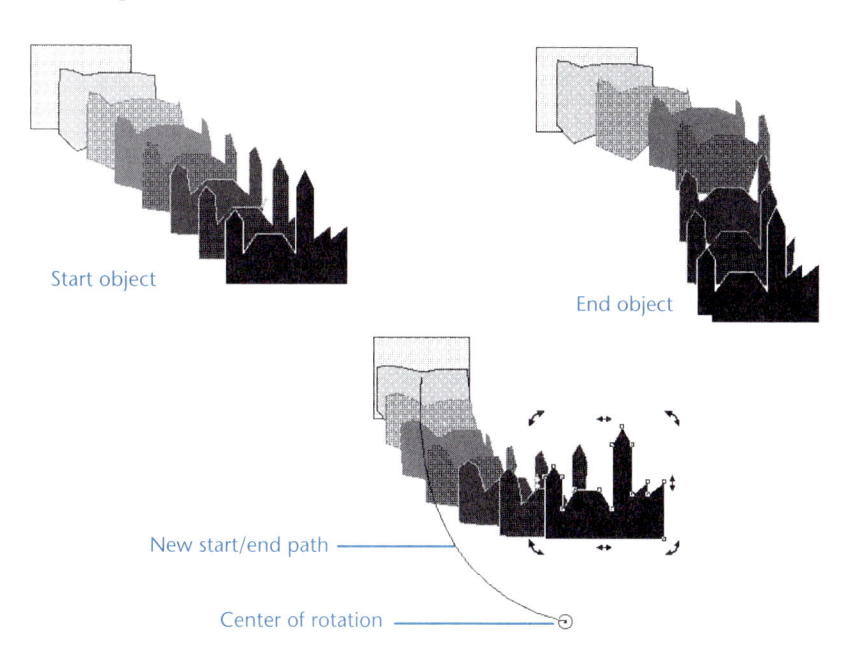

Fig. 16.15
With all parts identified, a blend looks pretty simple to create, and it is.

Finding the Start Object of a Blend

The Start object is important because it is the beginning of the blend. It controls the blend and what the objects start out looking like by being the control object for the beginning of the blend. An object that you draw and blend to another object is automatically the Start object. If you can't find the Start object, follow these steps:

452 Chapter 16—Creating Special Effects with Blending

1. Open the Effects menu and choose the Blend Roll-Up command, or press Ctrl+B.

2. Click the Start arrow button in the Blend roll-up window. The roll-up window shows a drop-down menu (see fig. 16.16).

Fig. 16.16
The Start button of the Blend roll-up window prompts a drop-down menu when you click it.

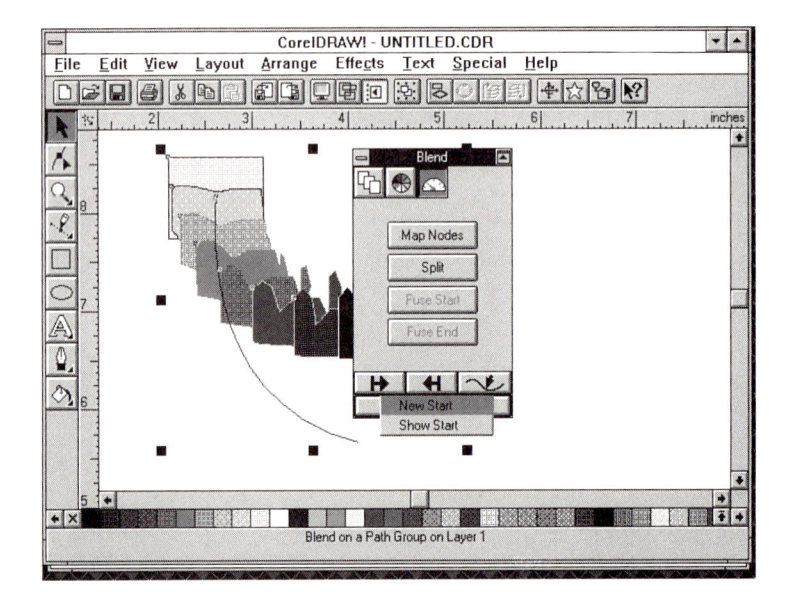

3. From the drop-down menu, choose Show Start. A bounding box surrounds the Start object for that blend.

Finding the End Object of a Blend

Finding the End object is nearly the same as the steps you followed for finding the Start object. The only difference is that you choose Show End from the drop-down menu of the End arrow button.

Making Just a Blend

Using the Blend Roll-Up command from the Effects menu makes blending easy. Follow these steps for creating a blend between two objects. In Chapter 22, "Combining and Reusing Effects," you can see that objects don't have to be even remotely similar in size or shape. They don't even have to be the same color, pattern, or texture.

1. Draw two objects that you want to blend together.

2. Open the Effects menu and choose Blend Roll-Up.

3. Select both objects.

4. Click the Apply button in the Blend roll-up window.

Splitting a Blend

Splitting is very useful if you want to incorporate a new image somewhere in the blend or if you want to send the blend in another direction with a new blend.

1. Open the Effects menu and choose the Blend Roll-Up command. Select the Blend group.

2. Click the Split button in the Map Nodes area.

3. Select one of the intermediate objects (not the one directly next to the Start or End object).

4. Click the Split button. A bounding box now appears around the object, indicating that it has been converted to a control object—the End object of the first blend and the Start object of the following blend.

> **Note**
>
> If you edit this new control object, both blends are affected.

Fusing a Blend

Now that you've broken the blend up, try these steps for putting it back together. You can fuse a Start or an End object since the split object makes up both the start of one blend and the end of another blend. Use the appropriate button for the direction you wish to fuse.

1. Open the Effects menu and choose the Blend Roll-Up command.

2. Using the Tab Key, select the Start/End object of the split (a control curve).

3. Hold down the Ctrl key and click an intermediate object.

4. Click the Fuse End or Fuse Start button. Results vary depending on the type of blend fused. If it was a blend not applied to a path and the blend was not in a straight line, a straight line is formed.

For fusing more than one blend, the steps vary slightly as follows:

1. Open the Effects menu and choose the Blend Roll-Up command.

2. Use the Tab Key to select the Start/End object of the split.

3. Hold down the Ctrl key and click an intermediate object of the blend group you want to fuse the control object with.

4. Click the Fuse End or Fuse Start button.

5. With the special Fuse pointer, click an intermediate object of the blend you want to fuse with. (Do not click an object directly next to the control object of the blend.)

Making a Blend Follow a Path

◀ See "Drawing Straight Lines," p. 63

◀ See "Drawing Curved Lines," p. 68

After a blend is made, it's a simple procedure to also make that blend follow a path. Use a drawing tool to draw a path to meld to and follow the steps. After attaching a blend to a path, click and drag one of the control objects to move the blend up or down the path (if you haven't selected the Full Path option).

1. Open the Effects menu and choose the Blend Roll-Up command.

2. Draw two objects and blend them in the manner described above.

3. Draw a path for the blended objects to follow.

4. Click Path in the Blend roll-up window. A drop-down menu appears.

5. Choose New Path from the drop-down menu. The cursor changes to a black arrow. (Methods for three other options are described following this series of steps.)

6. Click the path that you want to meld the blend to.

7. Click Apply.

Use one of these alternate methods for using the Full Path, Rotate All, and Spacing options.

5a. Choose Full Path.

6. Click Apply.

The blend is distributed evenly from end to end of the path, with CorelDRAW! adding even amounts of space between the objects. The beginning of the path is centered in the Start object, and the tail of the path is centered in the End object.

or

5b. Choose Rotate All.

6. Click Apply.

Working with Blends 455

The objects of the blend are rotated in sync with the angles of the line of the path. Without Rotate All, the objects retain their applied angle.

or

5c. Choose Spacing from the list box.

6. Click Apply.

Type a value in the field or use the Nudge buttons to specify a value of space between the objects.

Finding and Moving the Center of Rotation

When you attach a blend to a path, you have the option to offset the distance between the two and between the objects of the blend group. To do this, move the center of rotation of one of the control objects. Before you try to move the path, follow the steps above for blending objects along a path. Use the following steps to move the blended objects from the path.

◀ See "Rotating Objects," p. 200

1. Click the Pick tool.

2. Double-click a control object. The rotation arrows appear (see fig. 16.17).

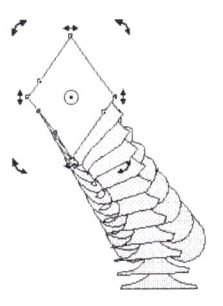

Fig. 16.17
When a control object is selected and double-clicked with the Pick tool, the Center of Rotation icon is visible. Drag it to move a blend from its path.

3. Click and drag the Center of Rotation of a control object. The center of rotation pulls away from the object.

4. Click the Apply button. The blended objects are moved away as the center of rotation aligns to the path.

Splitting a Blend from a Path

If you decide that the blend should not follow a path, or if you want to attach it to a different path, follow these steps for separating the two:

456   Chapter 16—Creating Special Effects with Blending

1. Select the blend attached to a path.
2. Click Path in the Blend roll-up window.
3. Click Detach from Path in the Blend roll-up window.

Making a Chain of Blends

After you create a blend, you can select an intermediate object and use it to create another blend, use one of those objects to create another blend, and so on. This process can produce some elaborately chained blends. Figure 16.18 shows an example of a chain of blends.

Fig. 16.18
Use intermediate objects as Start objects for other blends, thus creating a chain of blends.

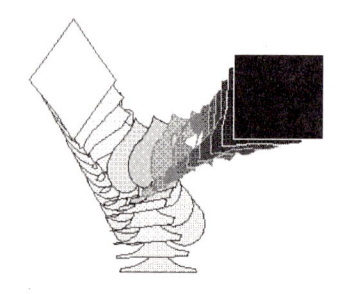

Making a Compound Blend

◀ See "Combining and Grouping Objects," p. 119

With CorelDRAW!, you're not limited to using a single object as the Start or End object of a blend. You are limited to using a group (not a blended group). So that's easy. Anytime you want to use more than one item, just group it first (Arrange menu). After you make a blend and flow it to a path, you can use that path as the path for another blend. Using shared paths, you can make what is known as a *compound blend*. In figure 16.19, the left footprint was blended three times and applied to a path. Then the right footprint (a flipped duplicate of the left) was blended twice and added to the same path.

Fig. 16.19
Here is an example of a compound blend made up of blends that share a common path.

Within a compound blend, clicking a single item of the blend selects the entire compound blend. Press Ctrl when you click to select one of the blends comprising the compound. To choose just a single object of a blend, click the Split command first in the Blend roll-up window, and click the individual item with the special cursor.

Selecting the path of a Compound blend is much easier—just click the path as you do normally. Change the path and the Compound blend objects attached to it rebuild and continue to follow the new path's shape.

You might find it useful to change blends into plain groups by selecting the blend, opening the Arrange menu, and choosing Group. This keeps blends from reblending or rebuilding if object shapes are changed.

Reversing the Direction of a Blend

Blends can easily change direction—and changing a blend's direction is much easier than deleting the blend and redrawing the objects. Click the blend. Open the Arrange menu and choose Order. From the resulting drop-down menu, choose Reverse Order.

Using Blends To Highlight

Blends make a wonderful tool for adding highlights (see fig. 16.20). Use the preceding steps for creating a blend; but for control objects, draw the first as an outline of the area you want to highlight (this outline is the background of the highlight) and fill it with the same color of the shape you're highlighting. Draw an End object inside the outline area with the shape of the object to contain the brightest color. Now blend the two objects together. You can expect results similar to those shown in figure 16.20.

Fig. 16.20
Use blends to add highlights to objects. (Doing so produces almost the same effect as the light source in Extrude.)

Clearing a Blend

When you clear or delete a blend, you do just that, take out the blend. To do this, click the blend; open the Effects menu; and choose Clear Blend. The blended objects are removed, leaving only the Start and End objects.

Copying a Blend

If you particularly like the type of blend you've created for a set of objects, you can apply those settings to another blend. Open the Effects menu and choose Copy. From the resulting drop-down menu, choose Blend From. You are not copying outline or fill colors from one blend to another, just the blend information. Follow these steps to copy the blend to another object.

1. Select the Start and End objects that you want to copy the blend information to. (These objects together are known as the *destination object*.)

2. Open the Effects menu and choose Copy. From the drop-down menu, choose Blend From. The cursor changes to an arrow.

3. Click the tip of the arrow next to the outline of the blend you want to copy from. (This blend is the *source object*.)

4. The destination object is redrawn with the blend settings of the source object.

Cloning a Blend

◄ See "Copying Objects," p. 105

Cloning is similar to copying, except that changes made to the original (master) object (from which you made the clone) are duplicated in the clone. But the clone can have fill and outline colors different from those of the master. If you change the outline or fill colors of the master, those changes do not affect the clone. The Rainbow button in the color portion of the Blend roll-up window does have an effect on the clone. It changes the clone's fill to Rainbow also, using the fill color of the clone's control objects. All other changes to the clone are locked into the master and must be adjusted there. To clone blend settings, follow these steps.

1. Use the preceding steps to create a blend with your choice of settings.

2. Draw the control objects that you want to apply the master settings to. Choose a fill and outline for the control objects if you want.

3. Select both control objects. They are surrounded by a bounding box with handles.

4. Open the Effects menu and choose Clone. From the drop-down menu, choose Blend From. The cursor changes into an arrow.

5. Click the source (master) object. The blend settings are now applied to the clone.

> **Troubleshooting**
>
> *Why is the color of the blend changing?*
>
> Colors of intermediate objects depend on the fill, outline, texture, and pattern of the control objects. Make sure you have selected the correct attributes for the control objects to attain the attributes you are looking for in the intermediate objects.
>
> *I can't select an intermediate object so that I can make changes.*
>
> Open the Arrange menu and choose Separate while the blend is selected. When the objects are separated, you can make changes to that object.
>
> *I have applied my blend to a path and the path is printing.*
>
> Go to the Outline tool and choose X (no outline) so that the line has no outline applied to it.
>
> *My blends are rough, with very distinctive steps.*
>
> Use more steps or move the steps closer together. Generally, the closer the steps are together, the smoother the blend looks. Also, adding an outline to an object tends to make it look more defined and less like a smooth blend.

From Here…

In this chapter, you learned to use CorelDRAW!'s Blend feature to create special effects. You learned techniques for transforming objects and flowing them along paths. You also learned to use the Blend feature to create highlights, add dimension to drawings, change fills, and create distinctive blends.

For information related to the topics covered in this chapter, refer to the following chapters:

- Chapter 3, "A Detailed Look at Object Drawing," and Chapter 4, "Mastering Object Manipulations," help you find your way around CorelDRAW!.

- Chapter 17, "Creating Special Effects with Extruding," uses a form of highlighting similar to the look you can achieve with blending, called light source.

- Chapter 18, "Creating Special Effects with Contouring," discusses the contour effect, which also is very similar to Blend. You have fewer options, but this might be just the effect you need.

- Chapter 22, "Combining and Reusing Effects," elaborates on this chapter's illustrations and explains the blending process in greater detail.

Chapter 17

Creating Special Effects with Extruding

by Cyndie Klopfenstein

Remember the moldable-clay factory you had as a kid? The one where you put the clay in the back, slid a template into the front slots, and then pressed the handle, and the clay pushed through the shapes and made long snakes of the shape it was pushed through? Well, that's CorelDRAW!'s special effect Extrude. It takes an object, a path, or even text and pulls it out as though you had pushed it through the clay factory. If you're a cook, think about running the object through a pasta machine—same effect.

The result of all this pushing and pulling is an object of depth and dimension. Technically speaking, CorelDRAW! is creating surfaces from your lines—surfaces that can contain a fill or a texture. These surfaces originally have the same fill and outline as the object, but of course, you can change them.

Figure 17.1 shows examples, simple and complex, of uses for the Extrude feature. Chapter 22, "Combining and Reusing Effects," has more examples along with a play-by-play description of how the steps of each illustration were tackled. The color section contains color examples and even more complex illustrations, so that you can make extrusions of your own and combine them with other special effects.

The two basic kinds of extrusions are wireframe (which look as though you were wearing x-ray glasses to see right through all the surfaces) and solid. Refer again to figure 17.1, which shows both kinds. You can create a wireframe by extruding a closed object or a path with no fill. Solid extrusions are the result of adding Extrude to an object with a fill (and perhaps an outline, too).

462 Chapter 17—Creating Special Effects with Extruding

Fig. 17.1
The word *Adventure* has a small back extrude but first was enclosed in a single-arc envelope. *Canada* is a wireframe parallel extrude. The leaf is a small front extrusion.

Working with the Extrude special effect is another way to add perspective to artwork. You learn about this effect in this chapter. You also learn to do the following things:

- Rotate an extrusion

- Adjust the light source directed at the extruded object

- Change the color and fill of an extrusion

- Gradate the color fill of an extrusion

- Control the way that fill and texture are applied to an extrusion

- Clone an extrusion style

Watching the Status Line

◀ See "Learning the Parts of the CorelDRAW! Screen," p. 18

So far, every chapter on special effects has referred to the status line. That's because the status line is an important feature of CorelDRAW!. Watching this line for prompts can help you remember what your next move should be. The status line also provides an up-to-date report about what is selected, what type of object it is, or what layer it's on. It won't take you long to make a habit of watching this area for help when you're crossing unfamiliar turf. When working with the Extrude roll-up window, your status line should look like the one shown in figure 17.2.

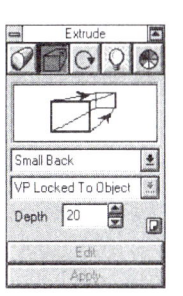

Fig. 17.2
The status line is providing information about the selected extrusion.

Working from the Menu

In the Effects menu, you find the Extrude Roll-Up command. Most of the extrude functions are performed here, but a few of the functions (such as copy, clone, and clear) bring you back to the Edit menu when you're ready to implement one. To use the menu, you usually select the object and choose the option from the menu, and the feature is applied. This is unlike many features of the Extrude roll-up window, which are not applied until you click the Apply button. You learn about the menu features later in this chapter when you go through the step-by-step instructions for creating extrusions.

Using the Extrude Roll-Up Window

Before we get into the steps for creating an Extrude, let's tour the Extrude roll-up window. This roll-up works like all the others in CorelDRAW!; you can collapse it, move it, close it, and even use keyboard shortcuts to choose it from the menu. Using this roll-up window, which follows you around the screen and applies changes at a click of the mouse, is preferable to using a menu—no more searching through several menus for the feature you need.

Figure 17.3 gives you your first look at the Extrude roll-up window. As you make your way through this chapter, come back to this illustration if you have difficulty finding a particular button in the window. Be aware, however, that the roll-up window changes dynamically depending on what object is selected and which buttons you click.

◀ See "Using Roll-Up Windows," p. 25

Fig. 17.3
The Extrude roll-up window is like other roll-up windows; it contains buttons, fields, windows, and (of course) a button for rolling it up.

464 Chapter 17—Creating Special Effects with Extruding

Extrude Preset Button

This button's simple enough; it's the Extrude Preset button. Click an object; click this button; choose an Extrude type from the drop-down list; and click Apply—that's it. After you apply an extrusion, you can use the other buttons to modify it. Read on for information about these options.

Figure 17.4 shows the extrusion options. Scroll through the list until you find the one that suits your project; then click.

Fig. 17.4
Here is the list of Extrude Preset options. Your list may look a little different if you've already saved custom extrusion settings, using the Save As button.

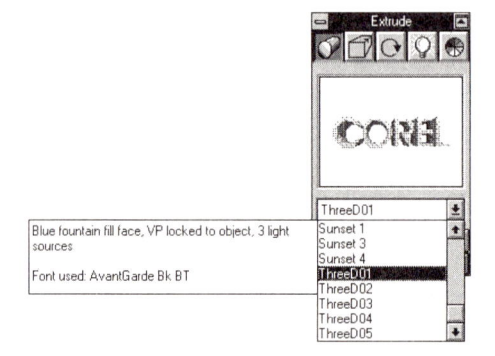

Depth Control Button

Clicking this button extrudes an object, but more than that, it also allows you to make choices about the type of extrusion to create. The first list box choice you'll make is whether you want a perspective or parallel extrusion. Select the type of extrusion from the drop-down list directly below the wireframe image of your object in the Extrude roll-up window. You actually have several options: Small Back, Small Front, Big Back, Big Front, Back Parallel, and Front Parallel. Choose any of the first four options to apply a perspective. Front or Back indicates the direction in which the extrusion moves. In the next few sections, you learn more about each of these types of extrusions.

◀ See "Using One-Point Perspective," p. 416

◀ See "Using Two-Point Perspective," p. 416

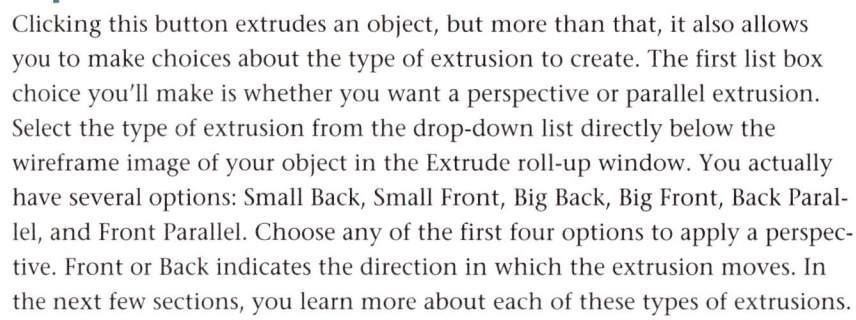

Perspective Extrusion

In Chapter 14, "Creating Special Effects with Perspective," you learned about using the perspective option to add one- and two-point perspective to objects. The Extrude feature relies heavily on perspective to create the appearance of depth. From the drop-down list, you can choose any of the first four options (Small Back, Small Front, Big Back, Big Front) to apply a perspective extrusion (see fig. 17.5).

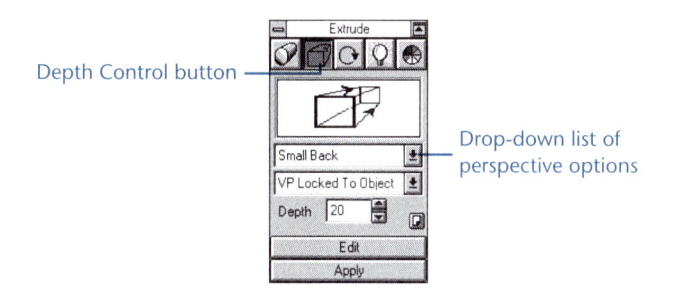

Using the Extrude Roll-Up Window   **465**

Fig. 17.5
Use the Depth Control button in the Extrude roll-up window to create a perspective extrusion.

Parallel Extrusion

Parallel extrusions differ from perspective extrusions in that they don't diminish in size. Look at figure 17.6, and notice the comparison of the two types. The × marks the *vanishing point*—the point to which the perspective diminishes. In the parallel extrusion, the vanishing point is in the center of the extrusion. You can edit this vanishing point by clicking and dragging. In the bottom half of figure 17.6, you can see the effect on each example when the vanishing point is moved. If this is the type of extrusion you want, select either the Back or Front Parallel from the drop-down list in the roll-up window.

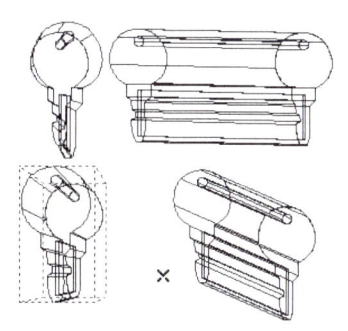

Fig. 17.6
The top two objects show a perspective extrusion on the left and a parallel extrusion on the right. In the bottom half of the figure, the vanishing point has been moved.

Depth of Extrusion

With the Depth Control button selected, you can type a value in the Depth field to move the vanishing point numerically. A higher number (99 is the maximum depth) moves the vanishing point farther away. A lower number (not smaller than 1) pulls the vanishing point toward the control object. In figure 17.7, you see the result of a value of 10 on the left and a value of 75 on the right.

◀ See "Understanding the Vanishing Point," p. 417

Fig. 17.7
Use the Depth field to numerically enter a long depth (on the left) and a short depth for the extrusion.

VP Locked to Object
Now that you understand the vanishing point and how you can move it, let's look at its other properties. By choosing VP Locked to Object, you are instructing CorelDRAW! to maintain the relationship of the vanishing point to the object. If you move the object around the page, the vanishing point moves with it, in direct proportion.

VP Locked to Page
VP Locked to Page produces the opposite result from VP Locked to Object. If you choose this option and then move the object, the vanishing point remains stationary; it maintains its relationship to the position on the page even when the object is moved. You might use this option if you are drawing a landscape and all the objects need to diminish to the same horizon, regardless of where they are moved.

Copy VP From
When you use either of the preceding options, you can copy that setting and, similarly, that position to another object. (You learn how to copy vanishing points later in this chapter.) In this section, suffice it to say that you simply select the object to which you want to copy the vanishing point (the *destination* object), choose the Copy VP From option, and then click the object from which you want to copy (the *source* object). CorelDRAW! applies the copied vanishing point to the destination object. When a vanishing point has been applied, it is separate from the source object and can be edited separately.

Shared VP
In realistic drawings, all objects share a vanishing point. Only one × appears on the page for a group of shared objects. You apply shared vanishing points in the same way that you copy them. The difference is that each object does *not* have its own point that can be edited separately from the others. When an object has a shared vanishing point, any edits to that vanishing point are applied to all objects that share it.

Using the Extrude Roll-Up Window   **467**

Rotating Perspective and Parallel Extrusions

Click the Rotate button, and the Extrude roll-up window changes to look like the one shown in figure 17.8. The sphere in the center is a representation of your extruded object. By clicking an arrow, you can spin the sphere (and, thereby, your object) in the direction in which the arrow points. If you change your mind, click the × in the center of the sphere; CorelDRAW! removes any applied rotation. To enter a rotation value numerically, click the small dog-eared page icon below and to the right of the sphere.

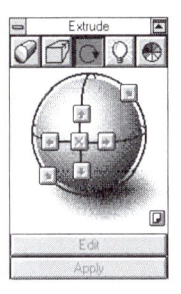

◄ See "Rotating Objects," p. 200

Fig. 17.8
This is the Rotate view of the Extrude roll-up window. Click an arrow to rotate the object in the direction of the arrow.

Light Source Button

Clicking the Light Source button changes the Extrude roll-up window again; click a light source button or two (the three buttons to the left of the wireframe box) and the roll-up should look like the one shown in figure 17.9. The sphere that you see in the figure (in the center of the wireframe) represents your object, as it did with the Rotate option. When the light source is turned on, the sphere appears inside the wireframe box. The light on the object is brightest; the extruded portion of the object receives the smallest amount of light.

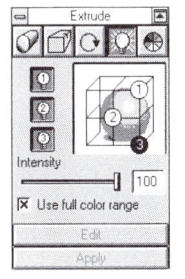

Fig. 17.9
Click the Light Source button to define directions for up to three light sources.

Turning on the Light Source

Three light-bulb buttons appear to the left of the wireframe image in the Extrude roll-up window (refer to fig. 17.9). These buttons technically are light switches; you click them to turn light sources on and off. Use the light bulbs to define a light source. The intersections of the wireframe box are where you click to change the direction of the light source. Click one of the light-bulb buttons and drag it to intersections on the wireframe image to define the direction from which the light should come. After a light source is turned on (by clicking the button), the sphere appears, with the brightest spot of the object being the intersection where the light source icon resides, and the Intensity control becomes available.

If you apply a light source and then rotate the object, you might hide the light source. If this happens and the object becomes too dark, you can use the Intensity control to lighten the object, or you can add another light source.

Moving the Light Source

After you apply light sources, numbers appear on the wireframe, each of which indicates the light source it represents. Click and drag one of the light-source markers to a new position to change the direction of the light source.

Controlling Brightness

Each of the three light sources can have a different intensity. Click the light-source marker that you want to brighten or darken, and use the Intensity slider (or the numeric field to the right of the slider) to make the adjustment. The Apply button is at the bottom of the Extrude roll-up window; click it to view the changes you made in brightness. The light-source markers themselves also change in intensity, depending on the brightness setting; the higher the number, the brighter (or whiter) the source. The default is 100, which also is the brightest setting. Move the slider to the left or type a number smaller than 49 to make the object darker.

Use Full Color Range

The Use Full Color Range option instructs CorelDRAW! to use the full spectrum of color to blend the beginning of the light source with the ending. You get a much smoother blend of the illusion of light when you choose this option. If you're converting CorelDRAW! 4 files to CorelDRAW! 5, however, disable this button; CorelDRAW! 4 doesn't support this option.

> **Troubleshooting**
>
> *When I click Apply, my object is so dark that I can no longer distinguish the pattern.*
>
> Increase the Intensity setting to brighten the object. You also might try adding another light source.
>
> *I can't get rid of my applied light sources.*
>
> Use the light-bulb buttons in the Light Source portion of the Extrude roll-up window. These buttons are also off switches; a click turns the light source off.

Color Button

The next option in the Extrude roll-up window changes the fill of surfaces. You add color to an object before extrusion the way you apply color to all other objects. If you need help with adding color, fills, or textures, refer to Chapter 5, "Modifying Object Outlines and Interior Fills." When you click the Color button, the Extrude roll-up window changes yet another time, and four new options are available. Each of these options takes effect only after you click the Apply button. Figure 17.10 displays the color options in the Extrude roll-up window.

Fig. 17.10
Use the Color button to prompt the Color fly-out in the Extrude roll-up window to change the fill of extruded surfaces.

Use Object Fill

The first option already is selected, because it is the default. Use Object Fill fills all surfaces of the extrusion with the same fill as the original object. If the original object doesn't have a fill, you get a wireframe effect.

Solid Fill

See "Working with Solid Fills," p. 150

Click this option button to display a color wheel, from which you can choose an extruded-surface fill. This option does not change the fill of the control object (the original object). Figure 17.11 shows examples of the ways that the Shade and Solid Fill options affect an object and its extrusion. The figure also shows how the Drape Fills option changes textures, patterns, and bitmap fills.

Fig. 17.11
These examples show the different fill possibilities: a solid fill (left), a shade fill (center), and a texture fill used on an object with the Use Object Fill and Drape Fills options (right).

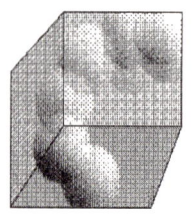

Shade

The Shade option works similarly to the Blend feature in CorelDRAW!. Use Shade to blend a fill between two colors. The From button in figure 17.12 (which appears when you click the Shade button) is for specifying the color of the object next to the control object. The To button specifies the color to which the extruded objects fade.

Fig. 17.12
When you click the Shade button, you can choose the two colors to be blended.

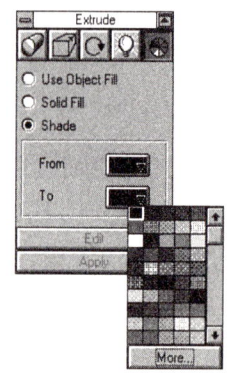

Drape Fills

See "Using Full-Color Patterns," p. 160

The Drape Fills option is used in conjunction with the Use Object Fill option. When you choose Drape Fills, you actually are instructing CorelDRAW! to treat the control object and the extrusion as a single object and to apply the fill to the entire group. If Drape Fills is not selected, each surface is a separate item, and the fill begins again with each surface. The example on the left in figure 17.13 shows how this option might affect your artwork.

Using the Extrude Roll-Up Window 471

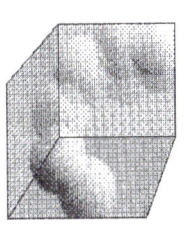

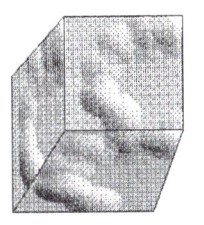

Fig. 17.13
On the left, the Drape option has been selected. On the right is an object fill without Drape.

All the Extrude options are affected by the intensity of light. Sometimes, the fills and textures you choose are just too dark when the extrusion is applied. Adjust these types of problems with the Intensity slide control in the Light Source window. Also remember that you might have rotated the brightest portion of your object out of view; you can rotate it back, add a new light source, or increase the brightness.

Save As Button

Now that you have used all the options to create the perfect Extrude, you might want to save these settings so you can apply them to other objects. Use the Save As button for this purpose. First, click the Extrude Preset button. A new dialog box appears like the one shown in figure 17.14. You can name the extrusion, as well as choose to save the outline, the fill options, and even tag notes about the settings. Click OK to save the extrusion as part of the Extrude Preset collection.

◄ See "Saving the Drawing," p. 46

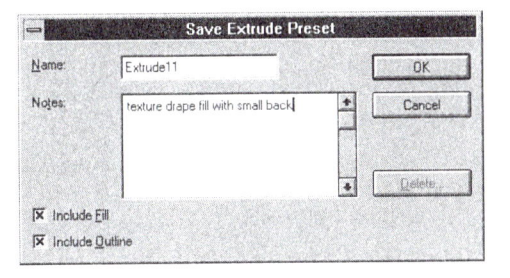

Fig. 17.14
Use the Save As button to prompt the Save Extrude Preset dialog box to save extrusion settings. You can apply saved settings to objects in any document.

Troubleshooting

I saved a preset extrusion, but when I applied it to another object, neither the fill nor the outline changed.

You must choose the Include Fill and Include Outline options in the Save Extrude Preset dialog box for these attributes to copy.

My buttons do not include a Save As option.

Make sure that you have clicked the Extruded Preset button to return the roll-up to the window for saving.

Apply Button

As you do in other roll-up windows, you usually have to click the Apply button in the Extrude roll-up window when you're ready to apply your changes. This feature can be a real time-saver if you're working with complex fills and textures, because the screen won't have to redraw every time you make a small change; it redraws only when you finish making changes and click Apply.

Working with Extrusions

Now that you've toured each of the buttons, it's time to apply what you know. In the upcoming sections, you can use the options of the Extrude roll-up window to create extrusions out of objects you've drawn, those from the Symbols roll-up, or those from the Corel Libraries on CD-ROM.

Extruding Objects

Spend just a moment planning your extrusion before you begin creating it. The fill of the object is the most important factor in the appearance of the end product. Suppose that you want either the wireframe look (start with no fill in the control object, only outline) or solid (start with a filled object) and that you want to apply a preset extrusion. To create this extrusion, follow these steps:

1. Select the object you want to extrude.

2. Open the Effects menu and choose the Extrude Roll-Up command, or press Ctrl+E. The Extrude roll-up window appears within the live area of the window.

3. Click the Extrude Preset button. A list of extrusions appears in the scrollable window.

4. Click the preset extrusion you want to use.

5. Click the Apply button. CorelDRAW! applies the preset extrusion settings to your object.

At this point, you can edit those settings further by choosing other options in the Extrude roll-up window.

Working with Extrusions   **473**

Troubleshooting

When I make changes to my extrusion, nothing happens.

Make sure that you click the Apply button. Many, but not all, of the options do not take effect until you click Apply.

Can I edit text after it has been extruded?

Use the Shape tool and click the nodes. You can edit the nodes as you can other nodes in modes other than Extrude. You cannot, however, edit the spelling and the like.

Editing an Extrude Node

Nodes, or handles, define the shape of a selected object. When you click an extruded control object with the Shape tool, you can edit or move the nodes. (Refer to Chapter 13, "Advanced Line and Curve Techniques," for detailed information on nodes and their manipulation.) If you previously applied the envelope or perspective special effect to the object, you must open the Effects menu and choose Clear Envelope or Clear Perspective before you can edit the nodes. If your object is a perspective extrusion and you rotated it with the 3D Extrusion Rotator, you must clear the extrude from the object before you can edit the nodes. If you like the extrusion settings of an item that you need to clear before editing the nodes, be sure to use the Save As button to store the settings *before* clearing them; when you finish editing the nodes, you can reapply the custom settings.

◀ See "Clearing Perspective," p. 420

◀ See "Clearing Applied Envelopes," p. 439

Changing the Center of Rotation

In figure 17.15, the center of rotation was moved from the control object. Now when the extrusion is rotated in the Extrude roll-up window, the object rotates from the new position.

◀ See "Rotating Objects," p. 200

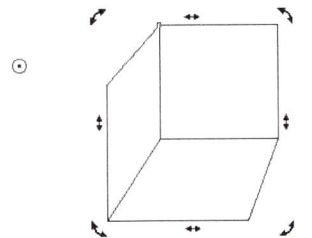

Fig. 17.15
Double-click an object to view the center of rotation. To move, click and drag the center of rotation marker (the dot inside circle), which identifies the exact center.

1. With the Pick tool, double-click the object (with parallel or perspective extrusion) for which you want to change the center of rotation. The control object is surrounded by arrows with the center-of-rotation marker at the exact center.

2. Click the center-of-rotation marker and drag it to a new location. The directional arrows move in proportion to keep the center of rotation at the exact center of the object.

3. Open the Effects menu and choose the Extrude Roll-Up command, or press Ctrl+E. The Extrude roll-up window appears somewhere in the active window.

4. Click the Rotate button. The roll-up window now displays the options for rotating the extrusion.

5. Click the arrows to move in one of the three directions. Click the × to remove rotation. Click the Dog-Eared-Page icon to type numeric values for the rotation.

6. Click the Apply button. CorelDRAW! applies the extrusion settings to your object.

Working with the Vanishing Point

◄ See "Understanding the Vanishing Point," p. 417

Choosing a vanishing-point style was explained in "Parallel Extrusion" earlier in this chapter. You don't have to follow a particular set of steps; just select one of the options in the scrollable window (directly below the Wireframe view in the Depth Control window) and click the Apply button.

Moving the Vanishing Point

When you click an object and the dark × appears, defining the vanishing point, you can use the Pick tool to click and drag the vanishing point to another location. Depending on the options you selected from the drop-down list, your extrusion(s) redraw according to your edit.

Sharing a Vanishing Point

One of the options in the drop-down list enables one object to share a vanishing point with other object(s). Follow these steps:

1. Use the Extrude roll-up to apply an extrusion to at least one of the objects on your page for which you want to share a vanishing point.

2. Select Shared Vanishing Point from the drop-down list as you apply extrusions to each object. The mouse pointer changes to a special cursor, indicating that it is waiting for you to click the source object (from which you are copying the vanishing point).

3. Click the source object.

4. Click Apply. CorelDRAW! redraws the destination object, using the same vanishing point as the source object.

> **Troubleshooting**
>
> *When I select the object, I cannot locate the vanishing point.*
>
> Check the status line, it may say that the vanishing point is Very Far. In other words, it may be off the edge of your page. Try reducing the view of the page and if you still can't see it, move the object as far down as possible. You also can use the Depth field to type in a value somewhat closer to the object.
>
> *I can't find the center of rotation on my selected object.*
>
> Sometimes you click on the object so fast that you click right past it. When you have an object selected, double-click. Try this until you get the hang of it.

Clearing an Extrude

Removing an applied extrusion is simple. But, it is not an option of the Extrude roll-up window. For this operation, you return to the Effects menu. To clear the applied extrusion, select the object; then open the Effects menu and choose the Clear Extrude command.

Copying an Extrude

Copying an extrusion setting is very much like using the Save As button in the Extrude roll-up window. Also, when you choose the Copy option from the Effects menu, the fill and outline of the destination object are not affected. With Save As, you can choose whether to include the fill and outline of the source object for later application to a destination object. The only reason to use Copy rather than Save As is if you want to use it only this one time. If you'll be applying an extrusion style to more than just one other object, it makes more sense to save it as a preset. If you do want to copy an extrusion style, follow these steps:

1. With the Pick tool, select the destination object.

2. Open the Effects menu and choose Copy; then choose Extrude From. The mouse pointer changes to a large black arrow.

3. Click the source object. CorelDRAW! redraws the destination object, using the settings of the source object.

Cloning an Extrude

◄ See "Copying Objects," p. 105

Clone differs from Copy (and Save As) in a major way: any change made in the master object is reflected in its clones. Similarly, you cannot edit a clone directly; you must make changes in the master. The only exceptions are changes to the fill and outline; the clone's fill and outline are not affected. After you make a change in the master, don't forget to click Apply so that changes are reflected in both the master and the clone.

Follow these steps to clone an extrusion:

1. Select the destination object.

2. Open the Effects menu and choose the Clone command; then choose Extrude From. The mouse pointer changes to a large black arrow, ready for you to select a master (source) object.

3. Click the source object. CorelDRAW! redraws the destination object, using the settings of the master object (except for the fill and outline, which do not change).

From Here...

All special effects complement one another well. Turn to any of the other special effects chapters in this section for ideas on how to connect them.

- Chapter 5, "Modifying Object Outlines and Interior Fills," helps you to add fill and outline to your Extrude so that you don't wind up with unexpected results.

- Chapter 14, "Creating Special Effects with Perspective," covers another special effect for adding perspective. Even though Extrude has a perspective button of its own, you might find helpful information about perspective in general in this chapter.

- Chapter 22, "Combining and Reusing Effects," walks you through the steps and shows great examples for using Extrude and the other special effects.

Chapter 18

Creating Special Effects with Contouring

by Cyndie Klopfenstein

The Contour feature is quite similar to Blend. The difference is that a contour does not blend along a path, and you do not blend between two objects. You can gradate an object to its center or in a specified number of steps. Figure 18.1 shows three examples of a contour: a contoured path, a circle contoured to the exact center, and a square contoured to the outside.

In this chapter, you learn

- How to create a contour
- What a contour looks like applied to objects and open paths
- How to break contours apart so that you can use the pieces
- How to control the amount of spacing and the number of steps used in a contour

You can edit the parts of a contour and can assign separate outline and fill colors. To generate smoother contours, remove the outline. Notice that the objects in figure 18.1 are individual objects; you cannot apply contour to a group of objects.

◀ See "Making Just a Blend," p. 452

◀ See "Changing the Outline Color," p. 141

◀ See "Adding a Solid Color Fill," p. 151

◀ See "Combining and Grouping Objects," p. 119

Fig. 18.1
On the left is a contoured path; in the center is a contoured circle with To Center chosen; and on the right is a square contoured to the outside.

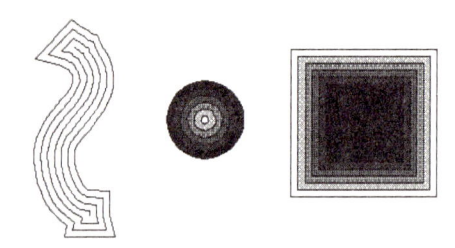

Watching the Status Line

A contoured object reports the information you see in figure 18.2 when it is selected. The status line is a good place to look for prompts that define the selected object and that sometimes tell you what the next step should be. If you blend similar objects, they can look the same as a contour, and you may have difficulty determining how you can edit the object; in such a case, look to the status line for help.

Fig. 18.2
Watch the status line for prompts when you are applying special effects or selecting objects made up of special effects.

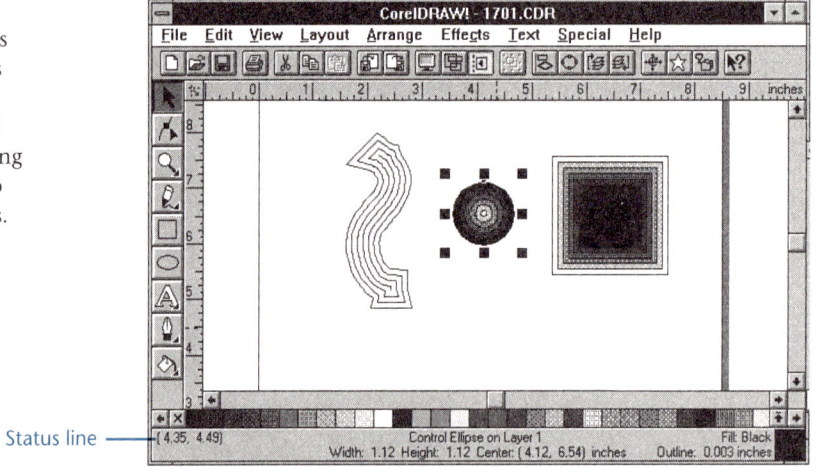

Working from the Menu

When you create contours, you will work primarily with commands located in the Effects menu. To edit individual steps of a contour, however, you first need to separate the group by using a command in the Arrange menu. The Effects menu also contains the commands for copying and cloning a contour. Later sections of this chapter explore these commands more fully.

◀ See "Using Roll-Up Windows," p. 25

Using the Contour Roll-Up Window

To access the Contour roll-up window, open the Effects menu and choose Contour Roll-Up. Like all other roll-up windows, the Contour roll-up window is movable, collapsible, and convenient. To add contour to a selected object, you need only click the appropriate button and then click Apply. The following sections of this chapter describe the options in the Contour roll-up window (see fig. 18.3).

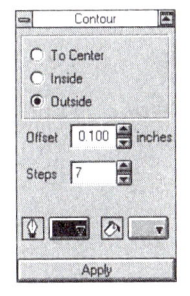

Fig. 18.3
Use the options in the Contour roll-up window to add contour to a control object (the selected object to which you applied the contour).

To Center

The first option you'll find in the roll-up window is To Center. When this option is selected, the contour moves toward the exact center of the selected control object. The value in the Offset field (described in the "Offset" section later in this chapter) determines the amount of space between each step. The Steps field is dimmed because CorelDRAW! figures how many steps are necessary based on the number you chose for the Offset setting. For an example of this option, refer to the middle object in figure 18.1.

Inside

This option is similar to the To Center option, except that if you define more steps than are necessary to reach the center, CorelDRAW! uses only the number of steps required to reach the center and spaces them according to the amount in the Offset field. The result is that CorelDRAW! places the intermediate objects (those objects that are created to make the contour) the correct distance apart (as you specified) but might do so in fewer steps than you defined.

Outside

The Outside option causes CorelDRAW! to draw the steps (whatever number you specify) and the offset from the control object outward. The square shown in figure 18.1 was created with this option selected.

Choosing Outside increases the size of the control object by the number of steps you specified multiplied by the amount of offset between steps. Make sure that you have enough room for the final product. If you selected an open path (a line that is not connected to its beginning), this is the only option available.

Offset

You can set the Offset amount by selecting or typing the amount of distance (in inches) you want between contours. Use a number between 0 and 10. Don't forget that unless you define an Outside contour, the Offset value always overrides the number of steps you specify.

Steps

The number of steps between intermediate objects can be very important. As a general rule, the more steps you have, and the closer together they are, the smoother the contour will be. Conversely, if you want more definition between steps, specify fewer steps with greater space between them. An outline color that contrasts sharply with the fill color also helps define the intermediate shapes.

To specify steps, select or type a number up to 999. In figure 18.4, the object on the left was stepped four times with a black outline; the object on the right was stepped 10 times with no outline color applied.

Fig. 18.4
More steps, closer together, make for a smoother contour, like the one on the right.

Outline

At the bottom of the Contour roll-up window are the buttons for selecting color for the fill and outline. Click the Color button next to the Pen icon, and the color palette drops down, revealing a preset list of colors. Click the More button to display a dialog box that displays additional colors.

◀ See "Changing the Outline Color," p. 141

Fill

As you do with Outline, click the color button to display a preset list of colors, and click the More button for additional choices. If the control object has no fill, the intermediate objects will have no fill either. This might be exactly the look you're trying to achieve—a wireframe look like the one shown in figure 18.5.

◀ See "Working with Interior Fills," p. 146

Fig. 18.5
This is an example of a contour without a fill in the control object.

Apply

The last button in the Contour roll-up window is the same as the last button in all the other special-effects roll-up windows: the Apply button. You must click this button to apply the options you chose in the roll-up window. This button will save screen-redraw time if you're making several adjustments to a contour; CorelDRAW! won't stop to redraw the object until you click Apply.

Creating Contours for Objects

Now that you understand the functions of the options in the Contour roll-up window, creating a contour will be simple. (If you can't remember the effect of one of the options, refer to the appropriate section earlier in this chapter.)

To create a contour, follow these steps:

1. Open the Effects menu and choose the Contour Roll-Up command or press Ctrl+F9. The Contour roll-up window appears in the active window.

2. Select the object to which you want to add contouring.

3. In the roll-up window, select the type of contour you want: To Center, Inside, or Outside.

4. Specify Steps and Offset.

5. From the Outline and Fill color buttons, choose the color you want to apply.

6. Click the Apply button. CorelDRAW! creates the contour.

Troubleshooting

My contour won't blend along a path.

Contours are unlike blends in that they do not blend along paths. Choose the object, remove the contour, and try adding a blend instead.

How can I tell the difference between a blend and a contour?

Click the object and check the status line. The object will be identified.

Editing Contours

◀ See "Combining and Grouping Objects," p. 119

You can edit the intermediate shapes in a contour, changing their color, fill, size, and rotation. To do this, you first must separate the dynamically linked group. With the Pick tool, click the contour. Then open the Arrange menu and choose Separate. Click the intermediate object that you want to change, and make the appropriate edits. Some types of objects remain grouped even after you have separated them. If this happens, return to the Arrange menu and choose Ungroup.

Copying Contours

To copy a contour style from one object (the source) and apply it to another object (the destination), you have to make a trip to the Effects menu. Follow these steps:

1. Select the destination object. A bounding box surrounds the object.

2. Open the Effects menu and choose Copy; then choose Contour From. The mouse pointer changes to a large black arrow.

3. Click the source object. CorelDRAW! applies the contouring to the destination object.

> **Note**
>
> The fill and outline colors of the destination object do not change to match those of the fill. The destination object picks up only the attributes of the contour itself.

Cloning a Contour

Cloning is very similar to copying. As in copying, fill and outline are not cloned—only the contour attributes. The procedure for cloning also is very similar to copying. Follow these steps:

◀ See "Copying Objects," p.105

1. Select the destination object. A bounding box surrounds the object.

2. Open the Effects menu and choose Clone. A drop-down menu appears.

3. Choose Contour From. The mouse pointer changes to a large black arrow.

4. Click the source object. CorelDRAW! clones the contouring to the destination object.

Clearing a Contour

Now that you've created a contour, you can remove it. Click the contoured object; then open the Effects menu and choose the Clear Contour command.

From Here...

Refer to the following chapters for some ideas about how you can use contouring.

- Chapter 3, "A Detailed Look at Object Drawing," helps you to learn more about the types of objects you can draw and add contouring to.

- Chapter 16, "Creating Special Effects with Blending," provides an in-depth look at using blending for highlighting.

- Chapter 22, "Combining and Reusing Effects," gives you ideas and step-by-step instructions for using Contour along with other effects.

Chapter 19

Creating Special Effects with PowerLine

by Cyndie Klopfenstein

Even without a stylus or a digitizing pen and pad, you can create drawings that have the look of traditional tools. With PowerLines, drawn lines can take on the look of wood engraving, brush strokes, or even calligraphy. Figure 19.1 shows a simple illustration that uses several preset PowerLine styles. The labels show the exact name of the type of PowerLine.

In this chapter, you learn how to

- Add PowerLine styles to previously drawn art
- Edit PowerLine nodes
- Select from the preset list of PowerLines
- Change the width, speed, and ink flow with which your lines are drawn

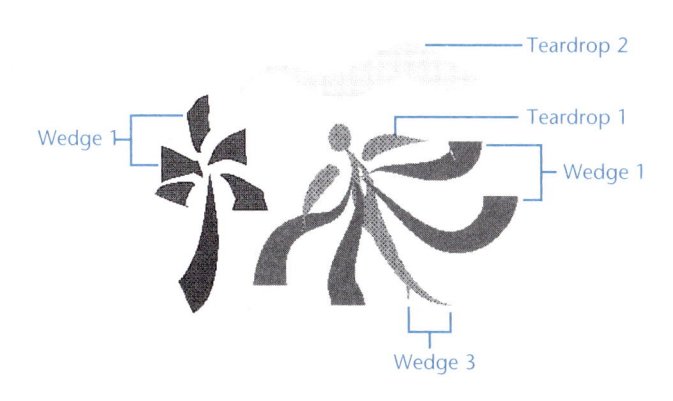

Fig. 19.1
This fairly simple illustration uses several different types of preset PowerLines.

Watching the Status Line

◄ See "Learning the Parts of the CorelDRAW! Screen," p. 18

As always, the status line is the perfect place to go to find out what you've selected and what you're supposed to be doing with it. If you've added a preset PowerLine style to a line, your status line should look like the one in figure 19.2. CorelDRAW! users often refer to this area for information about the type of object, the layer, and the group status—it's a good habit to get into.

Fig. 19.2
Refer to the status line for information about a selected object.

Working from the Menu

With the exception of Perspective and PowerClip, each of the special effects has a Roll-Up command. Each of these commands is found in the Effects menu or in the View menu under Roll-Ups. Other menus play a minor part in special effects, such as the Arrange menu. The Effects menu also is where you travel to when you want to clone or copy the PowerLine effect.

Using the PowerLine Roll-Up Window

◄ See "Using Roll-Up Windows," p. 25

This section discusses the options that are available in the PowerLine roll-up. The PowerLine roll-up has quite a few buttons, and some of them prompt the roll-up to take on a different view for further options. Most options require you to select that option or a series of options, and then click the Apply button in the PowerLine roll-up window. Figure 19.3 shows the buttons that are discussed in this section.

Fig. 19.3
Use the PowerLine roll-up for adding special effects to previously drawn lines or to lines as they are drawn.

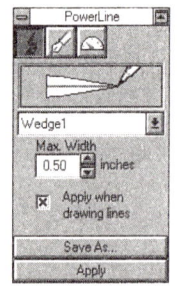

PowerLine Button

To draw PowerLines, you first need to display the PowerLine roll-up in the active window area and ensure that the PowerLine icon at the top left is selected. To the right of the button, you have several options that affect the PowerLines. We need to skip around on the buttons a bit, in order to logically explain their usage. So first let's move to the lower portion of the roll-up.

Apply When Drawing Lines

Use the check box Apply When Drawing Lines to make lines into PowerLines as each line is drawn. There are two modes of the Pencil tool to which you can apply PowerLines: the Freehand mode and the Bézier mode. Both make rather interesting PowerLines. You're not limited to adding PowerLines to just simple lines; try adding them to objects also.

◄ See "Drawing Straight Lines," p. 63

◄ See "Drawing Curved Lines," p. 68

Preset List Box

Add PowerLines to previously drawn lines by choosing the line with the Pick tool and then selecting a preset style from the drop-down list. Click Apply after making a selection to see it applied to your line. This list may look different from the one pictured in figure 19.4 if you already saved a few custom lines of your own. We get to Save As in a moment. For now, look to table 19.1 to see an example of the PowerLine and the name. These are the default PowerLines installed along with the CorelDRAW! program from the original disks. Use the Preset titled None to remove applied PowerLines from a selected line.

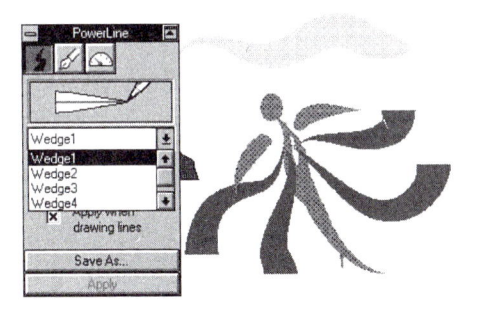

Fig. 19.4
The drop-down list allows you to choose a preset style and previews that style in the window above.

Table 19.1 Samples of Each of the Preset PowerLine Styles

Sample	Style
	Wedge 1
	Wedge 2
	Wedge 3
	Wedge 4
	Woodcut 1
	Woodcut 2
	Woodcut 3
	Woodcut 4
	Trumpet 1
	Trumpet 2
	Trumpet 3
	Trumpet 4
	Bullet 1
	Bullet 2
	Bullet 3
	Bullet 4
	Teardrop 1
	Teardrop 2

Maximum Width

In the Maximum Width field, you can type a numeric entry between .01 and 16 inches, with .5 inch being the default. You'll soon get to know the feel of a half-inch line as opposed to something narrower or thicker, and you'll feel confident about selecting a width that's proper for the current project. To see the effect of a maximum width setting, you must click Apply.

Nib Shape

Changing the nib shape can totally alter the look of a PowerLine. You can immediately go from soft rounded endings to lines to sharp, angled precision endings. When you click the Nib icon, it also changes the PowerLine roll-up to look like the one in figure 19.5.

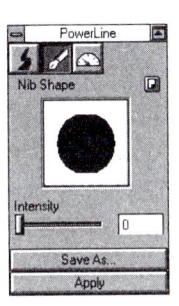

Fig. 19.5
When you select the Nib icon, the view or page of the roll-up changes so that you can define the nib shape.

You make changes to the nib by moving the cursor over the nib shape in the center of the window. When you do, the cursor changes to a cross-hair cursor. Click the image and drag to change the shape and angle. Click the Apply button as you make these changes to see them applied to a selected line.

Intensity

The intensity of a line is the width at which it draws at the widest point. To change the intensity of a line, type a number into the field or use the slider bar. You can enter a number up to 100, with the effect that a 90-degree angled line is at the maximum intensity or width.

Page Icon

The small dog-eared page icon allows you to change the Angle, Nib Ratio, and Intensity in a more precise manner. When you click this icon, the page of the roll-up shown in figure 19.6 appears. Here you can type a number rather than click and drag the nib shape. The ratio, angle, and intensity are interrelated in the same way here as in the primary view of nib shape editing.

Angle

When you change the angle of the nib, you will see the difference most in the ends and curves of lines. Changing the nib angle gives the same result as if you angled your paintbrush or calligraphy pen. To change the angle, you can type a value in the Angle field or use the click-and-drag method. The changes you make are applied to the view of the nib shape in the primary page of the nib shape roll-up.

Fig. 19.6
Click the dog-eared page icon to see this page of the PowerLine roll-up.

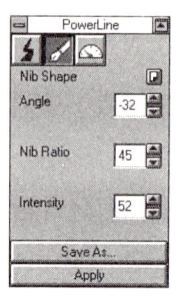

Nib Ratio

The Nib Ratio is how fast the line thins out. Choose a number up to 100 to give CorelDRAW! instructions on how far from the end of the line you want to start diminishing to a point. A smaller number makes for a shorter diminish distance.

Intensity

This works the same as the Intensity slider in the primary page—just type in a number. After you select values for the three fields, click Apply (or use Apply as you go). Changing even one of the values may have a pretty drastic effect on the lines that it is applied to.

Speed, Spread, Ink Flow, and Scale With Image

Click the Speed, Spread, and Ink Flow button to display the next page of the PowerLine roll-up. It should look like the one in figure 19.7, though your fields may contain different values. This page is actually two separate sections that aren't dependent on one another. The Speed and Spread work together, but the Ink Flow is a setting independent of those two.

Fig. 19.7
This is the page view of the roll-up when Speed, Spread, and Ink Flow is selected.

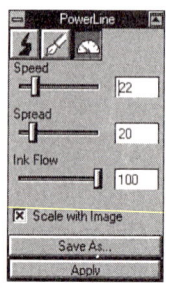

Speed

For a visual idea about the Speed setting, think about ice skating or roller skating around a curve. The faster you go, the wider the arc you make as you round the corner. With the Speed setting, you're actually widening the line at sharper curves to make up for the wide arc. When you draw curves sharper (slower Speed), you're actually making a thinner line.

A setting of more than zero in Nib Ratio or Speed is how line endings and curves are controlled. With a zero value in both ratio and speed, lines are drawn with pointed sharp turns and triangles at very sharp turns. If you have a ratio of zero and a speed of more than zero, sharp and very sharp curves are rounded and more smooth. If the speed is zero and the ratio is more than zero, sharp curves and line endings are trimmed to the value you entered in the nib angle field. If both ratio and speed are more than zero, the nib value takes precedence over speed and the curves are trimmed.

Spread

Entering a value of more than zero in the Speed field affects the Spread also. Larger values in this field make for a smoother-looking line, while smaller values make for rougher lines. This is partially the way that CorelDRAW! lines tend to imitate traditional tools such as pens and brushes. Brushes lay down smoother lines (higher spread value), because a brush stroke is made with a swash. Using a Rapidograph pen or ink pen requires more control, and, if drawn freehand, is usually less smooth (a lower spread value) than a brush stroke. Of course, with all the intermediate numbers between zero and 100, you can create almost any feel you're looking for. Take a look at figure 19.8 for an example of different Speed and Spread values added to the same lines.

◀ See "Reshaping a Curve or Object by Changing Its Nodes and Control Points," p. 72

Fig. 19.8
The Speed and Spread settings are most apparent at the ends of these lines. The line on the left has a speed of 100 and a spread of 8. The line on the right has a speed of 3 and a spread of 100.

The bumps in the lines are caused by nodes. So it could be said that a node is placed each time it feels a bump that you make with the mouse or stylus. The sensitivity of CorelDRAW! to the movements of your hand is basically what's in control here. You might also note that lines you draw with a stylus have fewer nodes and so are smoother in general than lines drawn with a mouse.

Because Speed and Spread depend on one another, Spread is dimmed if you have a zero value in the Speed window.

Ink Flow

Setting the ink flow rate is like having a slider scale on the side of a fountain pen or marker. How much ink flows through the point onto the paper? Once again, your options are between zero and 100. Use a value of zero and you'll have no ink in the pen, or the flow is cut off. Thinner portions of the line at a low number might also have no ink, or at least very little, or your closed-path shape may become a number of separate shapes. A value of 100 ensures that you have a full pen all the way to the end and through the thinner portions of the PowerLine. In figure 19.9, similar lines were drawn with different values in the Ink Flow field.

Fig. 19.9
On the left, an example of the line without PowerLine applied; in the center, the line is drawn with a low ink flow of 10. On the right, a similar line with a fuller pen: 80.

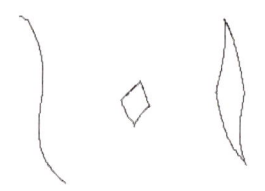

Scale With Image

After a PowerLine is added to a line, it becomes editable. The most primary edit is whether you want the maximum width of a PowerLine to scale in proportion to any scaling you apply to a line (we discuss other ways later in this chapter). If you check this box, the line width reduces in direct proportion to the reduction applied to the overall line. Remember that this scaling only works when you drag a corner handle of the object's bounding box to scale it (see fig. 19.10).

◀ See "Scaling and Sizing an Object," p. 184

> **Note**
> The Scale With Image characteristic is assigned when the PowerLine is first created. You can't change it later, so make sure you set it right the first time, especially if the object is difficult to re-create.

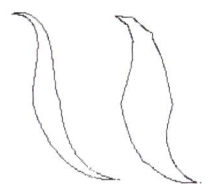

Fig. 19.10
The line on the left was scaled with the Scale With Image option checked; the one on the right didn't have this option checked.

Save As

With all these settings to go through, it's unlikely that you'd remember each of them exactly if you wanted to apply the same style PowerLine to another line.

Thankfully, there's Save As. Here you can save a set of options so the PowerLine you created appears in the Preset list. You can even edit one of the Presets and add it here. Click the Save As button, and you see the dialog box shown in figure 19.11.

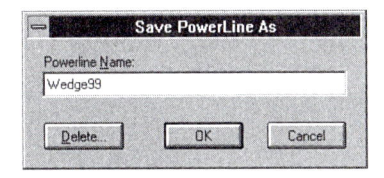

Fig. 19.11
With the Save PowerLine As dialog box, you can save your own custom PowerLines as presets.

Apply

Click the Apply button at the bottom of the PowerLine roll-up after you've chosen the options you want. If you don't like the results, use the buttons and options previously described above to alter the look, or choose a different style from the preset list.

Drawing with PowerLines

The step-by-step instructions are pretty simple for a PowerLine. You can add a PowerLine before or after you draw the line, but the steps are the same in either case with one exception. Both ways are listed here. Here's how to apply a PowerLine to already-drawn lines.

1. Choose the PowerLine roll-up from the Effects menu or press Ctrl+F8.

2. Select the line. The line is surrounded by handles.

3. Click the PowerLine icon and choose the PowerLine settings from each of the pages of the roll-up. If you need help, look for the option earlier in this chapter.

4. Click Apply. The line is redrawn with the settings you chose applied.

To apply PowerLines before they're drawn, follow these steps:

1. Choose the PowerLine roll-up from the Effects menu or press Ctrl+F8.

2. Click the Apply When Drawing Lines check box near the bottom of the roll-up.

3. Click the PowerLine icon and choose the PowerLine settings from each of the pages of the roll-up. Refer back in this chapter to the heading matching the option if you need help.

◀ See "Reshaping a Curve or Object by Changing Its Nodes and Control Points," p. 72

Troubleshooting

The PowerLines that I draw have very sharp corners.

The Speed setting needs to be adjusted lower. You might also lower the Intensity level if the Speed setting doesn't yield the required results.

The thin portions of the line are too thin.

Adjust the Ink Flow to a number closer to 100. You may be running low on ink in these areas. Adjusting the Intensity to a higher number will also help.

When I scale the image, my PowerLines don't scale proportionately.

You must select the Scale With Image option in the PowerLine roll-up (when you first create the image), and you must scale by dragging a handle.

Node Editing PowerLines

◀ See "Reshaping a Curve or Object by Changing Its Nodes and Control Points," p. 72

With the Shape tool and the Node Edit roll-up, you can make other modifications to a PowerLine without adjusting the settings that you chose. You're limited to staying within the maximum width setting any time the Nib intensity and the Speed are set to numbers above zero. You'll be reminded that these particular nodes cannot be edited by the caps that appear on the handles. The Node Edit roll-up is shown in figure 19.12. To node edit the PowerLine, use these steps:

1. Double-click a node with the Shape tool. The Node Edit roll-up appears in the active window.

2. Using the Shape tool, click the object to be edited.

Fig. 19.12
Using the Node Edit roll-up you can make changes to a PowerLine.

3. Click the Pressure Edit check box at the bottom of the Node Edit roll-up.

4. Select the options from the Node Edit roll-up as necessary.

5. Click on nodes of the PowerLine and edit them in the usual manner. Pressure-edit nodes allow you to adjust the thickness or width of your PowerLine shape.

> **Troubleshooting**
>
> *When using the Node Edit roll-up, I cannot seem to edit some of the handles.*
>
> You cannot edit handles past the maximum width when Speed and Nib Intensity are set to zero.

Copying a PowerLine

With the Effects menu, you can copy a PowerLine from one line to another. This is similar to saving it as a Preset and then Applying it, but it's a few less steps, and if you're not planning on ever needing these settings again, it's a good shortcut. As with all other Copy Effects modes, the outline and fill colors of the destination object (the object you're copying settings to) are not affected. To copy PowerLine settings to another line, use this numbered list:

1. Select the destination object.

2. Open the Effects menu, choose Copy, and then choose PowerLine From. The cursor changes to a black arrow.

3. Click the source object (the object that has PowerLine settings you want to copy). The destination object is redrawn with the settings of the source object.

Cloning a PowerLine

◄ See "Copying Objects," p. 105

Cloning is very similar to copying. In cloning, however, you have a master object (the source) and a clone (the destination). You can't make changes to a clone; changes must be made to the master, and then changes affect both the master and the clone. If you want to assure consistency throughout all the PowerLines and to have changes ripple through each of the PowerLines uniformly, this is great. Use these steps to clone a PowerLine.

1. Select the destination object.

2. Open the Effects menu and choose Clone; then choose PowerLine From. The cursor changes to a black arrow.

3. Click the master object (the object with PowerLine settings you want to clone). The clone is redrawn with the settings of the master object.

Removing a PowerLine

Removing a PowerLine is the same as applying a preset—you simply select None from the Preset list. Here are the steps:

1. Select the object for which you want to apply a Preset. (Even if the Preset is None.)

2. Choose the PowerLine roll-up from the Effects menu.

3. Click the PowerLine icon.

4. Use the up and down arrows of the drop-down Preset List to find None and select it.

5. Click the Apply button. The previously applied PowerLine styles are removed.

From Here…

Adding PowerLines to a completed drawing is an easy and effective way to dress it up. Try different PowerLines until you find one that compliments the look. If you develop a line style of your own, don't forget to add it to the preset list so that you can use it again. You may want to turn to these other chapters for help with object drawing and other special effects.

- For more information about the Node Edit roll-up go back to Chapter 3, "A Detailed Look at Object Drawing." The lessons that you learn there are easily applied to node editing here.

- If you're unaccustomed to working with lines, review Chapter 4, "Mastering Object Manipulations."

- You might want to start with a scan of an image that you trace and then add PowerLines to. Turn to Chapter 11, "Scanning Images into CorelDRAW!," if you need help digitizing the image.

- PowerLines, and all other special effects, have been gathered into a gallery along with the instructions for creating the examples in Chapter 22, "Combining and Reusing Effects."

Chapter 20

Creating Special Effects with Lens

by Cyndie Klopfenstein

Imagine looking at the world through rose-colored glasses—that's the lens effect. But with these lenses, you have more options than you get in a sunglass store. You have lenses that remove color, some that add color, those that change color, and even one that magnifies.

The *lens* is an object that is in front of another object or objects, from which it filters the colors. You cannot make a lens out of a group, but you can place a lens over a group. The lens must be a closed path, and it may or may not have a uniform fill, depending on the type of lens with which you are working. If the lens has no fill, the objects that are below it appear unchanged. An outline color applied to a lens will make the borders visible, though this may not be the style you're striving for. With the multilayer option, you can even apply lenses to objects on different layers.

◀ See "Working with Interior Fills," p. 146

Working with Lens is probably the simplest of the special effects. It doesn't help you draw, add perspective, or even blend, but it is a great way of looking at things. A lens over your art can add color, limit the color showing through, or magnify the artwork. In this chapter, you learn to do the following:

- Change the opacity of lenses
- Apply lenses over different patterns and textures, and predict the results
- Copy the lens settings from one object to another
- Remove applied lenses

◀ See "Learning the Parts of the CorelDRAW! Screen," p. 18

Watching the Status Line

The status line, which by default is at the bottom of the active window, will dynamically track your moves. As it watches what you're up to, it reports what objects are selected. This will help you to know what is selected, and with that you'll know what your options are. With lens, you have not just the lens but also the objects that it filters. The status line below, in figure 20.1, is a result of selecting a lens with the Pick tool.

Fig. 20.1
For information about the selected object, look to the status line.

Working from the Menu

▶ See "Combining and Reusing Effects," p. 515

Like other special effects, the roll-up for the Lens is in the Effects menu. You'll also return to this menu for Copy and Clone, which is about the only reason to come back once you have the roll-up open on the screen. Besides, the roll-up can follow you around to wherever you're working, something you can't even train a menu to do.

Using the Lens Roll-Up Window

▶ See "Combining and Reusing Effects," p. 515

Using the filter options of the Lens roll-up is very difficult to illustrate in black and white. That's one of the reasons for the color insert. Feel free to turn to that section as you work through the rest of this chapter to see some examples of Lens effects.

Before we get to the instructions on how you actually create a lens, we need to explore the options available. With the exception of drawing the objects over which the lens is placed, all of the lens functions are found in the Lens roll-up pictured in figure 20.2.

Fig. 20.2
Use the Lens roll-up for making a lens out of an object.

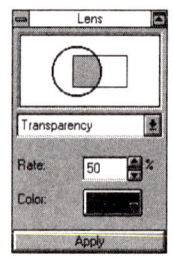

Type of Lens

From this drop-down list you can choose one of nine different lens styles. As discussed in the first paragraph, each lens style has a different function, but some share similarities. By using the drop-down list, clicking to select, and then clicking Apply, the type of lens you select is applied to the active object.

Transparency

This is the default lens type. It creates an illusion of a transparent sheet laid over the top of your artwork. The opacity, or the clearness, of the transparency is controlled by the Rate. The higher the rate number, the more transparent (clear) the object. At 100% the object is perfectly clear—as though you are viewing the objects below through a pane of glass. By decreasing the rate number, the opacity increases. The lens obscures the art behind it as though you are looking through frosted glass. Since this type of lens can have only a uniform fill color, the color becomes more obvious the lower the opacity rating is. The objects below this lens can have a uniform fill, fountain fill, two-color fill, full-color pattern, or bitmap fill. Each of these objects are affected by the lens over the top of it. At 0% the object is so opaque that the objects below it are not visible. Use the numeric field to type a number in or use the nudge arrows to select a number.

◀ See "Using Patterned Fills," p. 152

Magnify

This one's rather obvious. The objects below this lens are enlarged (see fig. 20.3), and you choose the value by typing it in the field or using the nudge arrows to select a value. Use any value between 1.0 and 10.0 in one tenth of a percentage. The higher the amount setting is, the smaller the area encompassed by the lens due to increased magnification. The Magnify lens shouldn't have a fill since the information is disregarded.

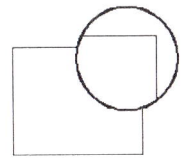

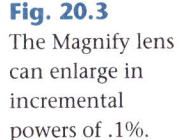

Fig. 20.3
The Magnify lens can enlarge in incremental powers of .1%.

Brighten

To darken or lighten objects below a lens (like the light source of the Extrude effect), use the Brighten lens option. Your lens can have a fill, but the fill is ignored with this type of lens. The Rate field in this lens type ranges from

–100% to 100% with zero being the turning point. Numbers above zero brighten the objects and numbers below zero darken the objects. The closer you get to 100%, the brighter the objects get. The closer you get to –100%, the darker the object gets. Look at figure 20.4 for an example of a brighter lens.

Fig. 20.4
Use the Brighten lens to add or remove the lightness of an illustration or picture.

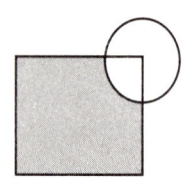

Invert

An Invert lens converts objects containing a uniform fill underneath to their CMYK representative and then changes the colors to the object's exact opposite. If you have a bitmap image made up of only black and white, the object appears as a negative image, much like a negative piece of film. If an Invert lens is placed over a pattern fill, the colors of the pattern are transposed.

Tip
In CorelDRAW! 5, the Color Limit lens allows objects drawn in some other colors to shine through a lens, even when the rate is set to 100%.

Color Limit

Color Limit is somewhat like the Transparency lens except that the Color Limit lens hides all the color below. Black and the color of the lens are the only colors not hidden by the Color Limit lens. White and light colors of the filtered objects are changed to match the lens color. The color that is allowed through the lens is limited, as the name implies. When the Rate field is 0%, there is a clear lens, no color is filtered out, and the lens itself shows no color. At 100% only, the lens color and black show through. Use the field to type in a value or use the nudge arrows to raise or lower the percentage in 5% increments.

▶ See "Working with Color," p. 616

Color Add

Color Add adds the color value of the lens to the colors below it. A red lens over yellow objects would produce orange. Color Add uses the rules you learned in kindergarten about primary and secondary colors. Entering a value of 0% in the Rate field adds no color to the objects below, and the lens fill cannot be seen. At 100%, the full color of the lens is added to the objects below. Type a number in the field or use the nudge arrows to change the value in increments of 5%. Colors made of light are different from colors made of pigment. All colors mixed together in light create white rather than a muddy brown. Therefore, if you place a colored lens over white objects, the lens turns white. The colors below must be colors other than white in order for the lens to have an effect.

Tinted Grayscale

If your document contains a color photo, the Tinted Grayscale lens can convert this photo to a halftone. Lighter colors are converted to light grays while darker colors are converted to dense grays. Black remains black. If you color the fill of the lens, you can create a single-color halftone in the color of your choice. Applying this lens to a bitmap changes the blacks of the bitmap to the lens color and changes the shades of the bitmap to similar shades of lens color, whereas white remains white. When the Tinted Grayscale lens is applied to a pattern, the colors of the pattern alternate between the lens color and white.

Heat Map

The Heat Map lens duplicates the effect of looking at an image through infrared glasses. This lens takes the regular color wheel of CorelDRAW!, tosses away all warm colors except yellow, orange, and red, and eliminates all cool colors except blue, violet, and cyan. White is also a retained color. A color wheel arranges these colors with the cool colors at the top of the color wheel. In this arrangement, 0 and 100% become the same value. The bottom of the color wheel is for the warm colors, with red at 50%. When you type a number in the Rotation field, you are moving around the color wheel. Using 50% changes the cool colors of the filtered object to red. When you choose Heat Map, a new page appears in the Lens roll-up. Figure 20.5 illustrates this feature of the Heat Map.

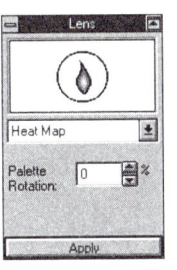

Fig. 20.5
The Heat Map option adds a Rotation field to the page of the Lens roll-up.

None

This choice from the scrollable drop-down list will remove any applied lens effect added to an object.

Color

Fill color can be added to lens objects using the Lens roll-up. To add a uniform fill to a lens object, click the More button. (This button appears if Transparency, Color Limit, Color Add, or Tinted Grayscale lenses are selected.) Take a look at table 20.1 to see which lenses can contain a fill, and how fill, or lack of fill, affects the objects below.

See "Working with Solid Fills," p. 150

See "Using Patterned Fills," p. 152

See "Working with Gradated (Fountain) Fills," p. 170

Table 20.1 The Result of Adding a Filter

Lens Type	Fill of Lens	Fill Types that Can Be Filtered
Transparency	Any color	Uniform, fountain, two-color or full-color pattern, bitmap fill
Magnify	Fill color ignored	Uniform, fountain, two-color or full-color pattern, bitmap fill
Color Limit	Any color	Uniform, two-color or full-color pattern, bitmap fill
Color Add	Any color	Uniform, two-color or full-color pattern, bitmap fill
Brighten	Fill color ignored	Uniform, two-color or full-color pattern, bitmap fill
Invert	Fill color ignored	Uniform, two-color or full-color pattern, bitmap fill
Grayscale	Any color	Full-color pattern, bitmap fill
Heat Map	None	Uniform, fountain, two-color or full-color pattern, bitmap fill

Apply

When you select an option from the Lens roll-up, you must click the Apply button for that option to take effect. Some effects don't require the Apply button, such as Copy and Clone, but these options are from the Effects menu. Effects from the roll-up menu are controlled by the Apply button.

Creating a Lens for Objects

To apply a lens to an object, you first need to draw the object and then draw another object to be used as the lens. Use the steps below to take it from here.

1. Select the lens object.

2. Choose Lens Roll-Up from the Effects menu. The roll-up appears in the window area.

Tip
Although you can't save the Lens settings you choose, as you can Envelope and PowerLine settings, you can save them to the Presets or Styles roll-ups.

3. Choose the type of lens you want from the drop-down list.

4. If you choose a lens style that requires a rate, type it in or use the nudge buttons to set Rate.

5. Use the Color button to apply color to the lens object when you choose a lens that uses color.

6. Click the Apply button.

Troubleshooting

When I choose a lens from the scrollable list, nothing happens.

Make sure that you click the Apply button after making your choices.

I can't see any of the objects behind my transparent lens.

The opacity of the lens is controlled by the Rate field. 0% makes the lens completely opaque.

I've added color to my Brighten lens but it doesn't show.

Fill color is ignored when the Brighten lens is chosen.

Copying Lens Effect

The settings that you have chosen for a lens can be copied to another lens object. The fill and outline settings, however, cannot be copied. To copy the lens, use these steps:

1. Select the destination object (to what you want to apply the settings) with the Pick tool.

2. Open the Effects menu, choose Copy, and then choose Lens From. The cursor changes into a black arrow.

3. With the special cursor, click the source object (from where you want to get the settings). The destination object is redrawn with the settings of the source object.

A lens is an object independent of the objects below it which the lens filters. For this reason, you can freely edit the lens without affecting your drawing. Using the handles, the lens can be resized or stretched. With the Pick tool, you can move the lens to a new location and the objects that now reside below it will be filtered.

From Here...

Working with lenses requires a piece of artwork. Lens is not a stand-alone feature—you must have something below it to view. Turn to these other chapters if you need help creating art or want to get a preview of a particular lens effect.

- For help with drawing objects to which you want to apply the Lens feature, go back to Chapter 3, "A Detailed Look at Object Drawing."

- If you need help with color, see Chapter 5, "Modifying Object Outlines and Interior Fills."

- More so than with the other special effects chapters, you need to go from here to Chapter 22, "Combining and Reusing Effects." Since the Lens special effect works primarily with color, that chapter shows you how these options affect objects.

- Lens works great with CorelPHOTO-PAINT, which you can find out more about in Chapter 25, "Photograph Touch-Up with CorelPHOTO-PAINT."

Chapter 21

Creating Special Effects with PowerClip

by Cyndie Klopfenstein

Take a piece of artwork, or even several layers of artwork, and call this the dough. Make yourself a cookie cutter (also known as a PowerClip) and then punch it down on your artwork. Pull the cookie cutter away, and you have a trimmed piece of artwork, exactly the same shape as the cutter. You also can create a cookie cutter made up of individual shapes and group them all together before you punch the dough. After you pull away the cutter, you can separate the pieces—maintaining the cut shape and the integrity of the contents. Figure 21.1 shows examples of what you can do with a PowerClip.

◀ See "A Detailed Look at Object Drawing," p. 61

Fig. 21.1
PowerClip is much like a cookie cutter, punching your trimmed artwork from the sheet of dough.

The contents (the objects that are clipped) and the container (the object that is used to clip the contents) can both have the full gamut of fills available in CorelDRAW!—no fill, uniform fill, fountain, two- and four-color patterns, or textures. Each can be either a closed path, grouped objects, or artistic text. The contents can also be a bitmap image.

PowerClip is somewhat similar to a mask. You use an object to mask away items you don't want to show, or to accent the objects under the clip. In this chapter, you learn the following:

- About each of the types of PowerClips
- How to reduce a complex drawing to only the part that you need by using a PowerClip
- How to make a PowerClip from an existing object
- What happens to the fill of a PowerClip
- Cloning and copying the PowerClip special effect to other containers

Watching the Status Line

When you work with a PowerClip, the status line should look like the one shown in figure 21.2. The status line will help you to identify a PowerClip after you've clicked on it. When a PowerClip is formed, it's often difficult to see it for exactly what it is, especially in the Wireframe view. Use the status line when you work with multiple layers to be clipped, or when you try to edit a PowerClip within a PowerClip—using the status line is much easier than guessing what you grabbed hold of.

Fig. 21.2
The status line helps you to find objects that might have a PowerClip applied.

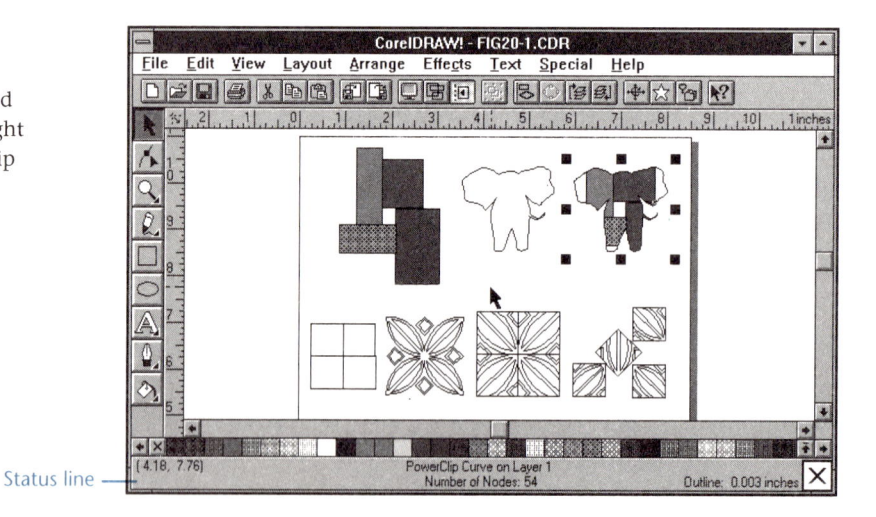

Working from the Menu

PowerClip doesn't have a roll-up window. Each of its options is listed in the Effects menu, although some other roll-ups can be used with PowerClip. The primary menu function is, of course, PowerClip. From this, you get a submenu from which you can choose Place Inside Container or Edit Contents, among other things. This chapter walks you through the steps for creating a PowerClip, but now you can take a look at the menu to get an idea of the options and their location.

Making a PowerClip

Making a PowerClip is quite simple. You need an item to clip (the *content object*) and an item to clip with (the *container object*). The contents can be anything that CorelDRAW! either draws or supports. For instance, it might be art that you created in CorelPHOTO-PAINT or something that you drew with the Pen tool. Whatever the item, follow these steps to add a PowerClip:

1. Select the Content object. It will be surrounded by a bounding box.

2. Open the Effects menu and choose PowerClip; then choose Place Inside Container. The cursor changes to a black arrow.

3. Click the Container object. The contents are placed into the center of the Container object.

In figure 21.3, you can see the end result of a simple PowerClip. The contents and container are from the Symbol roll-up window of CorelDRAW!. A PowerClip is nearly the opposite of an envelope, which would force the contents to follow the shape of the envelope. With a PowerClip, the content retains its shape, but the excess is clipped away.

Fig. 21.3
Use the Effects menu after you select content to apply a PowerClip. The contents here were made by drawing several boxes of different color placed side by side.

Making a PowerClip from a Group

◄ See "Grouping Objects," p. 120

PowerClips also can be made from groups of objects by selecting all the objects to be grouped and then choosing Group from the Arrange menu. After the items are grouped, you can clip contents with the group, just as you would with a single container. After you apply the PowerClip, you can separate the items by choosing Ungroup from the Arrange menu and pulling the separated objects to different locations, still maintaining the clip. See figure 21.4 for ideas on how to use this feature.

Fig. 21.4
This PowerClip started as a group applied to a graphic. Then the parts were moved apart.

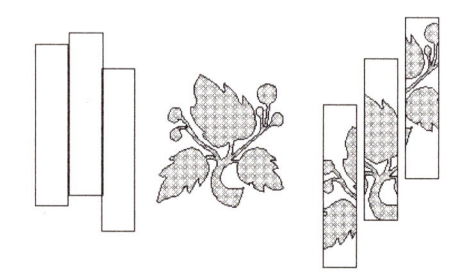

Locking and Unlocking PowerClip

◄ See "Selecting Objects," p. 94

When you use the Lock Contents option from the Object menu, exactly that happens: the contents are locked to the container. The benefits of locking the two together are that any rotation, move, or scale applied affects both the content and the container equally and proportionally. When you disable this feature, the container can be moved without taking the contents along for the ride. You can use this feature to move the content around inside the container. To unlock the two objects, follow these steps:

1. Select the container object.

2. Using the right mouse button, open the Effects menu and choose PowerClip. Point to the container object and press the right mouse button to display the Object menu.

3. From the resulting drop-down menu, select Lock Contents to PowerClip by clicking on it.

4. Move the container to the new position.

5. Choose Lock Contents to PowerClip again. This fastens the two back together so that you don't inadvertently drag the container off to some new location, leaving the contents behind.

Editing the Contents of a PowerClip

After you apply a PowerClip, the contents can still be edited. While you're in the editing mode, a temporary layer for the container and the contents is created. You can see the layers if you access the Layers roll-up window, but they are not part of the drawing layer. While you're editing a PowerClip, the drawing and page control operations are unavailable. You can use the drawing layer, but only on the entire PowerClip, not while it's separated for editing. To make edits to a PowerClip, follow these steps:

◀ See "Reshaping a Curve or Object by Changing Its Nodes and Control Points," p. 72

1. Select the PowerClip object on the page. The object is surrounded by a bounding box.

2. Open the Effects menu and choose PowerClip; then choose Edit Contents.

3. Make the changes to the content object(s).

4. Open the Effects menu and choose PowerClip; then choose Finish Editing this Level.

If you have more than one layer of PowerClips (because you can clip a PowerClip, and then clip that PowerClip, and so on), choose Edit Contents until you reach the layer you need to edit. After you make all the edits, choose Finish Editing this Layer to return to the previous layer and so on until you exit the editing mode altogether. You can stop at a layer and make an edit before returning to each previous layer.

Combining a PowerClip with Other Special Effects

PowerClip can create even more complex clipping by combining the clipping with special effects such as Blend, Contour, and Extrude. Chapter 22, "Combining and Reusing Effects," is dedicated to the use of this and other special effects. In Chapter 22, you find several examples of how special effects complement one another, and how they complement your artwork. Figure 21.5 shows several examples of combined special effects, but for more extensive work turn to Chapter 22.

Fig. 21.5
PowerClip combined with Perspective (top left), Extrude (top right), Blend (middle left), Contour (middle right), and the Magnify Lens (bottom).

Copying a PowerClip Effect

You can copy a PowerClip in two ways. First, you can open the Edit menu and choose Copy. The resulting duplicate PowerClip is of both the container and the contents. In the second method, you use the Effects menu, and the steps are somewhat more complicated. Follow this numbered list for help in copying in this manner.

1. Click on a new content object.

2. Open the Effects menu and choose Copy, and then choose PowerClip From in the drop-down menu.

3. When the cursor changes to a black arrow, click the PowerClip from which you want to copy the style. The selected contents are placed in a duplicate container of the style you clicked.

As with all other special effects you copy from, the object fill and outline don't change when you apply a duplicate PowerClip.

Cloning a PowerClip Effect

Cloning, which is similar to copying, is also found in the Effects menu. The difference between a clone and a copy is that you cannot make edits directly to a clone; you must edit the master (the item the clone was made from). Cloning is similar to copy in the Edit menu because the changes made to the master's contents aren't reflected in the clone, only in the container.

Removing a PowerClip

When you want to delete a PowerClip, you actually split the container from the contents. The contents take on their original full size after the PowerClip is removed. To remove a PowerClip, follow these steps:

1. Use the Pick tool to select the PowerClip.
2. Open the Effects menu and choose PowerClip.
3. From the drop-down menu, choose Extract Contents.

Troubleshooting

I'm in the Edit Contents mode, but I'm unable to edit the objects with the drawing tools.

All drawing edits made to a PowerClip must be made outside the editing mode, while the content and container are still joined.

I've tried several times to place my contents within the container in order to trim at a specific location, but the contents are placed in exactly the same position each time.

PowerClip contents are always clipped to the exact center of the content and the container. To change this, open the Effects menu and choose Edit Contents.

I've placed my contents inside an open path, but now I can't find the contents.

The PowerClip enables you to place contents inside a path, but the object cannot be seen until the path is closed.

From Here...

You can use nearly any object as a PowerClip container, and you can have nearly any object as the contents. Other chapters of this book help you to draw container and contents objects, to use the PowerClip in combination with other special effects, and to use PowerClip with other CorelDRAW! applications. Turn to these chapters as a place to begin exploring.

- Chapter 4, "Mastering Object Manipulations," gives you a refresher course in using the drawing tools.

- Chapter 22, "Combining and Reusing Effects," shows full-color samples of PowerClip and illustrates how it can be used with other special effects.

- Chapter 26, "Advanced CorelPHOTO-PAINT," shows you useful ways to create contents for containers.

Chapter 22

Combining and Reusing Effects

by Cyndie Klopfenstein

In Chapters 13 through 20, you learned how to use and apply each of the different special effects included with CorelDRAW!. In this chapter, you walk through the creation of illustrations that combine and mix the different effects. As you look at these illustrations and read through these steps, not only will you learn how to make them work for your own drawings, but you'll get ideas from them. If you turn to the first section of color plates in this book, you find the final illustrations in full color.

Sometimes the most difficult part about using any electronic application is that you learn a way to use a tool and then never expand on that basic knowledge. With this chapter, you see several ways to use each of the special effects tools, and perhaps then you'll challenge yourself to find even more.

You progress through the tools, accumulating special effects skills as you go. Feel free to turn back to the special effects chapter of the same title for more in-depth information about the buttons and options of the roll-ups.

Special effects are probably the most empowering part of CorelDRAW!. By applying everything from extrusions to perspective, you can easily add mild accents or dramatic flair to your hand-drawn or scanned artwork. In this chapter, a combination of all the special effects chapters, you learn to:

- Use one special effect to pick up where another has shortcomings
- Add perspective without using the Perspective special effect, or in addition to the Perspective special effect

- Add in objects from other roll-up windows that do not control the special effects, such as Text and Presets

- Use the templates, styles, and presets for reapplying custom sets of special effects

Diminishing with Perspective

Adding Perspective, probably the simplest of the special effects, doesn't even have a roll-up window, but don't underestimate this effect. When you're trying to create a realistic look to a drawing, getting the vanishing points of the objects to align would be difficult if it weren't for the automation of Perspective. Just getting perspective added to an object is quite a task sometimes, especially if you're working with a group of objects. In the next sections, you explore the task of adding perspective to single and grouped objects, and then take that knowledge even farther by adding other special effects.

Simple Perspective with a Blend

Figure 22.1 starts out with a house. It's particularly easy to draw because it's a symbol dragged from the Symbols roll-up window (see fig. 22.2). To create an effect like the one you see here, you need to be able to add color to a chosen symbol. Some symbols are a single object; other symbols, like this house, are a group of objects or surfaces. Each can be filled or outlined. To do this, drag the symbol you want from the Symbols roll-up (Ctrl+F11). After placing the illustration of the house on the document area, open the Arrange menu and choose the Break Apart (Ctrl+K) command. This separates the individual surfaces so that they can be filled or outlined with different colors and shades.

Fig. 22.1
The house is a symbol pulled from the Symbols roll-up in the Buildings category. (See color plate 1.)

With the Pen and Rectangle tools, you can add and fill a lawn. To create a row of houses like those in figure 22.3, select the house and lawn and duplicate them several times. Use the Pick tool to select and move each duplication, placing them side by side. Figure 22.4 shows the result of duplicating and moving the objects. You might find it easiest to group the house and lawn together using Group (Ctrl+G) from the Arrange menu before you begin duplicating.

Diminishing with Perspective **517**

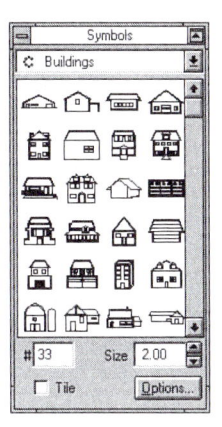

Fig. 22.2
Most of the illustrations in this chapter use symbols dragged from the Symbols roll-up.

After you finish duplicating and moving the objects, group the entire set together using the Group command again. Choose the Pick tool, click on the group, open the Effects menu, and choose Perspective. Move the vanishing point cross hairs so the village fades toward the horizon.

Use the Pen tool to draw the street and add perspective to it in the same way, possibly grouping together several lines or shapes used to make the street. In this example, a little extra perspective is added to the lawn and street to help with the effect. The perspective is made more drastic—in fact, even somewhat out of sync—with the houses by choosing Ungroup (Ctrl+U) from the Arrange menu to separate the houses and lawns and making a new group of the lawns and street. Once done, the vanishing points of this new group are moved independently of the house.

◄ See "Grouping Objects," p. 120

Fig. 22.3
After completing a house and lawn, use the Pick tool to marquee the objects, group them, and duplicate them. (See color plate 2.)

Fig. 22.4
After several duplications, you have a row of houses. (See color plate 3.)

518   Chapter 22—Combining and Reusing Effects

◄ See "Making Just a Blend," p. 452

In the final stage (see fig. 22.5), duplicate the entire row of houses again, move them to a lower layer (To Back, Shift+Pg Dn, in the Arrange menu) and to the left, and fill them with gray to give the illusion of depth. For the background, draw two ovals, one small and the other large enough to span as much background as you like. Use the Blend roll-up (Ctrl+B) to make a blend from two ovals and move entire blend to the back layer (see fig. 22.6).

Fig. 22.5
The final illustration also uses the Blend roll-up to create a background. (See color plate 4.)

Fig. 22.6
With the Blend roll-up, you can use blended tints for background color.

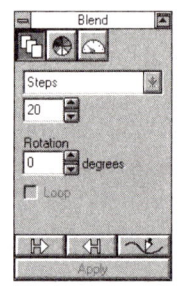

Perspective for Artistic Text

◄ See "Working with Artistic Text," p. 212

To create perspective for Artistic text, type the characters and use the Text roll-up (Ctrl+F2) window (in the Text menu) to choose a font and size. Figure 22.7 shows the Text roll-up window with the CorelDRAW! library of fonts loaded. After this step, you can add perspective to stretch the text by choosing Perspective from the Effects menu (see fig. 22.8). After you do this, the Perspective bounding box surrounds the text and is ready for editing. Click and drag one of the handles at the corners of the bounding box, or click and drag one or both of the vanishing points.

To create the cover and pages, use the Pen tool or Rectangle tool to draw the cover. For pages, select the cover with the Pick tool and duplicate it several times. Click and drag each page to move it into position if you don't like where it was placed during duplication. While continuing to use the Pick tool, click every other page as you hold down the Shift key. This allows you to make a multiple selection and change the fill color of only the selected pages to black.

Color Plate 1
The house is a symbol pulled from the Symbols roll-up. (See fig. 22.1.)

Color Plate 2
After completing a house and lawn, use the Pick tool to marquee the objects and duplicate them. (See fig. 22.3.)

Color Plate 3
After several duplications, you have a row of houses. (See fig. 22.4.)

Color Plate 4
To create the final illustration, you use the Blend roll-up to create a background. (See fig. 22.5.)

All The News That's Fit to Print

Color Plate 5
Add text by using the Type roll-up and then add perspective. (See fig. 22.7.)

All The News That's Fit to Print

Color Plate 6
Choose Perspective from the Effects menu to add depth to the box. (See fig. 22.8.)

Color Plate 7
Several elements here contain added perspective. (See fig. 22.9.)

Color Plate 8
To complete the illustration, more symbols (the hand and the face) were dragged from the Symbols roll-up. (See fig. 22.10.)

Color Plate 9
Completely finish the art before adding an envelope. (See fig. 22.13.)

Color Plate 10
The envelope makes subtle changes to the illustration, but the result is a vastly different look. (See fig. 22.14.)

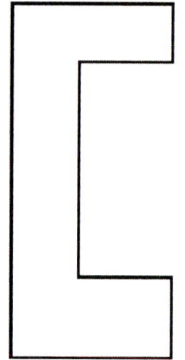

Color Plate 11
First, an envelope is copied from the object on the right to the man. (See fig. 22.15.)

Color Plate 12
The result of adding a sharp-edged envelope to a free-form object should look something like this. (See fig. 22.16.)

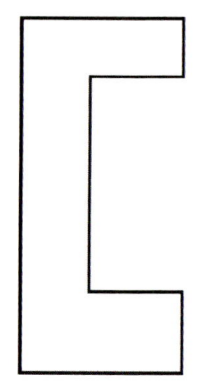

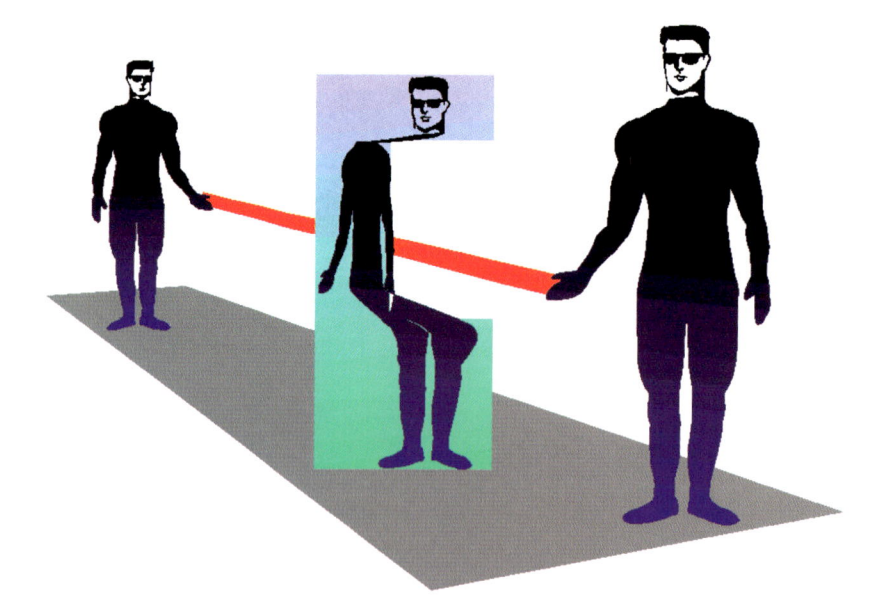

Color Plate 13
Duplicating the man and accenting with additional elements gives this drawing a three-dimensional illusion. (See fig. 22.17.)

Mapping Nodes Off *Mapping nodes On, Nose to nose*

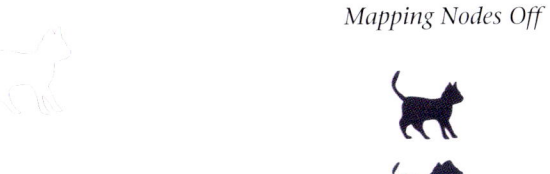

Color Plate 14
Cat and dog symbols from the Symbols roll-up. (See fig. 22.18.)

Color Plate 15
Two tries were needed to achieve the desired results. It was also necessary to map the nodes at the tips of the noses. (See fig. 22.19.)

Color Plate 16
By moving the control object to the right, you angle the blend. Additional objects are added and filled to achieve the final illustration. (See fig. 22.20.)

Color Plate 17
A house chosen from the Symbols roll-up. (See fig. 22.22.)

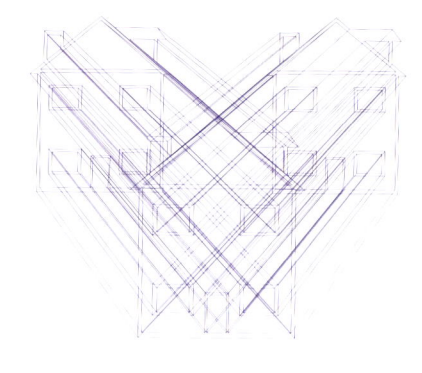

Color Plate 18
After applying two separate extrusions and moving the vanishing points to reside opposite each other. (See fig. 22.23.)

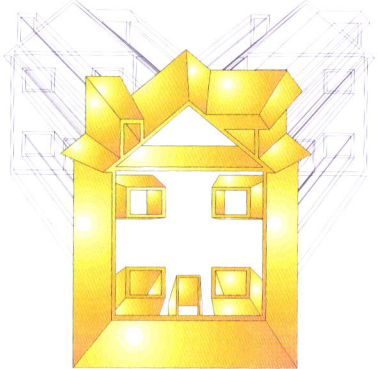

Color Plate 19
Since Extrude makes surfaces from the selected objects, the surfaces can be filled. (See fig. 22.24.)

Color Plate 20
Using the Blend roll-up, the bushes were rotated around the bottom of the house. (See fig. 22.25.)

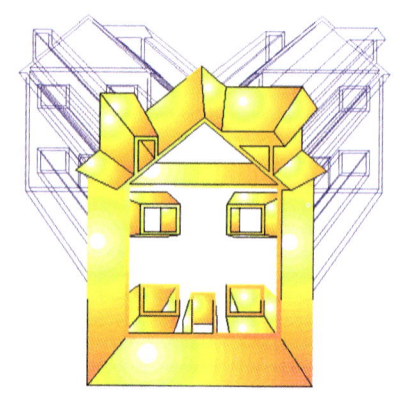

Color Plate 21
To begin an illustration like this one, type the letters and then choose a font and size from the Text roll-up. (See fig. 22.26.)

Color Plate 22
Add the extrusion (small back) and move the vanishing point to the upper-right corner. Use a Shade fill from the Extrude roll-up. (See fig. 22.27.)

Color Plate 23
The extrusion is then separated (Arrange menu), and the surfaces are pulled away from the main body of the extrusion. (See fig. 22.28.)

Color Plate 24
Contouring was added to the musical note with a setting of To Center. (See fig. 22.29.)

Color Plate 25
The PowerLines were added before and after these lines were drawn. (See fig. 22.30.)

Color Plate 26
Applying an invert lens changes colors to their opposites. (See fig. 22.31.)

Color Plate 27
Applying a magnify lens zooms in on that portion behind the lens. (See fig. 22.32.)

Color Plate 28
Applying a brighten lens at a 35-percent rate makes that portion of the drawing brighter. (See Chapter 22, "Combining and Reusing Effects.")

Color Plate 29
Applying a color lens, with light blue color and a 50-percent rate. (See Chapter 22, "Combining and Reusing Effects.")

Color Plate 30
Applying a color limit lens with light blue color and a 50-percent rate. (See Chapter 22, "Combining and Reusing Effects.")

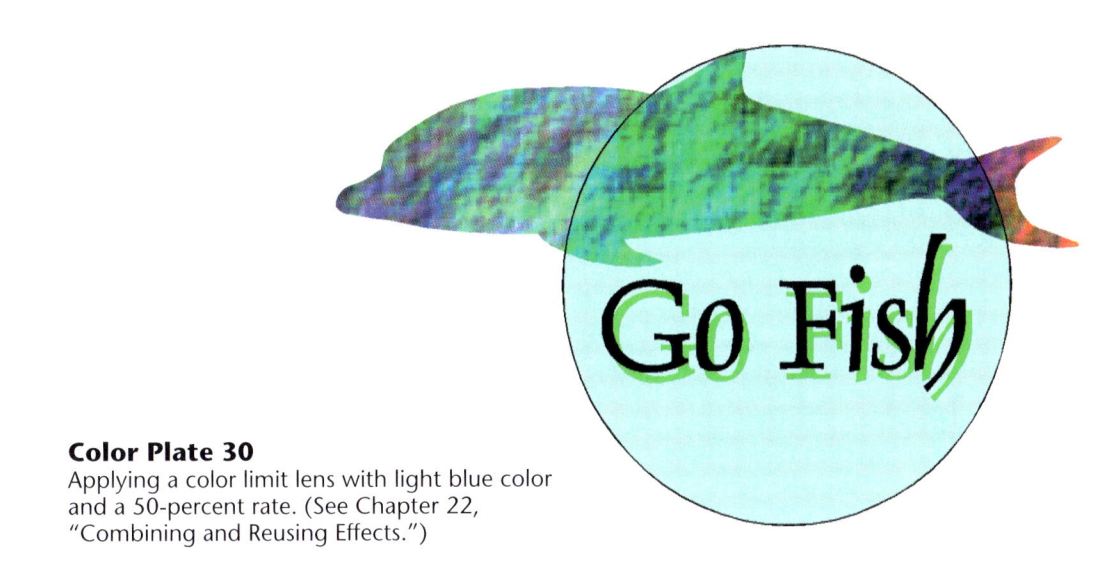

Color Plate 31
This is a heatmap lens with a 90-percent palette rotation. (See Chapter 22, "Combining and Reusing Effects.")

Color Plate 32
This is a transparency lens with a 75-percent rate. The fish has a rainbow surface. (See Chapter 22, "Combining and Reusing Effects.")

Color Plate 33
This is a tinted grayscale lens using a light blue tint. (See Chapter 22, "Combining and Reusing Effects.")

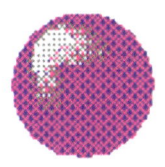

Color Plate 34
Draw a smaller crescent-shaped object inside the circle and color with a light shade. Blend the two objects together. Wireframe view is on the left. (See fig. 22.33.)

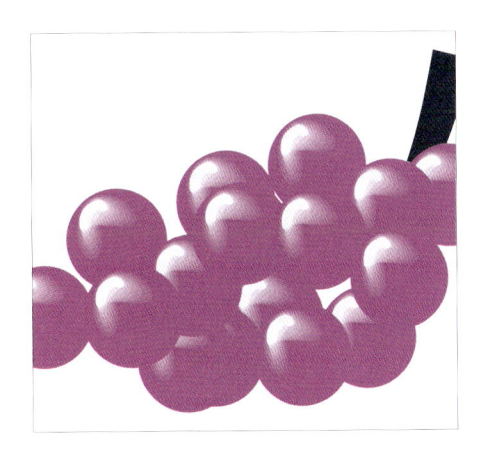

Color Plate 35
This illustration uses a blend, a PowerLine, and a PowerClip. (See fig. 22.34.)

Color Plate 36
The original photo of the circuit board, imported from Photo-CD. (See fig. 22.35.)

Color Plate 37
With the circle for the blow-up drawn, the drawing is ready to apply a PowerClip and then a lens. (See fig. 22.36.)

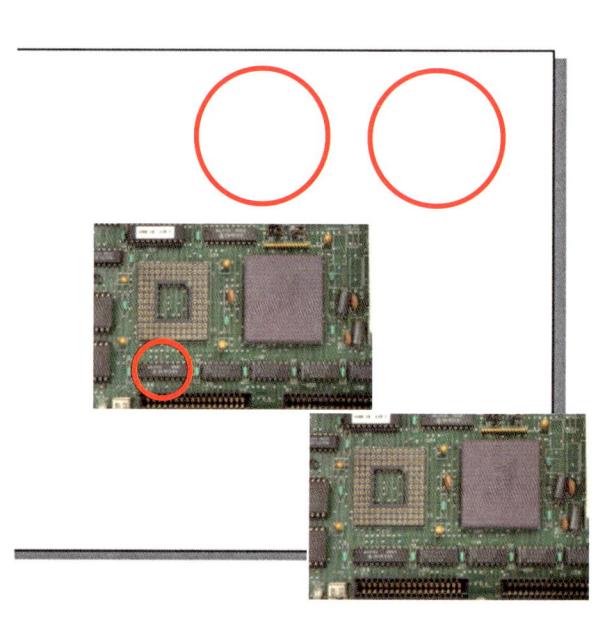

Color Plate 38
The final drawing shows the original photo and a blow-up of an individual chip. (See fig. 22.37.)

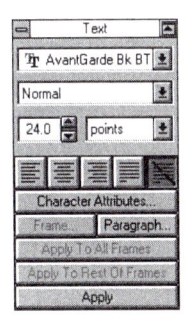

Fig. 22.7
Type the text using the Text roll-up window to add perspective. (See color plate 5.)

Fig. 22.8
Choose Perspective from the Effects menu to add depth to the text. (See color plate 6.)

◀ See "Copying Perspective," p. 419

Now, to add perspective that matches that already applied to the Artistic text, select all the pages and the cover, and group them using the Group command (Ctrl+G) in the Arrange menu. From here, open the Effects menu and choose Copy Perspective From. With the special cursor (black arrow), click the Artistic text, and the pages take on the angle of Perspective copied from the text.

Fig. 22.9
Several elements here contain added perspective. (See color plate 7.)

When you finish the right side, select, duplicate, and flip vertically the entire group of cover and pages to make the left side of the book. Additional elements (such as shapes and symbols) can be added to complement the finished piece. In the example, these were drawn using the Pen tool, the Symbols roll-up (Ctrl+F11) window, and ovals. The oval in the upper-left corner has been further modified by making it a lens. To create a lens, select an object and choose the Lens roll-up (Alt+F3) window from the Effects menu (see fig. 22.10).

◀ See "Mirroring an Object," p. 188

◀ See "Creating a Lens for Objects," p. 504

Fig. 22.10
In the finished piece, more Symbols (the hand and the face) were dragged from the Symbols roll-up to complete the illustration. (See color plate 8.)

> **Troubleshooting**
>
> *Why can't I add Perspective to my group of objects?*
>
> You can, but you need to group the objects together first (not just select them all) with the Group command (Ctrl+G) in the Arrange menu.
>
> *Is there a way to more precisely align the position of my vanishing points?*
>
> Yes. Click the object that has the correct perspective. Drag horizontal and vertical ruler guides out to align with one or both of the vanishing point markers. Use these guides for aligning other vanishing points to the same position.

Fig. 22.11
Use the Lens roll-up to add one of ten different lens effects to objects.

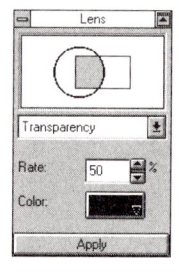

Fitting to Envelopes

◀ See "Reshaping a Curve or Object by Changing Its Nodes and Control Points," p. 72

Use Envelopes to change the shape of your artwork. The example in the next section walks you through an envelope that just barely adds a little extra overall shape to artwork. Then, in the section immediately following, you see a hard-edged envelope that has made drastic and obvious changes to the artwork. Both are created in the same manner. The sharpness of the envelope is up to you (see fig. 22.12).

Subtle Envelopes

In this example, different symbols were used from the Symbols roll-up (Ctrl+F11) window to create the man and woman objects shown in figure 22.13. The heads are separate symbols that are joined at the neck by editing the nodes with the Node Edit roll-up window in the View menu. Use standard shapes from the toolbox to create a circle and diamond to add as background. Use the Fill fly-out menu to choose an object fountain fill.

◀ See "Grouping Objects," p. 120

When you finish drawing all the objects that you want to include in the envelope, select them all by dragging a marquee around them with the Pick tool. Group (Ctrl+G) them and add an envelope using the Envelope roll-up (Ctrl+F7) window in the Effects menu.

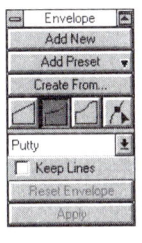

Fig. 22.12
The Envelope roll-up is similar to the other special effects roll-ups.

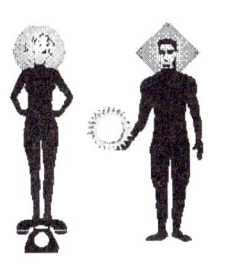

Fig. 22.13
Completely finish the art before adding an envelope. (See color plate 9.)

Several Envelope styles were applied, edited, and removed before the Two Curve style was determined. The envelope is pulled to the left and right to give an arc to the bodies. Figure 22.14 illustrates this arc. A background starburst (from the Symbols roll-up, Ctrl+F11) is added for highlight, and text (using the Text tool and Text roll-up, Ctrl+F2) is added below.

Fig. 22.14
The envelope made subtle changes to the illustration, but created a vastly different look. (See color plate 10.)

Defined Envelope Styles

◀ See "Mapping," p. 430

In this example of an envelope, the changes are much more obvious. To create similar artwork, use the man symbol from the Symbols roll-up (Ctrl+F11). Fill and duplicate the object. With the Pick tool, drag each object into the desired position. With the Pick tool, select the man in the background and reduce it in size by dragging a corner handle.

◀ See "Reshaping a Curve or Object by Changing Its Nodes and Control Points," p. 72

Select the Bézier pen tool from the toolbox and draw a shape like the one you see here. You will copy an envelope from this shape. With the Pick tool still chosen, select the man in the foreground and choose Copy From in the Envelope roll-up (Ctrl+F7) found in the Effects menu. Click the shape you just drew to create an envelope of similar proportions, and click Apply. If necessary, use the Shape tool and the Node Edit roll-up (View menu) to add, delete, and move nodes until you have an envelope shape like the one you see here. The right side of figure 22.15 shows the shape of the applied envelope. Once applied, the man takes on the shape that you see in figure 22.16.

Fig. 22.15
First, an Envelope is copied from the object on the right to the man. (See color plate 11.)

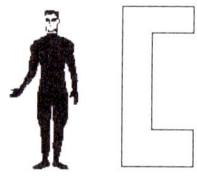

Fig. 22.16
The result of adding such a sharp-edged envelope to a free-form object. (See color plate 12.)

◀ See "Moving the Vanishing Points," p. 474

Using the Pen tool and other tools from the toolbox, additional shapes are added, such as the flooring shape. It's drawn with the Rectangle tool, and then Perspective is applied from the Effects menu. The vanishing points are moved to give the floor a diminish-to-horizon effect.

Bringing all these steps together results in the illustration in figure 22.17.

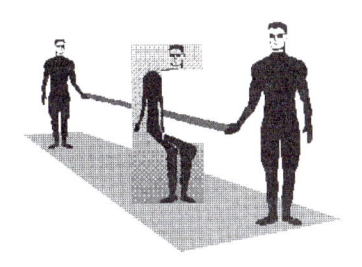

Fig. 22.17
Duplicating the man and accenting with additional elements gives this drawing a three-dimensional illusion. (See color plate 13.)

Troubleshooting

Is there a way to edit both sides of my envelope so that they remain proportional?

Hold the Ctrl key down while you drag the node of a Two Curve envelope, and the opposite node will move proprotionally in the opposite direction.

What if I don't like the way the envelope makes the enclosed symbol look?

Remove the envelope and choose another symbol, or edit the nodes of the envelope until you are happy with the results.

Using Blend Between Objects

Changing one object into another is a simple process with the Blend roll-up (Ctrl+B) (see fig. 22.18). In the first step, choose a cat and a dog from the Symbols roll-up (Ctrl+F11) window. Position the symbols so there's plenty of space between the two objects. This allows the steps of the Blend to be clearly defined.

◄ See "Making Just a Blend," p. 452

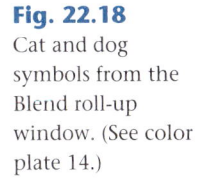

Fig. 22.18
Cat and dog symbols from the Blend roll-up window. (See color plate 14.)

◄ See "Identifying the Parts of a Blend," p. 451

◄ See "Start Nodes," p. 446

To create a simple blend like this one, select both control objects (the beginning and ending objects), choose Blend Roll-Up (Ctrl+B) from the Effects menu, and then click Apply. Figure 22.19 shows the positioning of both the control objects and the initial blend as it was created from the roll-up. On the right of the figure, the blend was made without mapping nodes. Because this created an undesirable effect, the blend was removed and retried by mapping the nodes at the tips of the noses. You can change the way nodes map by clicking the Map Nodes button in the Blend roll-up window. The left side of figure 22.19 illustrates the results of mapping the cat's and dog's noses to one another.

Fig. 22.19
Two tries were needed to achieve the desired results. It was also necessary to map the nodes at the tips of the noses. (See color plate 15.)

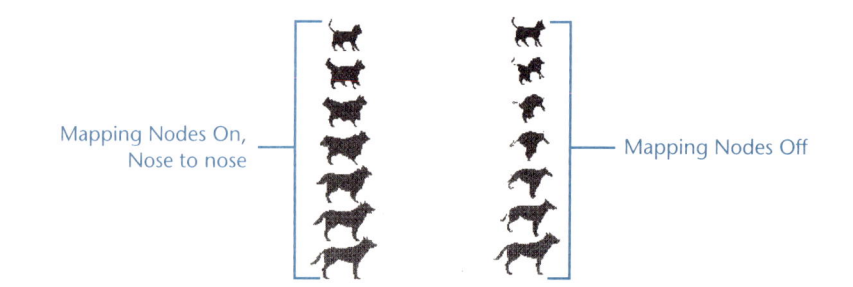

Mapping Nodes On, Nose to nose

Mapping Nodes Off

◄ See "Working with Artistic and Paragraph Text," p. 226

To create the final illustration you see in figure 22.20, move the control object (the cat) slightly to the right so that the rain falls at an angle. Duplicate the entire blend across the page and use the Pen tool to draw lightning strikes. From the Symbols roll-up (Ctrl+F11), pull a cloud onto the page and use a fountain object fill to color it. Add text below using the Text tool from the toolbox and the Text roll-up (Ctrl+F12) from the Text menu (see fig. 22.21).

Fig. 22.20
Move the control object to the right to angle the blend. Additional objects are added and filled to achieve the final illustration. (See color plate 16.)

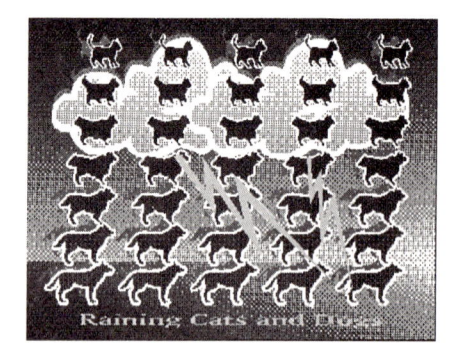

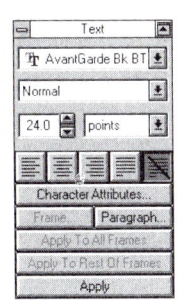

Extruding for Depth   **525**

Fig. 22.21
With the Text roll-up window, you have easy access to text options such as font, size, and so on.

Extruding for Depth

Another way to add depth to a drawing is to extrude it. Using Extrude, surfaces are added to the art that can be filled or outlined. Using the Extrude roll-up window (Ctrl+E), you can also move the light source (the brightest part of the drawing), and rotate the object. To create something similar to the example in figure 22.22, select a house from the Symbols roll-up (Ctrl+F11). Do not fill the surfaces of the house; use as a wireframe.

◄ See "Adding Symbols," p. 55

Fig. 22.22
A house chosen from the Symbols roll-up. (See color plate 17.)

To create this beginning step, apply two extrusions to the house using the Extrude roll-up. As each extrusion is applied, the vanishing points are moved—in one case to the upper left and in the other, to the upper right (see fig. 22.23). The vanishing points are the place to which the object diminishes—its horizon. Apply the first extrusion, click the vanishing point (marked by a ×), and drag it to the upper left. The second extrusion is applied after the house is separated. Click the house object and choose Separate from the Arrange menu. Apply a new extrusion and move that vanishing point to the upper right corner. Your object should now look something like the example in figure 22.23.

◄ See "Working with Extrusions," p. 472

◄ See "Moving the Vanishing Points," p. 474

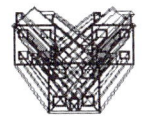

Fig. 22.23
After applying two separate extrusions, and moving the vanishing points to reside opposite each other, your art should resemble this illustration. (See color plate 18.)

To prepare for the next extrusion (the third), select the house and choose Separate again. In figure 22.24, you can see the results. After this final extrusion, separate one more time. The surfaces after separation become independent objects and the main part of the house is filled with the Yellow Plastic

526 Chapter 22—Combining and Reusing Effects

◀ See "Using the Blend Roll-Up Window," p. 443

texture of CorelDRAW!. Access the fill options using the Fill fly-out menu in the toolbox. Here you can choose a texture or fill to your liking.

In the final step, shown in figure 22.25, drag a bush from the Symbols roll-up (Ctrl+F11) and use the Pick tool to place it at the bottom. While it is still selected, duplicate the bush for the right side, and drag it to position. Select the Blend roll-up (Ctrl+B) window from the Effects menu and use it to create the series of bushes that appear at the bottom. Check Rainbow, and Loop, and type in a value of 50° in the Rotation field of the Blend roll-up. This causes the bush to diminish in size and to curve along the bottom edge of the house.

Fig. 22.24
Because Extrude makes surfaces from the selected objects, the surfaces can be filled. (See color plate 19.)

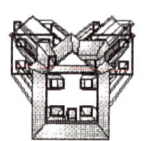

Fig. 22.25
With the Blend roll-up, you can rotate the bushes around the bottom of the house. (See color plate 20.)

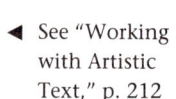

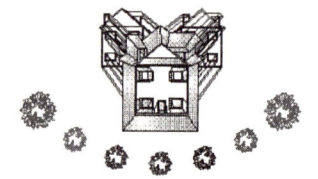

◀ See "Working with Artistic Text," p. 212

A more typical example of Extrude is in figure 22.26. The Artistic text word *Move* is extruded using the Extrude roll-up. When you type characters for an extrusion, kern them apart so that the final extrusion surfaces are more defined. After you apply Extrude, separate the entire extrusion with the Arrange menu (see fig. 22.27). Return to the Arrange menu and choose Ungroup (Ctrl+U). Use the Pick tool to select individual pieces of the surfaces and pull them in the same direction as the vanishing point. This gives the illusion of breaking up during movement (see fig. 22.28). To further define the initial characters, pull the front control object (the word *Move*) down and to the left to separate it from the extrusion surfaces.

Fig. 22.26
To begin an illustration like this one, type the letters and then choose a font and size from the Text roll-up window.

Fig. 22.27
Add the extrusion (small back) and move the vanishing point to the upper-right corner. Use a Shade fill from the Extrude roll-up window.

Fig. 22.28
The extrusion is then Separated (Arrange menu) and the surfaces pulled away from the main body of the Extrude. (See color plate 23.)

Troubleshooting

The front face of my extruded object is so dark I can't decipher it from the surfaces of the Extrude. How can I make this more legible?

Try applying a lighter color to the original object and moving the light source behind the object. Or separate the extrusion by using Separate from the Arrange menu, and then pulling the control object away from the other surfaces.

When I try to make a Blend across the bottom of the houses, the bushes overlap one another in a straight line. How can I make them further apart and curve around?

You used too many steps in the blend. Choose fewer steps and mark the Loop check box to make them curve along the bottom of the illustration.

Adding Contours to an Object

The effects of an applied Contour can look very similar to Blend. In figure 22.29, you can see the effects that contour has on the note in the center. Instead of drawing two control objects and blending them, use Contour to diminish to the center or grow outward. Each step of a Contour is a separate object and can be moved around independently of the group. To do this, select a completed Contour and choose Separate from the Arrange menu.

◀ See "Creating Contours for Objects," p. 482

528 Chapter 22—Combining and Reusing Effects

Fig. 22.29
Contouring was added to the musical note with a setting of To Center. (See color plate 24.)

◄ See "Making Just a Blend," p. 492

For figure 22.29, Contour, Envelope, *and* Blend were used. The musical symbols are from the Symbols roll-up. Place them on the page, assign each a fill color, and then select just the note. Select the Contour Roll-Up (Ctrl+F9) from the Effect menu and apply a Contour using the To Center option. Choose an outline and fill color from the Color buttons, if you like.

Use the Free-Hand Pen tool to draw a curved line for the staff, like the one in the illustration. After the first line, select it with the Pick tool, duplicate it, and move it into position for the top row of the staff and the duplicate line into position for the bottom row. Choose an outline color for each line.

To make the blend between the two lines, choose the Blend roll-up (Ctrl+B) window from the Effects menu. Apply a blend with Rainbow checked. Choose a distance between the blend steps that suits you. If you don't like the number of steps, choose a new setting and click the Apply button.

◄ See "Enveloping Objects," p. 434

To make the treble clef follow the same curves as the staff, choose the Envelope roll-up (Ctrl+F7) and apply a Two Curves Envelope to the treble clef symbol. Pull the nodes of the envelope to force the treble clef to arc in the same directions as the staff lines drawn with the Pen tool.

> **Troubleshooting**
>
> *I try using the Contour roll-up to make the lines for the staff, but they close up around the ends. What can I do to open them up?*
>
> Contour is different from blend. There aren't two control objects, only one. With an open path, the Contour starts at the path and draws the next shape all the way around the outside of the line. This continues until it has exhausted the requested number of steps. For open-ended lines, use blend and two control objects.
>
> *I want to pull apart the segments of a Contour—can this be done?*
>
> Yes, choose Break Apart from the Arrange menu and use the Pick tool to place the individual segments where you want them. This is also a good tip to get several sizes of circles or squares in an easy move.

Making Powerful Lines

In the illustration of the horse (see fig. 22.30), the mane and forelock are both drawn using the PowerLine special effects. You can add PowerLine before you begin a drawing or any time after. In fact, you can add PowerLine to a drawing that you did weeks ago when you just want to add some additional flair.

◄ See "Drawing with Power-Lines," p. 493

Fig. 22.30
The PowerLines were added before and after these lines were drawn. (See color plate 25.)

In this example, the main part of the illustration was completed with the Bézier pen tool before the PowerLine roll-up was selected from the Effects menu. To add the PowerLine effect before you draw, check the Apply When Drawing Lines option, and then draw the lines.

Try many different line styles in your illustrations for a varied effect. Here, Wedge 1 and Wedge 3 PowerLine styles were primarily used to draw the mane. A Trumpet 3 was added to the outline of the ear, followed by a Teardrop 2 on the nose, and a Trumpet 1 for the outline of the eye.

To try these out, draw your illustration wholly or partly and choose the PowerLine roll-up window (Ctrl+F8) from the Effects menu. Add PowerLine as you go, or choose a style to be applied before the lines are drawn. Click the Apply button if you are adding a PowerLine to an existing line.

◄ See "Modifying Object Outline Characteristics," p. 137

For additional highlights in the eyeball, use the Blend roll-up (Ctrl+B). Draw the outside object for the eye, perhaps using the oval tool in the toolbox. Draw a second smaller shape inside the oval to act as the point of highlight. This highlight object should be crescent shaped and can be drawn with the Bézier pen tool from the toolbox. Fill both objects. The oval should have a dark color, while the highlight shape should be very light, if not white. Make sure that neither object has an outline by choosing no outline color from the Outline fly-out menu in the toolbox. Apply the blend. Use many steps (about 15) so that the blend looks smooth.

For the text, after drawing an H, several PowerLines were applied before settling on Trumpet4. The Artistic Text tool from the toolbox was used to add the remaining characters in Bellevue type style.

◄ See "Working with Artistic Text," p. 212

Looking at Art Through Lenses

◄ See "Creating a Lens for Objects," p. 504

Most of the Lens effects work best with color, and are therefore best displayed in color. Turn to color plates 28–33 to see more examples of the multicolored fish with different lenses applied. In figure 22.31, you see the invert lens and in figure 22.32, the magnify lens applied to the circle object overlaying the object below. Use the Lens roll-up (Alt+F3) to add the Lens effect to an object.

Fig. 22.31
Applying an invert lens changes colors to their opposite. (See color plate 26.)

Fig. 22.32
Apply a magnify lens to zoom in on that portion behind the lens. (See color plate 27.)

Using the Power of Clipping

◄ See "Making a PowerClip," p. 509

Applying a PowerClip to an illustration does just that—you clip away any part of the illustration that falls outside the PowerClip object. Any object you can draw can be a PowerClip. In fact, you can even make a Lens a PowerClip or even a Contour. Many other special effects can be applied to an object followed by a PowerClip. In the following sections, we'll look at some of those options.

Figure 22.33 is another good example of the ways to combine special effects. For the grapes, draw a circle with the Ctrl key held down as you draw an oval with the Oval tool from the tool box (the Ctrl key constrains the oval to a perfect circle). Fill the circle with purple from the color wheel of the Fill fly-out menu in the toolbox. Draw a smaller, crescent-shaped object inside the circle and fill it with a very light purple, pink, or white. Choose the Blend roll-up window (Ctrl+B) from the Effects menu and blend the two objects together (see fig. 22.33). Use several steps to the blend and be sure that neither object contains an outline color.

Using the Power of Clipping 531

Switch to the Wireframe (Shift+F9) mode if you're not already working in that view (so the screen redraws faster). Select all the objects of the grape and choose Group (Ctrl+G) from the Arrange menu. With the Pick tool, select the group and Duplicate (Ctrl+D) it. Move the duplicate to the desired position. Continue to duplicate and move until you've shaped a bunch.

Use the Bézier pen tool to draw a stem, and choose the PowerLine roll-up (Ctrl+F8) window from the Effects menu to apply a PowerLine style that resembles a stem. In the illustration, Wedge1 is used, but, depending on how your line is drawn, some other style might work best for you. Select all the grapes and the stem and Group (Ctrl+G) them using the Arrange menu.

To clip the bunch, as shown in figure 22.34, draw a rectangle with the Rectangle tool in the toolbox. Choose an outline and a fill color for the rectangle PowerClip. Select the grouped bunch and choose PowerClip from the Effects menu. From the drop-down menu, choose Place Inside Container. Using the special cursor, click the rectangle; the grapes will center inside the rectangle, and all excess that falls outside the rectangle will be trimmed away.

Fig. 22.33
Draw a smaller crescent shaped object inside the circle and color it with a light shade. Blend the two objects together. Wireframe view is on the left (See color plate 34.)

◀ See "Viewing Your Work," p. 20

> **Troubleshooting**
>
> *When I place the grapes inside the rectangle with PowerClip, nothing is trimmed. What am I doing wrong?*
>
> Make sure that the PowerClip you draw is smaller than the item you want to clip. If it's not, reduce the size of the container or enlarge the size of the contents before applying PowerClip. (If you've already applied the PowerClip, go back to the Effects menu and choose Extract Contents from the PowerClip drop-down menu.)

Fig. 22.34
This illustration uses a Blend, PowerLine, and PowerClip. (See color plate 35).

One very useful application of the Magnify Lens is to combine it with a PowerClip to create a blown-up view of a small portion of the drawing, which is offset from the drawing itself. This is often useful in technical drawings (and computer books).

Figure 22.35 shows a Photo-CD image that has been imported into CorelDRAW!. To show some detail, a small portion of this image is enlarged. Using CorelDRAW! to automate this process is far simpler than creating the illustration twice, in two different sizes.

Fig. 22.35
The original photo of the circuit board, imported from Photo-CD. (See color plate 36.)

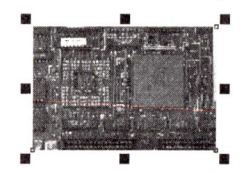

◀ See "Copying Objects," p. 105

To create this type of special effect, you need to use the Lens and PowerClip special effects—the Lens to zoom in on the part you want to enlarge, and the PowerClip to trim away the parts of the photo that aren't enlarged. If you look ahead to figure 22.36, you'll see that there needs to be two images of the photo—one at the correct size, and another to add the Lens and PowerClip to. So start by selecting the image; open the Edit Menu and choose Duplicate.

Now to add a Lens and PowerClip, draw a circle using the Oval tool from the toolbox; then Duplicate (Ctrl+D) it. Drag one of the circles out of the way for now (this one will become the PowerClip later) and make the first circle a Magnify Lens by using the Lens roll-up (Alt+F3) in the Effects menu. Place the Lens over the portion of the duplicate illustration you want to zoom in on, as you see in figure 22.36.

Select the Lens and the photo with the Pick tool, and use the Group (Ctrl+G) command in the Arrange menu. Then, while they are still selected, choose PowerClip from the Effects menu and choose Place Inside Container from the drop-down menu. With the special cursor, click the duplicate circle that you dragged out of the way.

To position the contents inside the PowerClip correctly, use the right mouse button and click the PowerClip. From the drop-down menu, choose Lock Contents to PowerClip. (This switch toggles this feature on and off.) You can now move the PowerClip directly over the Lens circle, and the remainder of the photo is clipped away (see fig. 22.37). It's best to use the right mouse button again to relock the contents to the PowerClip so that if you need to move the objects, the contents will move along with the container.

> **Troubleshooting**
>
> *When I choose Place Contents in Container, my entire photo and lens disappear. Where have they gone?*
>
> They are still there, but using these features, you cannot work in the Wireframe view. Turn off Wireframe in the View menu, and all of the contents are now visible.
>
> *After I completed my PowerClip, I moved it closer to the original photo and now the contents have disappeared. What did I do wrong?*
>
> You forgot to use the right mouse button on the PowerClip to Lock Contents to Container. When you moved the PowerClip the contents stayed in the same place and now you can't see them. Use Ctrl+Z to undo the last move, click the PowerClip with the right mouse button, and relock the contents.

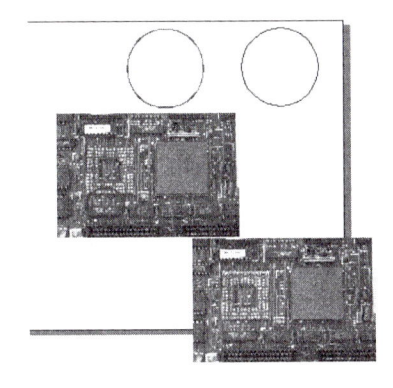

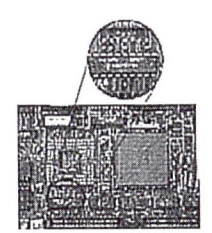

Fig. 22.36
With the photo duplicated, the circles for the Magnify Lens and PowerClip drawn, the photo is ready to apply a Lens and then a PowerClip. (See color plate 37.)

Fig. 22.37
The final drawing shows the original photo and a blow-up of an individual chip. (See color plate 38.)

Creating Preset Templates, Styles, and Macros

Most artists develop a style uniquely their own. CorelDRAW! planned and even prepared for you to do this. If, for instance, you create a particular PowerLine and combine it with a specific lens, you can save this combined effort as a single style or as a macro, whichever you prefer. A group of styles can be saved as a template. So, as you can see, you have many options available to you other than just copying effects to other objects. Using one of these three methods, you can apply a collection of attribute changes and even have them available in other CorelDRAW! documents.

Styles

Styles can be saved individually in the Styles roll-up of the Layout menu (see fig. 22.38), where both styles and templates are accessed. Styles are specific to the type of object to which they are applied (Artistic Text, Paragraph Text, or Graphics). For instance, you can save a series of attributes that you apply to an object, perhaps special effects, but when you apply that style, it can only be applied to an object that accepts those settings. You can't add a bold type style to a rectangle; conversely, you cannot add blend to paragraph text.

Fig. 22.38
Use the Styles roll-up, accessed from the Layout Menu, for working with templates and styles.

Use the Styles roll-up window to quickly find and apply a style to a selected object. In this section, we discuss the steps for saving applied special effects as styles that can be applied to Graphics. Follow these steps for adding a style to the list in the Styles roll-up.

1. Make sure that you finish applying the special effects that you want to save.

2. Choose the Pick tool from the toolbox, and click the object with the right mouse button. The object menu will drop down.

3. From the Object menu, choose Save As Style. The Graphics Save As Style dialog box in figure 22.39 appears because you selected a graphic to which special effects have been applied.

4. Type a name in the field provided.

5. Click the applicable attributes buttons. Some options are dimmed because you haven't selected that type of object. (If you selected text, the text options would be available and the graphics buttons would be dimmed.)

6. Click OK. The style name is now added to the list in the Styles roll-up window.

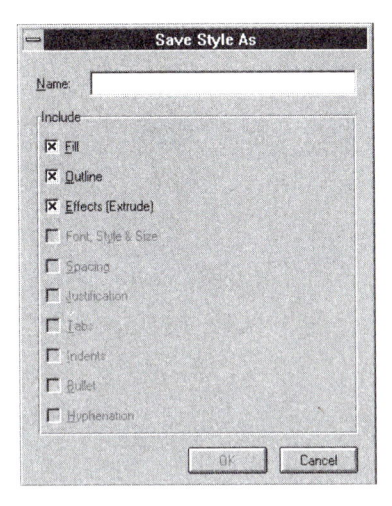

Fig. 22.39
Type a name into the field provided and click the appropriate attributes buttons.

Applying Styles to Graphics Objects

After a style is saved, it can be applied to objects in the same document or other documents. There are two methods for applying a style, and both are listed here. To apply a style, follow the steps for the method of preference.

1. Click the object from which you want to copy styles with the right mouse button. The object menu appears.

2. Click Apply Styles. A drop-down menu appears with a list of all the styles applicable to the selected object.

3. Choose a style name from the drop-down menu.

For an alternate method of applying a style, try these steps:

1. Using the Pick tool, click on the object to which you want to apply styles. The object is surrounded by a bounding box.

2. Choose the Styles roll-up from the Layout menu. The Styles roll-up is placed in the active document area.

3. Choose a style name from the scrollable list.

4. Click Apply.

> **Troubleshooting**
>
> *When I click with the right mouse button, nothing happens. My Object menu does not appear. What am I doing wrong?*
>
> Your mouse may be programmed so that it's necessary for you to hold down the mouse button and wait for the Object menu.
>
> *When I try to save a style, some of the attributes buttons are dimmed. Why can't I select them?*
>
> You can only save attributes that are part of that object. If it's a graphic, the text options are dimmed. If it's text, the graphics options are dimmed.

Templates

Templates can be opened into current documents so that you can apply your style choice to a selected object. Templates are stored at a selected destination, just like a regular CorelDRAW! file. Templates have a three-letter extension of CDT following the file name, which holds up to eight characters. You can load, save, and assign hot keys for templates using the Styles roll-up in the Layout menu. To work with a template, follow these steps:

1. Click the Templates icon at the right margin of the Styles roll-up in the Layout menu. A drop-down menu appears with the options for working with templates.

2. From the drop-down list, choose Load or Save Template. If you choose Load, a dialog box appears so that you can locate the template containing the styles you need for this document. If you choose Save, the save dialog box appears. In the appropriate field, name the template you're saving with no more than eight characters. Choose the destination to which you want to save the template.

3. Click OK.

Tip
If you try to load a template with style names exactly like those already included in your document, a warning dialog box asks how you want to resolve the issue.

Templates can store hot key information for individual styles, up to ten different ones. You can also choose the Revert command to return an object to its state before the last-applied style. In addition, styles can be deleted and searched.

There are two ways to access the dialog for saving and applying styles. Click the right mouse button on an object to prompt the Object menu (see fig. 22.40), or use the Styles roll-up. Either command produces the same result; choose whichever is most comfortable for you.

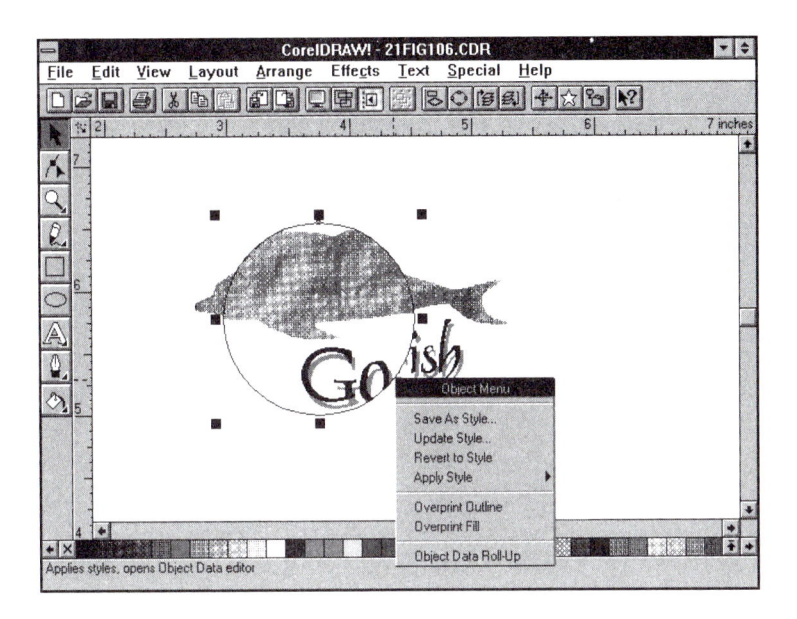

Creating Preset Templates, Styles, and Macros   **537**

Fig. 22.40
Use the right mouse button to click an object if you want to prompt the Object menu.

Macros

Macros are similar to styles and templates, but they're saved in the Macro Presets roll-up window, along with a thumbnail preview of how the applied macro looks. Macros, like styles and templates, are available to each CorelDRAW! document you create. Corel has even included some macros along with the program. Try these macros first if you want to get a feel for how macros affect your art.

Unlike styles, macros don't require you to apply special effects until you activate the macros' recording function. To begin recording a macro that's accessible from the Presets roll-up (see fig. 22.41), follow these steps:

1. With the Pick tool in the toolbox, select a single object (you cannot record macros for effects applied to groups). This object is the control object, and anything applied to it is recorded into a macro.

2. Select the Macros Preset roll-up (Alt+F5) window from the Special menu.

3. Click the Start Recording button.

4. Apply special effects such as blend, extrude, or contour; or apply attributes such as fill, outline, rotate, skew, stretch, mirror, duplicate, move, nudge, align, order, or convert to curves; or create another object.

Becoming an Expert

V

Fig. 22.41
Use the Start Recording and Stop Recording buttons of the Macros Preset roll-up window to store special effects macros.

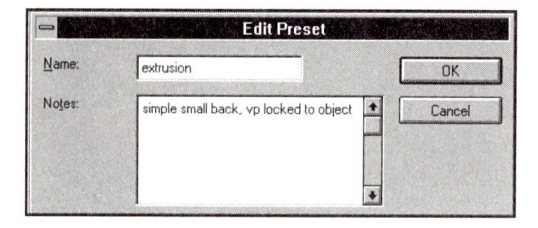

5. Click the Stop Recording button in the Macros Preset roll-up window. The Edit Preset dialog box appears (see fig. 22.41).

6. Type a name for the Preset in the name field.

7. Type a note describing the Preset in the Notes box, if you want.

8. Click OK. The Preset name and a thumbnail representation are saved into the list of available Presets.

If you want to edit the name or notes of a particular Preset, use the Macro Preset roll-up window and follow these steps:

1. Choose a Preset from the list and click the Edit button.

2. Enter a new name for the selected Preset or change the notes.

3. Click OK. The Preset edits are saved.

If you want to remove a Preset from the list, use the Edit button and click the Delete button.

> **Troubleshooting**
>
> *When I edit the name of a chosen Preset, the Preset I clicked on is removed from the list. I didn't want to delete the other Preset, just make a new one. What am I doing wrong?*
>
> Editing the name of a Preset overwrites the Preset you chose. If you want a new Preset you must begin from the beginning. Refer to the preceding section for recording a Preset.
>
> *I tried to record a Macro for Perspective but it won't allow me to. What steps do I need to take?*
>
> You cannot store a macro for any effect that requires an intermediate step, like stretching the bounding box in Perspective. Use the list in the preceding numbered steps for saving a macro as a guideline for the types of attributes and effects that can be stored.

From Here...

If you need help with any of the special effects, Perspective, Envelope, Blend, Contour, Extrude, PowerLine, Lens, or PowerClip, return to the chapters with those titles. These are the most obvious places for assistance with the special effects roll-up windows. Some other topics that were used often in this chapter can be found in the chapters listed below.

- Chapter 7, "Adding Text to a Drawing," will help you understand the Text roll-up if you have trouble entering text.

- Chapter 3, "A Detailed Look at Object Drawing," and Chapter 4, "Mastering Object Manipulations," both provide a refresher course in working with the objects.

Chapter 23

Multipage Documents and the Object Data Manager

by Stephen R. Poland

CorelDRAW!'s capability to edit images that cover more than one page is a terrific feature. With the multipage editing capability, up to 999 pages of a newsletter or other document can be edited as a single image. Using this single-file approach offers a major benefit: it frees you from the task of keeping track of the point where text ends in one file and begins in another. Text automatically flows across multiple pages, making document editing substantially easier.

The Object Data Manager is useful for people who need to correlate database information (weight, size, price, and so on) with an image of some kind. Examples of this sort of application include catalogs that use product descriptions and pictures, and personnel rosters that associate a person's picture with his or her personal information. The Object Data Manager makes this type of integration possible. Most Windows OLE-based data managers can link an image with a text source (that is, select a person's name and the person's picture appears). CorelDRAW! reverses this process by displaying text information when the image is selected.

In this chapter, you learn how to do the following:

- Create and manage multipage documents
- Create master layers in multipage documents
- Use the Object Data Manager's basic features
- Add, edit, and print object data

Multipage Document Fundamentals

In general, basic CorelDRAW! operating principles apply equally well to multipage documents. The one exception, perhaps, is that you must make more efficient use of the page layout and layering options, or your screen refresh times may become unbearably slow. To create and work with a multipage document, follow these steps:

1. Open the **F**ile menu and choose **N**ew to create a document from scratch; choose **F**ile New **F**rom Template to use a CorelDRAW! supplied template; or choose **F**ile **O**pen to use a previously created document with the desired formatting information already embedded.

2. Open the **L**ayout menu, choose Pa**g**e Setup, and define a page layout style that includes decisions about the assumed page size and the way in which you plan to use it for paste-up layout purposes.

3. Set up the master layer of the document, which includes all the information that is to appear on each page.

4. Add the desired text and image information to the document.

> **Tip**
> You can use any document template as a starting point for a multipage document.
>
> ◀ See "Sharing Drawings—Export, Import, and the Clipboard," p. 268
>
> ◀ See "Merging Text into a Corel Drawing," p. 310

The steps in this process are explained in detail in the next few sections.

There's good news and bad news about the CorelDRAW! multipage document feature. The good news is that this feature allows you to import CorelDRAW! graphic images directly into your document and to spread document stories over multiple pages. The bad news, however, is that the multipage feature currently doesn't include a utility for importing Aldus PageMaker documents. Many of your current multipage documents may have to be re-created using the CorelDRAW! formats. And text must be imported in a supported format such as ASCII text, RTF, Microsoft Word, Ami Pro, or WordPerfect. Text formatting is preserved, but the associated graphic images in the original document will probably be lost.

Choosing a Page Layout and Display Style

CorelDRAW! provides numerous page layout styles that are used to automate the actual *paste-up* procedures necessary to optimize the printing process. The best page layout style for a particular job depends on the size of the paper the images will be printed on, the method of folding and binding to be used, and the page numbering scheme. The CorelDRAW! options used to determine the relationship between the actual page size and the layout of the designed pages are located in the Layout Page Setup menu selection. When you choose this menu option, the dialog box shown in figure 23.1 appears.

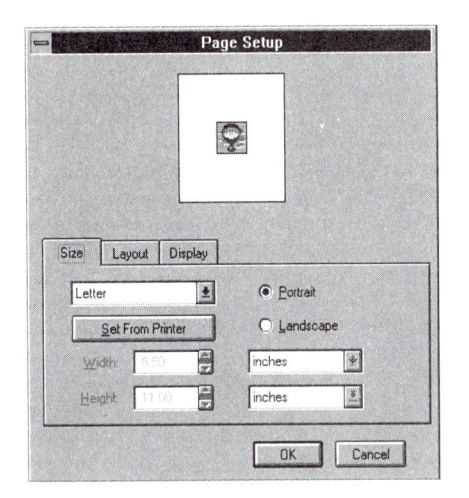

Fig. 23.1
The Page Setup dialog box.

The initial options displayed in the Page Setup dialog box enable you to choose one of several standard paper sizes, such as letter, legal, and tabloid, or create your own custom paper size.

To choose the correct paper size for your page layout design, follow these steps:

1. Choose Layout, Page Setup to open the Page setup dialog box, if it is not already open. Click the arrow to display the paper size pull-down list; then choose the desired size from the choices provided (tabloid, letter, legal, and other sizes). The Width and Height settings reflect your paper size choice in the specified units (*inches* in the figure provided).

2. Select either **P**ortrait or **L**andscape to determine whether the paper is to be printed with the long side vertically oriented (portrait) or turned on its side (landscape).

3. Choose Set From Printer to adopt a paper size with dimensions equal to that currently set as the currently active printer paper size.

To select the options that define the orientation and size of the pages of your document, follow these steps:

1. Click the Layout tab in the Page Setup dialog box. The layout options are displayed in the dialog box (see fig. 23.2).

Fig. 23.2
Page Layout options in the Page Setup dialog box determine how the printable page is divided into smaller sections.

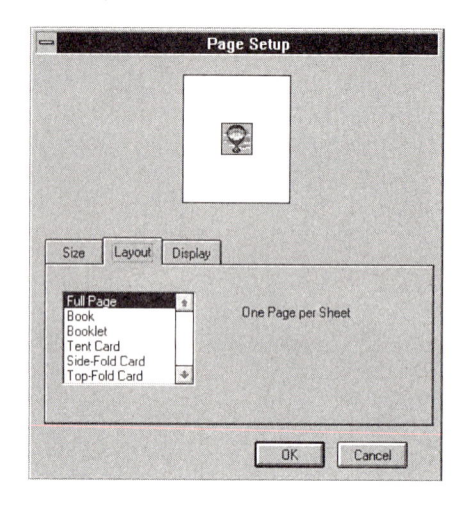

2. Select one of the basic layout styles from the list displayed, such as Full Page, Book, Booklet, Tent Card, Side-Fold Card, and Top-Fold Card. Each one has a different effect on how the paper size is subdivided into the smaller page layout areas.

> **Note**
>
> Notice that a sample of the layout style is displayed at the top of the dialog box. The sample shows how each piece of paper is subdivided to create the selected layout. A description of the layout option is also displayed to the right of the layout selection.

If you plan to create a document with folds, make certain the pages are upside down with respect to the others because of the folding and cutting (trimming) operations required to create the final document. Those operations align them correctly. Under certain circumstances, pages that follow each other may not even print on the same piece of paper because the actual printing, folding, and trimming processes require that they print on opposing pieces of paper. But whatever the paper dimensions, the layout design divides the physical page into the sections required to meet these folding needs.

To select the Display options for your page setup, follow these steps:

1. Click the Display tab of the Page Setup dialog box. The display options appear in the Page Setup dialog box (see fig. 23.3).

2. Click the Paper Color selection to set a background color for the editable preview display area. You might want to set this color to the paper color on which you plan to print; doing so helps you to determine whether your choice of colors is appropriate.

Fig. 23.3
Display options in the Page Setup dialog box enable you to select a paper color, facing pages, and whether or not to display a page border in the Editable Preview view.

3. Select the Show Page **B**order option to display the actual page border, based on the paper size you selected, in the Editable Preview view.

4. Click **A**dd Page Frames to place a rectangle the size of the printable page around the page border.

5. Choose **F**acing Pages to display your document two pages at a time. The choice of Left First or Right First depends on whether you plan to start your document on the left or right page. This feature is typically used for book layouts.

Changing, Adding, and Deleting Pages

After you select the size, orientation, and other page setup options for your document, you can add pages to create a multipage document. CorelDRAW! creates a single-page document by default, so you'll need to insert new pages to create a multipage document. If you started your document using a document template, the template may already be set up with several pages. Remember, you can always add or remove pages as needed.

▶ See "Using CorelDRAW! Templates," p. 581

To add pages to a document, follow these steps:

1. From the **L**ayout menu, choose **I**nsert Page from the menu bar. The Insert Page dialog box appears (see fig. 23.4).

Fig 23.4
The Insert Page dialog box enables you to add single or multiple pages to a document.

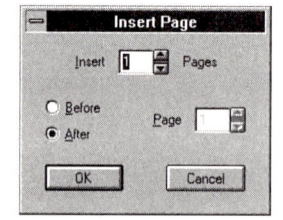

2. Click the up arrow or down arrow in the **I**nsert Pages section of the dialog box to indicate the number of pages to insert.

3. Choose **B**efore to insert the new pages before the current page, or choose **A**fter to insert the new pages after the current page. If the document already has multiple pages, specify which page the pages should be inserted before or after by clicking arrows for the **P**age indicator.

4. Click OK to insert the new pages in the document.

You can move around in your multipage document and add pages by using the icons located on the left end of the horizontal scroll bar.

> **Note**
>
> The multipage control icons appear only when your document has more than one page.

The triangle moves you forward or backward through the document, depending on the triangle's direction. You can also press the PageUp or PageDown keys on the keyboard. To move to a specific page, from the Layout menu, choose Go To Page to display a dialog box in which you can enter the desired page number. Press Ctrl as you click the Page Forward/Back icons to move to the first or last page of the document, respectively. Clicking the Page Forward/Back icons with the right mouse button moves you in the respective direction by five pages for each click. If the Facing Pages option is active, each right mouse button click moves you 10 pages.

If the first page or last page of the document is displayed, a small + icon appears next to the black triangles. Clicking the small + icon opens the Insert Page dialog box, which allows you to insert a specified number of pages before or after the current page, depending on the location of the + when selected. The plus appears on the left side when you're on the first page of the document and appears on the right side when you're on the last page. You delete a page by choosing Layout-Delete Page, selecting the page range for deletion, and then clicking OK.

Designing a Master Layer

The *master layer* contains all the information that will appear on each page of the document (unless you specifically turn off the display for that particular page as outlined later in this section). Any created layer can be designated as a master layer. You can also have multiple master layers by naming them differently when you designate them as master layers in the Edit Layer dialog box. See Chapter 4, "Mastering Object Manipulations," for more information about using layers in CorelDRAW!.

Follow these steps to establish your master layer(s):

1. From the **L**ayout menu, choose **L**ayers Roll-Up (Ctrl+F3) to open the Layers roll-up window.

2. Click the solid triangle that points to the menu to open the menu, and select New to add a new layer to the drawing. The New Layer dialog box appears (see fig. 23.5).

Fig. 23.5
The New Layer dialog box contains the option for creating a master layer in your drawing.

3. Type the desired layer name in the **N**ame area, choose **M**aster Layer, and then click OK. A master layer with the designated name is added to the drawing.

> **Note**
>
> If you display the document with facing pages, the master layer information displayed on the left-hand page is repeated on all left pages, and the right-hand master layer page information is repeated on all right pages. Each must be set up separately.

You can hide Master Layer information on specific pages by following this procedure:

1. From the **L**ayout menu, choose **G**o To Page and type the page number in the Go To Page dialog box. Go to the page for which you want to hide the Master Layer information; then open the Layers roll-up window.

2. Double-click the master layer containing the information you want to hide. The Edit Layers dialog box appears.

3. Click the Set Options For **A**ll Pages option to disable it. This keeps your selections from being applied to all pages.

4. Click the **V**isible check box to disable it. This makes the master layer invisible on this page. Click OK. The currently selected page(s) will not display the information contained on the disabled master layer.

> **Note**
>
> CorelDRAW! doesn't provide automatic page numbering. You can add page numbers to your pages manually.

Printing and the Page Layout Styles

Determining the proper layout of pages to accommodate specific printing situations is tricky business, and you can easily get confused if you don't clearly understand the process. Luckily, CorelDRAW! does lots of the work for you when it prints the final documents. It determines the proper sequencing of pages so that they print on their respective sheets and line up properly when finally printed.

In a 12-page document printed in the booklet style, for example, pages 1 and 2 wouldn't appear on the same sheet of paper. Instead, pages 1 and 12 would print on one sheet, pages 2 and 11 on another sheet (or the back of the first sheet), and so on. When the pages print this way, they align perfectly and give the desired page numbering in the bound booklet. This process is tricky, so you're encouraged to let CorelDRAW! make the decisions for you. Just don't be alarmed if you see non-sequential pages coming out of your printer. Check with your print shop operator before finalizing your output. The operator works with the final product and can tell you exactly what he needs.

Troubleshooting

Each time I print a drawing, I get a warning that says Paper Orientation does not match document.

The paper orientation you selected in the Page Setup dialog box does not match the orientation selected in the Print Setup dialog box. You can choose to have CorelDRAW! adjust the difference automatically by choosing Yes in the warning dialog box, or you can change the orientations in Page Setup and Print Setup to match.

I selected a Legal size page for Paper Size in the Size section of the Page Setup dialog box, but when I return to draw in the drawing window, I can't tell where the edges of the paper are supposed to be.

To show the page board for any paper size choice, open the Page Setup dialog box and click the Display tab. Click Show Page Border to select this option. Click OK to complete the change. The border of the printable page is displayed in the drawing window.

I'm working with a multipage drawing and I want to print page numbers at the bottom of each page. Can CorelDRAW do this automatically?

Unfortunately, CorelDRAW does not support automatic page numbering. You must place page numbers on your pages using the Artistic Text tool.

Object Data Manager Basic Concepts

The Object Data Manager is a CorelDRAW! feature that allows you to access database information through images (instead of accessing images by way of textual information). Most databases present a text representation of some type (name, location, and so on) and then present the image if requested. CorelDRAW! turns this process around by presenting the image first and recovering the textual database information as a secondary action.

Assume that you're an interior designer, for example, and you're working with a house floor plan. You're using various symbols in your drawing to represent the pieces of furniture to be placed (as well as their dimensions, costs, and purchase locations). With the Object Data Manager, the database information for each object in the drawing can be retrieved by clicking the object itself. The Object Data Manager also provides some simple mathematical operations to sum columns of information for objects formed into groups using the CorelDRAW! Arrange-Group command.

◀ See "Combining and Grouping Objects," p. 119

Remember that in this case, you start with the objects and create the database around them, not the other way around. To group database information, group the objects. To separate database information, separate the objects. This procedure is contrary to most conventional database operations, and you're encouraged to shift your thinking so that you can take full advantage of the benefits associated with image- or object-oriented database operations.

Designing the Object Database

Begin with a CorelDRAW! object to which you want to attach data. Assume that you're working with a floor plan for a conference room and want to create a database of information related to the interior design project (see fig. 23.6).

Fig. 23.6
A conference room floor plan to be used to track object data using the Object Data Manager.

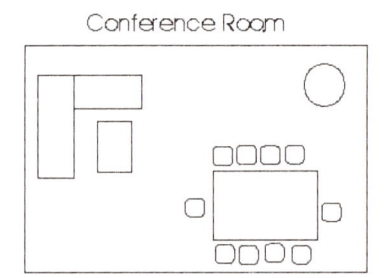

Follow these steps to use the Object Data Manager:

1. Create or open the drawing that contains the objects to which you want to attach information. In this example, the drawing consists of four basic objects: a sofa, a coffee table, a plant (in the corner), and a conference table.

2. Decide what types of information you want to track. For the purpose of this example, track each object's Name, Purchase Price, Purchase Location, and Color. These categories of information are called *field names*. Each field name is a general category of information that pertains to each object in an image. Once again, you can make this list of field names as detailed as necessary to meet your needs.

3. Position the mouse pointer on an object, and then click the right mouse button. The Object Data menu appears.

Object Data Manager Basic Concepts 551

4. Choose Object Data Roll-Up, and the Object Data roll-up window appears (see fig. 23.7).

Click here to open the Object Data pull-down menu.

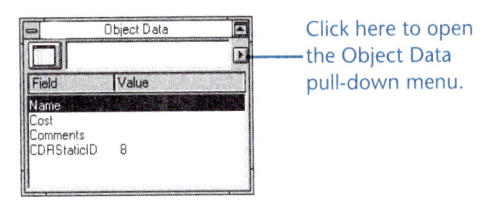

Fig. 23.7
The Object Data roll-up window.

5. Notice that the default field names are listed in the Object Data roll-up. They can be edited by clicking the small, black triangle to reveal a pull-down menu. Choose Field Editor from the resulting list, and the Object Data Field Editor dialog box appears (see fig. 23.8).

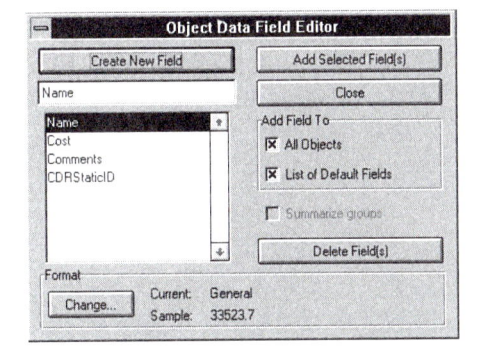

Fig. 23.8
The Object Data Field Editor dialog box lists the data fields and their contents for the selected object.

6. Edit a field name by clicking the appropriate name in the text area window and editing the name in the text area box located at the top of the window. Remember that you're not dealing with the actual data associated with an object at this point; you're simply setting up the general fields under which the data will be stored.

Tip
Double-click any of the field names in the Object Data dialog box to open the Object Data Field Editor dialog box.

To add any fields you need to meet your requirements, choose Create New Field. If you don't give new fields names, they're created with the names Field0, Field1, and so on.

The Add Field To All Objects option adds the fields that you selected at the left side of this dialog box to each of the objects contained in the currently active image. You can select all the fields by pressing Shift while clicking at the beginning and end of the listing of field names, or you can select a group of fields that appear randomly in the list by pressing Ctrl as you click the group of field names.

Add Field To List of Default Fields adds the selected field names to an overall listing of field names that appears each time you create a new document and use the Object Data Manager. To remove fields from the database for the currently active image, select the appropriate field names and then choose the Delete Field(s) option.

If the All Objects option isn't selected, use the Add Selected Fields option to add individual fields to the image objects currently selected. Until you're familiar with the Object Data Manager's operation, you're encouraged to leave All Objects selected.

The Summarize Groups option instructs CorelDRAW! to total the numbers contained in any set of objects grouped by the Arrange Group menu command. You might occasionally get strange results when this option is selected because CorelDRAW! simply adds whatever numbers appear in the columns and places the total in a cell at the end of the list. Remember that CorelDRAW! lists the objects as they are grouped, and summarizes the column listing for that group. Make sure to select Show Group Details on the Object Data Manager Preferences menu.

Format Change is used to present data in a desired format such as currency, comma separated, percent, and so on. You can also change data and distance formats using the Change option. This opens the Format Definition dialog box shown in figure 23.9.

Fig. 23.9
Use the Format Definition dialog box to select how the data in an object database is displayed.

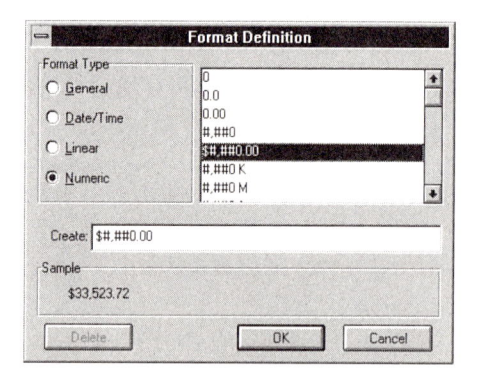

You can see CorelDRAW!'s numerous General, Date/Time, Linear dimensional unit, and Numeric display formats by clicking the appropriate button in the Format Type section of this dialog box. You can also create a custom format by entering the proper symbols in the Create text box. See table 23.1 for a listing of the most frequently used formatting characters.

Table 23.1 Formats and Their Uses

Type of Format	Format	Use
General		Adds text just as you enter it, except all leading and trailing zeroes are dropped and commas separating thousands are not recognized
Date/Time	M	Month in numeric form
	MMMM	Month in full text form
	d	Day of the month as a number
	dddd	Day of the week in full text form
	yy	Year in two digits
	yyyy	Year in four digits
	h	Hour as a number
	mm	Minutes with a leading zero as required
	am/AM	Shows AM or PM, as required
Linear	Feet	Single quotes or ft
	Inches	Double quotes or in
	Miles	MI
	Kilometers	KM
Numeric	0	Keeps a place for this number of digits to display
	#	Designates comma separator location
	,	Used with # to determine comma separator location
	$	Currency (Use $$"x" to show another currency symbol where x represents the symbol)
	.	Decimal separator
	K	Thousands abbreviation

Note

You can mix formats, but you must enter the minor format, or the units of smallest measure. For example, to display 1 ft 6 in, you must enter 18 (inches) as the value in the Object Data roll-up window with a 00ft00-in formatting definition.

554 Chapter 23—Multipage Documents and the Object Data Manager

If you choose the two decimal point currency option, for example, you can then edit it to remove the two decimal places. Simply enter **$#,###** over the format displayed in the Create entry box to do so. Choose OK to return to the Object Data Field Editor, and click Close to return to the CorelDRAW! image and the Object Data roll-up.

Tip
Detailed explanations of the symbols used in these formats and the way they're used can be obtained by using the Help Search for Help On Formats for Object Data.

In the Object Data roll-up, you can reorder the field names by dragging a selected field to a new location and dropping it there. A double arrow appears to indicate that CorelDRAW! is ready to move the field to a new location.

Now that the fields are defined, you can enter object data into the Object Data roll-up.

Adding, Editing, and Printing Object Data

Select any of the objects in your drawing to display a listing of its associated field names and their contents in the Object Data roll-up. At this point in the process, no data has been entered for the objects, so the Object Data roll-up window displays the field names without any value entries. If no object is selected, the window comes up empty.

To enter data associated with an object, follow these steps:

1. Select the object by clicking on it.

2. Select the appropriate field name from the Object Data roll-up window and type the desired field contents in the entry box at the top of the window. The data shown in figure 23.10, for example, was entered by clicking the Name field and entering **Sofa**, clicking the Purchase Price field and typing **1100**, clicking the Purchase Location field and typing **Jacobson's**, and then clicking the Color field and typing **Blue**.

Fig. 23.10
The object data for the Sofa object is displayed in the Object Data roll-up.

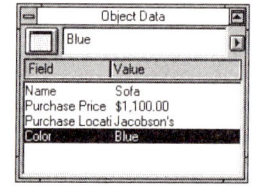

The data associated with the other objects could be entered in the same manner, but CorelDRAW! provides an easier method using the Object Data Manager. First select the Sofa, Coffee Table, Conference Table, and Plant objects using the Shift-click or marquee techniques. Then click the Object Data Manager icon located just to the left of the entry box in the Object Data roll-up window. The Object Data Manager data entry screen appears (see fig. 23.11).

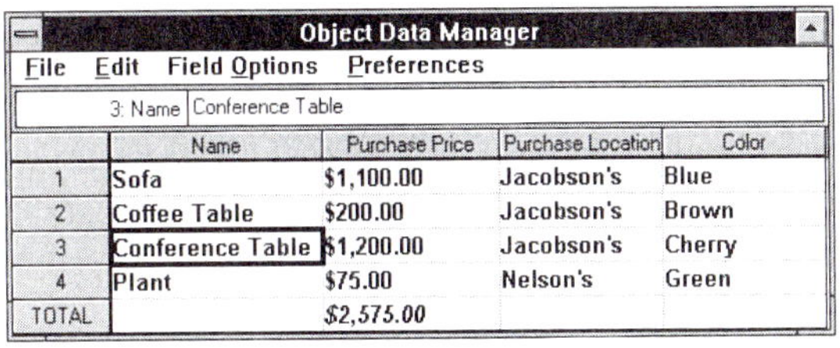

Fig. 23.11
The Object Data Manager data entry screen presents data in a spreadsheet format.

The data is stored in a spreadsheet format with the object number and name shown on the left side. Notice that each of the columns represents one of the field names that you defined earlier. The listing order of the objects depends on their order of creation and any Front/Back reordering you might have applied after initial creation. To determine which object corresponds to each database row number, click the row of interest to highlight the associated object.

You can enter data by clicking the cell of interest and typing in the desired information. If the columns aren't wide enough for the information you enter, drag the dividing line between the field names on the top row until the width meets your needs.

You can turn the column totals on or off by opening the Field Options menu and choosing Show Totals. To turn on column totals, select a column by clicking its field name, and then select Field Options Show Totals. If you don't want the field totals shown, as in the case of the color column in the example, repeat the procedure for the color column to turn off the Show Totals option. If your column totals are erratic, total the columns before summarizing the group to avoid adding the summary numbers to the column total.

Edit Cut, Copy, Paste, and Delete work just as they do in other Corel applications; they can be used to copy and move data in the Data Manager screen.

To print the object data, choose File Print Setup to determine how the data will print. You can determine whether grid lines, row and column headers, page numbers, and file names print and whether the data will be centered on the page based on your selections from this dialog box. Margins are also set from within this dialog box.

Choosing File Print opens the Print Options dialog box which is used to determine the number of copies printed, scaling of the data on the printed page, whether CorelDRAW! should size the output to fit the selected cells on one page, and whether the entire database should be printed or just the selected cells.

Tip
Make sure that you select the objects of interest before entering the Object Data Manager screen, or you might not have access to the objects you need.

Refer to Chapter 10, "Printing and Merging Files," for more information on printing. You can also print the database to a disk file for use with other spreadsheet products such as Lotus 1-2-3 or Microsoft Excel. The database is automatically given a PRN extension that is readable by most spreadsheet products.

Grouping and Data Hierarchy

Object data is grouped in the Object Data Manager in accordance with the image grouping defined in the CorelDRAW! image using the Arrange Group functions. For example, if we group all the objects to be purchased at Jacobson's into one CorelDRAW! group (the sofa, coffee table, and conference table), they appear together with their own subtotal within the Object Data Manager.

You can also define a name for any group of objects (*Jacobson's Purchases*, for example) and create up to 10 hierarchical group levels. The number of hierarchy levels displayed in the Data Manager is determined by the Preferences Show Group Details menu selection of the Data Manager.

The basic procedure for creating a group is as follows:

1. Make sure all data is correct for the objects to be grouped.

2. Select the objects to be grouped.

3. Group the objects by choosing **A**rrange **G**roup (Ctrl+G).

4. Type the desired group name into the text entry box of the Object Data roll-up window.

5. Open the Object Data Manager and verify that the new group was created (see fig. 23.12).

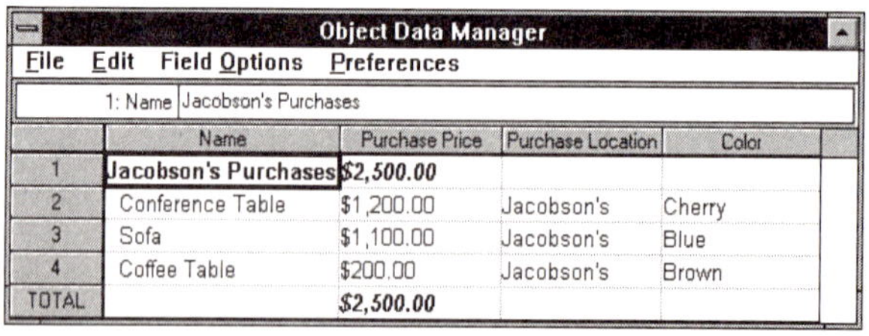

Fig. 23.12
Data Manager information using a hierarchy.

	Name	Purchase Price	Purchase Location	Color
1	Jacobson's Purchases	$2,500.00		
2	Conference Table	$1,200.00	Jacobson's	Cherry
3	Sofa	$1,100.00	Jacobson's	Blue
4	Coffee Table	$200.00	Jacobson's	Brown
TOTAL		$2,500.00		

You can still change Object Data from within the Object Data Manager if required. You can also create groups of groups (just as with CorelDRAW! objects). Selecting an object or group from the Object Data Manager selects the object on the image screen and shows the circles as handles, which is characteristic of a child object or group.

Objects placed in a group are indented two spaces to set them off from the others in the database. In addition, a space is left at the top of the group for a group name definition. You can set all Top Level (or first level) group titles or objects to have a boldface text appearance, once again for easy recognition. This is done using the Preferences, Highlight Top Level Objects menu selection. Preferences, Italicize Read-Only Cells displays all noneditable cells (such as calculated totals) in italic form.

The Data Manager information shown in figure 23.12 shows the Jacobson's purchases formed into a group using the standard CorelDRAW! Arrange Group command, Highlight Top-level Objects, and Italicize Read-Only Cells. The Jacobson's Purchases text in Row 2 was typed in as a group name. Field Options Show Totals was enabled for Purchase Price and disabled for Purchase Location and Color.

> **Troubleshooting**
>
> *I attempt to edit the field names in the Object Data roll-up by clicking the field name and entering a new name, but when I type a new name, it gets entered in the Value area of the roll-up. How do I edit field names?*
>
> To edit field names in the Object Data roll-up, double-click the field name to open the Object Data Field Editor dialog box. You can now enter a new field name by clicking on a field name and editing it in the text box at the top of the dialog box. Click Close when you complete your editing process.
>
> *My drawing has several objects, and each object should have the same field names associated with it, but each time I draw a new object and attempt to enter data for a field I created for previous objects, I have to re-create the field name and then add the data.*
>
> To create a field that will be present for all the objects you draw, the All Objects option under the Add To section of the Object Data Field Editor dialog must be selected.
>
> *Using the Object Data Field Editor, I deleted a field from the list of fields, but it deleted the field from all of the objects in my drawing. How can I delete a field from a single object?*
>
> You cannot delete a field for a single object. The Delete Fields option deletes the selected field from all of the objects.

From Here...

The multipage document feature of CorelDRAW! 5 is a valuable feature, and one you'll probably use quite often. Object Database Manager is a clever tool with a multitude of uses. The ability to link database information to a graphical image is becoming more important in today's computer environment.

For other information related to the topics in this chapter, consider these chapters:

- Chapter 3, "A Detailed Look at Object Drawing." This chapter gives detailed instructions for using and understanding CorelDRAW's drawing tools.

- Chapter 10, "Printing and Merging Files." This chapter explains in detail printing and merging options.

Chapter 24

Customizing CorelDRAW! to Fit Your Needs

The power of CorelDRAW! would be a potential curse if you constantly needed to define *all* a new object's attributes. The length of time involved in creating new objects would increase substantially, and you wouldn't enjoy creating images as much. Fortunately, CorelDRAW! comes with a number of customization options that make the display appear more to your liking while speeding up the drawing process. This chapter leads you through the customization characteristics that keep you from having to reinvent the wheel each time you work and help you increase your drawing productivity. A section on templates is included because CorelDRAW! provides several standard page layout designs, and you may want to use some of your own to leverage the time spent on prior projects.

In this chapter, you learn about the following:

- Customizing CorelDRAW! at Windows startup
- Setting positioning, constraint, and undo defaults
- Customizing the mouse
- Customizing screen display characteristics
- Establishing grid-related and display dimension defaults
- Customizing the toolbox
- Defining defaults for object attributes

- Setting default dimension line attributes
- Using CorelDRAW! templates
- Customizing text attributes
- Setting curve preferences

Customizing CorelDRAW! at Windows Startup

You can customize CorelDRAW! in Program Manager so that, when you start Windows, the CorelDRAW! program group is minimized to an icon at the bottom of the screen. Minimizing program groups reduces screen clutter. You can also place the CorelDRAW! icon in the Startup program group so that the CorelDRAW! program automatically starts when Windows starts. You'll work more efficiently if your most frequently used programs are already running when you start your work sessions. You can switch from one to another with ease.

Minimizing the CorelDRAW! Program Group

If you installed numerous Windows applications on your computer, you may want to minimize the program group windows to make the appearance of the Program Manager screen more neat, and to make it easier to search for the groups you want. To minimize any group window, including the CorelDRAW! program group, to an icon, click the Minimize button (the button with the arrow pointing down in the top right of the group's window).

Starting CorelDRAW! When You Start Windows

You can start CorelDRAW! automatically whenever you start Windows by including the CorelDRAW! icon in the Windows Startup application group. This feature is a Windows function, but you may find it useful if you start CorelDRAW! every time you use your computer. To have CorelDRAW! start whenever you start Windows, follow these steps:

1. From the Program Manager, open the Startup program group window and then the Corel 5 program group window.

2. While pressing the Ctrl key, click and drag the CorelDRAW! icon from the Corel 5 program group to the Startup program group.

3. Release the mouse button and Ctrl key. A copy of the CorelDRAW! icon appears in the Startup program group window.

The next time you start Windows, the CorelDRAW! application will start automatically. Thereafter, any time you want to switch to CorelDRAW! from another application, you can use the **S**witch To feature in the Control Menu box. You don't have go to Program Manager and open CorelDRAW! because it is always running when Windows is running.

Program Startup Defaults

A few characteristics apply every time you start CorelDRAW!. The page setup always appears as the last design used in your most recent CorelDRAW! session. If you last edited in Tabloid-Landscape page layout mode, for example, that page setup mode is adopted by CorelDRAW! for the next session. In addition, CorelDRAW! always starts a session in the Editable Preview mode. In this mode, you can see colors and outline attributes on your drawing and you can edit the drawing. (This mode is toggled with Wireframe mode in the View menu, which lets you see and edit only the outlines of your drawing.)

After you close CorelDRAW!, the program retains the default settings you specify in the menus described in this chapter. The next time you open the program, your defaults remain in effect.

Many user preferences can be changed in CorelDRAW! in the Preference menu property sheets (similar to dialog boxes). You no longer need to modify the CORELDRW.INI file to change preferences as in previous versions. You can access all Preference property sheets by opening the Special menu and choosing Preferences (or pressing Ctrl+J). The Preferences dialog box appears with the General Preferences property sheet in view, as shown in figure 24.1. To view any property sheet of options, you can click one of the five tabs across the top of the dialog box: General, View, Curves, Text, or Advanced.

Setting General Preferences

Options in the General Preferences property sheet allow you to specify how certain commands and operations will work. After you select **P**references from the Special menu, the Preferences dialog box appears with the General tab selected, showing the General property sheet (see fig. 24.1). This sheet provides positioning and constraint settings, Undo levels, and right mouse button options. These are described in the following sections.

Fig. 24.1
The General property sheet of the Preferences dialog box. The General tab is selected. The other tabs—View, Curves, Text, and Advanced—open other preference property sheets.

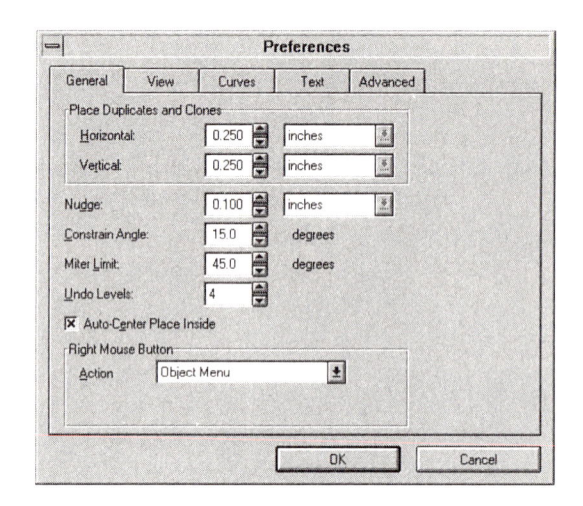

Setting Positioning, Constraint, and Undo Defaults

Positioning options on the General property sheet allow you to determine how far objects will be moved or placed. Constraint options allow you to specify the increments certain transformations or adjustments will be held to. One of the most important of the options on this sheet sets the levels of Undo. This feature allows you to experiment without worrying about ruining your drawing. The following positioning, constraint, and Undo options are available:

- The Place Duplicates and Clones Horizontal/Vertical option allows you to specify how far and in what direction duplicates and clones move away from the original object when you choose Duplicate or Clone in the Edit menu.

    Enter a positive value in the Horizontal box to place the copy to the right of the original.

    Enter a negative value in the Horizontal box to place the copy to the left of the original.

    Enter a positive value in the Vertical box to place the copy above the original.

    Enter a negative value in the Vertical box to place the copy below the original.

You can specify Horizontal and Vertical settings in inches, millimeters, picas/points, and picas.

- The Nudge option allows you to specify the distance your arrow keys move selected objects or curve nodes. Each time you press an arrow key, the objects or nodes move the distance you entered. If you hold down the arrow key, the items move in steps continuously. You can specify Nudge settings in inches, millimeters, picas/points, and picas.

  ◄ See "Copying Objects," p. 105

  > **Note**
  >
  > The hourglass may display when you nudge a large, complex drawing. After a delay for each press of the arrow key, the object will jump the specified nudge distance.

- The Constrain Angle option allows you to specify the degree increments at which certain actions will be constrained (held in position). This option affects skewing, rotating, drawing straight lines in freehand mode, and adjusting control points as you draw in Bézier mode. The Constrain Angle default is 15 degrees. With this default setting, when you rotate an object by moving its rotation arrows, the object will "jump" to the nearest 15-degree angle. The Constrain Angle can be set so that objects jump in degree increments as small as 1.0 degree to increments as large as 90 degrees.

  ◄ See "Moving Objects with Nudge," p. 101

  ◄ See "Rotating an Object," p. 189

  ◄ See "Skewing an Object," p. 192

  ◄ See "Drawing Straight Lines," p. 63

- The Miter Limit option affects how smoothly lines join at corners (miter joints). You can see the results of this setting only in the preview modes. Experiment with this setting to see the effect it makes on corner joints at different angles.

- The Undo Levels option allows you to reverse the results of your actions a specified number of "backtracks." This option affects the Undo and Redo commands in the Edit menu. The default is 4 levels. The maximum number of undo levels is limited only by the amount of available memory your computer has. The more undo levels you specify, the more memory is required. The capacity of your computer, the complexity of your art, the number of roll-ups open, and the number of other applications running are a few of the factors that determine the number of undo levels you can have without running out of memory.

> **Troubleshooting**
>
> *I keep running out of memory when I work on my bitmap files. Could my seven levels of undo be the problem? I have 8 megabytes of RAM.*
>
> Eight megabytes of RAM may not be enough memory to handle seven levels of undo for a file with large bitmaps or texture fills. Try setting the undo level at five or six.

- The Auto-Center Place Inside option affects the location of PowerClip contents objects pasted inside extrusions (container objects). When this option is checked (the default setting), you can select an object and choose Paste in the Edit menu to paste the Clipboard contents centered inside the extruded object. Only the part of the contents object inside the container object's boundary will be seen. If the option is unchecked, an object will be placed randomly inside the extrusion and you won't be able to see the contents object if it doesn't overlap the container. To make it visible, you have to unlock the container object and reposition the contents object so that you can see it.

> **Troubleshooting**
>
> *When I duplicate or clone an object, the copy is placed so close to the original that I have trouble selecting the correct one.*
>
> On the General tab of the Preferences dialog box, increase the Horizontal or Vertical value, or both, in Place Duplicates and Clones. (Try doubling the value.) This separates the objects more and makes it easier to select them individually.
>
> *I made a long, narrow triangle with a thick outline. The long tip of the triangle is blunted. How can I get a sharp point?*
>
> On the General tab of the Preferences dialog box, decrease the value of the Miter Limit. Try lowering the setting in increments of 5 degrees until the triangle has a sharp point.

Customizing the Mouse

The right mouse button can greatly increase your drawing efficiency. You can set it to perform specific menu-related functions automatically with a simple click. This short section introduces you to the mouse-related options.

Using the Right Mouse Button

Open the Special menu and choose Preferences. The Preferences dialog box appears, showing options available on the General property sheet (refer to fig. 24.1). The list box under Right Mouse Button lists options that enable you to associate various actions with a click of the right mouse button. These options are shown in figure 24.2.

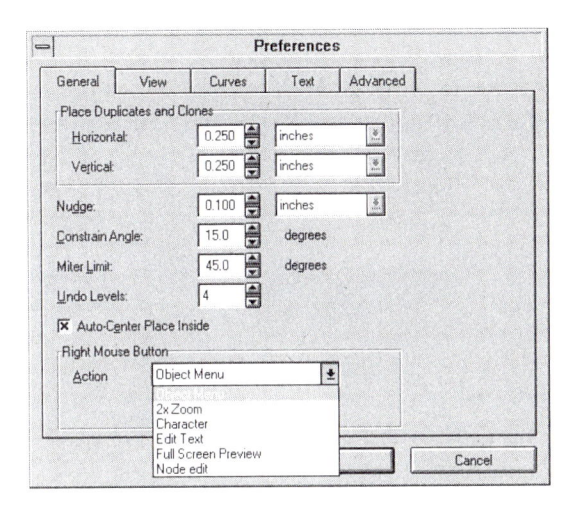

Fig. 24.2
The right mouse button default options. When you set the default to one of these options, a click of the right mouse button will perform an action associated with the option.

The first option, Object Menu, is the default. Clicking an object selects the object and displays the Object Menu for that particular object, shown in figure 24.3. With this menu, you can apply an object style, determine whether the outline prints on top or under the interior fill, or display the Object Data roll-up window, which you use with the Data Manager functions.

The Object menu is available with all other right mouse button selections. If you selected another button option as the default and you want to open the Object menu, simply place the cursor on the object and hold the button for a longer period of time before the menu displays.

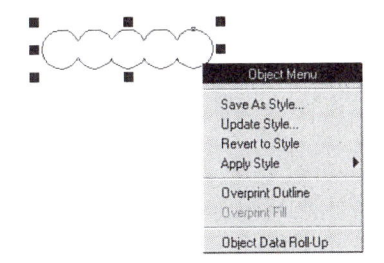

Fig. 24.3
If Object Menu is selected as a preference in the Action list, you can open this menu by clicking the right mouse button on a selected object.

The 2x Zoom option in the General Preferences property sheet Action list instructs CorelDRAW! to apply a two-times zoom-in to the image when you click at the mouse pointer location. You can repeat this action to zoom to the limit of magnification on your screen. Use the Zoom-out tool or double-click the right mouse button to zoom out.

With Character selected, you can highlight one or more characters of text and click the right mouse button to display the Character Attributes dialog box.

If you choose Edit Text in the Action list as the preferred action for the right mouse button, you can select text using the Pick tool, and then you can display the Edit Text dialog box simply by clicking the right mouse button (see fig. 24.4).

Fig. 24.4
The Edit Text dialog box. If Text is selected as a preference in the Action list, you can select text with the Pick tool and click the right mouse button to display this dialog box.

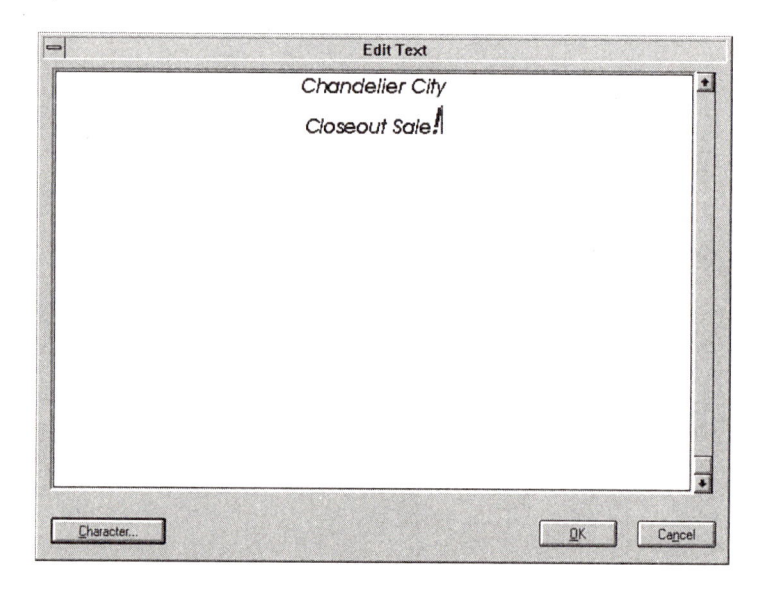

Select Full Screen Preview in the General property sheet Action list if you want CorelDRAW! to display the image in Full Screen mode when you click the right mouse button. (Full Screen mode is otherwise accessed from the View menu or by pressing F9.) Press Esc or the right mouse button again to return to the previous editing screen.

The Node Edit option is a shortcut to the Shape tool. Select this option in the Preferences-General property sheet Action list so that switching from any drawing tool to the Shape tool can be done with one click of the right mouse button. For example, if you want to work on nodes after creating an object with the Pencil, Bezier, Text, Rectangle, or Ellipse tool, simply click the right mouse button to switch to the Shape tool. (Of course, you'll have to convert rectangles and ellipses to curves before you can edit their nodes.)

Calibrating Mouse Speeds

You set the mouse double-click speed and level of tracking sensitivity not in CorelDRAW!, but in the Windows Main application group Control Panel Mouse option. After you select this option, the Mouse dialog box shown in figure 24.5 appears. Play with the settings until you find the right combination for you. Your Windows documentation describes this dialog box in detail. If you're left-handed, try the Swap Left/Right Buttons option to be more comfortable while using the mouse.

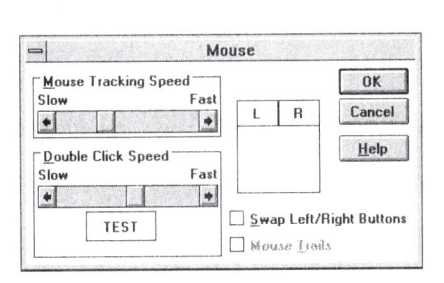

◀ See "Reshaping a Curve or Object by Changing Its Nodes and Control Points," p. 72

Fig. 24.5

The Mouse dialog box. This Windows dialog box is accessed in Program Manager through the Main application group Control Panel.

Customizing Screen Display Characteristics

The screen display is integral to effective CorelDRAW! operation. If the display isn't set up properly, you can be frustrated by small screens, insufficient area to accommodate your images, poorly aligned objects and text, and time-consuming refresh of the screen after any major change.

This section describes the following ways to customize the screen display:

- Positioning roll-up windows on the display using the View Roll-Ups dialog box.

- Positioning rulers on the display.

- Changing screen-related options that are located in the View property sheet of the Preferences dialog box.

Positioning the Roll-Up Windows

You can customize the way that CorelDRAW! appears when you start it by specifying options in the Roll-Ups dialog box. The options in this dialog box automate the standard step-by-step procedures that you might follow to set up your display with roll-ups for a drawing session.

You have some flexibility in the way the roll-up windows display when you initially start CorelDRAW!. These selections are particularly valuable if you consistently perform the same type of operations and use the same roll-up windows. You set the roll-ups in the Roll-Ups dialog box (see fig. 24.6). To access this dialog box, click **V**iew in the menu bar, and choose Roll-**U**ps. The Roll-Ups dialog box appears.

The Roll-Ups list box lists all the available roll-ups for the program. You can use this box to select just the roll-ups you want for the current drawing session, or you can use it with the Custom Option described below to select the roll-ups you want to appear every time you open the program.

To select each roll-up you want displayed, follow these steps:

1. Click the roll-up you want in the **R**oll-Ups list box. This highlights the roll-up.

2. Click the **V**isible option to the right of the list box. A small roll-up icon appears to the left of the roll-up to show it's selected. An X appears in both the Visible option and the **A**rranged option. When an X appears in both boxes, the roll-ups are arranged in straight rows at the left and right corners of the drawing area. If you prefer a cascaded arrangement, click Arranged to remove the X.

3. Click the **R**olled Down option to the right of the list box if you want the roll-ups to be displayed rolled down. CorelDRAW! stacks the rolled-down roll-ups with the title bars visible so that you can click the title bar to bring the entire roll-up to the surface.

4. If you decide you want all the roll-ups on your screen, choose the **S**elect All button below the Roll-Ups list box. You'll probably not use this feature because the numerous roll-ups obscure the screen and consume memory (see the tip about roll-ups and memory that follows in this section). Choose the Deselect button to deselect all your choices.

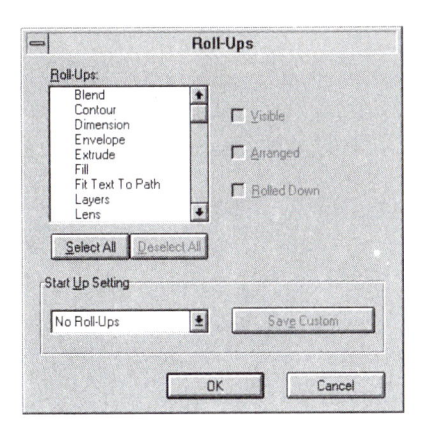

Fig. 24.6
The Roll-Ups dialog box. Use the options in this dialog box to customize the appearance of your display when CorelDRAW! opens.

The Start Up Setting list box in the Roll-Ups dialog box provides the following four options for customizing the start-up appearance of your CorelDRAW! screen.

◀ See "Using Roll-Up Windows," p. 25

- Choose No Roll-Ups in the Start Up Setting list box to tell CorelDRAW! to close all roll-up windows whenever you exit and to make sure that all are closed whenever you start the program again.

- Choose All Roll-Ups Arranged in the Start Up Setting list box to open all roll-up windows automatically and stack them, in closed form, in the upper right and left corners of the window.

- Choose Save on Exit in the Start Up Setting list box to tell CorelDRAW! to retain the roll-up information at the time of exiting and to display that roll-up configuration whenever you start the program again. This option is useful when you want the screen to appear exactly as you left it last (even if it was messy).

- Choose Custom to save the roll-up windows as they currently appear and to have CorelDRAW! display this arrangement the next time you start the program. If you choose Custom and do not select any roll-ups, the effect is the same as choosing No Roll-Ups.

> **Note**
>
> Roll-up windows consume memory. If you notice that CorelDRAW! is running slowly, do not choose All Roll-Ups Arranged. Instead, in the Roll-Ups list box, select only the roll-ups you use frequently and then choose the Custom option in the Start Up Setting list box. Users with 8M of RAM or less should use the Save On Exit or Custom option.

Positioning Rulers on the Display

You can add and remove the screen rulers by checking and unchecking the Rulers option in the View menu. In addition, you can relocate a ruler to another part of the screen by following these steps:

1. Press and hold the Shift key while dragging the ruler itself. (Note: You must press the Shift key before selecting the ruler.)

2. After the ruler is where you want it positioned, release the Shift key and the mouse button to lock the ruler into place.

To move the rulers back to their original positions, use this same technique.

Many times you want to measure an object from the zero point (0,0) of the rulers. You can change the zero point to new locations on the rulers by clicking on the icon at the left of the horizontal ruler and dragging the cursor to the location where you want the zero point to begin. When you release the mouse button, the zero point changes in the rulers. To reset the zero point, double-click the ruler icon.

Defining Display Preferences

Open the Special menu and choose Preferences (or press Ctrl+J). Click the View tab to display the View property sheet shown in figure 24.7. These options determine the quality of the displayed image, which has a direct effect on the screen refresh time. In addition, the options allow you to display and position the status line, display the cursor as a crosshair, display the ribbon bar, and enable the Pop-Up Help feature.

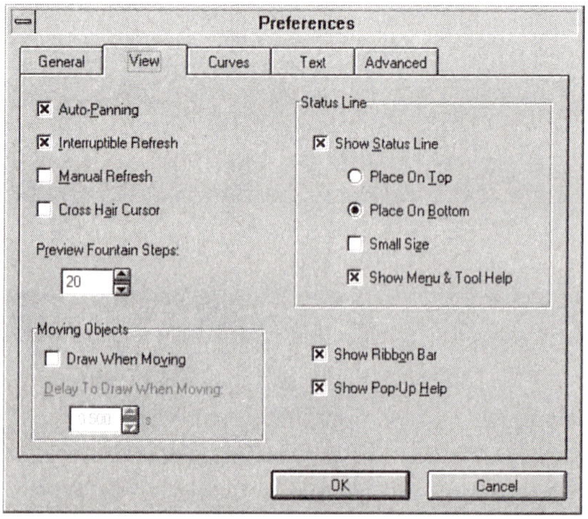

Fig. 24.7

The View property sheet of the Preferences dialog box. The options will affect your screen refresh and the display of the cursor, status line, ribbon bar, and pop-up help fly-outs.

- Choose Auto-Panning to instruct CorelDRAW! to move the underlying image one direction or the other, as required, while you drag with the mouse. This feature enables the cursor to stay on the image page and is particularly handy when you're working in Zoom mode because the image and objects are often larger than the display area. It's suggested that you work with Auto-Panning activated. It is enabled as a default when CorelDRAW! is installed.

- Choose Interruptible Refresh to instruct CorelDRAW! to stop the screen refresh when you click either the left or right mouse button or press a key. You can still click to select an object, even though its refresh has not completed. If you take no actions such as moving or stretching, the refresh resumes in a few seconds. When working in Wireframe mode, you can initiate the redraw of a specific object—one that's not part of a group—before the others by first selecting the object. This feature is particularly helpful with complex art, which takes a long time to refresh. It's suggested that you work with Interruptible Refresh activated. It is enabled as a default when CorelDRAW! is installed.

- When you choose Manual Refresh, screens will not refresh until you choose Refresh Window from the View menu, or until you choose Ctrl+W. This allows for a longer period of inactivity when you interrupt the display refresh by clicking the mouse button. When you need time to analyze a complex drawing before or after you perform an action on an object in it, this feature is helpful.

- Choose Cross Hair Cursor to replace the standard CorelDRAW! cursor with a set of lines that extend from top to bottom and left to right across the screen. These lines are occasionally handy for alignment purposes when you begin drawing an object.

Click the scroll buttons in Preview Fountain Steps to specify the number of steps used to display a fountain fill. This setting has no effect on the printed version of the fountain fill but affects how the fill appears on-screen. (You access the printed fountain fill options in the Print Options dialog box.) While creating the initial drawing, you may want to set this option to a number under 15 to improve the refresh time and later change it to 20 for the final drawing stages. The refresh time also depends on the speed of your system.

◀ See "Working with Gradated (Fountain) Fills," p. 170

Check the Draw When Moving option in the Moving Objects section to delay the redrawing of an object after you move it. After you check this option, the Delay To Draw When Moving area becomes active. You can then specify how long you want the delay to be (in seconds) in the Delay To Draw When Moving scroll box.

The Show Status Line box is enabled by default. You'll probably never want to disable this option because the status line shows information that you need for drawing. You can specify whether you want the status line on the top or bottom of your screen and whether you want it to appear in a smaller size. You can also enable the Show Menu & Tool Help option so that a description of a selected tool or menu item appears in the left corner of the status line. This works best if the status line is at the bottom of the screen.

The Show Ribbon Bar is also enabled by default. The ribbon bar is the line of icon buttons beneath the menu bar (see fig. 24.8). The buttons are shortcuts to menu bar commands. Though the ribbon bar buttons are convenient to use, you may want to disable this option when you have many roll-ups and objects on your screen and you want more room.

Fig. 24.8
The Ribbon Bar. The icon buttons are shortcuts to menu bar commands.

Show Pop-Up Help is also enabled by default. With this option checked, small descriptive fly-out labels appear when you rest the cursor on a tool or ribbon bar button, as shown in figure 24.9.

Fig. 24.9
Pop-Up Help fly-out labels. Descriptive labels appear when you rest the cursor on a tool or ribbon bar button.

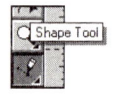

Establishing Preview Color Defaults

You can access preview color display options in the Preferences dialog box by clicking on the Advanced tab. The property sheet shown in figure 24.10 appears. The bottom half of the sheet shows available options for the preview modes.

The Preview Colors options determine the quality of color used to display the image in Editable Preview mode and Full-Screen Preview mode. These settings have nothing to do with the final printed output.

Windows Dithering is the only option provided for display devices (such as black and white displays, and displays in 8-color/gray shades mode) that do not support 256 colors/gray shades.

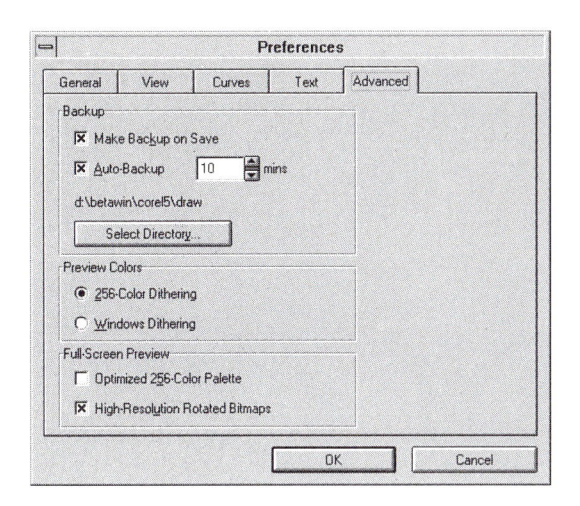

Fig. 24.10
The Advanced property sheet of the Preferences dialog box. The options affect the backup features and the quality of the display color in preview modes.

256-Color Dithering is automatically selected if your display does support the full 16-bit color range and/or 24-bit range.

> **Note**
>
> *Dithering* is a method of substituting colors to give the illusion of continuous color or gray. CorelDRAW! can support 16 million colors/grays, but display devices are limited in the colors/grays they can display. So CorelDRAW! uses a combination of supportable colors to approximate other colors.

Tip
You can refresh the screen more quickly if you set it to Windows Dithering, even if you have a 256-color display device.

Two options are available for full-screen previews:

- High-Resolution Rotated Bitmaps, if checked, will allow you to preview rotated bitmaps—even photobitmaps—at high resolution. This requires additional memory and screen refresh time. Leave this option unchecked if you want faster refresh or if memory is low. If you do not check this box, bitmaps may show a little graininess on-screen after being rotated. This feature in no way affects output.

- Optimized 256-Color Palette in the Full-Screen Preview box instructs CorelDRAW! to make its best estimate of the ideal colors to use for a full-screen image preview. 256-Color Dithering is used if the hardware supports it.

Customizing Backup Defaults

If you've ever accidentally erased a word-processed document, you know what a bother it is to re-create. Drawings may be even more difficult to re-create because of the numerous and varied curves, fills, and outlines.

To help you avoid inadvertently erasing or overwriting your drawings, CorelDRAW! provides two automatic backup options that can be accessed from the Preferences dialog box. Click Special in the menu bar and choose Preferences. The Preferences dialog box displays. Click the Advanced tab. The Advanced property sheet appears in figure 24.12, which appears in a following section.

Make Backup On Save creates a backup file when you use Save or Save As. The file is given the extension BAK. This option is enabled as a default.

AutoBackup creates a backup at periodic intervals. You specify how often you want the AutoBackup feature to save your file. You also specify which directory the file is to be saved under by using the Select Directory button. You can specify any directory you want. CorelDRAW! defaults to the \COREL50\DRAW directory. Your autosaved files receive the extension BAK. When you select Save, Save As, File New, or File Exit, the automatic backup files are deleted by CorelDRAW!. To safeguard against losing data between automatic backups, save frequently using the Save command. The AutoBackup option is enabled as a default for saving every 10 minutes.

To restore your most recent autobackup file, use File Manager to find the BAK file under the AutoBack directory you specified. Rename the BAK file to file name CDR so that you can find it easily when you return to CorelDRAW! and try to open it.

Because many factors such as electrical disturbances can cause computer problems, it's always wise to make backups on diskettes, tapes, or other off-disk backup media.

Tip
To restore the backup copy of a damaged file, use File Manager to find the BAK file. Rename the BAK file to file name CDR so that you can find it easily when you return to CorelDRAW! and try to open it.

Troubleshooting

When I am working on a drawing, the hourglass sometimes appears and I can't do anything for a few seconds. Why does this happen?

When the hourglass displays and freezes actions for a few seconds, CorelDRAW! is making an automatic backup of your file. The default backup interval is 10 minutes. If you want to disable the feature or change the backup interval, open the Special menu and select Preferences. In the Preferences dialog box, choose the Advanced tab. On the Advanced property sheet in the Backup area, change the number of minutes you want as the interval between backups. If you don't want the program to save backups of your work, click Auto-Backup to remove the X from the box.

Caution

It's not recommended that you disable the Auto-Backup feature. This helpful feature will save your masterpiece from oblivion if you damage it or lose data for some reason. If you do disable the Auto-Backup feature, make a habit of saving your work frequently in the active file and as a separate new file.

Establishing Grid-Related and Display Dimension Defaults

You use the grid to align objects along predefined intersecting divisions. A grid helps tremendously when you want to ensure a regular pattern and alignment for image objects. Detailed grid usage is covered elsewhere in this book, but the basic grid concepts are covered here in this description of how to set the defaults. The grid displays on-screen as lines of regularly spaced dots. The default preference options for setting the location and spacing of these dots and the way they affect objects near them are located in the Grid & Scale Setup dialog box. This dialog box also controls the drawing scale preference settings that help you create page measurements equivalent to actual floor plan measurements.

Open the Layout menu and choose Grid & Scale Setup to display the Grid & Scale Setup dialog box shown in figure 24.11. You use this dialog box to establish the grid-related defaults.

In the Drawing Scale text boxes, you can enter the value and units for Page Distance and World Distance. You'll be specifying the measurement on the page that is equivalent to a measurement on the plan. For example, if you're drawing house floor plans, you might decide that one inch on your drawing page (Page Distance) is equal to twelve inches on the floor space (World Distance). The Typical Scale list shows typical scale ratios used in plans. When you click a ratio in this list, the values in the Page Distance and World Distance fields are automatically updated. To use the Drawing Scale text boxes, you must click Use Drawing Scale. An X will appear in the box and the Drawing Scale text boxes will be activated.

Tip

You can also double-click the ruler to open the Grid & Scale Setup dialog box.

Fig. 24.11
The Grid & Scale Setup dialog box. Options in this box determine the location and spacing of grid dots and the way they affect objects near them. Other options determine the scale that matches your page measurements to your floor plan measurements.

◄ See "Establishing the Grid," p. 109

Tip
Always change the unit of measurement (inches, millimeters, picas, points, feet, yards, and so on) before changing the numerical value.

◄ See "Establishing the Grid Origin," p. 112

Tip
Another way to activate the Snap To Grid feature is by choosing Layout, Snap To Grid (or by pressing Ctrl+Y).

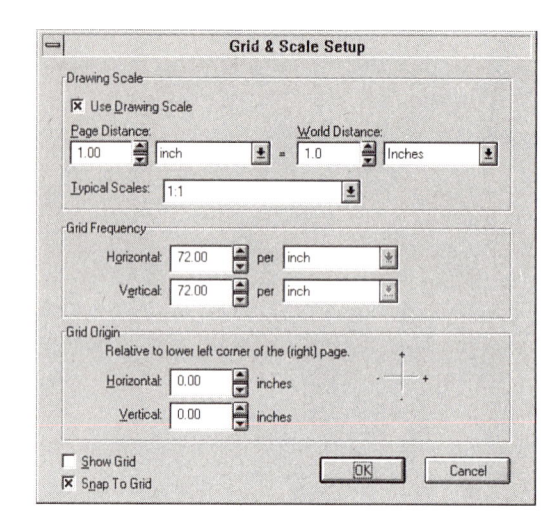

- The Vertical and Horizontal Grid Frequency settings in the Grid Frequency section determine the number of grid lines per dimension unit in each direction. For example, 16.00 per inch causes 16 grid lines to be inserted for every inch of image distance. The horizontal and vertical frequencies don't have to be the same number. The inch, millimeter, pica, and point dimensional units are provided.

  Use the scroll buttons to change a value or highlight the numbers and type in a new value. Values must be between .01 and 100 for Page distance, and .01 and 1563 for World distance.

- The grid origin is the position where the x-y coordinates are 0,0. By default, the grid origin in CorelDRAW! is in the lower left corner of the image page. You're encouraged to leave it there unless you have a specific reason to change it and really know what you're doing. If you reset the origin, the cursor position and object position information on the status line are affected. You can reset the grid origin by dragging the intersection point between the horizontal and vertical rulers to the new grid origin location.

Show Grid and Snap To Grid determine whether a representation of the grid displays on-screen and whether objects snap to, or are attracted to, the grid dots in the grid lines.

Customizing the Toolbox

You also can customize the location and contents of the toolbox in CorelDRAW!, and you can even make it disappear from your screen. This section describes the commands that allow you to customize the toolbox to make your workspace more suitable for your needs.

Relocating the Toolbox

You can relocate the toolbox from its normal position at the left side of the screen. Open the View menu, choose the Toolbox option, select Floating, and drag the toolbox to any location of your choice. Figure 24.12 shows a floating toolbox. You can return it to the standard position by double-clicking the toolbox's Control menu, or by once again choosing Toolbox from the View menu and deselecting Floating.

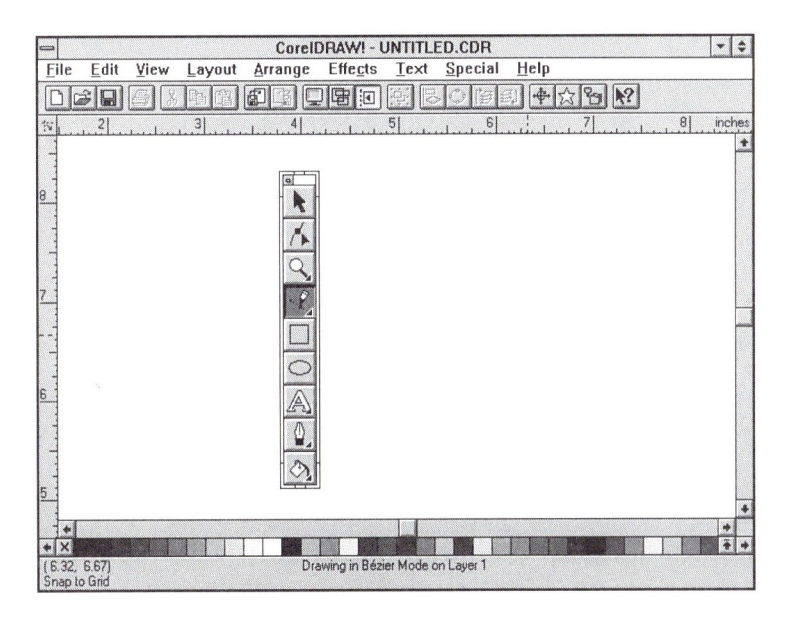

Fig. 24.12
A floating toolbox. You can drag it to any location on your screen.

Making All Tools and Icons Appear on the Toolbox

If you want all 48 tools and tool fly-out icons to appear in one floating toolbox, you can click the Control Menu box at the top left corner of the floating toolbox and select Grouped from the fly-out menu. The grouped toolbox is shown in figure 24.13. To ungroup the menu, click Grouped again, and the smaller floating toolbox appears.

Fig. 24.13
The grouped toolbox. All tools and fly-out tools are grouped on one floating toolbox.

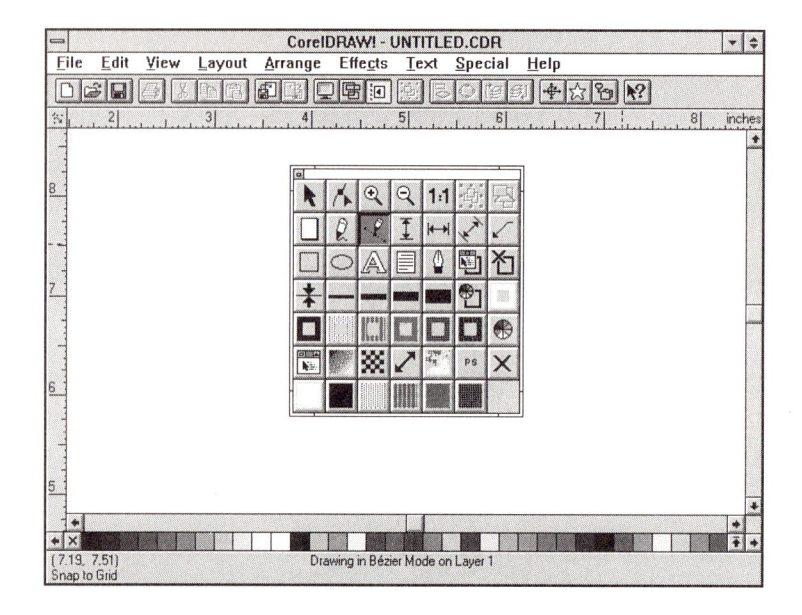

Hiding the Toolbox

If you don't want the fixed or floating toolbox to show at all on-screen, click Visible in the View-Toolbox fly-out menu. The toolbox disappears. To make it reappear, click Visible again in the View-Toolbox fly-out menu. To make the floating toolbox disappear, you can also click Close in the Control Menu box of the toolbox. The floating toolbox will disappear. To make it reappear, click Visible in the View-Toolbox fly-out menu.

Defining Defaults for Object Attributes

Setting the defaults for object attributes early in the drawing process saves you a great deal of time and aggravation. In addition, it better ensures a consistent look to your drawings. As an example, if you want most of the lines in your drawing to have rounded caps and a .02-inch line width, make these attributes default settings so that every time you draw a line, it will have these characteristics. You can later change attributes for any lines that you want to be different from the default. Setting object attribute defaults is an easy procedure that you can accomplish by following these steps:

1. Make sure that no objects are selected. When you do this, CorelDRAW! saves any settings you make as a default or global attributes, and they are applicable until you change them again. In fact, these attributes remain in effect after you exit and restart CorelDRAW!.

2. Click the Outline Tool fly-out menu and choose the Outline Roll-Up tool. This displays the Pen roll-up.

3. Set the various outline attributes you want by selecting each element of the roll-up and choosing a setting or attribute, such as color, arrowheads, line style, and so forth.

4. Click Apply. CorelDRAW! opens the Outline Pen dialog box shown in figure 24.14.

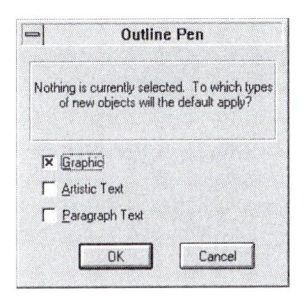

Fig. 24.14
The Outline Pen dialog box. You set outline defaults for new objects in this box.

5. You can assign the attributes you just set to any or all of the three object types in CorelDRAW!: **G**raphic, **A**rtistic Text, or **P**aragraph Text.

    You probably want different defaults for graphic objects and text because an outline appropriate for an object could make text characters illegible.

You can also apply attribute settings in a similar manner for fills. To do so, follow these steps.

◀ See "Modifying Object Outline Characteristics," p. 137

1. Make sure that no objects are selected.

2. Click the Fill tool fly-out menu and choose the Fill Roll-Up tool. This displays the Fill roll-up.

3. Set the various Fill attributes you want by selecting each element of the roll-up and choosing a setting or attribute. Click each of the tool buttons, such as Fountain Fill, Two-Color Fill, and so on, and set the attributes you want.

4. Click Apply. This displays the corresponding dialog box for the fill attribute you have set.

5. You can assign the attributes you just set to any or all of the three object types in CorelDRAW!: Graphic, Artistic Text, or Paragraph Text.

◄ See "Working with Interior Fills," p. 146

◄ See "Establishing a Default Outline Style," p. 145

All attributes you set in this manner are global—that is, they remain permanent until you change or reset them. You can learn how to change or reset them in Chapter 5, "Modifying Object Outlines and Interior Fills."

Now watch how your new default attributes are applied to all new objects you create.

Setting Default Dimension Line Attributes

Dimension lines are used primarily in technical drawings. They can save you a tremendous amount of time if you set them up properly. After you set them, these defaults apply to all subsequently created dimension lines.

◄ See "Using Dimension Lines," p. 403

To set default dimension line attributes, follow these steps:

1. Choose Roll-Ups from the View menu. Select Dimensions from the Roll-Ups list.

2. Select Visible, Arranged, and Rolled Down; then click OK. The Dimension roll-up appears (see fig. 24.15).

Fig. 24.15
The Dimension roll-up with unit options displayed.

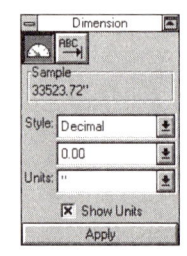

3. Set the dimension line's style to Decimal, Fractional, U.S. Engineering, or U.S. Architectural.

4. Enter the number of decimal places needed for the dimension label.

5. Set the units. Use " for inches, ' for ft, or mi. By default, the Show Units box is marked with an X and the unit appears after the dimension numbers.

6. Select the Text (ABC) button to display the options for positioning the text at the endpoints (see fig. 24.16).

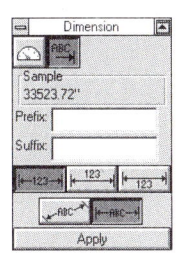

Fig. 24.16
The Dimension roll-up with text options displayed.

7. Select the appropriate button to position text on, above, or below the endpoint line.

8. Select the horizontal button if you want the text placed horizontally. If this button isn't selected, the text is positioned on the same angle as the line.

9. Select the center button if you want the text centered on the line when you drag it inside the extension lines. If this is not selected, the text will be placed at the location of your last click.

10. Click Apply to return to your drawing. The settings take effect the next time you draw dimension lines.

To break the link between a dimension line and its label object, select Separate in the Arrange menu. The only way you can relink the two is by using Undo or redrawing the dimension line.

Using CorelDRAW! Templates

CorelDRAW! comes with a set of standard templates that represent a combination of page layout design and text styles.

After a template is created, it can make updating a drawing or document a trivial task and greatly increase your efficiency. The designs and styles in the template can easily be applied to the objects in a new or old drawing. Finally, you can save a custom drawing as a template for later use. Why reinvent the wheel, when you can use a template instead?

You can load a template file to use with your drawing by following these easy steps:

1. Open the File menu and choose New From Template to display the standard directory dialog box. Notice that all files have the CDT extension and are stored in the COREL50\DRAW\TEMPLATE subdirectory (see fig. 24.17).

Tip
Even if a template is not perfectly suited to your drawing, you may be able to start with the template, make the modifications necessary for your needs, and still greatly increase the speed of drawing creation.

Fig. 24.17
The New From Template dialog box. You can use this dialog box to find the template that has the styles that most closely fit the styles you want for a new document.

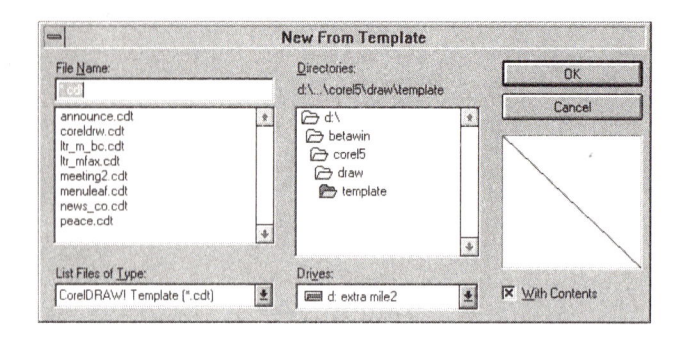

2. Scroll through the various designs until you locate the template design you want. Notice that several templates are provided with the CorelDRAW! program.

3. You can see a representation of the image in a small preview window on the right side of the dialog box. If you want to load the contents of the template as well as its styles and designs, click an X in the With Contents box.

4. Click OK. CorelDRAW! loads the drawing into the editing area for your use.

Save a currently active image as a template by following these steps:

1. Open the **F**ile menu and choose Save **A**s.

2. Choose the Template (CDT) option in the List Files of Type pull-down list.

◀ See "Using Styles and Templates," p. 236

3. Select the COREL50\DRAW\TEMPLATE subdirectory.

4. Type a file name in the File Name text box.

5. Click OK to save the file as a template.

Customizing Text Attributes

CorelDRAW! offers several preference options that control how text can be displayed or manipulated on-screen. To access these options, open the Special menu and choose Preferences. The Preferences dialog box displays. Click the Text tab. The Text property sheet shown in figure 24.18 appears.

Customizing Text Attributes 583

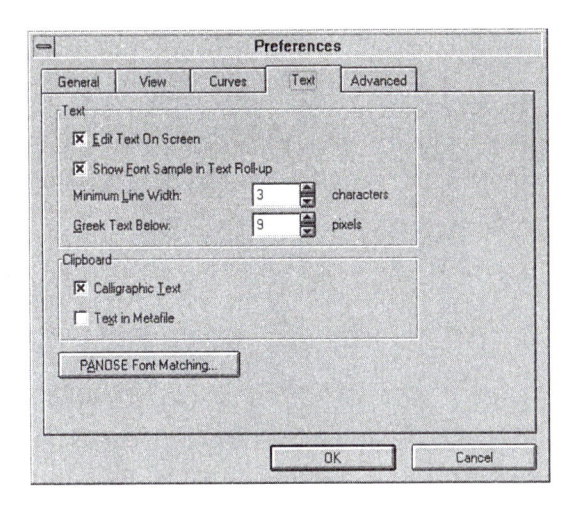

Fig. 24.18
The Text property sheet of the Preferences dialog box. The options determine how text can be displayed or manipulated on-screen.

- Edit Text on Screen is enabled by default. It allows you to edit text on-screen (except for text fitted to a path or changed with some of the Effects features). You'd want to disable this feature only if you were running a slow computer. Disabling Edit Text on Screen allows you to edit text faster in the Text dialog box, which automatically appears when the Text tool is selected and you select a location for the text.

- Choose the Show Font Sample in Text Roll-up option to have CorelDRAW! display, to the side of the Text roll-up window, a fly-out window that contains a sample display of the highlighted typeface (see fig. 24.19). By dragging the mouse across the listed typefaces, you can survey the various designs until you find the one you want. Deselect this option to remove the typeface display box from the Text roll-up window. This option is enabled by default.

    ◄ See "Working with Artistic Text," p. 212
    ◄ See "Working with Paragraph Text," p. 218
    ◄ See "Fitting Text to a Path," p. 240

- Use the Minimum Line Width scroll buttons to specify the minimum number of characters that can be located at the end of a line in paragraph text placed in an envelope. For example, if you set the value at the default of 3, a sentence can flow onto the next line if there are at least three characters that will flow onto the line. If there are only two, the two characters remain on the line with the preceding text.

- Use the Greek Text Below text box to specify the character-size threshold, in pixels, where text is displayed as small gray boxes rather than text. If a great deal of paragraph text is involved with an image, and you don't need to see the text itself (such as during page layout), you can set this option to a high value (such as 30 or more) so that the

584 Chapter 24—Customizing CorelDRAW! to Fit Your Needs

screen refreshes substantially faster. Any text under the specified number of pixels is drawn as gray boxes but can be viewed as text if you zoom in on it with the Zoom tool. When you're in the final editing mode, set this option to a smaller number (such as 9 pixels), and view the final document. The maximum Greek value is 500 and the minimum is 0.

- The Calligraphic Text option allows you to retain calligraphic pen outlines when you cut or copy them to the Clipboard or export them to vector applications. This option is enabled as a default. If you uncheck this box, drawings export or cut/copy to the Clipboard faster. The calligraphic outlines aren't retained on the Clipboard. They may or may not be retained on export, depending on the vector export filter.

- With the Text in Metafile option enabled, text cut or copied to the Clipboard is pasted as text. If you leave the box blank (the default), text cut or copied to the Clipboard is pasted as curve objects.

Fig. 24.19
The Text roll-up window showing a font sample in the fly-out window.

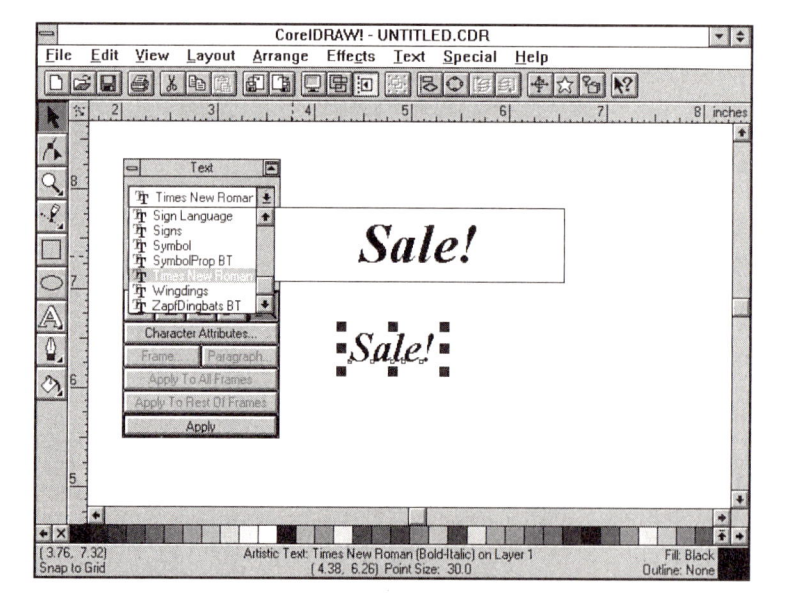

Setting Curve Preferences

Option items in the Preferences Curves property sheet affect nodes and curves (see fig. 24.20). They determine whether a segment is treated as a line or a curve, whether a node is treated as smooth or a cusp, how closely CorelDRAW! should track hand movements when drawing, and when two nodes should be joined automatically. One of the most useful settings is the setting for the Auto-Reduce Feature which helps you eliminate excess nodes on freehand curves.

This section describes how to set preferences for the Auto-Reduce Feature, freehand and autotrace tracking, corner and straight line thresholds, autojoin, and the minimum extrude facet size.

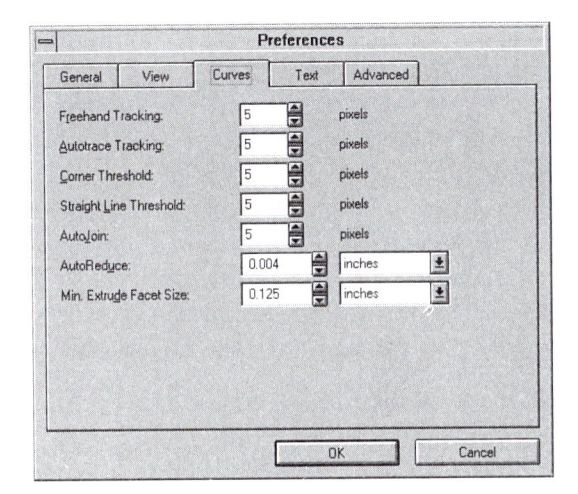

Fig. 24.20
The Curves Property Sheet of the Preferences dialog box. The options in this property sheet affect curves and nodes.

Setting the Auto-Reduce Feature Default

The Auto-Reduce option provided in the Node Edit roll-up window deletes unneeded nodes within a curve segment and reduces the number of nodes used to fit the curve.

When you choose Auto-Reduce from the Node Edit roll-up window, CorelDRAW! looks to the Auto-Reduce (min-max) setting in the Curves property sheet of the Preferences dialog box (refer to fig. 24.20) and determines which nodes are required to maintain the general direction of the curve, and deletes the rest for those segments you selected.

The Auto-Reduce option has a default setting of .004 inches. The lower the number, the less the curve changes with Auto-Reduce and a lesser number of nodes are removed. You probably need to experiment with this setting until you find the correct level for your applications.

Setting Tracking and Threshold Defaults

The tracking and threshold default settings in the Curves property sheet tell CorelDRAW! to keep the pixels (dots) of the lines you draw within certain limits as you draw or autotrace a line. The settings also determine how close pixels of separate nodes need to be before they're joined into one node. In addition, these default settings give the program the information needed to determine the type of node (smooth or cusp) or line (straight line or curve) to be created.

The *Freehand Tracking* setting specifies a threshold for the number of display pixels within which CorelDRAW! should ignore the line variations and not insert a node. If this number is low (1 to 3 pixels), CorelDRAW! attempts to match the complexities of the curve precisely and create the number of nodes required to make that happen. The result is often a large number of unnecessary nodes and a jagged-looking line. A high setting (6 to 10 pixels) gives a wider margin and creates fewer nodes and a smoother curve. For most drawings, a setting of 6 to 8 is adequate, but you need to experiment for yourself to determine the level that matches your needs. The default value is 5 pixels.

▶ See "Using Manual Tracing and AutoTrace," p. 661

Autotrace Tracking has to do with the level of accuracy you want when tracing a bitmap. The default value is 5 pixels.

Corner Threshold sets the level at which a cusp node turns into a smooth node. A low setting (1 to 3 pixels) creates many cusp nodes because the sharp line-direction changes are required to match the smaller hand movements. A higher number (7 to 10 pixels) causes more smooth nodes rather than cusp nodes and creates a smoother curve that may not exactly match the curve drawn or traced. Once again, you need to experiment to determine the proper level setting for your needs. The default value is 5 pixels.

Straight Line Threshold sets the number of pixel variations allowed before CorelDRAW! treats a straight line as a curve when you use the Freehand tool or AutoTrace feature. This threshold setting simplifies a drawing by ignoring small variations and making the drawing as elementary as possible. On the other hand, you may want a complicated drawing that exactly matches your hand movements. You would then set this level between 1 and 3 pixels and deal with the curves rather than lines. If you want more lines than curves, set the threshold level between 7 and 10 pixels. The default value is 5 pixels.

AutoJoin determines the number of pixels within which CorelDRAW! naturally assumes that two nodes are the same point and does not create separate objects or leave an open path. This feature generally comes into play with the double-clicking involved in multi-segment objects. If the second click is within the pixel radius, the two nodes are joined. If the click is outside the pixel boundary, a new segment is started, and the two nodes are treated as distinct and not joined. The default value is 5 pixels.

◄ See "Drawing Curved Lines," p. 68

Min Extrude Facet Size should be set to a high value as you are drawing extrusions. This makes the redraw time faster. When you're ready to print, change the setting to a lower value for a smoother, more accurate final output. Facet size represents the distance between shades of color in extrusions. Experiment with the settings for drawings of different complexity. The default value is .125 inches.

Customizing INI Files

One nice thing about CorelDRAW! 5 is that you no longer need to modify the INI files to customize the program. All customizing can now be done from within CorelDRAW! in the various dialog boxes described in this chapter.

> **Caution**
>
> If you try to modify an INI file and accidentally damage the data in the file, CorelDRAW! may not run as expected, if at all. You may need to reinstall the application. If you must edit an INI file, use any ASCII text editor such as the Windows Notepad.

If you need additional instructions on editing INI files, choose Search For Help On from the Help menu and search for CORELDRW.INI to find the most current definable commands and their parameters.

From Here...

For information relating directly to the various procedures affected by setting customizing preferences, you may want to review the following major sections of this book:

- Chapter 1, "An Overview of CorelDRAW! 5," provides basic information about CorelDRAW! including how to use roll-up windows.

- Chapter 3, "A Detailed Look at Object Drawing," describes how to draw lines and shapes and how to manipulate their nodes.

- Chapter 4, "Mastering Object Manipulations," describes object selection, alignment, transformation, duplication, and arrangement. It includes a detailed section on using the grid.

- Chapter 5, "Modifying Object Outlines and Interior Fills," describes how to add fills and outlines to objects. It includes detailed sections on using the Fill and Outline roll-ups.

- Chapter 7, "Adding Text to a Drawing," describes how to add and work with artistic and paragraph text. It includes descriptions of Templates, the Text roll-up, and the Edit Text dialog box.

- Chapter 12, "Advanced Line and Curve Techniques," describes advanced techniques for creating and manipulating curves. It provides a detailed description of node and curve manipulation and the Node Edit roll-up window. It also describes how to draw dimension lines.

Part VI

Using the Other Corel Applications

25 Photograph Touch-Up with CorelPHOTO-PAINT

26 Advanced CorelPHOTO-PAINT

27 Tracing Bitmap Images with CorelTRACE

28 Creating Presentation Charts with CorelCHART

29 Making Presentations with CorelSHOW

30 Adding Animation with CorelMOVE

Chapter 25

Photograph Touch-Up with CorelPHOTO-PAINT

by Ed Paulson

CorelPHOTO-PAINT, a painting and photo-retouching utility is included with the CorelDRAW! package. CorelPHOTO-PAINT enables you to create new bitmap images with tools that emulate paint brushes, airbrushes, and other conventional drawing tools. CorelPHOTO-PAINT also allows you to manipulate and compile bitmap images—especially photographs—that have been captured using a monochrome or color scanner.

This separate software utility from CorelDRAW! works very much like other PC paint programs, but it provides a variety of sophisticated effects that the other programs don't. You can use the images you create or rework in CorelPHOTO-PAINT directly, or you can export them for use as bitmap images in other CorelDRAW! 5 suite application images. You can also export CorelPHOTO-PAINT images to CorelTRACE, another utility program included in this package, to convert the bitmap image to a vector image. (This topic is covered in Chapter 24, "Customizing CorelDRAW! To Fit Your Needs.")

This chapter covers the following topics:

- Basic CorelPHOTO-PAINT operation
- Selecting image areas
- Fundamentals for effective image editing
- Applying CorelPHOTO-PAINT special features
- Color versus grayscale editing

Understanding Memory Limitations

CorelPHOTO-PAINT is a memory-intensive program; the usefulness of some of its features depends upon how much random-access memory (RAM) and virtual memory the computer has at its disposal. The more memory you have, the larger the picture you can handle and the more colors you have to work with. Available memory is reduced when you display a single document multiple times or when you open multiple CorelPHOTO-PAINT documents at the same time. If the available memory is low when you open a new document in CorelPHOTO-PAINT and attempt to set its dimensions, choosing a large image may limit the number of colors available to you in the program. Starting with 4M will be frustrating, and moving to 8M will help. Effective editing really requires 16M or more of RAM.

In the best possible scenario, you have enough memory to support *24-bit color*, the CorelPHOTO-PAINT setting that gives you the most options and effects (and uses all the 16.7 million colors available in the CMYK commercial printing model). Realistically, however, you can choose the 256-color mode because it requires less video memory, increases screen refresh speed, and doesn't degrade the color of the final output because the display (which itself is a temporary output medium) is separate from the actual printed page. If you plan to have the CorelPHOTO-PAINT picture commercially printed in a four-color process and want to use the electronic prepress functions of CorelPHOTO-PAINT and/or CorelDRAW!, 24-bit color gives you a great deal of control over the final printed piece because what you see on the display matches the output. 24 bit is a must for people performing high-quality image processing because accurate control is only provided with the higher storage capability. This is particularly true when using the 32-bit CMYK printing processes. (See Chapter 12, "Using Color for Commercial Success," for the details of color use.)

Tip
With only 4M RAM, you need to quit all Windows applications, including CorelDRAW!, before launching CorelPHOTO-PAINT. With 8 or 16M RAM, you can probably run one or two other applications and still edit a decent-sized picture.

> **Note**
> There are trade-offs between the amount of video memory, the desired resolution, and the number of colors displayed. The higher the resolution and number of colors, the more video RAM (VRAM) required. More than 2M of VRAM is required to display 24-bit color in 1,024 by 768 SuperVGA mode.

Basic CorelPHOTO-PAINT Operation

It's beneficial to be familiar with several basic CorelPHOTO-PAINT features before you attempt any advanced editing with the drawings. This section covers starting a CorelPHOTO-PAINT application, opening an image for editing, and saving and printing images.

Starting CorelPHOTO-PAINT

A completely installed CorelDRAW! includes an icon for CorelPHOTO-PAINT; this icon is placed in the Corel 5 group. To start CorelPHOTO-PAINT from Windows, double-click this icon. The screen shown in figure 25.1 appears.

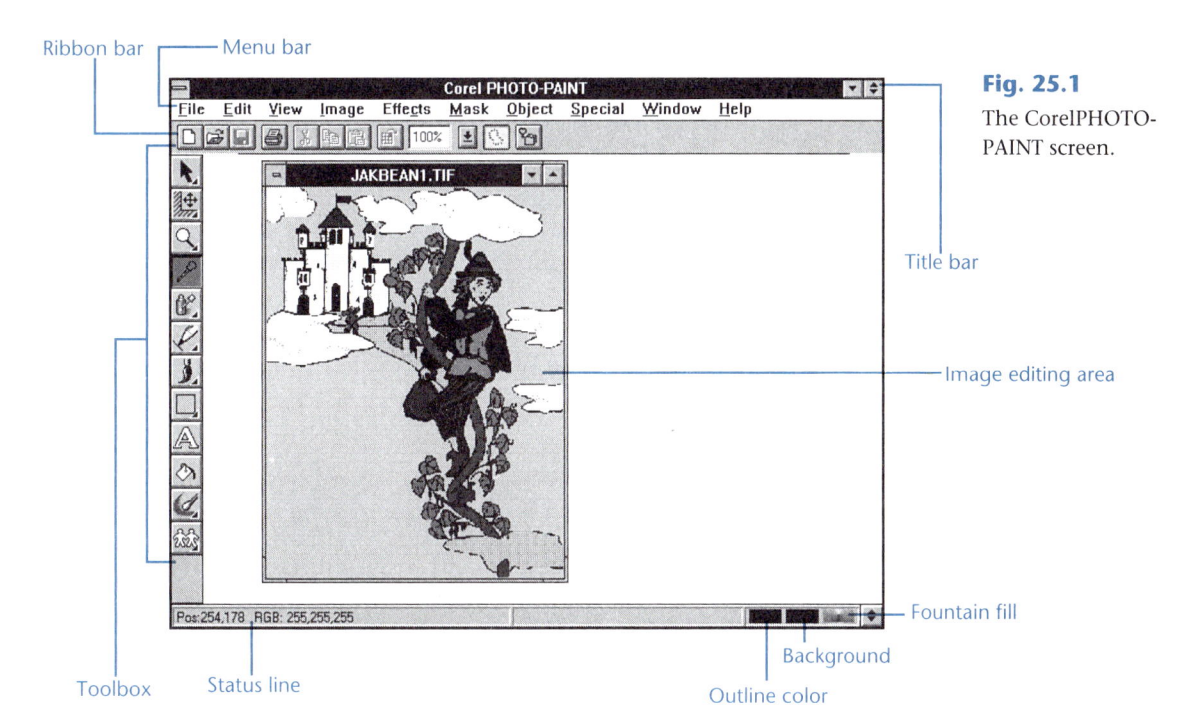

Fig. 25.1
The CorelPHOTO-PAINT screen.

Notice that this screen does not contain an open file for editing or an image area in which to work. A new or existing file must be opened before proceeding. To open a new file, follow these steps:

1. Open the **F**ile menu and choose **N**ew. This opens the Create a New Image dialog box, shown in figure 25.2.

Fig. 25.2
The Create a New Image dialog box.

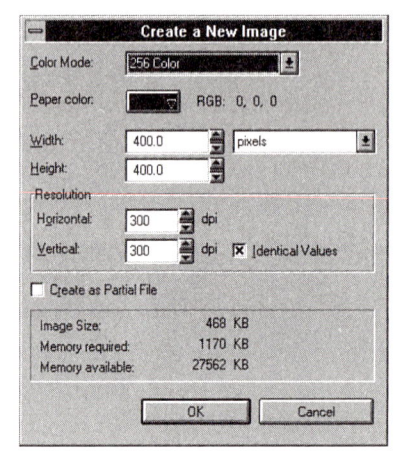

2. Enter the desired dimensional units for the image using the drop-down list to the right of the Height and Width box. Image sizes can be set in pixels (default), inches, millimeters, and picas, among others.

3. Choose the type of image (black and white, gray scale, 16 color, 256 color, 24-bit or 32-bit CMYK color) by clicking one of the options in the Color **M**ode drop-down list.

4. In the H**o**rizontal and **V**ertical boxes, set the resolution of the image in dpi (dots per inch), where you have the option of using identical values for your dpi settings. Image sizes can be set in pixels (default), inches, millimeters, and picas, among others.

5. The **P**aper Color setting defines the background color for the page. The drop-down color list works exactly the same as in the other CorelDRAW! applications.

6. Set the resolution in the H**o**rizontal and **V**ertical boxes, with 300 by 300 (a good working standard) as the default. It's generally a good idea to check the **I**dentical Values box to keep the image size with a 1:1 aspect ratio when printing.

> **Note**
>
> Remember that image dimension, resolution, and type are limited by the amount of RAM in the computer. CorelPHOTO-PAINT monitors the memory available and the memory required by the choices. If the choices require more memory than is currently available, you'll be required to reduce some of the settings. The memory information at the bottom of the dialog box indicates the estimated file size, memory size required to edit the file, and the total memory available. If the available memory is smaller than the memory required, it just won't work. Create as Partial File allows you to break the final image into multiple pieces.

7. After you make the choices, choose OK to create the new image area, or choose Cancel to leave the dialog box without opening a new file. The actual appearance of the screen depends upon the size and image type.

Earlier versions of CorelPHOTO-PAINT use a default PCX file format, whereas version 5 uses a new CPT file format. To save the image as a PCX file, choose Save As from the File menu. Then select the PCX format from the Save as File Type drop-down list.

To access an existing file (one that's been previously saved), choose the File menu's Open command to access the Open an Image dialog box. You can view on-screen bitmap representations of the available files and display textual information about them. To open a file, follow these steps:

1. Open the **F**ile menu and choose **O**pen to display the Open an Image dialog box.

2. From the List Files of Type list box, choose the desired file format.

3. Select the proper drive and directory that contains the desired file.

4. Click Preview to display the selected file in the preview window at the right of the dialog box.

5. Select the desired level of image cropping from the drop-down list below the Preview selection. Options include Crop, Full Image, Resample, and Partial Image. Full Image opens the entire image as a single file. Choosing Resample opens a dialog box within which the new resolution and image sizes are defined. This option is used to create another image of different resolution and size from that being opened. The Crop option opens a dialog box that contains the image with the familiar scaling handles. The outlined box, defined by the handles, defines the

image section to include in the opened file. Partial Area opens a dialog box within which the desired grid spacing is defined from within the Grid Size list. The finer the grid (for example, 8x8), the smaller the image portions available. Selecting a segment and then clicking OK opens the file with only the selected section displayed. Images of over 16M are opened automatically using Partial Image.

Saving an Image

Whether saving a scanned-in photograph, a piece of line art, or a picture created within CorelPHOTO-PAINT, the saving process is the same. It's also possible to save a portion of a CorelPHOTO-PAINT picture and process only that portion. All images created or reworked in CorelPHOTO-PAINT are saved as bitmap images. To save an entire CorelPHOTO-PAINT picture, follow these steps:

◀ See "Saving and Retrieving Files," p. 261

1. If the image has been previously saved, open the **F**ile menu and choose **S**ave. If the image has not been previously saved, the Save An Image To Disk dialog box appears.

> **Note**
>
> Choosing **F**ile Save **A**s displays the same dialog box.

2. Choose a file type from the Save Files of **T**ype box in this dialog box.

3. Specify a new drive and directory in which to save the file, as required.

4. Click the backup box to tell CorelPHOTO-PAINT to save a backup copy of the file by adding a $ to the end of the extension (cp$). These backups are also created at preset intervals.

> **Note**
>
> This action (backup) puts another copy of the file on disk. You may want to skip this option if the file is very large and disk space is at a premium.

5. Name the new file, and then choose OK.

Printing an Image

At some point, the image must be printed. The basic steps are the same no matter what type of image is printed or what type of printer is used. To print the image, follow these steps:

1. Open the **F**ile menu and choose **P**rint. The Print dialog box appears (see fig. 25.3).

> **Note**
>
> A Print paper orientation does not match document. Adjust printer automatically. Yes or No? message indicates a discrepancy between the default printer orientation and that which is defined for the currently active image. Clicking Yes adjusts the printer to match the image's page orientation.

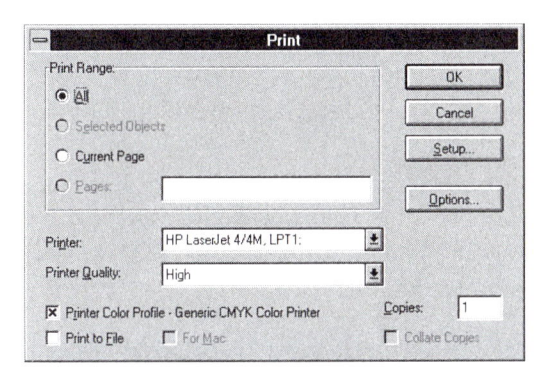

Fig. 25.3
The Print dialog box provides access to various output device settings.

> **Note**
>
> Many of the features and options in this dialog box are the same as those provided in the CorelDRAW! Print dialog box. See Chapter 11, "Scanning Images into CorelDRAW!," for a complete discussion of this dialog box.

2. The default printer appears in the Printer text box. Select an alternate printer from the drop-down list.

3. With the (Print) options button, you can change the location, size, and units of measurement for the image, if necessary.

4. Choose Pri**n**ter, **O**ptions, or **S**etup to make any changes to the printer setup.

> **Note**
>
> Options are covered in a later chapter entitled "Advanced CorelPHOTO-PAINT." The Printer option is covered in Chapter 11, "Scanning Images into CorelDRAW!."

5. After setting all the options as desired, choose OK to print.

Getting To Know the CorelPHOTO-PAINT Screen

The CorelPHOTO-PAINT screen isn't the same as the CorelDRAW! Screen. Some screen elements might be familiar to people who use other types of paint programs. The uninitiated should get to know the CorelPHOTO-PAINT screen— it only takes a few minutes. Understanding the CorelPHOTO-PAINT tools screen and knowing how to navigate from one area or option to another are the keys to producing quality art and retouched photos (see fig. 25.4). Remember, double-clicking the CorelPHOTO-PAINT icon contained within the Corel application group opens CorelPHOTO-PAINT to a display similar to that shown in figure 25.4.

Fig. 25.4
The CorelPHOTO-PAINT screen with an image open for editing.

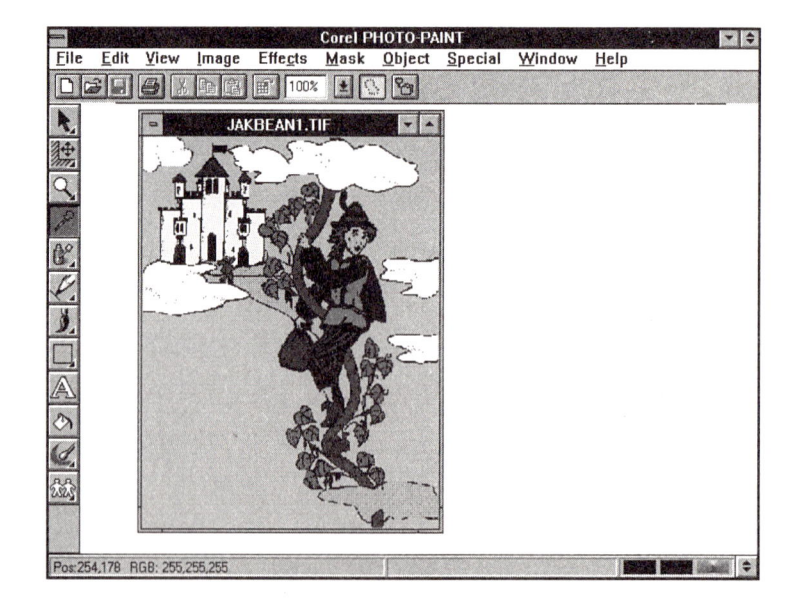

Getting To Know the CorelPHOTO-PAINT Screen

The CorelPHOTO-PAINT screen has many of the same features as the CorelDRAW! screen (and both screens have features similar to those provided in many other Windows-based graphics programs). These shared features include the title bar, the toolbox, the pull-down menus on the menu bar, and the roll-up windows.

The CorelPHOTO-PAINT *image-editing area* is different from the one provided in CorelDRAW! in a few key ways. First, as covered in the previous section, no image area opens automatically when you start CorelPHOTO-PAINT. Second, more than one image area can be open at the same time. You can work on different images at the same time in different windows, or on different parts of the same image in different windows.

The *status line* at the bottom of the window works like the status line in CorelDRAW!; and it provides information about the *x* (horizontal) and *y* (vertical) coordinates of the pointer position, using pixels as measurement units (although these units can be changed by choosing the Special dialog box from the Preferences menu). The 0,0 position indicates the upper left corner of the screen. If the cursor is placed over the icon without clicking, the status line also provides information about the currently selected tool, including its name and function.

The three color boxes at the bottom right corner of the screen correspond to the outline color, the background color, and the currently active fill type as shown from left to right, respectively.

For information concerning the current image, open the **I**mage menu and choose **I**nfo. The information box shown in figure 25.5 appears.

Fig. 25.5
The Image Info dialog box displays file size, type, and other important information about the currently active image.

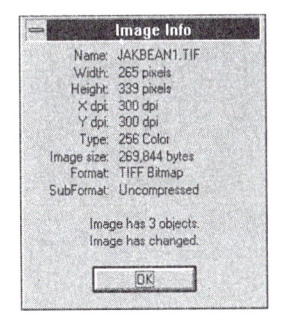

This box provides you with the name of the image, its width and height, its resolution in dpi, and its type and size. It also shows whether the image has been altered since the last save and provides the image's format and

600 Chapter 25—Photograph Touch-Up with CorelPHOTO-PAINT

subformat (if any). The number of selected objects refers to the number of image sub-areas selected as masks.

◀ See "Using CorelMOSAIC," p. 282

◀ See "Using Roll-Up Windows," p. 25

Like CorelDRAW!, CorelPHOTO-PAINT also uses *roll-up windows*. Choose the View menu to see its list of available roll-up windows: Color (F2), Canvas (F3), Fill (F6), and Tool Settings (F8). The File menu also contains the Mosaic roll-up. The Object menu contains the Layers/Objects roll-up (F7), and the Mask menu contains the Color Mask roll-up (F4). These windows provide most of the command buttons, list boxes, and options found in regular dialog boxes; but, they remain open after you choose an option, and they're consolidated in a single place, which makes program operation more efficient.

Sizing and Rearranging Windows

CorelPHOTO-PAINT offers some flexibility when you're choosing how to display information and graphics. To provide more work area on the monitor for a large picture, pull down the View menu and choose the Maximize Work Area command. This command uses the space normally reserved for the CorelPHOTO-PAINT title bar and menu bar. You can still access menu commands by holding down the Alt key and selecting each command's underlined letter (use Alt+F to open the File menu, for example). To return to the regular CorelPHOTO-PAINT screen, press Alt+V, E to activate the View menu's Restore Screen option. The quickest way to maximize work area is by clicking on the double arrow at the right side of the status line.

To remove everything from the screen except the active CorelPHOTO-PAINT picture, open the View menu and choose Full Screen Preview (F9) (The same as in CorelDRAW!). This mode, unlike the maximized work area mode just described, does not allow image editing. To return to the regular CorelPHOTO-PAINT screen, press Esc.

Tip
Pressing Ctrl+F6 cycles the display through the open image windows.

Working on more than one image at once or with parts of an image in several windows requires switching between and rearranging the windows. To change the active picture, click any part of the desired image window (it's safer to click on the image's title bar) or choose the desired window from the list offered at the bottom of the Window menu. The separate numbered items in the Window menu are the various displayed and minimized pictures and copies currently available. The active picture is indicated with a check mark.

CorelPHOTO-PAINT can arrange image windows in several ways designed to make the work area neater and the images easier to find. To arrange the windows, simply choose **W**indow and then choose one of the following four menu options:

- *Cascade.* Layers the CorelPHOTO-PAINT picture windows so that each title bar is visible.

- *Tile Horizontally.* Tiles the CorelPHOTO-PAINT picture windows horizontally across the screen.

- *Tile Vertically.* Tiles the CorelPHOTO-PAINT picture windows vertically across the screen (Shift+F4).

- *Arrange Icons.* Arranges already minimized pictures (now shown as icons) across the bottom of the CorelPHOTO-PAINT desktop.

Occasionally, ghost images appear in your drawing, or parts of the screen become jumbled. These images typically look like deleted information or appear left over from other sections of the display as the view was changed. To correct this type of problem, open the Window menu and choose Refresh (Ctrl+W).

Magnifying and Reducing the Image View

When you're editing an image, it's often useful to *zoom in* or *zoom out* so that you can either see more detail or get a better view of the big picture. These techniques are particularly useful if you want to draw large shapes or cut and paste large areas while viewing the entire picture on-screen.

> **Note**
>
> When you open a picture, it's at 100% (no zoom), even if it's larger than the display area. Zoom out presets are at 25%, 33%, and 50% when you zoom to fit available screen area. CorelPHOTO-PAINT chooses whichever zoom out setting gives you the full picture.

To zoom in or out on the active picture, choose View **Z**oom. A submenu appears, offering zoom percentages from 25% to 50% (smaller than actual size; used to shrink the picture or zoom out), and from 200% to 1600% (larger than actual size; used to magnify the picture or zoom in). CorelPHOTO-PAINT provides the 1600% for individual pixel editing. The title bar of the active window and the CorelPHOTO-PAINT status line indicate the current zoom percentage. The zoom is also easily set using the Zoom drop-down list located on the ribbon bar.

Tip
Press Ctrl+1 to activate 0% (no zoom).

To zoom in on a specific portion of the image, choose the Zoom tool from the toolbar, move the cursor to the desired area, and then click the left mouse button (to zoom in) or the right mouse button (to zoom out). A custom zoom level also can be set by dragging a marquee around the desired zoom area that the Zoom tool activates. The Zoom text box located on the ribbon bar indicates the

602 Chapter 25—Photograph Touch-Up with CorelPHOTO-PAINT

currently active zoom level percentage. The cursor looks like a magnifying glass when the Zoom tool is selected. Clicking the right mouse button while the Zoom tool is activated reverses the most recent Zoom action.

To show the actual size of the picture, choose View 100% (No Zoom), press Ctrl+1, or double-click the Zoom tool.

To magnify or shrink the image to fit the desktop, choose View Zoom to Fit.

The scroll bars at the left and bottom of the window are used to view other portions of a picture larger than the CorelPHOTO-PAINT window. The Zoom flyout menu's Hand tool is used to drag the display to the desired section when in an expanded view.

Working with Duplicate Windows

It's often useful to simultaneously work with more than one view of an object in CorelPHOTO-PAINT. You can do some detailed retouching work on the image of someone's eyes, for example, while still viewing the entire face in another window. To facilitate this sort of work, CorelPHOTO-PAINT provides the option of using *duplicate windows*.

To copy a specified picture, open the **W**indow menu and choose **D**uplicate, or press Ctrl+D. A second window opens, showing the original image at its original magnification level. The title bar of the second window indicates that it shows view 2 of the image (see fig. 25.6).

Fig. 25.6
The CorelPHOTO-PAINT screen with entirely duplicated windows as reflected by the title bar's name.

Original window

Duplicate after zoom

Indicates view #2 of the image

The second window can be changed without affecting the first. Use the Save As command with a different file name to ensure that changes made in the second window do not affect the first window's underlying file contents. Up to 20 different views of the same image can be open at the same time.

Corel provides the Locator tool to highlight the same area in duplicated windows. Simply choose the Locator tool from the Zoom tool fly-out and click the desired editing area in the currently active window. All other windows with the same image in varying magnifications then display that area. Select the window showing the view that you want to use for editing purposes and make the desired changes. This procedure is particularly handy when you're making progressive images where one image is based on slight variations from another.

CorelPHOTO-PAINT Tools

The CorelPHOTO-PAINT toolbox has over 50 tools that perform various tasks related to drawing, painting, editing, and choosing colors and patterns. The toolbox itself can be turned on or off (use the View menu's Toolbox Visible command), can be set up as a fixed or floating location, and can be rearranged to display the tool icons in different ways.

When the toolbox is fixed, it appears at the left side of the window, and icons are accessed by flyout menus. Click the toolbox control menu to access the toolbox layout options, which include the Grouped option used to combine related tools under a lead icon as seen in the normal toolbox arrangement. Turning the Grouped option off displays all the icons in a window that can be sized just like any window. When the tools are grouped, certain buttons appear with a small triangle in the corner. These triangles indicate that these buttons have more tools you can view and select. Hold down the mouse button as you select the button so the fly-out menu for that group of tools comes up.

The Tool Settings roll-up windows, accessible from the View menu, control how each of these tools works when creating different effects.

Tip
To display all icons, access the toolbox's control menu. It appears only when the toolbox is floating as set by the View menu's Toolbox Floating command.

Chapter 25—Photograph Touch-Up with CorelPHOTO-PAINT

Display Tools

Tool	Icon	Tool	Icon
Zoom		Hand	
Locator			

Selection Tools

Tool	Icon	Tool	Icon
Pick		Lasso	
Polygon Object		Magic Wand	
Rectangle Object		Circle Object	
Freehand Object		Object Brush	
Object Node Edit			

Painting Tools

Tool	Icon	Tool	Icon
Paintbrush		Airbrush	
Impressionist Brush		Pointillist Brush	
Spraycan		Flood Fill	
Artist Brush		Impressionist Clone	
Clone		Pointillist Clone	

Mask Tools

Tool	Icon	Tool	Icon
Mask Picker		Rectangle Mask	
Circle Mask		Freehand Mask	
Polygon Mask		Lasso Mask	
Magic Wand Mask		Mask Brush	
Mask Node Edit			

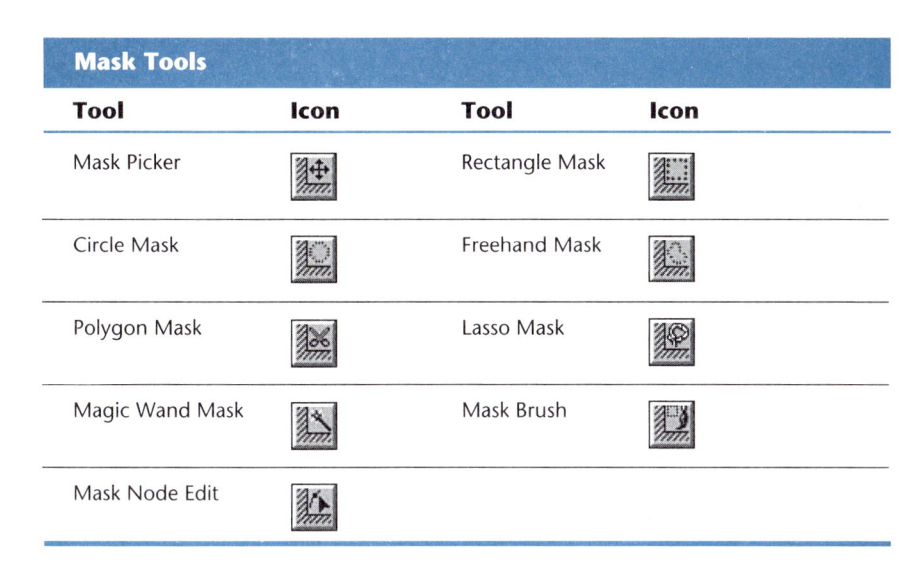

Drawing Tools

Tool	Icon	Tool	Icon
Line		Curve	
Pen		Text	
Rectangle		Ellipse	
Polygon			

Retouch Tools are specific for types of paintbrushes, so the name of an icon may change (that is, Freehand Contrast, Pointillist Contrast, and so on). These tools are in the following table:

Tool	Icon	Tool	Icon
Freehand Contrast		Freehand Brighten	
Tint		Freehand Blend	

(continues)

Tool	Icon	Tool	Icon
Smear Paintbrush		Freehand Smudge	
Sharpen		Eyedropper	
Local Undo		Eraser	
Color Replacer		Hue	
Saturation			

Editing Images in CorelPHOTO-PAINT

Painting and photo-retouching are done in CorelPHOTO-PAINT through a combination of menu commands and tool functions. The basic editing commands—Copy, Cut, Undo, and Paste—are similar to those used in CorelDRAW! and other Windows applications. They are covered briefly here; if you need more information about these basic commands, see Chapter 3, "A Detailed Look at Object Drawing," for a complete discussion of the CorelDRAW! commands.

After covering the basic tools briefly, this section discusses the commands and tools used to edit color, transform parts of images, and touch up images in CorelPHOTO-PAINT.

Before you can use any of these commands or tools, you need to know how to select objects in CorelPHOTO-PAINT.

Selecting Image Areas

CorelPHOTO-PAINT provides six basic object selection tools that can be used to define the areas of an image to include in a cutout:

- *Rectangle Object Tool.* Defines a rectangular or square area by dragging the icon on the image until the marquee surrounds the desired area.

- *Lasso Object tool.* Defines irregular areas when you drag the tip of the lasso around the desired area.

- *Polygon Object tool.* Defines multisided geometric areas (polygons). The shape can have three or more sides of any length, but must be an enclosed figure. The sides must be straight; no curved lines are allowed.

- *Irregular Freehand Object tool.* Used to select an irregular-shaped area that contains all image elements within the marquee.

- *Magic Wand Object tool.* Defines irregular areas with similar colors as determined by the Color Tolerance settings.

- *Paintbrush Object Brush tool.* Selects areas based on brush strokes of the currently active brush size.

The most basic of these tools is the Rectangle Object tool, which appears on the fly-out displayed by clicking and holding down the mouse button on the Object Picker icon that looks like the CorelDRAW! Pick tool. To select an image area using the Rectangle Selection tool, follow these steps:

1. Select the Rectangle Object tool.
2. Click at one corner of the area to be defined, and then hold the mouse button down while dragging to the opposite corner. The left mouse button gives you an opaque cutout; the right mouse button gives you a cutout with a transparent background color.
3. When you get to the opposite corner, release the mouse button. A marquee appears around the selected area.

Tip
Hold down the Ctrl key during this operation to constrain the cutout to a square shape.

To select an area using the Lasso, follow these steps:

1. Click once to define the area to be selected, and then drag the pointer while holding down the mouse button to create any shape you want.
2. When the shape has been defined, release the cursor. The area is selected.

To select an area using the Polygon Object tool (Scissors), follow these steps:

1. Click once at one of the corners or turning points of the area you want to select.
2. Click the next corner or turning point; the two points you defined connect with cut-out lines. Repeat this step until you have only one more turning point or corner to go.
3. Double-click the last corner. It connects to the first; the area is selected.

Tip

Use this tool when you are zoomed in close enough to the image to see individual pixels, or you may accidentally click an undesired color.

To select an area based on color, the Magic Wand Object tool is the tool you need. Simply choose the tool and click the desired color with the Wand's point. Be warned, however, that this is a tricky tool to master. It selects all adjacent pixels of a similar color as defined by the Color Tolerance Comparison settings.

To refine the color selections of the Magic Wand, you must adjust its color tolerance. Choose **S**pecial **C**olor Tolerance to open the Color Comparison Tolerance dialog box (see fig. 25.7), or use the shortcut method of double-clicking the tool itself.

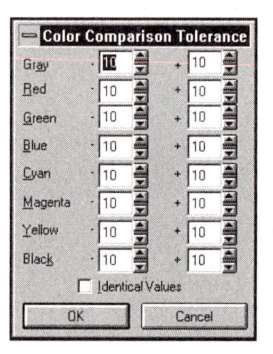

Fig. 25.7

The Magic Wand's Color Comparison Tolerance dialog box used to set the variance allowed when using the Magic Wand and Lasso tools.

Enter or select a +/–percent color tolerance range for red, green, and blue. Click Identical Values to set all the ranges to the same values. Set the values to low numbers to fill, replace, or select a single, narrowly defined color range. Higher numbers indicate a higher tolerance, which include more colors and subsequently more image area.

Using this feature requires a certain amount of experimentation to meet specific acceptance criteria. After the area is chosen, its interior fill can be set using the Fill tool and default color. This is a handy feature for changing the color of irregular shapes, deleting a specific colored area, or even adding a custom fill, such as a fractal or fountain fill, to an image area.

> **Note**
>
> Even the shapes of the cursors of these irregular tools are irregular. The bottom tip of the Lasso indicates its position, the top of the Scissors is the cursor point, and the furthest tip of the Wand indicates its position.

A number of new area selection tools are included with the release of CorelPHOTO-PAINT 5.0. They allow for greater speed and flexibility when selecting image areas. The operation of most of these tools, such as the rectangle and ellipse select tools, is obvious. The Freehand Object tool is operated in the same manner as the Lasso tool, except that the Freehand tool includes the entire image contained in its perimeter, while the Lasso tool includes only a specified range of colors. The Object Brush tool is used to paint over the area to be selected by using a brush size set in the Tools roll-up window. The Object Node Edit tool is similar to the Node Edit tool in CorelDRAW!, and allows for precise modification of the selected object's perimeter.

To select an area using the Freehand tool, follow these steps:

1. Select the Freehand selection tool.

2. Click on the image once to start defining the area to be selected, and then drag the pointer while holding down the mouse button to create any shape you want.

3. When the shape is defined, release the cursor. The entire contents of the defined area is selected.

The Object Brush tool allows for very precise selection of image areas not easily accessed using the Freehand tool. It is used by following these steps:

1. Select the Object Brush tool.

2. Move the cursor, which now looks like a circle, to the image area and then drag it until the desired region is selected.

Manipulating Image Cutouts

After a portion of a CorelPHOTO-PAINT picture has been selected, it becomes a *cutout*. Cutouts can be manipulated in many ways:

- To move the cutout to another location, place the mouse pointer inside its boundaries, and then click and drag it to the desired location. To leave a single copy behind, hold down the Shift key while you click and drag it.

- To resize the cutout horizontally or vertically, click and drag one of its corner handles.

- To resize the cutout proportionally in all directions, hold down the Shift key while you click and drag one of its corner handles.

- To make the cutout opaque, drag holding down the left mouse button.

- To move the cutout one pixel at a time, use the arrow keys.

Of course you can also manipulate the cutout in a variety of other ways using the Edit, Image, and Effects menus.

Cutting, Copying, and Pasting Parts of an Image

Like CorelDRAW!, CorelPHOTO-PAINT allows you to alter images by cutting, copying, and pasting parts of them. These are the most basic image-editing skills, and they are used frequently.

Tip
It's often easier to copy a portion of an image to another area in the same image from one CorelPHOTO-PAINT to another using the Clone tool.

Like many other applications, CorelPHOTO-PAINT uses the Clipboard as a temporary storage area to hold text and graphics. From the Edit menu, use Copy to duplicate or Cut to remove the contents of the selected area and place them on the clipboard. Then use Paste to copy the contents of the clipboard into the current CorelPHOTO-PAINT picture.

To cut or copy a portion, follow these steps:

1. Select the desired portion of the image using any of the available image selection techniques and tools (Rectangle, Lasso, Scissors, Magic Wand, and so forth).

2. Open the **E**dit menu and choose **C**opy to copy the selection and leave the original in place.

   or

   Open the **E**dit menu and choose Cu**t** to cut the selection from its original place.

In either case, the selected image area is now placed on the Clipboard. To paste it somewhere else, follow these steps:

1. Move the cursor to the desired location (another part of the same image, another image, or another Windows application).

2. Choose Edit Paste. You have two options at this point.

3. Choose As New Object to place the image in the center of a picture, surrounded by the marquee. This way you can then drag the image to any area in the picture. Or choose As New Image to place the image into its own window and treat it as a new file.

> **Note**
>
> If you change your mind immediately after cutting, copying, or pasting something, you can reverse the most recent editing action by choosing Edit Undo (Ctrl+Z). Only one undo level is available. Edit Undo also can be used to reverse the transformations covered in any of the following sections on editing.

To save a defined area of a CorelPHOTO-PAINT picture, follow these steps:

1. Define the portion of the picture to be saved using one of the object selection tools. A marquee appears around the selected portion.

2. Open the **E**dit menu and choose Cop**y** to File. The Save An Image to Disk dialog box appears.

3. Select a file type from the Save File as Type box. If applicable, select other options from the File Sub-Format drop-down list.

4. Set the Drive and Directory to which the file should be saved.

5. Give the picture a file name.

6. If you want CorelPHOTO-PAINT to save a backup copy of the file in either EP$ or BM$ format, check the Backup box.

7. Click OK.

Replacing Colors

You can replace colors with another color one at a time by using the Color Replacer tool. Follow these steps:

1. Select the Fill color box, the color you want to change. This is the foreground color box in the Color roll-up (see fig. 25.8), and is easily and exactly set by using the eyedropper on the color targeted for replacement. Simply click the Eyedropper tool and then click the desired image color to set that color exactly within the Color roll-up window. This color will be used for outline and paint.

Fig. 25.8
The Color roll-up window with eyedropper on outline color.

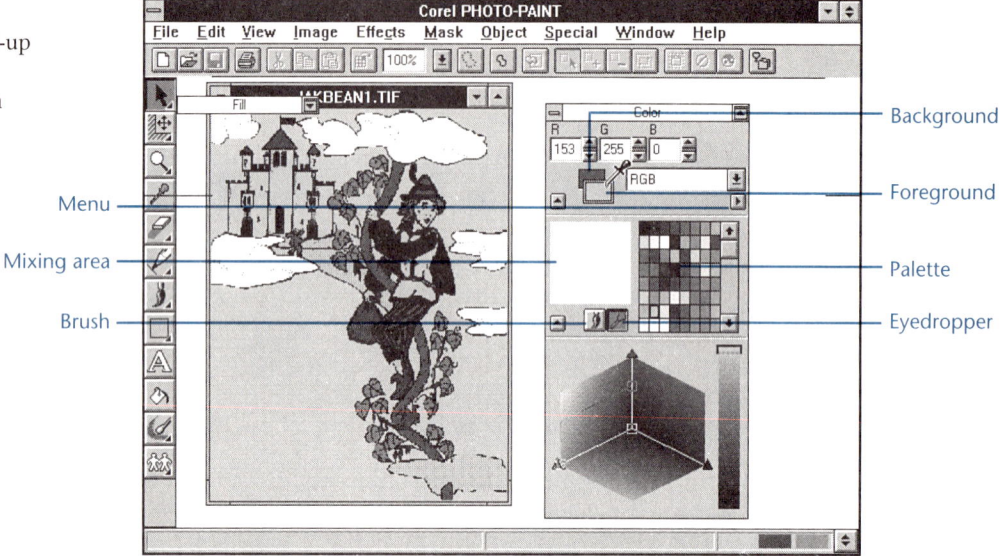

Labels on figure: Menu, Mixing area, Brush, Background, Foreground, Palette, Eyedropper

2. Select another color, the new color you want to use as the replacement for the background color box in the Color roll-up. It is easily set using the eyedropper. The background color box is behind the Fill color box. The background color is used by the Eraser tool, for example.

3. Adjust the shape and width of the Color Replacer's tool next to the Eraser tool. To do this, use the Tool Settings roll-up menu. You don't need to be too precise with this setting because the color tolerance settings combined with the outline/fill selections in the Color roll-up will filter out most colors that shouldn't be changed.

> **Note**
>
> If the Tool Settings roll-up window isn't open, choose View Tool Settings Roll-Up (F8) to display it or double-click on a draw or paint tool, for example.

4. Adjust the range of colors to replace in the Special Color Tolerance dialog box. Click Identical Values if an exact color match is desired. Otherwise, set the +/- percentage tolerance ranges to higher values to allow more deviation from the base color used.

5. Drag the cursor over the image areas in which automatic color replacement is desired. Watch as CorelPHOTO-PAINT automatically selects the colors within the specified tolerance range and replaces them with the new color. You may not see any colors replaced until you increase the color tolerances.

> **Note**
>
> Hold down the Shift key to constrain tool movement to vertical or horizontal. Press the space bar to change the direction of the constraint.

Troubleshooting

Why can't I just click on an object and edit it as I do in CorelDRAW!?

CorelDRAW! works with vector graphic images, and CorelPHOTO-PAINT works with bitmap images. A bitmap is simply a special configuration of dots that comprise an image object. A vector graphic, on the other hand, is an arrangement of nodes connected to form an object. That object can be edited. The closest you can come to editing an object in CorelPHOTO-PAINT is to use the Magic Wand (or other object selection tools), which selects matching colors in a specified tolerance range, and forms the final group of pixels into an object that can be shaped or edited.

I am frustrated with having to perform all my pixel color editing by hand. Is there an automated procedure for changing those colors?

Use the Color Replacement tool, because it's designed to automatically select the colors from a specified range and replace them with the colors in the color roll-up. The Special menu's Color Tolerance settings determine how closely the selected colors match the one selected. To best ensure that your colors match, use the Eyedropper tool to select the color to replace directly from the image itself.

Acquiring Images

One of the most useful features of CorelPHOTO-PAINT is its capability to retouch and edit photographic images with many sophisticated tools, effects, and color choices. Now you can use the File Acquire command to scan and place an image into CorelPHOTO-PAINT in one step, instead of performing the scanning outside the program. (See Chapter 11, "Scanning Images into CorelDRAW!," for detailed information on scanning.) Another good use of CorelPHOTO-PAINT is to edit and annotate screen images captured with CorelCAPTURE.

Scanning a Picture with CorelPHOTO-PAINT

You can still import photographs and other images into CorelPHOTO-PAINT, but now you can also use CorelPHOTO-PAINT's resident scanning program to capture images directly from a scanner attached to the PC. To access the

614 Chapter 25—Photograph Touch-Up with CorelPHOTO-PAINT

scanning program, first make sure the driver software for the scanner is set up according to Microsoft Windows requirements. The options that appear under the File Acquire Image Acquire dialog box (resolution, size, cropping, and so on) are determined by the type of scanner and driver software you have. Some scanners require manual resetting of resolution or gray scale; others are controlled by software commands. The scanner has to be supported by both Windows and Corel. Please consult the scanner documentation for details.

After setting up the driver software, follow these steps to scan in a photograph or other artwork:

1. If using a flatbed scanner, place the photograph or artwork on the scanner bed. If using a hand-held scanner, have the scanner and photograph or artwork aligned so that the image is scanned directly from top to bottom as the scanner is dragged over the image.

2. Open the **F**ile menu and choose Acquire **I**mage. A submenu appears.

3. Choose **S**elect Source to specify the device (usually a TWAIN-compatible scanner).

4. Choose **A**cquire to activate the scanner attached to the PC. A scanning dialog box appears (see fig. 25.9).

Fig. 25.9
The scanning Acquire dialog box. The settings that appear in this window depend on the driver software you install for the scanner.

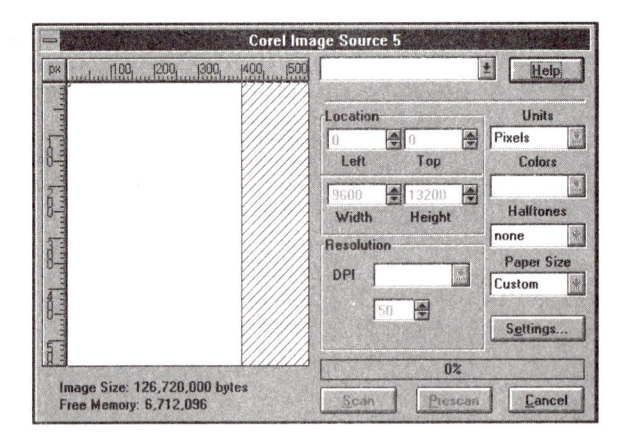

5. A Setup Scanner dialog box appears. Choose Setup, if available, to adjust resolution, gray scale, and so on. (You may need to use manual controls on the scanner itself to reset these parameters.)

   Make any necessary changes to the information in this dialog box (see the scanner documentation for detailed instructions), and then choose OK.

6. Click the Scan button to complete the scan of the image. The image appears in the CorelPHOTO-PAINT window, ready for reworking.

Scanned images come into CorelPHOTO-PAINT as bitmaps. Large bitmaps use a great deal of memory and disk space, so previewing them can be a very slow process. In general, the higher the resolution of the scan, the more detailed and accurate the bitmapped image and the larger the resulting file. You have to weigh the importance of the detail in the bitmap against the realities of working with large, memory-hogging files. An oversized file can cause problems with printing or importing, and after it's imported into CorelPHOTO-PAINT, it may also be harder to edit.

After retouching the photograph in CorelPHOTO-PAINT, you can convert it to vector form using CorelTRACE if you plan to use it in CorelDRAW! or another drawing or page layout program. See Chapter 24, "Customizing CorelDRAW! To Fit Your Needs," for details on how to use CorelTRACE.

Capturing a Screen

CorelDRAW! 5 comes with a screen capture package titled CorelCAPTURE. This program allows the acquisition of information displayed on the computer screen such as the currently active window, the entire screen, or a subsection of the screen. The information is copied to the Windows Clipboard and must be retrieved using the Edit Paste commands integral to the destination application. Start CorelCAPTURE by double-clicking the CorelCAPTURE icon located in the Corel application group. The window shown in figure 25.10 appears.

The entire screen, the desktop, is captured by pressing Print Screen. The currently active window is captured by pressing Alt+PrintScreen. The entire window of the currently active Window's application, or Client Area, is captured by pressing Alt+Pause. Pressing Alt+Shift+F2 captures a rectangular area to the Clipboard.

Fig. 25.10
The CorelCAPTURE window showing the capture keyboard shortcuts and their effects.

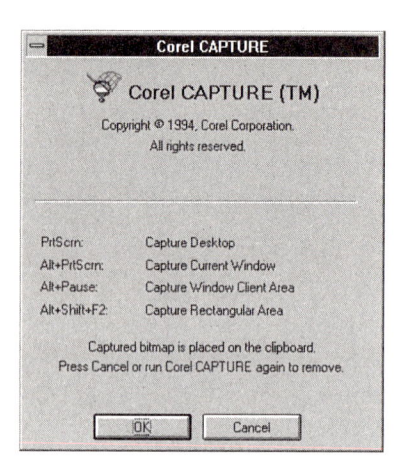

[Screenshot of Corel CAPTURE window showing:]

Corel CAPTURE (TM)
Copyright © 1994, Corel Corporation.
All rights reserved.

PrtScrn: Capture Desktop
Alt+PrtScrn: Capture Current Window
Alt+Pause: Capture Window Client Area
Alt+Shift+F2: Capture Rectangular Area

Captured bitmap is placed on the clipboard.
Press Cancel or run Corel CAPTURE again to remove.

[OK] [Cancel]

> **Note**
> The Clipboard files are lost unless saved to another application or from the Clipboard directly using the Windows Clipboard Viewer.

CorelCAPTURE is disabled by either clicking Cancel from within the CorelCAPTURE window, or by again double-clicking the CorelCAPTURE icon. Rerunning CorelCAPTURE terminates its operation.

Working with Color

Tip
To improve the way CorelPHOTO-PAINT shows 256 color or less on-screen images, open the View menu and choose Dithering Ordered.

CorelPHOTO-PAINT supports up to 32-bit CMYK color, grayscale, and black-and-white pictures. The CorelPHOTO-PAINT filters and retouch tools, however, work most quickly with 24-bit color or grayscale. If you open a CorelPHOTO-PAINT picture in gray or with fewer than the most common 256 colors, it's automatically converted into 256-color display. Even though the on-screen colors don't appear to change when you make color changes in CorelPHOTO-PAINT, the program remembers the underlying file changes. You can create and edit pictures that have more colors than the hardware supports because CorelPHOTO-PAINT simulates the enhanced colors on-screen.

Working with Color Images

24-bit color mode is also called *true color*, because it supposedly gives you all the color choices found in nature (nearly 17 million). In CorelPHOTO-PAINT, 24-bit color has better detail and depth than the other color modes; all the retouch tools, painting tools, and filters work best in this mode. Even if the monitor doesn't display 24-bit color, CorelPHOTO-PAINT simulates the colors on-screen and retains the original detail. The palette you see for 24-bit color contains 256 of the almost 17 million colors available. The CMYK process color options provide a larger number of color options, which require 32 bits to represent properly.

A *256 colors* picture is made up of 256 solid colors, with a color set in the palette that defines the colors available for the picture. Use 256 Colors mode if you're creating pictures to view on-screen or if you don't have the memory to support 24-bit color. Even if the monitor doesn't support 256 colors, CorelPHOTO-PAINT simulates all colors on-screen and retains the original detail.

No matter which color mode you choose, you can use the Color roll-up window to adjust individual colors or to change all the colors in the palette together. The Eyedropper tool enables you to click a colored area in the picture and then change another spot in the picture to that color or recreate the color in another place.

Working with Grayscale Images

Think of gray and black and white as shades of colors. Often, the output device is a monochrome printer, and working with grays is a good way to ensure output quality.

Grayscale mode is the best setting for providing tone shadings in the picture without adding the complexity of the color modes (or requiring the large amount of free RAM). A grayscale picture is made up of 256 solid grays; any grays not supported by the monitor are simulated on-screen with the original detail retained. All the filters and tools of CorelPHOTO-PAINT are available in Grayscale mode.

Another color choice is *Black and White* mode, which is useful for high-contrast pictures. Black and white also requires the least amount of memory. When you convert to black and white, you can choose a conversion type such as halftone or line art. Because most of CorelPHOTO-PAINT's tools and filters are not available for Black and White mode, you can convert the image to another mode for editing purposes and then convert it back to black and white as a final step.

Automatically Changing Color Modes

To convert an image from one color format to another, choose the **I**mage Con**v**ert To command. As mentioned earlier, the choices are Black and White [1-bit], Grayscale [8-bit], 256 Colors [8-bit], RGB Color [24-bit], and CMYK color [32 bit]. If an application or device requires grayscale or 24-bit color images, you can convert the picture to the required format, edit it, then convert it back to the format you need.

If you convert to black and white, you have three more options from which to choose. If you don't want halftones, choose the Line Art setting. If you want gradations of black in a picture that has a coarser dot pattern, you can choose the Screen Halftone option.

The converted picture is loaded into a window and named *New*; you can then save it using the Save As command from the File menu.

Painting the Photo

One of the most exciting and useful things about CorelPHOTO-PAINT is that any scanned photograph can be enhanced and saved as a bitmap. Colors can be changed. Areas can be modified using the artistic filters to transform a photograph into a painted representation of the same image. Contrast can be changed to brighten an image, or to eliminate distracting flaws. Naturally, images can be skewed, scaled, or rotated. You can modify the original photographic image in thousands of different ways.

At the most basic level, painting photographs using CorelPHOTO-PAINT is quite simple. To paint a photograph, follow these general steps:

1. Choose the drawing or selection tool (for example, the Paintbrush) you want to use for the job at hand.

2. Make desired tool dimensioning adjustments using Tool Settings and menu commands to create precisely the effect you want. Different tool definition options are available depending upon the tool currently in use.

3. Choose an outline color from the Color roll-up window.

4. Point to the location in the image where you want to start, and paint away!

The next few sections introduce you to the details specific to the use of several of these tools.

Painting with the Brushes and Spray Tools

Several painting tools all work from the basis of a drawn line, but apply a special artistic effect to the line after the path is defined. The tools are basically paintbrushes and spraycans, which are all available under the Paintbrush tool's fly-out menu.

The brushes perform different artistic effects based upon which brush is selected before the line is drawn. The first brush in the fly-out is the Paintbrush tool, which is the most basic of tools. It can be rectangular, circular, or one of several other shapes as displayed when the Paintbrush icon at the top of the dialog is selected (see fig. 25.11). Scrolling through the designs reveals the wide variety provided. A particular design is deleted by first selecting it and then clicking the Delete Brush (garbage can) icon.

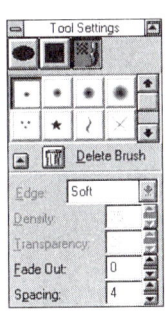

Fig. 25.11
The Paintbrush Tool Settings roll-up showing the various brush designs and the options associated with Paintbrush.

The next two brushes are the Impressionist and Pointillist designs, and each has its own settings within the Tool Setting roll-up. The brush designs are similar to those shown in figure 25.11, but several variances are provided to control the number of lines or dots drawn and their relative placement with respect to the originally drawn line.

The fourth brush, the Artistic Brush, contains a Flatbrush, Fanbrush, and Knife option (see fig. 25.12). Each has its own distinctive style, which is modified in pixels by the Size setting, and by the Fade setting. The larger the number, the quicker the drawn image utilizes the imaginary paint contained on the brush.

Fig. 25.12
The Tool Settings for the Artistic Brush tool with the Knife design displayed in the preview window.

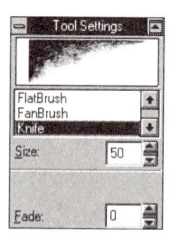

The final two icons represent the Airbrush and Spraycan tools. These tools simulate the effect of spraypainting an image. The Tool Settings roll-up displays the various aperture designs, flow rates, transparency, and amount of image Fade Out desired from the beginning to the end of a spraying tool's use.

The point of providing all these tools is to allow accurate simulation of actual graphic designer painting techniques. Experimenting with the various sizes, orientations, and designs is fun.

Drawing Lines with the Line, Curve, and Pen Tools

Objects are also drawn on the image surface by using several tools located in the toolbox under the Line tool fly-out menu, which contains the Line, Curve, and Pen tools. After the line is drawn, it becomes part of the image. Undo the latest drawing modification by pressing Ctrl+Z or selecting the Edit menu's Undo option. All these tools have a Transparency option included in their Tool Setup roll-up window. A high transparency makes the drawn line more translucent, which allows more of the underlying image to show through.

The Line tool draws straight lines and is used similarly to the Pencil tool in CorelDRAW!. Simply move the cursor to the image surface and click to anchor the beginning of the line. Move to the desired endpoint and click again to finish the line. Clicking and dragging the cursor anchors the beginning point and draws a straight line between the initial anchor point and the location at which you release the mouse button. A new line is automatically started at the second click location. End the series of lines by double-clicking at the termination point.

The Curve tool is used to draw curved lines. It is operated by simply clicking and dragging the cursor on the image surface until the desired effect is achieved. The curve tool draws a line similar to the CorelDRAW! wireframe, complete with nodes, and then adds the outline attributes to the underlying line after a new line is started or another tool selected.

The Pen tool draws a line that directly tracks on the cursor movements, but you will find the line less fluid than with the Curve tool. Simply click and drag the cursor on the image surface until the desired line is drawn.

Adding Shapes to the Photo

You can add shapes to the picture, perhaps as background for text. CorelPHOTO-PAINT offers many of the same square, ellipse, polygon, line, and curve drawing tools provided by CorelDRAW!; the only difference is that in CorelPHOTO-PAINT, these tools create bitmap images instead of vector graphic ones. That means you won't see any nodes or Bézier curves in CorelPHOTO-PAINT. Still, the process of drawing a rectangle or circle is the same as it is in CorelDRAW!. You simply click and drag the mouse to create the shape, using the Ctrl key to constrain it to a square. See Chapter 4, "Mastering Object Manipulations," if you need to refresh your skills in these areas.

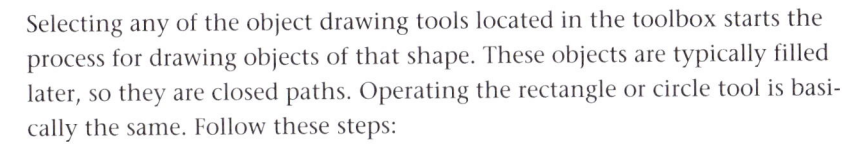

Selecting any of the object drawing tools located in the toolbox starts the process for drawing objects of that shape. These objects are typically filled later, so they are closed paths. Operating the rectangle or circle tool is basically the same. Follow these steps:

1. Click the Rectangle or Circle tool.

2. From the Tool Settings roll-up, set the desired amount of corner round (rectangle only) and outline thickness in points. A zero points thickness creates an object with no outline that can still have a fill when initially drawn. In addition, a transparency setting is provided to set the desired level of translucence for the object.

3. Set the desired outline, background, and fill designs and colors. The current defaults applied to all newly drawn objects are displayed at the bottom right corner of the screen.

4. Move to the image surface and drag the desired shape just as you would with a CorelDRAW! tool. Pressing Ctrl while dragging constrains a rectangle to a square and an ellipse to a circle. The size of the object is displayed on the status line.

The Polygon tool is used to draw multisided objects with straight lines. Simply click the polygon's first corner location and then click each other desired corner location, making sure to double-click on the final corner. The object is outlined and filled with the currently active default colors and designs. Transparency and various line-joining options are provided under the Tool Settings roll-up window.

Filling Objects

The CorelPHOTO-PAINT Fill tool is used to add an interior fill to closed path sections of an image. The closed path is not a single object, but an image area completely surrounded by pixels. In this way, CorelPHOTO-PAINT can determine the intended area's overall shape and then apply the fill to that area. The Fill tool in conjunction with the Fill roll-up window's Gradient selection, for example, creates an effect in which the color(s) filling an area change gradually from one shade or tint to another.

The Fill roll-up window allows you to specify a pattern (CorelPHOTO-PAINT gives you several from which to choose) to fill an object. It operates almost identically to the CorelDRAW! Fill roll-up window, which provides access to the solid, fractal, gradient, and bitmapped fills.

After the desired fill is established with the Fill roll-up window, an area is filled by following this procedure:

1. Set the desired fill type.

2. Select the Fill tool.

3. Click the image with the tail-end of the Fill tool which is located within the area to be filled. The area should fill as desired.

4. If the area does not fill, press Ctrl+Z immediately and look for breaks in the outline of the area. Use the Paintbrush, Line, or other tool to close the gap and repeat the fill procedure.

> **Note**
>
> It is easier to fill solid-color screen areas that do not contain a previously applied fill. Trying to fill an already filled area causes erratic results.

To use bitmap patterns or textures as fills with the View menu's Fill, open **V**iew menu and choose **F**ill Roll-Up (F7). This roll-up window gives you access to all the texture and pattern fills used in CorelDRAW! (see Chapter 5, "Modifying Object Outlines and Interior Fills"); it also provides access to bitmaps, which can then be used to create patterns.

In this roll-up window, you also can set the color and grayscale gradient fills available with the Fill tool. Again, each type of fill tool provides its own set of options. Figure 25.13 shows the Fill roll-up window with the Cosmic Energy fill selected by using the small triangle at the bottom right corner of the preview window, and then selecting the desired pattern.

Fig. 25.13
The Fill roll-up showing how the Cosmic Energy fill was applied to the clouds.

Cloning

To paint an image section by dragging the mouse a few times, you can use the Cloning tools. These tools paint whatever portion of the image you select onto another area you specify, including special painting effects attached to the tool used. For example, suppose that you want to apply an image of a moon contained in one image against a sky backdrop contained in another. The clone tools are used for just this type of operation. Follow these steps:

1. Open the files that contain the image to be cloned and the destination file for the cloning operation.

2. Select the desired clone tool. CorelPHOTO-PAINT provides a Straight Clone, Pointillism, and Impressionist clone tools. The Straight Clone tool simply copies the image exactly as it appears in the original image. The other clone tools apply their respective special effects to the clone's image to provide an additional level of flair.

3. Right click in the center of the section of the original image that is to be cloned. Make sure that you click at a convenient reference point as pertains to the next step.

4. Click in the destination image at the point that corresponds to the reference point of the original image.

5. Drag the cursor on-screen and notice that the original image is copied to the destination file, but referenced to the original point.

Effective use of the reference point can save a great deal of rework time in obtaining the desired proper alignment between the underlying image and the cloned section.

Smudge, Smear, and Sharpen Tools

Other tool effects include smudging and smearing colors. *Smudging* blends the colors in the neighboring pixels to provide a similar effect to that achieved by mixing water colors. *Smearing* is similar to dragging an object over oil paints of different colors where the final result is not a blending of the two colors, but more a run-off of the two.

Fuzzy photographs can be sharpened and sharp ones can be blurred. The Smudge and Smear tools enable you to rework the edges of shapes, pixel by pixel if you want. The tools are used to take the coarseness from an image by selectively smearing or smudging image components into each other. The effect is easily accomplished by first selecting the desired tool and then dragging the cursor over the area to be modified.

Changing the Effects of Brushes and Tools

You can customize CorelPHOTO-PAINT tools and brushes in numerous ways to meet your needs. Most of this customization is done using roll-up windows. To open a roll-up window, open the **V**iew menu and then choose one of the roll-up windows from the list.

To change the shapes, sizes, and effects of brushes and tools, open the **V**iew menu and choose Too**l** Settings roll-up window (F8) (see fig. 25.14). The options available in this window vary, depending on the tool you're working with. If the active tool doesn't have any associated settings, the roll-up isn't displayed.

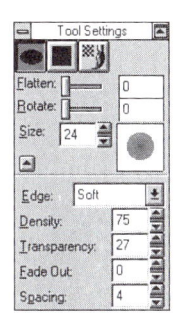

Fig. 25.14
The Brush Tool Settings roll-up window.

Defining the Drawing Canvas

All CorelPHOTO-PAINT images are drawn on a background canvas. CorelPHOTO-PAINT comes with numerous canvas designs that provide an additional level of texture to the drawn image. The canvas designs vary from canvas to concrete to tweed. When the drawings are applied to this canvas surface, interesting three-dimensional effects are achieved.

To load previously saved canvas patterns, open the **V**iew menu and choose **C**anvas Roll-Up (F6). CorelPHOTO-PAINT provides an error message, unless canvas files are square, 8-bit, or 24-bit color, and sized between 16 and 128 pixels (in multiples of 16) on each side.

To use the canvas as the background or as an overlay on the image, click the Apply button. To view the canvas pattern, click the Load button. Make sure that the Preview option is activated in the Load A Canvas from Disk dialog box. The Merge button only works if you're using the canvas as an overlay; it combines the canvas and the picture it overlays into one image that can then be painted on, and the paint will adopt the underlying texture of the canvas. Until the picture and canvas are merged, they're treated as separate images. After they're merged, they become a single image with the characteristics of both.

Changing Color Palettes

Color palettes are used to ensure consistency of color across different images. For example, if a project requires a custom blend of colors, the colors are saved in a palette with a distinctive name. This named palette could then be loaded at a later date, and the exact same blend of colors would be available. All CorelPHOTO-PAINT palettes are stored with a CPL extension and are accessible from the Color roll-up windows selection list.

To select and revise the color palette, do the following:

1. Open the View menu and choose Color Roll-Up (F5). The Color roll-up window appears (see fig. 25.15).

Fig. 25.15
The Color roll-up window with custom colors being mixed.

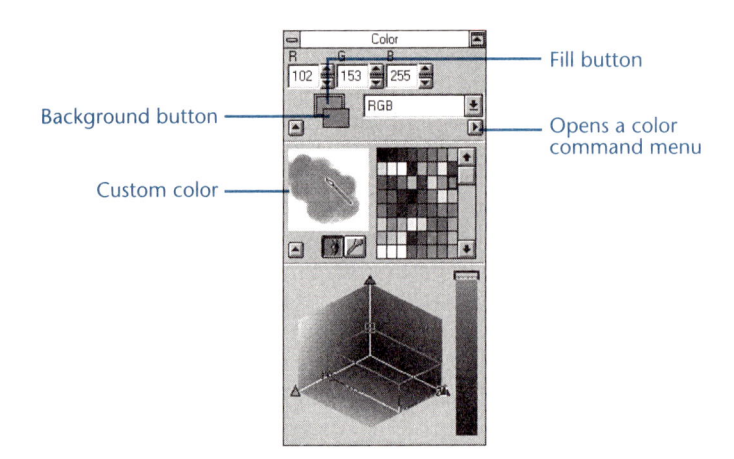

Fill button
Background button
Opens a color command menu
Custom color

2. Click the Background/Fill buttons to choose different colors for the outline/paint and image background. CorelPHOTO-PAINT uses the outline color with the painting, drawing, and text tools. You can use the Color Replacer tool to set the outline image area to another color.

3. To mix custom colors, first select the brush and then click the desired colors. Drag the brush on the mixing area to allow for combinations of several colors until the exact shade is achieved. Using the Eyedropper tool, that color is then applied to images to set either the paint, background, or outline color.

Palettes can be loaded and saved. To clear the paint mixing area, click the small right-pointing triangle (refer to fig. 25.15) and select as necessary from the menu. Choose Load Palette to set the current color defaults in accordance with the loaded palette. Choose Save Palette to save the currently active color palette under a name for use at a later date. The Add Color and Delete Color options either add or remove the currently selected color to and from the color palette. Custom mixed colors can be cleared, saved or retrieved using the Paint Area related options shown at the bottom of this menu. The same color model choices as seen in CorelDRAW!—RGB, CMYK, HSB, the standard palette (process colors)—and a special image palette are available here.

Adding Text to the Picture

CorelPHOTO-PAINT gives you very sophisticated control over the process of adding text to the picture. You may want to add labels to images in the CorelPHOTO-PAINT picture, or add titles and author's names. CorelPHOTO-PAINT gives you advanced control over the text size, font, and style; it supports all the installed Windows fonts. In version 5, text is now entered directly to the picture, rather than in a dialog box. Text is entered in the outline color. To add text to the picture, follow these steps:

1. Click the Text tool; then click the image and type the desired text.

2. Click the Pick tool to end the text entering phase.

3. Click the text with the Pick tool and notice that the customary scaling handles appear. Drag the handles of this text frame until it's the size you want. To move the entire text frame, place the pointer inside it and click and drag. To edit the text, click with the Text tool in the text frame and perform the desired editing functions.

4. To change the text font, select the text string using the Pick tool. Then use the Font menu selection, which displays the dialog box shown in figure 25.16. To merge the text object with the image, press Ctrl+G.

Fig. 25.16
The Font dialog box.

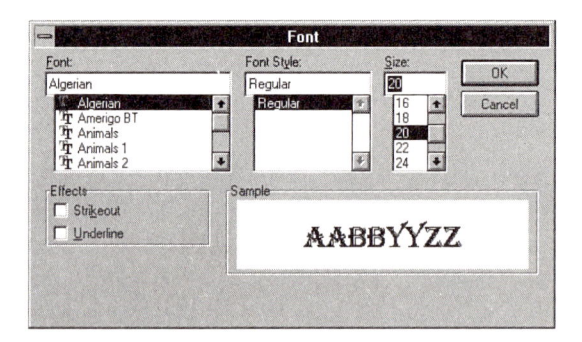

From Here...

This chapter introduced you to CorelPHOTO-PAINT and showed you how to create new bitmap images with tools that emulate paint brushes, airbrushes, and other conventional drawing tools. It also showed you how to manipulate, edit, and compile bitmap images—especially photographs—including those captured with a monochrome or color scanner.

For information related to the topics covered in this chapter, refer to the following:

- Chapter 26, "Advanced CorelPHOTO-PAINT," deals with many of CorelPHOTO-PAINT's more advanced features including the mask and other 3-D features. It also investigates the techniques for using CorelPHOTO-PAINT to quickly create interesting images.

- Chapter 27, "Tracing Bitmap Images," covers CorelTRACE, which converts bitmap images into vector graphic images. This procedure can be used after you have already created a CorelPHOTO-PAINT image that you now want to scale or substantially modify without degrading the image quality. In addition, vector graphic images take up substantially less disk space than bitmaps, which affects the day-to-day practicality of working with image files.

- Chapter 29, "Making Presentations with CorelSHOW," introduces CorelSHOW, which you can use to present your CorelPHOTO-PAINT images as part of a larger presentation.

Chapter 26

Advanced CorelPHOTO-PAINT

by Stephen R. Poland

In Chapter 25, "Photograph Touch-Up with CorelPHOTO-PAINT," you learned the basics of photo touch-up using CorelPHOTO-PAINT, as well as how to use CorelPHOTO-PAINT's paintbrushes to create new paint images. In this chapter, you learn how to use some of CorelPHOTO-PAINT's advanced tools to further enhance your photo images and paintings.

In this chapter, you learn to:

- Adjust image color using Color Effects commands
- Control image sharpness and contrast
- Transform images using the Flip, Rotate, and Stretch commands
- Add special effects to images
- Create image, color, and transparent masks
- Create custom brush shapes using the Mask tools

Editing Image Color

As you learned in the preceding chapter, CorelPHOTO-PAINT offers color palettes that enable you to choose a wide array of colors to add to and change in your images. As you become comfortable with basic color commands, you'll want to explore additional color control options available on the Effects menu.

To adjust the way that colors are displayed, open the Effects menu and choose Color. This menu offers four options, and the dialog box associated with each option provides a Preview choice that enables you to see the effect of that option on the image before you actually apply it. The four options are in the following list:

- *Brightness, Contrast, and Intensity.* Lightens or darkens a picture (the brightness control) and changes the distinction between light and dark areas (the contrast control). The intensity control affects the brighter parts of the picture more than the darker parts by increasing the overall intensity level.

- *Gamma.* Enhances detail by adjusting the midtones without affecting the shadows and highlights.

- *Hue and Saturation.* Adjusts colors without affecting brightness. Hue is the particular color (red, blue, orange); saturation is the amount of the color. You can adjust this by using sliding controls or by entering values for the colors. A negative color value usually gives a grayscale image.

- *Tone Map.* Presents a histogram display of the various color tones contained within an image.

> **Note**
>
> All these options are available only when working with 24-bit and 32-bit color or grayscale images. Some effects do not apply to black-and-white or 256-color images.

Working with Detail and Sharpness

To add more definite edges to boundaries and detail to your images, you can use the Sharpen filters available on the Effects menu. These filters give a broad range of control over the appearance of your images.

> **Note**
>
> All the detail and sharpness options are available only when working with 24-bit and 32-bit color images or grayscale images. Some do not apply to black-and-white or 256-color images.

To examine the Sharpen options, open the Effects menu and choose Sharpen. This menu option opens a submenu, containing the options detailed in the following list. Each submenu option opens a dialog box that enables you to adjust the parameters of the Sharpen filter.

- *Adaptive Unsharp Mask* (usually more apparent in high-resolution color images), accentuates edge detail without affecting the rest of the image.

- *Directional Sharpen* applies an edge to many of the interior boundaries of colored segments, giving the appearance of an intense light source applied from a specific direction, which sharpens boundaries.

- *Edge Enhance* sharpens the outlines of an image. The degree of edge enhancement is controlled by entering a percentage in the resulting dialog box.

- *Enhance* analyzes the values of the pixels in different directions to determine where to apply the most sharpening. Control this by setting percentage with the slide control.

- *Sharpen* enhances edges and brings out detail; the higher the number, the greater the sharpness. Choosing Wide Aperture enlarges the affected area.

- *Unsharp Mask* (usually more apparent in high-resolution color images), accentuates edge details as well as sharpening the smooth areas. This command works by blurring the contrast zones and then eliminating them from the original. You control this by setting a percentage on the slide control.

When pixels change radically from one color or level of darkness to another, they create a harsh transition that shows up in the image. To change the appearance of the pixels in the image, choose the following Soften options from the Effects menu:

- *Diffuse* scatters the colors and makes the image fuzzier. The higher the percentage, the greater the scatter or fuzziness.

- *Directional Smooth* smooths out the image transitions so that they appear to transition in the same general direction on the image.

- *Smooth* tones down differences in adjacent pixels, so that only a slight loss of overall detail occurs.

- *Soften* tones down transition harshness without losing detail.

To adjust for lighting and the light/dark of the colors in the picture, use the Effects menu's Tone selection. The option for Tone is as follows:

- *Equalize* makes the darkest colors black and the lightest colors white and then distributes the other colors in between. Choosing this filter displays a dialog box containing a histogram that represents the shades in the current picture (see fig. 26.1).

Fig. 26.1

The Tone Equalization dialog box displays a histogram plot of the current image.

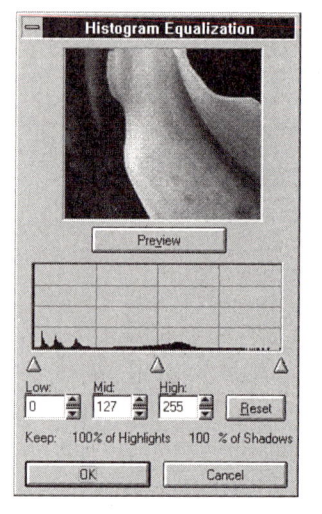

The photograph used in this chapter's figures is by Aris Multimedia Entertainment, Inc.

To adjust the colors, simply drag the arrows or enter numbers. It is difficult to improve an overexposed photograph where the histogram shows most of the shades at or near full white or full dark. Dragging the lower and upper limits defines the desired shading range to include in the image. Dragging all triangles to the lower limits makes the image lighter, whereas dragging all triangles to the upper range makes the image darker.

Changing Overall Photo Contrast Characteristics

Often a photograph looks less than perfect as a graphic image, so some of the most useful features of CorelPHOTO-PAINT help to improve a mediocre photograph. Contrast, highlights, and shadows can be added to the photograph to enhance detail or emphasize certain images. Contrast has little to no effect on non-photographic image. To add contrast to selected areas of the picture, follow these steps:

1. Use the Selection tools to select the area(s) to be changed.

2. Click and hold down the Smear tool to open the Effects tools fly-out menu.

3. Click the Contrast tool.

   ◄ See "Selecting Image Areas," p. 606

   > **Note**
   >
   > If you have the entire toolbox displayed instead of grouped, you can click the Contrast tool directly without clicking Smear first.

   ◄ See "Corel-PHOTO-PAINT Tools," p. 603

4. Double-click the Contrast tool to open the Tool Settings roll-up window. Adjust the size and shape of the tool in the Tool Settings roll-up window.

5. At the bottom of the Tool Settings roll-up window, drag the arrow in the Contrast section of the roll-up window to adjust the tool's effect (the amount of contrast).

6. Finally, move the Contrast tool to the image area and click and drag over the area to be changed.

To adjust an image's overall brightness, contrast, and intensity, on the other hand, open the Effects menu and choose Color Brightness and Contrast. The Brightness and Contrast dialog box that appears contains controls for brightness, intensity, and contrast. The higher the number, the greater the effect. You should usually increase contrast about one tenth the amount you increase brightness. Check the effects using Preview, and then click OK.

Sometimes portions of a photograph appear to have too much contrast (overexposed) or to be too dark (underexposed). To fix these conditions, follow these steps:

1. Open the **E**ffects menu and choose Tone Equalize filter. This filter works on either selected areas (make sure that you select the area before choosing the filter) or the entire picture.

2. In the dialog box that appears, drag the arrows at the bottom of the graph to adjust the low, mid, and high values. Shades to the left of the low arrow are black. Shades to the right of the high arrow are white. Highlights are the shades between the high and mid values, and shadows are the shades between the low and mid values.

3. Check the effects by clicking Pre**v**iew. Repeat step 2 as necessary.

4. When you are satisfied with the preview, choose OK.

   If you decide to return to the original values (the default values do provide good results in most cases), choose **R**eset in the Equalize dialog box.

Image Transformations

The image transformations available in CorelPHOTO-PAINT are similar (but not identical) to those available in CorelDRAW!.

To transform the orientation or appearance of an entire picture (or a selected area of a picture), open the Object menu and choose Flip. The submenu that appears enables you to flip the image horizontally (along the side-to-side axis) or vertically (along the up-and-down axis). A vertical flip creates a mirror image of the picture; a horizontal flip creates an upside-down version of the picture.

To rotate the picture, open the Object menu and choose Rotate. The submenu that appears enables you to rotate the image 90 degrees at a time in a clockwise or counterclockwise direction, or to rotate it 180 degrees. Choose Custom to rotate in one-degree increments.

To rotate a subsection of the image manually by dragging it, choose the Object menu's Free Rotate selection. This option enables you to use the curved corner areas to rotate the image to the desired location. Freeform rotations are similar to the rotation possible in CorelDRAW! when you click a second time on an object. You can change the point of rotation exactly the same way you change it in CorelDRAW!, by moving the bull's eye. A moving, dotted-line box surrounds the object; to grab the corner arrows, you must move the image in the window. Click the Arrow tool, and select an area in one of the corners of the window. When the corner of the dotted line appears, you can stop dragging. Place the cursor over the curved arrows and rotate the image as you want. The screen redraw on this rotation is slow, so be patient. Also, when you use Custom at 45 degrees, it displays a new image box.

To manipulate an image by stretching it in one or more directions, open the Object menu and choose Distort. The image is selected and bounded by a marquee with corner handles. Drag the corner handles in any direction to change the image into different shapes. Figure 26.2 shows the result of distorting a figure by dragging two corner handles in and leaving the other two fixed.

Fig. 26.2
A distorted image created using the Distort command on the Object menu.

To create a new image of a different size (in pixels) and/or resolution, follow these steps:

1. Open the **I**mage menu and choose **R**esample. The Resample Image dialog box appears (see fig. 26.3).

Fig. 26.3

The Image menu's Resample dialog box enables you to change the size and resolution of an image.

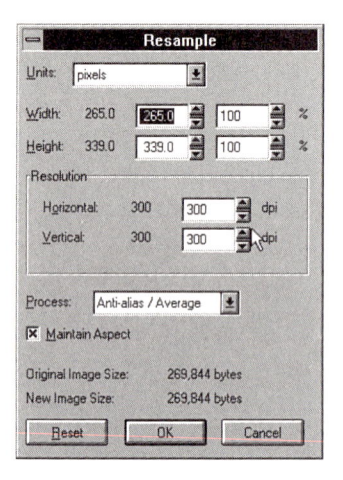

2. Define the change by selecting the appropriate values in either the Resample By Size or Resample By Percentage box. The changes made in one box are reflected automatically in the other.

3. When the Maintain Aspect box is checked, the height-to-width ratio of the image is maintained through all changes. The height automatically changes in relation to the width and vice versa. Deselect this box by clicking to enter both values yourself.

4. To change the resolution (in dpi) for the image, change the value in the Resolution box. This procedure has an effect on the output, but does not change the on-screen image.

5. The Process box provides the following tools that you can use to affect the quality of the resampled image:

    Anti-alias removes jagged edges, making a smoother image.

    Stretch/Truncate creates a jagged image by separating duplicated pixels and removing duplicated pixels, which creates a rougher image.

6. After making all the choices, choose OK. A new window opens and displays the resampled image.

To change the resolution of the image (in dpi), open the Image menu and choose Resolution. This relates the image dimension in pixels to the image dimension in inches. This creates a new file and a separate window for the new image with the new resolution. You may not see a difference on-screen, but you can with the output and file size.

Working with Special Effects

CorelPHOTO-PAINT comes with numerous special effects filters that can dramatically alter (and hopefully enhance) the images. To use any of these special effects on an entire image, open the Effects menu and choose the desired effect. To use the effect on only part of an image, select the appropriate area before choosing the desired effect from the Effects menu. The effects are located in cascading menus with multiple options. All are listed and described briefly in table 26.1. Click Preview while in the dialog box to see the results of the chosen effect. Click Cancel to not apply the effect, or click Apply to apply the effect to the active image.

> **Note**
>
> All these effects are available only when working with 24-bit and 32-bit color images or grayscale images. Some do not apply to black-and-white or 256-color images.

Table 26.1 CorelPHOTO-PAINT Effect Filters

Effect Name	Result
Artistic	
Pointillist	Adds colored dots to the picture so that the image appears to have been created with dabs of colored paint.
Impressionist	Adds colored brush strokes to the picture so that the image appears to have been created with big swaths of paint.
Color	
Brightness and Contrast	Adjusts the lightness and darkness of the overall image.
Gamma	Enhances image detail by adjusting midtones.
Hue/Saturation	Adjusts image color without affecting brightness.
Tone Map	Adjusts the overall image colors. Covered earlier in the chapter.

(continues)

Table 26.1 Continued

Effect Name	Result
Fancy	
Edge Detect	Creates an outline effect by adjusting the sensitivity to edges.
Emboss	Creates a 3D raised relief effect.
Invert	Switches all colors to their opposites, like in a negative image.
Jaggie Despeckle	Scatters colors in a picture, making the image appear diffused.
Motion Blur	Creates the appearance of an image moving so fast that the picture is blurred.
Outline	Outlines all or the selected parts of a picture.
Mapping	
Glass Block	Applies a wavy effect like that seen when looking through a thick glass block.
Impressionist	Makes the image look like an oil painting.
Map to Sphere	Makes the image look as though it is being viewed through or reflected off a sphere or cone.
Pinch/Punch	Makes the image look squashed.
Pixelate	Adds a block-like effect to the image.
Ripple	Creates vertical and horizontal waves in an image.
Smoked Glass	Adds a dark tint to the image to make it look smoky.
Swirl	Makes the image appear as though it has been rapidly rotated around its center point.
Tile	Creates a pattern of smaller versions of the initial image. Similar to Tile in CorelDRAW!.
Vignette	Gives an old-world feel by applying a soft white effect to the center of the image.
Wet Paint	Makes the image look like dripping wet paint.
Wind	Applies thin lines that make the image look windblown.

Effect Name	Result
Noise	
Add Noise	Puts a granular texture on the image.
Maximum	Lightens an image by adjusting pixel values to decrease the number of colors in an image.
Median	Removes noise from scanned pictures with a grainy texture.
Minimum	Darkens an image by adjusting pixel values to decrease the number of colors in an image.
Remove Noise	Softens edges and reverses a grainy effect (like the unwanted noise from a bad scan).
Sharpen	
Adaptive Unsharp Mask	Makes the image look very high resolution.
Directional Sharpen	Applies the greatest amount of sharpening based upon image processing analysis.
Edge Enhance	Highlights color and intensity transitions.
Enhance	Smooths and sharpens the image.
Sharpen	Adds a higher level of detail to an image.
Unsharp mask	Sharpens both the edges and smoother image areas.
Soften	
Diffuse	Scatters the colors within the image.
Directional smooth	Results in a slight loss of detail.
Smooth	Tones down the image harshness with minimal loss of detail.
Soften	Smooths transitions from one contrast to another.

(continues)

Table 26.1 Continued

Effect Name	Result
Special	
Contour	Creates lines to outline the edges of a picture.
Posterize	Takes away the color gradations, re-creating the image as large sections of solid colors or solid grays.
Psychedelic	Creates a 1960s psychedelic look by randomly changing colors.
Solarize	Creates a negative (reversed image) of the image.
Threshold	Makes the image lighter or darker.
Tone Equalize	Allows for color correction to improve imbalances.
Transformations	Makes the image appear as though it has been rotated in three dimensions.
3D Rotate	Use the slides to vary the amount of rotation.
Mesh Warp	Changes the image shape by dragging nodes on a mesh to which the image conforms.
Perspective	Distorts the entire image to provide an illusion of depth.

These effects cannot be adequately described with words. To see how they really work, apply them to images and consider the results. Figures 26.4 to 26.10, and color plates 39 to 41, show images treated with several of these effects.

Each effect employs a menu or a dialog box to determine how to transform the image. The best way to get to know them is to experiment and watch the images on the preview screen.

> **Troubleshooting**
>
> *It seems as though many of the tools perform the same functions as the selections under the Effects menu. When should I use the tools rather than the menu selections?*
>
> The menu selections apply to the entire image or a smaller region defined by the Selection tools. The Artistic tools themselves are designed to work in a more freehand mode and provide a less "computer-generated" effect when done.

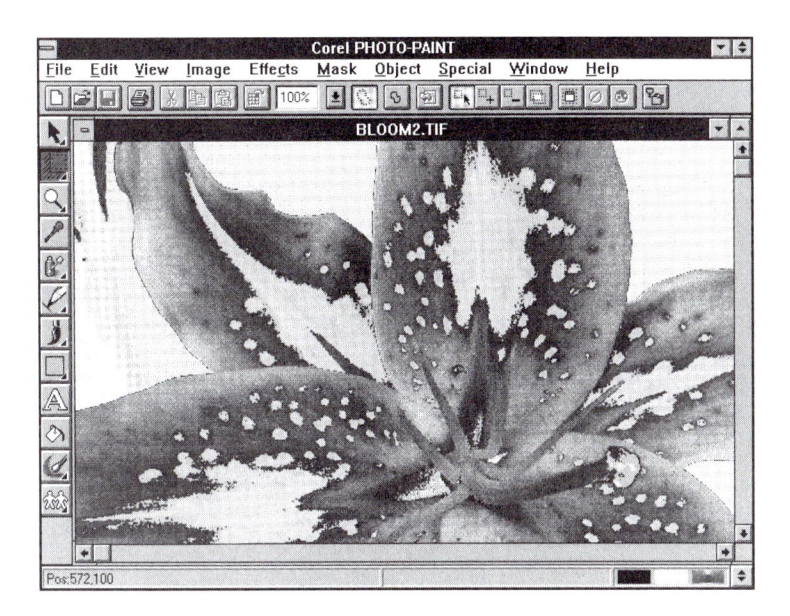

Fig. 26.4
The Solarized effect in action.

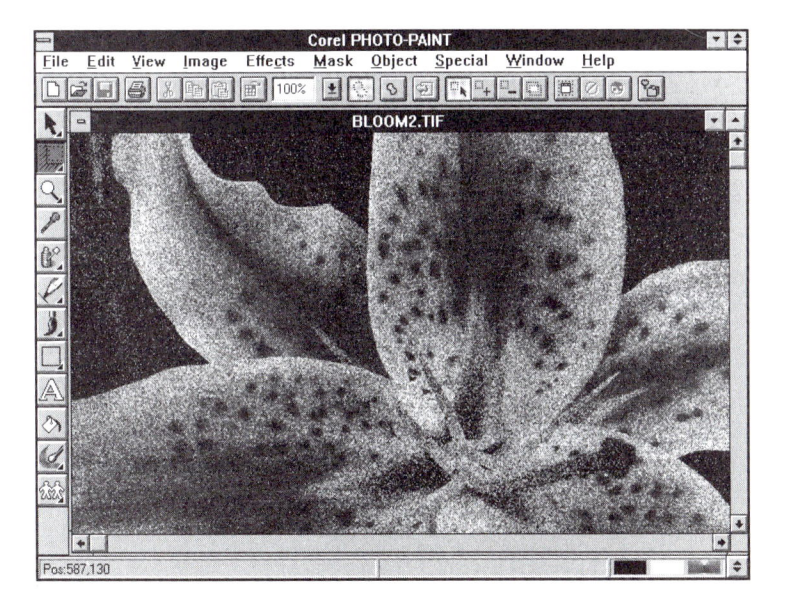

Fig. 26.5
Add Noise gives an image a rough appearance.

Fig. 26.6
The Emboss effect gives a 3D look and removes color variation from the image. (See color plates 39 and 41.)

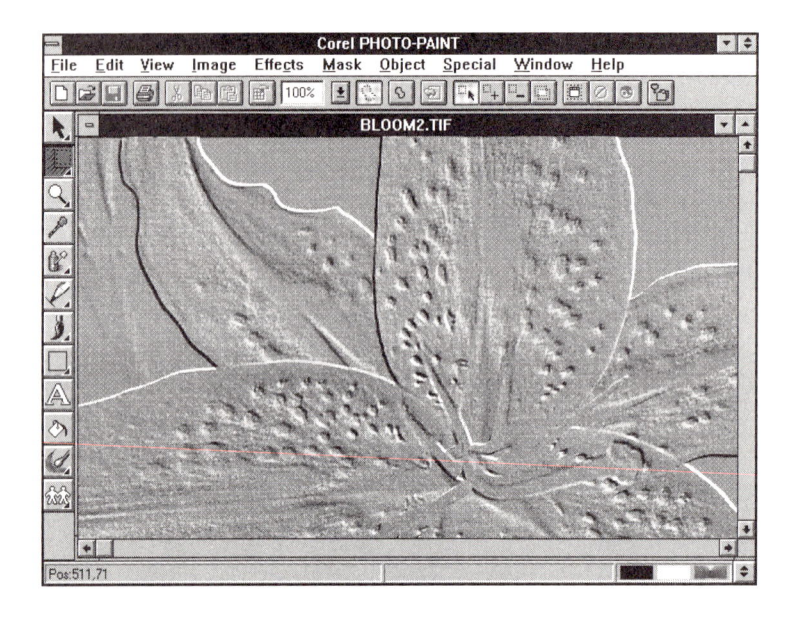

Fig. 26.7
Applying the Swirl effect twists the image from its center.

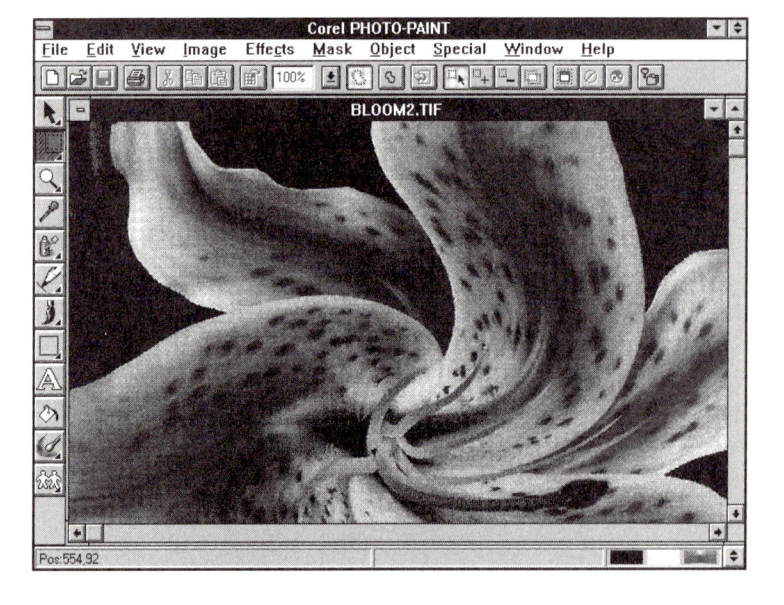

Working with Special Effects **643**

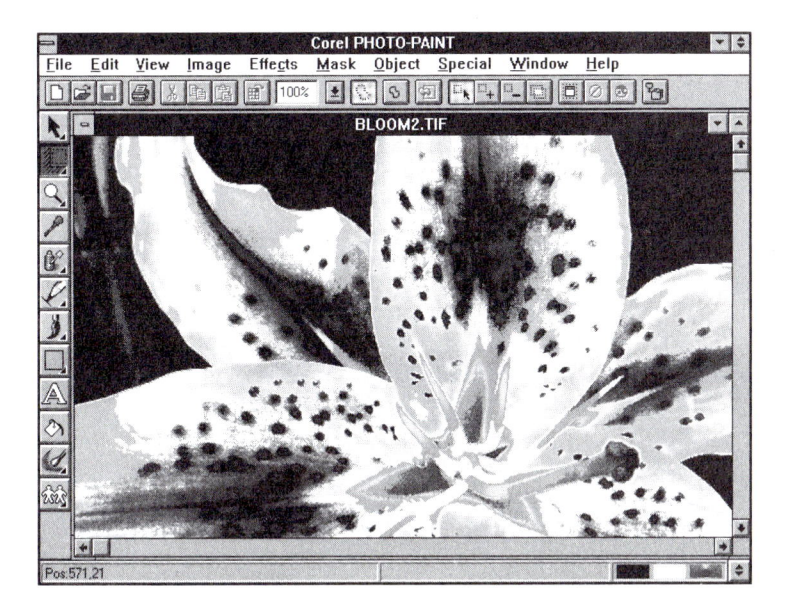

Fig. 26.8
The Psychedelic effect gives images a 60's feel.

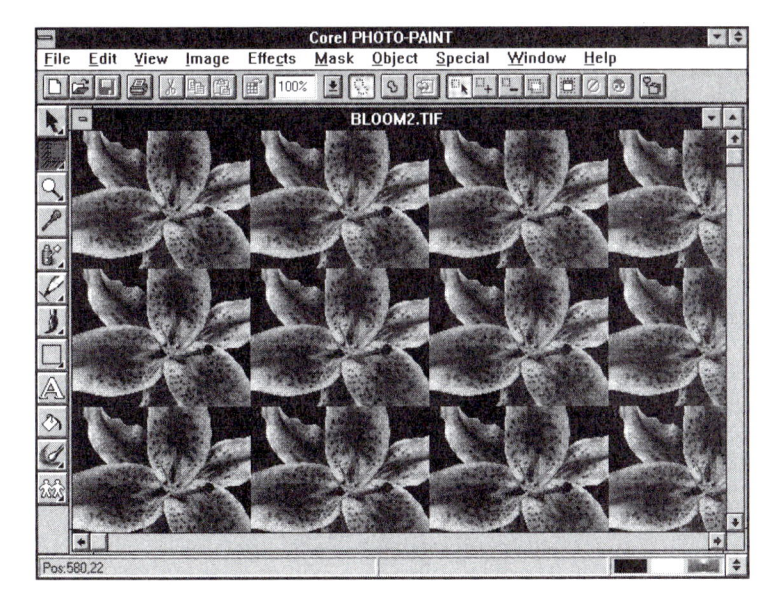

Fig. 26.9
Apply the Tile effect to break an image into several smaller versions of the entire image.

VI

Other Corel Applications

Fig. 26.10
The Posterize effect reduces the number of colors in the image, giving it a painted poster appeal.

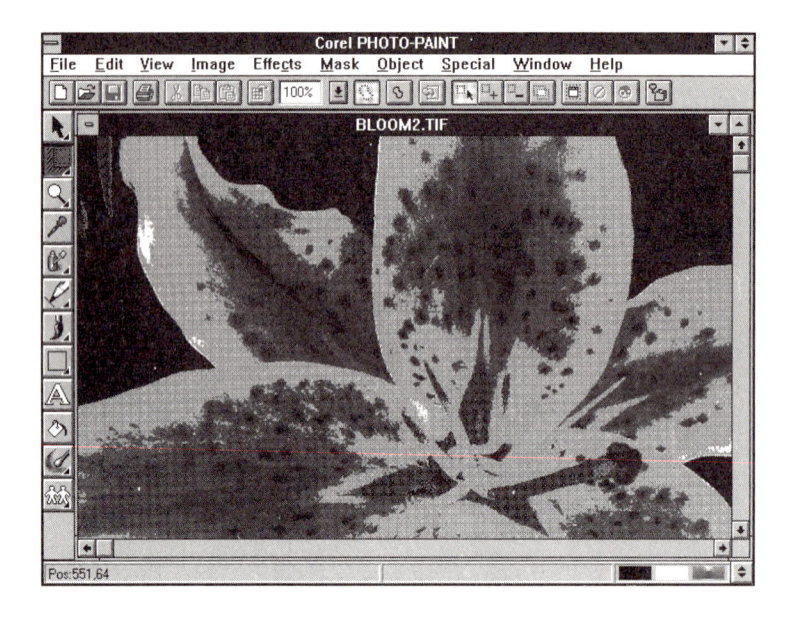

Using CorelPHOTO-PAINT Masks

As you become more experienced with CorelPHOTO-PAINT, you'll find the Mask tools and commands to be some of the more important elements of CorelPHOTO-PAINT. A mask enables you to protect a portion of your image, allowing changes to be made only to the region inside or outside a masked area. CorelPHOTO-PAINT provides several kinds of specialized masks. In this section, you learn how to create and use masks, color masks, and transparent masks to control the effects applied to your images.

CorelPHOTO-PAINT masks define an area of an image similar to the way the Selection tools select image areas; like the Selection tools, masks appear as marquee.

Using CorelPHOTO-PAINT Mask Tools

CorelPHOTO-PAINT provides numerous tools to create masks of every shape and size. Like the Selection tools, the Mask tools fly-out menu contains equivalent tools to create masks. The following list gives a brief description of each mask tool available on the Mask tools fly-out menu.

- *Mask Picker* enables you to select and move an existing mask. To select an existing mask, click the marquee of the mask. The mask's bounding rectangle appears, as well as its sizing handles.

Using CorelPHOTO-PAINT Masks 645

- *Rectangle Mask* creates a rectangular shaped mask. Click and drag to draw a rectangular mask. Release the mouse button to complete the mask.

- *Circle Mask* creates a circular shaped mask. To use this tool, click and drag to create the circular mask shape. Release the mouse button to complete the mask.

- *Polygon Mask* creates multisided geometric masks. To use this tool, click to place points of the polygon. Double-click to complete the polygon mask shape.

- *Freehand Mask* enables you to draw a freehand mask of any random shape. To use this tool, drag in a freehand shape over the area to be masked. A mask is created around the area defined by dragging.

- *Lasso Mask* creates an irregular mask shape with similar colors. To use this tool, drag in the shape of the desired mask. A mask is created around the similar colors in the region created while dragging.

- *Magic Wand Mask*, like the Magic Wand Selection tool, the Magic Wand Mask tool creates a mask over an entire area of similar color. To use this tool, position the tool over the desired color to be masked and click the left mouse button. A mask is created around the area of the similar color. The color tolerance for the Magic Wand Mask tool is adjusted the same way the color tolerance for the Magic Wand Selection tool is adjusted.

  ◄ See "Editing Images in PHOTO-PAINT," p. 606

- *Brush Mask* creates a mask marquee the shape of the current paintbrush. To use this tool, choose a paintbrush shape from the Tool Settings roll-up window; choose the Brush Mask tool; move the pointer to the image area to be masked; and click to mask a brush shaped area.

- *Mask Node Edit* enables you to reshape a mask by dragging its nodes. To use this tool, select the mask to be edited using Mask Picker tool; click the Mask Node Edit tool and drag the mask nodes to reshape the mask.

VI

Other Corel Applications

Chapter 26—Advanced CorelPHOTO-PAINT

To create a mask to limit the effects of a CorelPHOTO-PAINT tool, follow these steps:

1. Click and hold down the Mask Picker tool in the toolbox. The Mask tool fly-out menu appears. Release the mouse button.

2. Click the Mask tool for the shape of the mask you want to create.

3. Move the Mask tool to the painting window and drag or click to create the mask shape desired. As you drag or click, a marquee appears defining the region of the mask (see fig. 26.11).

Fig. 26.11
A mask created using the Polygon Mask tool surrounds a brushstroke in CorelPHOTO-PAINT.

You now can apply a CorelPHOTO-PAINT effect or operations such as painting with the Pointillist brush to the masked area. The effect will affect only the region inside the masked area.

Editing Mask Sizes and Shapes

After you create a mask, you might find it helpful to enlarge or reduce the area covered by the mask. Using the Mask Picker tool, you can select and resize a mask using its sizing handles.

To edit a mask size, follow these steps:

1. Click the Mask Picker tool in the toolbox and click the mask to be edited. The mask's bounding rectangle and sizing handles appear.

2. Drag the mask's corner handles to resize the mask proportionally.

3. Drag the mask's side sizing handles to resize vertically or horizontally.

Tip
To cause the CorelPHOTO-PAINT operation or effect to affect everywhere but the masked area, choose Mask Invert to invert the masked area.

You also can reshape a mask using the Mask Node Edit tool. Because masks are created as outlines similar to object outlines in CorelDRAW!, you can manipulate a mask's shape using its control nodes. Although you cannot add and delete nodes as in CorelDRAW!, reshaping a mask using its nodes gives you a great deal of flexibility in controlling its shape.

To edit a mask shape, follow these steps:

1. Click the Mask Picker tool in the toolbox and click the mask to be edited. The mask's bounding rectangle and sizing handles appear.

2. Click the Mask Node Edit tool on the Mask tools fly-out menu. Control nodes appear on the selected mask (see fig. 26.12).

Fig. 26.12
Clicking the Mask Node Edit tool causes control nodes to appear on the selected mask.

3. Drag the control nodes to reshape the mask. Click the Mask Picker tool to complete the reshaping of the mask.

Combining Mask Designs

You can combine mask shapes to create custom mask shapes that may be difficult to draw using one of the freehand Mask tools. For example, your image editing process might require a keyhole-shaped mask—a rectangular mask with a circle for one end. Drawing this shape using the freehand Mask tool is difficult and somewhat inaccurate. By combining a rectangular mask and circular mask, you can create the desired shape quickly and accurately.

Follow these steps to combine mask shapes:

1. Use the Mask tools on the Mask tools fly-out menu to create the first shape of the combination.

2. Open the **S**pecial menu and choose **A**dd to Selection, or click the Add to Mask or Build Object button on the ribbon bar.

3. Use the Mask tools to draw a second mask that intersects the first mask. When you release the mouse button to complete the second mask, the mask marquee surrounds the two mask shapes created. Any mask path on the interior of the two shapes is eliminated (see fig. 26.13).

Fig. 26.13
With the Add to Selection option selected on the Special menu, mask shapes can be combined to create a unique mask.

Tip
To take bites out of a mask shape, use Remove from Selection on the Special menu. Instead of adding a second mask outline to an existing mask, any overlapping sections are removed from the shape.

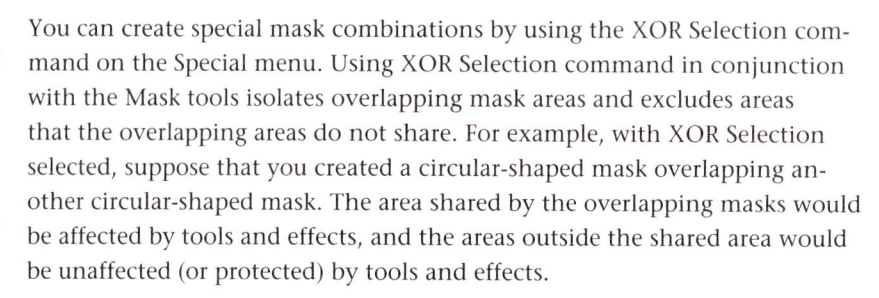

You can create special mask combinations by using the XOR Selection command on the Special menu. Using XOR Selection command in conjunction with the Mask tools isolates overlapping mask areas and excludes areas that the overlapping areas do not share. For example, with XOR Selection selected, suppose that you created a circular-shaped mask overlapping another circular-shaped mask. The area shared by the overlapping masks would be affected by tools and effects, and the areas outside the shared area would be unaffected (or protected) by tools and effects.

> **Troubleshooting**
>
> *I want to combine two mask shapes, but each time I draw the next mask, the first mask disappears.*
>
> Open the **S**pecial menu and choose **A**dd to Selection to tell CorelPHOTO-PAINT to add masks to the image. You also can click the Add to Selection button on the ribbon bar (the small marquee with a plus sign icon).
>
> *Each time I draw a mask shape and release the mouse button, the mask disappears.*
>
> The Remove From Selection option is selected on the Special menu. To change the option to add or combine masks, choose **A**dd to selection or one of the other special object options.
>
> *I want to affect everything outside a circle mask I created, but tools affect the area inside the circle mask.*
>
> The circle mask you created is restricting changes to the area inside the circle. To reverse the area affected, open the **M**ask menu and choose **I**nvert. A mask marquee is added around the parameter of the entire image, and the circle mask marquee remains as it was. You can now modify the area outside the circle.

I attempted to use the Magic Wand mask to select an area of color, but the mask created surrounds too small of an area—not the color range that I want.

Experiment with the color tolerance of the Magic Wand Mask tool. To do this, select the Magic Wand Mask tool and double-click it. The Color Comparison Tolerance dialog box appears. Enter higher color tolerance numbers in the color boxes to make the Magic Wand Mask tool pick up a wider range of color shades. Lower values restrict the tool to a smaller range. Click OK to accept the changes and try the Magic Wand Mask tool again.

Creating Color Masks

Just as a mask enables you to protect or affect a particular region of an image, color masks enable you to select a color to protect or modify. For example, suppose that you want to change a highlight color in the image of an apple from white to light red. You could attempt to use the Paintbrush tool to paint over the individual dots of color with a new color, but this is tedious and extremely time consuming. A better way is to use a color mask to select the color you want to change and paint over the masked area with a new color. The color mask lets the paintbrush change only the colors selected when you created the color mask.

To create a color mask, follow these steps:

1. Open the **M**ask menu and choose Color **M**ask Roll-Up. The Color Mask roll-up window appears (see fig. 26.14).

Fig. 26.14
The Color Mask roll-up window enables you to select and mask up to ten specific colors in an image.

650 Chapter 26—Advanced CorelPHOTO-PAINT

2. Choose Modify Selected Colors from the drop-down list at the top of the roll-up window. If you want to create a mask that enables you to modify all colors except a particular color, choose Protect Selected Colors from the drop-down list.

3. Click the first Color button. The pointer becomes the Eyedropper tool.

4. Move the Eyedropper tool to the image and click the color you want to mask. As you move the eyedropper over the image, the Color button in the Color Mask roll-up window changes to the color under the Eyedropper tool.

5. Click in the On check box to turn on the modification or protection mode for the color you selected. If On is not checked for a color, no mask is created for that color.

6. Adjust the Tolerance for the selected color. The higher the values, the greater the range of colors affected.

7. Click Preview Mask to show the colors affected by the mask (see fig. 26.15).

Fig. 26.15
Selecting Preview in the Color Mask roll-up window displays the image with the colors affected by the mask changed to a different color.

> **Note**
>
> Note that the color applied to the image when you click Preview Mask in the Color Mask roll-up window can be changed in the Preferences dialog box. After you create a color mask, you can choose which color or effect to apply to the mask region; Preview only shows you how the image looks with the preselected color applied to the mask region.

8. Click Apply when you are satisfied with the color mask settings.

> **Note**
>
> Unlike masks created using the Mask tools, color masks cannot be selected, resized, reshaped, or moved.

After you select a color for the color buttons in the Color Mask roll-up window, that color stays the same until you reassign a new color to that button. If you need to mask several colors in an image, set up a button for each color and use the On check boxes for each color to turn on and off the mask for the colors you need to mask. This will speed up the editing of the image in the future.

You can remove a color mask by clicking Remove in the Color Mask roll-up window.

Troubleshooting

I created a color mask, but I don't see a marquee defining the mask shape.

Color masks do not use a marquee to show the masked area. To view the colors affected by the color mask, you must use the Preview button in the Color Mask roll-up window.

I attempted to paint portions of an image, but only certain pixels change to the new paint color.

A color mask is over the image. To change all the colors of the figure, you must turn off or remove the color mask. Open the Color Mask roll-up window and click the On check boxes to turn off any active colors, or click remove to delete the color mask from the image.

I created a mask so that I can change only the red colors of my image, but when I attempt to paint over the image, every color but red gets changed.

The mask you created was set to Protect Selected Colors rather than Modify Selected Colors. To change the mask so that only the red colors can be changed, click Modify Selected Colors in the Color Mask roll-up window and click Apply to apply the mask.

Using the Transparency Masks

Like other masks, transparency masks limit the effect that tools have on an image. For example, a transparency mask can limit the amount of paint applied by the paintbrush or another Paint tool; the amount of paint removed using the Eraser tool; and even the effect of image enhancement tools, such as the Smudge and Sharpen tools. Transparency masks cover the entire image area and cannot be edited with the Mask Shape tools.

Think of the transparency mask as a filter on your image. If the filter is thin (high transparency), changes you make to the image affect the image greatly. If the filter is thick (low transparency), changes you make have little effect on the underlying image.

To add a transparency mask to an image, follow these steps:

1. Open the **M**ask menu and choose Create **T**ransparency Mask. The Transparency Mask Creation dialog box appears (see fig. 26.16).

Fig. 26.16
The Transparency Mask Creation dialog box enables the selection of uniform and gradient transparent masks.

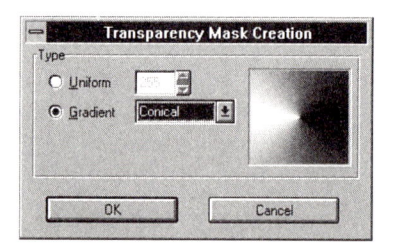

2. Choose **U**niform if you want a uniform mask over the image. Choose a transparency level for the mask. Remember that high transparency numbers (light preview image) make a mask that allows more change to the image. A low number (dark preview image) creates a mask that allows less change to the image. A preview of the mask is displayed at the right of the dialog box.

3. Choose **G**radient to create a mask with one of the gradient types. Choose a gradient type from the drop-down list. A preview of the mask is displayed in the dialog box.

4. Click OK to apply the selected mask to the image.

After a transparency mask is created, you can save the mask to disk using the Save Transparency Mask command on the Mask menu. You can later load a saved mask using the Load Transparency Mask option on the Mask menu.

You can remove a transparent mask from an image by using Remove Transparency Mask on the Mask menu. Remember, removing a transparent mask only removes the mask; it does not undo any changes made since you added the mask to your image.

Troubleshooting

I want to add a transparency mask of high transparency to one part of my image and another transparency mask of low transparency to another part of my image.

You can use only one transparency mask at a time. To apply a different transparency mask to a image, you must remove the current transparency mask by using the Remove Transparency Mask option on the Mask menu.

I can't tell whether a transparency mask covers my image. How do I tell if a transparency mask is in effect?

A transparency mask does not appear as marquee; so it is difficult to determine if a transparency mask is applied to an image. To judge whether an image has a transparency mask, open the **M**ask menu. The Save, Remove, and Invert options are active if a mask is present; they are dimmed if no mask has been created.

Loading and Saving Masks

You may spend a great deal of time drawing and combining masks to encompass a specific region of an image, so you need to be able to save a mask after it's created. Throughout the image editing session, you apply and remove masks frequently.

Furthermore, color masks should be saved and loaded because selecting an exact color tolerance can be time consuming, and it may be difficult to reproduce the exact color range of a mask.

To save a mask created using the Mask tools, follow these steps:

1. Create the mask you want to save, or select the mask using the Mask Picker tool.

2. Open the **M**ask menu and choose **S**ave. The Save an Image to Disk dialog box appears (see fig. 26.17).

3. Type a descriptive name for the mask in the File Name box. Click OK to save the mask.

When a mask is saved, you can load the mask using the Load command on the Mask menu.

Fig. 26.17
To save a mask to disk, open the **M**ask menu and choose **S**ave. The Save an Image to Disk dialog box appears.

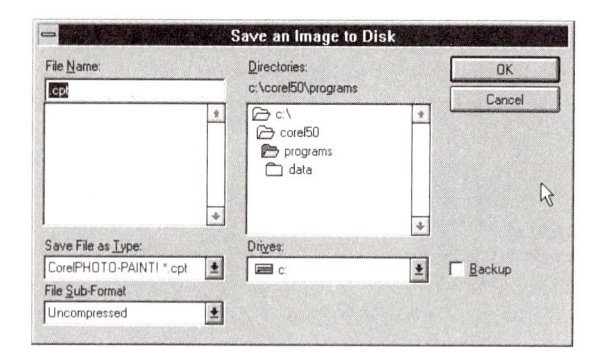

Designing Your Own Brushes

CorelPHOTO-PAINT has many default paintbrush shapes. You learned in Chapter 25, "Photograph Touch-Up with CorelPHOTO-PAINT," how to select a paintbrush shape for the various Paintbrush tools using the Tool Settings roll-up window. Now that you know how to create and modify CorelPHOTO-PAINT masks, you can design your own custom brush shapes for the various Paintbrush tools.

◄ See "Corel-PHOTO-PAINT Tools" p. 603

To create a custom brush, follow these steps:

1. Using the Paint tools and other tools in CorelPHOTO-PAINT, create an image that has the attributes you want your new brush to have. Gradients and color changes are common brush attributes. Alternatively, open an image that has the attributes you want to apply to a brush.

> **Note**
>
> When a custom brush is created, the new brush is created with the shading of the image selected using the Mask tools. If a rectangular mask is drawn over a dark yellow to light yellow gradient, the brush created from the mask applies paint shaded from dark to light—in the currently selected paint color.

2. Using the Mask Selection tools, draw a mask the shape of the image in step 1. The mask should be the approximate size you want the brush to be.

3. Open the **S**pecial menu and choose Create **B**rush. The Create a Custom Brush dialog box appears (see fig. 26.18).

Designing Your Own Brushes

Fig. 26.18
After you've used the Mask selection tools to draw a unique mask shape, use the Create a Custom Brush dialog box to choose a size for the new brush.

4. Enter the size of the custom brush in the **S**ize setting box. Click OK to complete the creation of a custom brush.

The new brush is added to the Custom Brush section of the Tool Setting roll-up window.

To use the newly created brush, open the View menu and choose Tool Settings Roll-Up. Click the Custom brush icon at the top of the roll-up window. Icons of the available custom brushes appear in the roll-up window. Scroll through the list of icons to locate the new brush and click the brush to select it. You now can paint using your new brush.

After you create a custom brush, you can edit some of the brush's attributes. Brush attributes such as Fade Out and Spacing can be edited using the Tool Settings roll-up window. Other brush attributes, such as Edge, Density, and Transparency, cannot be edited for custom brushes.

Troubleshooting

I created a new brush shape with a mask covering a red, white, and blue image area; but when I paint with the new brush, it only paints in shades of the current color selection, not in red, white, and blue.

Custom brushes only pick up the shades and gradients of the image contained in the mask outline. To define a multicolored-colored brush, explore customizing the Pointillist and Impressionist brushes.

I created a custom brush using the Mask tools, but when I try to paint with the new brush, nothing happens.

Make sure that you remove any masks that cover the image. The brush creation process leaves a mask the shape of the new brush over the image until you remove it.

I can't find the custom brush I just created. How do I locate the new brush?

Open **V**iew menu and choose **T**ool Settings Roll-up; then choose the Custom brush icon. Scroll down the icon list to reveal your new brush icon. Click the new icon to use the new brush shape.

From Here...

In this chapter, you learned to use PHOTO-PAINT special effects filters as well as advanced tools such as Masks. You also learned to create your own unique brushes using the mask tools. With a little practice (and patience), these advanced PHOTO-PAINT operations will become second nature. For information relating to advanced image enhancement and masks, consider these chapters:

- Chapter 20, "Creating Special Effects with Lens," describes the CorelDRAW! Lens feature that enables you to add photographic-like effects to CorelDRAW! objects.

- Chapter 25, "Photograph Touch-Up with CorelPHOTO-PAINT," helps you learn the basics of the CorelPHOTO-PAINT tools and commands.

Chapter 27

Tracing Bitmap Images with CorelTRACE

by Ed Paulson

CorelDRAW! helps you create sophisticated illustrations by allowing you to import images into your drawing from other sources. You can, for example, import images such as logos, architectural drawings, illustrations from paint programs, and scanned-in photographs and line art. These imported images, however, usually come in as bitmaps, which can be difficult to rework. If you convert your imported bitmap images into vector-based images (like those created in CorelDRAW!), they print smoother and faster, take up less disk space, and can be resized without distortion.

This chapter introduces you to the three basic methods (which range from fairly simple to very sophisticated) for converting a bitmapped image to a vector-based image:

- Tracing an outline with the Pencil tool from within CorelDRAW!
- Using the AutoTrace features of CorelDRAW!
- Running the CorelTRACE utility program

CorelTRACE also offers Object Character Recognition (OCR). This feature allows you to trace scanned text, convert it to vector form, and then edit the text using a word processing program or using the text functions in CorelDRAW! or CorelPHOTO-PAINT. The Forms tracing option allows you to convert paper-based forms into computer-based graphic images that are easily edited in CorelDRAW!.

Some Considerations before Tracing

Tracing is a processor/memory-intensive operation. CorelTRACE analyzes dot patterns and determines objects from the pattern's relationship. If the starting bitmap is very complex, many objects will have to be sensed and created which makes the tracing time lengthy. If the bitmap is simple, the tracing time is reduced along with the number of objects created.

You should now understand that the quality of the scan greatly determines the quality of the images created by CorelTRACE. Try to capture the essence of your image when scanning and trace the bitmap so that the essential information of the starting image is converted to vector form. This procedure is often an experimental process where the scanning resolution and the scanned details are intimately linked. In general, the higher the scanned resolution, the more likely you are to be successful when tracing.

What Are the Advantages of Tracing?

You can trace imported images to turn them into vector form so that you still get high-quality resolution and sophisticated image manipulation features when working with those images in CorelDRAW!. Many non-CorelDRAW! images are created or imported as bitmaps, or as arrangements of dots that form pictures of certain sizes.

The major drawback of bitmaps is that they have a fixed resolution, or number of dots per image inch. Printing the image to a high-resolution output device or substantially enlarging the image causes jaggedness and distortion due to the images fixed resolution. The problems occur because the bitmap contains no encoded information explaining how the dots are placed in relation to each other to create the perceived objects.

In comparison, each node and line in a vector-based object carries with it invisible data about its placement and connection with the other nodes and lines that make up the object. As a result, you can scale and even rotate the object without distortion, because CorelDRAW! maintains a consistent relationship among all its components. A vector-based image can still be revised and reworked, even when it's placed in a page layout program or in a drawing program. Vector-based images also take up less disk space and print faster than bitmaps.

Generally, you trace an image to enhance and change it. When you edit bitmap images, you change dots from one color to another as you do in CorelPHOTO-PAINT. You can also use many interesting special effects that are specifically related to bitmap editing technology, such as blurring. Tracing the bitmap image, on the other hand, enables you to rework it using the powerful editing features of CorelDRAW!. You can add nodes to a scanned object, change the fill and outline type, and apply the PowerLines along with the various special effect transformations. After an object is traced, it becomes an arrangement of lines and nodes that you can revise and edit using the features covered in previous chapters.

Tracing can also be used in other ways to enhance your work in CorelDRAW!. For example, you can create a rough sketch with pen and paper and then transfer it to CorelDRAW! by scanning the sketch, tracing it, and importing it into CorelDRAW! for editing. After the illustration has gone from paper to a vector-based computer image, you can experiment more easily with outlines, fills, stretching, scaling, and other revisions. This technique is ideal for people who work best with paper and pen sketches for initial conceptualization, but want the precision of the computer for their final product.

Tracing text in the OCR mode in CorelTRACE converts it from a single bitmap image containing the text block into a set of individual vectors for each letter. This method is used in type management programs; it allows you to edit and format the resulting image as regular text. CorelTRACE can read many fonts (including artistic fonts); it also maintains to a high degree the position, style, and size of the scanned text. OCR tracing is often used, with some degree of success, on fax image files to allow conversion of a received fax into an editable text file.

Scanning Hints for Improving CorelTRACE Results

A high-quality bitmapped image gives you better results when you're tracing. Though some flaws can be fixed after the image is imported, try to maximize image quality when scanning. A major disadvantage of bitmapped files is their size; scanning in a bitmap at a high resolution results in many dots per inch (dpi), or can create so large a file that you have difficulty importing it or tracing it. Too low a resolution, however, results in a loss of detail and an inaccurate image. Apply the following tips to best ensure properly scanned images that will successfully trace.

Scan black-and-white images (without grayscale shading) at the highest resolution possible, such as 300 or 400 dpi, to ensure more accurate tracings.

Scan color and grayscale images at 150 dpi or less because higher resolutions only increase the size of these files without giving you much improved quality.

Although CorelTRACE does detect 256 levels of gray, scanning at 16 levels is usually sufficient for tracing and also keeps the image file size to a reasonable level.

> **Note**
>
> You can open a 24-bit color bitmap in CorelTRACE, but it will reduce the number of colors to 256 or less, depending on what is set in Trace Edit options. CorelTRACE can detect a maximum of 256 colors or grayscale, so never scan color or photographic images at a setting higher than this. In fact, if the shape of the image is more important than its colors or shading, scan for 8 or 16 colors or grayscale levels only. Otherwise, your scanned files will be too large to easily manage.

The artwork you scan should be as clean and sharp as possible. Make sure that you scan black-and-white and color images at their respective optimum settings.

When scanning black-and-white artwork, adjust the contrast or intensity controls of the scanner to get a sharper image. If the image is too dark, the tracing functions have difficulty distinguishing between shades of gray or color.

Original artwork should be no smaller in size than 4 by 5 inches, and no larger than 10 by 10 inches. If the original image is smaller, enlarge it by using the scanner's scaling feature.

Tip
Bitmap editor programs such as CorelPHOTO-PAINT or PC Paintbrush can correct problems that occur because of poor alignment, such as broken or jagged lines. (See Chapter 25, "Photograph Touch-Up with CorelPHOTO-PAINT.")

Make sure the artwork is positioned at right angles to the edges of the scanning bed so that straight lines scan in straight. If you're using a sheet-fed scanner, you may want to mount the artwork on a sheet of 8 1/2-by-11-inch paper.

Scan only the portion of the image that you need for your specific purposes by cropping any unnecessary white space around the image before tracing it.

Working with Large Bitmap Files

Large bitmaps gobble up the computer's RAM memory and disk space and can be painfully slow to preview. Tracing a large or complex bitmap can create a very large file. In general, the more detail in the bitmapped image, or the more accuracy, the larger the traced file. You have to weigh the importance of retaining detail in your bitmap against the realities of working with large, memory-hogging files.

The CorelTRACE setting contained under the Trace menu's Edit Options dialog box affects both the detail and the accuracy of your tracing. The options contained under the Lines tab selection determine the level of definition that CorelTRACE will apply to the bitmap-to-vector graphic conversion.

These options also affect the final size of the traced file. An oversized file can cause problems with printing or importing, and can also be more difficult to edit. Even the conversion process uses a fairly large amount of temporary disk space. If you don't have enough temporary disk space to accommodate tracing as defined by the combination of your Windows swap file, RAM memory, and temp file space, CorelTRACE halts and notifies you of the problem.

CorelTRACE's conversion process also uses up a great deal of memory. To cut down on conversion time and prevent computer lock-up problems, it's recommended that you quit all other Windows applications before using CorelTRACE.

Tip
For a rough estimate of the kilobytes of RAM and temporary disk space it will take to convert an image, multiply the underlying bitmap file size by ten.

Using Manual Tracing and AutoTrace

The AutoTrace feature of CorelDRAW! was implemented in version 2.0 as a replacement for manually tracing an image. It was designed for simple black-and-white graphics. AutoTrace only traces images with colors that map to black, so color bitmaps give you unacceptable results. If you encounter this color-to-monochrome conversion problem, you can manually trace the object in CorelDRAW! using the Pencil tool, just as you would use a pencil and tracing paper. You can also try using AutoTrace to trace the inner and outer edges of an object and then define the fill and outline for the resulting object.

If you're working with a complex image or a color image, you're better off using the CorelTRACE application instead of the CorelDRAW! AutoTrace feature. CorelTRACE offers you greater speed and accuracy, and it requires less work on your part than the Trace and AutoTrace features of CorelDRAW!. CorelTRACE is covered later in this chapter.

Manually Tracing an Object with the Pencil Tool

Tracing an object in CorelDRAW! is simply a matter of using the Pencil tool in either Freehand or Bézier mode to set nodes and/or draw the lines that make up the outline of the object (see fig. 27.1).

This process works just as hand-tracing with a pencil and tracing paper does, so it's appropriate for only the most simple objects (or when image accuracy is not very important). Remember to join the beginning and final nodes to make a closed path if you plan to fill or color the object later.

◀ See "Understanding Line Segments and Nodes," p. 379, and "Joining and Breaking Nodes," p. 392

662 Chapter 27—Tracing Bitmap Images with CorelTRACE

Fig. 27.1
A bitmap image manually traced using CorelDRAW!'s Pencil tool. Notice the familiar nodes and line segments.

Creating an object outline

Tracing a Simple Drawing with AutoTrace

AutoTrace is a feature provided under the CorelDRAW! Pencil tool. It allows you to scan areas of a selected bitmap image and convert the scanned area into a vector graphic outline of that area. The bitmap image can be scanned and touched up using CorelPHOTO-PAINT and then imported into CorelDRAW! for autotracing.

To AutoTrace a simple drawing, follow these steps:

1. Open the **F**ile menu and choose the **I**mport command. Then find and select the bitmap image to be traced. The Import dialog box appears (see fig. 27.2). Typical bitmap image formats include BMP, TIF, and PCX.

2. If you are using CorelDRAW! 4, select the For Tracing option to display the bitmap at a higher resolution so AutoTrace can be more accurate. In CorelDRAW! 5, this step is automatic.

3. Choose OK to import the image into CorelDRAW!.

4. Use the Zoom tool to zoom in on the area to be traced—usually the outer edge of the bitmap.

5. With the Pick tool, click the bitmap image to select it, if it is not already selected when imported. The standard CorelDRAW! handles appear at the edges and Bitmap appears on the status line, indicating that the bitmap has been selected.

Using Manual Tracing and AutoTrace   663

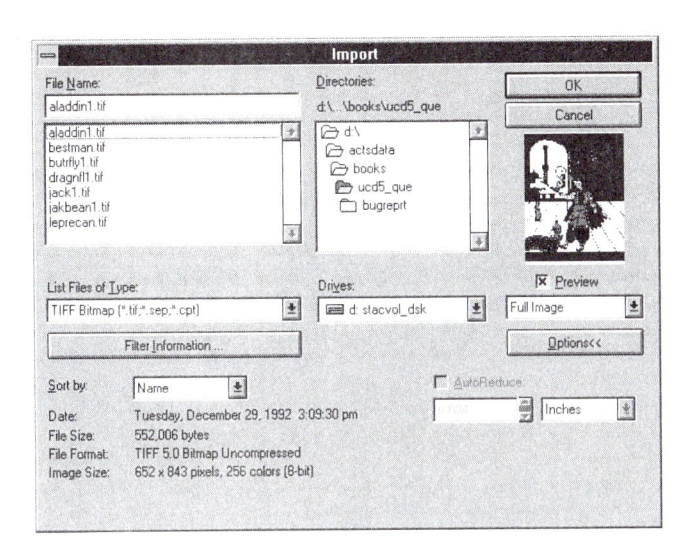

Fig. 27.2
The Import dialog box with Preview activated and the options displayed.

6. Now click the Freehand tool. This step automatically puts you in AutoTrace mode (see fig. 27.3); the special AutoTrace cursor appears on-screen.

Fig. 27.3
The AutoTrace cursor shown overlayed on an imported bitmap image prior to image section tracing.

7. To begin the automatic tracing, click just to the left of the bitmap area to be traced. (see fig. 27.3). AutoTrace evaluates the area and then applies its best guess to the desired object's outline. It is generally rough, at best, as seen before and after in figure 27.4.

664 Chapter 27—Tracing Bitmap Images with CorelTRACE

CorelDRAW! automatically finds the black bitmap image and begins to trace around it. Nodes appear along the contour of the object created by the AutoTrace procedure.

8. Trace as many regions of the bitmap as necessary to define the major black-and-white areas of the image (see fig. 27.4).

Fig. 27.4
The image and several traced segments. The bitmap was moved to the right to display the sections.

◄ See "Combining and Grouping Objects," p. 119

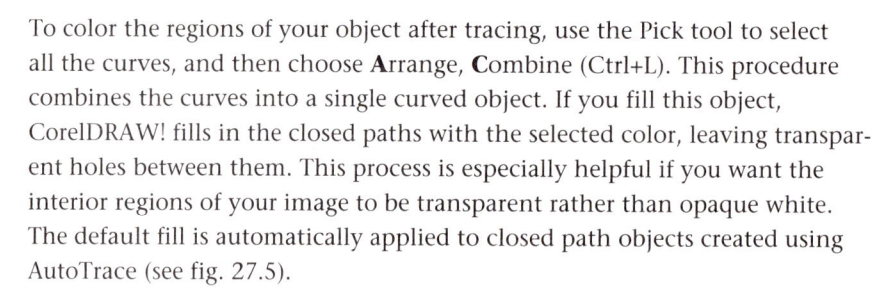

To color the regions of your object after tracing, use the Pick tool to select all the curves, and then choose **A**rrange, **C**ombine (Ctrl+L). This procedure combines the curves into a single curved object. If you fill this object, CorelDRAW! fills in the closed paths with the selected color, leaving transparent holes between them. This process is especially helpful if you want the interior regions of your image to be transparent rather than opaque white. The default fill is automatically applied to closed path objects created using AutoTrace (see fig. 27.5).

◄ See "Modifying Object Outlines and Interior Fills," p. 137

The other way to color the regions of your image is to select each of the closed paths and click the desired fill color from the color palette with the left mouse button. To move quickly and easily from one part of the drawing to another, use the **A**rrange **O**rder menu commands To **F**ront, To **B**ack, Forward **O**ne, Back O**n**e, and **R**everse Order.

Using Manual Tracing and AutoTrace   **665**

Fig. 27.5
The AutoTraced regions with the facial features combined and then filled.

Regions with fill applied

> **Note**
>
> After you trace a bitmap image, select the bitmap and delete it to keep your CorelDRAW! document small. To keep the bitmap itself, assign it to a non-printable invisible layer in the drawing.
>
> Then select all the objects and group them using Arrange Group. This procedure keeps the components of the converted image from being dragged apart accidentally.

◀ See "Understanding CorelDRAW! Layers," p. 131

◀ See "Combining and Grouping Objects," p. 119

Customizing the AutoTrace Operation

Setting the options available under the Preferences command can make AutoTrace perform more accurately. To customize the AutoTrace operation, follow these steps:

1. From the **S**pecial menu, select **P**references.

2. Click the Curves tab to access the settings that affect AutoTrace. The Preferences dialog box appears (see fig. 27.6).

VI

Other Corel Applications

Fig. 27.6
The Special menu's Preferences Curves settings tab which determines the accuracy with which the AutoTrace tracks the underlying image.

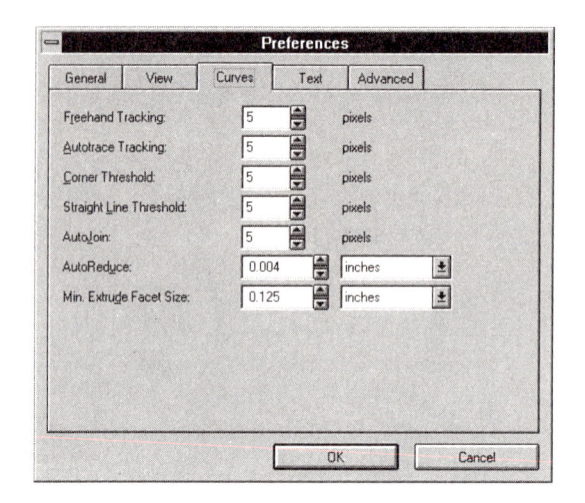

3. If you want, change the setting in the **A**utoTrace Tracking, **C**orner Threshold, and Straight **L**ine Threshold text boxes. See table 27.1 for explanations of the effects of these settings. For these settings, low numbers (1–3) produce more accurate results.

> **Note**
>
> The **C**orner Threshold and Straight **L**ine Threshold settings apply to both AutoTrace and Freehand Drawing modes.

4. Choose OK twice to return to the drawing screen. You can see the results obtained with Autotrace Tracking in figure 27.7.

Table 27.1 Curve Settings on AutoTrace

Option	Low Setting	High Setting
Autotrace Tracking	Rough curve with many nodes	Smooth curve with fewer nodes
Corner Threshold	More cusp nodes for crisp changes in direction	Smooth corners for flowing look
Straight **L**ine Threshold	More curves and fewer straight lines	More straight lines and fewer curves

Fig. 27.7
AutoTrace Tracking with one pixel (left) and 10 pixel (right) settings. Notice the higher level of detail on the left images outlines.

> ### Troubleshooting
>
> *I position my cursor on-screen and click, but nothing happens. Why does this occur, and what can I do to avoid this situation?*
>
> If you click to begin tracing and nothing happens, move your cursor slightly and click again. Usually, this means there are hidden pixel clusters that do not appear at your current zoom factor. A hidden pixel cluster is a group of pixels large enough to be sensed during tracing, but too small to show on the display. There's a good chance that the section was AutoTraced, but the object is too small to appear on the display. If problems continue, zoom in to find these hidden pixel clusters. You may also need to move the cursor point closer to an outline so that CorelDRAW! can determine the desired image portion.

Tracing an Image with CorelTRACE

CorelTRACE provides much finer control over tracing options than either hand tracing or the AutoTrace function of CorelDRAW!. In addition, CorelTRACE can trace color and grayscale images as well as monochrome bitmaps, and can extract words from a bitmap to convert them to editable text. CorelTRACE is a utility program that installs automatically with a conventional full CorelDRAW! installation. It can also be installed separately.

Refer to Appendix A, "Installation Considerations" for additional information.

The general tracing procedure is as follows:

1. Open CorelTRACE.
2. Either open the bitmap image to be traced, or scan a new image for tracing.
3. Define the various tracing options that determine the accuracy of the traced image.
4. Select the tracing method to use, such as Woodcut or Outline, and trace the bitmap
5. Save the traced image as a vector graphic file EPS format file.
6. Repeat the process for additional images, or use the Batch roll-up window to process multiple images at one time.
7. Exit CorelTRACE.

To open CorelTRACE, use the Windows Program Manager to open the COREL application group window, and then double-click the CorelTRACE icon.

To close the CorelTRACE window and application, choose E**x**it from the **F**ile menu.

Placing Images into CorelTRACE

Tip
TRACE is disk and memory-intensive, so exit your other Windows programs, including CorelDRAW!, before starting it.

Tip
HiJaak, DoDot, and Collage convert images from a variety of formats into TIFF or PCX format.

Images in several bitmap file formats, including TIFF, TGA, BMP, Photo CD and PCX, can be traced in CorelTRACE. Acceptable sources for these images include digital scanners, paint programs (such as CorelPHOTO-PAINT, PC Paintbrush, or Publisher's Paintbrush), bitmapped clipart, and screen capture programs (such as CorelCAPTURE, Collage, and HiJaak).

One of the advantages of TIFF files is that they can be created at any resolution (whatever settings on your scanner you think best: 150 dpi, 300 dpi, and so forth), and can have any number of gray levels or colors. But TIFF files can also be very large; some scanning software automatically compress monochrome TIFF images by as much as 75 percent. Because CorelTRACE expands these files to their original size before tracing them, large or complex images can take up lots of disk space during the tracing process. You may need up to ten times the number of kilobytes for the bitmap file you're tracing. This is a RAM-intensive, and perhaps expensive, process that can be aided by the use of the Windows swap file on the computer hard disk.

PCX is a format compatible with most bitmap editors. PCX can also handle monochrome, grayscale, and color images. Some scanners are limited to 16 levels of gray when saving in PCX format. Either format can be used by most graphics oriented packages, with PCX being a common favorite.

You can import images to be traced, or you can use CorelTRACE's resident scanning program.

The scanning option allows you to capture images for use in CorelTRACE directly from a scanner attached to your PC.

To access the scanning program, follow these steps:

1. Make sure the driver software for your scanner is configured according to Microsoft Windows requirements as outlined by your manufacturer's installation procedures.

2. From the File menu, choose Acquire Image.

3. Choose Select Source to specify a standard image input driver (usually a TWAIN-compatible scanner); the Corel Image Source is a default, and the driver for your particular scanner should appear as an option at the top of the Corel Image Source dialog box.

or

Choose Acquire to control your scanner without leaving the CorelTRACE program. A scanning dialog window like the one shown in figure 27.8 appears.

Tip
Zoom in to precisely view a section of the image. CorelTRACE, however, traces the image based on the actual data file contents, not screen resolution.

◀ See "Using TWAIN Technology," p. 321

Fig. 27.8
The scanning Obtain Image dialog box used to scan directly from CorelTRACE.

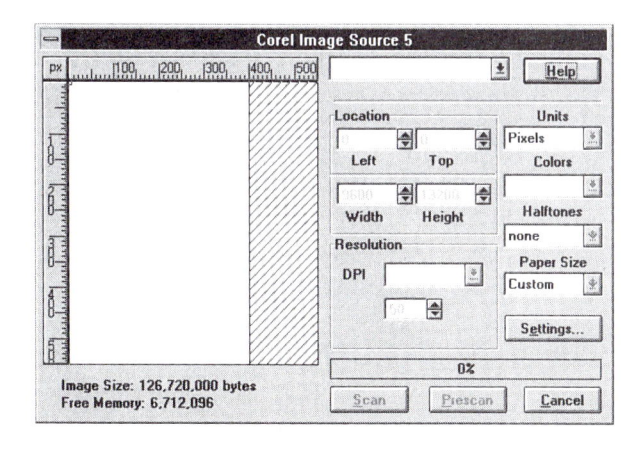

The group of options (resolution, size, cropping, and so on) that appears in this window is determined by the scanner and driver software you're using. Some scanners require manual resetting of resolution or gray scale; others are controlled by software commands.

4. Choose Prescan, if provided with your equipment, to test scan the entire image area. After setting options for color, resolution, brightness, and contrast (see settings), drag the marquee around the area in which you want to perform your final scan and click Scan. This technique is primarily used with flatbed scanners and is valuable for keeping the image sizes small as discussed previously in this chapter.

Use **F**ile **O**pen to access a BMP, TIFF, PCX, or TGA bitmap image for tracing. If you select more than one file, the Batch roll-up window automatically opens. The Open command brings up a dialog box. Clicking on a file and then the Options button displays the expanded dialog box shown in figure 27.9.

Fig. 27.9
The Open dialog box with Options activated for opening image files for tracing.

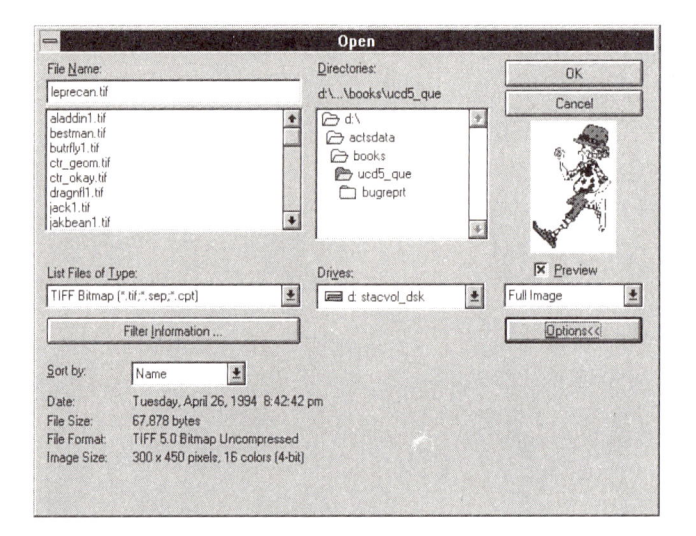

To see a small bitmap picture of the selected file displayed in the Preview Window, click **P**review. Choosing Options lets you sort by name, date, or other criteria; in addition, it gives you such information on the selected file as date, file size, file format, width, height, and color depth.

Understanding the CorelTRACE Window

The CorelTRACE dialog window is basically a split screen; the left side displays the source image (to be traced) and the right side displays the newly traced image. The CorelTRACE interface window also provides five pull-down menus, several buttons in the ribbon at the top, and six buttons at the left side of the screen (see fig. 27.10).

Tracing an Image with CorelTRACE   **671**

Fig. 27.10
The CorelTRACE screen showing the initial bitmap image (left), the scanned resulting image (right), the various tools, and the Batch roll-up.

Batch Files roll-up

The File-Related Icons

The file-related buttons are shown on the left side of the ribbon located at the top of the screen. You use these buttons to perform file and Clipboard-related operations with a simple click of the button.

The *Open File* button is used to access the File Open dialog box, which is used to select the bitmap for intended tracing.

The *Save Trace* button is used to save the traced image as an Encapsulated PostScript (EPS) file. This is the default saved file type for all CorelTRACE created files. The name of this EPS file will be the same as that of the original bitmap file.

The *Cut* button is used to remove the selected image section from the traced portion of the screen and place it on the clipboard in Windows Metafile (WMF) format. This is generally used to immediately transfer the traced portion to another application, such as CorelDRAW!.

The *Copy* button is used to load a duplicate of the selected traced image portion onto the Clipboard while leaving the original traced image intact.

The *Paste* button is used to transfer a device-dependent bitmap image from the Clipboard into CorelTRACE.

VI

Other Corel Applications

The *Settings* list box contains the grouped default settings, or tracing Styles, used to trace the currently open image. Setting styles are defined and saved using the Trace menu's Edit Options dialog box selections.

The *Batch Files* button displays the Batch Files roll-up, which provides control over the batch-tracing process and ready access to the various tracing tools. Those tools are covered in detail in the next section.

The *MOSAIC* button opens CorelMOSAIC for visual access to files using their image instead of their text name.

The Tracing Method Buttons

The *Outline* button is used to trace the edge of each element or shape in the bitmap. The resulting outlined closed-path object can then be filled to emulate the source image.

The *Centerline* button is used to trace lines as lines instead of objects to be filled. This tracing method is not available on color images, and is used only on monochrome image.

The *OCR* button is used to convert scanned text into editable text format, maintaining most of the relationships between different font styles and sizes. It only works with black text on a white background.

The *Form* button is used to convert scanned text in a form or convert other ruled and lined documents into editable format, keeping the boxes, rules, and so on. It only recognizes black text on a white background

The *Woodcut* button is used to create a special effect on the traced image that emulates the lines across woodcuts; you can specify the angle of the lines.

The *Silhouette Trace* button is used to trace the outline of a specified area and fill it with a single silhouette color, which is selected with the Eyedropper tool or the Magic Wand.

Other Buttons and Tools

The *Color Selection* button gives you the color palette, from which you can choose a tracing fill color when in Silhouette or Woodcut mode.

The *Image Info* button opens a dialog box that contains information about the bitmap image being traced and the number of objects and nodes contained in the traced image (see fig. 27.11).

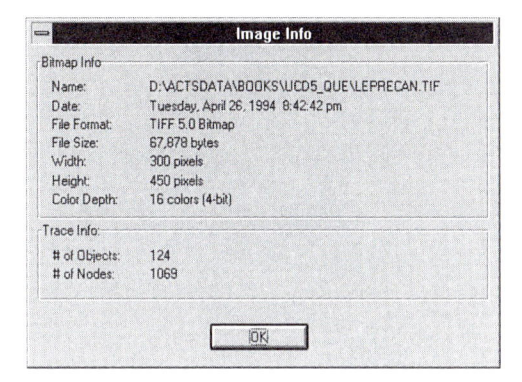

Fig. 27.11
The Image Information dialog box with information about the bitmap image and the complexity of the traced image.

The *Online Help* button provides direct access to the CorelTRACE help facility's Table of Contents window.

The *Pick* tool is used to select certain areas of the source image for tracing. Selection is accomplished by clicking and dragging the tool across the desired tracing area. You can specify more than one area by holding down the Shift key while selecting.

The *Magic Wand* tools are used to select (icon with a +) and deselect (icon with a –) areas of the source image for scanning that share a similar color range. These tools are generally used when you want to simultaneously work with similar shades of a color. You can specify multiple areas by holding down the Shift key while selecting.

The *Zoom* tools are for magnifying (icon with a +) and minimizing (icon with a –) the display of the image.

The *Eyedropper* tool lets you pick up color from the source image for use in the traced image. Defines the color used in the Color Selection button.

The Batch Files Roll-Up Window

The Batch Files roll-up window allows you to select several files for automatically tracing as a group, saving you time and allowing you to take care of other business while CorelTRACE performs its magic (see fig. 27.12). The Batch Files roll-up opens automatically if you select more than one file using the File menu's Open Files selection and the standard Windows multiple file selection operations. You can also open the Batch Files roll-up by choosing the File menu's Batch Roll-Up option or by clicking the Batch Files button located on the ribbon bar.

Fig. 27.12
The Batch Files roll-up window used for automatically tracing many images in sequence.

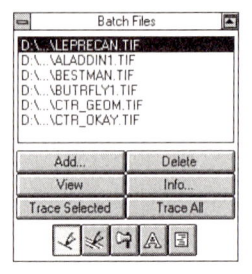

Some of the buttons in this roll-up window perform the same functions as commands found elsewhere in CorelTRACE; others are unique to this menu.

The file names box shows a list of the files you have selected. Click the Add button to open a dialog box that lets you open one or more files for tracing by way of an Open Files dialog box, like the one provided under the File menu. To select groups of files to add, hold down the primary mouse button and drag over several consecutive names, or hold down the Shift key as you click consecutive file names. Ctrl-clicking allows you to select non-consecutive files.

If you choose an image file and then decide that you do not want to use it, simply highlight it and click the Delete button. To display a bitmap representation of a file, click the View button or double-click any file in the File Names box. Click the Info button to see a given file's date, size, file format, width, height, color mode, resolution, and compression. This information is important if you want to export the tracing to CorelDRAW!.

To trace only one file or a subset (choose multiple files using the Shift key with the mouse button) of all the files listed, click the Trace Selected button. To begin tracing all the files in the File Names box, click the Trace All button. The files chosen for batch tracing do not all have to be the same type of file. The tracing method and parameters must be the same, however, for all files traced by a single command. Five of the six tracing method buttons—Outline, Centerline, Woodcut, OCR, and Form—appear at the bottom of the Batch Files roll-up window. Silhouette tracing is not available in Batch mode.

The CorelTRACE Menus

The menus in CorelTRACE differ from the CorelDRAW! menus. In the far right corner of the CorelTRACE window is the on-line Help menu, which allows you to choose from a general overview, a list of commands, step-by-step instructions on different procedures under How To, and a list of the tools and their functions. Access this menu by clicking Help in the upper-right corner of the screen or by pressing F1. A Help Index gives an overview of the available topics; you can see detailed Help information on any of these topics by double-clicking the topic name. Some topic explanations contain hypertext entries—underlined words or phrases—that you can click to get related information. You can also Browse the help topics or Search for a specific topic. To exit Help, click the Exit command in the File menu.

Choosing a Tracing Method

The various tracing options included with CorelTRACE are provided to most accurately, and automatically, replicate the underlying bitmap image. Certain bitmap image types are better suited to Centerline tracing, while others are traced better with the Outline method. The Silhouette and Woodcut tracing options provide artistic flair to your tracing activities. The OCR and Form tracing methods can make your life a lot easier, and save hours of typing, if used effectively to change documents into editable text.

You can use the following guidelines to determine which CorelTRACE tracing method is appropriate for a job:

- To simply turn a bitmap image into a vector-graphic image, use either the Centerline or Outline method.

- To turn a bitmap image into a vector-graphic image with special effects applied to the traced outlines, use either Woodcut or Silhouette.

- To turn words into editable text, use either OCR or Form.

Centerline and Outline

The two basic tracing methods in CorelTRACE are Centerline and Outline (see figures 27.13 and 27.14). Clicking a method's button starts a trace of the currently active bitmap using that tracing method. Think of the Centerline method as producing a traced image that consists of a number of lines with varying thicknesses and minimal interior fills; while the Outline method provides a number of different objects with narrow outlines and large interior fills.

Both these methods can be used with almost any image that contains solid areas, fine lines, or a combination of both. Centerline is the best choice for images with many thin black lines, such as technical illustrations or architectural drawings. The original bitmap image must consist of black lines on a white background for optimal conversion.

676 Chapter 27—Tracing Bitmap Images with CorelTRACE

Fig. 27.13
An image traced using the Outline mode.

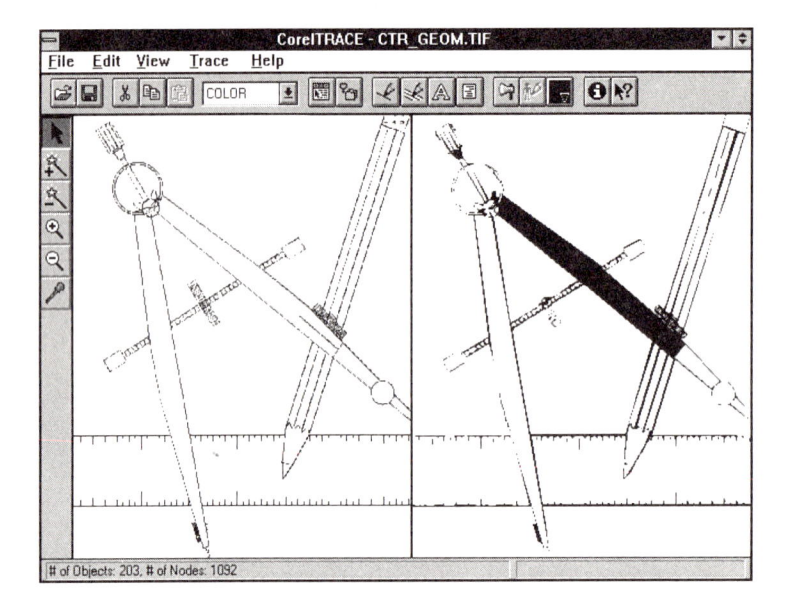

Fig. 27.14
The same image traced using the Centerline method.

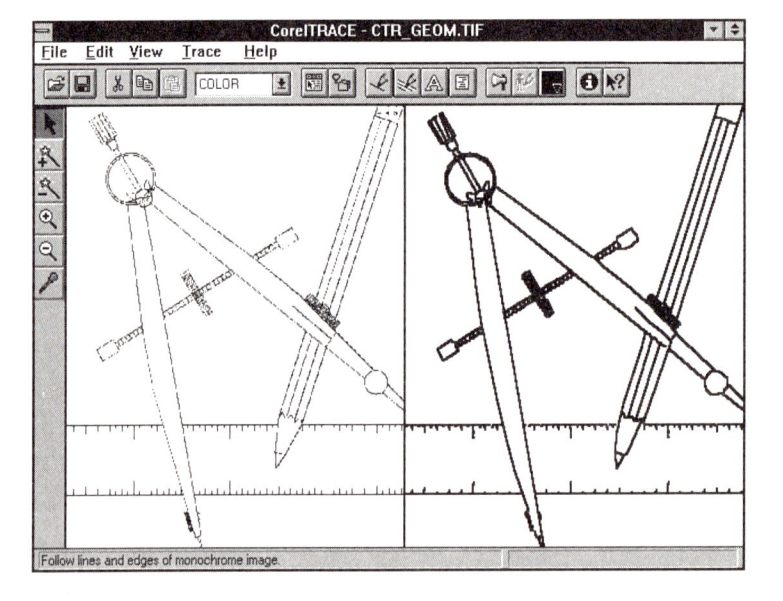

Outline is the best choice for tracing images with many thick filled objects, images in gray scale, color images, or images made up of white lines on a black background. The Outline method traces the edges of the elements in a bitmapped image—the equivalent of the Wireframe display—and then fills in the resulting outline. If you're tracing a black-and-white image, the areas that are black in the original will be black in the converted image, too.

If you're tracing color or grayscale images, CorelTRACE decides which grays or colors are the closest match to the original and uses those colors up to 256 colors for the interior fills.

The Centerline method treats thin bitmapped lines as objects having a certain thickness but no fill. As a result, the line itself is traced instead of its outline. Any lines that exceed the pixel threshold set in the Trace menu's Edit, Options, Lines tab (the Centerline method's Maximum Line Width setting) are traced using the Outline method (see fig. 27.15).

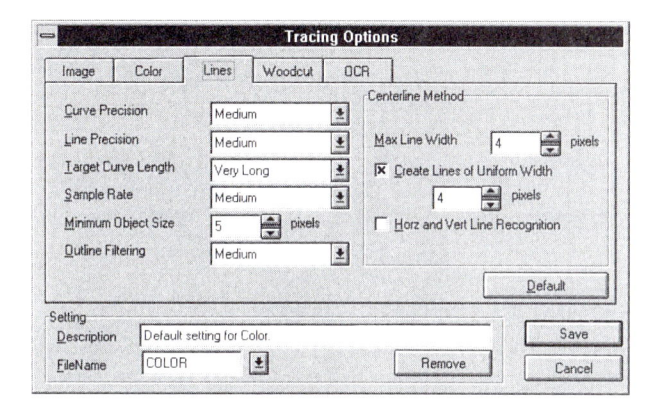

Fig. 27.15
The Tracing Options Lines dialog box used to set thresholds and line thicknesses for the Centerline method.

> **Note**
> When the Outline method is used, each element in a bitmap image is treated as a filled area. So lines may appear as elongated ovals or rectangles when the vector image is exported to CorelDRAW!. The letter O, for example, becomes a black circle with a white inner circle layered on top.

Woodcut and Silhouette

To create special effects, try the Woodcut or Silhouette methods. Both these methods add a special visual appearance to the vector version of the bitmap image that they create.

The Woodcut method puts lines or cuts across the image at a specified angle (see fig. 27.16). You can control the appearance of these cuts, including whether they obscure or enhance the original image.

Fig. 27.16
Tracing the same image in Woodcut mode.

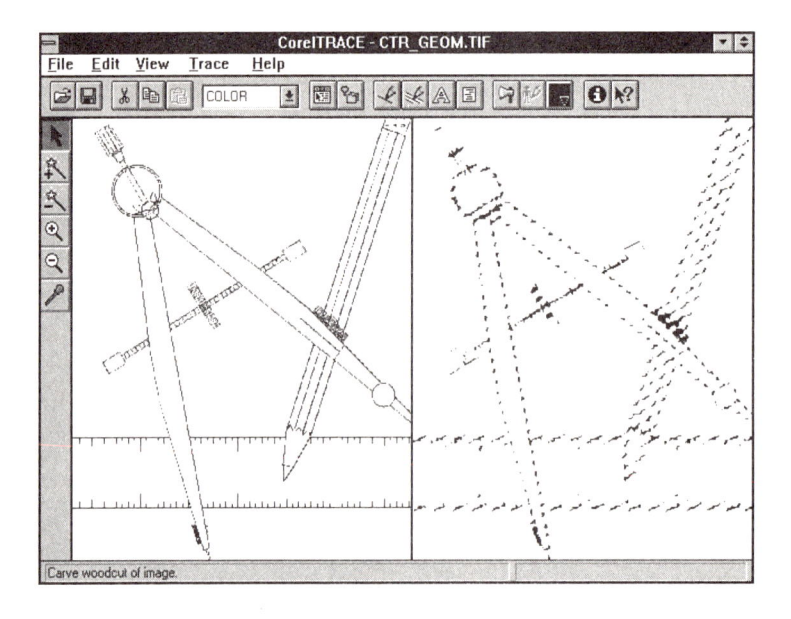

The Silhouette method drops out the interior of objects; it traces just an outline and fills it with a color that you specify using the color selection button (see fig. 27.17). The silhouette shown in figure 27.17 was created by first selecting the individual areas of the bitmap with the Magic Wand tool, and then clicking the Silhouette button.

Fig. 27.17
Tracing in Silhouette mode provides an interesting artistic effect.

OCR and Form

To convert bitmap words to editable text, CorelTRACE offers an Optical Character Recognition (OCR) feature. You can turn scanned text into vectors that can be manipulated as normal text. You can even re-create other graphic elements with editable text by using the Form tracing method. CorelTRACE scans an image and converts the contents into text, then into lines for the form rules, and then makes its best attempt at re-creating any remaining objects that it discerns from the scanned image.

The OCR method provides you with several options. To display these options, choose the **T**race menu's **E**dit Options, OCR tab to reveal the OCR dialog box shown in fig. 27.18.

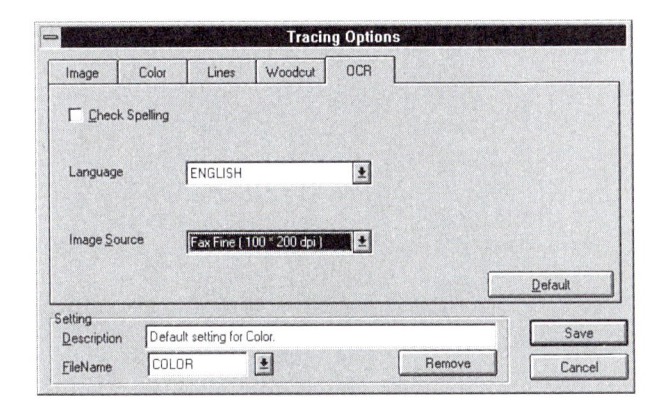

Fig. 27.18
The Tracing Options dialog box, with the OCR tab selected.

Activating Check Spelling sets CorelTRACE to ignore all incorrectly spelled words—not a recommended procedure, because this can make your final text document difficult to decipher since whole sections of text may be ignored by CorelTRACE during the conversion process. The Image Source option defines the source of the original copy so that CorelTRACE can apply special recognition features to improve accuracy: Normal is used for 300-dpi printed text, such as text from a laser printer; Fax Fine is used to scan a fax and improve its readability; and the Dot-Matrix option improves the readability of dot-matrix printed text.

The Language setting defines the character set and spelling dictionary that CorelTRACE uses when recognizing words, which becomes important when you're dealing with languages that use accents and special characters. The CD-ROM includes the French, German, Spanish, and Swedish dictionaries in addition to the English dictionary. The dictionaries are also available from the Corel Tech Support bulletin board. The phone number is listed in the Corel Documentation. Be careful to select the correct dictionary before OCR scanning a foreign document; otherwise, accents and special symbols won't trace.

The Form option on the Trace menu converts a scanned bitmap of a preprinted form and changes it into text, lines, and objects so that the form can be reused or modified. It's really a combination of OCR, for the text, Centerline, for the form lines, and Outline for all remaining objects. The accuracy with which the Form method traces the underlying image depends on the Tracing Edit Options dialog box's Lines and OCR tab settings, as outlined in the next section. You're generally better served by converting a color image to monochrome before attempting a Form trace. The conversion is accomplished using the Trace menus Edit Options, the Image tabs Convert to Monochrome option, and then clicking on Save.

Defining the Accuracy of the Traced Image

CorelTRACE provides different levels of tracing accuracy through its various parameters, which enable you to control the results of its automated tracings. The best settings for these parameters depend on the image to be traced and how you plan to use it. Use this four-step procedure to help you choose the settings that yield the best results in the least amount of time. Ultimately, you'll find the best method through trial and error.

1. Evaluate the composition. Is the image you are tracing made up of mostly lines (Centerline), mostly filled shapes (Outline), or a combination of both (Form)? Are the lines thick (Outline) or thin (Centerline)? Are the lines straight or curved? If you're scanning an image containing words (OCR), are the words the most important element, and do you plan to edit the text later? Do you want only the text, or do you also want to trace some of the rules, lines, and boxes (Forms)?

2. After analyzing composition, choose between Outline or Centerline tracing. Or if you want a special effect applied to the trace, choose Woodcut or Silhouette. If you're scanning text for editing later, choose between OCR and Form. Use the Form setting to keep the graphic elements (lines, rules, and so on) with the text.

3. Decide how much detail you want to include in the traced image. As much as possible? Some detail, but a final image with smooth edges? Or just the general shape and features of the bitmapped image?

4. Determine how the traced image will be used. Will it be used as-is, brought into a page layout program, or transferred into a drawing program for editing? Will it be used as text or as a graphic?

When you know answers to these questions, you can review the settings information provided next in this chapter to apply CorelTRACE to your job.

Modifying Additional Image Settings

In the discussion "OCR and Form," earlier in this chapter, you looked at the settings presented when you choose the OCR tab in the Tracing Edit Options property sheet. This dialog box provides access to Image, Color, Lines, Woodcut and OCR default settings. Using these settings effectively will make your relationship with CorelTRACE a lot smoother.

Image Filtering

CorelTRACE works best on high-resolution (300 dpi) black-and-white line art. This category includes technical illustrations, architectural drawings, and logos.

CorelTRACE converts the shades of gray in a grayscale image into either black or white. This procedure may create problems; not all grayscale images yield satisfactory results when traced. The best candidates are simple images with distinct outlines, rather than images where the object tends to blend into the background. You can improve the grayscale tracing by using your scanner's 4-bit grayscale scanning mode, reducing the scanner resolution to at least 150 dpi to get a smaller file, and adjusting your scanner's contrast and intensity to more sharply define the darker and lighter portions of the image.

Images made of solid color also trace well; when the colors change gradually instead of changing at clearly defined borders, tracing problems can arise. Smooth Dithering can help you avoid some of these problems. To access this setting, choose the **T**race menu's **E**dit Options and then click on the Image tab. The Image property sheet, which contains the Smooth Dithering option, appears (see fig. 27.19).

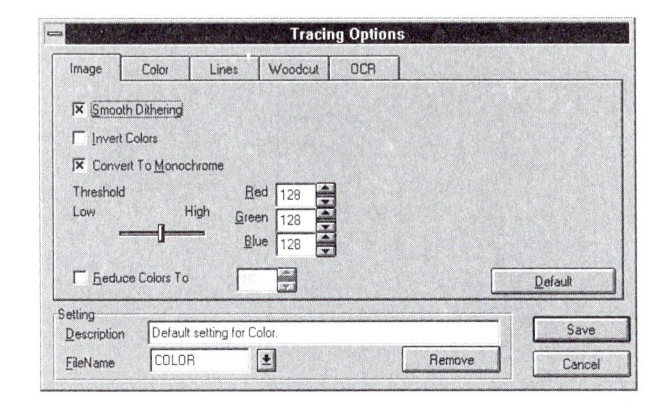

Fig. 27.19
The Image property sheet, in the Tracing Options dialog box, contains color transition and filtering options.

Image filtering controls how CorelTRACE reads the source image. It provides the following setting options:

Smooth Dithering. Improves the traced image by smoothing the dithered display pixels (creating pure color areas from dithered or approximated color areas) to produce a clearer image when traced.

Invert Colors. Specifies a numeric inversion of the RGB values of the colors (reassigns each initial color value to the difference between that color value and 255). In actual color terms, this procedure turns white to black and other colors to their corresponding inverted, or complementary, colors.

Convert to Monochrome. Controls how colors are converted to a series of grays by letting you set values for various RGB shades. Convert to Monochrome must be selected before the Threshold levels can be set.

Threshold. Activates controls over the darkness and lightness of the converted image by establishing a point at which black-and-white levels are determined. Low threshold values tend to generate conversions in which only the very dark colors convert to black, which makes the overall image appear lighter. High threshold values tend to generate darker conversions in which only very bright colors convert to white. You can also use the Red, Blue, and Green (RGB) boxes provided with this setting to enter individual values for RGB—the default button specifies an RGB value of 128. These numbers are relative and vary the value at which the selected colors are recognized and turned into black or white.

Reduce Colors To. Controls the number of colors used for the tracing. CorelTRACE examines all the colors in the image and selects the best ones to perform the reduction. The common setting of 16, for example, displays the image using only 16 representative colors.

The Setting options located at the bottom of the tab are used to define defaults that are applied to the image being traced. The drop-down list contains a listing of all available preset tracing default files. You can define your own by establishing the settings you want and then clicking in the **FileName** text box and entering the desired name. CorelTRACE comes with default files (CTR) that provide excellent starting points for tracing Color, Dithered, Form and Monochrome image files. You might want to use these as a starting point for creating your own custom files. Make your desired setting changes and then save the new settings under your own custom filename. These setting files contain information from all of the Options tabs and can be selected from each of the Edit Option tabs.

The Description line provides information about the file selected. This information is entered by modifying the text in the description line, just as you would with any other Windows application. Remove a file by first selecting it and then clicking on the Remove command button. The Default command button is used to reset all values associated with the currently active file to their stored, default values.

Adjusting Color Tolerance

Color property sheet settings adjust the Magic Wand tools and the tracing tolerance that enable CorelTRACE to distinguish objects of different color (see fig. 27.20). You can think of the color tolerance as a measure of color similarity, and colors perceived as similar will be treated as the same color. Low tolerance values result in a greater number of different objects that all vary slightly in color. High values allow many different colors to fall into a color range, resulting in a smaller number of objects that are of different colors.

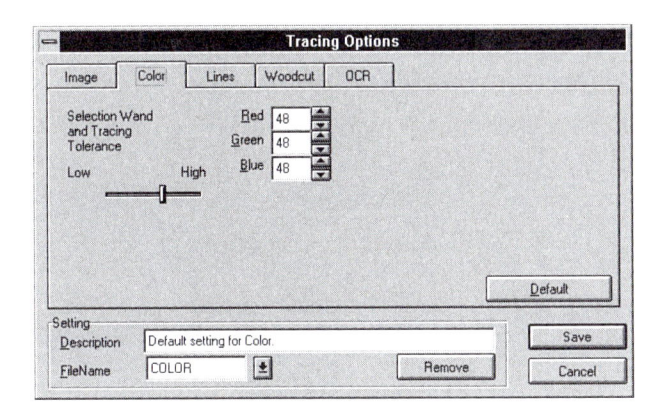

Fig. 27.20
The Color property sheet in the Tracing Options dialog box lets you adjust color tolerance as seen during tracing and with the Magic Wand tool.

The default RGB tolerance in CorelTRACE for the Magic Wands is plus or minus 48. Numbers lower than 48 give you a more detailed final image that takes longer to trace and creates more objects. You can specify your own RGB tolerance values by clicking in the R, G, or B buttons and entering a value. Experimentation will lead you to the tradeoff between image complexity and tracing clarity. Clicking on Default resets the values established in the currently active Style.

Setting Line Tracing Attributes

Selecting the Line tab from the Edit Options dialog box displays the Lines property sheet (see fig. 27.21). It lets you define Outline tracing related parameters for the Outline tracing method. The following options are provided:

Fig. 27.21
The Lines property sheet in the Tracing Options dialog box is used to define the level of tracing line tracking and tolerances used in the Centerline, Outline and Form tracing method.

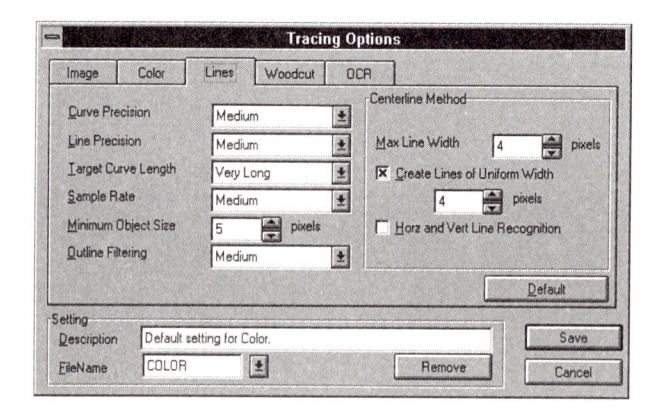

Curve Precision. Controls how tightly the trace output follows the curves of the original image.

Line Precision. Controls how straight a line must be before CorelTRACE converts it to a line. CorelTRACE first attempts to convert all edges to simple uncurved linear paths. The default value captures as much detail in the source image as possible.

Target Curve Length. Limits the length of individual curves in the traced image (limits the distance between the nodes placed to emulate the bitmap curves of the source image). The default setting of Very Long is adequate for most types of images. For more detail, choose Short or Very Short. The shorter the curve length, however, the more nodes are required. Be aware that a short curve length generates a larger image file due to the additional data required to represent the increased number of nodes.

Sample Rate. Tells CorelTRACE how closely to match the bitmap. Medium is the default setting. Fine gives the closest match possible; Coarse averages some connecting points.

Minimum Object Size. Affects the way that CorelTRACE counts the pixels in the object outline. A higher number filters out small objects; a lower number gives greater detail.

Outline filtering. Determines the level of smoothness applied to the traced object's outline. Smooth Points provides the most smoothing of object outlines, and None provides no smoothing at all and tends to provide a more jagged edge. Medium is in the middle between Smooth and None.

Centerline Method Accuracy Settings

The Centerline method related options provided in the Tracing Options Lines property sheet determine the level of accuracy obtained from a Centerline method trace.

Maximum Line Width. Defines the widest object that can be accepted for a centerline traced object. If the ends of lines in the traced image look distorted, reduce the line width setting in this property sheet and retrace. If the curves have gaps, increase line width and retrace. To trace all lines in the source image as lines instead of as filled objects, set the line width to match the width of the heaviest line. If the majority of lines are wider than 20 pixels (in an image at 300 dpi), use the Outline method instead.

Create Lines of Uniform Width. Assigns a specific weight (1 to 50 pixels) to all lines in the image. The default is 4 pixels.

Horizontal and Vertical Line Recognition. Rotates the entire page to get the lines perfectly vertical and/or horizontal for better recognition. Used when the scan is slightly rotated, and you want the traced image perfectly vertical and horizontal.

Default. Resets all parameters to the default attached to the currently active style.

Setting the Woodcut Style

When you use the Tracing Options dialog box and click the Woodcut tab, you get the options shown in figure 27.22 and described in the following list. These options apply whenever you perform a Woodcut trace.

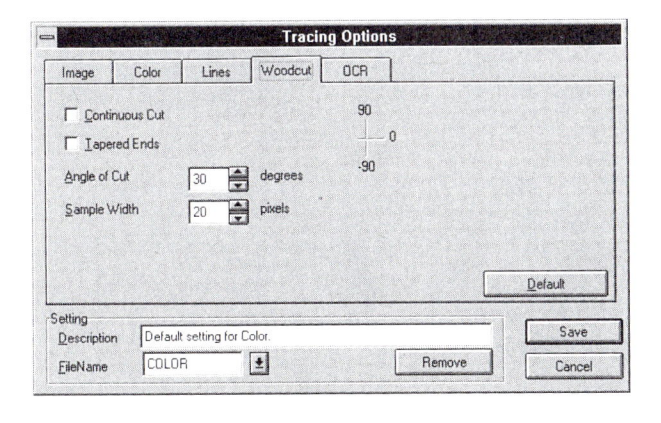

Fig. 27.22
The Woodcut property sheet in the Tracing Options dialog box lets you control the effect you achieve when you click on the Woodcut tool.

Continuous Cut. Makes cuts with no breaks; otherwise, the cuts fade in bright areas to give the illusion of highlights. The default is No Continuous Cut.

Tapered Ends. Creates a gradual narrowing effect at the end of each line. The default is No Tapered Ends.

Sample Width in Pixels. Specifies the width of each line. Lower numbers create more lines in the tracing. The default is 20 pixels.

Angle of Cut in Degrees. Determines the angle of the lines; a negative number creates a mirror image of the positive angle. The default is 30 degrees.

Clicking on Default sets all Woodcut values to their defaults.

Customizing OCR Traces

The OCR property sheet in the Tracing Options dialog box (refer to fig. 27.18) provides options enabling you to specify the source of the document and to have CorelTRACE check the spelling of the traced text (misspelled words are not traced). By default, the Check Spelling option is disabled.

Spell checking is specified by the combination of the Language drop down box and selecting the Check Spelling option. This instructs CorelTRACE to check the spelling of each traced word and ignore those that are incorrectly spelled according to the selected language dictionary.

OCR text can come from the following sources as selected from the Image Source drop-down list:

Normal. Documents with standard fonts and a resolution of 300 dpi (the default).

From Dot Matrix. A scanned dot-matrix printout, which takes longer and produces less reliable results. Try to avoid dot-matrix source documents if possible.

Fax Fine (100x200 dpi). A standard scanned fax at an expected resolution of 100 by 200 dpi.

Clicking on the Default button sets the OCR values to their default values.

Save Options for Batch Output

Selecting the File menu's Save Options displays the dialog box shown in figure 27.23. It works in conjunction with the Batch roll-up window discussed earlier in this chapter. First select the drive and directory into which you want to save the traced images. The dialog box contains additional instruction on what to do in the case of a name conflict between the traced image and an existing file (Always Prompt for instructions or Always Replace), on whether to Make file Read Only and whether to Save text as *.TXT file (see fig. 27.23).

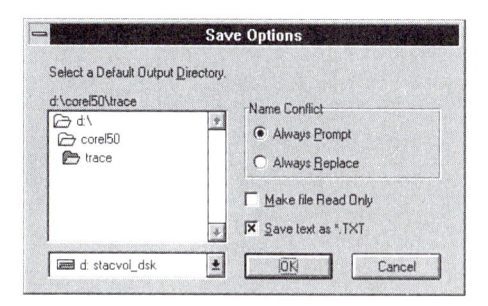

Fig. 27.23
The Save Options dialog box used to set parameters that work with the Batch roll-up window operation.

Saving the Traced Image

CorelTRACE allows you to save tracings in three different formats, depending on the type of image you create. All three choices are accessed by choosing Save from the File menu:

Trace As. Choose this option for a bitmap successfully traced and converted to vector form. It saves an EPS (Encapsulated PostScript) file using the path and file name you specify.

Text As. Choose this option for scanned text successfully converted to an editable text file. It saves a TXT format file using the path and file name you specify.

Image As. Choose this option for an edited bitmap image that hasn't been scanned or converted to vector form. It saves the image as a BMP document using the path and file name you specify.

Save Trace. Choose this option to store the trace under the directory and path previously specified. It saves an EPS file, which is readable by CorelDRAW! and can be imported there and exported in whatever file format you need.

Tracing Only Part of a Bitmap

In many cases, you might want to trace only a part of a bitmap. Because bitmaps are such large files, selecting only part of the image to trace can save you time and disk space. CorelTRACE provides two ways to do so. You can use the Pick tool to draw a rectangular marquee around the area(s) you want to trace. You can select several areas at once by holding down the Shift key; all areas selected will be traced at the same time.

If you are working with non-geometric shapes, on the other hand, you can use the Magic Wand tools to select (or deselect) portions of the image that have the same or similar colors. The color tolerance for these selections can be set using the Color tolerance settings contained in the Trace menu's Edit Options, Color property sheet display.

You can use the Magic Wand tools and the Silhouette setting to piece together a tracing using different colors for different shapes. This procedure allows you to approximate the source image without having to go back later and choose fill colors. To use it, follow these steps:

1. Click the Magic Wand Select tool.

2. Click an area on the source (bitmap) image. A marquee appears around the area that is in the color tolerance range you set earlier (under the Color property sheet).

3. Click the Color Selection button located on the ribbon bar, and choose a tracing color similar to the original bitmap color from the drop-down colors list (or choose a different but appealing color, if you want to make changes). You can also use the Eyedropper tool to click on an image color that matches the desired traced objects interior fill. The color displayed in the color selection button becomes the default fill color for all subsequently created objects.

4. Click the Silhouette Trace button. The tracing of the selected area appears as a solid filled shape.

5. Click the Magic Wand Select tool again, and then click another area of the source image. Another marquee appears. Choose a color similar or complementary to the bitmap, and continue with the steps above.

6. After you piece together a complete image, you can save it to disk or copy it to the Clipboard and paste it into another program.

Tracing and Saving Multiple Files Simultaneously

CorelTRACE makes it easy for you to perform repetitive tasks by using a few simple commands. You can trace and save multiple files at once, for example, by choosing all the bitmap files to be traced, specifying the path for the traced images, and then issuing a single command to start the tracing.

CorelTRACE then scans the images consecutively, leaving you free to catch up on reading or eat dinner. CorelTRACE gives the tracings it produces the same root names as the original bitmap images, but changes each extension to EPS.

Batch Trace begins automatically with the same CorelTRACE settings. CorelTRACE loads the files and creates the traced images. Pressing Esc stops the batch process. To trace a complete batch of files at once, follow these steps:

1. Activate the Batch Files roll-up by clicking the Batch Files button.

2. Click the Add button to get a list of directories and files. Deactivate Preview in the Open Files dialog box if you are using it. Select the files you want to trace, using standard Windows selection techniques. You can add several file formats (PCX, TGA, TIFF, BMP, and so on) to the list at the same time. After you finish, click OK.

3. Select the files that you want to trace from within the Batch Files roll-up, using any of the standard Windows selection techniques. Click a button for the tracing method to use at the bottom of the roll-up.

4. Click the Trace Selected button to trace the files in the list you have highlighted. Click the Trace All button to trace all the files listed in the roll-up window. All traced images will go to the same drive and directory location, saved with the same file name and an EPS extension.

5. To halt the entire process of tracing and saving, press the Esc button. To restart, repeat the steps, beginning with step 3 above.

Using the Bitmap Header Information

A header is a bitmap representation of an image that is required by some programs (such as PageMaker 5.0) to correctly size and position the vector-based image. Without the header, you get a screened box in PageMaker. To see the image on-screen and manipulate it, you need the header. After CorelTRACE finishes tracing a bitmap, it saves the vector-graphic image as an EPS file without a header. So when you look up CorelTRACE files in programs like PageMaker 5.0, your screen displays an × in the preview box instead of an image.

If you want to add a header to an EPS file created by CorelTRACE, follow these steps:

1. Import it into CorelDRAW!. (See "Using Traced Images in CorelDRAW!" later in this chapter.)

2. Export the image from CorelDRAW! as a PostScript file with an image header included.

3. Specify the size of the header you want to include (a dimension that affects the resolution of the bitmap only and has no impact on the quality of the printed image). See Chapter 9, "File-Related Operations and CorelMOSAIC," for detailed information on exporting PostScript files.

To minimize the increase in document size, choose the 128×128 header setting (which adds only 2K or so). Size is important because some programs that use these image headers also have maximum importable file sizes of about 64K.

Using CorelTRACE Images with Other Applications

A traced bitmap rarely becomes the final document; the image is generally edited to its final form in CorelDRAW! or some other application. But the images created by CorelTRACE can be quite complex; at times they can lock up the application program attempting to load them for use. Somewhat less complex images can still take up to several minutes to load, and may not print correctly after being loaded. To remedy these problems, experiment with the following suggestions:

- Reduce the size of the file by tracing only a portion of the bitmap instead of the entire object. CorelTRACE reproduces fine details by creating many short line segments; some programs, like CorelDRAW!, have a maximum number of line segments and nodes that they accept in an imported document.

- Scan the image to be traced at a lower resolution. You reduce the number of line segments and nodes this way; you also lose some of the detail of your image.

- Choose **E**dit Options from the **T**race menu. Click the Image tab, select **R**educe Colors, and change the value to 8 or less. Then click the Lines tab and reset **T**arget Curve Length to Very Long and/or Minimum Object Size to a higher number until the image is of the desired complexity. When finished, choose save.

- After the converted image is in CorelDRAW! or another vector-based drawing program, simplify it by deleting groups of nodes, breaking apart long lines, and eliminating unnecessary objects.

> **Note**
>
> CorelDRAW! accepts a maximum of 3000 objects and limits the nodes to between 1000 and 2000 per object, depending on your printer. You might have to trace a smaller portion of the image or adjust the parameters to lower the node and/or object count on complex bitmapped images.

Using Traced Images in CorelDRAW!

It's common to use CorelTRACE images in CorelDRAW!. The procedure for bringing the traced images into CorelDRAW! is similar to importing any other image format.

To import a CorelTRACE image into CorelDRAW!, follow these steps:

1. Choose Import from the File menu, and then click CorelTRACE (*.EPS) as the import type. A list of EPS files appears.

2. Choose the one you want and click OK.

3. After the image appears, you can rework it just as you can any object created within CorelDRAW!. To make revisions, the first step is usually to Ungroup the elements. Then you can add a fill, change the outline, add or subtract nodes and line segments, or issue other desired object manipulation commands.

4. Save the file as CDR to automatically work with the files in their native CorelDRAW! format from that point forward.

Using Traced Images in Other Applications

CorelTRACE is made expressly to be used with CorelDRAW!, but files created with CorelTRACE can also be imported into other IBM PC programs or even to the Macintosh if you use the PostScript file format. It's best to use the graphics file conversion capabilities of CorelDRAW! to put the traced image into a format acceptable to another program. Read the documentation for the source program to see what formats are needed. Printing CorelTRACE images placed into other programs usually requires a PostScript printer. If you have a non-PostScript printer, import the traced image into CorelDRAW! first and save it in a file format acceptable to the target printer, such as Windows MetaFile (WMF) or WordPerfect Graphic (WPG).

The OCR and Form settings turn scanned words into text that can be edited in CorelDRAW! or CorelPHOTO-PAINT using the Text tools. Text tracings made with the OCR and Form settings can also be exported as ASCII text files, which can be opened and edited by most major word processing programs.

Conceptual Overview: Tracing a Logo

The scanning and placement of photographs or drawings rarely require tracing. If you include a photograph of a product in a flyer or brochure, for instance, the bitmap image, though large, works fine. Tracing is important, however, when converting a graphic image into a form that you want to scale, skew, and rotate without distortion. This process comes in handy, for example, when you create a new paper system—letterhead, business envelopes, business cards, pocket folders—and want to use your company's logo in many sizes and orientations. You want the logo to reproduce on your laser printer without jaggedness, and you want to be able to give your CorelDRAW! file to your commercial printer and know the logo will appear clear at any resolution. Most logos begin as black-and-white images, but maybe you can only find the already printed three-color version (green, red, and orange). How would you trace the logo?

If you care only about retaining the logo shape, the AutoTrace function in CorelDRAW! may be enough. As you remember, AutoTrace cannot see colors, so the logo will trace as an outline that you can then fill with colors from the color palette. If the logo is elaborate, delicate, or has great variations in color, use CorelTRACE and adjust the settings in the Tracing Options dialog box for the best effect. If you use the Silhouette setting and the Magic Wand tools, you can even scan each of the red, green, and orange areas in matching colors.

When you have your traced logo, you can place it at one-fifth the original size on your business card layouts, at six times the original size on the cover of your pocket folder, and at 45 degrees rotation on your business envelopes. No matter how you treat it, you will get a crisp image with a smooth outline. Plus, each of these graphic files will be smaller than if they had the appropriately sized bitmap image included and will be easier and faster to rework in CorelDRAW!.

> **Troubleshooting**
>
> *I traced my images, but cannot read them into my destination application. What is the problem?*
>
> It could lie in two possible areas. First, make sure that you are using the CorelTRACE EPS format when working with CorelDRAW!, and the Adobe Illustrator EPS file when working with everything else. Making this work may require you to import the CorelTRACE file into CorelDRAW! and export it as an Adobe Illustrator EPS file. A little arcane, but it should work. You may also have a file that is too complicated for the destination application. Try reducing the number of nodes using the CorelDRAW! utilities, and try your luck then.
>
> *I always wind up with thousands of nodes and hundreds of objects whenever I trace an image. This makes the process slow and sometimes crashes my system. What can I do to get around this situation?*
>
> The answers to your problems lie in the Trace menu's Edit Options dialog box. The Lines property sheet contains numerous options that determine the accuracy and complexity of the traced image. Set the Curve Precision and Line Precision to Very Loose, the Target Curve Length to Very Long, and the Minimum Pixel Size to a larger number. These settings make the tracking as loose as possible and should reduce the complexity of the trace, which reduces the number of objects and nodes.
>
> *Can I trace subsections of the bitmap without having to trace the entire image? Also, I want certain sections to adopt a different color after tracing. Can I do both at once?*
>
> Yes and yes! To change a color after tracing, first set the Color Selector on the ribbon to the desired color by either clicking on a color contained in its color palette, or by selecting the target color with the eyedropper. Then use the Magic Wand tool to select the desired image area and click on the Outline Tracing tool. The selected area appears on the right side of the screen filled with your selected color.

From Here...

This chapter introduced you to the three basic methods for converting a bitmapped image to a vector-based image. You learned to trace an outline with the Pencil tool, use the AutoTrace features, and run the CorelTRACE utility program. You also learned about Object Character Recognition (OCR), which allows you to trace scanned text, convert it to vector form, and then edit the text using a word processing program or the text functions in CorelDRAW! or CorelPHOTO-PAINT. Finally, you learned how the Forms tracing option allows you to convert paper-based forms into computer-based graphic images that are easily edited in CorelDRAW!.

For related information, see the following chapters:

- Chapter 9, "File-Related Operations and CorelMOSAIC," covers the details of file manipulation and conversion.

- Chapter 5, "Modifying Object Outlines and Interior Fills," discusses the ways to change the color, shape, and texture of outlines and interiors of objects.

- Chapter 13, "Advanced Line and Curve Techniques," deals with a more advanced description of editing nodes, working with different line styles, and dimensioning a drawing.

Chapter 28

Creating Presentation Charts with CorelCHART

by Ed Paulson

CorelCHART integrates CorelDRAW!'s graphic capabilities with a versatile charting package. With CorelCHART's 54 chart types, you can create dozens of variations to meet virtually any charting need. In addition to standard chart titles, headings, and legends, CorelCHART enables you to place text annotations anywhere on the chart to explain the data or highlight specific points. Custom graphics can be created within CorelCHART or imported from other applications (such as CorelDRAW!) to give your charts visual interest and a personalized touch.

After you complete this chapter, you will have learned the following:

- The basics of CorelCHART file management, including opening and saving charts
- The intended use for the Chart and Data Manager views
- Techniques for entering chart data
- The way to use the automation features for data entry
- Methods for performing calculations on entered data
- Techniques for modifying the chart characteristics to achieve your intended artistic and presentation goals
- The way to customize your charts

You can easily import data from many other applications into CorelCHART. In addition, data created in Windows-based applications can be dynamically linked to CorelCHART via dynamic data exchange (DDE) so that the chart is updated each time the source data changes. After a chart is created in CorelCHART, it can be exported or linked in graphic format to a number of other graphics and word processing packages including CorelSHOW!. These DDE related features become important when the underlying data changes frequently, but the overall chart appearance stays the same. The underlying data is changed in the spreadsheet application, such as Excel, and the CorelCHART graphic automatically adopts the new data and presents it using the previously established format. The time saving involved by not reinventing the chart each time the data changes can be substantial, and you're encouraged to become familiar with the standard Windows-based data exchange procedures.

CorelCHART offers features that set it apart from the charting packages that come with spreadsheet, database, and word processing software. Its capability for customizing chart presentations using graphics and text annotations, for example, represents a major advantage over other charting packages. CorelCHART uses CorelDRAW!'s artistic tools to enable you to move, size, color, and fill titles, backgrounds, and other chart elements. CorelCHART enables you to store these basic characteristics as templates that can be applied to charts you create later. This feature makes it easier for you to maintain consistency in your reports and presentations even when working with large numbers of charts. CorelCHART's easy interface with CorelSHOW enables you to quickly produce professional presentations that integrate charts with images and text generated in other applications (such as CorelMOVE! animation).

CorelCHART does not have an extensive text editing capability because the Text tool is primarily used for annotation purposes. Items such as bulleted text lists for use in CorelCHART must be imported from another application such as CorelDRAW!. In most cases, however, you probably will use CorelCHART's tremendous flexibility to design and create your chart before transferring it to another application where it can be integrated with text lists and other images.

Understanding How CorelCHART Works

CorelCHART uses the following two windows to create a chart:

- The Data Manager window contains the data that generates the chart, including chart titles and headings.

- The Chart View window displays the chart and provides tools to customize the chart presentation.

Figures 28.1 and 28.2 show what a simple chart looks like in each of these windows.

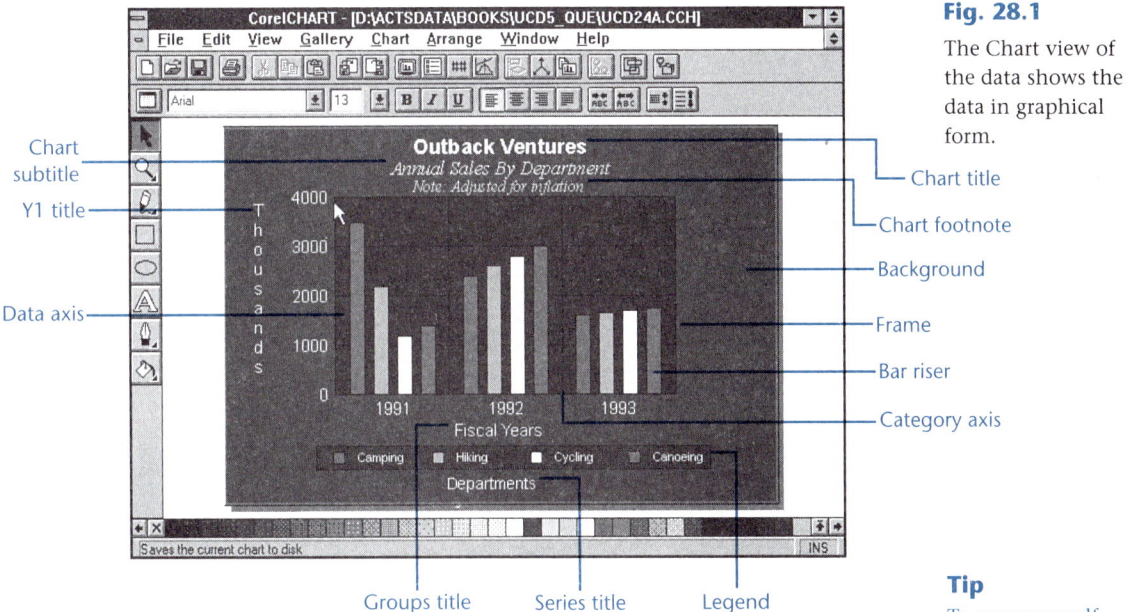

Fig. 28.1 The Chart view of the data shows the data in graphical form.

Only two simple steps are required to create a chart. First, specify the type of chart that you want to create (bar, pie, or line, for example). Second, enter the data to be charted in the Data Manager window. After entering your data, you can view the resulting chart in the Chart View window.

If you want to change anything about the way the chart is presented, the Chart View window provides the tools. You can change almost any aspect of the chart presentation, including font styles and sizes, legend and title positions, colors and patterns, and many other elements. You also can add text

Tip
To save yourself aggravation and time, follow the CorelCHART Data Manager's data orientation conventions outlined later in this chapter.

and graphic annotations (imported or created in CorelCHART) to your chart. You might scan your company logo in CorelPHOTO-PAINT!, for example, and then add it to your chart.

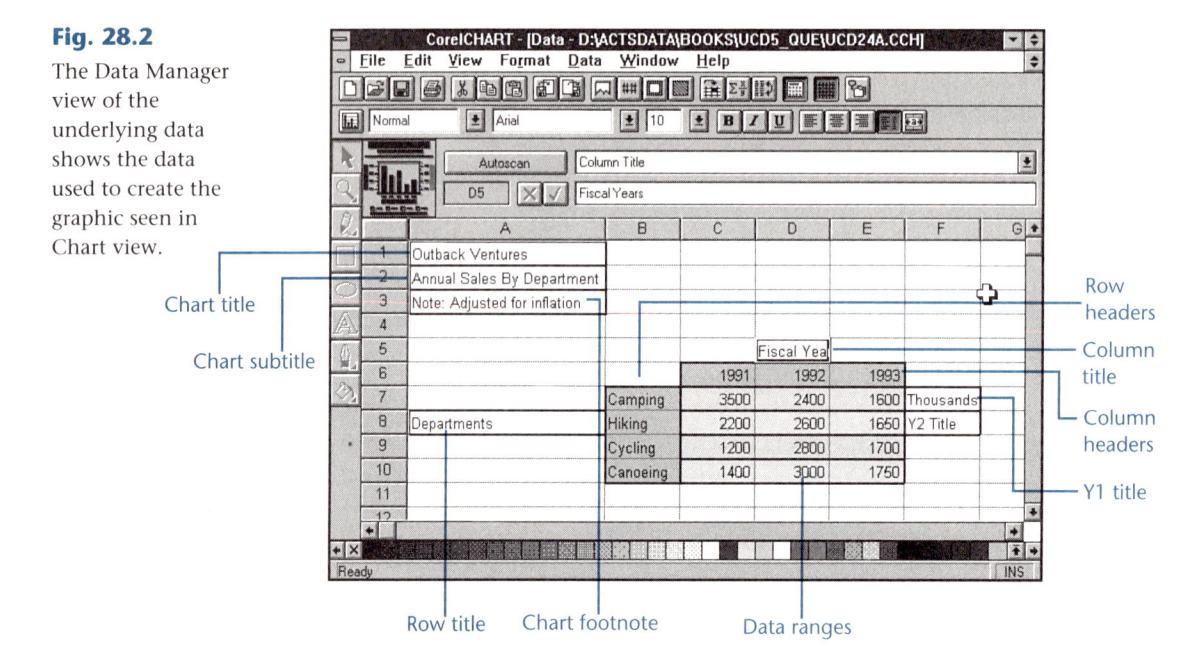

Fig. 28.2
The Data Manager view of the underlying data shows the data used to create the graphic seen in Chart view.

Learning Basic CorelCHART Concepts and Terminology

Before getting into the details of creating a chart, you should be familiar with some basic CorelCHART terminology.

The Chart View window in figure 28.1 shows a chart with its numerous elements labeled. Charts are generally divided into several components. In this chart, the horizontal or x axis is the category axis, and the vertical or y axis is the data axis. The category axis shows the different data groups being charted. The data axis enables you to read the value of each data point. The vertical bars that represent data points are called *risers*.

The chart also includes a footnote and data labels. The data classifications labeled along the category axis are called *groups*. Individual data items within each group are called *data series* and are labeled in the legend.

> **Note**
>
> Think of the series as data you plot, and the groups as the intervals at which data was acquired. For example, Annual Sales data acquired over a three-year period consists of a data series divided into four groups (1991, 1992, and so on).

Each chart element can be individually sized, placed, and colored. For the most part, these steps can be handled with simple point and click techniques. To change the color of the title, for example, click the title and then click the color you want to apply from the palette at the bottom of the screen. To move the title to a different location, click the title and drag it to the new location. See the "Modifying Chart Elements Using Chart View" section of this chapter for more details on these techniques. You can also see the section "Tagging the Data Cels," later in this chapter.

All the items shown in the sample chart came from data entered in the Data Manager worksheet. The Data Manager window in figure 28.2 shows a data worksheet with its various parts labeled. The Data Manager works much like a spreadsheet. Text, numbers, and formulas are first entered into individual cels and then are tagged or identified as titles, headings, data, and so on. If you use the Autoscan feature, data entered in the format shown in the figure is recognized and automatically tagged by CorelCHART. If you need to analyze your data before charting it, CorelCHART provides a formula editor with a full range of statistical functions. Hundreds of new functions were added to release 5, providing a wide variety of new capabilities. For example, release 4 included seven statistical functions, and release 5 includes over 50 including Poisson probability distributions, Chi-squared probabilities, and many more! See the section in this chapter "Entering Data Using the Data Manager," for more information.

Starting CorelCHART

To start CorelCHART from the Program Manager window, open the Corel 5 program group and then double-click the CorelCHART icon. Click the File option, and the screen shown in figure 28.3 appears.

Only the File and Help menu choices appear on the menu bar of the opening screen; other menu items appear as needed, depending on the selections you make as you create your chart.

Fig. 28.3
The CorelCHART opening screen with the File menu options displayed.

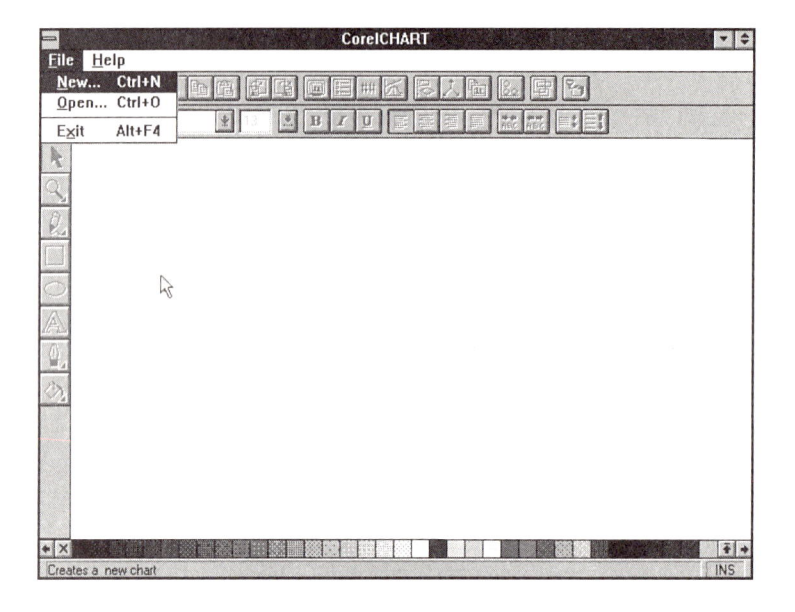

◀ See "Understanding CorelDRAW! 5's Color Management System," p. 359

A chart is created or opened by using the New or Open options in the File menu, respectively. The New option provides a series of standard templates, including sample data, to guide you through the process of creating a new chart. These materials are particularly handy when you initially create a chart. The Open option enables you to access an existing chart. The MOSAIC Roll-Up option opens the MOSAIC roll-up and provides direct access to MOSAIC's visual file management capabilities. The same effect is achieved by clicking on the MOSAIC button located on the toolbar. The Color Manager option is used to define the color templates, or profile, used while editing from within CHART. It operates similarly to that seen in the other Corel 5 applications. The Preferences option opens the CHART preferences dialog box within which the various general editing and display properties can be defined. Exit is used to leave CorelCHART completely.

Creating a New Chart

To create a new chart, open the **F**ile menu and choose **N**ew. The dialog box shown in figure 28.4 appears.

You must first specify the kind of chart you want to create. The 16 chart styles supported by CorelCHART are listed in the Gallery window on the left side of the dialog box.

Each basic chart style comes in several different flavors. For example, Bar chart data can be graphed horizontally or vertically, or bars can be stacked instead of being placed side by side. These variations are called *chart types*, of which there are 54.

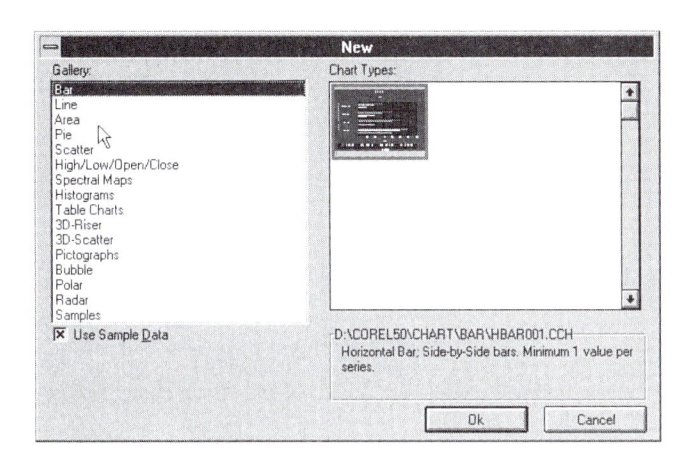

Fig. 28.4
The Chart Gallery displays the various chart designs associated with various chart styles.

To view the chart types available for a particular chart style, click the chart style in the Gallery window. Previews of each chart type appear in the Chart Types window at the right side of the dialog box. Table 28.1 summarizes the 16 chart styles and the chart types related to each style.

Tip
The file information box below the Chart Types window lists the path and file name of the selected chart as well as other basic information about the chart.

Table 28.1	Chart Styles and Types	
Chart Style	**Chart Types**	**Use**
Bar Graph	Horizontal or Vertical, Stacked or Side-By-Side, Dual Axis, Bipolar, Percent	Compare the behavior of several groups of data over time; best used for a limited number of data groups and observation points (usually not more than 4-5 of either); stacked bars show parts of the whole.
Line Graph	Horizontal or Vertical, Absolute Lines or Stacked, Lines, Dual Axis Absolute, Bipolar Absolute, Percent	Compare the behavior of several groups of data over time; especially good for long time periods; large numbers of data groups can be confusing on these charts.

(continues)

Table 28.1 Continued

Chart Style	Chart Types	Use
Area Graph	Horizontal or Vertical, Absolute or Stacked, Bipolar Absolute, Bipolar Stacked, Dual Axis Absolute, Dual Axis Stacked, Percent	Show parts of the whole in a continuous fashion; can be more appealing visually than stacked bars.
Pie Graph	Standard or Ring Pie, Single or Multiple Pies, Proportional Pie	Show parts of the whole effectively; multiple pies allow comparisons over time or between different categories.
Scatter Graph	Dual Y, With or Without Data Labels	Show the correlation between two variables.
High/Low/Open/Close Graph	High/Low or High/Low/Open/Close Data Dual Y	Show multiple data items at a single point in time or a single data item at a series of time points; standard stock market graph.
Histogram	Horizontal or Vertical	Show the individual values of each item in a data group; frequently used for reports on exam scores.
Table Chart	Colored by Row, Colored by Column, or Not Colored	Show the actual data points in table form rather than a graph; good when there is much disparity between sample points.
Spectral Map	No options available	Show the occurrence of an item across a geographic area; these maps are unique in that they show value using color intensities rather than numeric quantities.
Pictograph	Horizontal or Vertical, Dual Y, Bipolar	Strengthen the visual identity of data categories and increase interest in the chart; best used with a very limited number of data categories and observation points.
3D Riser	3D Riser, 3D Connected Group, 3D Connected Series or 3D Floating Bars, Ribbon, Floating Cubes or Area	Highlight the interrelationships among multiple data categories; rotating the chart with the 3D tool can create very dramatic presentations.
3D Scatter	With or Without Tie Lines to Floor and Walls, With or Without Data Labels	Show the correlation among three variables; this is an extremely effective way of presenting these types of relationships.

Chart Style	Chart Types	Use
Polar	Single Axis; Dual Axis; Color; Dual Axis, Gray Scale	Used to plot data represented in polar coordinate form where each data point represents a unique polar angle and distance from the center, or radius. Typically used in point-source radiation field intensity plots.
Bubble charts	Three Values per Series; Three Values per Series with Dual Axis; Four Values per Series; Four Values per Series with Data Lables; Three Values per Series, Grayscale	Show data with an X and Y format just like a scattergram, with the size of the bubble representing a third dimension.
Radar	One Value per Series; Stacked; Dual Axis; Grayscale	Show data occurrences with respect to each other; similar to a line graph, except plotted along a radial axis. Multiple data series can be represented on a single radar chart with the different series data points connected by lines. CorelCHART offers regular, stacked radar, and dual axis radar charts.
Gantt	Color and Grayscale	Show the starting and ending points of an event, which provides duration information. Typically used in project management.

To select a specific type of chart, click the preview sketch of the chart in the Chart Types window. Each chart type comes with sample data; you can simply type your own information over the data provided by CorelCHART.

If you don't want the sample data included in your chart, click the Use Sample Data box to deselect it. But make sure that you match the overall data layout structure used by the CorelCHART sample data; if you don't, you may get unpredictable results.

After you select the appropriate chart type, click OK to load the chart. If you loaded the file with sample data, the Chart View window appears first. If you loaded the file without sample data, the Data Manager window appears instead.

The Chart Types window shows files located in subdirectories in the CorelCHART directory (the full path name, shown at the top of the file information box, is usually C:\COREL50\CHART), but it can be an alternate directory if the user defines it as the desired directory name during installation.

Tip
It's a good idea to include the sample data and then replicate the provided layout for additional rows and columns as needed for your specific charting situation.

Each chart style has its own subdirectory; my chart subdirectory contains sample charts that include graphic annotations and other customized features. You can customize the chart types provided by CorelCHART or add your own chart type to this group simply by saving it in the appropriate subdirectory. This way, your personal chart designs are included as a starting point for future designs.

Opening an Existing Chart

To open an existing chart, open the **F**ile menu and choose **O**pen, or press Ctrl+O. The Open Chart dialog box appears (see fig. 28.5).

Fig. 28.5
The Open Chart dialog box used to open an existing chart.

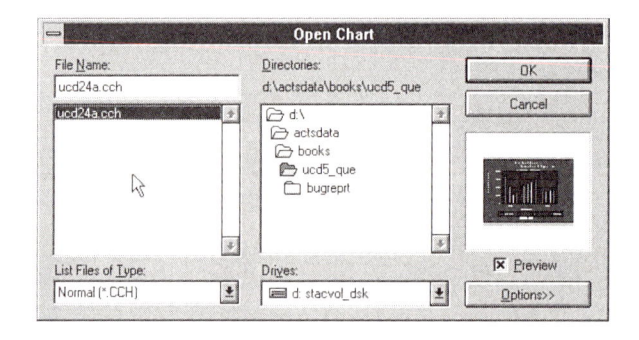

Tip
Use the Notes section for entering information you need to understand the significance of the charted data, such as the revision level of the currently selected chart.

All CorelCHART files have a CCH extension. To list all the CorelCHART files in a particular disk location, use the Drives and Directories boxes to specify that location. CorelCHART lists all files with the appropriate extension in the files window. Click on **O**ptions to display additional options for defining the file sort order as by Name or last saved Date. Any notes attached to the selected file are displayed in the Notes section of the dialog box. Notes information is entered by simply clicking in the Notes section and typing the desired information. Check Preview, as shown in figure 28.5, to view a thumbnail image of the selected chart. Double-click the file name, or single-click the file name and then click OK to open the selected chart file.

Entering Data Using the Data Manager

Generally, it is easier to start chart creation from within the Data Manager because it provides quick access to the contents of all Chart view components except for specially annotated text that points to the various chart components. Work in the Data Manager to lay the foundation and walls of a house by adding data and any required numeric processing using the provided functions, and use Chart view to add the decorations that make the data more attractive.

Use the Data Manager window to enter data to be charted, chart titles, and labels. This information can be entered directly into the Data Manager spreadsheet, imported from another file, pasted from the Clipboard, or dynamically linked to files from other Windows-based applications. Figure 28.6 shows the Data Manager window.

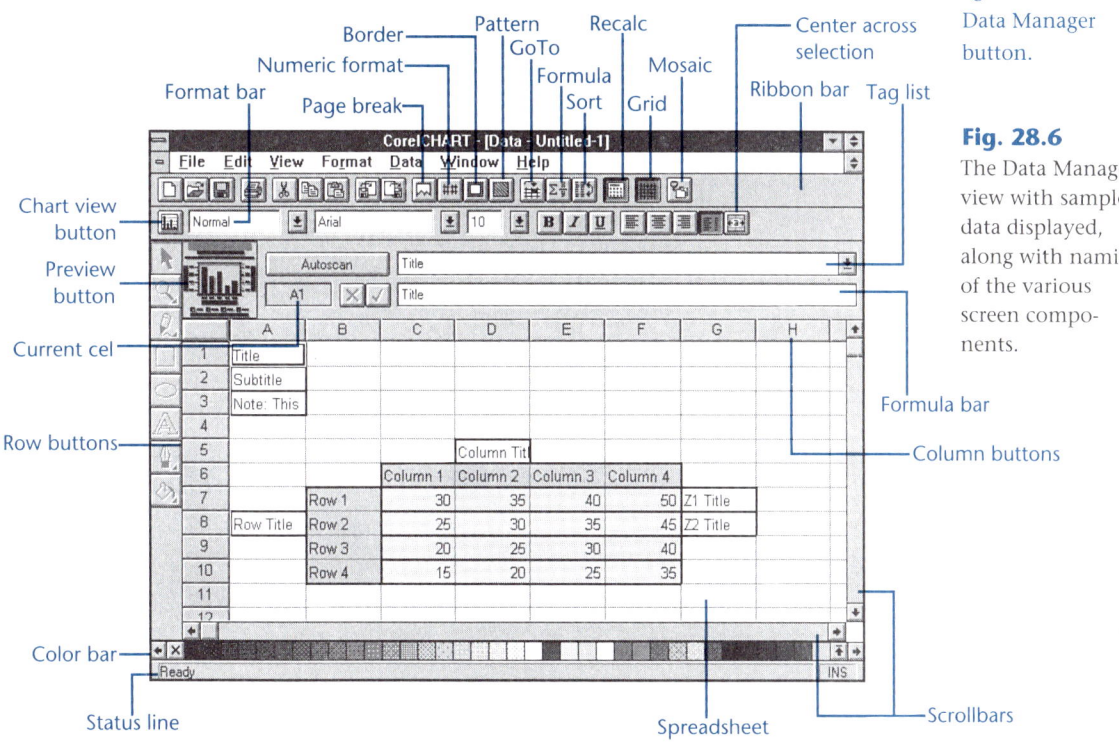

Tip

If you start a chart with sample data, CorelCHART displays the Chart View window. To display the Data Manager, choose View, Data Manager or click the Data Manager button.

Fig. 28.6

The Data Manager view with sample data displayed, along with naming of the various screen components.

Entering Data

Entering information in the Data Manager is much like entering data in a spreadsheet. Information is entered in cels that are referenced by their column letter and row number (A1, C6, F12, and so on).

To enter information into a particular cel, follow these steps:

1. Click the cel and begin typing. As you type, the characters appear in the selected cel and in the Formula bar at the top of the Data Manager window.

2. To enter the information in the cel, press Enter; press one of the arrow keys; click the Enter Data button; or simply click another cel.

To make corrections to existing data, follow these steps:

1. Click the cel to be corrected; the contents of the cel display in the formula bar.

2. Click the text in the formula bar at the point where you want to make the change.

3. Make your corrections using the standard editing keys.

4. Press Enter or click the check mark. Pressing Esc or clicking the × mark cancels the changes.

To completely overwrite old information, simply click the cel and begin typing. The old information is replaced by the new information.

To clear the cel completely, select the cel or range of cels and then press the Delete key; or open the **E**dit menu and choose Clear. The Cut and Clear Options dialog box (see fig. 28.7) appears, displaying the various options feautures that will be deleted with this action. Select those you want deleted and click OK. The default setting clears all data and formatting from the cel.

> **Note**
>
> You can delete the data from a cel and retain its formatting by unchecking the Formats All option and clicking OK. When a new number is entered into this cel, it adopts the previously existing formatting because that formatting was not deleted. Notice that individual formatting items, such as borders and patterns, can be retained or deleted to meet your needs.

Fig. 28.7
The Cut and Clear Options dialog box used to select the precise cel-related attributes, such as formulas or formatting, to delete.

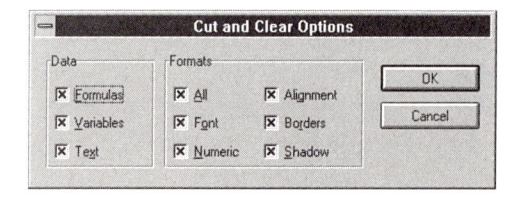

Selecting Data Cel Ranges

Many CorelCHART operations require the selection of a single cel or a range of cels. To select a single cel, click the cel or use the **D**ata menu's **G**o To Cel command. To select an entire column, click the column's letter designation at the very top of the column. Select a complete row by clicking the row's number designation as shown at the far left of the row. Drag across a number of row or column designations to select several consecutive rows or columns. Select a range of cels by dragging the mouse diagonally across the cel range.

Tip
The Windows standard Shift- or Ctrl-click to select consecutive or random cels does not work with CorelCHART.

Speeding Up Data Entry

You can substantially speed up the data input process by using CorelCHART's data range entry feature. To do so, follow these steps:

1. Select the data range into which you plan to enter data.

2. Begin entering the data in the upper-left corner of the range and press Enter after each entry.

CorelCHART automatically moves the cursor down the column for you until it reaches the end of the currently active column. At the end of the column, CorelCHART moves the cursor to the beginning of the next column. The process repeats itself until you reach the end of the selected data range.

Automatically Filling Ranges of Cels

CorelCHART provides several automation features that can greatly increase your data entry efficiency if used properly. You can fill a range of cels with the same information by using the repetitive fill operation covered in the next section. A more practical automation tool is the Series Fill command, which fills a range of cels in a progressive manner based on the initial data selected. This provides a quick way to add cel data that progresses in a routine manner such as the days of the week, the numbers in a sequence, or the months of the year.

Filling in Repetitive Data

The Fill Right and Fill Down commands in the Edit menu enter the same value in all cels within a highlighted range. For Fill Right or Fill Down to work, the fill value must initially be entered in the top- or leftmost cel in the range. Follow these steps to fill a range with repetitive data:

1. Select the range including the cel(s) with the intended fill value or text.

2. From the Edit menu, click either the Fill Right or Fill Down option as desired.

All cels in the range now are identical to the first cel(s) selected.

Applying the Fill Series Command

Charts often contain progressive information such as the months of the year, days of the week, hours of the day, and so on. It is tedious to manually enter this information. CorelCHART saves you from this chore by providing the Fill Series command under the Data menu.

The Fill Series feature is a form of artificial intelligence. It recognizes the initial information that you enter, determines some type of progression pattern to the information, and applies that pattern to the balance of selected cels. Follow these steps to use the Fill Series command:

1. Enter the information into the first cel. If it is a day of the week or month of the year, only one cel of information is required since CorelCHART can easily recognize it and increment accordingly. If, on the other hand, a series of data points that increment by 20 each is desired, at least two cels separated by a 20 increment must be entered or CorelCHART cannot determine the desired pattern.

2. Select the range of cels into which you want data series entered; make sure that you select the initially entered data cel.

3. Open the **D**ata menu and choose the Fi**l**l Series command to reveal the dialog box shown in figure 28.8.

4. Select the desired fill options, and click on OK to create the fill.

Fig. 28.8
The Fill series dialog box used to define the various defaults used by CorelCHART when creating the series' fill data.

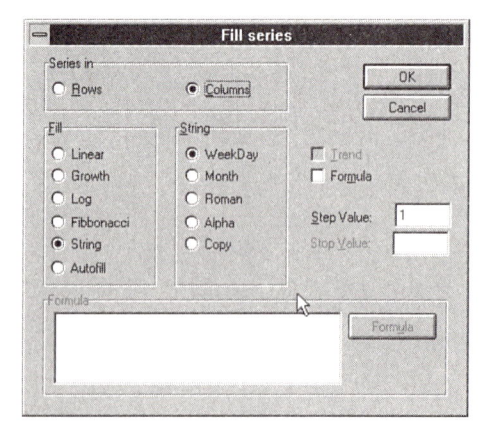

The Series In option determines whether the series fills along the rows or in a column. This is automatically selected based upon the orientation of the initially selected cels.

The various Fill types are listed at the left of the dialog box. They provide a number of different progression techniques and are as follows:

- **Linear** automatically increments the cel contents by the Step Value entered at the left (a linear progression), up to the value you specify.

- **Growth** increments the cel contents as a multiple of the number entered as the Step Value (a geometric progression).

- **Log** increments the initial number based upon a logarithmic progression.

- **Fibonacci** increments the values as the sum of the two numbers immediately preceding the destination value.

- **String** recognizes the text string as a day of the week, month, or year and increments it in accordance with the Step Value or based upon the cels of data already entered. If the Step Value is 2, for example, it skips every other month.

- **Autofill** makes its best guess about the series and applies it to the rest of the selected range. Sufficient progression information must be included for Autofill to sense the incremental value or its results will be unpredictable.

The Stop Value setting ends the series fill operation even if more cels initially were selected for filling. This feature is particularly handy when you are filling a large series and do not want to count the number of selected cels before performing the Fill Series operation such as with the days in a month. You could select more than 31 cels, but define the stop value as 31 to ensure that the remaining extra 9 cels did not get filled.

The String sections Weekday and Month increment the series based on days of the week or months of the year in accordance with the Step Value, respectively. Roman and Alpha increment the range in either Roman Numeral (I, II, III, IV, and so on) or Alpha (A, B, C, and so on) form. The underlying contents are replaced with the sequential number scheme chosen. Copy simply takes whatever already exists in the range and copies it as many times as possible to fill the selected cel range.

The Trend reviews the selected data, determines the amount of offset between cel contents, and automatically applies that differential when calculating series cel contents.

Selecting the Formula option activates the Formula section located at the bottom of the dialog box. An incremental formula can then be entered in the Formula section's editing area or using the Formula dialog box, which is activated by clicking the Formula command button. The formula should use relative cel referencing to ensure that the increment works as desired. This is a handy feature when the progression is based upon some complicated algorithm not easily recognizable by Autofill. See the next section for details regarding creating and entering formulas.

> **Note**
>
> Cels are referenced as either absolute or relative in spreadsheet-type products such as the Data Manager. Absolute referencing designates a specific location by its intersection of a column and row number. Relative referencing refers to a cel location relative to the currently active cel location. Notice that absolute references are clearly defined where relative references are determined by the cel doing the referencing.

Performing Calculations in the Data Manager

Release 5 includes hundreds of new spreadsheet functions that perform scores of financial, engineering, and statistical operations, among others.

A welcome addition to CorelCHART 5 is the wide array of arithmetic operations that you now can perform within CorelCHART. The variety is substantial enough that you can probably use their features without having to perform your calculations in another spreadsheet product, such as Excel or 1-2-3, and then import the data into CorelCHART for display. The formulas and functions are entered directly in the destination cel or are accessible from the Enter Formula dialog box. Find this dialog box by pressing F12 or by selecting Enter Formula from the Data menu. If the equation to be entered uses a number of the functions, you are probably better served by using the Formula dialog box; if not, entering the data directly into the cel is probably faster.

Entering Formulas

The procedure for entering formulas is similar to that used in any Windows-based spreadsheet product, but CorelCHART requires more extensive use of the Formula bar than products like Excel or 1-2-3.

Add, subtract, multiply, and divide numbers by either typing the desired formula with its associated cel references into the destination cel or by typing the arithmetic operators (+, -, *, /,^) and then selecting the cels or range of cels with the mouse. For example, the formula =2+4+6 displays the value 12 and =4*2 displays a value of 8. A more complicated formula would appear as =2+(5*6)-12, which displays 20. The formula =25*AVG(A1:A4) displays a value that represents 25 times the average of the values contained in cels A1, A2, A3, and A4. The AVG() component can be typed directly into the formula or selected from the available functions provided in the Enter Formula dialog box. Table 28.2 shows a list of the arithmetic operators and their respective effects. For more information, see the section "Selecting Data Cell Ranges" in this chapter.

Tip

The underlying cell must be empty or contain a formula for the Enter Formula option to operate. Select the cell and press Delete to clear the cell before entering a new formula.

Note

All formulas must begin with an equal (=) sign, or CorelCHART treats the characters that follow as a text string and does not perform the desired arithmetic operations.

Table 28.2 The CorelCHART Arithmetic Operators

Operator	Effect
+	Adds two numbers or arguments. If the + sign separates two text strings enclosed in double quotations ("), then the two text strings are linked together one after the other.
-	Subtracts the two numbers or arguments.
*	Multiplies the first number or argument by the second (for example, 5*8=40). If the first argument is a number and the second is a text string enclosed by double quotes ("), the text string is repeated the number of times indicated by the first number (for example, 2*"Uh-Huh!" = Uh-Huh!Uh-Huh!).
/	Divides the first number by the second (for example, 6/3=2).
^	Raises the first number to the exponential power indicated by the second number (for example, 2^3=2*2*2=8).

(continues)

Chapter 28—Creating Presentation Charts with CorelCHART

Tip
If a syntax error occurs, count the left and right parentheses in the formula. If they aren't equal, add or delete a parenthesis to correct the formula.

Table 28.2 Continued	
Operator	**Effect**
( )	Separates sections of the formula. This ensures that the different arithmetic operations are performed as desired. For example, =(5+6)/5 displays a result of 2.2 because 5+6=11 and 11/5=2.2. On the other hand, =5+6/5 displays a result of 6.2 because 6/5=1.2 when added to 5 equals 6.2. Using parentheses is a good way to ensure that calculations are performed as you desire.

Enter a formula by following this generic procedure:

1. Select the empty cel into which the calculation result is to be placed.
2. Type = to start the formula.
3. Type the required numbers, cel locations, operators, and parentheses to perform the desired calculation. Cell locations are referred to by their column and row titles (for example, A3, B7, F15, and so on).
4. Press Enter to complete the formula entry process.

Using the Functions in Formulas

CorelCHART comes with a wide array of preinstalled functions that address the vast majority of conventional spreadsheet operations. These functions are included in your formulas to make formula creation faster and more accurate. For example, instead of manually creating the proper mathematical steps to calculate the average of several numbers, you could use the AVG(range) function, where the average is automatically calculated on the cels contained within the designated range. Functions are accessed from the Enter Formula dialog box, which is activated by opening the **D**ata menu and choosing Enter For**m**ula, clicking on the Formula tool, or pressing F12 (see fig. 28.9).

Tip
Enter a formula that refers to specific cels by clicking the cel or dragging across a range of cels, instead of typing the cel designations directly into the destination cel.

The various function groups are listed in the Functions drop-down list box below the Paste button. Table 28.3 shows the various function groups.

Table 28.3 The Standard CorelCHART Function Groups	
Function Group	**Typical Use**
Conversion	Converts common units from one form to another such as Celsius temperature measurements into Fahrenheit.

Function Group	Typical Use
Date and Time	Converts serial date values into their respective months, days, and years. Also contains functions for entering the current date, time, and so on.
DDE/External	Provides tools for connecting to various other Windows-based applications using the Dynamic Data Exchange (DDE) and Object Linking and Embedding (OLE) features, which are important automation tools integral to the Windows environment.
Engineering	Provides easy access to Bessel and Delta functions.
Financial	Provides numerous functions used to calculate note principal payments, interest rates, dividends, yields, and other common financial parameters.
Information	Provides information about a cel in a true/false 1/0 format, depending on comparison parameters chosen.
Logical	Uses the common And, Or, and other logical operators required for automated decision making.
Lookup and Reference	Finds information contained within a table automatically.
Math and Trig	Provides an extensive list of common mathematical and trigonometric functions, including automated summation.
Statistical	Provides another extensive list of statistically related functions, including the average, standard deviation, median, linear regression, and others.
Text	Performs a number of text-related operations, including converting text from one case to another, removing inter-word spaces, substituting one text string for another, and others.

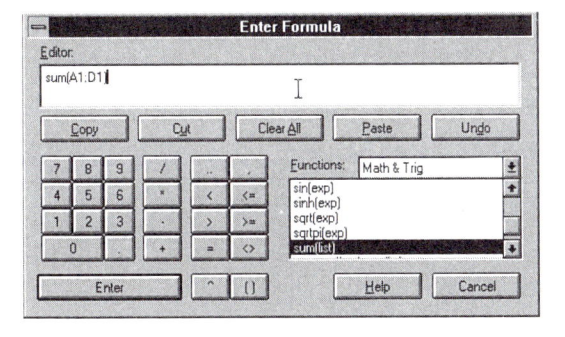

Fig. 28.9
The Enter Formula dialog box is used to create formulas and provides access to the various included functions. The Math and Trig formulas are activated in the figure.

Using the Separators

Formulas and functions contain various items upon which operations are to be performed. These items are referred to as *arguments*, and CorelCHART must have some way of separating one argument from another. The comma, colon, space, semicolon, and double period are used for just this purpose. Table 28.4 shows the separators and their purpose.

> **Tip**
> The Recalculate button (F7) causes all formulas to update to the most current values. If Auto Recalc in the Data menu (Shift+F7; also an icon in the toolbar) is active, this button serves no purpose.

Table 28.4 The Formula and Function Separators

Separator	Purpose	Example
,	Separates different arguments	AVG(5, 10, A1:B2)
: or ..	Designates a range of cels	A1:A3 or A1..A3
;	Separates the sections of a conditional numeric formatting statement (formats positive numbers as bold, with one decimal place and displays "Neg" in cels holding negative values).	#.#; "neg"

Moving, Copying, and Pasting Data

You can easily move data within the Data Manager using either the Clipboard or the new drag-and-drop features of CorelDRAW 5. To move data using the Clipboard, follow these steps:

1. Highlight the desired data range.

2. Open the **E**dit menu and choose Cu**t**, or press Ctrl+X. Click OK in the Cut and Clear Options dialog box.

3. Click the cel that represents the upper-left corner of the new location for the data that was cut.

4. Open the **E**dit menu again and choose **P**aste, or press Ctrl+V.

The data is transferred from the Clipboard onto the Data Manager screen, and all internal cel references are automatically updated.

Moving data is even simpler with the new drag-and-drop feature. Follow these steps:

1. Highlight the range of cels to be moved.

2. Move the cursor until it points at the top line of the selected range. Notice that the cursor changes from a cross to an arrow. This indicates that CorelCHART is ready to drag the selected cels.

3. Drag the cels until the upper-left corner of the gray box surrounding the cursor rests within the target cel, and then release the mouse button. The cels now appear in their new location. Once again, all cel references are automatically updated.

To copy data using the Clipboard, follow these steps:

1. Highlight the desired range of cels.

2. Open the **E**dit menu and choose **C**opy, or press Ctrl+C; this copies the cel data to the Clipboard.

3. Move the cursor to the location that corresponds to the new upper-left corner of the copied cel range.

4. Open the **E**dit menu again and choose **P**aste, or press Ctrl+V.

The underlying formulas are copied to the new location, leaving the initial data range in place.

You also can use a drag-and-drop feature for copying cels from one portion of the spreadsheet to another, as outlined in the following steps:

1. Highlight the range of cels to be copied.

2. Move the cursor until it points at the top line of the selected range. Notice that the cursor changes from a cross into an arrow. This indicates that CorelCHART is ready to drag the selected cels.

3. Drag the cels while simultaneously pressing Ctrl until the upper-left corner of the gray box surrounding the cursor rests within the target cel. Then release the mouse button. The cels now appear in their new location. Once again, all cel references are automatically updated.

Tip
Make sure that your cursor is precisely on the edge of the highlighted area and that the cursor arrow shows, or these procedures may not work. Be patient with slower systems.

Paste Special enables you to perform arithmetic operations on data as it is transferred from one location in the Data Manager to another. For example, sales, cost, and expense data for a number of products over a period of time might need to be combined to calculate annual total profit. Instead of entering formulas to calculate the profit for each product, use Paste Special to copy all the data sets to a new location, one on top of the other, with Add selected as the operation and Paste All as the default. The values are combined by the operation selection, and the result displays as the new numbers. Selecting Transpose reverses the order of rows and columns when the paste operation is performed.

Choose Paste Special from the Edit menu; the Paste Special dialog box appears (see fig. 28.10).

Fig. 28.10
The Paste Special dialog box showing the various information to be pasted and the arithmetic operations provided with the paste operation.

Manipulating Columns and Rows

To select a column or row, click the button that appears to the left of the row or above the column. The entire column or row is highlighted. Multiple columns and rows are selected by clicking and dragging across multiple buttons.

Inserting and Deleting Columns and Rows

To insert a column or row, select the row below the desired location for the new row (or the column to the right of the desired location for the new column). Open the **E**dit menu and choose Insert. To delete a row or column, simply select the entire row or column; then open the **E**dit menu and choose **D**elete.

Changing Column Widths and Row Heights

Although the column widths and row heights used in the Data Manager window do not affect the presentation of your chart, your data is much easier to work with when your column width settings match the types of data being entered.

To change the width of a column, move the cursor to the vertical line separating the header of that column from the one to its right. Notice that the cursor changes from a cross to horizontal bars with arrows. Click and drag the bar to the right until the column is wide enough to accommodate its longest data entry.

You also can change the column width by opening the F**o**rmat menu, choosing Column Width, and setting the entry box to the desired value. You can change the row height by following similar procedures. Simply use the appropriate row selection button at the left side of the screen, or the Format menu's Row Height selection. Direct access to the Column Width dialog box is provided by moving the cursor to the column header and pressing the right mouse button to reveal the pop-up shown in figure 28.11.

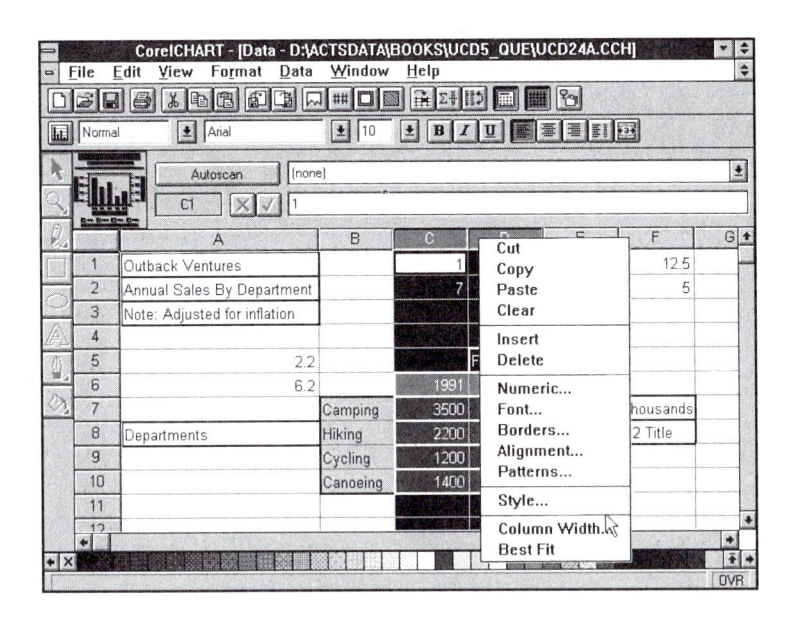

Fig. 28.11
The Right Mouse button pop-up is displayed by placing the cursor over the desired item and pressing the right mouse button. The various applicable options are displayed for selection.

Importing Data from Other Applications

If the data you want to chart is already entered in another application, you can import the existing data to CorelCHART instead of manually reentering it in the Data Manager window. You also can link your chart to the source application data so that changes to that data are automatically reflected in CorelCHART.

CorelCHART accepts data imported from CorelCHART 4 Table (TBL), Tab Separated Text (TXT), Comma Separated Text (CSV), Comma Separated Values (CSV), and Rich Text Format (RTF).

The imported data must be arranged in a specific fashion for CorelCHART to make use of it efficiently. If the format of incoming data is not consistent with the standard CorelCHART format, you may get unexpected results. See the "Automatic Tagging" section later in this chapter for tips on organizing your data after it arrives in CorelCHART.

Tip
Use the File Export command in CorelCHART to export data in any of the five import formats or in Tab Separated Values (TXT) or Rich Text Format (RTF) file formats.

To import a data file, follow these steps:

1. From the Data Manager window, open the **F**ile menu and choose Import. The dialog box that appears queries you for the drive and directory location of the source file to be imported.

2. Select the file and then click OK to import the file into the Data Manager.

CorelCHART always starts entering imported data at cel A1; it erases anything in the Data Manager window prior to the import. If you need data from several files to produce a chart, combine the data in a single source file before importing it to CorelCHART.

If the source application for your data is a Windows application such as Excel or Lotus for Windows, you can use dynamic data exchange (DDE) to link the data in the source program to CorelCHART. DDE is helpful if you plan to update your source information frequently and want to have an updated chart available at all times. With DDE, all changes in the source document are reflected in the linked document.

To set up DDE links in CorelCHART, use the Paste Link option as follows:

1. Start up both applications (CorelCHART and Excel, for example) and open the files to be linked. Make sure that the Data Manager window is open in CorelCHART. Before setting up the links, check your spreadsheet program documentation to make sure that it supports DDE.

2. Select the range of cels to be linked to CorelCHART in the source spreadsheet program. Open the **E**dit menu and choose **C**opy to copy these cels to the Clipboard.

3. Switch back to CorelCHART and click the upper-left cel of the range location at which you want to place the linked data.

4. Open the **E**dit menu again and choose Paste Link. The linked data appears in the Data Manager.

Tip
You also can use Paste Link to link together related CorelCHART documents.

Obtaining Database Information with CorelQUERY

It's often useful to chart database information to see trends and other changes associated with the data. It's often difficult or impossible to directly access the database, which means that the database file can't be accessed from within the application that created it—for example, Microsoft Access exported in one of CorelCHART's compatible formats would be difficult to access. Instead, you need to access the data as a viewer, copy the desired information into a separate file, and then save the file in a CorelCHART importable format. This is CorelQUERY's function: to view a database of information and extract the desired information for use in other applications.

Think of a query as a request, or questioning, of the database for its record information. To access the database information, it must conform with the Windows Open Database Convention (ODBC) standard and be registered as such with the computer system. Registration should happen automatically when the database application is installed; CorelQUERY automatically

Importing Data from Other Applications

recognizes the available formats. The query is issued against the underlying data in the industry standard System Query Language (SQL), and CorelQUERY essentially creates the necessary SQL commands for you after you instruct it regarding your intended information extraction purposes. Here is a general query procedure that should provide basic guidelines for your specific application needs.

> **Note**
>
> It's well beyond the scope of this book to cover database operations in detail. The intention of this section is to introduce you to basic CorelQUERY operation and provide a foundation for obtaining more detailed information on your own.

Start CorelQUERY from the Corel 5 program group by double-clicking on the CorelQUERY icon.

The general query creation procedure is as follows:

1. Start a new query by selecting New from the File menu, which displays the Data Source dialog box.

2. Click the ODBC Data Sources heading shown in the left hand window. Click the Add button under Data Source to display the CorelQUERY compatible database applications: dBASE, FoxPro, Microsoft Access, and Paradox.

3. Click on the application that created the targeted database of information. Notice that Add, Configure, and Remove appear. Use **A**dd to add another ODBC database applications. Use Remove to remove the currently selected ODBC application from the list. Configure sets up the currently selected application for database access.

4. Click on Co**n**figure to open the Setup dialog box for that particular application as shown in figure 28.12. This dialog varies among database applications; the Microsoft Access related dialogs are presented in this section.

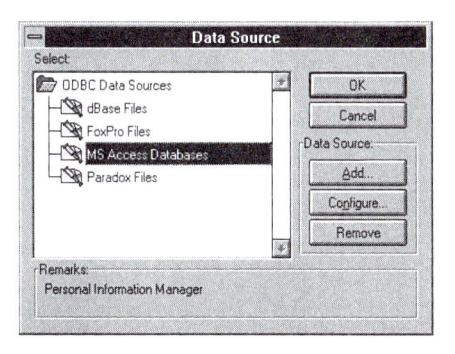

Fig. 28.12
The ODBC application setup dialog box after clicking on the Options button. This dialog is used to define the overall query parameters.

720 Chapter 28—Creating Presentation Charts with CorelCHART

5. Click Select Database to pick a database file. Click Create Database to open the target application and create a new database. Fill in the Description information as desired, leave the other selections at their defaults, and click OK to return to the Data Source dialog.

6. Click OK to open the Query Builder dialog shown in fig. 28.13. The relations shown are those available from the database selected in step 5.

Fig. 28.13

The Query Builder dialog box with associated tabs as displayed for a Microsoft Access directed query.

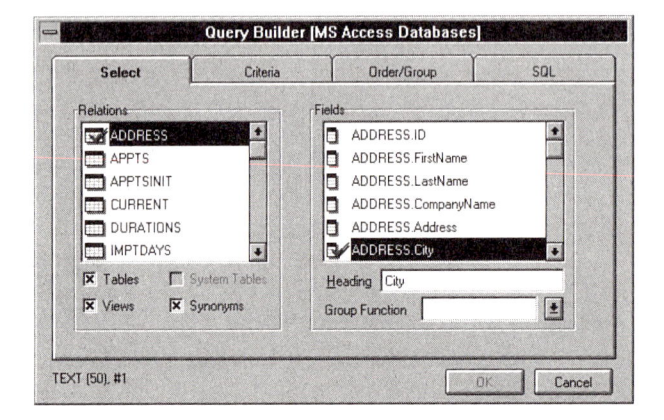

7. Double-click each of the relations that contains information to be queried. The fields associated with the general relations heading appear in the right hand window.

8. Double-click the fields that you want included as part of the query. You can select as many of the fields as necessary.

9. Click the Criteria tab to display the dialog shown in figure 28.14. This dialog defines the fields on which to select the record information, and determines what criteria the fields must meet to be selected. Leave the criteria blank to extract all records.

Select a Field Name from the list box. From the list box, select the Operator to apply to the comparison such as less than, equal to, greater than, and so on. Click List Values to include the total number of possible comparison values contained in the selected field's data records, and then select the desired match criteria from the list. Click Add to place that criteria in the criteria list area of the dialog. And and Or are used to determine whether a match must comply with all the listed criteria (And) or any one of the criteria (Or). Selecting a criterion and clicking Remove deletes that criterion from the list.

Importing Data from Other Applications 721

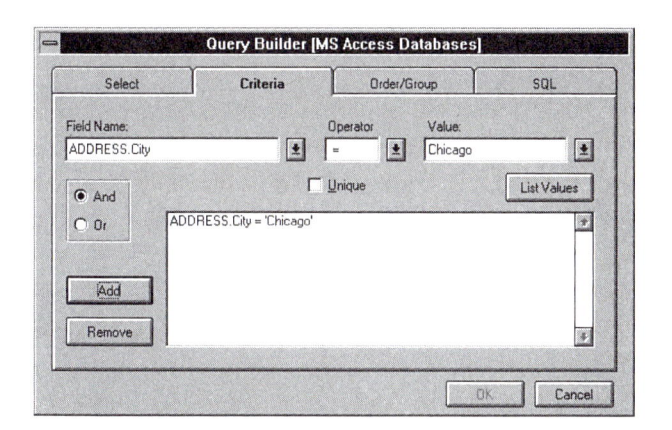

Fig 28.14
The Criteria property sheet used to establish database record extraction fields and match criteria. This criteria instructs to select all records with the City field matching the city name of Chicago.

10. Click the Order/Group tab to display the property sheet shown in figure 24.15.

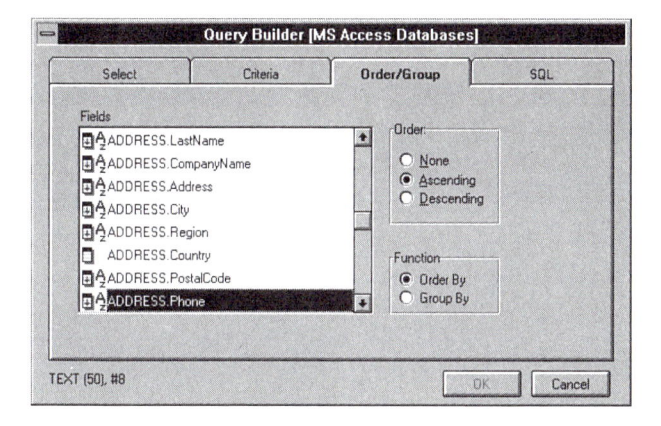

Fig. 28.15
The Order/Group dialog used to define the order in which the fields are included in the query and how the finished data is to be grouped and ordered.

Double-click each of the desired fields, in the order that you want them to appear on the finished query, if the Order By option is selected. You do not have to include all fields. Select **A**scending or **D**escending as fits your purposes. Click Group By if you want only the extracted records included in groups by the chosen selection criteria, such as city names.

11. Click on SQL to display the dialog shown in figure 24.16.

    Click Build to create the proper SQL commands to extract the desired information. Click Load to activate an already existing SQL query. Click Save to save the currently active query for future use.

Chapter 28—Creating Presentation Charts with CorelCHART

Fig. 28.16
The SQL property sheet after clicking on Build to generate the necessary SQL commands to retrieve the desired information.

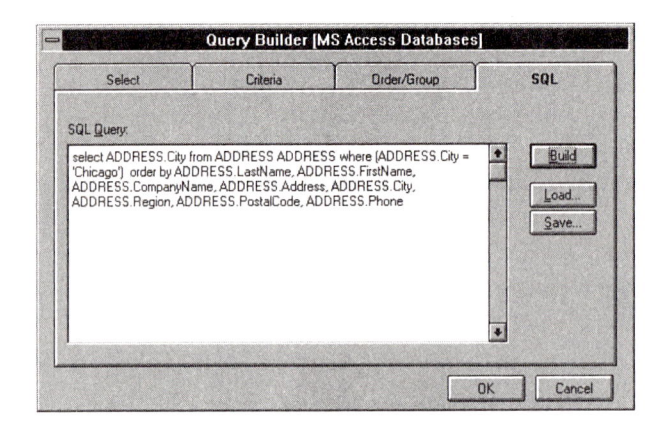

Tip
OK isn't accessible until the SQL command is generated.

Fig. 28.17
The CorelQUERY screen displays the desired information in spreadsheet form.

12. Click OK to perform the query and display the information on the CorelQUERY screen, as in figure 28.17. Columns, rows, and cels are selected just as in CorelCHART. Clicking at the upper-left corner intersection of the columns and rows selects the entire data field.

The resulting query can now be saved using the File menu's Save and Save As commands. All queries are given a DSQ extension.

The window contains several icons in addition to the standard New, Open, Save, and Copy tools provided with every Windows application. From left to right, from the Copy tool, are the Grid Toggle, which activates/deactivates the grid; the Font tool for changing text fonts and colors; the Move To tool, which displays a dialog box when clicked (within which a record number is entered to move to that particular record); and the SQL command editor, which is activated by clicking on the SQL tool.

13. Move data into CorelCHART by selecting the desired records, or all records, and clicking the Copy tool. This copies the records to the clipboard.

14. Return to CorelCHART and create a new Table style of chart without sample data. Activate the Data Manager view and choose Paste from the Edit menu. The data is added to the Chart and can now be charted just like any other CorelCHART data.

Formatting Text, Numbers, and Cells

CorelCHART's formatting options can make your data easier to understand in the Data Manager window (and easier to read on your printouts). You can change the font of any of the text items in the Data Manager window; you also can apply bold, italic, or underline type characteristics to these items. Release 5 has an augmented text ribbon bar that contains text styles and direct access to the typeface and size (see fig. 28.18).

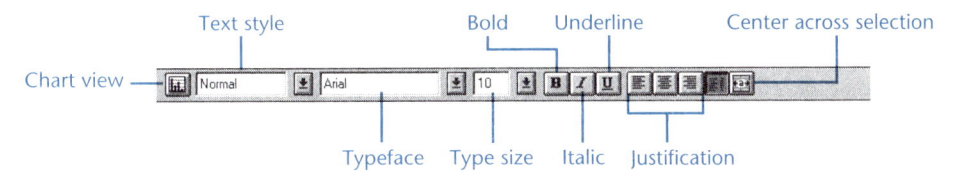

Fig. 28.18
The text ribbon bar, which makes formatting tools readily accessible through their respective icons.

These various formatting options are applied by first selecting the data range to be formatted. You then click the desired style, typeface, and point size, or select B (bold), I (italic), or U (underline) from the Format button bar to apply the desired trait.

Styles are defined by selecting the Style option in the Format menu to display the Style dialog box shown in figure 28.19.

Click in the Name box to define a new style name. The text displayed under Descriptions reflects the current setting for the selected style. Clicking the various command bars (Font, Alignment, Number, Border, and Patterns) allows access to the various features where they can be defined specifically for the selected style. Click Add to add the style to the currently active CorelCHART template (CCT file). Click Save to save the currently active set of styles to a new template that can be recalled for future use using the Load button shown in this dialog box. Click Close to return to the editing screen without changing the template. Click OK to apply the style to the selected cels.

Fig. 28.19
The Style dialog box used for creating styles for numeric, text, and graphic formatting.

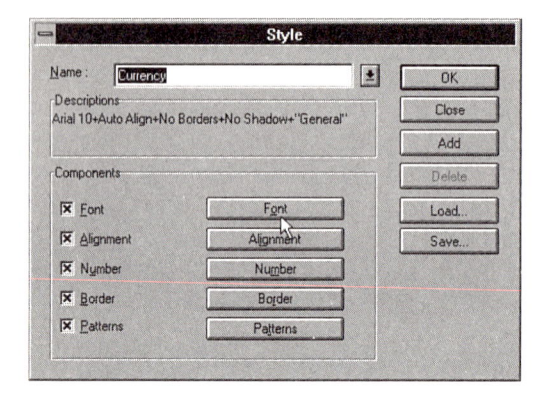

Centering Text across Several Cells

A popular technique for adding a professional touch to your work is to center a large heading at the top of a spreadsheet. A few steps make this addition easy to accomplish:

1. Enter the heading text into the left hand cel of the final range.

2. Drag across the range of cels in which the text is to be centered.

3. Click the Format bar icon or open the Format menu and choose Center Across Selection. The text centers on the cels.

To define the way your numeric entries are displayed, select the range of cels to be formatted and then choose the Numbers (##) button (or open the Format menu and choose Numeric). The Numeric dialog box appears, where you can create your own format and then add it to the list. The format you create becomes available the next time you access the Numeric dialog box.

To define the formatting of the cels themselves, open the Format menu and choose Border (or click the Borders button on the ribbon bar). In the Borders dialog box that appears, you can define a border line style and color. You also can determine whether the border surrounds the highlighted cels or only appears on selected sides of the data range. Click the Patterns icon located on the ribbon bar; open the Format menu and choose Patterns; or press Ctrl+F to access the Patterns dialog box, from which you can color the interior of your data range. From within the dialog box, select a shading pattern and a foreground and background color, and then click OK to apply that shading to your selected cels.

To align data in a cel or range of cels, select the data range and then click the appropriate button (left, center, right, or no justification) at the right side of the text ribbon bar.

Tagging the Data Cells

Different cels in the Data Manager window contain different types of data that serve different purposes. Some cels contain title data, for example, and others contain data to be charted. For CorelCHART to work correctly, these data items must be correlated with their corresponding Chart View window components. CorelCHART calls this correlation process *tagging*, and enables you to perform it in either manual or automatic modes.

Tip
Formatting data in the Data Manager affects only the way text displays and prints in the Data Manager; it doesn't affect the way text appears in the chart itself.

> **Note**
>
> The Preview box is in the upper-lefthand corner of the Data Manger window. It represents a snapshot view of the overall chart layout, based on the most current settings. It provides a convenient means for you to quickly determine the macroscopic effect of any formatting changes you make. If you select a cel that is tagged as one of the chart elements, the corresponding part of the Preview box is highlighted.

Manual Tagging

Using manual tagging to identify the elements of your chart is a simple and straightforward process. To tag your chart title, for example, follow these steps:

1. Click cel A1 (or whichever cel contains the title) to select the title.

2. Click the down arrow on the drop-down Tag list box located just above the Formula bar at the top of the Data Manager window. The drop-down menu lists the various chart elements (see fig. 28.20).

3. Click Title. The Tag list box displays Title as the tag for this cel.

Repeat this procedure as often as necessary, tagging data items until all required chart components are identified.

Fig. 28.20
The Data Manager view showing the options provided when manually tagging cells.

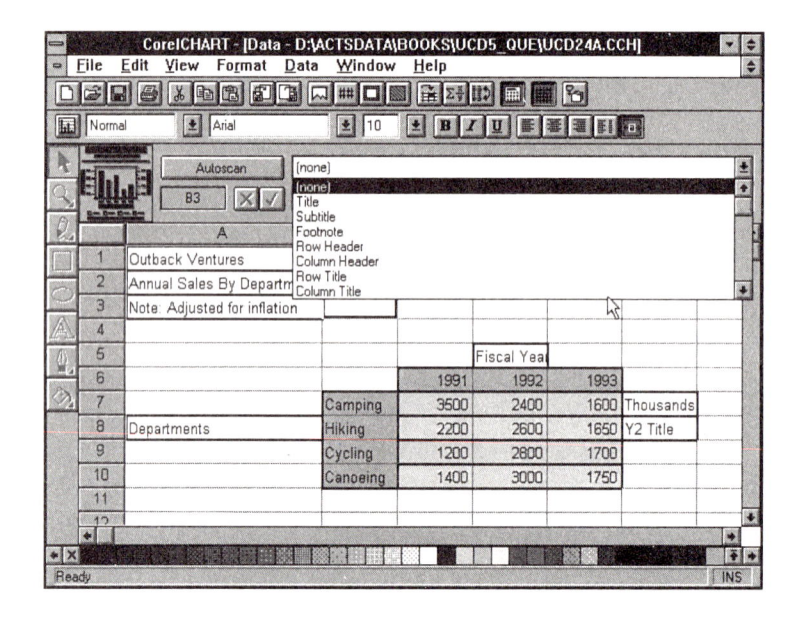

Automatic Tagging

Tagging data manually is a tedious process. But as long as your data is arranged within certain parameters, CorelCHART can automatically tag the data for you using its Autoscan feature. The sample data provided with each chart type are arranged in a format that Autoscan can use; these formats are fairly consistent from one chart type to another. Figure 28.21 shows a typical data format.

Fig. 28.21
Typical Autoscan data arrangement for most Corel-CHART types.

Title					
Subtitle			Column Title		
Footnote			Column Headers		
		Row	Data Range	Data Range	Data Range
Row Title		Headers	Data Range	Data Range	Data Range	Y (Z) Title #1
			Data Range	Data Range	Data Range	Y (Z) Title #2

After your data is in the proper format, simply click the wide Autoscan button next to the Tag list box. CorelCHART automatically tags the data and highlights the column headers, row headers, and data range. Click some of the highlighted cels to see how the tags are assigned.

Printing Data from the Data Manager Window

To print the information you enter in the Data Manager without printing the chart it creates, open the Data Manager's **F**ile menu and choose **P**rint, or press Ctrl+P.

The Page option enables you to set page margins and control the printing of cel borders, grids, and highlights. With the Setup option, you specify a printer and set the characteristics of the printed page.

Print Pre**v**iew (F9) enables you to interactively place your data on the page by using the mouse to drag the margins to your desired locations. Both the Page Setup and Print Setup options are available from Print Preview.

Sometimes you might want to break the printed output at a specific place, vertically or horizontally, to ensure that certain sets of data appear on their proper pages. You can do this in several ways: select the cel just below the desired page break and click the Page Break icon located on the ribbon bar, or open the F**o**rmat menu and choose Set Page Break (Ctrl+Q). A gray line appears on the spreadsheet to indicate the page break location. The page break is deleted by selecting a cel just beneath the page break indicator and once again clicking the Page Break icon.

Reversing the Orientation of Data

Data orientation refers to the Data Manager information that CorelCHART uses to create the category, or horizontal, axis. *Data categories* are frequently points in time such as months or fiscal quarters. A *data series* is the item graphed at each point in the data categories. When more than one item is graphed at each category point, those items form a *data group*. The Data Orientation command on the Data menu enables you to choose which part of the chart data you want as a series and which part you want as a group (see fig. 28.22).

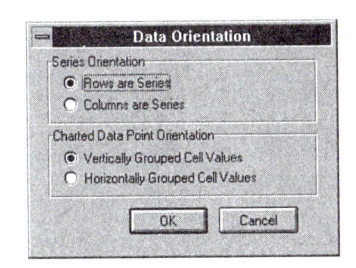

Fig. 28.22

The Data Orientation dialog box, which provides options for making the columns or rows the categories.

728 Chapter 28—Creating Presentation Charts with CorelCHART

Reversing the orientation of the data on your chart highlights different aspects of the data. Figures 28.23 and 28.24 show the results of reversing data. Notice that the legend and horizontal axis information has reversed, indicating that the category-to-series relationship was reversed. Row as series makes rows appear as the series data, which makes the first row's text heading appear as the x-axis categories and the first column appear as the legend points. Column as series reverses this orientation.

Fig. 28.23
Chart with Row As Series orientation before data series reversal.

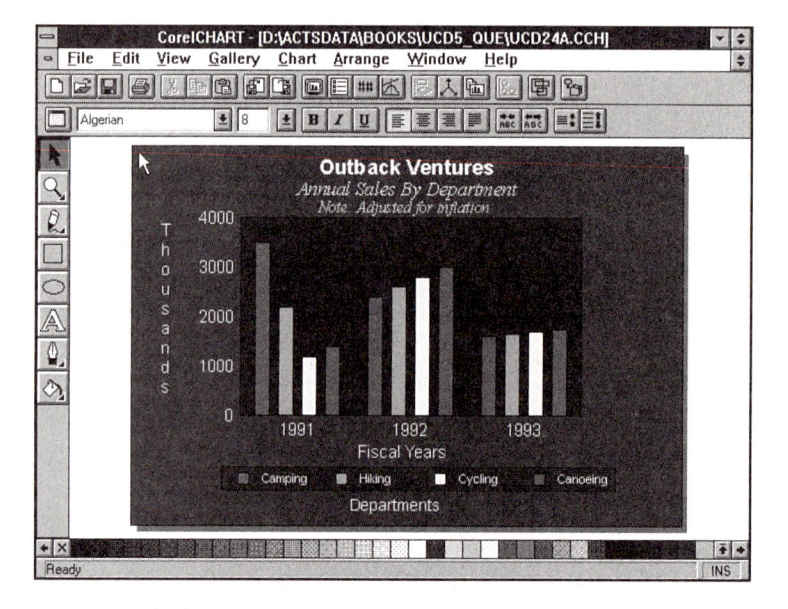

Fig. 28.24
Same data after data series reversal to make Column As Series active.

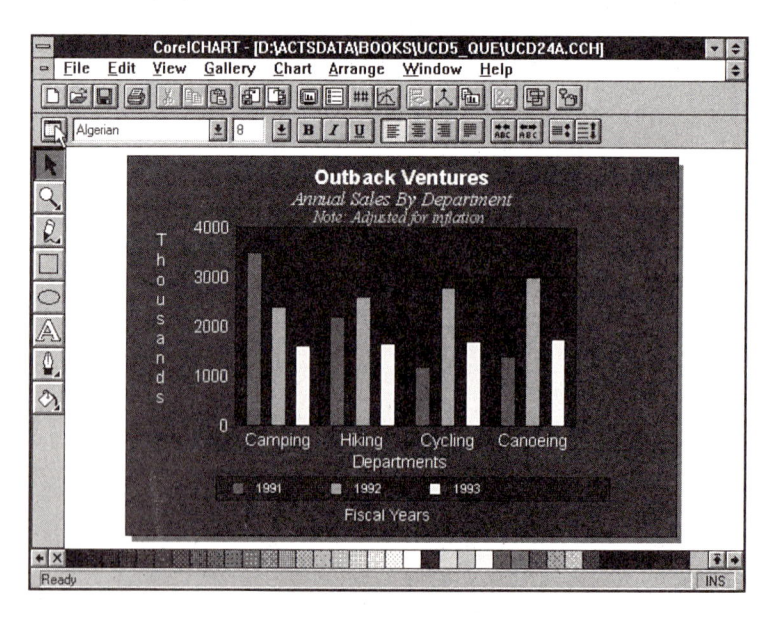

Sorting Data Items

Insert Sorted Item on the Data menu is a handy feature if you frequently add new items to your sorted chart data. Click and drag over the range in which you want the new item inserted, open the Data menu and choose Insert Sorted Item, and type in the item you included. CorelCHART automatically inserts the item in the correct alphabetic sequence and inserts a row or column as designated. The key defines the row/column at which the sort begins.

Modifying Chart Elements Using Chart View

The Chart View window displays the charted data (see fig. 28.25).

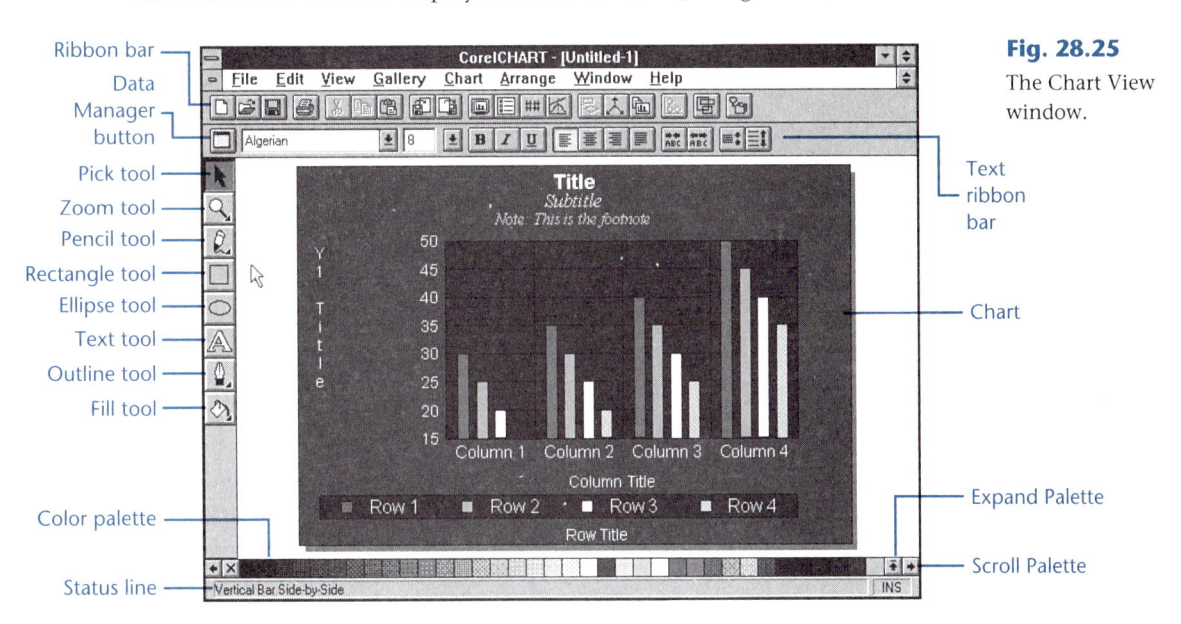

Fig. 28.25
The Chart View window.

In this window, you can edit all aspects of the chart presentation and add text and graphic annotations. The toolbox found at the left side of the screen works almost exactly like the one in CorelDRAW!. It enables you to add, select, and move chart elements, graphic objects, and text. The ribbon bar found at the top of the screen enables you to define typefaces, point sizes, and text formats. The menu bar provides commands that enable you to change chart types and rearrange the data within your chart. The commands on the Chart View menu bar are similar to those found on the Data Manager menu bar; the main difference is that they work with graphic files and objects rather than text.

Using the Toolbox

◄ See "Reviewing the Toolbox Tools," p. 23

Most chart objects are edited or created by one of the tools found at the left side and top of the screen. With these tools, you can move and size objects, place graphic and text annotations, and select colors for chart elements. Table 28.4 provides a list of the toolbox devices and their functions. Most function just like their counterparts in CorelDRAW!.

Table 28.4 The Chart View toolbox showing the names of the various tools

Icon	Tool Name	Function
	Data Manager/ Chart View button	Toggles between the Data Manager screen and the Chart View screen.
	Pick tool	Selects, scales, and moves CorelCHART objects.
	Zoom tool	Magnifies or reduces the chart; unlike the CorelDRAW! Zoom tool, the CorelCHART Zoom tool magnifies the entire graph as a unit.
	Pencil tool	Draws lines, curves, and arrows.
	Rectangle tool	Draws rectangles and squares on the annotation layer.
	Ellipse tool	Draws ellipses and circles on the annotation layer.
	Text tool	Adds and edits text information entered in the chart.
	Outline tool	Changes color, width, and pattern of borders around objects.
	Fill tool	Changes the interior color and fill of an object.

Several tools have fly-out menus that provide additional options.

The Zoom fly-out menu works similarly to CorelDRAW!'s (see fig. 28.26). You might find it helpful to zoom portions of the chart when you are adding text or graphic annotations.

Fig. 28.26
The Zoom fly-out menu showing its various options.

The Pencil fly-out menu provides tools for drawing lines, polygons, and curves (see fig. 28.27). All three tools work in the same general fashion. Click the tool to select it; click the chart where you want the line to begin; and drag to the end point. The polygon tool is a little different because you don't hold down the mouse button as you drag. Instead, you click the end point of each side of the polygon and double-click to join the final side to the starting point.

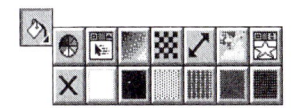

Fig. 28.27
The Pencil tool fly-out menu looks similar to that seen in CorelDRAW!.

The Outline fly-out menu (see fig. 28.28) enables you to specify an object's outline width, color, and pattern. You can control the outline width of chart elements, such as chart riser bars and frames, as well as objects drawn on-screen with the drawing tools. The menu works almost exactly like the comparable menu in CorelDRAW!.

Fig. 28.28
The Outline fly-out menu used to define object outlines, and appears similar to that seen in CorelDRAW!.

To change outlines, use the Pick tool to select the object that you want to modify; click the Outline tool; and then click the modification you want to make. The first row of the fly-out menu specifies the outline width; the first tile allows custom widths; the second provides access to the outline roll-up; and the third tile removes the outline entirely. The second row specifies the color of the outline: a custom color as created by the color wheel, or white, black, and shades of gray.

The Fill fly-out menu enables you to fill any CorelCHART element with the color, pattern, texture, or graphic of your choice (see fig. 28.29). It includes two roll-up windows—the Fill roll-up and the Pictograph roll-up—discussed in detail later in this chapter in the "Adding Pictographs" section.

Fig. 28.29
The Fill fly-out menu.

The first row of tiles, from left to right, enables you to apply uniform fills; use the Fill roll-up window; apply fountain fills, two-color patterns, or bitmap textures; apply full-color fill; and use the Pictograph roll-up window. The second row permits black, white, and various patterned fills. Except for the Pictograph roll-up menu, the use of this menu is almost identical to its use in CorelDRAW!. See Chapter 5, "Modifying Object Outlines and Interior Fills," for more information.

Selecting Chart Elements

You can select most chart elements as objects in much the same way you select objects in CorelDRAW!. To use the Pick tool to select any item on the chart, click the Pick tool and then click the object you want to select. The object's outline and handles appear. You can select multiple objects by holding down Shift while clicking the additional items.

After you select an item, you can move it by clicking and dragging it to the new location. You can resize the chart itself, as well as the titles and legends, by clicking the object's handles and dragging the item to its new size.

Using the Context-Sensitive Pop-Up Menu

Although you can modify some chart elements directly by clicking and dragging the object frame, you must use menu selections to modify other chart elements. One way to modify these elements is to use the right mouse button to display a pop-up menu related to that element's attributes. When you select a chart item with the Pick tool and the right mouse button, a menu pops up to give you access to various options that relate to that specific item. Figure 28.30 shows the pop-up menu for the data axis legend. Choose the modification you want, and it is automatically applied to the selected object.

◀ See "Scaling and Sizing an Object," p. 184

Moving and sizing text in CorelCHART is similar to moving and sizing text in CorelDRAW!. Follow these steps:

1. With the Pick tool, click the text item you want to modify. The scaling handles appear around the text, indicating that it is selected. Handles will not appear around data values or category axis text.

2. To move the text, click the text box and drag it to the new location.

3. To size the text, click a scaling handle and drag the box to the desired size. CorelCHART adjusts the text to fit inside the box.

   Alternatively, after the box is selected, you can use the Font Size box on the Format Text ribbon to enter the desired point size.

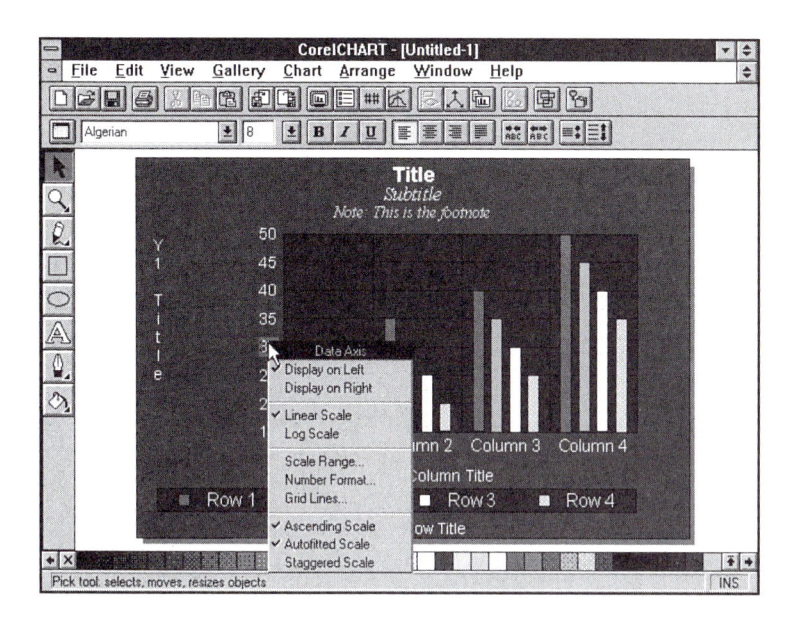

Modifying Chart Elements Using Chart View   **733**

Fig. 28.30
The Data Axis pop-up menu is activated by clicking the data axis with the Pick tool and the right mouse button.

Occasionally, the box containing the text may be larger than actually required to hold the text, which may prevent you from repositioning the text because the frame of the box cannot extend past the edge of the chart. To correct this problem:

1. Click the text with the right mouse button. The context-sensitive pop-up menu appears.

2. Choose Fit Box to Text.

3. Click the text again. The box is sized so that it exactly matches the text length.

4. Click and drag the text to the desired chart position.

Formatting Numbers

Numbers usually are most valuable when they have the proper formatting, such as currency, and the proper number of commas and decimal places. To reformat numbers, follow these steps:

1. Highlight any of the values along an axis.

2. Click the right mouse button. The context-sensitive pop-up menu appears. From this menu, you can choose the Number Format menu option, or click on the Format Number button from the ribbon.

3. Scroll through the formats listed until you find the format you want.

4. Choose the format and click OK. The highlighted numbers are now displayed in the desired format.

Adding Color with the Color Palette

To change the color of any chart item, select the item and then click the desired color on the color palette located at the bottom of the screen.

To choose the outline color when working with objects such as a bar in a vertical bar chart, click the object and then choose the desired outline color from the palette by clicking it with the right mouse button.

Modifying a Chart Using a Template

Apply Template from the File menu is a handy tool for applying a standard chart format to the currently active chart. Use this feature to give charts a similar appearance without recreating the underlying Data Manager contents, which is commonly done to present several different data sets with the same overall graphic colors, sizes, and attributes to make them appear similar in style. To use this feature, open a chart and insert the desired data using the Data Manager. Go to Chart view. Open the **F**ile menu and choose Apply Template to open a standard Windows file directory dialog box, where you choose the desired CorelCHART template file (which is another CorelCHART file with a CCH extension). CorelCHART applies the formatting and graphic information (but not the data) contained in the template file to the currently active chart.

Importing Graphics into a Chart

◀ See "Adding a Graphic Symbol," p. 250

◀ See "Sharing Drawings—Export, Import, and the Clipboard," p. 268

You can take advantage of the vast CorelDRAW! clipart library or graphics created in CorelDRAW! or other graphics applications to include graphic files in your chart. (The procedure is virtually identical to that discussed in Chapter 8, "Advanced Text Techniques.") To import a graphics file into a chart, follow these steps:

1. Open the **F**ile menu and choose Import. The Import dialog box appears.

2. From the List Of File Types list box, choose the graphic file format type you want to import. A wide assortment of file types is supported.

3. Select the proper drive and directory.

4. Double-click the desired file, or click the file and then click OK. The graphic appears on-screen.

5. Move and scale the graphic as needed.

Exporting Charts into Other Applications

The File menu's Export command enables you to convert the charts you create in CorelCHART to a format usable by other applications. CorelCHART provides a number of bitmap and vector graphic file formats, including Windows MetaFile (WMF). Choose the export format based upon the import capabilities of the application into which you want to insert the chart.

Editing Chart Objects

The Edit menu options operate similarly within CorelCHART as they do in all other Corel applications. Undo only applies to the last action taken. Cut (Ctrl+X), Copy (Ctrl+C), and Paste (Ctrl+V) work with Clipboard data and function just as they do in other applications.

You can use the Paste Inside command to copy an object from the Clipboard and have CorelCHART automatically size it to fit the inside dimensions of the CorelCHART page. (Click the printable page, using the Pick tool, to select it before using the Paste Inside command.) You can then move the object to the back using Arrange To Back to create a backdrop against which the chart data is displayed. For example, if you present a chart to investors concerning a new building, you could transfer a drawing of the building to the background of the chart by using Paste Inside. Paste Inside is not available unless the source file is in CMF, WMF, BMP, or DIB format.

Clear (Del) erases the highlighted information from the CorelCHART screen. Duplicate (Ctrl+D) makes an exact copy of the highlighted information as long as the information is not created in, or used by, the Data Manager.

Copy Chart automatically selects the entire chart and copies it to the Clipboard. You can then open another application (such as CorelDRAW!, CorelSHOW!, or Word for Windows) and paste the chart information into that application.

Changing the Chart Style

You may want to change the chart style after the data is entered to determine whether another style (for example, line chart rather than bar chart) might better match your presentation needs. To change styles, use the options on the Gallery menu. When you choose a chart style from this menu, a fly-out menu appears, listing the types associated with that style.

The Chart menu options deal with the attributes of the currently selected style. Use these options to edit the current chart.

Controlling the Display of the Underlying Chart Data

All options on the Chart menu deal with the display of the underlying chart data contained within the Data Manager. Remember that the category and data axes change from horizontal to vertical depending on the style of chart selected, and the menu options vary with the type of chart being created.

Choosing the Category Axis option from the Chart menu opens a menu you use to determine where and whether the category headings are displayed. A vertical bar chart provides a top and bottom choice, and a horizontal bar chart provides a left or right choice. Activating the Show Grid Lines option displays the lines that divide the different categories along the category axis. The line thickness is set using the Outline tool. Autofitted Text, when selected, controls the type size of the legend data so that it all fits on a single line. Staggered Text displays alternate category titles on different horizontal lines so that very long titles can be displayed without overlapping each other.

Choosing the Data Axis option opens a menu with options that deal with the formatting and orientation of the data axis information. You can define the location of the axis (top/bottom, left/right), the scale (logarithmic/linear), the data scale range (lower-and-upper range bounds), the formatting of the numbers, and the grid line display characteristics.

Figure 28.31 shows the dialog box that appears when you choose the Grid Lines option.

Fig. 28.31
The Grid Lines dialog box showing the various grid options, including tick mark options and intervals.

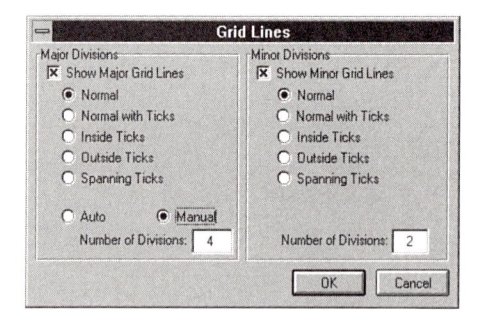

You can choose to display either or both of the major and minor grid lines. You also can determine whether the number of subdivisions within the major and minor grid lines should be automatically determined by CorelCHART or conform to a set number that you define in the text entry box. The Normal grid line display is simply a line that extends from one side to the other side of the chart area. Normal with Ticks displays a small line outside the chart across from the grid line and next to the data value. Inside Ticks and Outside Ticks removes the Normal Line and display the tick mark either inside or outside the chart area, depending on which is selected. Spanning Ticks spans the chart frame barrier and does not include the Normal line. It is common practice to include Normal for the major grid lines and to use Inside Ticks for the minor grid lines.

The options at the bottom of the Data Axis menu enable you to determine whether the scales are displayed in Ascending/Descending order; whether the scale ranges should be automatically determined by CorelCHART (overrides the Scale Range option); and whether the scale labels should be staggered similarly to that described in the Category Axis section.

The 2nd Data-Axis command performs the same function as the standard Data Axis menu selection, except it deals with those instances when a dual, or Y1 and Y2, axis chart type exists, for example, in the Vertical Line Dual Axis Stacked chart type.

> **Note**
>
> Use the dual axis design when you have two related quantities on a substantially different scale. Dual axis works well when you want to compare company profits against production volume for specific quarters. Profit in dollars (millions) would be on one axis and production volume (thousands) would be on the other. Without this dual axis approach, the production volumes would appear insignificant when plotted on the millions scale.

Be cautious when you set your grid lines for the two axes; you want to be able to easily determine which grid lines are associated with which data axis. When working with dual axis charts, you also can define which scale range (Y1 or Y2) appears on the left or right axis by choosing the Axis Assignment menu option. The displayed dialog box enables you to switch the current axis assignment if you choose.

The Data Reversal option does not switch the series-group relationship; it only reverses the ordering of the information contained in the group or series. For example, choosing the Data Reversal Reverse Groups option causes the category heading on the left side of a vertical bar chart to swap with the heading on the right side, and all categories in between to swap positions accordingly. Using the Data Reversal Reverse Series option reverses the ordering of the series data displayed in each category, but the category location remains the same.

Chapter 28—Creating Presentation Charts with CorelCHART

Clicking a data series and choosing Data Analysis displays the dialog box shown in figure 28.32.

Fig. 28.32
The Data Analysis dialog box is used to define the various curve fitting, or regression, options that can be applied to the selected data range.

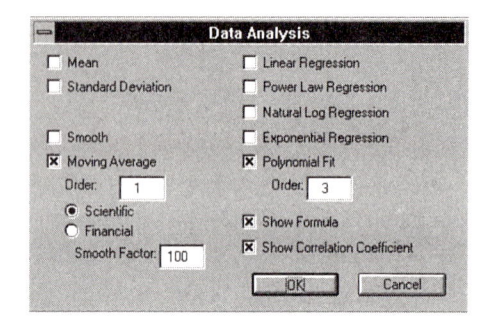

A number of different data analysis procedures are provided with CorelCHART. Using these tools properly keeps you from having to perform this analysis in another spreadsheet type product and then import the information into CorelCHART for final display. You can work with the raw data within the CorelCHART application's framework.

Choosing Mean and/or Standard Deviation in the Data Analysis dialog box displays the result of the calculation on the chart as straight lines. Both scientific and financial data series smoothing are provided, and you can set the order and smooth factor used in performing the calculations when you choose Moving Average. Linear, common log, natural log, and exponential regression analysis also are available. If polynomial fit is chosen, you can define the order of the equation used in the text entry box. Choosing Show Formula and Show Correlation Coefficient displays the information used in calculating the equation fit (see fig. 28.33). You can then move the displayed correlation information to the desired location on the chart.

> **Note**
>
> Use the regression analysis to not only get a "best curve" fit to your actual data, but also to give you an equation that you can use to predict future events. For example, plotting sales (Y) versus production (X) with regression analysis applied to the resulting data provides an equation into which other values for X can be inserted to get other values for Y. This procedure enables you to predict sales for different levels of production.

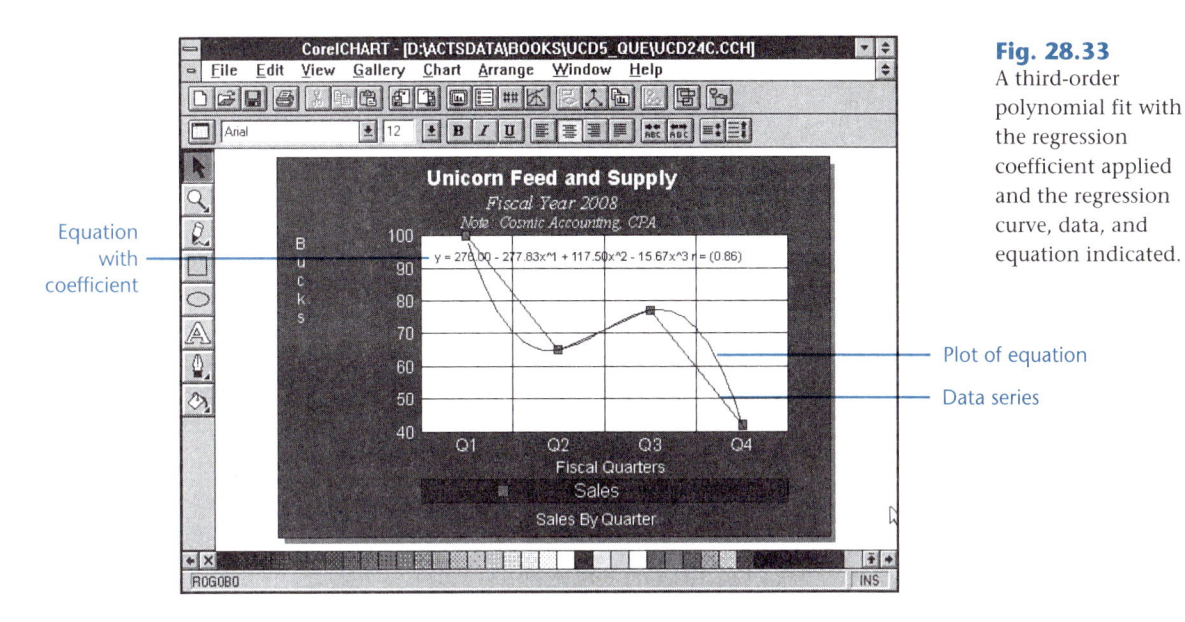

Fig. 28.33
A third-order polynomial fit with the regression coefficient applied and the regression curve, data, and equation indicated.

The content of the menu section below Data Analysis changes with the type of chart selected. In general, you can modify attributes associated with the display of the actual data (the bar chart riser thickness and spacing, line chart data markers, and so on). Clicking an attribute reveals a fly-out menu within which you can change the designs and preview the final effects on your chart.

The contents of the next section of the Chart menu also vary with the chart type selected. A bar chart type enables you to create a pictograph, which uses a graphic image such as an airplane in place of the bar. If you are working with a line chart, selecting a data series and then choosing Display As Bar enables you to make combination charts because one section can be a line chart and the other a bar chart. If you are working with a bar chart, this option becomes Display As Line and performs a comparable function. Emphasize Bar also is provided with bar charts, and enables you to select a data point out of a series and give it special emphasis by modifying the bar outline. This feature is useful for drawing attention to particular data points presented within your chart.

Clicking on Legend displays the Legend dialog box shown in figure 28.34. Clicking on the Legend tool also displays the same dialog box.

740 Chapter 28—Creating Presentation Charts with CorelCHART

Fig. 28.34
The Legend dialog box indicates the various legend-related placement and design options.

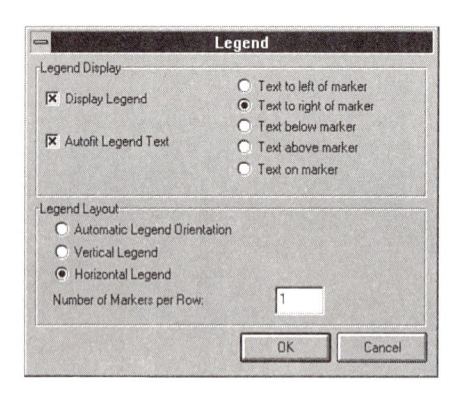

Display Legend enables you to enable/disable the legend function. When this option is enabled, you have a number of options provided with respect to orientation of the text to the legend marker. These options are displayed to the right of the dialog box; you can designate the orientation as left, right, below, above, or on the marker itself. Autofit Legend Text automatically fits the text to appear on the line in accordance with the Legend Layout criteria set at the bottom of the dialog box. You can set the legend to automatically determine its orientation, to display vertically, or to display horizontally. The Number of Markers per Row option defines the number of legend entries allowed on a single line and affects the legend text size.

Choosing Display Status from the Chart menu or clicking the Display Status tool on the ribbon reveals a dialog box where you determine which chart elements are displayed or hidden (see fig. 28.35).

Fig. 28.35
The Display Status dialog box, where many of the overall chart appearance characteristics are defined.

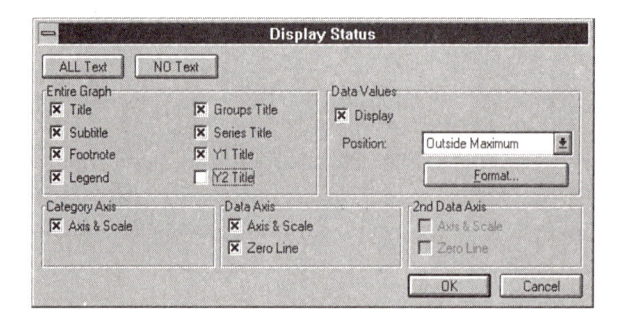

Most of the options in the Display Status dialog box are self-explanatory, but several require elaboration. Choosing ALL Text displays all chart-related text items, and NO Text hides all text items. The Display option in the Data Values area affects the entire chart and enables you to display the numeric value of the data points at a number of different locations with respect to the specific data point. The location definition is consistent for all data points within the chart.

Clicking Format enables you to define the format in which the numbers are displayed. The Zero Line option under the Data Axis section adds an emphasis to the zero line as either a different color and/or a different thickness. The 2nd Data Axis options are available when a dual axis chart is created.

Controlling the Alignment of Graphics and Text

The Arrange menu enables you to control the presentation of graphic and text annotations on the chart. The upper part of the menu is used to order the layering of objects when multiple objects exist. Any number of objects can be arranged together. To change the order of a particular object, select the object and choose the desired option from the Arrange menu using the Order fly-out menu.

◀ See "Laying Objects on Top of or beneath Each Other," p. 102

You can also align objects with each other or on the page. To align two objects, first select the item to be aligned, and then hold down Shift while you select the object on which to align. (When aligning more than two objects, the last item selected should be the object on which the other objects should be aligned.) With both items selected, open the **A**rrange menu and choose Align (Ctrl+A) or click the Align button located on the ribbon bar. The Align dialog box shown in figure 28.36 appears.

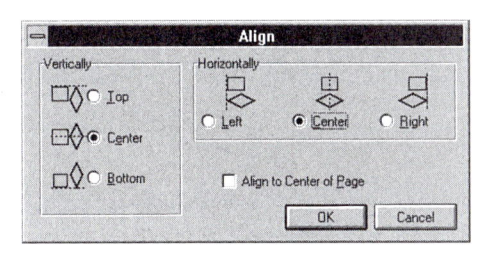

Fig. 28.36
The Align dialog box operates identically to that seen in CorelDRAW!.

You can choose to align the items with each other horizontally, vertically, or both, matching tops, bottoms, or centers. Alternatively, the items can be aligned on the page. (This procedure is identical to that used in CorelDRAW!.)

◀ See "Aligning Objects," p. 109

The Arrange menu also contains a Make Same Size option. Clicking this option opens another menu that allows for sizing of the objects so that they are the same horizontal or vertical—or both—size. This feature is handy when importing objects that you want to appear similar in size and importance. Simply select the object and then select the desired menu option.

Refreshing a Window

The Refresh Window option on the Window menu is helpful when you are making custom annotations and text adjustments to a chart. CorelCHART sometimes leaves ghosts on-screen when working with these types of changes. The Refresh Window option redraws the screen, eliminating these problems.

The Cascade and particularly the Tile options also are extremely helpful in enabling you to move from window to window when working with multiple charts. With the edges of each window displayed, you can click the windows you want to make current. All the currently active windows are listed at the bottom of the Window menu. You can make a chart current by clicking its title in the Window menu. (This tiling procedure is not available with CorelDRAW!.)

Formatting Text with the Text Ribbon

The text ribbon bar immediately above the chart window enables you to choose the typeface and size of the chart text. The first text box on the left is the Font List box. Click the down arrow beside the box to choose from a list of available typefaces. The second text box on the text ribbon bar is the Point Size box, which also has a down arrow that you can use to choose from a list of point sizes.

The text ribbon bar also provides the capability to add emphasis with bold or italicized type. It has icons you use to justify the text and control the spacing between letters and lines. The functions of the various text ribbon bar icons are described in table 28.5.

Table 28.5 Text Ribbon Button Functions

Icon	Function
B	Bold the selected text
I	Italicize the selected text
U	Underline the selected text
≡	Left-justify the selected text
≡	Center the selected text
≡	Right-justify the selected text
≡	Fully-justify (right and left) the selected text

Icon	Function
	Decrease kerning (interletter spacing)
	Increase kerning (interletter spacing)
	Decrease leading (interline spacing)
	Increase leading (interline spacing)

To use these tools, you must first select the text to be modified with the Pick tool or the Text tool. To select text with the Pick tool, select the text box by simply clicking the text to be changed. To select with the Text tool, highlight the text to be changed by dragging the cursor over it. After you select the text, click the appropriate button(s) to change the text. Selected buttons appear darker or lighter than unselected buttons.

Customizing Your Charts

When you have the basic data charted, you can add the final touches that draw attention to important characteristics. Text, graphic objects, fill types, and other artistic features standard with CorelDRAW! also are available with CorelCHART. These attributes make a conventional-looking chart into something worth noticing. You apply them using Chart view.

Creating Text Annotations

Text annotations are text strings added to the chart in addition to the titles and legend. To enter the annotation, follow these steps:

1. Select the Text tool from the toolbox on the left side of the chart and click in the area to the left of the chart. The cross hairs become an I-beam cursor.

2. Type in the annotation, pressing Enter at the end of each line to preserve the line spacing. Don't worry about correct text sizing at this point.

3. When you finish typing, choose the Pick tool. Click the text you just entered and drag the text box so that the first line is located in the desired chart position.

4. Position the cursor over the lower-left corner of the box until the cursor changes to a double-headed arrow. Drag the box corner until it is the desired size and release the mouse button. The text size changes to fit into the box, just as it does in CorelDRAW!.

Tip
If the text does not change immediately after you apply the formatting, click anywhere on the chart background and then click the text box again.

The text formatting procedures outlined earlier can be applied to the text annotation to make it bold, italicized, a different font or color, and justified the way you want.

Creating Graphic Annotations

You can use the Pencil, Ellipse, Rectangle, Fill, and Outline tools just as they are used in CorelDRAW!. Together they combine to create as varied a combination of graphic objects as you can imagine.

To create a backdrop to highlight the text, for example, choose the Ellipse tool from the toolbox. Choose a bright yellow color from the Palette. Click and drag an ellipse around the text. Don't worry if they don't line up correctly. When you release the mouse button, a yellow ellipse covers most of the text. Open the **A**rrange menu and choose Backward One (Page Down). The text is now superimposed on the ellipse.

To center the text in the ellipse:

1. Choose the Pick tool and click the ellipse if it's not already selected.
2. Hold down Shift and click the text. Both the ellipse and the text are now selected.
3. Open the **A**rrange menu and choose Align, or click the Align tool from the ribbon bar.
4. Click Center Vertically and Center Horizontally in the Align dialog box and then click OK. The text is now centered within the ellipse.

Creating Customized Fills

Any CorelCHART element, except text, can have any of the various CorelDRAW! fill types applied to it. For example, the bars on a bar chart can all contain a fountain fill or a bitmap pattern. The method of application is identical to that used in CorelDRAW!. You can read more about fills in Chapter 5, "Modifying Object Outline and Interior Fills."

Fills fall into several basic categories as follows:

- **Uniform.** The same percentage of shading occurs across the entire object.
- **Fountain.** The fill density varies in a linear or radial pattern across the object.
- **Two-color pattern.** The applied pattern contains two colors in a format consistent with any of the CorelCHART-compatible formats.
- **Full-color pattern.** The color and pattern of the object are virtually unlimited.
- **Bitmap textures.** A bitmap image is used to create a three-dimensional effect to the surface of the fill.

A wide variety of fill types, colors, and patterns are provided with CorelDRAW!, and you can use any of them to add an artistic effect to CorelCHART objects.

It is generally faster to use the Fill roll-up window to apply object fills. Access the Fill roll-up window by choosing the Fill tool and then the Roll-Up icon. After the roll-up is activated, you can access the fill types by clicking the appropriate icon in the roll-up window.

Adding Pictographs

Bar charts and histograms enable you to add pictographs so that the conventional lines and rectangles associated with the chart are replaced by graphic images (see fig. 28.37). The number of images placed in each bar is related to the height of the bar and its width. The same image is used in each of the bars associated with the selected series, and pictographs are only available on vertical and horizontal bar charts and histograms.

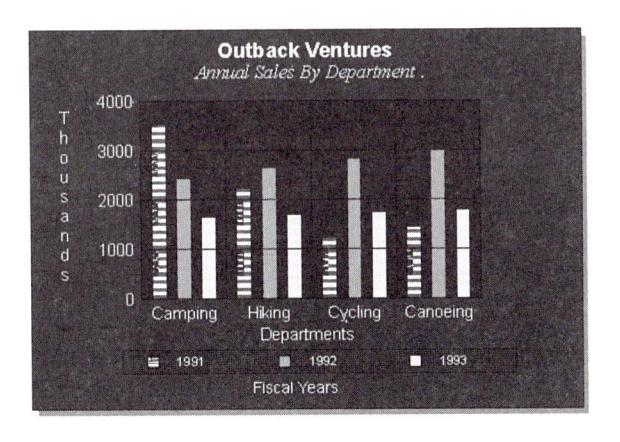

Fig. 28.37
A pictograph using the United States flag in the first data series, while leaving the others as they are.

To add a pictograph, follow these steps:

1. After you create your bar chart or histogram, choose the Chart menu's Show as Pictograph option to divide the bars into smaller subsections that exist between the grid lines.

2. Using the Pick tool, click a bar of the series to which you want to apply the pictograph; then open the Pictograph roll-up by clicking the Fill tool and selecting the upper-right icon in the fly-out menu. The Pictograph roll-up now opens to display the currently active pictograph image.

3. If the pictograph image is acceptable, click the roll-up's Apply button to create a pictograph of the currently selected bar using this pictograph image.

    If it is not acceptable, click the small arrow in the bottom right of the image box to display the variety of images readily available for pictograph creation. Double-click the image you want and then click Apply to create the pictograph using your selected object.

Tip
It's faster to create the pictograph using the File New Pictograph process if you know that the final product will end up as a pictograph.

You also can import an image using the Import option provided in the Pictograph roll-up. Follow the standard importing procedures to import graphic objects such as logos, clipart, symbols, and other CorelDRAW! objects you might want to use. (Importing is covered in the "Importing Graphics into a Chart" section earlier in this chapter and in Chapter 9, "File-Related Operations and CorelMOSAIC".) When they are included in the roll-up, click Apply to create the pictograph.

Creating 3D Charts

The extent of CorelCHART's power becomes clear when you use the 3D Tool roll-up window. The features in this roll-up only work on 3D charts.

To use this window, first create your 3D chart using any of the Gallery 3D menu options. Then open the 3D roll-up by opening the **C**hart menu and choosing 3D Roll-Up, which appears on the menu only when you are working on a 3D chart. The roll-up shown in figure 28.38 appears.

The 3D Tool roll-up window is used to vary perspective effects, modify the thickness of walls and the length of chart axes, rotate the chart in virtually any direction, and move it diagonally on the chart surface. By using this roll-up window, you can modify most orientation and design features associated with a 3D chart.

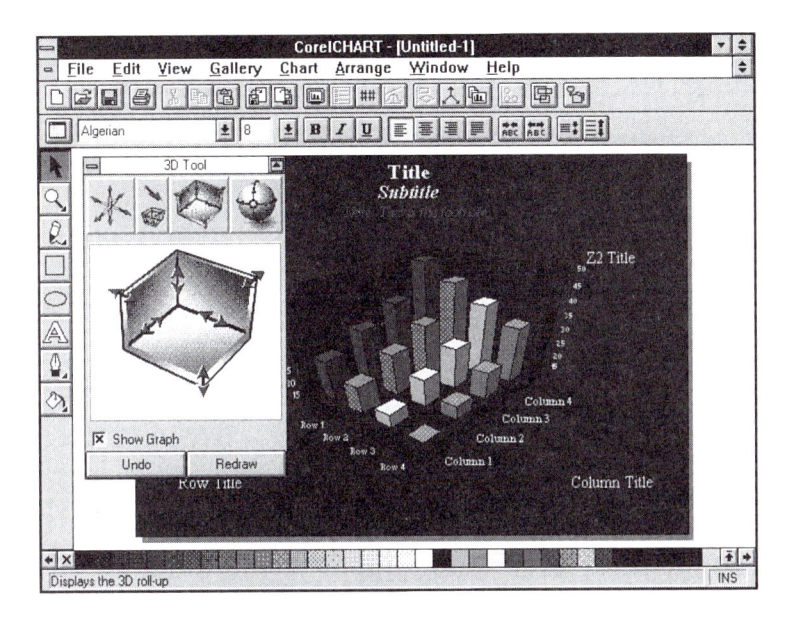

Fig. 28.38
The 3D Tool roll-up window with 3D chart displayed.

The upper-left icon moves the entire chart at an angle across the page; the next icon adds perspective to the entire chart by creating the illusion of depth; the third enables you to change the individual axes' lengths and wall thickness; the upper-right icon enables you to change the orientation of the entire chart in virtually any dimension. The procedure for operating these icons is to choose the icon and then click the appropriate arrows attached to the center object to make the chart perform as you expect. Make sure that Show Graph is activated so that you can monitor the changes. When you are satisfied with the chart, click Redraw to change your original 3D chart to look as the preview does. If you click Undo, no changes are made to your chart, and you are returned to the Chart view.

> **Troubleshooting**
>
> *Every time I create a new chart, I end up adding all the graphic images such as logos and text. How can I get around this problem?*
>
> Create a template that contains the images you need and then apply that template to new sets of data by using the File menu's Apply Template command.
>
> *I don't get the same result when I change the series or category orders while in the Chart view as when I am in the Data Manager view. What is the problem?*
>
> People often confuse the Chart view's Reverse Order commands contained under the Chart menu with the Data Manager's Data Orientation settings. The Data Manager determines whether the rows or columns are treated as the data series. The Chart view settings determine the order in which the categories or series are displayed and does not reverse the orientation of the categories and series data points.
>
> *I can't get reliable results from my laserjet printer when printing my charts. The gray shades all blend together, and it is difficult to tell one bar chart series from another. Can I do something about this situation?*
>
> This problem becomes more pronounced when you photocopy the chart a few times. You get around it by using pattern fills rather than shaded fills. The patterns do not lose their "color" when copied and can withstand more generations of copying before losing their effectiveness.
>
> *My data analysis operations rarely produce a close fit between my initial series data and the computed regression equation. What am I doing wrong?*
>
> Your procedure is probably right, and you should use a different type of regression analysis tool or setting. Many naturally occurring phenomenon are fit best using a natural or regular logarithmic fit. In addition, the more complicated your initial data series, the higher the polynomial fit order that it requires. Try a third or fourth order fit and see if the results are better. It is rarely cost effective or necessary to get an exact fit with a complicated curve.
>
> *Am I better off performing my spreadsheet operations in CorelCHART or in Excel and then importing the data into CorelCHART for final display?*
>
> It really depends on the complexity of the spreadsheet. CorelCHART in CorelDRAW! 5 has many spreadsheet capabilities, but CorelCHART is still not a replacement for Excel. On the other hand, Excel does not have CorelCHART's image-processing capability. Perform your complicated analysis in Excel and then import the salient data into CorelCHART for final processing—that is, data analysis and fancy display. If you do not own another spreadsheet product, CorelCHART presents a convenient and cost-effective alternative to purchasing a separate spreadsheet product.

From Here...

Charting is a lot of fun, and a tremendous productivity tool when used in conjunction with presentations and general data analysis. Make sure that you use your charts in presentations and other graphic arts projects.

- Chapter 4, "Mastering Object Manipulations," shows you how to change additional object characteristics and work with many objects at once.

- Chapter 5, "Modifying Object Outlines and Interior Fills," covers the ways to change the color, shape, and texture of outlines and interiors of objects.

- Chapter 9, "File-Related Operations and CorelMOSAIC," deals with importing and exporting files. It contains useful information for using charts in other applications.

- Chapter 29, "Making Presentations with CorelSHOW," covers the creation of formal presentations. Charts are usually an integral part of business presentations, and necessary to make a presentation effective.

Chapter 29

Making Presentations with CorelSHOW

by Paul Bodensiek

Quite often, you create charts, logos, images, scanned images, animation, and screen shots to make a formal presentation. It can be in the form of a computer-based display (a screen show), a set of 35mm slides, a set of overhead projections, or a collection of images on paper. CorelSHOW enables you to combine materials created in all the other Corel applications into a single unified presentation that can become a rallying point the other applications revolve around. This chapter introduces you to the operation of CorelSHOW and covers some recommended procedures for making the most out of your presentations.

This chapter covers the following topics:

- Building a CorelSHOW file by defining the slide page
- Adding common and individual backgrounds to a slide
- Incorporating images from other programs into a presentation
- Adding text and bulleted lists to a slide
- Including slide-to-slide transition effects
- Making sophisticated event timing within slides
- Working with interactive, stand-alone, and formal presentations
- Using Object Linking and Embedding (OLE) and Dynamic Data Exchange (DDE)

A *show* consists of a series of *slides* containing images and text. The slides are generally unified in appearance by similar fonts, colors, and bullets.

Tip
Remember that CorelDRAW! objects can be used in CorelSHOW presentations. Try to use the provided clipart and images that you already created to make the most efficient use of your time and effort.

> **Note**
>
> A drawback to CorelSHOW is that it has little intrinsic processing power and relies on the source applications for all modifications other than simple sizing and moving. This means that you often have several applications running at the same time, which drains processing power and makes computer operation very slow. If you plan to use CorelSHOW along with the other Corel applications on a regular basis, get a high-power machine (486/66 type minimum) with at least 12M RAM (16 recommended) and at least 200M free hard disk space. Otherwise, it is frustratingly slow to work with several applications at once.

Starting CorelSHOW and the CorelSHOW Screen

◄ See "Saving and Retrieving Files," p. 261

To start CorelSHOW, double-click the CorelSHOW icon located in the Corel application group. The blank CorelSHOW screen appears.

Opening an Existing Presentation

Tip
For a new presentation, set the page size you intend to use right away. Later changes affect object layout on-screen and may require substantial rearrangement.

To work with an existing presentation, open the **F**ile menu and choose **O**pen. A standard Windows file access dialog box opens, where you find the desired file and double-click it to begin the editing process.

Starting a New Presentation

To begin a new presentation, open the **F**ile menu and choose **N**ew. The New Presentation dialog box opens (see fig. 29.1). Here you can set the number of slides you initially want to include in your presentation, define the Printer Setup parameters, and define the Page Setup for the new presentation.

Fig. 29.1
Set the number of initial slides, define the printer setup parameters, and define the page setup in this dialog box.

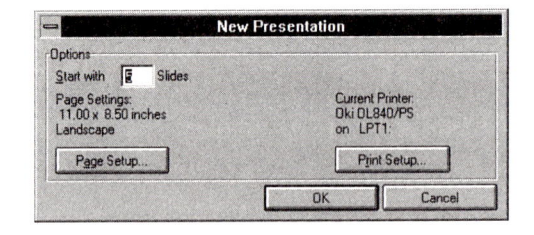

To define the page size and characteristics for your presentation, follow these steps:

1. Choose P**a**ge Setup. The Page Setup dialog box appears (see fig. 29.2).

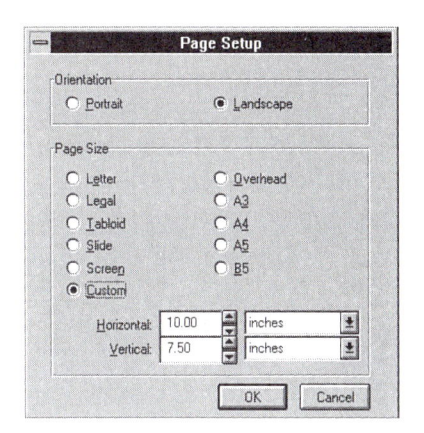

Starting CorelSHOW and the CorelSHOW Screen 753

Fig. 29.2
Use the Page Setup dialog box to specify what media you will use to present your show. Choose from slides, the computer screen, and many standard paper sizes.

2. Choose the desired page size from the numerous Page Size options available. After you make your choice, the corresponding page dimensions are shown in the Horizontal and Vertical boxes. Switching from Portrait to Landscape (or vice versa) automatically switches the Horizontal and Vertical dimensions.

3. After you make your page size choice, click OK. The CorelSHOW editing window appears with the desired page setup displayed (see fig. 29.3).

Tip
Stick with a landscape page for on-screen presentations, because most monitors are landscape.

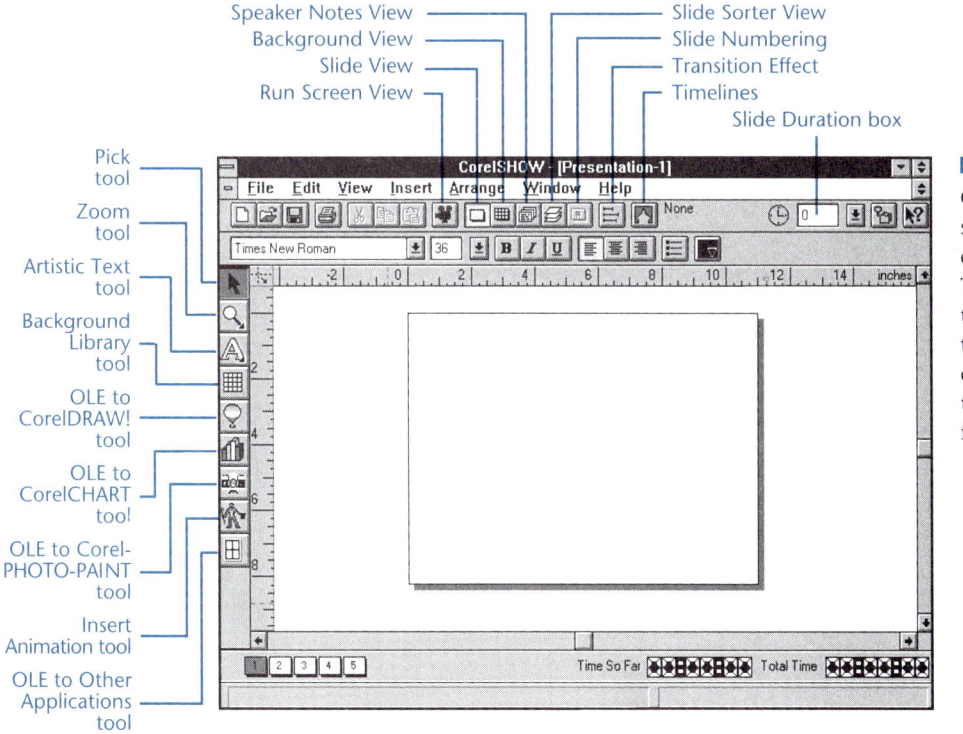

Fig. 29.3
Create individual slides in the editing window. The ribbon bar, text bar, and toolbox, provide direct access to the most used features.

Callouts (Fig. 29.3):
- Speaker Notes View
- Background View
- Slide View
- Run Screen View
- Slide Sorter View
- Slide Numbering
- Transition Effect
- Timelines
- Slide Duration box
- Pick tool
- Zoom tool
- Artistic Text tool
- Background Library tool
- OLE to CorelDRAW! tool
- OLE to CorelCHART tool
- OLE to Corel-PHOTO-PAINT tool
- Insert Animation tool
- OLE to Other Applications tool

VI Other Corel Applications

Setting Up the Printer

See "General Printing Procedures," p. 298

You set up the printer in CorelSHOW much as you do in any other Corel application. Open the **F**ile menu and choose **P**rint Setup to open the Print Setup dialog box. If you are starting a new presentation, simply click **P**rint Setup in the New Presentation dialog box to open the Print Setup dialog box. From this dialog box, you can access the default printer, select a special printer for a particular operation, or use print options such as print orientation.

The CorelCHART Screen

Along the left side of the new display is a set of tools used to create CorelSHOW objects and images. The Pick and Zoom tools operate much like those in CorelDRAW!. Clicking with the right mouse button on an object or on the screen itself displays a pop-up menu with various options associated with the selection. The menu contains various framing options when an object is selected and contains page setup or background options when you click on the screen itself (see fig. 29.4).

Fig. 29.4
The context-sensitive pop-up menu provides access to only those options appropriate to the object clicked with the secondary mouse button.

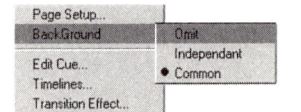

With this menu, you can access the Page Setup menu, select a background, edit cues, show timelines, and set up transition effects for objects and slides. You can, of course, use the pop-up tool, icons, or menu selections to achieve the same results. At the bottom of the toolbox at the left of the screen are buttons that provide direct OLE access to objects created in CorelDRAW!, CorelCHART, CorelPHOTO-PAINT, CorelMOVE, or other (non-Corel) OLE-compatible Windows applications.

Information about total and elapsed presentation times, slide selection, cue management, and object timelines appears along the bottom of the screen. Icons related to background editing, slide viewing (individually or in groups), and slide and object transition effects associated with the currently active slide appear at the top of the screen, along with a box noting the slide show's total viewing duration.

> **Troubleshooting**
>
> *I want to use my presentation for multiple formats (a screen show, handouts, and overhead transparencies). What should I set the page layout to?*
>
> Set the page layout to Screen. A presentation set up for the computer screen and printed on paper still looks OK because the paper's margins make differences in the size and shape of the slide less apparent. You will want to consider, however, whether you will be printing your handouts in black and white or color and adjust the colors on your slides accordingly.
>
> *After I created my presentation, I realized that all my slides are the wrong size. How do I resize my slides?*
>
> Click the Background View button on the ribbon bar. Then size all the backgrounds so that they match the new page size. When you are done, return to the Slide view and resize and reposition the various text and graphics objects on each slide. The resized backgrounds will give you a visual cue on the size of the slide.

Creating CorelSHOW Presentations

Easy access to slide show creation technology does not create an effective presentation any more than using a word processor automatically makes a best-selling novel. Planning, design, and a clear vision of the purpose and audience are essential to a useful presentation. This section is a primer on the rules of good presentation design and some techniques that streamline the creation process.

Understanding Design Principles

No matter how effective you are with CorelSHOW's operation, the presentation is only as effective as its basic design. Whenever you create a presentation, consider the following design principles:

- Know your audience and what its members expect from the presentation.

- Determine the three essential concepts that you want to drive home and make sure that they are reinforced throughout the presentation. Three concepts are generally the optimum number for an audience to concentrate on during a presentation.

◄ See "Working with Artistic Text," p. 212

◄ See "Working with Paragraph Text," p. 218

Tip
You might find it easier to work with Artistic text rather than Paragraph text because the number of characters and lines are generally small with slide text.

- Outline the flow (storyboard) of the presentation before you create it in CorelSHOW.

- Determine the proper output media type before you start designing. If the output goes to a monochrome printer, for example, color considerations do not apply.

- Keep the amount of slide text to a minimum. Use seven lines of text or fewer per slide and never more than seven words to a text line. Use bullets for emphasis and text of at least 18-point size. (Don't forget to check for grammar and spelling errors.)

- Use charts, graphs, and graphic images to reinforce a point.

- Keep the presentation flow consistent and on track toward your ultimate goals.

Adding Text

In many ways, text is even more important in a presentation than graphics are. This is the meat of your show.

To add Artistic text to a slide, follow these steps:

1. Click the toolbox's Text tool. The cursor changes to cross hairs.

2. Position the cursor where you want to begin a line of text and click the mouse button.

3. Type the text that you want.

4. End the particular piece of text by clicking the cursor on another part of the screen to begin a new line of text, or click the Pick tool in the toolbox.

Follow these steps to add Paragraph text to a slide:

1. Click and hold down the toolbox's Text tool. The Text fly-out menu opens.

2. Click the Paragraph Text tool. The cursor changes to cross hairs.

3. Starting at one corner of where you want the text to appear, click and drag the cursor to create a bounding box for the text. Release the mouse button when the box is the size you want.

4. Type the text you want.

5. End the particular piece of text by making a new bounding box in another part of the screen to begin a new string of text, or click the Pick tool in the toolbox.

To change the text style and color, click the appropriate button on the text ribbon bar at the top of the screen.

To add a bullet to a string of text, simply select the text with the Pick tool and then click the Bulleted Text button on the ribbon bar.

Troubleshooting

Bulleted lists indent, but do not display bullets when used with light colored text.

This probably is not based on the light color of the text, but on the dark background that light text is generally used with. The bullets are automatically set to be black, so they don't show up against very dark backgrounds.

One solution for this is to place a light-colored rectangle behind the text so that the bullet shows up against it. Another is to import a circle filled with the appropriate color to show up against the background from CorelDRAW! and place copies of it at the beginning of each piece of bulleted text.

I want to change all the text on my slides from one typeface to another.

Using the Pick tool, draw a rectangle around all the text on a slide (a marquee box). When you release the mouse button, the text will have eight handles in a square pattern around it. Select the typeface you want to use from the Font Name pull-down menu on the Text ribbon. All of the text will be changed to the new typeface without changing the size. Don't worry if you also include graphic objects in the marquee because they will not be affected by text commands.

Including Graphic Objects

CorelSHOW can include graphic objects from most OLE/DDE-compliant Windows applications, including CorelDRAW!, CorelPHOTO-PAINT, and Microsoft Graph, to name a few.

The following example specifically shows how to insert a CorelDRAW! graphic into a slide, but the method is essentially the same for any appropriate application.

To add a CorelDRAW! object to a slide, follow these steps:

1. Click the CorelDRAW! icon in the toolbox. CorelDRAW! opens, and you have access to the full range of CorelDRAW! tools.

◀ See "Sharing Drawings—Export, Import, and the Clipboard," p. 268

2. Import a piece of clipart or an existing drawing, or create a graphic from scratch as you normally would in CorelDRAW!.

3. Exit CorelDRAW! by choosing **F**ile, E**x**it and Return to CorelSHOW or Alt+F4. The graphic you just worked with is imported directly into CorelSHOW.

4. If necessary, resize the object by dragging the control handles or move it by dragging the object itself.

If you want to edit an object after placing it in CorelSHOW, double-click it. CorelDRAW! opens and enables you to edit the object using all CorelDRAW!'s formidable features. After completing your edit, exit CorelDRAW! to return to the CorelSHOW editing window with the modified object.

Both objects shown in figure 29.5 are clipart imported from CorelDRAW! using the preceding method.

Fig. 29.5
Clipart can greatly enhance the appearance and ease of creating a slide. Both the graphic objects in this slide are clipart available on the CorelDRAW! CD-ROM and imported using CorelDRAW!.

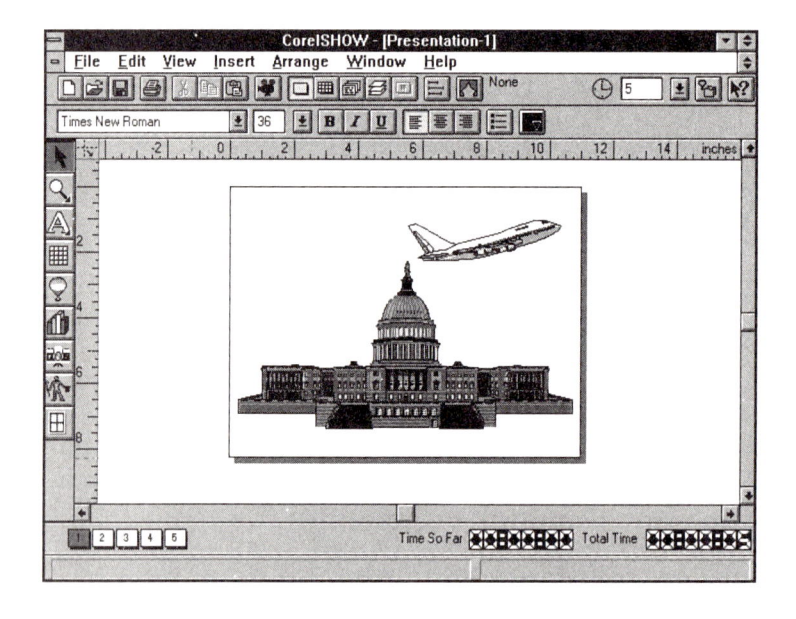

CorelSHOW does not differentiate between CorelDRAW! objects imported at the same time. Although CorelDRAW! may treat a circle and a square individually, CorelSHOW deals with them as one object.

To work with applications that do not have specific icons in the toolbox, follow these steps:

1. Click the OLE To Other Applications tool. The Insert Object dialog box opens (see fig. 29.6).

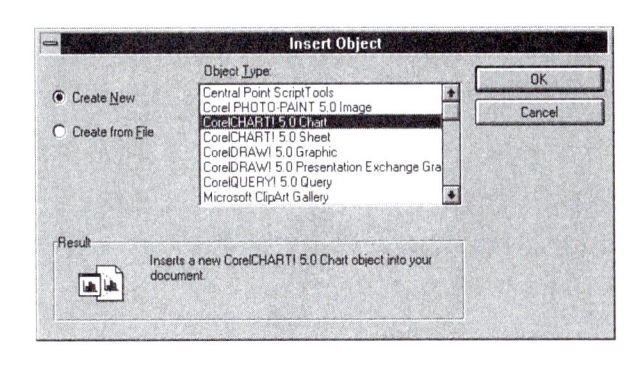

2. Make sure that the Create New button is selected.

3. Select the desired application from the Object **T**ype box.

4. Click OK. The application opens.

5. Edit or import a new graphic or text object and edit it according to the procedures used in that application.

6. When you are finished, exit the application. The object is added to the current slide.

To import an existing graphic file without opening the source application, use these steps:

1. Click the OLE To Other Applications tool. The Insert Object dialog box opens (see fig. 29.6).

Fig. 29.6
Use the Insert Object dialog box to select graphic and text objects to import into CorelCHART.

2. Click the Create From **F**ile button.

3. Click the Browse button. The Browse dialog box opens.

4. Using standard Windows file practices, find the file you want to include in your show.

> **Note**
>
> To link your show to the file you are importing so that changes to the file are automatically incorporated in your presentation, click the **L**ink box in the Insert Object dialog box so that an × appears in it. For more information, see the section "Using OLE with CorelSHOW," later in this chapter.

5. Click OK. The file is included in your show.

> **Troubleshooting**
>
> *I opened CorelDRAW! from SHOW and drew a background. I sized the background exactly to the page in CorelDRAW!, but when I brought it back into SHOW, the size was totally wrong.*
>
> CorelDRAW!'s page setup is determined by the most recent CorelDRAW! file that was edited, not by the SHOW page setup. When you start CorelDRAW!, make sure that you change the page setup.
>
> *I created a new object from a graphic file via the OLE to Other Applications tool, and its source application will not load when I double-click the object.*
>
> When you insert a file, you are not able to load the application directly from CorelSHOW. To edit the graphic object, open the file from the source application, make your changes, and save the file again. If you linked your SHOW to the file, the show will update automatically. If not, you will have to reinsert the graphics file. See the section "Using OLE with CorelSHOW" later in this chapter for more details.

Creating Chart Slides

Charts can quickly convey complex information in a way that makes it seem simple. Effective use of charts is important to a successful presentation. CorelSHOW makes including charts and graphs from CorelCHART an almost effortless task.

> **Note**
>
> In most cases, a chart is the main object of the slide in which it appears. One way to make sure that the chart does not obscure other information on the slide is to use the background as the slide. If you want to do this, click the Background View button in the toolbox and proceed according to the following procedure.

Creating CorelSHOW Presentations **761**

Follow these steps to add a chart to a presentation:

1. Select the slide in which you want to place a chart.

2. Click the OLE to CorelCHART tool. The New dialog box opens.

3. Select the graph category and type and click OK. CorelCHART opens.

4. Create a chart using the standard CorelCHART tools. (For more information, see the section "Creating Presentation Charts with CorelCHART" later in this chapter.)

5. When you are finished, open the **F**ile menu and choose **E**xit & Return to CorelSHOW. The chart is inserted into the current slide.

Organizing the Presentation

To rearrange the order in which slides are presented during your screen show, click the Slide Sorter View button at the top of the screen. A view showing thumbnail images of your slides in their current order appears (see fig. 29.7).

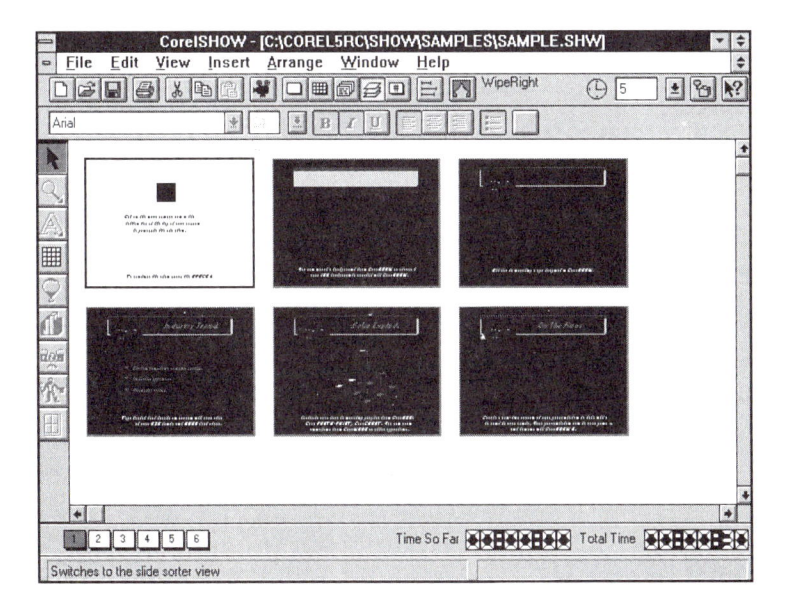

Fig. 29.7
Slide Sorter view provides a quick way to review a slide presentation, as well as make it easy to rearrange the order by simply dragging the slides into position.

To place a slide in a new sequence position, simply drag it to the correct point relative to the other slides. Notice that a vertical bar appears on-screen at the point where the slide is now located.

762 Chapter 29—Making Presentations with CorelSHOW

To rearrange the order of all slides at once, follow these steps:

1. Click the Slide Sorter View button. The Slide Numbering button becomes active (changes from being grayed out to being visible).

2. Click the Slide Numbering button. The prompt No: ??? appears on each slide.

3. Click each slide in the desired presentation order. The ??? changes to a number indicating the sequence.

4. The slides are automatically rearranged after all the slides are picked.

Display and Timing of Slide Object Transition Effects

When creating a show to be presented on the computer screen, you can use a number of *transition effects* that enable you to determine the way the show moves from one slide to the next. In addition, you can choose whether you want the show to proceed from one slide to the next automatically or under interactive control.

Transition Effects

Transition effects include fades, wipes, and other interesting transitions. The opening effect for one slide is the closing effect for the preceding slide.

To apply a transition effect, follow these steps:

1. Select a slide to work with (in either Slide Sorter view or Individual Slide view).

2. Click the Transition Effects button. The Transition Effects dialog box, shown in figure 29.8, appears. Numerous effects are provided; experiment with them to see exactly what each one does.

Fig. 29.8
When presenting a show on the computer screen, you can use transition effects to greatly enhance the visual impact of individual slides by being selective about their use.

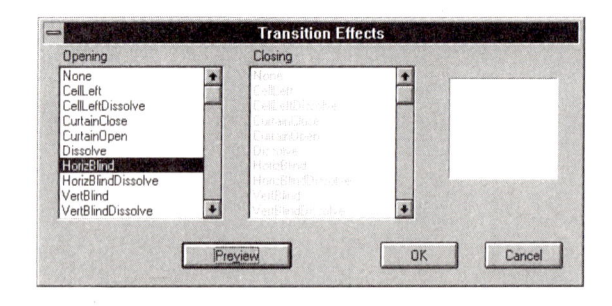

3. Choose an Opening transition effect for your slide from the Opening box. Click Pre**v**iew to see the transition effect in action before applying it to the slides.

4. After making your choice, click OK. Repeat the process for as many slides as necessary.

Transition effects can even be applied to individual objects within a slide. To define transition effects for a particular object contained within a slide, simply select that object and then follow the preceding steps. In either case, the transition effects are applied when your screen show is created. For more information, see the section "Adding Cues and Using the Timeline" later in this chapter.

Automatic versus Manual Advance Mode

When running a presentation on-screen, you can have the slides proceed from one to the next automatically or under interactive control. The timing of events related to a particular slide is determined by the timelines in both modes. For more information, see the section "Adding Cues and Using the Timeline" later in this chapter.

In *Automatic Advance mode*, the slide opens with the defined transition effect (if any), stays on-screen the designated number of seconds, and then closes with the transition effect defined for the opening of the following slide. To set the length of time that you want the slide to appear on-screen, click the Slide Duration box (next to the clock icon toward the right end of the ribbon bar) and set it to the desired number of seconds.

In *Manual Advance mode*, you determine the display duration. Manual Advance mode determines only when the specific slide display starts and stops.

Table 29.1 Manual Advance Mode Keyboard Options

To Move	Press
Forward one slide	Right cursor arrow key Down cursor arrow key PageDown key F10 key Double-click the left mouse button
Backward one slide	Left cursor arrow key Up cursor arrow key PageUp key F5 key Double-click the right mouse button

(continues)

Table 29.1 Continued	
To Move	**Press**
To first slide	Home key
To last slide	End key

> **Troubleshooting**
>
> *I set up my presentation to run in Automatic Advance mode, but I want to run it in Manual Advance mode sometimes.*
>
> When you want to run the presentation in Manual Advance mode, open the **F**ile menu and choose Pre**f**erences to open the Preferences dialog box; then select **M**anual Advance to next slide and press OK. When you want to run in Automatic Advance mode, select **A**utomatic Advance to next slide from the Preferences dialog box.

Working with Backgrounds

The overall graphic design, set behind the text and any other graphic elements in a slide, is the *background*. Information about the background appears on each slide of the presentation unless you specifically choose to omit it. This feature helps to give overall consistency to your presentation.

> **Note**
>
> Do not modify the standard backgrounds that come with CorelSHOW until you have worked with the program for a while. It takes some practice to determine which backgrounds are effective and which are too confusing.

To add a common background to a show, perform the following steps:

1. Click the Background Library Access tool. The Background Library dialog box opens. Move to the \Corel50\SHOW\backgrounds directory to show a library of CorelSHOW background files. Click a file name and click to turn on the Preview Option to see the file in thumbnail format (see fig. 29.9).

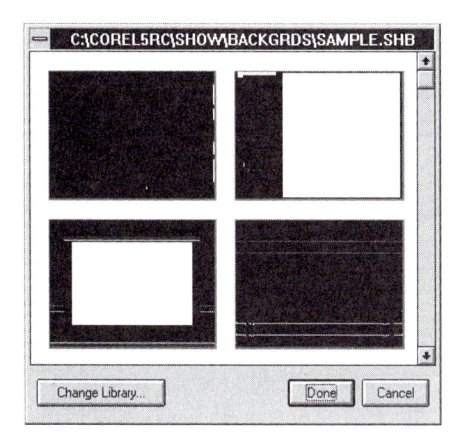

Fig. 29.9
CorelSHOW comes with a large number of ready-made backgrounds that can be incorporated into your presentation. The Background Library dialog box provides access to collections of backgrounds, both those included with CorelSHOW and ones you create yourself.

2. Double-click the desired background file (or select it and then click OK) to add it to the show.

3. In the library dialog box, click the background to add to the current slide, and then click Done to close the dialog box.

To view another library, click the Change Library button and then select the appropriate directory and library file.

To add a specific background to a particular slide, follow these steps:

1. Click the Slide Number button at the bottom of the screen to select the appropriate slide.

2. Click the clear open area outside the slide with the secondary mouse button to open the pop-up menu (see fig. 29.10).

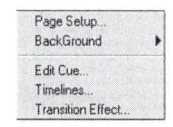

Fig. 29.10
The pop-up menu provides direct access to many commands based on the object that is selected.

3. Click Background and then choose Independent. If there was a common background, it disappears from that slide.

4. Select a background as outlined in the preceding set of steps. It appears only in this particular slide.

Perform the following steps to turn off the background for a particular slide:

1. Click the Slide Number button at the bottom of the screen to select the appropriate slide.

2. Click the clear open area outside the slide with the secondary mouse button to open the pop-up menu (refer to fig. 29.10).

3. Click Background and then choose Omit. The background disappears from the slide.

4. To turn the background back on for a particular slide, activate the slide; open the pop-up menu and choose Background; then choose Omit once again.

To create a custom background, follow these steps:

1. Click the Background Edit View button on the tool bar at the left side of the screen.

2. Click the OLE to CorelDRAW! icon on the toolbox at the left side of the screen. CorelDRAW! opens, and you have access to the full range of CorelDRAW! tools.

> **Note**
>
> To work with applications that do not have specific icons on the ribbon bar, click the OLE To Other Applications tool in the toolbox and make sure that the Create New button is selected. Select the appropriate application from the list in the dialog box and click OK.

Tip
You can create very effective backgrounds by creating a rectangle the size of the slide and filling it with a fountain fill, texture, or bitmap.

3. Import a piece of clipart, edit an existing drawing, or create a graphic from scratch as you normally would in CorelDRAW!.

4. Choose **F**ile Exit and return to CorelSHOW. The graphic you just worked with is imported directly into CorelSHOW (see fig. 29.11).

5. If necessary, resize the object by dragging the control handles, or move it by dragging the object itself. After you return to Individual Slide view, you can no longer edit the background (without returning to Background Edit view once again).

You also can use images in the CorelDRAW! clipart directory for your backgrounds. Use the extensive drawing capability (and the ready-made resources) of CorelDRAW! to make the presentation backgrounds and other objects look professional and attractive.

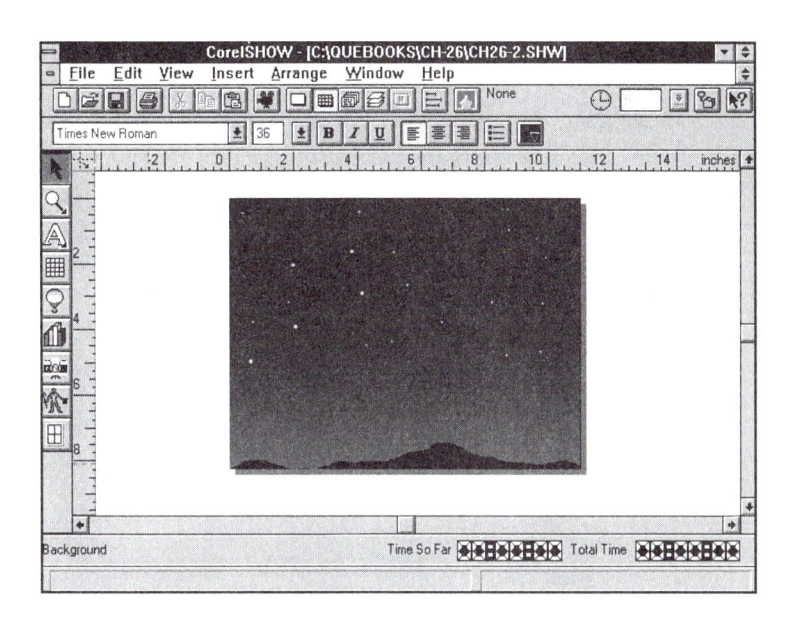

Fig. 29.11
This background was created in CorelPHOTO-PAINT; then brought into CorelSHOW as a TIFF format file and resized to match the current presentation page size.

Using OLE with CorelSHOW

Much of the power associated with CorelSHOW comes from the Windows *Object Linking and Embedding (OLE)* feature. CorelSHOW has very little object creation capability in and of itself, but it provides tremendous flexibility for displaying objects created in other applications.

Applications that create objects for use in CorelSHOW are called *source* applications; CorelSHOW is the *destination* application for those objects. Similarly, the original file created by the source application is called the *source file,* and the presentation file in CorelSHOW is called the *destination file.*

After an object is transferred to a destination file, it can be embedded so that the destination file retains a record of the source application and file name. Double-clicking the object in the destination file then automatically opens the source application, loads the source file, and enables you to edit the file or object within the source application. After you finish editing, the image of the object within the destination file is updated to reflect the most current changes. If you do not want the changes you made included in your show, click No when you're asked by the Windows dialog box.

Object linking sets up a path between the source object and the destination object so that any time the source object is modified, the destination object is updated automatically. Linking makes life much easier when the underlying objects are going through substantial revision. Embedding ensures that you always have access to the original application so that object modifications are possible.

One critical thing to remember about links: *files should not be moved around after they are linked*. Doing so breaks the link because the computer has no way to recognize the change of locations and can no longer make the connection between the source and destination files and applications.

Saving and Retrieving a Presentation or Background

You save a presentation just as you would save any Windows application file—by opening the **F**ile menu and choosing **S**ave or Save **A**s. The Save option works just as it does in other Windows applications.

A few special options appear, however, when you use the Save As option in CorelSHOW (see fig. 29.12). Most of the features of the Save Presentation As dialog box should be familiar by this point, with the exception of the following options unique to CorelSHOW:

Fig. 29.12
The Save Presentation As dialog box contains a number of options that enable you to customize a saved presentation in addition to the standard Windows options for name and location.

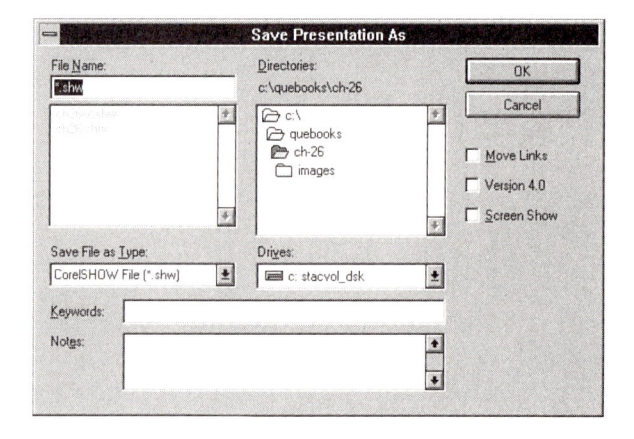

Tip
Files saved in Screen Show Only format cannot be edited. Make sure that you save your presentation file in CorelSHOW (SHW) format before saving it as a Screen Show Only file.

- Because you are saving the file under a different name and possibly to another directory, the OLE/DDE links must be updated for the new file. To update the location of all linked files relative to the file you are saving so that linked objects still appear in the new presentation, choose the **M**ove Links option.

- To save your file in a CorelSHOW 4-compatible format for use by someone who does not have the latest version of the CorelSHOW, select the Vers**i**on 4.0 option.

- To create a stand-alone presentation by saving to a file format that can be used in conjunction with CORELPLR.EXE, choose the Screen Show Only option. (For more information, see the section "Running a Stand-Alone Screen Show" later in this chapter.)

To save the background for use with other presentations, open the **F**ile menu and choose Save **B**ackground. This command enables you to save the background file as a stand-alone file or to include it in the background library (choose Insert In **L**ibrary) for easier access with less disk storage space required. If you save to the background library, your background appears as one of the options when you click the Background Library Access tool in the toolbox.

Presenting Your Work

CorelSHOW creates a screen show from the slides contained in the currently active file. The recommended procedure for creating a screen show involves the following steps:

1. Design the slides.

2. Place them in the desired presentation order using Slide Sorter view.

3. Open the **F**ile menu and choose Pre**f**erences; then set the desired options within the dialog box that appears (see fig. 29.13).

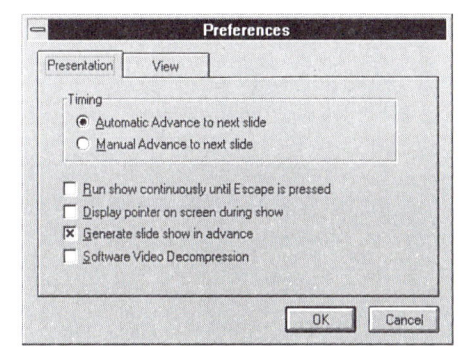

Fig. 29.13
Running a presentation directly from CorelSHOW is fairly straightforward. The dialog box shown in this figure contains all the options necessary to make the show display the way you want.

The Run Show Continuously Until Escape Is Pressed option simply loops the show back to the beginning when the final slide is reached. The Display Pointer On Screen During Show option makes the pointer accessible during the show so that you can use it to address portions of the screen. The Generate Slide Show In Advance option instructs CorelSHOW to process the entire show before displaying it, which is advisable when displaying on a slower system in which processing power is limited and creating each slide as it is displayed may cause flickering or slow transitions.

4. After choosing your presentation options, save the presentation.

5. Click the Screen show Preview button. CorelSHOW assembles the screen show, and then asks if you want to see it. Click OK to watch your work come alive.

You can stop the presentation by pressing Esc, whether you are in Automatic or Manual Advance mode.

You can also have 35mm slides and/or overhead transparencies made of your CorelSHOW presentation. If you will not be showing your presentation on a computer screen, don't add animations, sounds, or transition effects because these cannot be translated to slides or tranparencies. See Chapter 35, "Painless and Powerful Slide Production," for more information.

Adding Sound

You can add sound to your presentation just as you add any other object type. Follow these steps to do so:

1. Select the slide to which you want to add the sound object.

2. Open the **I**nsert menu and choose **S**ound. The Insert Sound dialog box opens.

3. Select the sound object you want to insert. Click the Play button to preview the sound before including it in the presentation.

   If Embed is checked, the object is embedded in the presentation, which allows ready access to the application that originally created it if sound editing is desired. Disable Embed if you want to add the sound in nonembedded mode.

4. To make your final choice, double-click the desired sound object, or click OK when it is highlighted.

The sound object is added to the CorelSHOW timeline associated with this particular slide. As of this writing, only WAV file formats are accessible and supported. You must have a sound card installed with the proper Windows compatible drivers for the WAV files to play properly.

Adding Animation

Animation can be included in a presentation to add extra dash. You can choose from CorelMOVE, Autodesk Animator, or QuickTime for Windows animation files.

▶ See "Adding Animation with CorelMOVE," p. 779

To add animation to a presentation, follow these steps:

1. Select the slide in which you want the animation to begin.

2. Click the Insert Animation Tool in the toolbox. The Insert Animation dialog box opens (see fig. 29.14).

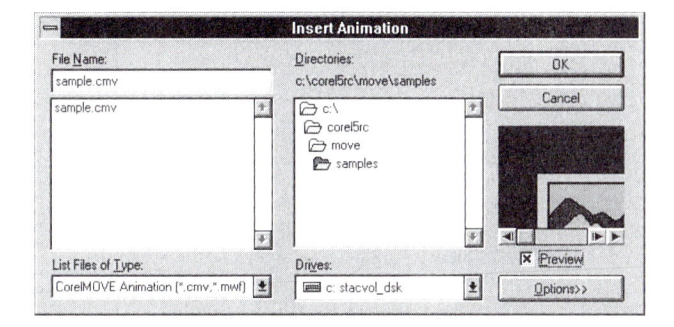

Fig. 29.14
Animation can add an extra spark to a presentation. The Insert Animation dialog box enables you to pick a specific animation to use as well as set options for how that animation displays in your presentation.

3. Select the animation file you want to include by using standard Windows file loading techniques.

4. For additional control over the display of the animation, click the **O**ptions button.

   To repeat the animation indefinitely, choose Repeat **F**orever. To repeat the animation a specified number of times set the number next to **R**epeat. To display the last frame of the animation until the slide is advanced to the next one, choose **H**old after Last Frame.

   You can specify the speed of playback as a percent of the normal frame per second speed.

   Choose N**a**tural Size or F**u**ll Screen, depending on which size you want to set the animation.

5. Click OK after you choose the appropriate file and set the options that you want.

6. After the animation is on-screen, move its location by dragging the box that outlines the animation.

Adding Cues and Using the Timelines

The overall timing of a presentation is recorded graphically on *timelines*. The Timelines chart shows the relationship between the various slides used, including when they open and close, what objects each slide contains, and the transition effects applied to each. To view or edit the timelines, click the Timelines button on the ribbon bar. The window shown in figure 29.15 appears.

Fig. 29.15
Timelines enable you to control when and how slides and the individual objects within them are presented during the course of your show.

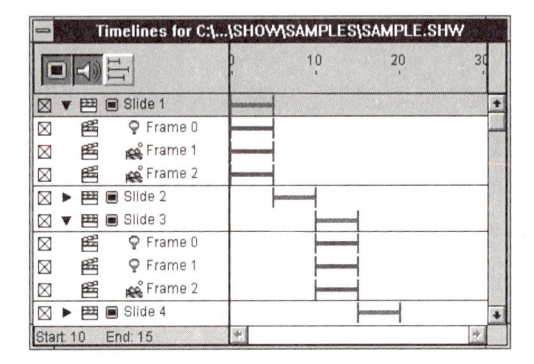

To open a slide sooner, drag the left side of the appropriate timeline. To make a slide stay on-screen longer, drag the right side of the timeline. You can move an entire slide by grabbing the timeline in the center and dragging it left or right. The duration time of the slide on-screen cannot be shorter than the duration time of its underlying objects.

To view the underlying slide objects, click the black triangle to the left of the appropriate slide. Notice that a timeline list of the objects is displayed. Like the overall slide, these objects are adjusted by dragging the endpoints around on the lines so that, for example, you can have a graphic appear on-screen three seconds after the slide opens, giving you time to describe what is going to happen. As you move the slide timings around, notice that the overall presentation timing also changes. Manual or Automatic Advance mode determines when a slide transition occurs, but the timing of events in the slide is determined by the timeline's relationship for that particular slide.

▶ See "Adding and Editing Cues," p. 802

Cues can be included with a slide. A cue is an action that takes place when a certain set of conditions exists, such as the user clicking a tool to move the presentation in a different logical direction. The slate (a movie clapper) on each line of the timeline indicates whether a cue has been set for that line. If the slate is open, no special cues are included with a slide. If the slate is closed, a special set of cue conditions exists for that particular slide. The logical cue procedure used with CorelSHOW is identical to that used in CorelMOVE.

The interesting thing about cues is that they allow for viewer interaction with the presentation. Based upon a user selection such as clicking an icon, a cue can display another slide, play a sound object, or display an animation. The cues make the show more personalized, and you should get to fully understand their capability after you become familiar with the other, more conventional CorelSHOW functions.

Troubleshooting

I would like to view a frame on for just an instant, but it won't display for any less than one second.

The smallest unit of measurement on the timeline is one second. You cannot specify a slice of time any smaller than that.

A section of music that has been inserted in a frame cuts off at a weird point and I can't adjust the timeline closely enough to make the ending of the music sound pleasant.

Open the file in Sound Recorder, the sound editing program that comes with Windows. Cut some of the music from the file to give it a pleasing ending and save it. If you linked the presentation to the sound file, the change will be automatic. If you did not link it, delete the original sound and load the newly altered sound file.

An animation is too short in length to fill the duration of a slide, so the screen just goes blank when it is finished.

Either set the playback speed to a lower percentage of the normal frame rate, repeat the animation, or have the animation hold on the final frame. The options must be set when the animation is first being inserted.

Running a Stand-Alone Screen Show

After you finish your presentation, you might want to distribute it for display on computers running Windows 3.0 or higher without CorelSHOW loaded. This is often the case with canned sales presentations in which the sales rep has access to a computer, but not to CorelSHOW. The *stand-alone* screen show option provides a solution to this problem.

To prepare your stand-alone screen show, follow these steps:

1. Open the **F**ile menu and choose Save **A**s (see the section "Saving and Retrieving a Presentation or Background," earlier in this chapter.

2. In the dialog box, choose **S**creen Show and enter the file name, drive letter, and directory name.

Tip

Save your presentation as a standard CorelSHOW file before saving it as a stand-alone screen show. Then it can be available for later editing.

Tip

If your CorelSHOW file is small enough, save it to a floppy disk for easy transportation. If it is not small enough, save it to the hard drive and use a compression program such as PKZIP to make it fit on a floppy disk.

Tip

You may want to create a temporary directory on the hard disk to make it is easier to delete CORELPLR.EXE and the data file when you are through.

Fig. 29.16

CorelSHOW PLAYER allows a presentation to run on any computer running Windows 3.0 or higher.

3. Copy the CORELPLR.EXE file from the COREL\PROGRAMS subdirectory to a floppy disk that can be inserted into the target computer.

4. On-site, copy CORELPLR.EXE and the screen show to the hard disk of the target computer.

5. If you compressed the CorelSHOW data file, load it on the hard drive and decompress it.

Perform the following steps to run your show:

1. Start Windows 3.0 or higher.

2. Start the CORELPLR.EXE application using any of the standard Windows techniques (choose the Run option in the File menu from within Program Manager, or double-click CORELPLR.EXE from within File Manager). The CorelSHOW PLAYER dialog box opens (see fig. 29.16).

3. Select the CorelSHOW file and set the options as applicable. The options include: Advance Slides Manually, Play Continuously until 'ESC', Display Pointer on Screen, and Software Video Decompression.

4. Click Play to begin the presentation.

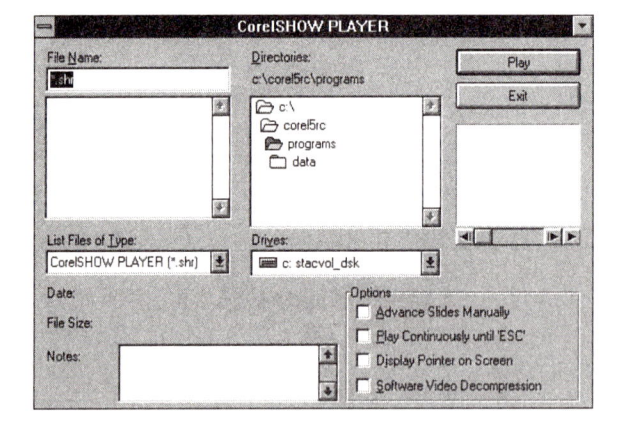

The target computer must have the proper hardware to support the presentation objects included. If the computer does not have a sound card, for example, it cannot play the sound parts of your presentation. In addition, the presentation may play at different rates on different computers due to RAM and processor limitations.

> **Troubleshooting**
>
> *Animations included in shows do not play when the file is saved in Screen Show Only format.*
>
> When animations are used in conjunction with CORELPLR.EXE, the program that created the animation (CorelMOVE, Autodesk Animator, and so on) must be installed on the computer running the show.

Printing Speaker Notes and Audience Handouts

Many times a presentation is not a complete entity in and of itself. A speaker often narrates each slide, expanding on the information given in the graphics and text. CorelSHOW has a simple method of compiling notes for the speaker by providing the Speaker Notes view, which has a thumbnail of each slide with space for adding the additional information needed. These notes can be printed out for use by the speaker and also provide a quick way to create audience handouts for future reference.

To create speaker notes, perform these steps:

1. Click the Speaker Notes View button on the ribbon bar. The display changes to show a thumbnail view of the current slide with a large border (see fig. 29.17).

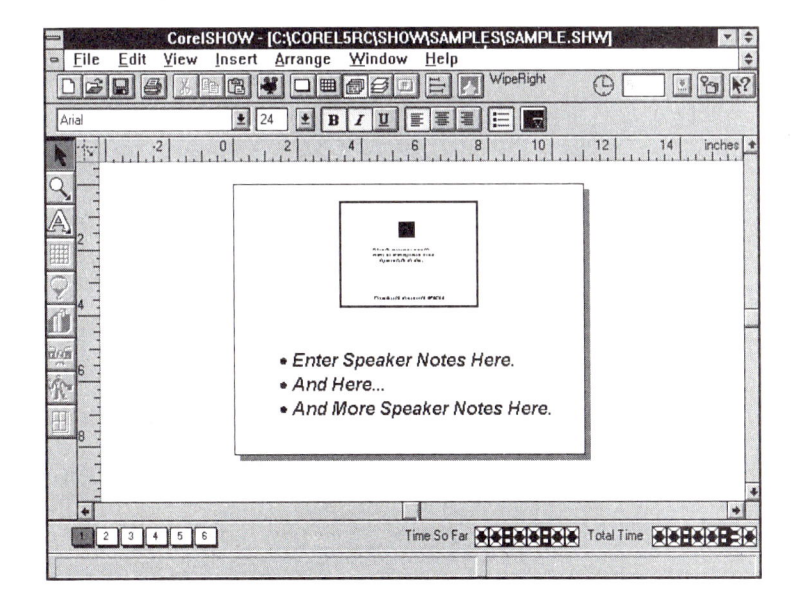

Fig. 29.17 Speaker notes added in Speaker Notes view make it easy to narrate a presentation and provide an excellent way to create audience handouts for later review.

2. Add text in any area outside the thumbnail of the slide using the techniques outlined earlier in this chapter.

3. Navigate through the presentation using the Slide Selection buttons at the bottom of the screen.

4. Return to the standard slide view by clicking the Slide View button on the ribbon bar.

Tip
Speaker notes are an excellent place to add information about cues and the way to run the presentation.

To print the speaker notes, enter Speaker Notes view and print as usual.

From Here...

Ultimately, the images and text that you create must be printed or displayed; SHOW provides a way for you to do that with flair. This chapter discussed the role that SHOW plays as a central clearinghouse for the other Corel applications.

This chapter covered the basics of effective presentation design, the use of OLE/DDE for adding text and graphic objects, various methods of displaying the presentation, and how to create a stand-alone presentation.

■ Chapter 30, "Adding Animation Using CorelMOVE," discusses how to gain attention during a presentation by adding movement. The tools explained in this chapter enable you to create sophisticated animations for use by themselves or as part of a complete presentation.

Chapter 30
Adding Animation with CorelMOVE

by Ed Paulson

CorelMOVE unleashes the power of the Corel application group. By using this program, you can add movement to objects so that the graphics you create in CorelDRAW! can communicate to the viewer through action and sound. The concepts associated with animation are a little foreign and the jargon is new, but the excitement this program generates is hard to describe.

The addition of morphing, which is essentially a bitmap version of the CorelDRAW! blend feature, adds another level of challenge to the imagination.

The complex process of creating animation requires prior planning. This chapter introduces you to the basic operational principles behind CorelMOVE and shows you how to use CorelDRAW! to simplify the tedious yet rewarding task of creating animation.

A picture may tell a thousand stories, but animation gives the story a life of its own. Animation is typically used in formal presentations in which the presentation introduces itself with animated characters talking with a sound overlay. Animation is useful for kiosk-type applications, such as self-guided information booths common in airports and railroad stations. Users select a series of screen icons, and an animated character takes them to their destination. Animation also is commonly used as a teaching tool for computer-based training. Regardless of the application, animation adds life to a presentation and provides a challenging development tool to the animation designer.

In this chapter, you learn the following:

- How to give life to your previously created CorelDRAW! and CorelPHOTO-PAINT images through animation
- How to add objects that move and objects that remain in one place
- Methods for moving your images on and off the screen with flair using the transition effects
- Detailed information about relative object timing
- How to add sound to the animation
- How to use Cues to guide the presentation based on viewer input

Understanding CorelMOVE's Basic Concepts

Animations are essentially relationships between objects and paths of action that happen over a predefined time. Animation objects fall into three basic categories: actors, props, and sound. *Actors* are objects that change location during the movie. As they change location, a new actor image appears that differs slightly from the others. These images are called *cels*, or frames, and provide the illusion of movement when played rapidly in sequence. Actors are either single cel or multicel. Single cel actors retain the same shape during their acting progression. Multicel actors change shape from one cel to another. *Props* are objects that remain stationary during the movie presentation, although they may appear or disappear during the movie. *Sound* objects are in the WAV file format that you can add to the movie timeline, which is CorelMOVE's visually oriented method for precisely arranging object timing. Sound adds a lot to the presentation, so you should consider adding sound to your animations when possible.

What Is CorelMOVE?

CorelMOVE is the application designed to create animation movies. It enables you to create and edit actors and props and provides a convenient mechanism for establishing the relationship between various objects. Suppose, for example, that you want to create an animation about a magician, and you want the magician to make things appear and disappear. The timeline enables you to define the precise time at which a prop appears and disappears. The animated magician actor can snap his fingers and make a hat or other prop disappear. The timeline also enables you to determine what the hat looks like as it appears and disappears. You can add music and sound effects to the animation for added drama. CorelMOVE provides the mechanism through which object creation, movement, and integration occur.

An Overview of the Animation Process

Animation, in its most basic form, is a backdrop against which actor objects are superimposed and moved. The backdrop can be any static object related to your animation—a pasture, a mountain, or the surface of the moon. The backdrop is generally displayed for the duration of the movie and is one form of prop; it may actually be composed of many props.

The actors move across the stage of the animation in a series of steps. Each step advances the actor in the desired direction. You can specify a different actor design for each step (multicel), or you can have the actor remain the same shape from step to step (single cel).

The sun moving across the screen, for example, is an actor with a shape that does not change and, consequently, requires only one cel to display properly. In this case, the actor is a single-cel actor following a path across the screen. The same cel is displayed at each point of the actor's action path.

It also is possible to specify a different actor shape for each step along the action path, which adds life-like attributes to actor objects. You can give a bird different wing shapes in each cel, for example, to give a more life-like illusion of a bird flapping its wings as it moves along its path. Each cel appears at node points designated along the movement path. Each node causes a change to the next cel of the animation for that particular actor, and the combination of subsequently played cels and the action path provides the desired level of animation to the actor.

Tip
Cels are called *frames* when editing an actor in CorelDRAW!.

After specifying the objects, they are automatically or manually arranged along a timeline that sets the timing relationship among them during the movie's course. Prop objects move on and off the screen with specified transition effects, actor objects interact as they move around, and sound objects play as defined on the timeline.

Starting, Saving, and Retrieving a Movie

The animation procedure is useless unless you know how to start CorelMOVE and how to save and retrieve the work you create. This section outlines these basic procedures.

To start CorelMOVE, double-click the CorelMOVE icon located in the Corel program application group. When CorelMOVE starts, the screen appears empty except for a few items on the menu bar. From this blank screen, you can start a new animation or open an existing animation for editing. The names of the last four edited CorelMOVE files are displayed at the bottom of the File menu.

Retrieving a Movie

After creating an animated movie, you may want to make changes, such as changing your magician's bird from a dove to an eagle. A movie must first be retrieved before it can be edited.

To open an animation, open the **F**ile menu and choose **O**pen (Ctrl+O). It is possible to open CorelMOVE (CMV) files or ProMotion (MWF) files by changing the file type selection that appears beneath the listing of file names. Selecting the proper directory and file name and then clicking OK opens the desired animation file. The CorelMOVE screen shown in figure 30.1 appears.

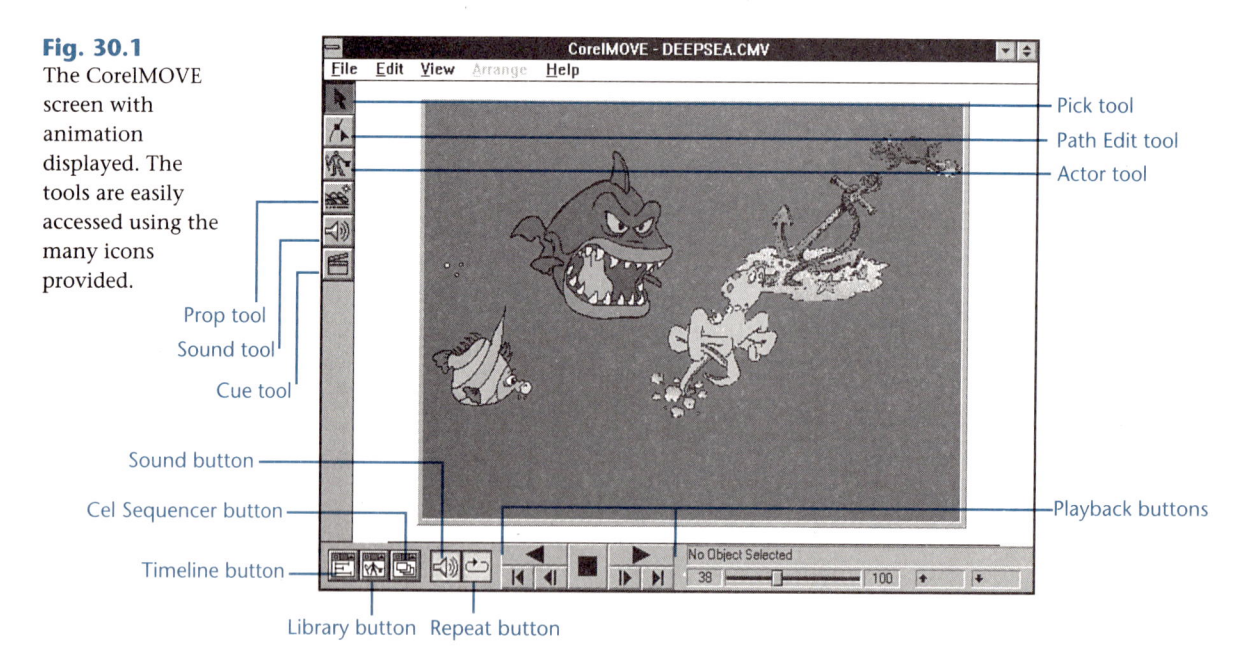

Fig. 30.1
The CorelMOVE screen with animation displayed. The tools are easily accessed using the many icons provided.

Table 30.1 explains how to use the tools along the left margin of the CorelMOVE screen.

Table 30.1	CorelMOVE Tools
Tool	Use
Pick tool	Selects objects.
Path tool	Creates and edits actor paths.
Actor tool	Creates and edits actors.
Prop tool	Creates and edits props.
Sound tool	Creates and edits sound objects.
Cue tool	Adds and edits the insertion of events, or cues, to the timeline. A typical event is the display and removal of an object, the start and finish of an actor's actions, and the start or finish of a sound cue.

The center of the screen contains the editing area in which you design the animation. Object placement and path definition happen in this screen.

Along the bottom of the screen are various other buttons, controls used to play or rewind the animation, and information about selected objects. Clicking the Timeline button reveals the relationship among objects in the current animation (see fig. 30.2). The Timeline window is discussed in detail in the section, "Viewing and Editing Animation Timing," later in this chapter.

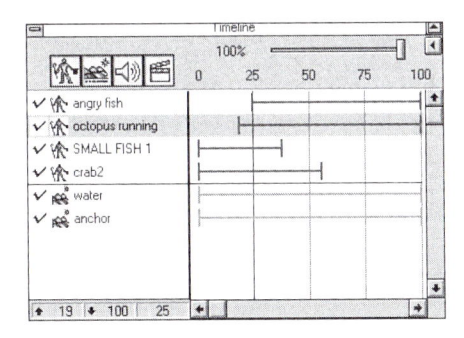

Fig. 30.2
The Timeline roll-up window expanded to display the entire timeline.

Starting a New Movie

Choosing **N**ew (Ctrl+N) from the **F**ile menu displays the Select Name For New File dialog box (see fig. 30.3).

Fig. 30.3
Naming a new animation file when first creating animations from scratch.

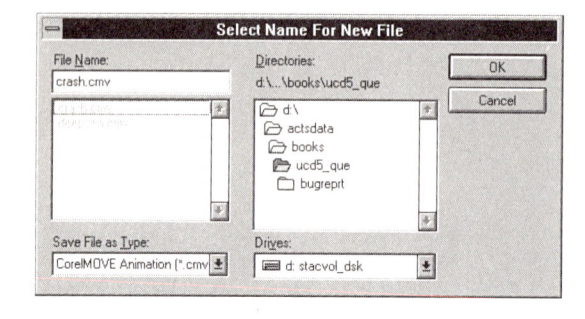

> **Tip**
> Avoid reinventing the wheel by using previously created animation props and actors in new projects. Either open an existing animation and use Save As in the File menu to store under the new name, or insert the new objects as needed.

Until a name is entered for the animation, the file name is UNTITLED.CMV. (The CMV extension indicates a CorelMOVE file.) Enter a file name, drive, and directory location, and click OK to save a spot for the animation where you specified. Now every time the movie is saved, which you should do frequently to avoid information loss, CorelMOVE stores the most recently edited animation file in the specified disk location. Note that this procedure is the same as in CorelDRAW!.

Saving a Movie

Save your animations by choosing File Save (Ctrl+S). CorelMOVE stores the animation in the drive and directory location you specified during the File New procedure. The File Save As command is more limited in CorelMOVE as compared to other applications because files can be saved only in CMV format. Save As is generally used to save the currently active animation under another name.

Setting the Animation Window Size and Playback Attributes

You should set the animation window size at the beginning of the animation process because the size of the window determines the amount of room available for props and actors. The default window size is 480-by-360 pixels (screen dots). Other standard sizes are 320-by-200 and 640-by-480 pixels. The smaller the window size, the less overall system demand it places on the computer, and the smoother the animation appears.

> **Note**
>
> Creating the animation at a 480-by-360 size, and then viewing it on a 1024-by-768 display shrinks the image substantially. Create the image at the same size as the intended viewing screen resolution to avoid later complications and surprises.

You set the animation window size by opening the Edit menu and choosing Animation Info (Ctrl+A). The Animation Information dialog box appears (see fig. 30.4).

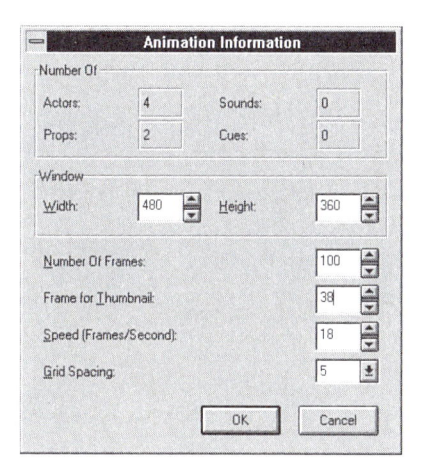

Fig. 30.4
Overall animation settings are displayed in the Animation Information dialog box.

The number of actor objects, prop objects, sound objects, and cues included in the current animation appear at the top of the window. Below this area are the boxes you use to enter the width and height, in pixels, of the animation window. Set the dimensions to the sizes mentioned previously in this section until you are familiar with CorelMOVE's operational constraints.

The bottom portion of the Animation Information dialog box includes the Number Of Frames option, which determines the total number of frames in the animation. The default value is 100, but the animation can be any length from 1 to 9,999 frames. Enter the frame number that best represents the contents of the animation into this box. The frame number appears at the bottom of the screen when viewing the animation in the editing window. The Frame for Thumbnail option sets the desired animation frame to display as the thumbnail (rough bitmap) image used in preview operations in MOSAIC and other Corel applications.

> **Note**
>
> The animation length can always be changed later using the Animation Info dialog box, but the timing of all objects and actors will change. Make sure that the overall frame length is firmly established before starting, to save yourself substantial rework at a later date.

The Speed (Frames/Second) option determines the speed of the animation. The higher the setting, the faster the animation progresses. The speed range extends from 1 to 18 frames per second, and the actual playback speed depends on the processor type, complexity of animation, hard disk access time, and amount of RAM memory.

> **Note**
>
> Dividing total frames by frames per second gives the time of the animation. Playing 100 frames at 10 frames per second yields a 10-second animation. Fifteen to 18 frames per second provides adequate speed to make the actor's movements appear reasonably smooth.

The Grid Spacing option determines the precise screen pattern along which objects and nodes are placed. If set to OFF, no grid is applied and objects can be placed anywhere. The grid is best used when structured alignment is desired, but can be aggravating to work with in more artistic animations because it constrains possible actor and prop locations to grid coordinates. The other grid pop-up menu settings determine the number of pixels used for grid intersection definition. Objects are automatically moved to the grid intersection point when added to the animation.

Clicking OK establishes these settings for the current animation.

Creating Props and Single-Cel Actors

You can create props and actors in CorelMOVE using the Paint window. (Don't confuse the Paint window with the CorelPHOTO-PAINT application.) Or you can create the objects in another drawing application—such as CorelDRAW!—and transfer the object to CorelMOVE. In this section, you learn how to create a prop or actor, and then you move on to applying painting techniques for special effects.

Creating a New Prop or Actor

Props are stationary objects that appear and disappear on the screen. They do not move while on-screen. The basic object creation process is as follows:

1. Click the Prop or Actor tool to indicate your intention to create a new actor or prop object.

2. Select the application in which the object creation is to occur (that is, CorelDRAW!, CorelMOVE, CorelPHOTO-PAINT, and so on).

3. Create the object and add it to the animation.

4. Set the entry, exit, and total framing information pertaining to the actor or prop object using the Edit menu's Object Info option. Actors and props have different options provided.

5. Position the props and actors, and then add motion to the actors.

This overall process is generally the same with modifications as needed for specific prop or actor object attributes.

To begin the process of creating a prop, choose the Prop tool from the toolbox or open the Edit menu and select Prop from the Insert Object options. The New Prop dialog box appears (see fig. 30.5).

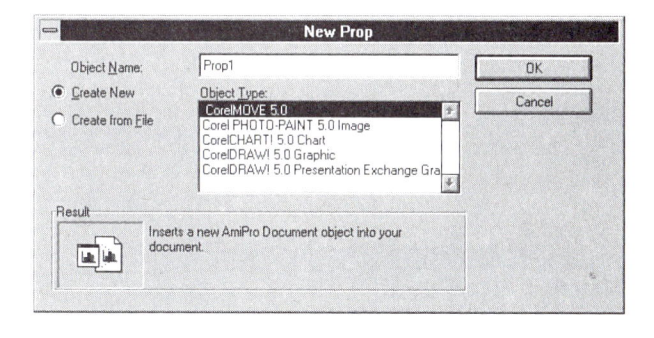

Fig. 30.5
The New Prop dialog box indicates the desired prop name and available prop creation applications.

To name the prop or actor object you want to add to your animation, use the Object Name box located at the top of the New Prop dialog box. Always use a unique name to prevent the object from being confused later with other objects you create.

Tip
Give each object a name that you will understand so that you will know which object to select when working later in the timelines display. Otherwise, CorelMOVE assigns names like Prop1, Prop2, and so on, which aren't very helpful.

The options available in the Object Type list box refer to the application you intend to use for creating the prop object. All OLE-compatible applications are listed.

The MOVE option uses the bitmap-oriented Paint utility included with CorelMOVE. CorelDRAW! Graphic instructs CorelMOVE to open CorelDRAW! so that you can edit in CorelDRAW! using its more sophisticated tools. CorelPHOTO-PAINT Picture refers to a bitmap obtained from the PHOTO-PAINT application. All objects are converted into CorelMOVE-compatible format before they can be used in CorelMOVE.

Choose Create New if you want to create a new object after you open the application. Choose Create from File if you want to use an already existing image in the designated Object Type format.

After you use the CorelMOVE Paint facility to draw the object, choose File Exit and follow the instructions to save the prop object under its designated name; then add it to the current animation.

To create a new actor, you follow an almost identical procedure except you begin by choosing the Actor tool rather than the Prop tool. The New Actor dialog box appears. It operates identically to the New Prop dialog box. The Paint-related editing operations for single-cel actors are the same as for props. Working with multicel actors is a little more complicated. You learn more about that topic after you learn about the basic operation of the Paint facility. See the section, "Using the CorelMOVE Paint Facility," later in this chapter.

You can examine detailed object information by double-clicking the object, or after selecting the object, choosing Edit Object Info. The Object Information dialog box appears (see fig. 30.6).

Fig. 30.6
The Actor Information dialog box shows the number of frames, entry and exit information, object name, and path information.

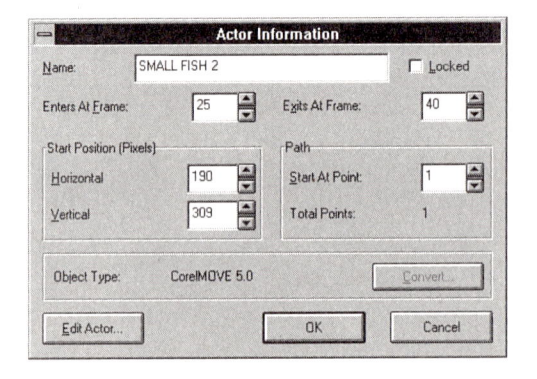

The Prop Information dialog box displays the prop's name, the enter and exit frame numbers, pixel location relative to the upper-left corner (which is 0,0), and the type of prop object as determined by the application used to create the object. You can edit any of these items. Choosing Locked, which is located in the upper-right corner of the dialog box, fixes the prop's screen position, preventing you from dragging the prop around the window by using the mouse.

CorelMOVE provides several transition effects to control the style with which an object enters and exits the screen. These effects appear in the Transitions for Prop dialog box (see fig. 30.7), and you can edit them by clicking the Edit button contained within the Prop Information dialog box. Selecting the desired transition type for Enter and Exit, and then choosing Preview, enables you to view the effect of your transition choice on that particular object.

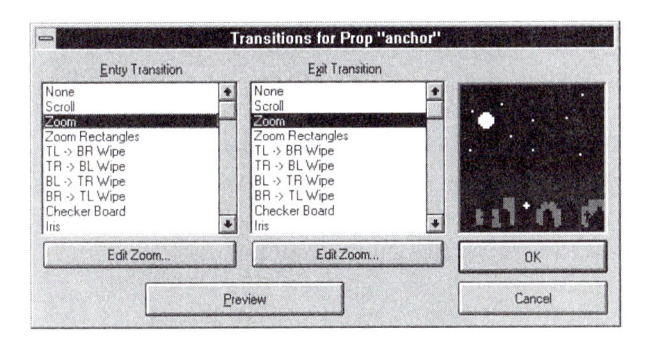

Fig. 30.7
The Transitions for Prop dialog box.

One of the easiest, yet effective, ways to add life to your props is to use the Zoom transition. It causes the object to appear at a reduced size at a specific point on the screen, and then increase in size over a number of steps until it is at the desired screen location and at the desired size. Select the Zoom transition effect, and then click on Edit Zoom. The EditZoom dialog box appears (see fig. 30.8).

The Prop Origin setting determines where the prop enters the screen on its way to appearing in its final position. You set this point by directly entering pixel numbers into the Horizontal and Vertical entry boxes, or by dragging the cross hairs on the thumbnail with the mouse to the desired entry position. The Horizontal and Vertical settings adjust accordingly. The Steps setting does not correlate to a certain number of frames, but is an arbitrary number that determines how long the animation playback is stopped while the prop entry steps are executed. You should take this playback interruption into account when designing your animation, or unwanted temporary stoppages will occur.

Fig. 30.8
The EditZoom transition editing dialog box.

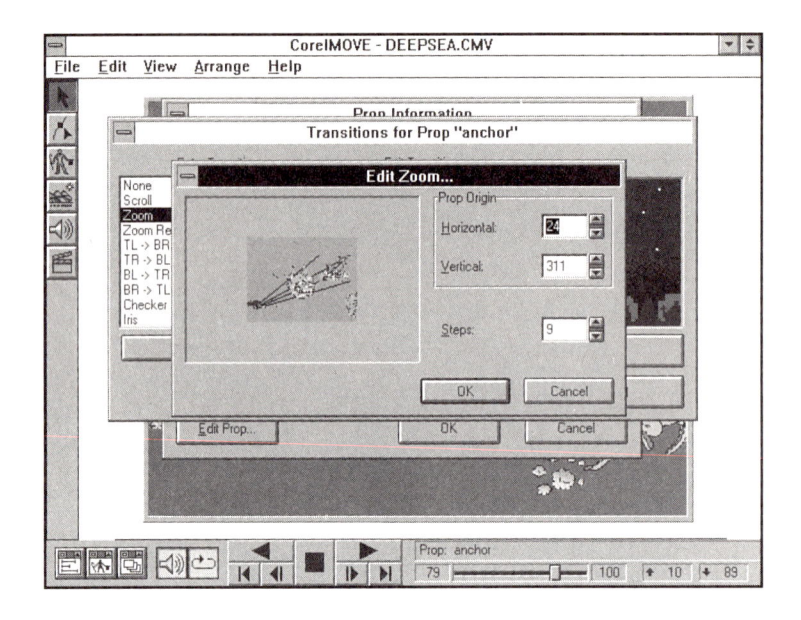

Using the CorelMOVE Paint Facility

Drawing objects using CorelDRAW! is covered later in the chapter. For now, assume that you are going to create a new prop object using the CorelMOVE Paint facility. Follow these steps to create a new object:

1. Click the Prop tool to display the New Prop dialog box.
2. In the dialog box, choose CorelMOVE 5.0 from the Object Type list box.
3. Choose Create New.
4. Click OK.

The Paint window shown in figure 30.9 opens so that you can begin creating a prop object.

To draw various objects, follow these steps:

1. Use the Background and Foreground tools to select the desired color.
2. Set the desired line thickness.
3. Set the desired fill pattern.
4. Select the appropriate graphics tool.
5. Draw the object.

Creating Props and Single-Cel Actors   **789**

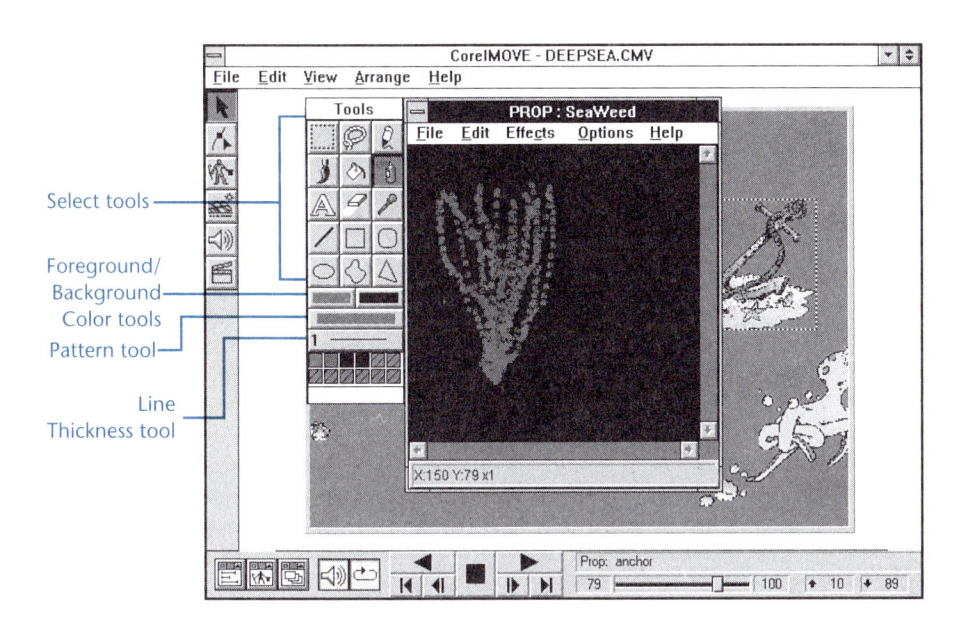

Fig. 30.9
The CorelMOVE Paint facility editing window, which shows the editing area and editing tools.

Remember that Paint works with bitmapped images and does not have the same object-related orientation of CorelDRAW!. The object must be shaped properly the first time or it will need to be erased and redrawn until it appears as desired.

The Marquee and Lasso tools are in the upper-left corner of the toolbox. You use Marquee to draw a square around the selected image sections, and you use the Lasso to draw an irregular shape around the selected image sections. Lasso selects all pixel dots contained within the selected area. When selected, you can drag the area to other parts of the screen, and delete, cut, or copy it.

You use the Pencil tool to draw freehand lines, which adopt the color and line thickness set in the Line Width Selector and Foreground/Background tool sections. If you draw with the left mouse button, the line is drawn in the foreground color; the right mouse button draws in the background color.

The Brush tool draws where you drag the mouse, but uses the pattern and color defined by the Pattern Selector tool. You edit the Paint Brush shape by double-clicking the Paint Brush tool. The pop-up menu displays several different shapes. Click on a shape to make it the new brush shape default.

You use the Paint Bucket tool to fill the interior of objects with the currently selected foreground color and selected pattern. The object should have a solid outline or the fill spills onto the rest of the page and colors it as one object. If the fill doesn't work as desired, immediately open the Edit menu and choose Undo (Ctrl+Z) to return to the prior state. Open the Options menu and choose Zoom to find the break in the line, and use the Pencil tool to fill the break. Then the object can be refilled.

> **Note**
>
> The solid section of a pattern fill adopts the foreground color. The background color is used for the rest of the fill pattern.

The Spray Can tool acts just like a normal spray can. Double-clicking the tool displays a pop-up dialog box with a setting for the thickness of the line (called the *aperture*) and the density of the color (called the *pressure*). Experiment with these settings to get the desired coverage and effect.

> **Tip**
> Press the Tab key to toggle between the current and previously used tools.

Use the Text tool to add text to the drawing. Double-click the tool to display a Font dialog box, which enables you to set the typeface, style, and size of any text added after you make this change. The text adopts the currently active foreground color. You must edit the text before clicking anywhere else on-screen. After you click the screen, the text becomes part of the bitmap image and must be erased and reentered to be edited.

If you use the Paint utility regularly, the Eraser tool will likely become an old friend. You use it to erase the pixels so that you can modify the image. To erase, drag the Eraser over the desired area. Double-click the Eraser to remove the image currently in the Paint window. To perform fine erasures, use Zoom in the Outline menu to increase the image size. That way, you can eliminate the desired pixels without disrupting the rest of the image.

You use the Color Pick-up tool to select a color from the drawing and to make it the currently selected color. This tool is most useful when working with complicated drawings that contain more than 12 colors (the limit of the Recent Color Pick-up Palette). The selected color becomes the current default and exactly matches the color from which it was selected by using the Color Pick-up tool.

The next two rows of the toolbox contain the tools you use for drawing various shapes. The functions include, from top left to bottom right, drawing lines, rectangles, rounded-corner rectangles, ellipses, curves, and polygons. All but the last two are simple click-and-drag operations to obtain the desired shape. You use the Curve tool to draw an irregularly shaped object that ends with a flat side. You first drag the desired shape, and then release the mouse button. A straight line connects the starting point with the point where you release the mouse button. You can fill the resulting object. You use the Polygon tool to create multisided objects in which all sides are flat. You click at the first corner point, and then click at each other corner point. At the final point, you double-click to end the object. You can fill the resulting object.

> **Note**
>
> You draw color-filled objects by first selecting the desired color from the Pickup Log, and then double-clicking any of the object shape tools. The object drawing tools fill in as displayed on the toolbox and objects are subsequently drawn with the selected interior fill color and pattern.

Creating Special Effects with Paint

You can rotate, scale, mirror, tint, define the opacity, or smooth out selected Paint image areas. These special effects are located in the Effects menu. The various display-related options such as Zoom and Transparency are located in the Options menu (see fig. 30.10).

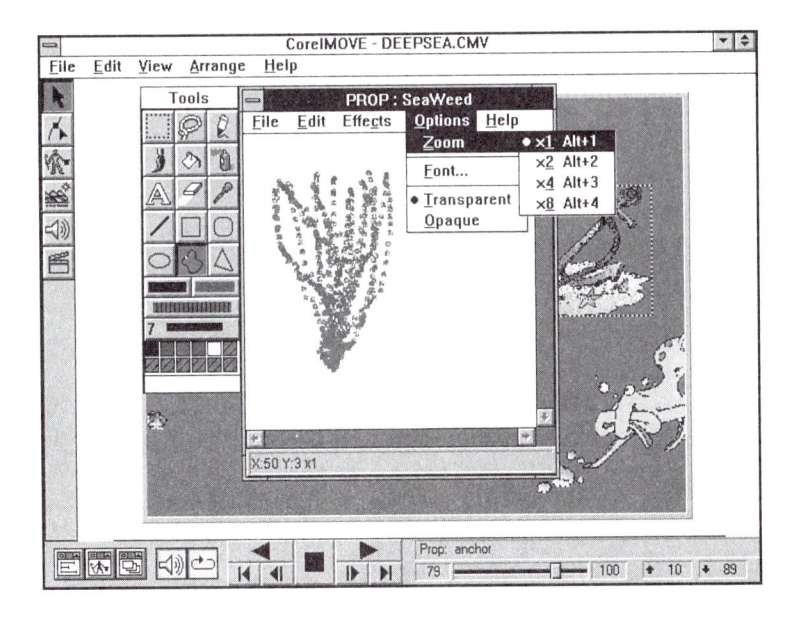

Fig. 30.10
The Options menu.

Zoom enables for x1, x2, x4, and x8 zoom on the current Paint image. The keyboard shortcuts for the zoom options are Alt+1, Alt+2, Alt+3, and Alt+4, respectively. Move to the desired section of the image using the scroll bars at the bottom and on the sides of the editing window.

You define the default text font by opening the Options menu and choosing Font. You set the font design, style, and size in the Font dialog box and click OK.

The two translucency effects are Transparent and Opaque. If an object or a selected subsection is transparent, any object beneath it shows through. If it is opaque, any underlying object is not visible.

Several other object-manipulation tools are provided under the Effects menu, shown in figure 30.11.

Fig. 30.11

The Effects menu.

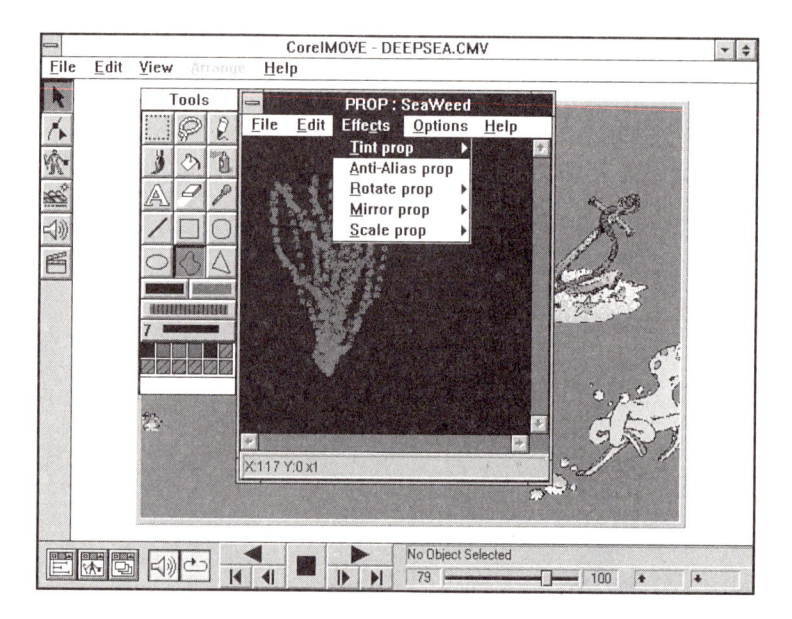

You use the Tint option to add a specific color tint to an entire object or to a specific section of the object. Towards Foreground adds a tint that shades the colors to that defined as the foreground color. Towards Background adds a tint that shades the colors to that defined as the background color. If you select a section of the Paint image, the Tint Selection option appears on the Options menu. If you do not select a section of the Paint image, the Tint All Cels menu option appears for an actor object, and the Tint Prop menu option appears for a prop object.

The Anti-Alias prop option smooths the outline of color objects and is most useful when printing to a video device.

The Rotate, Mirror, and Scale options deal with major movements of the object or a smaller subsection. Either the entire object or a smaller section of the object can be rotated left by 90 degrees, right by 90 degrees, or by a specific number of degrees (By Degrees) clockwise or counterclockwise. If you select a smaller section of the object, you can rotate that section around the center of the selected area by dragging on the small handles in the corners of the selection outline border.

You use the Mirror option to change the object, or its selected subsection, into a mirror image of the original. You use the Vertical option to turn the object upside down. The Horizontal option turns it left to right.

Use Scale to change the size of the object. You can change the size of the entire object from 5 to 200 percent of the original size by using the Scale By Percent dialog box opened by selecting the Custom Scaling option. Selecting the Free Scaling option allows scaling by dragging the corner handles of the smaller subsection selection outline.

A nice feature of CorelMOVE 5 is the Edit menu's Keep Paint and Revert Paint options. You use these options to protect the work already accomplished before this editing session. Keep Paint temporarily stores the current object design and allows all new editing to be accomplished on top of what was already there without affecting the underlying image. If you don't want the changes, simply select Edit Revert Paint to return to the image that existed when you used the Keep Paint command.

Adding Multicel Actors, Movement, and Sound

Animation is created through a series of images with minor changes that, when displayed in rapid succession after each other, give the illusion of movement. Each separate image containing any modification is called a *cel*, and a number of cels together compose an actor's animation. Consequently, a multicel actor (one requiring multiple cells that vary slightly from each other) is required to animate the actor. The actor can either remain in one place and animate (a tree blowing in the wind), or it can move along a predefined path while animating (a boy running down the street). A single-cel actor can move along a predefined path. The actor itself does not change shape, but its location changes (the sun tracing its path across the sky).

A multicel actor is animated as its components change location and shape during replay. The movement of the actor across the screen is caused by the relationship between the actor's cels, the predefined path that it is to follow. The speed with which the actor appears to move across the screen is determined by the number of path nodes as related to the number of multicel actor's cels. Remember that each cel correlates to a node on the action path.

If you are getting the impression that creating animation requires a great deal of advance planning, you're right. Little happens spontaneously in animation, although it looks that way on-screen. A great deal of creative effort goes into making animation look effortless. This section covers the creating actors, creating actor paths, object alignment, adding sound, and editing cues. The wonderful news is that the final product is fun to watch, and you have a real sense of pride watching people enjoy your creation.

Creating Multicel Actors Using Paint

The process of creating a multicel object is the same as that used to create a single-cel object. Start with the basic object, copy it to the next cel of the animation, and make the desired changes. Then repeat the copying process until the desired actor animation is obtained.

Because Paint is bitmap-oriented, the object must be redrawn often. If actors are created in CorelDRAW!, you find that CorelDRAW!'s node editing features greatly speed up the frame-to-frame image changing and editing process.

Follow this procedure to create a multicel actor object:

1. Double-click the actor object you want to animate. The Actor Info dialog box appears.

2. Click the Edit Actor button.

3. Choose Edit Insert Cels (Ctrl+T) to display the Insert Cels dialog box, shown in figure 30.12.

Fig. 30.12

An actor's Insert Cels dialog box is used to add cels to a multicel actor.

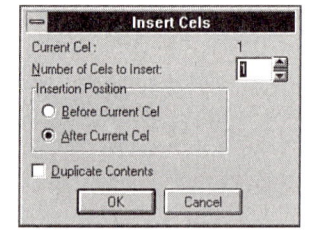

4. Click **B**efore Current Cel or **A**fter Current Cel to designate whether the additional cels are added before the current cel or after. In general, you add the cels after the current cel.

5. Enter a number in the **N**umber of Cels to Insert text box to define how many cels you want to add before or after the current cel.

Adding Multicel Actors, Movement, and Sound 795

6. Click **D**uplicate Contents if you want to copy the contents of the current cel to the inserted cels. This makes modification of the contents in the other cels easier because you don't create the initial object from scratch on each cel.

7. Click OK to insert the designated number of cels.

8. At the bottom of the Tools palette, use the scroll bar to select the cel you want to alter.

9. Edit the actor with the paint tools.

10. Repeat steps 8 and 9 as needed to edit all the cels.

11. Choose **F**ile **A**pply Changes.

12. Choose **F**ile **E**xit to close Paint and return to your animation.

13. If needed, use the Actor Information dialog box to adjust when the actor enters and leaves the animation.

To delete cels, move to the cel just before those to be deleted and choose the Edit Remove Cels menu option to display the Delete Cels dialog box. Set the number of cels after the currently selected cel that you want to delete and click OK.

Viewing the prior cel's contents while creating the current cel is often useful to monitor the amount of change that takes place from one cel to the next. Choose the Options Onion Skin menu option to display a menu with Previous Cel, Next Cel, and None as options. Choosing Previous Cel displays the prior cel at 30 percent of its actual translucency. Thus, you can view the current cel's changes against the cel from which it is supposed to have moved. Choosing Next Cel performs the same function except that the following cel instead of the prior cel appears at 30 percent saturation. None displays only the current cel.

You can change the size and the orientation of all cels associated with an object by applying the special effects to the entire image of any of the cels without selecting a subsection of the cel. After you apply these special effects, they can't be removed or undone. If you want to change a certain cel only, select a subsection of the cel or the entire cel by using Edit Select All and apply the desired change. You can verify the change by using the Onion Skin effect. The images shown in figure 30.13, for example, are roughly the same fish with the current cel's contents rotated and scaled in the vertical and horizontal dimensions.

Fig. 30.13

Viewing another multicel actor's cel using the onion skin effect to verify cel-to-cel changes.

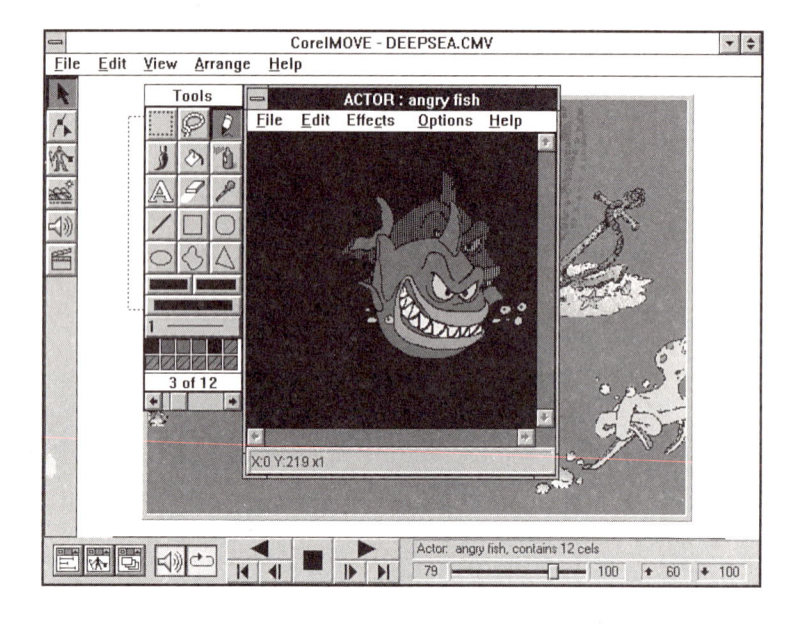

Repeat this copy-modification process until the desired number of cels with the proper modifications are obtained. Choose File Exit to return to the editing window. Select Yes, No, or Cancel as appropriate in the Save Related dialog box.

Setting the Path Registration Point

Tip

Registration points can be changed only on CorelMOVE Paint objects. Objects created in other applications must move along paths using their respective default registration points.

When an actor object moves along a path, it must have some orientation point that determines where the object lines up with respect to the path. This mark is called a *registration point* and appears aligned with the active node as shown in figure 20.14. You can move this registration point by opening the Paint window for the actor object in question and choosing Edit Registration (Ctrl+R). A blinking registration point marker appears on the Paint screen.

To move the registration point, simply click the new registration point location and select Edit Registration to disable the registration operation. The object aligns along the path using the new registration point location while moving after you return to the animation editing screen.

Arranging Object Orientation

CorelMOVE places every new object on top of those created previously, which makes them appear more toward the foreground when displayed. This feature can create problems for the actors as they move across the screen because they may be in front of or behind other objects simply because of the order of creation.

To remedy this situation, first select the object of interest, and then use the Arrange menu selections, which operate similarly to those seen in CorelDRAW!. Forward One (Ctrl+PgUp) moves an object one layer forward than it is currently. Back One (Ctrl+PgDn) moves an object one layer back, or under, than it is currently. To Back (Shift+PgDn) moves the selected object to the very back of all other objects. To Front (Shift+PgUp) moves the object to the top of all other objects.

In addition, you can change the location of an object by simply clicking it with the Pick tool and dragging it to the new location.

Adding Actor Movement

Actors move along a path, which you define using the Path tool. Each node of the path corresponds to a cel on the actor's animation sequence. A correspondence between the number of nodes and the number of actor cels is important for many animated effects. If the actor only has one cel, it proceeds along the entire length of the path.

Start creating a path by first selecting the actor, and then choosing the Path tool from the toolbox. The Path Edit roll-up appears, as shown in figure 30.14.

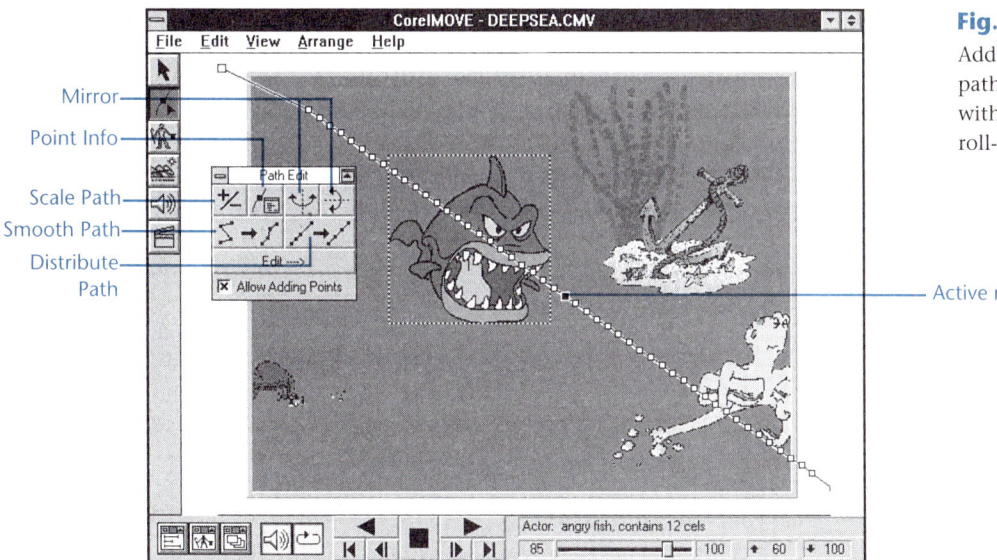

Fig. 30.14
Adding action paths and nodes with the Path Edit roll-up.

Make sure that you select Allow Adding Points before proceeding with the path-creation process. Disable this feature when you want to edit the path node so that clicking with the mouse does not add another node point.

When an actor is first created, it is automatically given a path with only one node that is located at the actor-object's registration point.

> **Note**
>
> You use the Edit Registration point feature to change the actor's registration point in the Paint facility. Only CorelMOVE-created objects have a definable registration point. Other actors must use the default registration point given when the object was created.

The Path Edit roll-up window automatically appears once you select the Path tool. You use the Path tool to add more nodes to the path, which makes the object move. To add a node, simply click at the next location along the desired path of the actor's movement. A line forms to connect the two points. This second point is the next location for object display, which is the actor's second cel if it is a multicel actor. Continue to click along the desired path until the full extent of movement is defined. The last point along the path is a circle, and the other node points are all small squares.

Choosing the Scale Path button from the Path Edit roll-up window displays the Scale Path dialog box, which enables you to set the number of nodes you want along the path. The current number of points is displayed, and you change the number by entering a value in the desired box. You can apply scale to the entire path by default or to a subsection of the path by Shift clicking the starting and ending node points, and then scaling the points between using the Scale Path button.

> **Note**
>
> You can have an actor appear to stop during your animation by inserting a large number of points between two existing ones along the path. Select the two points by clicking the first point, and then pressing Shift while clicking the second point. Choose Scale and add a large number of points between the two you selected. The actor takes a long time to traverse this large number of points, giving the impression that it has stopped. Conversely, placing a few points over a large distance makes the object appear to move quickly.

Clicking the Point Information button, or double-clicking a node point, displays the dialog box shown in figure 30.15.

The Point Information box shows the total number of nodes, the number of the node currently selected, and its location in pixels on the editing window. The zero point is in the upper-left corner of the editing window. Selecting

Loop To Here causes the actor to continuously loop back to this point after it has traversed the entire path. This process continues until the actor's timeline ends or the animation terminates. Double-clicking any point displays the Point Information window for that particular node.

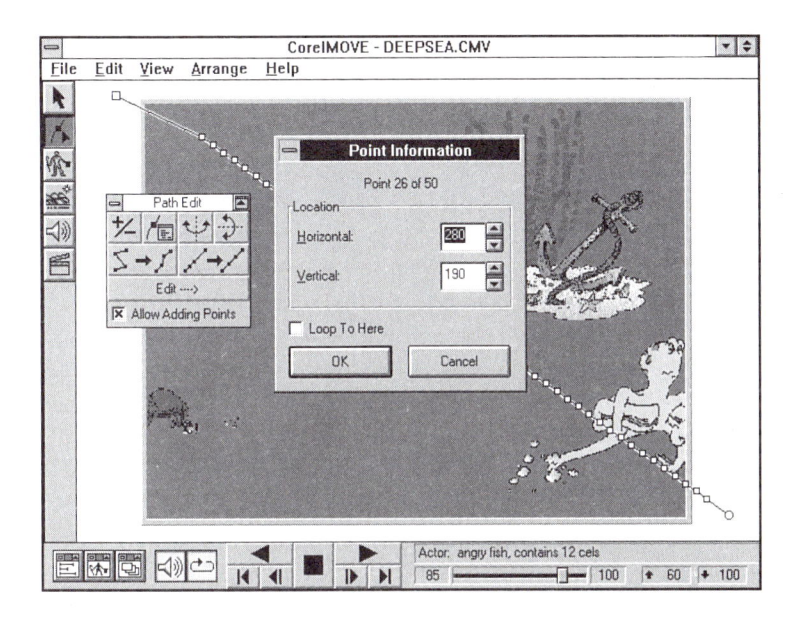

Fig. 30.15
The actor animation Point Information dialog box is used to change action path node point attributes.

The Path Edit dialog's Mirror Vertical and Horizontal buttons simply replace the original path with a mirror copy in their respective directions.

The Smooth Path option removes the sharp changes from the path. If you select this option several times, the curve begins to flatten. Use Distribute Path to evenly distribute the nodes along the entire path or a specific subsection using the Shift+click point-selection process. Clicking on the Path Edit's Edit command button displays the Edit fly-out menu. It provides access to point-editing tools that allow for copying, cutting, pasting, clearing, and selecting points. The Clear Path option is useful for removing the entire path associated with an actor so that it can be recreated from scratch.

Adding Sound to the Animation

Sound adds a professional touch to animation. In traditional animation, you first create the sound track, and then animate the actors to go along with the soundtrack. You must have properly working sound capture and playback equipment for the CorelMOVE sound features to work. Typical equipment includes a sound card, a microphone, speakers, and associated software. Commonly available products include the Pro Audio Spectrum and Sound Blaster cards.

To start the Sound Editor, either click the Sound tool located in the toolbox, or choose Insert Object Sound from the Edit menu. The New Wave dialog box appears. Be sure to give the sound a distinct object name in the Object Name text box for use when working with the timelines. Click on Create New, and then select the desired sound editing application, such as Sound Editor. Click OK and the Wave Editor program will open for use in creating the desired sound object. When you edit and save the sound and close the application, CorelMOVE inserts the object in the CorelMOVE animation.

> **Note**
>
> There are many sound recording software packages on the market such as those that come with the ProAudio Spectrum or Sound Blaster cards. These applications also come with a wide array of prerecorded sounds that can be incorporated into the animation. Only waveform (WAV) file formats are usable by CorelMOVE. MIDI files will not play.

Sounds are recorded by clicking the Record button. To stop recording, click the Stop button; click Play to hear the recording. Choose File Exit to return to the editing window and save the sound object under its currently active name.

The Effects menu provides many special effects including the capability to flatten the sound (Silence), Fade Up from zero to a set percentage of the total volume, Fade Down to an established percentage of the current volume level, and Amplify from 0 to 9,999 percent. (Numbers less than 100 percent make the sound quieter and those more than 100 percent make it louder.) Other special effects include Reverse, which plays the sound backward (sometimes with amusing effects), and Echo, which makes the sound echo as though it originated in a cave. CorelMOVE applies these effects to the entire wave by default, but you also can apply them to subsections of the sound by first selecting the section by dragging the mouse over the desired area and then selecting the desired effect.

After exiting from the Wave Editor, you get sound file information by opening the timeline, clicking the Timeline button, and then double-clicking the sound object of interest. The Sound Information dialog box appears, as shown in figure 30.16.

The name of the sound object appears at the top of the window. You can edit this name if you want. The Starts At Frame and Ends At Frame numbers indicate the animation frame numbers at which the sound starts and stops playing. The Start frame cannot be a number greater than the total number of

Adding Multicel Actors, Movement, and Sound 801

frames in the animation. The end frame can be any number greater than the start frame. If the sound length is less than the total number of animation frames, though, the sound terminates before the end of the animation unless you choose the Repeat Sound option. If the sound length is greater than the total number of frames, the animation ends and stops the sound replay at that point.

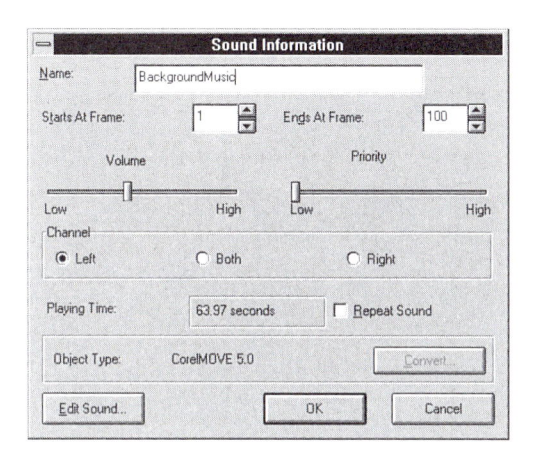

Fig. 30.16
The Sound Information dialog box, showing details associated with the currently selected sound object.

The sound can be designated as left-, right-, or both-channel resident. If you want to play more than one sound at a time, you might consider putting one sound on the left channel and the other on the right channel. Putting it on both provides stereo sound but does not allow for flexible overlay of multiple sound signals. The Volume control sets a volume level for the sound wave and relates to the Priority setting. The higher the priority, the higher the sound volume relative to lower priority items. You should keep background music, for example, at a low priority (lower sound level) while making the narrator's voice a higher priority (louder sound level). The length of recording time appears in the Playing Time section of the dialog box. Choose Edit Sound to display the Wave Editor or other generating application as shown in the Object Type list box in the New Wave dialog box.

Tip
Merging two digital files into a single file makes CorelMOVE playback more consistent because fewer files are involved. This requires a third-party sound editing application.

Note
Remember, the Wave Editor is not very sophisticated and cannot perform some special functions, such as merging two sounds into one soundtrack. You may want to look around for more extensive sound-editing packages, such as Microsoft Quick Recorder or EZ Sound FX, for more capability—and more fun!

Adding and Editing Cues

Cues are used to initiate segments of the animation. They provide a way for the person viewing the animation to interact with it and guide it in desired directions. Each Cue has its own name, which allows for its own specific definition. The basic Cue insertion sequence is to open the Cue tool, name the cue, define its enter and exit frame locations, designate the conditions under which events should happen (for example, clicking a prop), and, finally, define the action you take after meeting the predefined conditions.

Choosing the Cue tool opens the Cue Information dialog box shown in figure 30.17.

Fig. 30.17
The Cue Information dialog box is used to create viewer-initiated presentation actions.

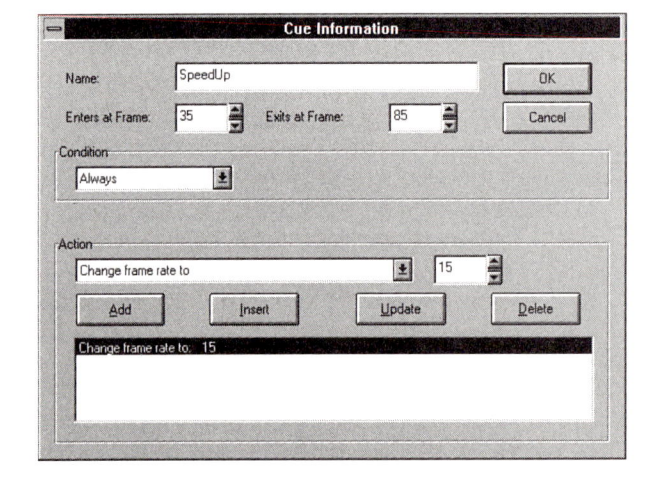

The Name field contains the name under which the cue is accessed for later editing. The Enters At Frame and Exits At Frame fields designate the animation frames at which the designated cue starts and stops.

The Condition field defines the criteria used to determine if and when to initiate the cue. Clicking the displayed button presents a listing of various condition types. Each of these conditions, except for Always, leads to other conditional lists. Actions can be initiated after a time delay, after a mouse click anywhere on-screen, or after pressing a key.

Pause until/for stops the animation until one of the actions shown in the Second List (Time Delay, Mouse Click, or Key Down) occurs. Choosing Time Delay displays another box that enables you to enter the desired time delay (up to a 30-second maximum). Choosing Mouse Click displays a list including Anything and the names of included actors and props. These options define which mouse click type initiates the designated action.

Selecting Anything from the list means that a click anywhere on-screen initiates the actions. Selecting one of the actor or prop names means that a click on that object initiates the indicated action specified later in the dialog box. Key Down, from list two, opens a third-level entry point that designates the pressed key action that starts the action. The currently active key selection is displayed in the command button and is changed by clicking on the command button and then pressing the desired new key.

The If/After option specifies that the cued action starts only when the designated conditions are met. If the specified conditions are met, the action designated in the Then section is initiated. If the conditions are not met, nothing happens. After indicates the amount of time (0-600 minutes) before initiating the specified Then actions.

The action field provides several options: Continue with the Animation as It Is; Goto Frame, which jumps the animation to a specific frame from which it continues; Pause Until Condition Occurs Again, which causes the animation to pause until the previously defined conditional statement becomes true; End Animation, which stops the animation completely; Change Frame Rate, which changes the speed at which the animation plays to the frame rate set in the attached box; Play a Sound Object; Stop a Sound Object's Playback; or Execute Another Cue.

CorelMOVE inserts cues on the timeline just like the other prop and actor objects, but grouped with the Cue tool. Make sure that the Then conditions are specified when you are setting the first action, or subsequently confusing results may occur.

Viewing and Editing Animation Timing

The timing of when props appear, actors start, and sounds play are all related in the timelines. This timing relationship is graphically displayed, which allows for easy modification.

Clicking the Timeline button from the main CorelMOVE screen reveals the Timeline roll-up. Clicking the resize button at the top right of the Timeline roll-up displays the relative timing of each animation event on a timeline, as shown in figure 30.18.

Fig. 30.18

The Timeline display with props, actors, cues, and sound object timings indicated.

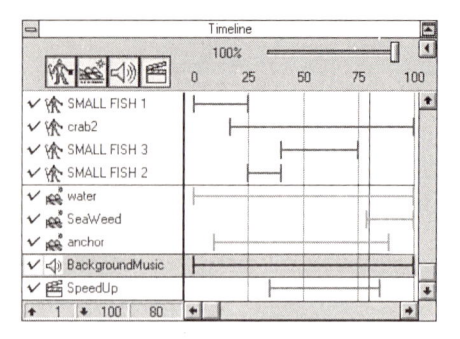

Along the left side of the display are the objects with the object-type icon shown to the left of the object name (such as prop or actor). To the right of the objects is a timing display that shows the starting and ending point for each of the objects. The frame numbers are at the top of the Timeline window, and the Enter and Exit frames for each selected object appear at the bottom left of the window on the status line. The up arrow indicates the Enter frame, and the down arrow indicates the Exit frame. The currently selected frame number appears to the right of the Exit frame number.

Above the object names are icons representing, from left to right, actors, props, sound, and cues. Clicking one of these icons causes CorelMOVE to display that type of object or removes it from the display depending on the current display status. The Zoom Slider displays a specified percentage of the timeline. Set the Zoom Slider to 100 percent to view the entire timeline. Setting it to 50 percent displays only half of the timeline but in much finer detail. This Zoom In mode is useful when precise timing between objects is critical.

The left side of an object's timeline represents its enter frame, and the right side represents its exit frame. Move the left and right ends of the timeline to new locations by dragging the left or right side of the line to the desired location. Dragging the entire line to a new location by dragging at the center of the line changes the timing of both starting and ending times.

Delete an object from the timeline by first selecting it and then pressing Delete.

Morphing: Blending from One Bitmap into Another

Morphing is a technique for blending bitmapped objects into each other. Just as the CorelDRAW! blend feature transitions from one object into another over a specified number of steps, morphing transitions from one bitmap image into another over a specified number of frames. It is particularly handy when working with actors because each stage of the morph is actually a new cel that changes as the actor moves along its action path. Morphing is accomplished from within the Paint facility and can be performed only on CorelMOVE 5.0 objects. Non-CorelMOVE 5.0 objects can be converted into CorelMOVE 5.0 objects by double-clicking on the object and clicking the Convert command button in the Actor Information dialog box.

Morphing is accomplished in the Paint facility and requires two images in separate cels to function. The details of how to morph specific images is heavily dependent on your specific artistic needs, so what follows is a general procedure that should apply to most situations.

1. Click on the Actor tool and select Create New or From File depending on whether a new actor or existing actor is being morphed. It is a good idea to give this actor a new, morph-related name so that you can keep track of it later.

2. Select the actor cel that represents the morph starting point.

3. Remove all other cels from an existing actor so that you have a single-cel actor that contains the desired starting image.

4. Insert a cel so that the actor has two cels.

5. Move to the second cel and insert the terminating morph image into this cel. The Edit Copy and Paste options are useful to add a completely separate image like that shown in figure 30.19.

6. Return to the original cel, open the Effects menu, and choose **M**orph Cel. The Morph editing box opens (see fig. 30.19).

7. Set the Cels to Create value to reflect the number of intermediate cels required for the specific effect. The maximum number is 200.

Fig. 30.19
The Morph editing box with starting and ending images displayed.

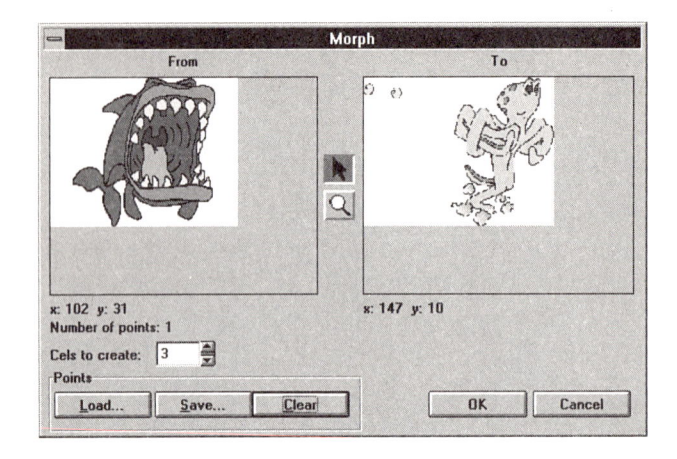

8. Define the alignment points by first selecting a point in one image and then dragging the second image's alignment point to the desired location. For example, the eyes would be used as alignment points to morph from one facial image to another while giving the effect of a personal transformation. Clicking on Clear removes the alignment points.

9. Click on the magnifying glass, and then on the image to zoom in on the desired close-up region. Click the right mouse button to zoom out.

10. Click Save to retain the current alignment point configuration as a file that can be retrieved later for future morphing activities. Clicking Load opens the standard Windows dialog box with the MPH extender files displayed.

11. Click OK to display the Morph Imaging Options dialog box. Select the desired color for the intermediate transparencies (white, black, or none) and select the Perform High Quality Dithering option to improve the quality of the transition colors.

12. Click OK to perform the morph operation. The procedure ends with an actor containing the desired number of morph cels and two more cels representing the starting and ending images.

13. Click File Apply Changes to return to the animation that now includes the recently morphed image-actor.

The newly created actor can be applied to an action path just like any other actor.

Animation Design Considerations

Planning goes a long way in creating an effective animation. Remember that animated objects appear more real when they have realistic characteristics. To compress a ball in the vertical direction when it hits a wall, for example, is one way to animate, but a real ball compresses vertically and expands horizontally. This combined effect makes animated objects appear more real.

You also can have fun with animation by setting up the characters—and the audience—for the next action. A slight pause, for example, may be very effective in increasing the awareness of the next activity. A slight wavering indicating the intention to walk makes the actual walking actions more effective. Don't be afraid to exaggerate an actor's movements, and don't minimize the number of frames at the expense of adequate follow-through on the actor's part. It also helps to keep things less square and more rounded. Real objects are rarely square, but because computers make squares so easily, many computer-generated objects have square edges. Try to avoid this tendency.

Timing also is a critical aspect of animation. You make things slow down or speed up based on the number of frames contained in that particular part of the animation. The more points included along the path, the slower the object moves. The fewer points, the faster the object will move. If you want a man to move slower than a dog that is chasing him, for example, you give the dog actor's path fewer points than the path for the man and adjust the point spacing so that the dog moves a larger distance with each path point compared to the man's distance.

The more appealing the characters, the more fun the audience has in watching them in their excursions. Take the time to make the characters meet your desired audience objectives, and your viewers will receive the animations better.

> **Tip**
> You can get interesting effects by using the same image in the two cels, with one image scaled and distorted from the first.

Creating and Using Libraries

Many images are stored in the CorelMOVE libraries, which are accessible from the Libraries roll-up. The library is a special storage area where you can consolidate your props, actors, and sound files for future access and use.

808 Chapter 30—Adding Animation with CorelMOVE

The library roll-up is activated by clicking on the Library button located at the bottom of the screen or by choosing the View menu's Library roll-up option. The roll-up with the most recently accessed library is displayed, as shown in figure 30.20.

Fig. 30.20
The Library roll-up allows access to a wide assortment of included CorelMOVE objects.

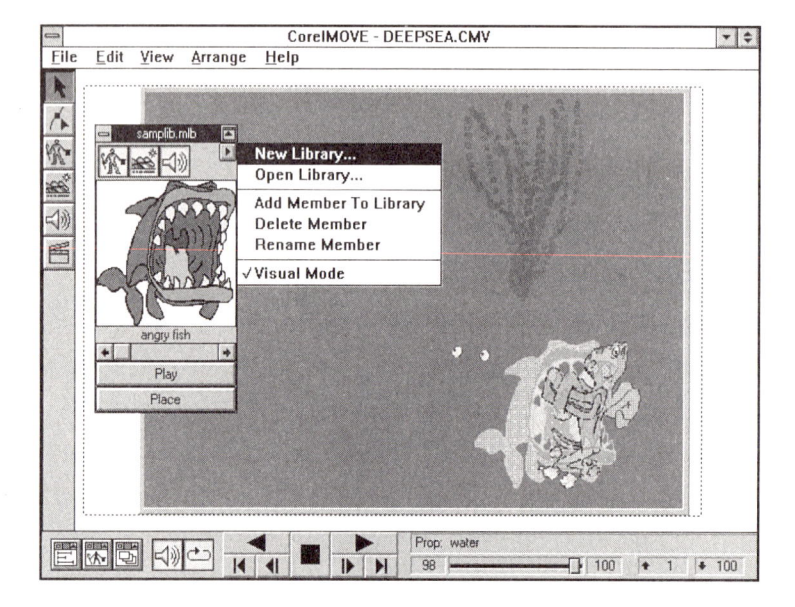

The icons at the top of the roll-up determine whether the displayed library members are props, actors, or sound objects. To display only props, turn off the other two icons by clicking on them. You can play actors and sound objects by scrolling through the library until the desired object is displayed, and then clicking on Play. Click on Stop Play to terminate the playback. Click on Place to include the currently active library object in the animation.

The fly-out button at the top right of the roll-up displays a menu that includes options for creating a new library, opening an existing library, adding a member to the currently active library, deleting the displayed member from the currently active library, or renaming the currently active member object. Activating the Visual Mode option causes the members to be displayed, and actors and sound objects play automatically. You may find that it is faster to work with visual mode disabled when searching for a particular object. You can click the object and Play to view its contents.

Applying the Cel Sequencer

Making objects stand still, reverse direction, or perform timeframe-related activities often requires the creation of multiple, identical actors, and then adjusting their timing and arrangement so that they coincide with each other as desired. The Cel Sequencer addition to release 5 provides a handy tool for correlating a specific actor's cels with animation frames while also including special effects.

First select an actor, and then select the View menu's Cel Sequencer option to display the window shown in figure 30.21.

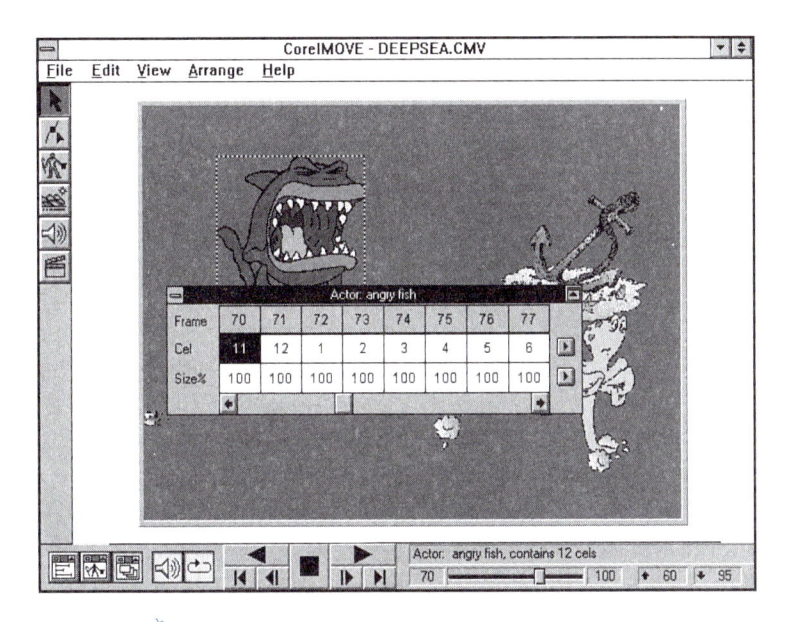

Fig. 30.21
The Cel Sequence roll-up applied to the Angry Fish.

The top row of the sequencer corresponds to the frame of the overall animation. The center row corresponds to the cel of the actor object selected. The bottom row is the size that is applied to that actor's particular cel for that frame.

It is possible to define the specific actor cel that should display at a particular frame by simply selecting the actor cel designation under the desired cel and typing in the actor cel number. This feature makes it easy to retain the same image over a number of frames. Shift clicking on a range of cels, preferably the entire actor sequence, activates the items listed in the Sequence Effects fly-out menu, which is activated by clicking on the small triangle located in the upper-right corner of the dialog box. Menu items include Normal Cycle (obvious), Reverse Cycle (reverses the sequence of cel display), Ping Pong (makes the sequence forward then backward, then forward, and so forth), Slow Forward and Reverse (carries the same cel over two playback frames, effectively slowing the action in either forward or reverse mode), and Random (takes cels at random and displays them over the selected range). Select All selects the cels associated with the entire time that the actor is on the screen.

The Size% of each cel is determined by the number displayed in the small box below the Cel number. 0% causes no display, 5% is considered small, 100% is the normal size, and 200% is considered large. The maximum size is 500%. The fly-out menu at the right of the window includes several other sizing options that are applied to the selected range of cels: Normal Size, Small to Large, Large to Small, Normal to Large, Large to Normal, Small to Normal, Normal to Small, Constant, and Random, which shifts the size from 5% to 200% in no particular order or sequence. Cels outside of the selected range always appear at 100% unless previously set otherwise.

Using CorelDRAW! Images in CorelMOVE

The Paint facility included with CorelMOVE is bitmap-oriented, and has only a fraction of CorelDRAW!'s editing capabilities. In addition, moving the object's parts (the feet or hands, for example) is much more difficult in Paint than in CorelDRAW!. CorelDRAW! allows for object node movements, whereas Paint requires a substantial redraw effort for each frame of an actor's animation movie because it does not use a vector graphic approach.

The layering aspects of CorelDRAW! allow for easy copying of information from one layer (or frame) to another while showing the previous or following layer in a specially selected outline color. You are strongly encouraged to use the editing capabilities of CorelDRAW! while making your animated actors. In addition, the extensive CorelDRAW! clipart and symbol library provides a tremendous base from which to create professional yet simple animations.

This section shows how you use CorelDRAW! to create actors and why you are better served working with CorelDRAW! than Paint.

To create a prop or actor in CorelDRAW!, choose Insert New Object Prop or Actor from the Edit menu to display the New Actor or Prop dialog box. Choose the Create New and CorelDRAW! 5.0 Graphic options; then click OK. CorelDRAW! opens and prepares for creation or editing of the desired object. In figure 30.22, a seahorse was pulled in from CorelDRAW!'s symbols library.

You have access to the CorelDRAW! symbols library and drawing tools while creating and modifying your actor and prop objects. Having this access makes life simpler when creating actors because moving object nodes around is much easier and faster than redrawing the object for each frame of the animation as is required with Paint.

The animation opens with a single frame, as shown in the Frame Select roll-up. Additional frames are added by selecting the menu's Insert Before or Insert After commands to add frames before or after the currently selected frame. The menu's Make Common Before and After options enable you to add a selected object to frames before or after the currently selected frame, respectively. To make an object common to other layers, select it from its currently active frame and then select the Make Common Before or After menu command. Enter the desired number of frames in the dialog box that appears and click OK. The object automatically appears on the other layers.

In figure 30.22, you can see the seahorse from the CorelDRAW! Animals symbol library.

Fig. 30.22
A CorelDRAW! symbol being used as a starting point for creating a CorelMOVE actor.

The To Next option, when selected, copies certain of the effects added to the object on the current layer to the next layer.

The process for adding objects to frames includes adding a frame and then copying the object to that frame. To add objects to frames, follow these steps:

1. To add a frame, first select Frame 1 in the Frame Select roll-up.

2. Click the black triangle in the upper-right corner of the Frame Select window to display the fly-out menu.

3. Choose New to display the Append New Frames dialog box, in which you can define the number of new frames to insert. When the frames are inserted, they have no objects on them. You add the objects after the frames are inserted.

4. Click OK to add a single frame, or change the number, and then click OK.

5. To copy an object from one frame to another, first move the frame containing the object for copying.

6. Select the object(s).

7. Select Copy To from the fly-out menu in the Frame Select roll-up. The cursor changes to an arrow.

8. Move the arrow to the desired destination frame and click to copy the object to that frame level. Notice that the same object now appears on each frame level.

Alternatively, choosing Move To from the fly-out menu moves the selected object(s) to the destination frame.

Seeing the prior frame's contents is often valuable when editing the current frame's objects. You can determine the level of desired change from one frame to the next. CorelDRAW! provides an easy way of determining one frame's contents from the next by allowing you to view the underlying, or following, frame in another color and at a reduced intensity. You access these settings from the fly-out menu's Options command, which displays the Frame Options dialog box (see fig. 30.23).

Fig. 30.23
The Frame Options dialog box is used for setting the prior and following frame's onion skin colors.

The onion skin is like a transparency that enables you to view the underlying (Previous) or following (Next) frames in a color you select by clicking the small triangle in the color boxes to the right. In Front tells CorelDRAW! to display the other layer's object outlines in front of the objects on the currently selected layer. Selection Wire Color defines the color used to display an object selected on a specific layer while viewing another layer of the actor's animation. If you set Wire Color to green, for example, and you have selected an object on frame 4 but are currently viewing frame 2, the frame 4 object appears in green. You can activate Previous and Next at the same time. Figure 30.24 displays the frame 2 view of the seahorse symbol copied to frame 2 and reduced in vertical height, and then copied to frame 3 and reduced again.

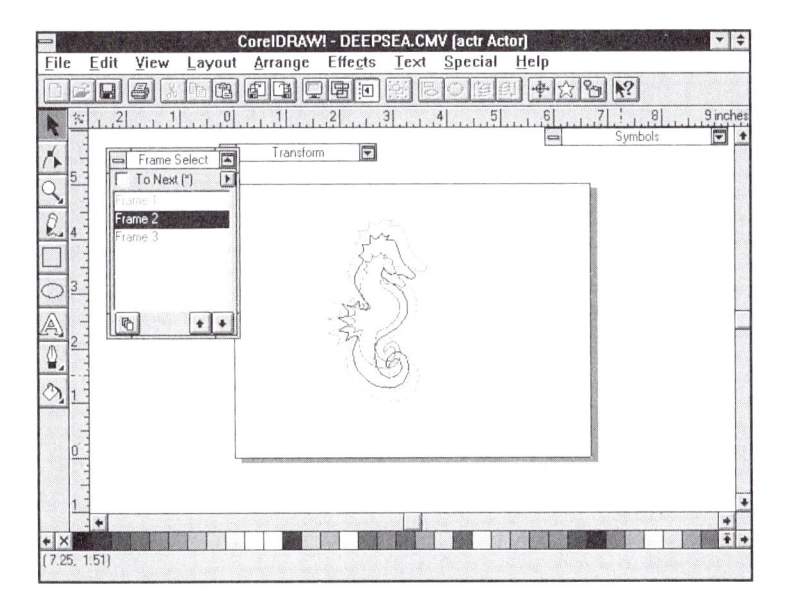

Fig. 30.24
A CorelDRAW! object with the Previous and Next onion skin in effect.

The Preview button is located in the bottom-left corner of the Frame Select dialog box. Clicking it displays the Previewing Frame dialog box and plays the animation for this particular actor. The arrows move the animation frame display forward and backward. This is a convenient way to survey the effect of the various editing changes between frames. Click OK to return to the Frame Edit display. Click the desired Frame level, and perform any editing necessary to get the actor into the desired form.

Open the File menu and choose Exit Revert To to save the actor under its designated name and return to the CorelMOVE editing window. The CorelDRAW! actor is treated as an OLE (Object Linking and Embedding) object while in CorelMOVE. Selecting Object from the Edit menu or clicking

Tip
If you want to save a copy of the object while in CorelDRAW! and in a CorelDRAW! format, open the File menu and choose Save As; then type a file name and directory, and choose OK.

on Edit in the Actor Information dialog box instructs CorelMOVE to open CorelDRAW! so that you can edit the object. Changes made to the object in CorelDRAW! are automatically updated and added to the CorelMOVE animation.

You are encouraged to use the power of CorelDRAW! to create and edit animation objects. The clipart library is extensive, and the node-editing tools make object modification much more efficient. The drawback is that to make it work at a reasonable speed requires a substantial amount of system resource. If your system is not powerful enough to perform up to desired speeds, you may be better off importing the objects into the Paint editor and making modifications there. A drawback is that the standard CDR format is not accepted by CorelMOVE, so you may need to export the image from CorelDRAW! into a PCX or other compatible format before using it in Paint. Importing is accomplished by selecting File Import Actor/Prop/Sound and then selecting the desired file.

Tip
From the Actor Information dialog box, you can convert a CorelDRAW! object into a CorelMOVE Paint-compatible object. All subsequent editing is done in Paint rather than CorelDRAW!.

Exporting Animation Objects

You can save your animation as a movie and view it without even operating CorelMOVE. This type of feature is useful for stand-alone kiosk displays like those seen at airports or sales presentations where you only need the movie, not the editing capability. Open the File menu and choose the Export To Movie command. After you type the name of the movie, make a drive selection and click OK. CorelMOVE makes a CMV movie playable by using the CorelPLAYER application. Installing the CorelPLAYER involves copying the executable files and modifying the INI files.

You can export animated movies in a CorelMOVE (CMV) file format, a Video for Windows (AVI) file format, or many other file format types. You can use the animation in another application as long as that application supports the selected file format. You can use CorelMOVE animations in CorelSHOW or export them as a stand-alone presentation when you use them in conjunction with the SHOWRUN.EXE file.

> **Troubleshooting**
>
> *My actors run over some of my props instead of running behind. How can I fix this problem?*
>
> You can fix this by arranging the drawing order using the Arrange menu's Front and Back options. Move the slider at the bottom of the screen so that the two objects are at the point in the animation where they overlap, and then apply the Arrange menu's options until the orientation is as desired. If you want to have the actor in front for one portion and behind on another, you may need to create a separate prop or actor and rearrange the new actor/prop combination.
>
> *I want my actor to run quickly across the screen to a certain point, then freeze for a few frames, and then proceed at a high rate of speed. How can I do this without creating multiple actors?*
>
> Use the Cel Sequencer to set the timing for your actor. Set the cel number for all frames in which the actor is standing still to the same number, and the actor will appear to stand still, as long as the action path does not pull it off in another direction.
>
> *I have two scanned images that I use as actor cels. I clean them up in PHOTO-PAINT, scan the images in TRACE, import them into CorelDRAW! for final cleanup, and then create actors using CorelDRAW! from them in CorelMOVE. Is there an easier way?*
>
> Yes. Morphing should provide the answer because it will work with your scanned bitmap images and transition them from one into the other. You will wind up with a bitmap image actor that contains the morphed intermediate cels.
>
> *My sound files degrade the animation playback. How can I avoid this?*
>
> Use smaller WAV files that are not recorded at a high quality sampling rate, and make sure that multiple WAV files are combined into a single file, which places less of a strain on the processor and enables the animation to proceed at normal speed.

From Here...

The level of image processing skill that you have acquired at this point is substantial, and it is now time to put it all together. The next part of the book deals with combining the various skills to make your work easier and more professional looking.

For information related to the topics discussed in this chapter, refer to the following chapters:

- Chapter 3, "A Detailed Look at Object Drawing," introduces the concepts associated with object drawing in CorelDRAW!. This is useful for creating the images needed for props and actors.

- Chapter 13, "Using Advanced Line and Curve Techniques," deals with a more advanced description of editing nodes, working with different line styles, and dimensioning a drawing. This is useful information when creating multicel actors in CorelDRAW!.

- Chapter 29, "Making Presentations with CorelSHOW," covers the procedures for incorporating CorelMOVE animations and other CorelDRAW!-created images into a formal presentation.

- Chapters 31–35 comprise the "Learning from the Pros" part of this book. These chapters contain interviews with professionals who use CorelDRAW! in their work and detail some of the ways in which they actually use the program.

Part VII

Learning from the Pros

- 31 Fast and Sure: Getting the Job Done
- 32 One-Page DTP Design with CorelDRAW!
- 33 Artful Type: Depth and Dimension
- 34 Pattern Making with a Master Mask Artist
- 35 Painless and Powerful Slide Production

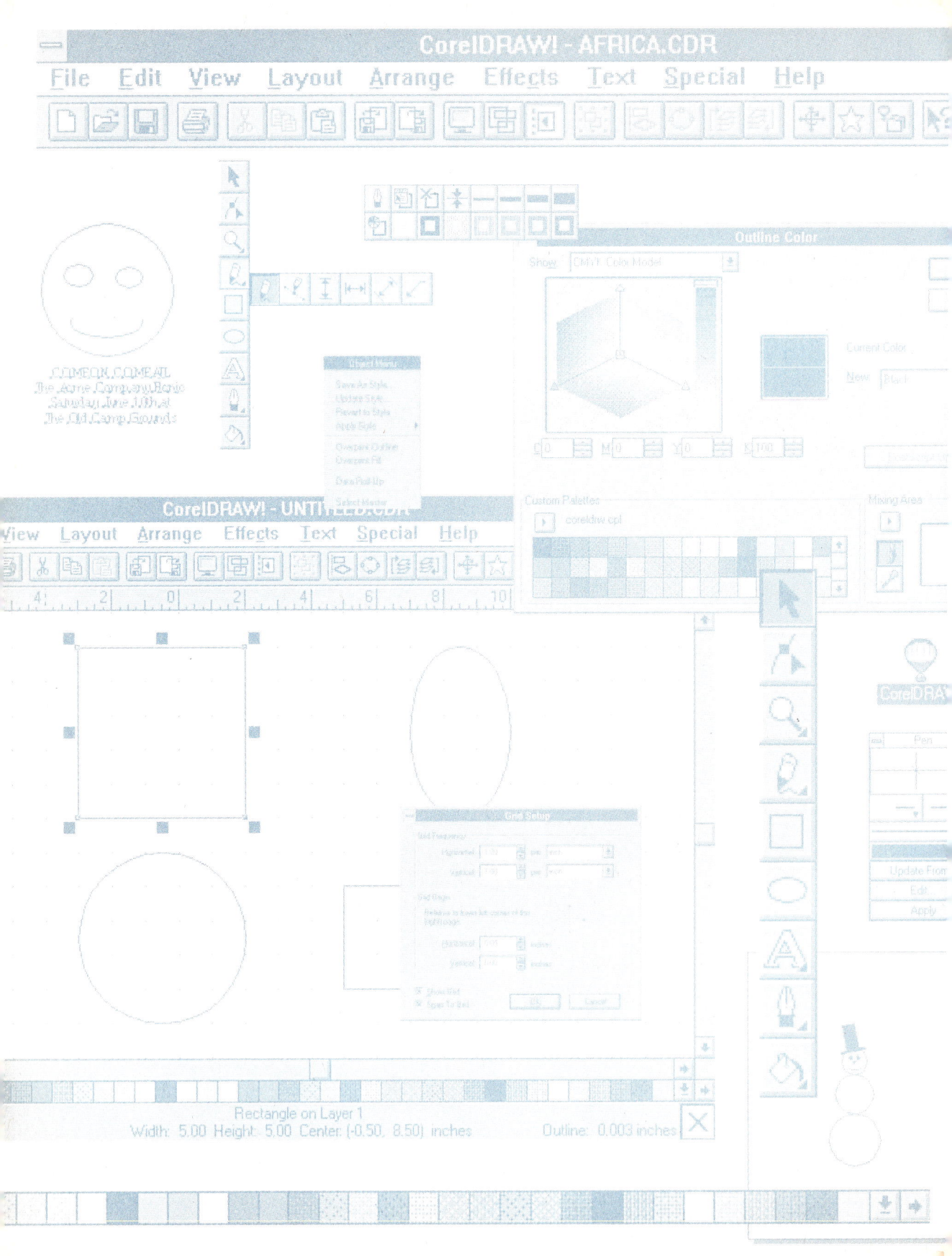

Chapter 31

Fast and Sure: Getting the Job Done

by Rick Wallace

Randy Tobin, President, Association of Corel Designers and Artists, Burbank, California

"I'm a production person and I push it to the limit!" says Randy Tobin, president of the rapidly growing international user group network Association of Corel Designers and Artists (ACAD). He goes out of his way to explain that he's a designer rather than an illustrator. But he does, without question, push the program to the limit, and in his role as the organizer of a widespread consortium of users groups, he helps others to do the same.

Like most of the contributors to this "Learning from the Pros" section, Randy did not start out to be a CorelDRAW! expert. He started out in the music business as a musician and a composer. In fact, years ago, when he was in the service, he was with a band that went to the worldwide finals of the Air Force Talent Contest. Today he still owns a Burbank recording studio that specializes in music—everything from scores for TV shows to rock groups cutting CDs.

That's what started it. Here he was, running a recording studio and paying for graphic arts services for cassette labels and promotional materials. He decided he'd try a do-it-yourself approach.

Randy had taken a print shop class in junior high where they set publications with movable metal type. Yes, they used real lead for leading, and that background helped him understand and evaluate quality typography.

He bought his first PC in 1984, and really didn't know what to do with it, although he learned fast. As Randy pointed out about himself, "You are really coming from nowhere when you don't know how to get the demo started." (He called the computer store and was told to type the word "demo" and press Enter.)

He's been interested in getting good type for quite a while. He simply had to have proportional spacing, so he bought Microsoft Word for DOS, which supported proportional spacing on his daisywheel impact printer. Ultimately he even figured out how to hook up an Apple LaserWriter to his PC to get even better type quality.

The next step was desktop publishing using Ventura Publisher. And in seeking help to get the most out of that program, Randy joined a users group, the Southern California Ventura Publisher Users Group. Randy became chairman of that organization, which eventually led to him being selected to head up ACAD. And these days Randy spends most of his time helping other people "push it to the limit."

ACAD is a fast growing group, with 100 chapters around the world at last count. ACAD has headquarters in Burbank, at (818) 563-ACAD. The group holds three major conferences a year around the country, and runs two-day seminars in enough cities and often enough that there's no room to mention them all here. There's also a full-color quarterly magazine called *Corelation*.

Stretching a program to its limits sometimes also means creating illustrations that blow up when they hit the imagesetter. For example, this cover of *Corelation* magazine you produced looks like it had the potential to cause a burp or two (see fig. 31.1).

Yes, this one had the potential for choking the imagesetter. Notice that it has a lot of blends and gradations. But we use some methods that allowed this job to run smoothly.

Fig. 31.1
A *Corelation* magazine cover, a bit of a test for the imagesetter, but output all the same thanks to some nearly surefire techniques for setting up CorelDRAW! and running a job. (See color plate 42.)

So what are Randy's top three ways to make sure a job will output at service bureau time?

Well, first, imagesetting means PostScript, so the first thing is to set the PostScript complexity threshold. You'll find it in CorelDRAW!'s CORELPRN.INI file, located in the CONFIG directory (see fig. 31.2). Open the CORELPRN.INI file in a text editor (not a regular word processor, unless you do a Save As on the file and make sure it is saved without any proprietary word processor formatting, as pure ASCII text). Find the line that says "PSComplexityThreshold=1500" and change the setting to 100.

Fig. 31.2
Set your PS Complexity Threshold down to 100 by editing this location in the CORELPRN.INI file. And leave Download Type 1 Fonts unchecked.

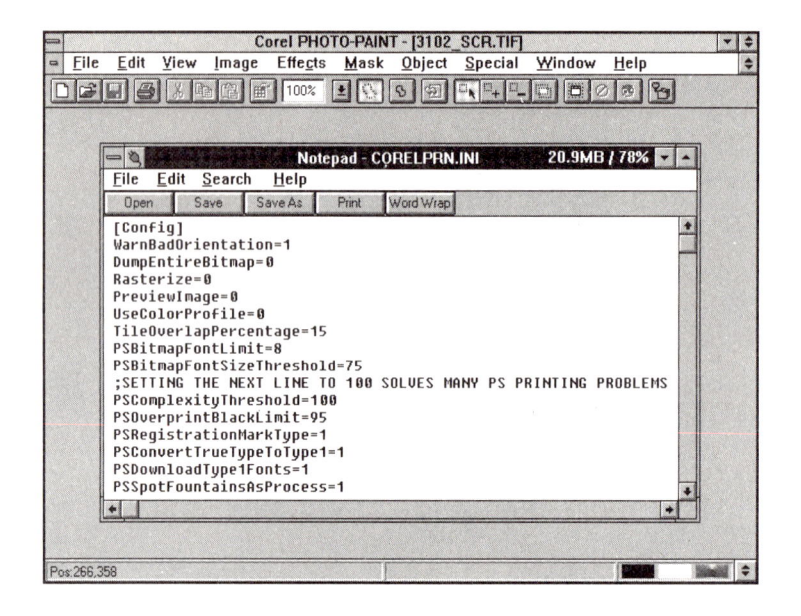

The new version of CorelDRAW! also lets you set the PS Complexity Threshold in a dialog box. It's in Print Options and it is called Number of points in curves.

Whichever way you choose to make this setting change, in the CORELPRN.INI file or in the Print Options dialog box, it forces CorelDRAW! to reduce the complexity of objects, sending them to the imagesetter in small, digestible chunks. They are then tiled together in the imagesetter's RIP.

If you are submitting PRN PostScript files to the service bureau, this will make your files larger, but they will print, even if they contain fountains and graduated fills.

Imagesetting means PostScript, so the first thing is to set the PostScript complexity threshold.

It's important to work closely with your service bureau so that they'll help out when you hit a tough job. And if you submit native CDR files, this can be especially important. For example, if a job won't run, think about making this suggestion to the bureau staff if they haven't already made the modification.

Okay, what's number two in the top three ways to be sure your file will make it through the imagesetter?

Fonts are a constant worry, so never check the Download Type 1 Fonts setting in the Print Options dialog box (see fig. 31.3). As with the suggestion about setting PostScript complexity very low, unchecking Download Type 1 Fonts causes your PRN files to be bigger, but all the text characters will be treated as graphic objects. That insulates you from any problems such as CorelDRAW! font names not matching the names of fonts at the service bureau, or maybe the service bureau not even having the font. I never get Courier substituted in my film output, because there's no font information in the files I send to the service bureau, just pre-drawn graphic objects.

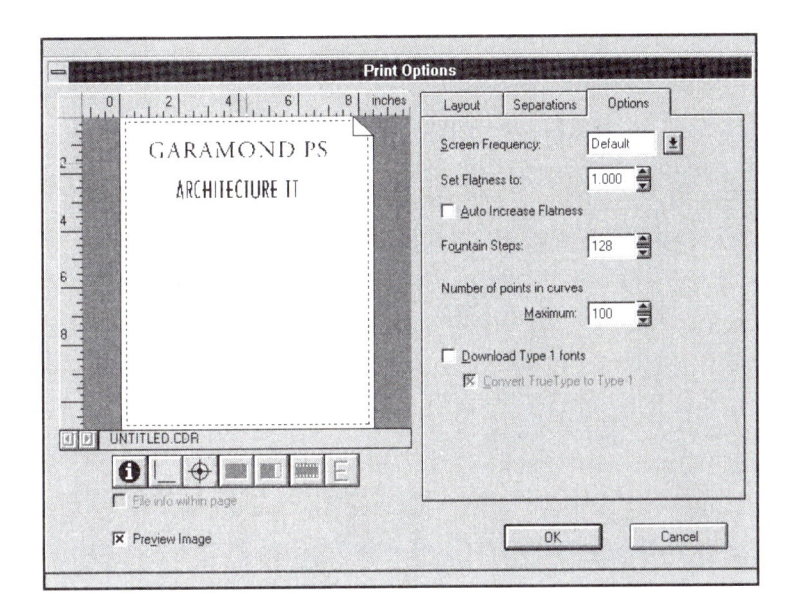

Fig. 31.3
Never set Download Type Fonts to On in the Print Options dialog box.

And on the subject of font substitution, you should consider disabling PANOSE, one of the new additions to CorelDRAW! 5. It is a font substitution engine, and it makes it easier to exchange documents even if you don't have the same fonts as the person sending the file. But substituted fonts aren't the same as the ones you chose as a designer. If typography is critical on your project, okaying a PANOSE suggestion could result in a font substitution that's far enough off to cause you some client problems. This could be especially bad if your service bureau inadvertently used PANOSE on one of your CDR files. PANOSE is a technological breakthrough, and it may be fine for casual file-sharing support in general business situations, but not for final work. You can simply try to

> *Fonts are a constant worry, so never check the Download Type Fonts setting in the Print Options dialog box*

reject the propose font substitutions when the PANOSE window comes up for a missing font. Or, better yet, turn it off by going into the Special Preferences dialog box and clicking on the Text tab. Click on the PANOSE button and deselect Allow Font matching to turn off PANOSE.

And the third tip preventing that sinking feeling when your expensive film comes back all wrong?

Run your file through a PostScript laser printer before taking it to the service bureau. This is especially important when you submit PRN PostScript files, but it also helps to check the ruggedness of your design even if you submit native CDR files to the service bureau.

If your file won't run through a laser printer, chances are high that it won't run through an imagesetter. The lower resolution of a laser printer should make complex, tough-to-output files easier to run, whereas an imagesetter must digest eight times the resolution density.

Sending your print file to the laser printer also allows you to check all sorts of things, things you can't see when you've run the Print to File command and have created a PRN file that can't be proofed in any other way. For example, you can check to see that your Print dialog settings were correct. And you can check your laser proof of a PRN file to see that separated colors are showing up on the right layers of film.

Much of this advice has the most value if the person going to the service bureau is submitting a print file, a PRN file, not the native CDR file. Is that your approach?

I'm a staunch believer that everyone has their system set up in a particular way—including the service bureau—and that it is likely my system won't perfectly match theirs. That's why I always submit a PRN file, not the native CDR file. If nothing else, this approach smooths out the differences in all the CorelDRAW! versions, as well as a myriad of other potential system mismatches. The bureau may not have the same fonts, may have a different version of ATM, possibly is Macintosh oriented, and may not even be working with the same version of CorelDRAW! as you are.

If your file won't run through a laser printer, chances are high that it won't run through an imagesetter.

On the other hand, you should work with your service bureau and find out what they prefer. If you don't feel comfortable that your project is absolutely bulletproof, submit the native CDR file instead of a PRN file.

If you don't feel comfortable that your project is absolutely bulletproof, submit the native CDR file instead of a PRN file.

Actually, some people submit both, including a CDR file, as a backup technique even when they are sending in a PRN file. The point is, everything depends on your service bureau. If you have the kind of relationship with them that they'll go into your job and fix it if it isn't running through the imagesetter, it makes sense to give them the opportunity to give you that kind of service. For that, they'll need the CDR file.

Now let's save some time. Give us the three top timesaving features of CorelDRAW!.

Version 5 comes with a new feature called Presets. It's a new roll-up that is sort of like a macro recorder (see fig. 31.4). Presets may seem similar to Styles, but Presets are much richer, and are capable of doing much more than assigning color, fill, and line width. With one selection, you can apply very complex sets of commands. The program comes with such prebuilt settings as Chrome, Bevel, and Plaque.

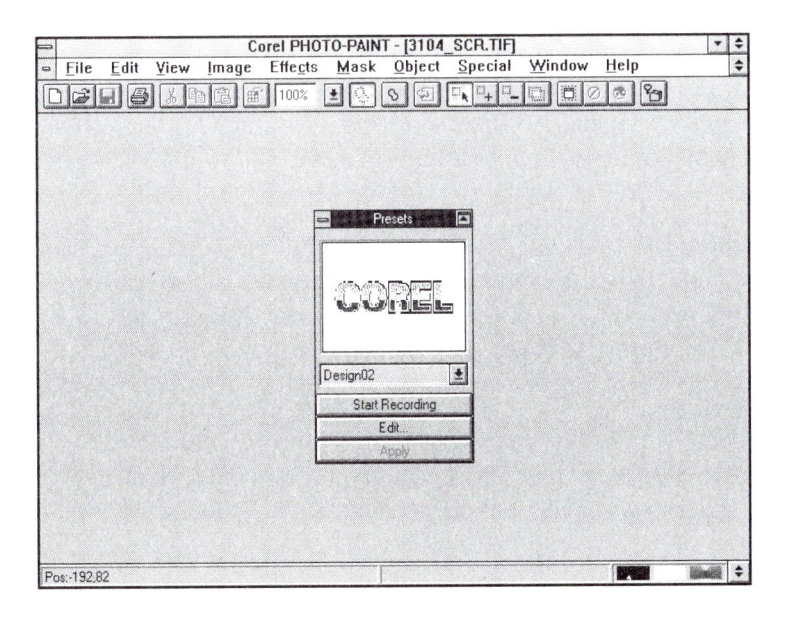

Fig. 31.4
Version 5's new Presets roll-up.

The new Presets may seem similar to Styles, but Presets are much richer...

A lot of us will simply use the Presets that come with the program, without exploring further. But if you learn how to record your own Preset macros, you'll save a lot of time applying effects and performing functions that you use frequently.

And the number two timesaver?

Use keystroke shortcuts.

I haven't touched the magnifying glass button in years, for example, because my most commonly used keystrokes are F2, F3, and F4. F2 is selective zoom. F3 returns you to the previous view. F4 shows you all the objects on a page.

I haven't touched the magnifying glass button in years....

Next, I rely often on the space bar, which toggles between the current tool and the Pick Selection tool. And F10 is the Node Edit shortcut key. Of course, you also have all the Control key shortcuts shown on the menus.

How about the new ribbon bar as a candidate for number three on the list?

It's a good idea and may be workable for many users. However, on hi-res monitors the icons get pretty small and therefore hard to see. For some time I've been using SuperBar. It's shareware from William J. Wood of Newport Beach and you can find it in most on-line services. SuperBar lives on my CorelDRAW! screen all the time (see fig. 31.5).

Thanks to SuperBar, I've had the new Delete All Guidelines feature for a couple of years, even though it is just coming into version 5. I've programmed this function as an item on my SuperBar. And instead of a simple delete all command, since I rarely want to do that, I've got one to delete the two most recently created guidelines.

By the way, we already did three timesavers, but I also believe the new color calibration in version 5 will save people a lot of time. A color management system will help you get accurate color results, and will save you the time of rerunning proofs or rerunning a job.

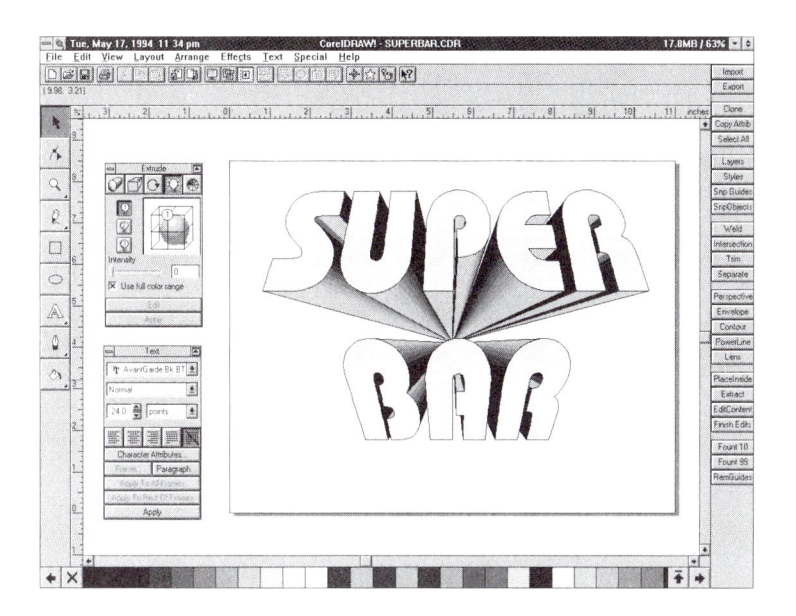

Fig. 31.5
A shot of Randy's CorelDRAW! screen, complete with the omnipresent SuperBar.

Finally, let's close with some advice for upgraders. You and your users group members struggled through some of the early problems with version 4, so you must have developed some ways to handle upgrades safely.

Let me just say that all of my answer here applies to any software upgrade situation. The concepts are the same whether or not you are using CorelDRAW!.

So, that being said, there's one main thing to remember about upgrading. Almost anyone using a program like CorelDRAW! is using it as a tool to make money. That means upgrade problems cost money, so you must do everything you can to make sure you have the tools to do your job.

> *Thanks to SuperBar, I've had the new Delete All Guidelines feature for a couple of years...*

Most important of all, you should leave the existing version on your system until you've completely tested out the new upgrade version. And, in the beginning, use the new version only on projects where you can afford to spend time trying to correct any unexpected problems.

Get as much information as you can before making the switch and find out how other users have solved problems that have come up. Check the reviews in the trade magazines and check out the program in person if you can. You might attend a live demo with a factory rep at a user group meeting or a conference. Ask probing questions about the issues that are important to your particular design business. Log on to the Corel forum on CompuServe, or check out the DTP Forum to see what other professionals are saying.

Of course, I think one of the best sources of information is the ACAD chapter meeting in your area.

Chapter 32

One-Page DTP Design with CorelDRAW!

by Rick Wallace

Robert Davis, Owner, Davis Advertising, Inc., Roswell, Georgia

Robert Davis says he first knew he had a career in design ahead of him when he spent time in high school classes impressing the girls with his drawings. (What we couldn't quite figure out is why drawings of hot rod cars would have such an attraction.)

He also impressed a classmate, who took some of the illustrations to his dad. The classmate's dad owned a commercial printing shop, and Robert quickly found himself—in the tenth grade—working in the shop's creative department.

At the print shop, he learned practically everything there is to know about the fundamentals of our business. Working weekends, after school, and summers, in addition to his duties as graphic artist, he was setting type, shooting film, using an X-Acto knife to strip separations and flats, running a press, and working in the bindery. Out of high school, he went full-time as the shop's art director, continuing his education by earning a degree in commercial art and graphic design.

At the print shop, a journeyman typesetter taught him to run a Linotype machine, setting hot lead. Strips of lead cut with a special saw were used to set leading. For headlines, the shop had a Ludlow, so he pulled type out of drawers and set characters one by one into a composing stick, which he then used to mold lead galleys. He also ran a Phototypositor.

Now, Robert isn't as old as this may make him seem. His print shop work was in the seventies. That will give you some idea of how quickly the phototypesetting revolution swept the graphic arts business, and then was quickly supplanted by digital type.

He ventured into advertising after the print shop experience, working at a furniture company putting together retail advertising. That job was followed by a position as art director at one of the country's largest printing companies, printers of Sunday newspaper advertising inserts, where he ran a graphics department that fed half a dozen of the company's 15 printing plants. It was during this time that Robert received a marketing degree at Georgia State University, with a minor in computer science.

Using his combined marketing, graphic art, and computer expertise, he went to work for an ad agency doing marketing research, strategic planning, and media planning and buying. This was in addition to overseeing the creative department, where he drew up storyboards and marker comps. In 1985 he bought the agency's first computer for performing analysis of broadcast (TV and radio) ratings and media planning.

"I knew that sooner or later somebody was going to come out with programs that would let you do typesetting on a PC," Robert says. And he was right. He discovered a company that would take his modem transfer of typesetting files and send galleys back overnight. In effect, he was using MultiMate to set type by inserting arcane typesetter codes into the text. But it was computerized typesetting and a big breakthrough. He later purchased Ventura Publisher and CorelDRAW! as soon as they were available.

About four years ago, Robert went into business for himself. "Back then, everyone thought desktop publishing was a toy, and that you could tell something had been set on a PC by just looking at it," he recalls. "But I had found Ventura Publisher by then, and I knew as a typesetter that it had real power, far beyond what PageMaker had at the time."

In addition to his advertising business, Robert is president of North Atlanta Association of Corel Artists and Designers. He also holds seminars on designing with CorelDRAW! and teaches CorelDRAW! at an Atlanta business school.

You use CorelDRAW! for practically all your work, it seems. Why? Take this advertisement and logo for the rug company. Why not do that in a page layout program (see fig. 32.1 and fig. 32.2)?

Robert Davis   **831**

Fig. 32.1
A one-page DTP project, an advertisement for a rug company, done entirely in CorelDRAW!.

I now use PageMaker, QuarkXPress, and Ventura Publisher, along with Photoshop, Fractal Design Painter, and many other graphics programs, plug-ins, and utilities. But for a one-page job, it just makes more sense to stay right in CorelDRAW!.

In this ad, working in CorelDRAW!, I had total control. I created that map at the same time I was creating the rest of the layout, and manipulated the type on the map while I was setting the body type and headlines. There's a seamless design process that way, when you create everything all in the same program.

Also, it saves some time, I think, because I don't end up switching back and forth between programs. Mainly, to tell the truth, I just like the tight CorelDRAW! user interface. It works for me. Maybe it's because I started as an artist and CorelDRAW! is, after all, a drawing program.

I especially like the elegant Snap To Grid function and the way I can double-click a guideline and type in a super precise coordinate. Also, I can put things on layers and turn off layers that I don't need, which means I can cut redraw time down to nothing. That's critical if you've got a bitmapped photo or a gradated background on the page.

> *...for a one-page job it just makes more sense to stay right in CorelDRAW!. In this ad, working in CorelDRAW!, I had total control. I created that map at the same time I was creating the rest of the layout....*

I occasionally use the Wireframe mode to speed things up. I can easily stretch and otherwise manipulate type, photos, and artwork while creating my layout, too. Bitmapped photos are embedded, resulting in a high-resolution, on-screen image. CorelDRAW!'s nudge function is also quite useful, as is the Zoom tool.

Also, I have found that CorelDRAW! prints out an accurate proof on an inexpensive non-PostScript printer and works well with my fax board for faxing proofs directly to clients.

Fig. 32.2
The logo Robert Davis created for the rug company featured in the newspaper ad in figure 32.1. (See color plate 43.)

If they had all of those features in any one desktop publishing program, I'm sure I'd use it instead of a draw program. That's why I'm excited about Ventura Publisher becoming part of the Corel family, because of the potential for welding together the Corel user interface with Ventura's DTP capabilities.

You said the CorelDRAW! interface may appeal to you because of your illustration background. Do you draw on the computer or do you sketch on paper first?

They are just two very different processes.

I don't draw in CorelDRAW! like I draw on paper. Mostly I work with nodes, rather than gestures. I do occasionally scan in sketches or images and trace them, but when I do that it is really a lot like tracing manually. I go through the resulting CorelTRACE image and do a lot of manual node reduction and manipulation of Bézier curves.

> *You sit at a computer all day long and you become a zombie, and I find that a graphics tablet is just a lot less taxing.*

I recently got a digitizing tablet, and that makes the CorelDRAW! user interface even more intuitive. You sit at a computer all day long and you become a zombie, and I find that a graphics tablet is just a lot less taxing. Besides, it's like sketching because you are using a pen.

But even with the graphics tablet I don't sketch on the computer the same way I do on paper.

These RE/MAX cards are some of the slickest and most colorful promotional cards I've ever seen. But how could agents afford to put their pictures on them (see fig. 32.3)?

The affordability and speedy turnaround on this project come from the production process I worked out.

Fig. 32.3
Promotional cards for real estate agents, produced on tight turnaround deadlines and on a budget. (See color plate 44.)

After the agent chooses from several designs and sales messages, the photos are duped to slides and scanned to Photo CD. I bring the photos into Photoshop for color correction, enhancement, and editing, and then drop the image into CorelDRAW!.

Once I drop the photos and the specific agent information into the layout, I can quickly duplicate the design and lay out four up flat, right in CorelDRAW!. I then upload the files via modem directly to the printer, who has an in-house service bureau.

After the agent chooses from several designs and sales messages, the photos are duped to slides and scanned to Photo CD.

The agents get double use out of the cards because the printing company makes them with laser safe ink and varnish. They can print customized information on the back so that they become *farming* postcards. Farming is what real estate agents call prospecting for listings.

These cards seem unusually crisp. There's a lot of snap to the design.

To some extent that's because everything is a vector graphic, with the exception of the photographs, of course.

I redid the RE/MAX logo in CorelDRAW!, for example, instead of scanning it in. I'm really a stickler about getting everything possible into vector format. Sometimes it is hard to convince the client that this is important, but it is.

I'm really a stickler about getting everything possible into vector format.

I read one time that one reason the Disney animated films are so good and so powerful is the attention to detail. Even something that will be seen on the screen for a split second gets enormous attention and precision. That's the way I feel about getting every possible part of a design into a vector drawing.

At first glance, this point of purchase display back card for the "Relief Center" seems like something that could easily have been done in a page layout program. Why did you do it in CorelDRAW! (see fig. 32.4)?

The decision to do this one in CorelDRAW! had a lot to do with the complicated blue gradation in the background. If I had done it in a page layout program, I would have had to create the gradation in CorelDRAW! and then import it into the layout program. But matching up the type with the locations of the gradations was an important part of this project. It saved a lot of effort to simply set the type right where I was creating the gradation.

Once the gradation had been created, I could turn off that layer to save time. That way I wouldn't be sitting there watching the screen redraw endlessly instead of designing the piece.

Fig. 32.4
A three-foot-wide point of purchase display card, executed in CorelDRAW!. (See color plate 45.)

I also stretched the "Relief Center" type to blend with the layout, and added the shadow effect to provide added dimension. Since I did everything in CorelDRAW!, I could work with all the elements as the design began to take shape, including experimenting with various shades of color.

By the way, all the art on this piece is from the CorelDRAW! CD clipart collection. The butterfly was simplified considerably to get it into three colors, but it's clipart. The flowers come from a clipart border, and I duplicated a section that I selected to create the border effect you see here, with the tall flowers on the outside edges.

> *By the way, all the art on this piece is from the CorelDRAW! CD clipart collection.*

And the typeface is Adobe's Bodoni Poster. Sometimes you have to blow letters up to appreciate them. I think, at this size, the beauty of these letterforms becomes more apparent.

I've seen a newsletter article you did for your users group about design basics. In it you talked about five design fundamentals. Entire books have been written on this subject, but how about talking us quickly through those design points for this "Relief Center" piece?

The five basics are balance, proportion, unity, emphasis, and sequence or eye travel.

First, the words "Relief Center" show the principle of emphasis. Those words are the most important thing on this product display riser card. Ad copy should show the benefit, which is *relief*. Design, in this case, emphasized the benefit to be the first thing you see. It dominates the design.

Of course, the sequence of eye travel closely interrelates with emphasis. Your eye travel begins with the item that dominates the design. On this display piece, your eye first goes to "Relief Center," and then to "Anti-Itch/Allergy." From there you probably pick up all these spring symbols for itching and allergy that need relief, such as the bee and flower pollen.

Balance can be formal, with complete symmetry between the left and right side of the ad. Or balance can be asymmetrical and more informal, with the weight distributed in different parts of the ad. To evaluate balance, find the optical center of your ad and think about how it can act as a sort of pivot for the ad. The optical center is just above the center line and slightly to the left. If you drilled a hole and inserted a pivot at the optical center, would the ad balance on it?

Proportion has to do with relationships. For the most interesting ad, avoid creating obvious mathematical relationships and aim for unequal dimensions and distances. Compare the width and depth of an ad element, relative size of two elements, and the width and height of the ad itself. Also, look for dynamic proportion between light and dark areas of the ad.

And the fifth basic is unity, right?

Unity is more important than any of the other four fundamentals. The first mistake I notice in a bad-looking ad is a violation of unity. Everything will be fighting for attention.

Advertising designers and their clients, for example, often make the mistake of making the company logo too big, so it ends up visually fighting with everything else in the ad. In this piece, the consumer sees the Big B Drugs logo across the top, but it is subdued enough that the benefit line about relief gets delivered as the dominant factor in the ad.

> *The first mistake I notice in a bad-looking ad is a violation of unity. Everything will be fighting for attention.*

Sometimes you have to struggle with the client over this issue, but as designers it is our job to explain the need to put the benefit forward as the most important item.

You mentioned an optical pivot concept for evaluating balance. Any handy trick you can offer for evaluating unity?

I had an art school teacher who told me this one. If you black in all the elements in the ad, leaving the open space or white space alone, the elements ought to look unified. They don't have to physically connect but they must relate to each other visually. I've blacked out all the design elements in this display back board, so you can see how this works (see fig. 32.5).

The white space or open space in this piece is the blue sky with the background blend. Notice how the blacked-in elements all associate with one another. They have unity.

If you black in all the elements in the ad, leaving the open space or white space alone, the elements ought to look unified.

Take a look at the bee in this blacked-in version. If the bee was a couple of inches higher, it would lose its unity with the benefit line.

Another way to look at this is to examine the white space. Ask yourself if any of it is trapped by the ad elements. There should be an outlet for any white space area.

One more thing. An advertising artist must also be sensitive to strategic marketing considerations, such as the target market definition, mission statement, positioning statement, and the objectives and strategies of the overall advertising plan. I have found few who fully understand the importance of building these marketing factors into an advertising design, but those who do are worth their weight in gold.

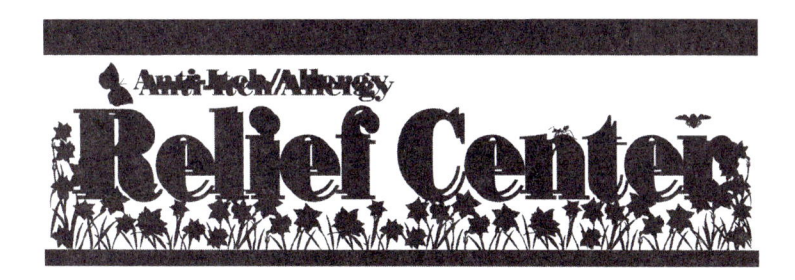

Fig. 32.5
Blacking in all the elements in an ad to check for visual unity.

Roger Goldingay

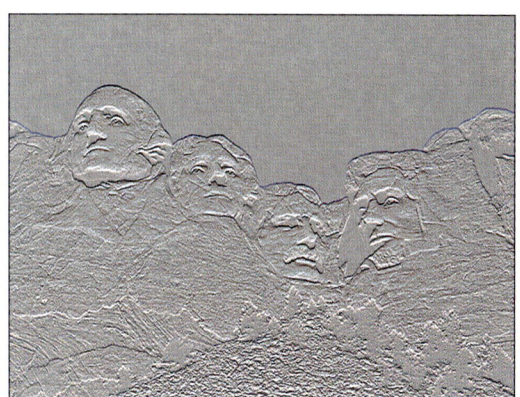

Color Plate 39
The original photograph is shown in the upper-left corner. The upper-right photo shows the inversion special effect. Vignette is shown in the lower left, and an embossed version is shown in the lower right. (See Chapter 26, "Advanced CorelPHOTO-PAINT.")

Color Plate 40
The original photograph is shown in the upper-left corner. The upper-right photo shows the glass block special effect. Impressionist is shown in the lower left, and a pixelated version is shown in the lower right. (See Chapter 26, "Advanced CorelPHOTO-PAINT.")

Tom Atwood

Color Plate 41

The original photograph is shown in the upper-left corner. The upper-right photo shows the inversion special effect. Contour is shown in the lower left, and a distorted version is shown in the lower right. (See Chapter 26, "Advanced CorelPHOTO-PAINT.")

Color Plate 42
A *Corelation* cover, a test for the imagesetter, but it output all the same thanks to some nearly surefire techniques for setting up CorelDRAW! and running a job. (See fig. 31.1.)

Color Plate 43
The colorful logo Robert Davis created for the rug company featured in the black-and-white newspaper ad in figure 32.1. The logo did extra duty in the company's television commercials. (See fig. 32.2.)

Color Plate 44
Promotional cards for real estate agents, produced on tight turnaround deadlines and on a budget. (See fig. 32.3.)

Color Plate 45
A three-foot wide point of purchase display card, executed in CorelDRAW!. (See fig. 32.4.)

Color Plate 46
A direct mail brochure showing the use of stacked blocks of type fitted to a curve. (See fig. 33.1.)

Who Should Attend?

Everyone involved in planning, developing, designing or delivering business presentations of any kind will benefit from Justin Joseph's Power Presenter Seminar. Past attendees include CEOs; marketing, advertising and public relations professionals; sales people; corporate trainers; desktop publishers; association executives; teachers; AV department supervisors; graphic artists and creative directors.

"FUN AND INFORMATIVE"
Corie Austin
Phoenix

1994 JUSTIN JOSEPH SEMINARS POWER PRESENTER TOUR

CITY	DATE	CITY	DATE
Dallas	Mar. 30, 1994	Cincinnati	July 27, 1994
Houston	April 6, 1994	Chicago	Aug. 3, 1994
Atlanta	April 20, 1994	Milwaukee	Aug. 10, 1994
Washington D.C.	April 27, 1994	Minneapolis	Aug. 17, 1994
Baltimore	May 4, 1994	St. Louis	Aug. 31, 1994
Philadelphia	May 18, 1994	Denver	Sept. 14, 1994
White Plains	May 25, 1994	Salt Lake City	Sept. 21, 1994
Boston	June 8, 1994	Vancouver	Oct. 5, 1994
Ottawa	June 15, 1994	Seattle	Oct. 12, 1994
Montreal	June 22, 1994	San Francisco	Oct. 26, 1994
Toronto	June 29, 1994	San Jose	Nov. 9, 1994
Cleveland	July 13, 1994	Orange County	Nov. 16, 1994
Detroit	July 20, 1994		

THE POWER PRESENTER SEMINAR

More than 20,000 people have attended The Power Presenter Seminar, North America's most popular presentation skills seminar.

Anyone involved in planning, developing, organizing, designing or delivering business presentations will benefit from this unique program.

What You Will Learn

- ☐ The critical differences between public speaking and business communication
- ☐ Strategies for each type of business communication
- ☐ The four communications styles and how to interact with them
- ☐ Listening skills as a power tool
- ☐ The essentials of an effective presentation
- ☐ Design principles for business graphics
- ☐ Powerful negotiation skills
- ☐ Rules for effective meetings
- ☐ Successful meeting planning
- ☐ Telephone techniques to improve communication
- ☐ The importance of the presenter as a visual
- ☐ How to match the medium to the message
- ☐ How to identify your audiences' "hot buttons"
- ☐ Plus, visit exhibits to see the best in presentation technology

"THIS SEMINAR IS JUST WHAT I WAS LOOKING FOR"
Phyllis Siwin
New York

"ALL THE INFORMATION IS APPLICABLE, IMMEDIATELY USEFUL"
Ken Kaley
Chicago

"THE MOST PROFESSIONALLY DONE AD PRESENTATION I HAVE EVER EXPERIENCED"
Tom Lyon
Salt Lake City

How to Register

Simply fax the enclosed Ticket Request Form to Justin Joseph Seminars at 817/285-8513 or mail it to Justin Joseph Seminars, 1848 Norwood Plaza, Suite 100, Hurst, TX 76054. Remember to select both the city and date of your choice. Also include your complete address, telephone and FAX numbers, with area codes. Your tickets will be mailed to you by Justin Joseph Seminars and paid for by your sponsoring company.

Door Prizes! A drawing for door prizes worth in excess of $2,000 will be held at the close of each seminar. Your seminar sponsors have provided the newest versions of presentation software, clip art, publication subscriptions, gift certificates for the best in presentation technology, desktop publishing accessories and much more! Of course, you must be present to win.

SEMINAR SCHEDULE

7:30am	Registration and exhibits
8:30am	Seminar
10:00am	Coffee break and exhibits
10:30am	Seminar
11:45am	Lunch (on your own)
1:15pm	Seminar
2:15pm	Stretch break and exhibits
2:30pm	Seminar
3:00pm	Door prizes
3:30pm to 4:00pm	Exhibits

Color Plate 47
Inside spread of Janie Owen-Bugh's brochure design, showing her stacked lines of text fitted to a curved path and her custom stippled background for putting oomph behind boxes of text. Together, these two design techniques unify the entire design of the brochure, while visually highlighting the all-important testimonial quotes that make this brochure really sell as a direct mail piece. (See fig. 33.3.)

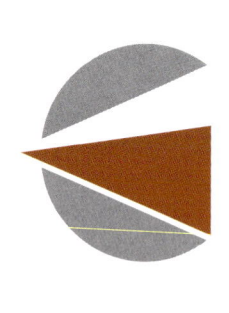

Color Plate 48
Stage one of Janie Owen-Bugh's method for creating a quick-and-dirty embossing effect for text, setting up a light-colored drop shadow. (See fig. 33.6.)

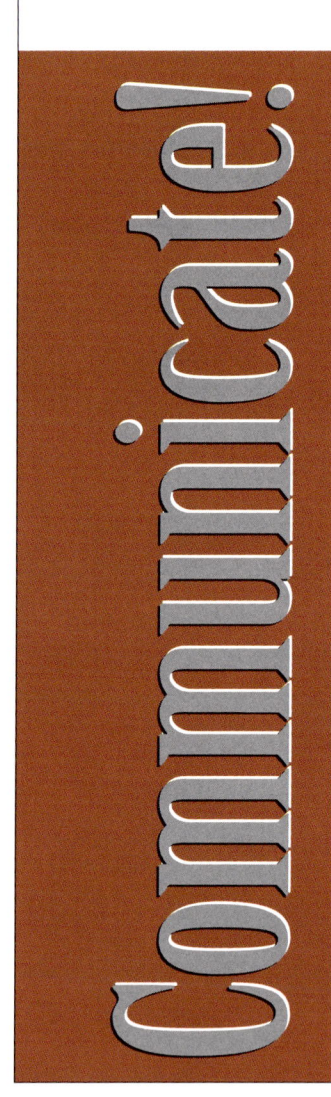

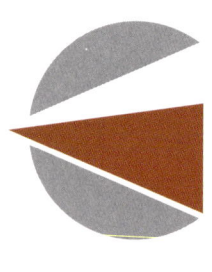

Color Plate 49
The completed quick-and-dirty text embossing effect. (See fig. 33.7.)

Color Plate 50
Janie's type-based company logo for a video post-production company, and the way she incorporated it into a newsletter nameplate. (See fig. 33.9.)

Color Plate 51
One of Nick Pregent's Mardi Gras mask creations, made from a pattern constructed in CorelDRAW!. (See fig. 34.1.)

Color Plate 52
A finished computer sketch of the mask, before distorting it to allow for turning it into a three-dimensional pattern for the leather pieces. (See fig. 34.4.)

Color Plate 53
A metallic effect was added to the text for this Gold Club award show, not easy to do in a regular presentation program. (See fig. 35.1.)

Main text

Color Plate 54
An exploded view of the gold metallic text effect in the Gold Club slide. (See fig. 35.2.)

Drop shadow

Color Plate 55
Using a repeating logo effect as a slide show background. (See fig. 35.3.)

Color Plate 56
A build slide with 15 steps, all built in CorelDRAW!. (See fig. 37.4.)

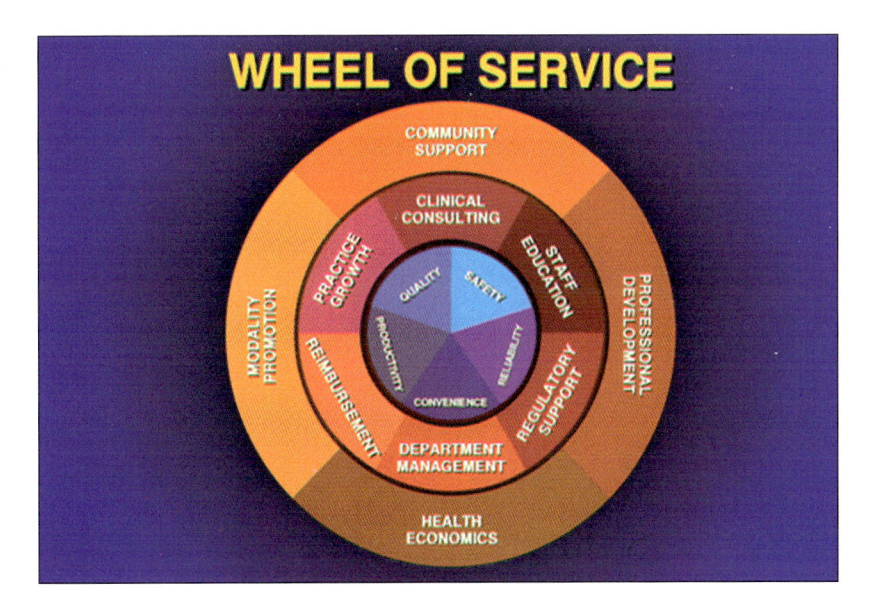

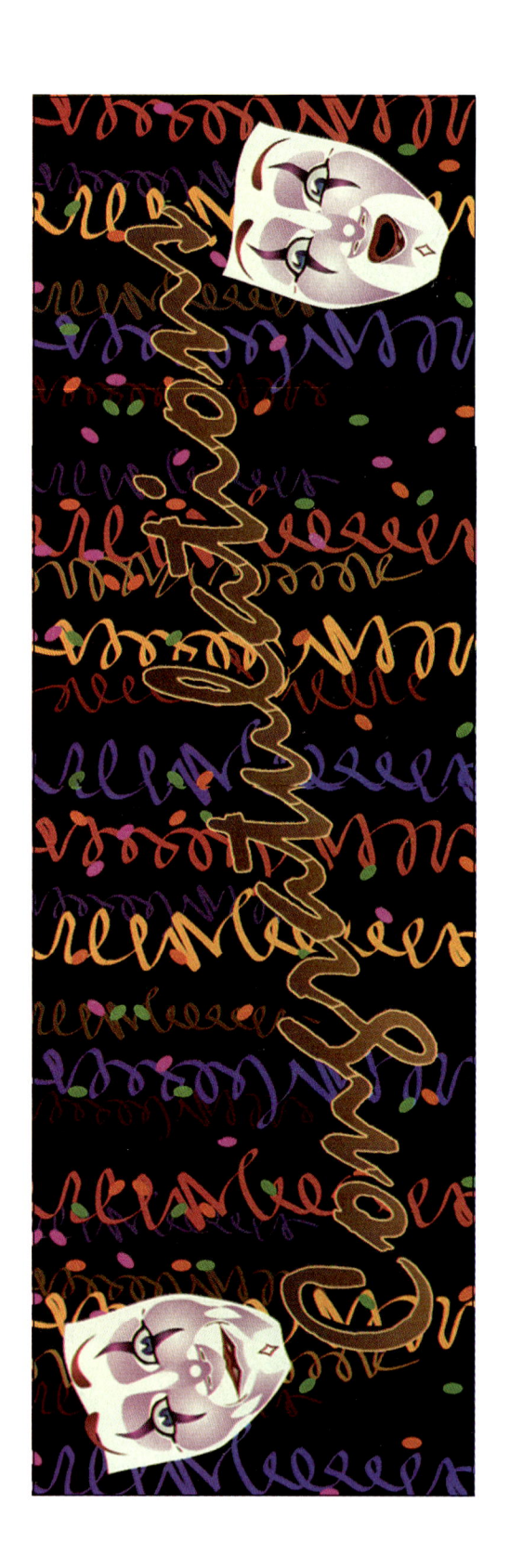

Color Plate 57
A double-wide slide, with no seams because it is cast on the screen from three projectors. (See fig. 35.5.)

Chapter 33
Artful Type: Depth And Dimension

by Rick Wallace

Janie Owen-Bugh, Janie Owen-Bugh Electronic Publishing, Dallas, Texas
It's always fun to hear about the sometimes quirky path that a designer follows to come to his or her profession. Janie, in fact, started out training as an architect, and that provided a direct connection leading to her love of typography and desktop design.

You see, at one point after leaving school, she went to work for a sign company, using her architectural skills to design those big monuments to commerce you see in front of burger stands and such. Of course, you can't design a sign without including the lettering. Drawing those letterforms onto the plan sheets was the beginning of a career for Janie.

It's worth noting that she grew up around the graphic arts, because her parents are both in the printing business. She had always claimed, she says, that she would never go into that business.

Right, you guessed it. Her career route next took her to a printing company, where she worked for the in-house art department. That's where she learned typesetting, using an old CompuGraphic phototypesetter, one of the ones where you insert plastic disks to image the type—maximum of four font families at a time in four weights.

She spent some time as art director of an ad agency, followed by a stint as editor/designer of a tabloid monthly called *Living Around Richardson* (Texas). She also worked as designer/desktop publisher for an arm of J C Penney where she did statement stuffers, direct mail pieces, and in-house newsletters.

During this 13-year journey, Janie moved through the various drawing and desktop publishing programs of the day (including CorelDRAW! version 1.2). Today she has her own design business and uses CorelDRAW! and Ventura as her primary tools to produce type-oriented publications such as brochures and newsletters. She's also president of the Dallas Association of Corel Artists and Designers.

The module of curved type on the cover of this brochure not only conveys information, but also acts as a design element to pull the whole piece together because you carry the technique over onto the inside pages. How did you line up these three lines of curved type (see fig. 33.1)?

Almost everybody knows how to fit text to a path and the fundamental operations of stacking multiple lines of text on a path are the same. Like all fit-to-path situations, you must first draw your path, in this case a curved line. Then type out your text into a single text block. Select both the text and the line, and use the Fit Text To Path command. That gets the job done if you just have one line of text, but it won't serve you very well if you need to precisely align three stacked lines of text like the one about Joe Montana on this brochure's front cover.

Making three paths and trying to make them all match takes too much time to create, and time is always critical in a production environment.

A lot of people would simply use three copies of the curved line and match them all up, but you don't do that, right?

No. Making three paths and trying to make them all match takes too much time to create, and time is always critical in a production environment. You also severely reduce your flexibility for editing and believe me, text always needs to be edited! Plus, if you have to adjust the shape of the curved line, you are forced to start all over again because you can never make the same precise adjustment to all three lines.

The answer is to fit all three lines to the same path, a single curved line in this case. To do that, you must create each line of text as a separate block. Then individually apply the Fit Text To Path command to each block and your single path.

Fig. 33.1
A direct mail brochure showing the use of stacked blocks of type fitted to a curve. (See color plate 46.)

As you fit each block to the path, use the roll-up menu to choose attributes such as alignment, rotation, and whether to align the type on baseline, top, bottom, or middle. Then, use the Edit button to specify the offset.

Which attributes did you use for each of the three lines shown here (see fig. 33.2)?

Do the middle line first and give it center alignment, to the middle of the type.

Then make the top line of type align left and the bottom one align right. Unless you are trying for some special effect, fit the path to the middle of the type.

In turn, select the top and bottom blocks of type and click the Edit button in the Fit Text To Path roll-up, which opens the Fit Text To Path Offsets dialog box. Now type the Distance From Path amount for both the top and bottom lines of text. The Distance From Path is measured from the baseline of the text to the path. The amount you push the top and bottom lines away from the middle line of type is a subjective judgement. Use whatever amounts look right.

Fig. 33.2
Stacking three lines of type to a curved path.

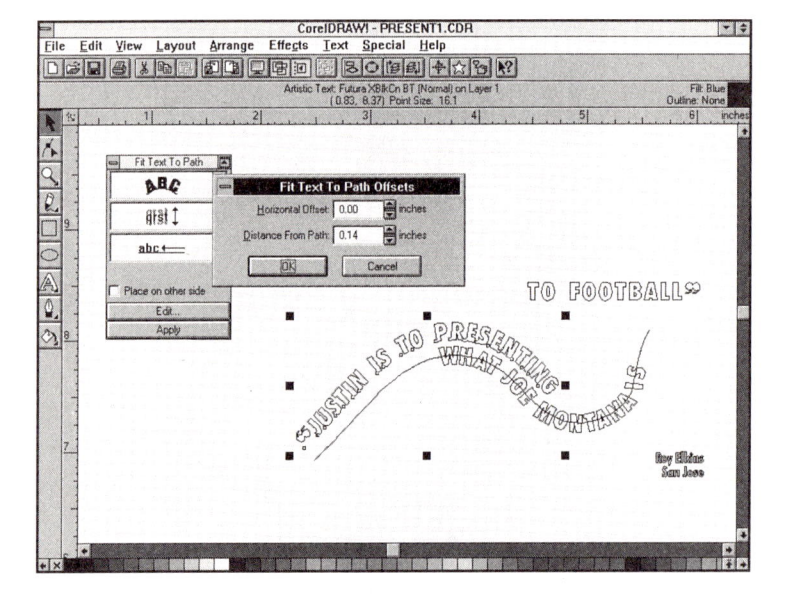

Then there's one last thing. Because you gave it center alignment, the center line of text will be mathematically centered on the path, between the extreme left of the top text block and the extreme right of the bottom one. But that doesn't mean the center line of text has been centered visually. The reader's eye will be trying to align the middle text in the interior space between the top and bottom lines. So now use your eye to check the look, and you probably will want to use some Horizontal Offset in the Fit Text To Path Offsets dialog box to get the proper visual effect.

As you are trying to make these adjustments, of course, you can always edit the line breaks between each of the three text blocks to get the best look. Sometimes swapping words between the various lines is really the best way to get visual alignment to work out correctly.

> *The reader's eye will be trying to align the middle text in the interior space between the top and bottom lines.*

You will notice that the Text tool doesn't seem to work when you've fitted text to a path and that makes it seem as if you must break the text back away from the path to edit. Well, you can edit it right where it is. Select the block of text you want to edit by using the Select tool while holding down the control key. This selects the *child object*. Once you do this, you can get the Text tool. Then when you click the text, the Text Edit dialog box appears and you can make your changes in there.

There's another element you've used for wedding together this brochure design while highlighting testimonial quotes. It's this stippled background you've used behind the quotes inside these rotate boxes (see fig. 33.3, also color plate 47). You've also used it on the cover of the brochure.

Sometimes you get the best communication by not messing with the text at all. These testimonial quotes leap off the page in a bold and direct manner, but they are very readable and haven't been manipulated at all except for putting them in color. One reason for that is the stippled background, which visually pops the text forward.

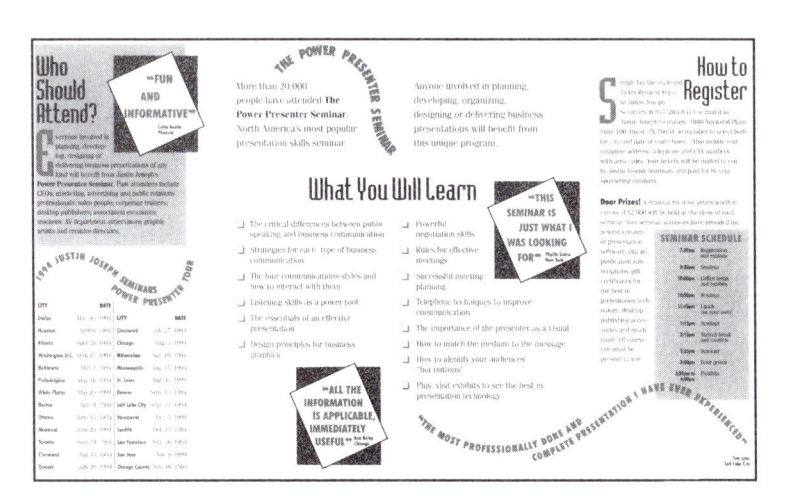

Fig. 33.3
Inside spread of brochure shows the custom stippled background used to highlight some of the testimonial quotes. The stippled background text boxes and the use of the curved type work together to unify the brochure design. (See color plate 47.)

Fig. 33.4
Using the Two-Color Pattern Editor to create your own two-color pattern for a flashy text box background.

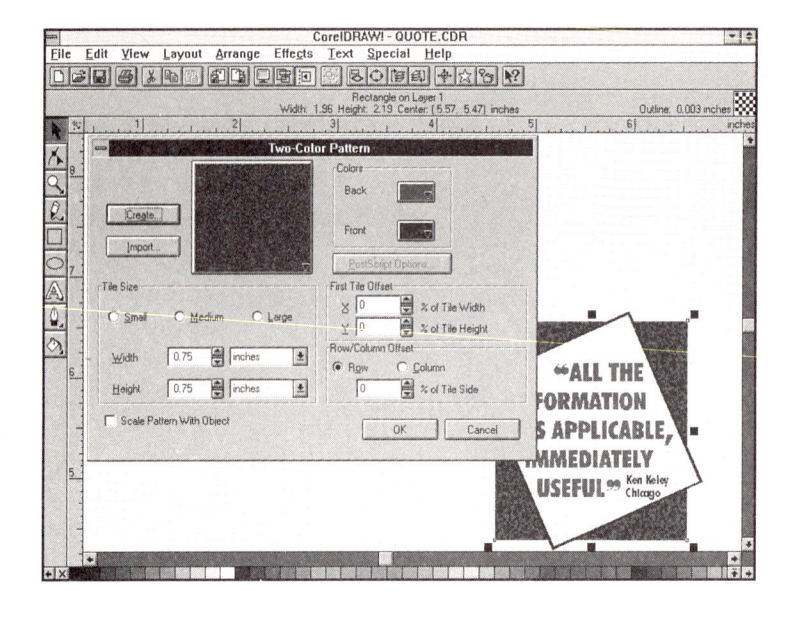

Creating this custom pattern was easy, even for somebody like me who doesn't consider herself an illustrator. And it's more inventive and fun than simply dropping a gray shadow or tint box behind a block of text.

First draw a box. With the box selected, click the Fill tool to open the Fill fly-out menu. Clicking the Checkerboard icon gets you the Two-Color Pattern dialog box. Click the Create button and just start scribbling to create your custom background (see fig. 33.4).

Once you have scribbled your stipple effect, or whatever you want to create as a backdrop, click OK and choose the back and front colors, which will be black and white by default.

Sometimes you get the best communication by not messing with the text at all. These testimonial quotes leap off the page in a bold and direct manner...

When back in the Two-Color Pattern dialog, pick whatever colors you want for the back (white) and front (black) layers of the pattern.

Click the Tiling button to make the same sorts of adjustments you might make for any patterned fill, such as proportional width and height and tile offset. Your new custom pattern gets stored in the library, ready for you to use again in another project, or to use as a starting point for a new pattern.

The rest of this text enhancement is simple as can be. Draw a box filled with white and rotate it in front of your custom background. In this case, I then grouped the two boxes so I could easily duplicate them for use as a repetitive design element for highlighting the testimonial quotes.

How about sharing your embossed text technique, like the one in this newsletter nameplate (see fig. 33.5).

Well, this isn't strictly speaking an embossed effect, but it sure is fast, and it does create a nice embossed-style feel of depth.

Fig. 33.5
Embossed-styling for the type in this nameplate gives the newsletter power to "Communicate."

Some people create a sort of embossed look by using the Effects menu's Extrude roll-up to apply a light amount of Large Back extrusion to the entire text block. However, to really make extrusion work for an embossing effect, you have to go through and put every letter in its own text block and then individually apply the extrusion to each one. Then you must select the extruded blocks and assign light source shading and colors to each letter individually to complete the embossing effect. For this block of type with the word "Communicate!," that would mean a dozen text blocks, a dozen applications of the effect to each letter, after I was done experimenting to find the right settings, including extrusion, shading and colors. That's not to mention the agony of lining up and spacing a dozen tiny text blocks. For really critical work it is worth it, but it sure takes a lot of time.

Well, this isn't strictly speaking an embossed effect, but it sure is fast, and it does create a nice embossed-style feel of depth.

Instead, this quick-and-dirty embossing technique manipulates the entire text block at one time by using the same sort of method you'd use for doing a drop shadow text effect, but it adds a highlight which gives it the right finishing touch.

Start by setting your text block, and then set your nudge preference to 1/2 point.

Press the + key on the keypad and you get an exact duplicate, precisely on top of the first text block. It's already selected so send it to the back and it will stay selected.

Give this duplicate text block a color of white if you are working in black and white. If you are working in color, assign it a dramatically lighter color or tint of the color you are assigning to your foreground text block. Nudge this back block to the right and down two or three times (see fig. 33.6). Don't use too much offset. That's the biggest mistake people make, overdoing the offset. This is a lot like the drop shadow effect we've all made at one time or another on any number of objects. Now you need to add a dark layer, between the main letters and the background light letters.

Be sure the light-colored drop shadow text block is still selected and use the + key again to create another duplicate. It's important to do it in this order so that the main letters and the shadow letters will be stacked on the correct layers. By duplicating the drop shadow, you get a third text block that sits on a layer between the foreground letters and the drop shadow letters. Now nudge your shadow up and to the left by doubling the number of nudges you used to position the first shadow (see fig. 33.7).

Fig. 33.6
The first stage of creating a quick-and-dirty embossing effect for text, setting up a light-colored drop shadow. (See color plate 48.)

Color the second shadow in a much darker shade than the first one, but be sure it contrasts adequately with the foreground text block, otherwise the effect won't work to give you the feeling of depth you need for an embossed look.

Again, the most common mistake is to go too far, so it doesn't look embossed, and ends up looking more like a drop shadow.

Notice, around the serifs, the embossing effect breaks down a bit, but this takes about 30 seconds and three major steps, which is a lot easier than individually extruding and coloring each letter in a text block.

Fig. 33.7
The completed quick-and-dirty text embossing effect. (See color plate 49.)

I know I said we'd work with text effects, but I notice the table of class schedules on the inside spread of this newsletter, where all these icons have been used to enhance the categories. You said you aren't an illustrator, but this looks pretty slick (see fig. 33.8).

Fig. 33.8

A table, enhanced by icons, produced by someone who says she "isn't an illustrator."

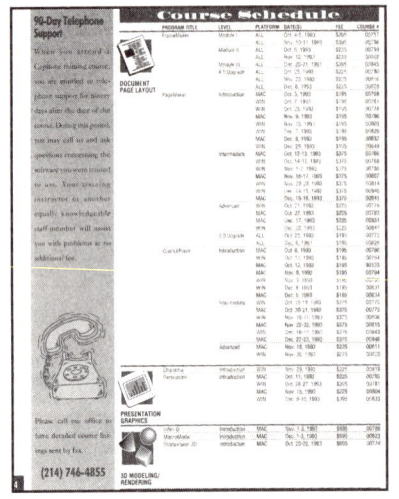

Thanks, but I stole almost every one of these from clipart that came with CorelDRAW!.

I drew a few of them, but there's nothing fancy here. The Document Page Layout icon was a matter of drawing series of lines and a drop shadow behind a box. The shapes in the 3D Modeling/Rendering icon were drawn and then I used extrude and gradated or radial screens to add some depth.

> *Thanks, but I stole almost every one of these from clipart that came with CorelDRAW!.*

For the Image Editing icon, I brought a clipart TIFF into PHOTO-PAINT, selected the face portion of the art, and then used CorelTRACE to get the icon effect and to turn it into a vector-type image so it could be easily manipulated and finalized in CorelDRAW!.

The Illustration (Draw/Paint) icon is two pieces of clipart combined, a drawing and the frame. The Multimedia Authoring icon is also a pasted together combination of clipart images.

One thing you do a lot of is to create nameplates and type-based company logos. How about taking us through the process of developing this company logo for *The Production Facility* (see fig. 33.9)? We see it here used in a newsletter nameplate, and as a stand-alone logo.

As much as anything, designing a company logo involves getting to know about the company, and that's the biggest suggestion I'd make to anybody who has to come up with a logo or a nameplate for their company.

In this case, I didn't know much about video post-production services and the process of making videos and I had to learn what they do. As you can see from this series of versions of the logo, well, there was quite an evolution before we got to an answer that satisfied both me and the client (see fig. 33.10).

> *As much as anything, designing a company logo involves getting to know about the company...*

Fig. 33.9
A company logo based on type, and the way it was incorporated into a newsletter nameplate. (See color plate 50.)

This company finds all its function in serving those who make movies and videos. They have editing services, equipment rental, and a special effects studio. I experimented with a number of different ideas for symbols, including strips of film, before centering on the spotlight feel you see in the final result.

Also, I wanted to do something that would be adaptable for different purposes but also work well by itself. The blocky overall shape of the logo helped, as did the reversed out word in the horizontal bar. Ultimately, when I had to wed the logo into a nameplate, the bar made it all fit together.

And I guess that's my final bit of advice. It's easy to get carried away but restrain the impulse. You can really hurt the ability of type to communicate, especially if you do something that harms its readability. Extrude and type on a path are great, but don't let anything get in the way of the type being able to say what it has to say to the reader. Don't overuse drop shadows and embossing, for example. And sometimes it is better to just let plain type display against a background that makes it stand out, or to highlight and categorize with icons.

Fig. 33.10
The evolution of a logo for a video services company, finally arriving at a spotlight theme.

Chapter 34

Pattern Making with a Master Mask Artist

by Rick Wallace

Nick Pregent, Creative Imagery, North Hills, California

Nick Pregent started out training as an architect, as did one of our other contributors for the "Learning from the Pros" section, Janie Owen-Bugh. Like Janie, his circuitous path turned him into a CorelDRAW! expert, but in his case, he uses the program as an artist to make the patterns for his leather Mardi Gras-style masks.

After switching out of architecture, Nick moved into photography, earning a degree in industrial photography at the prestigious Brooks Institute in Santa Barbara.

It wasn't long before Nick began using his photography skills to produce slide and multimedia shows. And that set him on the road to becoming an artist. Nick began constructing sets and scenery for photo shoots. Of course they had to be designed and painted.

"At some point in there, I began using a computer to sketch set designs. Suddenly I could draw a straight line! The computer enabled and empowered me," Nick told us, remembering the days when he started out working with such pioneer PC drawing packages as Lumina and TimeArts. "Eventually I could even shade objects," he says.

This discovery of the power of computers set Nick on a path of growth. Finding out he could shade objects on the computer made him comfortable enough to do it in his hand-drawn sketches. Advancing his skills with an air brush led him to try new techniques on the computer; his skills in each medium grew as he switched back and forth between working by hand and working on the computer.

As it happens, Nick had worked in high school for a company that manufactured machinery for making boxes for soap and cereal. That experience fell into place one day when he tossed a computer sketch down onto the workbench being used to construct a table top model, just to show someone what the model ought to look like.

Then he realized, "Why not use the sketch to construct the table top set?" So he made multiple copies of the printout, cut the sketch into pieces, and used them to make the table top set's group of miniature buildings.

This pattern construction led to another twist in his path toward master mask maker, as he helped a friend who needed some computer assistance in making patterns for beaded jewelry—and got turned on to making jewelry himself. He began making computer-generated patterns for making lost wax molds for silver jewelry.

Ultimately, that led to molding leather into three-dimensional shapes, where the wet leather would be stretched over or pounded into the curves of a relief mold.

In addition to his work as an artist, Nick also puts his expert CorelDRAW! skills to work as a staff member at the Burbank headquarters of the Association of Corel Designers and Artists users group. He's the friendly, helpful voice most members end up reaching when they are trying to crack some intractable problem. He also writes and designs most of the Tips and Tricks sheets handed out at chapter meetings, and assists with the design for *Corelation* magazine.

Not everyone makes Mardi Gras masks like this one (see fig. 34.1). Do your pattern-making techniques have any general applications?

Anybody who designs packaging, for instance, ought to be able to apply the broad concepts of my work...

I think so. Anybody who designs packaging, for instance, ought to be able to apply the broad concepts of my work to the designing of a pattern for die-cutting an unfolded box. I know someone who uses CorelDRAW! to make patterns for making quilts. I started out making patterns for table top photography sets, which are a lot like model railroad layouts or architectural models. And my friend is still using CorelDRAW! to construct bead patterns for her jewelry fabricators.

Fig. 34.1
One of Nick Pregent's Mardi Gras mask creations, made from a pattern constructed in CorelDRAW!. (See color plate 51.)

That's a lot longer list of applications than I expected! Let's establish a fundamental concept. What makes a drawing program such as CorelDRAW! so suitable for this kind of pattern-making work?

Two things. First, it is a vector-based drawing program, so you can draw a sketch of what you want the object to look like and then break it up into parts, so the parts become the pieces of your pattern. Second, the CorelDRAW! user interface, at least for me, makes sense to my artistic side. There's a lot of this that's kind of mechanical, so you might think that a CAD program would make more sense, being designed for this sort of thing in the first place. But for me, a drawing program feels more like something I'd use to…well, draw.

S o how does someone start making a pattern for a complex object like this mask?

I think there are basically two kinds of people. One type just starts out working on the computer, creating their object from scratch. But I can't work that way and I'm an example of the second type. I start with a hand-drawn sketch, which I then experiment with until I've got the mask to the point where I think I can move to the computer (see fig. 34.2).

Fig. 34.2
Nick's thumbnail sketch, his starting point for making a complex and multi-dimensional mask pattern.

> *I start with a hand-drawn sketch, which I then experiment with until I've got the mask to the point where I think I can move to the computer.*

The ideas for my masks come from almost anywhere—a statue, an image on TV, alien creatures in movies. So, the sketch helps me to conceptualize and develop an idea. Through my hands I just intuitively note my thoughts on paper. I need to develop the original core idea into my artistic vocabulary, my idiom. For example, this one started out, as do a lot of my masks, with a notion about the Celtic green man, who has to do with the spirit of harvest, rebirth, and change.

O nce you have your idea developed to a certain point, how do you get the sketch onto the computer?

I use a scanner. I import the TIFF into CorelDRAW! and trace it by hand, because the tracing is part of the process of advancing the design (see fig. 34.3). I do a lot of changing while I'm tracing my scanned sketch. The sketch is really a lot like working notes or an outline for a writer. I've outlined the core thoughts, and on the computer I actually finish the job.

So, the sketch helps me to conceptualize and develop an idea.

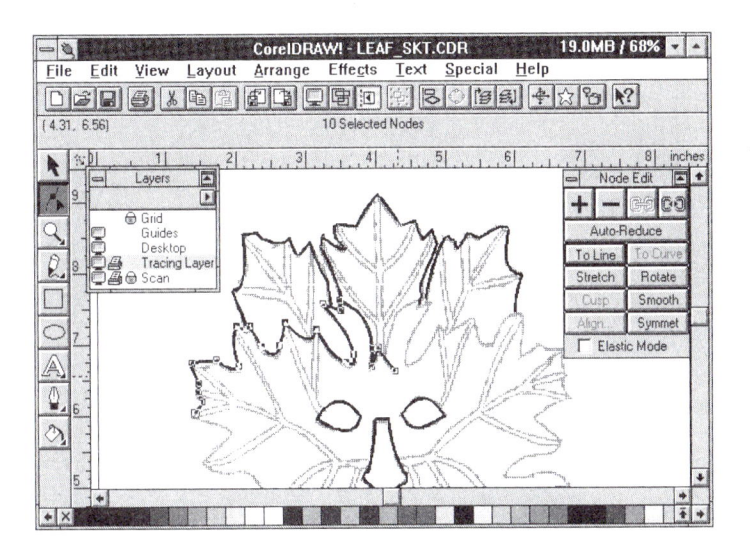

Fig. 34.3
A screenshot as Nick hand-traces the scanned developmental sketch for the mask. The darker lines are Nick's trace.

So you end up with a finished computer drawing of what the mask will look like (see fig. 34.4). But you are still working in only two dimensions. How do you get the depth?

Good question, because this next step in the process is fundamental to all three-dimensional pattern making. It's as important as being able to use the draw program to break the drawing into pattern pieces.

As you can see, I achieve the appearance of depth with shading techniques in the computer sketch. But that's an artistic illusion and doesn't actually give me the dimensionality of a pattern.

Once I have developed the mask into this face-on, two-dimensional artistic rendering, I intentionally distort it to allow for the bending that will need to happen when it gets converted into a three-dimensional pattern. For example, the average adult's eyes are three inches apart, center to center.

But to allow for the depth of the mask so that it can curve over the nose, the eyes really must be around five inches apart. I simply group the mask and stretch it horizontally until the eyes are the right distance apart. The result ends up resembling the map "projections" we used to study in school, where someone flattened a globe of the Earth into a map page in an atlas; the distances seem distorted to the eye but would be accurate if wrapped back around the globe.

Once I have developed the mask into this face-on, two-dimensional artistic rendering, I intentionally distort it to allow for the bending that will need to happen...

There are two elements that go into this process. First, I have a basic template that has the proper distortion dimensions for eyes, nose, and mouth and I can stretch the mask to fit that template for starters. Second, I just know by experience some of the issues I'll face when breaking the mask drawing into pattern pieces for the leather mask itself, so I make subtle adjustments by eye. Anybody making patterns will need to go through this kind of experimentation and learning curve, I think.

Fig. 34.4
A finished computer sketch of the mask, before distorting it to allow for turning it into a three-dimensional pattern to cut out the leather pieces. (See color plate 52.)

It helps that I design Mardi Gras-style masks, meaning the eyes are extra large and the mouth area is open. That's so the person wearing the mask can be comfortable for many hours and partake in one of the key features of partying, which is eating and drinking. These open areas mean that one mask fits many face sizes, so tolerances for such dimensions as eyehole distance aren't so critical. Anyone making patterns might want to keep that concept in mind, that you can design your project in such a way that it gives you this kind of leeway.

Next, I guess you break the distorted rendering down into pattern pieces, right?

The first step, though, is to rename the file and explode it into individual elements. In the case of this particular mask, there are pieces for the ears, the eyes, and so on (see fig. 34.5).

But I use an experimental, trial-and-error approach. I keep printing out the pattern pieces and cutting them out of paper instead of leather, trying them repeatedly until they fit properly on my face or on a model head I use for molding the leather. You could do the same thing for any pattern you were making, like a box or some type of sculpture, for example. It's better to get the mechanics worked out with pieces of paper before actually cutting into leather.

CorelDRAW! really makes this trial-and-error process tolerable. Do a print out, check the fit, and then use the computer to reshape and resize the vector-drawn pattern pieces until they have passed the test trials. I often use duplicate and mirror operations when I have a piece on one side of the face right, since faces are symmetrical.

During this step I take into account the overlap needed to attach all the pieces together. And, by the way, that's an important reason for me to do the gradation rendering, because it helps me visualize the layers and contours for the individual pieces when they are broken away from the main mask drawing.

You could do the same thing for any pattern you were making, like a box or some type of sculpture, for example.

When the pieces are shaped just right, I do a final printout and lay them out on leather to make the best use of the material at hand, taking into account holes and defects, the grain, and any need I may have for different textures of leather. Often the layout isn't on one sheet, like you see it here, but on bits and pieces of material I have lying around.

Then it is a matter of dampening the leather and stretching, hammering, and molding it into the contours of my model head, sometimes using a hair dryer or heat gun to fix the leather into shape before I stitch or glue the pieces together.

Fig. 34.5
Pattern pieces, broken out of the artist rendering in CorelDRAW!.

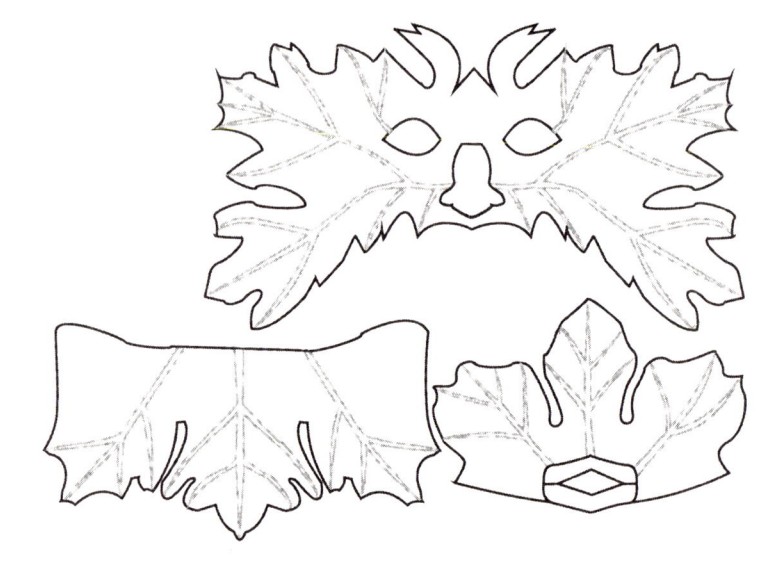

The final touch is dying the leather and sometimes using an airbrush to add shading and highlights to emphasize the contours of the mask.

And the result is the beautiful mask we showed at the beginning of the interview (refer to fig. 34.1). Let's close by hitting the high points of the concepts you've learned as a mask artist, fundamentals that would apply for anyone wanting to use CorelDRAW! to make patterns.

Use the artistic tools in CorelDRAW! to maximum advantage and don't just treat it like a CAD program. Use shading, for example, to indicate contours. That'll help you implement your vision as you make the translation into paper pattern pieces.

Start any way you're comfortable, of course, but I find it really helpful to work out my ideas to a certain point on the sketch pad and then scan that in. Others just start on the computer, but not me.

Once you have your two-dimensional, head-on view, distort it and break it up into pieces to help you make the transition to a three-dimensional object.

I fit my pattern to some pretty complicated contours, the human face, so this is a big part of my operation. Making a box pattern so it can all fold together for assembly may be a little less complicated but the concept is still the same.

And, finally, use a trial-and-error technique with laser printouts of the pieces to test the mechanical aspects of your design. Test your mechanics with laser printouts before spending time or money on making a final pattern.

Chapter 35

Painless and Powerful Slide Production

by Rick Wallace

David Wood, Director, Graphic Computer Services, Woodland Hills, California

Graphic Computer Services does just what their name would imply. They produce 35-millimeter slide shows, and also offer imaging services to other computer-based slide show producers. Suffice it to say that they keep both of their film-processing lines humming.

They also produce electronic presentations, multiprojector slide shows, special effects, and computer animation.

Their work has been commissioned by many major corporations, including Apple, Baskin-Robbins, Blue Cross, Honda Motorcycles, J. D. Power and Associates, Lockheed, Nestle, Pritikin, Prudential, Redken, and SuperCuts.

One of the tough things about the interviews in this "Learning from the Pros" section is being unable to give you, the reader, the pleasure of actually hearing the voices. Robert Davis, for example, has a mellow but authoritative Georgia drawl. And if you listen to Janie Owen-Bugh, you would know instantly that she comes from Dallas.

David Wood, the subject of this interview, has a voice full of enthusiasm, and a British accent. But, as David pointed out, this interview probably ought to be with a chorus of voices, since a team of designers at Graphic Computer Services participated in creating each of these projects.

Fig. 35.1
A metallic effect was added to the text for this Gold Club award show, not easy to do in a regular presentation program. (See color plate 53.)

David, why would you have produced this Gold Club slide show in CorelDRAW!? It seems, at first glance, to be pretty straightforward and text oriented (see fig. 35.1).

Richard Mednick was the designer in our shop for this one, and he decided to use CorelDRAW! because it would have been very tough to do this gold metallic effect in Persuasion or PowerPoint. Richard's also the president of the company, so we didn't argue.

Well, there was no need to argue, because there were more than 60 slides in this project, and you can imagine what a struggle it would have been to create each type block in CorelDRAW!, or some other drawing program, and import all those images into the presentation program. And, of course, inevitably we had to edit the text and that would have meant double steps all over again.

> *As you can see, it goes together like an embossed effect, not easy to do in a presentation program, especially if you want to work with the colors as we did here.*

Here's the metallic lettering, broken down into pieces and exploded so that you can see how they fit together (see fig. 35.2).

As you can see, it goes together like an embossed effect, not easy to do in a presentation program, especially if you want to work with the colors as we did here. Of course, you can create drop shadows in presentation programs and get some depth that way, but I think applying the gradated fills to the letters would be the biggest challenge if you tried to do this in something other than a drawing program.

Fig. 35.2
An exploded view of the gold metallic text effect in the Gold Club slide. (See color plate 54.)

— Main text

— Drop shadow

The foreground text has a gradient fill. The gold outline has to be added, which is easy in a drawing program. And the background drop shadow has also been gradated with a lighter set of shades.

The zigzag design in the background also was done in CorelDRAW!. It is actually a rotated version of the company logo, so it works as a background but also establishes the company's identity for the audience attending this awards show.

How did you know what to choose for the range of colors in the gradations?

Ah, well, what you see on the screen is often not exactly what you get on the slides. We know from experience what to expect, but we still do a test, probably more than one. We often will make up a run of a number of experiments when working on a job like this, noting the color choices for each slide. Then we can show the results to the client for final approval and there's no second guessing about the outcome.

There's another point I'd like to make about slide production. You really must focus on how slides are different from print. They are on the screen for as little as four seconds, and no more than one minute. That means slides must be easy to read, and at the same time have high impact. That's something else to look for when running your experiments—readability and impact.

> *...what you see on the screen is often not exactly what you get on the slides.*

What's the best way to image all these slides? A presentation program automates the process, but CorelDRAW! doesn't work in the same way.

We output each slide as a PostScript print file. For this awards show job we did more than 60 files. We have the advantage of having Autographix imaging equipment, so the driver gives us a way to compile all the images into one job and the gear clicks them off overnight. In this case the files were very big, so we obviously couldn't fit all 60 plus slides into one job order, but the principle still holds and makes it a great deal easier than imaging them one by one.

The issue of driver compatibility—that's another reason to run a test with your imaging bureau.

The issue of driver compatability—that's another reason to run a test with your imaging bureau. You need to work this sort of thing out with them. The Autographix driver comes with CorelDRAW!, but in past versions it hasn't always been able to image multipage files. We advise our clients to play it safe and image each page separately, but your imaging bureau may have different advice.

Tell us about this shampoo presentation. You used CorelDRAW! for the embossed logos in the background, right (see fig. 35.3)?

Fig. 35.3
Using a repeating logo effect as a slide show background. (See color plate 55.)

Yes. The embossed yellow logo in the corner was duplicated and converted into a gray version. The gray logo was then grouped and then duplicated and precisely positioned in a pattern for the slide background.

> *I think this logo usage, for the background, is a great example of how a drawing program can be used to enhance a slide program.*

The shampoo bottle photograph was, of course, imported into CorelDRAW! as a TIFF.

Sarah Rhee, the designer, worked in collaboration with the company's in-house design department to produce this speaker support show for a national meeting.

I think this logo usage, for the background, is a great example of how a drawing program can be used to enhance a slide program. Although this is certainly a slide that could have been done in Persuasion or PowerPoint, you would still have had to resort to a drawing program to produce this logo for the embossed background.

This wheel of service show looks incredibly complex. What's the story behind this one (see fig. 35.4)?

This may be the world's longest build slide. Every one of these wedges was popped onto the screen until a ring was complete, and then the ring shrank to allow room for the next ring to build onto the bull's-eye.

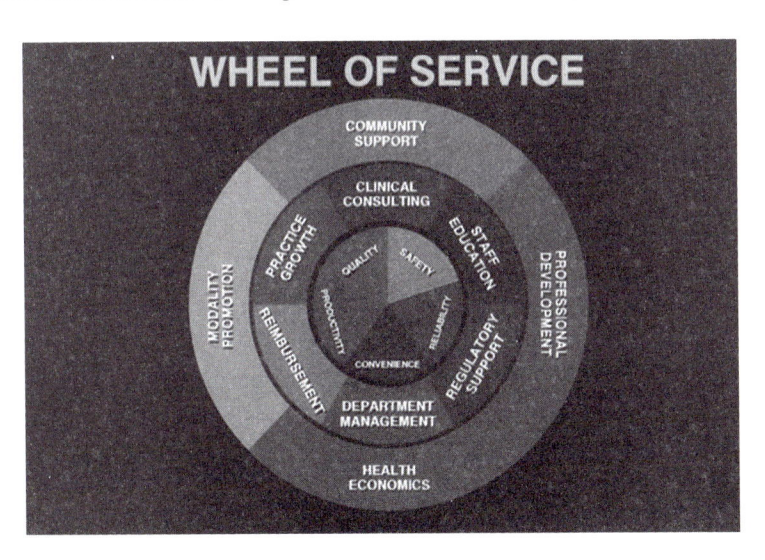

Fig. 35.4
A build slide with 15 steps, all built in CorelDRAW!. (See color plate 56.)

I wanted to show this one because it is certainly an example of something that would have been impossibly tedious to do in a presentation program, especially with all those gradations.

Vince Kernaghan, the designer, built the master image first and then simply subtracted the wedges one by one, doing a print file of each step. As a ring was removed, the remaining ring or two could then be expanded to fill the screen. Then the wedge removal step could continue. At the end, the center circle completely filled the screen as the wedges were removed.

For the show, the order was reversed so it looked like it was being built, instead of being removed.

Dimensionality was added by using gradient fills. And there's a lesson in that. At one point we added a bevel edge to the rim of the circles, sort of like a 3D pie chart. You just couldn't read it on-screen. The extra depth was too visually confusing and distracting. The rim edge cluttered up the show's ability to communicate. Strive to keep slides straightforward with clean lines, especially when it is a topic that ends up with an image that is this complicated. They must communicate right away when they come on-screen, or they won't work.

This may be the world's longest build slide.

This set of three slides ends up as a double-wide display (see fig. 35.5). How do you pull that off?

We produce multiprojector slide shows and this wide image is called a panorama. The designer on this one, Vince again, built this as one image to start. Then it is imaged three times, each time to capture a different section of the slide.

The page size in CorelDRAW! for a 35-millimeter slide is 11" wide and 7.33" high. But this one was created as an image that is 22" wide, so you get twice the width of a normal slide on the screen.

Once the image is finished, it is grouped and centered on the page area, left to right. With the image centered, make a PRN file, which takes the center section of the slide, clipping off the left and right ends. We need this middle image to join together the left and right half, to eliminate the visible seam that can appear where the two outside images join.

Then set nudge preferences to 5.5" and nudge the image to one side and snap that end of the slide. Nudge twice in the opposite direction and do another PRN file.

Fig. 35.5
A double-wide slide with no seams because it is thrown up on a wide screen from three overlapping slides, from three projectors, using a special CorelDRAW! technique. (See color plate 57.)

Once you have imaged the three slides, you need some glass slide mounts and some soft edge masks. The masks have gradated black areas that allow the image to be overlapped during projection and, along with the middle image, act to prevent any sharp line from being visible where the two sides join to form a complete image.

Again, build yourself some insurance on this type of project and run some tests. In this case, however, don't stop at testing the slide output, see how they actually project, and double-check the alignment of your projectors first!

Appendixes

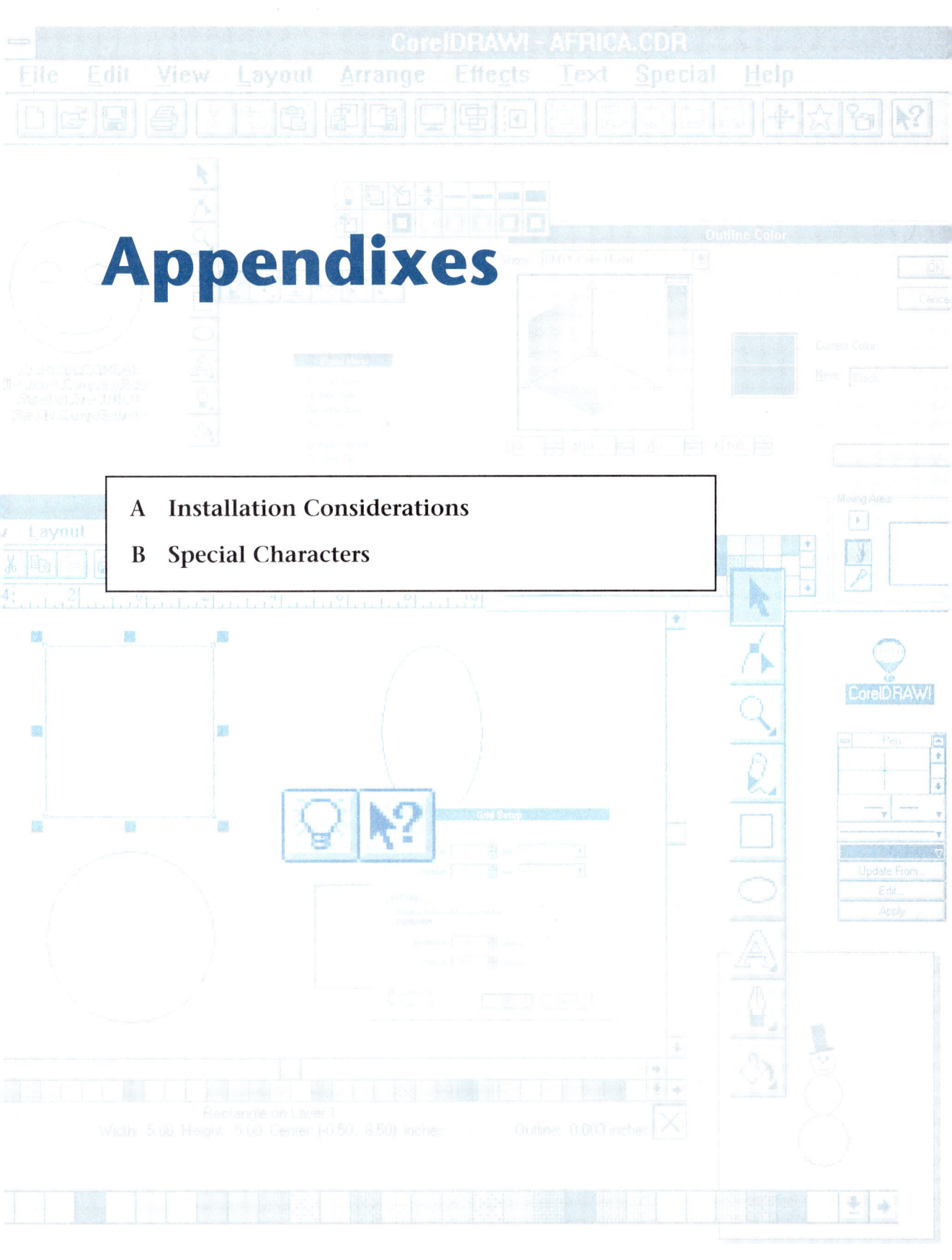

A Installation Considerations

B Special Characters

Appendix A
Installation Considerations

This section of the book provides you with the overall information you need to perform an initial installation of CorelDRAW! 5. If you have very specific problems with the installation procedure, refer to the *CorelDRAW! 5 Installation Guide*, or review the README.WRI file located on floppy disk 1, on the CD1 root directory, or in the COREL50 directory once the program is installed. Also check the various application subdirectories for additional README files that contain the most current information available at the time of product shipment. You also can call Corel Technical Support at (613) 728-1990.

Finally, to run CorelDRAW! at an adequate speed, you need a system with at least an 80386/33 processor with 8M RAM, particularly if you plan to open more than one application at a time, such as CorelDRAW! and CorelCHART. To achieve acceptable performance, use a super VGA monitor with 1M video memory, upgrade your RAM to 16M, and run on an 80486DX processor with at least a 200M hard disk drive and one high-density 3 1/2-inch drive. You need a sound card, such as the Pro Audio Spectrum, to play sound objects.

Windows 3.1 is required for CorelDRAW! 5 operation, and the SHARE.EXE file must be installed unless running under Windows for Workgroups. In addition, you can store the various sections of CorelDRAW! on different disk drives, but the first fixed disk drive (usually C) must have 939K free for use by the ~COREL.T temporary file. This file is deleted automatically after the installation is complete. Finally, make sure that the SMARTDRV.EXE is installed with your Windows installation, or loading CorelDRAW! can take an eternity (about two and a half hours). To install SMARTDRV.EXE, add the following line to your AUTOEXEC.BAT file:

```
C:\WINDOWS\SMARTDRV
```

Understanding the Basic Installation Options

You can install CorelDRAW! 5 from floppy disks or from the CD-ROM. You can install CorelDRAW! 5 to run from a hard disk or from the CD-ROM.

To install from floppy disks or a CD-ROM, follow these steps:

1. Insert floppy disk 1 or CD disc 1 in the 3 1/2-inch drive (usually A or B) or your optical drive (for example, D).

2. Open Windows Program Manager.

3. Open the **F**ile menu and choose **R**un. Type *<drive letter>*:**\SETUP**. The setup program starts and leads you through the rest of the installation procedure.

The program asks you to choose between Full Install or Custom Install. The following sections detail these options.

> **Note**
>
> You can run earlier versions of CorelDRAW! (2.x, 3, or 4) and version 5 on the same system if they are stored in separate directories. If you are installing to a system that already has version 4 installed, delete the PROGMAN.COR, REG.COR, and WIN.COR files from the \WINDOWS subdirectory before performing the installation so that the version 5 installation creates the proper files and backups. CorelDRAW! makes backups of prior files by leaving them with the same file name, but adding a BAK extension to designate it as a backup.

Full Installation

Full Install installs all applications and offers a choice of specific import and export filters, fonts, and scanner drivers. Files are installed under the COREL50 subdirectory on the default drive on which Windows is installed, unless you specify otherwise at the beginning of the installation procedure. If you choose to install a scanner, the TWAIN.DLL file is copied to the \WINDOWS\TWAIN directory. The directory is created if it does not already exist. A full installation requires around 50M of hard disk space.

Custom Installation

Custom Install enables you to specify precisely which applications are installed and where they are installed. If you decide to install CorelCHART,

Understanding the Basic Installation Options 873

CorelDRAW! is automatically installed because the two share some files. At the bottom of the Custom Install dialog box (see fig. A.1) is a reading of the total disk space free on the target disks and the amount of disk space required for the installation selected. You also can edit the path name and directory name for each application you want to install, but the default path names are the recommended settings.

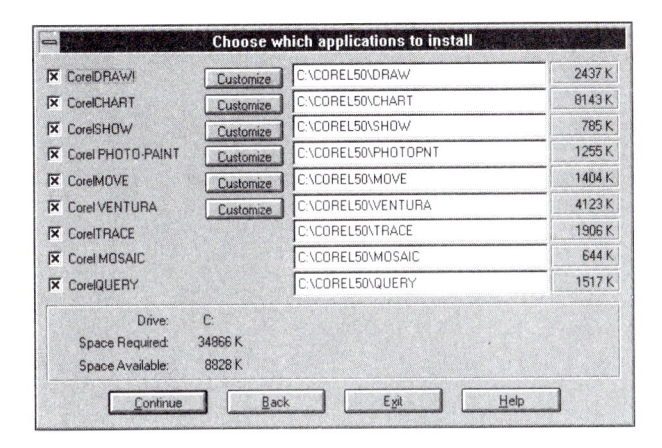

Fig. A.1
The Custom Installation dialog box enables you to choose which Corel applications to install.

Clicking the Custom button next to each application name opens a dialog box (see fig. A.2) that enables you to select which file groups to install for that application. Program files, help files, and sample files are some of the options available. Check the check box next to each file group to indicate that you want to add that group to the files to be installed.

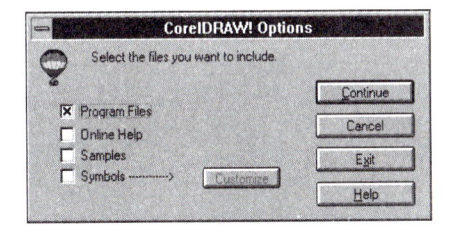

Fig. A.2
The Customize dialog box enables you to choose which files to install for each Corel application.

> **Note**
>
> If you are performing a Custom installation, make sure that you check the Customize options for each application you want to install. The default settings install only the program files for the application, not the help files and sample files.

A minimum installation of CorelDRAW! requires only between 15 and 20M of hard disk space. Loading only CorelDRAW! makes the installation procedure faster and easier; so if you don't plan to use the other applications, don't install them.

If you need to change your installation at a later date, choose the Custom Install option and install only the options you want.

SETUP makes changes to the AUTOEXEC.BAT, CONFIG.SYS, and WIN.INI files as needed to make the packages run correctly.

Installing Fonts

Because Windows applications scan the TrueType font list while loading, a large number of installed TrueType fonts can slow down your applications. You may want to keep the number of fonts to a minimum and load only those you need.

Full Install installs up to 50 TrueType fonts under the \WINDOWS\SYSTEM subdirectory. Note that CD disc 1 contains over 775 additional TrueType fonts that also can be installed using the FONTINST.EXE file located on the CD-ROM root directory. You may find that the larger the number of installed fonts, the slower your system runs.

The TrueType fonts are installed from the Windows File Manager. Follow this procedure:

1. Open the Windows File Manager.

2. Insert CD disc 1 in your optical drive.

3. Open the **F**ile menu and choose **R**un. Type **D:\FONTINST.EXE** (assuming that D is the letter for your optical drive). The TrueType Font Options dialog box appears with a number of different font categories.

4. Choose the font category you want, or select Customize to pick exactly the fonts for your needs.

5. Click OK to install the fonts you selected as FOT files in the \WINDOWS\SYSTEM subdirectory.

Installing CorelDRAW! to Run from the CD-ROM

You can install CorelDRAW! applications so that they run from CD-ROM rather than your hard disk. This saves a great deal of disk space, but slows down the overall speed at which the program runs.

To install CorelDRAW! to run from the CD-ROM, follow these steps:

1. Insert CD disc 1 into the CD-ROM drive.

2. Open the Windows File Manager.

3. Open the **F**ile menu and choose **R**un.

4. Type ***<drive letter>*:\SETUP2**, in which *<drive letter>* is the CD-ROM drive.

The CD disc 1 must remain in the CD drive while running the applications because the program files are not on the hard disk, but on the CD.

Although running CorelDRAW! directly from the CD-ROM gives you access to features that you don't get on the floppy disks, the access times are slower. CD-ROM access times are 10 to 15 times slower than a standard IDE hard drive. The best way to take advantage of the CD-ROM and still achieve acceptable performance is to install the program to the hard drive using SETUP and then access the CD-ROM as needed for clipart and so on.

Installing CorelDRAW! on a Network

CorelDRAW! 5 comes completely local area network (LAN) ready. LAN users can concurrently access all modules after they are installed. To perform the installation, you must have access to Windows and the intended CorelDRAW! installation subdirectories. When you want to perform a network installation, run \SETUP /A. Without the /A, a non-network installation is accomplished.

After CorelDRAW! is installed on the server, you must run \COREL50\SETUP\SETUP.EXE on the server from the user's station. This action installs the necessary files on the user's hard disk. This procedure takes around 3M of hard disk space. You also can install CorelDRAW! on the server so that the users can install a stand-alone version on their own PC from the server. The CorelDRAW! license allows this type of operation.

Appendix B
Special Characters

You often will need to include characters other than the standard alphabetical and numeric (*alphanumeric*) characters in your CorelDRAW! documents. You can insert any of the characters from any Windows, TrueType, or Adobe (if you have Adobe Type Manager) font you have installed. You also can insert any of the characters from the Corel WFN fonts you have installed. The WFN fonts are font versions of the symbol sets. (Refer to Chapter 8, "Advanced Text Techniques," for details on working with symbols.)

There are three ways to enter a character in CorelDRAW!:

- Type it from the keyboard.
- Enter the three- or four-digit Corel character code.
- Use the Windows Character Map.

Because not all characters are on the keyboard, you need to use the second two methods for the *extended* (nonkeyboard) characters.

To enter a character by using the three- or four-digit Corel code, choose either the Artistic or Paragraph Text tool, and press and hold down the Alt key while typing the character code from the numeric keypad. Release Alt after you type the code; the character is inserted at the text insertion point.

Figure B.1 shows the character codes for a typical character set. Blank spaces in the table indicate that there is no character in this font for that code. Remember that different fonts may have different characters.

> **Note**
>
> The Quick Reference booklet provided with the CorelDRAW! package lists character codes for six of the Corel fonts, including symbol fonts.

Fig. B.1

Character codes for a typical font (Times New Roman). The codes for text fonts will be similar to one another, but symbol fonts will vary.

Code	Char	Code	Char	Code	Char	Code	Char	Code	Char	Code	Char
033	!	071	G	0109	m	0147	"	0185	¹	0223	ß
034	"	072	H	0110	n	0148	"	0186	º	0224	à
035	#	073	I	0111	o	0149	•	0187	»	0225	á
036	$	074	J	0112	p	0150	–	0188	¼	0226	â
037	%	075	K	0113	q	0151	—	0189	½	0227	ã
038	&	076	L	0114	r	0152	˜	0190	¾	0228	ä
039	'	077	M	0115	s	0153	™	0191	¿	0229	å
040	(	078	N	0116	t	0154	š	0192	À	0230	æ
041	)	079	O	0117	u	0155	›	0193	Á	0231	ç
042	*	080	P	0118	v	0156	œ	0194	Â	0232	è
043	+	081	Q	0119	w	0157		0195	Ã	0233	é
044	,	082	R	0120	x	0158		0196	Ä	0234	ê
045	-	083	S	0121	y	0159	Ÿ	0197	Å	0235	ë
046	.	084	T	0122	z	0160		0198	Æ	0236	ì
047	/	085	U	0123	{	0161	¡	0199	Ç	0237	í
048	0	086	V	0124	|	0162	¢	0200	È	0238	î
049	1	087	W	0125	}	0163	£	0201	É	0239	ï
050	2	088	X	0126	~	0164	¤	0202	Ê	0240	ð
051	3	089	Y	0127		0165	¥	0203	Ë	0241	ñ
052	4	090	Z	0128		0166	¦	0204	Ì	0242	ò
053	5	091	[	0129		0167	§	0205	Í	0243	ó
054	6	092	\	0130	‚	0168	¨	0206	Î	0244	ô
055	7	093	]	0131	ƒ	0169	©	0207	Ï	0245	õ
056	8	094	^	0132	„	0170	ª	0208	Ð	0246	ö
057	9	095	_	0133	…	0171	«	0209	Ñ	0247	÷
058	:	096	`	0134	†	0172	¬	0210	Ò	0248	ø
059	;	097	a	0135	‡	0173	-	0211	Ó	0249	ù
060	<	098	b	0136	ˆ	0174	®	0212	Ô	0250	ú
061	=	099	c	0137	‰	0175	¯	0213	Õ	0251	û
062	>	0100	d	0138	Š	0176	°	0214	Ö	0252	ü
063	?	0101	e	0139	‹	0177	±	0215	×	0253	ý
064	@	0102	f	0140	Œ	0178	²	0216	Ø	0254	þ
065	A	0103	g	0141		0179	³	0217	Ù	0255	ÿ
066	B	0104	h	0142		0180	´	0218	Ú		
067	C	0105	i	0143		0181	µ	0219	Û		
068	D	0106	j	0144		0182	¶	0220	Ü		
069	E	0107	k	0145	'	0183	·	0221	Ý		
070	F	0108	l	0146	'	0184	¸	0222	Þ		

If you are working with a Windows, TrueType, or Adobe font, the Windows Character Map is an easy way to insert characters, especially characters from nonalphanumeric fonts such as Symbol and Wingdings. To use the Character Map to insert a character, follow these steps:

1. Open the Accessories group and start Character Map.

2. Drop down the Font list, and select the font containing the characters you want to use.

3. Select the character (or characters) you want to insert. The selected characters appear in the Ch**a**racters to Copy box, in the upper right of the Character Map window (see fig. B.2).

4. When you have selected all the characters you want to use, choose **C**opy.

5. Return to the CorelDRAW! document; then open the **E**dit menu and choose **P**aste. The characters are pasted into place. You then can edit or move them as you would any other CorelDRAW! text.

Tip
The keyboard code for entering the selected character appears in the bottom-right corner of the window.

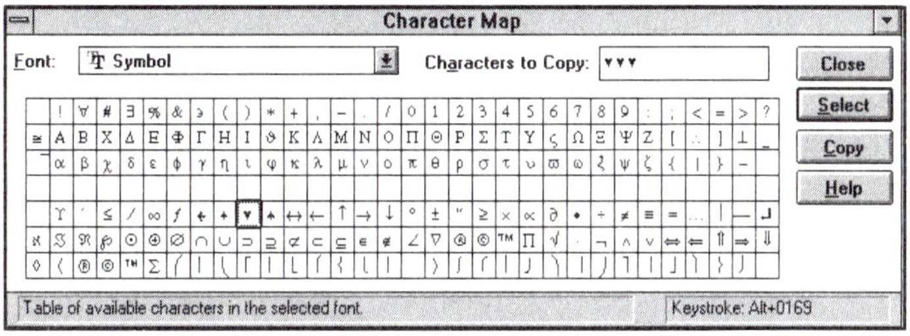

Fig. B.2
Windows Character Map. You can use this window to insert characters from any Windows font.

Index of Common Problems

CorelDRAW!	
If you have this problem...	**You'll find help here...**
Application error message appears after typing a large amount of text and clicking the Pick tool	p. 218
Accidentally select Redo	p. 100
Arrowhead is added at the end of a callout	p. 143
Arrowhead is too small to see in the final drawing	p. 143
Arrowheads appear at every node on the curve of an open path object	p. 143
ASCII characters have only three numbers to fill in instead of four in the DOS manual chart	p. 252
Bézier tool creates a single object with several straight lines instead of two separate lines	p. 67
Bézier tool doesn't draw a straight line; it gives a line that's slightly curved at one end	p. 67
Bulleted list text crowds the bullets	p. 226
Callout line and callout text are too close together	p. 88
Callout line disappears before typing in the callout text	p. 88
Callout line moves when moving callout text	p. 88
Can I have the pattern rotate with an object?	p. 160
Can Not Open Help message appears	p. 31

(continues)

Index of Common Problems

CorelDRAW! Continued

If you have this problem...	You'll find help here...
Can't change the shape of a line by dragging even though the nearest node is a smooth node	p. 385
Can't create an arrowhead in a design with a circle and curved line	p. 400
Can't delete a corner node from a square to make it a triangle	p. 381
Can't delete a field for a single object using the Object Data Field Editor	p. 557
Can't edit the field names in the Object Data roll-up by clicking the field name and entering a new name	p. 557
Can't find the outline color of an existing object in the color palette to apply it to other objects	p. 346
Can't get the center of rotation back to the center of an object	p. 192
Can't line up the edge of a circle along two lines	p. 86
Can't round the corners of a rectangle by moving one of the corner nodes	p. 381
Can't see or pick any of the objects behind a newly-filled object	p. 152
Can't select individual characters to change their typeface	p. 245
Can't select two nodes at one time to align them	p. 396
Can't skew an object to an even degree number	p. 194
Can't stretch an object by dragging a corner handle; the handle moves away from the cursor	p. 189
Changing the curve segment on one side of a node changes the other side, too	p. 77
Changing the curve segment on one side of a node makes a sharp corner	p. 77
Clicking a roll-up window button doesn't work	p. 27
Combined objects end up with the same fills and outlines instead of looking as they did before combining	p. 127
Control points on a corner node aren't visible	p. 390

Index of Common Problems

If you have this problem...	You'll find help here...
CorelDRAW! won't let me merge back my text file after grouping some objects, including text	p. 247
Cross hair cursor won't fall on the exact edges of objects when clicking to make the dimension lines, and accurate readings are needed	p. 408
Cursor snaps between grid points even when the grid is set	p. 119
Curve won't select even when surrounded with the marquee	p. 97
Data from the text file lands in the wrong fields in the drawing	p. 314
Dimensions come out different when drawing a circle	p. 86
Drawing a circle with the Ellipse tool and the Ctrl key doesn't work	p. 47
Drawing a rectangle from the center with Shift doesn't work	p. 81
Drawing a square with Ctrl doesn't work	p. 81
Drawing an ellipse from the center doesn't work	p. 86
Drawing windows doesn't show edges of paper when Legal size page is selected for Paper Size in the Size section of the Page Setup dialog box	p. 549
Duplicated or cloned object appears too close to the original	p. 546
Editing the curve segment on the other side of a smooth node doesn't work when there's only one control point	p. 77
Extracted text file includes all the text from the drawing; need to find the correct section of text to edit	p. 247
Field created for previous object won't appear for new object and has to be recreated	p. 557
File is hard to find because list of file names in File Open dialog box is too long	p. 268
File Open doesn't list enough files	p. 268
Filling an object with color doesn't work	p. 47
Find Next doesn't work when selected	p. 230

(continues)

CorelDRAW! Continued

If you have this problem...	You'll find help here...
Fountain fill contains many more stripes when printed than when displayed	p. 175
Frame with multiple columns ends up being twice as wide	p. 239
Freehand tool makes a wiggly curved line instead of a straight line	p. 67
Halftone pattern doesn't rotate with object	p. 160
Help menu won't open while a dialog box is open	p. 31
Hourglass appears randomly, stopping work	p. 574
Last parts of Paragraph text disappear from the frame	p. 225
Letters (individual) won't stay in line when changing their spacing with the Shape tool	p. 218
Letters like "b" get all filled in when text is converted to curves and broken apart	p. 250
Line needs to be vertically straight	p. 67
Lines sections don't link when drawing a single object using the Freehand tool	p. 67
Memory runs out when working on bitmap files; undo levels might be the problem	p. 564
Merging edited text back into a drawing changed some of the character attributes	p. 248
Mirroring an object with the mouse displays a new object that isn't the same size	p. 189
Mouse won't draw a line to a specific length, such as 1 inch	p. 67
Moving a node changes the curve instead	p. 77
Multiple objects won't align to the center of the page properly	p. 119
Need a draft output of a PostScript halftone but only have a non-PostScript printer	p. 170
Need to automatically print page numbers for a multipage drawing	p. 549
Nodes don't align when Arrange Align is selected	p. 396

Index of Common Problems

If you have this problem...	You'll find help here...
Object fill pattern gets cut off and looks jagged	p. 160
Object fill pattern looks jagged when printed	p. 160
Object needs to look as though it has no fill without revealing objects under it	p. 152
Object pattern doesn't rotate with object	p. 160
Object pattern has half a tile cut off, but needs to line up within the object	p. 165
Objects appear on every page of a multipage document, not just one page	p. 134
Objects appear on-screen as dashed outlines and won't print	p. 134
Objects are created but can't be seen	p. 144
Objects are created with an unwanted fill pattern	p. 149
Objects filled with a solid color block need to be translucent instead of opaque	p. 152
Objects snap to points slightly away from guidelines instead of aligning	p. 119
Objects with many nodes won't print or create a printer error	p. 127
"Oh" (as in, "oh, my!") is replaced with the word Ohio when typed	p. 232
Only part of the drawing prints	p. 305
Opened a new drawing without saving and Undo won't bring back the old drawing	p. 100
Operation Cannot Be Completed. The active layer "layername" is locked or invisible appears when creating objects	p. 134
Paper Orientation does not match document appears when printing	p. 549
Pie wedge lines don't appear	p. 86
PostScript Halftone that is a light shade "fades out" when printed	p. 170
PostScript Texture doesn't display on the screen	p. 167

(continues)

CorelDRAW! Continued

If you have this problem...	You'll find help here...
PostScript Texture doesn't print	p. 166
PostScript Textures take too long to print to check the effect of changing parameters	p. 167
Pressing plus (+) to leave the original of the object being transformed doesn't work	p. 197
Preview in the File Open dialog box shows a diagonal line, not a preview picture	p. 268
Print asks for a file name	p. 305
Print quality of an imported image is poor	p. 282
Printout is "garbage" characters, and lots of paper comes out of the printer	p. 305
Roll-up window setting changes don't affect the selected object	p. 27
Scaling a rectangle with rounded corners distorts the corners to ellipses instead of circles	p. 81
Scaling an object by dragging a handle only scales the object in that direction, not overall	p. 189
Scaling Paragraph text scales the frame but not the text	p. 226
Scaling with Shift doesn't work	p. 197
Scrolling won't work when zoomed in and when copying the fill style from an object that is outside the visible page	p. 149
Segments between aligned nodes didn't align, leaving gaps between the lines	p. 396
Selected multiple nodes don't move together the same distance as the node when dragged	p. 390
Small text looks indistinct or muddy	p. 218
Special characters change when the typeface changes	p. 252
Square fountain fill won't work right when applied to a circle	p. 346
Status line says only two objects are selected after ungrouping a large number of objects	p. 127
Status line says that more objects are selected than shown in the marquee	p. 98

If you have this problem...	You'll find help here...
Text Frame Envelope text goes outside the envelope	p. 239
Text looks muddy or mottled	p. 144
Text pasted from another application with the Clipboard is placed on the drawing as a "Document Object" that can't be edited	p. 231
Text that has been fit to a path gets all bunched up at some top points	p. 245
Text with a linear fountain fill turns to a solid color when rotated	p. 174
Tip of a long, narrow triangle with a thick outline is blunted rather than having a sharp point	p. 564
Transform dialog box in a positive setting skews an object to the left (negative direction)	p. 194
Undo Levels is set to 10, but only the last 4 actions can be undone	p. 100
Unfilled object changes shape when moving it is attempted	p. 47
When rotating an object with the mouse, the object is deselected when trying to drag the handles	p. 192
When typing two sets of numbers in inches (such as 15" and 20"), the first quotation mark gets turned backwards	p. 233
Wrong file format or could not open message appears during Print Merge	p. 314

CorelDRAW! Special Effects and Styles

If you have this problem...	You'll find help here...
Applying the extrude makes object so dark that can't pull handles out equally in edit modes	p. 432
Attributes buttons are dimmed when saving a style	p. 536
Blend applied to a path isn't printing; the path is	p. 459
Blend caused objects to overlap and come out in a straight line; the objects need to be controlled and curved	p. 527

(continues)

CorelDRAW! Special Effects and Styles   Continued

If you have this problem...	You'll find help here...
Blend color is changing	p. 459
Blends are rough with very distinctive steps	p. 459
Can't add Perspective to a group of objects	p. 520
Can't edit some of the handles when using the Edit Node roll-up	p. 495
Can't find the center of rotation on a selected object	p. 475
Can't find the Perspective roll-up window	p. 417
Can't find the vanishing point for an object	p. 418
Can't find the vanishing point for selected objects	p. 475
Can't remove all envelopes because Effects Clear Transformations is dimmed	p. 439
Can't see objects behind a transparent lens	p. 505
Can't select an intermediate object to make changes	p. 459
Can't tell the difference between a blend and a contour	p. 482
Color added to a Brighten lens doesn't show	p. 505
Contents placed inside an open path disappear	p. 513
Contour doesn't blend along a path	p. 482
Contour roll-up closed up ends of parallel lines; the ends need to be opened	p. 528
Contour segments need to be pulled apart	p. 528
Edit Contents mode doesn't allow editing with the drawing tools	p. 513
Editing a Preset name deletes it from the list rather than creating a new Preset	p. 538
Envelope makes the enclosed symbol look bad	p. 523
Envelope shape changes don't take effect	p. 434
Extruded object's front face is so dark it's indecipherable from the surfaces of the Extrude and needs to be more legible	p. 527
Extrusion changes don't take effect	p. 473

Index of Common Problems

If you have this problem...	You'll find help here...
Getting one-point perspective but need to get two-point perspective	p. 417
Macro for Perspective doesn't record	p. 538
Must every envelope shape be drawn?	p. 433
Need to add additional nodes to envelope bounding box	p. 433
Need to change envelope style chosen	p. 432
Need to edit both sides of an envelope so they remain proportional	p. 523
Need to edit text after it has been extruded	p. 473
Nothing happens after choosing a lens from the scrollable list	p. 505
Object lines bend when an envelope is added	p. 434
Object menu doesn't appear when right mouse button is clicked	p. 536
Object placed inside the PowerClip isn't trimmed	p. 531
Pattern is indistinguishable	p. 469
Place Contents in Container makes entire photo and lens disappear	p. 533
PowerClip container won't allow contents to be placed at a specific location for trimming; contents are always placed in same position	p. 513
PowerClip contents disappear when moved closer to the original photo	p. 533
PowerLines don't scale proportionately when the object is scaled	p. 494
PowerLines have very sharp corners	p. 494
Preset extrusion won't take effect on another object	p. 471
Save As option isn't available when extruding	p. 471
Text fit to an envelope doesn't match the bounding box of the envelope	p. 438
Thin portions of a line are too thin	p. 494
Vanishing points need to align more precisely	p. 520

Index of Common Problems

CorelDRAW! Scanning and Tracing

If you have this problem...	You'll find help here...
Adjusting the brightness makes halftones look posterized	p. 337
Can't find CorelTRACE or CorelPHOTO-PAINT	p. 323
Destination application won't read traced images	p. 693
Need to trace only subsections of a bitmap or to have certain sections adopt a different color after tracing	p. 693
Nothing happens when clicking the PreScan button after choosing a scanner from Select Source	p. 323
Nothing happens when clicking to start tracing	p. 667
Scanned image is too big for a floppy disk to take to a service bureau	p. 337
Scanner won't work	p. 336
Traced image has thousands of nodes and hundreds of objects; their numbers need to be reduced	p. 693
When accessing Select Source from CorelTRACE or CorelPHOTO-PAINT, no scanners are listed in the drop-down menu	p. 323

CorelPHOTO-PAINT

If you have this problem...	You'll find help here...
Can't find a new custom brush	p. 655
Can't select the desired color range with the Magic Wand mask	p. 649
Can't tell whether a transparency mask is in effect	p. 653
Clicking on an object doesn't select it for editing	p. 613
Custom brush created using the Mask tools doesn't work	p. 655
Is there an automated procedure for changing pixel colors?	p. 613
Marquee disappears after creating a color mask	p. 651
Mask disappears when the mouse button is released	p. 648

If you have this problem...	You'll find help here...
Mask doesn't change the desired color; it changes all other colors instead	p. 651
Need to add a high transparency mask to one part of an image and a low transparency mask to another part of an image	p. 653
New brush shape paints in shades of the current color selection, not the colors the mask was created with	p. 655
Only certain pixels change when painting portions of an image	p. 651
Tools affect the area inside the circle mask rather than area outside the mask	p. 648
What's the difference between the tools and Effects menu selections?	p. 640
When combining two mask shapes, the first mask disappears when drawing the second mask	p. 648

CorelCHART, CorelSHOW, and CorelMOVE

If you have this problem...	You'll find help here...
Actor needs to run quickly across the screen to a certain point, freeze for a few frames, then proceed at a high rate of speed; can this be done without multiple actors?	p. 815
Actors run over some props instead of running behind them	p. 815
All slides need to be resized	p. 755
Animation is too short in length to fill the duration of a slide, so the screen just goes blank when it is finished	p. 773
Animations included in shows don't play when the file is saved in Screen Show Only format	p. 775
Background sized exactly to the page in CorelDRAW! is the wrong size when brought back into CorelSHOW	p. 760
Bulleted lists indent, but don't display bullets when used with light colored text	p. 757
Changing the series or category orders while in the Chart view gives a different result than doing so in the Data Manager view	p. 748

(continues)

Index of Common Problems

CorelCHART, CorelSHOW, and CorelMOVE Continued	
If you have this problem...	**You'll find help here...**
Data analysis operations rarely produce a close fit between initial series data and the computed regression equation	p. 748
Frame doesn't display for less than one second	p. 773
Is it better to perform spreadsheet operations in CorelCHART, or in Excel and then import the data into CorelCHART for final display?	p. 748
LaserJet printer doesn't give reliable results when printing charts; gray shades blend together, and it's difficult to tell one bar chart series from another	p. 748
Music inserted in a frame cuts off at a weird point; can't adjust the timeline closely enough to make the ending of the music sound pleasant	p. 773
Need to change all the text on slides from one typeface to another	p. 757
Need to create new charts with all the graphic images such as logos, text, and text used before, without placing all the graphics for every new chart	p. 748
New object is created from a graphic file via the OLE to Other Applications tool, and the source application doesn't load object when double-clicked	p. 760
Presentation is set up to run in Automatic Advance mode; need to run it in Manual Advance mode sometimes	p. 764
Presentation is to be used for multiple formats (a screen show, handouts, and overheads). What should page layout be set to?	p. 755
Sound files degrade the animation playback	p. 815
To use scanned images as actor cels, is there an easier way than cleaning them up in CorelPHOTO-PAINT, scanning the images in CorelTRACE, importing them into CorelDRAW! for final cleanup, and then creating actors using CorelDRAW! from within CorelMOVE?	p. 815

Glossary

Active window A region of the display ready and waiting to receive user input.

Actor An object in CorelMOVE contained within an animation that moves during the animation. Composed of a number of cels.

Actor cel A series of images that creates the illusion of movement in CorelMOVE when displayed quickly in succession.

Additive primary colors Red, green, and blue. The three colors used to create all other colors if direct or transmitted light is used (as on television, for example). See also *primary colors* and *subtractive primary colors*.

Alignment The positioning of lines of text on a page or in a column: aligned left (flush left, ragged right), centered, aligned right (flush right, ragged left), or justified (flush on both left and right).

Animation path The path over which the actor moves during the animation.

Animation path points The prompting point for displaying the next cel in the actor's movement.

Annotations Text added to a chart to further explain its contents. Can also annotate Corel's HLP file.

Anti-alias The process of adding dots adjacent to existing dots to make a jagged line appear more smooth.

Artistic text Strings of text in CorelDRAW! that can be manipulated as objects.

Ascender The part of a lowercase letter that rises above its main body. Technically, only three letters of the alphabet have ascenders: b, d, and h. Uppercase letters and the lowercase letters f, k, l, and t also reach the height of the ascenders. See also *descender*.

ASCII A standard format for storing text files, which stands for American Standard Code for Information Interchange. The form in which text is stored if saved as Text Only; an Export/Import command option, as well as a Save command option, available for most databases, spreadsheets, and word processors. ASCII files include all the characters of the text itself (including tabs and carriage returns), but not the non-ASCII codes used to indicate character and paragraph formats. See also *text-only file*.

Aspect ratio A fractional number that represents the ratio between horizontal and vertical measurements of dots relating to printing and screen display resolutions.

Attributes The characteristics applied to an object, including font, size, spacing, style, color, line thickness, and fill.

Autoflow Text placement in which the text continuously flows from column to column and page to page.

Auto-panning A CorelDRAW! feature that automatically scrolls the drawing window when an object is moved beyond the window's borders.

Autotrace The conversion by CorelTRACE of a fixed resolution bitmap image into a structured graphic that is not of fixed resolution. In other words, the bitmap becomes a scalable vector graphic image.

Bad break Term referring to page breaks and column breaks that result in widows or orphans, or to line breaks that hyphenate words incorrectly or separate two words that should stay together (for example, *Mr. Smith*).

Baseline In a line of text, the lowest point of letters, excluding descenders. (The lowest point of letters such as *a* and *x*, for example, but not the lower edges of descenders on *p* and *q*.)

Bézier curve A curve created in CorelDRAW! comprised of nodes connected by line segments whose slope and angle can be altered by moving related control points.

Binding margin Additional margin space added to the inside edge of pages to allow for binding of the pages into book or booklet format.

Bitmap A graphics image or text formed by a pattern of dots. PC Paint, Windows Paint, and PC Paintbrush documents produce bitmapped graphics, as well as scanned or digitized images. Low-resolution images are sometimes called *paint-type* files, and these images usually have a lower number of dots per inch (dpi) than high-resolution images.

Bitmap texture A representation of surface irregularity that can be applied to an object in CorelDRAW! to change its appearance.

Bleed A printed image extending to the trimmed edge of the sheet or page.

Blend Changing one image into another over a series of steps to provide a transition type of visual illusion. Used for highlighting objects.

Block See *text block*.

Blue lines A preliminary test printing of a page to check the offset printer's plates. This test printing is done by using a photochemical process (rather than printer's inks) that produces a blue image on white paper. See also *prepress proofs* and *press proofs*.

Blue pencil/blue line Traditionally, a guideline drawn with a blue pencil or printed in light blue ink on the boards and used as a guide for manually pasting up a page layout. The blue ink is sometimes called *nonrepro blue* because the color is not picked up by the camera when a page is photographed to make negatives for offset printing. In CorelDRAW!, you can create nonprinting margins, column guides, and ruler guides on-screen to help you position text and graphics; these lines do not appear when the page is printed. See also *board*.

Board A sheet of heavyweight paper or card stock onto which typeset text and graphics are pasted manually. See also *blue pencil/blue line*.

Body copy The main part of the text of a publication, as distinguished from headings and captions. See also *body type*.

Body type The type (font) used for the body copy. See also *body copy*.

Boilerplate See *template*.

Bounding box The imaginary outline that surrounds an object after the object is selected.

Brightness In the Hue, Saturation, Brightness color model, Brightness is the setting that determines the amount of black in the color.

Brochure A folded pamphlet or small booklet.

Bullet A symbol or large dot that precedes a line of text used to add emphasis to the line.

Calibration bar A band of color printed in the margin of a color output, used to judge the color accuracy of the color output.

Calligraphic A drawing effect that varies the line thickness of objects. Calligraphic objects have a hand drawn appearance.

Callouts Text that points out and identifies parts of an illustration. Also refers to headings that appear in a narrow margin next to the body copy. See also *pull-out quote*.

Camera-ready art The complete pages of a publication assembled with text and graphics and ready for reproduction. Literally refers to pages ready to be photographed as the first step in the process of making plates for offset printing. See also *mechanicals* and *offset printing*.

Cap height The distance measured from the top of an uppercase character to its baseline.

CDR File name extension that indicates CorelDRAW! as the associated tool.

Center of rotation A point relating to an object or group in CorelDRAW! around which the group or object can be rotated.

Chained text Blocks of text connected across the columns on a page and across pages from the beginning to the end of an article. CorelDRAW! chains all text blocks that are part of a story. As you edit chained (or threaded) text, CorelDRAW! moves words from one text block into the next text block in the chain to adjust to the new text length. See also *text block*.

Chart The graphical display of data as a line, bar, or other type of chart design.

Check box The small square to the left of certain options in dialog boxes; you click a check box to turn an option on or off (to select or deselect it). An X appears in the check box after it is selected, or turned on. The check box is empty if is it deselected, or turned off.

Child object A member of a group that is individually selected without ungrouping that object.

Choke A trapping technique where the outline of a background object is extended or enlarged to overlap with a foreground object.

Cicero A unit of measure equivalent to 4.55 millimeters, commonly used in Europe for measuring font sizes.

Click To press and release a mouse button quickly.

Clipart Originally, predrawn art ready for cutting from a book to be pasted into a design layout. Now, ready-to-use digital art provided for easy paste-up into designs and projects.

Clipboard   A feature of Microsoft Windows, the Clipboard temporarily stores text or graphics cut or copied by the commands on the Edit menu. The Paste command brings the contents of the Clipboard to the page. The Clipboard command displays the contents of the Clipboard. See *Copy*, *Cut*, and *Paste*.

Clipping holes   Holes resulting from the combination of two or more objects using the Combine command. Overlapping portions of the objects become clipping holes.

Clone   In CorelDRAW!, a command used to create an exact copy of the original including the attributes of the original. Clones are actively linked to the original and reflect any changes made to the original object. See also *duplicate*.

Close   To choose the Close command from the Control menu and leave CorelDRAW!. Close is also used to close some dialog boxes.

CMYK   The letters that represent each of the ink colors used in four-color process printing—Cyan, Magenta, Yellow, and Black. Printers use K to represent black to avoid confusion with blue. See also *subtractive primary colors*.

Coated stock   Paper that has a light clay or plastic coating. A glossy or slick paper is often coated.

Collated   Printed in numerical order with the first page on top of the stack that comes out of the printer. This is an option in the Print dialog box. Multiple copies are grouped into complete sets of the publication.

Color keys   A color overlay proofing system produced by the 3M Company. See also *overlay proofs*.

Color Manager   A Corel 5 feature that uses specific parameters of your system's monitor, printer, and scanner to more accurately display, print, and capture color.

Color palette   The grid of color boxes along the bottom of the Corel screen that enables you to fill selected objects with color, and change outline colors of selected objects.

Color separations   In offset printing, separate plates used to lay different colors of ink on a page printed in multiple colors. You can create masters for color separations by preparing the drawing by choosing the Print Separations option from the Options dialog box in the Print menu of CorelDRAW!.

Column rules   Vertical lines drawn between columns.

Command button A large rectangular area in a dialog box that contains a command such as OK or Cancel. You can activate command buttons surrounded by a thick black line by pressing Enter.

Comp Traditionally, a designer's comprehensive sketch of a page design, showing the client what the final page is to look like after being printed. Usually a full-sized likeness of the page, a comp is a few steps closer to the final than a pencil rough and can be composed by using ink pens, pencils, color markers, color acetate, pressure-sensitive letters, and other tools available at art supply shops. The comp is used as a starting point in building the final document.

Composite A printing process that includes all colors on a page, as in CorelDRAW!'s Print Options feature.

Compound blend A blend created using one object of an existing blend and a new object.

Condensed type A narrow typeface having proportionally less character width than a normal face of the same size. Although you can achieve this effect by graphically scaling characters from the normal font, condensed characters are usually individually designed as a separate font. Condensed typefaces are used where large amounts of copy must fit into a relatively small space (such as in tabular composition). See also *kerning*.

Constrain To restrict an object's movement while drawing or moving it to an angle that is a multiple of degrees. You constrain the movement by holding down Ctrl as you drag the mouse. See also *X axis* and *Y axis*.

Continuous-tone image An illustration or photograph, black-and-white or color, composed of many shades between the lightest and the darkest tones and not broken up into dots. Continuous-tone images usually need to be converted into dots, either by scanning or by halftone, to be printed in ink or on a laser printer. See also *halftone*.

Contour A blend that an object performs on itself.

Control menu The Microsoft Windows menu listing commands for working with Windows and leaving an application.

Control Menu box Small square displayed in the upper left corner of a window. Click this box to display the Control menu.

Control Panel A Microsoft Windows utility program used to add or delete fonts and printers, change printer connections and settings, and adjust mouse and screen settings.

Control point   A point relating to a node whose position determines the shape of the object containing that node.

Copy   To place an exact copy of an object or text on the Clipboard. See also *Clipboard*, *Cut*, and *Paste*.

Copy fitting   Determining the amount of copy (text set in a specific font) that can fit in a given area on a page or in a publication. You make copy fit on a page in CorelDRAW! by adjusting the line spacing, word spacing, and letter spacing.

CorelCAPTURE   The Corel screen capture utility.

CorelCHART   The Corel charting application.

CorelDRAW!   The Corel drawing and illustration application.

CorelMOSAIC   Visual file manager used to organize, manage, manipulate, and view graphic files.

CorelMOVE   The Corel animation application.

CorelPHOTO-PAINT   The Corel bitmap modification application.

CorelQUERY   The Corel utility that enables the extraction of database information from spreadsheets and databases, for use in CorelCHART.

CorelSHOW   The presentation application that allows for the integration of CorelCHART and CorelMOVE images into a unified presentation.

CorelTRACE   The Corel application that converts bitmap images into vector graphic images.

Corner style   Rectangular objects that have either square or rounded corners.

Crop   Trimming the edges from a graphic to make the image fit into a given menu, or removing unnecessary parts of the image.

Crop marks   Lines printed on a page to indicate where the page is to be trimmed after the final document is printed. These marks are printed if the page size is smaller than the paper size and if the Crop Marks option in the Print options dialog box is selected.

Cross hairs   A mouse pointer style that resembles the cross hairs of a gun sight. See also *pointer*.

Cues   In CorelMOVE, decision points within a timeline that steer the sequence of events in particular directions based upon user actions.

Curve object   A Bézier or Freehand curve created with CorelDRAW!.

Cusp node   A node where the line is independently controlled on each side.

Custom   A word to describe attributes or characteristics that do not conform to an existing standard reference.

Custom color   An ink color that you assign to objects in your publication. Using custom color, you produce one negative for each color used in your artwork. Treated the same as spot color.

Cut   To remove an object or text from the working page to the Clipboard. See also *Clipboard*, *Copy*, and *Paste*.

Cutout   See *knockout*.

Cyan   The subtractive primary color that appears blue-green and absorbs red light. Used as one ink in four-color printing. Also known as process blue. See also *subtractive primary colors*.

Data sheet   Similar to a spreadsheet, a document for storing information in cels arranged in rows and columns.

Data range   A group of neighboring cels in a column and/or row in the Object Data Manager in CorelDRAW!.

Database   An organized collection of information pertaining to a topic or image. Corel's Object Database Manager enables you to store information about each object you draw.

Default   The initial setting of a value or option when you first display or create it (as when a dialog box opens). You can usually change default settings.

Descender   The part of a lowercase letter that hangs below the baseline. Five letters of the alphabet have descenders: g, j, p, q, and y. See also *ascender* and *baseline*.

Deselect   To select another command or option or to click a blank area of the screen to cancel the current selection. Also to turn off (remove the X from) a check box. See also *select*.

Desktop publishing   Use of personal computers and software applications to produce material ready for reproduction.

Dialog box   A window that appears in response to a command that calls for setting options. See also *window*.

Digitize To convert an image to a system of dots that can be stored in the computer. See also *scanned-image files*.

Dimension lines Lines and labels adjacent to an element that describe an object's dimensions.

Dingbats Traditionally, ornamental characters (bullets, stars, flowers) used for decoration or as special characters within text. The laser-printer font Zapf Dingbats includes many traditional symbols and some untraditional ones.

Directory A user-named area, or an area created by an application, on the hard disk where a group of related files can be stored together. Each directory can have subdirectories. See also *hierarchical filing system*.

Display type Type used for headlines, titles, headings, advertisements, fliers, and so on. Display type is usually a large point size (several sizes larger than body copy) and can be a decorative font.

Dithered color On a computer monitor, a color created by mixing dots of two or more colors to approximate a color the monitor cannot display.

Dot gain In the printing process, color separations are made of dots. If the dots increase in size or shape when the image is printed, the image turns out darker than desired.

Dot-matrix printer A printer that creates text and graphics by pressing a matrix of pins through the ribbon onto the paper. These impact printers usually offer lower resolution (dots per inch) than laser printers and are used only for draft printouts from CorelDRAW!.

Dots per inch (dpi) See *resolution*.

Double-click To quickly press and release the main mouse button twice in succession.

Drag To hold down the main mouse button, move the mouse until the object is where you want it, and then release the button.

Drag and drop Dragging a selected item from one open publication to another open publication.

Drawing window Window appearing after you start CorelDRAW!. Displays a view of one or two pages, page icons, pointer, scroll bars, title bar, menu bar, and toolbox window.

Drop-down menu A list box activated by clicking an icon in a dialog box. See also *pull-down menu*.

Dummy publication Traditionally, a pencil mock-up of the pages of a publication, folded or stapled into a booklet, that the offset printer uses to verify the correct sequence of pages and positions of photographs.

Duplicate In CorelDRAW!, a command used to create a copy of an object, not linked to the original. See also *clone*.

Edit To alter the text of a written work. See also *Copy*, *Cut*, and *Paste*.

Editable Preview The default display mode in CorelDRAW! that enables you to interactively work with objects and shows outlines, fills, and text attributes as they appear when printed. See also *wireframe view*.

Ellipse A regular-shaped oval created by using the Ellipse tool.

Em Unit of measure equaling the size of the capital letter M. The width of an em dash or an em space. See also *en*.

Emulsion The photosensitive layer on a piece of film or paper. Emulsion side up or down can be specified in the Print command dialog box.

En One-half the width of an em. The width of an en dash or an en space. See also *em*.

Encapsulated PostScript (EPS) format A file format that describes a document or graphic written in the PostScript language and contains all the codes necessary to print the file.

End node A point at the end of a line or curve. In CorelDRAW!, it is denoted as a small square.

Enter key Key you press to break a line if the Text tool is active, or to confirm the selected options in a dialog box. Also called the Return key. Usually has the same effect as the Return key on a typewriter.

Envelope A shape applied to an object in CorelDRAW! that acts like a mold to form that object.

Export To convert text or an image to another file type for use with another application.

Export filter A process that defines how to convert an exported file so that the file can be understood by the program that imports it.

Extrude To give an object the illusion of depth by adding dynamic three-dimensional forms in CorelDRAW!.

Facing pages The two pages that face one another if a book, brochure, or similar publication is open. Also an option used in double-sided publications.

Field   In CorelDRAW's Object Database Manager, a column of cels.

Field Type   The format type of a field in the Object Database Manager. Examples include currency, data, time, and percentage.

Fill   To paint an area enclosed by a border with a gray shade, pattern, and/or color. You can only fill a closed path.

Fill tool   The toolbox item used to define an object's fill attributes.

Film   Photosensitive material, generally on a transparent base, that receives images and can be chemically processed to expose those images. In phototypesetting, any photosensitive material, transparent or not, can be called film. See also *negative*.

Flow text   To place text on a page.

Flush   Aligned with, even with, or coming to the same edge as. See also *alignment*.

Flush right (or right justified)   Text in which lines end at the same point on the right margin. Opposite of ragged right or left justified. See also *alignment*.

FOCOLTONE   A printing industry standard color system that provides a range of spot colors built with CMYK process color model.

Folio   Page number on a printed page, often accompanied by the name of the document and date of publication.

Font   One complete set of characters (including all the letters of the alphabet, punctuation marks, and symbols) in the same typeface, style, and size. A 12-point Times Roman font, for example, is a different font from 12-point Times Italic, 14-point Times Roman, or 12-point Helvetica. Screen fonts (bitmapped fonts used to display text accurately on-screen) can differ slightly from printer fonts (outline fonts used to describe fonts to the laser printer) because of the differences in resolution between screens and printers.

Footer   See *folio* and *running foot*.

Footnote   Text at the bottom of a page that further explains or clarifies a sentence or term in the main body of text. Footnotes are referenced to the sentence on the page by a number or symbol.

Format   Page size, margins, and grid used in a publication. Also, the character format (font) and paragraph format (alignment, spacing, and indentation).

Formatting Using the type and paragraph attributes to modify the page.

Fountain fill Fill pattern applied to objects in CorelDRAW! to create three-dimensional effects.

Four-headed arrow Shape of the pointer if used to drag a selected text block or graphic. See also *pointer*.

Fractal texture A representation of surface irregularity applied to an object in CorelDRAW!. This effect is based on the fractal number set for chaotic events.

Frame In CorelDRAW!, this defines the boundaries for paragraph text on the drawing page.

Freehand drawing mode A mode of drawing in CorelDRAW! appropriate for rough sketches, analogous to pencil-on-paper techniques.

Gamut The range of colors a display, input, or output device or medium can reproduce or sense.

Ghosting The shift in ink density that occurs when large, solid areas interfere with one another. Also, a procedure in which two images are combined together electronically. The images are given specific weight in relation to each other to create the effect.

Graphic A line, box, or circle that you draw in CorelDRAW! or a group thereof. An illustration brought into a CorelDRAW! publication from another application.

Graphic boundary The dotted line around a graphic that limits how close text can get to the graphic.

Grayscale image An image made up of various shades of gray.

Greek text (greeked text) Traditionally, a block of text used to represent the positioning and point size of text in a designer's comp. Standard greeked text used by typesetters looks more like Latin: "Lorem ipsum dolor sit amet..." See also *greeking*.

Greeking The conversion of text to symbolic bars or boxes that show the position of the text on-screen, but not the real characters. Text usually is greeked in the Fit in Window view in CorelDRAW!; small point sizes can be greeked in closer views on some screens. See also *greek text*.

Grid The underlying design plan for a page. You can use the grid for object alignment by using the Snap To Grid option in the Layout menu.

Grid origin   The intersection of the two CorelDRAW! rulers at 0 (zero). The default zero point is at the intersection of the left and top margins, but can be moved.

Gripper   The top part of a page.

Group   Several objects combined into a single unit that accepts modifications as a whole entity.

Guide   A nonprinting line (margin guide, ruler guide, or column guide) created to help align objects on a page. Nonprinting guides look like dotted lines, dashed lines, or blue lines, depending on the screen's resolution and color settings.

Gutter   The inside margins between the facing pages of a document; sometimes describes the space between columns in a frame setting. In some word processors, the gutter measure is entered as the difference between the measures of the inside margin and the outside margin. See also *margin*.

Hairline   The thinnest rule you can create. (Some laser printers do not support hairline rules.)

Halftone   The conversion of continuous-tone artwork (usually a photograph) into a pattern of dots or lines that looks like gray tones when printed by an offset printing press. See also *continuous-tone image*.

Handles   The eight small, black rectangles enclosing a selected shape; the two small rectangles at the ends of a selected line; the small black rectangles at the four corners; and the loops at the center of the top and bottom of a selected text block. You can drag the handles to change the size of the selected object. Also called *sizing squares*. See also *windowshades*.

Hanging indent   A paragraph in which the first line extends to the left of the other lines. You can use a hanging-indent format to create headings set to the left of the body copy. See also *indentation*.

Hard disk   Disk storage built into the computer or into a piece of hardware connected to the computer. Distinguished from removable floppy disk storage.

Header   See *running head*. See also *folio* and *running foot*.

Hierarchical filing system   Disk storage system in which files can be stored in separate directories that in turn can contain subdirectories. See also *directory*.

Highlight To distinguish visually. Usually reverses the normal appearance of selected text, graphics, or options (black text on a white background, for example, appears as white text on a black background after it is highlighted).

Hue In the Hue, Saturation, Brightness color model, the individual color—for example, blue, green, or brown.

Hyphenation The dividing of text words as they reach the end of a line (the right margin). If hyphenation is not used, the entire word moves to the next text line. Using hyphenation divides the word in accordance with accepted conventions, keeps the first half of the word (pre-hyphen) on the initial line, and moves the post-hyphen word section to the next line. A "Hot Zone" is defined within which hyphenation application is determined.

Icon Graphic on-screen representation of a tool, file, or command.

Image header Part of an EPS graphic file that allows the screen viewing of the image.

Import To bring in text or graphics from other programs, such as text from a word processing program or clipart from a graphics program.

Import filter A processor that tells how to convert files brought in from other programs.

Increment Distance between tick marks on a ruler. See also *measurement system*.

Indentation Positioning the first line of paragraph text (or second and following lines) to the right of the left-column guide (to create a left indent); or, positioning the right margin of the paragraph text to the left of the right-column guide (to create a right indent), relative to the other text on the page.

Insertion point A blinking vertical bar where text is to be typed or pasted.

Inside margin Margin along the edge of the page that is to be bound. In single-sided publications, this is always the left margin. In double-sided publications, the inside margin is the left margin of a right-hand page and the right margin of a left-hand page. See also *gutter* and *margin*.

Integral proof A color proofing system that bonds all four process colors to a single sheet. Also called a *composite*.

Inter-character spacing The amount of spacing between characters of text.

Inter-line spacing The amount of spacing between lines of text.

Inter-paragraph spacing   The amount of spacing between paragraphs of text.

Inter-word spacing   The amount of spacing between words in a line of text.

Invert   A CorelPHOTO-PAINT filter used to produce a negative photo offset. See *Reverse*.

Italics   Letters that slope toward the right, as distinguished from upright, or Roman, characters.

Jump line   Text at the end of an article indicating on what page the article is continued. Also, the text at the top of a continued article, indicating from where the article is continued. Also called a *continued line*.

Justified text   Text that is flush at both the left and right edges. See also *alignment*.

Kern   To adjust the spaces between letters with the Shape tool, usually to move letters closer together. See also *kerning*.

Kerning   The amount of space between letters, especially certain combinations of letters that must be brought closer together to create visually consistent spacing around all letters. The uppercase letters AW, for example, may appear to have a wider gap between them than the letters MN unless a special kerning formula is set up for the AW combination. See also *kern*.

Knockout   A generic term for a positive or overlay that "knocks out" part of an image from another image. The most obvious example of this is white type on a black background. The white type is knocked out of the background.

Landscape printing   The rotation of a page to print text and graphics horizontally across the longer measure of the page or paper (11 inches on a conventional 8 1/2" x 11" page).

Laser printing   Term used to describe printing on a toner-based laser printer. These printers use laser technology—light amplification by stimulated emission of radiation—to project an intense light beam in a narrow bandwidth (1/300 inch in 300-dpi printers). This light creates a charge on the printer drum that picks up the toner and transfers it to the paper. Some typesetters (such as the Linotronic 300 and 500) also use laser technology in their photochemical processing, but usually are referred to as phototypesetters or imagesetters rather than laser printers. See also *phototypesetting*.

Layer One plane that contains one object or group of objects in CorelDRAW!. Used to place objects in front of other objects to provide depth and to provide more control during drawing construction.

Layering order Order in which overlapping text and graphics are arranged on the page and on-screen.

Layout The process of arranging text and graphics on a page; a sketch or plan for the page; also the final appearance of the page. (In plate making, a sheet indicating the settings for the step-and-repeat machine.)

Leaders Dotted or dashed lines that can be defined for tab settings. Other symbols may be used also.

Leading Historically, the insertion of thin strips of metal (made of a metal alloy that included some lead) between lines of cast type to add space between the lines and to make columns align. In modern typography, the vertical space between the baselines of two lines of text. Leading is measured from ascender to ascender between two lines of text and is entered in points or percentage in the Type Specifications dialog box. To give an example of the terminology, 12-point Times with 1 point of leading added is called 13-point leaded type; also called 12 on 13 Times and sometimes written as 12/13 Times.

Lens A CorelDRAW! feature that gives objects photographic qualities such as transparency.

Letterspacing Space between letters in a word. The practice of adding space between letters.

Library A collection of commonly used text and graphic elements which may be displayed in the CorelMOSAIC palette.

Ligatures Character combinations often combined into special characters in a font. Some downloadable fonts, for example, come with the combinations fi and fl as special characters.

Line spacing See *leading*.

Line style The type of a line, as in dotted, dashed, or solid lines.

Linked file A graphic or text file imported using the Place or Paste command in conjunction with the option to link the original file to the current publication, rather than store it as part of the publication. Linked files can be managed through the First Links command. See also *Object Linking and Embedding*.

List box   Area in a dialog box that displays options. See also *drop-down menu*.

Lock   Use the Lock Guides on Layers command to anchor column guides and ruler guides on the current page or to anchor the zero point of the rulers. Locked guides cannot be inadvertently moved while laying out text and graphics.

Logo   A company trademark. Also, the banner on the front cover of a magazine or newsletter. See also *masthead*.

Luminosity   The brightness of a color.

Magenta   The subtractive primary color that appears blue-red and absorbs green light. Used as one ink in four-color printing. Also known as *process red*. See also *subtractive primary colors*.

Manual text flow   Manually placing text on the page so that the text flows to and stops at the bottom of the column or the first object that blocks the text. See also *Autoflow*.

Margin   Traditionally, the distance from the edge of the page to the edge of the layout area of the page. Margins are normally used to define the limits of text. See also *gutter* and *inside margin*.

Margin guides   Dotted nonprinting lines displayed near the borders of the screen page to mark the margins of a page as specified in the Page Setup dialog box. See also *margin* and *nonprinting master items*.

Marquee   A dashed rectangular region that appears when you drag the Pick tool to select multiple objects. See also *bounding box*.

Marquee select   The process of using a marquee to encompass and thus select an object or group of objects.

Mask   A shape that can be applied to an image in CorelPHOTO-PAINT to isolate a region from/for effects of filters.

Master items   Items on a master page; can include text (running heads), graphics (rules), and nonprinting guides (column guides). See also *master page* and *nonprinting master items*.

Master layer   A plane that holds all objects common to all layers or pages of a project.

Master page   Page containing text, graphics, and guides you want repeated on every page in a publication. See also *master items*.

Masthead Section of a newsletter or magazine giving its title and details of staff, ownership, advertising, subscription, and so on. Sometimes the banner or wide title on the front cover of a magazine or the front of a newsletter or newspaper. See also *logo*.

Measurement system Units chosen through the Preferences command on the Edit menu: inches, decimal inches, millimeters, picas and points, or ciceros and points. The chosen units appear on the rulers and in all dialog boxes that display measurements. You can enter a value in any unit of measurement in many dialog boxes. See also *pica*.

Mechanical separations Color separations made based on black-and-white art. If using CMYK process color separations, for example, each of four plates represents a different color (cyan, magenta, yellow, and black), but is given to the press/printer as a black-and-white print on paper or film.

Mechanicals Traditionally, the final pages or boards with pasted-up galleys of type and line art, sometimes with acetate or tissue overlays for color separations and notes to the offset printer. See also *camera-ready art* and *offset printing*.

Memory Area in the computer where information is stored temporarily while you work; also called *RAM*, or random-access memory. You can copy the contents of the memory onto disk by using the Save or Save As command.

Menu A list of choices presented in a fly-out, pull-down, or pop-up window.

Menu bar Area across the top of the publication window where menu commands appear.

Merge Combining text information with an image so that the resulting merged file is a combination of the two.

Mirror To create a mirror image of an object.

Moiré pattern An undesirable pattern that occurs if two transparent dot-screen fill patterns are overlaid or a bitmapped graphic with gray fill patterns is reduced or enlarged.

Monochrome A single color (usually black) image or display device.

MOSAIC See *CorelMOSAIC*.

Mouse buttons The main, or primary, mouse button (usually the left button) used to carry out most actions. Use the Control Panel to specify the main button as the left or right button of a two- or three-button mouse. Some commands also use the secondary mouse button on a two- or three-button mouse. See also *Control Panel* and *secondary mouse button*.

Movie   A completely finished and self-contained animation.

Multiple select   To choose more than one object in sequence with the Shift key as a modifier. See also *marquee select*.

Negative   A reverse image of a page, produced photographically on a clear sheet of film as an intermediate step in preparing offset printing plates from camera-ready mechanicals. See also *film*.

Node   Object locations that designate the start and end of line segments and a possible change in curve direction. Nodes can be moved to change object shapes. See also *cusp node*, *end node*, *smooth node*, *start node*, and *symmetric node*.

Nonbreaking space   A special space used to keep words from being separated at the end of a line of text.

Nonprinting master items   The ruler guides and column guides on a master layer. See also *margin guides*, *master page*, and *ruler guides*.

Object Data Manager   The CorelDRAW! feature that correlates database information with an image so that clicking on the image displays the information.

Object Linking and Embedding (OLE)   A feature of Windows 3.1 (and later versions), whereby objects created in one application that supports OLE can be pasted into another application that supports OLE either as embedded objects (that is, part of the document into which they are pasted) or as linked objects (that is, linked to the external source and updated when the source changes). In either case, the objects can be edited by double-clicking on them, thereby activating the application that originally created them. See also *linked file*.

Object-oriented files   Vector graphic files consisting of a sequence of drawing commands (stored as mathematical formulas). These commands describe graphics (such as mechanical drawings, schematics, charts, and ad graphics) that you would produce manually with a pencil, straightedge, and compass. Usually contrasted with paint-type files or bitmaps. See also *bitmap*.

Offset printing   Type of printing done using a printing press to reproduce many copies of the original. The press lays ink on a page according to the raised image on a plate created by photographing the camera-ready masters. See also *camera-ready art*, *laser printing*, and *mechanicals*.

OLE See *Object Linking and Embedding*.

One-point perspective Using CorelDRAW!'s Perspective command, adding a three-dimensional effect to an object so it appears as if it is receding from view to a single point on the horizon.

Onion skin A special view of the animation actor's cels so that the underlying or following cels can be viewed while modifying the currently active cel.

Option boxes The square area to the left of certain options in a dialog box; click the option box to turn on, or select, its option. Click it again to deselect the option. See also *Control Panel* and *secondary mouse button*.

Orientation Refers to the portrait or landscape page position options. Portrait pages and columns run down the longer measure of the page. In landscape orientation, text runs horizontally across the wider measure of the page, and columns run down the shorter measure of the page. See also *landscape printing* and *portrait printing*.

Orphan The first, or first and second, line of a paragraph that falls at the bottom of a column or page. See also *widow*.

Outline font A printer font in which each letter of the alphabet is stored as a mathematical formula, as distinguished from bit mapped fonts, which are stored as patterns of dots. PostScript and TrueType fonts, for example, are outline fonts. See also *bitmap* and *font*.

Outline tool The toolbox item used to define the object outline attributes.

Outside margin The unbound edge of a page. In single-sided publications, the outside margin is the right margin. In double-sided publications, the outside margin is the right margin of a right-hand page and the left margin of a left-hand page. See also *inside margin* and *margin*.

Overhead transparency An image printed on clear acetate and projected onto a screen for viewing by an audience.

Overlay A transparent acetate or tissue covering a printed page; contains color specifications and other instructions to the offset printer. Also, an overhead transparency that is intended to be projected on top of another transparency. See also *color separations*.

Overlay proofs A color-proofing system that uses transparent overlays for each of the colors in the publication.

Overprint To specify that a colored object shows through an overlapping colored object. Normally, the object underneath is hidden by the object in front.

Oversized publication   Publication in which page size is larger than standard paper sizes. See also *page size* and *tile*.

Page Control box   An icon displayed in the bottom left corner of the publication window. Icons represent the master pages and every regular page. See also *icon*.

Page size   The dimensions of the pages of your publication as set in the Page Setup dialog box. Page size can differ from paper size. See also *margin* and *paper size*.

Paint-type file   See *bitmap*.

Pair kerning   The process that changes the amount of space between two letters to create visually consistent spacing between all letters. See also *kerning*.

Palette   The color bar located at the bottom of the screen that is used to define outline and interior colors.

PANTONE Matching System   A widely-used, standard system for choosing colors, based on ink mixes. Also referred to as PMS colors.

Paper size   The size of the printer paper. Standard paper sizes are letter (8 1/2 by 11 inches), legal (8 1/2 by 14 inches), European A4 (210 by 297 millimeters), and European B5 (176 by 250 millimeters).

Paragraph text   A block of text in CorelDRAW! to which many attributes can be applied, always placed in a text frame. See *artistic text*.

Paste   To place cut or copied objects or text from the Clipboard to the working page. The object or text is left in the Clipboard.

Pasteboard   The on-screen work area surrounding the pages on which you are working. You can move text and graphics to the pasteboard, where they remain after you turn to another page or close the publication.

Paste-up   See *mechanicals*.

Perspective   Provides the illusion of depth by forcing all lines to merge at a selected vanishing point.

Phototypesetting   Producing a page image on photosensitive paper or film negative, as when documents are printed on a Linotronic 300 or 500. This process is sometimes referred to as cold type to distinguish it from the older method of casting characters, lines, or whole pages in lead (called *hot type* or *hot metal*). See also *laser printing*.

Pica   A unit of measure equal to approximately 1/6 inch, or 12 points. See also *cicero*, *measurement system*, and *point size*.

Pick tool   The tool used for selecting and manipulating text and graphics. If the Pick tool is selected, the pointer looks like an arrow. See also *pointer*.

PICT format   A format used to store graphics on a Macintosh computer. Usually converted to PIC format when transferred to an MS-DOS/Windows system.

Pictographs   Bar charts created with outlines and fills derived from images rather than patterned or shaded interior fills.

Pixel   The smallest unit on a computer display. Monitors can have different screen resolutions (pixels per inch) and different sizes (total number of pixels).

Point   To place the mouse pointer on an object on-screen.

Point size   The smallest unit of measure in typographic measurement and the standard unit of measure for type. Measured roughly from the top of the ascenders to the bottom of the descenders. A pica has 12 points; an inch, approximately 72 points; a point equals 1/12 pica, or 1/72 inch. See also *cicero*, *measurement system*, and *pica*.

Pointer   The on-screen icon that moves as you move the mouse.

Portrait printing   The normal printing orientation for a page: horizontally across the shorter measurement of the page or paper (usually, 8 1/2 inches).

PostScript   A page-description language (PDL) developed by Adobe Systems used to control an output device for the placement of text and graphics on a printed page.

PostScript textures   A representation of surface irregularity defined in a PostScript device that can be applied to an object to alter its appearance.

PowerClip command   The PowerClip command creates PowerClip objects by placing a contents object inside another object, the container object. A container object acts as a window, displaying only the portions of the contents object that fall within the boundaries of the container.

PowerLines   A CorelDRAW! tool used to give lines a hand-drawn look or a variable line width.

PPD and PDX files   PostScript Printer Description and Printer Description Extensions files. These files provide information used to set the default information for the type of printer or other PostScript output device you are using.

Preferences The command on the Special menu used to select the unit of measure displayed on ruler lines and in dialog boxes, display characters, mouse options, and other options. See also *measurement system* and *pica*.

Prepress proofs Sometimes called blue lines, these proofs are made by using photographic techniques. See also *blue lines* and *press proofs*.

Press proofs A test run of a color printing job through the printing press to check registration and color. See also *blue lines* and *prepress proofs*.

Preview A CorelDRAW! mode that allows you to view the work as it will appear when printed.

Primary colors Elemental colors of either pigments or light. Red, green, and blue are additive primaries. White light is produced when red, green, and blue lights are added together. Cyan, magenta, and yellow are subtractive primaries, the inks used to print in the three-color process (or four-color process with black). See also *additive primary colors* and *subtractive primary colors*.

Print area The area on a piece of paper where the printer reproduces text and graphics; always smaller than the paper size. See also *margin*.

Print Manager A Microsoft Windows utility for sending files to the printer. The Print command sends the publication to Print Manager (a spooler), and not directly to the printer. If enabled, Print Manager holds files in a print queue and prints them in the order in which they are received. You can continue working on other files while a file is being printed. See also *print queue*.

Print queue Files in a print spooler waiting to be sent to the printer. Files are sent in the order received. See also *Print Manager*.

Printer font A bitmapped or outline font installed in the printer or downloaded to the printer as a publication is printed. Usually distinguished from the screen font, which displays the text on the computer screen. See also *bitmap*, *font*, and *outline font*.

Process color Cyan, Magenta, Yellow, and Black. The four primary colors used to create all other colors in four-color process printing.

Process separations Four-color separations made from color artwork.

Proofread To read a preliminary printout of a page and check for spelling errors, alignment on the page, and other features.

Prop Background objects for animation.

Pull-down menu   A list of commands that appears after you select a menu item. The menu items appear on the menu bar along the top of the screen, and the menu commands drop down in a list below the selected menu title.

Pull-out quote   Quotation extracted from the text of an article and printed in larger type, often set off by ruled lines. Also called a pull quote.

Ragged right   Text in which lines end at different points near the right margin. Opposite of flush right or justified text. See also *alignment* and *flush right*.

RAM   See *memory*.

Record   A complete set of information in a database that relates to one topic, such as name, address, and phone number.

Rectangle tool   The tool used to create squares and rectangles.

Registration   The accuracy with which images are combined or positioned, particularly in reference to multicolored printing where each color must be precisely aligned for the accurate reproduction of the original.

Registration mark   A mark added to a document for lining up color separations of the same page to aid the printer in positioning color overlays. Often appears as a circle with an X in it.

Release   To let go of a mouse button.

Resolution   Number of dots per inch (dpi) used to create an alphanumeric character or a graphics image. High-resolution images have more dots per inch and look smoother than low-resolution images. The resolution of images displayed on-screen is usually lower than that of the final laser printout. Laser printers print 300 dots per inch or more; phototypesetters print 1,200 dots per inch or more.

Reverse   Text or a graphic on the printed page that appears opposite of normal. Usually, text and graphics are black on a white background; if reversed, they are white on black.

RGB   Shorthand notation for red, green, and blue. See also *additive primary colors* and *primary colors*.

Ribbon bar   Bar that appears at the top of the CorelDRAW! screen below the menu bar. It contains buttons you can click to perform common operations, such as cutting, pasting, saving, and printing.

Right justified   See *alignment* and *flush right*.

Roll-up window Small window that provides quick access to a number of related object attributes that can be applied quickly to selected objects.

Roman Upright text styles, as distinguished from italic.

Rotate To revolve an object around a given point.

Roughs Traditionally, the preliminary page layouts done by a designer using pencil sketches to represent miniature page design ideas. See also *thumbnail*.

Ruler guides Nonprinting extensions of the tick marks on the rulers, which form horizontal and vertical dotted, dashed, or blue lines on the page. Used to align text and graphics on the page. See also *nonprinting master items*.

Rulers Electronic rulers are displayed across the top of the publication window and down the left side. Rulers show measurements in inches, picas, millimeters, or other undefined units. Increments (tick marks) on the rulers depend on the size and resolution of your screen, as well as on the view. See also *measurement system*.

Ruling lines In page layouts, horizontal and vertical graphic lines used to separate text or frames from the surrounding paragraphs of text.

Running foot One or more lines of text appearing at the bottom of every page. The running foot is entered on the master pages. Also referred to as the footer. See also *folio*.

Running head One or more lines of text appearing at the top of every page. The running head is entered on the master pages. Also referred to as the header. See also *folio*.

Sans serif Typefaces without serifs, such as Helvetica and Avant Garde. See also *serif*.

Saturation In the Hue, Saturation, Brightness color model, the amount of color. A high saturation creates an intense color, a low saturation creates a weak, pale color.

Scale To change the size of an object vertically, horizontally, or both. You scale a graphic by selecting it with the Pointer tool and then dragging one of the square handles.

Scanned-image files Bitmapped files created by using hardware that digitizes images (converts a two- or three-dimensional image to a collection of dots stored in the computer's memory or on disk). See also *bitmap* and *digitize*.

Scanner Electronic device that converts a photo, illustration, or other flat art into a bitmap. A video camera is a scanner that converts three-dimensional objects into bitmaps.

Screen font See *font*.

Screen ruling The number of lines per inch in a screen tint or halftone. See also *halftone*.

Screen tint A screened percentage of a solid color.

Script fonts Type designed to look like handwriting or calligraphy, such as Zapf Chancery.

Scroll bar Gray bars on the right side and bottom of the publication window. Scroll arrows at both ends of each bar enable you to scroll the document horizontally or vertically. Each scroll bar has a scroll box that you can drag to change the view within the publication window. Drop-down list boxes can also have scroll bars for viewing long lists of files or options.

Secondary mouse button On a multiple-button mouse, the button that is not the main button. (Usually the right button.) See also *mouse buttons*.

Segments The lines between the nodes of a Corel curve object.

Select To click or drag the mouse to designate the location of the next action. Also, to turn on (or place an × in) a check box (or other options) in a dialog box. See also *deselect*.

Selection area Area of a text block or graphic defined by the handles displayed after you select that text block or graphic.

Selection marquee A dashed rectangular region drawn by dragging the Pointer tool to enclose and select more than one graphic or text block at a time. See also *drag*.

Serif A line crossing the main stroke of a letter. Typefaces that have serifs include Times, Courier, New Century Schoolbook, Bookman, and Palatino. See also *sans serif*.

Shape A drawn object such as a square, rectangle, circle, or oval.

Shape tool A toolbox icon used to modify object shapes and attributes primarily by working with the nodes.

Signature In printing and binding, the name given after folding to a printed sheet of (usually) 16 pages. The term is sometimes applied to page spreads printed adjacent to each other in the sequence required for offset printing of smaller booklets.

Size   To make a graphic smaller or larger by dragging the handles. See also *handles*.

Skew   To slant an object vertically or horizontally.

Slide   A CorelCHART image.

Smooth node   A node where a line enters and leaves the node at the same angle.

Snap   To force objects to a predefined point on grid lines or guides for alignment purposes.

Snap To   The effect of various types of alignment options, such as margin guides, object, and column guides. These guides exert a "magnetic pull" on the pointer, text, or a graphic that comes close to the guides. Useful for aligning text and graphics accurately.

Snap To guides   Command that causes margin guides, column guides, and ruler guides to exert a "magnetic pull" on the pointer or any text or graphic near the guides.

Sound icon   A small picture that represents a sound file for use in CorelSHOW.

Spacing   The amount of space, in points, that is added or removed between every pair of characters or lines in a type block. Spacing affects the amount of white space in a type block. See also *leading* and *white space*.

Spooler   See *Print Manager*.

Spot color   A process that adds solid areas of colored ink to a publication.

Spot-color overlay   A page prepared so that each color on the page is printed separately and then combined by a commercial printer to form the completed page.

Spreads   A trapping technique where the outline of a foreground object is extended or enlarged to overlap with a background object.

Standoff   Distance between the graphic boundary and the graphic.

Start node   A point at the beginning of a line represented by a hollow square larger than an end node square.

Story All the text from one word processing file; all the text typed or compiled at an insertion point outside existing text blocks. Can be one text block or several text blocks threaded together. See also *text block*.

Stretch The application of horizontal or vertical expansion to an object, usually by use of sizing handles.

Style A variation within a typeface, such as Roman, bold, or italic. See also *font* and *typeface*.

Subpath A segment or line drawn by CorelDRAW! between nodes.

Subtractive primary colors Cyan, yellow, and magenta. The three colors used to create all other colors if reflected light is used (for example, in printed material). See also *additive primary colors*, *CMYK*, and *primary colors*.

Symmetric node A node where the curve is exactly the same on each side of the node.

Target printer The printer on which you intend to print the final version of your publication. If no target printer is selected, CorelDRAW! uses the default printer chosen when Windows was installed.

Template A collection of text and object styles that are applied to newly created objects and/or text to provide design consistency between drawings.

Text block A variable amount of text identified, when selected with the Text Pointer tool, by handles (small squares at the four corners of the text block) and windowshades. See also *story*.

Text-entry box The area in a dialog box in which you type text.

Text-only file Text created in another application and saved without type specifications or other formatting. See also *ASCII*.

Text tool Tool used to insert text into a drawing.

Text wrap Automatic line breaks at the right edge of a column or at the right margin of a page. Also, the capability to wrap text around a graphic on a page layout. You can wrap text around a graphic by changing the envelope of a text block.

Texture fill The application of a bitmap, fractal, or PostScript pattern to the interior of an object.

Thumbnail A miniature version (mosaic) of a page that is created by using the Thumbnails option in CorelMOSAIC.

Tick marks Marks on the rulers showing increments of measure. See also *measurement system*.

Tile Used in oversized publications. A part of a page printed on a single sheet of paper. For a complete page, the tiles are assembled and pasted together.

Timeline The overall timing sequence of events for animation and presentations.

Time-out error Printer stops because it has not received information for awhile. Usually occurs while you print complex pages, and the printer takes a long time to print a large bitmapped image. Saving before printing helps reduce chances of data loss. Time-out value may be adjusted upward.

Tint A percentage of one of the process or custom colors.

Toggle switch An on/off switch, command, or option. Used to describe cases in which the same command is invoked to turn a feature on and off. As they appear in pull-down menus, these commands display a check mark if they are on.

Tones The shades of a photograph or illustration that are printed as a series of dots. Tones are percentages of black; lower percentages produce lighter tones.

Toolbox window Window that overlaps the publication window and contains icons for the tools you use to work with text and graphics.

Tracking The adjustment of horizontal spacing between a range of characters or words for better readability.

Transitions The process of adding or removing an image from the screen. This applies to animation props and CorelCHART slides.

Transparency See *overhead transparency* and *overlay*.

Trap Color overlap needed to ensure that a slight misalignment or movement of the color separations does not affect the final appearance of a print job.

Trim command Applying the Trim command to two (or more) overlapping objects separates the paths at points where the objects overlap.

TrueType Font definitions from Windows that allow sizing and alteration of text without losing resolution quality. See also *outline font*.

TRUMATCH A standard method of exactly matching colors in the print industry.

TWAIN An industry-standard scanning image driver that allows for various manufacturers to provide compatible scanning devices.

Two-point perspective Using CorelDRAW!'s Perspective command, adding a three-dimensional effect to an object so that it appears as if it is receding from view to two points on the horizon.

Typeface A single type family of one design in all sizes and styles. Times and Helvetica, for example, are two different typefaces. Each typeface has many fonts (sizes and styles). Sometimes the terms typeface and font are used interchangeably. See also *font* and *style*.

Uniform color A solid color applied to the fill or outline of CorelDRAW! objects.

Unit of measure The units marked on display rulers and division files such as inches, picas and points, millimeters, or ciceros.

Vector graphics See *object-oriented files*.

Weight The thickness of the outlines of CorelDRAW! objects.

Welding The process of reducing many overlaid objects into a single object with a combined outline of the previous group of objects.

WFN The font used with early versions of CorelDRAW!. You can convert it to an Adobe Type 1 font using the WFNBoss utility.

White space Empty space on a page, not used for text or graphics.

Widow Last line of a paragraph that falls at the top of a column or page.

Window On-screen area in which a Windows application or a dialog box runs. Each application window has a title bar, menu bar, and scroll bars. Some dialog boxes also include a title bar. See also *dialog box*.

Windowshades Horizontal lines, each with a small hollow square at each end, that span the top and bottom of a text block.

Wireframe view View in which only the outline of an object is shown, and the fill is not displayed. Useful in displaying drawings faster.

Word spacing The space between words in a line or a paragraph. See also *kerning* and *letterspacing*.

Word wrap The automatic adjustment of the number of words on a line of text according to the margin settings. The carriage returns that result from automatic word wrap are called soft carriage returns to distinguish them from hard carriage returns, which are entered to force a new line after you press Enter. See also *text wrap*.

Wrap   See *text wrap* and *word wrap*.

WYSIWYG   "What You See Is What You Get" (or *wizzy-wig*). Term describes systems that display all text and graphics on-screen in a good facsimile of how it will actually look when printed. The Corel applications are good WYSIWYG programs. Some computer systems are more WYSIWYG than others in the accuracy of the display.

X axis   The horizontal reference line to which objects are constrained. See also *constrain*.

X-height   A distinguishing characteristic of a font. The height of lowercase letters without ascenders or descenders, such as *x*, *a*, and *c*. Also called the body of the type.

Y axis   The vertical reference line to which objects are constrained. See also *constrain*.

Yellow   The subtractive primary color that appears yellow and absorbs blue light. Used as one ink in four-color printing. See also *subtractive primary colors*.

Zoom   To magnify or reduce your view of an object or drawing.

Index

Symbols

() (parentheses) arithmetic operator, 712
* (multiplication sign) arithmetic operator, 711
^ (exponent sign) arithmetic operator, 711
+ (plus sign) arithmetic operator, 711
– (subtraction sign) arithmetic operator, 711
.. (double periods) argument separator, 714
, (comma) argument separator, 714
/ (divide sign) arithmetic operator, 711
: (colon) argument separator, 714
; (semicolon) argument separator, 714
= (equal sign) formulas, 711
3D charts, 746-747
　　riser charts, 702
　　scatter charts, 702
3D effects
　　CorelPHOTO-PAINT images, 625
　　curved lines, 587
　　object fills, 170-179
　　patterns, 855-858
　　see also extrude effect
3D Roll-Up command (CorelCHART Chart menu), 746
3D Rotate Special Effect filter (CorelPHOTO-PAINT), 640
3D roll-up, 746-747
24-bit color mode (CorelPHOTO-PAINT), 592, 616-617
35mm slides, printing color drawings, 307
256 color mode (CorelPHOTO-PAINT), 617

A

About CorelDRAW! command (Help menu), 31
absolute referencing (spreadsheet cells), 710
ACAD (Association of Corel Designers and Artists), 819-820
Acquire command (CorelPHOTO-PAINT File menu), 322
Acquire command (CorelTRACE File menu), 322
Acquire Image command (CorelPHOTO-PAINT File menu), 614
Acquire Image command (CorelTRACE File menu), 669
active window, 893
Actor Info dialog box, 794, 814
Actor tool (CorelMOVE), 781
actors (animations), 778-779, 893
　　animating, 793-794, 797-799, 809-810
　　cues, 802-803
　　deleting, 804
　　drawing, 810-814
　　entrances, 787, 804
　　exits, 787, 804
　　libraries, 807-810
　　looping movement, 799
　　morphing, 815
　　moving, 797, 815
　　multicel actors, 778-779, 793-794
　　　　drawing, 794-796
　　　　speed of movement, 793
　　naming, 785
　　paths, 793-794
　　single cel actors, 778-779
　　　　drawing, 785-793
　　stopping, 798
　　timing, 807, 815
　　tinting colors, 792

Adaptive Sharpen Effect filter (CorelPHOTO-PAINT), 639
Adaptive Unsharp Mask dialog box, 631
Add Noise Noise Effect filter (CorelPHOTO-PAINT), 639
Add Perspective command (Effects menu), 415
Add to Selection command (CorelPHOTO-PAINT Special menu), 647-648
additive primary colors, 893
Adobe fonts, 209
　　Adobe Type 1 Font export filter, 273
　　customizing, 253-258
Adobe Illustrator
　　export filter, 273
　　import filter, 275
Adobe Type 1 Export dialog box, 255-256
Advanced property sheet, 572-575
AI files, 273-275
Airbrush tool (CorelPHOTO-PAINT), 604, 620
Aldus PageMaker files, importing, 542
Align command (Arrange menu), 116, 131, 396
Align command (CorelCHART Arrange menu), 741
Align dialog box, 116, 131
Align dialog box (CorelCHART), 741
Align to Baseline command (Text menu), 244
alignment, 893
　　alignment lines, 130-131
　　nodes to objects, 393-396
　　text, 44
　　vanishing points (perspectives), 418
Ami Pro files, importing, 226, 542

Ami Professional import filter, 275
Amplify command (CorelMOVE Wave Editor Effects menu), 800
anchor points, *see* nodes
Animation Info command (CorelMOVE Edit menu), 783
Animation Information dialog box, 783-784
animations, 13-14, 771, 777-779
    actors, 778-779, 893
        animating, 793-794, 797-799, 809-810
        cels, 893
        deleting, 804
        drawing, 785-796, 810-814
        entrances, 787
        exits, 787
        morphing, 14, 805-806, 815
        moving, 797, 815
        multicel actors, 793-794
        naming, 785
        paths, 793-794
        stopping, 798
        tinting colors, 792
    cels, 793
    cues, 802-803, 899
    exporting, 814
    frames, 778, 783, 811
        copying objects to another frame, 812
        inserting, 812
        inserting objects, 811
        speed, 784
        viewing several simultaneously, 813
    grids, 784
    libraries, 807-808
    looping, 799
    naming, 782
    nodes, 779
    paths, 798-799, 893
    pixels, 782-784
    props, 778-779, 915
        animating, 797-799, 809-810
        deleting, 804
        drawing, 785-793, 810-814
        editing, 786-787
        entrances, 787
        exits, 787
        moving, 797
        moving to back, 796-797
        moving to front, 796-797, 815
        naming, 785
        saving, 786
        stopping, 798
        tinting colors, 792
        zooming in/out, 787
    realism, 807
    running, 814
    saving, 782
    sound, 778, 799-801, 815
    thumbnails, 783
    timelines, 778-779, 921
    timing, 803-804, 807, 815
    transitions, 921
    windows, 782-784
annotations (charts), 893
    annotation layer, 731
    graphic annotations, 744
    text annotations, 743-744
Anti-Alias prop command (CorelMOVE Paint Effects menu), 792
anti-alias smoothing, 893
Anti-alias tool (CorelPHOTO-PAINT), 636
Append New Frames dialog box, 812
applications
    CorelCAPTURE, 615-616, 899
    CorelCHART, 13, 695-749, 899
    CorelMOSAIC, 13, 282-295, 306, 899
    CorelMOVE, 13-14, 777-816, 899
    CorelPHOTO-PAINT, 14, 591-656, 899
    CorelPLAYER, 814
    CorelQUERY, 15, 718-723, 899
    CorelSHOW, 14, 751-776, 899
    CorelTRACE, 14, 335-337, 667-694, 899
    file extension associations, 306
    OLE, 32-33
    reducing to icons, 19, 560
    switching between applications, 561
Apply Styles command (Object menu), 535
Apply Template command (CorelCHART File menu), 734
arcs, drawing, 84-86
area charts, 702
arguments (formulas), 714
arithmetic operators, 711-712
Arrange Icons command (CorelPHOTO-PAINT Window menu), 601
Arrange menu commands
    Align, 116, 131, 396
    Break Apart, 124, 250, 395, 516
    Combine, 90, 124-125, 393
    Convert To Curves, 250, 380, 388
    Group, 45, 120, 457, 516
    Intersect, 128-129
    Order, 103-104, 457
    Order Forward One, 55
    Order To Back, 55
    Separate, 88, 236
    Trim, 128, 130
    Ungroup, 50, 122, 517
    Weld, 128-129, 204
Arrowhead Editor dialog box, 398
arrowheads
    creating, 399-400
    editing, 398-399
    lines, 396-400
    object outlines, 142-143
    open path objects, 143, 385
    selecting, 397, 401
art
    camera-ready art, 896
    charts, importing, 734
    clipart, 47-53, 896
        Clipart CD, 49
        copyright restrictions, 57
    envelopes, 424-425, 435
    line art
        scanning, 333-335
        tracing, 335
    pixel-based art, 333
    scanning, 319, 333
    symbols, 47-48, 55-56
    vector-based art, 333
Artist Brush tool (CorelPHOTO-PAINT), 604, 619
Artistic Effect filters (CorelPHOTO-PAINT), 637
Artistic text, 211-212, 893
    aligning, 215
    baselines, 244

bitmapped images 927

bolding, 215
character limit, 212, 218
chrome effects, 170
Clipboard, 281
converting to curves, 249-250
curved lines, editing, 380
editing, 212-213
em shift, 244
envelopes, 436-437
extrude effects, 526
fills, 217-218
hanging indents, 905
inserting in drawings, 212
italicizing, 215
kerning, 216-218
node points, 114
outlines, 217-218
paths, 240-245
perspective effects, 518-519
PowerClip effects, 507
quotation marks, 232
replacing words or phrases, 228, 232
rotating, 240
scaling, 239
searching, 227-228, 231
skewing, 240
spacing, 216
special characters, 877-879
Spelling Checker, 228-230
straightening, 244
styles, 215
    applying, 237-239, 535
    copying, 245
    creating, 237
    saving, 237
subscript, 244
superscript, 244
Thesaurus, 228, 230
Type Assist, 231-233
underlining, 215
Artistic Text tool, 27, 41-42, 212
ascenders (letters), 893
ASCII editors, 311
ASCII text files, 894, 920
    characters, 252
    fields, 311-312
    importing, 226-227, 542
    merging with drawings, 310-314
    records, 311
aspect ratio (resolution), 894
Associate command (File Manager File menu), 306

Association of Corel Designers and Artists (ACAD), 819-820
associations (files), 289
auto-panning drawings, 894
AutoBackup, 574-575
AutoCAD DXF, 273-275
Autofitted Text command (CorelCHART Chart menu), 736
autoflowing text, 894
Autographix driver, 864
automatic transition (slides), 763-764
AutoTrace, 661-665, 894
    color, 664
    curve settings, 666
    customizing, 665-667
    Pencil tool, 661
    troubleshooting, 667
axes (charts), 736-737
    category axes, 698, 736
    data axes, 698, 736
    dual axes, 737
    X axis, 923
    Y axis, 923
Axis Assignment command (CorelCHART Chart menu), 737

B

Back One command (CorelMOVE Arrange menu), 797
Background Library dialog box, 764
Background tool (CorelMOVE), 788
backgrounds
    charts, 735
    CorelSHOW, 764-766
    stippled effects, 843-845
backing up files, 262, 574-575, 596, 611
Backward One command (CorelCHART Arrange menu), 744
balance (design), 835-836
banding (fountain fills), 368
bar charts, 701, 745-746
baselines (text), 244, 894
Batch Files roll-up, 670, 673-674
BBSs (Bulletin Board Systems)
    PostScript drivers, 308
    shareware typefaces, 209

Bessel functions, 713
Bézier curves, 894
Bézier mode (Pencil tool), 63
    drawing curved lines, 69-71, 383
    drawing straight lines, 64-67
binding margins (pages), 894
Bitmap Export dialog box, 271
bitmapped images, 894
    backing up, 596
    black and white, 617
    canvas backgrounds, 625
    canvas overlays, 625
    cloning, 623-624
    colors, 592, 616-617
        brightening, 630
        darkening, 630
        gamma, 630
        histogram, 630
        hue, 630
        intensity, 630
        saturation, 630
        tone, 632
    continous-tone images, 898
    cutouts, 609-610
    drawing over surface image, 620-621
    editing, 32, 601-603
    enlarging, 635
    exporting, 271-273
    flipping, 634
    grainy effects, 639
    importing, 282, 668
    jagged edges, 636
    mirroring, 634
    node points, 114
    object fill patterns, importing, 158-160
    pixels
        cutting, 610
        pasting, 610-611
        saving, 611
        selecting, 606-609
        selecting by color, 608
    PowerClip effects, 507
    printing, 310, 597-600
    reducing, 635
    resolution, 573, 635-636, 658
    retouching, 605-606, 611-613
    rotating, 634
    saving, 596
    scanning, 669-670
    sharpening details, 630-631
    smearing, 624

928 bitmapped images

smudging, 624
softening details, 631-632
stretching, 635
tracing, 586, 658-659
zooming in/out, 601-602
bitmapped patterns (fills), 345, 622
bitmapped textures (fills), 745, 895
Bitstream fonts, 209
black-and-white mode (CorelPHOTO-PAINT), 617
black-and-white drawings, printing, 32, 298
bleed effects, 364, 895
blend effects, 441-442, 523-524, 895
chaining blends, 456
cloning, 458-459
colors, 444-446, 459
compound blends, 456-457, 898
copying, 458
creating, 452-453
deleting, 458
end points
finding, 452
selecting, 449
fills, 344
fuse blends, 448, 453-454
highlights, 457
loops, 444
objects, 526-528
closed path, 446-451
open path, 446-451
paths, 449-450, 454-456, 459
perspective effects, 518
rotating, 444, 457
smoothing, 443, 459
space between objects, 444
split blend, 447-448, 453
start points
finding, 451-452
selecting, 446-448
status line, 442
steps, 527
see also contours
Blend roll-up, 442-450, 518
Blend Roll-Up command (Effects menu), 442, 452, 524
blocks (text), 920
blue lines, 895
BMP files, 273, 276, 668
boards, 895, 910
body copy (text), 895

body type (fonts), 895
boilerplates, *see* **templates**
bolding text, 215
booklets, 544
binding margin, 894
pagination, 548
see also documents
Border command (CorelCHART Format menu), 724
borders
drawings, 42-46, 54-55
pages, 545
spreadsheet cells, 724
Borders dialog box (CorelCHART), 724
boundaries of objects, lining up, 393-396
bounding boxes, 895
Break Apart command (Arrange menu), 124, 250, 395, 516
Brighten lens, 501-505
Brightness and Contrast Color Effect filter (CorelPHOTO-PAINT), 637
Brightness and Contrast dialog box, 633
brochures, 895
see also documents
Brush Mask tool (CorelPHOTO-PAINT), 645
brushes
CorelPHOTO-PAINT
designing custom brushes, 654-655
finding, 655
selecting sizes, 609, 624
shapes, 619, 624
CorelMOVE Paint, 789
drawing lines, 403
PowerLines, 489-490
bubble charts, 703
Bubble Help, 29
builds (slides), 865-866
bullets, 224-226, 895
charts, 696
CorelSHOW, 757
indents, 225-226
point size, 225
buttons
Maximize, 19
Minimize, 19, 560
Restore, 19
roll-ups, 27

C

calculations (CorelCHART), 710-712
calibration (colors)
calibration bar, 895
monitors, 359-361
printers, 359-361, 365
scanners, 359-361
calligraphy effects (text), 403, 584
Callout tool, 86-88
callouts, 896
drawing, 86-88
lines, 86-88
moving, 88
node points, 114
text, 86
camera-ready art, 896
`Can Not Open Help` **error message, 31**
Canvas roll-up, 600
Canvas Roll-Up command (CorelPHOTO-PAINT View menu), 625
cap height (text), 896
capturing screen displays, 615-616
cards, 544
see also documents
Cascade command (CorelCHART Window menu), 742
Cascade command (CorelPHOTO-PAINT Window menu), 601
catalogs (CorelMOSAIC), 283-284
creating, 284
drawings
deleting, 288-289
editing, 289-290
importing graphics, 290
inserting, 285-288
keywords, 291-292
thumbnails, 290-291
opening, 285
category axes (charts), 698, 736
Category Axis command (CorelCHART Chart menu), 736
CCH files, 704
CD-ROM installation, 5, 875
CDR files, 19, 263, 275, 824-825, 896

circles 929

CDs
    Clipart CD, 49, 835
    Kodak Photo CD, 277-278
    TrueType fonts, 874
    typefaces, 209
CDT files, 238, 536
Cel Sequencer (CorelMOVE), 809-810, 815
Cel Sequencer command (CorelMOVE View menu), 809
cells (spreadsheets)
    borders, 724
    clearing, 706
    copying, 714-716
    cutting, 714-716
    editing, 706
    entering data, 705
    numbers, formatting, 724
    pasting, 714-716
    patterns, 724
    ranges, 900
        designating, 714
        filling automatically, 707-710
        selecting, 707
    referencing, 710
    tagging, 725-726
    text, aligning, 724-725
    text strings, 709
    values, 709
    see also spreadsheets
cels (animations), 778, 793, 893
Center Across Selection command (CorelCHART Format menu), 724
center of rotation, 896
centering
    spreadsheets, 555
    text, 44
        Artistic text, 215
        Paragraph text, 220-221
Centerline button, 672
Centerline method (tracing objects), 675-677, 685
CGM files, 273-275
chained text, 896
Character Attributes dialog box, 214-215, 221, 243
Character command (Text menu), 215
Character Map, 878-879
Chart Types window (CorelCHART), 703

Chart View window (CorelCHART), 697-698, 729-732
charts, 695-696, 896
    3D charts, 746-747
        riser charts, 702
        scatter charts, 702
    analyzing data, 738, 748
    annotations, 731, 893
    area charts, 702
    axes, 736-737
        category axes, 698, 736
        data axes, 698, 736
        dual axes, 737
        X axis, 923
        Y axis, 923
    backgrounds, 735
    bar graph charts, 701
    bubble charts, 703
    bulleted lists, 696
    copying, 735
    creating, 697, 700
    customizing, 704
    data categories, 727
        reversing, 737
        sorting, 729
    data group, 727
        reversing, 737
        sorting, 729
    data points, 698, 740
    data series, 698, 727
        reversing, 737
        sorting, 729
    DDE (dynamic data exchange), 696
    directories, 703-704
    elements
        colors, 699, 734
        copying, 735
        cutting, 735
        displaying, 740
        duplicating, 735
        fills, 731-732, 744-745
        hiding, 740
        moving, 699
        outlines, 731
        pasting, 735
        selecting, 732
        zooming in/out, 730
    exporting, 696, 735
    Gantt charts, 703
    graphics
        aligning, 741
        annotations, 744
        importing, 734
    grid lines, 736-737
    groups, 698

    high/low/open/close graph charts, 702
    histograms, 702
    labels, 698
    legends, 736, 739
    line graph charts, 701
    loading, 703
    logos, 698
    numbers, formatting, 733-734
    opening, 704
    pictographs, 702, 745-746, 914
    pie graph charts, 702
    polar charts, 703
    presentations, 696
    printing, 748
    radar charts, 703
    refreshing display, 741
    risers, 698
    rotating, 747
    sample data, 703
    scales, 737
    scatter graph charts, 702
    selecting type, 703, 735
    spectral map charts, 702
    spreadsheet data, orienting, 727-728
    tagging, 725-726
    table charts, 702
    templates, 696, 734, 748
    text
        aligning, 741
        formatting, 742-743
        kerning, 743
        moving, 732-733
        sizing, 732-733
        text annotations, 743-744
    titles, 736
    zero lines, 741
check boxes, 896
child objects, 122-124, 896
choke effects, 896
chrome effects, 170
cicero (fonts), 896
Circle Mask tool (CorelPHOTO-PAINT), 605, 645
Circle Object tool (CorelPHOTO-PAINT), 604, 621
circles
    arcs, 84-86
    colors, 41
    copying, 40

circles

drawing, 40-41, 47, 81-86
  CorelPHOTO-PAINT, 621
  from a center point, 83
  from a corner point, 82
moving, 41
nodes, 114, 381
outlines, 41
pie wedges, 84-86
selecting, 40
shading, 41
sizing, 40
CLB files, 284
CLC files, 284
Clear All command (CorelMOSAIC Edit menu), 288
Clear Blend command (Effects menu), 458
Clear command (CorelCHART Edit menu), 706, 735
Clear Envelope command (Effects menu), 439
Clear Perspective command (Effects menu), 420
Clear Transformations command (Effects menu), 196, 439
clicking
  mouse, 896
  objects, 23
clipart, 47-48, 835, 848, 896
  Clipart CD, 49
  copyright restrictions, 57
  deleting portions, 51
  drawing portions, 52-53
  editing, 50-53
  inserting
    charts, 734
    drawings, 48-49
  printing, 48
  saving, 49
Clipboard, 100, 280, 897
  CorelCAPTURE, 615-616
  CorelMETAFILE, 281
  CorelPHOTO-PAINT, 610-611
  fountain fills, 281
  inserting
    objects, 107
    text, 281, 584
  Windows Metafile format, 281
clipping holes (combined objects), 897
  see also masks
clipping objects, 530-533
  see also PowerClip

Clone command (Edit menu), 107-108, 562
Clone command (Effects menu), 458, 496
Clone tool (CorelPHOTO-PAINT), 604, 623
cloning
  bitmapped images, 623-624
  objects, 897
  photographs, 623-624
closed path objects, 89-91, 385
  converting to open path objects, 91
  drawing, 90
  fills, 385
CMP files, 273
CMYK (Cyan, Magenta, Yellow, Black) color model, 342, 349, 352-355, 617, 897
coated stock paper, 897
collating documents, 897
collections (CorelMOSAIC), 284
Color Add lens, 502-505
Color Brightness and Contrast command (CorelPHOTO-PAINT Effects menu), 633
Color command (CorelPHOTO-PAINT Effects menu), 630
Color Comparison Tolerance dialog box, 608
Color Correction command (View menu), 361
Color dialog box, 401
Color Effect filters (CorelPHOTO-PAINT), 637
Color keys (3M), 897
Color Limit lens, 502-505
Color Manager, 359-361, 897
Color Manager command (CorelCHART File menu), 700
Color Manager command (File menu), 359
Color Mask roll-up, 600, 649-651
Color Mask Roll-Up command (CorelPHOTO-PAINT Mask menu), 649
color masks (CorelPHOTO-PAINT), 649-651
  creating, 649-650
  deleting, 651
  loading, 653
  previewing, 650-651
  removing, 651
  saving, 653

Color Palette command (View menu), 20, 356
color palettes, 20, 139, 897, 913
  CorelPHOTO-PAINT, 626-627
  displaying, 357
  dithering, 348
  process color palettes, 348-349
  rearranging colors, 357
  resetting, 356
  selecting, 356-357
  spot color palettes, 348-352
Color Pick-Up tool (CorelMOVE Paint), 790
color printers, *see* printers
Color Replacer tool (CorelPHOTO-PAINT), 606, 611-613
Color roll-up, 600, 611
Color Roll-Up command (CorelPHOTO-PAINT View menu), 626
Color Selection button, 672
Color Tolerance dialog box, 612
Color Tolerance command (CorelPHOTO-PAINT Special menu), 608
colors
  AutoTrace, 664
  bitmapped images, 592, 608, 611-613
  bleed effects, 364
  blend effects, 444-446, 459
  brightness, 353-354, 895
  calibration bar, 895
  chart elements, 734
  Color keys (3M), 897
  color schemes, 355-357
  CorelPHOTO-PAINT, 616-617, 629-630
  CorelTRACE, 682-683
  customizing, 900
  cutouts, 610
  dimension lines, 407
  dithering, 572-573, 901
  drawings, 341-342, 545
  fountain fills, 172-179
  gamut, 904
  gradation, 834
  hue, 353, 354
  illustrations, 341-342
  intensity, 353-354
  layers, 133
  Lens, 499-505
  lines, 401-402

luminosity, 909
models
   CMYK (Cyan, Magenta, Yellow, Black), 342, 349, 352-355, 897
   HSB (Hue, Saturation, Brightness), 353-354, 895, 906, 917
   RGB (Red, Green, Blue), 353-354, 916
monochrome, 910
naming, 355
objects
   fills, 23, 39, 47, 150-151, 343-344
   outlines, 23, 41, 139-141, 344-346
Paint (CorelMOVE), 790
patterns (fills), 152-155, 160-165
photographs, 592, 608
   Kodak Photo CD, 277
   retouching, 611-613
primary colors, 915
   additive primary colors, 893
   subtractive primary colors, 920
printing, 32, 298, 307
   accuracy, 359-361
   color printers, 347
   commercial printers, 342-343, 347, 362-369
   composite printing, 898
   costs, 368-369
   registration, 369, 916
   spot color vs. process color, 348-351
process colors, 349, 915
   customizing, 352-355
   fountain fill banding, 368
   printing, 349, 357-361, 372-374
   selecting, 370-374
proofing, 906, 912
saturation, 353-354
saving, 355
screen display, 347, 572-577
separations, 349, 362-369, 897
   layers, 304
   mechanical separations, 910
   printing, 15, 363-367
   process color separations, 915
   registration marks, 365, 367, 916

spot colors, 348-349, 919
   converting to process color, 350-351
   selecting, 370-374
   tints, 351-352
swatching systems
   Focoltone, 359, 903
   PANTONE Matching System (PMS), 343, 359, 913
   swatch books, 359
   TRUMATCH, 353, 359, 921
tints, 921
tones, 921
trapping, 366-367, 919, 921
Column Width command (CorelCHART Formula menu), 716
Column Width dialog box, 716
columns
   pattern pixels, 157-158
   rules, 897
   spreadsheets, 716-718
   text, 233-234
Combine command (Arrange menu), 90, 124-125, 393
command button, 898
commands
   Arrange menu
      Align, 116, 131, 396
      Break Apart, 124, 250, 395, 516
      Combine, 90, 124-125, 393
      Convert To Curves, 250, 380, 388
      Group, 45, 120, 457, 516
      Intersect, 128-129
      Order, 103-104, 457
      Order Forward One, 55
      Order to Back, 55
      Separate, 88, 236
      Trim, 128, 130
      Ungroup, 50, 122, 517
      Weld, 128-129, 204
   Arrange menu (CorelCHART)
      Align, 741
      Backward One, 744
      Make Same Size, 741
   Arrange menu (CorelMOVE), 797
   Chart menu (CorelCHART)
      3D Roll-Up command, 746
      Autofitted Text, 736
      Axis Assignment, 737

      Category Axis, 736
      Data Axis, 736
      Data Reversal, 737
      Display Status, 740
      Show as Pictograph, 746
      Show Grid Lines, 736
      Staggered Text, 736
   Data menu (CorelCHART)
      Data Orientation, 727
      Fill Series, 707-710
      Go To Cell, 707
      Insert Sorted Item, 729
   Edit menu
      Clone, 107-108, 562
      Copy, 107
      Copy Attributes From, 145, 148, 245
      Cut, 100, 107
      Delete, 51, 100
      Duplicate, 40, 105-106, 562
      Object, 813
      Paste, 107
      Redo, 99-100
      Repeat, 99, 196
      Select All, 99
      Undo, 65, 99-100, 196
      Undo Curve Edit, 391
   Edit menu (CorelCHART)
      Clear, 706, 735
      Copy, 715, 735
      Copy Chart, 735
      Cut, 714, 735
      Delete, 716
      Duplicate, 735
      Fill Down, 707
      Fill Right, 707
      Insert, 716
      Paste, 714, 735
      Paste Inside, 735
      Paste Link, 718
      Paste Special, 716
      Transpose, 715
      Undo, 735
   Edit menu (CorelMOSAIC)
      Clear All, 288
      Delete, 288
      Extract Text, 292
      Import, 290
      Keywords, 292
      Select All, 288
      Select by Keyword, 288
   Edit menu (CorelMOVE)
      Animation Info, 783
      Insert New Object Actor, 810
      Insert New Object Prop, 810

commands

Insert Object, 785
Insert Object Sound, 800
Object Info, 786
Edit menu (CorelMOVE Paint)
  Keep Paint, 793
  Registration, 796
  Remove Cels, 795
  Revert Paint, 793
  Select All, 795
Edit menu (CorelPHOTO-PAINT), 610-611
Edit menu (Data Object Manager), 555
Effects menu
  Add Perspective, 415
  Blend Roll-Up, 442, 452, 524
  Clear Blend, 458
  Clear Envelope, 439
  Clear Perspective, 420
  Clear Transformations, 196, 439
  Clone, 458, 496
  Contour Roll-Up, 479, 528
  Copy, 419-420, 458, 495, 505
  Copy Perspective From, 519
  Envelope, 434
  Envelope Roll-Up, 424
  Extrude Roll-Up, 463
  Lens, 500
  Perspective, 517-518
  PowerClip, 509, 531
  PowerLine Roll-Up, 486
  Separate, 459
  Transform Roll-Up, 101, 186
Effects menu (CorelMOVE Paint)
  Anti-Alias prop, 792
  Mirror, 792-793
  Morph, 805
  Rotate, 792-793
  Scale, 793
  Tint All Cels, 792
  Tint Prop, 792
Effects menu (CorelMOVE Wave Editor), 800
Effects menu (CorelPHOTO-PAINT)
  Color, 630
  Color Brightness and Contrast, 633
  Sharpen, 631

Soften, 631
Tone, 632
Field Options menu (Object Data Manager)
  Show Totals, 555
File menu
  Color Manager, 359
  Exit, 31
  Export, 255, 269
  Export To Movie, 814
  Import, 226, 274, 691
  Mosaic Roll-Up, 48, 283
  New, 18, 48, 542
  New From Template, 542, 581
  Open, 265, 542
  Print, 56, 298-299
  Print Merge, 313
  Print Setup, 301
  Run, 872
  Save, 47, 262
  Save As, 46, 262-264
File menu (CorelCHART)
  Apply Template, 734
  Color Manager, 700
  Exit, 700
  Export, 735
  Import, 717, 734
  MOSAIC Roll-Up, 700
  New, 700
  Open, 700, 704
  Page Setup, 727
  Preferences, 700
  Print, 727
  Print Preview, 727
  Print Setup, 727
File menu (CorelMOSAIC)
  New Collection, 284
  Preferences, 290
  Print Files, 292
File menu (CorelMOVE)
  New, 782
  Open, 780
  Open Collection, 285
File menu (CorelMOVE Paint)
  Exit, 796
File menu (CorelPHOTO-PAINT)
  Acquire, 322
  Acquire Image, 614
  New, 594
  Open, 595
  Print, 597
  Save, 596
File menu (CorelQUERY)
  New, 719

Save, 722
Save As, 722
File menu (CorelSHOW)
  New, 752
  Open, 752
  Print Setup, 754
  Save, 768
  Save Background, 769
File menu (CorelTRACE)
  Acquire, 322
  Acquire Image, 669
  Exit, 668
  Open, 670
  Save As, 336
  Save Options, 686-687
File menu (Data Object Manager), 555
File menu (File Manager), 305-306
Format menu (CorelCHART), 723-724
Formula menu (CorelCHART), 716
Help menu
  About CorelDRAW!, 31
  Contents, 30
  Screen/Menu Help, 30
  Search For Help On, 30, 278
  Tutorial, 30
Image menu (CorelPHOTO-PAINT)
  Convert To, 618
  Info, 599
  Resample, 635
  Resolution, 636
Insert menu (CorelSHOW), 770
Layout menu
  Go To Page, 237, 546-548
  Grid & Scale Setup, 111-112, 405
  Grid Setup, 67, 109, 575
  Guidelines Setup, 118
  Insert Page, 546
  Layers Roll-Up, 304, 547
  Page Setup, 298, 542-543
  Snap to Grid, 80
  Snap To Guidelines, 117, 132
  Snap To Objects, 113-114, 404-405
  Styles Roll-Up, 237, 534
Mask menu (CorelPHOTO-PAINT)
  Color Mask Roll-Up, 649

Create Transparency
  Mask, 652
Invert, 648
Load, 653
Load Transparency Mask,
  652
Remove Transparency
  Mask, 653
Save, 653
Save Transparency Mask,
  652
Object menu
  Apply Styles, 535
  Save Style As, 534
Object menu (CorelPHOTO-
  PAINT)
  Distort, 635
  Flip, 634
  Rotate, 634
Options menu
  (CorelMOVE), 790
Options menu (CorelMOVE
  Paint)
  Font, 792
  Onion Skin, 795
  Tint Selection, 792
  Transparency, 791
  Zoom, 791
Options menu (Print
  Manager), 308
Preferences menu (Data
  Object Manager), 552, 556
PowerClip menu, 531-533
Special menu
  Create Arrow, 400
  Create Pattern, 164
  Extract, 246
  Macros Preset Roll-Up,
    537
  Merge Back, 247
  Preferences, 65, 99, 561,
    915
  Symbols Roll-Up, 23, 250
Special menu (CorelPHOTO-
  PAINT)
  Add to Selection, 647-648
  Color Tolerance, 608
  Create Brush, 654
  Remove From Selection,
    648
  XOR Selection, 648
Text menu
  Align to Baseline, 244
  Character, 215
  Edit Text, 213, 242, 438
  Find, 227
  Fit Text to Path, 240

Frame, 233
Paragraph, 220
Replace, 228
Spell Checker, 229
Straighten Text, 244
Thesaurus, 230
Type Assist, 231
Trace menu (CorelTRACE)
  Edit Options, 336, 681
  OCR B&W, 336
View menu
  Color Correction, 361
  Color Palette, 20, 356
  Full-Screen Preview, 22,
    299
  Refresh Window, 571
  Roll-Ups, 568
  Rulers, 570
  Toolbox, 577
  Wireframe, 21, 94
View menu (CorelMOVE),
  808-809
View menu (CorelPHOTO-
  PAINT)
  Canvas Roll-Up, 625
  Color Roll-Up, 626
  Full Screen Preview, 600
  Maximize Work Area, 600
  Restore Screen, 600
  Tool Settings Roll-Up,
    612
  Toolbox Visible, 603
  Zoom, 601
Window menu
  More Windows, 18
Window menu
  (CorelCHART)
  Cascade, 742
  Refresh Window, 741
  Tile, 742
Window menu
  (CorelPHOTO-PAINT),
  601-602
commercial printing service
  bureaus
  camera-ready art, 896
  color accuracy, 357, 365
  preparing documents,
    362-367
  printer calibration, 365
complexity threshold
  (PostScript printers), 821
composite printing, 898
compound blends, 898
CompuServe Bitmap, 273-275
Computer Graphics Metafile,
  273-275

condensed type, 898
conical fountain fills, 344
Contents command (Help
  menu), 30
context-sensitive help, 30, 732
continous-tone images, 898
Contour roll-up, 479-481
Contour Roll-Up command
  (Effects menu), 479, 528
Contour Special Effect filter
  (CorelPHOTO-PAINT), 640
contours, 477
  applying, 479-482
  center contours, 479
  cloning, 483
  copying, 483
  deleting, 483
  editing, 479, 482
  fills, 481-483
  inside contours, 480
  objects, 527-528, 898
  offset distance, 480
  outlines, 481-483
  outside contours, 480
  paths, 482
  smoothness, 480
  status line, 478
contrast (photographs),
  633-634
Contrast tool, 633
Control menu, 898
Control Menu box, 19, 898
Control Panel, 898
control points
  curved lines, 72-77, 378, 384
  nodes, 390, 899
conversion functions, 712
Convert To command
  (CorelPHOTO-PAINT Image
  menu), 618
Convert To Curves command
  (Arrange menu), 250, 380,
  388
Copy Attributes dialog box,
  145, 148
Copy Attributes From
  command (Edit menu), 145,
  148, 245
Copy Chart command
  (CorelCHART Edit menu),
  735
Copy command (CorelCHART
  Edit menu), 715, 735
Copy command
  (CorelPHOTO-PAINT Edit
  menu), 610

Copy command (Data Object
  Manager Edit menu), 555
Copy command (Edit menu),
  107
Copy command (Effects
  menu), 419-420, 458, 495,
  505
Copy Perspective From
  command (Effects menu),
  519
copy, *see* text
Copy Style dialog box, 245
Copy to File command
  (CorelPHOTO-PAINT Edit
  menu), 611
Copy tool (CorelQUERY), 722
copyright restrictions
  (clipart), 57
copyright symbol, 252
Corel application group,
  finding, 18
Corel forum (CompuServe),
  828
Corel icons, 18
Corel Image Source driver,
  669
Corelation magazine, 820
CorelCAPTURE, 615-616, 899
CorelCHART, 13, 695-696, 899
  Chart Types window, 703
  Chart View window,
    697-698, 729-732
  charts, 701-703
    analyzing data, 738, 748
    annotation layer, 731
    axes, 698, 736-737
    backgrounds, 735
    bulleted lists, 696
    colors, 699, 734
    copying, 735
    creating, 697, 700
    customizing, 704
    data categories, 727, 729,
      737
    data group, 727-729, 737
    data points, 698, 740
    data series, 698, 727-729,
      737
    directories, 703-704
    editing, 735
    exporting, 696, 735
    fills, 731-732, 744-745
    formatting numbers,
      733-734
    graphics, 741, 744
    grid lines, 736-737
    groups, 698
    hiding elements, 740
    importing graphics, 734
    labels, 698
    legends, 736, 739
    loading, 703
    logos, 698
    moving elements, 699
    opening, 704
    outlines, 731
    pictographs, 745-746
    printing, 748
    risers, 698
    rotating, 747
    scales, 737
    selecting elements, 732
    spectral map charts, 702
    table charts, 702
    templates, 696, 734, 748
    text, 732-733, 741-743
    titles, 736
    zero lines, 741
    zooming in/out, 730
  CorelSHOW, exporting
    charts, 696, 761
  Data Manager window, 697,
    704-705
    arithmetic operators,
      711-712
    calculations, 710
    database queries, 718-723
    entering data, 699
    Formula bar, 705, 711
    formulas, 710-712
    functions, 712-713
    importing files, 717-729
    spreadsheets, 705-706,
      714-716, 723-727, 748
  DDE (dynamic data
    exchange) links, 696, 718
  exiting, 700
  files
    importing, 696
    listing, 704
  formula editor, 699
  Gallery window, 700-704
  Help, 732
  menu bar, 699
  starting, 699
  tools
    Ellipse tool, 730
    Fill tool, 730-731
    Outline tool, 730-731
    Pencil tool, 730-731
    Pick tool, 730
    Rectangle tool, 730
    Text tool, 730
    Zoom tool, 730
  windows, 742
CorelCHART 4 files, importing
  to CorelCHART 5, 717
CorelDRAW! 5, 4, 12, 899
  compatibility with files from
    previous versions, 267-269
  exiting, 19, 31
  installation, 872-875
  importing objects to
    CorelMOVE, 813
  starting, 16, 560-561
  system requirements, 871
  upgrading, 827
  versions, 18
CORELDRW.INI file, 587
CorelMETAFILE, 281
CorelMOSAIC, 13, 282-283,
  899
  catalogs, 283-289
  files
    editing, 292
    printing, 306
  keywords, 291-292
  libraries, 283-284
    creating, 284
    deleting drawings,
      288-289
    editing drawings, 289-290
    importing graphics into
      drawings, 290
    inserting drawings,
      285-288
    opening, 285
  printing drawings, 292
  starting, 13, 283
  thumbnails, 290-291
CorelMOSAIC roll-up, 283
CorelMOVE, 13-14, 899
  animations, 777-779
    actors, 778-779, 793-794,
      893
    animating objects,
      797-799, 809-810
    cels, 793
    cues, 802-803, 899
    deleting objects, 804
    drawing objects, 785-796
    frames, 778, 783
    grids, 784
    length, 784
    looping, 799
    morphing actors,
      805-806, 815
    moving objects, 797
    moving objects to back,
      796-797
    moving objects to front,
      796-797

naming objects, 785
Paint, 784
paths, 796, 893
props, 778-779, 785
realism, 807
selecting screen size, 782
sound, 778, 799-801
speed, 784
stopping object movement, 798
thumbnails, 783
timelines, 778-779
timing object actions, 803-804
Cel Sequencer, 809-810, 815
files, 780-782
importing CorelDRAW! objects, 813
libraries (animation objects), 807-808
Paint, 788-791
Sound Editor, 800
starting, 780
tools
    Actor tool, 781
    Cue tool, 781, 802-803
    Path tool, 781, 797
    Pick tool, 781
    Prop tool, 781
    Sound tool, 781, 800
Wave Editor, 800-801
CorelPHOTO-PAINT, 14, 591, 629, 899
brushes, 654-655
canvases, 625
Clipboard, 610-611
color modes, 616-617
color palettes, 626-627
colors, 629-630
cutouts, 609-610
files
    backing up, 611
    creating, 594-595
    opening, 595-596
    saving, 595-596
filters, 632, 637-640
images
    blurring, 624
    cloning, 623-624
    contrasting, 632-634
    copying, 610
    cutting, 610
    drawing over, 620-627
    enlarging, 635
    flipping, 634
    inserting text, 627
    jagged edges, 636
    mirroring, 634
    painting, 618
    pasting, 610
    reducing, 635
    resolution, 635-636
    retouching colors, 611-613
    rotating, 634
    saving, 611
    scanning, 613-615
    selecting by colors, 608
    selecting pixels, 606-609
    sharpening, 624, 630-631
    softening, 631-632
    stretching, 635
masks, 644
    circle masks, 645, 648
    color masks, 649-651
    combining, 647-649
    creating, 645-646
    drawing, 645
    editing nodes, 645-646
    loading, 653
    moving, 644
    overlapping, 648
    polygon masks, 645
    rectangle masks, 645
    saving, 653
    selecting, 644
    sizing, 646
    transparency masks, 652-653
memory requirements, 592, 615
photographs, scanning, 322-323, 333-334
screen display, 598-603
starting, 593-596
tools, 603-609, 619-623
    Anti-Alias tool, 636
    Brush Mask tool, 645
    Circle Mask tool, 645
    Contrast tool, 633
    customizing effects, 624
    Freehand Mask tool, 645
    Hand tool, 602
    Lasso Mask tool, 645
    Locator tool, 603
    Magic Wand Mask tool, 645, 649
    Mask Node Edit tool, 645
    Mask Picker tool, 644
    Polygon Mask tool, 645
    Rectangle Mask tool, 645
    Stretch/Truncate tool, 636
    Zoom tool, 601-602
windows, 600-603

CorelPLAYER, 814
CORELPRN.INI file, 821
CorelQUERY, 15, 718, 899
SQL command editor, 723
SQL (System Query Language), 719
starting, 719
tools
    Copy tool, 722
    Font tool, 722
    Grid Toggle tool, 722
    Move To tool, 723
    SQL tool, 723
writing queries, 719
CorelSHOW, 14, 751-752, 899
animations, 771, 814
backgrounds, 764-766
charts, importing, 761
CorelCHART, 696
cues, 772-773
graphics, 757-760
OLE (Object Linking and Embedding), 767-768
presentations
    designing, 755-756
    saving, 768-769
screen shows, 769-770, 773-775
slides
    creating, 760-761
    sizing, 755
    sorting, 761-762
sound, 770
speaker notes, 775-776
starting, 752-755
text, 756-757
timelines, 772
transition effects, 762-764
troubleshooting, 755
    animation, 773
    cues, 773
    graphics, 760
    sound, 773
    stand-alone screen shows, 775
    text, 757
    transition effects, 764
windows, 754-755
CorelTRACE, 14, 667-668, 899
accuracy, 680
Autotrace, 894
bitmapped images, scanning, 669-670
BMP files, importing, 668
Centerline method, 675-677, 685
colors, 682-683

CorelTRACE

Data Manager window
 spreadsheet, 707-710
exiting, 668
exporting traced images,
 690-692
files
 importing, 276
 size, 660-661
Form method, 680
headers, 689-690
image filtering, 681-683
import filter, 275
importing images, 668-670
Kodak PHOTO CD files,
 importing, 668
line art
 scanning, 322-323, 333
 tracing, 335
line tracing attributes,
 683-684
menus, 674-675
Object Character
 Recognition (OCR), 657
OCR method, 679-680, 686
Outline method, 675-677
PCX files, importing, 668
ribbon bar, 671-672
saving images, 687
scanning, 659-660
Silhouette method, 677-678
simultaneously tracing and
 saving, 688-689
starting, 668
text files, scanning, 336-337
TGA files, importing, 668
TIFF files, importing, 668
tracing bitmap parts,
 687-688
troubleshooting, 693
windows, 670
Woodcut method, 677-678,
 685-686
corners
 lines, 402
 objects, 899
Create a Custom Brush dialog
 box, 654
Create a New Image dialog
 box, 594
Create Arrow command
 (Special menu), 400
Create Brush command
 (CorelPHOTO-PAINT Special
 menu), 654
Create New Collection dialog
 box, 284

Create Pattern command
 (Special menu), 164
Create Pattern dialog box, 164
Create Transparency Mask
 command (CorelPHOTO-
 PAINT Mask menu), 652
crop marks, 364, 899
cropping objects, 899
cross-hair cursors, 96, 571, 899
CT files, 273, 276
Cue Information dialog box,
 802-803
Cue tool (CorelMOVE), 781,
 802-803
cues
 animations, 802-803, 899
 presentations, 772-773
cursors
 cross-hair cursors, 96, 571,
 899
 I-beam cursor, 213
curve objects, 900
Curve tool
 CorelMOVE Paint, 790
 CorelPHOTO-PAINT, 605,
 620
curved lines
 Bézier curves, 894
 control points, 72
 converting to straight lines,
 382
 curves, editing, 388-390
 drawing, 68-77, 382-383
 extrude effects, 587
 joining, 69, 71-72, 587
 nodes, 72, 77, 378
 control points, 73-77,
 378, 384
 cusp nodes, 74, 77, 383
 deleting, 391-392
 editing, 76-77, 379,
 384-385
 moving, 73, 390
 smooth nodes, 74, 77,
 383
 symmetrical nodes, 74,
 77, 384
 scaling, 387
 segments, 918
 selecting, 97
 setting defaults, 584-587
 shaping, 72-77
 sine waves, drawing,
 408-410
 tracing, 586
Curves property sheet,
 584-587

curving text, 840-842
cusp nodes (curved lines), 74,
 77, 383, 900
Custom Install dialog box,
 873
Cut and Clear Options dialog
 box, 706
Cut command (CorelCHART
 Edit menu), 714, 735
Cut command (CorelPHOTO-
 PAINT Edit menu), 610
Cut command (Data Object
 Manager Edit menu), 555
Cut command (Edit menu),
 100, 107
cutlines (photographs), 627
cutouts (images), 609-610

D

daisy chaining SCSI boards,
 321
dashed lines, 142, 401, 403
Data Analysis dialog box, 738
data and time functions, 713
data axes (charts), 698, 736
Data Axis command
 (CorelCHART Chart menu),
 736
data catagories (charts), 727
 reversing, 737
 sorting, 729
data group (charts), 727
 reversing, 737
 sorting, 729
Data Manager window
 (CorelCHART), 697, 704-705
 arithmetic operators,
 711-712
 calculations, 710
 database queries, 718-723
 files, importing, 717-729
 Formula bar, 705, 711
 formulas, 710-712
 functions, 712-713
 spreadsheets, 699, 748
 aligning text across cells,
 724-725
 analyzing data with
 formula editor, 699
 automating data entry,
 707-710
 breaking pages, 727
 cell borders, 724
 cell ranges, 707-710
 copying cells, 714-716

dialog boxes   937

deleting columns and rows, 716-718
deleting data, 706
editing, 706
entering data, 705
fonts, 723
formatting, 706
inserting columns and rows, 716-718
moving cells, 714-716
patterns, 724
printing, 727
sizing columns and rows, 716
styles, 723
tagging cells, 725-726
Data Orientation command (CorelCHART Data menu), 727
data points (charts), 698, 740
Data Reversal command (CorelCHART Chart menu), 737
data series (charts), 698, 727
    reversing, 737
    sorting, 729
data sheet, *see* spreadsheets
Data Source dialog box, 719
databases, 900
    fields, 903
        creating, 557
        date, 553
        deleting, 552, 557
        editing, 551, 557
        inserting, 551
        inserting text, 552-554
        measurements, 553
        numbers, 553
        selecting, 551
        symbols, 553-554
        text, 553-554
        time, 553
    hierarchy levels, 556-557
    Object Data Manager, 541, 549
    objects
        counting, 552, 555
        inserting, 550-554
        naming, 551
        selecting, 554
    queries, 718
        creating, 719-723
        Open Database Convention (ODC), 718
        SQL (System Query Language), 719
    records, 916
    spreadsheets, 554-556

dates (spreadsheets), 709
Davis, Robert (Davis Advertising), 829-837
dBASE database queries, 719
DDE (dynamic data exchange) links (CorelCHART), 696, 718
DDE/external functions, 713
default settings, 25
Delete Cels dialog box, 795
Delete command (CorelCHART Edit menu), 716
Delete command (CorelMOSAIC Edit menu), 288
Delete command (Data Object Manager Edit menu), 555
Delete command (Edit menu), 51, 100
Delta functions, 713
depth
    charts, 747
    objects, 525-527
    see also extrude effects
descenders (letters), 900
design fundamentals, 835-837
Desktop control panel, 251
desktop publishing, 233, 831-837, 900
    columns (text), 233-237
    style templates, 237-239
desktop, *see* screen display
dialog boxes, 900
    Actor Info, 794, 814
    Adaptive Unsharp Mask, 631
    Adobe Type 1 Export, 255-256
    Align, 116, 131
    Align (CorelCHART), 741
    Animation Information, 783
    Append New Frames, 812
    Arrowhead Editor, 398
    Background Library, 764
    Bitmap Export, 271
    Borders (CorelCHART), 724
    Brightness and Contrast, 633
    Character Attributes, 214-215, 221, 243
    Color, 401
    Color Comparison Tolerance, 608
    Color Tolerance, 612
    Column Width, 716
    Copy Attributes, 145, 148
    Copy Style, 245
    Create a Custom Brush, 654
    Create a New Image, 594

    Create New Collection, 284
    Create Pattern, 164
    Cue Information, 802-803
    Custom Install, 873
    Cut and Clear Options, 706
    Data Analysis, 738
    Data Source, 719
    Delete Cels, 795
    Diffuse, 631
    Directional Sharpen, 631
    Directional Smooth, 631
    Display Status (CorelCHART), 740
    Edge Enhance, 631
    Edit Layer, 132, 304, 547
    Edit Outline, 139
    Edit Preset, 538
    Edit Text, 212, 219
    EditZoom, 787
    Enhance, 631
    Enter Formula, 711-712
    Equalize, 632-634
    Export, 269
    Export EPS, 270
    Extract, 246, 292
    File Acquire Image Acquire, 614
    File Open, 268, 671
    Fill, 149
    Fill Series, 709
    Find, 218, 227, 231
    Fit Text To Path, 242
    Fit Text To Path Offsets, 242, 842
    Font, 790, 792
    Format Definition, 552
    Formula, 710
    Fountain Fill, 170-172, 345-346
    Frame Attributes, 233
    Frame Options, 812
    Frame Select, 813
    Full-Color Pattern, 160
    Go To Page, 548
    Graphics Save As Style, 534
    Grid & Scale Setup, 112, 405, 575-576
    Grid Setup, 109, 112
    Guidelines Setup, 117
    Import, 158, 163, 226, 274, 662, 734
    Insert Animation, 771
    Insert Cels, 794
    Insert Object, 759
    Insert Page, 546
    Keyword Search, 266
    Legend, 739

938 dialog boxes

Load, 162
Load A Canvas from Disk, 625
Monitor Calibration, 360
Morph Imaging Options, 806
Mouse, 567
New Actor, 786, 810
New Layer, 547
New Presentation, 752
New Prop, 785, 788, 810
New Wave, 800
Node Align, 394
Node Edit, 77
Numeric, 724
Object Data Field Editor, 551, 557
Object Information, 786
OCR, 679
Open, 263
Open an Image, 595-596
Open Chart, 704
Open Collection, 285
Open Drawing, 264-265, 267-268
Options, 256-257
Outline Color, 139-141, 346
Outline Fill, 344
Outline Pen, 140-141, 397, 400-411, 579
Page Setup, 36, 543, 752
Paragraph, 220-221
Paragraph/Bullets, 224-225
Paragraph/Indents, 223
Paste Special, 716
Patterns (CorelCHART), 725
Photo CD Options, 277
PostScript Options, 167-169
PostScript Texture, 165
Preferences, 19, 99-100, 561
Preferences (CorelMOSAIC), 290
Previewing Frame, 813
Print, 56, 597
Print Merge, 313
Print Options, 299, 362-363, 555, 822-823
Prop Information, 787
Query Builder, 720
Replace, 228
Resample Image, 635
Roll-Ups, 568-569
Save A Mask To Disk, 653
Save An Image To Disk, 596
Save Drawing, 46, 262-265
Save Extrude Preset, 471

Save Full-Color Pattern, 164-165
Save Related, 796
Save Style As, 28, 237
Save Template, 238
Scale By Percent, 793
Scale Path, 798
Scanner, 323
Search, 30
Search (Help), 278
Select Name For New File, 782
Setup (CorelQUERY), 719
Sharpen, 631
Smooth, 632
Soften, 632
Sound Information, 800
Spell Check, 229
Style (CorelCHART), 723
System Color Profile, 359
Tabs, 225
Text, 583
Text Editing, 438
Text Paragraph Indent, 236
text-entry boxes, 920
Texture Fill, 180
Thesaurus, 230
Tile, 251
Tracing Options, 336, 686
Transition Effects, 762
Transitions For Prop, 787
Transparency Mask, 652
TrueType Export, 255-256
TrueType Font Options, 874
Two-Color Pattern, 153-155
Two-Color Pattern Editor, 159
Type Assist, 231
Uniform Fill, 147, 150, 167-169, 344
Unsharp Mask, 631
Windows Printer Setup, 301
DIB files, 273
dictionaries (Spelling Checker), 229
Diffuse dialog box, 631
Diffuse Soften Effect filter (CorelPHOTO-PAINT), 639
digitizing images, *see* scans
dimension lines, 403-408, 901
  angling, 404
  colors, 407
  deleting, 407
  floor plans, 404-405
  measurement units, 408

node points, 114
objects
  linking, 404-407
  separating, 581
  rotated objects, 408
  selecting, 407
  setting default dimension lines, 580-581
  text, 404, 407
dimensions (objects), viewing, 62
dingbats (text), 901
Directional Sharpen dialog box, 631
Directional Sharpen Sharpen Effect filter (CorelPHOTO-PAINT), 639
Directional Smooth dialog box, 631
Directional Smooth Soften Effect filter (CorelPHOTO-PAINT), 639
directories, 901
  charts, 703-704
  hierarchical filing system, 905
  searching by keywords, 265-266
disks (hard disks), 905
display screen, 567
  applications, 19
  bitmapped images, 573
  capturing, 615-616
  colors, 572-577
  Control Menu box, 19
  CorelMOVE
    Library button, 808
    Timeline button, 781
  CorelPHOTO-PAINT, 598-603
  cursors, 571
  fountain fills, 571
  grids, 575-576
  Maximize button, 19
  menu bar, 19
  Minimize button, 19
  page numbers in files, 20
  panning, 571
  Pop-Up Help, 572
  refreshing, 571
  Restore button, 19
  ribbon bar, 19, 572
  roll-up windows, 568-569
  rulers, 19, 570
  status line, 19, 572
  text, 582-584

drawings 939

title bar, 18
toolbox, 19, 577-578
wallpaper, 251
see also monitors
Display Status command (CorelCHART Chart menu), 740
Display Status dialog box (CorelCHART), 740
display type, 901
Distort command (CorelPHOTO-PAINT Object menu), 635
dithering colors, 348, 572-573, 901
documents
    bleed effects, 364, 895
    booklets, 544
    books, 544
    collating, 897
    creating, 542
    crop marks, 364, 899
    folds, 544
    layers, 542, 547-548
    pages
        borders, 545
        colors, 545
        deleting, 547
        editing simultaneously, 541
        facing pages, 545
        inserting, 546
        landscape orientation, 543, 549
        layout, 542-545
        moving between pages, 546
        numbering, 548-549
        pagination, 548
        portrait orientation, 543, 549
        size, 542-543, 549
    printing, 548-549
        colors, 372-374
        tiles, 921
    registration marks, 365
    scanning, 319, 336-337
    side-fold cards, 544
    templates, 536
    tent cards, 544
    text, importing, 542
    top-fold cards, 544
DOS files, printing, 306-307
dot gain (printing documents), 329-332, 901
dot-matrix printers, 901
dots (vector graphics), 24
dotted lines, 142, 401, 403
double-clicking mouse, 567, 901
dpi (dots per inch)
    aspect ratio, 894
    bitmapped images, 658
    dot gain, 329-330
    imagesetters, 328
    monitor display vs. printout quality, 327-328
    scans, 325-327
    see also resolution
drag-and-drop objects, 901
dragging mouse, 901
drawing
    actors (animations), 788-791, 810-814
        multicel actors, 794-796
        single cel actors, 785-787, 791-793
    arcs, 8486
    arrowheads, 399-400
    callouts, 86-88
    circles, 40-41, 47, 81-86
        CorelPHOTO-PAINT, 621
        from a center point, 83
        from a corner point, 82
    closed path objects, 90
    drawing window, 20
    ellipses, 40-41, 81-86
        CorelPHOTO-PAINT, 621
        from a center point, 83, 86
        from a corner point, 82
    freehand drawing mode, 904
    lines
        brush shapes, 403
        CorelPHOTO-PAINT, 620-621
        curved lines, 68-77, 382-383
        inflection points, 391
        straight lines, 63-67, 382-383
        vertical lines, 67
    masks, 645
    objects
        CorelPHOTO-PAINT, 621
        Paint (CorelMOVE), 790
        to scale, 110-111
    open path objects, 90
    paths (animations), 798
    pie wedges, 84-86
    polygons, 621
    PowerLines, 494
    props (animations), 785-793, 810-814
    rectangles, 37-39
        CorelPHOTO-PAINT, 621
        from a center point, 79-81
        from a corner point, 78-79
        rounded rectangles, 80-81
    rules, 44-45
    sine waves, 408-410
    squares, 37-39, 81
        CorelPHOTO-PAINT, 621
        from a center point, 79
        from a corner point, 78-79
        rounded squares, 80
    stars, 204
drawing tools, *see* tools
drawing window, 20, 901
drawings
    auto-panning, 894
    backing up, 262, 574-575
    bitmap format, editing, 32
    black and white, printing, 32
    blown-up view of portion of drawing, 532-533
    borders, 42-46, 54-55
    charts, importing, 734
    clipart, inserting, 48-49
    colors, 341-342
    continous-tone images, 898
    converting to version 5 format, 267
    CorelMOSAIC
        deleting, 288-289
        editing, 289-295
        importing, 290
        inserting, 285-288
        keywords, 291
        printing, 292
        thumbnails, 290-291
    envelopes, 424-425, 435
    exporting, 268-269
    faxing, 300
    finding, 264-266
    importing, 268-282
    layers, 304
    merging with text files, 310-314
    naming, 262
    notes, 264-265
    opening, 261, 265-266
    orientations, printing, 32, 36-37
    page size, 36-37
    perspective effects, 415, 420
    previewing, 56-57, 299, 302
    printing, 127, 300-304

drawings

35mm slides, 307
a selected portion, 300
alignment, 303
black and white, 298
colors, 32, 298, 307, 347, 357-361, 368-374
disk files, 301
DOS, 306-307
File Manager, 305
halftone screens, 307, 310
Macintosh computers, 301
margins, 303
multipage drawings, 300
multiple drawings simultaneously, 306
paper size, 298
Print Manager, 305
print quality, 300
resolution, 302, 310
scale, 303
speeding up printers, 308-310
spot color vs. process color, 348-351
tiled pages, 304
to fit to paper size, 303
proofreading, 303
saving, 46-47, 262-264
shadows, 54-55
sorting, 266-267
symbols, 55-56, 250-251
text, 207
    editing with CorelMOSAIC, 292
    importing, 226-227
    inserting, 23, 41-42
    inserting Artistic text, 212
    inserting Paragraph text, 219
vector-graphics formats, editing, 32
see also files

drivers
Autographix driver, 864
PostScript printers, 308
scanning drivers
    Corel Image Source driver, 669
    installation, 320
    TWAIN, 321

drop shadows, 54-55
drop-down menu, 901
drum scanner, 320
DSQ files, 722
DTP forum (CompuServe), 828
dual axes (charts), 737
dummy publications, 902
Duplicate command (CorelCHART Edit menu), 735
Duplicate command (CorelPHOTO-PAINT Window menu), 602
Duplicate command (Edit menu), 40, 105-106, 562
DXF files, 273-275

E

Echo command (CorelMOVE Wave Editor Effects menu), 800
Edge Detect Fancy Effect filter (CorelPHOTO-PAINT), 638
Edge Enhance dialog box, 631
Edge Enhance Sharpen Effect filter (CorelPHOTO-PAINT), 639
Edit Contents command (Effects menu), 511
Edit Layer dialog box, 132, 304, 547
Edit menu commands
    Clone, 107-108, 562
    Copy, 107
    Copy Attributes From, 145, 148, 245
    Cut, 100, 107
    Delete, 51, 100
    Duplicate, 40, 105-106, 562
    Paste, 107
    Redo, 99-100
    Repeat, 99, 196
    Select All, 99
    Undo, 65, 99-100, 196
    Undo Curve Edit, 391
Edit Options command (CorelTRACE Trace menu), 336, 681
Edit Outline dialog box, 139
Edit Preset dialog box, 538
Edit Text command (Text menu), 213, 242, 438
Edit Text dialog box, 212, 219
Editable Preview view, 20-22, 386, 902
EditZoom dialog box, 787
Effects menu commands
    Add Perspective, 415
    Blend Roll-Up, 442, 452, 524
    Clear Blend, 458
    Clear Envelope, 439
    Clear Perspective, 420
    Clear Transformations, 196, 439
    Clone, 458, 496
    Contour Roll-Up, 479, 528
    Copy, 419-420, 458, 495, 505
    Copy Perspective From, 519
    Edit Contents, 511
    Envelope, 434
    Envelope Roll-Up, 424
    Extrude Roll-Up, 463
    Lens, 500
    Perspective, 517-518
    PowerClip, 509, 531
    PowerLine Roll-Up, 486
    Separate, 459
    Transform Roll-Up, 101, 186
effects, *see* **special effects**
electronic prepress (commercial printing), 343
Ellipse tool, 23, 40-41, 47, 82-83
    CorelCHART, 730
    CorelPHOTO-PAINT, 605
ellipses, 902
    arcs, 84-86
    colors, 41
    copying, 40
    drawing, 40-41, 81-86
        CorelPHOTO-PAINT, 621
        from a center point, 83, 86
        from a corner point, 82
    moving, 41
    nodes, 114, 381
    outlines, 41
    pie wedges, 84-86
    selecting, 40
    shading, 41
    sizing, 40
    see also objects
em shift (text), 244
em space, 902
Emboss Fancy Effect filter (CorelPHOTO-PAINT), 638
embossing
    logos, 865
    text, 845-847
emphasis (design), 835-836
emulators (PostScript emulators), 307
emulsion (film), 332, 902
en space, 902

Encapsulated PostScript
  format files, 273-275, 902
end nodes (objects), 902
end points (objects), 62, 402
engineering functions, 713
Enhance dialog box, 631
Enhance Sharpen Effect filter
  (CorelPHOTO-PAINT), 639
Enter Formula command
  (CorelCHART Data menu),
  712
Enter Formula dialog box,
  711-712
Enter key, 902
Envelope command (Effects
  menu), 434
Envelope roll-up, 424-425
  Add New button, 424-425
  Add Preset button, 425
  Apply button, 433-434
  Create From button, 426,
    435
  Keep Lines option, 433-434
  Mapping option, 430-432
  Not Constrained edit mode,
    429-430
  Reset Envelope button, 427,
    432-433, 439
  Single Arc edit mode,
    427-428
  Straight Line edit mode, 427
  Two Curves edit mode,
    427-428
Envelope Roll-Up command
  (Effects menu), 424
envelopes, 423, 520, 902
  art, 424-425
  bounding boxes, 424, 429,
    433
  constrained envelopes,
    427-428
  customizing shapes, 522
  deleting, 439, 523
  drawings, 424-425, 435
  nodes, editing, 429-430
  objects
    fitting, 425, 434-435
    mapping, 430-433
    preventing lines from
      curving, 433
  shapes
    editing, 427-430
    selecting, 425-426, 433,
      437-438
    stretching proportionally,
      432
    status line, 424
    text, 435-436
    Artistic text, 436-437
      editing, 438
      fitting, 426, 435-438
      mapping, 432
      setting minimum
        characters in last line,
        583
    text frame envelopes,
      234-235, 239
    Two Curves style, 521-523,
      528
    unconstrained envelopes,
      427-430
EPS (Placeable), 273-275
EPS files, *see* Encapsulated
  PostScript (EPS) format files
Equalize dialog box, 632-634
Eraser tool
  CorelPHOTO-PAINT, 606
  Paint (CorelMOVE!), 790
errors
  messages
    Can Not Open Help, 31
    Paper orientation does not
      match document, 549
    Print paper orientation
      does not match document,
      597
  spelling, 228-230
  time-out errors, 921
Excel for Windows 3 import
  filter, 275
Exit command (CorelCHART
  File menu), 700
Exit command (CorelMOVE
  Paint File menu), 796
Exit command (CorelTRACE
  File menu), 668
Exit command (File menu), 31
exiting CorelDRAW!, 19, 31
Export command
  (CorelCHART File menu),
  735
Export command (File menu),
  255, 269
Export dialog box, 269
Export EPS dialog box, 270
export filters, 273, 902
Export To Movie command
  (File menu), 814
exporting
  animations, 814
  charts, 696, 735
files, 268-270, 902
  bitmap format, 271-273
  Encapulated PostScript
    (EPS) format, 270-271
  Help, 280
  traced images (CorelTRACE),
    690-692
extensions, *see* files
Extract command (Special
  menu), 246
Extract Contents command
  (PowerClip menu), 531
Extract dialog box, 246, 292
Extract Text command
  (CorelMOSAIC Edit menu),
  292
extracting text, 246
extrude effects, 461-462
  cloning, 476
  copying, 475
  creating, 472-473
  curved lines, 587
  deleting, 475
  depth, 465
  fills, 469-472
  lighting effects, 467-469
  light source, 525-527
  nodes, editing, 473
  objects, 525-527, 902
  parallel extrusions, 465
  perspective extrusions, 464
  rotating, 467, 473-475
  saving, 471
  solid extrusions, 461
  status line, 462
  text
    Artistic text, 526
    editing, 473
    embossed effects, 845-847
  vanishing points, 474
    copying, 466
    finding, 475
    locking to objects, 466
    locking to page, 466
    moving, 474
    sharing, 466, 474-476
  wireframe extrusions, 461
Extrude roll-up, 463-464,
  467-473, 525
Extrude Roll-Up command
  (Effects menu), 463
eye travel (design), 835-836
Eyedropper tool
  (CorelPHOTO-PAINT), 606,
  611

F

facing pages, 545, 902
   gutters, 905
   master layers, 548
Fade Down command (CorelMOVE Wave Editor Effects menu), 800
Fade Up command (CorelMOVE Wave Editor Effects menu), 800
Fanbrush option (Artistic Brush tool), 619
Fancy Effect filters (CorelPHOTO-PAINT), 638
faxes
   drawings, 300
   tracing, 659
fibonacci values (spreadsheet cells), 709
Field Editor (Object Data Manager), 551
fields
   ASCII files, 311-312
   Object Data Manager, 903
      creating, 557
      date, 553
      deleting, 552, 557
      editing, 551, 557
      inserting, 551
      measurements, 553
      numbers, 553
      selecting, 551
      sizing, 555
      symbols, 553-554
      text, 552-554
      time, 553
File Acquire Image Acquire dialog box, 614
File Manager, printing files, 305
File menu commands
   Color Manager, 359
   Exit, 31
   Export, 255, 269
   Export To Movie, 814
   Import, 226, 274, 691
   Mosaic Roll-Up, 48, 283
   New, 18, 48, 542
   New From Template, 542, 581
   Open, 265, 542
   Print, 56, 298-299
   Print Merge, 313
   Print Setup, 301
   Run, 872
   Save, 47, 262
   Save As, 46, 262, 264
File Open dialog box, 268, 671
File Print command (File Manager File menu), 305
files
   AI files, 273, 275
   Aldus PageMaker, 542
   Ami Pro files, 542
   ASCII files, 542, 894, 920
   associations, 289
   backing up, 262
   BMP files, 273, 276, 668
   CCH files, 704
   CDR files, 263, 275, 824-825, 896
   CDT files, 238, 536
   CGM files, 273, 275
   CLB files, 284
   CLC files, 284
   CMP files, 273
   converting to version 5 format, 267
   CorelCHART, listing, 704
   CORELDRW.INI file, 587
   CORELPRN.INI file, 821
   CT files, 273, 276
   DIB files, 273
   DSQ files, 722
   DXF files, 273, 275
   EPS files, 273, 275
   exporting, 269-270, 902
      bitmap format, 271-273
      Encapulated PostScript (EPS) format, 270-271
      Help, 278
   finding, 265-266
   FONTINST.EXE file, 874
   GEM files, 273, 275
   GIF files, 273, 275
   ICB files, 273, 276
   image headers, 263
   importing, 226, 274, 906
      bitmapped images, 282
      CorelCHART, 696, 717-729
      CorelTRACE, 276
      Encapsulated PostScript format files, 275
      Help, 278
   INI files, editing, 587
   JFF files, 273
   JPG files, 273, 275
   JTF files, 273, 276
   keywords, 264-265
   linking, 908
   merging, 297, 310-314
   Microsoft Word files, 542
   naming, 262
   notes, 264-265
   opening, 261, 265-266, 273
   page numbers (screen display), 20
   PAT files, 162-163
   PCT files, 273, 275
   PCX files, 273, 276, 668
   PDX files, 914
   PFB files, 273
   PHOTO CD files, 668
   PIC files, 275
   PIF files, 273, 275
   PLT files, 273, 275
   PPD files, 914
   printing, 300-307
      merged files, 313-314
      multiple files, 13
      Print Manager, 305
   PRN files, 824-825
   ProMotion files, 780
   PS files, 275
   README.WRI file, 871
   RLE files, 273
   RTF files, 276, 542
   SAM files, 275
   saving, 262-264
   SCD files, 273
   SEP files, 276
   sorting, 266-267
   TGA files, 273, 276, 668
   thumbnail images, 13
   TIFF files, 273, 276, 668
   TTF files, 273
   TXT files, 276
   VDA files, 273, 276
   version 3 format, 267
   version 4 format, 267
   VST files, 273, 276
   WK files, 275
   WMF files, 273, 276
   WordPerfect files, 542
   WP files, 276
   WPG files, 273, 276
   XLS files, 275
   see also drawings
Fill dialog box, 149
Fill Down command (CorelCHART Edit menu), 707
Fill fly-out menu, 147
   Fountain Fill button, 172
   Full-Color Pattern button, 160
   Texture Fill button, 180

formula editor (CorelCHART)   943

Two-Color Pattern button, 153
Uniform Fill button, 150
Fill Right command (CorelCHART Edit menu), 707
Fill roll-up, 147-148, 154, 170, 579, 745
   CorelCHART, 731
   CorelPHOTO-PAINT, 600, 622-623
Fill Series command (CorelCHART Data menu), 707-710
Fill Series dialog box, 709
Fill tool, 23, 147, 903
   CorelCHART, 730, 731
   CorelPHOTO-PAINT, 622-623
fills, 903
   3D effect, 344
   chart elements, 731-732, 744-745
   colors, 23, 39-40, 47, 150-151, 343
   contours, 481-483
   copying, 148-149
   CorelMOVE Paint window, 791
   CorelPHOTO-PAINT, 622-623
   defaults, 148-150, 579
   deleting, 344
   extrude effects, 469-471, 472
   fountain fills, 170-179, 344-346, 571, 904
      banding, 368
      Clipboard, 281
   fractal fills, 622
   gradients, 622
   Lens, 501-505
   lines, 402
   objects, 25, 62, 146
      closed path objects, 89-91, 385
      grouped objects, 122
      open path objects, 89-91, 385
   patterns, 23, 152-170
      bitmapped, 345, 622
      vector, 345
   PowerClip effect, 507
   symbols, 516
   rainbow effect, 178, 345
   screens, 167-170, 344
   text, 25, 211
      Artistic text, 217-218
      Paragraph text, 221

textures, 180-181, 920
transparent, 151-152
uniform, 344, 922
see also blend effects
film, 903
   emulsion, 332, 902
   printing, 332-333
filtering
   colors (Lens), 500-504
   fills (Lens), 500-504
filters
   CorelPHOTO-PAINT
      Artistic Effect filters, 637
      Color Effect filters, 637
      Fancy Effect filters, 638
      Mapping Effect filters, 638
      Noise Effect filters, 639
      Sharpen Effects filters, 630-631, 639
      Soften Effects filters, 639
      Special Effect filters, 640
      Tone Equalize filter, 634
   export filters, 273, 902
   import filters, 275-276, 906
financial functions, 713
Find command (Text menu), 227
Find dialog box, 218, 227, 231
Fit Text to Path command (Text menu), 240
Fit Text to Path dialog box, 242
Fit Text To Path Offsets dialog box, 242, 842
Fit Text to Path roll-up, 242-243
flatbed scanners, 320, 614
Flatbrush option (Artistic Brush tool), 619
Flip command (CorelPHOTO-PAINT Object menu), 634
flipping documents, 634
Flood Fill tool (CorelPHOTO-PAINT), 604
floor plans (dimension lines), 404-405
flowing text, 903, 909
flushing text, 903
fly-out menus, 23
Focoltone color swatching system, 349, 359, 903
folds (documents), 544
folio (pages), 903
Font Axcess CD (Quantum Axcess), 209

Font command (CorelMOVE Paint Options menu), 792
Font dialog box, 790-792
Font tool (CorelQUERY), 722
FONTINST.EXE file, 874
fonts, 208-209, 903, 922
   Adobe, 209
   Bitstream, 209
   body type, 895
   Character Map, 878-879
   cicero, 896
   condensed, 898
   CorelCHART Data Manager spreadsheets, 723
   creating custom fonts, 253-258
   Font Axcess CD (Quantum Axcess), 209
   Image Club Graphics, 209
   installation, 874-875
   ligatures, 908
   monospaced fonts, 210
   outline fonts, 912
   PANOSE font substitution engine, 823
   paragraph text, selecting, 221
   point size, 914
   PostScript printers, 308, 823-824
   printer fonts, 915
   proportional fonts, 210
   Roman, 917
   sans serif, 210, 917
   script fonts, 918
   selecting, 42
   serif, 210, 918
   shareware, 209
   styles, 920
   TrueType fonts, 209, 253, 921
   viewing, 583
   WFN, 209, 253
   WFN fonts, 922
   x-height, 923
footnotes, 903
Foreground tool (CorelMOVE Paint), 788
Form button, 672
Form method (tracing objects), 680
Format Definition dialog box, 552
forms, tracing, 657
Formula dialog box, 710
formula editor (CorelCHART), 699

formulas, 710
  arguments, 714
  arithmetic operators, 711-712
  calculating, 710
  entering, 711-712
  functions, 712-713
  separators, 714
forums (CompuServe), 828
Forward One command (CorelMOVE Arrange menu), 797
Fountain Fill dialog box, 170-172, 345-346
fountain fills, 344-346, 904
  banding, 368
  chart elements, 745
  Clipboard, 281
  colors, 172-176
    blending, 178-179
    gradations, 178-179
  conical fountain fills, 171-172
    angle, 176-177
    center offset, 177-178
  edge padding, 173-174
  linear fountain fills, 171-172, 176-177, 344
  printing, 175, 176
  radial fountain fills, 171-172, 177-178, 344
  rainbow fills, 178
  rotating, 174
  screen display, 571
  square fountain fills, 171-172
    angle, 176-177
    center offset, 177-178
  steps, 174-176
four-headed arrow pointer, 904
FoxPro database queries, 719
fractal fills, 622
fractal textures, 904
Frame Attributes dialog box, 233
Frame command (Text menu), 233
Frame Options dialog box, 812
Frame Select dialog box, 813
Frame Select roll-up, 811
frames, 904
  animations, 778, 783, 811
    copying objects to another frame, 812
    inserting, 811-812
  viewing several simultaneously, 813
  drawings, 42-46, 54-55
  paragraph text, 219
    columns, 233-234, 239
    deleting text, 236
    editing, 236
    flowing text between frames, 235-237
    margins, 223
    sizing, 219, 226
Freehand Blend tool (CorelPHOTO-PAINT), 605
Freehand Brighten tool (CorelPHOTO-PAINT), 605
Freehand Contrast tool (CorelPHOTO-PAINT), 605
Freehand Mask tool (CorelPHOTO-PAINT), 605, 645
Freehand mode (Pencil tool), 44, 63, 904
  AutoTrace mode, 663
  drawing curved lines, 68-69
  drawing straight lines, 63-64, 67
Freehand Object tool (CorelPHOTO-PAINT), 604, 607-609
Freehand Smudge tool (CorelPHOTO-PAINT), 606
freeware
  SuperBar, 826
  typefaces, 209
Full Screen Preview command (CorelPHOTO-PAINT View menu), 600
Full-Color Pattern dialog box, 160
Full-Screen Preview command (View menu), 22, 299
Full-Screen Preview view, 22
functions, 712-714

G

Gallery window (CorelCHART), 700-704
Gamma Color Effect filter (CorelPHOTO-PAINT), 637
gamut (colors), 904
Gantt charts, 703
GEM Files, 273-275
General Preferences property sheet, 561-567
geometric values (spreadsheet cells), 709
ghost images (screen display), 601
ghosting objects, 904
GIF files, 273-275
Glass Block Mapping Effect filter (CorelPHOTO-PAINT), 638
Go To Cell command (CorelCHART Data menu), 707
Go To Page command (Layout menu), 237, 546-548
Go To Page dialog box, 548
gradations (colors), 834
gradients (fills), 622
grainy effects (documents), 639
graphics, 904
  charts, 734, 744
  graphic boundary, 904
  presentations, 757-760
  see also objects
Graphics Save As Style dialog box, 534
grayscale images, 904
grayscale mode (CorelPHOTO-PAINT), 617
greek text, 904
Grid & Scale Setup command (Layout menu), 111-112, 405
Grid & Scale Setup dialog box, 112, 405, 575-576
grid lines
  charts, 736-737
  spreadsheets, 555
Grid Setup command (Layout menu), 67, 109, 575
Grid Setup dialog box, 109, 112
Grid Toggle tool (CorelQUERY), 722
grids, 109-110, 119, 904
  animations, 784
  grid lines per inch, 111-112
  layers, 132
  origin point, 112-113, 905
  scale settings, 110-111
  screen display, 575-576
  see also guidelines
gripper (pages), 905
Group command (Arrange menu), 45, 120, 457, 516
grouping objects, 45-46
groups (charts), 698

Impressionist Clone tool (CorelPHOTO-PAINT) 945

guidelines, 905
   aligning objects, 117-119
   blue lines, 895
   layers, 132
   lock guidelines, 909
   Snap To guides, 919
   see also alignment lines; grids
Guidelines Setup command (Layout menu), 118
Guidelines Setup dialog box, 117
gutters (pages), 233, 905

H

hairline rules, 401, 905
halftones, 905
   photographs
      dot gain, 330
      enlarging, 334
      reducing, 334
      scanning, lpi (lines per inch), 326
   PostScript haltones screens
      object fills, 167-170
      printing, 307, 310
Hand tool (CorelPHOTO-PAINT), 602-604
hand-held scanners, 320, 614
handles (objects), 38, 62, 95, 185, 905
hanging indents (text), 905
hard disks, 905
headers, 905
   CorelTRACE, 689-690
   image headers, 263, 906
   spreadsheets, 555
Heat Map lens, 503-505
Help, 29-31
   Bubble Help, 29
   context-sensitive help, 30
   CorelCHART, 732
   exporting files, 280
   importing files, 278
   installation (CorelDRAW! 5), 871
   pop-up Help, 572
   tutorials, 30
Help menu commands
   About CorelDRAW!, 31
   Contents, 30
   Screen/Menu Help, 30
   Search For Help On, 30, 278
   Tutorial, 30

Hewlett-Packard inkjet printers, 347
hierarchical filing system (directories), 905
high/low/open/close graph charts, 702
highlighting objects, 457, 906
histograms, 702
   CorelPHOTO-PAINT documents, 630
   pictographs, 745-746
hot keys (templates), 536
hot zone (paragraph text), 221
hourglass icon, 563, 574
HPGL Plotter File, 273-275
HSB (Hue, Saturation, Brightness) color model, 353-354, 895, 906, 917
hue (colors), 353-354, 906
Hue tool (CorelPHOTO-PAINT), 606
Hue/Saturation Color Effect filter (CorelPHOTO-PAINT), 637
hypenating text, 221, 906

I

I-beam cursor, 213
IBM PIF, 273-275
ICB files, 273, 276
icons, 906
   Corel icons, finding, 18
   hourglass icon, 563, 574
   magnifying glass icon, 602
   reducing applications to icons, 19, 560
   sound icons, 919
illustrations, *see* drawings
Image Club Graphics, 209
image filtering (CorelTRACE), 681-683
image headers (files), 263, 906
Image Info button, 673
imagesetters
   calibration, 331-332
   complexity threshold, 821
   dot gain, 329-330
   dpi (dots per inch), 328
Import command (CorelCHART File menu), 717, 734

Import command (CorelMOSAIC Edit menu), 290
Import command (File menu), 226, 274, 691
Import dialog box, 158, 163, 226, 274, 662, 734
import filters, 275-276, 906
importing
   bitmapped images for object fill patterns, 158-160
   BMP files into CorelTRACE, 668
   clipart, 48-49
   CorelDRAW! objects to CorelMOVE, 813-814
   CorelTRACE, 668-670
   drawings, 268-282, 290
   files, 274, 906
      Aldus PageMaker, 542
      Ami Pro files, 542
      ASCII text files, 542
      bitmapped images, 282
      CorelCHART, 696, 717-729
      CorelTRACE, 276
      Encapsulated PostScript format files, 275
      Help, 278
      Microsoft Word files, 542
      RTF files, 542
      WordPerfect files, 542
   full-color patterns for object fills, 162-163
   graphics into charts, 734
   Kodak PHOTO CD files
      CorelPHOTO-PAINT, 277-278
      CorelTRACE, 668
   PCX files into CorelTRACE, 668
   text into drawings, 226-227
   TGA files into CorelTRACE, 668
   TIFF files into CorelTRACE, 668
   traced images, 691
Impressionist Artistic Effect filter (CorelPHOTO-PAINT), 637
Impressionist Brush tool (CorelPHOTO-PAINT), 604, 619
Impressionist Clone tool (CorelPHOTO-PAINT), 604, 623

Impressionist Mapping Effect filter (CorelPHOTO-PAINT), 638
indents, 906
  bullets, 225-226
  hanging indents, 905
  paragraph text, 223-224, 234
inflection points (lines), 391
Info command (CorelPHOTO-PAINT Image menu), 599
INI files, editing, 587
inner negatives, 332
input resolution (scans), 325-327
Insert Animation dialog box, 771
Insert Cels dialog box, 794
Insert command (CorelCHART Edit menu), 716
Insert New Object Actor command (Edit menu), 810
Insert New Object Prop command (Edit menu), 810
Insert Object command (CorelMOVE Edit menu), 785
Insert Object dialog box, 759
Insert Object Sound command (CorelMOVE Edit menu), 800
Insert Page command (Layout menu), 546
Insert Page dialog box, 546
Insert Sorted Item command (CorelCHART Data menu), 729
insertion point (text), 906
inside margins, 906
installation
  CorelDRAW! 5, 871-874
  scanners
    drivers, 320-321
    SCSI boards, 321
  SMARTDRV.EXE file, 871
  TrueType fonts, 874-875
integral proof (color proofing), 906
inter-character spacing, *see* kerning
inter-line spacing, 906
inter-paragraph spacing, 907
inter-word spacing, 907
Intersect command (Arrange menu), 128-129
Invert command (CorelPHOTO-PAINT Mask menu), 648
Invert Fancy Effect filter (CorelPHOTO-PAINT), 638

Invert lens, 502-505, 530, 907
italicizing text, 215, 907

J

Jaggie Despeckle Fancy Effect filter (CorelPHOTO-PAINT), 638
JFF files, 273
joining
  lines, 69
    curved lines, 69, 71-72
    straight lines, 65-68, 67
  open path objects, 385
JPEG Bitmap, 273-275
JPG files, 273, 275
JTF files, 273, 276
jump lines (text), 907
justifying text, 220-221, 907

K

Keep Paint command (CorelMOVE Paint Edit menu), 793
kerning, 210, 907
  chart text, 743
  kerning pairs, 913
keys (Enter key), 902
keystroke shortcuts, 826
Keyword Search dialog box, 266
keywords (files), 264
  CorelMOSAIC files, 291-292
  searching directories, 265-266
Keywords command (CorelMOSAIC Edit menu), 292
Knife Brush option (Artistic Brush tool), 619
knockouts, 907
Kodak Photo CD Image import filter, 275
Kodak Photo CD photographs, 277-278

L

labels
  charts, 698, 737
  photographs, 627

LAN installation, 875
landscape orientation, 32, 36-37, 543, 907
laser printing, 907
Lasso Mask tool (CorelPHOTO-PAINT), 605, 645
Lasso tool
  CorelPHOTO-PAINT, 604-608
  Paint (CorelMOVE), 789
layers, 131, 908
  charts, 731
  drawings
    arranging, 132
    colors, 133
    color separations, 304
    combining, 133
    deleting, 132
    Desktop layer, 132-133
    grids, 132
    grouping, 133
    guidelines, 132
    inserting, 132
    layering order, 908
    master items, 909
    Master Layers, 132-134, 542, 547-548, 909
    naming, 132
  objects
    printing, 304
    viewing, 62
  selecting, 132-134
Layers roll-up, 132, 304, 547
Layers Roll-Up command (Layout menu), 304, 547
Layers/Objects roll-up (CorelPHOTO-PAINT), 600
layout (pages), 542-545, 902, 908
Layout menu commands
  Go To Page, 237, 546, 548
  Grid & Scale Setup, 111-112, 405
  Grid Setup, 67, 109, 575
  Guidelines Setup, 118
  Insert Page, 546
  Layers Roll-Up, 304, 547
  Page Setup, 298, 542-543
  Snap to Grid, 80
  Snap To Guidelines, 117, 132
  Snap To Objects, 113-114, 404-405
  Style Roll-Up, 237, 534
leading (text), 210, 908
Legend dialog box, 739
legends (charts), 736, 739

macros 947

Lens effects, 499, 530, 908
  applying, 504-505
  Brighten lens, 501-505
  Color Add lens, 502-504
  Color Limit lens, 502-504
  colors, 499
  copying, 505-506
  deleting, 503
  editing, 505
  fills, 503
  Heat Map lens, 503-504
  Invert lens, 502, 530, 907
  Magnify lens, 501-504, 530-533
  moving, 505
  selecting, 501, 505
  sizing, 505
  status line, 500
  stretching, 505
  Tinted Grayscale lens, 503-504
  Transparency lens, 501-505
Lens command (Effects menu), 500
Lens roll-up, 500-505
Lens tool, 152
letters
  ascenders, 893
  baseline, 894
  breaking apart, 250
  cap height, 896
  descenders, 900
  editing, 243-245
  kerning, 210, 907
  rotating, 244
  see also text
letterspacing, *see* kerning
libraries, 810, 908
  animation objects, 807-808
  CorelMOSAIC, 283-284
    creating, 284
    deleting drawings, 288-289
    editing drawings, 289-290
    importing graphics into drawings, 290
    inserting drawings, 285-288
    keywords, 291-292
    thumbnails (drawings), 290-291
    opening, 285
  fonts, 209
  object fill textures, 181
  text style templates, 238
Library roll-up, 808

Library Roll-Up command (CorelMOVE View menu), 808
ligatures, 908
light source (extrude effects), 525-527
line art
  scanning, 333-335
  tracing, 335
line graph charts, 701
line spacing, *see* leading
Line tool (CorelPHOTO-PAINT), 605, 620
line tracing attributes (CorelTRACE), 683-684
linear fountain fills (object fills), 344
linear values (spreadsheet cells), 709
lines
  applying PowerLine effects, 493-494, 529
  arrowheads, 396-401
  beveled corners, 402
  blending, 528
  brush shapes, 403
  colors, 401-402
  CorelPHOTO-PAINT, 620-621
  curved lines
    Bézier curves, 894
    control points, 72
    converting to straight lines, 382
    drawing, 68-77, 382-383
    editing, 388-390
    extrude effects, 587
    joining, 69-72, 587
    nodes, 72-77, 378-379, 383-385, 390
    scaling, 387
    selecting, 97
    setting defaults, 584-587
    shaping, 72-77
    tracing, 586
  dashed lines, 401-403
  dotted lines, 401-403
  end point line caps, 402
  fills, 402
  hairlines, 401
  inflection points, 391
  joining, 69
  mitered corners, 402
  nodes, 391
  rounded corners, 402
  segments, 918

straight lines
  converting to curved lines, 381-382
  drawing, 63-67, 382-383
  joining, 65-68
  nodes, 378-379, 385
  thickness, 401-402
  vertical lines, 67
lines per inch, *see* lpi
linking
  files, 908
  frames (paragraph text), 235-237
list boxes, 909
lithography printing, 342
Load A Canvas from Disk dialog box, 625
Load command (CorelPHOTO-PAINT Mask menu), 653
Load dialog box, 162
Load Transparency Mask command (CorelPHOTO-PAINT Mask menu), 652
Local Undo tool, 606
Locator tool, 603-604
Lock Contents to PowerClip command (PowerClip menu), 532-533
lock guidelines, 909
logarithmic values (spreadsheet cells), 709
logical functions, 713
logos, 909
  charts, 698
  designing, 849
  embossing, 865
  importing into charts, 734
  scanning, 322, 333
looping animations, 799
loops (blend effects), 444
Lotus 1-2-3 1A import filter, 275
Lotus 1-2-3 3.0 import filter, 275
Lotus PIC import filter, 275
lpi (lines per inch)
  scans, 326-328
  object fills, 168
luminosity (colors), 909

M

Macintosh PICT
  export filter, 273
  import filter, 275
macros, 533-534, 537-538

Macros Preset Roll-Up
  command (Special menu),
  537
MacWrite II import filter, 275
Magic Wand tool, 604,
  607-608
Magic Wand Mask tool, 605,
  645, 649
Magnify lens, 501-505,
  530-533
magnifying
  bitmapped images, 601-602
  objects, 23
  photographs, 601-602
magnifying glass icon, 602
Make Same Size command
  (CorelCHART Arrange
  menu), 741
manual transition (slides),
  763-764
Map to Sphere Mapping Effect
  filter (CorelPHOTO-PAINT),
  638
Mapping Effect filters
  (CorelPHOTO-PAINT), 638
margins, 909
  binding margin, 894
  inside margin, 906
  margin guides, 909
  outside margin, 912
  paragraph text, 223-224, 234
  printing, 303
marquee selection, 45, 96-98,
  909
Marquee tool, 789
Mask Brush tool, 605
Mask Node Edit tool, 605, 645
Mask Picker tool, 605, 644
masks, 644, 909
  circle masks, 645, 648
  color masks, 649-651
  combining, 647-649
  creating, 126, 645-646
  drawing, 645
  fountain fills, 173
  loading, 653
  moving, 644
  nodes, 645-646
  overlapping, 648
  polygon masks, 645
  rectangle masks, 645
  saving, 653
  selecting, 644
  sizing, 646
  transparency masks, 652-653
Master Layers, see layers
mastheads, 910

mathematical functions, 713
Matrix/Imapro SCODL export
  filter, 273
Maximize button, 19
Maximize Work Area
  command
  (CorelPHOTOPAINT View
  menu), 600
Maximum Noise Effect filter
  (CorelPHOTO-PAINT), 639
measurement units, 910, 922
mechanical separations
  (colors), 910
  see also colors, separations
mechanicals, 910
Median Noise Effect filter
  (CorelPHOTO-PAINT), 639
memory, 910
memory requirements
  CorelPHOTO-PAINT, 592,
    615
  printers, 305, 308
  roll-up windows, 569
  tracing, 658
  undo levels, 563-564
menu bar, 19, 910
menus, 910
  fly-out menus, 23
  pull-down menu, 916
Merge Back command (Special
  menu), 247
merging
  files, 297, 310-314
  text, 247-248, 910
Mesh Warp Special Effect
  filter (CorelPHOTO-PAINT),
  640
messages
  Can Not Open Help, 31
  Paper orientation does not
    match document, 549
  Print paper orientation does
    not match document, 597
Micrographx import filter,
  275
Microsoft Access database
  queries, 719
Microsoft Word files,
  importing, 226, 542
Microsoft Word import filters,
  275
MIDI files, playing in
  animations, 800
Minimize button, 19, 560
Minimum Noise Effect filter
  (CorelPHOTO-PAINT), 639

Mirror command (CorelMOVE
  Paint Effects menu), 792-793
mirroring, 910
  animation paths, 799
  bitmapped images, 634
  objects, 188-189, 199-200
    marquee outline, 196
    master object, 196-197
    Paint (CorelMOVE),
      792-793
    precision, 195
  paintings, 634
  photographs, 634
  text, 910
mistakes, undoing, 99-100
moiré patterns, 910
Monitor Calibration dialog
  box, 360
monitors
  calibration, 359-361
  colors
    displaying, 347
    dithering, 348
  pixels, 325
  see also screen display
monochrome colors, 910
monochrome printers, 32, 298
More Windows command
  (Window menu), 18
Morph command (CorelMOVE
  Paint Effects menu), 805
Morph Imaging Options
  dialog box, 806
morphing actors (animations),
  14, 805-806, 815
Mosaic roll-up, 600
Mosaic Roll-Up command
  (File menu), 48, 283, 700
Motion Blur Fancy Effect filter
  (CorelPHOTO-PAINT), 638
mouse
  buttons, 910, 918
    programming, 565-567
    switching left and right
      buttons, 567
  clicking, 896
  double-clicking, 567, 901
  dragging, 901
  dragging objects, 100
  pointer, 914
  tracking sensitivity, 567
Mouse dialog box, 567
MOVE, 13-14
Move To tool, 723
movies, see animations
music (animations), 778, 801

Object menu commands   949

N

negatives, 911
　photographs, 907
　printing, 332
　scans, 332
network installation, CorelDRAW! 5, 875
New Actor dialog box, 786, 810
New Collection command (CorelMOSAIC File menu), 284
New command (CorelCHART File menu), 700
New command (CorelMOVE File menu), 782
New command (CorelPHOTO-PAINT File menu), 594
New command (CorelQUERY File menu), 719
New command (CorelSHOW File menu), 752
New command (File menu), 18, 48, 542
New From Template command (File menu), 542, 581
New Layer dialog box, 547
New Presentation dialog box, 752
New Prop dialog box, 785, 788, 810
New Wave dialog box, 800
nib shapes
　drawing lines, 403
　PowerLines, 489-490
Node Align dialog box, 394
Node Edit dialog box, 77
Node Edit roll-up, 90, 379, 429-430
　Align button, 393-396
　AutoReduce button, 392
　AutoReduce option, 585
　Break icon, 392-393
　Elastic Mode, 389
　Join icon, 392-393
　PowerLines, 494-495
　Smooth option, 409
　Stretch button, 387
　Symmet option, 409
　To Curve button, 382
　To Line button, 382

nodes, 113-114, 911
　animation paths, 798-799
　animations, 779
　circles, 381
　control points, 390, 899
　curved lines, 72, 77, 378
　　control points, 73-77, 378, 384
　　cusp nodes, 74, 77, 383
　　deleting, 392
　　editing, 76-77, 379, 384-385
　　moving, 73, 390
　　smooth nodes, 74, 77, 383
　　symmetrical nodes, 74, 77, 384
cusp node, 900
ellipses, 381
end node, 902
envelope bounding boxes, 429, 433
envelopes, 429-430
extrusions, 473
lines
　deleting, 391
　inserting, 391
masks, 645-646
objects, 24
　aligning, 393-396
　breaking, 393
　deleting, 391
　deselecting, 386
　inserting, 391
　moving, 387-388
　selecting, 386-387, 396
　shaping, 23
　viewing, 62
smooth nodes, 919
start nodes, 919
straight lines, 378-379, 382, 385
subpaths, 920
symmetric nodes, 920
text letters, 381
Noise Effect filters (CorelPHOTO-PAINT), 639
nonbreaking space (text), 911
nonrepo blue, 895
Notepad, editing extracted text, 246-248
notes (files), 264
numbering pages
　documents, 548-549
　spreadsheets, 555

numbers
　charts, formatting, 733-734
　spreadsheet cells
　　filling automatically, 708-710
　　formatting, 724
Numeric command (CorelCHART Format menu), 724
Numeric dialog box, 724

O

Object Brush tool, 604
Object Character Recognition (OCR), 657
Object command (Edit menu), 813
Object Data Field Editor dialog box, 551, 557
Object Data Manager, 541, 549, 911
　data entry screen, 554
　Field Editor, 551
　fields, 903
　　creating, 557
　　date, 553
　　deleting, 552, 557
　　editing, 551, 557
　　inserting, 551
　　inserting text, 552-554
　　measurements, 553
　　numbers, 553
　　selecting, 551
　　symbols, 553-554
　　text, 553-554
　　time, 553
　hierarchy levels, 556-557
　objects
　　counting, 552, 555
　　inserting, 550-554
　　naming, 551
　　selecting, 554
　spreadsheets, 554-556
Object Data roll-up, 551, 554
Object Info command (CorelMOVE Edit menu), 786
Object Information dialog box, 786
Object Linking and Embedding, see OLE
Object menu commands
　Apply Styles, 535
　Save Style As, 534

950 Object Node Edit tool

Object Node Edit tool, 604, 609
Object Paintbrush tool, 607-609
object-oriented files, 911
objects
    alignment, 109
        alignment lines, 130-131
        grids, 117, 119
        guidelines, 117-119
        horizontally, 116
        to another object, 119
        to center of page, 116
        to grids, 109-113
        to other objects, 113-115
        vertically, 116
    applying PowerLines, 529
    attributes
        applying, 26-27
        setting defaults, 578-580
    blend effects, 442, 523-528, 895
        chaining, 456
        cloning, 458-459
        closed path objects, 446-451
        colors, 444-446, 459
        compound blends, 456-457, 898
        copying, 458
        creating, 452-453
        deleting, 458
        finding end points, 452
        finding starting point, 451-452
        fuse blends, 448, 453-454
        highlights, 457
        loops, 444
        open path objects, 446-451
        paths, 449-450, 454-456, 459
        rotating, 444, 457
        selecting ending points, 449
        selecting starting points, 446-448
        smoothing, 443, 459
        space between objects, 444
        split blends, 447-448, 453
    breaking apart, 124, 127
    callouts, 86-88
    child objects, 896
        deleting, 124
        selecting, 122-124

choke effects, 896
Clipboard, 107
clipping, 530-533
cloning, 107-109, 897
closed path objects, 385
combining, 119-120, 124-128, 897
constraining movement, 898
contours, 477, 527-528, 898
    applying, 479, 481-482
    breaking apart, 528
    center contours, 479
    cloning, 483
    copying, 483
    deleting, 483
    editing, 479, 482
    fills, 481, 483
    inside contours, 480
    offset distance, 480
    outlines, 481-483
    outside contours, 480
    paths, 482
    smoothness, 480
copying, 40, 899
corner style, 899
cropping, 899
curve object, 900
curved lines, 380-381
    converting to straight lines, 382
    nodes, 379-380
    scaling, 387
cutting, 100
deleting, 100, 124
deselecting, 96, 900
dimension lines, 403-408, 901
    linking, 404-407
    rotated objects, 408
    separating, 581
dimensions, viewing, 62
drag and drop, 901
drawing
    CorelPHOTO-PAINT, 621
    Paint (CorelMOVE), 790
    to scale, 110-111
duplicating, 105-106, 902
editing shape, 379-385
ending points, 62
envelopes
    creating, 435
    deleting, 439
    fitting, 425, 434-435
    mapping, 430-433
    preventing lines from curving, 433
    Two Curves style, 521

extrude effects, 472-473, 525-527, 902
fills, 25, 62, 146
    3D effect, 344
    bitmap patterns, 345
    closed path objects, 89-91
    colors, 23, 39, 47, 150, 343
    copying, 148-149
    CorelMOVE Paint, 791
    CorelPHOTO-PAINT, 622-623
    defaults, 148-150
    deleting, 344
    fountain fills, 170-179, 344, 346, 571
    grouped objects, 122
    open path objects, 89-91
    patterns, 23, 152-170
    rainbow effects, 178, 345
    screens, 167-170, 344
    solid-color fills, 151
    textures, 180-181
    transparent, 151-152
    uniform fills, 344
    vector patterns, 345
ghosting, 904
grouping, 45-46, 119-122, 127, 905
handles, 38, 62, 95, 905
    rotate/skew handles, 184
    stretch/mirror handles, 184
hidden objects
    deselecting, 98
    selecting, 98
highlighting, 906
layers, 62, 132-133, 908
Lens effects, 501-505
magnifying, 23
mirroring, 188-189, 199-200, 910
    CorelMOVE Paint, 792-793
    marquee outline, 196
    master object, 196-197
    precision, 195
moving, 39, 47, 100, 571
    nudges, 101-102
    to a specific page location, 101
    to back, 103-104
    to front, 102-104
    with mouse, 100
node points, 113-114
nodes, 24
    aligning, 393-396
    breaking, 393

Outline button

deleting, 391
deselecting, 386
inserting, 391
moving, 387-388
selecting, 386-387, 396
shaping, 23
viewing, 62
open path objects, 385
  arrowheads, 143
  contours, 528
  fills, 385
  inserting arrowheads on endpoints, 385
  joining, 385
outlines, 25, 62, 137-138
  applying PowerLines, 141
  arrowheads, 142-143
  colors, 23, 41, 139-141, 345-346
  copying, 144-145
  dashed outlines, 142
  defaults, 138, 145-146
  deleting, 344
  dotted outlines, 142
  endpoints, 23
  hiding, 144
  intersecting, 128
  patterns, 23
  PMS colors, 346
  showing, 144
  thickness, 23
  trimming, 128
  welding, 128
  widths, 142
perspective effects, 415, 520
  copying, 419
  deleting, 420
PowerClip effects, 507
reversing, 104, 916
rotating, 189-192, 200-201, 917
  center of rotation, 896
  center point, 191-192, 202
  CorelMOVE Paint, 792-793
  marquee outline, 196
  master object, 196-197
  precision, 195
scaling, 184-189, 197-198, 917
  anchor points, 187
  CorelMOVE Paint, 792-793
screen location of duplicate objects, 106-107

selecting, 23, 38, 94, 184, 386-387, 918
  all objects, 99
  marquee box, 96-98
  objects within groups, 122-127
  Pick tool, 94-95
  Shift key, 98-99
  Tab key, 95-96
shading, 39-40, 47
sizing, 37, 187-188, 919
skewing, 192-194, 203, 919
  marquee outline, 196
  master object, 196-197
  precision, 194-195
snapping, 919
starting points, 62
stretching, 184-189, 198-199, 387, 920
  marquee outline, 196
  master object, 196-197
  precision, 195
styles
  applying, 27, 535
  defining, 28-29
  saving, 28-29
tracing, 586
trimming, 921
undeleting, 100
ungrouping, 122
welding, 922
wrapping text around, 234-235, 239
see also art
OCR (Optical Character Recognition)
  CorelTRACE, 679-680, 686
  scanning documents, 336-337
  faxes, 659
OCR B&W command (CorelTRACE Trace menu), 336
OCR button, 672
OCR dialog box, 679
ODC (Open Database Convention) database queries, 718
offset lithography printing, 342
offset printing, 911
OLE (Object Linking and Embedding), 32-33, 911
  CorelMOVE, 813
  CorelSHOW, 767-768
one-point perspective, *see* perspective

Onion Skin command (CorelMOVE Paint Options menu), 795
Online Help button, 673
Open an Image dialog box, 595-596
Open Chart dialog box, 704
Open Collection command (CorelMOVE File menu), 285
Open Collection dialog box, 285
Open command (CorelCHART File menu), 700, 704
Open command (CorelMOVE File menu), 780
Open command (CorelPHOTO-PAINT File menu), 595
Open command (CorelSHOW File menu), 752
Open command (CorelTRACE File menu), 670
Open command (File menu), 265, 542
Open dialog box, 263
Open Drawing dialog box, 264-265, 267-268
open path objects, 89-91, 385
  converting to closed path objects, 90-91
  drawing, 90
  fills, 385
  inserting arrowheads on endpoints, 385
  joining, 385
operators (arithmetic operators), 711-712
Optical Character Recognition, *see* OCR
option boxes, 912
Options dialog box, 256-257
Order command (Arrange menu), 103-104, 457
Order Forward One command (Arrange menu), 55
Order to Back command (Arrange menu), 55
orientation (pages), 543, 549
orientations, 912
  landscape orientation, 907
  photographs, 634
  portrait orientation, 914
origins (grids), 905
OS/2 Bitmap export filter, 273
Outline button, 672

Outline Color dialog box

Outline Color dialog box, 139, 141, 346
Outline Fancy Effect filter (CorelPHOTO-PAINT), 638
Outline Fill dialog box, 344
Outline fly-out menu, 138, 400-401
outline fonts, 912
Outline method (tracing objects), 675-677
Outline Pen dialog box, 140-141, 397, 400-411, 579
Outline Pen tool, 23, 138
Outline tool, 345-346, 396, 730-731, 912
outlines
    chart elements, 731
    contours, 481, 483
    Lens effects, 499
    lines, hiding, 402
    objects, 25, 62, 137-138
        applying PowerLines, 141
        arrowheads, 142-143
        colors, 23, 41, 139-141, 344-346, 346
        copying, 144-145
        dashed outlines, 142
        defaults, 138, 145-146, 579
        deleting, 344
        dotted outlines, 142
        endpoints, 23
        hiding, 144
        intersecting, 128
        patterns, 23
        showing, 144
        thickness, 23
        trimming, 128
        welding, 128
        widths, 142
    symbols, 516
    text, 25, 144, 211
        Artistic text, 217-218
        Paragraph text, 221
    weight, 922
output resolution (scans), 325-327
outside margin (pages), 912
overhead transparencies, 912
overlay proofs (proofing colors), 912
    see also colors, separations
overprints, 912
Owen-Bugh, Janie, 839-849

P

Page Control box, 913
page numbers, *see* numbering pages
Page Setup command (CorelCHART File menu), 727
Page Setup command (Layout menu), 298, 542-543
Page Setup dialog box, 36, 543, 752
    Display tab, 544, 549
    Layout tab, 543
PageMaker files, importing, 542
pages
    bleed effect, 895
    borders, 545
    breaking, 894
    colors, 545
    deleting, 547
    facing pages, 545
    folio, 903
    gripper, 905
    gutters, 905
    inserting, 546
    layers, 547-548, 909
    layout, 542, 908
        book, 544
        booklet, 544
        displaying, 544-545
        facing pages, 902
        full page, 544
        side-fold card, 544
        tent card, 544
        top-fold card, 544
    margins, 909
        binding margin, 894
        inside margin, 906
        margin guides, 909
        outside margin, 912
    moving between pages, 546
    numbering, 548-549
    orientations, 543, 549
    pagination, 548
    print area, 915
    printing, 548-549
    signatures, 918
    size, 542, 549, 913
        customizing, 543
        legal, 543
        letter, 543
        tabloid, 543
    spreadsheets
        breaking, 727
        numbering, 555

pagination (documents), 548
Paint (CorelMOVE), 784, 788
    colors, 790-792
    importing CorelDRAW! objects, 814
    morphing animation actors, 805-806
    multicel actors, drawing, 794-796
    objects (actors, props)
        fills, 791
        mirroring, 792-793
        rotating, 792-793
        scaling, 792-793
        tinting colors, 792
        translucency effects, 792
        zooming in/out, 791
    text, 792
    tools
        Background tool, 788
        Color Pick-Up tool, 790
        Curve tool, 790
        Eraser tool, 790
        Foreground tool, 788
        Lasso tool, 789
        Marquee tool, 789
        Paint Brush tool, 789
        Paint Bucket tool, 789
        Pattern Selector tool, 789
        Pencil tool, 789
        Polygon tool, 791
        Spray Can tool, 790
        Text tool, 790
Paint Bucket tool, 789
Paintbrush
    export filter, 273
    import filter, 276
Paintbrush tool
    CorelMOVE, 789
    CorelPHOTO-PAINT, 604, 619
paintbrushes, *see* brushes
painting photographs, 618
painting tools
    CorelPHOTO-PAINT, 604, 619-620
paintings, *see* bitmapped images
pair kerning, *see* kerning
palettes (color palettes), 20, 139, 897, 913
    CorelPHOTO-PAINT, 626-627
    displaying, 357
    dithering, 348
    process color palettes, 348-349

rearranging colors, 357
resetting, 356
selecting, 356-357
spot color palette, 348-349,
    351-352
panning screen display, 571
PANOSE font substitution
    engine, 823
PANTONE Matching System
    (PMS), 343, 346, 349, 359,
    913
paper
    coated stock paper, 897
    emulsion, 902
    RC (resin coated) paper, 332
    sizes, 298, 913
Paper Orientation does not match
    document error message, 549
Paradox database queries, 719
Paragraph command (Text
    menu), 220
Paragraph dialog box, 220-221
Paragraph text, 211-212, 218,
    913
    aligning, 220-221
    baselines, 244
    bulleted lists, 224-226
    character limit, 212
    Clipboard, 281
    columns, 233-234
        gutter, 233
        wrapping, 234
    editing, 219
    em shift, 244
    fills, 221
    frames, 219
        deleting, 236
        editing, 236
        flowing text between
            frames, 235-237
        sizing, 219, 226
    hyphenating, 221, 906
    indents, 223-224, 234,
        905-906
    inserting in drawings, 219
    margins, 223-224, 234
    nonbreaking space, 911
    outlines, 221
    point size, 221
    quotation marks, 232
    replacing words or phrases,
        228, 232
    rotating, 211, 240
    scaling, 226, 239
    searching, 227-228, 231
    skewing, 240

spacing, 219-220, 907
special characters, 877-879
Spelling Checker, 228-230
straightening, 244
styles, 221
    applying, 238-239, 535
    copying, 245
    creating, 237
    saving, 237
subscript, 244
superscript, 244
tabs, 222-223, 234
Thesaurus, 228, 230
Type Assist, 231-233
widows, 922
Paragraph Text tool, 27, 219
Paragraph/Bullets dialog box,
    224-225
Paragraph/Indents dialog box,
    223
paragraphs, *see* text
parallelograms, 192-194, 203
Paste command (CorelCHART
    Edit menu), 714, 735
Paste command
    (CorelPHOTO-PAINT Edit
    menu), 610
Paste command (Data Objects
    Manager Edit menu), 555
Paste command (Edit menu),
    107
Paste Inside command
    (CorelCHART Edit menu),
    735
Paste Link command
    (CorelCHART Edit menu),
    718
Paste Special command
    (CorelCHART Edit menu),
    716
Paste Special dialog box, 716
pasteboard area (drawing
    window), 20
pasteboards, 913
PAT files, 162-163
Path Edit roll-up, 797-799
Path tool, 781, 797
paths
    animations
        actors, 793-794
        deleting, 799
        drawing, 798
        mirroring, 799
        points, 893
        registration point, 796
        scaling, 798
        smoothing, 799

contours, 482
text
    curving, 242, 840-842
    editing, 242
    fitting, 240-243, 245
    separating, 243
Pattern Selector tool, 789
patterns, 852-853
    3D effect, 855-858
    chart elements, 745
    moiré patterns, 910
    object fills, 23, 164-165, 345
        colors, 154-155
        creating, 153, 159-160
        full-color patterns,
            160-165
        importing bitmapped
            images, 158-160
        importing full-color
            patterns, 162-163
        jagged patterns, 160
        lining up, 165
        loading, 162
        outlines, 23
        PostScript haltones
            screens, 167-170
        PostScript textures,
            165-167
        rotating, 160, 165
        selecting, 153
        tile offset, 155-158
        tile size, 153-154
        two-color patterns,
            152-160
    screen display, 251
    spreadsheet cells, 724
Patterns command
    (CorelCHART Format menu),
    724
Patterns dialog box
    (CorelCHART), 725
PCD files, 275
PCT files, 273, 275
PCX files, 273, 276, 668-669
PDX files, 914
Pen roll-up, 25, 139, 141, 145,
    396, 400-401
Pen tool, 605, 621
pen-and-ink sketches, tracing,
    659
Pencil tool, 23, 63
    AutoTrace, 661
    Bézier mode, 63
        drawing curved lines,
            69-71, 383
        drawing straight lines,
            64-65, 67

CorelCHART, 730-731
Freehand mode, 44, 63
    drawing curved lines,
        68-69
    drawing straight lines,
        63-64, 67
    Paint (CorelMOVE), 789
Perspective command (Effects
    menu), 517-518
perspective effects, 413-414,
    516, 913
    Artistic text, 518-519
    blends, 516-518
    bounding boxes, 518
    charts, 747
    copying, 419
    deleting, 420
    drawings, 415
    objects, 415, 520
    one-point perspective,
        414-416, 912
    status line, 414
    text, 415
    two-point perspective,
        414-418, 922
    vanishing point, 413-414,
        417
        aligning, 418, 520
        finding, 417-421
        moving, 418
    see also extrude effects
Perspective Special Effect filter
    (CorelPHOTO-PAINT), 640
PFB files, 273
PHOTO CD files, see Kodak
    Photo CD
Photo CD Options dialog box,
    277
photo offset printing, 342
PHOTO-PAINT, 14
photographs
    backing up, 596
    black and white, 617
    canvas backgrounds, 625
    canvas overlays, 625
    cloning, 623-624
    colors, 592
        24-bit color mode, 616
        256 color mode, 617
        brightening, 630
        CMYK process colors, 617
        darkening, 630
        gamma, 630
        grayscale, 617
        histogram, 630
        hue, 630
        intensity, 630

saturation, 630
tone, 632
continous-tone image, 898
contrast, 632-634
cutouts, 609-610
drawing over surface image,
    620-621
editing
    by individual pixels, 601
    in duplicate windows,
        602-603
enlarging, 635
flipping, 634
grainy effects, 639
halftones, 905
    dot gain, 330
    enlarging, 334
    lpi (lines per inch), 326
    reducing, 334
    Tinted Grayscale lens,
        503
jagged edges, 636
Kodak Photo CD
    colors, 277
    importing, 275-278
    resolution, 277
mirroring, 634
negatives, 907, 911
outlines, 599
painting, 618
pixels
    copying, 610
    cutting, 610
    pasting, 610-611
    saving, 611
    selecting, 606-609
printing, 597-600
reducing, 635
resolution, 635-636
retouching
    colors, 611-613
    tools, 605-606
rotating, 634
saving, 596
scanning, 319, 322, 333-334,
    613-615
sharpening details, 630-631
smearing, 624
smudging, 624
softening details, 631-632
stretching, 635
text, inserting, 627
zooming in/out, 601-602
phototypesetting, 913
PIC files, 275
picas, 914
picas (text), 210

Pick tool, 23, 38, 94-95, 914
    CorelCHART, 730
    CorelMOVE, 781
    CorelPHOTO-PAINT, 604
    editing capabilities, 386
PICT format, 914
Pictograph roll-up, 731, 746
pictographs, 702, 745-746, 914
pictures, see photographs
pie graph charts, 702
pie wedges, drawing, 84-86
PIF files, 273, 275
Pinch/Punch Mapping Effect
    filter (CorelPHOTO-PAINT),
    638
pixel-based art, 333
Pixelate Mapping Effect filter
    (CorelPHOTO-PAINT), 638
pixels, 914
    animations, 782-784
    images
        copying, 610
        cutting, 610
        pasting, 610-611
        saving, 611
        selecting, 606-609
    monitors, 325
    patterns
        offset, 155-158
        sizing, 153-154
PLT files, 273, 275
PMS, see PANTONE Matching
    System
point size, 914
    bullets, 225
    text, 42, 210, 221
pointers, 904, 914
Pointillist Artistic Effect filter
    (CorelPHOTO-PAINT), 637
Pointillist Brush tool, 604, 619
Pointillist Clone tool, 604, 623
points (animation paths), 893
polar charts, 703
Polygon Mask tool, 605, 645
Polygon tool
    CorelPHOTO-PAINT,
        604-608, 621
    CorelMOVE Paint, 791
polygons, drawing, 621
portrait orientation, 32, 36-37,
    543, 914
Posterize Special Effect filter
    (CorelPHOTO-PAINT), 640
PostScript haltone screens,
    167-170
PostScript Options dialog box,
    167, 169

printers

PostScript printers, 307-310, 347
   complexity threshold, 821
   drivers, 308
   fonts, 308, 823-824
   laser proofs, 824
   non-PostScript printers, 15
   PostScript emulators, 307
PostScript Texture dialog box, 165
PostScript textures, 165-167, 914
PowerClip command (Effects menu), 509, 531
PowerClip effect, 507-508, 530-533, 914
   cloning, 513
   copying, 512
   creating, 509-510
   deleting, 513
   editing, 511, 513
   fills, 507
   layers, 511
   locking, 510
   paths, 513
   status line, 508
   unlocking, 510
PowerLine roll-up, 486-494, 529
PowerLine Roll-Up command (Effects menu), 486
PowerLines, 485, 529, 914
   cloning, 496
   copying, 495
   deleting, 496
   drawing, 487, 494
      ink flow, 492-494
      smoothness, 491-492
      speed, 491, 494
   editing, 492, 494-495
   nib shapes, 489-490
   objects
      applying, 529
      outlines, 141
   status line, 486
   styles, 487-488
      applying, 493
      saving, 493
   widths, 488-489
PPD files, 914
Preferences command (CorelCHART File menu), 700
Preferences command (CorelMOSAIC File menu), 290

Preferences command (Special menu), 65, 99, 561, 915
Preferences dialog box, 19
   Advanced property sheet, 572-575
   Constraint Angle box, 195
   Curves property sheet, 584-587
   property sheets, 561-567
   Text property sheet, 582-584
   Undo levels, 99, 100
   View property sheet, 570-572
Preferences dialog box (CorelMOSAIC), 290
Pregent, Nick (Creative Imagery), 851-859
prepress (commercial printing), 343, 915
presentations (CorelSHOW)
   animation, 771
   backgrounds, 764-766
   charts, 696
   cues, 772-773
   designing, 755-756
   graphics, 757-760
   importing from CorelCHART, 761
   OLE, 767-768
   saving, 768-769
   screen shows, 769-770, 773-775
   slides
      creating, 760-761
      sizing, 755
      sorting, 761-762
   sound, 770
   speaker notes, 775-776
   starting, 752-755
   text, 756-757
   timelines, 772
   transition effects, 762-764
   troubleshooting, 755
      animation, 773
      cues, 773
      graphics, 760
      sound, 773
      stand-alone screen shows, 775
      text, 757
      transition effects, 764
   window, 754-755
Presets roll-up, 537-538, 825
press proofs, 915
previewing drawings, 56-57
Previewing Frame dialog box, 813

primary colors, 915
   additive primary colors, 893
   subtractive primary colors, 920
print area (pages), 915
Print command (CorelCHART File menu), 727
Print command (CorelPHOTO-PAINT File menu), 597
Print command (Data Object Manager File menu), 555
Print command (File menu), 56, 298-299
Print dialog box, 56, 597
Print Files command (CorelMOSAIC File menu), 292
Print Manager, 305, 915
Print Merge command (File menu), 313
Print Merge dialog box, 313
Print Options dialog box, 299, 362-363, 555, 822-823
Print paper orientation does not match document error message, 597
Print Preview command (CorelCHART File menu), 727
print queues, 915
Print Setup command (CorelCHART File menu), 727
Print Setup command (CorelSHOW File menu), 754
Print Setup command (Data Object Manager File menu), 555
Print Setup command (File menu), 301
printable page (drawing window), 20
printer fonts, 915
Printer Setup command (Print Manager Options menu), 308
printers
   calibration, 331-332, 359-361
   color printers, 32, 298
      Hewlett-Packard inkjet printers, 347
      printing colors, 347
   dot-matrix printers, 901

imagesetters
    dot gain, 329-330
    dpi (dots per inch), 328
memory requirements, 305, 308
monochrome printers, 32, 298
non-PostScript printers, 15
PostScript printers, 15, 307-310
    color printers, 347
    complexity threshold, 821
    drivers, 308
    fonts, 308, 823-824
    laser proofs, 824
    PostScript emulators, 307
selecting, 298, 300, 305, 598
speeding up, 308-310
target printer, 920

printing
    bitmapped images, 310, 597-600
    black-and-white drawings, 32
    charts, 748
    clipart, 48
    color drawings, 32
    color separations, 15, 363-367
    colors
        accuracy, 359-361
        color printers, 347
        composite printing, 898
        costs, 368-369
        process colors, 349, 372-374
        registration, 369, 916
        spot color vs. process color, 348-351
    commercial printing, 342-343
        blue lines, 895
        boards, 895
        camera-ready art, 896
        color separations, 343
        colors, 342-343, 347
        electronic prepress, 343
        offset lithography, 342
        plates, 343
        prepress, 343
    CorelMOSAIC drawings, 292
    Data Manager (CorelCHART) spreadsheets, 727
    documents, 548-549

drawings, 127, 300-304
    35mm slides, 307
    a selected portion, 300
    alignment, 303
    black-and-white, 298
    color, 298
    colors, 307
    from DOS, 306-307
    halftone screens, 307, 310
    in tiled pages, 304
    layers, 304
    Macintosh computers, 301
    margins, 303
    multiple drawings simultaneously, 306
    orientation, 32
    Print Manager, 305
    print quality, 300
    process colors, 357-361
    resolution, 302, 310
    scale, 303
    speeding up printers, 308-310
    to a disk file, 301
    to fit to paper size, 303
files (File Manager), 305
film, 332-333
fountain fills, 175-176
laser printing, 907
merged files, 313-314
multipage drawings
    one page, 300
    selected page range, 300
multiple files, 13
negatives, 332
offset printing, 911
overprints, 912
page sizes, 298
photographs, 597-600
PostScript haltone screens, 170
scans
    dot gain, 329-330
    RC (resin-coated) paper, 332
slides, 863-864
spreadsheets, 555
tiles, 921
PRN files, 824-825
process colors, 349, 915
    commercial printing, 342, 357-361

converting spot colors to process colors, 350-351
customizing, 352-355
fountain fill banding, 368
palettes, 348-349
printing, 349, 372-374
selecting, 370-374
separations, 349, 915
see also colors
programs, see applications
ProMotion files, 780
proofreading drawings, 303, 915
Prop Information dialog box, 787
Prop tool, 781
property sheets, 561
    Advanced property sheet, 572-575
    Curves property sheet, 584-587
    editing, 561
    General Preferences property sheet, 561-567
    Text property sheet, 582-584
    View property sheet, 570-572
    viewing, 561
proportion (design), 835-836
props (animations), 778-779, 915
    animating, 797-799, 809-810
    cues, 802-803
    deleting, 804
    drawing, 785-793, 810-814
    editing, 786-787
    entrances, 787, 804
    exits, 787, 804
    libraries, 807-810
    moving, 797
    moving to back, 796-797, 815
    moving to front, 796-797, 815
    naming, 785
    saving, 786
    stopping, 798
    timing, 807, 815
    tinting colors, 792
    zooming in/out, 787
PS files, 275
Psychedelic Special Effect filter (CorelPHOTO-PAINT), 640
pull-down menu, 916
pulled quotes, see callouts

Q

queries (databases), 718
　creating, 719-723
　Open Database Convention
　　(ODC), 718
　SQL (System Query
　　Language), 719
Query Builder dialog box, 720
quotation marks
　straight (measurement)
　　quotation marks, 233
　typographic quotation
　　marks, 232
quotes, *see* callouts

R

radar charts, 703
radial fountain fills (object
　fills), 344
ragged text, 916
rainbow effect (blends),
　445-446
rainbow fountain fills
　(objects), 178
ranges (spreadsheet cells), 900
　borders, 724
　copying, 715-716
　cutting, 714
　designating, 714
　filling automatically,
　　707-710
　moving, 714
　numbers, formatting, 724
　pasting, 714-716
　patterns, 724
　selecting, 707
　tagging, 725-726
　text
　　aligning, 725
　　centering, 724
RC (resin-coated) paper, 332
README.WRI file, 871
records
　ASCII files, 311
　databases, 916
Rectangle Mask tool, 605, 645
Rectangle tool, 23, 37, 78-81,
　916
　CorelCHART, 730
　CorelPHOTO-PAINT,
　　604-607, 621

rectangles
　drawing, 37-39
　　CorelPHOTO-PAINT, 621
　　from a center point, 79,
　　　81
　　from a corner point,
　　　78-79
　　rounded rectangles, 81
　moving, 39
　node points, 114
　parallelograms, 192-194
　rounded rectangles, 80, 114
　selecting, 38
　shading, 39-40
　sizing, 37
Redo command (Edit menu),
　99-100
reference functions, 713
referencing spreadsheet cells,
　710
Refresh command
　(CorelCHART Window
　menu), 741
Refresh command
　(CorelPHOTO-PAINT
　Window menu), 601
Refresh command (View
　menu), 571
refreshing screen display, 571
registration (printing colors),
　369, 916
Registration command
　(CorelMOVE Paint Edit
　menu), 796
registration marks (color
　separations), 365-367, 916
registration point (animation
　paths), 796
relative referencing
　(spreadsheet cells), 710
Remove Cels command
　(CorelMOVE Paint Edit
　menu), 795
Remove From Selection
　command (CorelPHOTO-
　PAINT Special menu), 648
Remove Noise Noise Effect
　filter (CorelPHOTO-PAINT),
　639
Remove Transparency Mask
　command (CorelPHOTO-
　PAINT Mask menu), 653
Repeat command (Edit menu),
　99, 196
Replace command (Text
　menu), 228
Replace dialog box, 228

Resample command
　(CorelPHOTO-PAINT Image
　menu), 635
Resample Image dialog box,
　635
resident fonts, 308
resin-coated paper, 332
resolution, 916
　aspect ratio, 894
　bitmapped images, 635-636,
　　658
　CorelTRACE, 681-683
　Kodak Photo CD
　　photographs, 277
　paintings, 635-636
　photographs, 635-636
　scanning images, 659
　scans, 325
　TIFF files, 668
　see also dpi (dots per inch)
Resolution command
　(CorelPHOTO-PAINT Image
　menu), 636
Restore button, 19
Restore Screen command
　(CorelPHOTO-PAINT View
　menu), 600
retouching photographs
　colors, 611-613
　tools, 605-606
　working in duplicate
　　windows, 602
Reverse command
　(CorelMOVE Wave Editor
　Effects menu), 800
Revert Paint command
　(CorelMOVE Paint Edit
　menu), 793
RGB (Red, Green, Blue) color
　model, 353-354, 916
ribbon bar, 19, 916
　CorelCHART, 729
　screen display, 572
Rich Text Format import
　filter, 276
Ripple Mapping Effect filter
　(CorelPHOTO-PAINT), 638
risers (charts), 698
RLE files, 273
roll-up windows, 25-27, 917
　buttons, 27
　closing, 26
　memory requirements, 569
　moving, 26
　opening, 26
　screen display, 568-569
　styles, applying, 27

Roll-Ups command (View menu), 568
Roll-Ups dialog box, 568-569
Roman fonts, 917
Rotate command (CorelMOVE Paint Effects menu), 792-793
Rotate command (CorelPHOTO-PAINT Object menu), 634
rotate/skew handles (objects), 184
rotating
    bitmapped images, 634
    charts, 747
    objects, 189-192, 200-201, 896, 917
        center point, 191-192, 202
        marquee outline, 196
        master object, 196-197
        Paint (CorelMOVE), 792-793
        precision, 195
    paintings, 634
    photographs, 634
    text, 211, 240, 244, 917
roughs, 917
rounded rectangles
    drawing, 80-81
    node points, 114
rounded squares
    drawing, 80
    node points, 114
rows
    pattern pixels, 157-158
    spreadsheets
        deleting, 716
        inserting, 716-718
        sizing, 716-718
RTF files, 276, 542
rulers, 19, 917
    moving zero point, 570
    Paragraph text
        setting indents, 224
        setting margins, 224
    ruler guides, 917
    screen display, 570
    tick marks, 906, 921
Rulers command (View menu), 570
rules, 917
    columns, 897
    drawing, 44-45
    hairline rules, 905
    screen rules, 918
Run command (File menu), 872
running foots, 917
running heads, 917

S

SAM files, 275
sans serif fonts, 917
sans serif typefaces, 210
saturation (colors), 353-354, 917
Saturation tool, 606
Save a Mask To Disk dialog box, 653
Save An Image To Disk dialog box, 596
Save command (CorelPHOTO-PAINT Mask menu), 653
Save command (CorelPHOTO-PAINT File menu), 596
Save command (CorelQUERY File menu), 722
Save command (CorelSHOW File menu), 768
Save command (File menu), 47, 262
Save As command (CorelQUERY File menu), 722
Save As command (CorelTRACE File menu), 336
Save As command (File menu), 46, 262, 264
Save Background command (CorelSHOW File menu), 769
Save Drawing dialog box, 46, 262-265
Save Extrude Preset dialog box, 471
Save Full-Color Pattern dialog box, 164-165
Save Options command (CorelTRACE File menu), 686-687
Save Related dialog box, 796
Save Style As command (Object menu), 534
Save Style As dialog box, 28, 237
Save Template dialog box, 238
Save Transparency Mask command (CorelPHOTO-PAINT Mask menu), 652
Scale By Percent dialog box, 793
Scale command (CorelMOVE Paint Effects menu), 793
Scale Path dialog box, 798
scales (charts), 737
scaling
    animation paths, 798
    drawings for printing, 303
    objects, 184-189, 197-198, 917
        anchor points, 187
        CorelMOVE Paint, 792-793
    spreadsheets, 555
    text, 239, 917
        Paragraph text, 226
        TrueType fonts, 253
Scanner dialog box, 323
scanners, 918
    calibration, 359-361
    drivers
        Corel Image Source driver, 669
        installation, 320-321
        TWAIN, 321
    drum scanners, 320
    flatbed scanners, 320, 614
    hand-held scanners, 320, 614
    SCSI (Small Computer System Interface) boards, 321
        daisy chaining, 321
        installation, 321
    software, 321
    troubleshooting, 336
    TWAIN, 922
scanning
    CorelTRACE, 659-660
    images
        CorelPHOTO-PAINT, 613-615
    sketches, 855
scans, 319, 917
    art, 333
    bitmapped images, 669-670
    enlarging input resolution, 325
    halftones (photographs), 326
    input resolution
        dpi (dots per inch), 325-327
        line art, 335
    lpi (lines per inch), 326-328
    monitor display vs. printout quality, 327-328
    negatives, 332
    output resolution, 325-328

photographs, 333-334
    editing, 334
    scanning, 322-324
previewing, 323
printing
    dot gain, 329-330
    RC (resin-coated) paper, 332
reducing input resolution, 325
saving, 335
screens (lpi), 326
text files
    OCR (Optical Character Recognition), 336-337
    tracing, 657
scatter graph charts, 702
SCD files, 273
scissors tool, *see* Polygon Object tool
Scitex CT Bitmap
    export filter, 273
    import filter, 276
screen display, 567
    applications, 19
    bitmapped images, 573
    capturing, 615-616
    colors, 572-577
    Control Menu box, 19
    CorelMOVE
        Library button, 808
        Timeline button, 781
    CorelPHOTO-PAINT, 598-603
    cursors, 571
    fountain fills, 571
    grids, 575-576
    Maximize button, 19
    menu bar, 19
    Minimize button, 19
    page numbers in files, 20
    panning, 571
    Pop-Up Help, 572
    refreshing, 571
    Restore button, 19
    ribbon bar, 19, 572
    roll-up windows, 568-569
    rulers, 19, 570
    status line, 19, 572
    text, 582-584
    title bar, 18
    toolbox, 19, 577-578
    wallpaper, 251
    see also monitors
screen fonts, *see* fonts

screen shows, 769-770
    stand-alone screen shows, 773-775
screen tint, 918
Screen/Menu Help command (Help menu), 30
screens
    lpi (lines per inch), 326
    object fills
        angle, 169
        diamonds, 167-169
        dots, 167-169
        grids, 167-168
        lines, 167-169
        lpi (lines per inch), 168-170
        printing, 170
        resolution, 168
    PostScript haltones screens, 167-170
    spot colors, 351-352
script fonts, 918
scroll bars, 918
    drawing window, 20
    Editable Preview view, 22
    Wireframe view, 22
scrolling drawing window, 20
SCSI (Small Computer System Interface) board (scanners), 321
Search dialog box, 30
Search dialog box (Help), 278
Search For Help On command (Help menu), 30, 278
searching
    directories, 265-266
    text, 218, 227-228, 231
segments (lines), 918
Select All command (CorelMOSAIC Edit menu), 288
Select All command (CorelMOVE Paint Edit menu), 795
Select All command (Edit menu), 99
Select by Keyword command (CorelMOSAIC Edit menu), 288
Select Name For New File dialog box, 782
selection handles, 38
selection marquee, 918
selection tools (CorelPHOTO-PAINT), 604
SEP files, 276

Separate command (Arrange menu), 88, 236
Separate command (Effects menu), 459
separations (colors), 362-369, 897
    mechanical separations, 910
    printing, 363-367
    process color separations, 915
    registration marks, 365-367, 916
separators (arguments), 714
sequence (design), 835-836
serif fonts, 210, 918
service bureaus
    calibrating imagesetters, 331-332
    film, printing, 332-333
    paper, 332
    preparing output for printing
        CDR files, 824-825
        fonts, 823-824
        PostScript complexity threshold, 821-822
        PostScript laser proofs, 824
        PRN files, 824-825
Set Page Break command (CorelCHART Format menu), 727
Setup dialog box (CorelQUERY), 719
shading
    graphics, 39-40
    objects, 47
    text, 42
shadows (drawings), 54-55
Shape tool, 23, 379, 918
    curved lines, 72-77, 384
        editing curves, 389
    editing capabilities, 386
    editing text characters, 243-244
    moving object nodes, 387-388
    rounded rectangles, 80
    rounded squares, 80
    selecting object nodes, 386
shaping lines, 72-77
shareware
    SuperBar, 826
    typefaces, 209
Sharpen command (CorelPHOTO-PAINT Effects menu), 631

Sharpen dialog box, 631
Sharpen Effects filters
    (CorelPHOTO-PAINT), 639
Sharpen Sharpen Effect filter
    (CorelPHOTO-PAINT), 639
Sharpen tool (CorelPHOTO-
    PAINT), 606
SHOW, 14
Show as Pictograph command
    (CorelCHART Chart menu),
    746
Show Grid Lines command
    (CorelCHART Chart menu),
    736
Show Group Details command
    (Data Object Manager
    Preferences menu), 556
Show Group Details command
    (Object Data Manager
    Preferences menu), 552
Show Totals command (Object
    Data Manager Field Options
    menu), 555
side-fold cards, 544
signatures (pages), 918
Silence command
    (CorelMOVE Wave Editor
    Effects menu), 800
Silhouette method (tracing
    objects), 677-678
Silhouette Trace button, 672
sine waves, drawing, 408-410
sizing
    objects, 37
    slides, 755
    text, 42
sketches
    scanning, 855
    tracing, 659
skewing
    objects, 203, 919
        marquee outline, 196
        master object, 196-197
        precision, 194-195
    text, 240
Slide Sorter View button, 762
slides, 919
    builds, 865-866
    creating, 760-761
    double-wide display, 866
    embossed logos, 865
    metallic lettering, 862-863
    printing, 863-864
    sizing, 755
    sorting, 761-762
    transition effects, 762-764
    see also presentations

SMARTDRV.EXE file,
    installation, 871
Smear Paintbrush tool
    (CorelPHOTO-PAINT), 606
Smear tool (CorelPHOTO-
    PAINT), 624
smearing photographs, 624
Smoked Glass Mapping Effect
    filter (CorelPHOTO-PAINT),
    638
Smooth dialog box, 632
smooth nodes, 919
    curved lines, 74, 77, 383
Smooth Soften Effect filter
    (CorelPHOTO-PAINT), 639
smoothing, 893
smudging photographs, 624
Snap To Grid command
    (Layout menu), 80
Snap To Guidelines command
    (Layout menu), 117, 132
Snap To guides, 919
Snap To Objects command
    (Layout menu), 113-114,
    404-405
Soften command
    (CorelPHOTO-PAINT Effects
    menu), 631
Soften dialog box, 632
Soften Effect filter
    (CorelPHOTO-PAINT), 639
software, 321
Solarize Special Effect filter
    (CorelPHOTO-PAINT), 640
sorting
    files, 266-267
    slides (CorelSHOW), 761-762
Sound command (CorelSHOW
    Insert menu), 770
Sound Editor (CorelMOVE),
    800
sound icons, 919
Sound Information dialog
    box, 800
Sound tool (CorelMOVE), 781,
    800
sounds (animations)
    amplifying, 800
    animations, 778, 799-801
    background music, 801
    channels, 801
    CorelSHOW, 770
    cues, 802-803
    deleting, 804
    echos, 800
    editing, 800
    libraries, 807-808

naming, 800
playing, 800-801, 815
recording, 800
repeating, 801
silencing, 800
stereo sounds, 801
stopping recording, 800
timing, 804
volume, 800-801
speaker notes (presentations),
    775-776
Special Effect filters
    (CorelPHOTO-PAINT), 640
special effects
    Blend effect, 441-460
    contours, 477-484
    Envelope, 423-440, 520-523
    Extrude, 461-476, 525-527
    Lens, 499-506, 530
    masks, 126
    Perspective, 413-421,
        516-520
    PowerClip, 507-514
    PowerLines, 485-497, 529
    stippled backgrounds,
        843-845
Special menu commands
    Create Arrow, 400
    Create Pattern, 164
    Extract, 246
    Macros Preset Roll-Up, 537
    Merge Back, 247
    Preferences, 65, 99, 561, 915
    Symbols Roll-Up, 23, 250
spectral map charts, 702
Spell Check dialog box, 229
Spell Checker command (Text
    menu), 229
Spelling Checker, 228,
    228-230
spoolers, *see* Print Manager
spot colors, 348-349, 919
    commercial printing, 343
    converting to process colors,
        350-351
    palettes, 348-352
    selecting, 370-374
    tints, 351-352
Spray Can tool (CorelMOVE),
    790
Spray Can tool (CorelPHOTO-
    PAINT), 620
spreads (trapping colors), 919
spreadsheets
    cells, 900
    centering, 555

symbols 961

Data Manager
  (CorelCHART), 699
    aligning text across cells,
      725
    analyzing data with
      formula editor, 699
    automating data entry,
      707-710
    breaking pages, 727
    cell ranges, 707-710, 714
    centering text across
      cells, 724
    copying cells, 714-716
    deleting columns and
      rows, 716-718
    deleting data, 706
    editing, 706
    entering data, 705
    fibonaccio values, 709
    fonts, 723
    formatting, 706
    formatting numbers, 724
    geometric values, 709
    importing, 718
    inserting columns and
      rows, 716-718
    linear values, 709
    logarithmic values, 709
    moving cells, 714-716
    printing, 727
    referencing cells, 710
    sizing columns and rows,
      716
    styles, 723
    text strings, 709
  grid lines, 555
  headers, 555
  page numbers, 555
  scaling, 555
  text, 555
  see also cells
SQL (System Query Language),
  719
SQL command editor
  (CorelQUERY), 723
squares
  drawing, 37-39, 81
    CorelPHOTO-PAINT, 621
    from a center point, 79
    from a corner point,
      78-79
  moving, 39
  node points, 114
  parallelograms, 203
  rounded squares, 114
  rounding corners, 80
  selecting, 38

shading, 39-40
sizing, 37
Staggered Text command
  (CorelCHART Chart menu),
  736
stand-alone screen shows,
  773-775
standoffs, 919
stars, drawing, 204
start nodes, 919
starting
  CorelDRAW!, 16, 560-561
  CorelMOSAIC, 13
  CorelMOVE, 780
  CorelPHOTO-PAINT,
    593-596
  CorelSHOW, 752-755
  CorelTRACE, 668
starting points (objects),
  viewing, 62
statistical functions, 713
status line, 19
  Blend effect, 442
  contours, 478
  CorelPHOTO-PAINT, 599
  Envelope, 424
  Extrude effect, 462
  hiding, 19
  moving, 19
  perspective, 414
  PowerClip, 508
  PowerLines, 486
  screen display, 572
  Wireframe view, 22
status lines (Lens), 500
stippled backgrounds, 843-845
straight lines
  converting to curved lines,
    381-382
  drawing, 63-67, 382-383
  joining, 65-68
  nodes, 378
    deleting, 391
    editing, 379, 382, 385
Straighten Text command
  (Text menu), 244
stretch/mirror handles
  (objects), 184
Stretch/Truncate tool
  (CorelPHOTO-PAINT), 636
stretching
  bitmapped images, 635
  objects, 184-189, 198-199,
    920
    marquee outline, 196
    master object, 196-197
    precision, 195
  paintings, 635
  photographs, 635

strings (spreadsheet cells), 709
Style command (CorelCHART
  Format menu), 723
Style dialog box
  (CorelCHART), 723
Style Roll-Up command
  (Layout menu), 237
Style roll-up windows, 27-29
styles, 533-534, 920
  artistic text, applying, 27,
    535
  CorelCHART Data Manager
    spreadsheets, 723
  objects
    applying, 27, 535
    defining, 28-29
    saving, 28-29
  paragraph text, applying, 27,
    535
  saving, 534-535
  templates, 237
  text
    applying, 27
    defining, 28-29
    saving, 28-29
Styles roll-up, 237, 535-536
Styles Roll-Up command
  (Layout menu), 534
subpaths (nodes), 920
subscript text, 244
subtractive primary colors,
  920
SuperBar, 826
superscript text, 244
swatching systems
  Focoltone, 359, 903
  PANTONE Matching System
    (PMS), 359, 913
  process colors, 349
  swatch books, 359
  TRUMATCH, 359, 921
Swirl Mapping Effect filter
  (CorelPHOTO-PAINT), 638
symbols, 47-48, 877-879
  breaking apart, 516
  copyright symbol, 252
  dingbats, 901
  drawings, inserting, 55-56,
    250-251
  duplicating, 516
  fills, 516
  grouping, 516
  importing charts, 734
  ligatures, 908
  outlines, 516
  selecting, 56
  sizing, 251

symbols

    Symbols roll-up window, 55
    tiling, 251
    trademark symbol, 252
Symbols Roll-Up command (Special menu), 23, 250
symmetical nodes (curved lines), 74, 77, 384, 920
synonyms, *see* Thesaurus
System Color Profile (Color Manager), 359-361
System Color Profile dialog box, 359
System Query Language (SQL), 719

T

table charts, 702
tabs (paragraph text), 222-223, 234
Tabs dialog box, 225
tagging spreadsheet cells, 725-726
Targa Bitmap
    export filter, 273
    import filter, 276
templates, 237, 533-536, 920
    charts, 696, 734, 748
    creating, 581-582
    hot keys, 536
    loading, 536
    saving, 536, 582
    text styles, saving, 237-238
tent cards, 544
text
    aligning, 44
    annotating charts, 893
    Artistic text, 27, 211-212, 893
        aligning, 215
        applying styles, 27
        character limit, 212, 218
        converting to curves, 249-250
        editing, 212-213, 380
        extruding, 526
        fills, 217-218
        hanging indent, 905
        node points, 114
        outlines, 217-218
        paths, 240-243
        perspective effect, 518-519
        PowerClip effect, 507
        searching, 218
        spacing, 216, 218
        styles, 215

ASCII characters, inserting, 252
autoflowing, 894
baseline, 244, 894
blocks, 920
body copy, 895
calligraphy effect, 584
callouts, 86
cap height, 896
capitalization, 232
chained text, 896
chrome effects, 170
Clipboard, 281, 584
columns, 233
copying, 899
copyright symbol, 252
CorelSHOW, 756-757
dimension lines, 404, 407
dingbats, 901
display type, 901
drag and drop, 901
drawings, 207
    importing, 226-227
    inserting, 23, 41-42
    inserting Artistic text, 212
    inserting Paragraph text, 219
editing, 583
    extracted text, 246-247
embossed effect, 845-847
em shift, 244
Envelopes, 583
envelopes, 435-436
    Artistic text, 436-437
    editing, 438
    fitting, 426, 435-438
    mapping, 432
    shapes, 437-438
extracting, 246
extrude effect, 902
extrusions, editing, 473
fills, 211
flowing, 903, 909
flush, 903
fonts, 208-210
    selecting, 42
    viewing, 583
formatting, 904
frames
    deleting, 236
    editing, 236
    flowing text between frames, 235-237
greek text, 904
greeking, 904
highlighting, 906
hyphenating, 906

insertion point, 906
interior fill, 25
intersecting, 128
italicizing, 907
jump lines, 907
justifying, 907
kerning, 210, 907
leaders, 908
leading, 210, 908
letters
    ascenders, 893
    breaking apart, 250
    descenders, 900
    editing, 243-245
    rotating, 244
line spacing, 906
merging, 910
    extracted text, 247-248
mirroring, 910
mottled text, 144
node points, 114
nonbreaking space, 911
objects, wrapping around, 234-235
outlines, 25, 144, 211
Paint (CorelMOVE), 792
Paragraph text, 211-212, 218, 913
    aligning, 220-221
    bulleted lists, 224-226
    character limit, 212
    columns, 233-234
    editing, 219
    fills, 221
    frames, 219, 226
    hanging indent, 905
    hyphenating, 221
    indentation, 223-224, 906
    margins, 223-224
    outlines, 221
    rotating, 211
    scaling, 226
    selecting point size, 221
    selecting typefaces, 221
    spacing, 219-220, 907
    style, 221
    tabs, 222-223
    widows, 922
paragraphs, applying styles, 27
paths, 840-842
perspective, 415
    copying, 419
    deleting, 420
photographs, 627
point size, 914
    selecting, 42

quotation marks, 232
ragged, 916
replacing words or phrases, 228, 232
reversing, 916
rotating, 240, 917
scaling, 239, 917
screen display, 582-584
searching, 227-228, 231
selecting, 918
selection area, 918
shading, 42
sizing, 42
skewing, 240
slanting, 192
Spelling Checker, 228-230
straightening, 244
styles
 applying, 27, 238-239
 copying, 245
 creating, 237
 defining, 28-29
 saving, 28-29, 237
subscript, 244
superscript, 244
symbols, 877-879
Thesaurus, 228, 230
tracking, 921
trademark symbol, 252
trimming, 128
Type Assist, 231-233
typefaces, 208-209
 creating custom typefaces, 253-258
 point size, 210
vector graphics, 208
welding, 128
wrapping, 920, 922
wrapping around objects, 239
text annotations (charts), 743-744
Text dialog box, 583
Text Editing dialog box, 438
text files
 fields, 311-312
 merging with drawings, 310-314
 records, 311-312
 scans, tracing, 657
 see also ASCII files
text functions, 713
Text import filter, 276
Text menu commands
 Align to Baseline, 244
 Character, 215
 Edit Text, 213, 242, 438

Find, 227
Fit Text to Path, 240
Frame, 233
Paragraph, 220
Replace, 228
Spell Checker, 229
Straighten Text, 244
Thesaurus, 230
Type Assist, 231
Text Paragraph Indent dialog box, 236
Text property sheet, 582-584
Text roll-up, 214, 518
text strings (spreadsheet cells), 709
Text tool, 23, 41-42, 920
 CorelCHART, 730
 CorelPHOTO-PAINT, 605, 627
 editing text in envelopes, 438
 Paint (CorelMOVE), 790
text-entry box (dialog boxes), 920
Texture Fill dialog box, 180
textures
 bitmap textures, 895
 fills, 920
 fractal textures, 904
 object fills, 180-181
 PostScript textures, 914
  object fills, 165-167
 see also patterns
TGA files, 273, 276
 importing (CorelTRACE), 668
Thesaurus, 228-230
Thesaurus command (Text menu), 230
Thesaurus dialog box, 230
Threshold Special Effect filter (CorelPHOTO-PAINT), 640
thumbnails, 920
 animations, 783
 CorelMOSAIC drawings, 290-291
 images, 13
tick marks (rulers), 921
 increments, 906
ticks (grid lines), 737
TIF files, 273, 276
TIFF Bitmap
 export filter, 273
 import filter, 276
TIFF files, 668
Tile command (CorelCHART Window menu), 742

Tile dialog box, 251
Tile Horizontally command (CorelPHOTO-PAINT Window menu), 601
Tile Mapping Effect filter (CorelPHOTO-PAINT), 638
Tile Vertically command (CorelPHOTO-PAINT Window menu), 601
tiles
 documents, printing, 921
 patterns
  offset, 155-156
  sizing, 153-154
tiling
 drawings, 304
 symbols, 251
time (spreadsheets), 709
time and date functions, 713
time-out errors, 921
timeline (animations), 778-779
Timeline roll-up, 803-804
timelines
 animations, 921
 CorelSHOW, 772
timing (animations), 807
Tint All Cels command (CorelMOVE Paint Effects menu), 792
Tint Prop command (CorelMOVE Paint Effects menu), 792
Tint Selection command (CorelMOVE Paint Options menu), 792
Tint tool (CorelPHOTO-PAINT), 605
Tinted Grayscale lens, 503
 colors, 503-504
 editing, 505
 fills, 503-504
 halftones (photographs), 503
 moving, 505
 sizing, 505
 stretching, 505
tints (colors), 921
 objects, 344
 Spot color, 351-352
title bar, 18
titles (charts), 736
To Back command (CorelMOVE Arrange menu), 797
To Front command (CorelMOVE Arrange menu), 797

Tobin, Randy (ACAD president), 819-828
toggle switches, 921
Tone command (CorelPHOTO-PAINT Effects menu), 632
Tone Equalize Special Effect filter (CorelPHOTO-PAINT), 640
Tone Map Color Effect filter (CorelPHOTO-PAINT), 637
tones (colors), 921
Tool Settings roll-up (CorelPHOTO-PAINT), 600, 624
Tool Settings Roll-Up command (CorelPHOTO-PAINT View menu), 612
toolbox, 19
   CorelCHART, 729-732
   CorelPHOTO-PAINT, 603-606
   Ellipse tool, 23
   Fill tool, 23
   hiding, 578
   moving, 577
   Outline Pen tool, 23
   Pencil tool, 23
   Pick tool, 23
   Rectangle tool, 23
   Shape tool, 23
   Text tool, 23
   tools
      Artistic Text tool, 212
      Fill tool, 147
      Outline Pen tool, 138
      viewing, 577
   Zoom tool, 23
   Zoom In tool, 23
   Zoom Out tool, 23
Toolbox command (View menu), 577
Toolbox Visible command (CorelPHOTO-PAINT View menu), 603
toolbox window, 921
tools
   fly-out menus, 23
   toolbox, viewing, 577
   see also individual tool names
top-fold cards, 544
TRACE, 14
Trace menu commands (OCR B&W), 336
Trace Options dialog box, 336

tracing
   AutoTrace, 661-665
      color, 664
      curve settings, 666
      customizing, 665-667
      Pencil tool, 661
      troubleshooting, 667
   bitmapped images, 658-659
   CorelTRACE, 667-668
      accuracy, 680
      Centerline method, 675-677, 685
      color, 682-683
      exporting traced images, 690-692
      Form method, 680
      headers, 689-690
      image filtering, 681-683
      importing images, 668-670
      line tracing attributes, 683-684
      menus, 674-675
      OCR method, 679-680, 686
      Outline method, 675-677
      saving images, 687
      Silhouette method, 677-678
      simultaneously tracing and saving, 688-689
      tracing bitmap parts, 687-688
      troubleshooting, 693
      window, 670
      Woodcut method, 677-678, 685-686
   documents, 659
   faxes, 659
   forms, 657
   line art, 335
   memory requirements, 658
   objects, 586
   scans (text files), 657
   sketches, 659
Tracing Options dialog box, 686
tracking (text), 921
trademark symbol, 252
Transform roll-up, 184
   Apply button, 187
   Apply to Duplicate button, 196
   H (horizontal) box, 101, 187
   Move button, 101
   Relative Position box, 101
   Rotate button, 191
   Scale button, 186

   Size button, 188
   Skew button, 193
   V (vertical) box, 101, 187
Transform Roll-Up command (Effects menu), 101, 186
transition effects (presentations), 762-764
Transition Effects dialog box, 762
transitions (animations), 921
Transitions for Prop dialog box, 787
translucent lines (photographs), 620-621
translucent objects, 151-152
transparencies, *see* overhead transparencies
Transparency command (CorelMOVE Paint Options menu), 791
Transparency lens, 501
   colors, 504
   editing, 505
   fills, 501-504
   moving, 505
   opacity, 501, 505
   sizing, 505
   stretching, 505
Transparency Mask dialog box, 652
transparency masks (CorelPHOTO-PAINT), 652-653
Transpose command (CorelCHART Edit menu), 715
trapping colors, 366-367, 921
   spreads, 919
trigonometric functions, 713
Trim command (Arrange menu), 128-130
trimming objects, 530-533, 921
   see also PowerClip
troubleshooting
   AutoTrace, 667
   CorelTRACE, 693
   presentations, 755
      animation, 773
      cues, 773
      graphics, 760
      sound, 773
      stand-alone screen shows, 775
      text, 757
      transition effects, 764
   printers, 305
   scanners, 336

W

true color, *see* 24-bit color
True/False functions, 713
TrueType Export dialog box, 255-256
TrueType Font export filter, 273
TrueType Font Options dialog box, 874
TrueType fonts, 209, 253, 921
   customizing, 253-258
   installation, 874-875
   scaling, 253
TRUMATCH color swatching system, 349, 353, 359, 921
TTF files, 273
Tutorial command (Help menu), 30
tutorials, 30
TWAIN, 922
TWAIN scanning drivers, 321
Two-Color Pattern dialog box, 153-155
Two-Color Pattern Editor dialog box, 159
two-point perspective, *see* perspective
TXT files, 276
Type Assist, 231-233
Type Assist command (Text menu), 231
Type Assist dialog box, 231
typefaces, *see* fonts

U

underlining text, 215
Undo command (CorelCHART Edit menu), 735
Undo command (CorelPHOTO-PAINT Edit menu), 611
Undo command (Edit menu), 65, 99-100, 196
Undo Curve Edit command (Edit menu), 391
undo levels, 563-564
undoing mistakes, 99
Ungroup command (Arrange menu), 50, 122, 517
Uniform Fill dialog box, 147, 150, 167-169, 344
unity (design), 835-837
Unsharp Mask dialog box, 631
Unsharp Mask Sharpen Effect filter (CorelPHOTO-PAINT), 639
upgrading CorelDRAW! 4, 827

V

vanishing point (perspectives), 413-414, 417
   aligning, 418, 520
   finding, 417-421
   moving, 418
   one-point perspective, 414
   two-point perspective, 414
VDA files, 273, 276
vector graphics, 24-25
   delete object-oriented files, 922
   dots, 24
   text, 208
vector patterns, 345
vector-based art, 333
vector-graphics drawings, editing, 32
vertical lines, drawing, 67
View menu commands
   Color Correction, 361
   Color Palette, 20, 356
   Full-Screen Preview, 22, 299
   Refresh Window, 571
   Roll-Ups, 568
   Rulers, 570
   Toolbox, 577
   Wireframe, 21, 94
View property sheet, 570-572
viewing drawings, 56-57
views
   Editable Preview mode, 20
      selecting objects, 386
   Full-Screen Preview mode, 22
   Wireframe mode, 21
      selecting objects, 386
Vignette Mapping Effect filter (CorelPHOTO-PAINT), 638
VST files, 273, 276

W

wallpaper, 251
WAV files, playing, 800
Wave Editor (CorelMOVE!), 800-801
Weld command (Arrange menu), 128-129, 204
welding objects, 922
Wet Paint Mapping Effect filter (CorelPHOTO-PAINT), 638
WFN fonts, 209, 253, 922
white space, 837, 922
widows (Paragraph text), 922
Wind Mapping Effect filter (CorelPHOTO-PAINT), 638
Window menu commands (More Windows), 18
windows, 922
   active window, 893
   animations, 782-784
   Batch Files roll-up window, 673-674
   cascading, 742
   CorelPHOTO-PAINT
      activating, 600
      arranging, 600
      ghost images, 601
      sizing, 600
      working in duplicate windows, 602-603
   CorelSHOW, 754-755
   CorelTRACE, 670
   drawing window, 20, 901
   refreshing, 741
   roll-up windows, 25-27, 917
      CorelPHOTO-PAINT, 600
      memory requirements, 569
   screen display, 568-569
   tiling, 742
   toolbox window, 921
   windowshades, 922
Windows Bitmap
   export filter, 273
   import filter, 276
Windows Metafile format
   Clipboard, 281
   export filter, 273
   import filter, 276
Windows Printer Setup dialog box, 301
windowshades, 922
Wireframe command (View menu), 21, 94
wireframe extrusions, 461
Wireframe view, 21, 922
   facing pages, 22
   objects
      editing, 22
   scroll bars, 22
   selecting objects, 386
   status line, 22
   tools, 22
WK files, 275
WMF files, 273, 276
Wood, David (Graphic Computer Services), 861-867
Woodcut button, 672
Woodcut method (tracing objects), 677-678, 685-686

Word for Windows, 246-248
Word Perfect 6.0 import filter, 276
word spacing, *see* kerning
WordPerfect 5.0 import filter, 276
WordPerfect 5.1 import filter, 276
WordPerfect files, importing, 226, 542
WordPerfect Graphic
    export filter, 273
    import filter, 276
WP files, 276
WPG files, 273, 276
wrapping text, 920- 922
    around objects, 234-235, 239
    columns, 234
WYSIWYG (What You See Is What You Get), 923

X-Y

X axis (charts), 923
X-height (fonts), 923
XLS files, 275
XOR Selection command (CorelPHOTO-PAINT Special menu), 648

Y-axis (charts), 923
yellow, 923

Z

zero lines (charts), 741
Zoom command (CorelMOVE Options menu), 790
Zoom command (CorelMOVE Paint Options menu), 791
Zoom command (CorelPHOTO-PAINT View menu), 601
Zoom tool, 23, 923
    CorelCHART, 730
    CorelPHOTO-PAINT, 601-604
    Editable Preview, 22
    Wireframe view, 22
Zoom In tool, 23
Zoom Out tool, 23
zooming in/out (animations), 787